W9-AQL-970

AUTHORS, ILLUSTRATORS, AND REPRESENTATIVE BOOKS

1989 ED YOUNG
Lon Po Po:
A Red Riding Hood
Story from China

1988 PAUL FLEISCHMAN
Joyful Noise:
Poems for Two Voices
ILLUS. ERIC BEDDOWS

1988 ELOISE GREENFIELD
Nathaniel Talking
ILLUS. JAN SPIVEY GILCHRIST

1988 VIRGINIA HAMILTON
Anthony Burns:
The Defeat and Triumph
of a Fugitive Slave

1987 RUSSELL FREEDMAN
Lincoln: A Photobiography

1987 JOHN STEPTOE
Mufaro's Beautiful
Daughters:
An African Tale

1987 JANE YOLEN
Owl Moon
ILLUS. JOHN SCHOENHERR

1986 NICHOLASA MOHR
Going Home

1985 PATRICIA MACLACHLAN
Sarah, Plain and Tall

1985 CHRIS VAN ALLSBURG
The Polar Express

1982 TOSHI MARUKI
Hiroshima No Pika

1981 YOSHIKO UCHIDA
Jar of Dreams

1970S

1978 PAUL GOBLE
The Girl Who
Loved Wild Horses

1977 KATHERINE PATERSON
Bridge to Terabithia

1977 DAVID MCCORD
One at a Time

1976 JEAN FRITZ
What's the Big Idea,
Ben Franklin?
ILLUS. MARGOT TOMES

1976 BYRD BAYLOR
Hawk, I'm Your Brother
ILLUS. PETER PARNALL

1976 MILDRED TAYLOR
Roll of Thunder,
Hear My Cry

1975 TOMIE DEPAOLA
Strega Nona

1975 NATALIE BABBITT
Tuck Everlasting

1975 SHARON MATHIS
The Hundred Penny Box
ILLUS. LEO & DIANE DILLON

1975 LAURENCE YEP
Dragonwings

1974 VIRGINIA HAMILTON
M. C. Higgins, the Great

1973 SUSAN COOPER
The Dark Is Rising

1972 ARNOLD LOBEL
Frog and Toad Together

1971 MISKA MILES
Annie and the Old One
ILLUS. PETER PARNALL

1971 MURIEL FEELINGS
Moja Means One:
Swahili Counting Book
ILLUS. TOM FEELINGS

1970 BETSY BYARS
Summer of the Swans

1960S

1969 JOHN STEPTOE
Stevie

1968 DON FREEMAN
Corduroy

1968 URSULA K. LE GUIN
Wizard of Earthsea

1967 VIRGINIA HAMILTON
Zeely
ILLUS. SYMEON SHIMIN

1964 MAURICE SENDAK
Where the Wild Things Are

1964 LLOYD ALEXANDER
The Book of Three

1962 MADELEINE L'ENGLE
A Wrinkle in Time

1962 EZRA JACK KEATS
The Snowy Day

www.wadsworth.com

wadsworth.com is the World Wide Web site for Wadsworth and is your direct source to dozens of online resources.

At *wadsworth.com* you can find out about supplements, demonstration software, and student resources. You can also send email to many of our authors and preview new publications and exciting new technologies.

wadsworth.com
Changing the way the world learns®

CULLINAN AND GALDA'S

Literature and the Child

FIFTH
EDITION

Lee Galda

UNIVERSITY OF MINNESOTA

Bernice E. Cullinan

NEW YORK UNIVERSITY

WADSWORTH

THOMSON LEARNING™

Australia • Canada • Mexico • Singapore • Spain • United Kingdom • United States

Education Editor: Dan Alpert
Associate Development Editor: Tangelique Williams
Editorial Assistant: Alex Orr
Marketing Manager: Becky Tollerson
Project Manager, Editorial Production: Trudy Brown
Print/Media Buyer: Barbara Britton
Permissions Editor: Stephanie Keough-Hedges

Production Service: Joan Keyes, Dovetail Publishing Services
Text and Cover Designer: Kaelin Chappell
Copy Editor: Jane Townsend
Cover and Part Opening Illustrations: Lauren Stringer
Compositor: New England Typographic Service
Text and Cover Printer: Transcontinental

Printed in Canada

2   3   4   5   6   7   05   04   03   02   01

For permission to use material from this text, contact us by
Web: http://www.thomsonrights.com
Fax: 1-800-730-2215
Phone: 1-800-730-2214

Wadsworth/Thomson Learning
10 Davis Drive
Belmont, CA 94002-3098
USA

For more information about our products, contact us:
Thomson Learning Academic Resource Center
1-800-423-0563
http://www.wadsworth.com

International Headquarters
Thomson Learning
International Division
290 Harbor Drive, 2nd Floor
Stamford, CT 06902-7477
USA

UK/Europe/Middle East/South Africa
Thomson Learning
Berkshire House
168-173 High Holborn
London WC1V 7AA
United Kingdom

Asia
Thomson Learning
60 Albert Street, #15-01
Albert Complex
Singapore 189969

Canada
Nelson Thomson Learning
1120 Birchmount Road
Toronto, Ontario M1K 5G4
Canada

Library of Congress Cataloging-in-Publication Data
Galda, Lee
    [Literature and the Child]
    Cullinan and Galda's literature and the child.—5th ed. /
Lee Galda, Bernice E. Cullinan.
        p. cm.
    Cullinan's name appears first on earlier editions.
    Includes bibliographical references and indexes.
    ISBN 0-534-24683-4
    1. Children—Books and reading—United States. 2. Children's literature—Bibliography. 3. Children's literature, English—Bibliography. 4. Children's literature—History and criticism. 5. Children's literature, English—History and criticism.
    I. Cullinan, Bernice E. II. Title.

Z1037 .C946 2002
025.5'5—dc21   2001026128

FOR

Henry Pearson Woelflein

AND

Jamison Webb Ellinger

A NEW GENERATION OF READERS

Contents

chapter 3

The Art of Picture Books   67

chapter 4

The Content of Picture Books   99

chapter 8

Historical Fiction   203

chapter 9

Biography   231

PART TWO
Children and Books

Preface

About Children's Literature

The field of children's literature continues to grow and change as exciting new books are published each year. Of course, older books remain good reading fare—they are new to each child who reads them—but new books bring fresh voices and visions to the field. Twenty years after the first edition, revising *Literature and the Child* finds us rewriting, rethinking, and fine-tuning a message that grows in importance for classrooms around the world: Give children books. In these times of mandated high-stakes testing with teacher accountability linked to test scores, it is vital that we not lose sight of one important reason to become a fluent reader—books.

About the Fifth Edition

In this edition we have reorganized some chapters, added new ones, and refined features that readers have enjoyed in earlier editions. The book is divided into two parts: "The Books" and "Children and Books."

Part One begins with an introductory chapter that examines the past, the present, and the potential future of children's literature. Additional information on the history of children's literature is included in Appendix E. Part One then moves on to chapters that are organized by genre, beginning with poetry. We have divided the material on picture books into two chapters, one focusing on the art of the picture book, the other on the types of content that are common in picture books. Each genre chapter is organized similarly: We introduce and define the genre, discuss how children respond to it, present evaluative criteria, then look closely at exemplars of the genre. The organization of the discussion of the books in each genre reflects the variety of possibilities for discussing children's books. We end Part One with a chapter on selecting books to build a diverse literature collection. Culturally diverse literature is present in all chapters; Chapter 11 highlights authors and illustrators who are contributing to the development of an increasingly diverse corpus of books from which to select.

In Part Two, we devote a chapter to the readers themselves and how they develop as responsive readers. The last two chapters are focused on literature in use in classrooms. Real classrooms, real children, and real teachers are described to bring to life the range of choices that exist for materials, organization, and instruction when children's books are the basis of the curriculum.

Features in this edition include Profiles and Teaching Ideas, just as in the previous edition. The Appendices have been updated, with new children's and young adult book awards included. We moved the Booklists to the end of each chapter where they are organized according to headings within the chapter. We hope that having the Booklists together at the end of each chapter will make the text easier to use as a reference for finding appropriate books. The Booklists also appear on the text-specific Web site, which can be accessed through the CD that accompanies this book. These Booklists will be updated every six months for the life of this edition. Further, there is a new feature that uses Infotrac® College Edition, an online database of articles and readings from hundreds of journals and periodicals (including *The Horn Book Magazine*), to encourage students to read and respond to specific professional material. The suggestions that we make for Infotrac College Edition exercises adapt well to small group assignments, paper topics, or examination questions.

Acknowledgments

We are most grateful to Lauren Stringer, who interrupted her busy schedule as a children's book artist and mother to paint the cover and part openers for this edition. Before she did so, she read the fourth edition so that she could capture in art what we were saying in words. Her beautiful visions of children's books and children reading them surpass our meager words.

Another special thank-you goes to Taffy Raphael and Deborah Dillon, two people whose vision of teaching and learning literacy have contributed to our understanding of how children's literature functions in children's literate lives. Lee's colleagues at the University of Minnesota enrich her intellectual life. Susan Watts-Taffe, Michael Graves, Barbara Taylor, Rick Beach, and Carolyn Gwinn are sources of support and good ideas. Karen Nelson Hoyle, curator of the Kerlan Collection at the University of Minnesota, is an invaluable colleague, as are Dianne Monson, Betty Peltola, and other Kerlan friends. Rebecca Rapport, who shares good books and teaching stories, was an important part of this edition—especially when we'd talk over a good meal. Deb Kruse-Field, a Master of Arts student at the University of Minnesota, kindly shared her ideas for Chapter 14. Without Audrey Appelseis, a doctoral student at the University of Minnesota, this book would not be finished, and there would be no references! She has been an invaluable part of this long process. Joelle Tegwen did an outstanding job of cleaning up and formatting the references.

The following reviewers contributed valuable feedback for the fifth edition: Laura Apol, Michigan State University; Luther B. Clegg, Texas Christian University; Linda Degroff, University of Georgia; Julie M. Jensen, The University of Texas at Austin; Inga Kromann-Kelly, Washington State University; and Sylvia P. Maxson, California State University, Long Beach.

Many superb teachers and librarians contributed to this book as well. Karen Hankins, Terry Nestor, Karen Bliss, Betty Shockley Bisplinghoff, and Lisa Stanzi, all working in the Athens Clarke County public schools, continue to inspire us when we think of good teachers. Leslie Radloff, St. Paul Public Schools, is a wonderful librarian. From Kenwood School in Minneapolis, Susan Kalin is always ready with another inspiring book-and-child story, and Rene Goepfrich is kind enough to share her fourth graders with Lee once a week.

Bee was aided by the librarians at the Port Washington Library: Carey Ayres, Rachel Fox, Lucy Salerno, Joni Simon, Nancy Curtin, and Coirrine Comaradie, and Genie Craner at the Bryant Library. Her writers group is another source of support: Joie Hinden, Ann Lovett, Marilyn Scala, Ginnie Schroder, and Deborah Wooten. Other helpful friends and collaborators include Diane Person, Kaaren Sorensen, Kent Brown, Jody Taylor Brown, Joan Irwin, John Micklos, Allan DeFina, Lee Bennet Hopkins, Rebecca Dotlich, Jeri Kozobarich, Shelley Harwayne, Renay Sadis, Sharon Hill, Paula Rogovin, Sharon Taberski, Judy Davis, Regina Chiou, Pat Werner, Joanne Hindley, and all the other teachers who invite her into their classrooms.

Finally, the support of Lee's family—Tony, Adam, and Anna—meant that she could write past dinner-making time and still be welcome at the table. Bee's family—Marguerite, Webb, and Jamison Ellinger; Janie, Alan, and Trisha Carley; and Kali and Jason Ream—continues to offer love and support as she leads her busy life. To all, thank you.

Lee Galda
Bernice E. Cullinan

About the Authors and Illustrator

Lee Galda

After teaching in elementary and middle school classrooms for a number of years, Lee Galda received her Ph.D. in English Education from New York University. A former professor at the University of Georgia, she is now a professor at the University of Minnesota where she teaches courses in children's literature and language arts. Lee is a member of the National Reading Conference, the National Council of Teachers of English, the International Reading Association, the American Library Association, and the United States Board on Books for Young People and sits on the review boards of many professional journals. She was the Children's Books Department editor for *The Reading Teacher* from 1989 to 1993 and is currently a contributing editor for *The Riverbank Review*. Author of numerous articles and book chapters about children's books, Lee recently co-authored a chapter on research in children's literature in the *Handbook of Reading Research, Volume III*. She lives in Minneapolis, Minnesota, with her husband and two children.

Bernice E. Cullinan

Bernice E. Cullinan is known both nationally and internationally for her work in children's literature. She has written over 30 books on literature for classroom teachers and librarians, including *Literature and the Child* (5th edition), *Poetry Lessons to Dazzle and Delight*, and *Three Voices: Invitation to Poetry Across the Curriculum*. She has also written a book for parents, *Read to Me: Raising Kids Who Love to Read*. Bee is editor in chief of Wordsong, the poetry imprint of Boyds Mills Press, a Highlights for Children company, and has collected poems written by the recipients of the National Council of Teachers of English Award for Poetry in *A Jar of Tiny Stars*. She served as president of the International Reading Association, was inducted into the Reading Hall of Fame and The Ohio State University Hall of Fame, and selected as the recipient of the Arbuthnot Award for Outstanding Teacher of Children's Literature. Bee lives in Sands Point, New York.

Lauren Stringer

Lauren Stringer was born in Great Falls, Montana. She received her Bachelor of Arts in Art and Art History from the University of California, Santa Cruz, in 1980, and continued her art education with the Whitney Museum of American Art until 1982. Lauren lived in New York for eight years, exhibiting her work in museums and galleries, as well as designing sets and costumes for theater and dance. In 1984, she was an artist-in-residence at both the Edward Albee Foundation and the Millay Colony for the Arts, where she began sculpting. In 1986, she was an artist-in-residence in the Dominican Republic at Altos de Chavon. Minnesota became her home in 1988, where she taught in schools as an artist-in-residence. In 1991, she received the McKnight Foundation Fellowship for sculpture. In 1994, she illustrated her first children's book, *Mud* by Mary Lyn Ray, which won the Minnesota Book Award for illustration, the IRA Children's Choice Award, and the Crayola Kids Best Book of the Year Award. Since *Mud*, Lauren has painted illustrations for *Scarecrow* by Cynthia Rylant; *Red Rubber Boot Day* by Mary Lyn Ray; and *Castles, Caves, and Honeycombs* by Linda Ashman. Lauren continues to illustrate books, sculpt, and paint in a huge Victorian house in Minneapolis where she lives with her husband and their two children.

CULLINAN AND GALDA'S

Literature and the Child

FIFTH
EDITION

PART ONE

The Books

chapter **1**

Children's Literature Yesterday, Today, and Tomorrow

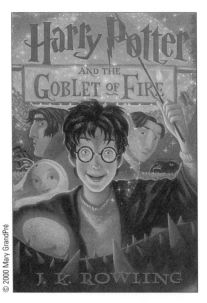

Harry Potter has captured the imagination of children and adults around the world.

Harry lay flat on his back, breathing hard as though he had been running. He had awoken from a vivid dream with his hands pressed over his face. The old scar on his forehead, which was shaped like a bolt of lightning, was burning beneath his fingers as though someone had just pressed a white-hot wire to his skin.

—J. K. ROWLING,
Harry Potter and the Goblet of Fire, p. 16

TWO OF THE MANY CHILDREN WHO HAVE BEEN CAPTURED BY THE Harry Potter books attend Churchill School in New York City. Churchill is a school for children with learning disabilities resulting from visual and auditory processing difficulties. Stephanie teaches a reading group with children who would be in fourth through sixth grade in general education settings. Her students have extremely advanced background knowledge, which gives them the ability to comprehend high-level material. However, their weak decoding skills and low sight-word recognition places them at a high second-grade reading level.

Despite this, two of Stephanie's students are reading the Harry Potter books at home, with the help of their parents. Although the books are written at a level too high for their decoding abilities, the boys are persisting. Even though they are having difficulties decoding, their desire to read these books remains strong.

Write me a letter explaining what is happening in the book you are reading at home.

Dear _____Stephanie_____,
I am reading the book _____Harry Potter and the chamber of secret_____
My favorite character right now is _____Harry_____
because _____he fun and he thinks his magic weak but it strong_____
Here are a few things I have read so far:
1) _____Dobby wants to stop Harry to go to Hogwarts._____
2) _____Dobby is saying there is bad Dangers._____
3) _____
I **predict** that _____Harry will beat tom ridle._____
_____
I will let you know if I am right!
Bye

Write me a letter explaining what is happening in the book you are reading at home.

Dear _____Stephanie_____,
I am reading the book _____Harry potter_____
My favorite character right now is _____Harry potter_____
because _____he is leaning to be a wister._____
Here are a few things I have read so far:
1) _____The praeinst dot like harry._____
2) _____The rell kid hads all the a tesh._____
3) _____Harry potter room is a closit_____
I **predict** that _____harry potter mite konn how to fly._____
_____
I will let you know if I am right!
Bye,

These letters were written by young readers who are determined to read the Harry Potter books.

The twenty-first century commenced with a series of books for children that made front-page headlines, broke all-time sales records, and caused major newspapers like the *New York Times* to start a separate list of best-sellers for children's books because the series had taken all the top spots in the comprehensive adult best-seller list. Those books were the Harry Potter books. The fourth book, *Harry Potter and the Goblet of Fire,* was released to the public on July 8, 2000. Many bookstores, wanting to comply with an agreed-upon opening date and yet take advantage of every minute of sales time, opened at one minute after midnight on July 7. Long lines of children, parents, and devoted readers formed outside bookstores waiting for doors to open; they couldn't wait to get inside to purchase the book.

Critics, educators, and politicians had proclaimed the death of reading. "Kids don't read anymore" was a common observation. The appearance of this series changed that perception. Teachers, librarians, and parents continually seek to find the right book for any particular child. Harry Potter proved to be the right book for millions of young readers, including those two boys for whom these books are a significant challenge. There are thousands more "right books" just waiting to be put into the hands of young readers. This text will help you learn how to do just that.

The Value of Literature

Literature entertains and it informs. It enables young people to explore and understand their world. It enriches their lives and widens their horizons. They learn about people and places on the other side of the world as well as ones down the street. They can travel back and forth in time to visit familiar places and people, to meet new friends, and to see new worlds. They can explore their own feelings, shape their own values, and imagine lives beyond the one they live.

Literature contributes to language growth and development. When children and young adults read or hear stories read to them, they learn new vocabulary. They encounter a greater variety of words in books than they will ever hear in spoken conversation or on television. Each learner builds an individual storehouse of language possibilities and draws upon that wealth in speaking, writing, listening, and reading. Young people who read literature have a broad range of experiences and language to put in their storehouse; they have greater resources upon which to draw than do people who do not read. Literature develops readers' facility with language because it exposes them to carefully crafted poetry and prose.

Literature helps students become better readers. Engaging stories, poetry, and information appeal to readers and entice them to read. The more they read, the better they get. The better they read, the more they learn. The more they learn, the more curious they become. Reading creates a self-fulfilling prophecy for success.

Literature helps students become better writers. When students read a lot, they notice what writers do. They see that writers use structured patterns in their writing. When readers write, they borrow the structures, patterns, and words from what they read.

Literature leads students to love reading. They seek out exciting stories, interesting information, and humorous poems. They turn to reading as a source of pleasure and entertainment.

Literature prompts students to explore their own feelings. They gain insight into human experience and begin to understand themselves better. When they explore their own feelings they also understand why others react as they do.

Literature reflects the millions of children and young adults worldwide who are diverse in their ethnicity, religion, nationality, and social and economic status but are united by commonalities of youth. Literature seeks to provide insights into the realities and dreams of young people and of the authors and illustrators who interpret those dreams and

realities. It reflects life throughout the course of time and across national boundaries. Literature keeps people's dreams alive through folklore, myths, legends, and fairy tales. It presents a vision of what is possible.

Books are a powerful force in the lives of children and young adults; teachers and librarians can take advantage of the force and power of books by shaping their curriculum around them. The richness and diversity that typifies literature today means that teachers, librarians, parents, and young people have a wealth of books from which to select.

Genres of Literature for Children and Young Adults

What is children's and young adult literature? A basic definition might state that it is books written for this particular audience; we might also add that it includes books that children and young adults enjoy and have made their own. Figure 1.1 summarizes the genres of children's and young adult literature discussed in this chapter.

There are many ways to categorize these books. One basic distinction can be made between narratives and nonnarratives. *Narratives* tell a story; they often have a character or

Figure 1 ✳ 1

Genres in Children's and Young Adult Literature

Category	Brief Description
Picture Books	Interdependence of art and text. Story or concept presented through combination of text and illustration. Classification based on format, not genre. All genres appear in picture books.
Poetry and Verse	Condensed language, imagery. Distilled, rhythmic expression of imaginative thoughts and perceptions.
Folklore	Literary heritage of humankind. Traditional stories, myths, legends, nursery rhymes, and songs from the past. Oral tradition; no known author.
Fantasy	Imaginative worlds, make-believe. Stories set in places that do not exist, about people and creatures that could not exist, or events that could not happen.
Science Fiction	Based on extending physical laws and scientific principles to their logical outcomes. Stories about what might occur in the future.
Realistic Fiction	"What if" stories, illusion of reality. Events could happen in real world, characters seem real; contemporary setting.
Historical Fiction	Set in the past, could have happened. Story reconstructs events of past age, things that could have or did occur.
Biography	Plot and theme based on person's life. An account of a person's life, or part of a life history; letters, memoirs, diaries, journals, autobiographies.
Nonfiction	Facts about the real world. Informational books that explain a subject or concept.

characters who encounter some kind of problem and work to resolve it. The narrative is developed through the *plot*—the temporal events or actions that lead to the solution of the problem—progresses to a *climax,* or solution to the prob-

lem, and ends with a *resolution,* or closure to the story. See Figure 1.2 for a summary of literary elements and how they function in narratives. *Nonnarratives* do not tell a story but rather present information. They may be argumentative,

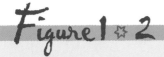

Literary Elements and How They Function in Narrative

Narratives contain certain literary elements that authors and illustrators work with to create memorable stories. They include setting, characterization, plot, theme, and style. We discuss criteria for each literary element.

Setting

Setting is the time and place in which the story events occur. Most stories are set in an identifiable place, but in others the setting is almost irrelevant. Broad brush strokes paint a picture of real or fanciful, rural or urban, home or school, and details are not necessary. Picture books with vague settings offer artists the opportunity to create images that the text does not define, to present their own vision of the physical surroundings of the story. In other stories setting is very important; details about a particular city, a part of the country, historical period, or a special place affect the development of the characters and the plot. Picture books supply information about the setting through illustrations, with art detailing the background the story demands.

Characterization

Characterization refers to the means by which an author establishes credibility of character. Characters are the personalities that populate literature. Like people, characters are multidimensional, with varied strengths and weaknesses, and over the course of time they grow and change. This change or development is most often due to the events that occur as the characters seek to resolve some kind of problem. Authors develop characters by describing how they appear, what they do or say, what others say about them or to them, what others do to them, and by what the narrator reveals. In picture storybooks, character is also interpreted by illustrators who reveal appearance, thoughts, and actions.

Plot

Plot refers to the sequence of story events. Most children want action in a story; they want something to happen, and happen fast. Most often, the plot is told in a straightforward chronology, but sometimes authors use a flashback, episodic, or alternating plot. Flashbacks provide background information about earlier events that led to the creation of the problem the character faces. Episodic plots highlight particular events in characters' lives, and alternating plots enable authors to tell stories from different points of view.

The plot usually revolves around a central conflict or conflicts. The most common conflicts are self against self conflicts in which the main character engages in an

internal struggle; self against other, in which the struggle is between the main character and one or more others; self against society, in which the main character combats societal pressures or norms; and self against nature, in which the main character struggles with the forces of nature.

Theme

A *theme* is a central, unifying idea. Often a theme is the reason authors write in the first place: A story allows them to say what they want to say. Many stories have several interwoven themes. Interpretation of themes varies among readers, with each student internalizing the theme in an individual way.

Style

Style is how an author writes—the vocabulary and the syntax that create the story. A tale is all in the telling, so style is an all-important criterion. The style needs to reflect the time, place, and characters in a way that is readable. Good dialogue sounds natural and descriptions are vivid and fresh.

Point of view is part of style. Many stories are told through the voice of the central character, who reports events in a first-person narrative, solely from his or her point of view. This allows readers to understand thoroughly the thoughts of the central character and often provokes a strong identification with that character. Another point of view, third-person limited, limits the information that is conveyed to what the central character could logically know, but it does so in a more detached tone, using third-person rather than first-person pronouns. Omniscient narrators, ones who are all knowing, can reveal the thoughts and inner feelings of several characters. They can move about in time and space to report events from an unbiased position. This point of view allows readers to know a great deal about what all of the characters are thinking and doing. It also puts more distance between the reader and the main character since the reader is viewing the protagonist through the narrator's eyes rather than viewing the story world through the protagonist's eyes.

Authors generally select one point of view and stick with it throughout the story, although some alternate between two or among several narrators. In a well-written story, the point of view provides a perspective that enriches the story.

Poets and authors who work with nonnarrative forms such as nonfiction also work with elements of style as they seek to illuminate the concept or idea that unifies their work. In the chapters that follow we discuss the unique qualities of the literary elements that define each genre.

descriptive, expository, or persuasive poetry, mood pieces, or nonfiction that presents concepts and information.

Another way that we categorize literature is by genre. A genre is a category of composition that has defining characteristics such as type of characters, setting, action, and overall form or structure. The defining characteristics of each genre help us to recognize the organization of the discipline of literature, provide a framework for talking about books, and help to guide our selection. The major genres include poetry, picture books, folklore, fantasy, science fiction, realistic fiction, historical fiction, biography, and nonfiction. These genres are based on content, with the exception of picture books, which are based on format. Each genre is discussed in detail in Chapters 2 through 10, but a brief overview is provided here.

Distinguishing features help readers recognize genres. For example, *poetry* contains short lines, rhyme, rhythm, and repetition. Ancient stories that were told by word of mouth are known as *folklore;* stories focusing on events that could happen in the real world today are works of *realistic fiction;* realistic stories set in the past are called *historical fiction;* *fantasy* stories could not happen in the real world; *science fiction* might happen in the future; and stories that tell the tale of a person's life are *biography.* Books that present information are called *nonfiction.*

Books may be narrative or nonnarrative, fiction or nonfiction, picture book or nonillustrated book. Fiction may be historical or contemporary, realistic or fantasy or science fiction. This textbook shows you how to recognize different genres; students will discover various types of books gradually, by reading them and by having them read to them. You will also learn to select books according to the grade level of students likely to enjoy reading them. In this text N = Nursery (birth to age 5), P = Primary (ages 5 to 8), I = Intermediate (ages 8 to 12), and A = Advanced (ages 12 and up).

POETRY AND VERSE

Poetry is the shorthand of beauty; its distilled language captures the essence of an idea or experience and encompasses the universe in its vision. Emerson suggests that poetry says the most important things in the simplest way. Lots of poetry is rhythmic and rhymed, appealing to the ear as well as to the mind and emotions. The best poetry and verse—from nonsense rhymes and limericks through lyrical and narrative poetry—shapes a taken-for-granted experience into thoughts extraordinary. X. J. Kennedy's *Uncle Switch: Loony Limericks* (P–I), John Ciardi's *The Reason for the Pelican* (I), Rebecca Dotlich's *Lemonade Sun* (P–I), Jane Yolen's *Color Me a Rhyme* (I), and Lee Bennett Hopkins's *Been to Yesterdays* (I–A) illustrate a range of poetic works.

Each year the number of books of poetry for children that are published is greater than the year before. The increase in quantity reflects an increase in interest over the past

DRAGONFLY

This sky-ballerina,
this glimmering
jewel,
glides in a gown
of lucid blue—
with wings that you
could *whisper* through.

© 1998 Jan Spivey Gilchrist

The most beautiful music I know
Is what Uncle makes, solemn and slow,
When a big violin
Tucks him under its chin
And then scrapes his bare chest with its bow.

© 1997 John O'Brien

"As all looks yellow to the jaundic'd eye."
— Alexander Pope

Yellow: A Haiku

One yellow leaf, yes!
But on the tree, in the woods,
One fades into all.

22

© 2000 Jason Stemple

Rebecca Dotlich's lyrics in **Lemonade Sun** are good for chanting, X. J. Kennedy's limericks in **Uncle Switch** lead to laughter, and Jane Yolen's beautiful language coupled with her son's breathtaking photographs cause us to look at color in a new way in **Color Me a Rhyme**.

decade. Parents have discovered that poetry lulls children to sleep at night. Teachers have discovered that poetry helps to teach beginning reading, to expand language development, and to enrich experiences across the curriculum. Researchers have found that poetry learned by heart in childhood stays in the mind for a lifetime. The National Council of Teachers of English Award for Poetry for Children, first awarded in 1977, calls attention to outstanding poets who write for children. See Appendix A for a complete listing of the winners. Today, publishers who once published only one or two poetry books per year create entire divisions devoted to poetry. Poetry is explored in Chapter 2.

PICTURE BOOKS

Picture books tell a story or develop an understanding of a concept through a unique combination of text and art. Unity between the text and the illustrations defines a high-quality picture book; together text and art create meaning greater than that conveyed by either art or words alone. The content of picture books may be realistic, historical, factual, or fanciful; format defines the genre.

The artistic possibilities of picture books attract skilled artists to the field. For instance, Marcia Brown, Maurice Sendak, Chris Van Allsburg, David Wisniewski, and Paul Zelinsky—talented artists who have won the Randolph Caldecott Medal—continue to produce beautiful books. Marcia Brown has received the Caldecott three times and adapts her artistic style to extend the meaning of each story. Compare her art in the three Caldecott winners: Perrault's *Cinderella* (P) (1954), *Once a Mouse* (P–I) (1961), and *Shadow* (P–I) (1982). Notice that she uses ethereal misty blues and pinks with delicate line for the dreamlike sequence of *Cinderella;* stylized woodcuts in earth tones for *Once a Mouse;* and collage silhouettes arising from black shadows in *Shadow.* Sendak also adapts his art to the story: He creates cartoonlike drawings of impish children for Krauss's *A Very Special House* (N–P) (1953); he draws ferocious adoring beasts in *Where the Wild Things Are;* and he develops elaborate romantic richness with subtle undertones in *Outside Over There* (P–I) (1981). Chris Van Allsburg is a talented draftsman who studied sculpture. His work shows solidity, mass, architectural forms, and play of light and shadow in *Ben's Dream* (P–I) (1982); he developed an exquisite storytelling art in *Polar Express* (P–I) (1985). A manuscript by Margret and H. A. Rey that preceded *Curious George* was discovered and published as *Whiteblack the Penguin Sees the World* (P) (2000). The penguin's curiosity and universal appeal is similar to that of Curious George.

Picture books for young children include small books made from cardboard that are just right for babies to grasp, look at, and chew. They also include pop-ups, cloth books, and alphabet books. Formerly, preschool and primary-

Everybody waved farewell to him.
"Come back with plenty of stories!" barked Seal.
"And bring us nice presents!" said Polar Bear.
"I promise!" shouted Whiteblack. "Good-bye!"

Margret and H. A. Rey created **Whiteblack** *before they wrote* **Curious George.** *Houghton editor Anita Silvey discovered the pre-1941 manuscript at the University of Southern Mississippi's de Grummond exhibit, "Curious George Comes to Hattiesburg: The Life and Work of H. A. and Margret Rey."*

grade children were the main audience for picture books, but today older readers also find picture books appropriate. We explore the art of picture books in Chapter 3 and the content of picture books in Chapter 4.

FOLKLORE

Folklore is composed of stories that were passed down through generations by word of mouth before they were ever written down. As such, they have no known author. As people told the stories to one another, they changed and molded them to suit their fancy. Eventually Charles Perrault and the Brothers Grimm, folklore collectors, wrote the stories down. Modern retellers continue to change the stories. Folklore reflects the values of the culture in which it grew; it encompasses universal experience as shaped by individual cultures.

Folklore comes in many shapes, including *nursery rhymes* from Mother Goose; *folktales* and *fairy tales* such as Cinderella or the Anansi stories; *tall tales* exaggerating the strength, and riches of America, such as John Henry and Paul Bunyan; *fables*—simply told, highly condensed morality tales—such as "The Boy Who Cried Wolf"; *mythology*, which explains the origins of the earth and the relation between humans and gods; *legends, epics,* and *hero tales* such as Robin Hood; *folksongs;* and *religious stories* from the Bible.

Folklore contains folktales from around the world and reflects an increasingly international view. Advances in transportation, communication, and technology have increased worldwide travel and global awareness; as a result we have more cross-cultural books for children that accurately portray other lands and cultures. This growth has occurred in all genres, but it is most notable in folklore. Similarly, as the composition of North America has become increasingly multicultural, folklore for children has expanded beyond

a predominantly Western European tradition to include folklore of many cultures, such as three recent Caldecott award winners. Simms Taback's ***Joseph Had a Little Overcoat*** (P) successfully combines text and illustrations to retell a Yiddish story. Paul Zelinsky draws upon French, Italian, and German origins for his version of ***Rapunzel*** (P–I). David Wisniewski retells a Jewish legend from Prague in ***Golem*** (P–I).

Internationally known artists lend their particular vision to traditional stories; they interpret classic tales in modern ways. Verna Aardema's interpretations of African folklore, Lawrence Yep and Jeanne Lee's Chinese lore, and Julius Lester and Virginia Hamilton's African-American folklore are among the fine stories that reflect today's global perspective. We discuss folklore in Chapter 5.

*Artists interpret folklore in ways that reflect the culture from which it arose. Zelinsky creates stunning oil paintings to reveal esoteric beauty, physical luxury, and a mother figure in **Rapunzel**. On page 13 (top), Taback uses die-cut pages in **Joseph Had a Little Overcoat** to show the holes in a worn-out overcoat that is being recycled into smaller garments. Wisniewski's **Golem** (bottom) masterfully uses layers of cut paper to create the saintly rabbi who brings to life a clay giant to help him watch over the Jews of sixteenth-century Prague. These artists all received the Caldecott Medal for their skillful aesthetic creations.*

The rabbi found Golem in the cemetery, gazing at the tombstones. "Joseph," he said softly. "Come here."

"No," said Golem.

"Why not?" asked the rabbi.

"The Jews are safe," Golem said. "Now you will return me to the earth."

"Yes," said Rabbi Loew. "Your purpose is at an end."

Golem regarded the setting sun. He raised his face to the fading light. "Father," said Golem, "will I remember this?"

"No," said Rabbi Loew. "You will be clay."

Golem leaned down to him. "Then I shall not obey you," he said.

"You have no choice, Joseph." The rabbi lashed out with his staff, erasing the first letter—*aleph*—from the word on Golem's forehead. At this, *emet*—Truth—became *met*: Death.

FANTASY

Fantasy is imaginative literature distinguished by characters, places, and events that could not happen in the real world. Animals can talk, inanimate objects have feelings, time follows the author's rules, and humans accomplish superhuman feats. Fantasy ranges from talking animal stories for very young children to complex novels that explore universal truths. Although fantasy stories could not possibly happen, they have carefully constructed plots, well-developed characters, and vivid settings to cause readers to suspend disbelief. Exemplary fantasy books include E. B. White's *Charlotte's Web* (P–I), Franny Billingsley's *The Folk Keeper* (I), Eva Ibbotson's *Island of the Aunts* (I), Kenneth Grahame's *Wind in the Willows* (I), and Maurice Sendak's *Where the Wild Things Are* (P). In *The Doll People* (I), Ann Martin and Laura Godwin tell the gripping mystery story of Annabelle, who tries to find her auntie who has been missing for 45 years.

The fantasy genre continues to grow as modern fantasy writers create powerful stories redolent with the legacy of folklore and ancient tales. Parodies of traditional tales, such as John Scieszka's *The True Story of the Three Little Pigs* (I) and *The Stinky Cheese Man and Other Fairly Stupid Tales* (I–A), enjoy tremendous popularity. Readers like books based on traditional folktales, such as Diane Stanley's *Rumpelstiltskin's Daughter* (P–I), Robin McKinley's *Beauty* and *Rose Daughter* (A), Gail Levine's *Ella Enchanted* (I–A), and Donna Jo Napoli's *Crazy Jack* (A). We explore fantasy in Chapter 6.

SCIENCE FICTION

Science fiction imaginatively extrapolates fact and theory: Stories project what could happen in another time through a logical extension of established theories and scientific principles. Science fiction describes worlds that not only are plausible, but also may exist someday. Scientific advances caused writers to speculate about the consequences of those advances; science fiction was the result. For example, space travel led to stories of space colonies and intergalactic wars. Garbage pileups led to stories of people and places drowning in garbage. In John Christopher's classic *The White Mountains* (A) a future world is reduced to a primitive society, and in Madeleine L'Engle's *A Wrinkle in Time* (I–A) Meg releases her brother from the grasp of evil. A Newbery Honor Book, *The Ear, the Eye, and the Arm* (A) by Nancy Farmer, reads like a detective mystery. Brian Pinkney has his major character in *Cosmo and the Robot* (P) take his damaged robot to an asteroid dump. Lois Lowry spells out a possible future world in *The Giver* (A) and *Gathering Blue* (A). A discussion of science fiction appears in Chapter 6. Teaching Idea 1.1 presents a way of helping young readers make the distinction between fantasy and realism.

REALISTIC FICTION

Realistic fiction (contemporary realism) is fiction set in modern times with events that could occur in the real world. Authors create characters, plot, and setting that stay within the realm of possibility.

Teaching Idea 1.1

Distinguish Between Fantasy and Realism

Choose two picture books—one realistic (it could possibly happen) and one fantasy (it could not happen). Read aloud both books; compare them on relevant points, as in the example below.

	Night Driving	The Blushful Hippopotamus
Genre:	Realistic	Fantasy
Characters:	Dad and son, nameless narrator	Roosevelt, Lombard, big sister, all talking animals
Plot:	Dad and son take a road trip at night	Big sister criticizes Roosevelt
Setting:	Highway	Any make-believe place
Theme:	Father-son relationship	Self-confidence gives courage
Details:	Where did the drivers go?	Are talking animals real or make-believe?
	How did the boy help Dad?	What gave Roosevelt confidence?

How did you know which story was real, and which one was make-believe? Which pictures and sentences prove it?

Coy, John, *Night Driving*. Peter McCarty, illustrator. Holt, 1996.
Raschka, Chris, *The Blushful Hippopotamus*. Jackson/Orchard, 1996.

Realistic fiction grapples with a wide range of human conditions and emotions. Writers address hunger, death, divorce, and homelessness as well as more traditional themes of growing up and making friends. They address the joys and complications of living in today's world. Katherine Paterson's *Bridge to Terabithia* (I) Cynthia Rylant's *Missing May* (I), Cynthia Voigt's *Homecoming* (I–A), Sharon Creech's *Walk Two Moons* (I–A), and Avi's *Nothing but the Truth* (A) explore serious issues such as death, abandonment, and freedom of speech. Carolyn Coman probes the pain of a grieving teenager in *Many Stones* (A). Joan Bauer follows a 16-year-old waitress, Hope Yancey, who tours the country in *Hope Was Here* (A).

Eve Bunting portrays homelessness in *Fly Away Home* (I), the Los Angeles riots in *Smoky Night* (I–A), and memories of the Vietnam War in *The Wall* (I), all realistic picture books. Realistic picture books also deal with happy times, as in *Sunflower* (P) by Miela Ford, and with personal concerns, as in *Hairs* (P) by Sandra Cisneros. Realistic fiction writers today write knowingly from many cultures and lifestyles. Many writers for the intermediate and advanced grades—Virginia Hamilton, Walter Dean Myers, Yoshiko Uchida, and Laurence Yep—produce books that reflect the true cultural diversity of America. We discuss realistic fiction in Chapter 7.

HISTORICAL FICTION

Historical fiction tells stories set in the past; it portrays events that actually occurred or possibly could have occurred. Authors create plot and character within an authentic historical setting. Today we are fortunate to have skilled authors writing from careful research and from various cultural perspectives. Historical fiction ranges from stories set in prehistoric times to those reflecting the issues and events of the twentieth century. The stories are usually told through the perspective of a child or young adult who is living life in a particular time and place. Taken altogether, historical fiction for children and young adults represents a broad range of voices and cultures. Teaching Idea 1.2 presents a way of helping students notice how setting helps distinguish contemporary fiction from historical fiction.

Although much historical fiction is written for intermediate and advanced-grade readers, such as Karen Hesse's *Stowaway* (I–A), there are many fine picture books—such as Eve Bunting's *Dandelions* (P–I), Yumi Heo's *Father's Rubber Shoes* (P–I), and Alice McGill's *Molly Bannaky* (illustrated by Chris Soentpiet) (P–I)—that bring the past to life for younger readers. We present historical fiction in Chapter 8.

*David Diaz creates bold paintings using various fabrics, torn paper, sections of corrugated cardboard, and textured collages to give a vivid intensity to the riot scenes that Eve Bunting describes in **Smoky Night**. In **Hairs**, a child describes how each person in the family has hair that is different—Papa's is like a broom, Kiki's is like fur, and Mama's smells like warm bread.*

Teaching Idea 1 ✿ 2

Distinguish Between Historical and Contemporary Realistic Fiction

Choose two books by the same author or two on the same topic. Choose one with a contemporary setting and one with a historical setting. Read and compare the books on relevant points. For example, compare two books by Lois Lowry, as shown here.

	Number the Stars	**See You Around, Sam!**
Genre:	Historical fiction	Contemporary realistic fiction
Characters:	Annemarie, Ellen Rosen	Sam, Anastasia Krupnik
Setting:	Denmark, 1939–1945	Suburb, contemporary time
Plot:	Nazi occupation encroaches	Sam tries to run away
Theme:	Friendship, courage	Home is the best place after all

How did you know which one was historical fiction and which one was contemporary realistic fiction? What evidence can you cite to prove your position/decision?

Lowry, Lois, *Number the Stars.* Houghton/Lorraine, 1989.
————, *See You Around, Sam!* Houghton/Lorraine, 1996.

BIOGRAPHY

Biography tells about a real person's life. The subjects of biography are usually people who were famous or who led exemplary lives, such as national leaders, artists, sports figures, writers, or explorers. Their stories may be told in picture books or in lengthy texts. In a book that contains biographies of several people (called a collective biography), author Judith St. George and illustrator David Small take a lighthearted look at 42 presidents in *So You Want to Be President?* (I–A). They point out some good things and some bad things about the job; they always take the humorous angle. Biographers also explore the lives of unknown citizens, as in Joan Hewett's *Hector Lives in the United States Now* (P–I).

Every biography bears the imprint of its author; although the story of the person's life provides the basic facts, the writer selects, interprets, and shapes elements to create an aesthetic work. Russell Freedman casts a new light on three famous people in his award-winning photobiography, *Lincoln* (I–A), and in *Eleanor Roosevelt* (I–A) and *The Wright Brothers* (A), both of which were Newbery Honor Books. He also creates vivid pictures of his subjects in *Martha Graham: A Dancer's Life* (A) and *Babe Didrikson Zaharias: The Making of a Champion* (A), both carefully researched biographies. Freedman describes how Lewis

Hine left teaching to become an investigative reporter in *Kids at Work: Lewis Hine and the Crusade Against Child Labor* (I–A).

Natalie Bober shows meticulous research in the way she interweaves excerpts from correspondence in *Abigail Adams: Witness to a Revolution* (A). Diane Stanley and her husband, Peter Vennema, bring life to historical figures in *William Shakespeare: Bard of Avon, Cleopatra,* and *Shaka, King of the Zulus* (all I–A). Albert Marrin explains how he acquires and verifies information about people and their times, and how he identifies recurring historical patterns, in *Sitting Bull and His World.* (A). Jim Giblin explains his subject's accomplishments and failures in *The Amazing Life of Benjamin Franklin* (I).

Like biographies, autobiographies are stories of a person's life, but they are written by the subjects themselves. A number of current authors have written their autobiographies: Lee Bennett Hopkins's *The Writing Bug* (P), James Howe's *Playing with Words* (P), and Laurence Yep's *The Lost Garden* (I–A). Helene Deschamps writes about her harrowing adventures as a spy for the French Resistance in *Spyglass* (A), and Anita Lobel discusses her childhood in Europe during World War II in *No Pretty Pictures* (A). The poet Juan Felipé Herrera tells about his own childhood in *The Upside Down Boy/El niño de cabeza* (P), a bilingual book. Tomie dePaola also tells his own story in *26 Fairmount Avenue* (P) and *Here We All Are* (P). Julie Cummins, formerly head of New York Public Library Services to Children, now editor in chief of *School Library Journal,* proposes the term *storyography* to describe a story built around a person's life. Storyographies may contain more story than biography, as in Jeanette Winter's *Georgia* (P), the life of the painter Georgia O'Keeffe. We discuss biographies in Chapter 9.

NONFICTION

Nonfiction books are informational sources that explain a subject. Children are naturally curious about the world they inhabit. They observe and explore, question and hypothesize about how this world works. Nonfiction outnumbers fiction 12 to 1 in most children's libraries and is available for children from preschool through the advanced grades.

Nonfiction presents information in a variety of formats: as picture books and photo-essays, as reproductions of original documents, as how-to-do-it manuals, or as direct expository texts. Nonfiction covers diverse topics, ranging from dinosaurs to endangered species, cathedrals to igloos, triangles to probability, artistic design to book construction. Many nonfiction books are works of art as well as works of fact. For example, David Macaulay's *Cathedral* and *Castle* (both I–A), Ron Hirschi's *Spring* (P), and Lynne Cherry's *A River Ran Wild* (I) are all as beautiful as they are informative. Rahel Musleah takes a standard Hebrew text for the Seder and adds stories, songs, dance, and drama in *Why on This Night? A Passover Haggadah for Family Celebration*

A President in your family tree is a plus. John Quincy Adams was John Adams' son. Theodore Roosevelt and Franklin Roosevelt were fifth cousins. Benjamin Harrison was William Harrison's grandson. James Madison and Zachary Taylor were second cousins.

The 2001 Caldecott Medal winner Author Judith St. George and illustrator David Small capture the humor behind the scenes in **So You Want to Be President?**

(1). She creates a meaningful and valued book. Illustrations in nonfiction books represent some of the best art to be found in children's books. For example, the *Eyewitness Books* series combines startlingly clear photographs and careful drawings to provide a wealth of information. Alphabet and counting books, once intended only for the very young, have sophisticated formats in which artists demonstrate their talents. Books designed to inform have evolved into books designed to inform and delight.

Informational books about any topic you might imagine appear on library shelves. Topics that become important in our lives appear in nonfiction for children; books about the environment reflect our growing concern for our planet. Outer space, world hunger, and natural science topics appear in children's books as rapidly as they appear in the daily newspaper. In *Liberty, the Statue of Liberty* (1) Lynn Curlee relates the story of the conception and completion of the Statue of Liberty; she describes Bartholdi's obsession with creating a monument that would compete with the Colossus of Rhodes. Five of Leonard Everett Fisher's excellent books about the craftsmanship of the colonial period were reissued in *The Architects, The Blacksmiths, The Limners, The Printers,* and *The Wigmakers* (1). We discuss nonfiction in Chapter 10.

These genres illustrate the breadth and depth of books available to children and young adults today, but it hasn't always been the case. The literature of yesterday looked quite different.

Children's and Young Adult Literature Yesterday

Literature written especially for children's pleasure is a recent development in history. In 1744 John Newbery (1713–1767) opened a bookstore in St. Paul's Churchyard, London, where he sold books for children. (He also published them.) Up until that time, children had been given chapbooks (crudely printed little books sold by peddlers or chapmen), battledores (folded sheets of cardboard covered with crude woodcuts of the alphabet or Bible verses), and hornbooks (small wooden paddles with lesson sheets tacked on with strips of brass and covered with a transparent sheet of cow's horn). These materials, like other books of their day, were intended for the instruction of children. One of Newbery's early books, *A Little Pretty Pocket-Book: Intended for the Instruction and Amusement of Little Master Tommy and Pretty Miss Polly,* contained the alphabet, proverbs, and rules of behavior. In 1765 Newbery published *The Renowned History of Little Goody Two Shoes,* a bittersweet story of orphan Marjorie Meanwell, who is overcome with gratitude when a

clergyman and his wife buy her a pair of shoes. She cries out, "Two shoes, Madam, see my two shoes." Newbery's books were meant to teach children proper behavior but did not threaten them with the standard fire and brimstone if they did not behave. The most prestigious U.S. award in children's books today is named in honor of John Newbery.

The Industrial Revolution helped to develop a middle class that had leisure time to read. Children, who had formed a large part of the workforce, were eventually released from the workplace and sent to school to learn to read and write. As child labor decreased, time to read increased, and children became literate; literature written especially for them became a reality.

Most children's books came to the United States from England. At first they were intended for instruction, but it soon became clear that the books nurtured children's imagination. The greatest among the imaginative books written for pleasure, Lewis Carroll's *Alice's Adventures in Wonderland* (1865), was soon reprinted in English-speaking countries all over the world. Other books from the same period, like George MacDonald's *At the Back of the North Wind* (1871) and Charles Kingsley's *The Water Babies* (1863), which described a make-believe world alongside a real one, are still read today. The revolutionary quality of Lewis Carroll's two books, *Alice's Adventures in Wonderland* (1865) and *Through the Looking Glass* (1871), derives from the fact that they were written purely to give pleasure to children. There is not a trace of a lesson or a moral in the books. Their publication gave rise to a new class of literature in English-speaking countries worldwide.

Early Canadian literature had a "survival" theme, something that is evident in Canada's first children's novel, Catharine Parr Traill's *Canadian Crusoes, A Tale of the Rice Lake Plains* (1852). Much later, allusions to Carroll's *Alice* books appeared in Dennis Lee's *Alligator Pie* (1974) and in Mordecai Richler's *Jacob Two-Two Meets the Hooded Fang* (1975). In Australia, the novels of Ethel Turner reflected the imitation of childhood rather than the realization of it. Her first and most famous book was *Seven Little Australians* (1894), which is still in print and is regarded as a classic. The best-known and best-loved talking animal (a koala) in Australian children's literature appears in Dorothy Wall's *Blinky Bill* (1933) and its sequels, but the first creatures invented for the bush were May Gibbs's Gumnut Babies in *Snugglepot and Cuddlepie* (1918) and its successors. During the 1920s a favorable climate for children's literature began to develop in New Zealand. Early books with a New Zealand setting had been preoccupied with the indigenous Maori people and with the land itself. Lady Barker, an early writer for adults, produced *Stories About* (1870), *A Christmas Cake in Four Quarters* (1871), and *Boys* (1874) for children. Esther Glen, a journalist, encouraged young writers and wrote *Six Little New Zealanders* (1917).

Nathaniel Hawthorne is considered the author of the first American book written specifically for children, *Won-*

Profile ☆ Louisa May Alcott

Louisa May Alcott Memorial Assoc.

Louisa May Alcott once said that she grew up in "genteel poverty." Her father held educational and social views that were ahead of his time. Her family's neighbors (Ralph Waldo Emerson, Henry David Thoreau, and Nathaniel Hawthorne) were outstanding intellectual leaders of the day. Although Louisa May Alcott was not rich in material things, her life was rich in books and ideas.

Louisa May Alcott began her life's work of rescuing her beloved family from chronic poverty by scribbling little stories for the ever-hungry magazine publishers. However, she was also deeply involved in the great social issue of her day: emancipation of the slaves.

She spent several months nursing wounded soldiers under deplorable conditions in a Civil War army hospital. Then, with her own health impaired, she returned home exhausted from this experience to produce her first serious book, *Hospital Sketches* (c. 1866). Its instant popularity inspired her to continue writing serious fiction. Her astute publisher, Thomas Niles, encouraged her to write "something for girls," and *Little Women* (1868) was the result. In its pages and in those of the several novels and dozens of short stories that followed, readers glimpse much of the popular culture of the times. *Little Women* is among the first and the finest examples of realistic fiction.

Louisa May Alcott herself was an avid reader. Through the character of Jo in *Little Women* we see the influence of John Bunyan's *Pilgrim's Progress* as well as that of Charles Dickens. Elsewhere in Alcott's work we hear the story of Rosamond (of *The Purple Jar*) retold and find occasional references to the novels of "dear Miss Yonge," one of Alcott's predecessors in writing family stories.

Many books followed *Little Women,* among them *An Old-Fashioned Girl* (1869), *Little Men* (1871), *Work* (1873), *Eight Cousins* (1874), *Rose in Bloom* (1876), *Under the Lilacs* (1877), *Jack and Jill* (1879), and *Jo's Boys* (1886). All have been reissued and are widely read. Alcott's short stories have also been reissued, including *Glimpses of Louisa: A Centennial Sampling of the Best Short Stories* by Louisa May Alcott (1968) and *An Old-Fashioned Thanksgiving* (1974, 1989).

Additional information about this important writer can be found in "Louisa May Alcott and the American Family Story" in *A Critical History of Children's Literature* by Cornelia Meigs et al.; in *Bronson Alcott: His Life and Philosophy* by F. B. Sanborn and W.T.A. Harris; in Cornelia Meigs's *Invincible Louisa;* and in Gretchen Anderson's *Louisa May Alcott Cookbook.* The cookbook, illustrated by Karen Milone, was started as a class project by a 9-year-old student. It re-creates recipes from nineteenth-century cookbooks for dishes mentioned in Alcott's books. Recipes for tarts, pies, plum pudding, and steak and potatoes accompany excerpts from the novels, while full-page drawings and text describe the life and work of Louisa May Alcott.

---

der Book (1851). However, England was the first and most continuous source of books for American children. It continued as a major source of literature for North American children for generations, and led the way to global publishing. American children made no distinction among British and American books or those from other countries. They read Carlo Collodi's *Pinnochio* (1833) from Italy, Johanna Spyri's *Heidi* (1881) from Switzerland, Selma Lagerlof's *The Wonderful Adventures of Nils* (1906–1907) from Sweden, and Antoine St. Exuperay's *The Little Prince* (1943) from France with equal enthusiasm.

The first child-labor laws, which were passed in 1907, freed children to go to school. As more children learned how to read and write due to universal first- through eighth-grade public schools, the quantity and the types of books published for them rapidly increased. At the same time new technology methods helped reduce publishing costs, and the public generosity of charitable individuals al-

lowed public library systems to rapidly develop, putting books in the hands of vast numbers of children worldwide. Howard Pyle (1853–1911) was considered a notable writer at the turn of the twentieth century. He published a story in *St. Nicholas* magazine and for many years continued to write fairy tales animated by the richness of the genuine folktale. Gradually he put more of his own thinking into the stories. His collection of fairy tales and verses, *Pepper and Salt* (1886), was followed by *The Wonder Clock* (1888).

Publishers began to establish departments of children's books. In 1919 the U.S. publishing house Macmillan launched a department devoted entirely to children's books. Louise Bechtel Seaman, who had worked as editor of adult books and who taught in a progressive school, was appointed department head. In 1922 Helen Dean Fish became the first children's book editor at Frederick A. Stokes and Company, and in 1923 May Massee took the leadership of the children's book department at Doubleday. In 1924, *The Horn Book*

Magazine was published by the Bookshop for Boys and Girls in Boston under the guidance of Bertha Mahony and Elinor Whitney. In 1933 May Massee moved from Doubleday to open a children's book department at Viking. Soon other publishers began to open children's book departments, and children's literature blossomed into the twentieth century. Modern picture books began to develop during the 1920s and 1930s, while in the 1940s through the 1960s, children's and young adult books became an increasingly important part of libraries, schools, homes, and publishing houses. Appendix E contains more details about the history of children's books, and Figure 1.3 lists some milestones in the history of literature for children and young adults.

Children's and Young Adult Literature Today

The spread of public libraries with rooms devoted to children's and teenagers' reading interests opened the floodgates, inviting an eager audience to read books and magazines and to listen to stories told aloud. Early publications sought to instill a community's values in the young, to socialize them, and to teach them. Over the past 150 years this approach has changed to reflect a broad spectrum of social values that

Figure 1 ☆ 3

Milestones in Literature for Children and Young Adults: Beatrix Potter to Harry Potter

1865	Lewis Carroll, *Alice in Wonderland*
1902	Beatrix Potter, *The Tale of Peter Rabbit*
	Rudyard Kipling, *Just So Stories*
	E. Nesbit, *Five Children and It*
	Walter de la Mare, *Songs of Childhood*
1904	J. M. Barrie, *Peter Pan*
1908	Kenneth Grahame, *The Wind in the Willows*
	L. M. Montgomery, *Anne of Green Gables*
1922	Margery Williams, *The Velveteen Rabbit*
1924	A. A. Milne, *When We Were Very Young*
1934	P. L. Travers, *Mary Poppins*
	Jean de Brunhoff, *The Story of Babar*
1936	Edward Ardizzone, *Little Tim and the Brave Sea Captain*
1938	Marjorie Kinnan Rawlings, *The Yearling*
1939	Ludwig Bemelmans, *Madeline*
	T. S. Eliot, *Old Possum's Book of Practical Cats*
1940	Maud Hart Lovelace, *Betsy-Tacy*
	Eric Knight, *Lassie Come-Home*
1941	Robert McCloskey, *Make Way for Ducklings*
	H. A. Rey, *Curious George*
1943	Esther Forbes, *Johnny Tremain*
1950	C. S. Lewis, *The Lion, the Witch, and the Wardrobe*
	Elizabeth Yates, *Amos Fortune: Free Man*
1952	Ben Lucien Burman, *High Water at Catfish Bend*
	Mary Norton, *The Borrowers*
	E. B. White, *Charlotte's Web*
1954	Lucy M. Boston, *The Children of Green Knowe*
	Rosemary Sutcliff, *The Eagle of the Ninth*
	J.R.R. Tolkien, *The Fellowship of the Ring*
1958	Philippa Pearce, *Tom's Midnight Garden*
1962	Joan Aiken, *The Wolves of Willoughby Chase*
	Madeleine L'Engle, *A Wrinkle in Time*
	Ezra Jack Keats, *The Snowy Day*
1963	Maurice Sendak, *Where the Wild Things Are*
1964	Louise Fitzhugh, *Harriet the Spy*
	Lloyd Alexander, *The Book of Three*
	Roald Dahl, *Charlie and the Chocolate Factory*
	Irene Hunt, *Across Five Aprils*
1968	Paul Zindel, *The Pigman*
	Ursula LeGuin, *A Wizard of Earthsea*
1971	Virginia Hamilton, *The Planet of Junior Brown*
	Robert C. O'Brien, *Mrs. Frisby and the Rats of NIMH*
1972	Richard Adams, *Watership Down*
1974	Robert Cormier, *The Chocolate War*
1977	Katherine Paterson, *Bridge to Terabithia*
1978	Janet and Allan Ahlberg, *Each Peach Pear Plum*
1983	Anthony Browne, *Gorilla*
	Mem Fox, *Possum Magic*
1985	Patricia MacLachlan, *Sarah, Plain and Tall*
1987	James Berry, *A Thief in the Village*
1998	J. K. Rowling, *Harry Potter and the Sorcerer's Stone*
2000	Philip Pullman, *The Amber Spyglass*

come from many cultures and cross international boundaries. Teaching Idea 1.3 describes a way to help young readers compare old and new books so they can understand how children's books have changed over the years.

INCREASING DIVERSITY

As books that reflected culturally diverse groups became an important issue in the book world, contemporary literature for children and young adults began also to reflect this diversity. The influx of immigrants to North America brought representative groups from all over the world. Readers wanted to see themselves in the books they read; unfortunately, that wish was slow to become a reality. Although we still have a long way to go before children's and young adult literature truly reflects the diversity of cultures within North America and around the world, we have made a great deal of progress. The scope of people represented in literature for children and young adults is broadening, and this

trend is gaining increasing strength as both established and new publishers stress cultural diversity in their lists. We discuss this in detail in Chapter 11.

We now have a global literature. Young people are able to view the experiences of those living in the midst of political turmoil and social upheaval. They can read about the emergence of alternate lifestyles. A global society gives voice to groups that were historically marginalized in previous literature, such as Native Americans, Aboriginals, African Americans, Asians, Maori, Inuit, women, and children. Organizations such as the International Board on Books for Young People and the International Reading Association, with members from around the world, help sustain a global perspective.

International coedition publishing ventures in which the same book is published simultaneously in several different countries are developed annually at the Bologna Book Fair, the Frankfurt Book Fair, the London Book Fair, and the Guadalajara Book Fair. Book editors dependent upon international coeditions must ensure that no distracting cultural

Teaching Idea 1 ☆ 3

Compare Picture Books of Past and Present

Ask students to gather picture books of the past from parents, grandparents, relatives, neighbors, friends, librarians, antique book dealers, flea markets, or garage sales. Visit a museum or library collection of historical children's books to examine the books at close range. If you cannot locate early books, select reprinted classics, such as *The Tale of Peter Rabbit, John Gilpin's Ride,* or *Peter Parley.* Choose early Newbery (*The Story of Mankind,* 1922) and Caldecott (*Animals of the Bible,* 1938) Medal winners. Also collect recent picture books, preferably award winners, to compare with the old. For instance, see *Emma's Rug* by Allen Say (Lorraine/Houghton, 1996), *Miss Bindergarten Gets Ready for Kindergarten* by Joseph Slate and illustrated by Ashley Wolff (Dutton/Penguin, 1996), or *Saving Sweetness* by Diane Stanley and illustrated by G. Brian Karas (Putnam, 1996). Prepare a comparison chart as shown here.

	Old Title	New Title
Color		
Style of Art		
Relation to Story		
Quality of Art as Art		
Attractiveness		
Visual Appeal		

Questions to Ask About the Books

* Do the books reflect the year they were published?
* Is the art coordinated with the text? Is it good art?
* How do children dress in the old and new books?
* Are the layout and design appealing?

indicators hinder a book's sales in other countries. For example, details such as whether cars drive on the left or right, whether milk bottles sit out on doorsteps, and whether government-funded schools are referred to as "private" or "public" must be correct or readers will be confused and possibly offended. The American editions of the Harry Potter books reflect this concern. The title of the first book was changed from **Harry Potter and the Philosopher's Stone** to **Harry Potter and the Sorcerer's Stone** for the American edition.

The increasing diversity in the book world is reflected in the establishment of awards that specifically recognize achievement in literature by and about particular cultural groups. For example, the Coretta Scott King Awards and the Pura Belpre Awards reflect the increasingly important presence of books by and about African Americans and Latinos.

BLURRING GENRE AND AGE BOUNDARIES

The genre boundaries of children's and young adult literature are blurred. Creative authors and illustrators ignore prior constraints and convention to expand genre, age-level appropriateness, and standard formats. Where does Louis Sachar's book *Holes* belong? Is it fantasy or realistic, historical or contemporary? Is it a spoof, or a coming-of-age story? Pam Muñoz Ryan's *Amelia and Eleanor Go for a Ride* (P) is a true story, but one that has been fictionalized. Increasing numbers of nonfiction books are written in a narrative frame; some call these "infostory" books. Is Jane Kurtz's *River Friendly, River Wild* (I)—a collection of poetry about the 1997 flood that devastated Grand Forks, North Dakota—

© 2000 Neil Brennan

*In free-verse poems, Jane Kurtz describes the Red River as a fat brown thread along a flat quilt stitching North Dakota and Minnesota together in **Run Friendly, Run Wild**. Melting snow changes the friendly river into a wild one, and homes are flooded to the roofs. Muted oil paintings soften the emotional impact of the poems.*

poetry, or a picture storybook? The same type of question can be asked regarding Karen Hesse's *Out of the Dust* (A)—Is it poetry or prose historical fiction?

Writers play with boundaries in format as well, as Paul Fleischman did in *Seedfolks* (A) and as Ellen Wittlinger did in *What's in a Name?* (A), both a series of interlocking stories. Walter Dean Myers blurred the boundaries in *Monster* (A), a combination of screenplay and journal entries. Diaries (both real and fictional), letters, and journals all provide a structure for books for young readers.

Can you give a picture book to preschool children and be confident that the story will not shock, offend, or be incomprehensible to them? The answer is *no*! Increasing numbers of picture books are being published for older readers, and many of them explore issues that are not appropriate for discussion by young children. Older children and young adults who look at lots of television, computer screens, videos, and movies become visual learners, and many of today's picture books are geared to their sensibilities. Although some worry about the amount of TV, video, and computer viewing done by older readers and claim that today's students do not read as well as students of two decades ago, comparison studies show that they read equally as well as earlier generations (Kamil, Mosenthal, Pearson, & Barr, 2000).

The market for young adult literature is expanding; this category of literature is enjoying an increase in both popularity and production. There are so many young adult novels published today that in 1999 the American Library Association established the Prinz Award specifically for young adult fiction. Along with the upsurge in popularity came a broadening of audience; now even august bodies such as the reviewers for *The Horn Book Magazine* distinguish between young adult fiction for middle school readers and that for high school readers. Generally, the fiction for middle grade readers is less intense, with less trauma than appears in books for older readers.

TECHNOLOGY AND COMMERCIALISM

Today's students are more familiar with icons, photographs, graphics, and visual displays than were students of the past. Technology makes it possible to illustrate fiction and nonfiction with strong, appealing visual images. Nonfiction is lavishly illustrated and often takes the form of a photoessay. We can view outer space photographs from NASA files and other images derived from digitalized cameras.

Commercialism has become dominant. The end of the twentieth century and the early years of the twenty-first century have been a time of dramatic change in the publishing world. We've seen mergers, buyouts, conglomerates, the establishment of new publishers, disagreements among

writers and publishers vying for electronic rights, and a continuous search for that one "big book" that would sell millions of copies and ensure financial success. Economics drives business in bookstores and in publishing companies that were once mom-and-pop operations. Once upon a time, the person who owned the publishing company also ran the company, made the publishing decisions, and knew the authors personally. No more. Big business practices make warm and friendly personal relationships between publishers and authors less likely.

Media plays a large role in the popularization of literature. Broadway plays (*The Lion King, Beauty and the Beast, The Little Mermaid*) add to the notoriety of books. Famous illustrators lend their skills to the big stage; Maurice Sendak designed the sets for the opera *For the Love of Three Oranges*. Television shows add to the popularity of *Clifford the Big Red Dog* and *Arthur*. Stuffed animals and other artifacts (Eric Carle's very hungry caterpillar, Lilly's purple plastic purse) can also be found for many book series with identifiable characters such as Winnie the Pooh, Peter Rabbit, Arthur, and D. W.

Increasingly, there's more to a book than just words and pictures. Books come with finger puppets and a finger puppet theater, felt board pieces to stuff into the tummy of the old lady who swallowed a fly, dress-up outfits such as the ones in the *To Be a Fairy Princess* book and gift pack. Lift the flaps and you can see all the animals on Old MacDonald's Farm. There are candy and cereal-related books: *Twizzlers Percentages Book* by Jerry Pallotta, *M & Ms Counting Book, Hershey Milk Chocolate Fractions Book, Hershey Milk Chocolate Kisses Addition Book, Reese's Pieces Count by Fives Book,* and *The Cheerios Counting Book*.

Children's and young adult literature now encompasses stories, poetry, and nonfiction in every medium. In

Children extend their imaginative play by pretending book characters come to life in stuffed animals and dolls.

© Marguerite Ellinger

addition to books, the media explosion offers computers, film, videos, CD-ROM products, videodiscs, microcomputer software, audiocassettes, interactive games, and the Internet to a visually oriented audience. What might this mean for tomorrow?

Children's and Young Adult Literature Tomorrow

The difficulty of predicting the future of children's books became easier when Roger Sutton, editor in chief of *The Horn Book Magazine,* devoted an entire issue (November/December 2000) to the topic. He asked several literary critics to hypothesize just how children's literature might look in the new millennium. He also asked a number of writers to choose one book from the twentieth century that he or she would most like to see survive into the twenty-second. Among those selected were Robert McCloskey's *Make Way for Ducklings* (P), selected by Natalie Babbitt; Phillipa Pearce's *Tom's Midnight Garden* (I), selected by Susan Cooper; Frances Hodgson Burnett's *The Secret Garden* (I), selected by Lois Lowry; T. H. White's *The Once and Future King* (A), selected by Jane Yolen; E. B. White's *Charlotte's Web* (I), selected by Katherine Paterson, and Natalie Babbitt's *Tuck Everlasting* (I–A), selected by Tim Wynne-Jones. Other professionals in the field of children's and young adult books selected 100 books that shaped the twentieth century. These are listed in the Booklist at the end of this chapter.

Leaders in children's and young adult literature also expressed their views about the future of the field. Stephen Roxburgh, president and publisher of Front Street, Inc., hopes that we will stop trying to "protect" children through censorship. He expresses concern, however, about the "few-holds-barred" application of mass marketing and merchandising techniques used to sell books. He says that we are reaching into young people's minds and pockets by whatever means possible, barraging them with powerful, exploitative, sophisticated media assaults and treating them as mature, fiscally responsible adults. Lolly Robinson, designer and production manager for The Horn Book, Inc., thinks positively about computer art, considering it to be a new medium that must be mastered skillfully to be good. Christine Heppermann, a reviewer for *The Horn Book Magazine* and member of the editorial board of the *Riverbank Review,* believes that e-books can make a contribution, because young folks associate computers with play, not work. She praises the possibilities of the links readers can make to check out the accuracy of an author's research. Betty Carter, professor of children's and young adult literature at Texas

Women's University, states that a choice between books and electronic sources is unnecessary. Each has already developed its strengths and we should use both. Writers print their e-mail addresses and home page URLs in books, they cross-reference Web sites, they go beyond books to give additional information and instruction. What is now considered nonfiction will come packaged in a variety of formats, including bound books, computer programs, Internet sites, and products yet to be imagined. Carter says that nonfiction books will survive all the electronics and the Internet, but they will change because of the vast array of easily accessible information the Internet provides. Betsy Hearne, professor of children's literature and folklore at the University of Illinois, believes that the oral tradition of storytelling will survive and that we can use the electrified global community to blur the boundaries between tellers and listeners.

Given the history and durability of children's and young adult literature, the future will encompass the best and the worst of the past. We will have more international literature, attempts at censorship will continue, global economics will play a stronger role, readers will have ready access to interviews with authors and illustrators on the Internet, and more culturally diverse writers and artists will present their culture more accurately.

Selecting Literature for Children and Young Adults

Books can play a significant role in the life of the young, but the extent to which they will do so depends upon the adults surrounding them. Books and children aren't made of velcro; they don't stick to each other without a little help from significant others, including parents, grandparents, teachers, librarians, community leaders, Scout leaders, hospital volunteers, and others who come into contact with them. Adults are responsible for determining a child's literary heritage by selecting and presenting nursery rhymes, traditional tales, and great novels. This selection process is neither easy nor without pitfalls. Knowing the literature is important. Knowing children and community is equally important.

CENSORSHIP OR SELECTION

Recently, books about topics that had never before been included in children's or young adult literature have been published. For example, Ann Turner's *Learning to Swim: A Memoir* (A) conveys in prose poetry the feelings of a girl who loses her sense of security and joy when an older boy who lives nearby sexually abuses her. Laurie Halse Anderson's main character in *Speak* (A) remains silent for most of the novel but finally reveals that she has been sexually abused and identifies her attacker. Walter Dean Myers's *Monster* (A) involves the murder of a Korean storekeeper and the trial for murder of a teenage boy.

The wide range of topics covered in children's and young adult literature gives young people access to a comprehensive picture of their world; it also invites serious attempts to censor what they read. Many people feel that the young should be allowed to grow as carefree children without facing difficult issues; others believe that difficult issues should be presented in books that reflect the real world children face. Most professional organizations, such as the American Library Association (ALA), International Reading Association (IRA), and the National Council of Teachers of English (NCTE) believe that parents have the right to decide what their own children read but not the right to tell other people's children what they should read. Banned Books Week calls attention to books that continue to be banned, such as *Catcher in the Rye* (J. D. Salinger), *Are You There, God? It's Me, Margaret* (Judy Blume), and *Harry Potter and the Goblet of Fire* (J. K. Rowling).

Sometimes books that teachers and librarians choose for school study provoke criticism from parents or community members. Often parents simply request that their child not read a particular book; it is easy to make provisions for that. Sometimes, however, an individual parent, school board member, or member of the larger community will request that no child be allowed to read a particular book; this is a bigger problem.

Suppressing reading material is *censorship,* a remedy that creates more problems than it solves. Choosing reading material that does not offend our taste, however, is *selection*—not censorship. Censorship is the attempt to deny others the right to read something the censor thinks is offensive. Selection is the process of choosing appropriate material for readers according to literary and educational judgments.

The National Council of Teachers of English differentiates between selection and censorship in five dimensions: (1) Censorship *excludes* specific materials; selection *includes* specific material to give breadth to collections. (2) Censorship is *negative;* selection is *affirmative.* (3) Censorship intends to *control* the reading of others; selection intends to *advise* the reading of others. (4) Censorship seeks to *indoctrinate and limit access* to ideas and information, whereas selection seeks to *educate and increase access* to ideas and information. (5) Censorship looks at specific aspects and *parts of a work in isolation,* whereas selection examines the relationship of *parts to each other and to a work as a whole* (1983, p. 18).

The controversy surrounding many books is rooted in a blatant attempt to impose censorship, to limit student access to materials, and to impose the religious and political views of a small segment of society on those whose views may differ. The International Reading Association, the National Council of Teachers of English, the American Library Association, and the National Coalition Against Censorship condemn attempts by self-appointed censors to restrict students' access to quality reading materials. Professional associations and most school districts have established procedures for dealing with attempts at censorship. School media specialists or principals need to have a standard process to follow if a book is challenged.

The National Council of Teachers of English states its beliefs about censorship in *The Students' Right to Read* (1972) and *The Students' Right to Know* (1982). The documents suggest procedures to follow when a book is challenged. The NCTE statement explains the threat that censorship poses to education, the teacher's role in challenging censorship, and the responsibility of the community. (A copy of the citizen's request form appears in Figure 1.4.) The procedures follow these general steps.

1. Establish book selection procedures *before* the censors come. Make your procedures public. Keep the community informed and involved. If you select wisely, you lessen the chances of an unpleasant experience.
2. Involve professional librarians, teachers, parents, administrators, and lay community members in the book selection process.
3. When complaints are registered, have them put in writing.
4. Ask the person who makes the complaint to read the entire book and put the incident or language in question in context.
5. Meet with the person who makes the complaint to discuss alternatives.

Never before have we had so many beautiful books and such high-quality books from which to choose. Children and young adults deserve to benefit from this wealth of treasures. There are wonderful books to share but we need informed judgment to select them. Once you become familiar with the various genres in contemporary children's and young adult literature, and once you learn the types of books your students prefer, you will find many ways to use books in the classroom. Part Two of this text discusses the interaction of children with books—specifically, how carefully selected, culturally diverse literature enhances children's appreciation of their world, and how literature can be used effectively across the curriculum.

It is important to build a diverse collection, because culturally diverse books portray the uniqueness of people while demonstrating a common humanity that connects us all. Human needs, emotions, and desires are similar; books can help us appreciate the similarities as well as celebrate the uniqueness of cultural groups. North America, once

Figure 1 ✲ 4

Citizen's Request for Reconsideration of a Work

Paperback _____

Author _____   Hardcover _____

Title _____

Publisher (if known) _____

Request initiated by _____

Telephone _____ Address _____

City _____ Zip Code _____

Complainant represents

_____ Himself/Herself

_____ (Name organization) _____

_____ (Identify other group) _____

1. Have you been able to discuss this work with the teacher or librarian who ordered it or who used it?

   Yes _____ No _____

2. What do you understand to be the general purpose for using this work?

   a. Provide support for a unit in the curriculum?

      Yes _____ No _____

   b. Provide a learning experience for the reader in one kind of literature?

      Yes _____ No _____

   c. Other _____

   _____

3. Did the general purpose for the use of the work, as described by the teacher or librarian, seem a suitable one to you?

   Yes _____ No _____ If not, please explain. _____

   _____

4. What do you think is the general purpose of the author in this book? _____

   _____

5. In what ways do you think a work of this nature is not suitable for the use the teacher or librarian wishes to carry out?

   _____

6. Have you been able to learn what is the students' response to this work?   Yes _____ No _____

7. What response did the students make? _____

   _____

8. Have you been able to learn from your school library what book reviewers or other students of literature have written about this work?   Yes _____ No _____

9. Would you like the teacher or librarian to give you a written summary of what book reviewers and other students have written about this book or film?   Yes _____ No _____

10. Do you have negative reviews of the book?   Yes _____ No _____

11. Where were they published? _____

12. Would you be willing to provide summaries of the reviews you have collected?   Yes _____ No _____

13. What would you like your library/school to do about this work?

    _____ Do not assign/lend it to my child.

    _____ Return it to the staff selection committee/department for reevaluation.

    _____ Other—Please explain.

14. In its place, what work would you recommend that would convey as valuable a picture and perspective of the subject treated? _____

    _____

Signature _____

Date _____

Figure 1 ✳ 5

Criteria for Good Books by Genre

	Text	Illustration
Poetry	Rhythmic, sensory images.	Interpret beyond literal meaning.
Folklore	Patterned language, fast-paced plot. Sounds like spoken language.	Interpretive of the tale and cultural origins.
Fantasy	Believable, consistent, logical world. Clearly defined conflict. Strong characterization.	Extends fanciful elements; reflects characterization and events.
Science Fiction	Speculative, extrapolation of fact. Hypotheses about life in untraveled worlds.	Visualizes imaginative worlds; reflects characterization and events.
Realistic Fiction	Story is possible, reasonable, plausible. Well-defined conflict; strong characterization.	Verisimilar; reflects mood, characterization, and events accurately.
Historical Fiction	Setting affects plot; details and language in keeping with period.	Authentic images of the period.
Biography	Story of a person's complete life or an interesting part of the person's life.	Authentic images of life segments.
Nonfiction	Clarity; factual accuracy.	Clarifies and extends concepts.

considered a melting pot where cultural differences disappeared, is more like a patchwork quilt today—patches of varying colors, textures, shapes, and sizes, all held together by a common thread of humanity (Jackson, 1992).

Children's books offer opportunities for building background knowledge and understanding about the world. Picture books, poetry, folklore, realistic and historical fiction, biographies, and nonfiction that celebrate cultural diversity are available for a wide range of readers. Culturally diverse books help achieve the goal of cross-cultural understanding. We discuss building a culturally diverse collection in Chapter 11, and we describe how these books can be used in the classroom in Chapters 13 and 14.

Selecting books to use in classrooms is a multidimensional task. First, think of all the excellent pieces of literature you want your students to know about, and, second, think of how literature can enrich your curriculum in every subject area. Because of the diversity and richness in children's literature today, your students' experiences with books can be infinitely varied. With so much to choose from, we, as teachers, can select high-quality literature: books that use interesting language in creative ways that develop important ideas that are potentially interesting to children and (through picture books) that contain illustrations that are

artistically excellent. Criteria for selecting each genre are summarized in Figure 1.5. We apply them in each genre chapter, and they form the basis for our discussion of building a culturally diverse collection in Chapter 11.

Keeping Up with New Books

The voluminous body of high-quality children's literature shows that the field attracts talented writers and illustrators. Creative people respond to and change their world; innovation is abundantly evident in the children's book world. The number of books published continues to grow, which makes selection even more difficult. Our job as teachers, librarians, and parents is to select the best from the vast array of books. The primary goal of this textbook is to help you recognize good literature and to develop your own criteria for selecting quality material. We can turn to review journals, awards, and other resources that call attention to new literature for children. As poet Walter de la Mare stated, "Only the rarest kind of best is good enough for children" (1942, p. 9).

REVIEW JOURNALS

Sources of information about new children's books include review resources: *Booklinks, Booklist, Bulletin of the Center for Children's Books (BCCB), The Horn Book Magazine, The Horn Book Guide, The New Advocate, Publisher's Weekly, The Riverbank Review, School Library Journal.* Although not primarily review journals, both *Language Arts* and *The Reading Teacher* contain book reviews written by teachers. Descriptions of these journals are found in Appendix B.

BOOK AWARDS

Excitement in the children's book world reaches fever pitch in mid January, when the Newbery and Caldecott Medal books are selected. Two separate selection committees, one for the Newbery and one for the Caldecott, read *all* the recommended books published during the year and meet for several days to decide which books will receive the prestigious awards. Waiting to hear who won the Newbery and Caldecott Medals is like waiting for the announcement of the winner of the Pulitzer Prize for Literature.

Why are these awards so important? Experts declare that the winners are the outstanding examples of children's literature for the year. The awards have significant educational, social, cultural, and financial impact. Books that receive the awards will be read by millions of children around the world. In America alone, every public and school library will purchase the award-winning books. Winning one of the awards, therefore, also guarantees considerable financial reward for the author, illustrator, and publisher. The awards receive widespread media attention, and winning authors and illustrators receive numerous speaking invitations.

The John Newbery Medal

Frederic G. Melcher, editor of *Publishers Weekly* magazine, donated and named the award as a tribute to John Newbery (1713–1767), the first English publisher and bookseller of children's books. The award, administered by the Association for Library Services to Children of the American Library Association, was established in 1922 and has been awarded annually ever since. The Newbery Medal is given for the most distinguished contribution to literature for children published in the United States during the year. Judgment is based on the literary quality of the text. See Appendix A for a listing of the Newbery winners and honor books.

The Randolph Caldecott Medal

In 1937, Frederic G. Melcher proposed an award for picture books named in honor of Randolph Caldecott (1846–1886), the English illustrator. Caldecott was one of the first to put action and liveliness into illustrations for children. This award, administered by the Association for Library Services to Children of the American Library Association, has been awarded annually since 1938. The Caldecott Medal is given annually to the illustrator of the most distinguished picture book published in the United States. See Appendix A for a listing of Caldecott winners and honor books.

There are several other major awards, such as the Coretta Scott King Awards, the Pura Belpre Awards, and the Prinz Awards, described above, given in the United States and other countries around the world. Many of them are described in Appendix A.

ELECTRONIC DATABASES FOR CHILDREN'S LITERATURE

Teachers and students can access an infinite amount of current information about children's books, authors, illustrators, professional publications, teaching ideas, library collections, conferences, and other activities through computerized databases, the Internet, and the World Wide Web. You need access to the Internet, a search engine (for example, InfoTrac College Edition®, Yahoo, Excite, Infoseek, AltaVista, or another one), and a few key terms. Once you are on the Internet, perform a simple search by typing in some key terms: "children's literature," "children's books," "children's authors," or "illustrators." You'll find numerous Web sites to help you in the study of children's literature.

Many authors, including Janet Stevens, Jane Yolen, and Lois Lowry, have a home page. At the home page you can initiate a conversation, ask questions, learn about the authors' new books, and find out about their speaking appearances. Many publishers have programs online that provide access to teaching ideas, books, and author information. Several publishers sponsor authors, illustrators, librarians, teachers, book reviewers, and editors for online interviews. See Figure 1.6 for helpful electronic sites.

Summary

The story of children's literature is intertwined with the social, political, and economic history of the world. Children's books are shaped by prevailing views of what adults believe children should be taught, by the amount of time children have to explore books, and by competing sources of entertainment available to children. Today we have a wealth of literature for children. We have moved from crude hornbooks and religious tracts to books with artistic and literary merit. Children are the beneficiaries of this wealth.

Exploring the field of children's literature can seem overwhelming at first, but knowledge about books is addictive: The more you know, the more you want to know and to share with children. With each new day there is more to know. Enjoy!

Figure 1 ☆ 6

Electronic Databases for Children's and Young Adult Literature

Beginning Literacy

These are good for children learning to read and write:

www.lil-fingers.com/abc/by/html

www.learningplanet.com/parents/alphabet

www.sesameworkshop.org/sesamestreet/coloringpages/
0.5903.00.html

Children's and Young Adult Literature

www.acs.ucalgary.ca/~dkbrown/　A reliable source with a search function for literature resources. Located at the University of Calgary, Canada.

www.ala.org　Access the American Library Association and the awards they administer.

www.bookwire.com　Switch back and forth among *School Library Journal, Publisher's Weekly,* and *Library Journal.* Book Reviews. You'll visit this Web site frequently.

www.britannica.com　Access to the *Encyclopedia Britannica.* Full-text articles free of charge.

www.carolhurst.com　Carol Hurst is an informed book person. She gives lively discussions of books to use with suggested thematic units.

www.lcweb.loc.gov　The Library of Congress is the place to find book titles by a specific author. Click on "using library catalog" and "other libraries' online catalog." Conduct a simple search by last name of author, first name. Click on "Search."

www.nationalgeographic.com/features/index.html National Geographic has several interactive activities such as finding the hidden animals in a forest and learning about them.

www.ncte.org　Access the National Council of Teachers of English and the awards they administer.

www.reading.org　Access the International Reading Association and the awards they administer.

Writing Resources

www.poetryzone.ndirect.co.uk/　Submit your own poetry here.

www.realkids.com/club.shtml　Young writers' clubhouse. Pick up tips and ideas for writing.

 Read the articles in the November/December 2000 issue of *The Horn Book Magazine.* Then discuss how you think literature might change within the next 10 years. What technologies will influence how children and young adults read? Will time on the Internet and at computer games impact time spent reading just as television did in the twentieth century?

Booklist

One Hundred Books That Shaped the Century

Four librarian book experts (Karen Breen, Ellen Fader, Kathleen Odean, and Zena Sutherland) chose 100 books that shaped the twentieth century. An asterisk (*) indicates the book was a unanimous first-round selection. A double asterisk (**) indicates the *author* was a unanimous first-round selection, but there were differences of opinion over which works to include.

Aardema, Verna, *Why Mosquitoes Buzz in People's Ears: A West African Tale*

**Alexander, Lloyd, *The High King*

Avi, *The True Confessions of Charlotte Doyle*

*Babbitt, Natalie, *Tuck Everlasting*

*Bemelmans, Ludwig, *Madeline*

Bishop, Claire Huchet, *The Five Chinese Brothers*

*Blume, Judy, *Are You There, God? It's Me, Margaret*

*Brown, Margaret Wise, *Goodnight Moon*

Bunting, Eve, *Smoky Night*

Burnett, Frances Hodgson, *The Secret Garden*

Burnford, Sheila, *The Incredible Journey: A Tale of Three Animals*

Burton, Virginia Lee, *Mike Mulligan and His Steam Shovel*

Byars, Betsy, *Summer of the Swans*

Carle, Eric, *The Very Hungry Caterpillar*

**Cleary, Beverly, *Ramona the Pest*

Cole, Brock, *The Goats*

Cole, Joanna, *The Magic School Bus at the Waterworks*

Cooper, Susan, *The Dark Is Rising*

*Cormier, Robert, *The Chocolate War*
Cresswell, Helen, *Ordinary Jack*
Crews, Donald, *Freight Train*
Dahl, Roald, *Charlie and the Chocolate Factory*
DePaola, Tomie, *Strega Nona*
*Fitzhugh, Louise, *Harriet the Spy*
Fleischman, Paul, *Joyful Noise: Poems for Two Voices*
Fox, Paula, *The One-Eyed Cat*
*Frank, Anne, *The Diary of a Young Girl*
*Freedman, Russell, *Lincoln: A Photobiography*
**Fritz, Jean, *And Then What Happened, Paul Revere?*
Gag, Wanda, *Millions of Cats*
Garden, Nancy, *Annie on My Mind*
*George, Jean Craighead, *Julie of the Wolves*
Grahame, Kenneth, *The Wind in the Willows*
**Hamilton, Virginia, *M. C. Higgins, the Great*
**Hamilton, Virginia, *The People Could Fly: American Black Folktales*
Henkes, Kevin, *Chester's Way*
Hesse, Karen, *Out of the Dust*
Hinton, S. E., *The Outsiders*
Hoban, Tana, *Shapes and Things*
Holling, Holling C., *Paddle-to-the-Sea*
*Keats, Ezra Jack, *The Snowy Day*
Kerr, M. E., *Dinky Hocker Shoots Smack*
Kipling, Rudyard, *Just So Stories*
*Konigsburg, E. L., *From the Mixed-Up Files of Mrs. Basil E. Frankweiler*
Lauber, Patricia, *The Eruption and Healing of Mt. St. Helens*
Lawson, Robert, *Rabbit Hill*
LeGuin, Ursula, *A Wizard of Earthsea*
*L'Engle, Madeleine, *A Wrinkle in Time*
*Lewis, C. S., *The Lion, the Witch, and the Wardrobe*
Lindgren, Astrid, *Pippi Longstocking*
*Lobel, Arnold, *Frog and Toad Are Friends*
**Lowry, Lois, *Anastasia Krupnik*
**Lowry, Lois, *The Giver*
**Macaulay, David, *Cathedral*
**Macaulay, David, *The Way Things Work*
*MacLachlan, Patricia, *Sarah, Plain and Tall*
Marshall, James, *George and Martha*
Martin, Bill, Jr., and John Archambault, *Chicka Chicka Boom Boom*
**McCloskey, Robert, *Make Way for Ducklings*
McCord, David, *Far and Few*

McKinley, Robin, *The Hero and the Crown*
McKissack, Patricia, *Mirandy and Brother Wind*
Merrill, Jean, *The Pushcart War*
*Milne, A. A., *Winnie-the-Pooh*
Minarik, Else, *Little Bear*
Montgomery, L. M., *Anne of Green Gables*
Myers, Walter Dean, *Fallen Angels*
*O'Dell, Scott, *Island of the Blue Dolphin*
*Paterson, Katherine, *Bridge to Terabithia*
Paulsen, Gary, *Hatchet*
Pearce, Philippa, *Tom's Midnight Garden*
Piper, Watty, *The Little Engine That Could*
*Potter, Beatrix, *The Tale of Peter Rabbit*
Raschka, Chris, *Yo! Yes?*
Raskin, Ellen, *The Westing Game*
Rey, H. A., *Curious George*
Rowling, J. K., *Harry Potter and the Sorcerer's Stone*
Scieszka, John, *The Stinky Cheese Man and Other Fairly Stupid Tales*
*Sendak, Maurice, *Where the Wild Things Are*
*Seuss, Dr., *The Cat in the Hat*
Silverstein, Shel, *Where the Sidewalk Ends: Poems and Drawings*
Singer, Isaac Bashevis, *Zlateh the Goat*
Slepian, Jan, *The Alfred Summer*
Slobodkina, Esphyr, *Caps for Sale: A Tale of a Peddler, Some Monkeys and Their Monkey Business*
**Steig, William, *Sylvester and the Magic Pebble*
Steptoe, John, *Stevie*
Sutcliff, Rosemary, *The Lantern Bearers*
Taylor, Mildred, *Roll of Thunder, Hear My Cry*
Tolkien, J.R.R., *The Hobbit*
Travers, P. L., *Mary Poppins*
**Van Allsburg. Chris, *The Polar Express*
**Voigt, Cynthia, *Homecoming*
Wells, Rosemary, *Max's First Word*
*White, E. B., *Charlotte's Web*
*Wilder, Laura Ingalls, *Little House in the Big Woods*
Young, Ed, *Seven Blind Mice*
Zelinsky, Paul O., *Rumpelstiltskin*
Zindel, Paul, *The Pigman*
Zolotow, Charlotte, *William's Doll*

"One Hundred Books That Shaped the Century," *School Library Journal* 46, no. 1 (January 2000): 50–58.

Poetry and Verse

BY MYSELF

When I'm by myself
And I close my eyes
I'm a twin
I'm a dimple in a chin
I'm a room full of toys
I'm a squeaky noise
I'm a gospel song
I'm a gong
I'm a leaf turning red
I'm a loaf of brown bread
I'm a whatever I want to be
An anything I care to be
And when I open my eyes
What I care to be
Is me

—ELOISE GREENFIELD, from *Honey, I Love*

MARILYN SCALA USES POETIC LANGUAGE TO DISCUSS POETRY WITH HER first-grade students, who are a multicultural mix of African Americans, Latinos, and representatives of other cultural groups. She chose the Greenfield poem because it enriches the theme of their studies, which is "All About Me." The goals for the students include learning to read and write, learning about themselves, learning to value cultural traditions, and appreciating their unique talents.

Marilyn printed Eloise Greenfield's poem on large chart paper for all the students to see. She points to each word as she reads the poem aloud several times.

Children chime in quite naturally to say some of the words along with her. Marilyn moves from reading aloud to shared reading as more student voices join the chorus of readers. They talk about Eloise Greenfield, this poem, and others she has written. They discuss some of the images the poet creates.

Marilyn says, "Close your eyes and think about what you would like to be." Jamal: "A parrot pecking at a tree." Maritza: "An angel in Mexico." Marilyn writes down each child's dream as they create their own "By Myself" poem. They discuss which lines should come in what order and continue working on the collaborative poem until it turns out this way:

BY MYSELF

When I'm by myself
And I close my eyes
I'm a heart on Valentine's Day
I'm an angel in Mexico
I'm a clown at a party
I'm a heart on a cake
I'm a red bird flying
I'm a parrot pecking at a tree
I'm a purple magic marker
I'm a black-and-white dog
I'm a yellow sun
I'm a star in heaven

STUDENTS IN ROOM 1-309

Marilyn prepares a poetry notebook for each student. A poetry notebook is a place to put copies of poems they read together and poems they discover that they like, and it is a place to write their own poems. Poetry is at the center of Marilyn's curriculum. She uses it in every subject area. All children receive a copy of Eloise Greenfield's poem and a copy of the collaborative poem written by the class. They put both poems in their poetry notebook and take them home to read to their family. The children are proud of their poem and proud of themselves.

Poetry in Children's Lives

Poetry is a poet's intuition of truth. Poetry combines rich meaning with sounds of language arranged in an interesting form. Poets select words and arrange them carefully to call attention to experiences we have not known or fully recognized. It is easier to say what poetry does than to describe what it is; poetry eludes precise definition. We know that poetry can make us chuckle or laugh out loud. It can startle us with insight or surprise us with its clarity. It can also bring a sense of peace and a feeling of repose. Some poems express feelings that we did not even know we had until we read them; then we say, "Yes, that's just the way it is." Poetry deals with the essence of life and experience. Poetry, says Gregory Corso (1983), is "the opposite of hypocrisy."

Understanding poetry is a continual process that evolves through the experience of hearing, reading, discussing, and writing poetry. Children develop understanding as they internalize poetry. They profit little from verbal definitions and descriptions. It is their firsthand experience of listening to, reading, writing, and discussing poetry that contributes the most to fostering their love of it. Children who live with poetry in their homes and in their schools turn to poems again and again for pleasure.

POEMS MAKE US SMILE

We all like to laugh; poetry gives us a chance. Poems contain every kind of humor. It may come from wordplay, from descriptions of preposterous situations and events, from an unexpected angle on an everyday concern; but it is not

Profile ✩ NCTE Award for Children's Poetry

The National Council of Teachers of English established an award to honor poets who write for children. The award, established in memory of Bee Cullinan's son, Jonathan (born 1969, died 1975), recognizes the outstanding contribution of a poet who writes expressly for children. Charlotte S. Huck (president of NCTE from 1975 to 1976), Alvina Burrows (colleague at New York University), John Donovan (director of the Children's Book Council), and Sister Rosemary Winkeljohann (director of the elementary section, NCTE) helped to

define the criteria for excellence in poetry for children; they developed the procedures used to select the recipients of the award. The award is given for the entire body of a poet's work for children. Beginning in 1977 and continuing until 1983, the award was given annually. The committees realized they would soon run out of poets; in 1983 a new policy was instituted to present the award every three years. The combined works of the twelve poets who have received the award form the foundation for poetry study in the field. Mini-profiles of the NCTE award winners,

David McCord, Aileen Fisher, Karla Kuskin, Myra Cohn Livingston, Eve Merriam, John Ciardi, Lilian Moore, Arnold Adoff, Valerie Worth, Barbara Esbensen, Eloise Greenfield, and X. J. Kennedy, appear throughout this chapter. After ten poets had received the NCTE Award for Excellence in Poetry, Cullinan conducted a national survey to discover children's favorite poems by each award recipient. Children's top five favorites for each poet appear in *A Jar of Tiny Stars* (Cullinan, 1996). All proceeds are used to support the NCTE Poetry Award.

---

malicious, sadistic, or hurtful. Humorous poems evoke laughter by taking delight in the absurd; they recognize the funny side of life. John Ciardi's (1964) "The Hairy-Nosed Preposterous," from his book *Someone Could Win a Polar Bear*, evokes belly laughs from primary-grade children who enjoy wordplay and exaggeration.

THE HAIRY-NOSED PREPOSTEROUS

The Hairy-Nosed Preposterous
Looks much like a Rhinosterous
But also something like a tank—
For which he has himself to thank.

His ears are the size of tennis shoes
His eyes the size of pins.
And when he lies down for a snooze
An orchestra begins.

It whistles, rattles, roars, and thumps
And the wind of it comes and goes
Through the storm-tossed hair that grows in clumps
On the end of his capable nose.

JOHN CIARDI

Douglas Florian (2000) creates humor by imitating the spelling of the word *aardvark* and creating laughable images in *Mammalabilia*. Florian says:

Aardvarks aare odd.
Aardvarks aare staark.
Aardvarks look better
By faar in the daark.

DOUGLAS FLORIAN

Poems for readers of all ages can bring a chuckle or a loud shout of laughter. Truly funny poems are often a child's first happy experience with poetry. Many good collections of humorous poems are listed in the Booklist at the end of the chapter.

POEMS CREATE IMAGES

Many poems create sensory images. Poets craft words in such a way that readers almost see, smell, taste, touch, or hear what a poem describes. For example, in *Creatures of Earth, Sea, and Sky* (I) Georgia Heard describes an eagle in flight.

© 2000 Douglas Florian

Florian's distinctive watercolor illustrations are as playful as his poems in **Mammalabilia**.

EAGLE FLIGHT

Eagle gliding in the sky
circling, circling way up high—
wind is whistling through your wings.
You're a graceful kite with no string.

GEORGIA HEARD

The Booklist at the end of the chapter lists collections that contain sensory poems.

POEMS EXPRESS FEELINGS

Poetry expresses our feelings in ways we have never thought about before. Good poetry is neither trite nor sentimental; it can help readers understand themselves and their emotions. Whether we experience joy, sadness, anger, jealousy, or loneliness, there is a poem that puts these emotions into words, as Mary Ann Hoberman (1991) does in "My Father" from the book *Fathers, Mothers, Sisters, Brothers*.

MY FATHER

My father doesn't live with us.
It doesn't help to make a fuss;
But still I feel unhappy, plus
*   I miss him.*

My father doesn't live with me.
He's got another family;
He moved away when I was three.
*   I miss him.*

I'm always happy on the day
He visits and we talk and play;
But after he has gone away
*   I miss him.*

MARY ANN HOBERMAN

The feelings expressed in poetry should have a ring of truthfulness. Whether evoking laughter, telling a story, or expressing an emotion, a poem is good only if its reader can understand it. The Booklist at the end of this chapter also includes poems that express feelings.

POEMS STIR EMOTIONS

As teachers and librarians, we need to go beyond surface-level features of poetry, such as poetic devices, form, or the way a poem looks on a page, to consider a deeper understanding of what poetry is and what a poet does. Meaning is everything; it's what we take from a poem that makes a lasting impression, that changes our thoughts and our language.

EAGLE FLIGHT

Eagle gliding in the sky,
circling, circling way up high—
wind is whistling through your wings.
You're a graceful kite with no string.

Georgia Heard creates memorable images in words that Jennifer Owings Dewey extends in art in **Creatures of Earth, Sea, and Sky.**

Although poetry's words can be familiar ones, they are carefully chosen and arranged in such a way as to capture our imagination. The experience conveyed in poetry may be commonplace, but it becomes extraordinary when seen through the poet's eye. As literary scholar Northrup Frye says, "The poet's job is not to tell you what happened, but what happens: not what did take place, but the kind of thing that always takes place" (1964, p. 63).

Poets themselves are often the best source for a definition of poetry. Many poets write about poems and the act of creating them. Bobbye Goldstein collected several of these poems in *Inner Chimes: Poems on Poetry* (P–I–A). Eve Merriam captures the essence of poetry and reveals some of its characteristics as she describes what is *Inside a Poem* (I). She says poetry has a beat that repeats, words that chime, an inner chime, and images we have not imagined before. Eleanor Farjeon (1951) gives a more elusive definition in her *Poems for Children*:

What is Poetry? Who knows?
Not the rose, but the scent of the rose;
Not the sky, but the light in the sky;
Not the fly, but the gleam of the fly;
Not the sea, but the sound of the sea;
Not myself, but what makes me
See, hear, and feel something that prose
Cannot: and what it is, who knows?

ELEANOR FARJEON

Poetry can make us laugh, give us something to think about, and help us put our feelings into words. Poetry captures the essence of experience.

POEMS PROMOTE SCHOOL LEARNING

Poetry does more than make children laugh or cry and create images; it helps students remember academic content. Poetry pays off in the hard currency of school learning. Think back: Did you learn a poem as a child? Can you recite it today? Probably. When students memorize poems, they can remember them for a lifetime. If you have information you want students to remember, give it to them in a poem. Who will ever forget the lines "Under the spreading Chestnut tree, the village smithy stands" from Longfellow's *The Village Blacksmith*; or "The wind was a torrent of darkness among the gusty trees, / The moon was a ghostly galleon tossed upon cloudy seas. / The road was a ribbon of moonlight over the purple moor, / And the highwayman came riding— / Riding—riding— / The highwayman came riding, up to the old inn-door. / from "*The Highwayman*" by Alfred Noyes; or "Listen, my children, and you shall hear / Of the midnight ride of Paul Revere, / On the eighteenth of April, in Seventy-five; Hardly a man is now alive / Who remembers that famous day and year. / from *Paul Revere's Ride* by Henry Wadsworth Longfellow; or "Why, who makes much of a miracle? / As to me I know of nothing else but miracles, / in *Miracles* by Walt Whitman.

Poetry draws students into listening. Students pay attention to poetry because it plays with the sounds of language, uses interesting, intriguing words, and deals with fascinating topics.

Poetry increases students' vocabulary. We all learn the language we hear; if we hear ordinary conversational language, we will use ordinary language when we speak. If we hear poetic language, we will use poetic language when we speak. Students recognize words in print more readily if they have heard those words spoken or read aloud. Since

book language often differs from spoken language, they need to hear book language, especially poetry, read aloud.

Poetry helps children learn how to read. Beginning readers can learn to decode print in verse more easily, because the lines are often short, the words rhyme, and the accent falls on meaningful words. These clues tell a reader what should be coming next in the text. When they hear "Sipping once, sipping twice, sipping chicken soup with _____," they know to fill in the word *rice*. Poetry is excellent material for developing phonemic awareness, the ability to segment and manipulate speech sounds. Children learn to discriminate sounds, hear parts of words, and make connections between sounds they hear and letters they see. Because poetry and verse are patterned, predictable, and repetitive, children know what a word should be and is probably going to be. When they recognize beginning consonants, they are likely to say the right word. Many poems have alliteration (words beginning with the same consonant sound), and they have rhyme (words ending with similar sounds). This ability to segment sounds is a prerequisite to learning phonics. These features help beginning readers decode print. Teaching Idea 2.1 suggests some poems that are appropriate for beginning readers.

Poetry helps students learn how to write by giving them warehouses of words to fulfill their language possibilities. Poetry presents students with a pattern or framework for writing; they see that writers often use a phrase repeatedly to structure a paragraph, story, or expository manuscript. The framework of poetry is visible because it is not hidden beneath layers of words; its skeleton shows.

Poetry helps students learn to think by showing students how to look at their world in a new way. It presents fresh perspectives on life and upends stereotyped ways of thinking. Poetry builds on paradox, ambiguity, contradictions; it sets these features in stark relief so they become apparent to naive readers. Slender poetic texts do not cloud issues or bury them under a pile of verbiage. Poetry brushes away the clutter and lets issues shine. Figure 2.1 shows how poetry promotes school learning. That is good reason to use poetry in the classroom.

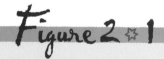

Poetry Promotes School Learning

Reading poetry helps students to:

* Read fluently
* Learn how language works
* Remember the content of a poem
* Develop speaking ability

* Increase writing skill
* Identify the essence of a subject
* Observe how writers use frameworks and structures
* Develop a large vocabulary

Teaching Idea 2 ☆ 1

Poems for Beginning Readers

Children learning to read need text that supports their early efforts to decode print. They need:

* A small number of words on a line
* Phrase-structured text (words said in a single phrase)
* Words that fall naturally from the tongue
* Predictable words that follow logically

These text characteristics describe poetry and stories in rhyme. Rhymed text helps children learn to read. The following books are good for beginning readers.

Easy-to-Read Poems and Stories in Rhyme

Agell, Charlotte, *Dancing Feet*

Ahlberg, Janet, and Allan Ahlberg, *Each Peach Pear Plum: An "I Spy" Story*

Appelt, Kathi, *Bayou Lullaby*

Asch, Frank, *Baby in the Box*

Baker, Keith, *Hide and Snake*

_____, *Who Is the Beast?*

Barracca, Debra, and Sal Barracca, *Adventures of Taxi Dog*

Bemelmans, Ludwig, *Madeline*

Brink, Carol Ryrie, *Goody O'Grumpity*

Bunting, Eve, *Flower Garden*

Cameron, Polly, *I Can't Said the Ant*

Cauley, Lorinda Bryan, *Clap Your Hands*

Christelow, Eileen, *Five Little Monkeys Sitting in a Tree*

Clifton, Lucille, *Everett Anderson's Christmas Coming*

Crews, Donald, *Ten Black Dots Revised*

Domanska, Janina, *If All the Seas Were One Sea*

Fleming, Denise, *Barnyard Banter*

Guarino, Deborah, *Is Your Mama a Llama?*

Hennessy, B. G., *School Days*

Hopkins, Lee Bennett, *More Surprises*

_____, *Surprises*

Kuskin, Karla, *Roar and More*

Kraus, Robert, *Whose Mouse Are You?*

Martin, Bill, Jr., *Brown Bear, Brown Bear, What Do You See?*

_____, *Polar Bear, Polar Bear, What Do You Hear?*

Martin, Bill, Jr., and John Archambault, *Chicka Chicka Boom Boom*

Sendak, Maurice, *Chicken Soup with Rice: A Book of Months*

Seuss, Dr., *I Can Read with My Eyes Shut*

Williams, Sue, *I Went Walking*

Other Resources

Learning Company, The, *Reader Rabbit 1, Reader Rabbit 2* (educational computer games on word recognition, phonetically rhyming words)

Miles, Betty, *I'm Reading! A How-to-Read Book for Beginners*

Profile ☆ Eloise Greenfield

HarperCollins Publishers

*W*riting was the farthest thing from my mind when I was growing up. I loved words, but I loved to read them, not write them. I loved their sounds and rhythms, and even some of their aberrations, such as *homonyms and silent letters, though the pluralizing of* leaf *to* leaves *annoyed me. I could think of no good reason for getting rid of that* f. . . .

There's a desperate need for more Black literature for children, for a large body of literature in which Black children can see themselves and their lives and history reflected. I want to do my share in building it.

Eloise Greenfield was born in Parmele, North Carolina, the daughter of Weston W. and Lessie Jones Little. Her family moved to Washington, D.C., when she was four months old. She grew up in Washington, attended Miner Teachers College, worked in the U.S. Patent Office, and served as codirector of adult fiction of the District of Columbia Black Writer's Workshop; as director of children's literature there, and as writer-in-residence with the District of Columbia Commission on the Arts. She was awarded an honorary doctorate from Wheelock College in Boston.

Greenfield has played a significant role in contributing to African-American literature in several genres; her poetry books are frequently cited by teachers and scholars. She received ALA Notable citations, the Coretta Scott King Award, and the Mary McLeod Bethune Award for her work, particularly for *Honey, I Love* and *Nathaniel Talking.* She received the NCTE Award for Poetry for Children in 1997.

Criteria for Evaluating Poetry

Poetry for children refers to things children know. We consider poems that have stood the test of time, ones that have won significant awards, and ones that have received positive reviews from literary critics. The final test, however, is the level of understanding of the child. While some poetry from the past still speaks to today's children, some does not. A wealth of excellent poetry has been written in the last decade. Individual poems can be judged on how well children understand them, on the emotions they elicit, on the images they create, on their rhythm and sounds, and on the appropriateness of their form. We can evaluate the overall quality of our collections in terms of the multicultural diversity of content, the mood, language use, and the variety of forms they contain. Figure 2.2 lists questions you might ask as you evaluate poems. Search for new poems instead of relying upon the ones you memorized in childhood. Keep the questions in mind when selecting poetry.

POETRY IS UNDERSTANDABLE

Children like poems they can understand. They also enjoy poems that expand their understanding, those that need to be read and discussed in the company of peers and adults who are interested in exploring poetry. Children respond to carefully selected poems that are geared to their intellectual development and that speak of their experiences. Poetry can evoke laughter, create images, and express feelings when it is about subjects and experiences that children understand.

POETRY IS APPEALING

Children want to read poetry—it appeals to them. When children begin to explore poetry, they like humorous poems with strong rhythm and rhyme more than they like free verse with abstract symbolism. They enjoy narrative poetry because it is based on their natural love of story. Children's responses to poetry depend heavily upon the way it is introduced to them. If initial encounters with poetry are happy ones, then a love for and understanding of poetry can grow.

Poetry is the natural language of childhood. Kornei Chukovsky (1963), a Russian poet, says that children are natural born poets. They play with the sounds of language; they like being bounced on a knee and hearing "Ride a little horsey up and down a hill. If you don't watch out, you'll take a little spill." During the early childhood years, they hear jingles and readily commit them to memory. They sing songs as they play and will join in to sing refrains with delight. Happy experiences with rhythm, rhyme, humor, and story shape children's preferences for poetry.

CHILDREN'S POETRY PREFERENCES

Researchers have studied the kinds of poems children like, as well as the kinds of poems teachers read to them. For example, in two national surveys, Terry (1974) studied the poetry preferences of students in the upper elementary grades, and Fisher and Natarella (1982) replicated her study with primary-grade children. These researchers found that children like

- Contemporary poems
- Poems they can understand
- Narrative poems
- Poems with rhyme, rhythm, and sound
- Poems that relate to their personal experiences

They also found that children dislike poems that have a lot of figurative language and imagery. They dislike highly abstract poems that do not make sense to them. Haiku was

Figure 2 * 2

Checklist for Evaluating Poetry

- Can students understand it? Can they understand it with help from adults?
- Does the poem stir emotions (laughter, sadness, thoughtfulness)?
- Does it create images of sight, touch, smell, taste?

- Does it play with the sounds of language? Does the sound echo the sense?
- Is the form one students can borrow or imitate?

consistently disliked. Girls like poetry more often than boys do. Favorite poems were humorous ones about familiar experiences or animals. John Ciardi's poem "Mummy Slept Late and Daddy Fixed Breakfast" in *You Read to Me, I'll Read to You* and limericks of all sorts were tops among the children's choices.

McClure (1984) extended Terry's study and found that classroom experiences change children's responses. In supportive environments, children respond more positively to a wider variety of poetry, showing that teachers' attitudes and practices make a tremendous difference. In other words, what you do with poetry in the classroom determines how your students respond to poetry. Birkman's (1973) research showed that elementary-grade students appreciated unrhymed poetry when they were read quantities of that type. Children can appreciate all kinds of poetry if the poems are well presented and if they are exposed to many forms.

Poetry grows increasingly popular; more poetry is published each year in appealing formats. Since 1973, the International Reading Association and Children's Book Council have annually conducted a national field test called Children's Choices; the results show that children consistently select poetry books as among their favorites. Preferences for poetry prevail amid opportunities to choose hundreds of other picture books, novels, and nonfiction. Children choose humorous poems about familiar things, poems that astonish them, and poems that help them to see the world in a new way. Generally preferences reflect Ann Terry and

Carol Fisher's early findings. See the Booklist at end of chapter for Children's Poetry Choices 1973–2000.

We may not know why a particular poem appeals to children, but we do know that poems read aloud with enthusiasm are likely to become their favorites. Teachers' choices soon become children's choices. Poet Eve Merriam (1995) said, "If we can get teachers to read poetry, lots of it, out loud to children, we'll develop a generation of poetry readers; we may even have some poetry writers, but the main thing, we'll have language appreciators." Results of the IRA Teachers' Choices project show that teachers frequently choose poetry as their favorite books for teaching. Teachers choose poems that reflect our multicultural heritage, poems with beautiful language, and poems that help them teach subject-area content. When teachers select poems that they like, their enthusiasm is apparent to their students. See the Booklist at the end of the chapter for Teachers' Poetry Choices 1982–2000.

Poetry Uses Language in Interesting Ways

Poets manipulate the elements of sound, rhythm, and meaning to create an impact more powerful than any found in prose. Sound and rhythm are more pronounced in poetry than in prose, and meaning is more condensed. Poets use language in

Profile ☆ X. J. Kennedy

Curtis Brown, Ltd.

*R*hyme and meter have been in the doghouse of adult poetry lately, and some have claimed that children, too, don't like such old-fangled devices. But children do. This makes me glad, for I have never been able to

write what is termed free verse. I love the constant surprise one encounters in rhyming things, and the driving urge of a steady beat. I have great fun in trading poems with grade-school audiences—tough audiences, for the most part, but full of fellow bards.

X. J. Kennedy was born in Dover, New Jersey, two months before the market crash of 1929. He began to scribble as early in life as possible. For years, he wrote poetry for children but kept it in the bottom drawer of his desk until Myra Cohn Livingston asked him to send some of it to her editor, Margaret McElderry. McElderry published his first book of poetry for children, *One Winter Night in August.*

Kennedy is the author of more than a dozen collections of verse for children, including a trio of books that began with *Brats,* followed by *Fresh Brats,* and *Drat These Brats!* He and his wife, Dorothy M. Kennedy, collected poems in *Knock at a Star: A Child's Introduction to Poetry,* which discusses what poems do, what's inside a poem, special kinds of poetry, and ideas for writing your own poems. Kennedy says that if you write for children, it helps to have an in-home audience. He was lucky with a girl and four boys, now all grown. X. J. Kennedy received the NCTE Award for Excellence in Poetry for Children in the year 2000.

unique ways. The terms that are used to describe these language techniques are defined in this chapter and are listed in the Glossary. Students will not need to learn the meanings of all the terms, but teachers should be comfortable enough with them to answer questions and discuss techniques of favorite poets. If, for example, children comment on the repetition of initial consonant sounds, you might say, "That's called 'alliteration.' Let's look to see how it works in this poem." Teachers who are willing to explore poetry become role models for children; they lead them to explore poetry. Teaching Idea 2.2 lists several books on language and wordplay. Also, see Harrison and Cullinan's *Easy Poetry Lessons That Dazzle and Delight* for accurate terminology.

WORDS AS SOUND

Of all the elements of poetry, sound offers the most pleasure to children. The choice and arrangement of sounds make poetry musical and reinforce meaning. Rhyme, alliteration, assonance, and onomatopoeia are among the language resources of sound.

Rhyme refers to words whose ending sounds are alike (despair/fair). Although poetry need not rhyme, children often prefer rhyme. Rhyme is not as fashionable with adults as it once was, but children still enjoy reciting it. It sticks better in the mind and lingers longer on the tongue. Generation after generation repeats the same jump rope jingles and rhyming street games.

Poets' ears are tuned to the repetition of consonants, vowels, syllables, words, phrases, and lines, separately and in combination. Anything may be repeated to achieve effect. Repeti-

tion is like meeting an old friend again; children find it reassuring. Repetition underscores meaning, establishes a sound pattern, and is a source of humor in many rhymes, as in this chant by David McCord from the book *One at a Time*:

III

The pickety fence
The pickety fence
Give it a lick it's
The pickety fence
Give it a lick it's
A clickety fence
Give it a lick it's
A lickety fence
Give it a lick
Give it a lick
Give it a lick
With a rickety stick
Pickety
Pickety
Pickety
Pick

DAVID MCCORD

Alliteration refers to the repetition of the initial consonant sounds of words at close intervals. Tongue twisters such as "Peter Piper picked a peck of pickled peppers. A peck of pickled peppers Peter Piper picked" and "rubber baby buggy bumpers" play with alliteration. Karla Kuskin uses alliteration effectively in her poem "The Meal" in the book *Dogs and Dragons, Trees and Dreams*:

Profile ✿ David McCord

Little, Brown and Company

One of my teachers told me, "'Never let a day go by without looking on three beautiful things." I try to live

up to that and find it isn't difficult. The sky in all weathers is, for me, the first to these three things.

Poetry, like rain, should fall with elemental music, and poetry for children should catch the eye as well as the ear and the mind. It should delight; it really *has* to delight. Furthermore, poetry for children should keep reminding them, without any feeling on their part that they are being reminded, that the English language is a most marvelous and availing instrument.

David McCord is considered the dean of children's poets. He was

born in Greenwich Village in New York City, was reared on Long Island, in Princeton, New Jersey, and on a ranch by the Rogue River in Oregon. McCord graduated from Harvard University and returned to work there for 37 years in various roles. His collected works appear in *One at a Time: His Collected Poems for the Young*. Other popular collections of his work appear in *Every Time I Climb a Tree, All Small Poems*, and *For Me to Say*. David McCord was the first recipient of the NCTE Award for Poetry for Children. It was awarded in 1977.

Teaching Idea 2 ☆ 2

Wordplay and Poetry

Poets are wordsmiths who play with the infinite possibilities of language. They make us listen to the repetition of similar sounds, they challenge us to probe double or triple meanings, they surprise us with unusual combinations of words and events. Poets savor language and pack their poems with multiple meanings, like firecrackers ready to explode. Poets craft their poems the way a potter shapes clay—turning, refining, polishing, smoothing until it satisfies. You can become sensitive to the nuances of words, too. Look at books about words. Discover what they offer. Here are some examples.

Agee, Jon, *Sit on a Potato Pan, Otis! More Palindromes*

Agee, Jon, *Who Ordered the Jumbo Shrimp? And Other Oxymorons*

Cleary, Brian P., *Give Me Bach My Schubert*

Heller, Ruth, *Many Luscious Lollipops: A Book About Adjectives*

_____, *Up, Up and Away: A Book About Adverbs*

Hoban, Tana, *Exactly the Opposite*

McMillan, Bruce, *Play Day: A Book of Terse Verse*

_____, *Super, Super, Superwords*

Merriam, Eve, *Chortles: New and Selected Wordplay Poems*

_____, *A Poem for a Pickle: Funnybone Verses*

Terban, Marvin, *The Dove Dove*

_____, *Hey Hay*

_____, *It Figures! Fun Figures of Speech*

_____, *Superdupers! Really Funny Real Words*

_____, *Time to Rhyme: A Rhyming Dictionary*

Young, Sue, *Scholastic's Rhyming Dictionary*

Create word walls, word maps, word balloons, and sunbursts. Put one word in the middle of a page. Encircle it with all the other words that come to mind. Cluster the words that go together in some way. Play with the words. Rearrange them on the page to see if they suggest a poem or verse. Try different combinations to try to create a tone or mood.

THE MEAL

Timothy Tompkins had turnips and tea.
The turnips were tiny.
He ate at least three.
And then, for dessert
He had onions and ice.
He liked that so much
That he ordered it twice.
He had two cups of ketchup
A prune, and a pickle.
"Delicious," said Timothy.
"Well worth a nickel."
He folded his napkin
And hastened to add
"It's one of the loveliest breakfasts I've had."

KARLA KUSKIN

Rhoda W. Bacmeister uses assonance, the repetition of vowel sounds at close intervals, and alliteration in the verses of "Galoshes" in the book *Stories to Begin On*:

GALOSHES

Susie's galoshes
Make splishes and sploshes
And slooshes and sloshes
As Susie steps slowly
Along in the slush.

They stamp and they tramp
On the ice and concrete
They get stuck in the muck and the mud;
But Susie likes much best to hear

The slippery slush
As it slooshes and sloshes
And splishes and sploshes
All around her galoshes!

RHODA BACMEISTER

She also makes use of *onomatopoeia*, or words created from natural sounds associated with the thing or action designated. For example, the word *murmur* resembles somewhat

Sky Scrape/City Scape

Sky scrape,
City scape,
High stone,
Steel bone,
Cloud crown,
Smóg gown,

Hurry up,
Hurry down.

Jane Yolen

© 1996 Ken Condon

6

*Jane Yolen captures the pace and rhythm of the city, which Ken Condon echoes and enriches in the art of **Sky Scrape/City Scape**.*

the sound of murmuring. Other words that sound like what they mean are hiss, bang, snap, and crack. Rhoda Bacmeister uses the onomatopoetic words slush, slooshes, sloshes, splishes, and sploshes. Onomatopoeia, in combination with other sound resources, can achieve poetic effect to light up any child's eyes.

An example of *end rhyme* in which the rhyming words appear at the ends of lines appears in Jane Yolen's *Sky Scrape/City Scape.*

SKY SCRAPE/CITY SCAPE

Sky scrape
City scape
High stone
Steel bone
Cloud crown
Smog gown

Hurry up
Hurry down.

JANE YOLEN

When the last word of one line rhymes with the first word of the next line it is called *run-over rhyme*. In **One at a Time**, David McCord gives us a beautiful example of this (together with end rhyme) in his "Runover Rhyme":

RUNOVER RHYME

Down by the pool still fishing
Wishing for fish, I fail
Praying for birds not present
Pheasant or grouse or quail.

Up in the woods, his hammer
Stammering, I can't see
The woodpecker, find the cunning
Sunning old owl in the tree.

Over the field such raucous
Talk as the crows talk on!
Nothing around me slumbers;
Numbers of birds have gone.

Even the leaves hang listless
Lasting through days we lose
Empty of what is wanted
Haunted by what we choose.

DAVID MCCORD

David Harrison calls his manipulation of the form *link rhymes*. In this link rhyme from *Easy Poetry Lessons That Dazzle and Delight,* he looks at the child he was and considers the person he will become:

Profile ✧ Karla Kuskin

HarperCollins Publishers

If there were a recipe for a poem, these would be the ingredients: word sounds, rhythm, description, feeling, memory, rhyme, and imagination. *They can be put together a thousand different ways, a thousand, thousand . . . more.*

Karla Kuskin was born in New York City and grew up in Greenwich Village. She graduated from the Yale School of Design and had her college project published as the book ***Roar and More***. She is an artist as well as a poet; she illustrated many of her own books. She designed the medallion for the NCTE Poetry Award; when she won the same award three years later, friends teased her about designing awards she would win. Her poetry appears in New York subways as part of the Poetry in Motion program. Her most popular books include ***Near the Window Tree***; ***Dogs and Dragons, Trees and Dreams***; ***The Upstairs Cat***; ***The Sky Is Always in the Sky***; and ***I Am Me***. Karla Kuskin received the NCTE Award in 1979.

THE FUTURE ME

Looking back, I see
Me, unafraid
Eager, teasing
Pleasing, first grade.

Part on the right
Light cowlick hair
Lopsided grin
Thin, blue eyes, fair.

Who am I now?
How am I to be?
Looking behind
To find the future me.

DAVID HARRISON

Children are willing explorers who will experiment with rhyme schemes when they are invited to the feast of poetry. They learn when to use rhyme to add to the meaning of a poem.

WORDS AS RHYTHM

Rhythm in language is created by the recurrence of specific beats of stressed and unstressed syllables. Human beings respond to regularity in the beat; this response may develop in the womb, when the fetus hears the mother's steady heartbeat. Rhythm is everywhere in life—in ocean waves, in the tick of a clock, in a horse's hoofbeats, in one's own pulse.

In poetry, rhythm refers to the repeated use of syllables and accents, and to the rise and fall of words spoken or read. In "Inside a Poem" from *It Doesn't Always Have to Rhyme*, Eve Merriam calls "the repeat of a beat . . . an inner chime that makes you want to tap your feet or swerve in a curve." All good poetry is rhythmical, as are other forms of high art from visual arts to dance, music, and even prose.

The rhythm in poetry is most often metrical. Meter is ordered rhythm, in which certain syllables are regularly stressed or accented in a more or less fixed pattern. "Meter" is defined as "measure," and metrical language in poetry can be measured. The meter in poetry can run from that of tightly structured verse patterns to loosely defined free verse. Whatever it is, rhythm helps to create and then reinforce a poem's meaning. In *Circus* (N–P), Jack Prelutsky adjusts his rhythms to the subject:

> *Over and over the tumblers tumble*
> *with never a fumble*
> *with never a stumble*
> *top over bottom and back over top*
> *flop-flippy-floppity-flippity-flop.*

The tumblers pass by, followed by the elephants, whose plodding walk echoes in the new rhythm:

> *Here come the elephants, ten feet high*
> *elephants, elephants, heads in the sky.*
> *Eleven great elephants intertwined*
> *one little elephant close behind.*

JACK PRELUTSKY

Prelutsky makes the rhythm in the elephant stanza plod along in the same lumbering way that elephants walk. He makes the sound echo the sense.

Word order contributes to the rhythm of poetry as well. Arranging words is central to creating a poem. Teachers, and perhaps interested students, should be aware of the ways poets manipulate syntax to make poetry distinctive from prose. One noticeable feature of poetic language is the way it varies from the straight declarative sentence. An example is Stevenson's "Where Go the Boats?" from *A Child's Garden of Verses:*

WHERE GO THE BOATS

Dark brown is the river
    Golden is the sand.
It flows along forever
    With trees on either hand.

ROBERT LOUIS STEVENSON

The literal meaning of the poem could probably be communicated in this way:

The river is dark brown
    The sand is golden.
The river keeps on flowing forever
    With trees on both sides.

Retaining Stevenson's words but rearranging them totally destroys the visual image. Poets manipulate syntax until they find an order and rhythm that is pleasing to them and that communicates more than the literal message. Inverted word order used for poetic effect may interfere with meaning; however, students grow in their ability to comprehend inverted sentences when they hear poetry read aloud.

WORDS AS MEANING

Poetry often carries several layers of meaning and, as with other literature, is subject to different interpretations. The meaning children create is directly related to what their experience prepares them to understand; background knowledge determines what we can see.

Terry (1974) read William Jay Smith's "The Toaster" to children of varying levels of development and asked them to draw a picture of what the poem was about. The poem describes the toaster as "a silver-scaled dragon." Children in the primary grades believed that it was an actual dragon and drew fiery-mouthed dragons to show that they understood the poem at a literal, concrete level. Older children, above the fourth grade, drew pictures of toasters that resembled dragons, suggesting that they understood the figurative language Smith used in the poem.

Not all poems have hidden meanings, but it is true that some poems carry subtle messages. Most poems, however, contain descriptions of characters, expression of emotions, or accounts of events. We chance losing our students if we continually send them searching for hidden messages. It is perfectly acceptable to assert, as Alice did, after reading "Jabberwocky," "Somehow it seems to fill my head with ideas, only I don't know exactly what they are."

Poetic devices used to convey meaning include figurative language, imagery, denotation, and connotation. Writers use poetic devices to suggest that the words mean more than meets the eye or ear. Something left unsaid is often as important as what is stated on the page, as in this poem from *Whistling the Morning In* by Lillian Morrison:

DAILY VIOLENCE

Dawn cracked;
    the sun stole through.
Day broke;
    the sun climbed over rooftops.
Clouds chased the sun
    then burst.
Night fell.
The clock struck midnight.

LILLIAN MORRISON

Figurative language produces a meaning beyond the literal meaning of the words used. In poetry, figurative language is used frequently. Figurative language affects meaning dramatically; metaphor, simile, and personification make the language of poetry different from that of prose. As poets create vivid experiences, they use language metaphorically; they help us to see or feel things in new ways. It is not enough just to have the idea; poets must also have the words. The special and particular words often involve figurative language, as in this poem from Eve Merriam's *It Doesn't Always Have to Rhyme:*

METAPHOR

Morning is
a new sheet of paper
for you to write on.

Whatever you want to say,
all day,
until night
folds it up
and files it away.

The bright words and the dark words
are gone
until dawn
and a new day
to write on.

EVE MERRIAM

Profile ☆ Eve Merriam

Bachrach

There is a physical element in reading poetry out loud; it's like jumping rope or throwing a ball. If we can get teachers to read poetry, lots of it, out loud to children, we'll develop a generation of poetry readers; we may even have some poetry writers, but the main thing, we'll have language appreciators.

I've sometimes spent weeks looking for precisely the right word. It's like having a tiny marble in your pocket, you can just feel it. Sometimes you find a word and say, 'No, I don't think this is it. . . .' Then you discard it, and take another and another until you get it right. I do think poetry is great fun. That's what I'd like to stress more than anything else: the joy of the sounds of language.

Eve Merriam was born in Philadelphia and graduated from the University of Pennsylvania. She did graduate work at the University of Wisconsin and Columbia University. Her poetry is widely anthologized. Some of her books include *It Doesn't Always Have to Rhyme, There Is No Rhyme for Silver, A Poem for a Pickle: Funny Bone Verses, The Singing Green: New and Selected Poems for All Seasons,* and *Higgle Wiggle: Happy Rhymes.* Eve Merriam received the NCTE Award in 1981.

Children need experience in using and understanding figurative language in order to fully appreciate poems that rely on it. How well they understand figurative language in a poem depends upon their background knowledge and experience. Young children understand a comparison made on a physical plane but not on a psychological one. Snow-covered bushes that look like popcorn balls and cars that look like big, fat raisins are more likely to make sense to young children than a prison guard's heart of stone. Young children interpret the prison guard's heart as being physically of stone. As children become more sophisticated language users they understand how figurative language contributes to meaning; poetry assumes a deeper dimension. Recognizing contrast, comparison, and exaggeration on a psychological level adds a richer interpretation. More complex comparisons can be made using the devices of metaphor and simile, which compare one thing to another or view something in terms of something else. The comparison in a *simile* is stated and uses the words *like* or *as* to draw the comparison. A comparison in a *metaphor* is inferred; something is stated as something else. Eve Merriam (1964) makes an unmistakable comparison by using the title "Metaphor" and by saying that morning is a new sheet of paper.

Personification refers to representing a thing or abstraction as a person. When we say "Fortune smiled on us" or "If the weather permits," we are giving human qualities

Profile ☆ Lilian Moore

HarperCollins Publishers

Poetry should be like fireworks, packed carefully and artfully, ready to explode with unpredictable effects. When people asked Robert Frost—as they did by the hundreds—what he meant by "But I have promises to keep/And miles to go before I sleep/And miles to go before I sleep," he always turned the question aside with a joke. Maybe he couldn't answer it, and maybe he was glad that the lines exploded in so many different colors in so many people's minds.

Lilian Moore was born in New York City, attended Hunter College, and did graduate work at Columbia University. She taught school in New York City and worked in publishing for many years. Her popular books include *I Feel the Same Way, Something New Begins, Poems Have Roots,* and *Adam Mouse's Book of Poems.* Lilian Moore received the NCTE Award for Excellence in Poetry in 1985.

to an idea—fortune—and to the weather. Poets often give human feelings or thoughts to plants and animals. In her poem "Crickets," Valerie Worth uses personification to make ideas more vivid or unusual. She says that crickets "talk" and dry grass "whispers." Langston Hughes uses personification in "April Rain Song" when he advises to let the rain "kiss" you and "sing you a lullaby." Lilian Moore uses personification in her poem "Construction," from *I Thought I Heard the City* and *Something New Begins*:

CONSTRUCTION

The giant mouth
chews
rocks
spews them
and is back for
more.

The giant arm
swings up
with a girder
for
the fourteenth floor.

Down there,
a tiny man
is
telling them
where
to put a skyscraper.

LILIAN MOORE

Poets create imagery through the use of words in ways that arrest our senses; we can imagine that we almost see, taste, touch, smell, or hear what they describe. Little escapes the poet's vision; nothing limits the speculations upon what he sees. Lilian Moore (1966) uses both imagery and personification to create her vision of September when she says that something is bleeding into the pond, leaving stains that are freshly red. In a poem from *All the Small Poems*, Valerie Worth creates imagery when she says that dandelions look like a cratered moon:

DANDELION

Out of
Green space,
A sun:
Bright for
A day, burning,
Away to
A husk, a
Cratered moon:

Burst
In a week
To dust:
Seeding
The infinite
Lawn with
Its starry
Smithereens.

VALERIE WORTH

Profile ✻ Valerie Worth

© Temple Studios

Never forget that the subject is as important as your feeling: The mud puddle itself is as important as your pleasure in looking at it or splashing through it. Never let the mud puddle get lost in the poetry—because, in many ways, the mud puddle is the poetry.

Valerie Worth's small poems are crystal clear images, luminous word jewels about the simplest things—coat hangers, pebbles, or marbles. Natalie Babbitt, a well-known fantasy writer, was in the same writer's group with Valerie. When she heard her poems read aloud, she asked if she could send them to her editor, who liked them, too. Babbitt created elegant but simple art to illustrate all of Valerie Worth's small poem books. Worth was born in Philadelphia, Pennsylvania. Her father was a field biologist who took the family to Bangalore, India, so that he could study malaria. Worth earned her B.S. degree in English at Swarthmore College. She received the NCTE Award in 1991.

Profile ☆ Barbara Esbensen

HarperCollins Publishers

As a child growing up in Madison, Wisconsin, I read everything in sight, and drew pictures on anything that looked like it needed decoration. I wrote stories with my two best friends, and we all intended to be writers. When I was 14-and-a-half, my teacher looked at a poem I had written and told me I was "a writer." When she introduced me to poets like Amy Lowell, Stephen Vincent Benet, and Emily Dickinson, she literally changed my life. Until then, I had not known that it was possible to use words in such exciting ways.

Barbara Esbensen wrote many informational books before she concentrated on poetry. She and her husband, Tory, had six children: Julie, Peter, Daniel, Jane, George, and Kai. Peter died when he was 19. The others are all grown. Barbara Esbensen received the NCTE Award for Excellence in Poetry for Children in 1994.

Barbara Esbensen creates imagery through word pictures when she says a frog goes splat and lands wet and squat upon the page. In *Words with Wrinkled Knees* she describes a frog:

> Touch it with your
> pencil
> Splat!   The word lands   wet
> and squat
> upon the page   F R O G
>
> Feed it something light
> With wings   Here's one!
> Tongue flicks   bright
> wing   caught!
> Small poem
> gone

BARBARA ESBENSON

Denotation refers to the literal meaning of a word or phrase. *Connotation* refers to the suggested meaning associated with the literal one, to the overtones of meaning. Connotations can vary with the individual person. Water, for instance, may have connotations of refreshment, cooling, beauty, pleasure, or cleansing, depending on which of its many aspects you are thinking of and where you have enjoyed water the most. But it might also arouse feelings of terror in a person who has been in danger of drowning. Poetry makes use of both denotative and connotative meaning, saying what it means but saying much more. Connotation enriches meaning. Sometimes the sounds of words combine with their connotations to make a very pleasing pattern. Georgia Heard uses the connotations of stained glass windows to make us think about dragonflies in a new way in *Creatures of Earth, Sea, and Sky*.

DRAGONFLY

> It skims the pond's surface
> searching for gnats, mosquitoes, and flies.
> Outspread wings blur with speed.
> It touches down
> and stops to sun itself on the dock.
> Wings flicker and still:
> stained-glass windows
> with sun shining through.

GEORGIA HEARD

Good poets make use of poetic devices that help them best express what they are trying to say. Children who hear and read poetry that contains excellent examples of these poetic devices will come to understand and appreciate their use as well as expand their language learning, as described in Figure 2.3. They will use these tools in their own writing.

Poetry Comes in a Variety of Forms

Poetry forms include narrative, lyric, free verse, haiku and cinquain, concrete, limerick, ballad, and sonnet. Teachers wisely begin with narrative poetry or with brief, humorous verses, and gradually expose children to a broader range of forms. As they expand students' experiences with poetry, they increase their potential for greater interest and understanding.

Poetry comes in many forms. Poems look different; the visual form, which reflects the poetic form, affects the way we read and comprehend the meaning of a poem. Poetic forms

Figure 2 ✸ 3

Poetry Promotes Language Learning

Poetry promotes language learning because it:

* Contains highly charged words
* Uses only a few words to say a great deal
* Is melodic; it sings as it says
* Contains rhythm, repetition, and rhyme

* Captures the essence of a concept
* Says more than it says
* Has layers of meaning
* Is the natural language of childhood

---

are clearly defined, although poets alter conventional and traditional forms as often as they manipulate word meanings.

One day, Myra Cohn Livingston, author of *Poem Making,* was looking at her daughter, who came in from a camping trip. Myra wrote a cinquain about her T-shirt:

> *T-shirt*
> *you're my best thing*
> *though you've faded so much*
> *no one knows what you said when you*
> *were new.*

MYRA COHN LIVINGSTON

NARRATIVE POETRY

Narrative poetry tells a story. Think about stories from childhood that you first heard through poetry. Perhaps "The Pied Piper of Hamelin," "Casey at Bat," "Hiawatha," "Paul Revere's Ride," or another rhymed story comes to mind. Many chil-

dren enjoy narrative verse, and this is not surprising—they enjoy and are familiar with stories of all kinds. A book-length narrative poem (one that is longer than a picture book) is called an epic, but most story poems for children are relatively short and relate one or more episodes.

Narrative poetry sets a story with characters, plot, and theme—like any other story—into a poetic framework, which can make even a humble story memorable. A. A. Milne, Henry Wadsworth Longfellow, and Rosemary and Stephen Vincent Benét are known for their narrative poems. Contemporary writers of narrative poems include Jack Prelutsky, Aileen Fisher, and Shel Silverstein. Teaching Idea 2.3 offers a variety of poems to help celebrate special occasions.

When poetry is read aloud, the words can truly sing, and listeners can savor the musical quality of the verse. Oral presentations accentuate the meaning in narrative poems. Listening to story poems helps children develop an appreciation for the charm of the spoken word and the melody of verse. They learn poems by heart after hearing them a number of times.

Poets experiment with the narrative form; several books, including Joyce Carol Thomas's *Gingerbread Days, Brown*

Profile ✸ Myra Cohn Livingston

Marilyn Sanders

Trained as a traditionalist in poetry, I feel strongly about the importance of order imposed by fixed forms, meter, and rhyme when I write about some things; yet free verse seems more suitable for other subjects. It is the force of what I say that shapes the form.

Myra Cohn Livingston was born in Omaha, Nebraska, and moved with her family to California at the age of 11. She graduated from Sarah Lawrence College and submitted

poems to publishers while a student. Her first book, *Whispers and Other Poems*, grew from work started at Sarah Lawrence. She published around 80 books of poetry or writings about poetry. Her work includes *Riddle-Me Rhymes, Lots of Limericks,* and *Call Down the Moon.* Myra Cohn Livingston received the NCTE Award in 1980.

Teaching Idea 2·3

Celebrate with Poetry

Whatever the occasion, celebrate with poetry — it captures the right feeling. Celebrate a holiday, the season, the weather, writers and poets. Poems make celebrations special and memorable.

Celebrate Holidays

Hopkins, Lee Bennett, *Good Morning to You, Valentine* (P)

_____, *My America* (P–I–A)

_____, *Ring Out, Wild Bells: Poems About Holidays and Seasons* (P–I)

Katz, Bobbi, *We the People* (P–I–A)

Livingston, Myra Cohn, *Halloween Poems* (P)

Moore, Clement C., *The Night Before Christmas* (P)

Yolen, Jane, *Best Witches: Poems for Halloween* (I)

Celebrate the Seasons

Adoff, Arnold, *In for Winter, Out for Spring* (P–I)

Bruchac, Joseph, *Thirteen Moons on Turtle's Back: A Native American Year of Moons* (I)

Frost, Robert, *Poetry for Young People* (I–A)

Hopkins, Lee Bennett, *Easter Buds Are Springing* (P)

Jacobs, Leland B., *Just Around the Corner: Poems About the Seasons* (P–I)

Morrison, Lillian, *Whistling the Morning In* (I)

Singer, Marilyn, *Turtle in July* (P–I)

Thomas, Joyce Carol, *Gingerbread Days* (P)

Turner, Ann, *Moon for Seasons* (P–I)

Updike, John, *A Child's Calendar* (I)

Yolen, Jane, Selector, *Weather Report* (I)

Celebrate Writers (Child and Adult)

Adoff, Arnold, *Street Music: City Poems* (I–A)

Hopkins, Lee Bennett, *Good Rhymes, Good Times: Original Poems* (P)

Merriam, Eve, *Bam, Bam, Bam* (P)

_____, *Blackberry Ink* (P)

Smith, William Jay, *Behind the King's Kitchen: Riddles* (I)

Stevenson, James, *Sweet Corn: Poems* (I)

Strickland, Michael, *Poems That Sing to You* (I–A)

Honey in Broomwheat Tea, and *I Have Heard of a Land* (all P–I) contain a series of short poems that, taken together, tell a story. Books like this, plus many beautifully illustrated, single editions of narrative poems are listed in the Booklist at the end of the chapter. With these books available we no longer need to settle for the simple, dull, and standardized verses often found in anthologies.

LYRIC POETRY

Lyric poetry is a statement of mood or feeling. It is probably the type of poetry most children read. It offers a direct and intense outpouring of thoughts and feelings. Any subjective, emotional poem can be called lyric, but most lyric poems are songlike and are expressive of a single mood. As its Greek name indicates, a lyric was originally sung to the accompaniment of a lyre. Lyric poems have a melodic quality to this day; they are songs, as Eleanor Farjeon's "Morning Has Broken" from her book *The Children's Bells* (P–I).

MORNING HAS BROKEN

Morning has broken
like the first morning
Blackbird has spoken
like the first bird.

Praise for the singing!
Praise for the morning!
Praise for them, springing
fresh from the Word!

Sweet the rain's new fall
sunlit from heaven
Like the first dew fall
on the first grass.
Praise for the sweetness
of the wet garden
Sprung in completeness
where His feet pass.

Mine is the sunlight!
Mine is the morning
Born of the one light
Eden saw play!
Praise with elation
praise every morning
God's re-creation
of the new day!

ELEANOR FARJEON

Many children's poems are lyrical because of their singing quality and their expression of personal feeling. Read and sing lyric poems many times over. Older students, with a rich understanding of symbolism, have a better appreciation for lyric poetry. Poetry in the lyric mode requires that children trust their own feelings in response to a poem; there is no one right interpretation when it comes to poetry. Joyce Carol Thomas collected *African American Lullabies: Hush Songs*, traditional songs sung by cradling mothers and caring fathers to lull a child to sleep. A soothing melody sung with comforting words works its magic on sleepy children:

ALL THE PRETTY LITTLE HORSES

Hush-a-bye
Don't you cry
Go to sleep
My little baby

When you wake
You shall have
All the pretty little horses

TRADITIONAL LULLABY

Collections of lyric poetry are listed in the Booklist at the end of the chapter.

FREE VERSE

Free verse is unrhymed verse with an irregular pattern or no visible metrical pattern. Elements that distinguish free verse include its arrangement on the page, the essence of its subject, and the density of thought. Teachers who encourage children to write in free verse help them avoid some of the difficulties of trying to rhyme. Lee Bennett Hopkins writes his autobiography in free verse in *Been to Yesterdays: Poems of a Life* (I–A). One poem celebrates a beloved teacher who recognized his desire to write:

"What
do you
want to be
when you grow up?"
asked my teacher
Miss Ethel K. Tway.

Down the rows
the kids called out:

"A cop."
"A nurse."

Brenda Joysmith's rich illustrations complement Joyce Carol Thomas's traditional lullabies.

"A soldier."
"A sailor."
"A scientist."
"Butcher."
"A firefighter."

When she got to me
I said

    "A writer."

Louis laughed
hysterically.

"A writer!"
he said.
"What a crazy thing
to want to be!"

"I don't think
that's funny, Louis."
said Miss Tway.
"Everyone's entitled

to sound
their own voice.
Becoming
a writer is a
fine life-choice."

That special moment
on that
red-letter day
I fell madly
in love
with
Miss Ethel K. Tway.

LEE BENNETT HOPKINS

Two collections by Gary Soto (1990; 1993), *A Fire in My Hands* (A) and *Neighborhood Odes* (I), contain poems written in free verse. Although children may initially prefer rhymed, metered poetry, they learn to appreciate free verse when they see it, say it, hear it, and experiment writing it. The Booklist at the end of the chapter cites examples of free verse.

Lee Bennett Hopkins describes memorable events during his thirteenth year—an autobiography in poetry—in **Been to Yesterdays.**

Profile ✿ Arnold Adoff

HarperCollins Publishers

I n the sixth grade, I loved to express myself through writing. If I'd never published a single poem in my life, I think I would always have been a

poet. I never wanted to follow rules. In poetry you must master the rules that have gone before, and then you make up your own rules. After that you are free to make or break them as you develop and change. Lee Bennett Hopkins, **Pass the Poetry, Please** (1998, p. 34)

I look for craft and control in making a form that is unique to the individual poem, that shapes it, holds it tight, creates an inner tension that makes a whole shape out of the words. Lee Bennett Hopkins, **Pauses** (1995, p. 219)

Arnold Adoff was born in the South Bronx, New York City. He attended City College of New York and did

graduate work at Columbia University. He taught in Harlem and on the Upper West Side in Manhattan. Many of his poetry collections and original works reflect African Americans including I Am the Darker Brother, Black Out Loud, Black Is Brown Is Tan, All the Colors of the Race, My Black Me, and Make a Circle, Keep Us In. Adoff's work consistently celebrates racial pride and strength of the family. He received the NCTE Award for Excellence in Poetry in 1988.

HAIKU AND CINQUAIN

The word *haiku* means "beginning." Haiku frequently refers to nature, to a particular event happening at one moment, and to an attendant emotion or feeling, often of the most fragile and evanescent kind. This Japanese verse form consists of three lines and seventeen syllables: The first line contains five syllables; the second line, seven; and the third, five. A haiku usually focuses on an image that suggests a thought or emotion. Students experimenting with the form should not stress counting syllables; instead they should feel free to think about the meaning they want to convey. Paul Janeczko notes that haiku often features nature in rural areas, but he sought out haiku that shows the natural beauty of everyday city streets in his collection *Stone Bench in an Empty Park*. Selected poems include these by Jane Yolen and Anita Wintz:

> Pigeons strut the rails
> Of the city reservoir
> Doing a rain dance.

JANE YOLEN

> from the tar papered
> tenement roof, pigeons
> hot-foot it into flight.

ANITA WINTZ

These two haiku by David McCord appear in his collection *One at a Time*:

> Take the butterfly:
> Nature works to produce him.
> Why doesn't he last?

> All these skyscrapers!
> What will man do about them
> When they have to go?

DAVID MCCORD

Poets who master the haiku form sometimes stretch its boundaries by varying the five-seven-five syllable count while maintaining the essence of its meaning. Issa (1969), a noted Japanese poet, demonstrates in *Don't Tell the Scarecrow* (I) the beauty of haiku in these two variations:

> Where can he be going
> In the rain,
> This snail?

> Little knowing
> The tree will soon be cut down
> Birds are building their nests in it.

Although haiku is a favorite with teachers, Terry's study of children's preferences in poetry shows that it is not always a favorite with children—a signal for teachers to handle it with care. Teachers who want to know the essence of haiku need to read *Wind in My Hand, The Story of Issa* (I), by Hanako Fukuda. Collections of haiku by Issa, cited in the Booklist at the end of the chapter, provide examples for students.

Stone Bench in an Empty Park

Selected by Paul B. Janeczko • *With photographs by* Henri Silberman

© 2000 Henri Silberman

A cinquain consists of five unrhymed lines usually in the pattern of two, four, six, eight, and two syllables. A simplified variation has five lines with one, two, three, four words with the fifth line just one word that is a synonym for the title. The pattern is as follows:

Line 1: One word, the title, usually a noun

Line 2: Two words describing the title

Line 3: Three words that show action

Line 4: Four words that show feeling or emotion

Line 5: One word, a synonym for the title

The following cinquains are variations that 9-year-old students wrote after studying the form:

SNIFFLES AND SNEEZES

Coughing
Sneezing a lot
Missing school, missing friends
I would feel bad at home a lot
Feel bored

ROY STUDNESS

WHERE I LIVE

Port Washington
Sleepy village
Busy and growing
Nice place to be
Home

JASON REAM

Haiku and cinquain are probably the most abstract poetry that children will experience. Since the symbolism and imagery of haiku and cinquain are elusive for many children, they need to have wide exposure to other forms before they meet these. Even then, they need a lot of experience exploring the form.

CONCRETE POETRY

Concrete poetry uses the appearance of words on a page to suggest or illustrate the poem's meaning. Children call these poems *shape* (or *picture*) poems. The actual physical form of the words depicts the subject, so that the whole becomes an ideogram, a graphic symbol used to represent a word; the work illustrates itself as the shapes of words and lines take form, as shown below:

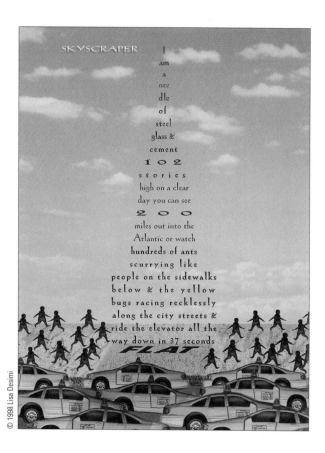

The end-of-chapter Booklist contains books of concrete poetry.

LIMERICK

Limerick, a form of light verse, has five lines and a rhyme scheme of a-a-b-b-a. The first, second, and fifth lines (which rhyme) have three feet (in poetic meter), whereas the third and fourth (which rhyme) have two feet.

Limericks appeal to children because they poke fun and have a definite rhythm and rhyme. Edward Lear (1812–1888) is credited with making limericks popular, although he did not create the form. Lear's *Book of Nonsense* (1), published in 1846, is still popular today. Limericks often make fun of those who take themselves too seriously. James Marshall's *Pocketful of Nonsense* pokes fun through words and illustration:

> There was an old man of Peru
> who dreamed he was eating his shoe.
> He woke in the night
> in a terrible fright
> and found it was perfectly true.

JAMES MARSHALL

Students with a good sense of humor devour limericks. Some limericks have become folklore; their original authorship is forgotten. One such is:

> A flea and a fly in a flue
> Were imprisoned, so what could they do?
> Said the fly, "Let us flee."
> Said the flea, "Let us fly."
> So they flew through a flaw in the flue.

ANONYMOUS

Children laugh at the nonsense primarily because the verses play with the idiosyncrasies of language; limericks encapsulate a joyful absurdity. The Booklist at the end of the chapter has collections of limericks.

BALLADS

A ballad is a story told in verse; it is often sung. Regular ballads, long ballads, and short ballads vary in pattern and rhyme scheme. A regular ballad has a four-line stanza where lines one and three are iambic tetrameter (four sets of da DA), lines two and four are iambic trimeter (three sets of da DA). The rhyme scheme is generally a-b-a-b (first and

There was an old man of Peru
who dreamed he was eating his shoe.
He woke in the night
in a terrible fright
and found it was perfectly true.

In Pocketful of Nonsense, *James Marshall's art spoofs the ridiculous situation described in the limerick.*

third lines end in a rhyme; second and fourth lines end in a rhyme) or a-b-c-b (only the second and fourth lines end in a rhyme). A long ballad is like a regular ballad except that every line has four feet (4, 4, 4, 4) instead of alternating (4, 3, 4, 3). Like the regular ballad, its rhymes may occur on the second and fourth lines (designated as a-b-c-b) and can also rhyme on the first and third lines as well (a-b-a-b). Ballads may be and frequently are written in couplets (a-a-b-b). Pat Lessie reinterprets Aesop's fables in *Fablesauce: Aesop Reinterpeted in Rhymed Couplets* (I). Christina Rossetti uses the short ballad form (the number of feet per line is 3, 3, 4, 3; the rhyme scheme is a-b-c-b) in "Who Has Seen the Wind?"

> *Who has seen the wind?*
> *Neither I nor you:*
> *But when the leaves hang trembling*
> *The wind is passing thro'.*
>
> *Who has seen the wind?*
> *Neither you nor I:*
> *But when the trees bow down their heads*
> *The wind is passing by.*

C H R I S T I N A   R O S S E T T I

Ballads are lyrical and tell a story relating a single incident or thought. Some poets use dialogue to tell a story in repeated refrains. Myra Cohn Livingston's *Abraham Lincoln: A Man for All the People: A Ballad* (1993) extols the trials and tribulations of Lincoln's life. Livingston's *Keep on Singing: A Ballad of Marion Anderson* (1994) focuses on the triumphs of the great singer.

There are folk ballads and literary ballads. Folk ballads have no known author; they have become anonymous and are handed down in song. "John Henry" is a well-known folk ballad. Modern vocalists, such as Beth Orton, Tracy Chapman, Van Morrison, James Taylor, k.d. lang, and Paul Simon express themselves through ballads.

Generally, ballads sing of heroic deeds and of murder, unrequited love, and feuds. Carl Sandburg's *The American Song-bag* (A) is a classic collection of the ballads of railroad builders, lumberjacks, and cowboys. Ernest Lawrence Thayer's *Casey at the Bat* (I) is a ballad young readers enjoy. It begins

> *The outlook wasn't brilliant for the Mudville nine*
> *that day:*
> *The score stood four to two, with but one inning more*
> *to play,*
> *And then when Cooney died at first, and Barrows did*
> *the same,*
> *A pall-like silence fell upon the patrons of the game.*
>
> *A straggling few got up to go in deep despair. The rest*
> *Clung to that hope which springs eternal in the*
> *human breast;*

> *They thought, "If only Casey could but get a whack*
> *at that—*
> *We'd put up even money now, with Casey at the bat."*

E R N E S T   L A W R E N C E   T H A Y E R

Ballads are listed in the Booklist at the end of the chapter.

RIDDLE POEMS

Students nurtured on poetry have meaningful experiences with complicated poetic forms like ballads, but many prefer simpler riddle poems. J. Patrick Lewis and Elizabeth Spires have contributed excellent material for riddle lovers. In *Riddle-Lightful* (P–I), Lewis says "The middle of table/The end of a tub///In front of a battleship/In back of a sub///A bus to start off with/A cab at the end///I hope you will be my/B-you-tiful friend. (Answer: The letter *b*) In *Riddle Road: Puzzles in Poems and Pictures* (P–I) Spires tells us: "I eat words wherever/I find them but am no wiser,/Keep your books under lock and key/or they'll be devoured by me! (Answer: Bookworm) Students enjoy creating their own riddles and delight in asking others to guess the answer. Riddle poems are listed in the Booklist at the end of the chapter.

Building a Poetry Collection

Teachers need to build their own poetry collection to fit their curriculum and their students. Poetry books come in different formats and sizes. Some poems are published in a single volume with beautiful illustrations; such books provide a good opportunity to explore fine poetry accompanied by fine artists' work. Teachers need anthologies and collections in order to provide a variety of poems and yet hold their collection to a manageable size. It is easy to locate a poem in a themed collection with subject, title, author, and first-line indexes.

Three types of anthologies are particularly useful in the classroom: the specialized anthology, with works by several poets on one subject; the generalized anthology, with works by many poets on many subjects; and the individual anthology, which contains the works of only one poet.

Specialized anthologies are popular. The plethora of collections of poems and verses about holidays, monsters, dinosaurs, horses, sports, and other special topics bear witness to this. Three excellent anthologists, Lee Bennett Hopkins, Paul Janeczko, and Jane Yolen, add immeasurably to the wealth of resources. Lee Bennett Hopkins has collected more than 100 specialized anthologies from easy-to-read verse to poetry by Carl Sandburg and Langston Hughes. Among his most popular collections are *Good Books, Good Times!* (P) (1990), *Hand in Hand: An American History Through Poetry* (I) (1994), *Side by Side: Poems to Read Together* (P–I) (1988), and *My America: A Poetry Atlas of the United States* (I–A) (2000). Paul Janeczko has collected many specialized anthologies, such as *The Music of What Happens, Poetspeak, The Place My Words Are Looking For, Poetry from A to Z, Brickward Summer, Wherever Home Begins,* and *I Feel a Little Jumpy Around You,* coedited with Naomi Shihab Nye (all I–A). Janeczko's individual anthologies include *Stardust Otel* (A) and *That Sweet Diamond: Baseball Poems* (P–I). Jane Yolen gives us multicultural collections in *Street Rhymes Around the World* (P–I) and *Sleep Rhymes Around the World* (P–I). She presents her own poetry along with that of others in *Alphabestiary* (P–I), *Sky Scrape, City Scape* (P–I–A), *Water Music* (I), *Weather Report* (I), *Color Me a Rhyme* (P–I), *Snow, Snow* (I), *Mother Earth Father Sky* (I), and *Once Upon Ice* (I). Jane Yolen has produced numerous individual and collective anthologies that enrich our poetry resources.

Alvin Schwartz uses a different kind of theme to organize his anthology (1992) *And the Green Grass Grew All Around* (P–I–A). This collection of more than 250 folk poems contains autograph rhymes, work poems, story poems, nonsense, and much more. The Booklist at the end of the chapter lists specialized anthologies.

A traditional generalized poetry anthology, originally May Hill Arbuthnot's *Time for Poetry,* now edited by Zena Sutherland in *The Scott Foresman Anthology of Children's Literature,* is a comprehensive volume with verse on many subjects. Best-loved poems of childhood include those about people, animals, adventures, games, jokes, magic and make-believe, wind and water, holidays and seasons, and wisdom and beauty. Anthologies help librarians and teachers make poetry central to children's lives. They often turn to general anthologies, whereas students prefer individual anthologies. Two books by X. J. Kennedy and Dorothy Kennedy, *Talking Like the Rain* (P–I) and *Knock at a Star: A Child's Introduction to Poetry* (revised edition 1999), contain poems arranged under informative headings. The books are a pleasure to skim, read, or savor. Several general anthologies are listed in the Booklist at the end of the chapter.

David McCord's book *One at a Time* (P–I–A) is an individual anthology comprised solely of his work. An impressive volume, it is a collection of most of his poetry. McCord's wit and thoughtful perception sing in the music of his words. *One at a Time* is a timeless resource to use for cultivating poetic taste and for producing children who will read poetry for pleasure. See the Booklist at the end of the chapter for general and individual anthologies.

All teachers and groups of students have personal favorite anthologies they like to use. We believe some poets' works are basic to the curriculum. These are listed in the Booklist; the age designations should be considered flexible. Poetry, especially, appeals to a wide age range.

Reading reviews in professional journals and noting the winners of the National Council of Teachers of English Poetry Award will keep you up-to-date on poetry for children. Being familiar with the body of work of the award-winning poets is a prerequisite for building a sound poetry curriculum in the classroom.

As described earlier, Cullinan (1996) conducted a national survey of 3,500 students to find out which poems among the award-winning poets' work they liked best. Children's top five favorites from each poet appear in *A Jar of Tiny Stars: Poems by NCTE Award-Winning Poets* (I–A). She also conducted a similar survey of Aileen Fisher's poetry. Published in 2001, the book is titled *Sing of the Earth and Sky: Poems About Our Planet and the Wonders Beyond.*

Using Poetry in the Classroom

All you need to do to create student poetry lovers is to love it yourself. Students will like what you like. Students need to feel comfortable using the books you have gathered; talk about the books and display their covers to attract readers. Shelve poetry with other books by the same author or the same subject. Your students need time and space to browse, to pull out several volumes at once, and to compare poems or look for favorites. Having tape recorders close by will stimulate oral interpretation of favorite poems. Give students time to browse through the poetry collection during a free period or to look up a poem for a particular occasion or for independent reading. Allowing and encouraging students to enjoy poetry together, and to talk quietly while doing so, forges strong bonds in a community of readers. It also helps students learn how to read poetry and increases contact with poetry and poets.

Children learn to love poetry when they are allowed to explore it freely. Unfortunately, some learn to dislike poetry because a teacher insists they search for elusive meanings or rhyme schemes that make no sense to them. Close attention to children's comments can supply a basis for thought-provoking questions that will lead children to discover the substance of poetry for themselves. The object is to develop a child's liking for the music of words; detailed analysis takes away the splendor of poetry. Explanation that destroys appreciation is no improvement over misconceptions. The magic that words can exercise on the imagination is more valuable than accuracy at the beginning stages. Appropriate discussions of poetry take children back into a poem, not away from it.

A love of poetry is contagious. The way you read and respond to poetry has a tremendous effect on the way students read and respond. If students see you enjoy poetry, they will be more likely to approach poetry with the expectation of joy. If you turn to poetry to illustrate the multicultural nature of our world, as in Isaac Olaleye's *The Distant Talking Drum* (I), students will be more likely to do the same. If they see you making connections to real experiences and feelings, they will be more likely to make poetry connections. Perhaps the most important thing that teachers can do with poetry is to make a human connection with a poet's words.

Naomi Shihab Nye (2000), a writer-in-the-schools poet, says, "In the midst of public jabber, high-velocity advertising, and shameless television, where is one true word? Where are three? Who will pause long enough to describe something truly and clearly? Where is the burn of speech, the sweet rub of language, the spark that links us? Poetry, poetry! It doesn't take long to weave it into our lives."

Two books, *Salting the Ocean: 100 Poems by Young Poets* (2000) and *What Have You Lost?* (1999), show the results of Nye's work with young people. She exposed students to excellent poetry and helped them to release their thoughts and feelings in poetry:

ONE

We had a
"Most commonly misspelled word"
Spelling test
Yesterday in English,
Fourth Period.
I commonly misspelled them all.
Except one.
Loneliness
was the only one I got right.

BUTCH MCELROY

Naomi Shihab Nye and Paul Janeczko chose selections from their poetry for a joint book, *I Feel a Little Jumpy Around You* (A), a collection that adolescents especially enjoy.

Poet Ralph Fletcher (2000) says, "Marinate students in poetry." Begin with poems that research shows to be favorites: humorous poems and narrative poems with strong rhyme, rhythm, and sound elements. Gradually expand children's experiences with poetry by exposing them to a broad range of forms. As students hear and read poetry, encourage them to experiment with oral interpretation such as paired reading, choral reading, choral speaking, and dramatization. Teaching Idea 2.4 gives suggestions for helping students to act out poetry.

Poems for two voices make good material for choral reading. Divide students into groups to read from Paul Fleischman's books *Joyful Noise: Poems for Two Voices* (I–A), *I Am Phoenix*, and *Big Talk: Poems for Four Voices* (both I). Also use Georgia Heard's poems for two voices in *Creatures of Earth, Sea, and Sky* (I).

Students explore how poetry works by examining what poets do, and they like to experiment with poetry in their own writing. Provide opportunities for students to play with various forms, elements, and devices of poetry to help them understand and enjoy a variety of poetry.

Children enjoy collecting their own favorite poetry, copying it onto Post-Its, file cards, or notebooks. Primary-grade teachers put favorite poems on charts to be read over and over; teachers of intermediate and advanced grades encourage students to create individual anthologies of favorite poems, adding to them throughout the year. Stu-

---

Teaching Idea 2 ☆ 4

Play with Poetry: Act It Out

Students like to perform poetry if we make it fun and nonthreatening. Here are some steps to follow.

* First, have the teacher perform the poem—model it for students.
* Next, invite students to recite the poem as a group.
* Then, invite individuals to say parts of the poem.
* Finally, ask individuals to recite poems of their own choosing.

At all stages, students should hold a copy of the poem in their hands—to use or not use as they choose. Performing poetry is not a test of memory. Brod Bagert, poetry performer, says in *Invitation to Read* that if children make the right face when they are ready to say a poem, everything falls into place. He suggests that we search for what a poem means and ask, "What face should I make when I say these words?" When we make a face to express feelings, we are bound to give the right expression to the words.

Books of Poems to Dramatize

All books and poems are at the P–I–A level.

Bagert, Brod, *Let Me Be the Boss*

Ciardi, John, *Mummy Slept Late and Daddy Fixed Breakfast*

Esbensen, Barbara, *Words with Wrinkled Knees*

Fleischman, Paul, *I Am Phoenix: Poems for Two Voices*

_____, *Joyful Noise: Poems for Two Voices*

Gunning, Monica, *Not a Copper Penny in Me House*

Olaleye, Isaac, *The Distant Talking Drum*

Service, Robert, *The Cremation of Sam McGee*

_____, *The Shooting of Dan McGrew*

Spilka, Arnold, *Monkeys Write Terrible Letters*

Springer, Nancy, *Music of Their Hooves*

Thayer, Ernest L., *Casey at the Bat: A Centennial Edition*

---

dents illustrate their anthologies, some with their own art, photographs, or pictures cut from magazines. Personal anthologies become part of the classroom library so that peers read and discuss each other's favorites. As anthologies grow, students experiment with classifying the contents.

When poetry is part of the daily life of the classroom, children spontaneously learn their favorite poems by heart. Do not require them to memorize and recite poems. Instead, casually recite your own favorites, and invite your students to do the same. They will soon be eager to share a poem with others. We discuss using poetry in the classroom in this Chapter and in Chapters 13 and 14.

IMMERSE STUDENTS IN POETRY

Teachers who want their students to develop an appreciation for poetry immerse them in it. They collect poems that they and their students like, read them aloud several times a day, put poems on charts for group reading, and sprinkle poetry throughout the curriculum. Teaching Idea 2.5 presents some ideas for integrating science and poetry. Beatrice Schenk de Regniers (1983) suggests one way to keep poetry ever-present:

Teaching Idea 2 ✩ 5

Integrate Science and Poetry

Acquaint students with unrhymed verse by reading several poems from Georgia Heard's *Creatures of Earth, Sea, and Sky* (I) and Pat Moon's *Earth Lines: Poems for the Green Age* (I). Such poems put students in a poetry mood and give them a sense of the poets' concern for the environment. Reread the poems, talk about the poems and the issues they raise.

When students complete informational reports about a science subject, ask them to think about their topic in a poetic way. The following examples show how you might lead off the discussion.

> TEACHER: We are going to look at the information in our reports in a new way. Let's go back to our reports and think about the seashore as poets.

TEACHER: Look at your report and locate five facts you learned about your subject. Write those five facts down.

TEACHER: The five facts are the essence of your subject. That's what poetry is—the essence—the distilled substance of a subject.

TEACHER: Put the five facts into phrases. Write them out on your page in different ways, with different line breaks. How do they look? How do they sound?

TEACHER: We can turn our science reports into poems. (*Then, the teacher can read examples of science and poetry.*)

Sources: The child-written examples came from Marilyn Scala's students. Developed by Marilyn Scala, Munsey Park School, Manhasset, NY.

```
① Horshoe crabs have been around for 400 millions
② They are called living fossils
③ There relatives are also very old
④ They eat small plants and animals
⑤ They molt
⑥ When babes get to big for there shell they molt

Horshoe crabs \ have been around \ for 400 million
years \ because they haven't \ been hunted
for any part of there \ body. \ Also they are
called \ living fossils \ because \ they have
around since the \ dinous \ Also thae
reletive the spider crab \ has been
around for \ so long because they haven'
been \ tampered with either \
```

The Fossil of the Sea

Horseshoe crabs
have been around
for 400 million years,
because they haven't
been hunted for any part of their body.
They are called

LIVING FOSSILS

because they have been around since the

DINOS!!!

Their relatives, the
spider crabs,
have been around for so long,
because they haven't been
tampered with either.

Pat Turano

(continued)

KEEP A POEM IN YOUR POCKET

Keep a poem in your pocket
and a picture in your head
and you'll never feel lonely
at night when you're in bed.

The little poem will sing to you
the little picture bring to you
a dozen dreams to dance to you
at night when you're in bed.

So—
Keep a picture in your pocket
and a poem in your head
and you'll never feel lonely
at night when you're in bed.

BEATRICE SCHENK DE REGNIERS

Each fall, teachers in the Cypress-Fairbanks School District in Houston, Texas, respond to a questionnaire from the district language and reading coordinator, asking if they would like to receive the monthly newsletter *Poetry Supplement*. To receive it, teachers must agree to establish a personal (not a team) poetry-card file to keep poems at their fingertips for convenient use. Each month, the *Poetry Supplement* contains 15 to 20 poems on a theme, with suggested activities for each. Patricia Smith, the creator of the newsletter, explains, "I gather an assortment of poems intended to promote an appreciation of poetry and at the same time facilitate teaching the essential elements of speaking, listening, reading, and writing."

Smith introduces the March issue by saying:

> March is sometimes marked as a month of contrasts. It enters loudly and goes out quietly. Your *Poetry Supplement* is organized into pairs of poems this month in a manner that will promote connections and reflections on likenesses and differences. A model for putting poems together is Bernice Wolman's book, **Taking Turns**. Ask your students to search for poems that belong together on some basis. The similarity might be topic, style, or poet. The amount and quality of reading and critical thinking for this task is immense. (1992, p. 1)

Following this introduction are seven pairs of poems with teaching suggestions for each.

There are Millions

There are millions
Of different kinds of seaweed,

Ribbon-like and delicate,

Hanging on to different things
Like boats, rocks and pinkish shells,

Living on either

The southern or Atlantic coasts.

There are
millions.

Cathy Perifimos

Profile ✳ Aileen Fisher

Thomas V. Crowell

*P*oetry is a rhythmical piece of writing that leaves the reader feeling that life is a little richer than before, a little more full of wonder, beauty, or just plain delight.

Aileen Fisher is a nature poet. She was reared in a big, square, white house on 40 acres of land near the Iron River on the Upper Peninsula of Michigan. She attended the University of Chicago for two years and then transferred to the University of Missouri to complete her degree in journalism. She worked at the Women's Journalistic Register and Labor Bureau before she returned to live in the country to write full-time. She lives near the mountains in Boulder, Colorado. Her most recent and popular books include *Sing of the Earth and Sky: Poems About Our Planet and the Wonders Beyond, Always Wondering, Anybody Home?, The House of a Mouse, Like Nothing at All, Out in the Dark and Daylight,* and *Rabbits, Rabbits.* Aileen Fisher received the NCTE Award for Poetry for Children in 1978.

HELP STUDENTS DISCOVER THE PLEASURE IN POETRY

Poetry is best understood when it is read aloud. Children who hear poetry read aloud and read it aloud themselves discover more about poetry. Children need to understand how to read this new style of written language. Work with your students to teach them how to read poetry aloud; it is not the same as reading prose. Illustrate the differences by reading poetry aloud in a number of ways. Read it by stopping at the end of every line regardless of the punctuation. Then read it from a prose format to demonstrate the impact of punctuation.

Remember that we communicate our own expectations through body language, gestures, and how and what we say. If a teacher reads poems in a spirited, enthusiastic manner, with a twinkle in the eye, children respond positively. If the reader is boring, children are bored. Demonstrate the effect of bad readings: Read it in a sing-song fashion. Read it in an icky sweet "poetry voice." Then read it to interpret the meaning. Work with poetry can link the experiences of listening, oral interpretation, silent reading, and writing. Experiences with poetry build on each other. Listening to a poem read aloud well provides insight into how poetry works, what a poem might mean to another reader, techniques for oral interpretation, and strategies for reading that can be employed silently. Lee Bennett Hopkins (1998), poet and teacher, suggests the following: (1) Before reading a poem aloud to an audience, read it aloud to yourself several times to get the feel of the words and rhythm. (2) Follow the rhythm of the poem, reading it naturally. (3) Make pauses that please you—pauses that make sense. (4) When reading a poem aloud, speak in a natural voice. (5) After a poem is read, be quiet. Don't feel trapped into asking questions such as "Did you like it?"

Writing poetry also helps children appreciate how poetry works and is best accomplished by building on a firm foundation of reading and listening experiences. Poetry writers read poetry with greater understanding. Poetry, perhaps more than any other genre, must be explored through both oral and written language activities. Choral reading can help students discover how important sound is to many poems as they experiment with different approaches, and explore how pitch, stress, and rate influence the overall effect of the poem.

These experiences can lead naturally to discussions of rhythm and other elements of sound. The rhythm of poetry is a natural springboard into movement. Young children will spontaneously move to the beat of highly metrical poetry, and older children can be encouraged to clap or tap pencils as they hear the beat in the poems they read. These experiences can lead to discussions of variations in rhythm, how rhythm contributes to meaning and overall effect, and word choice in relation to rhythm.

Drawing pictures in response to poems can help children formulate their own meanings. Poems that are rich in figurative language can lead to discussions of metaphor, simile, and imagery. Discussions of "how" a poem means can spring naturally from discussions of "what" a poem means to individual readers, especially when these readers are writers as well.

Children who read a lot of poetry will want to try writing it themselves. In the introduction to *Dogs and Dragons, Trees and Dreams* (1), Karla Kuskin says

The poetry reader often becomes a poetry writer. What could be better? No imagination is freer than a child's; no eye is sharper. The conversation of young children is a constant reminder that they are natural poets. But fitting unrestrained thoughts into rigid

Profile ☆ John Ciardi

Houghton Mifflin Company

Poetry and learning are both fun, and children are full of an enormous relish for both. My poetry is just a bubbling up of a natural foolishness, and the idea that maybe you can make language dance a bit.

John Ciardi was born in Boston, the only son of Italian immigrant parents, and grew up in Medford, Massachusetts. He graduated magna cum laude from Tufts University and received his M.A. degree in English literature from the University of Michigan. He began writing poetry for his own children. His first book was *The Reason for the Pelican.* Other favorites include *You Read to Me, I'll Read to You; You Know Who; The Monster Den* or *Look What Happened at My House and to It; The Man Who Sang the Sillies;* and *I Met a Man.* John Ciardi received the NCTE Poetry Award in 1982.

forms can be discouraging and may cramp the eccentric voice that makes a child's work (any work) unique. Read rhymes to children, but encourage them, as they begin to write, to write without rhyming. To write any way at all. And to read everything, anything . . . more poetry. (1980)

Just as children try on other forms of writing to suit their own purposes, they try on a poet's cloak when they feel comfortable with poetry. Sensitive teachers will encourage but not require them to do so. Professional references for teachers and students who write poetry are listed in the Booklist at the end of the chapter.

Creative teachers find many ways to involve children in poetry. One group of primary-grade teachers noticed their students' interest in studying weather and asked, "Why not have poetic as well as meteorological reports?" The teachers assigned a poetry reporter to select a poem that best expressed the foggy, sunny, windy, or rainy day; the poems extended the meaning of the weather symbols attached to the classroom calendar. Now Jane Yolen makes their search easier with *Weather Report* (P–I), a collection of poems about fog, rain, snow, wind, and sun.

Poets themselves have good suggestions for aspiring poets. When Eve Merriam accepted the NCTE Award for Poetry for Children, she encouraged children with these words:

Read a lot. Sit down with anthologies and decide which pleases you. Copy out your favorites in your own handwriting. Buy a notebook and jot down images and descriptions. Be specific; use all the senses. Use your whole body as you write. It might even help sometime to stand up and move with your words. Don't be afraid of copying a form or convention, especially in the beginning. And, to give yourself scope and flexibility, remember: It doesn't always have to rhyme. (1981)

You don't need gimmicks, elaborate plans, or detailed instructions. You do need lots of poetry books, time to savor them, and pleasurable experiences.

Poetry is a valuable tool for fully realizing life's many and varied experiences. It allows us to participate in the imaginative experience of others and thereby better understand our own experiences. The more readers participate, the more they create, and the more personal and enjoyable the experience of poetry becomes. The rewards are more than worth the effort.

Summary

Listening to, reading, and writing poetry helps us to learn about the world, about ourselves, and about the power and potential of language. Poems make us smile, create memorable images, and express feelings in an understandable way. Poets use devices of sound, rhythm, and meaning to present their own unique visions. Poetry comes in varied forms and is available in many formats. Children are attracted to poetry and teachers can build upon this attraction, providing experiences with poetry that will lead children to enjoy poetry and thus to consider how poetry works. Children who experience a poetry-rich environment will become lifelong readers and writers of poetry.

INFOTRAC Read the tribute to David McCord in the November/December issue of *The Horn Book Magazine.* Add to your knowledge of McCord and other poets you enjoy by using the reference aids presented in Appendix B and by discovering resources on the World Wide Web.

Booklist

Poems That Stir Emotions

Selections in the following sections are at the P–I level unless otherwise noted.

LAUGHTER

Bagert, Brod, *Chicken Socks and Other Contagious Poems*

_____, *Elephant Games and Other Playful Poems to Perform*

_____, *Let Me Be the Boss*

Cole, William, *A Zooful of Animals*

Fox, Mem, *Harriet, You'll Drive Me Wild!*

Florian, Douglas, *Beast Feast*

_____, *Bing Bang Boing*

_____, *Laugh-eteria*

_____, *On the Wing*

Giovanni, Nikki, *Shimmy, Shimmy, Shimmy Like My Sister Kate* (A)

Harrison, David, *The Boy Who Counted Stars*

_____, *Somebody Catch My Homework*

_____, *A Thousand Cousins*

Hughes, Shirley, *Rhymes for Annie Rose*

Kennedy, X. J., *The Forgetful Wishing Well*

_____, *Fresh Brats*

_____, *Ghastlies, Goops and Pincushions: Nonsense Verse*

_____, *Kite That Braved Old Orchard Beach*

Kherdian, David, *Beat Voices: An Anthology of Beat Poetry* (A)

Lewis, J. Patrick, *Ridicholas Nicholas: Animal Poems*

McNaughton, Colin, *Who's Been Sleeping in My Porridge? A Book of Wacky Poems and Pictures*

Merriam, Eve, *Poem for a Pickle*

Prelutsky, Jack, *Baby Uggs Are Hatching*

_____, *For Laughing Out Loud*

_____, *The New Kid on the Block*

_____, *A. Nonny Mouse Writes Again! Poems*

_____, *A Pizza the Size of the Sun*

Silverstein, Shel, *Falling Up*

_____, *A Light in the Attic*

_____, *Where the Sidewalk Ends*

Smith, William Jay, *Behind the King's Kitchen: A Roster of Rhyming Riddles*

Soto, Gary, *Neighborhood Odes: Poems* (A)

Steig, Jeanne, *Consider the Lemming*

SENSORY IMAGES

Adoff, Arnold, *In for Winter; Out for Spring*

Dickinson, Emily, *Poems for Youth* (A)

Esbensen, Barbara Juster, *Dance with Me*

_____, *Who Shrank My Grandmother's House?*

_____, *Words with Wrinkled Knees*

Fisher, Aileen, *Always Wondering*

Giovanni, Nikki, *Knoxville, Tennessee*

_____, *Spin a Soft Black Song*

Gordon, Ruth, *Pierced by a Ray of Sun: Poems About the Times We Feel Alone* (A)

Greenfield, Eloise, *Honey, I Love: And Other Poems*

_____, *Nathaniel Talking*

Gunning, Monica, *Not a Copper Penny in Me House*

Heard, Georgia, *Creatures of Earth, Sea, and Sky*

Huck, Charlotte, *Secret Places*

Hughes, Langston, *The Block,* selected by Lowery S. Sims and Daisy Murray Voigt (A)

James, Simon, *Days Like This: A Collection of Small Poems*

Janeczko, Paul, *Stone Bench in an Empty Park* (A)

Levy, Constance, *A Tree Place and Other Poems*

Livingston, Myra Cohn, *Call Down the Moon: Poems of Music*

_____, *Sea Songs*

Mado, Michio, *The Magic Pocket: Selected Poems*

Merriam, Eve, *Higgle Wiggle: Happy Rhymes*

Moore, Lilian, *Sunflakes: Poems for Children*

Morrison, Lillian, *Whistling the Morning In*

Osofsky, Audrey, *Free to Dream: The Making of a Poet: Langston Hughes* (A)

Smith, William Jay, *Around My Room*

Sneve, Virginia Driving Hawk, *Dancing Tepees*

Stevenson, James, *Candy Corn*

_____, *Cornflakes*

_____, *Popcorn*

_____, *Sweet Corn: Poems*

Worth, Valerie, *All the Small Poems*

FEELINGS (SCARY POEMS, THOUGHTFUL POEMS, AND POEMS ABOUT FAMILY LOVE)

Adoff, Arnold, *Black Is Brown Is Tan*

Berry, James, *Isn't My Name Magical? Sister and Brother Poems*

Bierhorst, John, *In the Trail of the Wind: American Indian Poems and Ritual Orations*

Brooks, Gwendolyn, *Bronzeville Boys and Girls*

de Regniers, Beatrice Schenk, *Way I Feel . . . Sometimes*

Dunning, Stephen, *Reflections on a Gift of Watermelon Pickle and Other Modern Verse*

Fletcher, Ralph, *I Am Wings: Poems About Love* (A)

_____, *Relatively Speaking: Poems About Family*

Gasztold, Carmen Bernos de, *Prayers from the Ark*

Goerge, Kristine O'Connell, *Little Dog Poems*

Glaser, Isabel Joshlin, *Dreams of Glory: Poems Starring Girls*

Greenfield, Eloise, *Nathaniel Talking*

_____, *Night on Neighborhood Street*

_____, *Under the Sunday Tree*

Grimes, Nikki, *A Dime a Dozen*

_____, *Hopscotch Love: A Family Treasury of Love Poems*

_____, *Meet Danitra Brown*

_____, *My Man Blue*

Hoberman, Mary Ann, *Fathers, Mothers, Sisters, Brothers*

_____, *The Cozy Book*

Hopkins, Lee Bennett, *Been to Yesterdays: Poems of a Life* (A)

_____, *Still as a Star: A Book of Nighttime Poems*

Hughes, Langston, *The Block,* selected by Lowery S. Sims and Daisy Murray Voigt

_____, *The Dream Keeper*

Janeczko, Paul, *Wherever Home Begins: 100 Contemporary Poems* (A)

Kurtz, Jane, *River Friendly, River Wild*

Livingston, Myra Cohn, *I Like You, If You Like Me: Poems of Friendship*

_____, *Roll Along: Poems on Wheels*

Margolis, Richard J., *Secrets of a Small Brother*

Medina, Jane, *My Name Is Jorge: On Both Sides of the River*

Newsome, Effie Lee, *Wonders: The Best Children's Poems of Effie Lee Newsome,* compiled by Rudine Sims Bishop

Nye, Naomi Shihab, *The Space Between Our Footsteps: Poems and Paintings from the Middle East* (A)

Ormerod, Jan, *Jan Ormerod's To Baby with Love*

Pomerantz, Charlotte, *If I Had a Paka: Poems in Eleven Languages*

_____, *The Tamarindo Puppy and Other Poems*

Prelutsky, Jack, *Nightmares: Poems to Trouble Your Sleep*

Rosenberg, Liz, *Light-Gathering Poems* (A)

Wong, Janet, *The Rainbow Hand: Poems About Mothers and Children*

Zolotow, Charlotte, *Snippets: A Gathering of Poems, Pictures, and Possibilities*

Children's Poetry Choices 1974–2000

Adoff, Arnold, *Chocolate Dreams*

Clarke, Gillian, *The Whispering Room: Haunted Poems*

Dakos, Kalli, *The Bug in Teacher's Coffee and Other School Poems*

_____, *The Goof Who Invented Homework: And Other School Poems*

dePaola, Tomie, *Tomie dePaola's Book of Poems*

Dotlich, Rebecca Kai, *Lemonade Sun: And Other Summer Poems*

Florian, Douglas, *Insectlopedia*

_____, *Laugh-eteria*

Griego, Margot C. et al., *Tortillitas Para Mama* (selected and translated)

Grossman, Bill, *My Little Sister Ate One Hare*

Harrison, David L., *A Thousand Cousins: Poems of Family Life*

Higginson, William J., *Wind in the Tall Grass: A Collection of Haiku*

Hoberman, Mary Ann, *A House Is a House for Me*

_____, *Miss Mary Mack*

Hopkins, Lee Bennett, *Good Books, Good Times*

_____, *Opening Days: Sports Poems*

_____, *Surprises*

Hubbard, Patricia, *My Crayons Talk*

Lee, Dennis, *Alligator Pie*

Lillegard, Dee, *The Big Bug Ball*

Lobel, Arnold, *The Book of Pigericks*

Merriam, Eve, *Blackberry Ink*

Morrison, Lillian, *Best Wishes, Amen: Autograph Verse*

Moss, Jeffrey, *Butterfly Jar*

O'Brien, John, *Mother Hubbard's Christmas*

Paul, Ann Whitford, *Everything to Spend the Night from A to Z*

Prelutsky, Jack, *Nightmares: Poems to Trouble Your Sleep*

_____, *Poems of A. Nonny Mouse*

Sandved, Kjell B. *The Butterfly Alphabet*

Siegen-Smith, Nikki, *A Pocketful of Stars: Poems About the Night*

Schwartz, Alvin, *And the Green Grass Grew All Around: Folk Poetry from Everyone*

Silverstein, Shel, *Falling Up*

Thayer, Ernest Lawrence, *Casey at the Bat*

Withers, Carl, *A Rocket in My Pocket: The Rhymes and Chants of Young Americans*

Worth, Valerie, *More Small Poems*

Teachers' Poetry Choices 1982–2000

Bruchac, Joseph, and Jonathan London, *Thirteen Moons on Turtle's Back: A Native American Year of Moons* (I)

de Regniers, Beatrice Schenk, *Sing a Song of Popcorn: Every Child's Book of Poems* (P)

Esbensen, Barbara, *Echoes for the Eye: Poems to Celebrate Patterns in Nature* (I)

Fleischman, Paul, *Joyful Noise: Poems for Two Voices* (I)

Florian, Douglas, *Beast Feast: Poems and Paintings by Douglas Florian* (P)

Glenn, Mel, *Who Killed Mr. Chippendale? A Mystery in Poems* (A)

Goldstein, Bobbye, *Inner Chimes* (P)

Granfield, Linda, *In Flanders Field: The Story of the Poem by John McCrae* (I)

Greenfield, Eloise, *Nathaniel Talking* (P)

Gunning, Monica, *Not a Copper Penny in Me House* (P)

Hastings, Selina, *A Selection from the Canterbury Tales* (A)

Hesse, Karen, *Out of the Dust* (A)

Hughes, Langston, *The Dream Keeper and Other Poems* (A)

Janeczko, Paul, *The Place My Words Are Looking For: What Poets Say About and Through Their Work* (A)

Krull, Kathleen, *Gonna Sing My Head Off!* (A)

Lee, Dennis, *Dinosaur Dinner (with a slice of alligator pie)* (P)

Lewis, J. Patrick, *Black Swan/White Crow: Haiku* (I)

Lindbergh, Reeve, *Johnny Appleseed* (P)

Livingston, Myra Cohn, *Let Freedom Ring* (I)

Myers, Walter Dean, *Brown Angels: An Album of Pictures and Verse* (P)

Nye, Naoami Shihab, *What Have You Lost?* (A)

Panzer, Nora, *Celebrate America in Poetry and Art* (I)

Prelutsky, Jack, selector, *The Beauty of the Beast: Poems from the Animal Kingdom* (I)

Rosen, Michael, selector, *Classic Poetry: An Illustrated Collection* (A)

Sandburg, Carl, *Poetry for Young People* (I)

Shannon, George, *Tomorrow's Alphabet* (P)

Siebert, Diane, *Mojave* (I)

_____, *Plane Song* (P)

Stevenson, James, *Popcorn* (I)

Thomas, Joyce Carol, *Brown Honey in Broomwheat Tea* (I)

_____, *Gingerbread Days: Poems* (I)
_____, *I Have Heard of a Land,* (I)
Whipple, Laura, *Eric Carle's Animals Animals* (P)
Wood, Nancy, *Spirit Walker* (A)
Yolen, Jane, *Sacred Places* (A)
_____, *Water Music: Poems for Children* (A)

Poetry in Many Forms

All entries in this section are at the P–I level unless otherwise noted.

NARRATIVE POETRY

Field, Rachel, *General Store*
Johnson, Angela, *The Other Side: Shorter Poems*
Kuskin, Karla, *James and the Rain*
Lear, Edward, *The Owl and the Pussycat*
_____, *The Pelican Chorus and Other Nonsense*
Leslie-Spinks, Tim, and Alice Andres, *Treasures of Trinkamalee*
Longfellow, Henry Wadsworth, *Paul Revere's Ride*
Moore, Clement C., *Grandma Moses Night Before Christmas*
_____, *Twas the Night Before Christmas: A Visit from St. Nicholas*
Nash, Ogden, *The Adventures of Isabel*
_____, *The Tale of Custard the Dragon*
Poe, Edgar Allan, *Annabel Lee*
Prelutsky, Jack, *The Mean Old Mean Hyena*
Whittier, John Greenleaf, *Barbara Frietchie*

LYRIC POETRY

de la Mare, Walter, *Peacock Pie*
Frost, Robert, *Stopping by the Woods on a Snowy Evening*
_____, *Swinger of Birches: Poems of Robert Frost for Young People*
_____, *You Come Too: Favorite Poems for Young Readers*
Hoberman, Mary Ann, *A House Is a House for Me*
Hollyer, Belinda, *Dreamtime: A Book of Lullabies*
Larrick, Nancy, *I Heard a Scream in the Street* (I–A)
O'Neill, Mary, *Hailstones and Halibut Bones*
Schertle, Alice, and Kathryn Sky-Peck, *Who Has Seen the Wind? An Illustrated Collection of Poetry for Young People*
Thomas, Joyce Carol, *Hush Songs: African American Lullabies*
Wolman, Bernice, *Taking Turns: Poetry to Share*

FREE VERSE

Adoff, Arnold, *Black Is Brown Is Tan*
_____, *Chocolate Dreams*
_____, *Eats*
_____, *Hard to Be Six*
_____, *In for Winter, Out for Spring*
_____, *Sports Pages*
Hopkins, Lee Bennett, *Been to Yesterdays: Poems of a Life*
Janeczko, Paul, *Pocket Poems*
_____, *That Sweet Diamond: Baseball Poems*
Soto, Gary, *Canto Familiar*
_____, *Neighborhood Odes*

HAIKU AND CINQUAIN

Atwood, Ann, *Haiku: The Mood of Earth*
Fukuda, Hanako, *Wind in My Hand, The Story of Issa*
Gollub, Matthew, *Cool Melons—Turn to Frogs! The Life and Poems of Issa*
Issa, *Don't Tell the Scarecrow*
Lewis, J. Patrick, *Black Swan White Crow: Haiku*
Livingston, Myra Cohn, *Sky Songs*
Schertle, Alice, *I Am the Cat*

CONCRETE POEMS

Adoff, Arnold, *Street Music: City Poems*
Esbensen, Barbara, *Echoes for the Eye: Poems to Celebrate Patterns in Nature*
Froman, Robert, *Seeing Things: A Book of Poems*
Graham, Joan Bransfield, *Flicker Flash*
_____, *Splish Splash*
Lewis, J. Patrick, *Doodle Dandies: Poems That Take Shape*
Livingston, Myra Cohn, *O Sliver of Liver*
Merriam, Eve, *Out Loud*
Morrison, Lillian, *The Sidewalk Racer and Other Poems of Sports and Motion*

LIMERICKS

Ciardi, John, *The Hopeful Trout and Other Limericks*
Hubbell, Patricia, *Boo!: Halloween Poems and Limericks*
Lear, Edward, *A Book of Nonsense*
Lewis, J. Patrick, *A Hippopotamusn't: And Other Animal Verses*
Livingston, Myra Cohn, *Lots of Limericks*
Lobel, Arnold, *The Book of Pigericks*
Marshall, James, *Pocketful of Nonsense*
McCord, David, *One at a Time*
Nims, Bonnie Larkin, *Just Beyond Reach and Other Riddle Poems*

BALLADS

Bryan, Ashley, *Sing to the Sun: Poems and Pictures*
Child, Lydia Maria, *Over the River and Through the Wood*
dePaola, Tomie, *Tomie dePaola's Book of Christmas Carols*
Fox, Dan, arranger, *We Wish You a Merry Christmas: Songs of the Season for Young People*
Key, Frances Scott, *The Star Spangled Banner*
Livingston, Myra Cohn, *Abraham Lincoln: A Man for All the People: A Ballad*
_____, *Keep On Singing: A Ballad of Marion Anderson*
_____, *Let Freedom Ring: A Ballad of Martin Luther King, Jr.*
Philip, Neil, *Singing America: Poems That Define a Nation*
_____, *Songs Are Thoughts: Poems of the Inuit*
Plotz, Helen, *Imagination's Other Place: Poems of Science and Mathematics*
_____, *A Week of Lullabies*

COUPLETS

Lessie, Pat, *Fablesauce: Aesop Reinterpreted in Rhymed Couplets*

RIDDLE POEMS

Lewis, J. Patrick, *Riddle-Lightful: Oodles of Little Riddle Poems*

Spires, Elizabeth, *Riddle Road: Puzzles in Poems and Pictures*

Smith, William Jay, and Carol Ra, *Behind the King's Kitchen: A Roster of Rhyming Riddles*

Swann, Brian, *The House with No Door: African Riddle Poems*

Specialized, General, and Individual Anthologies

All entries in this section are at the P–I–A level.

SPECIAL ANTHOLOGIES (WORKS BY SEVERAL POETS ON ONE SUBJECT)

Carter, Anne, *Birds, Beasts, and Fishes: A Selection of Animal Poems*

De Regniers, Beatrice Schenk, *So Many Cats!*

Duffy, Carol Ann, *Stopping for Death: Poems of Death and Loss*

Hopkins, Lee Bennett, *Hand in Hand: An American History Through Poetry*

_____, *Ragged Shadows: Poems of Halloween Night*

Huck, Charlotte S., *Secret Places*

Janeczko, Paul B., *Poetry from A to Z: A Guide for Young Writers*

_____, *Very Best (Almost) Friends: Poems of Friendship*

Livingston, Myra Cohn, *Dog Poems*

_____, *If You Ever Meet a Whale*

Rogasky, Barbara, *Winter Poems*

Strickland, Dorothy, and Michael Strickland, *Families: Poems Celebrating the African American Experience*

GENERAL ANTHOLOGIES (WORKS BY MANY POETS ON MANY SUBJECTS)

Cole, Joanna, *A New Treasury of Children's Poetry: Old Favorites and New Discoveries*

Hall, Donald, *The Oxford Book of Children's Verse in America*

Lalicki, Barbara, *If There Were Dreams to Sell*

MacKay, David, *A Flock of Words: An Anthology of Poetry for Children and Others*

Nye, Naomi Shihab, *This Same Sky: A Collection of Poems from Around the World*

Paladino, Catherine, *Land, Sea, and Sky: Poems to Celebrate the Earth*

Prelutsky, Jack, *The Random House Book of Poetry*

INDIVIDUAL ANTHOLOGIES (THE WORKS OF ONE POET)

Adoff, Arnold, *Sports Pages*

Angelou, Maya, *Soul Looks Back in Wonder*

Bodecker, N. M., *Water Pennies and Other Poems*

Cassedy, Sylvia, *Zoomrimes: Poems About Things That Go*

Ciardi, John, *Monster Den: Or Look What Happened at My House—and To It*

Dotlich, Rebecca Kai, *Sweet Dreams of the Wild: Poems for Bedtime*

Hillert, Margaret, *The Sky Is Not So Far Away*

Katz, Bobbi, *We the People: Poems by Bobbi Katz*

Kuskin, Karla, *Soap Soup and Other Verses*

Livingston, Myra Cohn, *Space Songs*

McCord, David, *One at a Time*

Prelutsky, Jack, *Beneath a Blue Umbrella*

_____, *Dragons Are Singing Tonight*

Ridlon, Marci, *Sun Through the Window*

Siebert, Diane, *Plane Song*

Silverstein, Shel, *Falling Up*

Spinelli, Eileen, *Where Is the Night Train Going? Bedtime Poems*

Willard, Nancy, *A Visit to William Blake's Inn: Poems for Innocent and Experienced Travelers*

Wong, Janet, *Behind the Wheel: Poems About Driving*

_____, *Night Garden: Poems from the World of Dreams*

A Basic Poetry Collection

Berry, James, *When I Dance* (A)

Clinton, Catherine, *I, Too, Sing America: Three Centuries of African American Poetry* (A)

Dunbar, Paul Laurence, *Jump Back, Honey: The Poems of Paul Laurence Dunbar,* selected by Ashley Bryan and Andrea Davis Pinkney (P)

Dyer, Jane, *Animal Crackers* (P)

Elledge, Scott, *Wider than the Sky: Poems to Grow Up With* (I)

Field, Edward, *Magic Words* (P)

Fleischman, Paul, *Big Talk: Poems for Four Voices* (I)

Gordon, Ruth, *Time Is the Longest Distance* (A)

Hall, Donald, *The Oxford Illustrated Book of American Children's Poems* (P)

_____, *The Oxford Book of Children's Verse in America* (I)

Hoberman, Mary Ann, *A House Is a House for Me* (P)

_____, *The Llama Who Had No Pajama: 100 Favorite Poems* (P)

Hopkins, Lee Bennett, *Climb into My Lap: First Poems to Read Together* (P)

_____, *My America: A Poetry Atlas of the United States* (I)

_____, *Side by Side: Poems to Read Together* (P)

_____, *Voyages: Poems by Walt Whitman* (A)

Hughes, Ted, *The Mermaid's Purse* (A)

Janeczko, Paul B., *Looking for Your Name: A Collection of Contemporary Poems* (A)

_____, *The Music of What Happens: Poems That Tell Stories* (A)

_____, *The Place My Words Are Looking For: What Poets Say About and Through Their Work* (A)

_____, *Preposterous: Poems of Youth* (A)

_____, *Stardust Hotel* (A)

Katz, Bobbi, *We the People: Poems by Bobbi Katz* (I)

Kennedy, X. J., and Dorothy M. Kennedy, *Talking Like the Rain: A First Book of Poems* (I)

_____, *Knock at a Star: A Child's Introduction to Poetry* (I)

Lawrence, Jacob, *Harriet and the Promised Land* (P)

Lear, Edward, *The Complete Nonsense of Edward Lear* (I)

Livingston, Myra Cohn, *I Like You, If You Like Me* (I)

Moss, Jeffrey, *Butterfly Jar* (I)

Myers, Walter Dean, *Brown Angels: An Album of Pictures and Verse* (I)

Nikola-Lisa, W., *Bein' with You This Way* (P)

Opie, Iona, *My Very First Mother Goose* (P)

Pomerantz, Charlotte, *Halfway to Your House: Poems* (P)

Prelutsky, Jack, *New Kid on the Block* (I)

_____, *Read-Aloud Rhymes for the Very Young* (P)

_____, *Something Big Has Been Here*

_____, *The 20th Century Children's Poetry Treasury* (P)

Rosen, Michael, *Classic Poetry: An Illustrated Collection* (P)

Sandburg, Carl, *Poems for Children Nowhere Near Old Enough to Vote* (I)

_____, *Poetry for Young People* (I)

Schertle, Alice, *How Now, Brown Cow?* (P)

Silverstein, Shel, *Falling Up* (I)

_____, *A Light in the Attic* (I)

_____, *Where the Sidewalk Ends* (I)

Stevenson, Robert Louis, *A Child's Garden of Verses* (P)

_____, *The Land of Nod: And Other Poems for Children* (I)

Wong, Janet S., *Good Luck Gold and Other Poems* (A)

Resources for the Poetry Teacher

Booth, David, and Bill Moore, *Poems Please! Sharing Poetry with Children*

Brown, Bill, and Malcolm Glass, *Important Words: A Book for Poets and Writers*

Chatton, Barbara, *Using Poetry Across the Curriculum*

Cullinan, Bernice, Marilyn Scala, and Virginia Schroder, with Ann Lovett, *Three Voices: An Invitation to Poetry Across the Curriculum*

Denman, Gregory A., *When You've Made It Your Own: Teaching Poetry to Young People*

Fox, Mem, *Radical Reflections*

Grossman, Florence, *Listening to the Bells: Learning to Read Poetry by Writing Poetry*

Harrison, David L., and Bernice Cullinan, *Easy Poetry Lessons That Dazzle and Delight*

Harwayne, Shelley, *Lasting Impressions: Weaving Literature into the Writing Workshop*

Heard, Georgia, *Awakening the Heart: Exploring Poetry in Elementary and Middle School*

_____, *For the Good of the Earth and the Sun: Teaching Poetry*

_____, *Writing Toward Home: Tales and Lessons to Find Your Way*

Hewitt, Geof, *Today You Are My Favorite Poet: Writing Poems with Teenagers*

Hopkins, Lee Bennett, *Pass the Poetry, Please*

_____, *Pauses: Autobiographical Reflections of 101 Creators of Children's Books*

Janeczko, Paul, *The Place My Words Are Looking For*

Kennedy, X. J., and Dorothy M. Kennedy, *Knock at a Star: A Child's Introduction to Poetry*

Larrick, Nancy, *Let's Do a Poem*

Livingston, Myra Cohn, *Climb into the Bell Tower*

_____, *Poem-Making: Ways to Begin Writing Poetry*

McClure, Amy, with Peggy Harrison and Sheryl Reed, *Sunrises and Songs: Reading and Writing Poetry in an Elementary Classroom*

McVitty, Walter, *Word Magic: Poetry as a Shared Adventure*

Nye, Naomi Shihab, *Salting the Ocean: 100 Poems by Young Poets*

_____, *What Have You Lost?*

Swartz, Larry, *Classroom Events Through Poetry*

The Art of Picture Books

The story of Rapunzel represents the struggle between good and evil. It matches 4- and 5-year-olds' level of moral development.

Rapunzel, Rapunzel, let down your hair.

—PAUL O. ZELINSKY, *Rapunzel*

CHILDREN AND PICTURE BOOKS ARE SPRAWLED ACROSS THE FLOOR. It is quiet book time. The children turn pages to study the pictures. Katie scowls at Ed Emberley's *Go Away Big Green Monster* (P). She bangs the book shut and says sharply, ". . . and don't come back! Until I say so!"

Four-year-old Daniel sits with his legs spread out, his mouth slightly ajar. He is staring intently at the picture of the black and white bull sitting peacefully among the flowers in *The Story of Ferdinand* (P) by Munroe Leaf. "Judy," he asks very seriously, "How can I be like Ferdinand?"

Nearby, four-and-a-half-year-old Gene has been eavesdropping. He's holding Maurice Sendak's *Where the Wild Things Are* (P). Gene shouts, "I don't want to be Ferdinand. I'm a wild thing . . . a wild thing!" He jumps up and down to demonstrate. Forgetting his wish, Daniel joins in. "I'm wild. I'm wild, too!"

Next to the bookcase Ismael lies on his stomach carefully examining *The Body Book* (P–I) by Melanie and Chris Rice. Five-year-old Jack grabs it out of his hands. "Jack," Judy says reproachfully, "that's not right! . . . give it back. You two can share it." Reluctantly, Jack returns the book. The two boys lie side by side, slowly lifting each page of acetate see-through paper to gradually reveal the mysteries inside the body.

Sam taps Judy's arm. He is holding Pete Seeger's *Abiyoyo* (P). "Read, Judy." "Me, too," says Sabrina. "Sure," Judy says. Sam and Sabrina sit on either side of her to study the pictures closely. They come to the page where father and son are banished from the village for making mischief. Sam asks sadly, "Why they no like Daddy?" Judy explains. Sam nods and says wistfully, "I love my Daddy," and, sighing, "but he works." The children come to the page with the giant Abiyoyo's picture. Sabrina looks apprehensive. "That giant's not real, right? . . . right?" Judy reassures her, and the three of them sing boisterously to chase the evil giant away, "Abiyoyo. Abiyoyo."

Later in the afternoon, following a reading of a version of *Rapunzel* (P), Judy asks who would like to be in a Rapunzel play. All hands go up. Jack laughs and says derisively. "No boys can be Rapunzel. See the picture? She's a girl!" "I don't care," says Brian. "I want to live in a tower." Brian walks to the makeshift stage. "Who wants to be the witch?" Judy asks. There are no takers. Perhaps witches are too scarey.

Judy Lipsitt says, "Clearly in our four's classroom, picture books are essential equipment for they address issues of vital concern and thus provide reasons for provocative dialogue. As preschoolers listen and look raptly at the pictures they learn that books give untold pleasure and are a vital means of understanding the world."

Picture Books in Children's Lives

Picture books enrich children's lives; they tell stories, elaborate concepts, or impart information—all things that learners need. Picture books are unique in the field of children's literature, because they are defined by format, not by genre. They are a combination of words and art.

Students of all ages read picture books. Preschoolers, as well as students in primary, intermediate, and advanced grades, read picture books appropriate to their interests. Young children, who are captivated by stunning illustrations and lyrical texts, anticipate what comes next and gradually memorize their favorite books. This is exactly what we want them to do. They begin by approximating reading, grow in their knowledge and confidence of what the words say, and develop a lifelong love for books.

The art children see should be good art. As picture book specialist Patricia Cianciolo states:

"The gratifying thing about good art is the longer one looks at it the more one sees, the more one sees the deeper one feels, and the deeper one feels the more profoundly one thinks. Looking at art is everything."

Picture books are the first books children see. Infants and toddlers grasp sturdy cardboard or cloth books with bright pictures that capture their attention. Nursery and primary-grade children listen as picture books are read aloud and develop concepts through the experience. Children most often hear their first stories and informational texts read aloud from picture books; these books are ideally suited for reading aloud, because large pages spread open wide across the parent's and child's lap can be shown to many children at once. Older students turn to picture books to see vivid examples of literary techniques and the writer's craft, and to explore difficult concepts presented in a concise manner.

Criteria for Evaluating Picture Books

In this section we discuss how to evaluate a picture book according to its genre, its text quality, and its artistic quality. Picture books span all genres. Many contain stories—realistic or fanciful, contemporary or historical—and some contain poetry, folklore, or information. The content of a picture book determines its genre. Picture books designed to present information and develop concepts differ from those designed to tell a story or present a poem. In order to read critically, we need to determine what genre we are reading, because we evaluate various genre differently. When you use a picture book, look first to see what genre it is. Refer to the questions in Figure 3.1 to determine picture book genre.

In subsequent genre chapters we present high-quality picture books for each particular genre. In this chapter we concentrate on books in several genre that exemplify the picture book format.

Evaluating Text in Picture Storybooks

Many picture books that are read aloud to children are narratives—books that tell a story. The narratives may be folklore, fantasy, contemporary realistic fiction, or historical fiction. Whatever the type of narrative, we evaluate the text quality of the literary elements—setting, character, plot, theme, and style. The literary criteria, discussed in Chapter 1, may vary somewhat; only elements unique to picture books are discussed here.

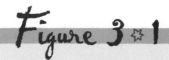

Determining Picture Book Genre

Fiction	Nonfiction
Folklore	Informational Books
Fantasy/Science Fiction	Concept Books
Realistic Fiction	Poetry
Historical Fiction	Biography/Autobiography

Picture books can be any genre. The questions listed here can help you to determine genre.

If fiction:

Are characters fanciful (fantasy, science fiction); believable (realistic fiction, historical fiction); stereotyped (folklore)?

Is the story set in the real world of the past (historical fiction); of contemporary times (realistic fiction); in a future time (science fiction)?

Is the story set in a make-believe world (fantasy)?

Could the events in the story happen in a real world (realistic fiction, historical fiction)?

Could the events happen in a fanciful world (folklore, fantasy)?

Could the events happen in a future world (science fiction)?

If nonfiction:

Does it present details about a concept (concept book)?

Does it present facts about a topic (informational book)?

Is it a realistic report about a person's life (biography, autobiography)?

Is it verse or poetic language (poetry)?

SETTING

Setting, the time and place of a story, is presented right up front in picture books, often through the illustrations. In this way visual details about time and place can be portrayed clearly and economically. Children are bored with lengthy word descriptions of setting. They want to know the time—present, past, or future—in which the tale is told, and the place—real or make-believe. Neil Waldman makes the setting and the illustrations critical to the story in *The Starry Night* (P–I–A). As a child dreams that Van Gogh comes to New York, he shows Van Gogh interesting landmarks to paint. Waldman then paints the scenes in Van Gogh's style. The illustrations reflect the setting through the artist's eyes. Waldman's students painted the art shown on the end papers.

Allen Say uses setting as a major plot complication in *Grandfather's Journey, Tea with Milk,* and *The Sign Painter* (all P–I). His characters speak with a delicate sense of melancholy, because they never feel totally at home either in Japan or in the United States. One of his characters says, "The funny thing is, the moment I am in one country, I am homesick for the other."

Good folklore settings reflect ethnic and cultural traditions associated with the origins of tales. David Wisniewski's illustrations of a traditional sixteenth-century Jewish legend in *Golem* (I) exemplify this in detail and style. He uses layers of cut paper to show a saintly rabbi bringing to life the humongous clay giant who helps him to watch over the Jews in Prague. Scenes from Prague and its culture show the rabbi miraculously bringing the Golem to life and illustrate the subsequent need to destroy him. According to legend, the Golem sleeps the sleep of dreamless clay, but when the need arises the Golem will come to life once more to protect the Jewish people.

Look for picture books with settings that are clearly identified in text and art, and are appropriate to the story.

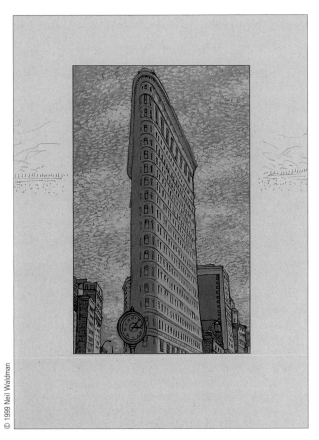

A young boy dreams that he gets to show Vincent Van Gogh around New York City to choose the sites he will paint. The Flatiron Building is a spot Van Gogh chooses in Waldman's **The Starry Night.**

CHARACTERIZATION

Characterization—establishing characters—varies according to genre in picture storybooks. In folklore, characters are usually stereotypes—the good princess, the brave prince, the wicked stepmother. In well-written realistic or fantasy narratives the characters are well-developed personalities that often show some evidence of growth and change across the story. Many fantasy picture books contain talking animal characters with habits, behaviors, thoughts, and feelings that are human rather than animal, such as Arthur in the popular series by Marc Brown. Brown's characters dress and act like people, but they have the heads of aardvarks and other animals. Their feelings reflect human feelings, as exemplified in *Arthur's Teacher Moves In* (P), in which Mr. Ratburn must stay at Arthur's home because his own roof has collapsed. All of Arthur's classmates call him teacher's pet, especially when he gets an A, but then Mr. Ratburn surprises them all by moving into each student's house for a stay. Mr. Ratburn's character is shown through the art as he unpacks his belongings.

Realistic books, whether contemporary or historical, contain recognizably human characters, such as Alice McGill's *Molly Bannaky* (P–I–A), illustrated by Chris K. Soentpiet. Molly, the main character, is a slave in England who is going to be hung because she allowed a cow to kick over a pail full of milk. She is saved from the gallows because she can read the Bible, but she is sentenced to a seven-year bondage in a colony across the ocean. She learns to cultivate the land, and when her bondage is served she stakes a claim for her own farm. Her grandchild is Benjamin Banneker. Historical notes reveal that Molly teaches her grandson Benjamin to read from the Bible. Teaching Idea 3.1 shows how to help students see the connections between *Molly Bannaky* and two other picture books.

Whether animal or human, characters in picture storybooks are usually childlike. They reflect the actions, thoughts, and emotions of children in the narration, the dialogue, and the art. Well-developed characters in picture storybooks are active rather than passive; they interact with their story worlds to solve their own problems.

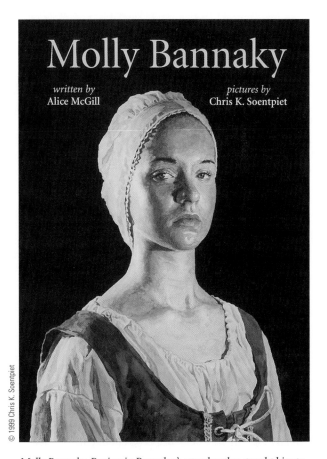

Molly Bannaky, Benjamin Banneker's grandmother, taught him to read the Bible. His ability to read changed his life and the lives of many others.

Teaching Idea 3·1

Making Connections with a Trilogy of Picture Books

Choose a week when you can read aloud all three of the following books: Alice McGill's *Molly Bannaky*, Andrea Davis Pinkney's *Dear Benjamin Banneker* (illustrated by Brian Pinkney), and James Cross Giblin's *Thomas Jefferson*. In discussions, recall that reading saved Molly Bannaky's life (she was to be hung for spilling a pail of milk). The story of *Molly Bannaky* ends with her teaching her grandson how to read. This story leads nicely to *Dear Benjamin Banneker*. Banneker was the first African American to publish an almanac. He taught other African Americans to read as his grandmother had taught him. Reading gave Banneker an opening into the publishing world. This caused him to write a letter to Secretary of State *Thomas Jefferson* concerning the injustice of slavery. These three books work together to tell the story of the struggles over gender, race, politics, and economics during the late seventeenth century.

Activities

Ask students to respond to each book by writing down how they connected to each book. Read the comments to the class and record them on a large chart. Use the following activities to make many different discoveries:

✳ Make the connection as you discover the accuracy of the illustrations. In Pinkney's book, the author researched the moon showing through the window so that it could be drawn in the same phase as the one it was in the very night that Benjamin Banneker wrote the letter to Thomas Jefferson.

✳ Make a "number" connection: Thomas Jefferson was our third president, and he is the third character portrayed in our trilogy of related literature. This could spark students' interest to learn the presidents in order. Numerous books will support this learning experience, including *Yo Millard Fillmore* and *So You Want to Be President*.

✳ Make a math connection: Subtract the year the story starts in Molly Bannaky (1683) from the year Benjamin Bannaker was born (1731) to find out how much time elapsed between those dates. Then work with other important dates, such as the year Ben wrote to Thomas Jefferson (1791).

✳ Create a time line for your classroom using these and other events as referral points.

✳ Discuss cause and effect. Historical events set the stage for student understanding of this concept.

✳ Write letters about the rights of all people.

✳ Tell students that these historical figures were scientists. Molly Bannaky planted seeds and did problem solving, and Benjamin Banneker was an astronomer and a surveyor. He worked on the team that planned Washington, D.C. He was a mathematician best known for calculating "ephemeredes" tables that use the sun, moon, and stars to measure time. How might their interest in science have influenced their actions and attitudes?

Developed by Deborah Wooten, author (1999), *Valued Voices: An Interdisciplinary Approach to Teaching and Learning*, International Reading Association.

Young children find it natural to identify with storybook characters. They recognize themselves and their friends in the books they encounter, and this recognition helps them become aware of who they are and how they feel. Look for picture storybooks that contain characters who are well developed in text and illustration and who actively make things happen.

PLOT

Plot, the sequence of events, is presented in picture storybooks in a straightforward chronological order. Children want action: They want something to happen and to happen fast. Plot often centers on a problem or conflict, generally a problem that children recognize: being too young, too small, or too scared to act; having to deal with changes in family structure; or facing new experiences. Children like well-defined, recognizable endings. If a problem is raised, it needs to be resolved in a logical manner. In Yumi Heo's **One Sunday Morning** (P) Minho and his father take the subway to the park. They walk paths, watch people sail remote-control boats on the pond, take a horse-and-carriage ride, eat pretzels and cotton candy. Only on the final page, when his father comes in to awaken him, do we find out that Minho's pleasure is all a dream.

Look for picture books in which a clear plot moves forward logically; the action is visible in both text and illustration; and the story comes to a recognizable climax and a satisfying resolution.

The Whispering Cloth (P–I) by Pegi Dietz Shea is a story about the Hmong refugee women who embroider the details of their lives in a pa'ndau, a tapestry that includes traditional images and a story. The story is the story of the life they live. The investment of time and work on the pa'ndau shows the great value they place upon their lives. The pa'ndau becomes a treasure that helps them hold a moment of time from their lives in the palm of their hand.

Minho got on the yellow carousel horse, and they went up and down and around and around.

A lovely day in the park turns out to be a dream one Sunday morning.

She helped Grandmother grow chilies and coriander.
Mai searched for empty glass bottles. When she
put them upside down in the ground around her hut,
they sparkled.
This is how Mai lived for many years.

Hmong refugee women embroider their life story in a pa'ndau, a tapestry with traditional symbols and images.

THEME

Theme, a major overriding idea, reflects a child's world. Picture books for children are often organized around the theme of growing up—increasing independence and self-reliance, increasing ability, increasing understanding. Memorable themes are neither blatantly stated, as in an explicit moral to a story, nor so subtle that they elude young readers. Look for picture books that have a readily identifiable theme that evolves naturally from plot and character, and a theme that permeates the illustrations and the plot.

STYLE

Style of language is essential to quality in a picture book; because words are limited, they must be carefully chosen. Style of art must also match the message. Picture books contain rich language because they are intended for reading aloud; they are read to children long before children can read them alone. Picture books are most often introduced to children by an adult reading *to* the child. The language in picture books is language that adults *can read* and children *can understand*. Thus it is not necessary to look for simple, easy-to-read language in picture books. Most picture books are not meant for beginning reading material. Look for picture books with interesting words used in interesting ways; with language that builds excitement and drama; or with images and language that has an internal rhythm and melody. If it sounds natural when read aloud, it's probably well written.

Evaluating Text in Nonfiction Picture Books

Evaluation of text quality of nonfiction picture books is based on the same criteria used for all nonfiction: The text should be readable, appropriate to the readers' age and developmental level, accurate, up-to-date, and consistent with current knowledge. See Chapter 10 for a full discussion of this topic.

READABILITY AND AGE APPROPRIATENESS

Today's classrooms contain gifted, special education, and regular students working at a variety of different levels. We need books that appeal to a wide range of abilities and interests. Nonfiction picture books, such as ***Bembo's Zoo: An Animal ABC Book*** (P) by Roberto de Vicq de Cumptich, ***The Graphic Alphabet*** (P) by David Pelletier, and ***Eat Your Words*** (I) by Charlotte F. Jones, illustrated by John O'Brien, help to reach that broad range of students. Producing picture books appropriate to the reader's age level creates a special challenge for nonfiction writers who ask, "How can I explain a subject simply enough to be understood and still be scientifically accurate?" Finding a subject of interest to a child and presenting authentic information in an understandable way—and keeping it appropriate to the age of the

*The intricate designs in the oversize **Bembo's Zoo** spread across both parent's and child's lap for shared reading.*

A traffic signal looks like the letter E *in Stephen Johnson's* **Alphabet City**.

satisfies children's craving to find the tallest (giraffe), the biggest (blue whale), the smallest (Etruscan shrew), the strongest for its size (ant), and the fastest (cheetah) creature. Jenkins gives detailed notes with specific facts in addition to his art. The book closes with a comprehensive chart that summarizes the animals' record, size, diet, and range; this supports lively discussions of comparisons.

Seymour Simon, notable science teacher turned science writer, has received outstanding ratings from the National Science Teachers Association and the Children's Book Council for more than half of the 200 books he has written. In an introduction to *Out of Sight: Pictures of Hidden Worlds* (I–A) he states that there are countless sights that our eyes cannot see. Simon explains that we first began to learn about hidden worlds nearly four hundred years ago when Galileo turned a small telescope to the night sky and saw the moons of Jupiter. Sixty-five years later Leeuwenhoek used a simple microscope to view tiny animals swimming in a drop of water. Seymour Simon shows some hidden worlds that can be viewed by instruments of today. His scholarship shows on every page.

Look for nonfiction picture books that contain language in which accurate words are used in precise ways and sentence patterns have an internal rhythm that makes them easy to comprehend when read aloud. Look for nonfiction picture books that have interesting topics presented in an understandable fashion for the intended audience; clear structure and illustrations that confirm and extend the verbal information; and accurate text and illustrations by an expert in the field.

child—is not an easy task. The same subject is treated differently for different age groups. For example, a book about trucks for young children might combine pictures and labels to identify various types of trucks; children a bit older would need more information about what the trucks can do; even older children might want a book that details the uses and the internal mechanics of trucks.

Informational picture books must convey a meaningful message with clarity and style through a lucid text and artful illustrations. Stephen T. Johnson's paintings in *Alphabet City* (N–P–I) show letters of the alphabet as he found them in urban settings. The art reflects the contemporary city scenes. Nonfiction picture books vary in structure, with the information itself determining the order of presentation.

ACCURACY AND RECENCY

Nonfiction picture books must be accurate, up-to-date, and consistent with current knowledge. Illustrations should match the text and provide extra details to enhance the verbal information. For example, Steve Jenkins describes record holders in the animal kingdom in *Biggest, Strongest, Fastest* (P–I) in vivid cut paper collage illustrations. Jenkins

Seymour Simon explores worlds we cannot see with the naked eye. His magnified photographs convince us that there is a world out of sight.

Biographies are among the many types of nonfiction picture books. Kathleen Krull's *Wilma Unlimited* (I–A), a biography of Wilma Rudolph illustrated by David Diaz, is dramatically visualized with collage and paintings created with acrylics, watercolor, and gouache. The runner's strength shows in the illustrations as well as in the words used to describe her talent.

Nonfiction picture books include content areas such as mathematics and farm life. For example, Bruce McMillan's *Eating Fractions* (P) is illustrated with close-up, focused photographs that explain why fractions are important in real life. Sandra Markle's *Measuring Up! Experiments, Puzzles, and Games Exploring Measurement* (I) challenges readers to measure distances, weights, heights, and temperatures. Bonnie Geisert's *Haystack* (P–I), illustrated by Arthur Geisert, shows that a haystack is more than just a place to pile hay. Examples of other fine nonfiction picture books are listed in the Booklist at the end of the chapter and are discussed further in Chapter 10.

Evaluating Text in Poetry and Song Picture Books

Some picture books present an artist's visual interpretation of a song, poem, or verse. In these books the artist arranges the text across the pages (often one or two lines per page) and then illuminates each thought that is expressed. In Ann Turner's *Rainflowers* (N–P), illustrator Robert Blake's vivid paintings display the power and splendor of the rainstorm that Turner captures in words. The paintings are full-color, double-page spreads, with the text superimposed at varying places, giving the effect of being surrounded by the storm. The paintings extend the poem; they show a young boy

going to pick a pumpkin, being caught in the storm, running to shelter in a barn, and resuming his walk home with his pumpkin when the storm subsides. Words and pictures combine to create a powerful picture book.

The song, poem, or verse should be interesting and understandable to the intended audience. Brief, rhythmic verses, narrative verses, and children's and folk songs make excellent picture book texts. Some books contain several separate texts; others present single poems or songs. In beautifully designed picture books the arrangement of the text across the pages reflects the natural breaks in the meaning and sound of the original. Illustrations depict both action and feeling, matching the mood established by the author, as interpreted by the artist.

Angela Shelf Medearis's *Skin Deep and Other Teenage Reflections* (I–A), illustrated by Michael Bryant, is an example of a poem illuminated by illustrations. The realistic drawings, framed in a sketched black border, face the text. Like the poems, the illustrations focus on the emotional upheaval of teenage problems and frustrations. Two visions of the teenage years, one expressed in words and the other in art, combine to present an experience that is made richer by both. Other examples of illustrated poems are listed in the Booklist and are discussed further in Chapter 4.

When evaluating poetic picture books, look for interesting ideas or stories that are presented in lyrical language, and for illustrations that interpret the text and illuminate its emotional content.

Human beings have a basic need to organize and substantiate their thoughts and feelings, to make sense of their experiences and ideas. They do this in practical and scientific ways, but in creating art they can be most expressive. The dictionary defines art as "the conscious skill and creative imagination in the production or creation of aesthetic objects." Authors and book illustrators who create picture books are literary artists. The authors tell their stories and create images with skillful and creative use of words, and the artists create images using line, shape, color, and other essential elements of art. An illustrator's pictures, however, are not simply judged as art but as a vital portion of a literary work. As such they enhance the author's meaning and mood and stimulate the imagination of the viewer.

Through art, David Diaz shows the determination Wilma Rudolph shows in her stride.

Evaluating Artistic Quality in Picture Books

ELEMENTS OF ART

Art in children's picture books involves the entire range of media, techniques, and styles used in all art. The *medium*—the material used in the production of a work—may be watercolors, oils, acrylics, ink, pencil, charcoal, pastels, tissue paper, acetate sheets, or fabric. The *technique* might be painting, etching, wood and linoleum cuts, airbrush, collage, photography, or many other means. The individual artist combines style, medium, and technique to evoke setting, establish character, convey theme, or create a mood presented in a picture book.

When illustrating a picture book, artists decide what media and techniques they will use, and they make other aesthetic choices as well. They must decide about color, style, and composition in their illustrations. They must make choices about line, shape, placement on a page, the use of negative space, and texture. These terms are discussed in this chapter and are also defined in the Glossary. Book illustration is an art; as such, it goes beyond the appeal of the literal to visual communication. Illustrations must be not only interesting and appealing but also imaginative and dramatic.

A beautifully illustrated picture book is a work of art. Artists use their talent and trained eye to arrange the art and text on a page. Visually appealing compositions are balanced; white space is used to set off various parts of a picture, and illustrations are balanced with the text. From one's first look at the dust jacket and endpapers to one's close scrutiny of the art on the pages, it should be apparent that the book is illustrated with skill and care. The illustration on the cover for *The Babe and I* (P–I), written by David Adler and illustrated by Terry Widener, draws the reader into the ballpark immediately. Terry Widener uses unusual perspective to convey meaning. Like voyeurs looking down from the sky on the 1930s Depression-era Bronx, we see the elevated subway lines and the dingy apartment rooftops, and we share a young boy's vision and sense his dismay when he sees his father selling apples on a street corner. The same overhead perspective makes the same boy appear small and defenseless as he tries to sell newspapers on the crowded city streets.

Artists work with the basic elements of art (line, shape, color, and texture) and with the principles of design (rhythm, balance, variety, emphasis, spatial order, and unity) to create a unified image that conveys meaning.

Line

Line is a mark on paper or a place where different colors meet. Each stroke starts with a dot that grows into a line that may be slow and rolling, sleek and fast, quiet or frenetic. Artists create lines that move in the direction in which they want to focus the viewer and that pull the eye in a particular direction. Lines can suggest delicacy (thin lines) or stability (thick lines). Artists use the angle, width, length, and motion of line to express the meaning they want to convey.

Peter Parnall's distinctive use of firm but delicate line, along with his use of space and color, gives his illustrations a clear, uncluttered feeling. His work is scientifically accurate; it appears in *Scientific American* and *Audubon* magazine. In *The Table Where Rich People Sit* (I) by Byrd Baylor the family feels wealthy when they assign a monetary value to themselves and to the beauties of nature they enjoy. Lines emanate from major images to express a sense of the breadth of the desert; Parnall treats the desert environment and its creatures with reverence and dignity.

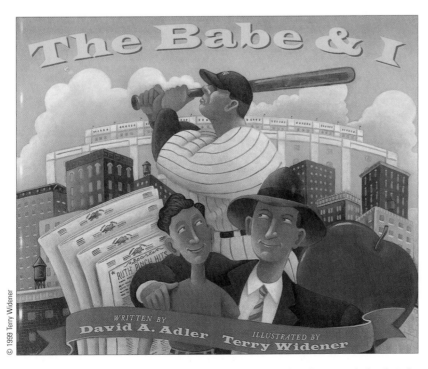

Artist Terry Widener chooses an unusual perspective from which to focus on a ballpark, Babe Ruth, and a fan.

Chris Van Allsburg uses bold carbon pencil drawings to create a sense of mass and to show the play of light and shadow in *The Garden of Abdul Gasazi* (I). In *Ben's Dream* (I) he uses black lines on white and white lines on black to accentuate light and shadow. He varies the lines' length, curve, and angle to create texture. His parallel lines, architectural forms, and exploration of perspective provide dimension and depth to his work.

John Steptoe uses line dramatically in all his books, especially in *Daddy Is a Monster . . . Sometimes* (P). Brittle lines almost crackle across the page to reflect broken glass and to capture the emotional tension of the relationship between a father and his children. Some lines slash diagonally across a wall or shirt to suggest a sense of frenzy and the father's exasperation with his children. In *Stevie* (P) Steptoe uses line to show Robert's alienation from and eventual affection for Stevie, the boy his mother baby-sits.

In *Zin, Zin, Zin, A Violin* (P) Marjorie Priceman uses wonderfully lyrical lines that complement the text. The charming story in verse by Lloyd Moss describes the humorous antics of assembling a chamber music group. Each element of Priceman's concert hall is drawn with a wiry, pulsating line, much like musical notations. One senses music in the air from the rhythm of the words to the terpsi-chorean gestures of the musicians with their animated instruments. Lines dance across the pages with increasing exuberance and syncopation, and the reader imagines the sound intensifying with the addition of each performer.

Molly Bang uses thick lines that become thicker and more brilliantly colored when emotions are heightened in *When Sophie Gets Angry—Really, Really Angry* (P). In this story, the little girl, Sophie, is initially outlined in a sunny yellow, but as she loses her temper the line registers her fury and gradually turns a flaming red. When Sophie actually has a screaming fit, multiple rich red pulsating lines surround her and create the impression that she is about to explode. As Sophie runs off into the woods, her anger gradually subsides, and she returns home her old self, with a sunny yellow outline.

In *Love as Strong as Ginger* (P–I) Stephen T. Johnson uses pastel and watercolor and a gentle caressing crayon outline to capture the poignancy in Lenore Look's beautifully written story based on her childhood memories of her Chinese immigrant grandmother. These tenderly rendered pictures resemble hand-tinted family photos. They carefully delineate the love between the older woman and the child, the pleasures of cooking and eating, and the pain and sacrifice in an immigrant's life.

The next day the doorbell rang. It was a lady and a kid. He was smaller than me. I ran to my mother. "Is that them?"
They went in the kitchen but I stayed out in the hall to listen.

*John Steptoe's art in **Stevie** has a strong black line to emphasize the alienation between the narrator and the child his mother baby-sits.*

© 1995 Marjorie Priceman

> Next, a TRUMPET comes along,
> And sings and stings its swinging song,
> It joins TROMBONE, no more alone,
> And ONE and TWO-O, they're a DUO.

Marjorie Priceman creates lyrical artistic lines to match the lyricism of the instruments and the text.

© 1999 Molly Bang

Molly Bang graphically depicts the intensity of Sophie's anger through facial expression and pulsating lines.

Shape

Shape is an area or form with a definite outline. It, along with line, directs the viewer's eye and suggests feelings and ideas. Shapes can be geometric (circles, triangles, squares), abstract (suggestive, less well-defined shapes such as clouds), or realistic and representational. Shape can contribute to the volume or three-dimensional quality of an illustration. In some illustrations, shapes seem to jut out from the front, or plane, of the picture, coming toward the viewer. Artists make decisions about the placement of shapes (positive space) on the background (negative space). Leo Lionni uses abstract and free-form shapes in *Little Blue and Little Yellow* (P). Gerald McDermott uses abstract and geometric shapes in *Arrow to the Sun* (P–I).

Lois Ehlert uses geometric shapes to convey a sense of vitality in *Cuckoo* (N–P), *Moon Rope* (P), *Snowballs* (N–P), *Top Cat* (N–P), and *Market Day* (P). Her books are marked by bright colors, clear, vivid lines, and shapes that seem to jump off the page. By transforming natural shapes into geometric forms she calls attention to the essential shape of the objects she depicts.

Trina Schart Hyman uses archways, windows, mirrors, and geometric print borders to frame her meticulously

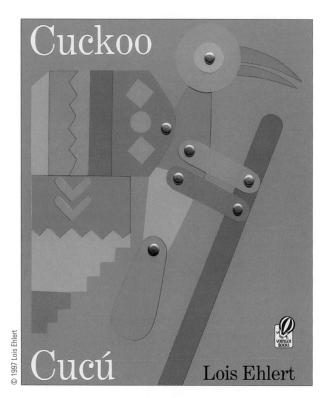

Lois Ehlert uses strong shapes and colors to convey a sense of strength and vitality in her art.

detailed illustrations. Look at *Snow White* (I), *The Sleeping Beauty* (I), *Little Red Riding Hood* (P), or *Saint George and the Dragon* (I) to appreciate her dramatic style. The borders confine her richly detailed paintings and increase the sense of lush romanticism. Jane Dyer's silhouettes and colored pencil art for Jane Yolen's *Piggins* (P–I) call our attention to character, action, and mood at a dinner party and a royal wedding.

In Ed Young's *Seven Blind Mice* (N–P) (a reinterpretation of the Indian fable of the blind man and the elephant) the large, empty, black, negative space filled with what is perceived as "different" shapes is an intrinsic part of the story. The tale is told from the perspective of the mice, and the reader is as mystified by these shapes as the mice are. Only when we see the whole shape on a double-page spread do we recognize it as an elephant.

In three separate stories describing snow, large amounts of lightly textured snow shapes reflect the text. Ezra Jack Keats's Caldecott classic, *The Snowy Day* (N–P), has pages filled with large white shapes that depict a snowy world. Denise Fleming piles lush heaps of snow for winter in *The Everything Book* (N–P). In Uri Shulevitz's *Snow* (N–P) a little boy wanders through a gray city landscape speculating on whether it will snow. Snow does actually fall and more of the landscape is obscured by it. At the end of the story, the boy's world has become white shapes and blue sky.

Eric Carle often uses large amounts of white space with simple, clearly rendered collage shapes that complement the text. In *The Clumsy Click Beetle* (P), Carle shows how small the beetle is by showing him standing next to large shapes of walls, tall grasses, and giant flowers. The beetle looks tiny when you see him beside grown animals and humans who fill the pages. When the beetle actually learns to click, he does three somersaults across the space of two pages, producing a clicking sound and landing upright on the third page. As he grows in skill, he acquires more space.

In David Pelletier's computer-generated or digitally enhanced alphabet book, *The Graphic Alphabet* (N–P), each black rectangular page has a letter shape. The letter is not only represented by a word or concept, but also has become the word or concept. For example, in U for universe, the moon is eclipsed so that only a U shape is apparent, and there are white dots representing stars on the black space. H has the word *hover*, and the letter actually hovers. K is for knot, and its shape is tied in a knot.

Texture

The surface of an illustration, whether actual or illusory, is its texture. Some illustrations seem smooth, others rough; some, like collage, do have a rough texture in the original art. Texture conveys a sense of reality; interesting visual contrasts or patterns suggest movement and action, roughness or delicacy.

Denise Fleming uses an unusual process to create illustrations for *Barnyard Banter* (N–P), *Lunch* (N–P), *In the Small, Small Pond* (N–P), *Where Once There Was a Wood* (P–I), and *The Everything Book* (N–P). She pours colored cotton pulp through hand-cut stencils, which results in handmade paper images. The art is satisfyingly textured and more softly edged than most cut-paper illustrations. The softness of the paper tempers the intense colors and active composition to make her art appealing to children and fascinating to adults.

In Brett Harvey's *My Prairie Year: Based on the Diary of Elenore Plaisted* (I) Deborah Kogan Ray creates a sense of isolation during a raging blizzard by using smudged lines, blanketed figures, and sparse furnishings in the prairie homestead. Ted Lewin's art captures the colorful clothing and reverence of Hindu worshippers who make pilgrimages to the Ganges River in *Sacred River* (I). Lewin's images of water seem to surge and splash across the page. Leo and Diane Dillon give a diaphanous, luminous, iridescent quality to fabrics in Leontyne Price's *Aida* (A). And David Diaz's collages for Eve Bunting's story, *Smoky Night* (P–I), convey the turmoil, fear, and anxiety caused by riots. Diaz won the Caldecott Medal for his book.

In *Snowflake Bentley* (N–I), Jacqueline Briggs Martin's biography of William Bentley, a photographer of natural phenomena, Mary Azarian's hand-colored woodcuts have a folksy, down-home quality that is appropriate for this story, which takes place in the Vermont countryside at the end of the nineteenth century. As we look at the rustic woodcuts, we can almost feel the rough wood furnishings, the scratchy wool knits, and the coarse weave of the lumber jacket. We can see the diversity of textures of fields and flowers and of course the beauty of the snowflakes that became Bentley's favorite subject matter.

Paul O. Zelinsky captures the exquisite textures in home and nature in his dramatic retelling of *Rumpelstiltskin* (P). Rendered in the style of early Renaissance art, these golden-toned oil paintings convey the majesty and mystery of a world of sorcerers and queens.

In Odd Bodkins's sea tale, *The Ghost of the Southern Belle* (I), Berni Fuchs creates exquisitely expressive oil paintings that convey the atmosphere at sea. In looking at the renderings, one can feel the eternal wind, the dense mist, the sea spray, and one can see the textures of the billowing clouds, the luminous ocean, and the reflected lights in Captain Le Nair's magic charm.

Color

Artists use color—or the lack of it—to express character, mood, and emotion. Color conveys warmth, coolness, personality traits, indifference, and feelings. Color can vary in *hue*—ranging across the rainbow of colors—and *intensity*. Subdued colors can express weariness, boredom, and serenity, whereas intense colors evoke feelings of energy, vibrancy, and excitement. Lizbeth Zwerger limits her palette to rustic tones in Grimm's *Hansel and Gretel* (P). She conveys foreboding through somber clothing, dark lines on faces, and swaths of brown through ecru and gray backgrounds. Colors can also vary in *value*, or the amount of light and dark. A range of values creates drama or movement; an absence of contrast creates a quiet or solemn mood.

Tomie dePaola uses color to help tell the story in *The Baby Sister* (P). His pages begin with black and white sepia tones of an old-fashioned photograph album and move to soft ecru, browns with a touch of red. The color red is significant because he wants his forthcoming baby sister to have a red ribbon in her hair. Sunny yellows accompany the getting-ready scene in which the characters paint the crib and prepare the baby's changing table. When the beloved baby sister arrives, she does wear the desired red ribbon in her hair! Tomie dePaola continues the family stories in *26 Fairmount Avenue* and *Here We All Are* (P–I), longer chapter books that give more details about the growing-up years, their victories and setbacks.

Tomie dePaola uses the bright, intense colors of the Southwest to establish Alice's character in Tony Johnston's *Alice Nizzy Nazzy: The Witch of Santa Fe* (P–I). Alice, a variation of Baba Yaga, is garbed in garish greens and purples with squash yellow skin and teeth as black as night. Strings

Tomie dePaola writes his autobiography or memoir in easily understandable prose.

of chili pods for hair and long red fingernails help to exaggerate her bizarre image.

In *Tea with Milk* (P) Allen Say, winner of the Caldecott award for *Grandfather's Journey* (P–I), once again uses color to convey emotions in a touching story of intercultural conflict. Say's American-born mother is sad about being forced to accept a new life in Japan; her sorrow is reflected in the artist's use of pale, somber colors. Once she leaves her Japanese parents' home in a red dress, and as she begins to live a more vigorous, independent, and Western lifestyle, there is a greater use of contrast and a greater use of vivid colors.

Dav Pilkey's use of color and light in *Paperboy* (P) is directly connected to this realistic story of a young night worker who performs his tasks in the dark, rich colors of night. The only bright lights are from the moon, the stars, the headlights of the delivery truck, the boy's bike, and the electric lights that he uses for illumination as he dresses and eats. As the night wanes and he completes his work, there is a gradual full-color sunrise as he returns home to sleep.

Bimba Landmann uses earthy warm colors and the gold leaf found in late medieval art to illustrate Paolo Guarnien's biography *A Boy Named Giotte* (P–I). In this story of a thirteenth-century artist's childhood in Florence, Italy, which uses the style and color of art of that period, one gains insight into the quality of life at that time. The steep umber hills, the ochres of the dry, barren plains, the terra cotta roofs on the windowless houses, the red and gold church interiors, and the quantity of religious art all describe a world very different from ours in the twenty-first century.

Harlem (P–I), a deeply moving descriptive poem by Walter Dean Myers, has highly expressive, many-hued collage illustrations created by his son, Christopher Myers. These emotional renderings perfectly convey the kaleidoscope of people and the cacophony of sounds that typify this vital ethnic neighborhood. Within the book, words and images come together to express the spirit of Harlem in its art, literature, and everyday life. Teaching Idea 3.2 offers a suggestion for helping students learn to recognize the art of notable illustrators.

Design

Artists use the basic elements of art to create meaning and feeling; they manipulate the elements through principles of design to express their own unique visions. Artists work to achieve unity, or a meaningful whole, through *composition*

© 1997 Christopher Myers

Christopher Myers uses strong collage shapes and colors to convey the images of Harlem.

Teaching Idea 3·2

Notable Illustrators

Read aloud books by the following illustrators, who are discussed in Pat Cummings's *Talking with Artists*, volumes 1 and 2. Ask listeners to respond to the art. Later, see if they (or you) can recognize the artist's style when you cover up the names and titles. Play "Name that Illustrator": Hold up an illustration and ask, "Who is the illustrator?"

From Volume 1

Victoria Chess
Pat Cummings
Leo & Diane Dillon
Richard Egielski
Lois Ehlert
Lisa Campbell Ernst
Steven Kellogg
Jerry Pinkney
Lane Smith
Chris Van Allsburg
David Wiesner

From Volume 2

Thomas B. Allen
Mary Jane Begin
Floyd Cooper
Julie Downing
Denise Fleming
Sheila Hamanaka
Kevin Henkes
William Joyce
Maira Kalman
Deborah Nourse Lattimore
Brian Pinkney
Vera B. Williams
David Wisniewski

Pat Cummings, compiler-editor, *Talking with Artists*, vol. 1, New York: Bradbury, 1992; *Talking with Artists*, vol. 2, New York: Simon & Schuster, 1995.

---

of their art. To achieve unity, artists make use of balance, repeated rhythms, variety, emphasis, and spatial order (Greenberg & Jordan, 1991, 1993, 1995). Balance means giving equal weight to the lines, shapes, textures, and colors in a picture; without it the picture seems awkward (Greenberg & Jordan, 1991, 1993, 1995). Greenberg and Jordan show examples of design in *Frank O. Gehry: Outside In* (all ages). Repetition in art helps to achieve visual harmony and balance, whereas variety sets up a paradox or a progression that leads the eye from one point to another. Artists draw attention to a particular part of their piece by emphasizing size, placement, color, or line; these elements work together to force our eyes to focus on a particular place in an illustration.

Peter Parnall uses white space to focus the viewer's eye on elements that he wants to emphasize in Byrd Baylor's books set in the Southwest. Lois Ehlert's bright, contrasting colors, shapes, and hard lines emphasize objects she chooses to feature in *Snowballs* (P). Chris Van Allsburg uses perspective to emphasize objects in *Two Bad Ants* (P), as does Don Wood in Audrey Wood's *The Napping House* (P). Steve Jenkins shows that perspective is everything by presenting what astronauts traveling in space would see if they looked at the earth in *Looking Down* (P). Gradually Jenkins brings the viewer closer and closer.

In picture books, principles of design relate to the overall design of a book as well as to individual pictures, and are integrated with the content. In *Strega Nona: Her Story* (P) Tomie dePaola uses strong black line to create sturdy figures arranged almost as if they were on a stage setting. His art reflects the sturdy folktale he retells and the pasta-eating grandmother in the story.

The cover design, text placement, typography, endpapers, illustrations, and white space are all elements of the total design. Arrangement and sequencing of design elements lead the eye effectively through a book. Lane Smith uses every inch of available space to increase the feeling of delighted shock in Jon Scieszka's *The Stinky Cheese Man* (I–A). The cover, title page, dedication page, table of contents, and typeface are all manipulated to achieve a playful sense of violating conventions. The text consists of hilarious versions of familiar folktales; the surrealistic art heightens the mockery of folktale conventions. Beyond that, the text and illustrations play with the format of the picture book itself, achieving a remarkable unity of text and illustration.

Simms Taback, author and illustrator of *There Was an Old Lady Who Swallowed a Fly* (N–P) received the Caldecott Medal for his elegantly designed *Joseph Had a Little Overcoat* (N–I). From a simple Yiddish folk song about a resourceful tailor who transforms his worn-out overcoat into smaller garments, Taback creates a unique and charming piece of art. The brightly painted and collaged pages, the playful use of folksy details, and the clever use of innovative die cuts all contribute to the raucous merriment. The comic gestures of all the characters and animals, the exaggerated perspective reminiscent of naive art, turn this simple story into a rich comic piece of literature.

In *The Starry Messenger* (I), a biography of Galileo, the sixteenth-century astronomer and philosopher, Peter Sis creates a beautiful and complex book using a combination of Galileo's original astronomical drawings, ancient maps, scientific manuscripts, and Sis's own illustrations, which are rendered in the style of Renaissance illuminations. Peter Sis tells Galileo's life story by presenting a simple text in type on the left side of each page, but above, in script, are additional facts that together contribute to a complex text. Halfway through the book on the upper portion of each page is a facsimile of Galileo's astronomical book of revelations, "The Starry Messenger." The extraordinary scope of the text and illustrations gives the reader a comprehensive picture of the life and work of the brilliant scientist–philosopher who

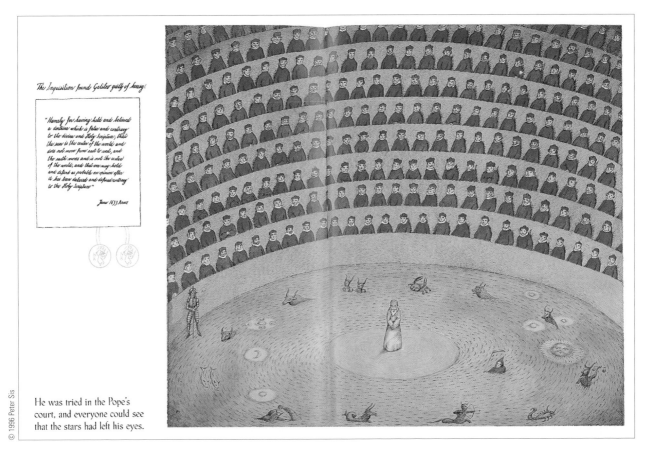

*Galileo faced trial before the Pope's jury because he challenged the prevailing belief that the earth was flat in Peter Sis's **The Starry Messenger**.*

Profile ☆ Peter Sis

HarperCollins Children's Books

Author and illustrator Peter Sis was born in Moravia, Czechoslovakia. His father, a filmmaker and explorer, and his mother, an artist, encouraged his creativity. Sis began drawing at age four or five and was soon a serious student of art. His parents gave him illustration assignments, complete with deadlines. This parental influence helped ensure what Sis remembers as a wonderful childhood, despite the dreary political times in Czechoslovakia. He earned an M.A. (1974) from the Academy of Applied Arts in Prague, then attended the Royal College of Art in London (1977–1979). The artistic freedom he enjoyed as a child caused some tension when he began

his more strictly guided formal training. When his teachers ranked their students' work, Sis's was always among the lowest in his class. After art school, Sis worked as a graphic designer for the Czech army's symphony orchestra. By the early 1980s, he had become a popular filmmaker in Europe. Sis came to the United States in 1982 to work on a film project connected with the 1984 Los Angeles Olympics. Although Czechoslovakia and other Soviet nations withdrew from Olympic competition, Sis stayed in Los Angeles to pursue his art. Because of his unique style, he had difficulty getting work as an artist. Instead, he taught art classes and painted decorative eggs that were commissioned by a Swiss woman. Sis sent samples of his work to artist Maurice Sendak, who arranged for him to meet the art director of Greenwillow Books. On the spot, Sis agreed to illustrate George Shannon's book *Bean Boy* (1984). In 1989, he became a U.S. citizen.

Sis believes that the illustrator's job is to complement the text, and his work is noted for effectively capturing the feeling and intent of other writers' words. His illustra-

tions for *Starry Messenger* (1996), a biography of Galileo, reflect Renaissance art and architecture. Through brief excerpts from Galileo's journals and diaries Sis evokes the excitement of the Renaissance and the fear of the Inquisition. In *Tibet Through the Red Box* (1998) he captures the downward spiral of chaos during the Communist takeover of Tibet, and he relates the disappearance of his father, who was there to report on events. Sis received American Library Association Caldecott Medal Honor Book citations for both books.

Peter Sis prefers to illustrate his own work in order to maintain artistic control. He gets story ideas from unfamiliar experiences and surroundings. For example, *Waving* (1988) grew from his observations of how people hail cabs in New York City. One of his best-known books, *Follow the Dream* (1991), is the story of Christopher Columbus's voyage. The book was inspired by Sis's father's explorations and by his own immigration to the United States.

Sources: Goldman, Linda. *The Encyclopedia of Children's Literature*, 2001; Silvey, Anita, ed. *Children's Books and Their Creators*. Boston: Houghton Mifflin, 1995.

stood up for his beliefs no matter what the cost. The illustrations show Galileo's strength of character through the trials before the Pope and his council.

Media and Technique

Artists make choices about the media, techniques, and styles they use. As mentioned earlier, *media* refers to the material used in the production of a work. *Technique* refers to the method used with the materials or media to create art. Artists can work with virtually any medium—clay, wood, metal, watercolors, oils, fabric, acrylics, ink, pencil, charcoal, pastels—or with any combination of media. An individual artist/illustrator may use the same medium as another artist, but he may produce a very different effect because he is using different techniques. As an example, Stephen T. Johnson uses pastels to create gentle, delicately colored drawings in Lenore Look's *Love as Strong as Ginger* (P–I),

while Jim La Marché in Louise Erdrich's *Grandmother's Pigeon* uses pastels to create highly luminous, richly hued painterly pictures. Reynold Ruffins uses acrylics in *Misoso* (I), as do David Shannon in *No! David* (N–P), Dav Pilkey in *Paperboy* (P–I), and Faith Ringgold in *Aunt Harriet's Underground Railroad* (P–I)—each with varying effects. James Ransome uses oils in *Dark Day Light Night* (P–I) and Floyd Cooper uses oils in *Brown Honey and Broomwheat Tea* (P–I) by Joyce Carol Thomas.

Paul O. Zelinsky uses full-color oil painting in *Rumpelstiltskin* (P), in *Rapunzel* (P), and in Anne Isaacs's *Swamp Angel* (P–I). Bernie Fuchs also uses oil in Odds Bodkin's *Ghost of the Southern Belle* (P–I). Artists also use a variety of techniques in addition to painting, such as etching, linoleum blocks, airbrush, collage, stitching, computer art, and photography.

Denise Fleming uses paper pulp to create art in *The Everything Book* (N–P), *In a Small Small Pond,* (P) and

© 1993 Floyd Cooper

Floyd Cooper creates an inviting scene showing a girl sipping a steaming hot cup of tea. He makes tea drinking seem appealing.

Barnyard Banter (P). Mary Azarian uses woodcuts in *The Garden Alphabet* (N–P) and in Jacqueline Martin's *Snowflake Bentley*, as does Stephen Huneck in *Sally Goes to the Beach* (N–P) and in J. Patrick Lewis's *Black Swan White Crow* (P–I).

Salley Mavor creates art through a process she calls *fabric relief* using stitchery, embroidery, and highly textured homespun fabrics in *Mary Had a Little Lamb* (P). Mavor also uses found objects like wood and stones to produce three-dimensional images. You Yang has embroidered tapestries designed by Anita Riggio for Pegi Deitz Shea's *The Whispering Cloth: A Refugee's Story* (I).

Many artists use collage materials but create different effects using different techniques and materials. Holly Meade uses torn paper collages in *Sleep, Sleep, Sleep: A Lullaby for Little Ones Around the World* (N–P) by Nancy Van Laan. Ed Young uses crisply cut collage shapes in *Seven Blind Mice*, as does Holly Meade in Min Fong Ho's story, *Hush! A Thai Lullaby* (N–P). David Wisnieski uses color-aid and coral and bark cloth papers in *Golem* (I). Artists may change the character of their collages by adding a variety of media. Christopher Myers uses ink and gouache with cut and torn pieces of collage in *Harlem* (P–I) by Walter Dean Myers. Simms Taback uses mixed media and collage on craft paper in *There Was an Old Lady Who Swallowed a Fly* (N–P), and in *Joseph Had a Little Overcoat* (N–P–I) he adds watercolor,

gouache, pencil, ink, and photography to his paper and fabric collages.

Some artists are known for their work with a particular technique or medium, like Ezra Jack Keats for collage in *The Snowy Day*, or Eric Carle for collages cut from handmade paper in *Stories for All Seasons* (N–P); Leo Lionni for collages in *Frederick's Fables* (N–P), Brian Pinkney for scratchboard art in *Jo Jo's Flying Sidekick* (I) or in *Duke Ellington: The Piano Player and His Orchestra* (I) by Andrea Davis Pinkney. Ken Robbins is known for his photographs. For *Fire: The Elements* (P–I–A) Robbins begins with photographs of the practical uses of fire—fireworks and candles—then moves to exquisite photographs of steel mills and cannons, which show fire in all its forms. He hand colors the photographs to produce a soft, romantic mood or a violent raging mood.

As in other areas of twenty-first century life, computers are making an impact. Although computer-generated art was initially considered inferior, enormous advances have been made in technology. Now, with proper training one can draw with a penlike stylus and approximate any medium that then appears on a monitor; the images can be corrected, adjusted, clicked, and saved. Artists such as Rachel Isadora in *ABC Pop* (N–P) or *Listen to the City* (N–P), Avis Harley in *Fly with Poetry* (P–I), and David Pelletier in the Caldecott Honor Book *The Graphic Alphabet* (N–P) have

Figure 3·2

Media and Techniques Used in Picture Books

Note: Some publishers now state the media, technique, and typography used in their books. Check the copyright page for this information.

Acrylic

Cooney, Barbara, *Miss Rumphius*

Pilkey, Dav, *Paperboy*

Roberts, Bethany, *A Mouse Told His Mother*, illustrated by Mary Jane Begin

Shannon, David, *No, David!*

_____, *When David Goes to School*

Chalk

Grifalconi, Ann, *Osa's Pride*

Conte Pencil

Van Allsburg, Chris, *Jumanji*

Collage

Carle, Eric, *The Very Lonely Firefly* (hand-printed collage paper)

_____, *The Clumsy Click Beetle* (hand-printed collage paper)

Ehlert, Lois, *Mole's Hill*

Fleming, Denise, *Barnyard Banter*

Fox, Mem, *Hattie and the Fox*, illustrated by Patricia Mullins

Ho, Minfong, *Hush! A Thai Lullaby*, illustrated by Holly Meade (cut paper collage and ink)

Keats, Ezra Jack, *The Snowy Day* (cut and torn paper collage)

Lionni, Leo, *Frederick's Fables* (collage and mixed media)

Wisniewski, David, *Golem* (color-aid/coral and bark cloth papers)

Young, Ed, *Seven Blind Mice*

Computer-Generated or Computer-Augmented Art

Eitan, Ora, *Astro Bunnies*

_____, *Dance, Sing, Remember: A Celebration of Jewish Holidays*

Harley, Avis, *Fly with Poetry!*

_____, *Leap with Poetry!*

Isadora, Rachel, *ABC Pop!*

_____, *123 Pop!*

_____, *Listen to the City*

Loomis, Christina, *Cowboy Bunnies*

Pelletier, David, *The Graphic Alphabet*

Stevens, Janet, *To Market! To Market!*

_____, *Cook-a-Doodle-Doo!*

_____, *My Big Dog*

Cut Paper

Wisniewski, David, *Sundiata: Lion King of Mali*

_____, *Rain Player*

_____, *Wave of the Sea-Wolf*

Gouache

Bang, Molly, *When Sophie Gets Angry . . . Really, Really, Angry*

Cousins, Lucy, *Katy Cat and Beaky Boo*

Kalman, Maira, *Max in Hollywood, Baby*

Moss, Lloyd, *Zin! Zin! Zin! . . . A Violin*

Graphite/Pencil

McDonald, Megan, *Tundra Mouse*, illustrated by S. D. Schindler (colored pencil on pastel paper)

Ryan, Pam Munoz, *Amelia and Eleanor Go for a Ride*, illustrated by Brian Selznick (pencil/colored pencil)

Mixed Media

Bunting, Eve, *Smoky Night*, illustrated by David Diaz

Johnson, Stephen T., *Alphabet City* (gouache and charcoal on hot pressed watercolor paper)

_____, *City by Numbers* (pastel, oil, watercolor)

Lester, Julius, *John Henry*, illustrated by Jerry Pinkney (pencil, colored pencil and watercolor)

McDermott, Gerald, *Raven: A Trickster Story from the Northwest* (gouache, colored pencil, pastel on heavyweight watercolor paper)

Myers, Walter Dean, *Harlem*, illustrated by Christopher Myers (ink, gouache, and cut paper collage)

used technology with great success. Ultimately technology will create other booklike forms that will not replace picture books but that will require publishers and editors who are skilled in new technology.

Other artists range across a variety of media and technique, selecting that which best suits the text they are illustrating. Figure 3.2 presents a variety of the media and techniques found in picture books.

Pinkney, Andrea Davis, *Duke Ellington: The Piano Player and His Orchestra*, illustrated by Brian Pinkney (scratchboard/gouache, luma dyes, and oil paint)

Sis, Peter, *Tibet: Through the Red Box* (oil pastel, watercolor, pen and ink)

Stevens, Janet, *Tops and Bottoms* (watercolor, pencil and gesso)

Stewart, Sarah, *The Garden*, illustrated by David Small (pen and ink and crayon)

Taback, Simms, *There Was an Old Lady Who Swallowed a Fly* (mixed media and collage on craft paper)

_____, *Joseph Had a Little Overcoat* (watercolor, gouache pencil, ink, collage)

Oil

Bodkin, Odds, *Ghost of the Southern Belle*, illustrated by Berni Fuchs

Isaacs, Anne, *Swamp Angel*, illustrated by Paul O. Zelinsky

Zelinsky, Paul O. *Rapunzel*

_____, *Rumpelstiltskin*

Zolotow, Charlotte, *The Old Dog*, illustrated by James Ransome

Opaque Paint

Politi, Leo, *Song of the Swallows*

Wise Brown, Margaret, *The Little Island*, illustrated by Leonard Weisgard

Pastel

Erdrich, Louise, *Grandmother's Pigeon*, illustrated by Jim LaMarche

Hendershot, Judith, *In Coal Country*, illustrated by Thomas B. Allen

Henderson, Kathy, *The Baby Dances*, illustrated by Tony Kirn

Look, Lenore, *Love as Strong as Ginger*, illustrated by Stephen Johnson (litho crayon line)

Lyon, George Ella, *One Lucky Girl*, illustrated by Irene Trivas

Shannon, George, *Climbing Kansas Mountain*, illustrated by Thomas B. Allen

Pen, Ink, and Watercolor

Falconer, Ian, *Olivia*

Feiffer, Jules, *Bark George*

Steig, William, *Wizzle*, illustrated by Quentin Blake

Scratchboard

Cooney, Barbara, *Chanticleer and the Fox*

Hooks, *Ballad of Belle Dorcas*, illustrated by Brian Pinkney

Pinkney, Brian, *Cosmo and the Robot*

_____, *Jo Jo's Flying Side Kick*

San Souci, Robert D., *The Faithful Friend*, illustrated by Brian Pinkney

_____, *Sukey and the Mermaid*, illustrated by Brian Pinkney

Stitchery

Ringgold, Faith, *Tar Beach*

Shea, Pegi Deitz, *The Whispering Cloth*, illustrated by Anita Riggio, stitchery by You Yang

Tempera

Sendak, Maurice, *Where the Wild Things Are*

Watercolor

Bunting, Eve, *Dandelions*, illustrated by Greg Shed (gouache)

Henkes, Kevin, *Owen* (ink and watercolor)

Lattimore, Deborah Nourse, *Why There Is No Arguing in Heaven*

McCloskey, Robert, *Time of Wonder*

Pinkney, Jerry, *The Ugly Duckling*

Polacco, Patricia, *Butterfly*

Say, Allen, *Tea with Milk*

Shulevitz, Uri, *Snow* (ink and watercolor)

Updike, John, *A Child's Calender*, illustrated by Trina Schart Hyman

Wiesner, David, *Tuesday, Sector 7*

Williams, Vera, *A Chair for My Mother*

Woodcuts

Azarian, Mary, *The Garden Alphabet*

Brown, Marcia, *Once a Mouse*

Emberley, Ed, *Drummer Hoff*

Huneck, Stephen, *Sally Goes to the Beach*

Lewis, J. Patrick, *Black Swan White Crow*, illustrated by Chris Manson

Martin, Jacqueline, *Snowflake Bentley*, illustrated by Mary Azarian

When evaluating picture books look at the artistic quality of the illustrations. The art should help to tell or extend the story, and it should present a fresh visual interpretation, one that enables the reader to look at the story, poem, or concept in a new way. A list of questions for evaluating picture books appears in Figure 3.3.

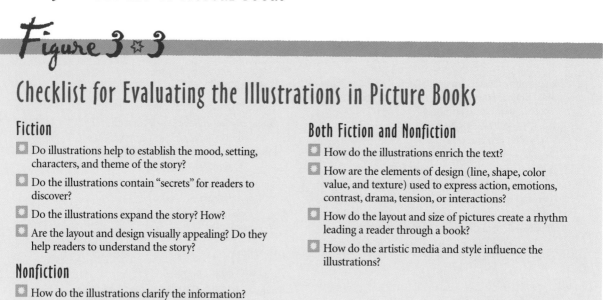

Figure 3 ✿ 3

Checklist for Evaluating the Illustrations in Picture Books

Fiction

- Do illustrations help to establish the mood, setting, characters, and theme of the story?
- Do the illustrations contain "secrets" for readers to discover?
- Do the illustrations expand the story? How?
- Are the layout and design visually appealing? Do they help readers to understand the story?

Nonfiction

- How do the illustrations clarify the information?
- What information do the illustrations impart?

Both Fiction and Nonfiction

- How do the illustrations enrich the text?
- How are the elements of design (line, shape, color value, and texture) used to express action, emotions, contrast, drama, tension, or interactions?
- How do the layout and size of pictures create a rhythm leading a reader through a book?
- How do the artistic media and style influence the illustrations?

Pictures and Text That Work Together

Whatever the genre or content, when illustrations are an equal or dominant partner with the text, the result is a picture book. In some picture storybooks, illustrations precisely verify the text, cotelling the same story. Barbara Cooney's illustrations in *Miss Rumphius* (P–I) visually support and verify the text. Illustrations in other picture books extend the text, adding visual information or meaning not presented in language, the way Susan Jeffers extends the poem in Robert Frost's *Stopping by Woods on a Snowy Evening* (P–I) and the way Stephen Gammell does in Jim Aylesworth's *Old Black Fly* (N–P). The art in some books parallels the text, presenting visual information that creates a story within a story, as in John Burningham's *Time to Get Out of the Bath, Shirley* (N–P) (Cianciolo, 1990; Nodelman, 1988). Shirley's imagination takes her down the bathtub drain and into a medieval world that is conveyed through the art, while her everyday world is conveyed through the text. In Ellen Raskin's *Nothing Ever Happens on My Block* (P), Chester complains of boredom and is totally unaware of a house burning, cops chasing robbers, and a parachutist landing behind him. Each of these books gives readers the opportunity to create meaning through language and art.

Books with pictures range from *wordless* books like Banyai's *Zoom* and *Re-Zoom* (P), which use close-ups and wide shots to show ever-widening surroundings, to *illustrated* books. Writing teachers use *Zoom* and *Re-Zoom* to teach focus and detail in writing; the visual example of expanding a moment makes sense to writers who try to do the same thing with words. An *illustrated book* consists of both text and illustrations, but the text carries the major responsibility for depicting the story or content while the illustrations contribute significantly, but not equally, to development, depth, and breadth of the story or content. In *The Sunday Outing* (I), written by Gloria Pinkney, Jerry Pinkney's art highlights significant aspects of setting, theme, mood, and character development. Another superb illustrated book, Sharon Bell Mathis's *The Hundred Penny Box* (I–A), features accomplished illustrations by Leo and Diane Dillon and makes artful use of language to explore aging. Art in illustrated books may enhance, enrich, and extend the text, but these books do not qualify as true picture books. In authentic picture books text and art are interwoven and inseparable. Words and pictures together create a meaning that neither could create alone (Nodelman, 1988). Figure 3.4 lists books that exemplify the ways in which art and text work together. Teaching Idea 3.3 gives ideas for considering works of art by prominent illustrators.

Styles of Art

Style refers to a configuration of artistic elements that together constitute a specific and identifiable manner of expression (Cianciolo, 1997). Style refers to a personal form of art that makes an artist's work recognizable because of his or her consistent treatment of details, composition, or handling of a

Figure 3 ❄ 4

When Pictures and Text Work Together

Extend

Peters, Lisa Westberg, *Cold Little Duck, Duck, Duck,*
  illustrated by Sam Williams
Mathers, Petra, *A Cake for Herbie*
Stuve-Bodeen, Stephanie, *Mama Elizabeti*

Verify

McCully, Emily Arnold, *Monk Camps Out*
Spinelli, Eileen, *Night Shift Daddy*

Parallel

Pinkney, Brian, *Cosmo and the Robot*

Wordless

Vincent, Gabrielle, *A Day a Dog*
Weitzman, Jacqueline Preiss, *You Can't Take a Balloon into
  the National Gallery*

Illustrated

Tudor, Tasha, *1 Is One*

Teaching Idea 3 ❄ 3

Studying the Art of Your Favorite Illustrator

Artists develop a characteristic way of presenting
ideas visually; some vary their style according to the
text. Collect several books by one illustrator and
compare them. Is the art similar across books? Do
they represent distinct approaches? Study some of
the following illustrators. Summarize your findings.
Describe each illustrator's work. How would you
characterize it? Use examples of the works to
illustrate your points.

  Patricia Polacco (watercolor, ink) Warm,
    inviting, integrated with story.
  Peter Sis (watercolor, pen and ink) Emotional,
    lots of detail, stories within art.
  Tomie dePaola (Naive, folk art) Strong outlines,
    sturdy people, hearts, birds.
  Marcia Brown (painterly techniques and
    collage) Each book has distinct style.
  Chris Van Allsburg (surrealist) Bull terrier in
    every book, surrealistic.
  David Macaulay (draftsman, architectural)
    Intricate line and composition.
  Jan Brett (representational) Makes use of
    intricate borders.
  Eric Carle (collage) Bold color, strong line.
  Ted Rand (representational) Varies light and
    shadow throughout his books.
  Maurice Sendak (from cartoon to high art)
    Portrays oversize hands and feet.

medium. Style reflects the individuality and artistic strength
of the artist; it is influenced by the content and mood of the
text and by the intended audience (Cianciolo, 1976). Artistic
styles available in books for children are many and varied.

REPRESENTATIONAL ART

Representational art consists of literal, realistic depictions of
characters, objects, and events. Greg Shed used live models
and traveled across the Nebraska prairie to find a sod house
in order to achieve realism in his paintings for Eve Bunting's
Dandelions (P–I). His art expresses the historical setting and
emotional tension of the story.

  Paul O. Zelinsky creates exquisite realistic oil paintings in
the style of the French and Italian Renaissance painters to illustrate the Grimm's fairy tale *Rapunzel* (P–I). Beautifully
rendered settings and emotionally filled portraits of the leading characters add drama and dimension to the old tale. The
same can be said for Jim La Marche's realistic, glowing art in
Louise Erdrich's magical story, *Grandmother's Pigeon* (P–I).

SURREALISTIC ART

Surrealistic art contains "startling images and incongruities" that often suggest an "attitude or mockery about
conventionalities" (Cianciolo, 1976, p. 40). Surreal pictures
are often composed of the kinds of images experienced in
dreams or nightmares or in a state of hallucination. Chris
Van Allsburg's surrealistic paintings in *Jumanji* (P–I) extend
the clever challenge of the text. His illustrations are full of
garishly funny details. Anthony Browne's surrealist paintings convey the idea of being encaged through the device of

vertical prison bars in both *Hansel and Gretel* (P) and *Gorilla* (P–I). In *Willy the Dreamer* (P–I), he has Willie the chimpanzee dreaming that he has been transformed into a variety of absurd roles from prima ballerina to superhero. Browne's books invite repeated viewing because he fills them with subtleties and the reader always finds something extra in each new reading. In David Wiesner's wordless books *Tuesday* (P–I) and *Sector 7* (P–I), strange phenomena occur, and totally surreal events appear in the skies. In Anne Isaac's tall tale, *Swamp Angel*, Paul O. Zelinsky portrays this mythical Bunyanesque superfemale engaged in superhuman feats. As she dwarfs all settings and all living creatures, there is a surreal quality to the illustrations.

IMPRESSIONISTIC ART

Impressionist artists emphasize light and color; they create an impression of reality. They may break an image into many small bits of color to mimic the way the eye perceives and merges color to create images. E. B. Lewis's watercolor paintings reflect the play of light and shadow in Alice Schertle's *Down by the Road* (I) and in Janet Kurtz's *Faraway Home* (I).

Emily Arnold McCully's paintings in *Mirette on the High Wire* (P–I) convey the almost lighter-than-air vitality of young Mirette; nineteenth-century Paris is romanticized with light and color suggestive of Toulouse Lautrec's work. The softly blurred lines of Carole Byard's acrylic paintings in Sherley Anne Williams's *Working Cotton* (I) suggest images of a day in the cotton fields, and convey the strength and exhaustion of those picking. Byard's paintings suggest rather than define reality.

Greg Couch's glowing watercolors in Jane Cutler's *The Cello of Mr. O* (I) capture the spirit of a war-torn European city and the resiliency of the human spirit. The devastated city is seen in a dull light, but when Mr. O. plays his cello and we sense the music in the air, the pages fill with radiant color and light. Lisa Desimini's vibrant oil paintings for Cynthia Rylant's book *Tulip Sees America* (N–P) capture the splendor and diversity of the American landscape and the pleasures of visiting places for the first time, particularly with a canine companion. From mist-laden green farmlands to golden prairies, from deserts with blooming cacti to brilliant, blue, foaming oceans, Desimini's art and Cynthia Rylant's vivid poetic words together give us a magnificent portrait of America.

Without using extraneous realistic detail, Ed Young creates the impression of a most eerie atmosphere and a most formidable beast in *Lon Po Po: a Red Riding Hood Story from China* (P–I). With just a few menacing shadows looming across the pages, and some touches of white for glowing eyes and sharp teeth, we have the essence of a threatening monster. In the scenes of imminent disaster we are totally sympathetic to the cowering girls.

FOLK ART

Folk art is a broad designation for the artistic expression of a particular ethnic group's style of representation. Folk art may simplify, exaggerate, or distort reality, but it does so in a way that is characteristic of the traditional art of a culture. This is often realized through the use of traditional motifs, symbols, and techniques (Cianciolo, 1990).

There are as many folk art styles as there are folk cultures. With the proliferation of folktale adaptations and original folktales told in the style of a particular culture, many artists illustrate these tales using the characteristics, motifs, and symbols found in the art of that culture (Cianciolo, p. 97). In a retelling of a Persian folktale, *The Girl Who Loved the Wind* (P–I), by Jane Yolen, the artist Ed Young uses a style of art found in Persian miniature paintings. Pegi Deitz Shea's *The Whispering Cloth: A Refugee's Story* (P–I), discussed earlier, uses pictures of embroidered tapestries designed by Anita Riggio and stitched by You Yang. This story about Chinese Hmong people uses a style of art common to the culture. There, Hmong women usually record significant events in their lives on embroidered tapestries called story cloths or pa'ndaus (Cianciolo, 1997). Baba Wagué Diakité, an author-illustrator from Bamako, Mali, in West Africa, uses the symbols and motifs of his culture in his folktale *The Huntsman and the Crocodile* (I). His bold primitively drawn ceramic tile paintings convey the voice and spirit of his African ancestors.

Deborah Nourse Lattimore's illustrations for *The Dragon's Robe* (I) include traditional Chinese motifs and symbols that reflect the art that marks the period of Chinese history in which the story is set. In Demi's *Liang and the Magic Paintbrush* (P–I) and in *The Empty Pot* (P), two Chinese folktales, the artist uses the fine line drawing and the skewed perspective typical of traditional Chinese art. Murv Jacob draws upon his own cultural heritage to illustrate Joseph Bruchac's retelling of *Flying with the Eagle, Racing the Great Bear* (I).

NAIVE ART

Naive art is technically unsophisticated but is marked by an artist's clear, intense emotions and visions. Artists may be self-taught or may give the impression of ignoring traditional academic standards of art. There is almost always adherence to frontal posture or profile and a disregard for traditional representation of anatomy and perspective. Naive art presents the essence of experiences and objects in a simplified fashion with clearly recognizable forms of people and places (Cianciolo, 1990).

Faith Ringgold's illustrations for *Tar Beach* (P) exemplify the naive style of art. Her paintings are simply bursting with joy and vitality as young Cassie flies up from the rooftop of her apartment building and out over New York City. In Ringgold's *Aunt Harriet's Underground Railroad in the Sky* (P–I), Cassie's brother BeBe joins her to travel over the same routes the runaway slaves traveled in the Underground Railroad. The brief but informative text and the dramatic, brightly colored naive paintings make it possible for young children to understand some facts about slavery and to appreciate the amazing accomplishments of Harriet Tubman and others associated with the Underground Railroad.

In *The Legend of the Poinsettia*, retold and illustrated by Tomie dePaola, the artist uses a naive style to tell the Mexican folktale of how this plant came to be called "flor de la noche buena" (flower of the holy night) and how the red and green plant traditionally associated with Christmas came to be called the poinsettia.

Ashley Bryan in *Sing to the Sun* (P–I) uses vivid colors, flat, frontal depiction of people, and a flattened perspective. In Monica Gunning's *Not a Copper Penny in Me House*, Frané Lessac creates brilliantly colored naive paintings that capture the charm and simplicity of life on the island of Jamaica. The vivid images conveyed in the words of the poems are perfectly complemented by the richly detailed naive pictures.

CARTOON ART

Cartoon art emphasizes line, reduces features to simplified shapes, and uses exaggeration in two dimensions to create caricature (Cianciolo, 1976). The artist may employ such techniques as slapstick and may use ludicrous distortions of characteristics to depict absurdities and incongruities of situations so that laughter or at least a smile is evoked. Both

adults and children are regularly exposed to cartoon art through comic strips, political cartoons, and of course, animated films and videos. Because of their exaggerated expressive qualities, cartoon art communicates most directly and can often be understood without words.

There may be a tendency to disparage cartoon art, perhaps because of its connection to comic books, comic strips, and animated films. Many of our greatest children's illustrators, however, were clearly inspired by cartoon art and they continue work in that style. Such brilliant author-illustrators as Maurice Sendak, creator of *Where the Wild Things Are* (N–P), William Steig, creator of *Sylvester and the Magic Pebble* (P–I), Tomie dePaola, creator of *Strega Nona* (P), Tomi Ungerer, creator of *The Moon Man* (P–I), and James Marshall, creator of a comic version of *Goldilocks and the Three Bears* (P) all use their cartooning skills to create award-winning books. Rosemary Wells, the author of *Max's Dragon Shirt* (N–P) and the many Max books uses her cartoon humor to tell the escapades of this mischievous boy bunny, Max.

Susan Meddaugh's *Hog-Eye* (P) combines bright, animated, expressive art with conversation balloons in a cautionary tale. Steven Kellogg is a master of cartoon humor, and his classic *Pinkerton, Behave* (P) exemplifies this style. A Great Dane who flunked obedience school, a burglar, and a quick-thinking dog owner create a situation as hilarious as the illustrations. In *No! David* and *David Goes to School* (both N–P) David Shannon uses full color cartoon art to create a portrait of a perfectly believable but impossible little boy. Edward Sorel, a caricaturist for *Time* magazine, *Atlantic*

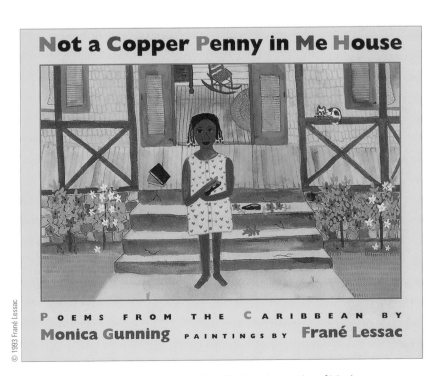

Frané Lessac's art extends the understanding of the Jamaican setting of Monica Gunning's poetry.

Figure 3 ✳ 5

Styles of Art in Picture Books

Surrealism

Browne, Anthony, *Willy the Dreamer*

Wiesner, David, *Sector 7*

Isaacs, Anne, *Swamp Angel*, illustrated by Paul O. Zelinsky

Realism

Erdrich, Louise, *Grandmother's Pigeon*, illustrated by Jim LaMarche

Johnson, Stephen T., *City by Numbers*

Zelinsky, Paul O., *Rapunzel*

Impressionism

Cutler, Jane, *The Cello of Mr. O*, illustrated by Greg Couch.

Rylant, Cynthia, *Tulip Sees America*, illustrated by Lisa Desmini

Young, Ed. *Lon Po Po: A Red Riding Hood Story from China*

Folk Art

Demi, *Liang and the Magic Paintbrush*

Diakite, Baba Wague, *The Hunterman and the Crocodile*

Shea, Pegi Dietz, *The Whispering Cloth*, illustrated by Anita Riggio

Yolen, Jane, *The Girl Who Loved the Wind*, illustrated by Ed Young

Naive Art

Gunning, Monica, *Not a Copper Penny in Me House*, illustrated by Frané Lessac

Ringgold, Faith, *Aunt Harriet's Underground Railroad in the Sky*

Cartoon Art

Shannon, David, *David Goes to School*

Marshall, James, *Goldilocks and the Three Bears*

Sorel, Edward, *Johnny on the Spot*

David Shannon often heard the word no *when he was a child. His memories convey the residue of feelings.*

Monthly, *The New Yorker,* and *New York* magazine has used his cartooning talents in ***Johnny on the Spot*** (I), a fanciful story of a Depression-era boy who is able to raise some well-needed cash when he temporarily becomes the owner of a time-traveling radio. Sorel's talents capture all the humorous possibilities in this tale of Depression-era New York City.

All these many styles of art—representational, surrealistic, impressionistic, folk, naive, and cartoon—can be found in picture books. Illustrations in the books cited in Figure 3.5 are examples of the variety of styles. Notice the variety of techniques and media.

A CLOSE LOOK AT

The Tale of Peter Rabbit

A picture storybook that has stood the test of time and is as beloved by children today as it was when it was published in 1902 is Beatrix Potter's ***The Tale of Peter Rabbit*** (N–P).

Synopsis

Peter is a young rabbit who lives with his mother and three sisters near Mr. McGregor's vegetable garden, a tempting but dangerous place where Peter's father met an untimely death. When Mrs. Rabbit goes to the baker's, disobedient Peter

*Peter turns his back to his family and faces the viewer, suggesting that he may not be listening to his mother's instructions. (**The Tale of Peter Rabbit** by Beatrix Potter)*

immediately squeezes under the garden gate and gorges himself on the treasures in Mr. McGregor's garden. Mr. Mc-Gregor spots him and chases Peter through the garden and into a shed, where Peter eludes him. Peter finally finds his way out of the garden and back home, where he is put to bed to recuperate from his excesses.

Setting

As in many fantasy narratives for young children, the setting in Peter Rabbit is briefly presented with words and is detailed in the illustrations. Potter introduces the story as follows:

> Once upon a time there were four little rabbits, and their names were—Flopsy, Mopsy, Cotton-tail, and Peter. They lived with their Mother in a sand-bank, underneath the root of a very big fir-tree. (p. 9)

This description is accompanied by a delicate, realistic watercolor illustration of the four rabbits and their mother peering at the reader from their fir tree home. Ears and tree trunk stand straight up, pulling the viewer's eye upward; the colors are muted browns and greens. Mother Rabbit is in the foreground, with her back to the viewer; her head is turned to look much as a real rabbit looks when startled by a person. Three small faces appear around the roots of the

tree. One set of hind legs and a tail are visible under the left-hand root; we infer later that this is Peter. The rabbits appear to be realistic—that is, they look like wild rabbits. The very next illustration shows the rabbits dressed in pink and blue human clothes, against a white background. The three girls are clustered around their mother, and Peter has his back to his family and is facing the viewer. His little blue jacket hides his front paws. The text contains Mrs. Rabbit's warning to her children to stay away from Mr. McGregor's garden. Thus, by the second page of the book, both text and illustration establish the place and the genre—this is a fantasy. Potter's fantasy, however, is special. Her animal characters may dress in human clothes and use language, but they act like animals. Everything Peter does is possible for a rabbit to do, but his personality is that of an irrepressible child.

Characters

The first three pages also establish the characters. In the first illustration we see the faces of three of the bunnies, and the tail of the fourth. Once readers get to know Peter, they guess that the tail must belong to Peter, as he is the naughty one. The second illustration shows Mrs. Rabbit leaning down to talk to her three daughters; Peter is turned away, obviously not listening. The third illustration again places the rabbits in the woods, but they are still in their human clothes. Mrs. Rabbit is leaning down toward Peter, whose head is tilted back. She is buttoning the top button of his jacket while Flopsy, Mopsy, and Cottontail are already going down the path. The text, "Now run along, and don't get into mischief. I am going out" (p. 13), is obviously directed toward Peter, the only one close enough to Mrs. Rabbit to hear her admonition. It is only by seeing the illustration and reading the text that the full implications of this double page can be understood.

Just in case the implications haven't been understood, the sixth illustration shows Peter, ears upright, squeezing under a gate, and the accompanying text reads, "But Peter, who was very naughty, ran straight away to Mr. McGregor's garden, and squeezed under the gate!" (p. 18). Thus a combination of text and art presents Peter as a naughty but endearing young rabbit who is recognizable as a human child—curious and apt to ignore a mother's restrictions in order to find out about the world. He not only goes into the garden, he loses his clothes—"The second little jacket and pair of shoes that Peter had lost in a fortnight!" (p. 54). Later in the story readers see him escaping from great danger and finding his way home again, all by himself.

Plot

The sequence of action in *Peter Rabbit* is straightforward, clear, and logical. Peter gets into the garden, eats a bit too much, is spotted by Mr. McGregor, is chased, gets caught in a gooseberry net, hides in a watering can in a shed, escapes

*We are aware of Peter Rabbit's small size and vulnerability as we see him knocking over flower pots when he tries to escape from Mr. McGregor's big foot. (**The Tale of Peter Rabbit** by Beatrix Potter)*

© 1987 Frederick Warne & Company

out the window, hides until McGregor gives up, finds the gate, and makes a mad dash for freedom and the safety of home, where Mrs. Rabbit puts him to bed with a spoonful of medicine, just as any good mother would. Readers view the action as they read it, seeing Peter eating carrots, coming face-to-face with McGregor, caught in the net, diving into the watering can, leaping out the window just as McGregor's boot is about to come down on him, and collapsed on the floor of the rabbit-hole. After he has lost his jacket he again looks like the wild rabbit that he is. The excitement builds twice: once when he is chased by McGregor, and again as he finds his way out of the garden. The resolution is clear—he is home, he is safe, and he is exhausted.

As the adventure occurs the illustrations heighten the sense of panic: Potter uses perspective to indicate how small Peter really is. When Peter is in the garden she is careful to place him with objects that make his small size apparent; we see him among plants, flower pots, by a watering can, and near Mr. McGregor himself. Perhaps the most vivid image of his vulnerability is when he flees out of a window, knocking over pots of geraniums, pursued by Mr. McGregor's hobnailed boot.

Theme

The theme, which is easily identified and understood by young readers, is established by text and extended by illustrations. The temptation to mischief, something that is very real to children, is exciting precisely because it is dangerous.

© 1987 Frederick Warne & Company

*Mother Rabbit makes sure that Peter hears her admonition as she buttons the top button of his jacket: "Run along and don't get into mischief." (**The Tale of Peter Rabbit** by Beatrix Potter)*

*Peter lies exhausted but relieved while Mother prepares food. The feeling of being safe at home brings comfort. (**The Tale of Peter Rabbit** by Beatrix Potter)*

Returning home to mother is reassuring. Both emotions are familiar ones to young readers, and these readers can see the excitement and the relief in the illustrations.

Illustrations

The illustrations are delicate, carefully wrought watercolors that, as we have seen, work in conjunction with the words to express the action, characterization, and theme. The delicacy and beauty of the illustrations are such that the publisher, Frederick Warne, recently published new editions using a more sophisticated printing technique that captures more closely the true colors of the original watercolors.

Potter was a keen observer of nature, and that fact is apparent in the detail that graces her illustrations. Peter consistently looks like a real rabbit, even when he is dressed in human clothes. The position of his ears, for example, is both realistic and indicative of his emotions. When Peter cries beside the locked door, he is standing like a sad child, one foot on top of another, with a paw in his mouth; like a tired and scared rabbit his ears are back rather than straight up (as they are throughout most of the story).

*A tear leaks out of a remorseful Peter's eye. His ears droop; he puts one foot on top of another. He could easily be chewing on his paw while he reflects upon his misbehavior and adventure. (**The Tale of Peter Rabbit** by Beatrix Potter)*

Potter's accurately detailed, realistic style, her delicate lines, and her glowing watercolors are unsurpassed. Other illustrators have tried to illustrate Potter's story, but none can compare with the original. Those who hear the story without seeing Potter's pictures do not experience the full meaning of *The Tale of Peter Rabbit*.

Language

Potter uses interesting words in imaginative ways and makes her story a delight to read aloud. *Mischief, naughty, dreadfully frightened,* and *exert* are but some of the interesting words and phrases Potter provides for her audience. The onomatopoeic words she uses—*kertyschoo* for a sneeze, *lippity* for a slow hop, *scr-r-ritch* for the sound of a hoe—all increase the vivid quality of the story. One sentence from the middle of the story, when Peter is caught in the gooseberry net, illustrates the complex and interesting quality of the language of this story: "Peter gave himself up for lost, and shed big tears; but his sobs were overheard by some friendly sparrows, who flew to him in great excitement, and implored him to exert himself" (p. 33). Children, delighting in these interesting words, will walk around chanting: "I implore you to exert yourself" after hearing the story.

Beatrix Potter's *The Tale of Peter Rabbit* exemplifies the criteria for excellent picture storybooks. Created through pictures and words, the story is captivating and understandable. The characters, seen through Potter's keen artistic eye, are vivid and engaging and the theme is identifiable and memorable. The pictures and the words are strong and elegant and serve to unify story, characters, and theme. Books like this offer children opportunities for wonderful experiences with literature.

Learning About Art in the Classroom

Children draw, paint, and learn how to view and talk about art by reading and responding to outstanding picture books. Certainly children use the illustrations in picture books to help them follow the story, to understand the concepts, and, in some cases, to read the text. Kiefer (1986) found that children were careful and critical viewers, noticing the "secrets" that artists often put in their illustrations, such as the small white dog that appears in all of Chris Van Allsburg's books.

Just as children notice the writer's craft, they notice the artist's craft and discuss it. In fact, a good question to ask students after reading a picture book is, "What do you notice?" Kiefer (1986) listened to students of all ages talk about

what they noticed about elements of design in picture books. First graders discussed line, shape, texture, and color with ease; older students considered the expressive qualities of illustrations. In every case teachers provided time for children to explore books, to discover and develop individual responses, and to share those responses with others. Teachers also provided a wide selection of books and gave children varied opportunities for response while sharing their knowledge of the elements of language and visual art, as well as their own critical aesthetic responses.

We often think of selecting books that contain similar themes, structures, or literary devices. We can also select books that demonstrate similarities and differences in visual art. Careful selection can lead students to compare the use of line and color, for example, or to note how different martists use texture, light, and space. A thoughtful selection of books that demonstrate particular qualities of visual art can educate students' eyes as well as their minds and hearts. Teaching Idea 3.4 gives ideas for exploring the media and techniques illustrators use. An extensive list of outstanding picture storybooks appears in the Booklist at the end of the chapter.

Summary

Picture books are artful books that hold a special place in the lives of children who read them. The books are the first exposure to fine art for many children. They can enrich children's worlds by providing opportunities for experiences through pictures and print. Picture book illustrators are a part of the wider field of visual art. Their books become a bridge to museum art. In fact, some books introduce them to museum art and to paintings by the old masters. Help children and adolescents to explore the fine arts by using the art of picture books as an introduction. As they become comfortable with the art in books, make connections with art in other places, espe-cially museums.

INFOTRAC Browse through the March/April 1998 issue of *The Horn Book Magazine,* which is devoted to the subject of the picture book. Of particular interest are the articles by Barbara Cooney (page 190), Jon Scieszka and Molly Leach (page 196), and the Studio Views that are sprinkled throughout the issue, in which illustrators talk about their tools and techniques. As you read, make note of information that would be of interest to young readers in terms of both art and process. Share a book by one of the featured illustrators with a colleague. Discuss the illustrator's comments about his or her art and how they influence the way you look at his or her books.

Teaching Idea 3 ✦ 4

Exploring Art Media

Experiment with the media and techniques illustrators use. Collect the following books as models.

Paper

Feelings, Tom, *Moja Means One, Jambo Means Hello* (tissue paper, oil, inks, tempera)

Keats, Ezra Jack, *The Snowy Day, Peter's Chair* (cut paper from textured paper)

Lionni, Leo, *Pezzetino* (torn paper, mosaic tile, type)

Wisniewski, David, *Golem* (cut paper with sharp blade knife)

Use tissue paper, construction paper, magazines, newspaper, wallpaper, and gift-wrap paper to make book illustrations, collages, mosaics, and paper sculptures.

Watercolors

Shulevitz, Uri, *Dawn*

McCloskey, Robert, *Time of Wonder*

McDermott, Gerald, *Arrow to the Sun*

Use watercolor paints, tempera, gouache, and water-base paint for book illustrations, landscapes, crayon-resist painting, seascapes, skyscapes, and backgrounds.

Crayons and Pastels

dePaola, Tomie, *The Baby Sister*

Spier, Peter, *Rain*, and *Noah's Ark*

Use crayons, craypas, pastels, water crayons, acrylics, and markers; include crayon scratch drawings, crayon resist, chalk paintings, crayon texture drawings, and any other combination of media.

Printing Techniques

Emberley, Barbara, *Drummer Hoff*, illustrated by Ed Emberley

Lionni, Leo, *Swimmy*

Use paper doilies, linoleum blocks, wood blocks, potato prints, styrofoam, cardboard, sandpaper, and yarn. Create shapes to dip into paints and stamp onto paper. Make relief prints, etchings, cardboard cuts, and potato prints.

Cartoons

Peet, Bill, *Bill Peet: An Autobiography*

Comic Strips

Aliki, *How a Book Is Made*

Ardizzone, Edward, *Little Tim and the Brave Sea Captain*

Write characters' dialogue in speech balloons. Illustrate the action.

Pen and Ink

Macaulay, David, *Cathedral: The Story of Its Construction*

Van Allsburg, Chris, *Ben's Dream*

Study the artists' use of line to create shapes, shadows, and texture. Experiment with black line on white to create movement and depth.

Computer-Generated or Computer-Augmented Art

Isadora, Rachel, *123 Pop!*

———, *ABC Pop!*

Harley, Avis, *Fly with Poetry*

Use computer program to create art. Illustrate a picture book or a poetry book with it.

Camcorder or Digital Camera

Make a picture book of any medium. Then make a video with sound using music as a background for reading aloud.

Booklist

Outstanding Picture Books

Bemelmans, Ludwig, *Madeline* (N–P)

Brooke, L. Leslie, *Johnny Crow's Garden* (N–P)

Bunting, Eve, *Smoky Night*, illustrated by David Diaz (I–A)

Burton, Virginia Lee, *The Little House* (N–P)

———, *Mike Mulligan and His Steam Shovel* (N–P)

Carle, Eric, *The Very Hungry Caterpillar* (N–P)

dePaola, Tomie, *The Legend of the Indian Paintbrush* (N–P)

Flack, Marjorie, *The Story About Ping*, illustrated by Kurt Wiese (N–P)

Ga'g, Wanda, *Millions of Cats* (N–P)

Goble, Paul, *Crow Chief: A Plains Indian Story* (I–A)

——, *Death of the Iron Horse* (I–A)

Gramatky, Hardie, *Little Toot* (N–P)

Hoban, Russell, *Bread and Jam for Frances*, illustrated by Lillian Hoban (N–P)

Keats, Ezra Jack, *The Snowy Day* (N–P)

Lasker, Joe, *Merry Ever After* (I–A)

Lionni, Leo, *Little Blue and Little Yellow* (N–P)

Macaulay, David, *Black and White* (I–A)

McCloskey, Robert, *Blueberries for Sal* (N–P)

McKissack, Patricia C., *Mirandy and Brother Wind*, illustrated by Jerry Pinkney (N–P)

Polacco, Patricia, *Aunt Chip and the Great Triple Creek Dam Affair* (I–A)

Potter, Beatrix, *The Tale of Peter Rabbit* (N–P)

Rey, H. A., *Curious George* (N–P)

Ringgold, Faith, *Tar Beach* (N–P)

Rylant, Cynthia, *Appalachia: The Voices of Sleeping Birds*, illustrated by Barry Moser (I–A)

Say, Allen, *Bicycle Man* (N–P)

Sendak, Maurice, *Outside Over There* (I–A)

——, *Where the Wild Things Are* (N–P)

Slobodkina, Esphyr, *Caps for Sale* (N–P)

Steig, William, *Amos and Boris* (I–A)

Steptoe, John, *Stevie* (I–A)

Thurber, James, *Many Moons*, illustrated by Marc Simont (I–A)

Van Allsburg, Chris, *The Garden of Abdul Gazasi* (I–A)

——, *The Polar Express* (I–A)

Wiesner, David, *Tuesday* (N–P)

Willard, Nancy, *William Blake's Inn*, illustrated by Alice and Martin Provensen (I–A)

Wisniewski, David, *The Warrior and the Wise Man* (N–P)

chapter 4

The Content of Picture Books

© 1982 Diane Goode

Diane Goode's art expresses Cynthia Rylant's words about family love in **When I Was Young in the Mountains.** *Goode received a Caldecott Honor for this book.*

When I was young in the mountains,
Grandfather came home in the evening
covered with the black dust of a coal mine.
Only his lips were clean, and he used them
to kiss the top of my head.

—Cynthia Rylant,
When I Was Young in the Mountains

Students in Elizabeth Ryan's second-grade class at P.S. 116 in Manhattan are engaged in a rich conversation about Cynthia Rylant, an author who enters into conversations like a friend passing through a room. Elizabeth has immersed her students in Rylant's books, reading them aloud and having students read them independently and with partners. Now the students are telling her what they notice about Rylant's writing. Elizabeth calls the comments "noticings" and lists them on a big chart about Cynthia Rylant that includes book titles, examples of beautiful language and stylistic techniques that the author uses, words that "wowed," sensory sounds, lines that are repeated, genre, and comments that have to do with the writer's passions. The children discuss the way Rylant writes in *When I Was Young in the Mountains* and *The Relatives Came.* Through her books, they can sense that Rylant has many passions in her life.

On day 3 of this author study, Elizabeth asks the students, "What do you notice about Cynthia Rylant as an author?" Justin says, "She loves her family and spending time in the mountains." Angelique says, "She writes beautiful books. Some books are filled with animals." Karl says, "Most books are memoirs." Michael adds, "*When I Was Young in the Mountains* and *The Relatives Came* are both country books. I think she may come from the country."

Each day, the students write what they notice about Rylant's work in their notebooks and share it in group discussion; it is evident that the children understand that Rylant is a writer who writes from personal experience. One child says she writes "from her heart." A child named Sheer sums it up by saying, "Her books are nice, she uses beautiful words, and her books are filled with her passions. She enjoys spending time in the country and spending time with her family. She mentioned her cousins and her grandparents in *When I Was Young in the Mountains* and *The Relatives Came*. Both books take place in the country and include the family." Then Ana says, "Well, her passion must be the country because she wrote *Night in the Country*." Joy adds, "She must like the mountains." Michael added, "Maybe she studied about the mountains."

Elizabeth plans to compare Rylant's "writerly life" with her "personal life" using a Venn diagram. The class will make their own "writing journey," going through the writer's process of revising and editing. They'll prepare for a publishing party where family and friends can join in a "Cynthia Rylant Publishing Celebration." Elizabeth hopes that all this will prompt her students to use Rylant's books as resources when they write about their own passions and families. Their understanding of her craft will also enrich their reading as they read the work of other authors with a keen eye toward the writer's craft.

Profile ☆ Cynthia Rylant

Courtesy Scholastic, Inc.

Cynthia Rylant was born in Hopewell, Virginia. She grew up in Appalachia and draws from family history to write some of her most poignant stories. Cynthia Rylant's parents separated when she was very young, and she spent most of her time until she was 8 years old with her grandparents in a coal-mining town in West Virginia. She then went to live with her mother in Beaver, West Virginia. She recalls going to school with friends, drinking Nehi grape pop, reading *Archie* comic books, and riding her bike around the small town. It wasn't until Cynthia attended college in Charleston, West Virginia, that she developed a love for books. She received a B.A. (1975), an M.A. from Marshall University (1976), and an

M.L.S. from Kent State University (1982). After receiving her degrees, Cynthia searched for a teaching job without any luck. She eventually worked as a clerk in the children's section of a public library. There she discovered writers she liked, including Randall Jarrell, Donald Hall, and E. B. White. As a young child growing up, she had never been to a library. Even the elementary school in Beaver that she loved so much had no library.

The roots of her first published book, *When I Was Young in the Mountains* (1983) (P), is grounded in her family experiences during the eight years with her grandparents. Cynthia Rylant writes with gentle emotion about the importance of family in many of her books, such as *Missing May* (1992) (I–A), the book that received the Newbery Medal. She also celebrates family reunions in *The Relatives Came* (1986) (P–I), allowing readers alike to reflect on their own family get-togethers. Rylant says that she writes when she senses a story. She observes closely what is around her and imagines a story to accompany the images. Books like *Night in the Country* (1986), which allows readers to imagine frogs singing in country settings and apples falling in yards,

were created this way. As she drove through stark, isolated mountains, Rylant sensed a lonely house trailer with two people missing someone they loved; that led to the story of *Missing May* (1992). She writes what she sees and feels, without adjusting the vocabulary or style to the age of the audience.

Cynthia Rylant received the following awards: ALA Caldecott Honor Book (1983) for *When I Was Young in the Mountains* (illustrated by Diane Goode) and (1986) for *The Relatives Came* (illustrated by Stephen Gammell); ALA Newbery Honor Book (1986) for *A Fine White Dust*; ALA Newbery Medal (1993) for *Missing May*; ALA Notable Book, School Library Journal Best Book (1984); National Council for Social Studies Best Book (1984) all for *Waiting to Waltz: A Childhood*; New York Times Best Illustrated Book, Horn Book Honor Book (1985) for *The Relatives Came*; Boston Globe-Horn Book Award (1991) for *Appalachia: The Voices of Sleeping Birds* and (1992) for *Missing May*; ALA Best Book for Young Adults (1990) for *A Couple of Kooks and Other Stories about Love*.

It is clear to readers of Cynthia Rylant books that she loves animals,
(continued)

especially big, friendly dogs that misbehave the way Mudge does in the easy-to-read **Henry and Mudge** series. Rylant writes other series for early readers, including **Mr. Putter and Tabby, Poppleton, The Everyday Books** (1993), and **The Cobble Street Cousins** (1998). Selected other works of Cynthia Rylant include *Miss Maggie* (1983); *This Year's Garden* (1984); *A Blue-eyed Daisy* (1985); *Every Living Thing* (1985); *Birthday Presents* (1987); *Children of Christmas* (1987); *All I See* (1988); *An Angel for Solomon Singer* (1992); *The Dreamer* (1993); *Gooseberry Park* (1995); *The Whales* (1996); *Margaret, Frank, and Andy: Three Writers' Stories* (1996); *A Little Shopping* (1998); *Bear Day* (1998); *Bless Us All: A Child's Yearbook of Blessings* (1998); *The Van Gogh Café* (1998); *Cookie-Store Cat* (1999); *Special Gifts* (1999); *Some Good News* (1999); *The Heavenly Village* (1999); *Dog Heaven* (1995); *Cat Heaven* (1997).

Sources:
http://www.rylant.com/Welcome.htm

Children's Literature Review 15 (1988), pp. 167–174.
Antonucci, Ron, "Rylant on Writing," *School Library Journal* 39, no. 5 (May 1993), pp. 26–29.
Rylant, Cynthia, "Appalachia," *The Horn Book Magazine* 68, no. 1 (January 1992).
_____, *Best Wishes* (Katonah, New York: R. C. Owen Publishers, 1992).
_____, *But I'll Be Back Again* (New York: Orchard Books, 1989).
_____, "Missing May," *The Horn Book Magazine* 69, no. 1 (January/February 1993).
_____, "Newbery Acceptance," *The Horn Book Magazine* 69, no. 4 (July/August 1993).
Ward Diane, "Cynthia Rylant," *The Horn Book Magazine* 69, no. 4 (July/August 1993).

Picture Books for Developmental Stages

Picture books are a powerful force in children's language and literacy development. Books provide models of language usage; they demonstrate meaningful concepts and represent the world a child is coming to know. Books build a foundation for reading as a pleasurable activity; children learn that good stories come from books. Concept development, language development, and children's storehouses of experiences are strengthened through books. Dorothy Butler, an educator from New Zealand, said simply, "Babies need books." Considering children's voracious appetite for language, almost any book can become a source for learning. We have many books available, however, so we can be selective in those we choose. Only the best are good enough for children.

PICTURE BOOKS FOR VERY YOUNG CHILDREN

Board Books

Board books that appeal to infants and toddlers up to 3 years of age are often 6 to 12 pages long. Many are made of sturdy cardboard. There are also cloth books, shape books, pudgy books, lift-the-flap books, toy books, and plastic bathtub books. Books of this type, appropriate for children in the picture identification stage, are also good for those in the earliest stages of reading. Children point to pictures and label them, creating meaning from texts. Eric Carle's *The Very Busy Spider* (N), reissued as a 24-page board book, has brightly colored collages and tactile renderings of the spider's growing web. Adults reading this book with children ask them to say the repetitive phrases with the onomatopoeic sounds and encourage them to feel the spider web. Rebecca Emberley created four board books in Spanish and English: *My Numbers/Mis Numeros; My Colors/Mis Colores; My Shapes/Mis Formas; My Opposites/Mis Opuestos* (N). Large, clear shapes shown in vivid colors with one word both in English and Spanish invite repeated pointing, labeling, counting, and recognizing of colors and shapes. Many other board books are listed in the Booklist at the end of the chapter.

Participation Books

Participation books provide concrete visual and tactile materials for children to explore—textures to touch, flaps to lift, flowers to smell, and pieces to manipulate. A classic in the field by Dorothy Kunhardt, *Pat the Bunny* (N), asks children to look in a mirror, play peek-a-boo, and feel a scratchy beard; babies love touching this book.

Pop-up books, a variation on participation books, use visual, tactile, and three-dimensional art. *Brooklyn Pops Up* (all ages) is an engineering tour de force that shows landmarks in Brooklyn, New York. The intricate pop-ups show Coney Island, Grand Army Plaza, the Brooklyn Museum of Art, and other lovely sights. Several artists and pop-up designers worked on the book, including Maurice Sendak and Robert Sabuda. These books involve young readers in the act of reading, requiring their active participation in the process. More excellent participation books are listed in the Booklist at the end of the chapter.

Storybooks and Poems

Stories to begin on have a simple plot line, are about familiar childhood experiences, and contain clear illustrations. Toddlers who enjoy participation books also enjoy simple

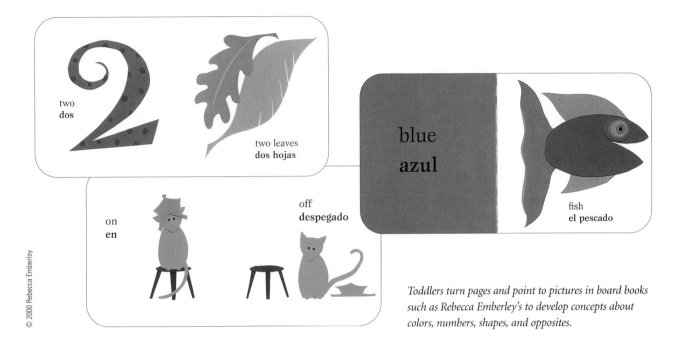

Toddlers turn pages and point to pictures in board books such as Rebecca Emberley's to develop concepts about colors, numbers, shapes, and opposites.

picture storybooks. Rosemary Wells's *Max's Breakfast* (N), shows a clever younger brother outwitting his bossy older sister in just a few pages. These books introduce children to stories by capturing and holding their interest even if they have short attention spans; they often are the books children turn to when they decide to read to themselves or to their toys. Author Laura Numeroff and illustrator Felicia Bond began a delightful series of books in which one thing leads to another with *If You Give a Mouse a Cookie* (N–P). The series continues the fun in *If You Take a Mouse to the Movies* (N–P).

There are many simple storybooks and poems that appeal to children who have outgrown books for babies but are not yet ready for longer stories. These books generally have a brief text and engaging illustrations. Examples of engaging stories are listed in the Booklist at the end of the chapter.

*A winsome mouse child has an endless list of requests in Laura Numeroff's **If You Take a Mouse to the Movies.***

PICTURE BOOKS FOR NURSERY- AND PRIMARY-GRADE CHILDREN

As children mature and their worlds expand, the number of books available to them also expands. Children in the nursery and primary grades have their choice of concept books, alphabet books and counting books, books that support their early attempts at independent reading, and books that relate to every facet of their world.

Concept Books

Concept books are simple nonfiction books. Nursery and primary school children are busy learning about the world, and a number of concept books engage these young readers. The books contribute to the child's expanding knowledge and language by providing numerous examples of an idea. Some books present abstract ideas such as shape, color, size, or sound through many illustrations, as Tana Hoban does in *Cubes, Cones, Cylinders, and Spheres* (N–P). Hoban, a master of the art of concept books and a skilled photographer, uses no words in the book about shapes. Instead, she uses crystal clear photographs of objects that children could find in their own environment. Children enjoy working with this book and often experiment with creating images using shapes and color on their own.

Other books tell stories that focus on specific concepts or involve the viewer by asking questions. Stephen Swinburne does this in *What's a Pair? What's a Dozen?* (P). First, Swinburne introduces number vocabulary in familiar contexts and then he invites the reader to play the game: Who is first in line? Where is the pair of boots? Much information about the concepts is supplied through the illustrations. Other outstanding concept books are listed in the Booklist at the end of the chapter.

Alphabet Books

We call books organized in ABC order alphabet books. Alphabet books serve many useful purposes, only one of which is related to learning the alphabet. Children 2 to 4 years old point to pictures and label objects on the page; 5-year-olds may say the letter names and words that start with each letter; 6-year-olds may read the letters, words, or story to confirm their knowledge of letter and sound correspondences. Whichever way they are read, alphabet books help children to develop an awareness of words on the page; they increase language learning and serve as a pleasurable activity for children.

No one should settle for a mediocre alphabet book, because there are magnificent ones available, such as *A Is for Salad* (P–I) by Mike Lester, *Tomorrow's Alphabet* (P–I) by

Tana Hoban, a photographer with imaginative vision, captures images that help children develop concepts in **Cubes, Cones, Cylinders, and Spheres.**

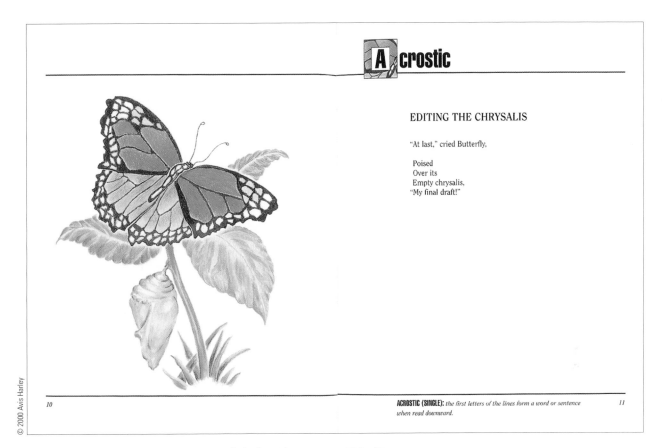

Learn about poetry through poetry in Avis Harley's **Fly With Poetry: An ABC of Poetry.**

George Shannon, *ABC for You and Me* (N–P) by Meg Girnis, *ABC Pop!* (N–P) by Rachel Isadora, *ABC T Rex* (N–P) by Bernard Most, *Bembo's Zoo: An Animal ABC Book* (P–I) by Roberto de Vicq de Cumpitch, *A Gardener's Alphabet* (P) by Mary Azarian, and *A Seaside Alphabet* (P) by Donna Grassby. In Helen Oxenbury's *The ABC of Things* (N), the elongated shape and simple format appeals to young readers. Each double-page spread contains both uppercase and lowercase letters, one or more words beginning with the letters, and objects associated with the letters. Children enjoy the way the illustrations place the objects in humorous situations, such as a cat and a cow sitting on a chair while a crow carries in a cake full of candles. Avis Harley uses the alphabet to present poetic forms in *Fly With Poetry: An ABC of Poetry* (P–I–A). She defines a form and writes a poem in that form to explain exactly what she means. For example, she explains what an acrostic poem is and then presents a poem in that format. Her book is an example of alphabet books that are not geared for young children. Authors use ABCs as a structure for information. For example, Kristen Joy Pratt uses the alphabet for *A Walk in the Rain Forest* and *A Swim in the Sea* (P). Other excellent alphabet books appear in the Booklist at the end of the chapter.

Counting Books

Some books help children learn numbers, numerical concepts, days of the week, months of the year, and the four seasons. Anita Lobel does all that and wraps it in an engaging story in *One Lighthouse One Moon* (P–I). Many counting books are available for the nursery and primary grades, starting with those that use simple pictures to illustrate the progression from 1 to 10, such as Rachel Isadora's *1 2 3 Pop!* (P) and Tasha Tudor's *1 Is One* (P). Other books count well beyond 10, or count in sets, such as *Anno's Counting Book* (P–I), which moves from 0 to 12 and from January to December, and which begins with an empty landscape that soon becomes a small village with 12 houses, 12 adults, and 12 children who go to church at 12 P.M. and spot 12 reindeer in the sky. Isadora and Tudor are at opposite ends of the spectrum of modern and traditional art, whereas Anno uses more complicated illustrations.

Molly Bang's *Ten, Nine, Eight* (N–P) counts backwards as a father helps his daughter get ready for bed, counting down from 10 toes to 1 sleepy child all ready for bed. The illustrations depict bedtime activities and invite young readers to find the numbered objects and to enjoy the loving story. Counting books help children develop concepts of quantity

NINE fisherfolk walked
home with their catch.

Counting books are works of art that tell stories and teach number concepts. They reflect many styles of art including those shown here: **One Lighthouse One Moon** *(Lobel),* **1 2 3 Pop!** *(Isadora), and* **1 Is One** *(Tudor).*

13 is thirteen candles

upon a birthday cake

and seriation through fine visual protrayal of numerical concepts. The best illustrations for young children avoid distracting clutter so that the objects can be identified and counted without confusion. Counting books are also listed in the Booklist at the end of the chapter.

Books for Emerging Readers

As children mature, their taste for books matures, as do their cognitive and linguistic capabilities and needs. Learning to read and being able to unlock the secrets printed on a page marks an important step toward maturity. Many books are available for developing readers, including those discussed above. There are also special kinds of storybooks—wordless books, predictable books, and beginning-to-read books, as well as easy, illustrated chapter books—that support children's attempts at independent reading.

Wordless books are appropriate for children who are developing a sense of story and learning language rapidly. Predictable books are ideal material for the child who is beginning to pay attention to print. Beginning-to-read books are perfect for children who have just become independent readers but still need the support of simple but interesting texts. Easy chapter books help newly independent readers make the transition from beginning-to-read books to full-length novels.

WORDLESS BOOKS Wordless books tell a story through illustration alone. Young children who do not yet read can retell a story from looking at the pictures; beginning readers, through their developing concept of story, are able to narrate the story with character and narrator voices. Struggling readers can grasp the story elements in wordless books. Good wordless storybooks contain all the important elements found in all good storybooks—except for the dialogue and narration, which are supplied by the reader. Some good wordless books are listed in the Booklist at the end of the chapter.

Wordless books provide a good opportunity to explore how stories work. Children produce narration for wordless books; their ideas can be written on large charts and used for reading instruction material. Moreover, children who watch their own words being put onto paper learn intuitively the relation between print and sound. This means of teaching, called the language experience approach, provides a meaningful foundation for reading, especially when accompanied by a strong reading-aloud program based on good literature.

Older students also enjoy wordless books. *You Can't Take a Balloon Into the National Gallery* (P–I–A) by Weitzman and Glasser gives readers several subplots, as well as background activity, art, geography, maps, people, architecture, and humorous detail. Intermediate-grade students use wordless books as models for story writing; middle-school students use them to delineate the elements of fiction. Students of all ages can enjoy David Wiesner's book *Sector 7* (N–P–I–A), each for different reasons. Young children enjoy looking at the world from atop the Empire State Building.

*The art tells the story and readers add their own words in David Wiesner's book **Sector 7**.*

Primary-grade children can supply narration, dialogue, and the magic of make-believe. The structure of the story, along with the character development, provides a good model for writers, and students can also explore the illustrations for the vivid visual characterization that Wiesner provides. Wiesner received the Caldecott Medal for this book.

PREDICTABLE OR PATTERNED BOOKS Predictable books have a strong rhythmic pattern in the language. This helps children to anticipate what is going to happen next, and to predict the next word to come. Many 4- and 5-year-old children can make predictions and can use their knowledge of phonics to read books on their own after hearing them read aloud once or twice. Lenny Hort replicated the pattern of a familiar song, turning the wheels on the bus into *The Seals on the Bus* (N–P) who go "errp, errp, errp" all around the town. In *Cold Little Duck, Duck, Duck* (N–P) Lisa Westberg Peters uses a similar pattern of repetition. A little duck comes to the pond only to find it still frozen. The text is written in large letters: "One miserable and frozen spring: brisk brisk brisk. A cold little duck flew in: Brr-ack Brr-ack Brr-ack. Her pond was stiff and white: creak creak creak." The interesting sounds Peters repeats make children want to read along.

Predictable books are structured using strong language patterns, such as repeated phrases, rhyme, and rhythm; cumulative story structures that add, or accumulate, information; and familiar concepts, songs, or sequences (like days of the week). Detailed illustrations reinforce the language patterns and provide a visual reproduction of the text. Characteristics of predictable books are listed in Figure 4.1.

Reading involves sampling, predicting, and confirming (Goodman, 1985; Smith, 1978). Fluent readers build hypotheses about text meaning as they read. They predict a probable meaning based on the information sampled and then confirm it by checking to see if it makes sense, matches the letter-sound correspondence in the print, and sounds like real language. For beginning readers, patterned books are ideal fare, because they match expectations every step of the way. Poetry also meets the criteria. Through rhythm, repetition, and rhyme, Jane Yolen creates a story in *How Do Dinosaurs Say Goodnight?* (P). It captures the childlike behavior in dinosaurs. Beginning readers chime in the second time through the book. Other outstanding patterned books are listed in the Booklist at the end of the chapter.

BEGINNING-TO-READ BOOKS Beginning-to-read books are ones that children who have just become independent readers can enjoy on their own; they combine controlled vocabulary with creative storytelling. Early books of this type were stilted, but today's authors have mastered the form. We have many excellent beginning-to-read books that tell good stories in a natural way.

Good beginning-to-read books have strong characterization, worthy themes, and engaging plots. The sentences are generally simple, without a lot of embedded clauses, and the language is often direct dialogue. Lines of text are printed so that sentence breaks occur according to natural phrasing, with meaningful chunks of language grouped together. Illustrations depict the characters and action in ways that reflect and extend the text, which contains a limited number of different words and tells an interesting story. Arnold Lobel's series, including *Frog and Toad Are Friends* (N–P), is a classic series and a favorite with newly independent readers. Frog and Toad, humanlike characters in animal form, solve understandable problems with naivety and wit. A

With predictable books, such as Lisa Westberg Peters's **Cold Little Duck, Duck, Duck,** *listeners join in to say repeated phrases. Gradually they become the readers.*

Figure 4 ✿ 1

Characteristics of Predictable, Patterned Stories

Bill Martin, Jr., created an ideal patterned book one morning on the train on the way to work. It was *Brown Bear, Brown Bear, What Do You See?* (N–P). What are the characteristics that make that book predictable? What do you look for in other texts that support beginning readers?

✴ Sounds like natural language

✴ Pictures illustrate the content literally

✴ Story line is simple and direct

✴ Repeated phrases, repetitive refrains

✴ Rhyming words

✴ Cumulative pattern of events

✴ Content appeals to children

✴ Plot events are understandable to children

---

theme of friendship pervades all of their intriguing stories. Illustrations depict the action and provide emotional details about the characters. Lobel chooses words wisely; his story is so well written that it's a pleasure to read aloud. Cynthia Rylant, another wizard with words, created a warm and wonderful series about a very large dog. In *Henry and Mudge and Annie's Perfect Pet* (P), illustrated by Suçie Stevenson, Henry and his cousin Annie love Mudge, but Annie wants her own pet—one that isn't wet, isn't scary, and doesn't fly. She chooses a bunny rabbit and, luckily, it gets along with Mudge. Other good beginning-to-read books are suggested in the booklist at the end of the chapter.

As children grow in their reading ability, they move beyond early easy-to-read materials into chapter books and then toward full-length texts. However, even though children outgrow reading about Frog and Toad and other characters from their early reading experiences, they remember their happy, successful experiences with these books. These strong, positive experiences propel them into more close and happy encounters with literature.

PICTURE BOOKS FOR INTERMEDIATE AND ADVANCED STUDENTS

At one time most picture books were published for students in the primary grades, but today publishers offer a variety of picture books that appeal to older students. Reasons for the change come from both sides of the supply-and-demand column: Teachers and librarians want books that appeal to visually sophisticated students. Teachers want picture books to use with struggling readers who learn more easily using books with more pictures and fewer pages of dense text than they do using traditional textbooks. Second-language learners also learn more readily using heavily illustrated texts and picture books instead of text-laden books. In an

integrated, literature-based curriculum, students explore topics in picture books that convey relevant information geared to their interest level. The publishing trend has been to produce more reader-friendly books with increased illustration and less densely packed texts. Picture books for older students are longer, have more complex text and themes, and deal with topics that are more abstract and more intellectually demanding. Some books are more accurately called illustrated books or photo-essays than true picture books, as the art actually drives most of the storytelling or the information-giving process.

In a true picture book for older students, Patricia Polacco's *Pink and Say* (I), African-American Pinkus saves Sheldon's life as they fight side by side on a Civil War battlefield. Pinkus takes his wounded white soldier friend to his own home, where his grandmother nurses him back to health. Despite his generous acts, Pinkus is hanged at Andersonville soon after arriving there as a Confederate prisoner. The story is handed down from Polacco's ancestor, Sheldon Curtis.

In a nonfiction photo-essay for older readers, *frank o. gehry: outside in* by Jan Greenberg and Sandra Jordan, readers meet the innovative architect who designed the Guggenheim Museum in Bilbao, Spain. Gehry, who revolutionized design by using computers, is praised internationally for unconventional architecture, but his neighbors in Santa Monica, California, objected when he remodeled his two-story pink bungalow with unorthodox materials. Greenberg and Jordan also bring art into the classroom with *Chuck Close, Close Up* (I–A), *The Painter's Eye: Learning to Look at Contemporary American Art*, *The Sculptor's Eye: Looking at Contemporary American Art*, and *The American Eye: Eleven Artists of the Twentieth Century* (all I–A). Some picture books for older readers are a visual treat, a stunning example of an artist's vision, such as Chris Van Allsburg's *The Polar Express* (P–I–A) and *The Wretched Stone* (I–A). *The Polar Express* is a magical Christmas story. The text of *The Wretched Stone* is excerpted from a fictional ship's log

Frank O. Gehry challenges readers to think in new ways—as he did about architecture—in **outside in**.

and tells a strange tale about men who are transformed into apes because they do nothing but stare at a glowing stone that is symbolic of a TV screen. When their captain reads to them, they begin to recover. Picture books that appeal to older readers are listed in the Booklist at the end of the chapter. As students become sensitive to design and artistic effect, they can profit from a study of styles, techniques, and media, discussed in Chapter 3. Greenberg and Jordan discuss elements of art, principles of design, well-known museum paintings, and artists' lives. They also present information in text supported by illustrations from contemporary art to demonstrate their point.

Forging Connections Between Life and Literature

Children forge connections between the books they read and the life they live because literature reflects every aspect of their expanding world. Children's language ability develops rapidly from birth through the primary grades; then their social ability grows as their world expands. They learn about themselves and their families, and they develop social knowledge as they form friendships and go to school. They also learn about the natural world and the aesthetic world of art, music, dance, and literature. Their imagination feeds on new experiences with life and literature. Picture books support and enrich this spiraling, expanding development; books offer opportunities for virtual experiences as well as imaginative language experiences. Figure 4.2 provides some outstanding examples of books which forge connections to a child's life.

THE CHILD'S INNER WORLD

In a supportive environment, children know that they are loved and unique; they are able to express themselves and to make choices. They understand that they are not the only people who have needs and feelings. They learn that others see the world differently from them, and they begin to develop self-esteem based on what others say to them. Many picture books address these important self-concepts.

Children in the preschool years are busy learning about themselves—who they are and what they can do—and about others. Their self-concept develops as a direct result of their interaction with the environment, including the reactions of others to their own actions. When children see that their actions meet with approval, they are encouraged to explore, to express their ideas, and to discover their world. Books mirror primary experiences that shape children's actions, reactions, and feelings; books can bring subtle issues to a conscious level, making it possible to discuss them. Books can play an important role for the child who is experiencing the conflicts of growing up; they enrich understanding when they can be related to real life. Issues such as sex-role stereotyping, childhood fears, and moral reasoning are some of the ideas that appear in picture storybooks for children. Kevin Henkes explores the idea of feeling special and liking your name in *Chrysanthemum* (P). Chrysanthemum knows that her parents think she is perfect and that the name they gave her is perfect. When she starts to school, however, things begin to change. Henkes explores the panic of being worried in *Wemberly Worried* (N–P). Wemberly worries about everything, especially going to school. With words and pictures Henkes explores emotional issues that are familiar to many children. Picture books that support children's developing understandings and inner feelings about themselves are listed in the Booklist at the end of the chapter.

THE CHILD'S FAMILY WORLD

Home is a child's first school; it has a lasting influence on a child's intellectual, personal, and social development. Children are affected by all of the events and relationships that involve the family, including new babies, adoption, mothers who stay at home, mothers who work outside the home, preschool, day care, divorce, grandparents, stepparents,

Figure 4 ✿ 2

Connections with Literature

Readers make at least three different kinds of connections to texts: text to self, text to life (world), and text to other texts.

Text to Self

Reading these books, children have this response: That story reminds me of my family. I feel the same way the character feels. I've been in the same situation as the character.

Haas, Jesse, *Hurry!* (N–P)
Kuskin, Karla, *I Am Me* (N–P)
Keller, Holly, *That's Mine, Horace* (N–P)
Johnson, Angela, *Down the Winding Road* (N–P)

Text to Life/World

Reading these books, children have this response: The same thing happened at my school. I see people like that on the street in my town. There was a story like that on TV.

Wong, Janet S., *Buzz* (N–P)
Uff, Caroline, *Lulu's Busy Day* (N–P)
Stuve-Bodeen, Stephanie, *Mama Elizabeti* (N–P)

Text to Text

Reading these books, children have this response: That reminds me of another book I read. I read about a girl just like that in another book. The same thing happened in one of Beverly Cleary's books. That story is just like the poem we read.

Henkes, Kevin, *Chrysanthemum* (P)
_____, *Lilly's Purple Plastic Purse* (P)

---

single parents, homelessness, death of a family member, and countless others. Books address these and many other issues that affect families. The best ones explore sensitive issues in family life and present a realistic picture of a variety of loving relationships. Three books show children developing a strong sense of self and working on their self-control in the midst of a loving family. In *Harriet, You'll Drive Me Wild* (P) by Mem Fox, Harriet spills things, breaks things, and is generally a messy child, but her mother refuses to yell at her. In *Olivia* (P) by Ian Falconer, the overly active young pig tests everyone's patience and is very good at wearing people out. She makes exasperating demands even at the end of the day, when she wants five books read to her at bedtime. Her mother says, "You know, you really wear me out. But I love you anyway." Olivia gives her a kiss and says, "I love you anyway too." Janet Wong shows in poetry how a young child can delay the start of the day in *Buzz* (N–P). The narrator is much more interested in watching a bumblebee buzzing around the garden than in keeping a morning schedule.

Stephanie Stuve-Bodeen received the Ezra Jack Keats Award for *Elizabeti's Doll* (N–P), illustrated by Christy Hale. When her mother cares for Obedi, her new baby brother, Elizabeti finds a huggable rock she names Eva. She pretends Eva is her doll and imitates her mother's loving care. In a sequel, *Mama Elizabeti* (N–P), her mother has another new baby and Elizabeti must now assume care for Obedi; he is not as easy to care for as the rock. Other books that explore family life are listed in the Booklist at the end of the chapter. Teaching Idea 4.1 presents ideas for exploring the family lore of children in your classroom.

When Elizabeti did her chores, she also tied Eva onto her back with a kanga. Mama had to help a little.

A child in Tanzania learns about caring for younger siblings, even though her "baby" is a cold, hard rock in Stephanie Stuve-Bodeen's **Elizabeti's Doll.**

THE CHILD'S SOCIAL WORLD

Social development intersects all other areas of growth; it reflects and influences a child's total development. Friendships with others develop slowly; they may not be truly possible until children develop an identifiable self-concept. By the time children enter school, they are beginning to know how to interact with others; they can identify with a peer group and slowly begin to sort out special friends within a group.

Friendship is a mixture of good and bad times; all friendships encounter some stumbling blocks. Oftentimes children experience internal and external conflicts as they try simultaneously to declare their independence as a person and to develop relationships with others. Lilly in Kevin Henkes's *Lilly's Purple Plastic Purse* (P) really likes her teacher, Mr. Slinger. One day, she takes her purple plastic purse, shiny coins, and sunglasses to school, because she wants to show them off. Mr. Slinger, however, takes them away from her because they make too much noise. Lilly's anger causes her to write a mean note to the teacher she no longer likes.

The one hundredth day of school is celebrated in many places, and books are often part of that celebration. In *100 Days of School* (P), Trudy Harris includes rhymes to show different ways to count to 100. "If 10 tired children take off their shoes what do you get? Lots of bare feet! And . . . (I suppose 100 toes)." Margery Cuyler describes Jessica's worries about finding 100 objects to take to school in *100th Day Worries* (P). Rosemary Wells shows many uses for the numbers up to 100 in *Emily's First 100 Days of School* (P). Other school stories are listed in the Booklist at the end of the chapter.

THE CHILD'S NATURAL WORLD

Children learn about nature as they explore their ever-widening worlds. Firsthand experiences are primary, of course, but books can deepen and extend children's awareness of the natural world. Books can draw attention to nature in sensitive and thoughtful ways; many do not so much tell a story as they do establish a mood or celebrate natural beauty through both words and pictures. Books explore seasonal change, special habitats and ecosystems, natural phenomena, and animals. They offer children experiences with the natural world that they wouldn't otherwise have and confirm the knowledge of nature that they have gained from their own life experiences. D. B. Johnson praises the beauty of the natural world in *Henry Hikes to Fitchburg* (P), which is based on a passage from Thoreau's *Walden*. In the

story, one friend chooses to earn money for a train ride to Fitchburg, but Henry chooses to walk the 30 miles in order to enjoy the beautiful landscape. The scenes suggest that the walker is the wiser person. Jeannie Baker creates elaborate collages to help us see parts of *The Hidden Forest* (P–I) that we might otherwise overlook. Illustrations often offer children visions of natural life that they wouldn't otherwise have, helping them to understand and appreciate the complex beauty of the natural world. Other books about the natural world are suggested in the Booklist at the end of the chapter.

Teaching Idea 4 ☆ 1

Create a Book of Family Lore or an Autobiography

Families in every culture have unique traditions and celebrate holidays in their own special ways. They have special foods to prepare, clothes to wear, services to attend, and stories to tell. Use your traditions to create a picture book about your family. Sections might include photographs of parents, grandparents, weddings, religious celebrations, favorite things to do, friends, favorite foods, favorite books, and stories we tell.

Family lore values the small details of life; realize that these details are important enough to write about. Read some of the following books to see what others wrote about:

Ada, Alma Flor, *Under the Royal Palms: A Childhood in Cuba*

Brinkloe, Julie, *Fireflies*

Carrick, Carol, *Left Behind*

Cooney, Barbara, *Miss Rumphius*

dePaola, Tomie, *Here We All Are*

_____, *26 Fairmount Avenue*

Friedman, Ina, *How My Parents Learned to Eat*

Hurwitz, Johanna, *A Dream Come True*

Keats, Ezra Jack, *Peter's Chair*

McPhail, David, *Lost!*

Rabinovici, Schoschana, *Thanks to My Mother*, translated by James Skofield

Rockwell, Anne, *My Doctor*

Rylant, Cynthia, *When I Was Young in the Mountains*

Zolotow, Charlotte, *Someone New*

THE CHILD'S AESTHETIC WORLD

As children's interests broaden, the aesthetic environment—art, music, dance, and literature—can add immeasurably to their overall sense of well-being. Many children first encounter the cultural arts through books; there they can discover the aesthetic world at an early age. Early and continued exposure to the arts lays a firm foundation on which children build an ever-increasing appreciation for their aesthetic world.

Picture books about the arts may be storybooks that explore a problem or theme related to the arts, such as a child's desire to practice an art, a child's effort to become good at an art, or a story in which the arts play an integral part in the main character's life. Nonfiction books about the arts often focus on explaining various aspects of particular art. Whether fiction or nonfiction, these picture books use both illustrations and text to create meaning. The illustrations may elaborate events and emotions, as in Emily Arnold McCully's *Mirette on the High Wire* (P–I), a story about a young girl who struggles to learn the art of tightrope walking and who seeks to restore her talented teacher's confidence in himself.

Petra Mathers appreciates a poet's attempts to create poems in *A Cake for Herbie* (N–P). Herbie sees a poster announcing a poetry contest and decides to enter. He tries very hard to create poems about foods from A to Z. He is laughed off the stage but he finds a more appreciative audience elsewhere.

Music, of course, is an integral part of an aesthetic life. Almost from the time they hear their first lullaby, young children can hum or follow along with favorite melodies. Every culture is replete with songs of its people. Many books—whether they are single-edition picture books or part of a collection—offer lavish visual interpretations of those rhymes or songs. Ashley Bryan is noted for his illustrations of African-American spirituals, which he highlights in *All Night, All Day: A Child's First Book of African-American Spirituals* (P–I). Bryan's beautiful interpretive illustrations accompany the words and arrangements for 20 spirituals, celebrating this musical form and the culture that created it.

Other books about music explore musical instruments, musical groups, and musicians' lives. Alan Blackwood's book *Orchestra: An Introduction to the World of Classical Music* (I) gives a history of the orchestra. It introduces classical composers, conductors, and instruments and presents a day in the life of an orchestra. Angela Shelf Medearis retells folklore in *Singing Man: Adapted from a West African Folktale* (I). After his manhood ceremony, Banzar decides to follow his love of music. The elders of the village expel him but he perseveres to fulfill his dreams.

Expressive movement is natural to children; they sway, tap their feet, and bounce, impelled by the pure joy of being and moving. Music, stories, and poems invite expressive participation on the part of children. Stories about dance and dancers intrigue young readers who wonder what it would be like. Andrea Davis Pinkney presents a dancer's life in *Alvin Ailey* (I), illustrated by Brian Pinkney. The Pinkneys also collaborated on an excellent biography on musician *Duke Ellington*. And Carol Greene presents a woman who inspired Ailey in *Katherine Dunham: Black Dancer* (I).

Children are sensitive to the visual art that surrounds them; much of that art is contained in picture books. When children have the opportunity to read and savor many picture books, they begin to recognize individual artists' styles and develop a sense of taste. Children who become interested in the lives of artists find some fine biographies of both contemporary children's book artists and important artists of the past. Lucy Micklethwait developed a series in which she presents fine art according to a unifying theme, as in *I Spy a Lion: Animals in Art* or *I Spy Freight Trains* (P–I). Students gain familiarity with art as they search for the animals or trains.

THE CHILD'S IMAGINARY WORLD

Imagination plays an important part in a child's early years. Adults can sometimes catch a glimpse of that fantasy world by observing the child at play with an imaginary friend, a favorite toy that has been invested with life, or other children. During these play episodes children create their own imaginative narratives. Parents and teachers can contribute to an environment that is conducive to children's imaginative play by playing "let's pretend" games, discussing dreams, and making up stories. They can also read imaginative stories. Peter Sis created two imaginative stories about children with vivid imaginations. In *Dinosaur!* (N–P) a young boy contemplates a bathtub filling up with water. When he gets into the tub, a small dinosaur comes up from the bottom, but then, all sorts of dinosaurs join him. Of course, they splash a lot of water and leave a mess. *Madlenka* (P), a young girl, discovers that she has a loose tooth and must tell all her friends. Her trip around the block is like a trip around the world as she announces her loose tooth to the French baker, the Indian news vendor, the Italian ice cream man, the German lady who sits by her window, the Latin American greengrocer, and the Asian shopkeeper. The art creates another level of imagination for readers.

Adults who fear that too much fantasy will affect a child's sense of reality need not worry; a lively imagination is a

Teaching Idea 4·2

Picture Books for Teaching Literary Concepts

Using picture books to teach literary concepts is a successful approach for a number of reasons:

❋ The books are slender, well-crafted pieces of literature.

❋ The literary elements shine through clearly.

❋ Students can see and understand the concept.

❋ The literary concept is visualized in a sparse text.

❋ The concept appears in an uncluttered environment.

Choose from the following books to prepare mini-lessons that focus on aspects of literature. The books can serve as models for demonstrating a literary concept.

Setting

The time and place (setting) are clearly identified and interact with the plot in good literature. The following books illustrate an effective use of setting.

Baylor, Byrd, *I'm in Charge of Celebrations*

Cameron, Ann, *The Most Beautiful Place in the World*

Carrick, Donald, *Dark and Full of Secrets*

Cooney, Barbara, *Miss Rumphius*

Martin, Bill, Jr., and John Archambault, *The Ghost Eye Tree*

Yolen, Jane, *Owl Moon*

Character and Setting

Character (who the story is about) is often shaped by the setting (where it takes place); further, character is revealed by the setting. All literary elements are intertwined; one affects another and they combine to affect still others. In the following books, characters are representative of the setting. They are, in fact, a part of their environment.

Hendershot, Judith, *In Coal Country*, illustrated by Thomas B. Allen

Radin, Ruth Yaffee, *High in the Mountains*, illustrated by Ed Young

Ringgold, Faith, *Tar Beach*

Rylant, Cynthia, *When I Was Young in the Mountains*, illustrated by Diane Goode

Schroeder, Alan, *Ragtime Tumpie*, illustrated by Bernie Fuchs

Surprise Endings

Surprise endings—a plot device that suddenly upends everything that was anticipated—leave the reader gasping with delight and shock. Picture book authors and illustrators engage in clever suprises in the following books.

Charles, Donald, *Paddy Pig's Poems*

Greene, Carol, *The Golden Locket*, illustrated by Marcia Sewall

Heide, Florence Parry, *The Shrinking of Treehorn*

---

central part of the developmental process. Imaginative stories provide a source of pleasure as well as a focal point for children's developing imagination and sense of story. In fact, children who have been deprived of traditional tales and other imaginative stories will create their own (Chukovsky, 1963). Some of the most distinguished literature for children builds upon the imaginative life of the central characters. In these stories stuffed animals come to life, fancy runs free, creatures hide under beds, and imaginary friends are real. Books that explore imaginative worlds are listed in the Booklist at the end of the chapter.

Using Picture Books in the Classroom

Picture books of all kinds are staples in primary, intermediate, and advanced-grade classrooms. Teachers and librarians have now discovered that picture books have an important place on classroom and library shelves. Picture books offer a unique opportunity for children to experience outstanding visual art, well-crafted language, and intriguing content. Picture books can support every area of the curriculum. Teaching Idea 4.2 demonstrates how to use picture books to teach literary concepts.

Excellent fiction, nonfiction, and poetry in picture book format is essential to any reading-writing program. Students naturally use the books they read as models for their own thinking and writing; picture books are resources for students' language production. They serve as fine examples of the author's craft. Excellent nonfiction gives children models for their own expository writing just as excellent stories and poems provide models for other modes. Literary devices such as imagery, foreshadowing, parody, metaphor, simile, and analogy are all found in picture storybooks and poetry. Talking about these devices can become a natural part of discussing favorite books when children are writers as well as readers; they constantly notice the choices that authors and illustrators make. Hall (1990) provides a source list of picture book titles that are good examples of a number of literary devices.

Kuskin, Karla, *Just Like Everyone Else*

Martin, C.L.G., *The Dragon Nanny*, illustrated by Robert Rayevsky

Steptoe, John, *Mufaro's Beautiful Daughters*

Udry, Janice May, *Let's Be Enemies*

Viorst, Judith, *Alexander and the Terrible, Horrible, No Good, Very Bad Day*

_____, *The Tenth Good Thing About Barney*

Zolotow, Charlotte, *The Quarreling Book*

Point of View

The point of view (who narrates) affects the telling of a story; it all depends on whose vantage point is used. These books illustrate how differently characters see things when events are told from their unique point of view.

dePaola, Tomie, *Helga's Dowry*

_____, *The Quicksand Book*

Friedman, Ina, *How My Parents Learned to Eat*

Lionni, Leo, *Fish Is Fish*

Scieszka, Jon, *The True Story of the Three Little Pigs*

Van Allsburg, Chris, *Two Bad Ants*

Viorst, Judith, *I'll Fix Anthony*

_____, *Rosie and Michael*

Plot Structure

Authors and illustrators manipulate plot structures to add variety, intrigue, and interest to their work. For example, in *Black and White*, David Macaulay continues four parallel

stories, which subtly become interrelated. In *Thirteen*, Remy Charlip presents 13 different illustrations on each double-page spread—numbered in reverse from 13 to 1—which are part of 13 wordless stories. The following books contain plot devices such as foreshadowing, parallel stories, and flashbacks.

Charlip, Remy, *Thirteen*

Macaulay, David, *Black and White*

McCloskey, Robert, *Blueberries for Sal*

Ness, Evaline, *Sam, Bangs, and Moonshine*

Van Allsburg, Chris, *The Garden of Abdul Gasazi*

Yorinks, Arthur, *Louis the Fish*, illustrated by Richard Egielski

Theme

The theme (an underlying message) is realized in many ways; the same or similar theme appears in very different stories. Read the following stories to see how the theme of "memories" can be visualized and dramatized.

Ackerman, Karen, *Song and Dance Man*, illustrated by Stephen Gammell

Fox, Mem, *Wilfrid Gordon McDonald Partridge*, illustrated by Julie Vivas

Martin, Bill, Jr., and John Archambault, *Knots on a Counting Rope*, illustrated by Ted Rand

Mathis, Sharon Bell, *The Hundred Penny Box*, illustrated by Leo and Diane Dillon

---

Picture books that support learning in social studies, science, art, music, and mathematics abound; many are discussed in Chapter 10. These books not only provide fine models of writing in the various fields but also explain concepts more clearly than traditional textbooks and encyclopedias. They provide numerous pictures, make comparisons easily available, and encourage critical thinking.

Children respond enthusiastically in classrooms that are rich with books and that offer the opportunity to read and respond to the books. In a year-long study of elementary school children responding to picture books in literature-rich classrooms, Kiefer (1986) discovered that a supportive, enriched classroom environment was an important factor in children's responses. Hickman (1995) found that teachers can create lively classrooms of book-loving children almost anywhere, but it takes planning and work. Teachers read aloud often, talk with children about the books, and make frequent comparisons to other books and to real life. They talk about authors and illustrators, refer to them by name, discuss information on the end flaps, and often study the works of single authors and illustrators. Teachers discuss all

aspects of books—dedication page, copyright page, title page—and use stylistic terminology to discuss the language and visual art.

Kiefer (1986), Hickman (1995), and Cianciolo (1997) note that, most important, good teachers provide the time and the opportunity for children to explore their own responses to the books they read—how they feel, what they are thinking about. This personal connection to a book seems to be a necessary first step toward critical aesthetic response (Cianciolo and Quirk, 1993). After teachers encourage children to clarify their understandings, reflect on what they like and dislike, and talk about feelings and personal connections, then children are ready to go "back to the book" to discover artistry in the language and the illustrations. Hickman (1995) says that book-loving classrooms are carefully constructed creations in which children respond to books because teachers invite response, because the books and materials to work with are there, because appropriate times and spaces are provided, and because the activities associated with being a reader are modeled, supported, and encouraged by a book-loving teacher.

Students vary in the way they select books, look at books, and respond to books. Some students, especially young ones, respond physically, moving their bodies in rhythm and saying the words they are reading or hearing (Kiefer, 1986). Children often choose to respond through drama, spontaneously reenacting a favorite story or planning an elaborate production. Some students write in journals, others adapt the language of books to their own writing. And many children choose to respond to picture books through art.

Summary

Picture books are artful books that hold a special place in the lives of children who read them. They are often children's first experience with fine art. They can enrich and extend children's worlds and provide experiences (through picture and print) that allow children to confirm their own worth, to learn about others, and to learn about the world. They provide stunning examples of art and language, and they become resources from which children draw as they develop their own abilities to shape and reshape their world.

Read Karla Kuskin's article "To Get a Little More of the Picture: Reviewing Picture Books" in the March/April 1998 issue of *The Horn Book Magazine*. Think about what she says about a picture book being a form of collaborative art, and about the quality that ought to be contained in any picture book for young readers. Then go back and look again at your five favorite picture books; ask yourself how Kuskin might review them. What have you learned about picture books that informs your own evaluation?

Booklist

Picture Books for Very Young Children

PARTICIPATION BOOKS

Ahlberg, Allan, *The Bravest Ever Bear*, illustrated by Paul Howard
Ahlberg, Janet, and Allan Ahlberg, *Each Peach Pear Plum*
_____, *Peek-A-Boo*
Ashbé, Jeanne, *What's Inside?*
Carle, Eric, *The Very Busy Spider*
Cousins, Lucy, *Katy Cat and Beaky Boo*
Hill, Eric, *Spot Goes Splash!*
_____, *Where's Spot?*
Isadora, Rachel, *Babies*
Kunhardt, Dorothy, *Pat the Bunny*
Miller, Margaret, *Whose Hat?*
Pomerantz, Charlotte, *Flap Your Wings and Try*, illustrated by Nancy Tafuri

BOARD BOOKS AND CAPTION BOOKS

Alexander, Martha, *Willy's Boot*
Cousins, Lucy, *Farm Animals*
Greenaway, Elizabeth, *Cat Nap*
Hawkins, Colin, and Jacqui Hawkins, *Hey Diddle Diddle*
Hoban, Tana, *What Is It?*
Hudson, Cheryl Willis, *Good Night Baby*, illustrated by George Ford
Leslie, Amanda, *Play Kitten Play: Ten Animal Fingerwiggles*
MacDonald, Amy, *Let's Pretend*

Maris, Ron, *Ducks Quack*
Oxenbury, Helen, *I Can*
_____, *I Hear*
_____, *I See*
_____, *I Touch*
Slier, Deborah, *Baby's Places*
Waddell, Martin, *Owl Babies*, illustrated by Patrick Benson
Wells, Rosemary, *Max's Bath*
_____, *Max's Birthday*
_____, *Max's Breakfast*
_____, *Max's First Word*
_____, *Max's New Suit*
_____, *Max's Ride*

SIMPLE STORYBOOKS AND CONCEPT BOOKS

Arnold, Katya, *Me Too!: Two Small Stories About Small Animals*
Baer, Gene, *Thump, Thump, Rat-a-Tat-Tat*, illustrated by Lois Ehlert
Barton, Byron, *Bones, Bones, Dinosaur Bones*
_____, *I Want to Be an Astronaut*
Brown, Margaret Wise, *Goodnight Moon*, illustrated by Clement Hurd
_____, *Red Light, Green Light*, illustrated by Leonard Weisgard
Bynum, Janie, *Otis*
Crews, Donald, *School Bus*
_____, *Truck*
Ehlert, Lois, *Color Farm*

Ehlert, Lois, *Color Zoo*

_____, *Red Leaf, Yellow Leaf*

Gibbons, Gail, *Trucks*

Hest, Amy, *In the Rain with Baby Duck*, illustrated by Jill Barton

Hoban, Tana, *Exactly the Opposite*

_____, *Of Colors and Things*

Jonas, Ann, *Color Dance*

Keller, Holly, *That's Mine, Horace*

McMillan, Bruce, *Super Super Superwords*

Meddaugh, Susan, *Hog-Eye*

Noll, Sally, *Watch Where You Go*

Oxenbury, Helen, *Good Night, Good Morning*

_____, *The Important Visitor*

_____, *Mother's Helper*

Rathmann, Peggy, *Goodnight, Gorilla*

Rockwell, Harlow, *My Nursery School*

Serfozo, Mary, *Who Said Red?* illustrated by Keiko Narahashi

Tafuri, Nancy, *Spots, Feathers, and Curly Tails*

Uff, Caroline, *Lulu's Busy Day*

Wells, Rosemary, *Edward in Deep Water*

_____, *Edward Unready for School*

_____, *Edward's Overwhelming Overnight*

Picture Books for Nursery- and Primary-Age Children

ABC, COUNTING, AND CONCEPT BOOKS

Anno, Mitsumasa, *Anno's Alphabet*

Aylesworth, Jim, *The Folks in the Valley: A Pennsylvania Dutch ABC*, illustrated by Stefano Vitale

_____, *Old Black Fly*, illustrated by Stephen Gammell

Bowen, Betsy, *Antler, Bear, Canoe: A Northwoods Alphabet Year*

De Vicq de Cumptich, Roberto, *Bembo's Zoo: An Animal ABC Book*

Ehlert, Lois, *Eating the Alphabet*

Fisher, Leonard Everett, *The ABC Exhibit*

Giganti, Paul, Jr., *How Many Snails? A Counting Book*, illustrated by Donald Crews

Girnis, Meg, *ABC for You and Me*, photos by Shirley Leamon Green

Grossman, Virginia, *Ten Little Rabbits*, illustrated by Sylvia Long

Hayes, Sarah, *Nine Ducks Nine*

Hughes, Shirley, *Lucy & Tom's 1 2 3*

Isadora, Rachel, *Listen to the City*

_____, *1 2 3 Pop!*

Johnson, Stephen T., *Alphabet City*

Katz, Michael Jay, *Ten Potatoes in a Pot & Other Counting Rhymes*, illustrated by June Otani

Kellogg, Steven, *Aster Aardvark's Alphabet Adventures*

Kitamura, Satoshi, *From Acorn to Zoo: And Everything in Between in Alphabetical Order*

Lester, Mike, *A Is for Salad*

Lobel, Anita, *Alison's Zinnia*

_____, *One Lighthouse, One Moon*

Lobel, Arnold, *On Market Street*

MacCarthy, Patricia, *Ocean Parade: A Counting Book*

MacDonald, Suse, *Alphabatics*

_____, *Puzzlers*, illustrated by Bill Oakes

Martin, Bill, Jr., and John Archambault, *Chicka Chicka Boom Boom*, illustrated by Lois Ehlert

McKenzie, Ellen Kindt, *The Perfectly Orderly House*, illustrated by Megan Lloyd

McMillan, Bruce, *Beach Ball—Left, Right*

Merriam, Eve, *Halloween A B C*, illustrated by Lane Smith

Owens, Mary Beth, *A Caribou Alphabet*

Paul, Ann Whitford, *Eight Hands Round: A Patchwork Alphabet*, illustrated by Jeannette Winter

Rankin, Laura, *The Handmade Alphabet*

Rockwell, Anne, *Bear Child's Book of Hours*

Ryden, Hope, *Wild Animals of Africa A B C*

Scott, Ann Herbert, *One Good Horse: A Cowpuncher's Counting Book*, illustrated by Lynn Sweat

Shannon, George, *Tomorrow's Alphabet*, illustrated by Donald Crews

Sis, Peter, *Waving: A Counting Book*

Sloat, Teri, *From Letter to Letter*

Tudor Tasha, *1 Is One*

Walsh, Ellen Stoll, *Mouse Count*

Wormell, Christopher, *An Alphabet of Animals*

Ziefert, Harriet, *Big to Little, Little to Big*, illustrated by Susan Baum

_____, *Clothes On, Clothes Off*, illustrated by Susan Baum

_____, *Count Up, Count Down*, illustrated by Susan Baum

_____, *Empty to Full, Full to Empty*, illustrated by Susan Baum

WORDLESS BOOKS

Aliki, *Tabby: A Story in Pictures*

Aruego, José, *Look What I Can Do*

de Paola, Tomie, *Pancakes for Breakfast*

Goodall, John, *Little Red Riding Hood*

Hoban, Tana, *Colors Everywhere*

Hutchins, Pat, *Changes, Changes*

Keats, Ezra Jack, *Pssst! Doggie*

Koren, Edward, *Behind the Wheel*

Mayer, Mercer, *Frog Goes to Dinner*

McCully, Emily Arnold, *Picnic*

Ormerod, Jan, *Moonlight*

_____, *Sunshine*

Sis, Peter, *Dinosaur!*

PATTERNED BOOKS

Carlstrom, Nancy White, *Jesse Bear, What Will You Wear?* illustrated by Bruce Degen

Cummings, Pat, *Angel Baby*

Ehlert, Lois, *Feathers for Lunch*

Fleming, Denise, *In the Tall, Tall Grass*

Fox, Mem, *Hattie and the Fox*, illustrated by Patricia Mullins

Gammell, Stephen, *Once upon MacDonald's Farm*

Guarino, Deborah, *Is Your Mama a Llama?* illustrated by Steven Kellogg

Hennessy, B. G. *Jake Baked the Cake*, illustrated by Mary Morgan

Hort, Lenny, *The Seals on the Bus*, illustrated by G. Brian Karas

Hutchins, Pat, *What Game Shall We Play?*

Katz, Michael Jay, *Ten Potatoes in a Pot: And Other Counting Rhymes*, illustrated by June Otani

Kovalski, Maryann, *The Wheels on the Bus*

MacDonald, Amy, *Rachel Fister's Blister*, illustrated by Marjorie Priceman

Martin, Bill, Jr., *Brown Bear, Brown Bear, What Do You See?* illustrated by Eric Carle

_____, *Polar Bear, Polar Bear, What Do You Hear?* illustrated by Eric Carle

Martin, Bill, Jr., and John Archambault, *Chicka Chicka Boom Boom*, illustrated by Lois Ehlert

Marzollo, Jean, *Pretend You're a Cat*, illustrated by Jerry Pinkney

Neitzel, Shirley, *The Jacket I Wear in the Snow*, illustrated by Nancy Winslow Parker

_____, *The Bag I'm Taking to Grandma's*, illustrated by Nancy Winslow Parker

Peters, Lisa Westberg, *Cold Little Duck, Duck, Duck*, illustrated by Sam Williams

Robart, Rose, *The Cake That Mack Ate*, illustrated by Maryann Kovalski

Rosen, Michael, *We're Going on a Bear Hunt*

Schaefer, Lola M., *This Is the Sunflower*

Shaw, Nancy, *Sheep in a Shop*, illustrated by Margot Apple

Stojic, Manya, *Rain*

Stow, Jenny, *The House That Jack Built*

Suteyev, Vladimir, *Chick and the Duckling*, translated by Mirra Ginsburg, illustrated by Jose Aruego and Ariane Dewey

Swope, Sam, *Gotta Go! Gotta Go!* illustrated by Sue Riddle

Waber, Bernard, *Do You See a Mouse?*

Walsh, Ellen Stoll, *Mouse Count*

_____, *Mouse Paint*

Walsh, Melanie, *Do Donkeys Dance?*

_____, *Do Monkeys Tweet?*

_____, *Do Pigs Have Stripes?*

Zelinsky, Paul, *The Wheels on the Bus*

BEGINNING-TO-READ BOOKS

Baer, Gene, *Thump, Thump, Rat-a-Tat-Tat*, illustrated by Lois Ehlert

Browne, Anthony, *I Like Books*

_____, *Things I Like*

Brown, Marc, *Play Rhymes*

Byars, Betsy, *The Golly Sisters Go West*

Caple, Kathy, *The Friendship Tree*

Carlstrom, Nancy White, *Better Not Get Wet, Jesse Bear*

Cushman, Doug, *Inspector Hopper*

Fleming, Denise, *In the Tall, Tall Grass*

Goennel, Heidi, *My Dog*

Lobel, Arnold, *Days with Frog and Toad*

_____, *Frog and Toad All Year*

_____, *Frog and Toad Are Friends*

_____, *Frog and Toad Together*

Mahy, Margaret, *The Horrendous Hullabaloo*, illustrated by Patricia MacCarthy

_____, *17 Kings and 42 Elephants*, illustrated by Patricia MacCarthy

Marshall, James, *The Cut-Ups Crack Up*

Martin, Bill, Jr., and John Archambault, *Here Are My Hands*, illustrated by Ted Rand

Marzollo, Jean, *Pretend You're a Cat*, illustrated by Jerry Pinkney

Minarik, Else, *Father Bear Comes Home*, illustrated by Maurice Sendak

_____, *A Kiss for Little Bear*, illustrated by Maurice Sendak

Noll, Sally, *Watch Where You Go*

Parish, Peggy, *Scruffy*, illustrated by Kelly Oechsli

_____, *Teach Us, Amelia Bedelia*, illustrated by Lynn Sweat

Porte, Barbara Ann, *Harry in Trouble*, illustrated by Yossi Abolafia

Ransom, Candace F., *Danger at Sand Cave*, illustrated by Den Schofield

Rosen, Michael, *We're Going on a Bear Hunt*, illustrated by Helen Oxenbury

Rylant, Cynthia, *Henry and Mudge and Annie's Perfect Pet: The Twentieth Book of Their Adventures*, illustrated by Suçie Stevenson

_____, *Henry and Mudge and the Bedtime Thumps*, illustrated by Suçie Stevenson

_____, *Henry and Mudge in Puddle Trouble*, illustrated by Suçie Stevenson

_____, *Henry and Mudge in the Sparkle Days*, illustrated by Suçie Stevenson

_____, *Henry and Mudge Take the Big Test*, illustrated by Suçie Stevenson

_____, *Henry and Mudge: The First Book*, illustrated by Suçie Stevenson

Shaw, Nancy, *Sheep in a Shop*, illustrated by Margot Apple

Thomas, Shelley Moore, *Good Night, Good Knight*, illustrated by Jennifer Plecas

Van Leeuwen, Jean, *Oliver, Amanda, and Grandmother Pig*, illustrated by Ann Schweninger

_____, *Oliver Pig at School*, illustrated by Ann Schweninger

Ziefert, Harriet, *The Gingerbread Boy*, illustrated by Emily Bolam

Picture Books for Intermediate and Advanced Readers

Adler, David, *A Picture Book of Sojourner Truth*

Adler, David, *Martin Luther King, Jr.: Free At Last*

Agee, Jon, *The Incredible Painting of Felix Clousseau*

Alexander, Sue, *Nadia the Willful*, illustrated by Lloyd Bloom

Anno, Mitsumasa, *Anno's Alphabet*

_____, *Anno's Britain*

_____, *Anno's Journey*

_____, *Anno's Math Games*

Base, Graeme, *Animalia*

Baylor, Byrd, *I'm in Charge of Celebrations*, illustrated by Peter Parnall

Bjork, Christina, *Linnea in Monet's Garden*

_____, *Linnea's Windowsill Garden*

Browne, Anthony, *Piggybook*

_____, *The Tunnel*

Bruchac, Joseph, *Crazy Horse's Vision*, illustrated by S. D. Nelson

Bunting, Eve, *Fly Away Home*, illustrated by Ronald Himler

_____, *Smoky Night*, illustrated by David Diaz

_____, *The Wall*, illustrated by Ronald Himler

Chorao, Kay, *Pig and Crow*

dePaola, Tomie, *Bonjour, Mr. Satie*

Dragonwagon, Crescent, *Home Place*, illustrated by Jerry Pinkney

Feelings, Tom, *Soul Looks Back in Wonder*

_____, *The Middle Passage*

Foreman, Michael, *War Games*

Garland, Michael, *Dinner at Magritte's*

Goble, Paul, *The Death of the Iron Horse*

Goffstein, M. B., *A Writer*

Heide, Florence Parry and Judith Heide Gilliland, *The Day of Ahmed's Secret*, illustrated by Ted Lewin

Hendershot, Judith, *Up the Tracks to Grandma's*, illustrated by Thomas B. Allen

Hooks, William, *The Ballad of Belle Dorcas*, illustrated by Brian Pinkney

Hooks, William, *Freedom's Fruit*, illustrated by James Ransome

Hopkinson, Deborah, *Sweet Clara and the Freedom Quilt*, illustrated by James Ransome

Houston, Gloria, *My Great Aunt Arizona*

Hunt, Jonathan, *Illuminations*

Innocenti, Robert, *Rose Blanche*

Johnston, Tony, *Yonder*

Lawrence, Jacob, *The Great Migration: An American Story*

Locker, Thomas, *The Boy Who Held Back the Sea*

_____, *Snow Toward Evening: A Year in River Valley: Nature Poems*

_____, *Where the River Begins*

Macaulay, David, *Black and White*

Maruki, Toshi, *Hiroshima No Pika*

McKissack, Patricia, and Frederick McKissack, *Christmas in the Big House, Christmas in the Quarters*

Medearis, Angela Shelf, *The Freedom Riddle*, illustrated by John Ward

Mendez, Phil, *The Black Snowman*, illustrated by Carole Byard

Mochizuki, Ken, *Baseball Saved Us*, illustrated by Dom Lee

Morimoto, Junko, *My Hiroshima*

Mullins, Patricia, *V for Vanishing: An Alphabet of Endangered Animals*

Polacco, Patricia, *Pink and Say*

Provensen, Alice, and Martin Provensen, *The Glorious Flight: Across the Channel with Louis Bleriot*

Rylant, Cynthia, *Appalachia: The Voices of Sleeping Birds*, illustrated by Barry Moser

Say, Allen, *Grandfather's Journey*

Shertle, Alice, *Down the Road*, illustrated by E. B. Lewis

Scieszka, Jon, *Math Curse*, illustrated by Lane Smith

_____, *The True Story of the Three Little Pigs*, illustrated by Lane Smith (P–I–A)

Sendak, Maurice, *Outside Over There*

Steig, William, *Caleb and Kate*

Thimmesh, Catherine, *Girls Think of Everything: Stories of Ingenious Inventions by Women*, illustrated by Melissa Sweet

Turner, Ann, *Dakota Dugout*

Van Allsburg, Chris, *Bad Day at River Bend*

_____, *The Polar Express* (P–I–A)

_____, *The Wretched Stone*

Willard, Nancy, *The Voyage of the Ludgate Hill: Travels with Robert Louis Stevenson*, illustrated by Alice and Martin Provensen

Yolen, Jane, *All Those Secrets of the World*, illustrated by Leslie Baker (P–I)

_____, *Encounter*

_____, *Owl Moon*, illustrated by John Schoenherr (P–I)

Picture Books About the Child's Inner World

Books in this section are appropriate for primary readers.

LOOSE TOOTH, TOOTH FAIRY

Birdseye, Tom, *Air Mail to the Moon*, illustrated by Stephen Gammell

Keller, Laurie, *Open Wide: Tooth School Inside*

McCloskey, Robert, *One Morning in Maine*

SELF-ESTEEM, PRIDE IN ONE'S NAME

Anholt, Catherine, and Laurence Anholt, *All About You*

Henkes, Kevin, *Chrysanthemum*

Martin, Bill, Jr., and John Archambault, *Knots on a Counting Rope*, illustrated by Ted Rand

RESOURCEFULNESS

Battle-Lavert, Gwendolyn, *The Shaking Bag*, illustrated by Aminah Brenda Lynn Robinson

Holabird, Katharine, *Angelina and Alice*, illustrated by Helen Craig

_____, *Angelina's Birthday Surprise*, illustrated by Helen Craig

Mathers, Petra, *A Cake for Herbie*

Mccully, Emily Arnold, *Monk Camps Out*

McKissack, Patricia, *Flossie and the Fox*, illustrated by Rachel Isadora

McPhail, David, *Emma's Pet*

_____, *Emma's Vacation*

_____, *Fix-it*

_____, *Pig Pig Gets a Job*

Nimmo, Jenny, *Esmeralda and the Children Next Door*, illustrated by Paul Howard

Schwartz, Amy, *Annabelle Swift, Kindergartner*

Segal, Lore, *Tell Me a Mitzi*, illustrated by Harriet Pincus

_____, *Tell Me a Trudy*, illustrated by Rosemary Wells

Seuss, Dr., *Oh, the Places You'll Go!*

Steig, William, *Brave Irene*

Viorst, Judith, *Alexander, Who's Not (Do You Hear Me? I Mean It!) Going to Move*, illustrated by Robin Preiss Glasser

_____, *Earrings!* illustrated by Nola Langner Malone

Wells, Rosemary, *Shy Charles*

FEARS

Bunting, Eve, *Ghost's Hour, Spook's Hour*, illustrated by Donald Carrick

Carrick, Carol, *Left Behind*, illustrated by Donald Carrick

Conrad, Pam, *The Tub People*, illustrated by Richard Egielski

Grifalconi, Ann, *Darkness and the Butterfly*

Henkes, Kevin, *Sheila Rae, the Brave*

McPhail, David, *Lost!*

Stolz, Mary Slattery, *Storm in the Night*, illustrated by Pat Cummings

Wells, Rosemary, *Max's Dragon Shirt*

HUMOR

Cronin, Doreen, *Click, Clack, Moo: Cows That Type*, illustrated by Betsy Lewin

Dumbleton, Mike, *Dial-a-Croc*, illustrated by Ann James

Fearnley, Jan, *Mr. Wolf's Pancakes*

Hale, Lucretia, *The Lady Who Put Salt in Her Coffee*, adapted and illustrated by Amy Schwartz

Kellogg, Steven, *Prehistoric Pinkerton*

Khalsa, Dayal Kaur, *How Pizza Came to Queens*

Kitamura, Satoshi, *Me and My Cat?*

Macaulay, David, *Why the Chicken Crossed the Road*

Mahy, Margaret, *The Great White Man-Eating Shark: A Cautionary Tale*, illustrated by Jonathan Allen

Meddaugh, Susan, *Hog-Eye*

Noble, Trina Hakes, *The Day Jimmy's Boa Ate the Wash*, illustrated by Steven Kellogg

BEDTIME BOOKS

Brown, Margaret Wise, *Goodnight Moon*, illustrated by Clement Hurd

Fox, Mem, *Time for Bed*, illustrated by Jane Dyer

Ginsburg, Mirra, *Asleep, Asleep*, illustrated by Nancy Tafuri

Hurd, Thacher, *The Quiet Evening*

Koide, Tan, *May We Sleep Here Tonight?* illustrated by Yasuko Koide

FUN, SPECIAL EVENTS

Ehlert, Lois, *Circus*

Goennel, Heidi, *The Circus*

Picture Books About the Child's Family World

Books in this section are appropriate for primary readers.

GRANDPARENTS

Ackerman, Karen, *Song and Dance Man*, illustrated by Stephen Gammell

Anderson, Lena, *Stina*

Dorros, Arthur, *Abuela*, illustrated by Elisa Kleven

_____, *Isla*, illustrated by Eliza Kleven

Farber, Norma, *How Does It Feel to Be Old?* illustrated by Trina Schart Hyman

Flournoy, Valerie, *Patchwork Quilt*, illustrated by Jerry Pinkney

_____, *Tanya's Reunion*, illustrated by Jerry Pinkney

Fox, Mem, *Wilfrid Gordon McDonald Partridge*, illustrated by Julie Vivas

Griffith, Helen V., *Grandaddy's Place*, illustrated by James Stevenson

Howard, Elizabeth Fitzgerald, *Papa Tells Chita a Story*, illustrated by Floyd Cooper

Johnson, Angela, *When I Am Old with You*, illustrated by David Soman

Lyon, George Ella, *One Lucky Girl*, illustrated by Irene Trivas

McMullan, Kate, *Papa's Song*, illustrated by Jim McMullan

Skolsky, Mindy Warshaw, *Hannah and the Whistling Teakettle*, illustrated by Diane Palmisciano

Stevenson, James, *We Hate Rain!*

Williams, Barbara, *Kevin's Grandma*, illustrated by Kay Chorao

SIBLINGS

Browne, Anthony, *The Tunnel* (P–I)

Graham, Bob, *Has Anyone Here Seen William?*

Henkes, Kevin, *Julius, the Baby of the World*

Hutchins, Pat, *Very Worst Monster*

_____, *Where's the Baby?*

Sheffield, Margaret, *Where Do Babies Come From?* illustrated by Sheila Bewley

Wells, Rosemary, *Max's Chocolate Chicken*

Williams, Vera B., *"More More More," Said the Baby*

_____, *Stringbean's Trip to the Shining Sea*, illustrated by Vera B. Williams and Jennifer Williams

Yorinks, Arthur, *Oh, Brother*, illustrated by Richard Egielski

PARENTS AND FAMILY AS A UNIT

Bunting, Eve, *The Mother's Day Mice*, illustrated by Jan Brett

Browne, Anthony, *Piggybook*

Carrick, Carol, *Mothers Are Like That*, illustrated by Paul Carrick

Fox, Mem, *Harriet, You'll Drive Me Wild!* illustrated by Marla Frazee

Keller, Holly, *Horace*

Loh, Morag, *Tucking Mommy In*, illustrated by Donna Rawlins

McPhail, David, E*mma's Vacation*

Pinkney, Brian, *Cosmo and the Robot*

Rayner, Mary, *Mrs. Pig Gets Cross: And Other Stories*

Scott, Ann Herbert, *On Mother's Lap*, illustrated by Glo Coalson

Steig, William, *Spinky Sulks*

Stuve-Bodeen, Stephanie, *Mama Elizabeti*, illustrated by Christy Hale

Weiss, Nicki, *On a Hot, Hot Day*

Wynott, Jillian, *The Mother's Day Sandwich*, illustrated by Maxie Chambliss

Picture Books About Ancestors and Intergenerational Bonds

Books in this section are appropriate for primary–intermediate readers.

Cooney, Barbara, *Hattie and the Wild Waves*

_____, *Island Boy*

_____, *Miss Rumphius*

Johnston, Tony, *Yonder*, illustrated by Lloyd Bloom

Houston, Gloria, *The Year of the Perfect Christmas Tree*, illustrated by Barbara Cooney

Palacco, Patricia, *The Keeping Quilt*

Pomerantz, Charlotte, *The Chalk Doll*, illustrated by Frané Lessac

Say, Allen, *Tree of Cranes*

Picture Books About the Child's Social World

Books in this section are appropriate for primary–intermediate readers.

Belpre, Pura, *Santiago*, illustrated by Symeon Shimin

Cohen, Miriam, *It's George!* illustrated by Lillian Hoban

_____, *See You in Second Grade!* illustrated by Lillian Hoban

_____, *Will I Have a Friend?* illustrated by Lillian Hoban

Fleischman, Sid, *Scarebird*, illustrated by Peter Sis

Henkes, Kevin, *Lily's Purple Plastic Purse*

Howard, Elizabeth Fitzgerald, *Virgie Goes to School with Us Boys*, illustrated by E. B. Lewis

Hughes, Shirley, *The Snow Lady*

Kellogg, Steven, *Best Friends*

Mathers, Petra, *Sophie and Lou*

Lacome, Julie, *Ruthie's Big Old Coat*

Rathmann, Peggy, *Officer Buckle and Gloria*

Tsutsui, Yoriko, *Anna's Secret Friend*, illustrated by Akiko Hayashi

Vincent, Gabrielle, *Merry Christmas, Ernest and Celestine*

Wells, Rosemary, *Emily's First 100 Days of School*

Winthrop, Elizabeth, *The Best Friends Club: A Lizzie and Harold Story*, illustrated by Martha Weston

The Child's Natural World

Books in this section are appropriate for primary–intermediate–advanced readers.

Baker, Jeannie, *The Hidden Forest*

Baker, Leslie, *The Antique Store Cat*

_____, *The Third Story Cat*

Baylor, Byrd, *The Desert Is Theirs*, illustrated by Peter Parnall

Bishop, Nic, *Digging for Bird-Dinosaurs: An Expedition to Madagascar*

Bjork, Christina, *Linnea in Monet's Garden*, translated by Joan Sandin, illustrated by Lena Anderson

_____, *Linnea's Windowsill Garden*, translated by Joan Sandin, illustrated by Lena Anderson

Budiansky, Satephen, *The World According to Horses: How They Run, See, and Think*

Cazet, Denys, *A Fish in His Pocket*

Floca, Brian, *Dinosaurs at the Ends of the Earth: The Story of the Central Asiatic Expeditions*

Florian, Douglas, *Mammalabilia*

Ford, Miela, *Sunflower*

French, Vivian, *Growing Frogs*, illustrated by Alison Bartlett

George, Jean Craighead, *How to Talk to Your Cat*, illustrated by Paul Meisel

_____, *How to Talk to Your Dog*, illustrated by Sue Treasdell

Gibbons, Gail, *Farming*

_____, *Zoo*

Haas, Jesse, *Hurry!* illustrated by Joseph A. Smith

Hadithi, Mwenye, *Crafty Chameleon*, illustrated by Adrienne Kennaway

Hoban, Tana, *Dots, Spots, Speckles, and Stripes*

Hurd, Edith Thacher, *Starfish*, illustrated by Robin Brickman

Johnson, D. B., *Henry Hikes to Fitchburg*

Keats, Ezra Jack, *The Snowy Day*

Kurtz, Jane, *River Friendly, River Wild*, illustrated by Neil Brennan

Lewison, Wendy Cheyette, *Going to Sleep on the Farm*, illustrated by Juan Wijngaard

Locker, Thomas, *Family Farm*

Lyon, George Ella, *Come a Tide*, illustrated by Stephen Gammell

McPhail, David, *Farm Boy's Year*

Rogers, Jean, *Runaway Mittens*, illustrated by Rie Munoz

Simon, Seymour, *Destination Mars*

Stevens, Janet, *Tops and Bottoms*

Yolen, Jane, *Owl Moon*, illustrated by John Schoenherr

The Child's Aesthetic World

Books in this section are appropriate for intermediate–advanced readers.

Agee, Jon, *The Incredible Painting of Felix Clousseau*

Beneduce, Ann Keay, *A Weekend with Winslow Homer*

Blizzard, Gladys S., *Come Look with Me: Exploring Landscape Art with Children*

Demi, reteller, *The Emperor's New Clothes: A Tale Set in China*

dePaola, Tomie, *The Art Lesson*

Dunrea, Olivier, *The Painter Who Loved Chickens*

Greenberg, Jan, and Sandra Jordan, *The Painter's Eye: Learning to Look at Contemporary American Art*

Greenfield, Eloise, *Under the Sunday Tree*, illustrated by Amos Ferguson

Heslewood, Juliet, *Introducing Picasso*

Levine, Arthur, *The Boy Who Drew Cats: A Japanese Folktale*, illustrated by Frederic Clement

Lyttle, Richard B., *Pablo Picasso: The Man and the Image*

Micklethwait, Lucy, *A Child's Book of Art*

Newlands, Anne, *Meet Edgar Degas*

Pinkney, Andrea Davis, *Alvin Ailey*, illustrated by Brian Pinkney

Roaf, Peggy, *Looking at Painters: Dancers*

Sturgis, Alexander, *Introducing Rembrandt*

Sufrin, Mark, *George Catlin: Painter of the Indian West*

Turner, Robyn Montana, *Frida Kahlo*

_____, *Georgia O'Keefe*

Zhensun, Zheng, and Alice Low, *A Young Painter: The Life and Paintings of Wang Yani—China's Extraordinary Young Artist*, photos by Zheng Zhensun

The Child's Imaginative World

Books in this section are appropriate for primary–intermediate readers.

dePaola, Tomie, *Bonjour, Mr. Satie*

_____, *Jamie O'Rourke and the Pooka*

Dorros, Arthur, *Abuela*, illustrated by Elisa Kleven

_____, *Tonight Is Carnaval*

Fox, Mem, *Possum Magic*, illustrated by Julie Vivas

Gauch, Patricia Lee, *Tanya and Emily in a Dance for Two*, illustrated by Satomi Ichikawa

Gordon, Gaelyn, *Duckat*, illustrated by Chris Gaskin

Gordon, Jeffie Ross, *Six Sleepy Sheep*, illustrated by John O'Brien

Hines, Anna Grossnickle, *It's Just Me, Emily*

Hoffman, Mary, *Amazing Grace*, illustrated by Caroline Binch

Howard, Elizabeth, *Aunt Flossie's Hats (and Crab Cakes Later)*, illustrated by James Ransome

Jeffers, Susan, *Brother Eagle, Sister Sky: A Message from Chief Seattle*

Johnson, Crockett, *The Carrot Seed*

_____, *Harold and the Purple Crayon*

Joosse, Barbara, and Barbara Lavallee, *Mama, Do You Love Me?*

Joyce, William, *Bently and Egg*

_____, *Dinosaur Bob & His Adventures with the Family Lazardo*

_____, *George Shrinks*

Karas, G. Brian, *Bebe's Bad Dream*

Kellogg, Steven, *Jack and the Beanstalk*

Krudop, Walter Lyon, *The Man Who Caught Fish*

Lobel, Anita, *The Dwarf Giant*

Martin, Rafe, *Will's Mammoth*, illustrated by Stephen Gammell

McGrory, Anik, *Mouton's Impossible Dream*

Pearce, Philippa, *Emily's Own Elephant*, illustrated by John Lawrence

Ringgold, Faith, *Tar Beach*

Speed, Toby, *Brave Potatoes*, illustrated by Barry Root

Steig, William, *Doctor De Soto Goes to Africa*

Van Allsburg, Chris, *The Wretched Stone*

_____, *The Mysteries of Harris Burdick*

Waber, Bernard, *Lyle, Lyle Crocodile*

Willard, Nancy, *Pish, Posh, Said Hieronymus Bosch*, illustrated by Leo and Diane Dillon

Yaccarino, Dan, *Deep in the Jungle*

Yolen, Jane, *Piggins and the Royal Wedding*, illustrated by Jane Dyer

Yorinks, Arthur, *Hey Al*, illustrated by Richard Egielski

Picture Books of Poetry, Verse, and Song

Aliki, *Go Tell Aunt Rhody* (P)

Brown, Marc, *Play Rhymes* (P)

Buffett, Jimmy, and Savannah Jane Buffett, *The Jolly Mon*, illustrated by Lambert Davis (I)

Clifton, Lucille, *Some of the Days of Everett Anderson*, illustrated by Evaline Ness (P)

Field, Rachel, *General Store*, illustrated by Nancy Winslow Parker (P)

Godwin, Laura, *Barnyard Prayers*, illustrated by Brian Selnick (P)

Goldstein, Bobbye, *Inner Chimes: Poems About Poetry*, illustrated by Jane Breskin Zalben (I–A)

Greenfield, Eloise, *Under the Sunday Tree*, illustrated by Amos Ferguson (P)

_____, *Night on Neighborhood Street*, illustrated by Jan Spivey Gilchrist (P)

Griego, Margot C., Betsy L. Bucks, Sharon S. Gilbert, and Laurel H. Kimball, editors and translators, *Tortillitas Para Mama: And Other Nursery Rhymes, Spanish and English*, illustrated by Barbara Cooney (P)

Gunning, Monica, *Not a Copper Penny in Me House*, illustrated by Frané Lessac (I–A)

Hamanaka, Sheila, *On the Wings of Peace* (I–A)

Harrison, David, *Somebody Catch My Homework*, illustrated by Betsy Lewin (I–A)

Hart, Jane, compiler, *Singing Bee: A Collection of Children's Songs*, illustrated by Anita Lobel (P)

Higginson, Vy, *This Is My Song!: A Collection of Gospel Music for the Family*, illustrated by Brenda Joysmith (P)

Hopkins, Lee Bennett, *Good Books, Good Times*, illustrated by Harvey Stevenson (P)

Hudson, Wade, and Cheryl Hudson, *How Sweet the Sound: African American Songs for Children*, illustrated by Floyd Cooper (P)

Hughes, Langston, *The Book of Rhythms*, illustrated by Matt Wawiorka (P)

Janeczko, Paul B., *Brickyard Summer*, illustrated by Ken Rush (I–A)

Krull, Kathleen, *Gonna Sing My Head Off!* illustrated by Allen Garns (I–A)

Livingston, Myra Cohn, *Sea Songs*, illustrated by Leonard Everett Fisher (I–A)

_____, *Sky Songs*, illustrated by Leonard Everett Fisher (I–A)

_____, *Space Songs*, illustrated by Leonard Everett Fisher (I–A)

Longfellow, Henry Wadsworth, *Hiawatha*, illustrated by Susan Jeffers (I–A)

_____, *Hiawatha's Childhood*, illustrated by Errol Le Cain (I–A)

_____, *Paul Revere's Ride*, illustrated by Nancy Winslow Parker (I–A)

_____, *Paul Revere's Ride*, illustrated by Ted Rand (I–A)

Metropolitan Museum of Art, *Go In and Out the Window: An Illustrated Songbook for Young People*, music arranged and edited by Dan Fox, commentary by Claude Marks (I–A)

O'Neill, Mary, *Hailstones and Halibut Bones*, illustrated by John Wallner (P)

Polacco, Patricia, *Babushka's Mother Goose* (P)

Prelutsky, Jack, selector, *A. Nonny Mouse Writes Again: Poems*, illustrated by Marjorie Priceman (P)

Raffi, *Raffi's Top Ten Songs to Read* (P)

Siebert, Diane, *Mojave*, illustrated by Wendell Minor (I–A)

Smith, William Jay, *Around My Room*, illustrated by Erik Blegvad (P)

Spier, Peter, *The Fox Went Out on a Chilly Night* (I–A)

Thomas, Joyce Carol, *Brown Hone in Broomwheat Tea*, illustrated by Floyd Cooper (P)

Van Laan, Nancy, *In a Circle Long Ago: A Treasury of Native Lore from North America*, illustrated by Lisa Desimini (I–A)

Wong, Janet S., *Buzz*, illustrated by Margaret Chodos-Irvine (P)

Zemach, Harve, and Margot Zemach, *Mommy, Buy Me a China Doll* (P)

Zemach, Margot, *Hush, Little Baby* (P)

Outstanding Picture Books Across the Curriculum: Science, Social Studies, Math, Art, Music, and Movement

Allen, Thomas B., *On Grandaddy's Farm* (P–I)

Arnosky, Jim, *Secrets of a Wildlife Watcher* (P–I)

Axelrod, Alan, *Songs of the Wild West*, arrangements by Dan Fox (A)

Berger, Melvin, *Why I Sneeze, Shiver, Hiccup, and Yawn*, illustrated by Paul Meisel

Blizzard, Gladys S., *Come Look with Me: Exploring Landscape Art with Children* (P–I)

Burleigh, Robert, and Mike Wimmer, *Flight: The Journey of Charles Lindbergh* (P–I)

Cole, Joanna, *Magic School Bus at the Waterworks*, illustrated by Bruce Degen (P–I)

Cooper, Floyd, *Mandela: From the Life of the South African Statesman* (I–A)

Cummings, Pat, editor, *Talking with Artists* (I)

_____, *Talking with Artists*, Volume II (I)

Heslewood, Juliet, *Introducing Picasso* (A)

Hoyt-Goldsmith, Diane, and Lawrence Migdale, *Pueblo Storyteller* (P–I)

Langstaff, John, *Climbing Jacob's Ladder: Heroes of the Bible in African-American Spirituals*, illustrated by Ashley Bryan (P–I)

Lauber, Patricia, *Get Ready for Robots*, illustrated by True Kelley (P)

Lavies, Bianca, *Backyard Hunter: The Praying Mantis* (P–I)

Macaulay, David, *Castle* (I–A)

_____, *Cathedral* (I–A)

_____, *Pyramid* (I–A)

_____, *The Way Things Work* (P–I–A)

McDonald, Megan, *Is This a House for Hermit Crab?* illustrated by S. D. Schindler (P)

Micklethwait, Lucy, *I Spy a Freight Train: Transportation in Art* (P–I)

Lourie, Peter, *Amazon* (I)

Musgrove, Margaret, *Ashanti to Zulu*, illustrated by Leo and Diane Dillon (P–I)

Richmond, Robin, *Introducing Michelangelo* (I)

Schwartz, David, *If You Made a Million*, Steven Kellogg (I)

Simon, Seymour, *Volcanoes* (P–I)

Yoshida, Toshi, *Young Lions* (P–I)

chapter **5**

Folklore

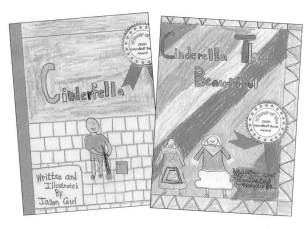

Students write their version of a Cinderella story.

Once upon a time there was a beautiful princess named Amrita. She lived with her mother in a beautiful palace, and they were very happy. They lived in India. One day, Amrita's mother died. Before she died, she gave Amrita a very special box. The box was made out of wood and it had animals and flowers carved on it. "Take this box with you, wherever you go," her mother said. "It will give you whatever you ask for."

—SHIRA KLAYMAN, *A Cinderella from India*, GRADE 4

Once upon a time there was a Chinese girl named Cinderella. She was 10 years old. She loved to draw and write. Her wish was to go to the palace and dance with a handsome prince. She lived in Taiwan and her favorite color was blue.

One day there was a parade and Cinderella went into a shop. She found a dragon kite. Next to it was a blue diamond that made wishes come true. She picked up the blue diamond and wished she could dance at the palace. Then she remembered she didn't have a dress. She wished for a dress but it never came. Just then Cinderella had a brilliant idea. She could wish for a magic genie that could make wishes come true.

—SHOSHANA KLAYMAN, *Cinderella and the Blue Diamond*, GRADE 4

N SANDY SWERDLOFF'S FOURTH-GRADE CLASS, THE STUDENTS begin their unit on Cinderella by discussing the elements of a fairy tale. The children brain-storm to come up with the elements they think constitute a "real" fairy tale. These usually include a prince, someone who is treated unfairly, a stepfamily, the number 3, animals that take on human characteristics, a problem and a resolution, and of course, a happy ending. They recognize that Cinderella-type stories usually center on one main character who is treated unfairly by members of a stepfamily. Sandy shows them her collection of Cinderella books, which come from countries all over the world. The children are amazed at the number and variety of stories and are excited about having the chance to write their own Cinderella stories.

Sandy and the children talk about the best way to begin writing a Cinderella story. Each child starts with a main character who has a problem, then plans a resolution and begins writing details that support the story. The children write complete descriptions of the main character, and they plan the events that will take the main character from the beginning of the story to the end. They learn the art of the writing process by editing, conferencing, and revising many times. When they are done, the children type their stories on a computer. Once the stories are printed, they are ready to be illustrated. The children take care to match the illustrations to the printed words. When the books are complete, each child compiles a cover page, a copyright page, a dedication page, and a page about the author.

When all the books are finished and bound, Sandy and her students celebrate by having a Cinderella Author's Tea. The children invite their families, and they hold the tea in the gym, where five or six children are seated at a round table along with their guests. Each child reads his or her story, and when all are finished reading, the group celebrates with a light breakfast of bagels, coffee, tea, and juice. It's a fitting ending for a unit on that most appealing form of literature, the fairy tale.

Defining Folklore: A Literary Heritage

The universal appeal of the Cinderella story reflects people's widespread embrace of folklore through the ages and across cultures. Folk literature is exactly what the words imply: stories of the folk that began as an anonymous, oral tradition and gradually became a part of our literary heritage. The roots of folklore in all societies lie in the quest for harmony with the world around us. Through our imaginations, through analogy and metaphor, we try to transform outer reality into a vision of life we can control. The timeless quality of folklore has inspired authors and illustrators today to create a rich treasury of new interpretations.

Storytelling began with the songs and tales early societies composed to describe their daily work. "The first primitive efforts," notes storyteller Ruth Sawyer (1962, pp. 45–46), "consisted of a simple chant set to the rhythm of some daily tribal occupation such as grinding corn, paddling a canoe or kayak, sharpening weapons for hunting or war, or ceremonial dancing."

As they speculated about the power of nature, the forces behind it, and human behavior, primitive societies also created stories about people and nature. These were the stories that grew into hero legends and myths. When the ancient Greeks, for instance, were frightened by thunder, they invented a story about an angry god who shook the heavens. When they did not understand how and why the sun moved, they imagined a god who drove a chariot across the sky. Love, hate, heroic acts, values, and morality play an important part in myths of all cultures. With the passage of time and the growth of tribes, the desire to preserve ancestral stories increased. The folklore that had been passed from one generation to the next became our cultural heritage.

At one time, common belief held that all folklore emerged from one prehistoric civilization. The Grimm brothers, who collected tales from all over Germany, ascribed to this view, speculating that as people migrated, they took their stories with them. This theory would account for regional differences in folktales, such as the evolution of West Africa's trickster *Ananse* the spider to *Anansi* in the Caribbean and *Aunt Nancy* in the United States. As folklorists studied the tales of many diverse cultures, however, it became apparent that some stories must have originated spontaneously in a number of separate places. "The themes were those . . . concerning human beings everywhere and the stories were bound to be invented wherever communities developed," according to the Director of the Center for the Book, Library of Congress, John Y. Cole (1982).

Today, cultural anthropologists believe that both theories about the origin of folktales are correct. Distinguished folklore scholars Iona and Peter Opie note that no one theory "is likely to account satisfactorily for the origin of even a majority of the tales. Their wellsprings are almost certainly numerous, their ages likely to vary considerably, their meanings—if they ever had meanings—to be diverse" (*Classic Fairy Tales*, p. 18).

Folklore in Children's Lives

Folklore is a rich source of literature for children. In the same way it explained the world to early people, it helps children today understand their world. Preschool children often believe that magic accounts for the things they do not understand. They even give inanimate objects human characteristics. André Favat, who studied the moral development of children, draws a parallel between the perceptions of morality in fairy tales and those held by children. Children under the age of six, he posits, have an "eye for an eye" mentality; because the fairy tale shares that vision, it is particularly suited for children in that developmental stage (1977, pp. 38, 50).

Psychoanalytic writers and psychologists have explored the meaning of folklore in children's lives. According to Freud, the characters in fairy tales symbolize a child's subconscious urges. Bettelheim, too, argues that fairy tales tap into unconscious desires—the well spring of repressed emotions. Fairy tales, he says, help children deal with emo-

tional insecurities by suggesting images about which they can fantasize. Jung suggests that dream, fantasy, imagination, and vision stem from the collective unconscious, a part of the mind common to all people. Because of the universal nature of the unconscious, he says, diverse people share common stories. The mythical figures and conflicts are archetypes of racial memories (1976, p. 6).

Researcher Arthur Applebee (1979), who has studied the child's concept of story, reasons that children search for structures and patterns that suggest order and consistency in the world around them. They are reassured by the repeated pattern of three characters, three events, and three trials. Stories are one means of transmitting these patterns. Children derive pleasure from mastering the rules, and this concept is a particularly important factor in formula stories such as folk and fairy tales. The pattern of going out from home, encountering three trials, and returning home successfully is a satisfying experience for a child.

Whatever the explanation, it is clear that similar archetypes—images, plot patterns, or character types that recur—appear in the myths, legends, and folktales of all peoples across time and place. For example, the normal process of maturing finds its psychological expression in the archetype of the hero's quest—slaying the dragon or winning a princess. Other familiar examples include the good mother (fairy godmother), the bad mother (wicked stepmother or old witch), and the evil underside of every person (the shadow). The same archetypes appear in realistic and fantasy novels; characters battle forces of evil to assure the survival of good. See Teaching Idea 5.1 for suggestions on exploring archetypes in folklore.

Criteria for Evaluating Folklore

When evaluating folklore, look for qualities of authenticity and excellence in both language and illustration, as presented in Figure 5.1.

These old tales are at their best when the language reflects their oral origins. Look for language that sounds natural,

Figure 5✳1

Checklist for Evaluating Folklore

Language
✳ Sounds like spoken language, with rich, natural rhythms
✳ Reflects the integrity of early retellings
✳ Avoids controlled, diluted, or trite vocabulary

Illustrations
✳ Serve as examples of artistic excellence
✳ Complement and extend the narrative
✳ Reflect the cultural heritage of the tale

Teaching Idea 5·1

Archetypes in Folklore

Reading a wide range of folklore helps students develop a sense of its basic elements. Gradually they become aware of various archetypes (images, plot patterns, or character types that occur frequently) in the folklore they read. To develop an awareness of archetypes in folklore, ask students to identify images, plot patterns, or character types that occur frequently, and to list them along with the titles of the stories. Compare and contrast the archetypes in class. Students can also compare different versions of the same story, such as the numerous retellings of the Baba Yaga tale. Possible elements to search for in folklore and novels, and some books that contain these elements, include the following:

Hero's Quest

Bond, Nancy, *String in the Harp*

Hodges, Margaret, *St. George and the Dragon: A Golden Legend*

Pyle, Howard, *The Story of King Arthur and His Knights*

Fairy Godmother

Ayres, Becky Hickox, *Matreshka*

Perrault, Charles, *Cinderella*

Rylant, Cynthia, *Missing May*

Wicked Witch/Wicked Stepmother

Grimm, Jacob, and Wilhelm Grimm, *Hansel and Gretel*

Levine, Arthur, *Boardwalk Princess*

Benevolent Crone

dePaola, Tomie, *Strega Nona*

Polacco, Patricia, *Babushka Baba Yaga*

Shadow/Evil Underside of Human Nature/ Good Versus Evil

Le Guin, Ursula K., *Wizard of Earthsea*

L'Engle, Madeleine, *A Wrinkle in Time*

Sendak, Maurice, *Where the Wild Things Are*

Yolen, Jane, *Tam Lin*

As you read, be aware of conventions, tasks, refrains, magical objects, and other folkloric elements. Many elements may appear in one folktale. For example, in Tomie dePaola's *Strega Nona* you find a noodlehead, an overflowing pot, a chant, and a benevolent crone, among other archetypes.

---

with vivid imagery and melodious rhythms, and that maintains the cultural integrity of early retellings. Avoid simplified, controlled vocabulary versions that reduce the stories to trite episodes.

Fortunately, talented illustrators often choose folklore to showcase their art. Artists present an immense amount of cultural detail in their illustrations—detail that the honed language of folklore may not provide. Further, they have a unique opportunity to create their own visions because the oft-told tales present only general descriptions of setting and character. Look for illustrations that are artistically excellent, complement and extend the narrative with accuracy, and reflect the cultural heritage of the tale.

A CLOSE LOOK AT

The Rough-Face Girl

Folklore structured around the basic Cinderella motif is common; approximately 1,500 versions of the tale have been recorded by folklorists. Rafe Martin retells the Algonquin Indian version of Cinderella in **The Rough-Face Girl** (I),

illustrated by David Shannon. In this retelling, both the Algonquin culture and the voice of the storyteller are apparent in illustrations and words.

Synopsis

The story begins "long ago" in a "village by the shores of Lake Ontario." Many women of the village want to marry the Invisible Being, but first they must be able to see him and answer questions that his sister asks. Two of the village women are cruel and haughty sisters who torment their younger sister, forcing her to keep the fire going, a job that results in scars on her face and hands. After the sisters fail in their attempt to marry the Invisible Being, the younger sister goes to his tent. When questioned by the Invisible Being's sister, the girl answers correctly. She is married to the Invisible Being and "they lived together in great gladness and were never parted."

Structure

The simple structure of an oral tale is preserved in this retelling. The story begins with a simple statement of setting and moves immediately to the problem: Only the woman

David Shannon captures the relationship between the human-sized Rough-Face Girl and the overwhelming grandeur and beauty of nature in **The Rough-Face Girl** *by Rafe Martin.*

who can see the Invisible Being can marry him. On the third page we are introduced to the characters: a poor man with three daughters, two cruel and heartless, one sweet and submissive. The story then moves immediately to the action, briefly detailing the unsuccessful attempts of the haughty sisters to convince the Invisible Being's sister that they have seen him, and the subsequent triumph of the Rough-Face Girl. This economy of detail reflects the oral origins of the tale: Brief statements of setting and the use of stereotypical characters allow the teller to get right to the exciting part—the action—thus holding the attention of his audience.

Language

The language, too, reflects the oral origins of the tale. The story makes use of dialogue and of prosodic features that indicate tone and volume when the sister of the Invisible Being speaks:

> "All right," she said quietly, "if you think you've seen him, then tell me, WHAT'S HIS BOW MADE OF?" And suddenly her voice was swift as lightning and strong as thunder!

There is also repetition: The Rough-Face Girl asks her father what her older sisters have already asked, she makes the same journey they did, and she is asked the same questions by the sister. Yet sharp contrasts are also made appar-

ent: Her father has nothing to give her, and the villagers laugh at her as she walks by in her odd clothing. Yet she answers the questions correctly. By repeating the events and the dialogue, the storyteller heightens the drama of the tale.

Perhaps the most moving passage comes when the Invisible Being enters his wigwam and sees the Rough-Face Girl:

> And when he saw her sitting there he said, "At last we have been found out." Then, smiling kindly, he added, "And oh, my sister, but she is beautiful." And his sister said, "Yes."

Read aloud, these words ring with emotion.

Illustrations

The voice of the storyteller comes through the words, but the culture of the people comes through both the words and the beautiful full-color realistic paintings that illustrate this tale. The first page, on which the setting is introduced in one sentence, exemplifies how text and illustrations work together to form this tale. Above the text is a painting of an Algonquin village. If you look closely you can see men in canoes and men carrying game, women carrying water, tending fires, scraping skins, and cooking, and children playing. Surrounding the village are tall pines and firs, and mist is rising from the lake. Thus, in one line the story is set, and the setting is elaborated in the detailed illustration.

© 1992 David Shannon

David Shannon's art quickly establishes the setting of a village by the lake. The time of "long ago" is reflected in the shelter and food preparation scenes in **The Rough-Face Girl** *by Rafe Martin.*

In subsequent illustrations we see wigwams and their symbolic decorations, details of clothing, and beautiful natural images that inspired much of Algonquin folklore. These images speak of the people and the culture that first told this haunting tale. We also see the pride and meanness of the two sisters, the humility of the Rough-Face Girl, and the awesome nature of the Invisible Being. The illustrations not only reflect but elaborate and extend the story, providing readers with details that are not easily incorporated in a brief oral text.

The Rough-Face Girl demonstrates the close relationship that the reteller and artist have with the original tale. The combination of a riveting story, a skillful retelling, and beautiful, detailed illustrations result in a book that children remember and reread numerous times.

Types of Folklore

Folklore has many categories. Those most commonly available to children include nursery rhymes, folktales, fables, myths, legends, folksongs, and Bible stories. Beginning in infancy, children delight in nursery rhymes. As they grow and develop a literary background, they understand and enjoy folktales, myths, legends, and the morals encoded in fables. Teachers often introduce children to folktales in the primary grades and subsequently move to legends and myths in the upper grades. Today's sophisticated retellings and artwork makes such age distinctions unnecessary. Primary-grade children enjoy myths presented in an appealing format; when they study myths later, they have a foundation on which to build their understanding. Similarly, students in the intermediate and advanced grades profit from a study of folktales, especially ones they are familiar with from childhood.

MOTHER GOOSE AND NURSERY RHYMES

Mother Goose and nursery rhymes form the foundation of a child's literary heritage. Surprising as that may sound, the rhythm and rhyme of the language, its compact structure and engaging characters produce bountiful models for young children learning language. As they chant the phrases, mimic the nonsense words, and endlessly recite the alliterative repetitions, children develop *phonemic awareness*—the ability to segment sounds in spoken words, something that is a prerequisite to phonics instruction. More important, children delight in language play. Poet Walter De la Mare (1962) declared that Mother Goose rhymes "free the fancy, charm the tongue and ear, delight the inward eye, and many of them are tiny masterpieces of word craftsmanship. . . . They are not only crammed with vivid little scenes and objects and living creatures, but, however fantastic and nonsensical they may be, they are a direct short cut into poetry itself" (1962, p. 21).

Mother Goose stories and nursery rhymes have been attacked through the years, but they continue to play a vital role in the lives of children. As early as the seventeenth century, our stern forefathers disparaged some of the tales as brutal, dishonest, and irresponsible, instead of viewing them as whimsical fun. In more recent years, the verses have been called sexist and violent. Despite this sometimes valid adult perspective, young children value the stories and verses for their rhythm, repetition, and rhyme, and for their nonsensical ways of viewing the world. Further, the stories and rhymes are but one part of children's literary experience. Children can read and hear other stories that reflect modern perceptions of gender equity and nonviolence. Researchers Maclean, Bryant, Bradley, and Crossland (1989) show that exposure to nursery rhymes improves children's phonological skills and thereby their later reading ability. Children learn basic story patterns, vivid plots, themes, and characters through the tales. These become the foundation stones for subsequent literary education.

Origins

As is true of all folklore, we do not have conclusive evidence of the origins of Mother Goose rhymes, nor do we know whether a person with that name actually existed. According to Iona and Peter Opie, authors of *The Oxford Nursery Rhyme Book*, *The Oxford Dictionary of Nursery Rhymes*, and *Tail Feathers From Mother Goose: The Opie Rhyme Book* (1988), the rhymes have been linked with social and political events, and numerous attempts have been made to identify the nursery characters with real people. "The bulk of these speculations are worthless," they write. "Fortunately the theories are so numerous they tend to cancel each other out" (1951, p. 27).

Many of the rhymes probably have a simple origin. They may have been written with the aim of teaching children to count, to recite the alphabet, or to say their prayers. Others—riddles, tongue twisters, proverbs, and nonsense—were probably intended simply for amusement. The name "Mother Goose" was probably first associated with Charles Perrault's 1697 publication of *Histoires ou Contes du Temps Passé, avec des Moralités (Stories or Tales of Times Past, with Morals)*. The frontispiece shows an old woman spinning and telling stories and is labeled *Contes de ma Mère l'Oye (Tales of Mother Goose)*.

Mother Goose and nursery rhymes know no regional, ethnic, cultural, or language boundaries. Our "Gingerbread Boy" is similar to "The Pancake" in Sweden and "The Bun" in Russia. Because the magic of Mother Goose is handed down by

Educators and researchers recognize Mother Goose rhymes as essential learning material for children.

word of mouth, it is essential to choose versions that maintain the original, robust language, not rewritten or abridged verses.

Most Mother Goose books are illustrated. Some illustrators develop an entire book around a single rhyme; others focus a collection of rhymes around a single topic, and still others present an entire collection through their particular artistic vision.

Characteristics

The pronounced beat of Mother Goose rhymes strengthens a child's sense of rhythm and language. The *rhythm* invites a physical response long before a child can attach meaning to the words. The cadence of the language—its beat, stress, sound, and intonation—is reinforced by the bounce of an adult's knee, as literary critic Northrop Frye points out:

> The infant who gets bounced on somebody's knee to the rhythm of "Ride a Cock Horse" does not need a footnote telling him that Banbury Cross is twenty miles northeast of Oxford. He does not need the information that "cross" and "horse" make (at least in the pronunciation he is most likely to hear) not a rhyme but an assonance. He does not need the value judgment that the repetition of "horse" in the first two lines indicates a rather thick ear on the part of the composer. All he needs is to get bounced. (1963, p. 25)

A second major characteristic of Mother Goose is the *imaginative use of words and ideas*. Nothing is too preposterous! Children delight in the images conjured up by

> *Hey diddle, diddle,*
> *The cat and the fiddle,*
> *The cow jumped over the moon;*
> *The little dog laughed*
> *To see such sport,*
> *And the dish ran away with the spoon.*

Anything can happen in the young child's unfettered world. The verses feed their fancy, spark their creativity, and stretch their imagination: Three wise men of Gotham go to sea in a bowl. An old woman is tossed up in a basket, 19 times as high as the moon. There was an old woman who lived in a shoe/She had so many children she didn't know what to do/She gave them some broth without any bread/She whipped them all soundly and put them to bed.

A third characteristic, the *compact structure*, establishes the scene quickly and divulges the plot at once. In four short lines we hear an entire story:

> *Jack Sprat could eat no fat,*
> *His wife could eat no lean,*
> *And so between them both, you see,*
> *They licked the platter clean.*

As in all folklore, the consolidation of action and the economy of words result from the rhymes being said aloud for many generations before being set in print. As the verses were passed from one teller to the next, they were honed to their present simplicity.

The *wit and whimsy* of the characters also accounts for the popularity and longevity of Mother Goose. Children appreciate the obvious nonsense in

> *Gregory Griggs, Gregory Griggs,*
> *Had twenty-seven different wigs.*
> *He wore them up, he wore them down,*
> *To please the people of the town;*
> *He wore them east, he wore them west,*
> *But he never could tell which he loved best.*

The humor appeals both to children and adults. Surprise endings provide clever resolutions, as in

> *Peter, Peter, pumpkin eater,*
> *Had a wife and couldn't keep her;*
> *He put her in a pumpkin shell,*
> *And there he kept her very well.*

Old favorites, namely, Alice and Martin Provensen's *Mother Goose*, Marguerite de Angeli's *Book of Nursery & Mother Goose Rhymes*, L. Leslie Brooke's *Ring O' Roses: A Nursery Rhyme Picture Book*, Blanche Fisher Wright's *The Real Mother Goose*, Arnold Lobel's *The Random House Book of Mother Goose*, and Iona and Peter Opie's *Tail Feathers of Mother Goose* (all N–P) are joined by multicultural editions with songs and stories from around the world. Patricia Polacco includes verses and images from her Russian grandmother in *Babushka's Mother Goose*. Judy Sierra retells *Nursery Tales Around the World*, Nancy Van Laan depicts a mother and a child from seven different continents in *Sleep, Sleep, Sleep: A Lullaby for Little Ones Around the World*, and Jane Yolen chooses *Sleep Rhymes Around the World* and *Street Rhymes Around the World* (all N–P). Rosemary Wells and Iona Opie worked together to produce *My Very First Mother Goose* and *Here Comes Mother Goose*.

Authors, editors, and publishers, aware of the international makeup of our population and the global-village view of our world, search for new books to reflect that vision. Schools need several Mother Goose and nursery rhyme collections for teachers to read aloud and for children to look at, hold, share, and love. Some popular collections today include *Michael Foreman's Mother Goose*, with a foreword by Iona Opie, and *Glorious Mother Goose*, selected by Cooper Edens and illustrated by many talented artists. Other excellent Mother Goose books in single editions and edited collections are listed in the Booklist at the end of the chapter.

THAILAND

Chao non bai
Yen pra-pai ma ruay-ruay
Mae cha pa pai non duay
Cha klom hai chao non
Mue-sai cha pad wee
Mue-kwa nee pen Chamorn
Sao-noy chao ya on
Chao puan-non kong mue—euy

Take an afternoon nap, my baby.
When the cool, constant breeze caresses you
I'll cuddle you to sleep, very near to me.
I'll lull you to sleep with my songs.
With my left hand as a fan I'll cool you,
With my right hand as a whisk I'll protect you.
Don't cry, my baby,
Dear sleeping friend of mine.

*Sleep rhymes work at bedtime all around the world. This illustration is from Jane Yolen's **Sleep Rhymes Around the World**.*

FOLKTALES

Origins

The transition from oral retelling to printed versions of folktales dates back centuries. Some Eastern stories appeared in print as early as the ninth century. Straparola (1480–1557), author and duchy of Milan, Italy, gathered one of the earliest and most important collections of traditional tales in mid-sixteenth century Venice in *Piacevoli Notti*, volumes 1 and 2 (published in 1550 and 1553). The work contains 20 folktales, including "Beauty and the Beast" and "Puss in Boots." Straparola's work was followed by Basile's *Pentameron or Entertainment for the Little Ones* in seventeenth-century Naples. Perrault's French publication of *Histoires ou Contes du Temps Passé* in 1697 helped folk literature flourish in Europe. Perrault included "Sleeping Beauty," "Little Red Riding Hood," "Cinderella," and "Puss in Boots." During the eighteenth century, La Fontaine's *Fables*, Countess d'Aulnoy's *Fairy Tales*, and Madame de Beaumont's *Beauty and the Beast* were published. Folklore has deep roots.

Toward the end of the eighteenth century, philologists studied folklore to find out about customs and languages in different societies. The German brothers Jacob and Wilhelm Grimm traveled through the countryside asking people to tell stories they remembered. The Grimms eventually wrote a German dictionary and a book of grammar, but they are best remembered for their retellings of the stories they heard. The two volumes of the first edition of *Kinder- und Hausmärchen* were published in 1812 and 1815.

German Popular Stories, an English translation of the Grimm's tales, illustrated by George Cruikshank, became an instant success when it was published in 1823. It raised the respectability of the old tales among scholars and educators who had held them to be "an affront to the rational mind" (Opie and Opie, 1974, p. 25). Wanda Gág illustrated *Tales from Grimm* in 1936 and Maurice Sendak illustrated *The Juniper Tree and Other Tales from Grimm* (I) in 1973.

Enthusiasm for collecting folklore spread around the world. Joseph Jacobs and Andrew Lang collected folktales in England; Jacob's *English Fairy Tales* includes many of the best-loved stories, and Lang's series, in which the books are identified by color—*The Blue Fairy Book*, for example—continues to serve as a primary source of British tales. Norse scholars Peter Christian Asbjornsen and Jorgen E. Moe collected most

of the Scandinavian tales we have today. Asbjornsen and Moe published a notable collection, *East O' the Sun and West O' the Moon* (I), during the 1840s. George Webbe Dasent translated the tales into English and retained the vitality of spoken language. Many of the same tales appear in Ingri and Edgar Parin d'Aulaire's *East of the Sun and West of the Moon* (I), which contains illustrations echoing Norwegian folk art.

Characteristics

Folk tales are *narratives* in which heroes and heroines triumph over adversity by demonstrating virtues like cleverness or bravery, or loveable vices like supreme silliness. Their *themes*, obvious though not stated explicitly, express the values of the people who created them.

The stories have an artistic yet simple form that derives from their oral tradition. The *plot lines* are clean and direct: The first paragraph establishes characters and setting, the body develops the problem and moves toward the climax,

*Patricia Polacco reflects her Russian heritage in her version of the Baba Yaga tale, **Babushka Baba Yaga** (P).*

© 1993 Patricia Polacco

Teaching Idea 5⋅2

Create a Folklore Performance

Folklore is ideal material for readers theatre, puppetry, story theater, or choral reading. Folktales contain clean plot lines, a limited cast of well-defined characters, and decisive endings. To create a folklore performance with your students:

1. Ask book groups to choose several folktales to read.
2. Have them choose one folktale to share through creative drama.
3. Prepare a script for readers theatre, a puppet play, story theater, or choral reading.
4. Share the performance with others.

"Fractured" folktales and myths add a note of hilarity to a story. Use these versions:

Scieszka, Jon, *The Stinky Cheese Man and Other Fairly Stupid Tales*

_____, *The True Story of the Three Little Pigs*

Wells, Rosemary, *Max and Ruby's First Greek Myth: Pandora's Box*

_____, *Max and Ruby's Midas: Another Greek Myth*

and the ending resolves the problem without complications. Folktales are, in fact, mini-dramas. See Teaching Idea 5.2 for ideas on involving students in folklore theatre.

Folktales unfold with little ambiguity: the good characters are supremely good, the evil ones are outrageously evil, and justice prevails without compromise. The conflict is identified early, and only incidents that build on the problem or add complexity to it have survived oral transmission. Problems are resolved decisively, with little denouement, resulting in classic "happily-ever-after" endings.

Because folktales are more concerned with situation than personality, *characters* are delineated economically. Few subtleties interrupt the intentional stereotyping that quickly establishes character traits. These one-dimensional or "flat" characters crystallize in the form of the foolish, the wise, the wicked, or the virtuous. All perform in predictable ways and rarely change throughout the course of a story. Children tolerate the idea that a different range of possibility existed in the past. In Applebee's study (1978) young children said, "Witches and giants lived a long time ago." They know that giants do not live in today's world, but they readily accept the possibility that they might have lived at one time.

The *language*—direct, vivid vernacular—is uncluttered by awkward constructions or convolutions. Gail Haley's retelling of *Mountain Jack Tales* (I) reflects the Appalachian regional dialect of their origin. Colloquialisms add to the flavor and reflect the heritage of the tale; they are tempered to the tongue, having been pruned and polished through centuries.

Themes in folktales, obvious although not stated explicitly, express the values of the people who created them and reflect their philosophy of life. Miserly Yoshi, the fan maker, lived next door to Sabu, who cooked delicious-smelling eels. Yoshi had no intention of paying Sabu for eels, and Sabu had no intention of giving eels to Yoshi even though he had leftovers every day. When Sabu suggests that Yoshi pay for the good *smell* of eels, Yoshi rattles his money box to say that he is paying for the *smell* of the eels with the *sound* of his money. Finally the two shopkeepers reach an agreement that leads to *Yoshi's Feast*. The theme that we can sometimes help ourselves by helping others is shown but never stated.

In folktales, if the language is precise, the *setting* remains geographically vague, leaving an impression of a world that is complete in itself. The stories take place in unidentified times, in places defined by minimal detail. Young children do not question the truthfulness of story—it is a *story* and it really happened. Paul Hazard, literary critic, observed that folktales know no geographic boundaries when we consider

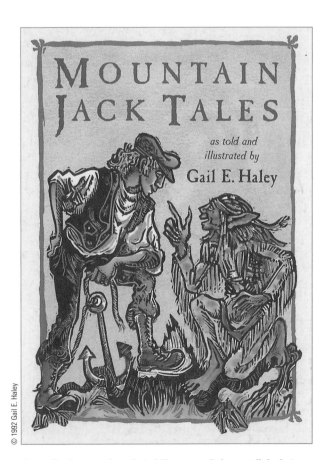

Storyteller Poppyseed speaks in hill-country dialect to tell the hair-raising adventures of Jack, a universal folk hero from the mountains.

Yoshi and Sabu learn the pleasure of give-and-take. In business as in life you often get what you pay for in **Yoshi's Feast**.

© 2000 Yumi Heo

that stories collected a century ago in Europe come to life everywhere for each new generation of children. Figure 5.2 summarizes folktale characteristics.

Types of Folktales

CUMULATIVE TALES Each incident in a cumulative tale grows from the preceding one, as in "This Is the House That Jack Built" and "The Old Woman and Her Pig." Jeanette Winter's version of *The House That Jack Built* (N–P) uses rebus characters in the text so that even younger children can predict what is coming next. These stories are often called "chain tales," because each part of the story is linked to the next. The initial incident reveals both central character and problem; each subsequent scene builds on the previous one, continuing to a climax and then unraveling in reverse order or stopping with an abrupt surprise ending. Chain tales often have repetitive phrases like "Run, run as fast as you can. You can't catch me. I'm the Gingerbread man," from "The Gingerbread Boy" and its variants, "Johnny Cake," "The Pancake," and "The Bun." More examples of cumulative tales are listed in the Booklist at the end of the chapter.

TALKING ANIMALS In this type of tale, animals talk with human beings or with each other. Like human characters, the talking animals may be good or evil, wise or silly. Those who are good and wise are rewarded. Nursery- and primary-grade children especially enjoy talking animals.

Perennial favorites include "The Three Little Pigs," "The Three Billy Goats Gruff," "Henny Penny," "Brer Rabbit," and the Anansi spider stories. Jessica Souhami retells a traditional tale from India in *No Dinner! The Story of the Old Woman and the Pumpkin*. With the help of her grand-

Figure 5✿2

Folktale Characteristics

* Heroes and heroines represent traits such as cleverness, bravery, or supreme silliness to triumph over adversity.
* Plot lines are direct and are uncluttered by side issues.
* Stories contain very little ambiguity: good is good, evil is outrageously evil.
* Conflict is identified early.
* Resolution is decisive.
* Characters are delineated economically.
* Themes express the values of the people who created them.
* Language is direct, vivid, vernacular.
* Setting is geographically vague; time is vague.

daughter, the old woman outsmarts a bear, wolf, and tiger that want to eat her for dinner. Children delight in the humorous situations and rhythmic language of Eric Kimmel's retelling of a West African trickster tale, *Anansi Goes Fishing* (P), an exemplary talking animal tale. Other talking animal stories appear in the Booklist at the end of the chapter.

NOODLEHEAD TALES Humorous noodlehead stories focus on characters who are pure-hearted but lack good judgment. In *Noodlehead Stories from Around the World* (I), M. A. Jagendorf describes a noodlehead as a simple blunderer who does not use good sense or learn from experience. Every cultural group has noodlehead stories that provoke hearty laughter: the wise men of Gotham in England, the fools in the Jewish ghetto of Chelm in Poland, Juan Bobo in Puerto Rico, the Connemara Man in Ireland, and the Montieri in Italy. Other examples of noodlehead stories are listed in the Booklist at the end of the chapter.

FAIRY TALES Fairy tales are simple narratives dealing with supernatural beings such as fairies, magicians, ogres, and dragons. They are typically of folk origin and are written or told for the amusement of children. Though fairy tales are structured like other folktales, their deeply magical character sets them apart. Wee people, fairy godmothers, and other magical beings intervene to make things happen. Enchantment aside, these stories paint an ideal vision of life based on the hope that virtue will be recognized and hard work rewarded. Fairy tales show children that courage, honesty, and resourcefulness are valued. Paul Hazard, literary critic and author of *Books, Children and Men*, said, "Fairy tales are like beautiful mirrors of water, so deep and crystal clear. In their depths we sense the mysterious experience of a thousand years" (1944, 1967, p. 157). Examples of fairy tales appear in Robert D. San Souci's *The Talking Eggs* (I), a Creole variant of Cinderella illustrated by Jerry Pinkney, and *The Turkey Girl* (I), a Zuni version retold by Penny Pollock and illustrated by Ed Young. Ellin Greene tells a variation of "The Golden Goose" in *The Little Golden Lamb*. A flute-playing shepherd wins the hand of the princess when he causes her to laugh: He walks by her with a string of people stuck to his little golden lamb. Other examples of fairy tales and their variants are listed in the Booklist at the end of the chapter.

TALL TALES Tall tales are indigenous to the United States and are a peculiarly American form of folktale. They are a combination of history, myth, and fact. Tall tales gave the early American settlers symbols of strength and offset the harsh realities of an untamed land with a little humor. The exaggerated strength and blatant lies in tall tales added zest and lightened a life of hard labor. As the settlers built a new country, they created heroes who were the mightiest, strongest, most daring lumberjacks, railroad men, coal miners, riverboat drivers, and steelworkers possible.

Many heroes of tall tales were real people, but their stories have made them larger than life. Davy Crockett, Daniel Boone, and Johnny Appleseed accomplished feats no mortal would dare. John Henry, Pecos Bill, and Mike Fink exemplify the Yankee work ethic, the brawn and muscle required to develop America. Jerdine Nolen relates the story told by Momma Mary about the time Addy was a house slave on a plantation and found *Big Jabe* (P–I). Addy loved to catch catfish, bass, and brim, but one day she caught a wicker basket. The basket held a little boy called Jabe who was about 5 or 6 years old. Jabe gave Addy a golden pear for rescuing him. After she ate the pear, Jabe planted the seeds, which grew into a huge tree. The story, part tall tale and part magical savior, tells how Jabe becomes Big Jabe who helps lighten burdens for slaves and helps them escape.

Children love the exaggerated humor and lies that mark the tall tales. They laugh when Paul Bunyan's loggers tie bacon to their feet and skate across the huge griddle to grease it. The thought of Slewfoot Sue bouncing skyward every time her bustle hits the ground produces giggles. And when the infant Pecos Bill falls out of the covered wagon, children can picture the abandoned baby scrambling toward the coyote mother, who eventually raises him with the rest of the coyote pack. Paul Bunyan's folks could not rock his cradle fast enough, so they put it in the ocean; the waves still pound today because of the strength of Paul's kicking. The hero in tall tales is all-powerful; therefore, readers know

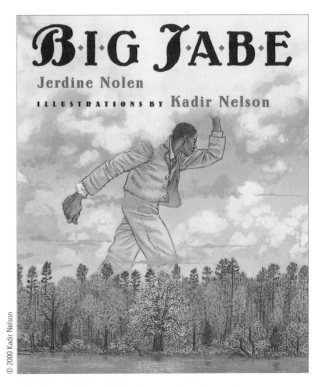

Big Jabe sees that justice is done on a slave plantation.

he will overcome any problem. The suspense is in *how* the problem will be solved.

Julius Lester describes the mighty battle between a steam drill and the legendary hero in *John Henry* (P–I), illustrated by Jerry Pinkney. Steven Kellogg's biography, *Johnny Appleseed*, and Reeve Lindbergh's poetic version, illustrated by Kathy Jakobsen, both tell the story of John Chapman, who traveled across the Allegheny Mountains planting apple orchards. Not all the heroes are male: Robert San Souci collected 20 tales that show women were *Cut from the Same Cloth: American Women of Myth, Legend, and Tall Tale* (I). Jane Yolen also shows strong women in a dozen tales entitled *Not One Damsel in Distress: World Folktales for Strong Girls* (I). Alvin Schwartz gathered his entertaining and informative research into the language, superstition and folk history of America's legendary past in *Whoppers: Tall Tales and Other Lies, Flapdoodle: Pure Nonsense from American Folklore*, and *Witcracks: Jokes and Jests from American Folklore* (all I). Other books of American lore are listed in the Booklist at the end of the chapter.

Patterns in Folklore Around the World

Students who read widely soon recognize recurring patterns in the folklore of many countries. As characters, events, and resolutions recur in their reading, students begin to recognize the themes, conventions, and motifs that form these tales. They then use this literary knowledge in their own writing. Brer Rabbit stories traveled from Africa and Jamaica to the American rural South. Originally popularized by storyteller Joel Chandler Harris, Van Dyke Park's outstanding renditions include *Jump! The Adventures of Brer Rabbit, Jump Again! More Adventures of Brer Rabbit*, and *Jump On Over: The Adventures of Brer Rabbit and His Family* (all I), all illustrated by Barry Moser. Julius Lester's retellings of the traditional tales, *The Tales of Uncle Remus, More Tales of Uncle Remus, Further Tales of Uncle Remus* (all I–A) are also marked by melodious language that reflects the authentic speech patterns of the culture that gave rise to the stories. *The Butter Tree: Tales of Bruh Rabbit*, retold by Mary Lyons and illustrated by Mireille Vautier, and William J. Faulkner's retelling of *Brer Tiger and the Big Wind*, illustrated by Roberta Wilson, show that Brer Rabbit is just as sly and tricky as ever.

Teachers and librarians can help students recognize the patterns, or archetypes, in folktales if they provide exposure to a wide array of stories that exemplify the characteristic structure.

CONVENTIONS Literary devices called *conventions* are the cornerstones of folktales. One of the easiest conventions children recognize and adapt in their own writing is the story frame, such as the one that begins with "Once upon a time" and ends with "They lived happily ever after." Open-

ing variations such as "Long ago and far away," which are used by storytellers in some cultural groups, contribute to children's ability to generalize the patterns; seeing a different frame serve the same purpose shows the device's flexibility. Early in their literary education, children search for formulaic patterns in language, plots, and characters that they can identify.

The repeated use of the number three is another familiar convention. In addition to three main characters—three bears, three billy goats, three pigs—there are usually three events. "Goldilocks and the Three Bears" contains three bears, of course, but also three more sets of three: three bowls of porridge, three chairs, and three beds. Other folktales feature three tasks, three adventures, three magical objects, three trials, or three wishes. The number seven appears frequently, too, as in "Snow White and the Seven Dwarfs," "The Seven Ravens," and "The Seven Swans." Teaching Idea 5.3 offers ideas for exploring numbers in folklore.

Teaching Idea 5 ☆ 3

Have Fun with Numbers in Folklore

Numbers in folklore are believed to have mythical qualities. Folktales center on numbers from 1 to 12, although there are more stories dealing with numbers 3, 7, and 12 than there are stories about other numbers. With your class, search for folktales with a numbers theme. Categorize them by number. Make a comparison chart for folktales and numbers. Can you identify any common themes or trends?

Folktales and Folk Songs with Numbers

1 Puss in Boots

2 Jorinda and Joringel
   Perez and Martina

3 Three Wishes
   Three Little Pigs
   Three Billy Goats Gruff
   Goldilocks and the Three Bears

4 Bremen Town Musicians
   Four Gallant Sisters

5 Five Chinese Brothers

6 Six Foolish Fishermen

7 Seven Blind Mice
   Her Seven Brothers
   Seven at One Blow
   Snow White and the Seven Dwarfs

12 Twelve Dancing Princesses
    Twelve Days of Christmas

MOTIFS A *motif* is a recurring salient thematic element: the intentional repetition of a word, phrase, event, or idea that runs through a story as a unifying theme. Characters—gods, witches, fairies, noodleheads, or stepmothers—behave in stereotypic ways. Readers learn to predict that some characters will behave in certain ways. A representative human (such as a busybody or a country bumpkin) is used to stand for a trait or type.

A second kind of motif focuses on magical objects, spells, curses, or wishes as the center of the plot. Beans tossed carelessly out a window lead the way to a magical kingdom in "Jack and the Beanstalk." "The Magic Porridge Pot" and its variants hinge on a secret ritual. Sometimes the magical element is a spell or enchantment. Both Snow White and Sleeping Beauty are victims of a witch's evil curse and are put to sleep until a kiss from a handsome prince awakens them. In some stories, the evil spell causes a transformation; only love and kindness can return the frog, donkey, or beast to its former state. "The Frog Prince," "The Donkey Prince," "The Seven Ravens," "The Six Swans," "Jorinda and Joringel," and "Beauty and the Beast" are all transformation tales.

A third type of motif involves trickery, or outwitting someone else. A spider man is the trickster in African and Caribbean tales. Trickery and cunning also appear in French and Swedish folktales like "Stone Soup" and "Nail Soup." The wiliest trickster of all, Brer Rabbit, traveled in one form or another from Africa to Jamaica to America.

THEMES The *theme* in a folktale revolves around a topic of universal human concern. Time and time again, the struggle between good and evil is played out: Hate, fear, and greed contrast with love, security, and generosity. The themes are usually developed through stereotyped characters that personify one trait. For example, the bad fairy in "Sleeping Beauty," the witch in "Hansel and Gretel," and the stepmother in "Snow White" all represent evil. Each is destroyed while the virtuous characters prevail. Such themes are reassuring to young children.

In enchantment and transformation tales, the struggle between good and evil materializes as a contrast between surface appearances and deeper qualities of goodness. A beautiful princess sees the goodness of the prince hidden beneath the loathsome or laughable guise of a beast, frog, or donkey. In other stories, such as some versions of "Sleeping Beauty," the entire world lies under an evil spell, veiled and hidden from clear view until goodness triumphs.

Another theme, that of a quest, centers on the hero's search for happiness or lost identity, which he undertakes in order to restore harmony to life. The hero succeeds only after repeated trials, much suffering, and extended separation, and he often exhibits courage, gallantry, and sacrifice.

Variants of Folktales

Although the origins of folktales are clouded in prehistory, variants can be traced to many cultures.

Profile ☆ Shirley Climo

Courtesy of Houghton Mifflin

Shirley Climo was born in Cleveland, Ohio, to a mother who was a children's author herself. Her childhood was filled with stories her mother told her as well as with those she made up on her own. A visit to Cornwall inspired her first book, a collection of Cornish folklore called *Piskies, Spriggans and Other Magical Beings* (1981). Folklore and legends underlie much of Climo's work. She is best known for retelling the Cinderella story. *The Egyptian Cinderella* (1989), set in sixth-century Egypt, is about a Greek slave girl, Rhodopis, who lived at that time and married a pharaoh. *The Korean Cinderella* (1993) is about a girl who is helped by a frog, a bird, and a black ox. *Irish Cinderlad* (1996) rescues a princess from a dragon; in his haste to leave, he loses a boot. The princess sends a royal messenger to search for the owner of the boot. Climo also collected, retold, and annotated *Treasury of Princesses: Princess Tales from Around the World* (1996) and *A Serenade of Mermaids: Mermaid Tales from Around the World* (1997). *Atalanta's Race: A Greek Myth* (1995) and *Stolen Thunder: A Norse Myth* (1994) are also picture books based on myths. Climo retold *The Little Red Ant and the Great Big Crumb*, a Mexican tale based on a fable found in Spain and France. *Someone Saw a Spider: Spider Facts and Folktales* (1985) and *Cobweb Christmas* (P) are further demonstrations of her interest in folklore. Climo's interest in folklore enriches the world for all readers.

CINDERELLA Folklorist M. R. Cox, a pioneer in folklore research during the 1890s, uncovered the Cinderella motif in his book for adults, *Cinderella: Three Hundred and Forty-Five Variants*. In the foreword to the Cox collection, Andrew Lang, a Scottish scholar who lived from 1844 to 1912 and who was noted for his own collections of fairy tales, states, "The märchen [fairy tale] is a kaleidoscope: the incidents are the bits of coloured glass. Shaken, they fall into a variety of attractive forms; some forms are fitter than others, survive more powerfully, and are more widely spread" (1893, p. x).

A romantic rags-to-riches version of "Cinderella," based on Charles Perrault's story, has been illustrated by noted artists Marcia Brown, Susan Jeffers, and Errol Le Cain. In the German version by the Brothers Grimm, *Aschenputtel*, illustrated by Nonny Hogrogian, the story takes on a macabre tone. In order to make their feet fit into the tiny glass slipper, the sisters take drastic measures: One cuts off her toe, and the other cuts off her heel. In the end they are blinded while their mother dances to her death in iron shoes. Other versions include Appalachian, Chinese, Creole, Egyptian, English, Indonesian, Irish, Korean, Persian, Spanish American, and Vietnamese, as well as the Algonquin variant, *The Rough-Face Girl*, discussed earlier in this chapter.

SLEEPING BEAUTY In *Once Upon a Time: On the Nature of Fairy Tales*, Lüthi (1970), a notable folklorist, presents an insightful analysis of the many variants of "Sleeping

Trina Schart Hyman's art in **The Sleeping Beauty** *reveals that Briar Rose has a few prickly thorns.*

Beauty." Lüthi speaks of fairy tales as remnants of primal myths, playful descendants of an ancient, intuitive vision of life and the world. The story of Sleeping Beauty, who is mysteriously threatened and who suffers a sleep similar to death but is then awakened, parallels the story of death and resurrection. The awakening of the sleeping maiden can also represent the earth's awakening from winter to blossom anew when touched by the warmth of spring. Trina Schart Hyman interprets *The Sleeping Beauty* (P–I–A) through elegant, mysterious art and graceful text. "The Princess grew up so gracious, merry, beautiful, and kind that everyone who knew her could not help but love her. And because she was mischievous and clever as well, she was called Briar Rose."

Lüthi describes how Sleeping Beauty is more than an imaginatively stylized love story portraying a girl whose love breaks a spell. The princess is an image for the human spirit: The story portrays her natural gifts, talents, and personal strengths; it describes the fall and the redemption not just of one girl but of humankind. Sleeping Beauty's recovery symbolizes the human soul, which can be revived, healed, and redeemed despite suffering repeated setbacks. The fairy tale is a miniature universe that reflects the wisdom of the ages in an enchanting tale.

GOOD SISTER–BAD SISTER More than 900 versions of the "kind sister–unkind sister" or "bad sister–good sister" theme have been recorded. Charlotte Huck's *Toads and Diamonds* (P–I), illustrated by Anita Lobel, shows the younger Reneé walking a mile and a half twice a day to carry water for her stepmother and stepsister. Along the path, Reneé feeds breadcrumbs to a friendly rabbit and to a bird that flies to her shoulder. One day an old peasant woman sits near the spring and asks for a drink. When Reneé quenches the old woman's thirst, the woman says, "Because you are as kind as you are beautiful, I have a gift for you. For every word you speak, a flower or jewel will drop from your lips. And this will happen as long as there will be a need for it." The stepmother sends her other daughter to receive the same gift, but her behavior—and the gifts she receives—are dreadfully different. John Steptoe's *Mufaro's Beautiful Daughters* (P–I) and Robert D. San Souci's *Talking Eggs* (P–I) are variants on this theme. Teachers at primary, intermediate, and advanced grade levels find that students are fascinated by discovering variants to familiar tales. Students gain an understanding of folklore, culture, literary structures, and genre characteristics. We discuss working with variants later in this chapter.

RUMPELSTILTSKIN The story of the little man who, for a cruel fee, helps a poor girl spin straw or flax into skeins of gold is another well-loved tale. The best-known version, Grimm's *Rumpelstiltskin* (P), tells the story of a dwarf who demands her firstborn child as payment. *Tom Tit Tot* (P), retold by Evaline Ness, is a version from Suffolk, England, in

Leo and Diane Dillon illustrate an elegant edition of an ancient tale in **The Girl Who Spun Gold***.*

which an impet (dwarf) spins five skeins of gold from flax. In Devonshire and Cornwall, England, the devil knits stockings, jackets, and other clothing for the Squire, as recounted in *Duffy and the Devil* (P), retold by Harve Zemach. The character that corresponds to Rumpelstiltskin is called Trit-a-Trot in Ireland and Whuppity Stoorie in Scotland. Each version's cultural origins are reflected in the clothing, dialect, and settings. Virginia Hamilton uses a colloquial style to present a West Indian variant in *The Girl Who Spun Gold* (P–I). Leo and Diane Dillon illustrate the book in magnificent paintings made with acrylic paint on acetate and over-painted with gold paint. The embossed paintings appear on pages edged with gold leaf. The gold of the art conveys the importance of gold in the story.

JACK AND THE BEANSTALK "Jack and the Beanstalk" first appeared in Joseph Jacob's collection of English folktales. It has been illustrated by many contemporary artists. Lorinda B. Cauley's beanstalk is a lush green forest peopled with dour folks who sense danger and are heavy with foreboding. In contrast, Paul Galdone's characters are oafish, laughing bunglers who create a light-hearted story.

Many Americanized versions of Old World tales revolve around a boy named Jack and are therefore known as "Jack Tales." One of the most familiar is a variant of "Jack and the Beanstalk" known as "Jack's Bean Tree." It is found in Richard Chase's *Jack Tales* (I) and in *Jack and the Wonder Beans* (P–I) by James Still. Appalachian dialect permeates

these versions of the familiar tale. For example, the giant's refrain in *Jack and the Wonder Beans* is "Fee, fie, chew tobacco, I smell the toes of a tadwhacker."

Gail Haley's Appalachian retelling, *Jack and the Bean Tree* (P), is set in the context of a storyteller's tale. Family and neighbors gather round Grandmother Poppyseed, who gives a local flavor to her tales: A banty hen lays the golden eggs; the giant chants "Bein' he live or bein'/he dead,/I'll have his bones/To eat with my pones." Haley paints her bold, energetic illustrations on wood, and the brilliant colors reflect the intensities of light and shadow.

Mary Pope Osborne chose a girl to climb the beanstalk in *Kate and the Beanstalk* (P–I), illustrated by Giselle Potter. Kate outsmarts the giant and makes a fortune for herself and her mother. Raymond Briggs wrote a parody of the Jack Tales in *Jim and the Beanstalk* (P–I). The giant has grown old and has lost his appetite, his teeth, and his eyesight. Jim helps him get false teeth and glasses. Variants of this tale and others appear in the Booklist at the end of the chapter.

In summary, contemporary writers and artists breathe new life into ancient folktales. To choose among the many versions available, look first for authenticity in language and cultural integrity. Old tales shine when they reflect their oral origins through symbols, imagery, and vocabulary. Dialogue should sound natural; the melodious and rhythmic narrative should maintain the cultural richness of early retellings and should quickly involve the reader or listener in the action. Avoid simplified, controlled-vocabulary

Kate and the Beanstalk by Mary Pope Osborne is a magnificent version of an old story with a female hero.

versions that reduce the stories to little more than trite episodes.

Talented illustrators often choose folklore to showcase their art. They fill their work with intricate cultural details that may not be reflected in the language. Look for illustrations that complement the narrative accurately and that enrich the text with details of setting, character, and cultures. See Figure 5.1 for suggestions on selecting folklore.

FABLES

A *fable* is a brief tale that presents a clear and unambiguous moral. Fables make didactic comments on human nature using dramatic action to make the ideas memorable. They differ from other traditional literature in that the moral of the story is explicitly stated.

Many common sayings come from fables. "Better beans and bacon in peace than cakes and ale in fear" derives from *Town Mouse, Country Mouse*, illustrated by Jan Brett. "Slow and steady wins the race" is based on "The Tortoise and the Hare," retold and illustrated by Jerry Pinkney in *Aesop's*

Fables. The philosophy "Knowing in part may make a fine tale, but wisdom comes from seeing the whole" is illustrated in *Seven Blind Mice* by Ed Young.

Such injunctions, explicitly stated as morals, are taught by *allegory*. Animals or inanimate objects take on human traits in stories that clearly show the wisdom of the simple lessons. Folklorists therefore relate fables to beast tales—stories in which characters are animals with human traits—that were used for satiric purposes (in some cases they taught a moral). In the single-incident story typical of the fable, we are told not to be vain, not to be greedy, and not to lie.

Australian-born English folklore scholar Joseph Jacobs (1854–1916) traces the origins of fables to both Greece and India. Reputedly, a Greek slave named Aesop used fables for political purposes, and though some doubt that he ever lived, his name has been associated with fables since ancient times. Jean de la Fontaine, a seventeenth-century French poet, adapted many of Aesop's fables into verse form. Brian Wildsmith illustrated several of these: *The Lion and the Rat*, *The North Wind and the Sun*, and *The Rich Man and the Shoemaker* (all P).

The source of early collections from the East is the Indian "Panchatantra" (literally five "tantras," or books), known to English readers as the "Fables of Bidpai" and "Jataka Tales." The Jatakas are stories of the Buddha's prior lives, in which he took the form of various animals. Each story is intended to illustrate a moral principle.

Several collections of fables for younger children are available, but some educators question whether primary-grade children understand the subtle abstractions. Because fables are short and are told in simple language, some teachers mistakenly give fables to children who are too young to comprehend or fully appreciate them. Researcher Arlene Pillar (1983) found that 7-year-olds often missed the point of widely used fables. Since fables are constructed within the oblique perspective of satire, allegory, and symbolism, their intent may elude young children's literal understanding. Examples of individual and collected fables appear in the Booklist at the end of the chapter.

MYTHOLOGY As folktales, fables, songs, and legends developed, the special group of stories we call myths developed as humans sought to interpret both natural phenomena and human behavior. Myths express the belief of ancient cultures and portray visions of destiny. Unlike other stories, myths relate to each other; taken together, they build a picture of an imaginative world (Frye, 1970).

The literary value of myths lies in their exciting plots, well-developed characters, heroic actions, challenging situations, and deep emotions. They are compelling stories of love, carnage, revenge, and mystery. At the same time, they transmit ancient values, symbols, customs, art, law, and language. Isaac Asimov explores the roots of hundreds of mythic images in *Words from the Myths* (I), a handy refer-

Jerry Pinkney gives a great gift to the field of literature through his art in **Aesop's Fables**.

ence for students interested in etymology. Penelope Prod-dow compiled *Art Tells a Story: Greek and Roman Myths* (I–A), a collection of myths accompanied by photographs of the artwork they inspired.

In myths, as in all folklore, a great deal depends upon the telling. Much also depends on the illustrating, and myths offer artists an excellent opportunity for presenting their own interpretation of some elemental stories.

Creation myths are popular and are suitable for students in elementary, middle, and junior high school. They describe the origin of the earth and the phenomena that affect it. They tell how the earth began and why the seasons change. Some books are collections of creation myths from around the world, while others focus on myths from one culture. Jacqueline Morley collected 11 creation myths in *Egyptian Myths* (I), illustrated by Giovanni Caselli. Her graceful retellings focus on the struggle between good and evil, the creation of the world, and the gods and humans.

Pourquoi *Stories*

The simplest myths are *pourquoi* stories, from the French word for "why." They tell how the earth began and why the seasons change, how animals got their colors, and so on.

Why the Sky Is Far Away: A Nigerian Folktale by Mary-Joan Gerson, illustrated by Carla Golembe, and *Why Mosquitoes Buzz in People's Ears* (P) by Verna Aardema, illustrated by Leo and Diane Dillon, are two execcellent examples. Pierre Grimal (1965) notes in his comprehensive *Larousse World Mythology* (I–A) that we humans lose our fear of things we can name and explain:

> Given a universe full of uncertainties and mysteries, the myth intervenes to introduce the human element: clouds in the sky, sunlight, storms at sea, all extra-human factors such as these lose much of their power to terrify as soon as they are given the sensibility, intentions, and motivations that every individual experiences daily. (p. 9)

Penelope Farmer, translator of many myths, describes their purpose this way:

> Myths have seemed to me to point quite distinctly—yet without ever directly expressing it—to some kind of unity behind creation, not a static unity, but a forever shifting breathing one. . . . The acquisition by man of life or food or fire has to be paid for by the acceptance of death—the message is everywhere, quite unmistakable. To live is to die; to die is to live. (1979, p. 4)

This great archetypal theme appears again and again throughout all cultures. Children are familiar with the rebirth of flowers and trees in the spring. Most of them have buried a seed in the ground and watched for it to sprout. In images and symbols, mythic themes reappear under many guises, and children can recognize them through their study of myth.

Literature throughout the ages echoes the themes of the ancient myths. Frye traces the origins of all literature back to one central story: how man once lived in a golden age or a garden of Eden or the Hesperides, or a happy island kingdom in the Atlantic, how that world was lost, and how we some day may be able to get it back again (1970, pp. 53 and 57). More *pourquoi* tales are listed in the Booklist at the end of the chapter.

Greek and Roman Mythology

Myths are only tenuously related to historical fact and geographical location. However, they played an important role in the lives of the ancients, especially in the art, music, and architecture and culture of ancient Greece.

The ancient Greeks believed that gods and goddesses controlled the universe. Zeus was the most powerful god. He controlled the weather—the lightning and thunder—and ruled over all the other gods who lived on Mount Olympus and the mortals who lived around it. Figure 5.3 lists the Greek gods and goddesses, the functions and powers attributed to them, and the names later given to them by the Romans, who adopted the Greek deities as their own.

Greek myths are replete with wondrous monsters. Children are fascinated by these half-human, half-beast creatures who frightened early people and wreaked havoc on their lands. Just as young children delight in tales of witches and giants, older students, too, love to read about Medusa, who grew hissing snakes on her head instead of hair, Cerberus, the huge three-headed dog, and the horrible one-eyed Cyclops.

Stories of individual heroes tell of great adventures, tests, victories, and losses. They feature relationships between gods and mortals and show how life must be lived with morality and conscience. Countless myths focus on the love between a god or goddess and a mortal, like that between Psyche and Cupid (named Eros by the Greeks, but commonly known today by his Roman name). Psyche, a mortal, incurs the wrath of Venus (Aphrodite) because Psyche is declared more beautiful. In a jealous rage, Venus summons her son Cupid to destroy Psyche by causing her to fall in love with a monster. Instead of obeying his mother's orders, Cupid himself falls in love with Psyche. Students familiar with this myth recognize its presence in many modern romances.

Figure 5 ✰ 3

Greek and Roman Gods

Greek Name	Title	Roman Name
Aphrodite	Goddess of love and beauty	Venus
Apollo	God of the sunlight, music, prophecy, and poetry	Apollo
Ares	God of war	Mars
Artemis	Goddess of the hunt	Diana
Athena	Goddess of wisdom	Minerva
Demeter	Goddess of the harvest	Ceres
Dionysus	God of wine	Bacchus
Eos	Goddess of the dawn	Aurora
Eros	God of love	Cupid
Hades	God of the underworld	Pluto
Hecate	Goddess of the dark and magic	Trivia
Hephaestus	God of fire/building	Vulcan
Hera	Goddess of marriage	Juno
Hermes	Messenger of the gods	Mercury
Hestia	Goddess of hearth and home	Vesta
Kronos	God of time	Saturn
Nike	Goddess of victory	Victory
Persephone	Goddess of spring	Prosperine
Poseidon	Lord of the sea	Neptune
Selene	Goddess of the moon	Luna
Zeus	King of the gods, Lord of the sky	Jupiter

In *Dateline: Troy* (I–A) Paul Fleischman shows that the ancient tabloids are as fresh as today's news. Fleischman sets the ancient myths and today's headlines side by side—they are strikingly similar!

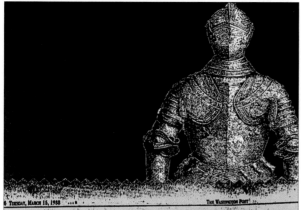

In **Dateline: Troy,** *Paul Fleischman shows that universal issues of the ancient past are still alive and appear in today's newspapers. His strategy makes the connection between the ancient story of Achilles and the armor being developed by the Pentagon.*

The first book to be printed in English appeared in 1475 and recounted the Trojan War. In 1873 the site of Troy was discovered in western Turkey, facing Greece across the Aegean Sea. The city long thought mythical was real. Listeners and readers had always found real human nature in what had transpired there. Envy-maddened Ajax, love-struck Paris, crafty Odysseus, and all the others have walked the earth in every age and place. They live among us today. Though their tale comes from the distant Bronze Age, it's as current as this morning's headlines. The Trojan War is still being fought. Simply open a newspaper. . . . (pp. 8–9)

Superior retellings of the Greek myths include Shirley Climo's *Atalanta's Race: A Greek Myth* (I–A), illustrated by Alexander Koshkin. Atalanta's extraordinary skill in running keeps any man from beating her until Aphrodite gives Melanion three golden apples to help him win the race as well as Atalanta's hand in marriage. In *Olympians: Great Gods and Goddesses of Ancient Greece* (I–A) Leonard Everett Fisher presents handsome portraits and describes the origins and characteristics of the deities. Philip Neil brings *King*

Midas to life in a book illustrated by Isabelle Brent, and Jane Yolen's *Wings* (I–A) tells the story of Daedalus, a mortal who is exiled to the island of Crete. He builds a great maze to hold the Minotaur but reveals the maze's secret to a Greek prince (1991 Harcourt). In *Wings* (P–I-A) Christopher Myers tells the modern story of Ikarus Jackson, who could fly but who was finally accepted even though he was different.

Most myths are seldom fully appreciated until the later years of elementary school. Even then, they may not be embraced by all students. The stories of King Midas, Pandora's Box, and Jason and the Golden Fleece are, however, basic material for students' literary education. Myths from many cultures appear in the Booklist at the end of the chapter.

Norse Mythology

Equally rich stories exist among other cultures, most notably the Vikings. The tales that grew from the cold, rugged climate of northern Europe burn with man's passionate struggle against the cruelty of nature and the powerful gods and monsters who ruled the harsh land.

Christopher Myers creates a modern story with ancient roots in **Wings.**

In *Favorite Norse Myths* (I–A) Mary Pope Osborne explains how the universe began, according to the creation story of Norway. She quotes from the *Poetic Edda*, the oldest written source of Norse mythology. In it, Odin, the Norse war god, trades an eye for all the world's wisdom. Thor, god of thunder, defeats a vicious giant with a hammer, and mischief-maker Loki creates trouble wherever he goes. Padraic Colum, an Irish poet and master storyteller, first published *The Children of Odin: The Book of Northern Myths* (I) in 1920; it remains available today.

Teaching Idea 5 ✳ 4

Search for Mythical Allusions

Students who read widely recognize frequently used allusions (references to a literary figure, event, or object) drawn from mythology. Classical allusions—such as an Achilles' heel, Pandora's box, the Midas touch, the Trojan horse, and the face that launched a thousand ships—appear in our language, literature, and culture; they are part of our common vocabulary. A winged horse (Pegasus) appears on gas station signs, Mercury delivers flowers, Vulcan repairs tires, and many of us wear our Nike shoes to work or play every day.

The English language reflects origins in Greek, Roman, and Norse myths: *erotic* comes from Eros, *titanic* comes from the Titans, and *cereal* comes from Ceres. The days of the week derive from myths: Sunday = Sun-day; Monday = Moon-day; Tuesday = Tiu's-day; Wednesday = Odin's-day; Thursday = Thor's-day; Friday = Freya's-day; Saturday = Saturn's-day. In *Words from the Myths*, Isaac Asimov presents many words that have their origins in myths. To encourage students to learn more about allusions:

1. Have students notice words, symbols, and allusions to myths as they read newspapers, magazines, and books, and as they watch television.
2. Instruct them to keep a list of words and mythological referents.
3. Have them find out who Odysseus, Medea, Achilles, Antigone, Oedipus, and Hector are and why their names are important to us today.
4. Have the class use the information they've gathered to prepare a quiz or a game similar to Trivial Pursuit.

Mythology from Other Cultures

Although Greek, Roman, and Norse mythology have traditionally been the most studied and the most readily available, today we have access to books of mythology from many cultures. Mythology from Africa and the Orient has taken its place alongside European stories, and hauntingly beautiful versions of Native American and Inuit tales are being published with increasing frequency.

Isaac Olaleye describes a contest on a rainfield in Africa in *In the Rainfield: Who Is the Greatest?* illustrated by Ann Grifalconi. Wind, fire, and rain are portrayed as regal Africans compete to determine who is the greatest in this *pourquoi* tale. Richard Lewis retells the Aztec myth that explains how music came to earth in *All of You Was Singing* (I–A), a poetic version that is infused with his own imagination. Ed Young's illustrations combine Lewis's images, Aztec cultural motifs, and his own vision. The result is a stunningly beautiful book that echoes the splendor of creation. Myths from non-European cultures are listed in the Booklist at the end of the chapter.

HERO TALES

Epics, also known as hero tales, are a specific type of myth that focuses on the courageous deeds of mortals in their struggles against each other or against gods and monsters. The heroes reveal universal human emotions and embody the eternal contest between good and evil. Hero tales contribute to an appreciation of world history and literature, to an understanding of national ideals of behavior, and to the knowledge of valor and nobility of humankind.

Epics are sometimes written in verse and consist of a cycle of tales that center on a legendary hero. Some well-known epics include King Arthur, Robin Hood, and the account of the Trojan War retold in Homer's *Iliad* and *Odyssey*. Language is often key in setting the drama of the tales, as is evident from the first line of Robert Sabuda's *Arthur and the Sword* (I): "Long ago in a time of great darkness, a time without a king, there lived a fair boy called Arthur." The elegant language foretells the majesty in the story.

Hero tales that are not technically epics are often referred to as *legends*. Legendary heroes may be real or imaginary people. Even if they have some factual basis, they are often so fanciful that it becomes difficult to tell where fact stops and imagination takes over. Many storytellers elaborated on reports of their hero's exploits until the stories became full-blown legends that interwove fact and fiction and contained a grain of truth at their core. Davy Crockett, Johnny Appleseed, and Daniel Boone were real people, but their stories have made them larger than life.

Arthur lifts his sword to regain England's power and glory in Robert Sabuda's **Arthur and the Sword.**

Legends also grow around places and phenomena. Barbara Esbensen's poem about the aurora borealis, ***The Night Rainbow*** (P), presents images from many cultures, including white geese, dancers, whales, and battles. Esbensen also provides scientific explanations as well as information about the legends in this celebration of the northern lights.

THE BIBLE AS LITERATURE

The Bible, one of the earliest forms of Western cultural literature, contains myths, legends, fables, parables, short stories, essays, lyrics, epistles, sermons, orations, proverbs, history, biography, prophecy, and drama. Teachers and librarians distinguish between using Bible stories to teach religious doctrine and using them in a secular context to explore literary content.

The Bible is still the best-selling book in the world. It is printed in every language and is known by all peoples. Northrop Frye discusses its basic value (1964):

> If we don't know the Bible and the central stories of Greek and Roman literature, we can still read

books and see plays, but our knowledge of literature can't grow, just as our knowledge of mathematics can't grow if we don't learn the multiplication table. (1964, p. 70)

One approach amenable to public schools and libraries is to examine how a contemporary author retells a biblical story. How does the author interpret the old tale? How is the character presented? How is the period portrayed? How is the theme realized? Since the source of the tale is the Bible itself, early versions of each story can be compared.

Some sections of the Bible reflect the oral tradition more dramatically than others: The use of lyric poetic forms, repetition, and measured metric schemes were aids to memory before the stories were written down. Although the verses may not rhyme in English, they probably did in Hebrew; although the metric scheme may vary in English, it was measured and pronounced in Hebrew, making it easier to remember.

Recent versions of Bible stories include Katherine Paterson's ***The Angel & the Donkey***, illustrated by Alexander Koshkin, Diane Wolkstein's ***Esther's Story***, illustrated by Juan Wijngaard, and Tomie dePaola's ***The Legend of the***

Brian Wildsmith creates a scene of ancient beauty in **A Christmas Story.**

Poinsetta (P). Noah's Ark stories still fascinate us today, as in Patricia Gauch's musical retelling, *Noah* (P–I), illustrated by Jonathan Green. Green used the sounds, songs, and models from his Hesbah Baptist Church in Gardens Corners, South Carolina, as inspiration.

FOLK SONGS AND WORK SONGS

Songs serve as powerful vehicles for both shaping and preserving our cultural heritage. Ballads and folk songs inform and unify people. Work songs, often developed as a diversion from boring work, capture the rhythm and spirit of the labor in which their creators were engaged. The songs sing of the values and lifestyles of the people who laid the railroads, dug the tunnels and canals, sailed the ships, and toted the bales.

Folklorist Benjamin A. Botkin observed in *A Treasury of American Folklore* that we sing folk songs for self-gratification, power, or freedom (1944, pp. 818–819). We also sing songs to lighten our labor, fill our leisure time, record events, and voice praise or protest. Civil rights marchers led by Martin Luther King, Jr., were united by the experience of singing "We Shall Overcome" together.

We use songs to teach young children to count or to say the ABCs and, most often, to soothe them and sing them to sleep. Joyce Carol Thomas collected *Hush Songs: African American Lullabies*, illustrated by Brenda Joysmith. These songs have worked their sleepy-time magic for generations. Jane Hart compiled 125 songs in her splendid *Singing Bee! A Collection of Favorite Children's Songs* (P–I), which is beautifully illustrated by Anita Lobel. She augments the nursery rhymes, lullabies, finger plays, cumulative, holiday, and activity songs with piano accompaniments and guitar chords. Lobel uses historical settings and eighteenth-century garb to illustrate the traditional songs, and creates stage production settings around others.

Children celebrate their own culture or learn about others through song; they can even learn a second language through song. The best published versions include guitar or piano scores, historical notes, and appropriate illustrations that coordinate with the text. Lulu Delacre selected and illustrated *Arroz Con Leche: Popular Songs and Rhymes from Latin America* (P), with English lyrics by Elena Paz and musical arrangements by Ana-Maria Rosada. Jose-Luis Orozco selected, arranged, and translated *De Colores and Other Latin-American Folk Songs for Children* (P), illustrated by Elisa Kleven. Gary Chalk chose humorous illustrations depicting events of the American Revolution to accompany the original verses of "Yankee Doodle" in *Yankee Doodle*. Other authors of folk songs include Robert Quackenbush, Aliki, Glen Rounds, John Langstaff, and Peter Spier.

Using Folklore in the Classroom

Because traditional literature is a foundation for future literary understanding, it is critical that children spend time reading from the vast body of folklore. We shortchange children if we deny them the background information necessary for understanding the countless references to folklore in contemporary books and society. Children who do not comprehend the significance of the wolf in folklore will not understand the meaning of the wolf-shaped bush in Anthony Browne's *Piggybook* (P–I). They will not know why their classmates say "uh-oh" when they discover that the baby-sitter in Mary Rayner's *Mr. and Mrs. Pig's Evening Out* (P) turns out to be a wolf. And they will not appreciate the humor of folktale parodies, like Jon Scieszka's *The True Story of the Three Little Pigs* (P–I).

Children should be aware that common phrases like "sour grapes" and "slow and steady wins the race" come from *Aesop's Fables*, and that "Pandora's box" and "the Midas touch" originated in mythology. See Rosemary Wells's *Max and Ruby's Midas: Another Greek Myth* for a variation on a well-known theme.

Good teachers give children opportunities to *discover* recurring patterns; they do not *tell* them what to recognize. Teachers who facilitate students' discovery of archetypes find that patterns become the structural framework for viewing all literature as one story. The most effective approach is to immerse students in traditional stories until they begin to recognize similarities, distinguish patterns, and make predictions. Children who have heard many folktales will tell you that they begin "once upon a time" and end "they lived happily ever after" and that the good people win and the youngest son gets the princess. These responses show that children recognize the motifs, themes, and story conventions of folklore. Teaching Idea 5.5 gives suggestions for helping children to identify folkloric style.

Folklore provides an opportunity for increasing multicultural understanding; it reflects the values, hopes, fears, and beliefs of many cultures. By recognizing recurring themes in folklore from around the world, we can begin to build a bridge of understanding among all people. The oral origins of folklore make it a wonderful resource for language development. Dramatic readings or performances offer one venue for creativity. Children who are familiar with folklore learn to use similar patterns and conventions in their own writing, borrowing and exploring folkloric frameworks for their own personal stories.

Teaching Idea 5 ☆ 5

Identify Folkloric Style

Contemporary stories are often written in a folkloric style: They contain elements, themes, or recurring patterns found in folklore. Read aloud and discuss stories containing folklore elements, motifs, or allusions to illustrate the idea. Encourage book discussion groups to continue the search for transformations, magic objects, wishes, trickery, and other folklore conventions. Do the following to help students learn about folkloric style:

❋ Collect stories written in folklore style.

❋ Discuss folklore elements. What characteristics suggest that a work is folklore?

❋ Have students work in groups to discover folklore elements.

❋ Discuss the devices, allusions, and patterns found. Make a list of commonly used folklore elements.

❋ Encourage students to use the elements in stories they write.

Consult the books listed below to get started.

Arnold, Caroline, *The Terrible Hodag*

Bang, Molly, *Dawn*

——, *The Paper Crane*

Della Chiesa, Carol, *Adventures of Pinocchio*

French, Fiona, *Anancy and Mr. Dry-Bone*

Gannett, Ruth, *My Father's Dragon*

Grant, Joan, *The Monster That Grew Small*

Gregory, Philippa, *Florizella and the Wolves*

Gregory, Valiska, *Through the Mickle Woods*

Gwynne, Fred, *Pondlarker*

Kimmel, Eric, *Bernal and Florinda: A Spanish Tale*

Mayer, Marianna, *The Prince and the Princess: A Bohemian Fairy Tale*

Melmed, Laura Krauss, *Rainbabies*

Morris, Winifred, *The Magic Leaf*

Paterson, Katherine, *King's Equal*

Wisniewski, David, *The Warrior and the Wise Man*

Summary

Folklore began as stories and poems told across the generations, as people sought to explain natural phenomena and transmit cultural values. Folklore helps us to understand ourselves and people from other cultures.

Each type of folklore has its own characteristics. Rhythmic Mother Goose tales and nursery rhymes delight young children. Folktales—which include fairy tales, talking animal stories, noodlehead tales, cumulative tales, and tall tales—have universal themes and motifs and appear in different guises around the world. Fables incorporate explicit moral statements that are intended to guide behavior. Myths explain the origins of the world, natural phenomena, and human behavior. Hero tales reveal cultural beliefs and values; the Bible contains many myths, legends, and parables that add depth to literary knowledge. Folk songs reveal the values and circumstances of those who first sang them.

Teachers in all grades recognize that folklore is a valuable resource for developing language, learning about literature, and learning about other cultures. As it did in the past, folklore today continues to educate and entertain.

In the May/June 1997 issue of *The Horn Book Magazine* Barbara Bader writes about one reteller's quest for authenticity in " 'They Shall Not Wither': John Bierhorst's Quiet Crusade for Native American Literature." Bader discusses Bierhorst's impeccable scholarship and laments the lack of popular recognition of his work. Often, people from one culture are unsure about judging the authenticity of folklore from another culture, especially when the reteller is a cultural outsider also. After reading Bader's article, read some of Bierhorst's retellings as examples of carefully reconstructed tales from various Native American cultures.

Booklist

Folklore from Around the World

NORTH, SOUTH, AND CENTRAL AMERICA

Aardema, Verna, *Borreguita and the Coyote: A Tale from Ayutla, Mexico* (P–I)

Ada, Alma Flor, *Mediopollito/Half Chicken* (P–I)

_____, *Three Golden Oranges* (P–I)

Anaya, Rudolfo, *My Land Sings: Stories from the Rio Grande* (I)

Bierhorst, John, *The People with Five Fingers: A Native Californian Creation Tale* (P–I)

Bruchac, Joseph, *Between Earth & Sky: Legends of Native American Sacred Places* (P–I)

_____, *The Boy Who Lived with the Bears and Other Iroquois Stories* (I)

_____, *Gluskabe and the Four Wishes* (P–I)

_____, *The Story of the Milky Way: A Cherokee Tale* (P–I)

Brusca, Maria Cristina, and Tona Wilson, *When Jaguars Ate the Moon: And Other Stories About Animals and Plants of the Americas* (P–I)

Bryan, Ashley, *The Cat's Purr* (P–I)

_____, *Turtle Knows Your Name* (P–I)

Duncan, Lois, *The Magic of Spider* (P–I)

Gershator, Phillis, *Tukama Tootles the Flute: A Tale from the Antilles* (P–I)

Gerson, Mary-Joan, *People of Corn: A Mayan Story* (P–I)

Goble, Paul, *Adopted by the Eagles: A Plains Indian Story of Friendship and Treachery* (P–I)

_____, *Crow Chief: A Plains Indian Story* (P–I)

_____, *Lost Children: The Boys Who Were Neglected* (I)

Hamilton, Virginia, *Her Stories: African American Folktales, Fairy Tales, and True Tales* (I–A)

_____, *When Birds Could Talk and Bats Could Sing* (I)

Hausman, Gerald, *Eagle Boy: A Traditional Navajo Legend* (P–I)

Hooks, William, *Moss Gown* (P–I)

Hunter, C. W., *The Green Gourd: A North Carolina Folktale* (P)

Jaffe, Nina, *The Golden Flower: A Taino Myth from Puerto Rico* (P)

Kimmel, Eric A., *The Two Mountains: An Aztec Legend* (P–I)

Lester, Julius, *John Henry* (P–I)

Lyons, Mary E., *The Butter Tree: Tales of Bruh Rabbit* (I)

Martin, Rafe, *The Rough-Face Girl* (P)

McDermott, Gerald, *Arrow to the Sun* (P–I)

_____, *Raven: A Trickster Tale from the Pacific Northwest* (P)

Oughton Jerrie, *How the Stars Fell into the Sky: A Navajo Legend* (P–I)

_____, *Magic Weaver of Rugs: A Tale of the Navajo* (P)

Pitcher, Caroline, *Mariana and the Merchild: A Folk Tale from Chile* (P–I)

Pohrt, Tom, *Coyote Goes Walking* (P–I)

Rockwell, Anne, *The Boy Who Wouldn't Obey: A Mayan Legend* (P–I)

Rodanas, Kristina, *Dance of the Sacred Circle: A Native American Tale* (I)

_____, *Dragonfly's Tale* (P)

Ross, Gayle, *How Turtle's Back Was Cracked: A Traditional Cherokee Tale* (P–I)

San Souci, Robert D., *The Faithful Friend* (P–I)

_____, *Six Foolish Fishermen* (P–I)

_____, *Sukey and the Mermaid* (P)

_____, *The Talking Eggs* (P–I)

Sierra, Judy, *Wiley and the Hairy Man* (P–I)

Stevens, Jane, *Old Bag of Bones: A Coyote Tale* (P–I)

Swamp, Chief Jake, *Giving Thanks: A Native American Good Morning Message* (P–I)

Van Laan, Nancy, *In a Circle Long Ago: A Treasury of Native Lore from North America* (I–A)

EUROPE, AFRICA, AND THE MIDDLE EAST

Aardema, Verna, *The Lonely Lioness and the Ostrich Chicks* (P)

_____, *Misoso: Once Upon a Time: Tales from Africa* (P–I)

_____, *Why Mosquitoes Buzz in People's Ears: A West African Tale* (P–I)

Blades, Ann, *Wolf and the Seven Little Kids* (P–I)

Bryan, Ashley, *Lion and the Ostrich Chicks* (I)

Cauley, Lorinda Bryan, *The Pancake Boy: An Old Norwegian Folk Tale* (P)

Climo, Shirley, *The Egyptian Cinderella* (P)

Cooper, Susan, *Tam Lin* (P–I)

dePaola, Tomie, *Tony's Bread* (P)

Gerson, Mary-Joan, *Why the Sky Is Far Away: A Nigerian Folktale* (N–P)

Greene, Ellin, *The Little Golden Lamb* (P–I)

Gregor, C. Shana, *Cry of the Benu Bird: An Egyptian Creation Story* (P–I)

Grifalconi, Ann, *The Village of Round and Square Houses* (P)

Haley, Gail E., *A Story, A Story* (P–I)

Hutton, Warwick, *The Trojan Horse* (P–I)

Kimmel, Eric A., *The Adventures of Hershel of Ostropol* (I)

_____, *Count Silvernose: A Story from Italy* (P–I)

McDermott, Gerald, *The Magic Tree: A Tale from the Congo* (P)

_____, *Tim O'Toole and the Wee Folk* (P)

McVitty, Walter, *Ali Baba and the Forty Thieves* (I–A)

Medearis, Angela Shelf, *Too Much Talk* (P)

Mollel, Tololwa M., *Subira Subira* (P–I)

Morley, Jacqueline, *Egyptian Myths* (I–A)

Olson, Arielle North, *Noah's Cats and the Devil's Fire* (P)

Onyefulu, Obi, *Chinye: A West African Folk Tale* (P–I)

Perrault, Charles, *Cinderella, Puss in Boots, and Other Favorite Tales* (P–I)

Philip, Neil, *Celtic Fairy Tales* (I–A)

Rayevsky, Inna, *The Talking Tree: An Old Italian Tale* (I)

Sanfield, Steve, *Strudel, Strudel, Strudel* (P–I)

Shute, Linda, *Clever Tom and the Leprechaun* (P–I)

Sierra, Judy, *The Beautiful Butterfly: A Folktale from Spain* (P–I)

Souhami, Jessica, *The Leopard's Drum: An Asante Tale from West Africa* (P)

Steptoe, John, *Mufaro's Beautiful Daughters: An African Tale* (P–I)

Williams, Sheron, *And in the Beginning* (P)

Wisniewski, David, *Elfwyn's Saga* (I)

Yolen, Jane, *Tam Lin* (I)

WESTERN ASIA

Bider, Djemma, *A Drop of Honey: An Armenian Fable* (I)

Brett, Jan, *The Mitten: A Ukrainian Folktale* (P)

Demi, *Firebird* (P–I)

Ginsburg, Mirra, *Good Morning, Chick* (P)

Hastings, Selina, *The Firebird* (P–I)

Hodges, Margaret, *The Little Humpbacked Horse: A Russian Tale Retold* (P)

Hogrogian, Nonny, *The Contest*, (P)

_____, *One Fine Day*, (P)

Hort, Lenny, *The Fool and The Fish* (I)

Kismaric, Carole, *The Rumor of Pavel Paali: A Ukrainian Folktale* (I–A)

Ransome, Arthur, *The Fool of the World and the Flying Ship: A Russian Tale* (P–I)

Sherman, Josepha, *Vassilisa the Wise: A Tale of Medieval Russia* (I)

Tresselt, Alvin R., *The Mitten: An Old Ukranian Folktale* (P)

Winthrop, Elizabeth, *Vasilissa the Beautiful: A Russian Folktale* (P–I)

THE FAR EAST

Climo, Shirley, *The Korean Cinderella* (P–I)

Demi, *The Empty Pot* (P)

_____, *The Magic Boat* (P–I)

Ginsburg, Mirra, *The Chinese Mirror* (P–I)

Greene, Ellin, *Ling-Li and the Phoenix Fairy: A Chinese Folktale* (P–I)

Heyer, Marilee, *Weaving of a Dream: A Chinese Folktale* (I)

Ho, Minfong, and Saphan Ros, *The Two Brothers* (P–I)

Ishii, Momoko, *The Tongue-Cut Sparrow*, translated by Katherine Paterson (I)

Johnston, Tony, *The Badger and the Magic Fan* (I)

Kajikawa, Kimiko, *Yoshi's Feast* (P–I)

McDermott, Gerald, *The Stonecutter: A Japanese Folktale* (P)

Paterson, Katherine, *The Tale of the Mandarin Ducks* (P–I)

Quayle, Eric, *The Shining Princess and Other Japanese Legends* (I)

Souhami, Jessica, *No Dinner! The Story of the Old Woman and the Pumpkin* (P–I)

Yacowitz, Caryn, *The Jade Stone: A Chinese Folktale* (I)

Yep, Laurence, *Tongues of Jade* (I–A)

Yolen, Jane, *The Emperor and the Kite* (I)

Young, Ed, *Seven Blind Mice* (P)

Mother Goose and Nursery Rhymes

Conover, Chris, *Mother Goose and the Sly Fox* (N–P)

Cooney, Barbara, *Chanticleer and the Fox* (N–P)

Craig, Helen, *I See the Moon, and the Moon Sees Me* (N–P)

dePaola, Tomie, *Tomie dePaola's Favorite Nursery Tales* (N–P)

_____, *Tomie dePaola's Mother Goose* (N–P)

Downes, Belinda, *A Stitch in Rhyme: A Nursery Rhyme Sampler with Embroidered Illustrations* (N–P)

Dyer, Jane, *Animal Crackers: A Delectable Collection of Pictures, Poems, and Lullabies for the Very Young* (N–P)

Edens, Cooper, *The Glorious Mother Goose* (N–P)

Gammell, Stephen, *Once upon MacDonald's Farm* (N–P)

Larrick, Nancy, *Songs from Mother Goose* (N–P)

Lobel, Arnold, *Random House Book of Mother Goose* (N–P)

Lodge, Bernard, *There Was an Old Woman Who Lived in a Glove* (N–P)

Marcus, Leonard, and Amy Schwartz, *Mother Goose's Little Misfortunes* (N–P)

Marshall, James, *James Marshall's Mother Goose* (N–P)

_____, *Old Mother Hubbard and Her Wonderful Dog* (N–P)

Mother Goose, *The Real Mother Goose* (N–P)

Opie, Iona, *Here Comes Mother Goose* (N–P)

_____, *My Very First Mother Goose* (N–P)

_____, *Tail Feathers from Mother Goose: The Opie Rhyme Book* (N–P–I–A)

Opie, Iona, and Peter Opie, *The Oxford Dictionary of Nursery Rhymes* (N–P–I–A)

Polacco, Patricia, *Babushka's Mother Goose* (N–P)

Potter, Beatrix, *Beatrix Potter's Nursery Rhyme Book* (N–P)

Sierra, Judy, *Nursery Tales Around the World* (N–P)

Slier, Debby, *The Real Mother Goose: Book of American Rhymes* (N–P)

Spier, Peter, *To Market! To Market!* (N–P)

Sutherland, Zena, *The Orchard Book of Nursery Rhymes* (N–P)

Watson, Wendy, *Father Fox's Pennyrhymes* (N–P)

_____, *Wendy Watson's Mother Goose* (N–P)

Yolen, Jane, *Jane Yolen's Mother Goose Songbook* (N–P)

Folktales of All Types from Around the World

FAIRY TALES

Grimm, Jacob, and Wilhelm Grimm, *Hansel and Gretel,* translated by Elizabeth Crawford, illustrated by Lisbeth Zwerger (N–P)

_____, *Rapunzel*, adapted by Barbara Rogasky (N–P)

_____, *Rumpelstiltskin* (N–P), retold by Paul O. Zelinsky

_____, *The Shoemaker and the Elves*, translated by Wayne Andrews (N–P)

_____, *Snow White and the Seven Dwarfs*, translated by Randall Jarrell (N–P)

Ness, Evaline, *Tom Tit Tot* (N–P)

Perrault, Charles, *Beauty and the Beast*, adapted by Nancy Willard (N–P–I)

TALKING ANIMALS

Asbjornsen, Peter C., and Jorgen Moe, *The Three Billy Goats Gruff* (N–P)

Galdone, Paul, *The Three Little Pigs* (N–P)

Grimm, Jacob, and Wilhelm Grimm, *The Bremen Town Musicians*, retold and illustrated by Ilse Plume (N–P)

Perrault, Charles, *Puss in Boots* (N–P)

Stevens, Janet, *The Three Billy Goats Gruff* (N–P)

NOODLEHEAD STORIES, SIMPLETON STORIES, AND DROLL TALES

Asbjornsen, Peter C., and Jorgen Moe, *The Squire's Bride* (N–P-I)

Cole, Joanna, *It's Too Noisy* (N–P-I)

Greene, Ellin, *The Little Golden Lamb* (N–P-I)

Hague, Kathleen, and Michael Hague, *The Man Who Kept House* (N–P-I)

Kellogg, Steven, *The Three Sillies* (N–P-I)

Lurie, Alison, *Clever Gretchen & Other Forgotten Folktales* (N–P-I)

McDermott, Dennis, *The Golden Goose* (N–P-I)

San Souci, Robert D., *Six Foolish Fisherman* (N–P-I)

Shulevitz, Uri, *The Golden Goose* (N–P-I)

Singer, Isaac Bashevis, *Mazel and Shlimazel, or The Milk of a Lioness* (N–P-I)

CUMULATIVE TALES

Aardema, Verna, *Bringing the Rain to Kapiti Plain: A Nandi Tale* (N–P)

Asbjornsen, Peter C., and Jorgen Moe, *The Runaway Pancake* (N–P)

Butler, Stephen, *Henny Penny* (N–P)

Galdone, Paul, *The Gingerbread Boy* (N–P)

Hogrogian, Nonny, *One Fine Day* (N–P)

Stobbs, William, *The House That Jack Built* (N–P)

Winter, Jeanette, *The House That Jack Built* (N–P)

TALL TALES

Davol, Marguerite W., *The Loudest, Fastest, Best Drummer in Kansas* (N–P-I)

Gershator, Phillis, *Tiny and Bigman* (N–P-I)

Gorbachev, Valeri, *Where Is the Apple Pie?* (N–P-I)

Johnson, Paul Brett, *Old Dry Frye: A Deliciously Funny Tall Tale* (N–P-I)

Kimmel, Eric A., *Grizz!* (N–P-I)

Nolen, Jerdine, *Big Jabe* (N–P-I)

Schroeder, Alan, *The Tale of Willie Monroe* (N–P-I)

White, Linda Arms, *Comes a Wind* (N–P-I)

Yolen, Jane, *Not One Damsel in Distress: World Folktales for Strong Girls* (P-I)

Variants of Folktales and Fractured Fairy Tales

BABA YAGA

Arnold, Katya, *Baba Yaga: A Russian Folktale* (N–P-I)

Mayer, Marianna, *Baba Yaga and Vasilisa the Brave* (N–P-I)

Polacco, Patricia, *Babushka Baba Yaga* (N–P-I)

Rael, Elsa Okon, *Marushka's Egg* (N–P-I)

BEAUTY AND THE BEAST

Brett, Jan, *Beauty and the Beast* (N–P-I)

Howard, Richard, *Beauty and the Beast* (N–P-I)

CINDERELLA

Climo, Shirley, *The Egyptian Cinderella* (N–P-I)

_____, *The Irish Cinderella* (N–P-I)

_____, *The Korean Cinderella* (N–P-I)

Greaves, Margaret, *Tattercoats* (N–P-I)

Hayes, Joe, *Little Gold Star/ Estrellita de Oro: A Cinderella Cuento* (N–P-I)

Hooks, William, *Moss Gown* (N–P-I)

Huck, Charlotte, *Princess Furball* (N–P-I)

Jacobs, Joseph, *Tattercoats* (N–P-I)

Jungman, Ann, *Cinderella and the Hot Air Balloon* (N–P-I)

Louie, Ai-Ling, *Yeh Shen: A Cinderella Story from China* (N–P-I)

Lowell, Susan, *Cindy Ellen: A Wild Western Cinderella* (N–P-I)

Martin, Rafe, *The Rough-Face Girl* (N–P-I)

Perrault, Charles, *Cinderella and Other Tales from Perrault* (N–P-I)

San Jose, Christine, *Cinderella* (N–P-I)

San Souci, Robert D., *Sootface: An Ojibwa Cinderella Story* (N–P-I)

FROG PRINCE

Cecil, Laura, *Frog Princess* (N–P-I)

Isadora, Rachel, *The Princess and the Frog* (N–P-I)

Ormerod, Jan, and David Lloyd, *The Frog Prince* (N–P-I)

Scieszka, Jon, *The Frog Prince Continued* (N–P-I)

Tarcov, Edith H., *Frog Prince* (N–P-I)

GOLDILOCKS AND THE THREE BEARS

Barton, Byron, *Three Bears* (N–P)

Marshall, James, *Goldilocks and the Three Bears* (N–P)

Muir, Frank, *Frank Muir Retells Goldilocks and the Three Bears* (N–P)

Tolhurst, Marilyn, *Somebody and the Three Blairs* (N–P)

Turkle, Brinton, *Deep in the Forest* (N–P)

GOOD SISTER–BAD SISTER

Huck, Charlotte S., *Toads and Diamonds* (N–P-I)

Mills, Lauren, *Tatterhood and the Hobgoblins: A Norwegian Folktale* (N–P-I)

San Souci, Robert, *Talking Eggs* (N–P-I)

Steptoe, John, *Mufaro's Beautiful Daughters: An African Tale* (N–P-I)

HANSEL AND GRETEL

Lesser, Rika, *Hansel and Gretel: A Tale from the Brothers Grimm* (N–P-I)

Marshall, James, *Hansel and Gretel* (N–P-I)

JACK TALES

Compton, Kenn, and Joanne Compton, *Jack the Giant Chaser: An Appalachian Tale* (N–P-I)

Haley, Gail E., *Mountain Jack Tales* (N–P-I)

JACK AND THE BEANSTALK

Briggs, Raymond, *Jim and the Beanstalk* (N–P)

Howe, John, *Jack and the Beanstalk* (N–P)

Kellogg, Steven, *Jack and the Beanstalk* (N–P)

Metaxas, Eric, *Jack and the Beanstalk* (videotape), read by Michael Palin, music by David Stewart (N–P)

Osborne, Mary Pope, *Kate and the Beanstalk* (N–P)

Wildsmith, Brian, and Rebecca Wildsmith, *Jack and the Meanstalk* (N–P)

RED RIDING HOOD

Crawford, Elizabeth D., *Little Red Cap* (N–P)

de Regniers, Beatrice Schenk, *Red Riding Hood* (N–P)

Ernst, Lisa Campbell, *Little Red Riding Hood: A Newfangled Prairie Tale* (N–P)

Hyman, Trina Schart, *Little Red Riding Hood* (N–P)

Langley, John, *Little Red Riding Hood* (N–P)

Perrault, Charles, *Little Red Riding Hood* (N–P)

Young, Ed, *Lon Po Po: A Red Riding Hood Story from China* (N–P)

Zeifert, Harriet, *Little Red Riding Hood* (N–P)

RUMPELSTILTSKIN

Sage, Alison, *Rumpelstiltskin* (N–P)

Stanley, Diane, *Rumpelstiltskin's Daughter* (N–P)

Zemach, Harve, *Duffy and the Devil: A Cornish Tale* (N–P)

SLEEPING BEAUTY

Early, Margaret, *Sleeping Beauty* (N–P-I)

Minters, Frances, *Sleepless Beauty* (N–P-I)

Perrault, Charles, *Story of Sleeping Beauty* (audiotape), read by Claire Bloom, adapted by Ward Botsford, music by Peter Tchaikovsky (N–P-I)

Yolen, Jane, *Sleeping Ugly* (N–P-I)

SNOW WHITE AND THE SEVEN DWARFS

French, Fiona, *Snow White in New York* (N–P-I)

Jarrell, Randall, *Snow White and the Seven Dwarfs* (N–P-I)

Watts, Bernadette, *Snow White and Rose Red* (N–P-I)

THREE BILLY GOATS GRUFF

Emberley, Rebecca, *Three Cool Kids* (N–P-I)

Wolff, Patricia, *The Toll Bridge Troll* (N–P-I)

THREE LITTLE PIGS

Bucknall, Caroline, *Three Little Pigs* (N–P)

Hooks, William H., *The Three Little Pigs and the Fox* (N–P)

Marshall, James, *The Three Little Pigs* (N–P)

Scieszka, Jon, *The True Story of the Three Little Pigs* (N–P)

Trivizas, Eugene, *Three Little Wolves and the Big Bad Pig* (N–P)

Zemach, Margot, *The Three Little Pigs: An Old Story* (N–P-I)

JUAN BOBO

Bernier-Grand, Carmen T., *Juan Bobo: Four Tales from Puerto Rico* (N–P-I)

ROSE RED

Andreason, Dan, *Rose Red and the Bear Prince* (N–P-I)

COLLECTIONS OF VARIANTS

Books in this section are appropriate for nursery–primary–intermediate readers unless otherwise noted.

Anno, Mitsumasa, *Anno's Twice Told Tales: The Fisherman and His Wife & the Four Clever Brothers*

Brooks, William, *A Telling of the Tales*

Galloway, Priscilla, *Truly Grim Tales*

King-Smith, Dick, *The Topsy Turvy Storybook*

San Souci, Robert D., *Cut from the Same Cloth: American Women of Myth, Legend, and Tall Tale*

_____, *Larger Than Life: The Adventures of American Legendary Heroes*

Scieszka, Jon, *The Stinky Cheese Man and Other Fairly Stupid Tales*

Segal, Lore, and Maurice Sendak, *Juniper Tree and Other Tales from Grimm*

Steig, Jeanne, *A Handful of Beans: Six Fairy Tales Retold*

Fables

Books in this section are appropriate for primary–intermediate readers unless otherwise noted.

Anno, Mitsumasa, *Anno's Aesop: A Book of Fables by Aesop and Mr. Fox*

Bierhorst, John, *Doctor Coyote: A Native American Aesop's Fables*

Brett, Jan, *Town Mouse, Country Mouse*

Cauley, Lorinda Bryan, *The Town Mouse and the Country Mouse*

Clark, Margaret, *The Best of Aesop's Fables*

Climo, Shirley, *The Little Red Ant and the Great Big Crumb: A Mexican Fable* (P–I)

Craig, Helen, *The Town Mouse and the Country Mouse* (P–I)

Hastings, Selina, *Reynard the Fox*

Heins, Ethel, *The Cat and the Cook and Other Fables of Krylov*

Holder, Heide, *Aesop's Fables*

Kherdian, David, *Feathers and Tails: Animal Fables from Around the World*

Kraus, Robert, *Fables Aesop Never Wrote*

La Fontaine, J. D., *The Hare and the Tortoise*

_____, *The Lion and the Rat*

_____, *The North Wind and the Sun*

Lessie, Pat, *Fablesauce: Aesop Reinterpreted in Rhymed Couplets*

Lobel, Arnold, *Fables*

MacDonald, Suse, and Bill Oakes, *Once Upon Another: The Tortoise and the Hare/The Lion and The Mouse*

McDermott, Gerald, *The Fox and the Stork*

Paxton, Tom, *Aesop's Fables*

_____, *Belling the Cat: And Other Aesop's Fables*

Pinkney, Jerry, *Aesop's Fables*

Reiser, Lynn, *Two Mice in Three Fables*

Stevens, Janet, *The Tortoise and the Hare: An Aesop Fable*

_____, *The Town Mouse and the Country Mouse: An Aesop Fable*

Storr, Catherine, *Androcles and the Lion*

Wallis, Diz, *Something Nasty in the Cabbages: A Tale from Roman de Renard, Written in the 12th Century by Pierre de Saint-Cloud*

Wang, M. L., *The Ant and the Dove: An Aesop Tale Retold*

Ward, Helen, *The Hare and the Tortoise: A Fable from Aesop*

Watts, Bernadette, *The Lion and the Mouse: An Aesop Fable*

_____, *The Wind and the Sun: An Aesop Fable*

Young, Ed, *Seven Blind Mice*

Pourquoi Tales, Myths, and Legends

Books in this section are appropriate for intermediate–advanced readers unless otherwise noted.

D'Aulaire, Ingri, and Edgar Parin, *Ingri and Edgar Parin d'Aulaire's Book of Greek Myths*

Esbensen, Barbara, *The Night Rainbow*

Fisher, Leonard Everett, *Olympians: Great Gods and Goddesses of Ancient Greece*

Goode, Diane, *Diane Goode's Book of Scary Stories and Songs*

Hamilton, Virginia, *The Dark Way: Stories from the Spirit World*

_____, *In the Beginning: Creation Stories from Around the World*

Huth, Holly Young, *The Son of the Sun and the Daughter of the Moon: A Saami Folktale*

Lattimore, Deborah Nourse, *Why There Is No Arguing in Heaven: A Mayan Myth*

Philip, Neil, *Fairy Tales of Eastern Europe*

Rosen, Michael, *How the Animals Got Their Colors: Animal Myths from Around the World*

Russell, William F., *Classic Myths to Read Aloud*

Shannon, George, *Still More Stories to Solve: Fourteen Folktales from Around the World*

Vogel, Carole Garbuny, *Legends of Landforms: Native American Lore and the Geology of the Land*

Mythology from Many Cultures

GREEK AND ROMAN

Books in this section are appropriate for intermediate–advanced readers unless otherwise noted.

Barth, Edna, *Cupid and Psyche: A Love Story*

Climo, Shirley, *Atalanta's Race: A Greek Myth*

Colum, Padraic, *Golden Fleece and Heroes Who Lived Before Achilles*

Craft, M. Charlotte, *Cupid and Psyche*

D'Aulaire, Ingri, *Ingri and Edgar Parin d'Aulaire's Book of Greek Myths*

Espeland, Pamela, *Story of Cadmus*

Evslin, Bernard, *Hercules*

_____, *Scylla and Charybdis*

_____, *Theseus and the Minotaur*

Fisher, Leonard Everett, *Olympians: Great Gods and Goddesses of Ancient Greece*

Fleischman, Paul, *Dateline: Troy*

Gates, Doris, *Lord of the Sky: Zeus*

_____, *Two Queens of Heaven: Aphrodite and Demeter*

Hawthorne, Nathaniel, *King Midas and the Golden Touch*

Hodges, Margaret, *The Arrow and the Lamp: The Story of Psyche*

Hutton, Warwick, *Odysseus and the Cyclops*

_____, *Persephone*

_____, *Theseus and the Minotaur*

Lattimore, Deborah Nourse, *The Prince and the Golden Ax*

McCaughrean, Geraldine, *Greek Myths*

McDermott, Gerald, *Daughter of the Earth: A Roman Myth*

Philip, Neil, *King Midas*

Orgel, Doris, *Ariadne, Awake!*

Weil, Lisl, *Pandora's Box*

NORSE

Books in this section are appropriate for intermediate–advanced readers unless otherwise noted.

Barth, Edna, *Balder and the Mistletoe: A Story for the Winter Holidays*

Climo, Shirley, *Stolen Thunder: A Norse Myth*

Colum, Padraic, *Children of Odin: The Book of Northern Myths*

Crossley-Holland, Kevin, *Beowulf*

_____, *Norse Myths*

D'Aulaire, Ingri, *Norse Gods and Giants*
De Gerez, Toni, *Louhi, Witch of North Farm*
Mayer, Marianna, *Iduna and the Magic Apples*
Osborne, Mary Pope, *Favorite Norse Myths*

AFRICAN

Books in this section are appropriate for primary–intermediate readers unless otherwise noted.

Aardema, Verna, *Princess Gorilla and a New Kind of Water*
_____, *Rabbit Makes a Monkey of Lion: A Swahili Tale*
_____, *Traveling to Tondo: A Tale of the Nkundo of Zaire*
_____, *Why Mosquitoes Buzz in People's Ears: A West African Tale*
Dayrell, Elphinstone, *Why the Sun and the Moon Live in the Sky: An African Folktale*
Dixon, Ann, *How Raven Brought Light to People*
Gerson, Mary-Joan, *Why the Sky Is Far Away*
Kimmel, Eric A., *Anansi and the Moss-Covered Rock*
Knutson, Barbara, *Why the Crab Has No Head*
Lester, Julius, *How Many Spots Does a Leopard Have? And Other Tales*
Mollel, Tololwa M., *The Orphan Boy: A Maasai Story*
Troughton, Joanna, *How Stories Came into the World: A Folk Tale from West Africa*

NATIVE AMERICAN

Books in this section are appropriate for primary–intermediate readers unless otherwise noted.

Connolly, James E., *Why the Possum's Tail Is Bare and Other North American Indian Nature Tales*
dePaola, Tomie, *The Legend of the Bluebonnet: An Old Tale of Texas*
Esbensen, Barbara Juster, *Ladder to the Sky: How the Gift of Healing Came to the Ojibway Nation*
Goble, Paul, *Her Seven Brothers*
_____, *Iktomi and the Boulder: A Plains Indian Story*
_____, *Star Boy*
Oughton, Jerrie, *How the Stars Fell into the Sky: A Navajo Tale*
Troughton, Joanna, *How the Birds Changed Their Feathers: A South American Indian Folktale*
_____, *How Rabbit Stole the Fire: A North American Indian Folktale*

Hero Tales and Epics

Books in this section are appropriate for intermediate–advanced readers unless otherwise noted.

Gretchen, Sylvia, *Hero of the Land of Snow*
Hodges, Margaret, *The Kitchen Knight: A Tale of King Arthur*
_____, *St. George and the Dragon*
Hodges, Margaret, and Margerey Evernden, *Of Swords and Sorcerers: The Adventures of King Arthur and His Knights*
Jaffrey, Madhur, *Seasons of Splendour: Tales, Myths, and Legends of India*
McKinley, Robin, *The Outlaws of Sherwood*
Malory, Sir Thomas, *Le Morte d'Arthur*

Perham, Molly, *King Arthur: The Legends of Camelot*
Philip, Neil, *Tale of Sir Gawain*
Pyle, Howard, *Merry Adventures of Robin Hood of Great Renown in Nottinghamshire*
Pyle, Howard, *Story of King Arthur and His Knights*
Running Wolf, Michael B., and Patricia Clark Smith, *On the Trail of Elder Brother: Glous'gap Stories of the Micmac Indians*
Sabuda, Robert, *Arthur and the Sword*
San Souci, Robert D., *Young Guinevere*
Sutcliff, Rosemary, *The Light Beyond the Forest*
_____, *The Road to Camlann*
_____, *The Sword and the Circle: King Arthur and the Knights of the Round Table*
Williams, Marcia, *King Arthur and the Knights of the Round Table*
Yolen, Jane, *Camelot*

American Folklore

Bang, Molly, *Wiley and the Hairy Man* (P–I)
Durell, Ann, *The Diane Goode Book of American Folk Tales & Songs* (P–I)
Faulkner, William J., *Brer Tiger and the Big Wind*
Forest, Heather, *The Baker's Dozen: A Colonial American Tale* (P–I)
Hamilton, Virginia, *In the Beginning* (P–I–A)
_____, *The People Could Fly: American Black Folk Tales* (P–I–A)
Isaacs, Anne, *Swamp Angel* (P–I–A)
Jaquith, Priscilla, *Bo Rabbit Smart for True: Tall Tales from the Gullah* (P–I–A)
Lester, Julius, *The Tales of Uncle Remus: The Adventures of Brer Rabbit* (P–I–A)
_____, *More Tales of Uncle Remus: Further Adventures of Brer Rabbit, His Friends, Enemies, and Others* (P–I–A)
_____, *Further Tales of Uncle Remus: The Misadventures of Brer Rabbit, Brer Fox, Brer Wolf, the Doodang, and Other Creatures* (P–I–A)
Lyons, Mary E., *The Butter Tree: Tales of Bruh Rabbit* (P–I–A)
Parks, Van Dyke, *Jump Again! More Adventures of Brer Rabbit* (P–I–A)
_____, *Jump On Over! The Adventures of Brer Rabbit and His Family* (P–I–A)
Parks, Van Dyke, and Malcolm Jones, *Jump! The Adventures of Brer Rabbit* (P–I–A)
San Souci, Robert D., *The Talking Eggs: A Folktale from the American South* (P–I)
Schwartz, Alvin, *I Saw You in the Bathtub and Other Folk Rhymes* (P–I)
Sierra, Judith, *Wiley and the Hairy Man* (P–I)

AMERICAN TALL TALES

Books in this section are appropriate for primary–intermediate readers unless otherwise noted.

Arnold, Caroline, *The Terrible Hodag*
Blair, Walter, *Tall Tale America: A Legendary History of Our Humorous Heroes*
Cohen, Caron Lee, *Sally Ann Thunder Ann Whirlwind Crockett*

Dewey, Ariane, *Gib Morgan, Oilman*

_____, *Pecos Bill*

Fleischman, Sid, *McBroom's Wonderful One-Acre Farm: Three Tall Tales*

Gleiter, J., *Paul Bunyan and Babe the Blue Ox*

Isaacs, Anne, *Swamp Angel*

Kellogg, Steven, *Mike Fink* (P–I–A)

_____, *Paul Bunyan, A Tall Tale*

Lester, Julius, *John Henry*

McKissack, Patricia C., *A Million Fish . . . More or Less* (P)

Nolen, Jerdine, *Big Jabe*

Osborne, Mary Pope, *American Tall Tales*

Rounds, Glen, *The Morning the Sun Refused to Rise: An Original Paul Bunyan Tale*

Shepard, Aaron, *Legend of Slappy Hooper: An American Tall Tale*

Stoutenberg, Adrien, *American Tall Tales*

_____, *American Tall-Tale Animals*

Walker, Paul Robert, *Big Men, Big Country: A Collection of American Tall Tales* (A)

Folk Songs

Aliki, *Go Tell Aunt Rhody* (P)

_____, *Hush Little Baby: A Folk Lullaby* (P)

Axelrod, Alan, *Songs of the Wild West* (P–I)

Bryan, Ashley, *All Night, All Day: A Child's First Book of African-American Spirituals* (P–I)

Chalk, Gary, *Mr. Frog Went A-Courting: Discover the Secret Story* (P–I)

Delacre, Lulu, *Arroz Con Leche: Popular Songs and Rhymes from Latin America* (P–I)

Durell, Ann, *The Diane Goode Book of American Folk Tales and Songs* (P–I)

Glazer, Tom, *Eye Winker, Tom Tinker, Chin Chopper: Fifty Musical Fingerplays* (P)

Goode, Diane, *Diane Goode's Book of American Folk Tales and Songs* (P–I)

Hoberman, Mary Ann, *The Eensy-Weensy Spider* (P)

Hort, Lenny, *The Seals on the Bus* (P)

Kellogg, Steven, *Yankee Doodle* (P)

Langstaff, John, *What a Morning! The Christmas Story in Black Spirituals*

_____, *Climbing Jacob's Ladder: Heroes of the Bible in African-American Spirituals* (P–N)

Larrick, Nancy, *The Wheels of the Bus Go Round and Round: School Bus Songs and Chants* (P)

Plotz, Helen, *As I Walked Out One Evening: A Book of Ballads* (I–A)

Sharon, Lois, and Bram, Sharon, *Elephant Jam* (P–I)

Staines, Bill, *All God's Critters Got a Place in the Choir* (P–I)

Watson, Clyde, and Wendy Watson, *Father Fox's Feast of Songs* (P–I)

Whippo, Walt, *Little White Duck* (P)

Yolen, Jane, *The Lullaby Songbook* (N–P)

_____, *Street Rhymes Around the World* (N–P)

Zemach, Harve, *Mommy, Buy Me a China Doll* (N–P)

Religious Stories and Songs

Adler, David, *A Picture Book of Hanukkah* (P–I)

_____, *One Yellow Daffodil: A Hanukkah Story* (P–I)

Armstrong, Carole, *Lives and Legends of the Saints* (P–I–A)

Bach, Alice, and J. Cheryl Exum, *Miriam's Well: Stories About Women in the Bible* (P–I)

_____, *Moses' Ark: Stories from the Bible* (P–I)

Bierhorst, John, *Spirit Child: A Story of the Nativity* (I–A)

Bierhorst, John, *The People with Five Fingers: A Native Californian Creation Tale* (I–A)

Brown, Susan Taylor, *Can I Pray with My Eyes Open?* (P–I)

Cohen, Barbara, *The Donkey's Story: A Bible Story* (I–A)

Cole, Joanna, *A Gift from Saint Francis: The First Creche* (I–A)

dePaola, Tomie, *Christopher: The Holy Giant* (I–A)

_____, *Francis: The Poor Man of Assisi* (I–A)

_____, *The Lady of Guadalupe* (P–I)

_____, *The Legend of the Poinsettia* (P–I)

_____, *Mary: The Mother of Jesus* (I–A)

_____, *Tomie dePaola's Book of the Old Testament: New International Version* (I–A)

Fisher, Leonard Everett, *The Seven Days of Creation* (I–A)

_____, *The Wailing Wall* (I–A)

Ganeri, Anita, *Out of the Ark: Stories from the World's Religions* (I–A)

Godwin, Laura, *Barnyard Prayers* (P)

Hample, Stuart, and Eric Marshall, *Children's Letters to God* (P–I–A)

Hennessy, B. G., *The First Night* (P–I–A)

Higginsen, Vy, *This Is My Song: A Collection of Gospel Music for the Family* (I–A)

Hodges, Margaret, *Brother Francis and the Friendly Beasts* (I–A)

_____, *St. Jerome and the Lion* (I–A)

Hutton, Warwick, *Adam and Eve: The Bible Story* (I–A)

Jacobs, William Jay, *World Religions: Great Lives* (I–A)

Johnson, James Weldon, *The Creation* (I–A)

Jonas, Ann, *Aardvarks, Disembark!* (P)

Kenna, Kathleen, *A People Apart* (I–A)

Kimmel, Eric A., *Bar Mitzvah: A Jewish Boy's Coming of Age* (I–A)

Kuskin, Karla, *Jerusalem, Shining Still* (P–I–A)

Laird, Elizabeth, *The Road to Bethlehem: An Ethiopian Nativity* (I–A)

Maccarone, Grace, *A Child Was Born: A First Nativity Book* (P–I)

Mayer, Marianna, *Young Mary of Nazareth* (I–A)

Mohr, Joseph, *Silent Night, Holy Night: A Christmas Carol* (P–I)

Muhlberger, Richard, *The Christmas Story: Told Through Paintings* (P–I–A)

Musleah, Rahel, *Why on This Night? A Passover Haggadah for Family Celebration* (P–I–A)

Rice, Edward, *The Five Great Religions* (I–A)

Rock, Lois, *Words of Gold: A Treasury of the Bible's Poetry and Wisdom* (I–A)

Salkin, Jeffrey K., *For Kids—Putting God on Your Guest List: How to Claim the Spiritual Meaning of Your Bar or Bat Mitzvah* (I–A)

Sawyer, Ruth, *The Remarkable Christmas of the Cobbler's Sons* (P–I–A)

Schur, Maxine Rose, *Day of Delight: A Jewish Sabbath in Ethiopia* (I–A)

Schwartz, Howard, and Barbara Rush, *The Sabbath Lion: A Jewish Folktale from Algeria* (I–A)

Segal, Lore, *The Book of Adam to Moses* (I–A)

Thompson, Lauren, *Love One Another: The Last Days of Jesus* (I–A)

Vivas, Julie, illustrator, *The Nativity* (P–I)

Wensel, Ulises, *They Followed a Bright Star* (I–A)

Westall, Robert, *The Witness* (I–A)

Wildsmith, Brian, *A Christmas Story* (P–I)

Wilner, Isabel, *B Is for Bethlehem: A Christmas Alphabet* (P–I)

Wilson, Elizabeth B., *Bibles and Bestiaries: A Guide to Illuminated Manuscripts* (I–A)

Winthrop, Elizabeth, *A Child Is Born: The Christmas Story* (P–I–A)

Wolkstein, Diane, *Esther's Story* (I–A)

NOAH STORIES

Baynes, Pauline, *Noah and the Ark* (P–I)

Emberley, Barbara, *One Wide River to Cross* (P–I)

Gauch, Patricia Lee, *Noah* (P–I)

Godden, Rumer, *Prayers from the Ark: Selected Poems* (I–A)

Hogrogian, Nonny, *Noah's Ark* (P–I)

Ludwig, Warren, *Old Noah's Elephants: An Israeli Folktale* (P–I)

Olson, Arielle, *Noah's Cats and the Devil's Fire* (P–I–A)

Ray, Jane, *Noah's Ark: Words from the Book of Genesis* (I–A)

Reid, Barbara, *Two by Two* (P–I)

Singer, Isaac Bashevis, *Why Noah Chose the Dove* (P–I)

Spier, Peter, *Noah's Ark* (P–I)

Stevens, Janet, *How the Manx Cat Lost Its Tail* (P–I)

Fantasy and Science Fiction

Jonas blurted out what he was feeling. "I was thinking that . . . well, I can see that it wasn't a very practical way to live, with the Old right there in the same place, where maybe they wouldn't be well taken care of, the way they are now, and that we have a better-arranged way of doing things. But anyway, I was thinking, I mean feeling, actually, that it was kind of nice, then. And that I wish we could be that way, and that you could be my grandparent. The family in the memory seemed a little more—" He faltered, not able to find the word he wanted.

"A little more complete," the Giver suggested.

Jonas nodded. "I liked the feeling of love," he confessed. He glanced nervously at the speaker on the wall, reassuring himself that no one was listening. "I wish we still had that," he whispered. "Of course," he added quickly, "I do understand that it wouldn't work very well. And that it's much better to be organized the way we are now. I can see that it was a dangerous way to live. . . . Still," he said slowly, almost to himself, "I did like the light they made. And the warmth."

—Lois Lowry, *The Giver,* pp. 125–126

Agroup of Joan Pearlman's fifth-grade students started on Susan Cooper's **The Dark Is Rising** (I) series and they just haven't stopped reading fantasy and science fiction. "The mold is cast during fifth grade: students become avid readers or else they fall into the MTV and computer habit," says Joan. "I introduce them to fantasy and science fiction—they might not find it on their own—and I think it's what hooks them as readers."

Joan reflects on the reading profile of each student. She looks at cumulative records, standardized test scores, portfolios, and letters students write to identify their goals for the year. For example, Jenny wrote about how much she enjoyed reading C. S. Lewis's **Narnia** (I) series; Joan makes a note to recommend Brian Jacques's **Redwall** (A) series to her. Christopher's record shows that he is not reading on grade level, but Joan wants him to enjoy fantasy like everyone else is reading. She suggests that he and his reading partner read Beverly Cleary's *The Mouse and the Motorcycle* (I). She can tell from Heather's letter that she is a science fiction fan and a computer whiz; she recommends Gillian Cross's book *New World* (A). Nick is interested in the environment; he will like *The Ear, The Eye, and the Arm: A Novel* (I–A) by Nancy Farmer. Joan talks about it with Nick, knowing that the descriptions of garbage heaps in a future world may very well mobilize him to political action. He will like the mystery, too. And, of course her students enjoy reading and discussing Lois Lowry's *The Giver* (A); they argue passionately about how the story really ended. Joan carefully introduces literature to create avid readers, to introduce new genres, and to correlate reading with the integrated curriculum in her classroom. That's good teaching!

Defining Fantasy and Science Fiction

Fantasy and science fiction are imaginative narratives that explore alternate realities. Science fiction explores scientific possibilities, asking and answering the question, "If this, then what?" Fantasy suspends scientific explanations and natural laws; it contains some element of character, setting, or plot not found in the natural world as it asks age-old questions about life, goodness, and balance. Both fantasy and science fiction are often set in worlds that do not correspond to present realities, but science fiction differs from fantasy in that the future realities it depicts are based on extrapolation from scientific principles. As Robert Heinlein describes it:

> The author takes as his first postulate the real world as we know it, including all established facts and natural laws. The result can be extremely fantastic in content, but it is not fantasy; it is legitimate—and often very tightly reasoned—speculation about the possibilities of the real world. (1953, p. 1118)

Some science fiction and fantasy is pure lighthearted fun: Creatures from other planets visit our world; miniature worlds exist within our own homes. Some, following the path of the hero, probes a deeper reality, an eternal truth.

Fantasy and science fiction spring from folklore but differ in that they are written by an individual author, rather than handed down by word of mouth.

Folklore encodes a culture's morality; the roots of fantasy and science fiction grow directly from folklore. These genres build on and derive their strength from traditions established in ancient myths and legends. Just as our ancestors created a myth to explain the sun's movement—describing how Apollo drove a chariot of fire across the sky—so modern writers spin imaginative tales to explain things we do not fully understand and to probe the dimensions of areas we do not know.

Just as the heroes of ancient legend confront great danger and rise to impossible challenges, modern heroes take on a larger-than-life nature as they are depicted in stories. For example, in Philip Pullman's magnificent trilogy *The Golden Compass, The Subtle Knife,* and *The Amber Spyglass* (all A), Lyra and Will, the youthful heroes, battle powerful forces as they seek to fulfill their own destinies. These stories and many others also rely on structural patterns found in the oral tradition. The characters go on a quest that turns out differently from what they expected, they rise to the occasion, and they return home transformed in some way. Jonas, in *The Giver* (A), sets out for Elsewhere and finds himself; Lyra and Will travel to the world of the dead and end up discovering the magnificence of love.

There is a significant difference, however, between stories that came to us through oral tradition and ones we now call fantasy or science fiction. Ancient tales were shaped and honed through cultural belief and the voice of the storyteller. Modern tales are shaped through the author's artistic vision and stylistic choices. Egoff (1981) calls this the difference between a public dream (folklore) and a private, metaphorical vision (modern fantasy and science fiction). For example, the appearance of the Holy Grail in Thomas Mallory's *Le Morte d'Arthur* was not taken as fantasy in the fifteenth century; it was a public dream, meant to be believed. Weaving this and other legends from Arthurian days into the fabric of modern life, Susan Cooper dramatizes the risks of not standing up for what is right and just. Cooper bases her stories on English and Celtic myth, beginning with *Over Sea, Under Stone,* and continuing with *The Dark Is Rising, Greenwitch, Silver on the Tree,* and *The Grey King* (all A).

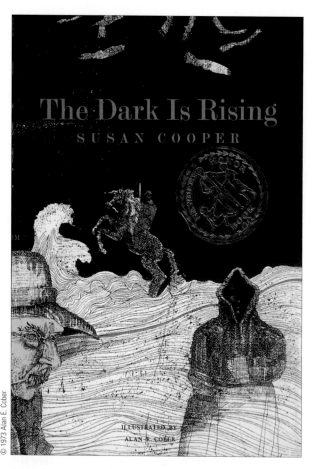

© 1973 Alan E. Cober

Susan Cooper spins a delicate web to create an elusive tension between physical reality and an imaginative world where good struggles against evil. Cooper's skill at manipulating myth and reality is unparalleled.

The Role of Fantasy and Science Fiction in Children's Lives

Fantasy and science fiction open doors to worlds of imagination. They enrich and illuminate children's lives because the stories deal with the great complexities of existence: the relativity of size, time, and space; the interdependence of the universe; good versus evil; the strength and courage of the individual; and self-integrity. Fantasy and science fiction writers treat problems of the universe with a high seriousness. They can also deal lightheartedly with capricious supernatural events, such as cars that fly through the air, as in *Chitty Chitty Bang Bang* (I) by Ian Fleming; adventures in space, as in Jane Yolen's *Commander Toad in Space* (P); or stuffed animals that talk, as in Margery Williams's *The Velveteen Rabbit* (P–I).

For many children fantasy is the first literature they love. Children in preschool and primary grades love books with animal characters who act like human beings. William Steig's *Sylvester and the Magic Pebble* (P), Russell Hoban's *Bread and Jam for Frances* (P), Rosemary Wells's *Max's First Word* (N), and many other beloved books for young children are fantasies—in this case books about characters who could not really exist. Children have no trouble understanding what the stories are about and what questions they raise about real life.

As they mature, children experience many kinds of literature. Sometime during the elementary school years some children become enraptured with realistic fiction, giving themselves completely over to this genre. Others become avid consumers of nonfiction and biography. Some continue to enjoy fantasy, moving from picture books to more fully developed narratives. As children mature they either move toward science fiction and fantasy or learn to avoid them entirely. By sixth or seventh grade, reader preference becomes markedly apparent (Cullinan, Harwood, and Galda, 1983; Galda, 1990). Those who like these genres love them passionately, and those who do not are equally as passionate. For some children, these genre preferences may last the rest of their lives; others will become more eclectic with development and will once again enjoy fantasy.

Why do some readers prefer this unrealistic and sometimes disturbing literature over any other genres? Susan Cooper, noted fantasy writer, speaks of fantasy as "the metaphor through which we discover ourselves" (1981, p. 16). She argues that rather than helping us to escape out of our selves and into a fantasy world, fantasy draws readers into themselves, pushing them to consider who they are and what the world is. Serious fantasy "is probably the most complex form of fiction [readers] will ever find" (p. 16) and demands a great deal from its readers.

Children don't expect fantasy to help them solve their daily social problems, but rather read and enjoy fantasy because it reaches for their souls (May, 1984). Lloyd Alexander, himself a much honored writer of fantasy, talks about the power of fantasy to encourage social change. He says, "The let's pretend of literature can have both an immediate and long range impact upon our lives . . . [it] influences our view of society and raises questions about it" (1970, p. 96). Fantasy literature can be a vital force for moral and spiritual growth.

The imaginative speculation that marks science fiction stretches the minds of readers as they consider ethical dilemmas that might result from physical and technological advances. Stories set in worlds never before known deal with problems that children may someday face—the rights of extraterrestrials whose planets are colonized, the consequences of diminishing resources in a world of rapidly growing populations—and thus prompt readers to rethink choices and directions of our society. Science fiction, a literature about change and the attendant moral issues that change brings, is appropriate for children of a rapidly changing world.

Criteria for Evaluating Fantasy and Science Fiction

As with all quality narrative literature, good fantasy and science fiction tells an interesting story, has well-developed characters, an engaging plot, and an identifiable theme. Authors manipulate these elements, particularly setting, character, and time, to create a fantasy world. If the writer is successful, readers willingly suspend disbelief. We judge the quality of a writer's private vision by how thoroughly it convinces us of its reality, by how long it haunts our memory, and by how deeply it moves us to new insights. Figure 6.1 lists criteria for evaluating fantasy and science fiction.

The science fiction community has established its own awards to recognize outstanding writers. The Nebula Award is chosen by a vote of the membership of the Science Fiction Writers of America. The Hugo Award is named in honor of Hugo H. Gernsback, who is credited with the development of modern science fiction. Both awards are given annually to books in several categories.

SETTING

Settings are believable, no matter how fantastic they are, when an author provides rich details that enable a reader to envision the setting. Some authors provide detailed maps of fantasy lands, complete with place names that are consistent with the fantasy. Others gradually lead readers from the real world into the fantasy world through some device, such as a magic door, a magic object, or the belief of realistic characters in the fantasy setting. In science fiction the setting is often the future, and that future has been shaped by a scientific possibility that has been realized. It may be a world that has become overcrowded due to medical advances or space travel, or a world in which genetic engineering has run amuck. Settings should be detailed and believable within the context of the story. Teaching Idea 6.1 suggests a way to look at believable settings with your students.

PLOT

What happens in a story must be logically consistent within the story world. If characters move through time, they do so for a reason; they may walk through a door, press a magic button, or visit a particular place. If the fantastic operates in the real world, then there must be consistency in how real people are affected by the fantastic events. In science fiction, the plot is usually driven by the problems that scientific

Figure 6 ✿ 1

Checklist for Evaluating Fantasy and Science Fiction

✿ Is the fantasy world detailed and believable within the context of the story?

✿ Are the story events imaginative yet logically consistent within the story world?

✿ Are the characters multidimensional, with consistent and logical behavior?

✿ Are there vivid images and solid, understandable structures?

✿ Are the themes meaningful, causing readers to think about life?

Teaching Idea 6 ☆ 1

Create Believable Settings

Good fantasy writers establish believable settings by carefully presenting them in intricate detail. Since the reader must envision the fantasy world, a writer's words ought to stimulate pictures in the mind's eye. Some writers add a map or some make a scale drawing of an area; some paint scenes that are so vivid you can smell them.

Read outstanding fantasies to savor the descriptive language used to establish setting. If you work with young students, read aloud scenes and ask them to create dioramas, paintings, or three-dimensional scenes of the ones described. Discuss examples of vivid writing in a writing workshop to show effective techniques. Ask students to describe the scene they envision.

Suggested books and pages where you will read vivid scenes:

Grahame, Kenneth, *Wind in the Willows.* See p. 9, the passage that begins: *The Mole had been working . . .*

Jacques, Brian, *Redwall.* See the frontispiece: *Redwall stood foursquare along the marches of the old south border, flanked on two sides by Mossflower Wood's shaded depths. . . .*

Jansson, Tove, *Tales from Moominvalley.* See p. 11: *The brook was a good one. . . .*

White, E. B., *Charlotte's Web.* See p. 13: *The barn was very large. It was very old. It smelled of hay and it smelled of manure. It smelled of the perspiration of tired horses and the wonderful sweet breath of patient cows.*

---

advances have created for the characters in the story world. However, such facts should not encumber the plot. Stories should contain imaginative events that are logical and consistent within the story world.

CHARACTERS

Excellent fantasy and science fiction stories contain characters, human and nonhuman, that are recognizable beings with strong emotions. They are multidimensional personalities who behave consistently, respond to events in a believable fashion, and grow and change across the course of the story. If a character who lives in a realistic story world enters a fantasy situation, the character does not magically change, but remains consistent across both worlds. Characters in

science fiction struggle with scientific advances as they try to live in a future world. Even if characters are superheroes within a story, they are so carefully delineated that readers accept their otherworldly powers. Characters should be well developed, with behavior that is consistent and logical within the story world.

STYLE

How a writer chooses to tell a story—through structure, syntax, and word choice—makes the difference between a mediocre book and an excellent one. Some of the best writing in children's books appears in fantasy and science fiction. Style works to establish the setting; rich images and vivid figurative language help readers envision the created world. Style makes the characters and the plot believable; authentic dialogue and clear structure help readers build characterizations and follow the action. Stories should have clear structures supported by vivid, interesting images and figurative language.

THEME

In fantasy and science fiction the theme often has great import. The monumental struggle between good and evil, what it means to be human, and the consequences of pride are all examples of recurring fantasy themes. The themes in science fiction make us consider the emotional, psychological, and mental effects of scientific advances; they help us keep an open mind so we can consider the unlimited possibilities science offers us. In both cases, these themes are woven throughout the story, logically radiating from character and plot. Other fantasy or science fiction stories are more lighthearted, using humor or fantasy or technological devices to reveal the absurd in the human condition or the thrill of life in space. At their best, these stories ask questions that arise naturally from the unity of character and action and are meaningful for readers, causing them to ask questions about life.

A CLOSE LOOK AT

Tuck Everlasting

Natalie Babbitt's *Tuck Everlasting* (I) is an outstanding example of a novel for intermediate-grade students, which illustrates excellence in fantasy quite well. It combines beautiful language, well-developed characters, a logical and consistent plot, and a richly detailed setting. The result is a believable and emotionally satisfying story.

Synopsis

Ten-year-old Winnie Foster struggles for independence against an overprotective mother and grandmother who devote all of their time to supervising her. Winnie lives beside a small forest and one day, as an act of courage, ventures into its woods. There she comes across a boy, Jesse Tuck, who is uncovering a fountain of water flowing from the ground. Although he takes a drink, he does not allow Winnie to drink from the spring. Jesse's family kidnaps Winnie to explain to her how they discovered the magical powers of the spring: Water from the fountain bestows eternal life on those who drink it. The Tucks also explain to Winnie the mixed blessing of everlasting life and leave her to make the choice about whether or not she will drink from the fountain.

Setting

The setting is believable. Natalie Babbitt uses a prologue to create a misty, surreal period of time when anything might happen, when people do things they might not normally do:

> The first week of August hangs at the very top of summer, the top of the live-long year, like the highest seat of a Ferris wheel when it pauses in its turning. The weeks that come before are only a climb from balmy spring, and those that follow a drop to the chill of autumn, but the first week of August is motionless, and hot. It is curiously silent, too, with blank white dawns and glaring noons, and sunsets smeared with too much color. Often at night there is lightning, but it quivers all alone. There is no thunder, no relieving rain. These are strange and breathless days, the dog days, when people are led to do things they are sure to be sorry for after.
>
> One day at that time, not so very long ago, three things happened and at first there appeared to be no connection between them.

Babbitt creates suspense by suggesting that this is an eerie time and foreshadowing things to come. Phrases such

Natalie Babbitt's prologue in **Tuck Everlasting** *foreshadows story events to come. Its language sounds like a legend and establishes the overarching metaphor of a turning wheel to represent the cycle of life and revolving seasons.*

as "one day at that time, not so very long ago" establish a story set in the not-so-distant past, yet in times gone by, a distancing that gives the illusion of a dream and the feeling of "once upon a time." The amount of time covered by the entire story is brief, perhaps a week, but that week will never be forgotten.

Characterization

Winnie is believable and changes in believable ways in the process of the narrative; like a real girl she affects and is affected by the events of the story. Babbitt presents Winnie as a realistic character, one that a reader can believe in. She is troubled and upset with her parents—a realistic picture of a young person straining for independence. It is this very situation that helps a reader believe in the magic that is introduced into Winnie's life once she meets the Tucks. Winnie is open to something new and different; she's fed up with being sheltered.

We watch her gathering the courage to take a forbidden walk in the woods. As Winnie sits on the bristly grass just inside the fence she speaks to a large toad squatting across the road.

"I will, though. You'll see. Maybe even first thing tomorrow, while everyone's still asleep."

Babbitt also shows why Winnie is exasperated with too much adult supervision in her life. From her grandmother:

"Winifred! Don't sit on that dirty grass. You'll stain your boots and stockings."

From her mother:

"Come in now, Winnie. Right away. You'll get heat stroke out there on a day like this. And your lunch is ready."

Winnie explains to the toad:

See? That's just what I mean. It's like that every minute. If I had a sister or a brother, there'd be someone else for them to watch. But, as it is, there's only me. I'm tired of being looked at all the time. I want to be by myself for a change.... I'm not exactly sure what I'd do, you know, but something interesting—something that's all mine. Something that would make some kind of difference in the world. It'd be nice to have a new name, to start with, one that's not all worn out from being called so much. And I might even decide to have a pet.... Do you know they've hardly ever let me out of this yard all by myself? I'll never be able to do anything important if I stay in here like this. I expect I'd better run away.... You think I wouldn't dare, don't you? I will, though. You'll see. Maybe even first thing in the morning, while everyone's still asleep.

When Winnie does venture into the woods she is ready for adventure.

Babbitt creates a totally believable character and when she reveals the element of make-believe—a sip of water from a spring that gives eternal life—we accept its truth because we have already accepted the character.

Winnie reacts to the magical water as a real person might react. As she learns about the life-giving powers of the spring water, she realizes her own immortality and blurts out, "I don't want to die."

"No," said Tuck calmly. "Not now. Your time's not now. But dying's part of the wheel, right there next to being born. You can't pick out the pieces you like and leave the rest. Being part of the whole thing, that's the blessing. But it's passing us by, us Tucks. Living's heavy work, but off to one side, the way *we* are, it's useless, too. It don't make sense. If I knowed how to climb back on the wheel, I'd do it in a minute. You can't have living without dying. So you can't call it living, what we got. We just *are*, we just *be*, like rocks beside the road."

Winnie may not fully understand the concept that Pa Tuck explains so vividly, but she thinks about it again and again. She—and the reader—begin to understand the complex issues involved in everlasting life.

Plot

What happens in *Tuck Everlasting* is logical and consistent. Winnie is unhappy, meets the Tucks, and enters the fantasy world in which one sip of water from the spring brings eternal life. But the real world is still apparent, as the Tucks worry about being found out and so move regularly around the country. The boys can't marry and have a normal family life because they don't age. And when Ma Tuck is put in jail, Winnie has to get her out, because if the authorities try to hang her, she won't die. The events in the story are all logically consistent with the magic—they are the result of drinking the spring water—and they operate within the contraints of the real world.

Style

Babbitt's vivid language makes the setting, characters, and plot believable. Vivid images and figurative language, like that in the prologue quoted earlier, paint a picture of a place and time when magic might happen. Authentic dialogue builds characters that are plausible. And images, like Tuck's image of life as a wheel, help to build a powerful theme.

Theme

Tuck Everlasting pushes readers to consider eternal life as a central theme. Like Winnie, we see the possibility of eternal life and ask ourselves, would we drink from the spring? We

Teaching Idea 6 ☆ 2

Everlasting Questions from Tuck

Powerful discussions arise from reading *Tuck Everlasting*. Here are some suggested book discussion group topics:

✳ Would you want to live forever? What age would you choose to be?

✳ If someone promised you everlasting life, would you do what was required to obtain it? What would you do with your life?

✳ Why does Winnie Foster confide in the toad?

✳ How does the toad help Winnie make up her mind about drinking the spring water, which promises eternal life?

✳ What does the man in the yellow suit represent?

✳ How does the Tuck family feel about Winnie Foster?

✳ Do you think Winnie made the right choice?

✳ What would you say to Winnie if you could meet her?

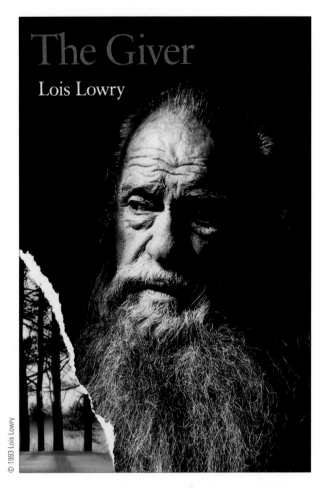

© 1993 Lois Lowry

The Giver, the receiver of memories in this planned community, tries to hand down those memories to his successor, Jonas.

see the consequences that eternal life has had for the Tucks, the greed with which some pursued it, and the consequences for the toad when he is sprinkled with water from the spring. Readers, drawn into the fantasy along with Winnie, are pushed to consider life, death, and the consequences of immortality. Teaching Idea 6.2 offers questions that help readers pursue this theme.

A CLOSE LOOK AT

The Giver

Lois Lowry unfolds an electrifying story of a possible future world in *The Giver* (A), a Newbery Medal winner. A world with no poverty, no conflict, and no problems seems ideal, but surface-level tranquillity lies like a thin veneer over deeper truths.

Synopsis

The Giver describes a possible future world in one community, a totally controlled society. Life seems perfect: There is no hunger, no below-level learners, no pollution, no hate, no

death. Old people and "newchildren" who do not thrive are simply released from the community; it's a time of celebration for the elderly and a time of resignation for the young.

Jonas, the protagonist, will become an adult when he receives his lifelong job assignment at the Ceremony of Twelve. He is surprised when he is assigned as the "Receiver of Memories," the person who keeps the memories of the past for the community. 'The Giver" is his mentor, an old man who was previously the Receiver, and who now must pass down the memories of the community to Jonas. As Jonas receives these memories, he begins to experience emotions, to see colors, and to realize ideas he had never before entertained. These experiences transform how he views his heretofore perfect community, and he and The Giver plan a way to force the community to change.

Setting

The setting is a nameless, utopian world in an unidentifed future time and place. Lowry immediately establishes the rules that guide the community. In the first chapter Jonas remembers an incident in which he saw a sleek jet fly over the community. He rushed inside the nearest building, obeying instantly rules that are alien to us but that are clearly part of Jonas's life. Everything is orderly, everyone does assigned jobs willingly. There is no conflict or deep emotion, no color, no love. Just sameness.

Characterization

A committee of anonymous Elders makes all the important decisions and resolves any conflict within the community; the members study community needs and individual talents so that they can assign lifetime jobs. Many characters are defined largely by their jobs. Jonas and his friends eagerly await their assignment; it determines their life. Some girls are chosen to become "Birthmothers" who produce three children and then work as laborers for the rest of their lives. Infants (newchildren) are raised in Childcare during their first year and are given a name only when they are assigned to a family. Nurturers, like Jonas's father, take full charge of all the "newchildren" in Childcare.

Lowry uses several techniques to establish the characters of Jonas and The Giver. She reveals Jonas's thoughts, shows what he says to others, shows what others say to him. She reveals his emotions and conveys his concerns by using a third-person limited point of view. We see the world through Jonas's eyes, as we watch him unquestioningly obey community rules in the beginning of the story, then grow to question them as he takes on his new job of Receiver.

We begin to understand him as he sits alone, having been passed over during the Ceremony of Twelve. He is ashamed, frightened, and totally confused.

> "Jonas," [the Chief Elder] said, looking down at him. "I apologize to you in particular. I caused you anguish."
>
> "I accept your apology, " Jonas replied shakily.
>
> "Please come to the stage now."
>
> Earlier that day, dressing in his own dwelling, he had practiced the kind of jaunty, self-assured walk that he hoped he could make to the stage when his turn came. All of that was forgotten now. He simply willed himself to stand, to move his feet that felt weighted and clumsy, to go forward, up the steps and across the platform until he stood at her side.
>
> Reassuringly she placed her arm across his tense shoulders.
>
> "Jonas has not been assigned," she informed the crowd, and his heart sank.
>
> Then she went on. "Jonas has been *selected*."
>
> He blinked. What did that mean? He felt a collective, questioning stir from the audience. They, too, were puzzled.

In a firm, commanding voice she announced, "Jonas has been selected to be our next Receiver of Memory." Then he heard the gasp—the sudden intake of breath, drawn sharply in astonishment, by each of the seated citizens. He saw their faces; the eyes widened in awe.

And still he did not understand.

Plot

Once Jonas begins his training, the plot begins to unfold. As he learns about the past through the memories that the Giver gives him, he begins to see all that his community lacks; he begins to understand that when you have safety and sameness you give up opportunities for other things. As he becomes increasingly restive in the community, he and the Giver plan a journey for Jonas that becomes a quest. As he searches for Elsewhere, he returns to the community that which is theirs—their memories—even as he discovers his own mettle.

> Now, through the memories, he had seen oceans and mountain lakes and streams that gurgled through woods; and now he saw the familiar wide river beside the path differently. He saw all of the light and color and history it contained and carried in its slow-moving water; and he knew that there was an Elsewhere from which it came, and an Elsewhere to which it was going.

Style

Lois Lowry's superb ability to create action through dialogue, build tension in mood, and still allow her readers plenty of room for interpretation leads to riveting prose. She creates a sense of unrest through subtle references to things that go unexplained but that nevertheless establish a sense of foreboding. There is a subtle and gradual development of imagery as Jonas comes to know and to see more, with the style reflecting his new vision. The juxtaposition of the richness and pain of the memories he receives with the sameness of life in his community builds a powerful theme.

Theme

The theme of this profound novel pushes readers to ask if opposite values can be balanced. The story echoes the folkloric moral that "beans and bread in peace are better than cakes and ale in fear," but turns it upside down to question the consequences. If security means a lack of freedom, is it worth it? If no hatred means no love or passion, would we want to live this way? What is the price of control? The contrast between the lives of those living in the controlled community and those who face the memories and terrors of a free world forces readers to consider questions about what it means to

Courtesy of Houghton Mifflin

Lois Lowry has been awarded the Newbery Medal twice: in 1990 for *Number the Stars* and in 1994 for *The Giver*. In 1978 she received the International Reading Association Children's Book Award for *A Summer to Die*, her very first book for children, and she has received numerous other awards since.

Lois Lowry writes broadly humorous and deadly serious stories in a variety of genres: realistic, historical, and science fiction. Her books include more than a dozen humorous *Anastasia Krupnik* stories, including a series about Anastasia's younger brother, Sam; the serious *Autumn Street*; and the gripping *Rabble Starkey*. She writes about eccentric relatives in *Us and Uncle Fraud*, about an adopted girl searching for a birth parent in *Find a Stranger, Say Goodbye*, and about a girl who baby-sits in *Taking Care of Terrific*, *The One Hundredth Thing About Caroline*, and *Your Move, J. P.* Her historical fiction novel *Number the Stars* and her science fiction novels *The Giver* and *Gathering Blue* demonstrate the breadth of this powerful writer.

In her acceptance speech for the Newbery Medal for *The Giver*, Lois Lowry describes Jonas, the protagonist, looking at the river from Elsewhere:

"Now he saw the familiar wide river beside the path differently. He saw all of the light and color and history it contained and carried in its slow-moving water; and he knew that there was an Elsewhere from which it came, and an Elsewhere to which it was going."

Lois Lowry portrays life as a river of memories that carries everything that comes from Elsewhere into our world, and then goes on to enter others. She describes her own process in writing *The Giver* by using a metaphor, saying that memories began to come to her as a spring bubbles up from the earth, and were added to by other memories until collected bits and pieces from the past mingled into a river that became *The Giver*.

How her life enters her stories is apparent when you read her autobiography, *Looking Back: A Book of Memories*. Lois Lowry splits her writing time between Boston and New Hampshire.

---

be human. More than just a novel about a future world, *The Giver* is a novel about the complexity of human life.

Both *Tuck Everlasting* and *The Giver* are outstanding examples of the genres of fantasy and science fiction at their best. Within these genres there are many types of stories, all of which offer their own special delights.

Types of Fantasy

As described above, fantasy can be deeply serious. This type of fantasy is sometimes called "high" fantasy. High fantasy lies closely beside ancient folklore and contains archetypal themes. It explores the struggle between good and evil or follows a quest for personal identity. More lighthearted fantasy uses a veil of unreality to disguise the real world in some way. The approach may be as simple as animals that act like humans or as complex as fully developed miniature worlds that reflect real life with a small twist. Often, it is marked by word play, wit, and humor. Fantasy writers use devices such as time slips and magic, fully developed unreal-world settings, or supernatural characters to create the fantasy. By creating a fantasy, writers are able to explore freely issues that might be too disturbing when considered in realistic settings. The metaphorical nature of fantasy allows children to consider prejudice, death, war, the consequences of beauty, and other serious issues in a manageable way. It is the seriousness of the questions that a story raises that determines whether or not a fantasy is "light" or "high." In either case, authors may create their fantasy in one or more of the following ways.

ANIMAL FANTASY

Animal fantasy attributes human thought, feeling, and language to animals. Children like to see animals dressed like people and believe in them readily. Actually, young children are often willing to invest any kind of creature or object with human characteristics. Because books that extend and enrich a normal developmental tendency strike a responsive chord in children, animal fantasy is a well-loved form. Like the folktale, it becomes part of children's literary experiences before they make clear distinctions between fact and fancy. This early pleasure in animal fantasy often continues as children mature into reading novels.

Some of the most memorable characters from children's literature are created in animal fantasy. Naive Wilbur, incorrigible Toad of Toad Hall, mischievous Peter Rabbit, Babar, and Winnie the Pooh call to mind many modern classics of this genre. Animal fantasies for older readers create an allegorical world in which the human scene is replayed to amuse and, often, to instruct. Authors of books like *Charlotte's Web* (I) by E. B. White, *Wind in the Willows* (I) by Kenneth Grahame, *Ratha's Creature* (A) by Clare Bell, and *Watership Down* (A) by Richard Adams use animal fantasy to comment on human frailties and foibles. In *Charlotte's Web*, for example, we find not only a delightful picture of the power of friendship and love, but also a reminder that in the midst of life there is also death. In *Watership Down* we confront, among other issues, the consequences of war.

Rat and Mole welcome the field mice carolers and treat them to warmth and a sip of mulled ale after enjoying their songs in **Wind in the Willows.**

Jill Barklem's **Brambly Hedge** (P) series presents realistic, everyday events, as experienced by a community of mice. The detailed, beautiful illustrations create a setting that heightens the pleasure. In books for slightly older readers, Dick King-Smith examines issues of individual difference in *Babe, the Gallant Pig* (I) and tolerance in *Martin's Mice* (I). Avi's **Tales from Dimwood Forest** series, which includes *Poppy, Poppy and Rye, Ragweed,* and *Ereth's Birthday* (all I), follows the adventures of one special mouse, Poppy, and her friends. As they seek to make a safe home in Dimwood Forest, they encounter many dangers from humans and other predators. The combination of humorous dialogue, notable characters, and a vividly detailed setting makes these books perfect for readers who enjoy animal fantasy and are ready for short novels. Once they have read this series, many will want to go on to Brian Jacques's **Redwall** (A) books, a multivolume series that provides high adventure, memorable characters, and intriguing descriptions of battles and weapons, all within an animal fantasy. These books are devoured by boys from fourth through seventh grade who enjoy animal fantasy. Because there are so many of them, many children never run out of good books to read! The Booklist at the end of this chapter contains a list of memorable animal fantasies.

MINIATURE WORLDS

Every cultural group has its folkloric sprites, elves, trolls, hobbits, or leprechauns, which go unseen about houses and villages. Tales about these small beings charm audiences, young and old alike. Just as older readers continue to enjoy novel-length animal fantasy, they also continue to respond to the call of miniature worlds. There is something compelling about smallness that pulls readers into a story world. What and how do small people eat, dress, move about? How does smallness transform daily life as we know it? What extra challenges does it pose? Miniature worlds, like animal fantasy, fascinate readers interested in details. Stories set in miniature worlds might take a lighthearted look at what life in miniature would be like, or a serious exploration of human needs and desires. Fantasies about toys or miniature beings highlight human emotions by displaying them in action on a miniscule scale. From Arriety in *The Borrowers* (I), by Mary Norton, to the Minnipins in *The Gammage Cup* and *The Whisper of Glocken* (both I), by Carol Kendall, the best and worst in human nature is magnified against a lilliputian backdrop where characters are memorable because of their size.

A secret world-within-a-world where dolls live *Behind the Attic Wall* (I–A) is created in Sylvia Cassedy's novel of a lonely, belligerent girl. Maggie, an incorrigible 12-year-old rebel who has been expelled from numerous boarding schools for "poor adjustment," hears whispers behind the walls and goes exploring. These whispers gradually lead her to two dolls who welcome her to their strange, secret life. The contrast between the tenderness Maggie shows to the dolls and her scathing response to humans around her is stark. In the Booklist we list memorable fantasy set in miniature worlds.

TIME SLIPS, UNREAL WORLDS, AND MAGIC

In some stories, time is the element that is carried beyond the realm of everyday experience, as characters move between their current reality and other times and places. For many writers, the past and future are part of the present; by challenging our understanding of time as sequential, these authors are making a statement about the meaning of time itself. One such writer, Eleanor Cameron (1969), describes a globe of time in which the past, present, and future are perceived as a whole.

Authors of fantasy invent a dazzling variety of devices to permit their characters to move in and out of conventional time. The children in C. S. Lewis's *The Lion, the Witch, and the Wardrobe* (I) enter the land of Narnia through a wardrobe door; while they are in Narnia, time does not pass in their real world. John Scieszka plays with time in his **Time Warp Trio** series (I) in which Joe, Fred, and Sam, ordinary boys all, manage to travel through time to a series of unlikely places. The eight books in this series, including *It's All Greek to Me*, are lighthearted fun.

Several time-slip fantasies focus on a central character going through a difficult adjustment period; loneliness, alienation, and extraordinary sensitivity seem to be associated with time travel. The time travelers in Anne Lindbergh's *Travel Far, Pay No Fare* (I) enter the world of stories with the help of a magic bookmark. Parsley's father is marrying Owen's mother, and they are not happy about this new family arrangement. When Parsley finds that she can enter the world of whatever story she happens to be reading by placing her bookmark in the book and beginning to read, she begins to visit various stories in an attempt to prevent the marriage. Owen gradually learns that Parsley really means it when she says that her cats are borrowed from Beatrix Potter, Charles Perrault, and Beverly Cleary.

Many books use time travel as a device for transporting characters into the past. These stories have a carefully researched, vivid historical story embedded within the time slip. Novels such as David Weisman's *Jeremy Visick* (I–A), Hans Magnus Enzensberger's *Lost in Time* (I–A) and Jane Yolen's *The Devil's Arithmetic* (A) use the device to propel readers into the past, where they confront the realities of history. In many cases, these books are more aptly categorized as historical fiction that uses the fantasy device of time slips; the important part of the story is not the fantasy, but the historical story.

Magic is a basic ingredient in fantasy. Often the magic is mixed with humor, and children respond avidly to both. Whether watching the evil spell cast by *The Dwarf Giant* (P) by Anita Lobel, delighting in the antics of Astrid Lindgren's *Pippi Longstocking* (I), or enjoying William Steig's *Sylvester and the Magic Pebble* (I), children recognize the possibilities that magic entails; they enter a world that does not operate by natural law. Bruce Coville's **Magic Shop** series (I) uses the device of a shop that caters to would-be magicians to allow realistic characters to enter fantasy worlds. Dragons figure prominently in *Jeremy Thatcher, Dragon Hatcher*, and talking toads are featured in *Jennifer Murdley's Toad*. In *Orwell's Luck* (I), Richard Jennings creates a setting that seems realistic except for the fact that a wounded wild rabbit is sending messages through newspaper horoscopes to the young girl who rescued him. David Almond's *Skellig* (A), a beautifully haunting, moving tale, involves a being that seems to be an angel, at least to the two young protagonists who see and talk with him.

John Scieszka transports characters and readers alike to ancient Greece, much to the delight of all.

J. K. Rowling's *Harry Potter and the Sorcerer's Stone* (I), *Harry Potter and the Chamber of Secrets* (I), *Harry Potter and the Prisoner of Azkaban* (I–A), and *Harry Potter and the Goblet of Fire* (A) make use of a vast array of magic devices, such as Harry's famous Quidditch broom, owls that deliver mail, invisibility cloaks, and maps that show people and their locations. They are also firmly anchored in the well-developed fantasy world of Hogwarts, a school for magic that is peopled by teachers and students who practice an assortment of bizarre and intriguing magic. All of this magic is carefully placed and the actions within the fantasy world are ultimately logical. Rowling never violates the rules she creates, and readers devour these books with a passion rarely seen. These and other fantasies that use magic are listed in the Booklist at the end of the chapter.

LITERARY LORE

The literary tale, a story deliberately crafted by a writer who intentionally imitates the traditional qualities of ancient folklore, has become increasingly popular over the past several years. Teaching Idea 6.3 offers suggestions for exploring these tales with students. Initially, these stories appeared as "fractured fairy tales," stories that were not cultural variants

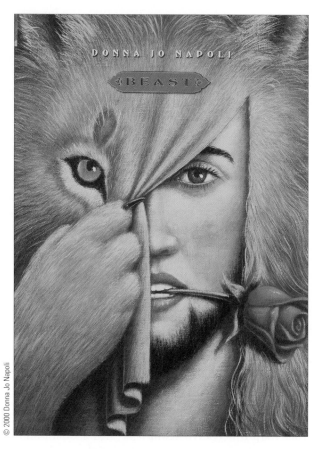

Donna Jo Napoli is a virtuoso of the literary tale. She weaves new stories out of old favorites, as in her retelling of "Beauty and the Beast."

Teaching Idea 6 ✩ 3

Literary Tales and Folkloric Themes

It is easy to confuse literary tales with folklore because the two genres are quite similar. Modern writers intentionally use folkloric elements in their stories, and sometimes they do this so well that their work is often mistaken for folktales. For example, Hans Christian Andersen captures the essence of folktales so artfully that it's hard to distinguish his work from the massive body of anonymous traditional literature. Other authors build upon essential elements of well-known folklore and craft novel-length stories around their central core. After you have read several literary tales with your students, ask them to consider the following questions:

✳ What folklore elements do they contain?

✳ How subtly does the author weave in the folklore elements? Give an example.

✳ Compare a literary tale to the original piece of folklore on which it was modeled.

of well-known folktales, but rather the deliberate construction of a writer intending to imitate, embellish, or alter traditional folktales. John Scieszka's *The True Story of the Three Little Pigs* and *The Stinky Cheese Man* (both I) are well-loved examples of this type of story for younger readers. Increasingly, writers for middle school and young adult readers have created stories that weave around traditional tales. Robin McKinley's *Beauty* (A), an early example of this phenomenon, has been followed by *Rose Daughter* and *Spindle's End* (both A). Donna Jo Napoli's *The Prince of the Pond* (I) is a delightful tale for intermediate-grade readers. Older readers, too, can appreciate her mastery of style in books such as *Crazy Jack, Beast, Spinners, Zel,* and *The Magic Circle* (all A). Gail Carson Levine's *Ella Enchanted* (I), a delightful twist of the Cinderella tale, won a Newbery Honor.

Stories that have a haunting mythic quality from writers such as Hans Christian Andersen, Jane Yolen, Natalie Babbitt, Mollie Hunter, and Susan Cooper remind readers of the ancient roots of tales. Mollie Hunter, noted fantasy writer, acknowledges her links with folklore, a "chain of communication through the centuries—the long unbroken line of folk memory stretching . . . from Megalithic times to the present day" (1976, p. 65). Stories that have a haunting mythic quality and echo the sounds from storytellers' tongues of ages past are literary lore.

In *A Stranger Came Ashore* (I), Mollie Hunter captures on the very first page a timeless moment reflecting this mythic quality:

> It was a while ago, in the days when they used to tell stories about creatures called the Selkie Folk. A stranger came ashore to an island at that time—a man who gave his name as Finn Learson—and there was a mystery about him which had to do with these selkie creatures. Or so some people say, anyway. . . . (1975, p. 1)

QUEST TALES

Boston Globe-Horn Book Award-winner Franny Billingsley also builds on the Selkie tales in *The Folk Keeper* (A), a hauntingly beautiful story of a young girl who disguises herself as a boy in order to keep herself safe as a folk keeper, a person who controls the damage that the folk can create when they are hungry and unhappy. When she moves to a wild island to control the folk there, she discovers her own heritage and her true powers, even as she is forced to acknowledge her femininity as she matures and falls in love. This quest tale epitomizes the depth of emotion and complexity of ideas that mark high fantasy.

Archetypal quest themes from folklore become vividly evident in high fantasy. Here again is the misty outline of a story in which we search for the golden age or lose—and seek to regain—our identity. Victory in the battle between good and evil depends upon finding the missing heir, recognizing a prince or princess in disguise, or achieving utopia under the rule of a king whose coming has been foretold. Quest stories that are most memorable describe characters' outer and inner struggles and may involve Herculean journeys where overcoming obstacles vanquishes evil. Quests often become a search for an inner, rather than an outer, enemy. Inner strength is required as characters are put to a variety of challenges that often seem endless and unbeatable. It is the indomitable goodness of character that prevails. Books such as Lloyd Alexander's **The Prydain Chronicles** (I), recently reissued in beautiful, matched editions, continue to enchant young readers eager to test their metaphorical mettle against all odds.

Some of the most remarkable books of this type published in the past few years are Philip Pullman's **His Dark Materials** trilogy (all A). Readers are introduced to Lyra, the young and engaging protagonist, in *The Golden Compass*. Lyra is an interesting blend: She is both a street urchin and a highly intelligent daughter of eminent and powerful people. She thinks herself an orphan but soon discovers to her horror who her mother and father really are. Lyra sets out on her quest to save herself and the children who are being kidnapped and sent north to be the victims of a horrible experiment. By the end of the story she has come to realize that her quest is bigger than this, and she unhesitatingly steps into a new world, determined to continue. Continue she does, in *The Subtle Knife*, where she meets her partner, Will, a hero not unlike herself but from a different world. They continue their struggles, moving between worlds, aided by witches and angels, running from the evildoers of the church, until the triumphant ending of *The Amber Spyglass*. This series has it all: child heroes, alternate worlds, time slips, magic objects, fantastic creatures, imagination at its height. It is all anchored within an overarching theme of the struggle between good and evil, mirrored in the story of *Paradise Lost*, and the overwhelming power of love. These and other quest tales are listed in the Booklist at the end of this chapter. Teaching Idea 6.4 offers a way to help children link their own lives and concerns with the heroes of some of these quest tales.

Philip Pullman's *magnificent trilogy,* **His Dark Materials**, *begins with the adventures of Lyra in* **The Golden Compass**.

Teaching Idea 6 ✵ 4

The Power of Naming

According to traditional lore there is power in knowing someone's true name; to know a true name is to hold that person's life in your hands. *Rumpelstiltskin* (Grimm) and *Duffy and the Devil* (Zemach) illustrate the folkloric power of naming. In high fantasy, the secrecy of a name and the true identity of a hero is heavily guarded. Only trusted friends know the hero's true name. Locate books in which naming is integral to the plot. Start with these:

Alexander, Lloyd, *The Book of Three*

_____, *The Black Cauldron*

_____, *The Castle of Llyr*

_____, *The High King*

_____, *Taran Wanderer*

LeGuin, Ursula, *The Farthest Shore*

_____, *Tombs of Atuan*

_____, *Wizard of Earthsea*

L'Engle, Madeleine, *Wind in the Door*

Sutcliff, Rosemary, *The Road to Camlann*

Questions for book discussion:

✳ If people who knew your name held power over you, who would you allow to know your name?

✳ What kind of people would you trust to know your true name?

✳ From what kind of people would you keep your name secret?

Types of Science Fiction

Most category systems, including ones for dividing science fiction into types, are arbitrary; some novels fit into more than one classification. There are, however, three major themes treated in science fiction: mind control, life in the future, and survival. As with fantasy, some science fiction is light; it relies on technological advances, such as space travel, to create the story. Many children are introduced to science fiction through some of these lighter stories. Science fantasy, that blend of fantasy and science fiction that is often set in other worlds but is uncomplicated by elaborate scientific theories, provides a good entree for beginning science fiction readers. As they read and enjoy these stories they will become interested in moving on to more complex stories that explore significant issues. Young readers enjoy Jane Yolen's

Commander Toad (P) series, and Dav Pilkey's **Captain Underpants** series (I), as well as books such as Betsy Duffey's *Alien for Rent* (P–I) or Louis Sachar's *Marvin Redpost: A Flying Birthday Cake?* (I), all humorous science fantasy.

Other science fiction for younger readers is more serious, while still not overly complex. In a beautifully written story by Jill Paton Walsh, young Pattie takes *The Green Book* (I) with her when she and her family escape from the dying planet Earth. When they arrive at their new settlement Pattie and her friends explore their new world. Their courage and perseverance lead the community to find a way to exist in their new world, and Pattie's green-covered blank book becomes the place where the community can write the story of their survival. The occasional soft illustrations by Lloyd Bloom help describe what life is like in Shine.

Science fiction for older readers offers the same kind of deep questioning that fantasy offers, although the questions asked are, in this case, scientific possibilities.

MIND CONTROL

Several science fiction writers deal with themes of mind control, telepathy, ESP, and other forms of communication across time and space. As computers, television, and other forms of communication reach more and more people across the globe, and advances in medicine make possible genetic and nervous system alterations, the potential for mind control on a grand scale grows.

One early example is John Christopher's **White Mountain** trilogy. This series about extraterrestial invaders of Earth appeals to today's readers in the upper elementary grades. *The White Mountains* (A), *The City of Gold and Lead* (A), and *The Pool of Fire* (A), are set in the twenty-first century in a world ruled by the Tripods, dreaded robots. When humans are 14, the Tripods implant steel caps in their skulls that keep them submissive, docile, and helpless. Will and his two friends learn that free people live in the White Mountains, and they make a hazardous journey to join them. Humane characters are pitted against hostile aliens in a series of bizarre encounters. Christopher's narrative impels readers to ponder the values of life and science.

Lois Lowry's *Gathering Blue* (A) continues her exploration of the possibilities of controlled communities that was begun in *The Giver* (A). When her mother dies, Kira is not sure how she is going to live; her deformed leg and lack of family make her a victim for vicious and hostile neighbors. When she is forced by her neighbors to be judged by the Council of Guardians, she expects to be cast out into the Field of Leaving, to be devoured by the Beasts that lurk there. Unexpectedly, her amazing skill with a needle and thread, something she learned from her mother, saves her life. She becomes The Threader, the one person in the com-

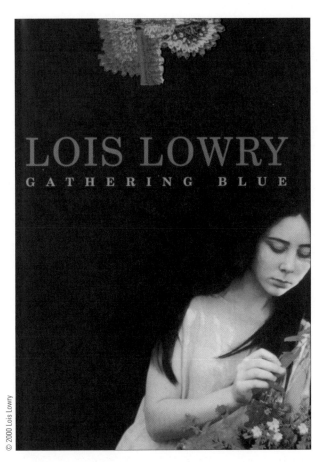

© 2000 Lois Lowry

Lois Lowry creates a future community in which the force of human nature pushes against control by powerful guardians.

munity who repairs the Singer's Robe and embroiders the community's future for them. Her startling discovery that the Singer is chained, and the possibility of life in another community that her father's reappearance brings, force Kira to consider issues of community values, creativity, and fear.

LIFE IN THE FUTURE

Some science fiction examines anthropological-sociological aspects of life in the future and considers questions of individual commitment and ethical behavior. The results of aggression and competition versus peace and cooperation, a consideration of what it means to be human, how to live in an increasingly crowded world, comparisons among cultures at different levels of development, and finding one's purpose in life are all ideas that science fiction writers explore. Peter Dickinson examines the possibility of brain transplants in *Eva* (A), a powerful story of a girl who wakes up in a hospital and realizes that something is terribly

wrong. She is horrified to discover that her brain has been implanted into a chimpanzee's body.

Helen Hoover has contributed a sizable body of science fiction that addresses sociological themes. In *The Shepherd Moon* (I–A), 13-year-old Merry Ambrose watches, in the forty-eighth century, for the rise of the five full moons circling the earth. Four of the moons were satellites built as space habitats; one, the Shepherd Moon, Terra II, was the first of the space satellites sent from earth hundreds of years earlier. Mikel Goodman, the product of genetic engineering on Terra II, lands near Merry's home and initiates his plan to rule the earth. His innocent appearance belies his malevolent amorality, and although he does not succeed in taking over the earth, his questions cause Merry to become aware of many social problems on earth. Hoover raises questions about the nature of the interaction between life on earth and life in space.

In Kate Gilmore's *The Exchange Student* (A), a student from another planet arrives on earth and is delighted to have been placed in a home that is full of animals, for he has a plan for these animals that he must conceal from his earth hosts. He and other exchange students are looking for DNA with which to repopulate their home planets. Mary Logue's *Dancing with an Alien* (A) is an unusual science fiction novel in that it is likely to appeal to girls who do not usually read science fiction. It is a romance, with a science fiction twist.

The Sterkarm Handshake (A), by Susan Price, winner of the 1999 *Guardian* Fiction Prize, blends the future and the past. The Elves, time travelers from the twenty-first-century, return to the sixteenth century to plunder the rich natural resources of the border country between England and Scotland. When Andrea, a twenty-first-century anthropologist, takes Per, her sixteenth-century lover, through time in order to save his life, she creates an unmanageable situation. Cultures clash, both societies and individuals, and there are no easy answers. Teaching Idea 6.5 describes a way to get students to think about the effects of scientific advances in their own lives, and how they might influence the future.

SURVIVAL

Both gloomy and hopeful views of the future are apparent in the literature of survival. Although most nuclear scenarios are both all-encompassing and extremely depressing, an entire body of books exists that show children surviving a nuclear war. Postnuclear holocaust books such as *Children of the Dust* offer young readers the opportunity to consider deep, abiding questions such as what it means to be human.

Stories about survival are not limited to the horrors of life after a nuclear war. The problems of life as it is today—the overcrowding, the pollution, the extinction of animal and plant species, and the question of an adequate food

Teaching Idea 6 ☆ 5

Technology Changes the World

Many people believe that each small change in our world results in a chain reaction of changes. We cannot foresee subsequent changes and we cannot control them; some may bring good results, some undesirable ones. Fantasy and science fiction writers take the possibility of change to its ultimate extreme.

Ask students to list kinds of new technology that they use. Describe their application in a possible future world. Consider pros and cons of their use. How will they affect life? Ask students to describe future life by extrapolating on changes brought about by new technology. Compare the changes.

List of Inventions	Good Changes	Bad Changes
Cellular phones		
CD players		
Computers		
Fax machines		
Laser		
Medical devices		
Photocopy machines		
Plane travel		
Printers		
Radiocarbon dating		
Scanners		
Television		
X-ray photography		

supply—provide science fiction writers with unlimited opportunities to project how humans will survive on earth. Some propose that the new frontier lies in outer space. Others propose that if we remain here on earth, the new frontier might be what we could do to make earth more livable.

Caroline Macdonald sets *The Lake at the End of the World* (A) in the year 2025. The world has been environmentally devastated and one family—young Diana and her parents—think that they are the only survivors until Diana sees a boy, Hector, near the mouth of a cave. Speaking in alternating chapters, the two young protagonists narrate the story of how Hector and some of his people escape from the underground colony in which they have been living. Issues of mind control and power intertwine with environmental issues in this fast-paced, exciting story.

The Ear, the Eye, and the Arm (A) by Nancy Farmer deals with life in the year 2194 when people live in armed fortresses and in tunnels under toxic waste dumps. Thirteen-year-old Tendai and his younger sister and brother are kidnapped and forced to work in miserable surroundings. Their parents engage the Ear, Eye, and Arm detective

agency to find them, but the detectives get near to the children only moments after they have moved on. The mystery and close calls keep readers turning the pages to find out what happens. These and other engaging science fiction stories are listed in the Booklist at the end of this chapter.

Fantasy and Science Fiction in the Classroom

Once children have enjoyed and made their own the many picture books that can also be classified as fantasy, it is an easy step into longer, more complex stories. Many children will find these stories on their own, moving naturally from books like Mem Fox's *Possum Magic* (N–P) to books such as E. B. White's *Charlotte's Web* (I) or Natalie Babbitt's *Tuck Everlasting* (I–A). As children develop as readers and thinkers, they discover the intellectual enchantment of

Ursula Le Guin's *Tehanu: The Last Book of Earthsea* (A), Robin McKinley's *The Hero and the Crown* (A), or Meredith Ann Pierce's *A Gathering of Gargoyles* (A). They are intrigued by the powerful questions that Sylvia Engdahl asks in *Beyond the Tomorrow Mountains* (A) and that Mary Caraker considers in *The Faces of Ceti* (A).

Some children, however, will leave fantasy behind as they grow older and will never discover the joys of science fiction unless they are helped into these genres by knowledgeable teachers. In many cases reading aloud is the very best way to encourage readers to expand their interests. The newfound interest in fantasy engendered by the **Harry Potter** series can be molded by teachers who know and enjoy fantasy and science fiction and who plan read-aloud programs that offer children the opportunity to experience books that move beyond magic into thoughtful considerations of some of life's most important questions. Intermediate-grade teachers might want to read some of the lighter fantasy and science fiction books, and upper-grade teachers might want to select science fiction short stories to read aloud. The books that we discuss and list in this chapter are well written and thought-provoking and are excellent choices to read aloud, both to pique and to fuel developing interest in these genres.

Fantasy and science fiction books can also be read and discussed by literature groups, an idea that is discussed in Chapter 12. These books fit well into genre studies as well as within many thematic units. The kinds of questions about values, selfhood, good and evil, and courage that fantasy and science fiction writers consider are also treated in some contemporary realism and historical fiction. Looking at books from various genres that contain similar themes can be a powerful reading experience.

Benefits of fantasy and science fiction include the flexibility of imagination that they encourage and the important questions that they push readers to consider. As children read stories about people and events that are real and familiar to them, they also need to read stories that make them wonder, that cause them to consider, and that stretch their souls. Fantasy and science fiction can do just that.

Summary

Fantasy is concerned with people, places, or events that could not occur in the real world. Science fiction is concerned with the impact of scientific possibilities on the world of the future. In both genres we find many excellent stories that are well written, that present multidimensional characters engaging in exciting plots, and that contain profound themes. Although some children move naturally from their favorite picture-book fantasies into more complex fantasies and science fiction, some need to be helped into the more complex books by their teachers. In either case the rewards are well worth the effort.

Locate the interview with Natalie Babbitt in the March/April 2000 issue of *The Horn Book Magazine*. After you have discussed *Tuck Everlasting* with your literature discussion group, read the interview and then talk again about any insights you gained or questions that were raised by hearing what Babbitt has to say.

Harry Potter and many other fantasy books have been the target of censorship for a long time. It is difficult for some to understand how someone might be upset by a fantasy that, after all, is not real. In an article in the May/June 2000 issue of *The Horn Book Magazine,* Kimbra Wilder Gish explains some of the reasoning behind the objections of certain religious groups to fantasy stories. Her article is quite informative and does not urge or even condone censorship. Read her piece and then consider, in class discussion or in an essay, how you would respond to these concerns if they were brought to you by the parent of a child you teach or work with in a library.

Booklist

Animal Fantasy

Adams, Richard, *Watership Down* (A)
Avi, *Ereth's Birthday* (I)
_____, *Perloo the Bold* (I)
_____, *Poppy* (I)
_____, *Poppy and Rye* (I)
_____, *Ragweed* (I)
Barklem, Jill, *Brambly Hedge* (P)
Bell, Clare, *Ratha's Creature* (A)
Brett, Jan, *Annie and the Wild Animals* (P)
_____, *Berlioz the Bear* (P)
Brown, Marc Tolon, *Arthur's Teacher Trouble* (P)
Burningham, John, *Mr. Gumpy's Outing* (P)

De Brunhoff, Jean, *The Story of Babar* (P)
Farmer, Nancy, *The Warm Place* (I)
Freeman, Don, *Corduroy* (P)
Grahame, Kenneth, *Wind in the Willows* (I)
Howe, James, *Bunnicula* (I)
Jacques, Brian, *Lord Brocktree* (A)
_____, *Marlfox* (A)
_____, *Redwall* (A)
Jarrell, Randall, *Animal Family* (I)
Jennings, Richard, *Orwell's Luck* (I)
King-Smith, Dick, *Babe: The Gallant Pig* (I)
_____, *Martin's Mice* (I)
Lawson, Robert, *Rabbit Hill* (A)
Lisle, Janet Taylor, *Forest* (A)
Lobel, Arnold, *Frog and Toad Are Friends* (P)
Lofting, Hugh, *The Story of Doctor Doolittle* (I)
MacDonald, Amy, *Little Beaver and the Echo* (P)
Milne, A. A., *Winnie the Pooh* (I)
Oppel, Kenneth, *Silverwing* (I)
_____, *Sunwing* (I)
Potter, Beatrix, *The Tale of Peter Rabbit* (P)
Selden, George, *Cricket in Times Square* (I)
_____, *Old Meadow* (I)
_____, *Tucker's Countryside* (I)
Soinbhe, Lally, *A Hive for the Honeybee* (A)
VandeVelde, Vivian, *Smart Dog* (I)
White, E. B., *Charlotte's Web* (I)

Miniature Worlds, Time Slips, Unreal Worlds, and Magic

Almond, David, *Kit's Wilderness* (A)
_____, *Skellig* (A)
Babbitt, Natalie, *Search for Delicious* (I)
_____, *Tuck Everlasting* (I)
Block, Francesca Lia, *I Was a Teenage Fairy* (A)
Bosse, Malcolm, *Cave Beyond Time* (A)
Boston, Lucy M., *Children of Green Knowe* (I)
Brittain, Bill, *Wizards and the Monster* (I)
Cassedy, Sylvia, *Behind the Attic Wall* (A)
_____, *Lucie Babbidge's House* (A)
Conrad, Pam, *The Tub People* (P)
_____, *Zoe Rising* (I)
Coville, Bruce, *Jennifer Murdley's Toad* (I)
_____, *Jeremy Thatcher, Dragon Hatcher* (I)
Curry, Jane Louise, *Dark Shade* (A)
Dahl, Roald, *Charlie and the Chocolate Factory* (I)
_____, *James and the Giant Peach* (I)
_____, *Matilda* (I)
Dexter, Catherine, *Mazemaker* (A)
Dunlop, Eileen, *Webster's Leap* (A)
Fleischman, Paul, *Time Train* (P)
_____, *Westlandia* (P)

French, Jackie, *Somewhere Around the Corner* (A)
Hamilton, Virginia, *The Magical Adventures of Pretty Pearl* (A)
James, Mary, *Shoebag* (I)
Jansson, Tove, *Finn Family Moomintroll* (I)
Jennings, Richard, *Orwell's Luck* (I)
Joyce, William, *George Shrinks* (P)
Juster, Norton, *The Phantom Tollbooth* (I)
Kendall, Carol, *The Gammage Cup* (I)
_____, *The Whisper of Glocken* (I)
King-Smith, Dick, *The Water Horse* (I)
Lewis, C. S., *The Lion, the Witch, and the Wardrobe* (I)
Lindbergh, Anne, *The Hunky Dory Dairy* (I)
_____, *Travel Far, Pay No Fare* (I)
_____, *Three Lives to Live* (A)
Lindgren, Astrid, *Pippi Longstocking* (P)
Lisle, Janet Taylor, *Lampfish of Twill* (A)
_____, *Afternoon of the Elves* (A)
Lobel, Anita, *The Dwarf Giant* (P)
Nesbit, E., *Enchanted Castle* (I)
Nickle, John, *The Ant Bully* (P)
Norton, Mary, *The Borrowers* (I)
Pearce, Phillipa, *Tom's Midnight Garden* (I)
Peterson, John, *The Littles* (I)
Rowling, J. K., *Harry Potter and the Sorcerer's Stone* (I)
Rubenstein, Gillian, *Under the Cat's Eye: A Tale of Morph and Mystery* (A)
Scieszka, Jon, *The Good, the Bad, and the Goofy* (P)
_____, *It's All Greek to Me* (I)
_____, *Knights of the Kitchen Table* (P)
_____, *The Not-So-Jolly Roger* (P)
_____, *Your Mother Was a Neanderthal* (P)
Sendak, Maurice, *Where the Wild Things Are* (P)
Steig, William, *Sylvester and the Magic Pebble* (P)
Turkle, Brinton, *Do Not Open* (P)
Van Allsburg, Chris, *The Garden of Abdul Gasazi* (I)
_____, *Jumanji* (I)
_____, *The Wretched Stone* (I)
_____, *The Wreck of the Zephyr* (I)
Waugh, Sylvia, *The Mennyms* (I)
Walsh, Jill Paton, *Chance Child* (A)
Wiesner, David, *Sector 7* (P)
Winthrop, Elizabeth, *Battle for the Castle* (I)
_____, *Castle in the Attic* (I)
Wrede, Patricia, *Dealing with Dragons* (A)
Wrightson, Patricia, *The Nargun and the Stars* (A)
Yorinks, Arthur, *Hey, Al* (P)

Literary Lore

Lamm, C. Drew, *The Frog Prince* (I)
Levine, Gail Carson, *Ella Enchanted* (I)
McKinley, Robin, *Beauty* (A)

_____, *Rose Daughter* (A)

_____, *Spindle's End* (A)

Morris, Gerald, *The Savage Damsel and the Dwarf* (A)

_____, *The Squire, His Knight, and His Lady* (A)

_____, *The Squire's Tale* (A)

Napoli, Donna Jo, *Beast* (A)

_____, *Crazy Jack* (A)

_____, *The Magic Circle* (A)

_____, *The Prince of the Pond* (I)

_____, *Spinners* (A)

_____, *Zel* (A)

Pullman, Philip, *I Was a Rat* (I)

Scieszka, Jon, *The Stinky Cheese Man* (I)

_____, *The True Story of the Three Little Pigs* (I)

Springer, Nancy, *I Am Mordred: A Tale from Camelot* (A)

_____, *Magic Steps* (A)

_____, *Wild Magic* (A)

_____, *Wolf Speaker* (A)

_____, *The Woman Who Rides Like a Man* (A)

Pullman, Philip, *The Amber Spyglass* (A)

_____, *The Golden Compass* (A)

_____, *The Subtle Knife* (A)

Tolkien, J. R. R., *The Hobbit* (A)

_____, *The Lord of the Ring* (A)

Wynne-Jones, Diana, *The Crown of Dalemark* (A)

_____, *Cart and Cwidder* (A)

_____, *Dark Lord of Dorkhdim* (A)

_____, *Drowned Ammet* (A)

_____, *The Spellcoats* (A)

Yolen, Jane, *The Dragon's Boy* (I)

Quest Stories

Alexander, Lloyd, *The Black Cauldron* (I)

_____, *Book of Three* (I)

_____, *The Castle of Llyr* (I)

_____, *Foundling and Other Tales of Prydain* (I)

_____, *The High King* (I)

_____, *Taran Wanderer* (I)

Barron, Thomas, *The Ancient One* (A)

_____, *Heartlight* (A)

_____, *The Merlin Effect* (A)

Billingsley, Franny, *The Folk Keeper* (A)

Cooper, Susan, *The Dark Is Rising* (A)

_____, *Greenwitch* (A)

_____, *The Grey King* (A)

_____, *Over Sea, Under Stone* (A)

_____, *Silver on the Tree* (A)

LeGuin, Ursula, *The Farthest Shore* (A)

_____, *Tehanu: The Last Book of Earthsea* (A)

_____, *The Tombs of Atuan* (A)

_____, *Wizard of Earthsea* (A)

Lewis. C. S., *The Lion, the Witch and the Wardrobe* (I)

_____, *The Horse and His Boy* (I)

_____, *The Last Battle* (I)

_____, *The Magician's Nephew* (I)

_____, *Prince Caspian* (I)

_____, *The Silver Chair* (I)

_____, *The Voyage of the "Dawn Treader"* (I)

Lisle, Janet Taylor, *The Lost Flower Children* (I)

McKinley, Robin, *The Blue Sword* (A)

_____, *The Hero and the Crown* (A)

Pierce, Meredith, *Darkangel* (A)

_____, *A Gathering of Gargoyles* (A)

Pierce, Tamora, *Alanna, the First Adventure* (A)

_____, *The Emperor Mage* (A)

_____, *In the Hand of the Goddess* (A)

_____, *Lioness Rampant* (A)

Science Fantasy and Short Stories

Alcock, Vivien, *Ghostly Companions* (A)

_____, *Monster Garden* (I)

Asimov, Isaac, *Norby the Mixed-Up Robot* (I)

Asimov, Isaac, Martin Harry Greenberg, and Charles Waugh, editors, *Time Warp* (A)

Atwater, Richard, *Mr. Popper's Penguins* (I)

Corbett, Scott, *Deadly Hoax* (A)

Duffey, Betsy, *Alien for Rent* (I)

Hildick, E. W., *Ghost Squad Breaks Through* (I)

Hitchcock, Alfred, *Alfred Hitchcock's Supernatural Tales of Terror and Suspense* (A)

_____, *Witch's Brew* (A)

Marshall, Edward, *Space Case* (P)

Marzollo, Jean, *Jed and the Space Bandits* (P)

_____, *Ruthie's Rude Friends* (P)

McKinley, Robin, *A Knot in the Grain and Other Stories* (A)

Pearce, Philippa A., *Who's Afraid? And Other Strange Stories* (I)

Pilkey, Dav, *Captain Underpants and the Invasion of the Incredibly Naughty Cafeteria Ladies from Outer Space (and the Subsequent Assault of the Equally Evil Lunchroom Zombie Nerds)* (I)

Pinkwater, Manus, *Lizard Music* (I)

Rubinstein, G., *Space Demons* (A)

Sachar, Louis, *Marvin Redpost: A Flying Birthday Cake?* (I)

Sargent, Sarah, *Watermusic* (I)

Service, Pamela F., *Stinker from Space* (I)

_____, *Weirdos of the Universe, Unite!* (A)

Sleator, William, *Duplicate* (A)

Slote, Alfred, *My Trip to Alpha One* (I)

_____, *Omega Station* (I)

Standiford, Natalie, *Space Dog the Hero* (P)

Turner, Megan Whalen, *Instead of Three Wishes* (A)

Wynne-Jones, Tim, *Some of the Kinder Planets* (A)

Yolen, Jane, *Commander Toad in Space* (P)

Yolen, Jane, editor, *Things That Go Bump in the Night: A Collection of Original Stories* (A)

Science Fiction

Asimov, Isaac, *Fantastic Voyage: A Novel* (I)

Brooks, Bruce, *No Kidding* (I)

Christopher, John, *City of Gold and Lead* (A)

_____, *Empty World* (A)

_____, *Pool of Fire* (A)

_____, *When the Tripods Came* (A)

_____, *The White Mountains* (A)

Coville, Bruce, *Aliens Ate My Homework* (I)

Cross, Gillian, *New World* (A)

Dexter, Catherine, *Alien Game* (I)

Dickinson, Peter, *Eva* (A)

Engdahl, Sylvia, *Enchantress from the Stars* (A)

_____, *The Far Side of Evil* (A)

Farmer, Nancy, *The Ear, the Eye, and the Arm: A Novel* (A)

Gilden, Mel, *Outer Space and All That Junk* (I)

Gilmore, Kate, *The Exchange Student* (A)

Heinlein, Robert A., *Citizen of the Galaxy* (A)

_____, *Door into Summer* (A)

_____, *Tunnel in the Sky* (A)

Hoover, H. M., *Away Is a Strange Place to Be* (A)

_____, *Only Child* (A)

_____, *Orvis* (I)

_____, *The Shepherd Moon* (A)

_____, *Winds of Mars* (A)

Howarth, Lesley, *Weather Eye* (I)

Hughes, Monica, *The Golden Aquarians* (I)

_____, *Invitation to the Game* (A)

_____, *Keeper of the Isis Light* (A)

Key, Alexander, *Escape to Witch Mountain* (I)

Lawrence, Louise, *Andra* (A)

_____, *Children of the Dust* (A)

_____, *Star Lord* (I)

L'Engle, Madeleine, *Swiftly Tilting Planet* (A)

_____, *Wind in the Door* (A)

_____, *Wrinkle in Time* (A)

Logue, Mary, *Dancing with an Alien* (A)

Lowry, Lois, *Gathering Blue* (A)

_____, *The Giver* (A)

Mahy, Margaret, *Aliens in the Family* (A)

_____, *Greatest Show Off Earth* (I)

McCaffrey, Anne, *Dragondrums* (A)

_____, *Dragonsinger* (A)

_____, *Dragonsong* (A)

O'Brien, Robert C., *Mrs. Frisby and the Rats of NIMH* (I)

_____, *Z for Zachariah* (A)

Ormondroyd, Edward, *Time at the Top* (I)

Paton Walsh, Jill, *The Green Book* (I)

Pinkwater, Daniel, A*lan Mendelsohn, the Boy from Mars* (I)

Price, Susan, *The Sterkarm Handshake* (A)

Rubenstein, Gillian, *Galax-Arena: A Novel* (I)

Seuss, Dr., *The Lorax* (P)

Sleator, William, *Others See Us* (A)

_____, *Duplicate* (A)

Fantasy Classics

Barrie, James M., *Peter Pan* (P–A)

Baum, L. Frank, *The Wizard of Oz* (P–A)

Carroll, Lewis, *The Adventures of Alice in Wonderland* (P–A)

Dickens, Charles, *A Christmas Carol* (P–A)

Hodges, Margaret, reteller, *Gulliver in Lilliput* (P–A)

Lofting, Hug, *The Story of Doctor Doolittle* (P–A)

Moses, Will, reteller, *The Legend of Sleepy Hollow* (P–A)

Thurber, James, *The Great Quillow* (P–A)

Contemporary Realistic Fiction

But Judd's out to teach me a lesson, and I'm out to teach him one. So I keep at it. Knew it takes me twice as long as Judd to split that wood, but I don't stop. And all the while, Judd sits on his porch, drinking his beer, watching me sweat. Sure does his heart good, I can tell.

Then he says somethin' that almost stops my heart cold. Laughs and says, "Boy, you sure are puttin' in a whole lot of work for nothin'."

I rest my back a moment, wipe one arm across my face. "Shiloh's somethin'," I tell him.

You think you're goin' to get my dog just 'cause you got some handwritin' on a piece of paper?" Judd laughs and drinks some more. "Why, that paper's not good for anything but to blow your nose on. Didn't have a witness."

I look at Judd. "What you mean?"

"You don't even know what's legal and what's not, do you? Well, you show a judge a paper without a witness's signature, he'll laugh you right out of the courthouse. Got to have somebody sign that he saw you strike a bargain." Judd laughs some more. "And nobody here but my dogs."

I feel sick inside, like I could maybe throw up. Can't think of what to do or say, so I just lift the sledgehammer again, go on splittin' the wood.

—Phyllis Reynolds Naylor, *Shiloh*, p. 137

A GROUP OF FIFTH GRADERS WERE DEEP IN A DISCUSSION OF Phyllis Reynolds Naylor's *Shiloh.* They've been reading and meeting in discussion groups for the past three weeks, and today they're having their final small-group discussion before presenting the novel to the rest of the class. Jamie and Adam really wanted to read this book, because they love animal stories, especially boy-and-dog stories. They've been surprised to find so much more than just a simple dog story in this book. Rebecca loved it, too. She's been writing in her journal about the moral dilemma that Marty struggles with. Maria and Louie have been reading with an intensity that delights their teacher; they've really connected with this book. All five of them say they're a little sad now that they've finished it. Maria changes the direction of the discussion.

> MARIA: I was so scared at the end when Judd told Marty he wasn't going to get to keep Shiloh because he didn't have a witness.
>
> LOUIE: Me, too. He was so mean.
>
> ADAM: But he did get nicer when he got the water and the dog collar.
>
> LOUIE: Yeah, but he still was mean inside.
>
> REBECCA: I don't know if he was mean inside. I thought maybe he was mean outside and wanting to be nice inside.
>
> JAMIE: What do you mean?
>
> REBECCA: Well, he did do some nice things, and he was worried about what other people thought of him. That's why he kept his truck so nice. And he could've just shot Shiloh instead of giving him to Marty in the end. And he did give him the collar.

They go on to talk about Judd and Marty, eventually agreeing to disagree about whether Judd is nice inside or not. They're all so satisfied with the happy ending that it doesn't matter, really, what Judd is like. He's done the right thing, at least.

Later in the discussion they talk about how to present the novel to the class. They've been keeping track of some of the ideas they've found in the novel, like "You can lie not only by what you say but what you don't say" (p. 57), "There's got to be times that what one person does is everybody's business" (p. 133), and "But there's food for the body and food for the spirit. And Shiloh sure enough feeds our spirit" (p. 132). They decide to make a series of posters with these ideas printed across the top and then look in magazines and newspapers to find pictures and articles that relate to them. Adam suggests that they list titles of other books that make them think about these ideas, and they all agree. Maria suggests putting *Bridge to Terabithia* by Katherine Paterson on the "food for the spirit" poster because of the way Leslie fed Jesse's spirit. They divide into two working groups and prepare for their presentation.

Characterization is the soul of great literature. When readers discover their own feelings in the character of a book, they experience the events of the story as though it were happening to them. Thus, through the magic of fiction, children accumulate the experience of many lives and grow wise beyond their years. These fifth graders grappled with moral and emotional issues as they lived through Marty's experience together. The group interaction gave them the opportunity to try out their ideas, to articulate their thoughts and use the ideas of their friends to strengthen and focus their own.

Defining Realistic Fiction

Realistic fiction has a strong sense of actuality. Its plausible stories are about people and events that could actually happen. Good contemporary realistic fiction illuminates life, presenting social and personal concerns in a fully human context.

Realistic fiction portrays the real world in all its dimensions; it shows the humorous, the sensitive, the thoughtful, the joyful, and the painful sides of life. By its very nature, it deals with the vast range of sensitive topics prevalent in today's world. "The raw materials of story," says Lloyd Alexander (1981), "are the raw materials of all human cultures. Story deals with the same questions as theology, philosophy, psychology. It is concerned with polarities: love and hate, birth and death, joy and sorrow, loss and recovery." Life's raw materials, questions, and polarities appear most starkly in realistic fiction. Consequently, controversy often surrounds realistic fiction for children and young adults.

Good literature does not resolve complex problems with easy answers; it considers these problems with the seriousness they require. Since literature reflects the society that creates it, children's contemporary realistic fiction reflects many of the problems that our society is concerned with today: drugs, alcoholism, divorce, abortion, death, homelessness, teenage sexuality, and child abuse. It also reflects the things that we value in our lives: love, personal integrity, family, and friends. Thus, many realistic novels are problem-laden. Many, however, are stories of courage in which people are not beaten down; instead, they transform their lives into something worthwhile by drawing on their inner strength. And many are accounts of ordinary people living ordinary lives; their stories are illuminated through the careful consideration of a talented author.

No definition of realism is simple, and to say that realism is fiction that could happen in the real world—as opposed to fantasy, which could not—is simplistic. Every work of fiction, like the stories we tell ourselves, is part fanciful and partly realistic. We selectively remember and reshape events of our past and present; the same thing happens in books. A realistic story is an author's vision of what might really happen (the plot) in a particular time and place (the setting) to particular people (the characters).

Realistic Fiction in Children's Lives

For many young readers the sense of actuality in realistic fiction makes it easy to live the story as it is being read, to have a virtual experience. Realistic fiction presents stories that can act as windows through which we see the world, and as mirrors in which we see ourselves. Readers who engage with these stories often report seeing themselves in a realistic fiction story: "The whole time I was reading I was thinking, 'Yes, that's right. That's exactly how I feel.'" This intense connection with a book causes many young readers to prefer realistic fiction above other genres. National surveys and librarians' reports (Monson and Sebesta, 1991) repeatedly show that intermediate-grade students choose realistic stories far more than any other type.

Children unabashedly ask for books "about a person just like me" who is confronting familiar issues. The connection between book and reader, however, hinges not upon age, time, or place, but upon the validity of the emotions presented. Feelings must ring true in the reader's mind; they are more important than surface actuality. Children and young adults who read widely, testing and tasting various circumstances and life experiences, have many opportunities to try out roles vicariously through realistic books. When they read books that show others searching for self, young readers find they are not alone. They learn that life will be what they make of it. They search for an identity and look for a yardstick against which to measure themselves, and they turn to realistic fiction to help them define the person they want to become.

While reading, we unconsciously participate in a story, drawing analogies between what we are reading and our own lives. These comparisons help us understand our lives and prepare us for the future by creating expectations and models. The expectations influence our reactions to real events. A fifth grader talked about this when she said: "When I wasn't reading, I was thinking what it would be like if that really happened, because it's such a big thing that happened, . . . like if it happened to me or something. Like if I had a sister, or if my mother died or something, how that would affect me." Younger readers also make connections between realistic fiction and life, asking questions or making statements that let you know they, too, are thinking about "what it would be like *if.*" As one young reader expressed after hearing Lucille Clifton's *My Friend Jacob* (P), "Mommy, if I had a friend who needed extra special help, I'd be very nice to him."

Realistic stories can cause us to reflect on life as well as illuminate lifestyles that are different from our own. We can try them on for size through the books we read. Realistic fiction helps us experience things we would never experience in real life, or practice what we might someday encounter. Realistic fiction allows us many experiences in the safe harbor of our role as reader: We can sail around the world without fear of shipwreck or suffer blindness without loss of sight, while still probing the emotions of the moment. We can also rehearse experiences we might live someday: We can meet new friends who bring love or sorrow to our lives. We can discover that others living in different environments have done, thought, and felt the same things that we ourselves have done, thought, and felt. Teaching Idea 7.1 shows how students can keep a writer's notebook, recording their own observations of life in a journal.

Teaching Idea 7 ☆ 1

Keep a Writer's Notebook

Authors of realistic fiction develop plotlines in which they portray real people with real feelings. To do this, they observe themselves and others living their lives and record their observations in journals—not only when they are working on a story, but every day.

Ask your students to collect material for future stories by recording their observations in small notebooks that they can carry around with them. Follow this procedure:

1. Have students start notebooks of their own by recording events that happen to them. Have them describe events they observe, as well as their feelings about what they see happening.

2. After they have kept the notebook for a period of time, have them go back through their notes and highlight items that might lead to a story. At the same time, read what established authors have to say about where they get their ideas for writing. The July/August issues of *The Horn Book Magazine* always contain Newbery acceptance speeches in which authors frequently talk about why they wrote their books.

3. Have students discuss in groups what ideas might lead to interesting stories. Then they can proceed to write.

Criteria for Selecting Realistic Fiction

Realistic fiction, like many other genres, should be evaluated in terms of the setting, characters, plot, theme, style, and point of view. The quality of the illustrations is important as well. General criteria for evaluation apply to a range of genres, but some are specific to realistic fiction. The plausibility of characters, plot, and setting, realized in both text and illustration, is especially important to this genre. It is this very quality of realism that also necessitates a consideration of community standards when selecting these stories.

SENSITIVITY TO COMMUNITY STANDARDS

In realistic fiction for children from nursery school through high school we can find explicit language, earthy dialogue, unseemly behavior, and sensitive issues. The issues that appear in literature for children reflect the concerns of the cul-

ture. For example, in the past few years a number of books that explore issues of sexuality have been published. Many of these novels, such as Marion Dane Bauer's *Am I Blue?: Coming Out from the Silence*, Francesca Lia Block's *Baby Be-Bop*, Paula Boock's *Dare, Truth, or Promise*, Nancy Garden's *Annie on My Mind*, *Holly's Secret*, and *The Year They Burned the Books*, M. E. Kerr's *Deliver Us from Evie*, Ellen Jaffe McClain's *No Big Deal*, Theresa Nelson's *Earthshine*, Barbara Ann Porte's, *Something Terrible Happened*, William Taylor's *The Blue Lawn*, Kate Walker's *Peter*, Ellen Wittlinger's *Hard Love*, Jacqueline Woodson's *From the Notebooks of Melanin Sun* and *The House You Pass on the Way*, and Lois-Ann Yamanaka's *Name Me Nobody*, all for advanced readers, grapple with the issues that surround homosexuality in today's culture. The publication of these books reflects the times; books about homosexuality were rare in the past.

Other sensitive topics, such as teenage sexuality and pregnancy, have been explored in books for older readers, such as Anna Fienberg's *Borrowed Light* (A), C. B. Christiansen's *I See the Moon* (A), and Berlie Doherty's *Dear Nobody* (A). In *A Dance for Three* (A), Louise Plummer employs multiple points of view as she explores the experience of one young girl and those connected to the baby that she births and gives up for adoption.

Sexuality is one of the issues that high school senior Jay McLeod is struggling with in Rich Wallace's *Playing Without the Ball* (A), a wonderfully introspective novel that appeals to adolescent males. Lori Aurelia Williams presents sexuality from several perspectives in *When Kambia Elaine Flew in from Neptune* (A), in which she contrasts adult and teenage sexuality, using both to present a disturbing picture of sexual abuse. The protagonist of Laurie Halse Anderson's *Speak* (A) is unable to communicate with others after she is sexually assaulted at a teenage drinking party. Her honesty and courage as she regains her ability to speak out are extraordinary.

Sexuality, both straight and gay, is an issue in the lives of many of the several adolescent narrators of Ellen Wittlinger's *What's in a Name?* (A), a powerful collection of 10 interlocking stories; it also is a recurring theme in E. R. Frank's *Life Is Funny* (A), another collection of interlocking stories that spans seven years in the lives of diverse adolescents.

Some adults prefer to shield children from subjects like these. Others believe that children can benefit from reading and having a safe experience that is removed from reality. Both positions have merit. It is important to consider books in light of what they *say* about the subjects they explore. For example, if a story is about children who take drugs, as in Melvin Burgess's *Smack* (A), what happens to them? Are drugs seen as good or bad? Is the general idea that children shouldn't take drugs because they're dangerous? Often adults who complain about a book that examines a controversial subject haven't looked to see what the author says about that topic. In many cases the "message" that a controversial realistic book contains is actually one that the community would approve.

Individual parents and communities will set the standards for what they believe to be suitable for their own children. We, as teachers and librarians, need to be sensitive to the standards of our community while at the same time protecting children's right to read books that stimulate, inform, and delight. This is an important and difficult task, and we discuss ways to respond sensitively to censorship in Chapter 1 because it is an issue that confronts teachers and librarians of all grades and concerns all genres.

When selecting realistic fiction, look for books that contain topics that are developmentally appropriate and use language, events, and themes that are in keeping with the community's standards. Think as well about how you are planning to use the books. Some are not good candidates for a read-aloud experience; others might be suitable as individual, independent reading, and some might work in a small-group setting. Also consider the literary quality of such books, and evaluate setting, characters, plot, theme, and style.

SETTING

Authors of realistic stories choose a time and place that actually does or could possibly exist as a setting. The setting may be general or specific, depending on the needs of the story. When evaluating setting in realistic fiction, look for a vivid, realistic setting that supports the events of the story.

CHARACTERS

Characters in realistic fiction reflect human beings we know; they are circumscribed by the natural powers and failings of a real person in a real world. When evaluating characterization in realistic fiction, look for main characters that are credible, authentic, and not stereotypic, are fully developed as multidimensional human beings, and show change or development during the course of the story.

PLOT

The central conflict in a realistic fiction story is one that is probable in today's world and that matters to today's children. When selecting realistic fiction, look for plot structures that can be understood by the target audience, and events that are probable given the setting and characters of the story.

THEME

Realistic fiction is often grouped by theme, which is how we discuss it later in this chapter. Themes in realistic fiction reflect important issues of contemporary society. When selecting realistic fiction, look for books that have themes that are woven intrinsically into the story situation and that matter to young readers' lives.

STYLE

The dialogue of the characters in realistic fiction should reflect today's language forms, including current slang and appropriate dialect variations. Yet strict adherence to current slang or faithful reproduction of dialect eventually can date a good story or make it inaccessible to many readers. Look for books that have a language style that engages the reader and an oral quality that is appropriate to the characters and their cultural milieu.

Figure 7.1 summarizes the criteria for evaluating a work of contemporary realistic fiction.

Figure 7 ✪ 1

Checklist for Evaluating Realistic Fiction

Setting
- Is there a vivid, realistic setting that supports the events of the story?

Characters
- Are the characters credible and lacking in stereotypes?
- Are the main characters multidimensional? Do they change and develop over time?

Plot
- Are the problems believable and solved in realistic, culturally grounded ways?
- Can the intended age group understand the plot structure?

Theme
- Is there a theme that is applicable to children's lives, and is it woven intrinsically into the story?

Style
- Do the dialogue and thoughts of the characters sound natural, with dialect and diction that does not overwhelm the reader?

A CLOSE LOOK AT

Shiloh

Phyllis Reynolds Naylor's *Shiloh* (I–A) is an outstanding example of realistic fiction. Winner of the 1992 Newbery Medal, *Shiloh* has been read by thousands of intermediate-grade students. What makes this book a favorite? Clearly, the Newbery committee felt this book was of outstanding literary merit according to the criteria presented above. Here, we closely examine the novel according to each criterion.

Synopsis

Marty Preston is 11 years old. He's enjoying summer in the West Virginia hills, where he lives with his parents and two sisters. His family doesn't have a lot of money, but they don't complain about it; they just work hard and love each other. Everything is peaceful until Marty finds a stray beagle who's clearly been abused. When he falls in love with the dog his life becomes complicated.

© 1991 Lynne Dennis

Marty struggles with the conflicting demands of his conscience and his heart in Phyllis Reynolds Naylor's **Shiloh**.

As Marty struggles to help the dog, he tangles himself in a web of lies and deceit that almost overwhelm him. His love for the dog and his desire to protect him from Judd Travers, the dog's abusive owner, conflict with his family and community ethics. When Shiloh is almost killed by roaming dogs because Marty has hidden him in a pen on the hill, Marty's secret is out and his fight to own Shiloh begins in earnest. A lucky discovery and hard work earn the dog for the boy. In the end, Marty has grappled with some profound moral dilemmas in his attempt to justify his own desires.

Setting

Shiloh is set in rural West Virginia in a community marked by pride, independence, and poverty. The nearest town, Friendly, is small, and the Prestons live several miles out, in a "little four-room house with hills on three sides." Marty calls his home "the best place to live" and describes the wildlife he sees as he explores the hills. The Friendly community is isolated, so much so that it seems almost as if the setting is the past rather than the present, although trucks, jeeps, and television mark the time as today.

The isolation of the community has made it independent and self-sufficient, with a strong behavioral code that governs adults and children. Adults do not pry into their neighbors' lives, children do not question adults, and outside authority is frequently resisted. This setting creates the conflict that propels the story.

Plot

The entire story is a flashback, with Marty recounting the events that occurred. After the opening sentence it proceeds chronologically from the first time Marty sees Shiloh, to his decision to keep him from his owner, to Shiloh's injury, and then to Marty's successful bid to become Shiloh's owner.

The conflicts that create the action occur on three levels; Marty struggles with himself, with Judd, and with the norms of his family and community. These conflicts occur simultaneously as he hides the dog from Judd and his family; argues with himself over the morality of keeping a dog that isn't his versus returning it to a life of abuse; lies and steals to protect the dog; worries about where his lies are leading him; and works to understand just when and how the community's rule about staying out of a neighbor's business should be violated.

Style

Naylor uses just the right amount of rural Appalachian dialect to reflect the setting and help create the characters, yet not overwhelm her readers. Since the story is told from Marty's first-person point of view, the dialect is reflected in his thoughts and in the spoken dialogue. The opening sentence demonstrates both the dialect and the vivid imagery with which Naylor makes her story come alive:

> The day Shiloh come, we're having us a big Sunday dinner. Dara Lynn's dipping bread in her glass of cold tea, the way she likes, and Becky pushes her beans up over the edge of her plate in her rush to get 'em down.
>
> Ma gives us her scolding look. "Just once in my life," she says, "I'd like to see a bite of food go direct from the dish into somebody's mouth without a detour of any kind."
>
> She's looking at me when she says it, though. It isn't that I don't like fried rabbit. Like it fine. I just don't want to bite down on buckshot, is all, and I'm checking each piece.
>
> "I looked that rabbit over good, Marty, and you won't find any buckshot in that thigh," Dad says, buttering his bread. "I shot him in the neck."

In her first four paragraphs, Naylor allows readers to hear, see, smell, and taste life in the Preston house as Marty knows it. This allows readers to enter Marty's world, to care about his problems, and to rejoice in the happy ending.

Characterization

The very next line of the opening chapter indicates one of the primary traits of Marty. In response to his dad's telling him that he shot the rabbit in the neck Marty thinks:

> Somehow I wish he hadn't said that. I push the meat from one side of my plate to the other, through the sweet potatoes and back again.
>
> "Did it die right off?" I ask, knowing I can't eat at all unless it had.

Readers soon learn that Marty is gentle and kind by the way he plays with his sisters, doesn't like to shoot animals, and reacts strongly to Shiloh's plight. He loves his mother, admires and respects his father, and clearly understands what they expect of him. His characterization as a happy and generally obedient child makes his decision to keep Shiloh all the more dramatic.

Both compassion and determination are evident in Marty's thoughts the night after he first sees Shiloh:

> I don't sleep more than a couple hours that night. When I do, I dream of Shiloh. When I don't, I'm thinking about him out in the rain all afternoon, head on his paws, watching our door. Thinking how I'd disappointed him, whistling like I meant something that first time, gettin' him to come to me, then taking

him on back to Judd Travers to be kicked all over again.

> By five o'clock, when it's growing light, I know pretty much what I have to do: I have to buy that dog from Judd Travers.

Later, when Shiloh runs away from Travers and back to Marty's place, Marty goes out to him knowing that he's made a decision:

> [I'm] not going to take him back. Not now, not ever.
>
> I don't have time to think how I had promised Judd if I ever saw Shiloh loose again, I'd bring him back. Don't even think what I'm going to tell Dad. All I know right then is that I have to get Shiloh away from the house, where none of the family will see him.

Because Marty is narrating the story, readers know exactly what he is thinking, and this internal dialogue gives the story its power, especially when Marty is grappling with his overwhelming moral dilemma. Lying on the couch where he sleeps after his family is in bed, Marty thinks about what he's doing:

> I'm thinking about lies again. I *hadn't* lied to Judd Travers when I said I hadn't seen his dog in the yard today. That was the honest-to-God truth, because Shiloh hadn't been anywhere near our yard. But I also know that you can lie not only by what you say but what you don't say. Nothing I'd told Judd was an outright lie, but what I'd kept inside myself made him think that I hadn't seen his dog at all.
>
> "Jesus," I whisper finally, "which you want me to do? Be one hundred percent honest and carry that dog back to Judd so that one of your creatures can be kicked and starved all over again, or keep him here and fatten him up to glorify your creation?"
>
> The question seemed to answer itself, and I'm pretty proud of that prayer.

As the story continues, Marty's lies weave a tangled web that eventually hurts both Shiloh and Marty's family as Marty continues to struggle with the question of what is right, just, and moral.

Theme

It is that very question that weaves the story together. Just what is the moral thing to do? Should Marty obey the rules of his community and the expectations of his family even when he feels, quite strongly, that they are wrong in this particular case? This question is worried over by Marty, discussed by his family, and clearly posed for readers to think about. Children in fourth to sixth grade, the optimal time to read this novel, are in the midst of developing their own moral code as they begin to encounter ideas and experiences that cause them to think about values, about right and wrong. *Shiloh* allows them to consider these important issues in safety.

Profile ✿ Phyllis Reynolds Naylor

Courtesy of Simon & Schuster

Phyllis Reynolds Naylor became an author early in her life. She wrote her first book when she was in kindergarten and sold her first story for $4.67 when she was just 16! She wrote her first book for children in 1965 and has written more than 80 books since then, including the 1992 Newbery Medal winner, *Shiloh*. Her books frequently appear on the Children's Choices lists issued by the International Reading Association and the Children's Book Council, and on the Notable Children's Book lists of the American Library Association.

Naylor writes in many genres. Her popular contemporary realistic fiction series about a teenager named Alice showcases her humor and grasp of contemporary life. She also writes gripping mysteries and has won the Edgar Allan Poe Award from the Mystery Writers of America.

In her Newbery Medal acceptance speech, Ms. Naylor talked about her writing:

*What shall I tell you about **Shiloh**? If it were my book **The Keeper** receiving the award, I could tell you how it was adapted from a chapter in my own life, and that would take up the rest of this talk. If it were **A String of Chances**, I could tell you about my struggles with faith. If it were **Send No Blessings**, I could talk of the numerous*

drafts it took to work out Beth's problems with self-esteem.

*But **Shiloh**—the first draft, that is—was written at breakneck speed. It was as though I were obsessed with getting to the end of the story and finding out just what happened between Marty and Judd Travers—as though Marty himself were perched on the arm of my chair, telling me the story in his own way.*

*As with most of my books, however, the roots of this one go deep. In many of my other books, I deal with problems I wrestled with as a child or teenager, but in the writing of **Shiloh**, I was dealing with discomfort that was still new.*

Many of you already know the story behind it—how my husband and I were visiting friends in West Virginia, and rose one morning for a long walk in the little community known as Shiloh. How we had passed the old grist mill and crossed the bridge, and how just beyond the school house, we found the hungry, trembling—and strangely silent—dog that was eventually to become Shiloh in my book.

How it was so frightened and beaten down it kept slinking away from us, but how finally, when I whistled, it inexplicably came bounding over, leaping up to lick my cheek. How it followed us back to the house of our friends, and sat out all day in the rain, head on its paws, watching the door. How I agonized all the way back to Maryland that evening, until finally my husband said, "Well, Phyllis, are you going to have a nervous breakdown, or are you going to do something about it?" The something, of course, meant writing, which was a catharsis for me, but did nothing for the dog. . . .

As for Shiloh, whatever saint looks out for strays must have had his eye on this one, because a few weeks into my writing the story, a note from our

friends said that they had encountered the dog again a few days after we left, brought it home, and named it Clover.

So why didn't I put my manuscript aside and say, "Fine. It's settled, then"? Because I got hooked on that dog, as Marty would say—whistling as though I meant something, then offering nothing. I felt I owed it more.

The second reason I couldn't let go of the story was that while we talked about the dog that day with our hosts . . . they had patiently explained that the animal sitting out in the yard was only one of many that owners abandon in those hills. . . . I wanted to write about how, once you become emotionally involved in a problem, all bets are off. Your perspective changes.

. . . And so I went on with my story. . . . As the novel progressed, I discovered that it also dealt with justice. Once reason that writing for children is satisfying is that they may, in reading your book, face a new idea for the first time. And when you consider that there can only be one "first time," you realize that the impact of that encounter may affect a child's thinking for the rest of his life.

If he sees the world as black and white, he may develop knee-jerk reactions to key words or slogans. If he determines that the end justifies the means, his ethics may tend to slip and slide. But if he sees that much of life is more complex than he thought, that each problem must be approached in its unique situation, and that he must base his actions not only upon his family's values but also upon his own innate sense of what is true and good, then he will get a taste of what being an adult really means. (Naylor, 1992, pp. 406–409)

Ms. Naylor lives in Bethesda, Maryland, with her husband, Rex, a speech pathologist. They have two grown sons and two granddaughters.

A CLOSE LOOK AT

Owl Moon

Picture storybooks can also be excellent realistic fiction, and Jane Yolen's ***Owl Moon*** (P–I) is a perfect example of a realistic story rendered outstanding by carefully selected words and evocative illustrations. Yolen tells the story of a father and his young child going out late one night to see owls. They walk together quietly into the woods, the father imitates the call of a great horned owl, and they see the owl. Afterward, they walk back home.

The story is deceptively simple, for poetic prose evokes powerful images of the cold, dark winter night, the silence, the beauty of the woods white with snow, and the adventure that child and father undertake. John Schoenherr's Caldecott Medal–winning illustrations take these images and transform them into an intensely beautiful visual experience. His pictures correspond to what the text is saying, but they also transcend it. His use of light and white space is extraordinary, making the dark spruce woods and winter night seem lit from within. In most of the pictures the father

and child are small, insignificant intruders in the forest of towering trees and pristine snow. In contrast, the mysterious majesty of the owl fills three-quarters of a double-page spread. The owl is shown poised for flight, intensely staring as it allows itself to be glimpsed by father and child and also by the reader.

The final picture shows the father carrying the child, whose arms are twined around his neck as they return to their farmhouse. The text is framed by two bare saplings that reach to the top of the white page like supplicating arms around these words:

> *When you go owling*
> *you don't need words*
> *or warm*
> *or anything but hope.*
> *That's what Pa says.*
> *The kind of hope*
> *that flies*
> *on silent wings*
> *under a shining*
> *Owl Moon.*

For one minute,
three minutes,
maybe even a hundred minutes,
we stared at one another.

John Schoenherr's strikingly dramatic watercolors evoke a sense of wonder on the cold, silent night that father and child go in search of owls in Jane Yolen's **Owl Moon.**

Text and pictures work together to create an unforgettable experience that many children will never have—unless they read this book.

Many other picture books contain wonderful realistic stories. Some are listed along with novels for intermediate- and advanced-grade readers in the Booklist at the end of this chapter; others are listed in Chapter 4.

Types of Contemporary Realism

Like other genres, realism includes a variety of types of literature. Many realistic stories are special types of realism, such as adventure stories, mysteries, animal stories, sports stories, humorous stories, romance, series books, and short stories. Of course, many books fall into more than one category, such as a mystery that is combined with an adventure story. Mysteries, adventures, animal stories, romance, and sports stories occur in other genres, such as historical fiction and fantasy, as well. We have chosen to discuss them in relation to the contemporary realistic fiction genre. No matter what type, good books for young readers measure up to the criteria discussed here. Some of the best are listed in the Booklist at the end of this chapter.

ADVENTURE STORIES

Marked by an especially exciting, fast-paced plot, adventure/survival stories captivate and hold readers who can't wait to discover what happens. Often the central problem is a conflict between person and nature. The best adventure stories also contain multidimensional characters who control much of the action and who change as a result of the action. Many young readers who enjoy the compelling nature of the plot prefer adventure stories.

Gary Paulsen's *Hatchet* (I–A) is one of the most popular adventure stories today. Captivated readers also enjoy *Brian's Winter* (I–A) and *Brian's Return* (I–A), in which Paulsen explores possible endings to this exciting adventure story set in the northwoods of eastern Canada. Donald Crews captures the sights, sounds, and feelings of a hair-raising adventure in the picture storybook *Shortcut* (P). Even though the children have been told not to walk on the railroad tracks, they decide to take the shortcut home, down the tracks. When they hear the whistle of an approaching train they have to decide what to do.

Sharon Creech's novel, *The Wanderer* (I–A), a Newbery Honor Book, revolves around several conflicts, one of which is person against nature—in this case the sea. Thirteen-year-old Sophie is sailing across the ocean with her

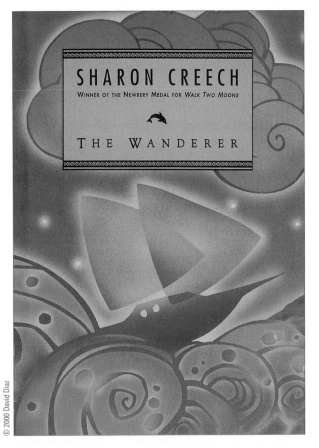

© 2000 David Diaz

David Diaz's striking cover and intriguing chapter-opening sketches enhance the drama in this multilayered adventure story.

uncles and two thirteen-year-old cousins, Cody and Brian, when a tremendous storm threatens their lives and calls forth courage that they did not know they possessed. Told in a series of journal entries from Sophie and Cody, this is a complex, beautifully crafted story.

MYSTERIES

A *mystery* is marked by suspense—Will the mystery be solved? The focus in a mystery story is a question—Who did it? Where is it? What happened?—and the action centers on finding the answer to that question and thus solving the mystery. The best mysteries revolve around an intriguing problem and contain characters who are well developed and who work to solve the problem. They feature fast-paced action and a logical solution that is foreshadowed through the careful presentation of clues. Many children go through a phase in which mysteries are all they want to read. Fortunately, there are some excellent mysteries for children of all ages.

Mysteries are often found as series books, and lucky young readers enjoy reading them. Elizabeth Levy, Donald Sobol, Seymour Simon, and Marjorie Sharmat are some of the writers who have provided younger readers with brief, exciting mysteries that satisfy their desire to figure things out. As these young readers mature they continue to enjoy series such as the very popular **Sammy Keyes** (I) books by Wendelin Van Draanen. These mysteries, like the **Herculeah Jones** books by Betsy Byars (I), keep intermediate-grade children reading and guessing.

Books by Eve Bunting, Joan Lowry Nixon's psychic mysteries, and Lois Duncan's eerie novels satisfy older readers. These and other books, such as James Howe's popular **Sebastian Barth** series, provide children with well-written alternatives to augment the many formula mystery series, such as the time-tested **Nancy Drew** and **Hardy Boys** books.

Two-time Newbery Medal winner E. L. Konigsburg's *Silent to the Bone* (A) has all the attributes of an excellent mystery. The characters are carefully crafted, the mystery is compelling, and the protagonist logically deduces the solution. All of these traits are skillfully embedded in a story of early adolescent issues with family and peers. This and other fine mystery stories and authors are listed in the Booklist at the end of this chapter.

ANIMAL STORIES

Animal stories are about realistic relationships between human beings and animals, most commonly horses or dogs, or about realistic animal adventures. When they focus on an animal-human relationship, this relationship is usually a vehicle for maturation by the central human character. Good animal stories have engaging characters that grow and change as a result of their experience with an animal. Many of these books are very moving, often provoking a strong emotional response. Teaching Idea 7.2 suggests questions to explore with your class after reading an animal story.

Johanna Hurwitz's *One Small Dog* (I) portrays the emotions surrounding the loss of a beloved pet in an unflinching, yet gentle fashion. *Not My Dog* (P), by Colby Rodowsky, is a brief novel just perfect for young readers who are moving beyond picture storybooks. Eight-year-old Ellie has been promised a puppy when she turns nine, and she knows exactly what she wants. When an elderly relative moves, however, Ellie inherits her dog, who doesn't look anything like the puppy she's been dreaming of. As Ellie gets to know Preston, she comes to love him, too.

The protagonist of Kate DiCamillo's *Because of Winn-Dixie* (I), 10-year-old India Opal Buloni loves her new dog from the first moment that she sees him in the Winn-Dixie grocery store. His canine companionship eases her loneliness for her mother, helps her develop new friendships in her new town, and opens up communication with her taciturn father. These and other fine animal stories are in the Booklist at the end of this chapter.

Teaching Idea 7 · 2

Animals in Realistic Novels

Wild animals and pets appear frequently in realistic novels. Read several stories about animals that are appropriate to the students' developmental level. Discuss questions like these with your students:

* How do the authors make you like the animal?
* What kinds of problems do the animals and/or humans face?
* What does the animal/human do to solve the problem?
* How does the animal show loyalty to humans?
* What kind of difference does the animal make in the lives of the humans?

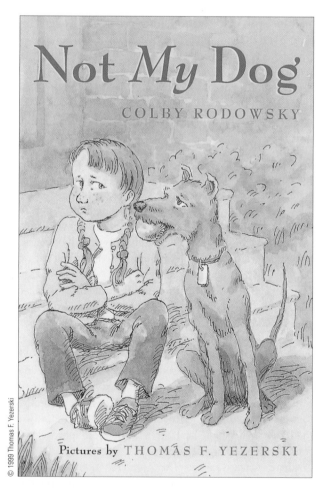

© 1999 Thomas F. Yezerski

Colby Rodowsky's easy-to-read novel is a delightful story of how a young girl comes to love a dog who is not what she hoped for.

SPORTS STORIES

In sports stories the action revolves around a sport and the thrills and tensions that accompany that particular sport. Like mysteries, many sports stories are series books as well. Also like mysteries, many of the available sports stories are not particularly well written, but they are devoured by young enthusiasts nonetheless. A small but increasing number of sports books with girls as the central character broaden the scope of the genre, and some recent sports stories examine social issues like sexism. The best of these books, such as Walter Dean Myers's *Slam!* (A) balance the descriptions of the sport with the development of the story, with the central character growing in some way as a result of the challenges he or she faces because of participation in the sport.

Rich Wallace writes sports stories that especially appeal to young adult males. His *Wrestling Sturbridge* (A) explores life in a small Pennsylvania town, the trials of adolescence, and the anxiety and exhilaration of being a member of a top-notch wrestling team in a sports-crazy town. He sets *Shots on Goal* (A), about an underdog high-school soccer team, and *Playing Without the Ball* (A) in that same small town. Jay, a senior in high school, is living alone in a room above a bar in *Playing Without the Ball*. His mother left him and his father several years before, and his father has gone to Los Angeles, leaving Jay to finish his senior year. He loves basketball but is not quite good enough for the high school team, so he plays in a church league; anything is better than not playing at all. He is also trying to discover who he is, especially when it comes to relationships with girls. The riveting descriptions of the basketball games and the outstanding character development make this a gem of a sports story. Other sports stories are listed in the Booklist at the end of this chapter.

HUMOROUS STORIES

Humorous stories present characters involved in funny situations, and the action that follows only heightens the humor. Monson (1966) studied the humor found in children's books and categorized five types: (1) character humor, (2) humor of surprise, (3) humor of the impossible, (4) humor of words, and (5) humor of a ridiculous situation. Each of these types can be found in contemporary fiction.

The real world has both laughter and tears, both happiness and sadness; children's books reflect them all. A world made up of all problems and no joy is just as unrealistic as the vision of the happily-ever-after world we gave children a generation ago, when so many books displayed the happy-ending-no-matter-what syndrome. Children need humorous books, and they want them. When you ask children, "What kinds of stories do you like to read?" the majority will answer, "*Funny* stories!" Many teachers choose a humorous story, such as Polly Horvath's *The Trolls* (P–I), to read aloud to remind children of the pure pleasure of enjoying a good book. In the annual Children's Choices sponsored by the International Reading Association and the Children's Book Council, humorous books repeatedly top the list.

Some of the best-known humorous stories for the elementary grades are Beverly Cleary's **Ramona** (P–I) series. Recently, other gifted authors have created characters who appear in a series of books that look with humor at some of the problems associated with growing up. Louis Sachar's **Marvin Redpost** books (P), such as *Marvin Redpost (#7): Super Fast, Out of Control*, offer children ready for simple chapter books the opportunity to read—and laugh—about someone they could easily know. Stephanie Greene's *Owen Foote, Frontiersman* (P–I) is the third in a funny series about Owen, an imaginative and irrepressible young hero. Betsy Duffey's *Cody Unplugged* (P–I) is also easily accessible to young readers who are comfortable with slim chapter books, as are Johanna Hurwitz's popular **Ozzie** books, such as *Ozzie on His Own* (I). These and other humorous books can be found in the Booklist at the end of this chapter.

ROMANCE STORIES

The action in romance stories centers on falling in love. Often an element of self-discovery is also involved, as when an intense relationship with another person helps the central character to come to know himself or herself better. Young adult readers, especially girls, often prefer romance stories, and there are a myriad of formula romance series, such as **Sweet Valley High**, for them to read. There are also some superbly crafted stories that can be classified as romance stories, such as Louise Plummer's *The Unlikely Romance of Kate Bjorkman* (A), in which romance is interwoven with themes of growing up and family and the characters are strongly drawn and multidimensional.

In the best of these books the main character is a well-developed, vivid personality—one with whom young readers identify and empathize. Jerry Spinelli's *Star Girl* (A) is an unusual romance in that it is told from a boy's point of view. It is also a thought-provoking novel about popularity and nonconformity, two major issues in the lives of many high school students.

BOOKS IN SERIES

Books that contain the same characters in varying situations across many different books are called *series books*. Obviously, series books may comprise animal, sports, humorous, adventure, mystery, romance, and other kinds of stories as well, but in this case their main characters appear in several books rather than in just one. The best of these books contain memorable, vivid characters that readers remember from book to book.

Many children like to read series books; the familiarity makes them comfortable. Feitelsen and colleagues (1986) studied the effects of reading series books on first-grade readers. They found that series books facilitate reading comprehension because the reader knows the character and setting, the framework, and the background of the story. Knowing the characters and what to expect from them makes reading easier; it's like meeting a good friend again. Recognizing that other books in the series are good stories increases the anticipation; if the first book was good, then the new one is sure to be.

While a number of series books are formula fiction, several high quality series are available, such as Cynthia Rylant's **Henry and Mudge** books (P), Lois Lowry's **Anastasia Krupnik** (I) series, the **Aldo** books by Johanna Hurwitz (P–I), and others mentioned above. Lois Lowry's **Anastasia** books are so popular that she has written several books about Anastasia's little brother, Sam, such as *Zooman Sam* (P–I). Phyllis Reynolds Naylor's **Alice** books, like Lowry's books, follow a young girl as she grows up. The books at the beginning of each of these series appeal to intermediate-grade readers; those at the end, especially in the **Alice** series, are more appropriate for advanced readers.

Themes in Contemporary Realism

The themes in contemporary realism are as many and varied as life itself. In fact, events in authors' own lives may influence what they write, as pointed out in Teaching Idea 7.3. Most books explore more than one theme. How would you classify *Shiloh*? Is it an "animal story," a "family story," or a "growing-up book"? It is all of these, and more, depending on the story an individual reader creates during reading. It is helpful, however, to group books loosely by themes since children often want to read several books that relate to a single theme; many teachers, too, enjoy constructing thematic units (discussed in Chapters 13 and 14) with their students. Some common themes in realistic fiction for children center on issues embedded in growing up, peer relations, and family relations.

GROWING UP

Not surprisingly, some of the most popular books for children and young adults are about growing up. Because our society has few formalized rites of passage, the way to adulthood is less clear for our children; they must mark their

Teaching Idea 7 ✩ 3

Study an Author's Works and Life

Choose an author who writes realistic fiction, both novels and picture storybooks, and who also has written an autobiography—for example, Jean Little, Cynthia Rylant, or Lois Lowry. With your students, read the autobiography and also some of the realistic fiction books and discuss how events in their lives influenced the authors' books. For example, there is a clear link between Cynthia Rylant's early years and some of her early picture books and novels; Lowry's autobiography makes clear connections between her life and her writing.

Some questions you might want to pursue include:

✳ What were the major influences in the author's life?

✳ How did events from the author's life influence her or his writing?

✳ What parallels can you find between her stories and her life?

own paths. Books that portray a character struggling toward adulthood allow readers to see themselves reflected and provide a rehearsal for real life. There are numerous picture storybooks for primary-grade readers that depict realistic characters trying to cope with growing up. Many of these books deal with children's increasing independence from adults, and with the fear and delight that accompany that independence. We discuss these in Chapter 4.

Older readers continue to struggle for independence, often confronting conflicting feelings, difficult moral choices, and personal challenges along the way. Young people are engaged in a process of trying to find out who they are, what they like and do not like, and what they will and will not do. They are passionately preoccupied with themselves and may look to literature for solutions to or escape from their preoccupations. They enter into books in ways they cannot with television, making reading a more personal and creative experience. When students want to understand themselves, they create images of themselves behaving nobly and are left with important memories. Stories that hinge upon the personal integrity of a character lead readers instinctively to grapple with envisaged tests of their own mettle.

In Gloria Whelan's *Homeless Bird* (A), winner of the National Book Award, growing up comes early. Like many

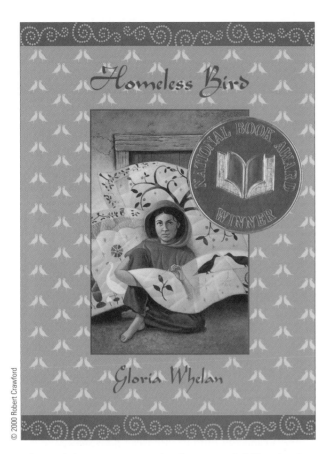

Gloria Whelan creates an engaging character and vivid settings in her National Book Award–winning novel **Homeless Bird**.

girls her age in India, Koly is married 13. Unlike most, however, she is almost immediately widowed, and thus doomed to a life of servitude or worse. Her artistry as an embroiderer, her thirst for knowledge, and her unquenchable spirit allow her to rise above the obstacles that modern Indian society set before her, and to craft herself a life as beautiful as her needlework.

Barbara Park's *The Graduation of Jake Moon* (I) and Colby Rodowsky's *Spindrift* (I) both revolve around young adolescents coping with the adults in their lives. Jake struggles to maintain his composure as his beloved Grandfather becomes increasingly erratic because of his Alzheimer's disease. Young Cassie faces the loss of her home while trying to understand how her older sister's husband is behaving. Both of these young protagonists are forced to confront issues they would rather ignore, and both rise to the occasion.

RELATIONSHIPS WITH OTHERS

Part of growing up involves learning to interact with ever-widening worlds and with a wide variety of people. Books that explore peer and family relations mirror many of the concerns that young readers have about their own lives.

Peer Relationships

You may remember as a child reading books that portrayed friendships as idyllic relationships of loyalty and noble sacrifice. Today's books explore a wide range of relationships among peers, with some characters noble, some loyal, but most simply ordinary beings. Because young people value acceptance by their friends, they are highly susceptible to peer pressure. The literature reflects their vulnerability and their strengths. Understandably, a number of realistic books dealing with peer relationships are set in school or revolve around a school-related problem.

Many picture storybooks involve peer relationships; making new friends, going to school, and learning to share are some of the things that children learn to do as they widen their circle of friends. These books are discussed in Chapter 4.

Many books about peer relationships for intermediate-grade students are easy to read and offer humor and satisfaction as well as reassurance that boys and girls are not alone in their feelings. Readers developing fluency can read them quickly and easily. They also form a solid foundation for the more complex stories and relationships that students will encounter as they mature. Writers who excel in capturing the spirit of an elementary classroom include Johanna Hurwitz, Robert Burch, Patricia Reilly Giff, Barbara Park, and Jamie Gilson. Their books often focus on a central character as he or she interacts within the classroom.

Not all books about friendships for intermediate-grade students are humorous. In Lynne Rae Perkins' *All Alone in the Universe* (I) Debbie is blindsided by the desertion of her best friend, Maureen. She retreats into herself, watching as Maureen grows close to another girl, mourning the loss of her friend. However, as in real life, the passage of time does help put things in perspective, and by the story's end, Debbie has made new friends and is, she realizes, not alone in the universe after all.

In his Newbery Medal–winning novel, *Holes* (I–A), Louis Sachar combines seriousness and humor as he tells the unlikely yet completely believable story of Stanley Yelnats, who is sent to a boys' juvenile detention center for a crime he did not commit. While there, he is forced to dig holes in the desert with his fellow prisoners. As he forms relationships with others, both fellow prisoners and guards, Stanley uncovers—literally—the key to the mystery of Camp Green Lake and the generations of bad luck that his family has suffered from. The engaging characters, complex plot structure, and dark humor make this book an outstanding book to read aloud to intermediate-grade readers.

As children mature, their relationships become more complex. Often the unevenness of the onset of adolescence creates gulfs between good friends: One is interested in the opposite sex, one isn't; one is physically mature, one isn't. Adolescence also brings with it increasing pressures to experiment with the dangerous side of life—drugs and alcohol, sex, brushes with the law—and books for advanced readers often contain characters who struggle with a personal crisis as they seek to stand up for what they value and at the same time maintain their friendships.

Because adolescents are concerned with these sensitive issues, books for adolescents examine them. In *Define "Normal"* (A), Julie Anne Peters explores the intersecting lives of two very different young women with seemingly different values. Antonia is fresh-faced and eager, an excellent student; Jazz is a punker and a druggie, someone who hangs around with gang members. When Antonia is asked to be a peer counselor to Jazz, she's not sure she can do it. As the year progresses, the girls find that they are actually a lot alike. An especially clever plot twist keeps this story from being saccharine.

Family Relationships

Family relationships are also important to children and young adults, and contemporary books present a varied picture of family life and probe new dimensions of realism. These books portray not only two-parent families but also communal, one-parent, and extended families, families headed by divorced or separated parents, families headed by homosexual parents, and children living alone without adults. Although there have always been books in which each family member stays in formerly culturally assigned roles, as these roles have evolved and changed, so, too, have books for young readers. Modern readers find both mirrors and windows in the wealth of family stories available today.

Family stories have changed in other ways as well. Fathers receive increasing attention in books for children and adolescents. Where they had once been ignored, they are now recognized as viable literary characters. Fictional mothers now run the full range of likeable to despicable characters just as they do in real life.

In Andrew Clements's *The Janitor's Boy* (I) fifth grader Jack Rankin gets in trouble when he smears chewing gum all over a desk. It is an act of revenge against his father: His dad is the janitor at his school, and some of his classmates are teasing him about it. As Jack painstakingly cleans the gum off of all of the desks and chairs in the school, he thinks about himself and his father. He discovers a key that lets him into the underground steam tunnel, an adventure that allows him to know his father in a new way.

Stories about siblings have also changed with the times. Children growing up in the same home must learn to share possessions, space, and parents or guardians. Stories of the idyllic relationships portrayed in books like *Little Women* (A) are seldom found in today's books. More often, contemporary novels treat subjects like sibling rivalry or learning to accept stepsisters or stepbrothers. In addition to happy, well-adjusted children from safe, loving homes, children are portrayed as victims of child abuse, abandonment, alcoholism, neglect, and a whole range of society's ills. These characters are often cynical, bitter, disillusioned, and despondent, but sometimes courageous and strong.

In Jean Thesman's *Calling the Swan* (A), 15-year-old Skylar is struggling to function in the world. Her parents don't want her to go out on her own, she retreats to her older sister's room whenever she has a problem, and she seems afraid to become friends with the kids who attend summer school with her. As the story unfolds, we gradually realize that Skylar's older sister is missing; she was abducted two years before when she was 15, and Skylar still has not accepted her loss. Although the family in this story is dysfunctional, the ending creates a sense of hope that, now that they've hit bottom, they can begin to recover.

Older relatives and friends, too, are increasingly visible in realistic stories for children and young adults. Often these friends and relatives die, and the central character must learn to accept this, as in Tim Bowler's *River Boy* (A), winner of England's Carnegie Medal. In this quietly moving and mystical tale, Jess must say goodbye to her beloved grandfather, as his heart is failing.

Grief is also a theme in Audrey Couloumbis's *Getting Near to Baby* (I), a Newbery Honor Book, in which two sisters learn to accept and move beyond the death of their baby sister. Teenaged Liza has to come to terms with her mother's cancer in Ruth Pennebaker's *Both Sides Now* (A), even though things like cancer just aren't supposed to happen to "people like them." As Liza and her mother struggle to be honest with one another, their relationship blossoms with new possibilities.

Teaching Idea 7.4 addresses the portrayal of parents in realistic fiction. Some books about family relationships for primary-grade readers are presented in Chapter 4. The Booklist at the end of this chapter contains additional titles for these readers as well as books appropriate for intermediate and advanced readers.

SPECIAL NEEDS

A small but growing number of books for children demonstrate society's increasing awareness of the emotional and physical demands and accomplishments of those with special needs. The trend in the field has been from nearly absolute neglect, to the appearance of occasional secondary characters, to the occasional book in which the main character has special needs. In today's literature, attitudes of those around people with special needs are not always positive and do not always improve; they often remain narrow and cruel. Happy endings are no longer automatic in children's books, and devoted attempts to teach, train, or help a character with special needs do not always result in progress, as they would have two decades ago. In today's

Teaching Idea 7 ☆ 4

Mothers and Fathers in Realistic Novels

Parents are portrayed in both positive and negative ways in realistic novels. Have students read some of the following books and compare the images of parents, discussing these questions:

✳ How do the girls get along with their fathers? Mothers?

✳ How do the boys get along with their fathers? Mothers?

✳ How would you describe the best parents? The worst?

✳ What descriptions or actions from the books best demonstrate what the parents are like? Why?

Fathers

Brooks, Bruce, *Midnight Hour Encores* (A)

Cleary, Beverly, *Ramona and Her Father* (I)

Creech, Sharon, *Walk Two Moons* (A)

Hamilton, Virginia, *A Little Love* (A)

Henkes, Kevin, *The Birthday Room* (A)

_____, *Protecting Marie* (A)

Houston, Gloria, *Littlejim* (A)

Oneal, Zibby, *In Summer Light* (A)

Mothers

Bauer, Marion Dane, *Like Mother, Like Daughter* (A)

Brooks, Bruce, *What Hearts* (A)

Bunting, Eve, *Is Anybody There?* (A)

Cleary, Beverly, *Ramona and Her Mother* (I)

Conly, Jane Leslie, *Trout Summer* (I)

Hamilton, Virginia, *Plain City* (A)

Henkes, Kevin, *Words of Stone* (A)

Lowry, Lois, *Rabble Starkey* (A)

Rylant, Cynthia, *A Fine White Dust* (A)

Smith, Doris Buchanan, *Return to Bitter Creek* (A)

helps an elderly teacher visit Italy in her "mind's eye," and discovers the power of her imagination.

Contemporary realistic fiction portrays many kinds of special needs: physical, mental, and emotional. Physical needs range from minimal muscular dysfunction to total paralysis, with as many causes as there are limitations on movement. Orthopedic problems are central or peripheral elements in children's books more frequently than any other type of disability. Children with physical disabilities have dreams and aspirations like any child; overprotection and patronage, no matter how well intended, can destroy these. In *Stuck in Neutral* (A), an unusual and disturbing novel, Terry Trueman takes readers inside the mind of a very bright boy with very bad cerebral palsy—he cannot control his muscles, which means he cannot speak. Those around him think that he is profoundly developmentally disabled, but instead he has the gift of almost total recall of everything that he hears. He's afraid that his father is planning to kill him, and he's telling us his story. Trueman tells readers in an afterword that he has a son who is very much like the protagonist in this novel.

Visually disabled children range from those who are totally blind and read braille to those who read large print or need the aid of special magnifying lenses or optical scanners. Deafness and speech and hearing impairments are an invisible disability; there are no obvious signs and, as a result, misunderstandings are frequent. Because the deaf look like everybody else, they are expected to cope with the environment normally. When this does not happen, strange inferences are made—most often about their intellectual abilities. In Morris Gleitzman's *Blabber Mouth* (I), Rowena Batts is the new girl at school, and the fact that she can't speak because of a birth defect doesn't make this difficult situation any easier. The first-person narrative makes readers forget that Rowena can't talk as her thoughts and feelings are so vividly real.

Mentally retarded characters appear in children's books less often than blind or emotionally disturbed ones, or those with orthopedic problems, but more often than the deaf or speech-impaired. Mental retardation was among the first special needs topics to appear in children's books. Books that portray mentally retarded characters often explore friendships between disabled and nondisabled characters, or family adjustment to a disabled family member. Nancy Hope Wilson's *The Reason for Janey* (I–A) is a sensitively written novel that explores mental retardation. In Jane Leslie Conly's *Crazy Lady!* (A), a Newbery Honor Book, Vernon, in peril of flunking seventh grade, becomes involved with an alcoholic recluse and her mentally retarded son. As he learns to see these outcasts as real people, he comes to accept his own sorrow and strength.

Emotional disturbance is often poorly understood, misdiagnosed, and feared. This happens because it is such a complex syndrome, with idiosyncratic manifestations.

books we find gradual improvement and partial resolution of problems, or totally open-ended conclusions. A character's progress results from training programs, therapy, rehabilitation programs, or schools, rather than from the actions of some deus ex machina. Moral strength and personal determination, however, continue to be attributes of the characters who succeed. The protagonist in Paul Fleischman's *Mind's Eye* (A) learns to transcend her paralysis when she

There are a few fine books that accurately portray this disability, such as Phyllis Reynolds Naylor's *The Keeper* (A), which describes a family with a manic-depressive father. Lucy Frank's *I Am an Artichoke* (A) explores anorexia triggered by emotional disturbance.

Some books explore specific learning disabilities. Jack Gantos writes from the point of view of a young boy with attention deficit hyperactivity disorder in the popular *Joey Pigza Swallowed the Key* and *Joey Pigza Loses Control* (both I). Gantos's breathless run-on sentences leave readers almost as frantic as Joey. The first-person point of view allows peers and adults to glimpse what life might be like for children with this disorder. *Joey Pigza Loses Control* is a 2001 Newbery honor book. These and other books about people with special needs are listed in the Booklist at the end of this chapter.

Contemporary Realism in the Classroom

Children enjoy contemporary realism, and this genre is often a way to entice reluctant readers to taste the joys of a good book. The books are often passed around from reader to reader as children discover themselves in these books. Such books can also open windows on other people and other worlds, offering children the opportunity to try on other lives for the space of time it takes them to read a book and to ponder it later.

Reading and discussing contemporary realism provides an opportunity to connect children's lives with the classroom, as children use their own experiences to help them understand the books they read. Many teachers find that discussing contemporary realism opens new paths of communication among students and between students and teachers.

Contemporary realism can also acquaint children with other cultures and communities. Reading contemporary realism that is set in different parts of the country or the world, contains characters that are culturally diverse, and explores the lives of a variety of people helps children learn about others. Knowing people from diverse cultures through books is a first step toward building understanding and tolerance. It is also a first step toward recognizing our common humanity—the wishes, fears, and needs we all share, regardless of culture. Culturally diverse titles are discussed in this chapter and many more are presented in Chapter 11.

Any well-stocked classroom library contains many contemporary realistic fiction titles. These books should represent a wide range of reading levels, a diversity of authors, and a range of types and themes. Comparing books of similar types or themes can help students learn about literature and writ-

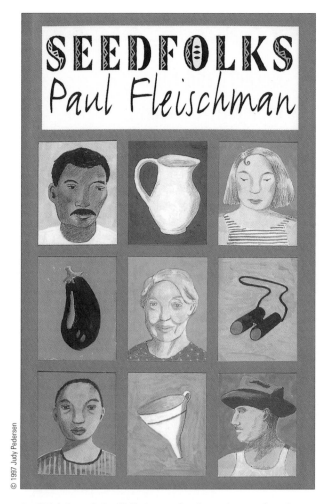

© 1997 Judy Pedersen

*Paul Fleischman's **Seedfolks** is one of an increasing number of outstanding novels that consist of linked short stories around a central theme.*

ing, as they closely examine how different authors approach comparable tasks. Reading a wide range of books can also help students develop knowledge of their own preferences.

Having many titles on hand means that teachers can readily incorporate realistic fiction in thematic units, building on students' interests or curricular demands by making available numerous appropriate and timely books.

Fine contemporary realistic fiction rings with truth. It offers readers multiple lenses through which to view the world and themselves, allowing them to become finer people—more compassionate, more knowledgeable, more heroic than they are in real life. Britton (1970) argues that the virtual experience possible through reading fiction is an important vehicle for constructing personal values. Freed from the necessity of action that real life demands, readers engaged with stories can contemplate feelings, consider actions, and make value judgments. Realistic fiction can be the mirror and the window in which we readers see our better selves.

Summary

Books of contemporary realistic fiction are plausible stories set in today's world. The characters often seem like people we know, and the plots consist of events and actions that could and do occur in everyday life. Realistic fiction includes adventure stories, mysteries, animal stories, sports stories, humorous stories, and romances. Several series are extremely popular with young readers, each with a memorable character who ties the books together. Contemporary realism explores a number of themes, including growing up, peer and family relationships, and life for persons with special needs. Sometimes sensitive issues are raised and discussed. Children enjoy realistic fiction, and teachers find these books an essential part of a classroom library.

Read Louis Sachar's Newbery Medal acceptance speech in the July/August 1999 issue of *The Horn Book Magazine*. In it he talks about how his life influences his writing. Use this information to develop a unit on *Holes* that combines ideas from Teaching Ideas 7.1 and 7.3.

Booklist

Adventure/Survival Stories

Crews, Donald, *Shortcut* (P)
Fox, Paula, *Monkey Island* (A)
George, Jean Craighead, *Julie of the Wolves* (A)
_____, *My Side of the Mountain* (A)
Hobbs, Will, *The Maze* (A)
Holman, Felice, *Slake's Limbo* (I–A)
Lester, Alison, *The Quicksand Pony* (I)
Marsden, John, *Tomorrow, When the War Began* (A)
Paulsen, Gary, *Brian's Return* (I–A)
_____, *Brian's Winter* (I–A)
_____, *Dog Song* (I–A)
_____, *Hatchet* (I–A)

Mystery Stories

Bauer, Marion Dane, *Ghost Eye* (A)
Bawden, Nina, *The House of Secrets* (I)
Byars, Betsy, *The Dark Stairs: A Herculeah Jones Mystery* (I)
_____, *Disappearing Acts* (I)
_____, *Tarot Says Beware* (I)
Crew, Gary, *Angel's Gate* (A)
Cross, Gillian, *Tightrope* (A)
Duncan, Lois, *Stranger with My Face* (A)
Griffith, Helen, *Cougar* (I)
Harrison, Michael, *It's My Life* (I–A)
Howe, James, *What Eric Knew* (I–A)
Joose, Barbara, *Ghost Trap: A Wild Willie Mystery* (P)
Konigsburg, Elaine, *From the Mixed-Up Files of Mrs. Basil E. Frankweiler* (I)
_____, *Silent to the Bone* (A)
L'Engle, Madeleine, *The Arm of the Starfish* (A)
_____, *Troubling a Star* (A)
Levin, Betty, *Creature Crossing* (I)
Naylor, Phyllis Reynolds, *Ice,* (A)
Nixon, Joan Lowry, *The Haunting* (A)
_____, *Spirit Seeker* (A)
Raskin, Ellen, *The Westing Game* (I)
Roberts, Willo Davis, *The View from the Cherry Tree* (I)
_____, *What Could Go Wrong?* (I–A)
Sharmat, Marjorie W., *Nate the Great* (P)
Sobol, Donald, *Encyclopedia Brown Takes the Cake* (I)
Stevenson, James, *The Bones in the Cliff* (I)
Van Draanen, Wendelin, *Sammy Keyes and the Hotel Thief* (I)
_____, *Sammy Keyes and the Skeleton Man* (I)
Wells, Rosemary, *When No One Was Looking* (A)
Werlin, Nancy, *The Killer's Cousin* (A)
Wright, Betty Ren, *The Ghost Comes Calling* (I)
_____, *A Ghost in the Family* (I)
Wynne-Jones, Tim, *Stephen Fair* (A)

Animal Stories

Blades, Ann, *Mary of Mile 18* (P)
Burnford, Sheila, *The Incredible Journey* (A)
Corcoran, Barbara, *Wolf at the Door* (I)
DiCamillo, Kate, *Because of Winn-Dixie* (I)
Farley, Walter, *The Black Stallion* (A)
George, Jean Craighead, *The Cry of the Crow* (I)
Godwin, Laura, *Forest* (P–I)
Haas, Jessie, *Beware and Stogie* (I)
_____, *Beware the Mare* (I)
_____, *Uncle Daney's Way* (I)
Hall, Lynn, *The Soul of the Silver Dog* (I)
Hearne, Betsy, *Eliza's Dog* (I)
Henry, Marguerite, *Misty of Chincoteague* (I)
Hesse, Karen, *Sable* (P)

Hurwitz, Johanna, *One Small Dog* (I)
Levin, Betty, *Look Back, Moss* (I)
Lewis, Kim, *Just Like Floss* (N–P)
Lyon, George Ella, *A Traveling Cat* (N–P)
Naylor, Phyllis Reynolds, *Shiloh* (I)
Rodowsky, Colby, *Not My Dog* (P–I)
Smith, Susan Mathais, *The Booford Summer* (I)
Strommen, Judith Bernie, *Champ Hobarth* (I)

Sports Stories

Avi, *S.O.R. Losers* (I)
Brooks, Bruce, *The Moves Make the Man* (A)
Christopher, Matt, *Catcher with a Glass Arm* (I)
Crutcher, Chris, *Ironman* (A)
_____, *Running Loose* (A)
Deuker, Carl, *Heart of a Champion* (A)
_____, *Night Hoops* (A)
Duder, Tessa, *In Lane Three, Alex Archer* (A)
Dygard, Thomas J., *The Rebounder* (I)
Farrell, Mame, *Bradley and the Billboard* (I)
Lipsyte, Robert, *The Brave* (A)
_____, *The Contender* (A)
Lynch, Chris, *Ice Man* (A)
_____, *Shadow Boxer* (A)
Myers, Walter Dean, *Slam!* (A)
Slote, Alfred, *Finding Buck McHenry* (I)
_____, *The Trading Game* (I)
Smith, Robert Kimmel, *Bobby Baseball* (I)
Spinelli, Jerry, *There's a Girl in My Hammerlock* (I)
Tunis, John R., *Highpockets* (A)
Wallace, Rich, *Playing Without the Ball* (A)
_____, *Shots on Goal* (A)
_____, *Wrestling Sturbridge* (A)
Willner-Pardo, Gina, *Jason and the Losers* (I)

Humorous Stories

Blume, Judy, *Tales of a Fourth-Grade Nothing* (I)
_____, *Superfudge* (I)
Byars, Betsy, *The Not-Just-Anybody Family* (I)
Conford, Ellen, *If This Is Love, I'll Take Spaghetti* (I–A)
Cutler, Jane, *'Gator Aid* (I)
Duffey, Betsy, *Cody Unplugged* (P–I)
Ferris, Jean, *Love Among the Walnuts* (A)
Gauthier, Gail, *A Year with Butch and Spike* (I)
Gilson, Jamie, *Hobie Hanson, You're Weird* (I)
Greene, Stephanie, *Owen Foote: Frontiersman* (P–I)
Honey, Elizabeth, *Don't Pat the Wombats!* (I)
Horvath, Polly, *The Trolls* (P–I)
Hurwitz, Johanna, *Adventures of Ali Baba Bernstein* (I)
_____, *Aldo Applesauce* (I)

_____, *Ozzie on His Own* (I)
Korman, Gordon, *No More Dead Dogs* (I)
Koss, Amy Goldman, *The Ashwater Experiment* (I)
Manes, Stephen, *Be a Perfect Person in Just Three Days* (I)
McKay, Hilary, *Dolphin Luck* (I)
Myers, Laurie, *Earthquake in Third Grade* (I)
Rennison, Louise, *Angus, Thongs and Full-Frontal Snogging: Confessions of Georgia Nicolson* (A)
Sachar, Louis, *Marvin Redpost: Super Fast, Out of Control* (P)
_____, *There's a Boy in the Girls' Bathroom* (I)

Romance Stories

Greene, Bette, *Philip Hall Likes Me. I Reckon Maybe.* (I)
MacLachlan, Patricia, *Unclaimed Treasures* (I)
McKay, Hilary, *The Exiles in Love* (A)
Oneal, Zibby, *In Summer Light* (A)
Plummer, Louise, *The Unlikely Romance of Kate Bjorkman* (A)
Spinelli, Jerry, *Star Girl* (A)

Stories About Growing Up

Adler, C. S., *Not Just a Summer Crush* (I)
Bauer, Cat, *Harley, Like a Person* (A)
Bauer, Joan, *Hope Was Here* (A)
_____, *Rules of the Road* (A)
Bauer, Marion Dane, *On My Honor* (A)
Blume, Judy, *Are You There God? It's Me, Margaret* (I)
_____, *Then Again, Maybe I Won't* (I)
_____, *Tiger Eyes* (A)
Bond, Nancy, *Truth to Tell* (A)
Brooks, Bruce, *What Hearts* (A)
Brooks, Martha, *Traveling on Into the Light and Other Stories* (A)
Clements, Andrew, *Frindle* (I)
_____, *The Janitor's Boy* (I)
_____, *The Landry News* (I)
Creech, Sharon, *Bloomability* (A)
_____, *Chasing Redbird* (A)
_____, *Walk Two Moons* (A)
Cutler, Jane, *Rats!* (I)
Duffey, Betsy, *Coaster* (I)
_____, *Cody Unplugged* (I)
_____, *Spotlight on Cody* (I)
Ferris, Jean, *Bad* (A)
Fleischman, Paul, *Whirligig* (A)
Fox, Paula, *The One-Eyed Cat* (I)
Frank, E. R., *Life Is Funny* (A)
Frank, Lucy, *I Am an Artichoke* (A)
Gantos, Jack, *Jack on the Tracks: Four Seasons of Fifth Grade* (I)
George, Jean Craighead, *Julie of the Wolves* (A)
Glassman, Miriam, *Box Top Dreams* (I)
Greene, Stephanie, *Owen Foote, Money Man* (P)

Hamilton, Virginia, *Plain City* (A)

Havill, Juanita, *Jamaica and the Substitute Teacher* (P)

Herman, John, *Deep Water* (A)

Johnson, Angela, *Gone from Home: Short Takes* (A)

Levitin, Sonia, *The Singing Mountain* (A)

Lisle, Janet Taylor, *The Afternoon of the Elves* (I)

Little, Jean, *Emma's Magic Winter* (P)

_____, *Mama's Going to Buy You a Mockingbird* (I)

Lowry, Lois, *Rabble Starkey* (A)

_____, *A Summer to Die* (A)

MacLachlan, Patricia, *The Facts and Fictions of Minna Pratt* (A)

Mahy, Margaret, *24 Hours* (A)

McNeal, Laura, and Tom McNeal, *Crooked* (A)

Mead, Alice, *Junebug* (I)

_____, *Junebug and the Reverend* (I)

Mills, Claudia, *You're a Brave Man, Julius Zimmerman* (I)

Moore, Martha, *Under the Mermaid Angel* (A)

Myers, Walter Dean, *Darnell Rock Reporting* (A)

_____, *Monster* (A)

_____, *145th Street Stories* (A)

Naylor, Phyllis Reynolds, *Achingly Alice* (A)

_____, *Alice the Brave* (A)

Park, Barbara, *The Graduation of Jake Moon* (I)

Pearson, Gayle, *The Fog Doggies and Me* (I)

Potok, Chaim, *Zebra and Other Stories* (A)

Randle, Kristen, *Breaking Rank* (A)

Rosenberry, Vera, *Vera's First Day of School* (P)

Singer, Marilyn, *Stay True: Short Stories for Strong Girls* (A)

Smith, D. James, *Fast Company* (A)

Tashjian, Janet, *Multiple Choice* (A)

Thesman, Jean, *The Rain Catchers* (A)

Weeks, Sarah, *Guy Time* (I)

Zemser, Amy Bronwen, *Beyond the Mango Tree* (I–A)

Stories About Peer Relationships

Aliki, *Marianthe's Story: Painted Words* (P)

Anderson, Laurie Halse, *Speak* (A)

Anderson, M. T., *Burger Wuss* (A)

Banks, Kate, *Howie Bowles, Secret Agent* (P)

Bloor, Edward, *Crusader* (A)

Boock, Paula, *Dare Truth or Promise* (A)

Burgess, Melvin, *Smack* (A)

Cameron, Ann, *Gloria's Way* (P–I)

Cole, Brock, *The Goats* (A)

Coleman, Michael, *Weirdo's War* (I)

Crutcher, Chris, *Staying Fat for Sarah Byrnes* (A)

Danziger, Paula, *Amber Brown Is Not a Crayon* (I)

DeClements, Barthe, *Liar, Liar* (I)

DeGroat, Diane, *Trick or Treat, Smell My Feet* (P–I)

Dessen, Sarah, *Someone Like You* (A)

Fiedler, Lisa, *Lucky Me* (A)

Fletcher, Ralph, *Flying Solo* (I)

Gorman, Carol, *Dork in Disguise* (I)

Greenfield, Eloise, *Koya Delaney and the Good Girl Blues* (I)

Grove, Vicki, *Reaching Dustin* (I)

Hamilton, Virginia, *Bluish* (I)

Hautman, Pete, *Stone Cold* (A)

Hewett, Lorri, *Dancer* (A)

Hurwitz, Johanna, *Roz and Ozzie* (I)

_____, *Starting School* (I)

Jukes, Mavis, *Planning the Impossible* (I)

Kerr, M. E., *What Became of Her* (A)

Kimmell, Elizabeth Cody, *Visiting Miss Caples* (I–A)

Koss, Amy Goldman, *The Girls* (I–A)

Lewis, Maggie, *Morgy Makes His Move* (I)

Marchetta, Melina, *Looking for Alibrandi* (A)

Marsden, John, *Letters from the Inside* (A)

Mills, Claudia, *Standing Up to Mr. O* (I)

Morgenstern, Susie, *Secret Letters from 0 to 10,* (I)

Myers, Walter Dean, *Me, Mop, and the Moondance Kid* (I)

Naylor, Phyllis Reynolds, *Alice on the Outside* (A)

_____, *The Grooming of Alice* (A)

_____, *Walker's Crossing* (A)

Nelson, Teresa, *The Empress of Elsewhere* (I)

Paterson, Katherine, *Bridge to Terabithia* (I)

_____, *Flip-Flop Girl* (I)

Perkins, Lynn Ray, *All Alone in the Universe* (I–A)

Salisbury, Graham, *Jungle Dogs* (A)

Spinelli, Jerry, *Crash* (I)

Vail, Rachel, *If You Only Knew* (I–A)

_____, *Not That I Care* (I–A)

_____, *Please, Please, Please* (I–A)

Voight, Cynthia, *Bad Girls* (A)

Walter, Mildred Pitts, *Suitcase* (I)

Willner-Pardo, Gina, *Jumping into Nothing* (P)

Winton, Tim, *Lockie Leonard, Scumbuster* (A)

Woodson, Jacqueline, *I Hadn't Meant to Tell You This* (A)

_____, *Last Summer with Maizon* (A)

Yee, Brenda Shannon, *Sand Castle* (N–P)

Yumoto, Kazumi, *The Friends* (A)

_____, *The Spring Tree* (A)

Stories About Family Relationships

Banks, Lynn Reid, *Alice-by-Accident* (I)

Bechard, Margaret, *If It Doesn't Kill You* (A)

Brooks, Bruce, *Everywhere* (I)

_____, *Vanishing* (I)

Brooks, Martha, *Being with Henry* (A)

Caseley, Judith, *Starring Dorothy Kane* (I)

Cassedy, Sylvia, *M. E. and Morton* (I)

Coloumbis, Audrey, *Getting Near to Baby* (I)

Conly, Jane Leslie, *Trout Summer* (I)

_____, *While No One Was Watching* (I–A)

Delton, Judy, *Angel Spreads Her Wings* (I)

Dessen, Sarah, *Dreamland* (A)

Fenner, Carol, *The King of Dragons* (I)

Fine, Anne, *Flour Babies* (A)

Griffin, Adele, *Dive* (A)

Hamilton, Virginia, *Second Cousins* (I)

Henkes, Kevin, *The Birthday Room* (I)

_____, *Protecting Marie* (A)

Hermes, Patricia, *Cheat the Moon: A Novel* (I–A)

Hobbs, Valerie, *Charlie's Run* (I)

Hughes, Shirley, *Alfie and the Birthday Surprise* (P)

Johnson, Angela, *Songs of Faith* (I)

Katz, Susan, *Snowdrops for Cousin Ruth* (I)

Lowry, Lois, *Zooman Sam* (I)

MacLachlan, Patricia, *Baby* (I–A)

_____, *Journey* (I–A)

Many, Paul, *My Life, Take Two* (A)

McDonnell, Christine, *It's a Deal, Dogboy* (I)

Mills, Claudia, *Gus and Grandpa and the Two-Wheeled Bike* (P)

Namioka, Lensey, *Yang the Third and Her Impossible Family* (I–A)

Nelson, Vaunda Micheaux, *Possibles* (A)

O'Connor, Barbara, *Me and Rupert Goody* (I)

Paterson, Katherine, *The Great Gilly Hopkins* (I–A)

_____, *Jacob Have I Loved* (A)

Paul, Anne Whitford, *Everything to Spend the Night from A to Z* (P)

Paulsen, Gary, *The Winter Room* (A)

Peck, Richard, *Strays Like Us* (I–A)

Pennebaker, Ruth, *Both Sides Now* (A)

Plummer, Louise, *A Dance for Three* (A)

Powell, Randy, *Tribute to Another Dead Rock Star* (A)

Rodowsky, Colby, *Hannah in Between* (A)

_____, *Sydney, Invincible* (A)

Ross, Adrienne, *In the Quiet* (I–A)

Rylant, Cynthia, *Missing May* (I–A)

Sachs, Marilyn, *Surprise Party* (I)

Saenz, Benjamin Alire, *A Gift from Papa Diego/Un Regale de Papa Diego* (P)

Thesman, Jean, *Calling the Swan* (A)

Weeks, Sarah, *Regular Guy* (A)

Woodson, Jacqueline, *Miracle's Boys* (A)

Special Needs Stories

Anderson, Rachel, *The Bus People* (A)

Banks, Jacqueline Turner, *Egg Drop Blues* (I)

Betancourt, Jeanne, *My Name Is Brain Brian* (I–A)

Birdseye, Tom, *Just Call Me Stupid* (I)

Byars, Betsy, *Summer of the Swans* (I–A)

Caseley, Judith, *Harry and Willy and Carrothead* (P)

Clifton, Lucille, *My Friend Jacob* (P)

Conly, Jane Leslie, *Crazy Lady!* (A)

Covington, Dennis, *Lizard* (I)

Gantos, Jack, *Joey Pigza Loses Control* (I)

_____, *Joey Pigza Swallowed the Key* (I)

Gleitzman, Morris, *Blabber Mouth* (I)

Johnson, Angela, *Humming Whispers* (A)

Lears, Laurie, *Ian's Walk: A Story of Autism* (P)

Little, Jean, *Mine for Keeps* (I)

Mazer, Harry, *The Wild Kid* (A)

Metzger, Lois, *Barry's Sister* (A)

_____, *Ellen's Case* (A)

Philbrick, Rodman, *Freak the Mighty* (A)

Sachs, Marilyn, *The Bear's House* (I)

_____, *Fran Ellen's House* (I)

Shreve, Susan, *The Flunking of Joshua T. Bates* (I)

_____, *Joshua T. Bates Takes Charge* (I)

Trueman, Terry, *Stuck in Neutral* (A)

Voigt, Cynthia, *Izzy Willy-Nilly* (A)

White, Ruth, *Belle Prater's Boy* (I–A)

_____, *Memories of Summer* (A)

chapter **8**

Historical Fiction

And Addie, at any time we could be sold by a fat man in a white hat in a tight white suit and we'd have to go, just like that. Dear Addie, Write soon, I miss you, and I have bad dreams at night. Love, Nettie.

—ANN TURNER, *Nettie's Trip South*

SILENCE FILLS THE ROOM AS JAMES LANGE CLOSES THE COVER OF *Nettie's Trip South.* In a soft voice he asks his seventh-grade students to write in response to the story they've just heard. "Just write how you're feeling and what you're thinking right now," he says. "Don't worry about making it pretty, just get your feelings down." All 27 heads bend to the task.

Later, when everyone is finished writing, the students move into small discussion groups. Soon passionate voices erupt from each group. "How could they treat people that way?" one queries. "I wanted to throw up, too!" another interjects. "Did they really tear families apart like that?" "Sure they did. Blacks weren't considered people, remember? It said that in the book."

When the small group discussions begin to slow down, James asks for summaries of what each group has talked about and invites students to share their written responses. One girl sums up what seems to be the response of the whole class when she says, "Now I can begin to know what slavery was really like—how it made you feel, and why it was so wrong."

In historical fiction the events of the past are told as the stories of people who seem real to us. As history becomes a story about someone we know, it gives us the opportunity to vicariously experience life in the past, and to consider historical events as issues that had real consequences for the people who lived them, rather than as abstract concepts. These seventh-grade students are about to embark on a study of the Civil War in their social studies class, and their language arts teacher is selecting literature to enhance their understanding of that historical period. Books like *Nettie's Trip South* by Ann Turner (I–A) help them connect with their history lessons in a way no textbook can.

Defining Historical Fiction

History is a story, the story of the world and its people and of cultures that rise and fall across time. Historical fiction tells the stories of history; as a distinct genre it consists of imaginative stories grounded in the facts of our past. It is not biography (discussed in Chapter 9), which focuses on the life of an individual; historical fiction has a wider scope. Historical fiction differs from nonfiction (discussed in Chapter 10) in that it not only presents facts or re-creates a time and place, but also weaves the facts into a fictional story. Historical fiction is realistic—the events could have occurred and people portrayed could have lived—but it differs from contemporary realistic fiction in that the stories are set in the past rather than the present.

Some books that we now classify as historical fiction began as contemporary realism. In 1868 Louisa May Alcott's *Little Women* (A) was a contemporary work of realism. The intervening years have made the story historical. Some historical fiction stories are more factual than others, as when authors include real events and/or people in their imaginative stories. Irene Hunt's *Across Five Aprils* (A) is a classic story of the Civil War with names, dates, newspaper accounts of real battles, and realistic political and social detail woven into a moving story.

Some authors set their stories in times past but do not specifically connect them with any particular historical events or people. Still, these authors know a great deal about the time and place in which their stories are set; it is the authentic social details that make the stories good history. Karen English creates a vivid picture of life in the Deep South of the 1950s in *Francie* (I–A), a Coretta Scott King Honor Book that explores issues of racism, human worth, and dignity that transcend time and place. Cynthia DeFelice's *Nowhere to Call Home* (I–A), set during the Depression, explores homelessness through entirely fictional characters and events. DeFelice provides a richly detailed setting without relying on specific people or events.

Other stories are memoirs of the authors' own lives or the lives of their relatives. The events of their lives have been sifted, artistically arranged, and presented as engaging stories. Louise Erdrich writes about her own family's history in *The Birchbark House* (I), the moving story of a year in the life of young Omakayas and her family, who lived on Madeline Island in Lake Superior in the mid-nineteenth century. Based on research by the author's mother and sister, this novel is full of the homely details of life in the Ojibwa community of that time and place. In the Newbery Medal–winning *Bud, Not Buddy* (I), Christopher Paul Curtis creates memorable secondary characters who are based on his grandfathers, but he notes in his afterword that most of what he knows about the Depression, he learned through research.

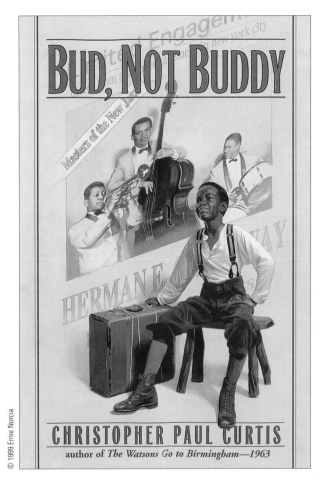

© 1999 Ernie Norcia

A spunky 10-year-old boy, memorable setting, and an engaging plot make Christopher Paul Curtis's Newbery Medal–winning **Bud, Not Buddy** *a wonderful book to read aloud to upper elementary and middle school students.*

Historical fiction sometimes surprises readers because it can also take the form of an adventure story, as in Will Hobbs's *Jason's Gold* (I–A); a mystery, as in Cynthia Voigt's *The Callender Papers* (I); or a romance, as in Richard Peck's *Amanda Miranda* (A). Historical fiction may be an animal story, as in Rosemary Wells's adaptation, *Lassie Come-Home* (I); it may be written in poetic form, as in Karen Hesse's *Out of the Dust* (A); or it may contain fantasy elements like time travel, as in Jane Yolen's *The Devil's Arithmetic* (A). What makes these books historical is their historical setting and the importance of the setting to the story.

In 1982 Scott O'Dell, a noted writer of award-winning historical fiction, established The Scott O'Dell Award for Historical Fiction, to be given to a writer from the United States for a meritorious book published the preceding year. O'Dell hoped that this award would interest new writers in working within the historical fiction genre and thus provide more books for young readers that will help them understand the historical background that has helped shape their world. It seems that his desire has been realized, for historical fiction seems to be enjoying renewed popularity; many new novels set in the past are published for young readers each year.

Several series, such as the Scholastic **Royal Diaries** (I) and the **Dear America** (I) books, or the Morrow **American Adventures** (I) series, have been developed and marketed to attract growing numbers of young readers to historical fiction. These books have created an interesting debate among children's literature scholars. Some of these books are very well done, written by outstanding authors and filled with a masterful blend of historical fact and period detail within an engaging fictional story. One such book is Kathryn Lasky's *Elizabeth I: Red Rose of the House of Tudor* (I), which presents Elizabeth's life in the years immediately preceding the death of her father, Henry VIII. Other books in these series are less well documented and may present misinformation to young readers. Native American scholars and children's book critics have faulted Ann Rinaldi's *My Heart Is on the Ground: The Diary of Nannie Little Rose, A Sioux Girl, Carlisle Indian School, PA 1880* (I) for glossing over the horrors of the Indian schools in nineteenth-century America. Others point out that Rinaldi has told one girl's story and does not presume to speak for all of the children at the Carlisle School. Still other critics decry the fact that the diaries are presented as real diaries, with some even containing a ribbon for marking the day's entry! On balance, however, these series, with their brief entries and engaging format, offer young readers an important entry into reading historical fiction. The best of them also offer readers a glimpse of life as it was lived by a historical, albeit fictional, *child,* someone whose voice is rarely heard in other histories.

No matter what form it takes, outstanding historical fiction shows that history is created by people, that people experience historical events in individual ways, that people living now are tied to those who lived in the past through a common humanity, and that human conditions of the past shape our lives today. Historical fiction offers readers the opportunity to travel across time and place and thus to find themselves.

Historical Fiction in Children's Lives

History is made by people—people with strengths and weaknesses who experience victories and defeats. It reflects what they do, what they say, and what they are. Authors of books set in the past want children to know historical figures as human beings—real people like themselves who have shortcomings as well as strengths. Historical events sometimes affected the common people even more than they did kings and battle leaders; the way the common folk responded to history's traumas shows adaptability and gives modern children a sense of reality concerning times past.

Today's children have a hard time imagining life without computers, video technology, rapid transportation, and modern communication. When they read good historical fiction, children can imagine themselves living in another time and place. They can speculate about how they would have reacted and how they would have felt. They can read about ordinary people acting heroically. By doing so, they begin to understand the impact one person can have on history.

There are strong links between children's family histories and the historical fiction that they read. Children are interested in finding out about what life was like in the "olden" days, and reading historical fiction is like listening to a grandmother's stories. Knowing stories of grandmother's childhood, of great-great-grandfather's escape from slavery through the Underground Railroad, or of a great-aunt's journey across the ocean to America is knowing history. Just as family stories help children discover their own place in the history of their family, historical fiction can help children discover their own place in the history of their world; it can give them a sense of the historical importance of their own lives. Well-written historical fiction can make the past alive, real, and meaningful to children who are living today and who will shape the world of tomorrow.

Historical fiction relates to children's lives both in and out of school. Stories of life in the past that are set in the place where they live help children to see their home with new eyes. Knowing the details of daily life in the past enables children to understand and appreciate the magnitude of the industrial, technological, and medical advances that shape their lives. So much good historical fiction is available that the study of virtually any time in history can be enriched.

By relating trade books to topics in the social studies, we strengthen children's understanding with a wealth of material that far exceeds the limited view of any single text. We can do the same in other curricular areas by reading stories, for example, that are set in times during which important scientific breakthroughs occurred. Poetry, biography and nonfiction (discussed in Chapters 2, 9, and 10) can also support historical fiction and extend children's understanding of our past. Books about important events in the history of science, mathematics, art, language, medicine, and many other fields provide factual information to add to the emotional information that historical fiction conveys. Historical fiction provides insights into the panoply of history; it is a lively and fascinating way to transmit the story of the past to the guardians of the future.

Criteria for Evaluating Historical Fiction

The best historical stories come from good storytellers who are well acquainted with the facts; good historical fiction is grounded in facts but not restricted by them. An author may use historical records to document events, but the facts merely serve as a framework for the story. Many books that present historical facts do not qualify as historical fiction. To do so, a text must meet the criteria for *all* good narratives: It must have well-developed characters and integral themes; it must tell an engaging story with well-crafted language; and, in the case of picture books, it must contain beautiful and accurate art. Beyond this, it must meet criteria that are particular to the genre. Figure 8.1 contains a brief list of questions to ask when evaluating historical fiction.

HISTORICAL ACCURACY

Historical fiction should be consistent with historical evidence. The story, though imaginative, must remain within the limits of the chosen historical background, avoiding distortion and anachronism. Historical accuracy, however, presents an interesting dilemma, one we discuss again in Chapter 9. While we can know so-called facts about our past, we know these facts only in light of the present. Every generation of historians, to some degree, reinterprets the past by using the concerns of the present as a lens. For example, a book like Esther Forbes's classic Revolutionary War story, *Johnny Tremain* (A), written during a time of great patriotic fervor (1946), is not at all critical of war. James Lincoln Collier and Christopher Collier's *My Brother Sam Is Dead* (A), written during the Vietnam Conflict (1974), presents a very different picture of the same war (Taxel, 1984). Both stories deal with the same set of "facts," but their implications are radically different because they are written from different perspectives. Any presentation of history is an interpretation, but good historical fiction creates as true a picture of the past as an author can craft. The interpretive nature of historical fiction is even more complicated when issues of "authority" are considered in terms of cultural group membership, which we discuss further in Chapter 11. Historical "accuracy", then, is always influenced by who the author is and when the author is writing, by how the author understands the historical experience within his or her own life.

Historical accuracy can create problems with racism and sexism. When writing about periods of time in which racism and sexism abounded, authors must take care to portray these social issues honestly while at the same time

not condoning them. In Ann Turner's *Nettie's Trip South* (I) the issue of slavery is foregrounded; it is slavery that marked the South before the Civil War and it is slavery that sickens young Nettie. In *Walks Alone* (I), Brian Burks describes the often vicious approach to the Apache taken by the United States army. Anne Isaacs's *Torn Thread* (A) and Carol Matas's *In My Enemy's House* (A) depict the racism and violence of Nazi-occupied Europe but do so in a way that helps readers understand how horrible it was as well as appreciate

Figure 8.1

Checklist for Evaluating Historical Fiction

General
- Does the work meet the criteria for all good narratives?

Historical Accuracy
- Are events and attitudes consistent with historical evidence and appropriate to the time period?
- Are social issues portrayed honestly, without condoning racism and sexism?

Setting
- Is the setting integral to the story?
- Does the story evoke a vivid historical setting consistent with historical and geographical evidence?

Language
- Are the language patterns historically authentic and in keeping with the mood and characterization?

Characterization
- Do characters' feelings, values, and behavior reflect the period?

Plot and Theme
- Is the plot based on authentic facts that are subordinate to the story itself?
- Is the theme an echo of larger historical concerns?

Illustrations
- Do the illustrations enhance an understanding of plot, setting, and characterization through the use of realistic details?

the personal courage of those caught up in the Holocaust. Historical fiction may have to portray racism and sexism for historical accuracy, but the stories themselves should not be racist or sexist.

Noteworthy historical novels do not *overgeneralize;* they do not lead the reader to believe, for example, that all Native Americans are like those portrayed in any one story. Each character is unique, just as each of us is, and while the novelist focuses on one person in a group, it should be clear that the character *is* only a person, and not a stereotype.

When evaluating historical fiction, look for events and attitudes that are appropriate to the time period and for stories that portray social issues honestly, without condoning racism and sexism.

SETTING

Setting is a crucial element in evaluating historical fiction, because it is this feature that distinguishes that form most dramatically from other literary forms. Details of setting must be spelled out so clearly that readers can create mental images of the time and place in which the events occur. These elements are integral to the plot of historical fiction; they determine characters' beliefs and actions. The setting must also be authentic and consistent with historical and geographical evidence. In evaluating historical books, look for settings that are integral to the story and are authentic in historical and geographical detail. See Teaching Idea 8.1 for one way to explore settings.

LANGUAGE

Language should be in keeping with the period and the place, particularly in dialogue. However, today's readers have difficulty understanding archaic language. Accomplished authors synthesize language that has the right tone or sound for a period but is understandable to contemporary readers. Rosemary Sutcliff explains how she works appropriate language into her writing:

> I try to catch the rhythm of a tongue, the tune that it plays on the ear, Welsh or Gaelic as opposed to Anglo-Saxon, the sensible workmanlike language which one feels the Latin of the ordinary Roman citizen would have translated into. It is extraordinary what can be done by the changing or transposing of a single word, or by using a perfectly usual one in a slightly unusual way: "I beg your pardon" changed into "I ask your pardon." . . . This is not done by any set rule of thumb; I simply play it by ear as I go along. (1973, pp. 307–308)

The character's thoughts should also reflect the time and place. Any metaphors, similes, or images that describe what

---

Teaching Idea 8✡1

Compare Literary Descriptions of Historic Sites

Authors and illustrators describe historical settings in narratives, biographies, poetry, and nonfiction. Select books to compare literary descriptions of historical sites.

Ask your students to:

1. Read several books that describe the same region or historical period.
2. Compare selections and illustrations.
3. Discuss which descriptions are more evocative, and which help them understand the place and time best.
4. Describe the place in their own words and/or art.

Use any of the books listed in this chapter, grouped by period or place. Some books with vivid settings are:

Avi, *The Barn* (A)

Cooney, Barbara, *Island Boy* (P)

Cushman, Karen, *Matilda Bone* (A)

_____, *Catherine, Called Birdy* (A)

_____, *The Midwife's Apprentice* (A)

Erdrich, Louise, *The Birchbark House* (I)

Holt, Kimberly Willis, *When Zachary Beaver Came to Town* (A)

Paulsen, Gary, *Harris and Me* (A)

Pinkney, Gloria, *Going Home* (P–I)

Smothers, Ethel Footman, *Moriah's Pond* (I)

Taylor, Mildred, *Song of the Trees* (I)

---

a character is thinking or feeling must be appropriate to the setting. In Michael Dorris's *Morning Girl* (I–A), set in 1492 on a Bahamian Island that will soon be visited by Christopher Columbus, Morning Girl, a young Taino, thinks about her brother:

> The world fits together so tightly, the pieces like pebbles and shells sunk into the sand after the tide has gone out, before anyone has walked on the beach and left footprints.
>
> In our house, though, my brother was the footprints.

Morning Girl's world is bounded by the sand and the sea; it is fitting that she think of life in those terms.

When evaluating language in historical fiction, look for language patterns and word choices that are authentic and in keeping with the mood and characterization.

CHARACTERIZATION

Characters in historical fiction should believe and behave in ways that are in keeping with the times in which they live. Authors who attribute contemporary values to historical figures run the risk of creating an *anachronism*, mistakenly placing something in the wrong historical period. Sometimes it's difficult to judge. When Karen Cushman's *Catherine, Called Birdy* (I–A) was published, several critics took Cushman to task for creating a character who was a literate female living in the Middle Ages. Women, they said, weren't literate and, what's more, didn't act independently. In fact, most women weren't literate and were completely under the control of men. However, some noted historical figures were different, and it was these that Catherine most resembled. She was not meant to represent "all" medieval women, but rather to stand as one specific, fictional woman. In historical fiction, the characters' feelings, behavior, values, and language should reflect the period, but also the individuality of the character.

PLOT AND THEME

History is filled with a tremendous amount of raw material for exciting plots and themes. Yet an abundance of historical facts may overburden a story. In *Talent Is Not Enough*, Mollie Hunter (1976), noted writer of historical fiction and other books, says that the facts of the past are needed to create a book, but it is the author's sense of history and his or her knowledge of people's dreams, realities, and passions that recreate some part of the past as a living link in the chain of human experience. None of the facts of the historical situation, she continues, may be relevant except that they serve the main function of source material, which is to yield a theme that has universal application and appeal (pp. 40–41). Teaching Idea 8.2 asks students to compare how historical topics are treated by writers of both fiction and nonfiction.

While the facts must be accurate, they should not bog down the plot. Instead, they should help to propel the narrative line. The themes that are developed through facts and narrative often reflect both the macrocosm of the era (for example, a war for independence) and the microcosm of the story (for example, a struggle for personal independence).

In evaluating historical fiction, look for books that blend factual background as subordinate to the story and that contain a theme that echoes larger historical concerns.

ILLUSTRATIONS

In recent years a number of excellent historical fiction picture storybooks have been published. These books contain not only well-written, riveting stories, but also beautiful illustrations that support and enhance the story. The

Chris Soentpiet's glowing watercolor paintings reveal details of time and place as they heighten the human drama in Alice McGill's **Molly Bannaky** *(P–I).*

Teaching Idea 8 ✷ 2

Compare Treatment of a Topic in Textbooks, Primary Sources, Contemporary Fiction, and Historical Fiction

Select a topic that crosses the boundaries of time, such as homelessness. Gather primary sources such as current or historical newspapers and magazines, and contemporary and historical fiction. Ask students to read and respond to their reading, then to compare these experiences to their reading of a textbook or encyclopedia on the same topic. Discuss the different ways of knowing that these readings generate. Fiction titles that deal with homelessness during the Great Depression and today are:

Contemporary

Bunting, Eve, *Fly Away Home* (I)
Fox, Paula, *Monkey Island* (I–A)
Tolan, Stephanie, *Sophie and the Sidewalk Man* (I)

Historical

Curtis, Christopher Paul, *Bud, Not Buddy* (I)
DeFelice, Cynthia, *Nowhere to Go* (A)

illustrations in picture storybooks of historical fiction must meet the criteria for quality of illustration in any picture book. In addition, they must be historically accurate, providing realistic details of life in the historical period as well as reflecting and interpreting character and action. Look for illustrations that enhance the story and that use realistic details to reflect an understanding of the setting, plot and characterization.

A CLOSE LOOK AT

Roll of Thunder, Hear My Cry

Synopsis

Roll of Thunder, Hear My Cry (A), the Newbery Award-winning novel by Mildred Taylor, chronicles the life of Cassie Logan and her family in rural Mississippi during the Great Depression. Young Cassie, her grandmother, mother, father, older brother, Stacey, and younger brothers, Christopher-John and Little Man, live on their own farm. Owning their own land—something that was unusual for African Americans in that place and time—is a source of pride for Cassie. However, she doesn't really understand why it is so important to her parents that her father leave the family and go in search of work. As the story unfolds it is apparent that Cassie, who feels free and indomitable among her own people, doesn't really understand the prejudice and hatred that surround her. It is only after she is publicly humiliated by a white girl, watches her mother lose her teaching job because of prejudice, sees her brother's friend arrested, and hears stories about the horrors of the "night men" that Cassie realizes the truth about where she lives and the reasons for holding on to the land.

Historical Accuracy

Taylor portrays the world in which Cassie lives as it would have seemed to African Americans living at that time. Indeed, much of Taylor's story is based on family stories passed down from her father and her extended family, many of whom lived in the South when she was growing up. Much of the historical context in *Roll of Thunder* is a matter of record. We know, for example, that most African Americans did not own land in the South, that many sharecroppers—both black and white—had to eke out an existence for their families any way they could, and that the Klan terrorized the Southern countryside, brutally killing African Americans. The small details of Cassie's life ring true within this larger historical context, in part because of the vividly painted setting, the authentic language, the well-developed characters, and Taylor's power as a story-teller.

Setting

Taylor's words paint such a vivid picture that it is hard not to feel that you have seen a photograph of the land and the house. The story opens as Cassie and her brothers make the long walk to school, stirring up red dust with each step:

> Before us the narrow, sun-splotched road wound like a lazy red serpent dividing the high forest bank of quiet, old trees on the left from the cotton field, forested by giant green and purple stalks, on the right. A barbed-wire fence ran the length of the deep field, stretching eastward for over a quarter of a mile until it met the sloping green pasture that signaled the end of our family's four hundred acres. An ancient oak tree on the slope, visible even now, was the official dividing mark between Logan land and the beginning of a dense forest.

Everything that Cassie sees, we see, as the story is told from her point of view. We see the well-kept grounds of the white children's school, the shabbiness of the black school ("a dismal end to an hour's journey"), and the Logan living room:

> It was a warm, comfortable room of doors and wood and pictures. From it a person could reach the front or the side porch, the kitchen, and the two other bedrooms. Its walls were made of smooth oak, and on them hung gigantic photographs of Grandpa and Big Ma, Papa and Uncle Hammer when they were boys, Papa's two eldest brothers, who were now dead, and pictures of Mama's family. The furniture, a mixture of Logan-crafted walnut and oak, included a walnut bed whose ornate headboard rose halfway up the wall toward the high ceiling....

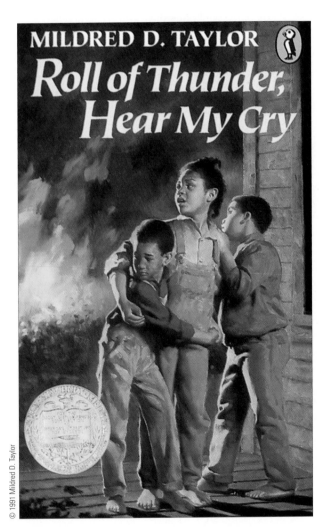

*Cassie Logan tries to shelter her brothers from the racism and hatred that enflame her 1930s rural neighborhood. (**Roll of Thunder, Hear My Cry** by Mildred Taylor.)*

The amount of physical details that Taylor supplies helps anchor this story in a real time and place, populated by real people. The details of actions and events that are revealed through the plot and the character development create an emotional reality as well.

Characterization and Language

Seen through Cassie's eyes, the story *sounds* like Cassie as well. Cassie and the other characters speak in a natural dialect. Taylor carefully allows her characters to sound realistic without making the dialogue difficult for readers to understand. As they walk to school, the Logan children meet their friend, T. J., who tells them about a neighbor who's been burnt by night riders:

> "I betcha I could give y'all an earful 'bout that burnin' last night."
> "Burning? What burning?" asked Stacey.
> "Man, don't y'all know nothin'? The Berrys' burnin'. I thought y'all's grandmother went over there last night to see 'bout 'em."....
> "What Berrys he talking 'bout, Stacey?" I asked. "I don't know no Berrys."

T. J., more interested in excitement than school, drops his final g's; Stacey and Cassie, children of a teacher, do not. They all speak in a dialect, but even within that dialect Taylor is careful to delineate the distinctive voice of each character.

Cassie, as the narrator, also must tell readers what she sees, thinks, and feels. Taylor is careful to keep within the boundaries of what a young girl would say.

Because we are privy to Cassie's thoughts and feelings we get to know her quite well. We feel her fear when the night riders come. We share her outrage when she is shamed by the storekeeper and forced off the sidewalk by Lillian Jean and her father. We certainly share her joyful satisfaction when she gets even with Lillian Jean in a way that is absolutely appropriate to her personality and the time in which she lives. Cassie seemingly apologizes to Lillian Jean, carries her books, and acts like her servant until one day when she lures her into the woods with the promise of a surprise. Once she gets Lillian Jean into the woods Cassie throws her books on the ground. When told by Lillian Jean to pick them back up, Cassie quietly says, "Make me."

> "What?" The shock on her face was almost comical.
> "Said make me."
> Her face paled. Then, red with anger, she stepped daintily across the clearing and struck me hard across the face. For the record, she had hit me first; I didn't plan on her hitting me again.

I flailed into her, tackling her with such force that we both fell.

After Cassie wins the fight, pinning Lillian Jean down and yanking on her hair, she makes her apologize for the torment she made Cassie endure:

> And she apologized. For herself and for her father. For her brothers and her mother. For Strawberry and Mississippi, and by the time I finished jerking at her head, I think she would have apologized for the world being round had I demanded it.

Cassie's pride, one of her primary traits, had been damaged, and she found a way to make it whole again.

When Lillian Jean threatens to tell her father what Cassie has done, Cassie has an answer for that, too. She threatens to tell everyone all of the hateful secrets that Lillian Jean has been telling her. Proud of herself, and secure in her safety from retaliation, Cassie begins to leave. And then:

Lillian Jean asked, bewildered, "But, Cassie, why? You was such a nice little girl." . . .

> I stared at her astonished. Then I turned and left the forest, not wanting to believe that Lillian Jean didn't even realize it had all been just a game.

This is just one of many incidents that reveal Cassie's pride, intelligence, and determination to hold her head high in a society that demanded that she look down.

Plot and Theme

The events that occur in this story are events that could, and did, happen in Mississippi during the Great Depression. The main action centers on the Logan family's struggle to live as honorable human beings in a forbidding society, to maintain their pride, their dignity, and their very lives. The land they seek to hold on to symbolizes their struggle for decency.

Profile ✡ Mildred Taylor

© Jack Ackerman

By the time I entered high school, I was confident that I would one day be a writer. . . . Once I had made up my mind to write, I had no doubts about doing it. It was just something that would one day be. I had always been taught that I would achieve anything I set my mind to.

In a talk cosponsored by the International Reading Association and the Children's Book Council, Mildred Taylor described her childhood memories in the vibrant countryside, and the vitality of black community life, with its revivals and courtings, prayer meetings and picnics. Where

there was beauty, however, there was also insufferable hatred and bigotry. She and her sister attended local schools, and she recalls how each book was marked, not only with previous owners' names, but with their race as well. Even as a child she sensed something wrong, so she scratched out the information.

As a child, Taylor wondered why the history books contained no stories about African Americans, when the stories from her own family's past were filled with heroic men and women who fought with valor against oppression and indignities. Her desire to tell the story of strong African-American families facing difficulties heroically and with integrity led her to write *Song of the Trees* (I); *Roll of Thunder, Hear My Cry* (I–A), winner of the 1977 Newbery Medal and the 1977 National Book Award; *Let the Circle Be Unbroken* (I–A); *The Gold Cadillac* (I); *The Road to Memphis* (A); *Mississippi Bridge* (A); *The Friendship* (I); and *The Well: David's Story* (A).

Taylor decries the conventional depiction of black ghettos as slums. The ghetto in which she grew up was

not a slum, and she has no recollection of fatherless families; rather, she remembers the protective presence of strong adults—somewhat like the Logans' protection of Cassie and her brothers in the **Roll of Thunder** series.

From her Peace Corps experience in Ethiopia, Taylor learned the price that independence exacts from an individual. Although her writing carries powerful themes about survival in a hostile society, Taylor's messages radiate rather than pummel:

> It is my hope that to the children who read my books, the Logans will provide those heroes missing from the schoolbooks of my childhood: Black men, women, and children of whom they can be proud.

Throughout, the strength and importance of the family is central. Taylor credits her father, a master storyteller, with having a powerful influence on her life. Her values and principles were shaped in a wholesome and loving family with strong and sensitive parents. Pride in one's heritage is a universal theme meaningful to all readers.

The events of the story are all linked to the drama of the struggle played out against the backdrop of a racist society. When Mrs. Logan chooses to lose her job rather than use textbooks that are offensive to her, she stands for pride in being African American. When Cassie and her brothers turn the tables on the white school-bus driver who torments them, they are fighting for their sense of pride. Faced with what seem to be unresolvable problems of prejudice and poverty, Cassie asks her father if they are "giving up too." David replies:

> "You see that fig tree over yonder, Cassie? Them other trees all around . . . that oak and walnut, they're a lot bigger and they take up more room and give so much shade they almost overshadow that little ole fig. But that fig tree's got roots that run deep, and it belongs in that yard as much as that oak and walnut. It keeps on blooming, bearing good fruit year after year, knowing all the time it'll never get as big as them other trees. Just keeps on growing and doing what it gotta do. It don't give up. It give up, it'll die. There's a lesson to be learned from that little tree, Cassie girl, 'cause we're like it. We keep doing what we gotta, and we don't give up. We can't."

Setting, plot, and characterization work together to present a family caught in a desperate struggle for their existence as human beings. In this family we recognize ourselves.

A CLOSE LOOK AT

Pink and Say

Like the stories about the Logans, the story of *Pink and Say* (I) is one that has been passed down over the generations in Patricia Polacco's own family. Her great-great-grandfather, Sheldon Russell Curtis, called Say, has been left for dead on a Civil War battlefield in Georgia when he is rescued by an African-American Union soldier, Pinkus Aylee. Pink takes Say to his home, where his mother, Moe Moe Bay, a slave, nurses Say back to health. The three become close. Say confides in Moe Moe that he is a deserter, and Pink tells Say that he knows how to read. Say tells Pink and his mother the story of how he shook the hand of Lincoln. Shortly after Moe Moe is killed by marauders, Pink and Say are captured and transported to Andersonville, where Pink is hanged.

I watched tears fill his eyes and cleaved my hand to his until they wrenched us apart. They smote him and dragged him away from me. He looked back at me and tried to say somethin' more but they crossed his back with knotted hemp and pushed him along.

Patricia Polacco's strong line and use of white space help readers feel the force with which Pink's and Say's hands are wrenched apart in **Pink and Say.**

Polacco's illustrations focus on the emotional highs and lows of the characters and provide enough details to anchor the story in the period visually. The story is told in Say's country dialect and the dialogue reflects the times without being overwhelming to the reader. The final few pages are an afterword, when we learn what happened to Pink and Say, and are asked to remember Pink.

One of the many strengths of this story is that no judgments are made. It is just a straightforward recounting of the events as lived and remembered by one 15-year-old Union soldier who was lucky enough to find a friend like Pink.

History Through Historical Fiction

Much historical fiction is set in one particular historical period, but a few excellent books are intergenerational sagas. Walter Dean Myers's *The Glory Field* (A) begins in 1753 with the harrowing story of a young man traveling from West Africa on a slave ship and ends at a family reunion in 1994. Each story he tells is rich with historical details reflecting the various times in the lives of the Lewis family, and each involves a turning point in an adolescent family member's life. Themes of family unity, pride, and freedom connect the stories into a unified whole.

Holding Up the Earth (A), by Dianne E. Gray, also spans a considerable amount of time, but the story is anchored in one place: the Nebraska farm that five different generations of young women have loved. Janet Hickman's *Jericho* (A) is yet another emotionally satisfying intergenerational story; it explores the lives of three generations of women—grandmother, mother, and daughter.

Historical fiction can be studied as a genre, by theme, by chronological period, or according to the topics in a social studies curriculum. In any case, well-written stories will "establish human and social circumstances in which the interaction of historical forces may be known, felt, and observed" (Blos, 1992). We present historical fiction chronologically, and then briefly consider how to explore themes across history.

PREHISTORIC AND ANCIENT TIMES

Prehistoric times, the ancient period before written records were kept, are wrapped in the shrouds of antiquity. Scientists theorize about the daily life and culture of ancient peoples by observing fragments of life and making inferences from bits of pottery, weapons, or scraps of bone. Authors draw from the findings of archaeologists, anthropologists, and paleontologists to create vivid tales of life as it might have been.

Many novels of prehistoric times are set in distant lands around the Mediterranean Sea or in ancient Britain. The best fiction about prehistoric people does more than re-create possible settings and events of the past. It engages itself with themes basic to all persons everywhere: the will to survive, the need for courage and honor, the growth of understanding, the development of compassion. Peter Dickinson's series, **The Kin**, which includes *Suth's Story, Noli's Story, Po's Story*, and *Mana's Story* (all I–A), takes readers back 200,000 years but grapples with issues important today. War and peace, the power of language and the thought it enables, loving relationships, and community are some of the themes that connect these stories with our own times. William Brooke takes a humorous approach to prehistory in *A Is for Aaarrg!* (I–A). Interestingly, he, too, explores the wonders—and pitfalls—of language. These and other stories of prehistoric times are listed in the Booklist at the end of this chapter.

Stories of ancient times often focus on life in the Mediterranean civilizations. Julius Lester's *Pharaoh's Daughter: A Novel of Ancient Egypt* (A) is a fictional account of the biblical story of Moses that contains well-developed characters and complex themes. Tracy Barrett's *Anna of Byzantium* (A) is a graphic novel of the life of a brilliant woman in the eleventh-century Byzantine empire, a difficult time in history for strong women. Susan Fletcher writes imaginatively of life in a Persian harem during the time of Sheherazade in *Shadow Spinner* (A), a suspenseful story with a resourceful female protagonist and intriguing details of time and place. Other books explore life in different parts of the world, such as Janet Rupert's *The African Mask* (A), set in eleventh-century Nigeria.

Some stories of ancient civilizations merge with mythology (Chapter 5), but often authors attempt to retain a more factual base for their work. Rosemary Sutcliff is distinguished among historical fiction writers for her ability to recreate an authentic picture of life in early Britain. She writes knowledgeably about the people and places of ancient Britain during the years it was occupied by Norsemen and, later, by Romans, Normans, and Saxons. Her books are marked by historical details that are smoothly integrated in a superb story.

The ring of authenticity is not the sole distinguishing feature of Sutcliff's work. While her novels of ancient Britain are masterful evocations of their time, they also provide sensitive insights into the human spirit. Each story reverberates with an eternal truth and lasting theme. Sutcliff's heroes live and die for values and principles that we embrace today. Much like high fantasy, a very different genre, her stories reveal the eternal struggle between goodness—that which we value—and evil—the forces that work to destroy it. Sutcliff's books, and other fine stories of ancient times, are listed in the Booklist at the end of this chapter.

THE MIDDLE AGES

The dissolution of the Roman Empire signaled the beginning of that part of the medieval period sometimes referred to as the Dark Ages. There is little recorded history of these times, which in Europe were marked primarily by the battles of barbarian tribes that swept across the continent. Writers breathe life into the shadowy figures of the novels set in this period—novels that blend fact and legend.

Karen Cushman's *The Midwife's Apprentice* (I), winner of the 1996 Newbery Medal, weaves an array of details about daily life into a compelling narrative. The mundane, often distasteful details of the lives of the common folk in the Middle Ages form the rich background against which a young girl discovers her worth. Cushman's other two books set in the Middle Ages, *Matilda Bone* (A) and *Catherine, Called Birdy* (A), are also filled with details that sweep readers into the midst of life in England at that time. Mollie Hunter's *The King's Swift Rider* (A) grapples with the conflicts that arise from having personal commitments to both nonviolence and a free Scotland. Other fine stories explore the Middle Ages in other parts of the world. Frances Temple's *The Beduins' Gazelle* (A) is set in the midst of a war between Beduin tribes in 1302. These and other stories are listed in the Booklist at the end of this chapter.

THE RENAISSANCE AND THE AGE OF EXPLORATION

Whether in real life or in books, mysterious or dangerous explorations of the unknown mesmerize us all. Accounts of navigations of the earlier world intrigue today's children as much as travels to the moon or Mars do. Explorers of the past and present need the same kind of courage and willingness to face the unknown. Stories of explorations range from tales of the early Vikings, such as Erik Haugaard's *Hakon of Rogen's Saga* (I), to stories set in the age of European exploration—Columbus and after.

In 1992, the 500th anniversary of Columbus's famous 1492 voyage brought forth many books to mark the anniversary. These books also reflected a growing trend in children's books: Some told the "other side" of the story, presenting Columbus from the point of view of the Native Americans who were present when he landed, or of Europeans who were skeptical of his motives. Books like Jane Yolen's *Encounter* (I–A) and Pam Conrad's *Pedro's Journal* (I) allow us to present a more balanced picture of the impact of the age of exploration. The powerful writing and clever structure of Michael Dorris's *Morning Girl* (I) allows young readers to

experience "firsthand" the shock of Columbus's invasion of the Taino Indian islands.

The Renaissance is a fascinating time in history, but few books for children explore this era in Europe, and even fewer are set in other parts of the world. Pilar Molina Llorente's *The Apprentice* (I) is set in Renaissance Florence and depicts the lives of middle-class merchants and famous artists alike. Linda Sue Park sets *The Kite Fighters* (I) in Seoul, Korea. These stories and others are listed in the Booklist at the end of this chapter.

COLONIAL THROUGH POST–REVOLUTIONARY WAR TIMES

Immigrants began sailing to America in the late sixteenth century, some seeking adventure and financial gain, some escaping religious persecution, some traveling as missionaries, and some seeking political freedom. Economic and social conditions made the New World attractive to people who were willing to sacrifice the known for the possibilities of a promising unknown. The settlements by the English at Roanoke, Jamestown, Plymouth, and Boston are vivid settings for stories based on early colonial life.

By 1692, the early settlers were well established in their new communities and were stern guardians of their religious views, pious behavior, and moral standards. The hysteria that gripped the people of Salem, Massachusetts, in the days of the witch hunts grew out of the political, economic, and social forces of the community. Kathryn Lasky's *Beyond the Burning Time* (A) explores some of the hidden passions that might have stoked the fires of Salem, and brings to life the way people lived, believed, and sometimes died in that place and time. In her classic *The Witch of Blackbird Pond* (I–A), winner of the 1959 Newbery Medal, Elizabeth George Speare reveals how guilt by association occurs in Old Salem when a young girl and the old woman she has befriended are accused of witchcraft. Both books artfully blend fact and fiction to create a vivid picture of people and their lives during colonial times.

The history of America is incomplete without stories of Native Americans. In the past their story was told, if at all, by European Americans who often characterized them in stereotyped ways. A growing number of writers now give more accurate portrayals of Native American cultures and a more objective picture of the 500-year clash between the European and Native American cultures. Stories for younger children may present a simple view of the interaction between Europeans and Native Americans, but this view should not rely on stereotypes. Stories for older readers often consider the complexities inherent in the clash between two cultures, such as Elizabeth George Speare's compelling novel about the faltering friendship of a white boy and an Indian boy in the 1700s, *Sign of the Beaver* (I–A).

Although some people criticize Speare for her non-Native point of view, others find the book to be a rewarding catalyst for discussion about the clash of cultures.

Stories that reflect a Native American point of view concerning these times, however, are still scarce, as are those that depict the lives and struggles of the many Africans brought as slaves before the turn of the century. Notable exceptions include Michael Dorris's *Guests* and *Sees Behind Trees* (both I), as well as Joseph Bruchac's *The Arrow Over the Door* (I). Teaching Idea 8.3 suggests a comparative way to examine versions of the first Thanksgiving.

A Stolen Life (A) by Jane Louise Curry brings to light a part of North American history of the mid-eighteenth century that most young readers are unaware of. The protagonist, a young Scots girl, is kidnapped by "spiriters" who sell their victims as bond slaves to planters and farmers in America. Once in Virginia, she endures through her courage and intelligence until, caught up in the destruction of the Cherokee by the British Army, she manages to escape.

Fiction set in the Revolutionary War period usually involves stories of war and, often, the divided loyalties in colo-

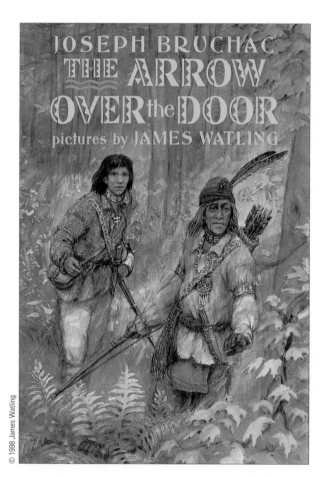

Joseph Bruchac bases his novel on an actual meeting between Quakers and Abenaki Indians during the American Revolution.

© 1998 James Watling

Teaching Idea 8 ✳ 3

Compare Versions of the First Thanksgiving

Collect several books, both fiction and nonfiction, that describe the first Thanksgiving. Read these together with your students. Compare them, considering questions such as:

✳ Who is telling the story?

✳ What is the mood at the feast?

✳ How does the narrator feel about the celebration?

Then ask students to role play, considering how point of view affects behavior. Books to use include:

Anderson, Joan, *The First Thanksgiving Feast* (P–I)

Dorris, Michael, *Guests* (I)

Sewall, Marcia, *People of the Breaking Day* (I–A)

---

nial families or communities. Janet Lunn, one of Canada's best-known writers for children, explores just this in *The Hollow Tree* (A), a gripping account of a young girl's harrowing journey north from New Hampshire to Canada to join other Loyalist families even though her own family is divided in its loyalties.

Historical fiction writers sometimes choose to tell more localized stories. *Fever 1793* (I–A), by Laurie Halse Anderson, graphically depicts the terrors of the yellow fever epidemic that killed nearly 5,000 people in Philadelphia. Anderson's heroine, a spunky and engaging 16-year-old, draws readers into her story; the informational notes at the end of the book offer the facts to interested readers. These and other stories that illuminate life in North America at this time are listed in the Booklist at the end of this chapter.

WESTWARD EXPANSION AND THE CIVIL WAR

The nineteenth century saw North America experiencing severe growing pains as the country expanded westward, national identity was seriously challenged, the question of slavery became a national debate, and immigrants from Europe, Africa, and Asia (both voluntary and involuntary) brought their despair and sometimes their hopes and dreams to a new land. It was an interesting century, filled with amazing contradictions. As the United States grew, the native people's lands shrank and their cultures were almost obliterated. As the nation expanded, indentured Chinese, lured to America by the promise of work, were exploited as they built the transcontinental railroad, a stunning achievement. As the new nation prospered, Africans and others were ripped from their homelands, forcibly transported, and doomed to endure a life of slavery. As the nation became industrialized, the quality of life improved for some, and grew worse for many. Children's books explore these contradictions from many viewpoints, telling the story of the growth of a nation and the consequences of that growth.

The Westward Migration

Americans were on the move from the beginning. Those moving called it expansion; those who were displaced saw it as invasion. In both cases, life required great physical strength and, often, the ability to endure loneliness. Pioneer families worked hard by necessity, providing their own food, clothing, shelter, and entertainment. Themes of loneliness, hardship, and acceptance of what life deals out are threaded through many excellent novels about the pioneers and their struggle to tame a wild land.

These themes are evident in D. Anne Love's *I Remember the Alamo* (A), a moving tale of one family's move from Kentucky to Texas. Readers feel the pain of 11-year-old Jessie when she is uprooted from her home, when her little sister dies on the way to San Antonio, and when she, her mother, and her younger brother are left behind by her father and older brother when they go off to fight Santa Anna. Unfortunately, the family takes refuge in the Alamo, and Jessie must call on all of her courage, as well as her friendship with a Mexican girl, to save their lives.

In a story for younger readers, Joyce Carol Thomas describes the courage and dignity of a young black woman determined to own her own land. *I Have Heard of a Land* (P–I) presents the inspiring story of one woman who symbolizes all who homesteaded the American West, braving isolation, the wilderness, and nature's vagaries to forge a home for themselves.

Jane Kurtz depicts the everyday sorrows and joys of life on the Oregon trail in *I'm Sorry, Almira Ann* (P–I). Young Sarah is thrilled that her best friend, Almira Ann is making

I have heard of a land
Where the pioneer woman still lives
Her possibilities reach as far
As her eyes can see
And as far as our imaginations
can carry us

Both Joyce Carol Thomas and illustrator Floyd Cooper have strong roots in Oklahoma, where their families fashioned new lives for themselves. **I Have Heard of a Land** *depicts the challenges of this homesteading.*

the journey to Oregon with her, but she finds life on the trail a trial. It's difficult for her to curb her unruly spirit and follow all of the rules. When she causes her friend to fall and break her leg, however, she is devastated. This is a lovely novel for young readers, who will recognize a kindred spirit in Sarah and enjoy seeing someone very much like themselves heading west in a covered wagon.

Adventure story lovers will enjoy Will Hobbs's *Jason's Gold* (A), a spine-tingling account of a young boy's adventures in the Klondike during the Alaskan gold rush. Hobbs includes a well-known character from this time and place, Jack London, in his very exciting story.

During these times, the clash of cultural values between European settlers and Native Americans resulted in numerous conflicts, from grisly battles in which hundreds were killed, to more personal conflicts in which individuals who had come to know each other as friends had to choose between friendship and loyalty to their own people.

The famous 1804–1805 voyage of Merriweather Lewis and William Clark is emblematic of the interest the United States government had in expanding westward. Until recently, stories of their expedition were told from the viewpoint of the two leaders or the soldiers who accompanied them. However, with the minting of the Sacajawea "gold" dollar came not one but several stories about this brave Native woman who led Lewis and Clark through a large part of the upstream Missouri River and into the Rocky Mountains. One, a biography by David Adler, is for primary-grade readers. One of the **Dear America** books, *The Journal of August Pelletier: The Lewis and Clark Expedition, 1804* (I), is an account of the journey told from the point of view of a fictional young man who joined the expedition. Peter and Connie Roop's *Girl of the Shining Mountains: Sacagawea's Story* (I) is an interesting account of the journey told from Sacajawea's point of view, with her capture, forced marriage, and the hardships she endured glossed over for a young audience. Joseph Bruchac's *Sacajawea* (I–A) is a brilliant, thoughtful recounting of the voyage told in alternating points of view— Sacajawea's and William Clark's. Clark's chapters begin with excerpts from the diaries he kept on the journey; Sacajawea's begin with stories that her people told. Each brings a unique perspective to the grand adventure, and their mutual respect and growing friendship are evident.

Working from knowledge of the place and time, Mary Pope Osborne has crafted a fictional story of Kit Carson's daughter by his Arapaho wife. *Adeline Falling Star* (I) has a name that reflects her dual heritage. Her father named her Adeline, her now-dead mother called her Falling Star. When Carson leaves his daughter with abusive relatives (racism toward "half-breeds" was quite strong in those days) Adeline runs away to find her father. Afraid that he has deserted her, the desperate girl sets off alone into the wilderness to find her mother's people.

On a more somber note, Cornelia Cornelissen writes of the forcible removal of the Cherokee to Oklahoma in *Soft Rain: A Story of the Cherokee Trail of Tears* (I). Racism and greed stand in contrast to the dignity and courage that Soft Rain and her family exhibit as they live through one of the more shameful episodes of this century. Destruction of a different kind is part of the story that Louise Erdrich tells in *The Birchbark House* (I), as the white man brings smallpox to the Ojibwa people. Noted writer Scott O'Dell's final novel (finished by E. Hall), *Thunder Rolling in the Mountains* (A), tells the moving story of Chief Joseph and the Nez Perce people, who were forced to leave their lands in the Wallowa Valley and resettle on a reservation. Some refused to go, choosing instead to flee to freedom in Canada. Their doomed flight and the battles that marked it are recounted through the eyes of the chief's daughter, who comes to understand why her father vowed, "I will fight no more forever."

These and other stories that reflect the negative aspects of the westward expansion, as well as those that depict the vigorous growth of a new nation, are listed in the Booklist at the end of this chapter.

Slavery, The Civil War, and Its Aftermath

Slavery was a part of American life from early colonial days until long after the Emancipation Proclamation. Many chapters of American history are grim, but those involving slavery and the Civil War are among the worst; the war was a long, savage contest that tore the country apart and caused many deaths. Historical fiction of this period describes antebellum life as well as the turmoil and tragedy of the bloody war years and the reverberations that are still felt today. The years immediately preceding the Civil War were a bleak period in American history, although individual acts of compassion and heroism did occur. A notable children's book that has captured the antebellum period is Ann Turner's *Nettie's Trip South* (I), which depicts the horror of slavery as seen through the eyes of a white girl from the North who is on a train trip to the South.

Many other books tell the story of slaves seeking freedom both before and during the war. One of the most gripping, Mary E. Lyons's *Letters from a Slave Girl: The Story of Harriet Jacobs* (A), is based on Jacobs's autobiography. This compelling novel focuses on the ordeal of Harriet's escape several years before the Civil War began. After hiding for seven years in the crawl space above her grandmother's ceiling, Harriet escapes to the North. But she is hunted and afraid there, as well, for she must evade the slave hunters who want to take escapees back to their owners. This story of the courage and perseverance of one young woman struggling to create a life for herself transcends time and place with its universal theme.

The Underground Railroad was a lifeline for many escaping slaves and a silent protest for those Southerners who disapproved of slavery. The heroine of Gloria Houston's *Bright Freedom's Song* (I–A), set in the North Carolina mountains, has strong feelings about freedom. She learned them from her father, a former indentured servant. Houston's endnote stresses the link between the slaves and those who, like Molly Bannaky and the protagonist of Curry's *A Stolen Life*, came to America because they were forced to.

Many stories set during the Civil War focus on the heart-wrenching conflicts inherent in the war, especially those that pitted countryman against countryman and, in some cases, brother against brother. Books written about this period do not paint an exciting picture or romanticize the battles; instead, they focus on the impact these battles had on individual lives, on injury and death, on divided loyalties, and, frequently, on the anguish of those who wanted no involvement in the war.

Irene Hunt's *Across Five Aprils* (I–A) is the classic novel of these times and explores the lives of a family divided among themselves just as the nation is divided. In Paul Fleischman's *Bull Run* (I–A), a series of brief stories and 16 different characters create vivid images of the war. This rich portrait of both the battle and the larger conflict is beautifully written. Gary Paulsen's *Soldier's Heart* (A) is a graphic reminder of the horrors of the Civil War, and all wars. "Soldier's heart" is the effect of war that came to be known as "shell shock" and, even later, "post-traumatic stress syndrome."

In Denise Lewis Patrick's *The Adventures of Midnight Son* (I–A) a young black man is forced to leave his home and run west toward safety. However, safety is not so easily obtained. He must elude the slave catchers, survive a tornado, and learn to be a cowboy, all the while missing his family and trying to learn how to be a man on his own. In the sequel, *The Longest Ride* (I–A), he struggles to help his Indian friends survive the end of the Civil War even as he struggles with issues of honor and adversity. These books connect the Civil War and the westward expansion through the character of a young, black cowboy, a very unique approach. Other notable stories about the Civil War period are listed in the Booklist at the end of this chapter.

IMMIGRATION AND THE INDUSTRIAL REVOLUTION

While the West was being explored, life in the cities of the east was full of interesting people and ideas. Kathleen Karr tells an intriguing story of them in *Skullduggery* (A), a tale of grave robbing, danger, and international intrigue, and a fascinating look at an unusual branch of medicine— phrenology.

By the end of the nineteenth century, thriving cities such as New York were fairly sophisticated, while rural and small-town America east of the Mississippi was less so, and the West was still wild. Several stories set at the end of the century give a glimpse of life as it was lived on the East Coast, away from the high drama of life on the frontier. Katherine Paterson's *Preacher's Boy* (I) is set in small-town Vermont at the turn of the century. Robbie, the preacher's son, is a memorable character, just as full of mischief as the proverbial preacher's kid should be. The details of life in this time and place, strong characterization, and knee-slapping humor make this a wonderful read-aloud. *Earthly Astonishments* (A), by Marthe Jocelyn, is also replete with the social details of time and place (late nineteenth-century New York) but presents a most unusual character. Josephine is the smallest girl in the world—to some, a freak—and life is not easy for her. When she is discovered by an entrepreneur eager to add to his curiosity show, her spunk and intelligence help her create a life that she can live with dignity.

Life in the tenements and the world of boxing in New York City in the 1880s is the setting for Kathleen Karr's *The Boxer* (A), a fascinating story of how one young man used the sport to move himself and his family out of poverty. Young Johnny starts out in prison (boxing was illegal in those days) and ends up in school, getting the education that he knows will help him to be successful.

These and other stories set at the end of the nineteenth and beginning of the twentieth centuries often show the effect of the Industrial Revolution, which changed the fabric of America by profoundly altering both economic and social structures. As jobs in factories became available, people left their family farms to seek their fortune in the cities, and the country moved ever more quickly away from an agricultural economy. However, those who left their farms were often unfortunate in what they found. Katherine Paterson tells the story of one young girl who leaves her Vermont farm to find a new and better life in *Lyddie* (A). Lyddie goes to Lowell, Massachusetts, to become a factory girl and earn the money she thinks will free her from debt and from being controlled by others. She finds that along with the money come new problems: dangerous working conditions, evil supervisors, and radical friends. Lyddie's struggle to be her own person is intensified by the social changes that marked the Industrial Revolution.

The story of America in the late nineteenth and early twentieth centuries includes the story of immigration. Millions of immigrants came from distant lands, dreaming of freedom and hoping to create a better life. Their stories are our stories, repeated over and over at family gatherings where young children gather around their elders, asking them to "tell us what it was like back in the olden days." Historical fiction contains a wealth of immigrant stories for all ages.

Many books describe the conditions that led families to leave one country and migrate to America; others focus on the difficulties and hardships endured during immigration. Patricia Reilly Giff sets *Nory Ryan's Song* (I–A) in 1845 in Ireland, just at the beginning of the potato famine. Although she is only 12, Nory's strength of character and gritty determination help her save her family and friends from starvation before she begins her own journey to America.

Other stories set around the turn of the century take place in small towns and farms around the growing nation. Jennifer Holm's *Our Only May Amelia* (I) is set in the Pacific

Northwest and is based on the author's own Finnish-American grandaunt's diary. Life for the only girl in a close-knit immigrant family of seven brothers is full of adventure, challenge, and sometimes frustration. Jesse Haas, known for her horse stories, sets *Unbroken* (I–A) in the Vermont countryside of 1910 as she explores a young woman's coming to terms with grief and self-doubts and, finally, with love itself. Julie Johnston's outstanding novel *The Only Outcast* (A) evokes life in Canada in 1904 as a boy grows into a young man.

Mildred Taylor's *The Well: David's Story* (A) is set in rural Mississippi and tells the story of David, the father in *Roll of Thunder, Hear My Cry* (A). Focused on discrimination and injustice, Taylor's story is emotionally draining and raises important issues for older readers to think about and discuss. Other stories set around the turn of the century are listed in the Booklist at the end of this chapter.

WORLD WAR I AND ITS AFTERMATH

There is a paucity of books set during World War I, in either picture book or novel form. One excellent novel, however, is Margaret Rostkowski's *After the Dancing Days* (A), a beautifully told story of a 13-year-old girl's growing awareness that the war is not over for its maimed and crippled veterans. Susan Hart Lindquist's *Summer Soldiers* (A) depicts life in a sheep ranching community on the California coast. Even being half a world away from the war in Europe doesn't insulate the town from prejudice, hate, and death.

Other stories are not directly concerned with the war but, rather, evoke the spirit of that and the postwar era. Kathleen Karr used her own father's childhood as the basis for *Man of the Family* (I), a brief, compelling story of one immigrant family's struggle to realize the American dream. In a collection of three stories set in the Appalachian Mountains, Rosemary Wells tells the moving story of Mary Breckinridge, the founder of the Frontier Nursing Service. *Mary on Horseback: Three Mountain Stories* (I) is a fascinating story of courage and selflessness in a setting that contrasts starkly with contemporary times. In *The Ornament Tree* and *Tree of Bells* (both A) Jean Thesman brings 1922 Seattle to life as she tells the story of a young girl on her way to womanhood.

THE GREAT DEPRESSION

Stories of the Depression years portray America in times of trouble. The beginning of the period is generally recognized as the stock market crash of 1929. Then, stories of ruined businessmen jumping from skyscrapers filled the headlines of daily newspapers. Now, stories for children describe the grim effect of living in poverty. Mildred D. Taylor's books about Cassie Logan and her family, *The Song of the Trees* (I), *Roll of Thunder, Hear My Cry* (A), *Let the Circle Be Unbroken* (A), *The Friendship* (A), and *Mississippi Bridge* (A) show rural poverty and prevailing racism. Karen Hesse's Newbery Medal–winning *Out of the Dust* (A) is unrelenting in its depiction of life in the Oklahoma dust bowl; the story is softened only by the sensitivity of its heroine and its own poetic form. Cynthia DeFelice depicts what might have happened to a young girl orphaned by the suicide of her father in *Nowhere to Call Home* (I–A). This painful story of life as a hobo during the Great Depression celebrates the resilience of the human spirit and echoes stories of homelessness today.

Other stories set during this time are less grim. While Christopher Paul Curtis's Newbery Medal–winning *Bud, Not Buddy* (I) does involve death, homelessness, and racism, its overall tone is one of hope mixed with poignant humor. Robert Cormier poetically describes life in 1938 as seen through the eyes of a boy on the brink of adolescence in a New England mill town in *Frenchtown Summer* (A). Richard Peck, in *A Long Way from Chicago: A Novel in Stories* (I), sets

Riding the rails is a frightening experience for a young girl during the Great Depression.

his seven mesmerizing stories in the Depression-era small-town Midwest. Characterization and humor, as well as sense of place and time, earned Peck a Newbery honor for this fine novel, which ends poignantly with the narrator's journey by train to fight in World War II.

WORLD WAR II AND ITS AFTERMATH

The years 1933 to 1946 encompassed Adolph Hitler's rise and fall in Germany and Japanese military activity in the Pacific. The Second World War brought into vivid awareness humanity's potential inhumanity, particularly toward its fellow human beings. The horrors of the period were so unthinkable that it was several decades before the story was told in books for young people. The children who read these books today are reading about the world that their grandparents and great-grandparents lived in; these stories connect with their family histories.

Stories Set in Europe and Asia

The familiar adage that those who do not know the past are condemned to repeat it is adequate cause for attending to the tragedy of the Holocaust. The books describing Hitler's reign of terror, with its effects ultimately on all people, are a good place to begin. Many emphasize—some in small ways, some in larger ways—that in the midst of inhumanity there can be humaneness.

Despite their grimness, some books are affirmative: Young people work in underground movements, strive against terrible odds, plan escapes, and struggle for survival. Some show heroic resistance, in which characters fight back or live with dignity and hope in the face of a monstrous future. Some teachers will agonize over the place of literature in teaching about the Holocaust. Valid questions for them to consider are: Is mass murder a suitable subject for a children's or young adult novel? What is the proper place for it in the school curriculum? What are the possible consequences of not informing young people about one of history's most bitter lessons?

Jane Yolen's *The Devil's Arithmetic* (A) is a graphic, moving account of living in the heart of the Nazi persecution, as is Lois Lowry's Newbery Medal–winning *Number the Stars* (I). Lowry tells the story of how one Danish family saved the lives of their friends, the Rosens. The young daughters of each family are best friends, and they are initially unaware of the danger in which they are living. The contrast between the implications of Nazi rule for the Jewish Ellen and the Danish Annemarie is striking.

Many other stories about World War II are set in the European Theater and focus on the consequences of war, especially for children. Anne Isaacs's *Torn Thread* (A) is based on the experiences of her mother-in-law, who spent the last two years of the war in a Nazi labor camp in Czechoslovakia. As sisters Eva and Rachel struggle to survive so that their family will live on, the tension mounts to an almost unbearable point. Throughout the graphic descriptions of the horrible events of the time, the love of a few good people shines through. Donna Jo Napoli's *Stones in Water* (A) depicts the struggle of a young Italian boy, Roberto, who is torn from his family by Nazi soldiers and sent, along with his best friend, Samuele, to a work camp. This dangerous situation is even more horrifying because Samuele is also a Jew.

Stories about life in Europe after the war explore how shattered lives began to mend. The 8-year-old protagonist of Vera Propp's *When the Soldiers Were Gone* (I) is out of danger but must learn to be a different person and use a different name when his biological parents come to take him home from the Dutch family that has been hiding him. Miriam Pressler's *Halinka* (A) explores the emotional damage of war through the eyes of a young girl sent to a home for troubled girls in Germany in the postwar years. This story, translated from the German, is truly a universal tribute to the power of love.

Despite the fact that American armed forces fought for four years in the Pacific, few children's and adolescent novels are set in this locale. Two especially outstanding novels, Yoko Kawashima Watkins's *So Far from the Bamboo Grove* and *My Brother, My Sister, and I* (A), are set in North Korea and postwar Japan. The horror and hardships that Watkins and her family face underscore the horror of war for those on both sides of the battle lines but also serve to illustrate the strength of love in adversity.

Stories Set in North America

Some stories that take place during the Second World War are set in North America. Many of these are about children who were evacuated from Europe. Others chronicle the shameless internment of Japanese Americans, and still others explore the lives of children whose fathers, uncles, and big brothers were fighting in the war abroad. Kit Pearson's *The Sky is Falling* (I) is set in England and Canada and tells the story of a brother and sister who are evacuated from England to Canada. They miss their family, and their adjustment is slow, but eventually they learn to live with their hearts in two worlds.

Some stories explore the ugly side of life in the United States during the war. Ken Mochizuki's *Baseball Saved Us* (I) describes how one Japanese-American family was uprooted and transported to an internment camp in the middle of the desert. In *Two Suns in the Sky* (A), Miriam Bat-Ami tells the story of the love developing between Adam, a Yugoslavian Jew in the Oswego, New York, refugee camp (the only such camp in the United States) and Chris, the child of a man who thinks of the refugees as "someone else's dirt." Janet Taylor Lisle's *The Art of Keeping Cool* (A), which takes place in a community located on the heavily fortified Rhode Island coast, explores the hatred in the community through the character of Abel Hoffman, a refugee artist. The story illustrates another historical situation by depicting the havoc that hatred has wreaked in the life of one family as well.

In *Star of Luis* (A), Marc Talbert describes how Luis, a young Latino growing up in East Los Angeles, discovers his roots when he and his mother return to the small New Mexican village where she and Luis's father grew up. Luis learns to love and live in two worlds, and to define who he is in each.

THE 1950S THROUGH THE 1980S: POLITICAL AND SOCIAL TURMOIL

The end of the Second World War brought with it a change in the social organization of the world and the lifestyles of many people. Peace was not long-lasting; soon the world was disturbed by the Korean, Vietnam, and Cambodian conflicts, as well as by other less publicized wars. In the United States the civil rights movement forever altered the status quo, and the role of women in society also changed dramatically. Although they are not yet plentiful, some excellent books are set amidst the issues and events of these decades.

People like Cassie Logan and her brothers were at the front of the line during the civil rights movement, and many authors now tell their stories. Christopher Paul Curtis's *The Watsons Go to Birmingham—1963* (A), a Newbery Honor Book, explores the experiences and feelings of 10-year-old Kenny and his family as they drive from Flint, Michigan, to Birmingham, Alabama, to visit Grandma. Alternately funny and deadly serious, the novel captures the tenor and the tragedy of the times.

Stories like Kirkpatrick Hill's *The Year of Miss Agnes* (I), set in a Native village in 1948 Alaska, and Jane Leslie Conly's *What Happened on Planet Kid* (I), set in the rural South in the late 1950s, seem almost more timeless than historical. The settings are rich and clear, but the stories transcend time. The same is true of Ruth White's *Memories of Summer* (A), set in the mid fifties. The migration of many Appalachian families from their beloved mountains to Michigan and its postwar-boom automobile industry provides the historical context for the move of Lyric's family. Lyric's agony in watching her older sister descend into mental illness is timeless, and is echoed in contemporary realistic fiction.

Similarly, Amy Gordon's *When JFK Was My Father* (A) is a poignant coming-of-age story set in the year that John Fitzgerald Kennedy was assassinated. Kimberly Willis Holt's

Kirkpatrick Hill captures life in Alaska and the love between students and their remarkable teacher.

When Zachary Beaver Came to Town (A), winner of the National Book Award, is set in a sleepy Texas town during the Vietnam conflict. In both books the historical details are rich, and the characters' lives reflect the times in which they live even as the novels focus on life issues rather than historical ones.

Historical fiction set during the conflict in Vietnam and the aftermath in Cambodia is becoming more plentiful. Like those about the Second World War, some of these books are set in the midst of the conflict and consider the lives of children in the war zones. Others are set in North America, Australia, or other countries and deal with issues such as children fleeing the war to find a new life; the experiences of children whose grandfathers, uncles, and fathers went to war; the impact of returning veterans on family life; and the deep divisions in America during the Vietnam conflict. Eve Bunting's picture storybook, *The Wall* (I), underscores the sorrow that reverberates across generations when someone is lost to them forever. Allan Baille's *Little Brother* (A) is set in Cambodia during the conflict there and graphically depicts the struggle of a young man seeking to escape the Khmer Rouge.

These stories set across the ages offer us a wonderful resource for helping children, and ourselves, discover our own connections with humanity throughout the ages.

Historical Fiction in the Classroom

Reading historical fiction can help children realize they are players on the historical stage, and that their lives, too, will one day become part of history. As they read historical fiction they come to realize the human drama inherent in history as well as the common themes that reach across time and cultures. Deborah Wooten (1991) found that students who used trade books and textbooks learned more than students who used only trade books or only textbooks. Both kinds of books supported student learning.

There are several ways to incorporate historical fiction into the curriculum. Middle school teachers can coordinate English language arts and social studies classes, assigning historical fiction that corresponds to the times and places focused on in the social studies curriculum. Elementary school teachers who have self-contained classes can easily link their students' reading material with the social studies topics that they explore. Groups of children can read and discuss books set in a particular period of history, individual children can read independently from a collection of historical fiction, and the teacher can read aloud from a book that explores the time and place that the class is studying. Teaching Idea 8.4 suggests a way to incorporate historical fiction with geography. In Chapter 14, we describe Book Club, an effective method for integrating the language arts and social studies curriculum.

Historical fiction can also be linked to poetry (Chapter 2), biography (Chapter 9), and nonfiction (Chapter 10). All four genres support each other and together enable children to understand history in a way that is not possible through a single textbook. Here are two examples:

The first time one fifth-grade teacher tried using historical fiction, poetry, biography, and nonfiction instead of the social studies text for the study of the American Revolution she was unsure of the possible outcomes. She asked students to read one novel, some poetry, one biography, and one informational book on that historical period. In addition, they read an encyclopedia account of one of the events described in the novel. The students then critically examined the presentations in the various sources. The teacher modeled the process, and they worked in collaborative learning groups to discuss their findings. The group concluded that no single book could have given them the basis for understanding that they gained from their wide reading. Even more exciting, the children begged their teacher to use the same approach for the next social studies unit.

Teaching Idea 8 ☆ 4

Compare the Literary Treatment of a Geographic Feature

Rivers, trails, and mountains provide settings for historical novels. Students might compare the way these settings are described in various genres of trade books.

✳ Collect several books that involve one geographic feature.

✳ Read the books and compare them on the following points: Which is most scientifically accurate? Which is the most appealing description? How would you use each type of book?

Rivers

Ancona, George, *Riverkeeper* (P–I)

Flack, Marjorie, *The Boats on the River* (P)

Locker, Thomas, *Where the River Begins* (P–I)

Lourie, Peter, *Hudson River* (P–I)

Michl, Reinhard, *Day on the River* (P–I)

Peters, Lisa Westberg, *Good Morning, River!* (P–I)

Twain, Mark, *The Adventures of Tom Sawyer* (I–A)

Mountains

Aylesworth, Jim, *Shenandoah Noah* (P–I)

Cleaver, Vera, *Where the Lilies Bloom* (A)

Hamilton, Virginia, *M. C. Higgins, the Great* (I–A)

Lyon, George Ella, *Borrowed Children* (I–A)

Radin, Ruth Yaffe, *High in the Mountains* (P–I)

Rylant, Cynthia, *When I Was Young in the Mountains* (P–I)

Showell, Ellen Harvey, *Our Mountain* (P–I)

Spyri, Johanna, *Heidi* (I–A)

White, Alana, *Come Next Spring* (I–A)

Another teacher worked with her third-grade children to develop a study plan for a unit on early settlers in America. She filled the room with many sources of information, including books, records, poetry, films, and pictures. The students spent several days exploring the material and making suggestions about topics that interested them. Their list included the Pilgrims, Plymouth Rock, the Mayflower, and the first Thanksgiving. The group organized the ideas into reasonably logical categories, and students chose topics they wanted to pursue, identified sources of information, and began the research for the study. Examining the past in this way helped students begin to understand human behavior, the ways that people and societies interact, the concept of humans as social beings, and the values that make people human.

Both teachers in the foregoing examples had help in identifying the books they wanted to use and finding research support for their plans. They consulted an annotated bibliography published yearly by the Children's Book Council and the National Council for the Social Studies: *Notable Children's Trade Books in the Field of Social Studies*. This is available from either organization and is also published in the April/May issue of the journal *Social Education*.

PRESENTING HISTORICAL FICTION BY THEME

Understanding human nature and social patterns can result from thinking about themes found in historical fiction and linking them to books in other genres and to our own lives. Teaching Idea 8.5 presents ideas for how to do this. People have common needs that must be met; these universal needs can be identified as themes that permeate social interactions. For example, the quest for freedom and respect, the struggle between good and evil or between love and hate, and the determination to seek a better life are themes that are as old as time and as current as today. Historical fiction contains the stories of many people caught up in such struggles. Reading a number of books that explore the same theme across different periods of history allows students to understand the similarities of human needs across time; looking at books that explore the same theme in different cultures allows students to understand the similarities of human needs across peoples. They recognize the meaning of universal themes.

Grouping by theme also encourages students to make connections between historical fiction and other genres. Themes about coming-of-age, learning self-reliance, and fighting for one's beliefs permeate contemporary realism, poetry, fantasy, and biography, as well as historical fiction. Many books, of course, contain more than one theme. For example, many books that explore issues of freedom or tell the story of immigration are likely to address prejudice as well. A sensitive discussion of some of these books illustrates how different cultural groups have struggled to overcome prejudice across the span of history.

Summary

When teachers put wonderful stories set in the past into the hands of children, the past comes alive for them. By reading historical fiction, students see that history was lived by peo-

ple who, despite their different dress, customs, and habits, were a lot like we are. Whether it's confronting the plague in Europe during the Middle Ages, fleeing from soldiers in the American West, or watching a young father go to war, readers of today can experience the events of the past. When children are immersed in a compelling story, history comes to life. It is only then that it becomes real and important for young readers.

Teaching Idea 8 ✳ 5

Explore Themes in Historical Fiction

Grouping historical fiction by theme allows students to see how people from diverse times and places grapple with common issues. Here are some titles to begin with. You can also add contemporary fiction and fantasy that explore the same themes.

Clash of Cultures

Conrad, Pam, *Pedro's Journal* (I)

Dorris, Michael, *Morning Girl* (I)

Meyer, Carolyn, *Where the Broken Heart Still Beats* (A)

Speare, Elizabeth George, *Sign of the Beaver* (I–A)

Yep, Laurence, *The Star Fisher* (A)

Yolen, Jane, *Encounter* (I)

Prejudice

Bunting, Eve, *Spying on Miss Muller* (A)

Curtis, Christopher Paul, *The Watsons Go to Birmingham—1963* (A)

Matas, Carol, *After the War* (A)

Mochizuki, Ken, *Heroes* (I)

Taylor, Mildred D., *The Friendship* (A)

_____, *Mississippi Bridge* (A)

_____, *Roll of Thunder, Hear My Cry* (A)

Find Christopher Paul Curtis's Newbery Medal acceptance speech in the July/August 2000 issue of *The Horn Book Magazine* and Karen Hesse's acceptance speech in the July/August 1998 issue. Compare what these authors have to say about their use of setting in their books. What kind of research did they do? How did this inform the story?

Booklist

Prehistoric Times

Brooke, William, *A is for Aaarrg!* (I–A)
Crowley, Marjorie, *Anoolia's Answer* (I)
Crowley, Marjorie, *Dar and the Spear Thrower* (I)
Denzel, Justin, *The Boy of the Painted Cave* (I–A)
Dyer, T. A., *A Way of His Own* (I–A)
Garcia, Ann O'Neal, *Spirit on the Wall* (I–A)
Pryor, Bonnie, *Seth of the Lion People* (I)
Steele, William O., *The Magic Amulet* (I–A)
Sutcliff, Rosemary, *Warrior Scarlet* (A)
Turner, Ann, *Time of the Bison* (I)
Wibberley, Leonard, *Attar of the Ice Valley* (A)

Ancient Times

Barrett, Tracy, *Anna of Byzantium* (A)
Bosse, Malcolm, *Tusk and Stone* (A)
Branford, Henrietta, *The Fated Sky* (A)
Carter, Dorothy, *His Majesty, Queen Hatshepsut* (I)
Fletcher, Susan, *Shadow Spinner* (A)
Haugaard, Erik Christian, *The Samurai's Tale* (A)
Lester, Julues, *Pharaoh's Daughter* (A)
Lord, Bette Bao, *Spring Moon* (I–A)
Lyon, George Ella, *Dreamplace* (P)
Manniche, Lise, *The Prince Who Knew His Fate* (I)
McGraw, Eloise Jarvis, *Mara, Daughter of the Nile* (I–A)
Paterson, Katherine, *The Sign of the Chrysanthemum* (A)
Paton Walsh, Jill, *Children of the Fox* (I–A)
Rupert, Janet E., *The African Mask* (A)
Speare, Elizabeth George, *The Bronze Bow* (A)
Sutcliff, Rosemary, *The Eagle of the Ninth* (A)
_____, *The Lantern Bearers* (A)
_____, *The Shining Company* (A)
_____, *The Silver Branch* (A)
_____, *Song for a Dark Queen* (A)
Yarbro, Chelsea Quinn, *Locadio's Apprentice* (I–A)

The Middle Ages

Aliki, *A Medieval Feast* (P–I)
Beatty, John, and Patricia Beatty, *Master Rosalind* (A)
Cadnum, Michael, *The Book of the Lion* (A)
Chaucer, Geoffrey, *Canterbury Tales* (I–A)
Cushman, Karen, *Catherine, Called Birdy* (A)
_____, *Matilda Bone* (A)
_____, *The Midwife's Apprentice* (A)
De Angeli, Marguerite, *The Door in the Wall* (I)
Gray, Elizabeth Vining, *Adam of the Road* (A)

Hilgartner, Beth, *A Murder for Her Majesty* (A)
Hunter, Mollie, *The King's Swift Rider* (A)
Kelly, Eric P., *The Trumpeter of Krakow* (A)
McCaffrey, Anne, *Black Horses for the King* (A)
Newth, Mette, *The Dark Light* (A)
_____, *The Transformation* (A)
Springer, Nancy, *I Am Mordred* (A)
Stolz, Mary, *Bartholomew Fair* (I)
Temple, Frances, *The Beduin's Gazelle* (A)
_____, *The Ramsay Scallop* (A)
Trease, Geoffrey, *Bows Against the Barious*

The Renaissance and the Age of Exploration

Blackwood, Gary, *The Shakespeare Stealer* (I)
Bosse, Malcolm, *The Examination* (A)
Bulla, Clyde Robert, *Viking Adventure* (I)
Burkert, Nancy Eckholm, *Valentine and Orson* (A)
Conrad, Pam, *Pedro's Journal* (I)
Cooper, Susan, *King of Shadows* (I)
Dorris, Michael, *Morning Girl* (I)
Farest, Antonia, *The Player's Bay* (A)
Garden, Nancy, *Dove and Sword: A Novel of Joan of Arc* (I–A)
Garland, Sherry, *Indio* (A)
Harnett, Cynthia, *Caxton's Challenge* (A)
Haugaard, Erik, *Hakon of Rogen's Saga* (I)
Hersom, Kathleen, *The Half Child* (A)
Hesse, Karen, *Stowaway* (I–A)
Konigsburg, Elaine, *A Proud Taste for Scarlet and Miniver* (A)
_____, *The Second Mrs. Giaconda*
Lasky, Kathryn, *Elizabeth I: Red Rose of the House of Tudor* (I)
Llorente, Pilar Molina, *The Apprentice* (I)
Merrell, Leigh, *Tenach* (I)
Park, Linda Sue, *The Kite Fighters* (I)
Pope, Elizabeth Mane, *The Perilous Gard* (A)
Smith, T. H., *Cry to the Night Wind* (I)
Sutcliff, Rosemary, *Knight's Fee* (A)
_____, *The Witch's Brat* (A)
Trease, Geoffrey, *A Cue for Treason* (A)
Yolen, Jane, *Encounter* (I–A)
Youlen, Jane, and Robert Hams, *The Queen's Own Fool* (A)

Colonial to Mid-Nineteenth Century

Anderson, Laurie Halse, *Fever 1793* (I–A)
Auch, Mary Jane, *Frozen Summer* (I)
Avi, *Encounter at Easton* (I)
_____, *Night Journeys* (I)
Borden, Louise, *Sleds on Boston Common* (I)
Bowen, Gary, *Stranded at Plimoth Plantation 1626* (I)

Bruchac, Joseph, *The Arrow Over the Door* (I)

Bulla, Clyde Robert, *A Lion to Guard Us* (P)

Clapp, Patricia, *Witches' Children* (A)

Collier, James Lincoln, and Christopher C., *My Brother Sam Is Dead* (A)

Curry, Jane Louise, *A Stolen Life* (A)

Dillon, Ellis, *The Seekers* (A)

Dorris, Michael, *Guests* (I)

_____, *Sees Behind Trees* (I)

Fleischman, Paul, *Saturnalia* (A)

Fleming, Candace, *The Hatmaker's Sign: A Story by Benjamin Franklin* (P)

Forbes, Esther, *Johnny Tremain* (A)

Greene, Jacqueline Dembar, *One Foot Ashore* (I–A)

_____, *Out of Many Waters* (I–A)

Krensky, Stephen, *The Printer's Apprentice* (I)

Lasky, Kathryn, *Beyond the Burning Time* (A)

Latham, Jean Lee, *This Dear-Bought Land* (I)

Levitin, Sonia, *Roanoke: A Novel of the Lost Colony* (I–A)

Lunn, Janet, *The Hollow Tree* (A)

McGel, Alice, *Molly Bannaky* (P–I)

Monjo, F. N., *The House on Stink Alley* (I)

Petry, Ann, *Tituba of Salem Village* (I)

Rinaldi, Ann, *A Break with Charity: A Story About the Salem Witch Trials* (A)

Speare, Elizabeth George, *The Sign of the Beaver* (A)

_____, *The Witch of Blackbird Pond* (A)

Revolutionary War Years

Avi, *The Fighting Ground* (I)

Collier, James Lincoln, and Christopher Collier, *My Brother Sam Is Dead* (A)

_____, *War Comes to Willy Freeman* (A)

Forbes, Esther, *Johnny Tremain*

Fritz, Jean, *Early Thunder* (A)

Gauch, Patricia Lee, *This Time, Tempe Wick?* (I)

Haley, Gail, *Jack Jouett's Ride* (P)

Hickman, Janet, *Susannah* (I)

O'Dell, Scott, *Sarah Bishop* (A)

Rappaport, Doreen, *The Boston Coffee Party* (P)

Rinaldi, Ann, *Time Enough for Drums* (A)

Roop, Peter, and Connie Roop, *Buttons for General Washington* (I)

Walkner, Sally M., *This Is Penny Goose* (P)

Wibberley, Leonard, *John Treegate's Musket* (I)

The Civil War

Alcott, Louisa May, *Little Women* (A)

Armstrong, Jennifer, *The Dreams of Mairhe Mehan* (I–A)

_____, *Mairhe Mehan Awake* (I–A)

_____, *Steal Away* (A)

Beatty, Patricia, *Charlie Skedaddle* (A)

_____, *Jayhawker* (A)

_____, *Turn Homeward, Hannalee* (A)

_____, *Who Comes with Cannons?* (A)

Blos, Joan, *A Gathering of Days: A New England Girl's Journal, 1830–32* (A)

Calvert, Patricia, *Bigger* (I)

Climo, Shirley, *A Month of Seven Days* (A)

Collier, James Lincoln, and Christopher Collier, *With Every Drop of Blood* (A)

Cox, Clinton, *Undying Glory* (I–A)

Fleischman, Paul, *Bull Run* (I–A)

Fox, Paula, *The Slave Dancer* (A)

Fritz, Jean, *Brady* (I–A)

Gaeddert, Louann, *Breaking Free* (I–A)

Gauch, Patricia Lee, *Thunder at Gettysburg* (I)

Hansen, Joyce, *The Heart Calls Home* (A)

_____, *Out from this Place* (A)

_____, *Which Way Freedom?* (A)

Hermes, Patricia, *On Winter's Wind: A Novel* (A)

Hesse, Karen, *A Light in the Storm: The Civil War Diary of Amelia Martin* (I)

Hopkinson, Deborah, *Sweet Clara and the Freedom Quilt* (P)

Houston, Gloria, *Bright Freedom's Song* (I–A)

Hunt, Irene, *Across Five Aprils* (A)

Hurmence, Belinda, *Tancy* (I–A)

Johnson, Dolores, *Now Let Me Fly: The Story of a Slave Family* (I)

Johnston, Tony, *The Wagon* (I)

Keith, Harold, *Rifles for Watie* (A)

Lester, Julius, *Long Journey Home* (A)

Lyon, George Ella, *Here and Then* (I)

Lyons, Mary E., *Letters from a Slave Girl: The Story of Harriet Jacobs* (A)

Monjo, F. N., *The Drinking Gourd* (P–I)

Paulsen, Gary, *Soldier's Heart* (A)

_____, *Novel of the Civil War* (A)

Polacco, Patricia, *Pink and Say* (I–A)

Ray, Mary Lyn, *Shaker Boy* (I)

Reeder, Carolyn, *Shades of Gray* (A)

Ruby, Lois, *Soon to Be Free* (A)

_____, *Steal Away Home* (A)

Turner, Ann, *Nettie's Trip South* (I–A)

Turner, Glennette Tilley, *Running for Our Lives* (I–A)

Winter, Jeanette, *Follow the Drinking Gourd* (P–I)

Wright, Courtney C., *Journey to Freedom: A Story of the Underground Railroad* (I)

_____, *Jumping the Broom* (I)

Westward Migration

Armstrong, Jennifer, *Black-Eyed Susan* (I)

Arrington, Francis, *Bluestem* (I)

Avi, *The Barn* (I–A)

Beatty, Patricia, *The Nickel-Plated Beauty* (A)

_____, *O the Red Rose Tree* (A)

_____, *Wait for Me, Watch for Me, Eula Bea* (A)

Brink, Carol Ryrie, *Caddie Woodlawn* (I–A)

Bunting, Eve, *Dandelions* (P)

Burks, Brian, *Runs with Horses* (A)

Cather, Willa, *My Antonia* (A)

_____, *Walks Alone* (I)

Coerr, Eleanor, *Buffalo Bill and the Pony Express* (P)

_____, *The Josephina Story Quilt* (P)

Conrad, Pam, *Prairie Songs* (A)

Cushman, Karen, *The Ballad of Lucy Whipple* (A)

Fritz, Jean, *The Cabin Faced West* (I)

Goble, Paul, *Death of the Iron Horse* (I)

Harvey, Brett, *Cassie's Journey: Going West in the 1860s* (P–I)

_____, *My Prairie Christmas* (P–I)

_____, *My Prairie Year: Based on the Diary of Elenore Plaisted* (P–I)

Howard, Ellen, *The Chickenhouse House* (P–I)

_____, *Edith Herself* (P–I)

_____, *Sister* (P–I)

Irwin, Hadley, *Jim-Dandy* (I–A)

Johnston, Tony, *The Quilt Story* (P)

Karr, Kathleen, *Oh, Those Harper Girls!* (A)

Kroeber, Theodora, *Ishi, Last of His Tribe* (I–A)

MacLachlan, Patricia, *Sarah, Plain and Tall* (I)

_____, *Skylark* (I)

_____, *Three Names* (P)

Meyer, Carolyn, *Where the Broken Heart Still Beats* (A)

Moeri, Louise, *Save Queen of Sheba* (I)

Myers, Ann, *Graveyard Girl* (I–A)

Myers, Walter Dean, *The Righteous Revenge of Artemis Bonner* (I–A)

O'Dell, Scott, *Sing Down the Moon* (A)

_____, *Thunder Rolling in the Mountains* (A)

Paulsen, Gary, *Call Me Francis Tucket* (I)

_____, *Mr. Tucket* (I)

Polacco, Patricia, *The Keeping Quilt* (P–I)

Putnam, Alice, *Westering* (I)

Ray, Mary Lyn, *Alvah and Arvilla* (P)

Roop, Peter, and Connie Roop, *Ahyoka and the Talking Leaves* (I)

Sanders, Scott, *Aurora Means Dawn* (P–I)

Sorensen, Henri, *New Hope* (P–I)

Stewart, Elisabeth, *On the Long Trail Home* (I)

Turner, Ann, *Dakota Dugout* (P–I)

_____, *Grasshopper Summer* (I–A)

Van Leeuwen, Jean, *Bound for Oregon* (I–A)

_____, *Going West* (P)

Whelan, Gloria, *Next Spring an Oriole* (I)

_____, *Night of the Full Moon* (I)

Wilder, Laura Ingalls, **Little House** series (I)

Wisler, G. Clifton, *Jericho's Journey* (I–A)

The New Century

Bartone, Elisa, *Peppe the Lamplighter* (P)

Baylor, Byrd, *The Best Town in the World* (P-I)

Blos, Joan W., *Brooklyn Doesn't Rhyme* (I)

Cameron, Eleanor, *A Room Made of Windows* (I)

_____, *Julia and the Hand of God* (I)

_____, *Julia's Magic* (I)

_____, *That Julia Redfern* (I)

_____, *The Private Worlds of Julia Redfern* (I)

Clifford, Eth, *Will Somebody Please Marry My Sister?* (I)

DeFelice, Cynthia, *Lostman's River* (A)

Dionetti, Michelle, *Coal Mine Peacher* (P)

Fleischman, Paul, *The Borning Room* (A)

Hall, Donald, *Lucy's Christmas* (P)

_____, *Lucy's Summer* (P)

Howard, Elizabeth Fitzgerald, *Aunt Flossie's Hats (and Crab Cakes Later)* (P)

_____, *Chita's Christmas* (P)

_____, *Papa Tells Chita a Story* (P)

Hyatt, Patricia Rusch, *Coast to Coast with Alice* (I)

Karr, Kathleen, *It Ain't Always Easy* (A)

Kroll, Steven, *The Hokey Pokey Man* (P–I)

Leonard, Laura, *Finding Papa* (I–A)

_____, *Saving Damaris* (I–A)

Levinson, Riki, *Watch the Stars Come Out* (P)

_____, *I Go With My Family to Grandma's* (P)

Levitin, Sonia, *Journey to America* (I)

_____, *Silver Days* (I)

Little, Jean, *His Banner over Me* (A)

Lovelace, Maud Hart, *Betsy-Tacy* (I)

_____, *Betsy-Tacy and Tib* (I)

Lucas, Barbara M., *Snowed In* (P)

Mayerson, Evelyn, *The Cat Who Escaped from Steerage* (I)

McDonald, Megan, *The Potato Man* (P–I)

McKissack, Patricia, *Mirandy and Brother Wind* (P)

Nagell, Judy, *One Way to Ansonia* (A)

Oneal, Zibby, *A Long Way to Go* (A)

Paterson, Katherine, *Lyddie* (A)

Sandin, Joan, *The Long Way to a New Land* (P)

_____, *The Long Way Westward* (P)

Skurzynski, Gloria, *The Tempering* (A)

Slepian, Jan, *Pinocchio's Sister* (A)

Taylor, Mildred D., *The Well: David's Story* (A)

Yektai, Niki, *The Secret Room* (I)

World War I and Its Aftermath

Frank, Rudolph, *No Hero for the Kaiser* (A)

Houston, Gloria, *The Year of the Perfect Christmas Tree* (P–I)

Ish-Kishor, Sulamith, *Our Eddie* (I)

Kinsey-Warnock, Natalie, *The Night the Bells Rang* (I)

Rostkowski, Margaret, *After the Dancing Days* (A)

Smith, Barry, *Minnie and Ginger* (P)

Voigt, Cynthia, *Tree by Leaf* (A)

Wells, Rosemary, *Waiting for the Evening Star* (P–I)

The Great Depression

Avi, *Smugglers' Island* (I)
Crew, Linda, *Fire on the Wind* (I)
Disher, Garry, *The Bamboo Flute* (I–A)
French, Jackie, *Somewhere Around the Corner* (A)
Green, Connie Jordan, *Emmy* (I)
Hendershot, Judith, *In Coal Country* (P–I)
Houston, Gloria, *Littlejim* (I–A)
Kinsey-Warnock, Natalie, *If Wishes Were Horses* (I)
Levinson, Riki, *Boys Here—Girls There* (I)
Mitchell, Margaree King, *Uncle Jed's Barbershop* (P–I)
Reaver, Chap, *Bill* (I)
Recorvits, Helen, *Goodbye, Walter Malinski* (I)
Reeder, Carolyn, *Grandpa's Mountain* (I–A)
_____, *Moonshiner's Son* (A)
Snyder, Zilpha Keatley, *Cat Running* (I–A)
Taylor, Mildred D., *Let the Circle Be Unbroken* (A)
_____, *Mississippi Bridge* (A)
_____, *The Road to Memphis* (A)
_____, *Roll of Thunder, Hear My Cry* (A)
_____, *Song of the Trees* (I)
Turner, Ann, *Dust for Dinner* (P)

World War II and Its Aftermath

Ackerman, Karen, *When Mama Retires* (P)
Anderson, Rachel, *Paper Faces* (A)
Avi, *Who Was That Masked Man, Anyway?* (A)
Bawden, Nina, *Carrie's War* (I)
Bergman, Tamar, *The Boy from Over There* (A)
Bunting, Eve, *Spying on Miss Muller* (A)
Cormier, Robert, *Other Bells for Us to Ring* (I–A)
Degens, T., *On the Third Ward* (A)
_____, *Transport 451-R* (A)
Gallico, Paul, *The Snow Goose* (A)
Glassman, Judy, *The Morning Glory War* (I)
Hahn, Mary Downing, *Stepping on the Cracks* (I–A)
Hautzig, Esther, *The Endless Steppe* (A)
Hest, Amy, *Love You, Soldier* (I)
_____, *The Private Notebook of Katie Roberts, Age 11* (I)
Holt, Kimberly Willis, *My Louisiana Ski* (I)
Hotze, Sollace, *Summer Endings* (A)
Houston, Gloria, *But No Candy* (P)
Innocenti, Robert, *Rose Blanche* (I–A)
Johnston, Julie, *Hero of Lesser Causes* (I–A)
Joose, Barbara M., *The Morning Chair* (P)
Kerr, Judith, *When Hitler Stole Pink Rabbit* (I–A)
Laird, Christa, *But Can the Phoenix Sing?* (A)
_____, *Shadow of the Wall* (A)
Lingard, Joan, *Tug of War* (A)
_____, *Between Two Worlds* (A)
Lowry, Lois, *Number the Stars* (I)

Magorian, Michelle, *Good Night, Mr. Tom* (A)
_____, *Back Home* (A)
Manley, Joan B., *She Flew No Flags* (A)
Matas, Carol, *After the War* (A)
_____, *Daniel's Story* (A)
Mochizuki, Ken, *Baseball Saved Us* (I)
Morpurgo, Michael, *Waiting for Anya* (A)
Oppenheim, Sulamith Levey, *The Lily Cupboard* (P)
Orlev, Uri, *The Island on Bird Street* (A)
_____, *The Lady with the Hat* (A)
_____, *Lydia, Queen of Palestine* (A)
_____, *The Man from the Other Side* (A)
Pearson, Kit, *The Lights Go On Again* (I–A)
_____, *Looking at the Moon* (I–A)
_____, *The Sky Is Falling* (I–A)
Ray, Deborah Kogan, *My Daddy Was a Soldier* (P)
Reiss, Johanna, *The Upstairs Room* (A)
Reuter, Bjarne, *The Boys from St. Petri* (A)
Rosenblum, Richard, *Brooklyn Dodger Days* (P–I)
Rudolfo, Anaya, *The Farolitos of Christmas* (I)
Rylant, Cynthia, *I Had Seen Castles* (A)
Say, Allen, *Tea with Milk* (P)
Schnur, Steven, *The Shadow Children* (I–A)
Stevenson, James, *Don't You Know There's a War On?* (P)
Thesman, Jean, *Molly Donnelly* (A)
Uchida, Yoshiko, *The Invisible Thread* (A)
_____, *Journey Home* (A)
_____, *Journey to Topaz* (A)
Vos, Ida, *Anna Is Still Here* (I–A)
_____, *Dancing on the Bridge of Avignon* (A)
_____, *Hide and Seek* (I–A)
Watkins, Yoko Kawashima, *My Brother, My Sister, and I* (A)
_____, *So Far from the Bamboo Grove* (A)
Westall, Robert, *Echoes of War* (A)
_____, *The Kingdom by the Sea* (A)
Wild, Margaret, *Let the Celebrations Begin!* (I)
Yep, Laurence, *Hiroshima* (A)
Yolen, Jane, *All Those Secrets of the World* (P–I)
_____, *The Devil's Arithmetic* (A)

The 1950s Through the 1980s: Political and Social Turmoil

Baille, Allan, *Little Brother* (A)
Bunting, Eve, *The Wall* (P–I)
Curtis, Christopher Paul, *The Watsons Go to Birmingham—1963* (I–A)
Davis, Ossie, *Just Like Martin* (A)
Haseley, Dennis, *Getting Him* (A)
Ho, Ming Fong, *The Clay Marble* (A)
_____, *Rice Without Rain* (A)
Look, Lenore, *Love as Strong as Ginger* (P)
Metzger, Lois, *Missing Girls* (A)

Mochizuki, Ken, *Heroes* (I)
Myers, Walter Dean, *Fallen Angels* (A)
Nelson, Theresa, *And One for All* (A)
Nelson, Vaunda Micheaux, *Mayfield Crossing* (A)
Oughton, Jerrie, *Music from a Place Called Half Moon* (I–A)
Paek, Min, *Aekyung's Dream* (P)
Paterson, Katherine, *Park's Quest* (A)
Paulsen, Gary, *Harris and Me* (A)

Qualey, Marsha, *Hometown* (A)
Ronder, Thomas Young, *Learning by Heart* (I–A)
Rostkowski, Margaret, *The Best of Friends* (A)
Slepian, Jan, *Risk n' Roses* (I–A)
Smothers, Ethel Footman, *Moriah's Pond* (I–A)
Talbert, Marc, *The Purple Heart* (I–A)
Thesman, Jean, *Rachel Chance* (A)
Whelan, Gloria, *Goodbye, Vietnam* (A)

chapter **9**

Biography

Above all, [Benjamin Franklin] would be honored for the role he played in helping America win its freedom, and then in writing the Constitution. He had proved himself a true patriot—even though it meant losing the love and respect of his only living son.

—JAMES CROSS GIBLIN, *The Amazing Life of Benjamin Franklin*, p. 40

TERRY NESTOR'S SECOND-GRADE CLASS IS WRITING BIOGRAPHIES. The students have chosen a variety of subjects: Adam H. is writing about his grandfather; his sources are mostly family memories, photographs, and mementos. Rebecca is studying the life of Rachel Carson, and she's found two biographies of the author's life. She's read the first and found it too brief; Rebecca wants more insight into what it was like to be a famous biologist as well as a famous writer. Adam P. is determined to find out all he can about Roald Dahl, his favorite author. He's read Dahl's autobiographical novel, *Boy*, and borrowed Dahl's title for his own autobiography. Bryce is writing about Michael Jordan and worries that he doesn't know enough about the famous basketball star's childhood to write a good biography.

These second-grade readers have become critical consumers of the biographies available to them. They've read and discussed many biographies of famous and not-so-famous people, such as James Cross Giblin's *The Amazing Life of Benjamin Franklin*, a richly detailed picture book that gives young readers much more than a superficial look at this famous American. They know which books are satisfying—those with pictures and rich details—and which are boring. They're determined to make their own efforts interesting to all.

Many people might think that second-grade children are too young to be interested in biography—but children enjoy telling about themselves, they like hearing the life stories of people important to them, and they like reading the biographies of famous people.

*Michael Dooling's beautiful oil paintings enhance the interesting story that James Cross Giblin tells in **The Amazing Life of Benjamin Franklin**.*

Defining Biography

A *biography* tells the story of a person's life and achievements; an *autobiography* recreates the story of the author's own life. Both biography and autobiography are embedded in the time and culture that shaped and were shaped by the subject of the biography. Some biographies are *chronological*; they recount the events of a subject's life in the order in which they occurred. Some are *episodic* and highlight only a certain period of a person's life. Other biographies are *interpretive* accounts in which "events are selected and arranged so as to bring out a particular aspect of the life or the essence of the personality of the subject. Autobiography, written from an inner perspective, may be particularly revealing of the personal, psychological, or poetic experiences of life" (Herman, 1978, p. 91). Autobiographies, which often take the form of memoirs, are increasingly popular with today's young readers. Many of them explore the experiences of people from parallel cultures who are living in North America.

Some biographies focus on a single individual, while others are *collective* biographies, or biographies about several individuals. These are usually focused around a theme or other unifying principle. Judith St. George takes this approach in ***In the Line of Fire: Presidents' Lives at Stake*** (A). Joyce Hansen creates a rich portrait of 13 strong African-American women who might inspire others to follow their visions in ***Women of Hope: African Americans Who Made a Difference*** (I–A). Any good biography illuminates the interaction between an individual and historical events, demonstrating how a person's time and culture influence life even as a person influences his or her time and culture. Vivid and accurate portrayals of the *people* of history make history come alive for readers.

Biography in Children's Lives

Biography was once regarded as an opportunity for young people to read about people they might emulate. For example, they might strive to be as honest as Abraham Lincoln or as brave as Charles Lindberg. Biographers in the nineteenth and early twentieth centuries wrote only about the good qualities of their subjects. In a self-conscious effort to provide children with a set of heroes to emulate, they deified America's heroes in a period of intense nationalism. Fortunately, contemporary biographers are more likely to consider their subjects in a less adulatory and more realistic manner. We now view biography not as an opportunity for moral enlightenment, but as a chance for children to learn about themselves as they learn about the lives and times of people who made a significant impact on the world (Herman, 1978). Students similar to Terry Nestor's second graders, who have embarked on their biographical study, have a wealth of excellent and entertaining books to read and enjoy.

Biography can help children develop their concepts of historical time; they can discover ideas and empathize with historical characters. Children who read biographies learn that all people have the same basic needs and desires. They begin to see their lives in relation to those of the past, learn a vast amount of social detail about the past, and consider the human problems and relationships of the present in the light of those in the past.

Milton Meltzer hopes that reading well-written biographies will help children learn that they, like the subjects of the biographies, can make a difference in their own lives and in the lives of others:

> I want to give young readers vision, hope, energy. I try to do it honestly, without concealing the weaknesses, the false starts, the wrong turns of my heroes and heroines. Even those who try their best not to engage in selfish attempts to outsmart their fellows can make tragic mistakes. Still, I write about them because they share a deep respect for the rights, the dignity, the value of every human being. (1989, p. 157)

Good biographies can enrich young readers' understanding of their history and potential. Meltzer hopes to "shape a world where every child may grow in the spirit of a community that fulfills the best in us" (1989, p. 157).

Criteria for Evaluating Biographies

Biographies are stories of people's lives and like all stories can be evaluated in terms of the characterization, the presentation of plot and setting, the style of the writing, the unifying theme, and, in the case of picture books or illustrated books, the quality and contribution of the illustrations. As biographies, they are also subject to special considerations. Biographies need to be portraits of real people rather than paragons. They must present historically accurate depictions of the time and place in which the subject lived. Grounded in source material, good biographies present authentic, verifiable facts about a person's life and times in an engaging style. Figure 9.1 presents a brief list of criteria for evaluating biographies.

ACCURACY

Although not all biographers for children rely solely on primary sources, good biographies are always grounded in research. Some, called *biographical fiction*, are more fictional than others; they consist entirely of imagined conversations and reconstructed events in the life of an individual. Robert

Figure 9 ☆ 1

Checklist for Evaluating Biography

Accuracy
- Is the story an authentic biography grounded in source material?
- If not, is there enough truthful information to make it worth reading?

Social Details: Setting and Plot
- Are facts and story line integrated?
- Are the social details interesting, accurate, and linked to the individual's accomplishments?

Portrayal of the Subject
- Is the subject's character well developed and multidimensional?
- Are stereotypes avoided?

Style
- Is the writing style comprehensible and engaging?
- Are complex topics explained adequately?

Theme
- Is there a unifying theme?
- Does the theme highlight the special qualities of the subject?

Illustrations
- Do the illustrations help the reader visualize the time and place?
- Do the illustrations illuminate the character of the subject?

Lawson's *Ben and Me* (P–I), a funny story about Benjamin Franklin narrated by a mouse, is grounded in fact but written in fictional form. Others, called *fictionalized biographies*, are grounded in research and fact but the dialogue is invented. F. N. Monjo's *Poor Richard in France* (P–I), a fictionalized biography, recounts Franklin's trip to Europe through the eyes of his grandson who travels with him. Still others, called *authentic biographies*, are well-documented stories about individuals in which even the dialogue is based on some record of what was actually said by particular people at particular times. Jean Fritz's *What's the Big Idea, Ben Franklin?* (I) is an authentic biography of Franklin, with documented evidence woven into an entertaining story. Biographies like this are anchored by primary sources: letters, diaries, collected papers, and photographs.

Biographies need to present both a vivid and an accurate picture of the life and the times of the subject. As is true of historical fiction, accuracy is a complex criterion. Careful biographers do not go beyond the facts as we know them today, but they do interpret these facts through the eyes of the present. Consider, for example, the D'Aulaires' biography *Columbus* (P–I), written in 1955, which refers to Native Americans as savages; the biographers seemingly saw no need to consider the humanity of the native people when assessing Columbus's life. Likewise, early biographies of Rosa Parks present her as a woman who sat down in the front of the bus because she was tired. Later biographies, such as *Rosa Parks: My Story* (I), were influenced by society's acknowledgement of the careful organization of the civil rights movement, and present her action as a planned, deliberate attempt to confront unjust practices and laws.

Judging the accuracy of a biographer's presentation is not easy unless one happens to be an expert on the subject. When evaluating a biography, ask these questions: What sources did the author use? Are these sources documented? Are unnecessary generalizations about the people of the time or stereotypes of gender, ethnic, or racial groups evident?

SOCIAL DETAILS: SETTING AND PLOT

A subject's personality and accomplishments are more understandable when they are presented against a rich and vivid depiction of the social details of life. Children often read for these social details, relishing the minutiae of another person's life. Careful biographers find a balance between telling everything and telling just enough to portray a person's life accurately. Many subjects of biographies for children had lives that were touched with pain, suffering, and great hardship; many great achievements were won at great cost. These issues must be carefully presented in biographies for children so as not to detract from the subject's most significant accomplishments. For example, the times

that shaped Dr. Martin Luther King were not happy times; he grew up in a country deeply divided by racism. In any biography of King written for young readers, the social climate needs to be honestly portrayed in a way that is understandable to children without being overwhelming. Balancing the needs of the audience and the accuracy of the story is especially difficult when writing for primary-grade readers. Rosemary Bray's *Martin Luther King* is an outstanding example of this balance. Look for settings that are clearly and accurately depicted, full of interesting social details, and linked to the development of the subject's character and accomplishments.

The particular events that shape a subject's life form the basis of a biographical plot. While some biographies are chronological and present the subject's entire lifetime, plodding through tedious detail about everything that happened in a subject's life makes a book unwieldy. However, oversimplification often results in an incomplete picture of both the individual and the times (Saul, 1986). Biographers have an array of facts available to them; how they select from those facts and craft an engaging story is up to them. Certainly whatever events are presented as facts should be accurate. Good authors document their facts and also differentiate between fact and opinion, or fact and legend. Diane Stanley and Peter Vennema do an excellent job of this in their biography *Bard of Avon, The Story of William Shakespeare* (I). In a foreword, they alert their readers to the problems of fact they encountered; not much is known about the details of Shakespeare's early life. In their text they make careful use of qualifying words and phrases such as *if so*, and *perhaps*, to alert readers to theory, opinion, and educated guesses.

Some biographers for young readers, like David Adler, choose to simplify the facts and present what is in effect an outline of the subject's life. Others, instead of attempting to recount a comprehensive survey of an individual's life, prefer to focus on an episode that illustrates the subject's character or contributes to the subject's development. Biographers focus on a brief period to present more details within a manageable length.

Books such as Floyd Cooper's *Coming Home: From the Life of Langston Hughes* (I) or William Miller's *Zora Hurston and the Chinaberry Tree* (P–I) are excellent examples of these types of biographies. Some teachers feel that these biographies are more rewarding for young children, since they avoid the problem of oversimplification and include the richness of detail that children enjoy (Carr, 1981).

Other biographers choose to present brief biographical sketches that combine basic biographical details with more interesting tidbits from the subject's life. Kathleen Krull is a master of this technique, as shown in her collective biographies, including *Lives of the Writers: Comedies, Tragedies (and What the Neighbors Thought)* (I). The combination of facts and quirky details makes an entertaining introduction to the lives of some of the world's great writers.

She followed boys to the edge of campfires,
listened while their fathers sang about John Henry:

a man so strong he swung a nine-pound
hammer from dawn till dusk.

She learned about Death, the great square-toed
one who lived in the west.

Death sat on a platform made of palm leaves
and ruled with a sword in his hands.

Zora learned about Africa, the place where
she and her people came from.

In Africa they had been kings and queens,
builders of cities that stood for thousands of years.

They worshipped Gods who ruled the sky,
the mountains and rivers, the stormy sea . . . .

*Zora defies her father and follows the boys to hear tales of her people in William Miller's **Zora Hurston and the Chinaberry Tree.***

Selecting key events in a subject's life and presenting them vividly illuminates the subject and keeps a reader's interest. Look for plots that blend factual background with a good story.

PORTRAYAL OF THE SUBJECT

Jean Fritz's biographies are especially well researched and, at the same time, quite entertaining. Fritz believes that we make history dull by presenting our national heroes as frozen statues, immersing them in stale facts and images:

> Sometimes it seems to me that we have forced our heroes to play the children's own game of Statues. We have twirled them about, called *time*, and then told them to hold their positions. Whatever stance they happen to assume is the one they must perpetuate. (1976, p. 191)

She believes that these stereotyped impressions carry over into adulthood and rob us of the full force of a person's character. Her own biographies about Revolutionary War heroes present a refreshing view. They are tinged with humor, one of the most effective ways of bringing a deeper understanding of a person from the past. She presents her subjects' foibles as well as their good deeds through character-revealing incidents and anecdotes.

Biographers must consider their subjects as individuals rather than as paragons, and individuals are multidimensional. The strengths *and* weaknesses of individuals are presented in excellent biographies, as in Jean Fritz's ***Why Don't You Get a Horse, Sam Adams?*** (I). Good biographies also avoid implying that the greatness of the subject was implicit from birth. They avoid weaving background knowledge or prescient knowledge of latent talents into unlikely conversations (Herman, 1978). Exaggerating the good qualities of a subject results in *hagiography*—the telling of the life of a saint—or the creation of a legend. Biographies are about real people, not legendary figures.

The biographer's point of view and interest in the subject should be apparent, as should the biographer's purpose. The same subject may be treated differently by different biographers. Teaching Idea 9.1 explores this idea. When selecting biographies, look for subjects that are well developed and multidimensional, brought to life through the presentation of vivid details.

Teaching Idea 9 · 1

Compare Biographies About One Person

Ask your students to compare and evaluate different biographies about the same person by doing the following:

1. Choose two biographies about the same person and read them.

2. Decide which biography gives the best idea of what the person was really like. How does it accomplish this.

3. Decide which tells the most about the person's accomplishments?

4. Decide which is more informative and which is more interesting.

Students can also compare biographies written from different perspectives:

1. Compare a biography written before 1970 with one written within the past five years.

2. Describe the differences in the way the subject is viewed or the way similar events are reported.

3. Decide which is more informative and which is more interesting.

STYLE

Authors make choices about what they say and how they say it. Even when a story is well grounded in verifiable fact, as in authentic biography, it still represents an author's choice of facts and can still be told in an engaging fashion. Good biographies incorporate the language and customs of the times. The dialogue should reflect how the subject is likely to have talked, with enough authenticity that readers get a true picture but are not overwhelmed by archaic or idiosyncratic speech patterns. For example, Joseph Bruchac's biography of Sitting Bull, *A Boy Called Slow: The True Story of Sitting Bull* (I), is told in the cadence of the storyteller and includes some Lakota words. Look for language that rings true to the characters but is not overwhelming.

THEME

The theme of a biography is the unifying element behind the story. Facts are merely facts until they are subordinated to a theme and a structure that allows them to make a statement with universal application and appeal. Fighting against injustice, struggling for independence, or working for human rights happens around the world and in many different ways. Each individual story builds its own theme; combined, the stories highlight the resilience and courage of human beings. Look for books that contain a theme with universal application and appeal.

ILLUSTRATIONS

If the biography is a picture book, the illustrations must present the setting and the subject in an accurate manner. Illustrations often provide the interesting details that the brief text of picture book biographies lacks. Illustrated biographies, like Diane Stanley's *Michelangelo* (I), present a great deal of information in the text but also rely on the illustrations to help children visualize the time, place, and people. In this case Stanley's detailed illustrations were enhanced by computer images of Michelangelo's works.

Biographers also make use of archival photographs, when they are available, to highlight their subject's personalities and lives. Ruby Bridges' Orbis Pictus Award–winning *Through My Eyes* (I) contains reproductions of photographs taken during the tense times when schools in the South were forcibly integrated. Look for illustrations that include interesting details and illuminate the character of the subject.

A CLOSE LOOK AT

Lincoln: A Photobiography

Russell Freedman's *Lincoln: A Photobiography* (I–A) won the Newbery Medal in 1988. This distinguished contribution to literature for children exemplifies the qualities of great biography. It is an outstanding example of the vivid re-creation of the life of a person who profoundly affected history, and thus our lives today.

Setting and Plot

Freedman chose to tell the story of Lincoln's entire life, from birth to death, but he carefully selected facts that would build on each other to present an accurate and vivid picture. The book begins with a brief chapter describing the personality and physical characteristics of Lincoln the adult; the chapter is aptly titled "The Mysterious Mr. Lincoln."

Freedman acknowledges that not much is known about Lincoln's early life, but he recounts what is known of his boyhood in just a few pages, telling of the way he lived, the places he lived, and the changes in his family. Accompanying this succinct description of Lincoln's childhood are photographs of Lincoln's father and stepmother, a replica of the cabin he was born in, and a page from his copybook. Text and illustrations present a picture of a poor, intelligent, hardworking youth—and one who was very tall.

After recounting Lincoln's young adulthood and the experiences that led him to become a lawyer, Freedman concentrates on Lincoln's expertise as a lawyer and his growing fascination with politics. The remainder of the book focuses on Lincoln's years as president, exploring the complex issues of emancipation and the Civil War. As in the earlier chapters, Freedman presents interesting details using text and illustration. In discussing the Lincoln-Douglas debates, Freedman says this:

> The striking contrast between Douglas and Lincoln— The Little Giant and Long Abe, as reporters called them—added color and excitement to the contests. Douglas was Lincoln's opposite in every way. Barely five feet four inches tall, he had a huge round head planted on massive shoulders, a booming voice, and an aggressive, self-confident manner. He appeared on the speakers' platform dressed "plantation style"—a navy coat and light trousers, a ruffled shirt, a wide-

brimmed felt hat. Lincoln, tall and gangly, seemed plain in his rumpled suit, carrying his notes and speeches in an old carpetbag, sitting on the platform with his bony knees jutting into the air.

This text is accompanied by two photographs, presented side by side, which dramatize the vast physical differences in the two men, differences that were mirrored by their opposing views on slavery.

Freedman grapples with the issue of slavery in a straightforward and sensitive fashion. Slavery was a part of life at the time and people held violently opposing views about it. Lincoln's character was shaped by the times in which he lived and by the events in his life. The increasing debate over slavery certainly played a part in the shaping of his character.

Portrayal of Subject

Perhaps the best example of Freedman's respectful and honest portrayal of Lincoln is how he presents Lincoln's views on slavery. Rather than simply labeling Lincoln "the Great Emancipator," Freedman explores the complex issues

Profile ✿ Russell Freedman

© Houghton Mifflin Company

Russell Freedman, a master of biography and nonfiction, worked as a journalist and television publicity writer before he became interested in children's books. He stumbled into the children's book field by chance when he read a newspaper article about a 16-year-old boy who was blind and who had invented a Braille typewriter. On further reading, he discovered that the Braille system itself had been invented by another 16-year-old boy who was blind, Louis Braille. Freedman was intrigued and began writing a collection of biographies

called *Teenagers Who Made History* (A).

Freedman does not look favorably on the type of biography that includes make-believe stories like George Washington cutting down a cherry tree or those that adopt a reverential tone toward the subject. His realistic biographies help shape the hero worship of the past into a more realistic approach. He sticks closely to documented evidence about his subject; his is a scholarly approach. He respects today's readers and knows that they prefer the facts. Freedman believes it is healthy for children to know that even the great figures of history often had doubts and fears.

Freedman approached writing his award-winning biography of Abraham Lincoln with trepidation; so many had already been written. A Lincoln scholar advised him about the best ones but firsthand research helped, too.

Freedman says:

Along with my reading, I had a chance to enjoy the pleasures of

eyewitness research. I visited Lincoln's log-cabin birthplace in Kentucky, his boyhood home in Indiana, and the reconstructed village of New Salem, Illinois, where he lived as a young man. I went to Springfield, with its wealth of Lincoln historical sites, and to Washington, D.C., for a firsthand look at Ford's Theatre and the rooming house across the street where the assassinated president died. There's something magic about being able to lay your eyes on the real thing—something you can't get from your reading alone. . . . I could picture the scene in my mind's eye, because I had walked down those same dusty lanes, where cattle still graze behind split-rail fences and geese flap about underfoot. When I wrote about Lincoln's morning walk from his house to his law office in downtown Springfield, I knew the route because I had walked it myself. (1988, p. 449)

Freedman's careful work helps young readers walk with Abraham Lincoln through some critical historical events.

that Lincoln had to face. He tells us that, although Lincoln was opposed to slavery, he was hopeful that confining it to the southern states would bring about its "natural death." He was not an abolitionist, and it wasn't until the Kansas-Nebraska Act of 1854 that Lincoln entered the political debate. Freedman says:

> Although Lincoln was determined to oppose the spread of slavery, he admitted that he didn't know what to do about those states where slavery was already established.

Freedman discusses Lincoln's eventual decision to proclaim emancipation within the context of the war and his duties as commander in chief; he shows how Lincoln's opposition to slavery and his military shrewdness both inform that decision.

Freedman is careful to separate legend from fact, and to portray Lincoln as a real man. His moodiness, his penchant for spoiling his children, his uncouth manners, and his reason for growing a beard are all anecdotes that bring life to this historical figure. So, too, are the descriptions of Lincoln's grief over the death of two of his sons and his bizarre, prescient dream of his own assassination. Freedman's Lincoln is a man to admire *because* he was human; he was a man who did the best job of living he could do.

Accuracy and Style

Freedman is always careful to distinguish fact from opinion and truth from legend. This distinction is made in a plain and forthright manner:

> He also fell in love—apparently for the first time in his life. Legend tells us that Lincoln once had a tragic love affair with Ann Rutledge, daughter of the New Salem tavern owner, who died at the age of twenty-two. While this story has become part of American folklore, there isn't a shred of evidence that Lincoln ever had a romantic attachment with Ann. Historians believe that they were just good friends.

He also presents a significant amount of interesting historical detail. We learn that Lincoln generally bought two suits a year—a significant detail because in those days most men had one suit that had to last their lifetime. We learn that Lincoln finished composing the Gettysburg Address after breakfast on the day he delivered it—writing it out on two pieces of lined paper—and that he felt the speech was a failure.

Freedman's text includes many direct quotations from Lincoln, all set off with quotation marks. These quotations, the historical facts, and social details are all taken from sources listed at the end of the book. A sampling of Lincoln's famous quotations, with sources indicated, and the sources for the quotations that begin each chapter immediately follow the text. These are followed by a list and description of

historic sites having to do with Lincoln's life, a description of source books about Lincoln, acknowledgments, and a useful five-page index. This end material, and the photographs of historical documents that appear throughout the text, all attest to the integrity and thoroughness of this biography.

Theme

The issue of slavery takes up a large portion of this book and indicates the way in which Freedman views Lincoln and his life. By presenting the events that resulted in Lincoln signing the Emancipation Proclamation, by exploring the complex issues that surrounded emancipation, and by acknowledging Lincoln's deliberation over the proclamation, Freedman encourages readers to think about freedom and slavery, and to see how divisive the institution of slavery was.

A CLOSE LOOK AT
Martin Luther King

Rosemary L. Bray and artist Malcah Zeldis present the life of another American hero through both text and illustration, in *Martin Luther King* (P–I). Like Freedman, Bray and Zeldis begin at the beginning, with the birth of their subject.

*Malcah Zeldis's folk-art paintings brilliantly depict the important moments of King's life in Rosemary Bray's **Martin Luther King**.*

Interesting details appear on the very first page as Bray explains that King's given name was Michael; his father changed both his own name and his son's name to Martin a few years after his son's birth. The defining issue of King's life is also presented on page one: inequality, exemplified by segregation. The complexities and varied forms of segregation are described in a manner that is understandable to primary and intermediate-grade children. As King develops a growing awareness of segregation, readers begin to understand how it must have felt to be Martin Luther King. Readers see his struggles against hate and despair, his boyishness, his growing faith, his early interest in Gandhi, and the powerful weapon of love.

The straightforward tone in which Bray presents the major events of the civil rights movement enables her to mention murder and hatred without being overly dramatic or inflammatory. King's gradual rise to become the central symbolic figure of the movement, and his eventual reaching out to all who were poor and needy, is reflected in the stunning folk-art paintings that face each page of text.

In a brief 48 pages, Bray and Zeldis evoke the spirit of the times and of the man himself. Not a saint, never a paragon, Martin Luther King was a human being struggling for justice for other human beings. Without oversimplification or equivocation, the illustrations and text of *Martin Luther King* make this clear to young readers.

Exploring Biography Chronologically

Looking at biography in terms of historical period is perhaps the most common way of using biography in the classroom. Like historical fiction, biography can help students envision what life was like in the past. Here we group biographies chronologically as we did for historical fiction.

PREHISTORIC TIMES THROUGH THE AMERICAN REVOLUTION

Biographies of people who lived prior to the eighteenth century are not numerous. There are no written records to provide information about prehistoric persons, and not much is known about those who lived before the eighteenth century, when we compare the wealth of data available on those who lived after. There are, however, some excellent new biographies that can support a study of the time periods between prehistoric times and the American Revolution.

Two excellent biographies of Joan of Arc appeared in 1998. Josephine Poole's *Joan of Arc* (P), beautifully illustrated by Angela Barrett, brings this young woman to life for pri-

mary-grade readers. Diane Stanley's outstanding *Joan of Arc* (I) provides more detail in both text and illustration, making it quite interesting for intermediate-grade readers. Both illuminate not only the subject but also the times in which she lived and died.

First published in 1986, Diane Stanley's *Peter the Great* (I), a biography of the Russian czar who built St. Petersburg and dragged Russia into the Western world, has recently been reissued. This book is a fascinating look at one of the most powerful—and determined—men of his time.

Elizabethan England is the setting for two other outstanding biographies. Jane Resh Thomas's *Behind the Mask: The Life of Queen Elizabeth I* (A) is a richly detailed account of this fascinating woman who ruled the British Empire, defeated the Spanish Armada, and supported the exploration of the new world. At once an icon and an enigma in her own time, Elizabeth I is a fascinating subject, and Thomas presents her as a woman of strength, and weakness.

Marc Aronson won the Boston Globe-Horn Book Award for nonfiction with *Sir Walter Ralegh and the Quest for El Dorado* (A), which was also the 2001 winner of the first Sibert prize for nonfiction. In presenting the life of the "first modern man," Aronson artfully blends factual information with compelling writing, and the result is a biogra-

Teaching Idea 9 ✳ 2

Study the Biography of a Biographer

Ask your students to do an author study on an eminent biographer such as Jean Fritz, Russell Freedman, Milton Meltzer, Patricia and Fredrick McKissack, or Diane Stanley. They should follow this procedure:

1. Find and read any biographical or autobiographical information on the author.

2. Try to determine how the author chooses his or her subject.

3. Try to determine how the author goes about collecting information for a biography.

Teachers may want to do the following:

✳ Read *Inventing the Truth: The Art and Craft of Memoir,* edited by William Zinsser, or *Extraordinary Lives: The Art and Craft of Biography,* also edited by William Zinsser. Share appropriate information with your students.

✳ Discuss with students how writers shape factual truth in writing biography, autobiography, or memoir, and how this affects the quality of the biography.

phy that is hard to put down. Additionally, Aronson includes archival maps and prints, a time line, 19 pages of endnotes and bibliography, and a complete index. Reading this book allows students not only to learn about Raleigh, but also to learn about the process of crafting an artful work of nonfiction. These and other biographies set during this time period are listed in the Booklist at the end of this chapter.

THE REVOLUTIONARY WAR PERIOD

There are many biographies that present the lives of those who were a part of the American Revolution. In 1976, the bicentennial of the beginning of the Revolution, a number of such biographies were published, including Jean Fritz's series of biographies for intermediate-grade readers. Biographies of American heroes continue to be published, and the best of them show men and women struggling for personal freedom as well as for freedom in the life of their country. Biographies about the people involved in the American Revolution give a serious view of their beliefs, sometimes a humorous glimpse of their shortcomings, and, ideally, a feeling that they were real people with blood in their veins.

Jean Fritz's series of biographies about the heroes of the American Revolution include *Why Not, Lafayette?* (I) and *Why Don't You Get a Horse, Sam Adams?* (I), a humorous look at a colorful hero. Fritz describes Adams in this way: "His clothes were shabby and plain, he refused to get on a horse, and he hated the King of England." Her series of biographies are all authentic and well grounded in documented sources; they are also funny.

Benjamin Franklin is the subject of numerous biographies. One of the most recent, and best, is James Cross Giblin's *The Amazing Life of Benjamin Franklin* (I). Giblin carefully presents facts about Franklin's life that allow readers to see the whole person, not just the patriot and inventor. We learn, for example, that Franklin had not seen his wife for 10 years prior to her death in 1774; he had been in London, working for the colonies he represented. This, coupled with Giblin's comment, a few pages later, that "At seventy-two, Ben still had an eye for the ladies," allows readers to draw their own conclusions. These and other biographies set during the American Revolution appear in the Booklist at the end of this chapter.

THE CIVIL WAR PERIOD AND LIFE ON THE FRONTIER

It is not surprising that a number of biographies about Abraham Lincoln are available for young readers. There are also biographies of those who, like Harriet Tubman, struggled for freedom and of those who served in the armies that fought the war. The best biographies about this period in history do not present the North as all good and the South as all bad. Rather, they present the individual subject as a human being, and the setting as a complex one, with heroes and villains on both sides.

Julius Lester uses first-person narratives in *To Be a Slave* (I–A), which consists of edited verbatim transcripts of accounts by blacks who escaped from the antebellum South. Lester also uses interviews, footnotes to history (such as bills of sale for slaves, letters, and marriage registers), and primary sources for six stories about slaves and freedmen in *Long Journey Home* (I–A). Lester says he tells the stories of minor figures because he feels that they are the true movers of history, whereas the famous exist as symbols of their actions. The stories are dramatic and sometimes bitter. They are always poignant.

Virginia Hamilton's *Many Thousand Gone: African Americans from Slavery to Freedom* (I–A) is a well-researched and beautifully written biography that tells 34 brief stories using a great deal of original testimony. The individual stories are brief, episodic biographies; the book as a whole becomes a biography of a people journeying from slavery to freedom.

While browsing in a rare books store in London, Walter Dean Myers discovered information about Sarah Forbes Bonetta, a young West African princess who was raised in England as the protégé of Queen Victoria. Fascinated, he set out to discover what he could about this young woman. The result, *At Her Majesty's Request: An African Princess in Victorian England* (I) is a highly readable, fascinating story.

The story of America during the latter half of the nineteenth century includes the great migration of people toward the western part of America. This migration, like other great events in history, has spawned many stories and many heroes. Recently, these stories and heroes have been reassessed and their place in history examined in light of the terrible destruction of the lives of Native Americans wrought by the westward expansion. While there are not yet enough biographies of Native Americans who lived in these times, heightened awareness of a need for these biographies is causing more and more of them to be written.

Joseph Bruchac's *A Boy Called Slow: The True Story of Sitting Bull* (I) and Albert Marrin's *Sitting Bull and His World* (A) both explore the life of one of the greatest Plains Indian leaders. Marrin's biography, a Boston Globe-Horn Book Award Honor Book, has been both praised and criticized for its scholarship and point of view. The controversy points out the difficulty inherent in presenting history to young readers.

In a collective biography, *My Heroes, My People: African Americans and Native Americans in the West* (I), Morgan Monceaux and Ruth Katcher present brief portraits of people of color in the West—both well-known and unsung heroes. Monceaux's paintings are striking and the biographical sketches make readers want to learn more about these interesting people.

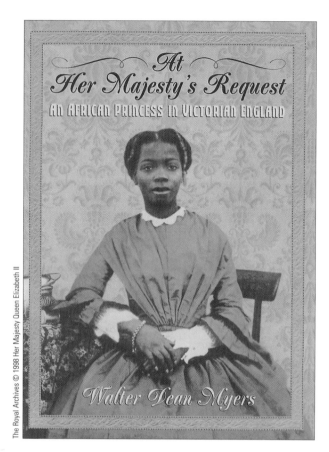

At
Her Majesty's Request
An African Princess in Victorian England

Walter Dean Myers

Walter Dean Myers has taken the few facts known about Sarah Forbes Bonetta and created a biography that explores race, identity, and the human longing for a place of one's own.

The Royal Archives © 1998 Her Majesty Queen Elizabeth II

IMMIGRATION, WORLD WAR I, AND THE GREAT DEPRESSION

Many of those who were part of the westward expansion had another story to tell as well—their immigration to America. As these new immigrants settled in and made new homes, the world was moving toward the First World War; this period was soon followed by the Depression. The stories of people who lived in these times reflect a courage and determination that enabled them to uproot their lives for another chance in new surroundings, to endure a world war, or to seek an opportunity for economic survival.

There are many biographies of those who were world leaders or important politicians, or who otherwise changed the world. There are also memoirs of ordinary people who lived during these times. One of the best of these is Alan Govenar's *Osceola: Memories of a Sharecropper's Daughter* (I). As collector and editor of Osceola Mays's stories, Govenar has shaped a portrayal that is redolent of the fear, pride, and eventual triumph of this granddaughter of a slave who was born in 1909 in Waskom, Texas. The strong voice of the

storyteller herself is present in the 20 brief chapters that comprise this oral history, making it a wonderful book to read aloud. Because Govenar shares the process he went through to compile this history, it is also a model of research that students can follow as they embark on their own oral histories. Teaching Idea 9.3 offers suggestions for getting students started on compiling oral histories or memoirs of their older friends and family members.

WORLD WAR II AND ITS AFTERMATH

The Great Depression ended and the Second World War began. Those who had been standing in bread lines soon stood in draft lines or on assembly lines as the world went to war. This war had its heroes, like all wars, but it also had more than its share of villains. Some biographies of the Second World War focus on notable figures, such as Russell Freedman's *Franklin Delano Roosevelt* and his *Eleanor*

Teaching Idea 9 ✳ 3

Help Write the Memoirs of an Older Friend or Family Member

After reading and discussing the process and structure of several memoirs, ask your students to do the following:

1. Think of an older friend or family member who has stories to tell.
2. Think of questions to ask that person. Write them down and share them with peers in order to gather feedback.
3. Arrange an interview with the subject. Use the questions as a guide during the interview. Record the conversation using a tape recorder. If this isn't possible, take written notes.
4. Write a draft relating the stories the subject has shared. When finished, ask the person for comments on the draft.
5. Collect photographs that illuminate the material.
6. Revise, edit, and combine text and illustrations. Audio recordings can also be included.
7. Present the final version to classmates and to the subjects of the memoirs, perhaps at a celebration in which the subjects visit the class.

Roosevelt: A Life of Discovery (both A), or Albert Marrin's *Hitler* (A). Some focus on those who suffered and died in the Holocaust. While biographies of the notable figures of the period are interesting and necessary, it is often the biographies of ordinary individuals, like Anne Frank's *Diary of a Young Girl* (I–A), or Mirjam Pressler's *Anne Frank: A Hidden Life* (A), that most effectively relate the tragedy of the war.

An account of one of the largest rescues of Jews during the Holocaust, Alison Leslie Gold's *A Special Fate: Chiune Sugihara: Hero of the Holocaust* (A), tells the story of Sugihara, a Japanese consul in Lithuania who defied his government and issued approximately 6,000 Japanese transit visas to Jews of Eastern Europe. Through his actions he saved the lives of those who received his aid and were thus able to leave Europe. This and other notable biographies of this period of history appear in the Booklist at the end of this chapter.

Chinue Sugihara quietly defied his own government and the other Axis powers when he issued 6,000 transit visas to Jews caught in the madness of Nazi Europe.

THE 1950S TO THE PRESENT

Since the end of the war, America and the world have changed considerably. We have suffered through armed conflicts in Korea and in Southeast Asia, watched governments rise and fall, seen new countries created, and received a new wave of immigrants to America. We have seen vast cultural changes spurred by the civil rights movement and the people who participated in it. We have entered the age of the celebrity, with sports and music superstars rocketing to fame almost overnight. All of these events are reflected in the books available for children.

Several biographies of notable figures of the civil rights movement are available, including many about Dr. Martin Luther King. Walter Dean Myers has written two about Malcolm X. *Malcolm X: By Any Means Necessary* (A) and *Malcolm X: A Fire Burning Brightly* (I) introduce today's children to the life and struggles of this complex and controversial figure in contemporary America.

Ruby Bridges tells her own story in *Through My Eyes*, a memoir of her early life, when as a first grader she was the only African-American child in a formerly all-white school in Louisiana. Photographs of the ugliness that surrounded school integration are presented in sharp contrast to the childlike, hopeful tone of the written text. *Through My Eyes* won an Orbis Pictus Award.

Quietly told stories of people who did not create headlines can also have a strong and lasting impact. Another memoir, *Leon's Story* (I–A), by Leon Walter Tillage with collage art by Susan L. Roth, won a Boston Globe-Horn Book Award for nonfiction. In this slim book Leon Tillage tells the story of his life as the son of an African-American sharecropper, growing up in North Carolina during the 1940s. As a young boy he learns to endure the racism and bigotry of his surroundings while keeping intact his own dignity and sense of worth. His experiences lead him directly to being involved in the civil rights movement. The way the story came to be written serves as a wonderful model for children, too; it began with Tillage telling his story to an assembly of seventh graders at the Baltimore school where he works as a custodian. When Roth's daughter came home from school and told her about Tillage, Roth began the process that turned his oral story into a written memoir.

Other books that tell the story of ordinary people sometimes focus on new immigrants, as does Diane Hoyt-Goldsmith's *Hoang Anh: A Vietnamese-American Boy* (I–A). The book's clear text and its color photographs by Lawrence Migdale present details in the life of a young adolescent who was a baby when his parents fled with him from Vietnam. The book explores how he is able to keep his Vietnamese traditions alive and still be an American kid. Mexican-American poet Juan Felipe Herrera recounts his experiences and feelings when he moved to the city and entered an English-speaking school in *The Upside Down Boy/El Niño de Cabeza* (P).

Many artists, musicians, athletes, and politicians who are in today's news become the subjects of biographies. Some of these biographies, like Tom L. Matthews's *Light Shining Through the Mist: A Photobiography of Dian Fossey* (I), Russell Freedman's *Martha Graham: A Dancer's Life* (A), and Maria Tallchief's *Tallchief: America's Prima Ballerina* (I), are carefully researched, well documented, and engagingly written. Others are quickly-thrown-together accounts of current superstars. Biographies of both the famous and the ordinary reflect life in today's world. Some of the best of these biographies are listed in the Booklist at the end of this chapter.

Biography in the Classroom

Biography can enliven a social studies curriculum; in conjunction with historical fiction and nonfiction, it can illuminate a time and place by telling the story of an individual. It can also support studies in music and art; many fine biographies of artists and musicians explore both their lives and their creative endeavors. An exploration of themes is enriched by including biographies.

Biography is the favorite reading material of many children. Intermediate- and advanced-grade children like biographies because they are real, not fictional, and present intriguing details of other people's lives. Children seem to choose biographies according to their interests. Those interested in music will choose biographies of musicians; baseball players will choose biographies of other baseball players (Herman, 1978).

Recent memoirs can serve as models for children as they develop their own or those of an older friend or family member. Other biographies serve as excellent examples of how to use source material to craft an engaging and accurate story. Some provide access to primary source material for students to use in their own research. A biography collection is an important part of any classroom or school library.

BUILDING A BIOGRAPHY COLLECTION

Individual biographies are judged according to the criteria explained at the beginning of this chapter. A collection of biographies needs to be assessed in terms of its scope and representativeness. As you gather biographies, be sure to evaluate the breadth of your selection in terms of gender and cultural representation. Biography for children was once dominated by the stories of white men. This has changed significantly in the past few decades and there are now good biographies available of women and people of color. Balancing your collection across gender and race is important, as we discuss in Chapter 11. If there are biographies of women and people of color that speak to your subject, be sure to include them in your collection. If there are not, you may want to consider with your students why there are no biographies of, for example, ancient female explorers, and why biographies of modern female explorers are now available. Taking into account the biographies and memoirs of ordinary people that are available today, consider with your students why someone might become the subject of a biography, an idea that is explored in Teaching Idea 9.4. Using this approach, children can begin to see how the world has changed and how historical and current social conditions influence individual potentials.

ORGANIZING BIOGRAPHY BY THEME

Biography, like historical fiction, includes stories of people who explore their world, fight for freedom, revolt against oppression, immigrate, establish new nations, and struggle for survival and human rights. Biographies can be used to complement historical and realistic fiction that studies similar themes; single themes can be explored primarily

Teaching Idea 9✳4

Who Becomes a Biographical Subject?

Ask your students to consider what types of people are most likely to become the subjects of biographies. What people are most likely to have several biographies written about them? Ask students to consider whether the subjects of biography have changed in the past 30 years. Have them follow this procedure:

1. Go to the library or on the Internet to find out how many biographies have been written about a particular individual. List authors, titles, and dates of publication.

2. Check the school library holdings to ascertain what kinds of people are subjects of biographies written within the past 30 years. List subjects, authors, titles, and dates of publication.

3. Summarize the data from items 1 and 2 and make generalizations based on the data.

through biographies. There are several biographical series, such as the Extraordinary People series, published by Children's Press, the Black Americans of Achievement series, published by Chelsea, and Enslow's African-American Biography series, Hispanic Biography series, World Writers series, and Historical Americans series, that present biographies about various people engaged in similar struggles. There are also collective biographies, mentioned earlier in this chapter, which present brief biographies of a number of people who are linked in some way. Nathan Aaseng's collective biography, *Black Inventors* (A), and Patricia Calvert's *Great Lives: The American Frontier* (A) offer readers a glimpse of the lives of people who share attributes, desires, and achievements. These and other series and collective biographies are listed in the Booklist at the end of this chapter.

You can also collect books that illustrate a particular theme, such as the struggle for human rights. By studying the lives of diverse people from around the world and across history, students can come to understand the universal struggles of humankind. Why do people around the world struggle for human rights? How are the struggles similar across nations and time? How do they vary according to age and culture? Exploring these kinds of questions can lead to a better understanding of humanity and one's place in it.

Many biographies focus on explorers, both ancient and modern. Sir Walter Raleigh explored the new world; Sally Ride explored space. The theme of exploration can be widened to include those who explore not only geography, but also science. Those people who have made scientific and technological breakthroughs are curious, dedicated individuals, just as many geographic explorers are. Biographies of famous scientists and inventors can enrich students' concepts of what it means to be an explorer. Artists and musicians who break new ground can also be considered explorers. Thus a general theme like exploration or human rights can be woven from many varying biographies as well as from fiction and nonfiction.

Biographies of artists and musicians also can support the study of art and music. They can be compared in terms of the driving force that shaped the lives of their subjects: What caused them to pursue their talents with such passion and success? Biographies of female artists and musicians can be explored as examples of triumph over discrimination and then related to the general theme of human rights.

Robyn Montana Turner's series, *Portraits of Women Artists for Children*, presents both the life and the work of famous women artists. The books also explore the effects of living in a discriminatory society and how each artist fought to pursue her talent. Andrea Davis Pinkney's biographies of artists such as Duke Ellington and Alvin Ailey do the same. The Booklist at the end of this chapter contains the titles of some biographies of scientists, artists, and musicians.

A great number of biographies and autobiographies of writers and illustrators of books for children also exist, including a series of autobiographies for primary-grade readers published by Richard Owens. These biographies can be read in any number of ways. For example, reading about Beatrix Potter's life yields knowledge about her as a writer; learning about the time and place in which she grew up allows us to appreciate how it affected her as a human being and especially as a woman. Thus a biography of Potter might be included in a study of people who pursued individual dreams despite significant obstacles. These biographies are also important resources for exploring what it means to be a writer, and for extending children's knowledge of the authors whose works they enjoy reading.

Another theme teachers can use to organize biographies is sports. People who single-mindedly pursue their talents as athletes are not fundamentally different from those who pursue their talents as artists, musicians, or writers. Some, like Arthur Ashe, who use their position as sports heroes to speak out against oppression, are linked to others who struggle for human rights. Good sports biographies are more than just sources of information about personal heroes; they can also serve as springboards for exploring themes that permeate other biographies as well as works of fiction. The Booklist at the end of this chapter contains the titles of some biographies of contemporary and historical sports figures.

Summary

Biographies tell the stories of the people who shaped our history. Reading fine biographies helps children understand that people lived and made history, and that these people had strengths and weaknesses, as we all do. Understanding the humanity behind the greatness allows children to dream of their own accomplishments, and to know they are possible.

Read the Boston Globe-Horn Book Award acceptance speech by Marc Aronson in the January/ February 2001 issue of *The Horn Book Magazine*. In that speech, Aronson makes some claims for the power of nonfiction. Think about what he says, about your own reading preferences, and about the implicit assumptions about fiction that guide much of what we do with books in school. Discuss this with peers in relation to some of the best authentic biography that you have read.

Booklist

The Period Before the American Revolution

Aronson, Marc, *Sir Walter Ralegh and the Quest for El Dorado* (A)

Blumberg, Rhoda, *The Remarkable Voyages of Captain Cook* (I)

Ceserani, Gian Paolo, *Marco Polo* (I)

Demi, *Buddha* (P–I)

_____, *Chingis Khan* (P–I)

Fisher, Leonard Everett, *Galileo* (I)

_____, *Gutenberg* (I)

Fritz, Jean, *The Double Life of Pocahontas* (I–A)

_____, *Where Do You Think You're Going, Christopher Columbus?* (I)

_____, *Who's That Stepping on Plymouth Rock?* (I)

Hodges, Margaret, *Brother Francis and the Friendly Beasts* (P)

Marrin, Albert, *The Sea King: Sir Francis Drake and His Times* (A)

Mayo, Margaret, *Brother Sun, Sister Moon: The Life and Stories of St. Francis* (P)

Poole, Josephine, *Joan of Arc* (P)

Provensen, Alice, and Martin Provensen, *Leonardo da Vinci: The Artist, Inventor, Scientist in Three-Dimensional Movable Pictures* (I–A)

Roth, Susan, *Marco Polo: His Notebook* (I)

Sis, Peter, *Follow the Dream: The Story of Christopher Columbus* (P–I)

_____, *Starry Messenger* (I)

Stanley, Diane, *Joan of Arc* (I)

_____, *Michelangelo* (I)

_____, *Peter the Great* (I)

Stanley, Diane, and Peter Vennema, *Cleopatra* (I)

_____, *Good Queen Bess: The Story of Elizabeth I of England* (I)

_____, *Leonardo da Vinci* (I)

_____, *Shaka, King of the Zulus* (I)

Thomas, Jane Resh, *Behind the Mask: The Life of Queen Elizabeth I* (A)

The American Revolution

Adler, David, *A Picture Book of Benjamin Franklin* (P)

_____, *A Picture Book of Thomas Jefferson* (P)

Aliki, *The Many Lives of Benjamin Franklin* (P)

Bober, Natalie S., *Abigail Adams: Witness to a Revolution* (A)

Fritz, Jean, *And Then What Happened, Paul Revere?* (I)

_____, *Can't You Make Them Behave, King George?* (I)

_____, *The Great Little Madison* (A)

_____, *Traitor: The Case of Benedict Arnold* (A)

_____, *What's the Big Idea, Ben Franklin?* (I)

_____, *Where Was Patrick Henry on the 29th of May?* (I)

_____, *Why Don't You Get a Horse, Sam Adams?* (I)

_____, *Why Not, Lafayette?* (I)

_____, *Will You Sign Here, John Hancock?* (I)

Giblin, James Cross, *The Amazing Life of Benjamin Franklin* (I)

_____, *George Washington: A Picture Book Biography* (P–I)

_____, *Thomas Jefferson: A Picture Book Biography* (P–I)

Jacobs, William Jay, *Washington* (I–A)

Lawson, Robert, *Ben and Me* (I)

McGovern, Ann, *Secret Soldier: The Story of Deborah Sampson* (I–A)

Meltzer, Milton, *The American Revolutionaries: A History in Their Own Words* (A)

_____, *George Washington and the Birth of Our Nation* (A)

_____, *Thomas Jefferson: The Revolutionary Aristocrat* (A)

Monjo, F. N., *Grand Papa and Ellen Aroon* (P–I)

_____, *Poor Richard in France* (I)

Osborne, Mary Pope, *The Many Lives of Benjamin Franklin* (A)

Pinkney, Andrea Davis, *Dear Benjamin Banneker* (I)

Wallner, Alexandra, *Betsy Ross* (P)

The Civil War

Adler, David, *A Picture Book of Robert E. Lee* (P)

Archer, Jules, *A House Divided: The Lives of Ulysses S. Grant and Robert E. Lee* (I–A)

Burchard, Peter, *Charlotte Forten: A Black Teacher in the Civil War* (I–A)

_____, *Lincoln and Slavery* (A)

Chang, Ina, *A Separate Battle: Women and the Civil War* (A)

Everett, Gwen, *John Brown: One Man Against Slavery* (I)

Freedman, Russell, *Lincoln: A Photobiography* (I–A)

Fritz, Jean, *Harriet Beecher Stowe and the Beecher Preachers* (I)

_____, *Stonewall* (A)

Hamilton, Virginia, *Anthony Burns: The Defeat and Triumph of a Fugitive Slave* (A)

_____, *Many Thousand Gone: African Americans from Slavery to Freedom* (I–A)

Lawrence, Jacob, *Harriet and the Promised Land* (P–I)

Lester, Julius, *Long Journey Home* (I–A)

_____, *To Be a Slave* (I–A)

Marrin, Albert, *Unconditional Surrender: U.S. Grant and the Civil War* (A)

_____, *Virginia's General: Robert E. Lee and the Civil War* (A)

McCurdy, Michael, *Escape from Slavery: The Boyhood of Frederick Douglass in His Own Words* (I)

McKissack, Patricia C., and Fredrick McKissack, *Sojourner Truth: Ain't I a Woman?* (I–A)

Meltzer, Milton, *Abraham Lincoln* (A)

_____, *Frederick Douglass: In His Own Words* (A)

Miller, William, *Frederick Douglass: The Last Day of Slavery* (P–I)

Reit, Seymour, *Behind Rebel Lines: The Incredible Story of Emma Edmonds* (I–A)

Rockwell, Anne, *Only Passing Through: The Story of Sojourner Truth* (P–I)

Schroeder, Alan, *Minty: A Story of Young Harriet Tubman* (P–I)

Stevens, Bryna, *Frank Thompson: Her Civil War Story* (I)

Warner, Lucille Schulberg, *From Slave to Abolitionist: The Life of William Wells Brown* (A)

Westward Expansion

Bruchac, Joseph, *A Boy Called Slow: The True Story of Sitting Bull* (P–I)

_____, *Crazy Horse's Vision* (P)

Conrad, Pam, *Prairie Visions: The Life and Times of Solomon Butcher* (I–A)

Freedman, Russell, *Indian Chiefs* (I–A)

_____, *The Life and Death of Crazy Horse* (I–A)

Fritz, Jean, *Bully for You, Teddy Roosevelt* (I–A)

_____, *Make Way for Sam Houston* (I)

Gilliland, Juidith Heide, *Steamboat! The Story of Captain Blanche Leathers* (P)

Harvey, Brett, *My Prairie Year: Based on the Diary of Elenore Plaisted* (P–I)

Jakes, John, *Susanna of the Alamo: A True Story* (P–I)

Katz, William Loren, *Black Women of the Old West* (I)

Klausner, Janet, *Sequoyah's Gift: A Portrait of the Cherokee Leader* (I–A)

Marrin, Albert, *Sitting Bull and His World* (A)

Miller, Robert, *Buffalo Soldiers: The Story of Emanuel Stance* (P)

Monceaux, Morgan, and Ruth Katcher, *My Heroes, My People: African Americans and Native Americans in the West* (I)

Pelz, Ruth, *Black Heroes of the Wild West* (I)

San Souci, Robert D., *Kate Shelley: Bound for Legend* (P)

Schlissel, Lillian, *Black Frontiers: A History of African American Heroes in the Old West* (I)

Yates, Diana, *Chief Joseph: Thunder Rolling Down from the Mountains* (I)

Immigration, World War I, and the Great Depression

Blumberg, Rhoda, *Commodore Perry in the Land of the Shogun* (I–A)

Burleigh, Robert, *Flight: The Journey of Charles Lindberg* (P–I)

Fradin, Dennis Brindell, and Judith Bloom Fradin, *Ida B. Wells: Mother of the Civil Rights Movement* (I–A)

Freedman, Russell, *The Wright Brothers: How They Invented the Airplane* (I–A)

Fritz, Jean, *You Want Women to Vote, Lizzie Stanton?* (I)

Govenar, Alan, *Osceola: Memories of a Sharecropper's Daughter* (I)

Greenfield, Eloise, *Mary McLeod Bethune* (I)

Giblin, James Cross, *Charles A. Lindberg: A Human Hero* (A)

Kerby, Mona, *Amelia Earhart: Courage in the Sky* (I–A)

Kraft, Betsy Harvey, *Mother Jones: One Woman's Fight for Labor* (I–A)

Lauber, Patricia, *Lost Star: The Story of Amelia Earhart* (I–A)

Levi, Steven C., *Cowboys of the Sky: The Story of Alaska's Bush Pilots* (I)

McKissack, Patricia, *Mary McLeod Bethune* (I)

World War II

Adler, David, *A Picture Book of Eleanor Roosevelt* (P)

Besson, Jean-Louis, *October 45: Childhood Memories of the War* (I)

Cooney, Barbara, *Eleanor* (P)

Faber, Doris, *Eleanor Roosevelt: First Lady of the World* (I–A)

Freedman, Russell, *Eleanor Roosevelt: A Life of Discovery* (A)

_____, *Franklin Delano Roosevelt* (A)

Gold, Alison Leslie, *A Special Fate: Chiune Sugihara, Hero of the Holocaust* (A)

Greenfeld, Howard, *The Hidden Children* (I–A)

Lobel, Anita, *No Pretty Pictures* (A)

Marrin, Albert, *Hitler* (A)

Pressler, Mirjam, *Anne Frank: A Hidden Life* (A)

Reiss, Johanna, *The Journey Back* (I–A)

_____, *The Upstairs Room* (I–A)

Rosenberg, Maxine B., *Hiding to Survive: Fourteen Jewish Children and the Gentiles Who Rescued Them from the Holocaust* (I–A)

Uchida, Yoshiko, *The Invisible Thread* (A)

Van der Rol, Ruud, and Rian Verhoeven, *Anne Frank: Beyond the Diary* (I)

The 1950s to the Present

Bray, Rosemary L., *Martin Luther King* (I)

Coleman, Evelyn, *The Riches of Oseola McCarty* (I)

Coles, Robert, *The Story of Ruby Bridges* (I)

Demi, *The Dalai Lama: A Biography of the Tibetan Spiritual and Political Leader* (P)

Filipovic, Zlata, *Zlata's Diary: A Child's Life in Sarajevo* (A)

Harrison, Barbara, and Daniel Terris, *A Twilight Struggle: The Life of John Fitzgerald Kennedy* (A)

Haskins, James, *Thurgood Marshall: A Life for Justice* (I–A)

Hoyt-Goldsmith, Diane, *Hoany Anh: A Vietnamese-American Boy* (I)

_____, *Pueblo Storyteller* (I)

Jaffe, Nina, *A Voice for the People: The Life and Work of Harold Courtlander* (I)

Matthews, Tom. L., *Light Shining Through the Mist: A Photobiography of Dian Fossey* (I)

McKissack, Patricia C., *Jesse Jackson: A Biography* (I)

McMahon, Patricia, *Chi-Hoon: A Korean Girl* (I)

Medearis, Angela Shelf, *Dare to Dream: Coretta Scott King and the Civil Rights Movement* (I)

Meltzer, Milton, *Winnie Mandela: The Soul of South Africa* (A)

Mills, Judie, *Robert Kennedy* (A)

Myers, Walter Dean, *Malcolm X: By Any Means Necessary* (I–A)

_____, *Malcolm X: A Fire Burning Brightly* (I–A)

Ringgold, Faith, *My Dream of Martin Luther King* (P–I)

Siegel, Beatrice, *Marian Wright Edelman: The Making of a Crusader* (I)

Tillage, Leon Walter, *Leon's Story* (I)

Winner, David, *Desmond Tutu* (A)

Collective and Series Biographies

Archer, Jules, *Breaking Barriers: The Feminist Revolution from Susan B. Anthony to Margaret Sanger to Betty Friedan* (A)

Bland, Celia, *Peter MacDonald: Former Chairman of the Navajo Nation* (North American Indians of Achievement series) (I)

Bryant, Jennifer Fisher, *Louis Braille: Inventor* (Great Achievers: Lives of the Physically Challenged series) (I)

Aaseng, Nathan, *Black Inventors* (A)

Calvert, Patricia, *Great Lives: The American Frontier* (A)

Caras, Roger, *A World Full of Animals: The Roger Caras Story* (Great Naturalists series) (I)

Cedeno, Maria E., *Cesar Chavez: Labor Leader* (Hispanic Heritage series) (I)

Elish, Dan, *James Meredith and School Desegregation* (Gateway Civil Rights series) (I)

Gulotta, Charles, *Extraordinary Women in Politics* (Extraordinary People series) (I)

Krull, Katherine, *Lives of the Presidents: Fame, Shame (and What the Neighbors Thought)* (I)

_____, *Lives of Extraordinary Women: Rulers, Rebels (and What the Neighbors Thought)*

_____, *They Saw the Future: Oracles, Psychics, Scientists, Great Thinkers, and Pretty Good Guessers* (I)

Lazo, Caroline, *Elie Wiesel* (Peacemakers series) (I)

Lyons, Mary, *Starting Home: The Story of Horace Pippin, Painter* (African-American Artists and Artisans series) (I)

McKissack, Patricia, and Fredrick McKissack, *African-American Scientists* (Proud Heritage series) (I)

Pinkney, Andrea Davis, *Let It Shine: Stories of Black Women Freedom Fighters* (I–A)

Turner, Robyn Montana, *Georgia O'Keeffe* (Portraits of Women Artists for children series) (P–I)

Whitelaw, Nancy, *Mr. Civil Rights: The Story of Thurgood Marshall* (Notable Americans series) (I)

Yolen, Jane, *Letter from Phoenix Farm* (Meet the Author series) (P)

Scientists and Inventors

Fisher, Leonard Everett, *Alexander Graham Bell* (I)

_____, *Marie Curie* (I)

Fleischman, Paul, *Townsend's Warbler* (I–A)

Gherman, Beverly, *The Mysterious Rays of Dr. Rontgen* (P)

Lucas, Eileen, *Jane Goodall: Friend of the Chimps* (I)

Matthews, Tom L., *Always Inventing: A Photobiography of Alexander Graham Bell* (I)

St. George, Judith, *Dear Dr. Bell . . . Your Friend, Hellen Keller* (A)

Severance, John B., *Einstein: Visionary Scientist* (I)

Towle, Wendy, *The Real McCoy: The Life of an African-American Inventor* (P–I)

Ventura, Piero, *Darwin: Nature Reinterpreted* (I–A)

Wadsworth, Ginger, *Rachel Carson: Voice for the Earth* (I)

Artists and Artisans

Bonafoux, Pascal, *A Weekend with Rembrandt* (I)

Cech, John, *Jacques-Henri Lartigue: Boy with a Camera* (P–I)

Cummings, Pat, *Talking with Artists: Volumes One and Two* (I)

Everett, Gwen, *Li'l Sis and Uncle Willie: A Story Based on the Life and Paintings of William H. Johnson* (P)

Greenberg, Jan, and Sandra Jordan, *The American Eye: Eleven Artists of the Twentieth Century* (I–A)

Greenfeld, Howard, *Paul Gauguin* (A)

Krull, Kathleen, *Lives of the Artists: Masterpieces, Messes (and What the Neighbors Thought)* (I)

Le Tord, Bijou, *A Blue Butterfly: A Story About Claude Monet* (P)

Lyons, Mary E., *Master of Mahogany: Tom Day, Free Black Cabinetmaker* (I)

_____, *Stitching Stars: The Story Quilts of Harriet Powers* (I)

Oneal, Zibby, *Grandma Moses: Painter of Rural America* (I–A)

Raboff, Ernest, *Albrecht Durer* (I–A)

_____, *Michelangelo* (I–A)

Rodari, Florian, *A Weekend with Picasso* (I)

Sills, Leslie, *Visions: Stories About Women Artists* (P)

Skira-Venturi, Rosabianca, *A Weekend with van Gogh* (I)

Turner, Robyn, *Mary Cassatt* (P–I)

Walker, Lou Ann, *Roy Lichtenstein: The Artist at Work* (I)

Winter, Jeanette, *Diego* (P)

Musicians and Dancers

Ferris, Jeri, *What I Had Was Singing: The Story of Marian Anderson* (I)

Freedman, Russell, *Martha Graham: A Dancer's Life* (A)

Jones, Hettie, *Big Star Fallin' Mama: Five Women in Black Music* (A)

Kamen, Gloria, *Hidden Music: The Life of Fanny Mendelssohn* (I)

Krull, Kathleen, *Lives of the Musicians: Good Times, Bad Times (and What the Neighbors Thought)* (I)

Medearis, Angela Shelf, *Little Louis and the Jazz Band: The Story of Louis "Satchmo" Armstrong* (I)

McKissack, Patricia, *Marian Anderson: A Great Singer* (P–I)

Nichol, Barbara, *Beethoven Lives Upstairs* (P)

Pinkney, Andrea Davis, *Alvin Ailey* (I)

_____, *Duke Ellington* (I)

Reich, Susanna, *Clara Schumann: Piano Virtuoso* (I)

Schroeder, Alan, *Satchmo's Blues* (P–I)

Tallchief, Maria, *Tallchief: America's Prima Ballerina* (I)

Winter, Jeanette, *Sebastian: A Book About Bach* (P)

Writers

Cooper, Floyd, *Coming Home: From the Life of Langston Hughes* (I)

Herrera, Juan Felipe, *The Upside Down Boy/El Nino de Cabeza* (P)

Krull, Kathleen, *Lives of the Writers: Comedies, Tragedies (and What the Neighbors Thought)* (I)

Lasky, Kathryn, *A Brilliant Streak: The Making of Mark Twain* (I)

Lowry, Lois, *Looking Back: A Book of Memories* (I)

Lyons, Mary E., *Keeping Secrets: The Girlhood Diaries of Seven Women Writers* (A)

_____, *Sorrow's Kitchen: The Life and Folklore of Zora Neale Hurston* (I–A)

Meltzer, Milton, *Langston Hughes: An Illustrated Edition* (A)

Miller, William, *Zora Hurston and the Chinaberry Tree* (P)

Murphy, Jim, *Into the Deep Forest with Henry David Thoreau* (I)

_____, *Pick and Shovel Poet: The Journeys of Pascal D'Angelo* (I–A)

Reef, Catherine, *Walt Whitman* (I–A)

Rylant, Cynthia, *But I'll Be Back Again* (I)

Shapiro, Miles, *Maya Angelou* (I)

Spinelli, Jerry, *Knots in My Yo-Yo String: The Autobiography of a Kid* (I)

Stanley, Diane, and Peter Vennema, *Bard of Avon: The Story of William Shakespeare* (I)

_____, *Charles Dickens: The Man Who Had Great Expectations* (I)

Walker, Alice, *Langston Hughes, American Poet* (A)

Wallner, Alexandra, *Laura Ingalls Wilder* (P)

Younger, Barbara, *Purple Mountain Majesties: The Story of Katharine Lee Bates and "America the Beautiful"* (P)

Sports

Adler, David, *Jackie Robinson: He Was the First* (P)

_____, *A Picture Book of Jesse Owens* (P)

Goedicke, Christopher J., *The Wind Warrior: The Training of a Karate Champion* (I)

Golenbock, Peter, *Teammates* (P–I)

Greenberg, Keith Elliot, *Magic Johnson: Champion with a Cause* (I)

Krull, Kathleen, *Wilma Unlimited: How Wilma Rudolph Became the World's Fastest Woman* (P–I)

Lipsyte, Robert, *Joe Louis: A Champ for All America* (A)

_____, *Michael Jordan* (I–A)

Littlefield, Bill, *Champions: Stories of Ten Remarkable Athletes* (I–A)

Macht, Norman L., *Christy Mathewson* (I)

Myers, Walter Dean, *The Greatest: Muhammad Ali*

Walker, Paul Robert, *Pride of Puerto Rico: The Life of Roberto Clemente* (I)

Weissberg, Ted, *Arthur Ashe* (A)

Nonfiction

Do iguanas eat frogs? The red-eyed tree frog does not wait to find out.

—JOY COWLEY, RED-EYED TREE FROG

EIGHTEEN KINDERGARTEN CHILDREN SIT, RAPT, AS THEIR TEACHER, Karen, reads Joy Cowley's **Red-Eyed Tree Frog** (N–P) aloud. They have been studying the natural world in science, and Karen has used that to structure her reading and writing times as well, providing a myriad of books, fiction and nonfiction, that allow her students to learn about various habitats and animals. The children are especially interested in the rain forest, with its exotic creatures, including the red-eyed tree frog with its brilliant colors and diminutive size. Cowley's book is perfect for read-aloud time. It has a brief but engaging text, fabulous close-up photographs, and high drama: Will the frog live through another harrowing day? The children are captivated by this nonfiction book, as they have been by others that Karen has shared with them.

Joy Cowley's text and Nic Bishop's photographs combine to make **Red-Eyed Tree Frog** *an engaging, exciting work of nonfiction for young readers.*

Defining Nonfiction

Children have a desire to *know,* and when they discover that books are a place to find answers, they embark on a journey of lifelong learning. They turn to nonfiction literature to feed their hunger for facts, ideas, and concepts. The term *nonfiction* describes books of information and fact. Nonfiction, or informational, books are distinguished from fiction by their emphasis. Both may tell a story and both may include fact. In nonfiction, the facts and concepts are uppermost, with storytelling perhaps used as an expressive technique; in fiction, the story is uppermost, with facts sometimes used to support it.

The nonfiction now being published has a direct appeal to the young reader. Writers select topics that interest children, and many of the topics they select fit nicely into an existing curriculum. Nonfiction today includes books with spacious, well-designed pages, and intriguing illustrations that enhance and extend the reader's understanding of the topic. The texts present writing at its best: interesting language used in varied ways. Metaphor and descriptive language allow readers to link what they are reading about with what they already know.

The structure of nonfiction varies widely. Some books, like Joanna Cole's popular **Magic School Bus** series (I), use fantasy devices and parallel texts to interest young readers. Others, such as Laurence Pringle's *An Extraordinary Life: The Story of a Monarch Butterfly* (I), winner of the 1998 Orbis Pictus Award, use a narrative frame to impart information. Lisa Westberg Peters's *The Sun, the Wind, and the Rain* (P) explores geology with young readers and includes a parallel narrative thread in which a young girl builds a sand castle on the beach. In *Dear Rebecca, Winter Is Here* (P), Jean Craighead George presents her information about the changing seasons in a letter from a grandmother to her granddaughter.

Because of these variations, nonfiction is sometimes difficult to distinguish from fiction. Indeed, children often wonder how books with talking dinosaurs or magic school buses can be called nonfiction. The key lies in the emphasis of the writer, which in nonfiction should be on the facts and concepts being presented. It is these that must be truthful, verifiable, and understandable.

Nonfiction available today is appealing, attractive, and abundant. Most collections in elementary school libraries and in the children's sections of public libraries are 60 to 70 percent nonfiction—a surprise to most people. Even so, nonfiction writers complain, justifiably, that their work receives less attention than fiction. The Orbis Pictus Award (presented annually since 1990 by the National Council of Teachers of English to the most outstanding work of nonfiction published in the preceding year) and the Boston Globe-Horn Book Award for nonfiction are attempts to balance the amount of attention, as is the Sibert Award. The American Library Association gave the first Sibert Award for nonfiction in 2001, honoring Marc Aronson's witty and informative *Sir Walter Ralegh and the Quest for El Dorado.*

Nonfiction In Children's Lives

Adults selecting books for children often give short shrift to nonfiction, assuming that stories and poetry are more appealing or are in some way superior to nonfiction. They aren't. Many children prefer nonfiction to fiction; their insatiable curiosity about the world is fueled by nonfiction books. As they mature, many young readers continue to prefer nonfiction, wanting to read to learn. When nonfiction books are well written, children learn not only about the topic being considered but also about good expository writing. And when the topics in nonfiction match children's interests, reading nonfiction is fun, just as reading stories is fun.

You probably remember only isolated fragments of information from your elementary school textbooks. You probably remember more from projects you associated with a special interest or had to research and develop for a presentation, a science fair, or a demonstration—perhaps a project like the one in Teaching Idea 10.1. We learn best when our emotions are involved and when we are actively engaged, and we learn more readily when we pursue our own—rather than someone else's—interests. We remember facts better when they are integrated into our conception of reality, and we often learn and retain them longer when they are part of a meaningful experience. Gardner (1965) stresses the interdependence of our intellectual and emotional life, stating:

> The basis of learning is emotion. . . . There is no intellectual interest which does not spring from the need to satisfy feelings. . . . Not only is learning fostered by the need to satisfy feelings but feelings themselves are relieved and helped by learning. (p. 34)

We learn best by fitting new information into a coherent frame or schema. Nonfiction makes information available to children in ways that facilitate the creation of meaningful category systems. The especially fine informational books published today illuminate children's path. When children seek out information for themselves, identify what is relevant, and use it for meaningful goals, they become more efficient at storing and retrieving facts. Furthermore, trade books are readily available on virtually any topic and for almost any level of understanding. This rich and vast array of materials generates an interest and excitement that encourages children to find out about their world.

Teaching Idea 10✳1

Make an Alphabet Book on the Topic of Study

Every discipline, topic, or subject area has a vocabulary of its own. In order to read and comprehend text, students exploring a new area need to become familiar with its vocabulary. One way to develop meaning for vocabulary related to a particular topic is to create an ABC book. This can be done as an individual or group project. For example, if the class is studying South America, each person in a group could be responsible for a different country. If students are studying animals, each person or group could be responsible for one class of animals or one animal within a class.

To create a topical ABC book, follow these guidelines:

1. List all the new words related to the topic under study.
2. Create an alphabet book that has a letter on each page.
3. On each page, list the words that begin with that letter.
4. Draw pictures, list synonyms, and write definitions for each word. Use each word in a sentence that explains something about the topic.
5. Read the book to peers or younger students.
6. Display the handmade books in the classroom.

Criteria For Evaluating Nonfiction

Each year, committees of subject area specialists and children's literature specialists select the outstanding examples of books in their respective disciplines. The work, coordinated by the Children's Book Council, involves the National Science Teachers Association, the National Council of Social Studies, the International Reading Association, and the National Council of Teachers of English. A list of outstanding books that can enhance teaching and learning in each discipline is published in the professional journals of each organization. These lists help teachers select quality trade books for their curriculum.

The science committee, for example, evaluates books using three criteria: (1) The book must be accurate and readable; (2) its format and illustrations must be pleasing; and (3) information must be consistent with current scientific knowledge. In areas where differences occur, a book should present different points of view, and information should not be distorted by personal biases or values. Facts

and theories must be clearly distinguished; generalizations must be supported by facts, and significant facts must not be omitted. If experiments are a feature of a book, the science committee considers whether they lead to an understanding of basic principles. Moreover, experiments discussed in the books must be appropriate for the reader's age group and must be both feasible and safe. The committee eschews anthropomorphized animals and plants. It also rejects books that are racist or sexist, or that extol violence.

The Orbis Pictus Award for Outstanding Nonfiction for Children is an award for nonfiction of all types, and thus the criteria are broad enough to be applicable to books from varied disciplines. The award committee considers four criteria: accuracy, organization, design, and style. The following discussion expands on those criteria. Figure 10.1 contains a checklist of general criteria for evaluating all types of nonfiction.

Figure 10✳1

Checklist for Evaluating Nonfiction

Accuracy

✳ Are facts current and complete, with a balance of fact and theory? Are differing viewpoints represented when appropriate?

✳ Is the scope appropriate to the audience and the subject?

✳ Are the author's qualifications and resources apparent?

Organization

✳ Is there a logical development of ideas and a clear sequence of ideas? Are they presented in an understandable and appropriate fashion?

✳ Are interrelationships between facts and between facts and theories indicated?

Design

✳ Is the format of the book attractive and reader-friendly, with appropriate illustrations that are strategically placed?

✳ Do the illustrations illuminate the facts and concepts?

Style

✳ Is the writing interesting, revealing the author's enthusiasm about the subject?

✳ Is the terminology appropriate? Does the writer use rich language that stimulates a reader's curiosity?

ACCURACY

The criterion of accuracy comprises several facets. First, the facts presented must be current and complete, with a balance between fact and theory, and authenticity of detail. If applicable, varying points of view should be presented. Stereotypes should be avoided. The scope of the book should be appropriate to the target audience and to the topic being presented. The author's qualifications should be adequate and should be stated in reference lists, acknowledgements, and notes describing the research process.

In excellent nonfiction, facts and theories are clearly distinguished. Highly qualified writers state clearly and succinctly what is known and what is conjectured; they do not mislead by stating as fact what is still a theory or hypothesis. Careful writers use qualifying phrases when they are tentative about the information. For example, some will use phrases like "many scientists (or historians) believe," "prob-ably could not," "we think that," and "the evidence to date suggests" to indicate that experts in the field are not certain about all things. Good writers also describe the changing status of information about a topic.

In **Wolves** (I), Seymour Simon lets his readers know what is fact and what is supposition: "Wolves make all kinds of sounds besides howling; they bark, growl, whine, and squeak. Barking seems to be a warning when a wolf is surprised at its den. Growling is common among pups when they play." A careful reader realizes that scientists suppose that barking serves as a warning, but know that pups growl when they play.

Nonfiction writers with integrity acknowledge other opinions of value; they present different views about their topic, discussing their strengths and weaknesses. For example, many books about dinosaurs present differing ideas about the extinction of the dinosaurs. Books about evolution acknowledge the controversy that this theory generates to this day.

Profile ☆ Seymour Simon

© William Gottlieb

Seymour Simon has written more than 100 science books for young readers since the late 1960s. Although the majority of his books are nonfiction, he is also the author of the popular **Einstein Anderson** fiction series, published in the early 1980s. Simon started writing while teaching in the New York City public schools, beginning with articles for *Scholastic* magazine. His first book, **Animals in Field and Laboratory,** was published in 1968.

One of his early, highly acclaimed books, **The Paper Airplane Book,** explains the principles of aerodynamics by asking readers to think about why certain things occur and encouraging them to think like scientists. Simon explains, "It's questions like these that occur to me and that have been asked of me by children that make me want to write science books. The books I write are full of such questions. Sometimes I'll provide an answer, but more often I'll suggest an activity or an experiment that will let a child answer a question by trying it out."

Simon left teaching in 1979 to write on a full-time basis. When he did so, his books became less science-oriented. "What I really wanted was to write the kind of books that a kid might pick up in a library or in a bookstore, and I found that I needed more time to do that kind of book," he explains.

The subjects of his books range from oceanography to birds, from air to food, from dinosaurs to computers. He has written several series, among them the **Discovering** series, including *Discovering What Puppies Do* (1977), the **Let's Try It Out** series, including *Let's Try It Out: About Your Heart* (1974), and the **Einstein Anderson** series, including *Einstein Anderson Lights up the Sky* (1982).

His **Space Photos** series includes *Jupiter, Saturn, Mars, Uranus, Neptune, Galaxies, Mercury,* and *Venus.* This series is marked by beautiful photographs and clear, lucid text that intrigue young readers by explaining interesting, and sometimes quite complex, concepts. These books are being updated, and *Destination: Mars* and *Destination: Jupiter* are recent releases. A new series about weather, which includes *Spring Across America,* continues Simon's outstanding contributions to the field of science trade books for children.

For these contributions, Simon has won awards from the National Science Teachers Association and Children's Book Council for outstanding science books for children. He won the Best Children's Science Book of the Year Award from the New York Academy of Sciences for *Icebergs and Glaciers* (1987), and the Eva L. Gordon Award from the American Nature Society for his contributions to children's science literature.

Seymour Simon was born in 1931 and is married with two grown sons. He lives in Great Neck, New York, where he enjoys reading history and poetry, collecting books and art, playing chess and tennis, traveling, listening to music, and exploring computers.

© Joe McDonald

Beautiful photography illustrates the way wolves live in the wild in Seymour Simon's **Wolves***.*

The appropriateness of the scope of a book is related to its target audience. What might be said about a topic for very young children is quite different from what might be said about the same topic for older children. For example, in Laurence Pringle's **Everybody Has a Bellybutton** (N–P), the topic of human reproduction is explored in a manner that is appropriate for young children. The information presented is accurate, but the level of detail is minimal in both text and illustration.

Seymour Simon's **Gorillas** (P) conveys information about these creatures in ways that young children can understand. He combines stunning photographs with a text that uses comparisons with humans that make sense to children.

When evaluating accuracy in nonfiction, consider the author's expertise, the sources the author used, the presentation of fact and theory, and the acknowledgment of alternate viewpoints, as appropriate to the scope of the book.

ORGANIZATION

The organization of a book refers to the logical development of the content. Ideas should be presented according to a clear sequence and pattern that informs the structure of the text. Interrelationships among facts or events should be clearly indicated.

How content is organized and presented affects the overall value of a piece of nonfiction. Good informational books are clearly organized. A brief look through a piece of nonfiction reveals how the content of a book is arranged. Does it illuminate concepts and build understanding? Does it have a table of contents to show readers what it contains? Some books have additional features such as a glossary, a subject and/or author index, a bibliography for further

reading, and appendixes with further information. Readers are able to retrieve information or build on the information presented in the book by going to other sources.

The unity of a book reflects the relations among the ideas in the text. The degree of unity hinges on how the author has organized ideas to convey information. Careful, logical development of concepts is essential. Ideas should follow a logical pattern, going, for example, from simple to complex or general to specific. Well-organized texts also make use of helpful transitions that guide the reader from one idea to the next. In **Blizzard! The Storm That Changed America** (A), Jim Murphy describes the blizzard of 1888 through the experiences of various real people who are representative of the demographics of the time and place. These individual stories stand alone, but strong tie-ins between events and connections between these events and the broader historical context create a story that is also a strong depiction of the political and social conditions of the time.

A book's organization, of course, should be related to its intended audience. Responsible writers respect their readers and know that children, no matter what their age, can understand important ideas and concepts if they are presented clearly, in an organized fashion. Look for books that have a logical development, with a clear sequence of ideas organized in an identifiable pattern.

DESIGN

The design of an excellent nonfiction book should be attractive, with illustrations that complement the text. These illustrations should be of an appropriate media and format to support and extend the ideas and concepts developed in the text. Further, this illustrative material should be appropriately placed.

Nonfiction books should be as appealing in layout and design as fiction books. As information is presented it can be supported by photographs, diagrams, maps, sketches, graphs, or other visual support. The illustrations help readers visualize the information contained in the text. Effective layout means that illustrations appear in close proximity to the text they illuminate, headings and subheadings are clearly presented, and the amount of text and illustration on a page does not make the page appear crowded or overwhelming. Russell Freedman's **Give Me Liberty! The Story of the Declaration of Independence** (A) is beautifully designed, with a lucid text complemented by carefully selected period art.

Many design variations are available today. The **Eyewitness** series and the **Visual Timeline** series use clear color photographs, small explanatory notes for each photograph, a brief introduction, and drawings on each double-page spread devoted to the topics in the book. For example, **Butterfly and Moth** (I–A) has sections on "caterpillar to pupa," "the pupa stage," and "an emerging butterfly." Far from being crowded or busy, each page is laid out so that eager

Jim Murphy's gripping account of a nineteenth-century storm makes it seem as if it's happening today.

readers are first drawn to the page by the exquisite photographs, and then intrigued by the well-written information.

Sandra Markle's **Outside and Inside Dinosaurs** (P) uses extraordinary photographs and illustrations, including micrographs, X-ray images, and computer-generated models, to frame a discussion of how dinosaur experts garner information about these extinct organisms.

Look for books in which the design enhances the presentation of information and is visually appealing.

STYLE

A work of nonfiction is also judged by style, or how the information is presented. The writing should be interesting and stimulating. It should reveal the author's enthusiasm for the subject. Appropriate terminology and rich language should generate curiosity and wonder in young readers.

Even when dealing with hard facts, graceful language and a fresh vision are important components of excellent literature. Descriptive words used in interesting yet precise ways are a mark of good nonfiction. The tone of a book reveals the thrust and significance of an author's work as well as the author's relationship to the subject. Milton Meltzer, an outstanding biographer and historian, puts it this way:

> What literary distinction, if any, does the book have? And here I do not mean the striking choice of word or image but the personal style revealed. I ask whether the writer's personal voice is heard in the book. In the writer who cares, there is a pressure of feeling which emerges in the rhythm of the sentences, in the choice of details, in the color of the language. Style in this sense is not a trick of rhetoric or a decorative daub; it is a quality of vision. It cannot be separated from the author's character because the tone of voice in which the book is written expresses how a human being thinks and feels. If the writer is indifferent, bored, stupid, or mechanical, it will show in the work. (1976, pp. 21–22)

A nonfiction book's literary value depends in large part on how much passion an author brings to a work. Laurence Pringle acknowledges that his passions enter his work:

> When I'm writing, I write about my values and feelings. Many people ask what nonfiction has to do with feelings. If you want feelings, they would say, turn to fiction. But I don't think that has to be true. (1986, p. 26)

Sophie Webb's ***My Season with Penguins: An Antarctic Journal*** (P–I) conveys Webb's delight in penguins through lively text and appealing watercolor illustrations. It also presents a model of a field-based research journal, complete with Webb's humorous commentary on life in the field.

Many nonfiction writers directly address their audience, using the pronoun *you* to draw readers into the book. Joanne Ryder asks readers to become a snail in ***The Snail's Spell*** (P). Other authors offer readers ideas for doing their own experiments or research, or challenge them to evaluate ideas and arguments based on facts presented. This technique creates active readers. Look for books that contain language that both conveys and generates excitement about the subject.

A CLOSE LOOK AT

Shipwreck at the Bottom of the World

Breathless excitement, intriguing characters, a captivating style, and a conflict with nature that almost defies belief make Jennifer Armstrong's ***Shipwreck at the Bottom of the World: The Extraordinary True Story of Shackleton and the Endurance*** (I) an outstanding work of nonfiction. Winner of the 1999 Orbis Pictus Award, this book exemplifies the standards of accuracy, organization, design, and style.

Accuracy

Even a cursory glance at the book indicates its accuracy and integrity. The cover shows a photo of the Shackleton expedition team pulling a boat across the ice. The title page, with its photo of the *Endurance* as it is being crushed by the ice, along with a subsequent photograph and list of the crew members, reproductions of the original plans of the *Endurance*, and maps of the expedition, entices readers into continuing on to the intriguing first chapter, which invokes the setting: the "most hostile place on earth." A glance at the end material reveals the acknowledgments, an extensive bibliography, and an index. Clearly, Armstrong has done her research, and this becomes even more apparent as one reads the text. Interesting, intriguing details pervade the story; the extensive preparations involved in preparing for and then conducting the expedition are clear, as is their importance to the success of the expedition.

Organization

The story begins at the end, with the author informing the reader that "in 1915 a British crew of twenty-eight men was stranded [in the most hostile place on earth], with no ship and no way to contact the outside world. They all survived" (p. 1). With the setting, conflict, and resolution stated, Armstrong moves, appropriately enough, to the planning stages of the expedition, introducing Sir Ernest Henry Shackleton himself. Subsequent chapters unfold sequentially, each steeped in detail and enhanced by photographs of the actual expedition, which were taken by one of the members of the party. The book ends with an epilogue that recounts the death of Shackleton in 1922, when he was on his way to the Antarctic.

Design

The design is superb. Even the title page, with its stark white background and sepia photograph, speaks of the cold and harsh landscape. The title, printed at the bottom of the cover, reinforces the location—the bottom of the world. Latitude and longitude lines grace the oversized white borders of the spacious pages, and the liberal use of archival photographs illustrate both the character of the men and the conflict that they endured.

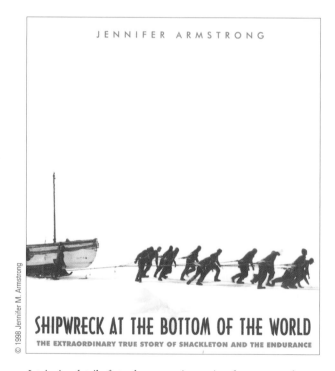

Intriguing details, factual accuracy, interesting characters, and a monumental conflict with nature make this story of the Shackleton expedition to Antarctica one that most book lovers read without stopping!

Style

Armstrong's writing is superb, keeping readers on the edge of their seats even though they know from the beginning that the outcome is a happy one. Details abound; the ice mustaches, the stink of rotting whales, the names of the sled dogs and how their "dogloos" looked, what the men ate, their sanitary conditions, and their entertainment are all part of the story Armstrong tells. Her tone is clearly admiring; Shackleton and his crew were brave, resourceful, and indomitable. Armstrong makes this clear without exaggeration; we also see their doubts, boredom, and peccadilloes. Concurrently, she maintains a constant movement forward, with the interdependence of the character of Shackleton and the conflict with nature driving the plot inexorably toward its exciting conclusion.

Nonfiction Across the Curriculum

So many wonderful books are available today that children can explore almost any topic that interests them using nonfiction trade books. Here we discuss nonfiction (excluding biography) that presents information about topics in science, social studies, mathematics, language study, and the fine arts.

SCIENCE

Science, as any other discipline, evolves over time, and books for children reflect the changes in the discipline. For example, books about environmental issues began to increase in number about 15 years ago, as environmental issues became important. As politicians and the public began to pay attention to environmental issues, the numbers of books about these issues decreased. Advances in science and technology also affect children's books.

Seymour Simon's wonderful series about the solar system, which includes **Mercury** and **Venus** (both I), is illustrated by stunning photographs taken during the many explorations of space that have occurred in the past several years. Patricia Lauber's **Seeing Earth from Space** (A) uses NASA photographs in conjunction with a well-written text to explain satellite photography and make a statement about taking care of our earth. The photographs are absolutely essential—no other kind of illustration would suit this topic—and they would not have been possible 20 years ago.

*This European weather satellite picture makes it obvious why our first astronauts called Earth "a big blue marble." The perspective from outer space helps students realize the interdependence of nations, the need for environmental protection, and the fragility of our planet. (**Seeing Earth from Space** by Patricia Lauber.)*

© NASA

Some books about timely topics such as space exploration have to be revised in light of new information. Seymour Simon's **Destination: Mars** (I), a revision of his 1987 **Mars,** became necessary because of recent exploration of and thinking about the red planet. Other books introduce entirely new topics, such as Franklin Branley's new addition to the **Let's-Read-and-Find-Out** series, **The International Space Station** (P).

Other science topics, such as plants, animals and their habitats, and dinosaurs, have remained popular across the years. As what we know changes, so, too, the books change to incorporate new information, yet the topics seem timeless. For example, a number of books about dinosaurs have been popular for years. Yet new dinosaur books continue to be written, such as Douglas Henderson's **Asteroid Impact** (I), Sandra Markle's **Outside and Inside Dinosaurs** (P), and Nic Bishop's **Digging for Bird-Dinosaurs: An Expedition to Madagascar** (I). It seems that some topics will never go out of favor as children continue to be intrigued by them.

A list of outstanding science trade books can be obtained from the Children's Book Council and is also published every March in *Science and Children,* a journal of the National Science Teachers Association for elementary and middle school teachers. Other journals, such as *The Reading Teacher, Language Arts,* and *The Horn Book Magazine,* regularly review books that treat science topics. The Booklist at the end of this chapter contains some titles of interesting books appropriate for a science curriculum. There are many more available.

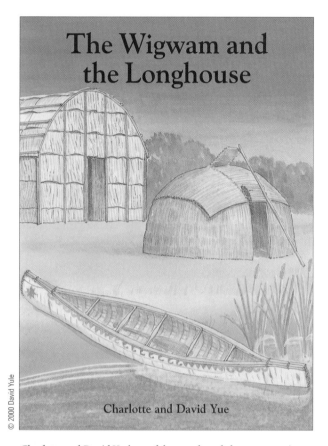

The Wigwam and the Longhouse

Charlotte and David Yue

Charlotte and David Yue's careful research and clear presentations make their books both accurate and interesting.

SOCIAL STUDIES

Just as in science, the content of social studies evolves as changes in the world result in new configurations of countries and people. New communications technology makes the world seem much smaller than it used to be and increases our interest in other people and places. Children have more books than ever to select from as they pursue their interests in the past and present.

In addition to the many fine biographies and works of historical fiction available, many nonfiction books cover topics such as geography and maps, life in the past, and the social structures and customs of various cultures. Children are quite naturally interested in who they are and where they come from; this natural curiosity and openness to people makes them receptive to books that explore the global community, past and present.

American history is presented from fresh perspectives in books such as Tom Feelings's **The Middle Passage: White Ships/Black Cargo** (I–A), and Patricia C. McKissack and Fredrick L. McKissack's **Christmas in the Big House, Christmas in the Quarters** (I). Charlotte and David Yue's **The Wigwam and the Longhouse** (I) is a chronicle of the

daily lives of the Woodlands Indians as they lived before the Europeans arrived in North America. The book ends with a description of what happened to these native people, and a brief summary of how some of them live today. The extensive bibliography and index add to the usefulness of this book. The Yues also collaborated on two other notable books, **The Igloo** and **The Pueblo** (both I).

Seemingly mundane topics are given depth and breadth in good nonfiction. Sylvia A. Johnson's **Mapping the World** (I) takes a historical and cultural perspective on maps and mapping. Rather than looking at maps as tools for getting from one place to another, Johnson sees them as artifacts that tell about the cultures that produced them. By taking a historical perspective, Johnson allows readers to understand how differences in scientific knowledge and in knowledge of the world are reflected in maps that span the course of time. By ending with a discussion of geography information systems (a computer mapping system) Johnson is able to invite her readers to join with Ptolemy and Mercator as cartographers of the world as they know it.

Current issues find their way into children's books, as Judith St. George's **So You Want to Be President?** (P–I) aptly demonstrates. David Small's funny cartoon-style illustra-

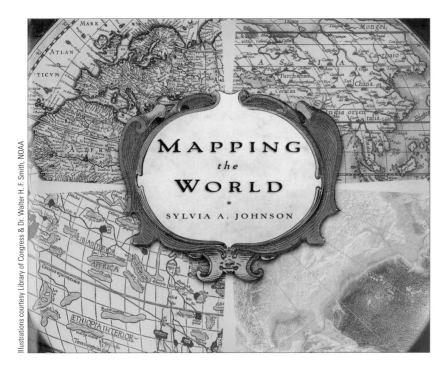

Reproductions of maps from across the ages create the visual appeal of this intriguing book.

tions perfectly match the witty text in which St. George imparts information about the office, offers humorous tidbits, and makes some forthright political statements.

In the Booklist at the end of this chapter, we list some books that indicate the breadth of choice that exists for the social studies teacher today. Other books that focus on various cultures are discussed in Chapter 11. Further, a list of Notable Trade Books in Social Studies is available from the Children's Book Council and is also published in the April/May issue of the journal *Social Education.*

MATHEMATICS

Fewer nonfiction books support a study of mathematics than support either science or social studies, although growing numbers are published each year. Mathematics programs today reflect a philosophy in which fiction and nonfiction literature fit naturally. Earlier mathematics instruction involved practicing isolated skills endlessly, calculating answers, memorizing combinations of numerals, and watching for a place to apply memorized routines. Today, we present mathematical problems in context, draw upon children's background knowledge to solve them, and model strategies for alternate ways to solve problems.

Today, many mathematics lessons begin with a story—a story with a problem that can be solved through a mathematical process. Teachers invite children to propose as many different strategies as possible to try to solve the problem. Together, they apply each strategy and evaluate its accuracy and efficiency. They learn that there are alternative ways to come up with the right answer. Stories that are structured around numbers and counting, such as Pat Hutchins's **The Doorbell Rang** (P), are especially useful for primary teachers who want to link mathematics and reading.

There are also many beautiful counting books and books that allow children to practice numeral recognition, such as Steve Jenkins's **Numbers in the City** (P). These books encourage children to develop their visual skills as they look for numerals or count items on the artistically beautiful pages.

Other books explain mathematical concepts, such as Bruce McMillan's **Eating Fractions** (P–I). McMillan illustrates fractions with mouth-watering photographs of children sharing—and eating—food. The concept of one-fourth is understandable when it means the difference between a whole pizza and only part of one!

Jon Scieszka's **Math Curse** (I), illustrated by Lane Smith, is a wonderfully funny book that underscores how we use mathematics in our daily lives and presents interesting mathematical puzzles for children to figure out. The outrageous humor in the book is so infectious that children enthusiastically engage in the mental arithmetic the book calls for.

The journal *Teaching Children Mathematics* reviews books that can be linked to mathematics instruction. The Booklist at the end of this chapter contains the titles of selected books for mathematics learning.

LANGUAGE STUDY

With writing and language study part of an integrated language arts curriculum, the need increases for children's books that explore language. Alphabet books, books about traditional parts of speech, histories of language, and books about writing are becoming more plentiful. Books such as these support the study of language, and, most importantly, support children's explorations of language as they are engaged in reading and writing.

Books like Brian Cleary's *Hairy, Scary, Ordinary: What Is an Adjective?* (P) help young readers understand the parts of speech. Ruth Heller is known for her brightly illustrated, eye-catching books about the parts of speech, such as *Mine, All Mine: A Book About Pronouns* (P–I). The rhyming text is surrounded by double-page illustrations visually depicting the pronouns. Heller's books give concrete and intriguing examples of what many students feel is boringly remote.

A series of books by Marvin Terban explore word play, such as *Guppies in Tuxedos: Funny Eponyms* (I–A). Jon Agee's books, such as *Elvis Lives! and Other Anagrams* (I) are also interesting to students exploring what we can do with the English language.

Studies of books and authors often accompany composition instruction. These studies work best if they transcend the usual biographical information to get at the essence of what writers do—write. Leonard Marcus does just that in a series of interviews with contemporary authors contained in *Author Talk: Conversations with Judy Blume, Bruce Brooks, Karen Cushman, Russell Freedman, Lee Bennett Hopkins, James Howe, Johanna Hurwitz, E. L. Konigsburg, Lois Lowry, Ann M. Martin, Nicholasa Mohr, Gary Paulsen, Jon Scieszka, Seymour Simon, and Laurence Yep* (I–A). Reading about childhood aspirations as well as details of these writers' contemporary lives helps make clear the human struggle inherent in writing.

In Chapters 13 and 14 we demonstrate how literature—both fiction and nonfiction—is a crucial component of a language arts program. In the Booklist at the end of this chapter we include a variety of books about language that indicate the breadth of materials available. Other books on this topic can be found by consulting any subject-organized reference source.

THE ARTS

In addition to the many fine biographies of musicians and artists listed in Chapter 9, a variety of nonfiction books explore aspects of music and art. Just as science, social studies, mathematics, and language study are enhanced when well-written and beautifully designed books become a part of the curriculum, the study of art and music is made more vivid when accompanied by beautiful books. Several series books that explore elements of art, including Philip Yenawine's *Line* (P–I), and books that help readers learn to look at paintings, such as Gladys Blizzard's *Come Look with Me: Animals in Art* (I–A), are excellent resources for those interested in learning more about fine art. Jean S. Tucker introduces children to photography in *Come Look with Me: Discovering Photographs with Children* (I), another book in the **Come Look with Me** series.

The **Looking at Paintings** series by Peggy Roalf is organized around what a viewer sees in a painting. Two books in this series are *Children* and *Flowers* (both I). Each volume contains 19 full-color reproductions of paintings accompanied by a text that presents a history of the artist and information about technique and style.

The Painter's Eye: Learning to Look at Contemporary American Art (A) is a fascinating book that explains complicated concepts in an understandable fashion. Jan Greenberg and Sandra Jordan define and give examples of the elements of art and principles of design that artists use to create paintings. They also present the postwar American artists themselves through conversations, photographs, and brief anecdotes about their childhoods and their work. The text begins with a useful table of contents and includes brief biographies of the artists, a list and description of the paintings discussed, a glossary, bibliography, index, and suggestions for further reading. Greenberg and Jordan's *The Sculptor's Eye: Looking at Contemporary American Art* (A) is an excellent introduction to the concepts of contemporary sculpture.

A number of books explain different artistic processes and the creation of different products, inviting children to create collages, make paper, or design structures. Others explore objects like bridges and buildings as architectural art. David Carter and James Diaz's *The Elements of Pop-Up* (I) is much more than just a how-to manual on pop-ups. It combines clever paper engineering with lucid explanations to create a book that inspires mechanically minded readers to create their own pop-ups.

By using nonfiction books about art in conjunction with picture books that contain fine art, teachers can help children become visually literate. The Booklist at the end of this chapter lists some books about art that will open children's eyes.

Books about music also are becoming increasingly available. Many of these books look at instruments, their development, and how they work; others explore musical groups such as the band or the symphony. The **Eyewitness** book *Music* (I–A) contains a wealth of information about how music is made. Topics range from "seeing sound" to detailed presentations of how specific instruments make music, from the evolution of early instruments to today's electric synthesizers. The photographs and sketches that illustrate the various instruments help to clarify some of the complex information. Other books about music are listed in the Booklist at the end of this chapter.

The ELEMENTS of POP-UP

A Pop-Up Book for Aspiring Paper Engineers
By David A. Carter and James Diaz

A glossary of terms and instructions for creating a variety of pop-up devices are enhanced by actual examples that allow readers to see how these devices are constructed.

Other arts, such as theater and dance, are also subjects of nonfiction books for children. In *Dance* (P), Bill T. Jones and Susan Kuklin add few words to visually stunning photographs of Jones dancing. Aliki's *William Shakespeare and the Globe* (I) brings alive Shakespeare's life, times, and theater as she tells the story of how Sam Wanamaker's desire to build an accurate replica of the Globe Theatre results in our being able to imagine theater as it was in Elizabethan England.

Whether the subject is science or social studies, language, or the arts, many beautiful nonfiction children's books present more depth of information than can be contained within the pages of a textbook. The well-written texts of these books not only inform but also provide models of good expository prose. The illustrations illuminate concepts and visualize information, bringing life and vitality to the topic under scrutiny. Teachers should encourage students to use their own voices when they transfer this information to written reports, an idea that is discussed in Teaching Idea 10.2. With the many fine nonfiction books that are available, children can learn many things, including how to be critical consumers of information.

Teaching Idea 10 ☆ 2

Read First, Write Later

Teachers often discover that students' science and social studies reports sound all too much like the entries in their encyclopedias. This teaching idea will help students write in their own voice, use a variety of resources, and synthesize information instead of copying it from an encyclopedia.

Collect many resources on science and social studies topics for the classroom library. Keep in mind the following suggestions for enriching students' learning experience:

1. Ask your students to keep journals as they read.
2. Ask them to write down what they are learning and what they think about what they are learning. They can do this by using the left-hand side of each double-page spread for notes, and the right-hand side for comments.
3. At regular intervals, ask students to answer these questions in writing: "What do I know already?" "What do I want to learn?"
4. Ask students to explain to a classmate what they have learned and what they are still trying to find out.
5. Use picture books, concept books, and books of all genres to search for answers to student questions.
6. As they read for a purpose—to find out specific information—ask students to jot down notes about their discoveries.
7. When they have read widely, talked about their discoveries, and written about what they are learning and how they feel about it, then it is time to have them draft a report. Talk with them about the importance of writing it in their own voice.

Nonfiction in the Classroom

Children learn best to think, read, write, speak, and listen when instruction in all curriculum areas is integrated—when, for example, a teacher exploring plant life in a science lesson grasps the opportunity to relate the term *phototropism* to other words with the prefix *photo*. This kind of integration in instruction parallels the way children actually learn—not by seeing facts in isolation, but rather by seeing them as parts of a meaningful whole.

Teachers fashion learning activities that cut across the curriculum and that draw upon books of fiction, nonfiction, and poetry in ways that encourage children in an active search for meaning. We discuss integrated instruction in Chapters 13 and 14. Children can also learn a lot by working collaboratively, as suggested in Teaching Idea 10.3.

Reading for information is related to other language uses; it is part of the scheme of the total language system. Children do read to learn in assigned textbooks, but they read to learn with enthusiasm and excitement in specialized trade books of quality. Compared to a textbook, a trade book can reveal the point of view of the author more directly, focus on an individual or a topic with a sharper light, and present specialized information that often gives readers a fuller understanding. Trade books provide reading and learning opportunities for readers of all ages and skill levels. Textbooks, written with a generic grade-level student in mind, cannot. Trade books also provide the opportunity for greater depth of study as a single book offers the possibility of more information about individual topics than any textbook could hold. Excellent nonfiction provides many rich opportunities for learning.

Learning is more than the laying on of discrete areas of information; it requires an active response from students, an interpretation or reconstruction of new information in relation to what they already know. Instead of teaching a body of facts for students to memorize, our goal is to help students learn to think critically.

LEARNING TO READ CRITICALLY

Critical reading and thinking are basic to a lifetime of learning. The schemata we develop as we learn to read and read to learn influence all subsequent knowledge. Thinking readers, called critical readers, evaluate new information in light of what they already know, compare many sources instead of accepting only one point of view, and make judgments about what they read. They can discriminate fact from opinion. If one goal of education is to develop informed, thinking, participating citizens, then helping children learn to read critically is essential.

The skill of reading critically is invaluable. The child who believes that anything found in print is the truth—the whole truth—is at a disadvantage relative to one who has learned to check sources, compare reports, and evaluate. Children do not question what they read when they are given one textbook that is held up as embodying the final and complete truth on its subject. They do learn to question and evaluate as they read if we encourage them to make comparisons among different sources, including nonfiction trade books.

We can engender unquestioning respect for the authority of the textbook by the way we respond to students' questions. Replies such as "Look it up in the book" or "What does the book say?" may inadvertently teach students to pay abject homage to textbooks in general, at the expense of their own thinking power.

Developmental differences in children's ability to think critically are not so much a matter of kind as of degree. Long before they turn to information found in books, very young children can make comparisons: They can consider ideas such as who is taller, which coat is warmer, which cookie is bigger. Listening to stories or looking at books, children, young and old alike, can attend to details, make comparisons, and draw inferences with the help of their teacher and peers. Children of all ages can, and do, think critically, especially when encouraged.

Verifying Information

Children of all ages can verify information found in books by checking it against observations made in real life, as when children compare the information in Joanna Cole's *My New Kitten* (P) with what their own new kitten does.

Teaching Idea 10.3

Develop Class Experts

Programs that intend for students to become independent learners are based on practices that include students learning collaboratively. Projects involving nonfiction topics and trade books provide an excellent opportunity to implement these practices. The purpose of this teaching idea is to promote collaborative learning and wide reading in trade books, and to develop independent learners. Follow this procedure to help students become "experts" in specific areas of study.

1. Have students explore a new area of study by having them read widely in nonfiction trade books.

2. Have students select an area within the broader topic in which they would like to specialize. Groups or individuals should make a list of questions that they would like to answer.

3. Have students begin their research independently.

4. On a chart, list each participant's name and his or her chosen topic of specialization. (At the top of the chart, write "_____ is becoming an expert in _____ ."

When the chart is made public, students can help each other with their research. They can watch for resources a classmate might need, and they can work collaboratively to answer questions. They can share information and insights as they work toward group and individual goals.

After completing the work, each student will have enough information to be able to make a short presentation on the topic and declare himself or herself "an expert."

Older readers also will evaluate authors' statements in light of their own experiences. They assess an author's qualifications, look at the documentation provided, and critically evaluate the books they read, much as we suggest in Figure 10.1, the evaluation checklist at the beginning of this chapter.

Many books encourage the reader to adopt a critical stance based on observing, collecting, and analyzing data, drawing conclusions, making inferences, and testing hypotheses. Carol Lerner's ***Backyard Birds of Winter*** (I) suggests that readers attract and observe the birds she discusses. Books that draw the reader into observation and hypothesis testing help children develop an observant critical stance that spills over from books into daily life.

Comparing Sources

Children can also compare one book with others and decide which they prefer—and why. Teachers can also assist them in comparing genres, as suggested in Teaching Idea 10.4. The spontaneous remarks of children show how natural it is for them to make comparisons. They also illustrate how useful informational books in the curriculum can be for fostering growth in critical reading and thinking.

Students in advanced grades deal with topics, compare sources, and use more complex skills than do younger students. Sixth-grade students in Iowa were learning all they could about what the world was like when Columbus sailed to America. They consulted many books—including encyclopedias and biographies of Columbus—to find the information they needed. One of the first books they read was Betsy and Giulio Maestro's ***The Discovery of the Americas*** (I–A), which provides information about the early inhabitants of America and how they might have traveled there; it also includes the stories of many famous explorers of whom the students had never heard. Armed with some astonishing new information, the students read Piero Ventura's ***1492: The Year of the New World*** (I), an overview of the world in Europe and America. Many students went on to read ***The World in 1492*** (A), with sections by Jean Fritz, Katherine Paterson, Patricia McKissack, Margaret Mahy, and Jamake Highwater. This book presents a great deal of information about Europe, Asia, Africa, Australia, and the Americas, including photographs of varied artifacts from around the world. It is much more comprehensive than the Ventura or the Maestro book, and students quickly began to compare earlier information with what they found in ***The World in 1492,*** using it as their definitive source. They discussed the footnotes and detailed bibliography that are included as reasons for trusting the information they were discovering. These students were practicing critical reading, and their understanding of the impact of exploration and conquest was enriched and extended.

Summary

When children are given excellent nonfiction books to explore topics of interest, they learn a great deal about those topics. They learn more because the intriguing formats of nonfiction books make them intrinsically more interesting to read and because trade books contain more detailed information than textbooks or encyclopedias. When reading nonfiction, children also have the opportunity to experience well-written, organized expository prose that can then serve as a model for their own informational writing. Further, reading several nonfiction books provides a perfect opportunity to think critically—evaluating and verifying information by making comparisons with experience and with other books. Children who learn to check multiple sources for the information they need are less likely to believe everything they see in print. Instead, they develop a healthy attitude of critical judgment.

Teaching Idea 10 ☆ 4

Compare Genres as Information Sources

By capitalizing on your students' interest in a particular topic, you can help them discover something about literary genres and learn how the same topic can be addressed in many different ways. Do the following with your students:

1. Read from several books of different genres.
2. Compare the kinds of information/ideas presented in each.
3. Discuss the relationship between the type of information presented and the literary genre represented.
4. Discuss what type of book students would choose to answer specific informational questions, to think imaginatively, or to dream poetically.

James Cross Giblin discusses the history of nonfiction in the twentieth century in the July/August 2000 issue of *The Horn Book Magazine.* Read this article and then examine two pieces of nonfiction about the same subject, one that is at least 20 years old and one that has been published within the past year. Compare these books in terms of content, design, and style, relating them to what Giblin says about the development of nonfiction.

Booklist

Books for a Science Curriculum

PLANTS AND ANIMALS

Aliki, *My Visit to the Zoo* (P)

Ancona, George, *Man and Mustang* (I)

Arnold, Caroline, *Camel* (I)

_____, *Elephant* (I)

Arnosky, Jim, *All About Owls* (P)

_____, *All About Rattlesnakes* (P)

_____, *I See Animals Hiding* (P)

_____, *Watching Desert Wildlife* (P)

_____, *Watching Waterbirds* (P)

Bash, Barbara, *Shadows of Night: The Hidden World of the Little Brown Bat* (P)

Bernhard, Emery, *Eagles: Lions of the Sky* (P)

_____, *Prairie Dogs* (P)

_____, *Salamanders* (P)

Bowen, Betsy, *Tracks in the Wild* (P)

Brandenburg, Jim, *To the Top of the World: Adventures with Arctic Wolves* (I)

Brenner, Barbara, and May Garelick, *The Tremendous Tree Book* (P)

Brown, Laurie Krasny, *What's the Big Secret: Talking About Sex with Girls and Boys* (P)

Brown, Mary Barrett, *Wings Along the Waterway* (I)

Budiansky, Stephen, *The World According to Horses: How They Run, See, and Think* (I)

Cerullo, Mary M., *Lobsters: Gangsters of the Sea* (I)

Clayton, Gordon, *Calf* (N–P)

Cole, Henry, *I Took a Walk* (P)

Cole, Joanna, *My New Kitten* (P)

Cowcher, Helen, *La Tigresa* (P)

Cowley, Joy, *Red-Eyed Tree Frog* (P)

Dewey, Jennifer Owings, *Poison Dart Frogs* (I)

Dowden, Anne Ophelia, *The Blossom on the Bough: A Book of Trees* (I)

_____, *Poisons in Our Path: Plants That Harm and Heal* (I)

Esbensen, Barbara Juster, *Playful Slider: The North American River Otter* (P)

Facklam, Margery, *Creepy, Crawly Caterpillars* (P)

_____, *What Does the Crow Know? The Mysteries of Animal Intelligence* (I)

French, Vivian, *Caterpillar, Caterpillar* (P)

_____, *Growing Frogs* (P)

George, Jean Craighead, *How to Talk to Your Cat* (P)

_____, *How to Talk to Your Dog* (P)

George, Lindsay Barrett, *Around the World: Who's Been Here?* (P)

Gibbons, Gail, *Bats* (P)

Giblin, James Cross, *The Mystery of the Mammoth Bones and How It Was Solved* (I–A)

Hodgkins, Fran, *Animals Among Us: Living with Suburban Wildlife* (I)

Hurd, Edith Thacher, *Starfish* (P)

Jackson, Donna, *The Wildlife Detectives: How Forensic Scientists Fight Crimes Against Nature* (I)

Jenkins, Steve, *Biggest, Strongest, Fastest* (P)

Jessel, Camilla, *The Kitten Book* (P)

_____, *The Puppy Book* (P)

Johnson, Sylvia A., *A Beekeeper's Year* (I)

_____, *Raptor Rescue! An Eagle Flies Free* (P)

King, Elizabeth, *Backyard Sunflower* (I)

King-Smith, Dick, *All Pigs Are Beautiful* (P)

_____, *I Love Guinea Pigs* (P)

Lasky, Kathryn, *Monarchs* (I)

Lauber, Patricia, *Who Eats What? Food Chains and Food Webs* (P)

Lavies, Bianca, *The Atlantic Salmon* (I)

_____, *A Gathering of Garter Snakes* (I)

Lerner, Carol, *Backyard Birds of Summer* (I)

_____, *Backyard Birds of Winter* (I)

_____, *My Indoor Garden* (P)

_____, *Plants That Make You Sniffle and Sneeze* (I)

Lewin, Ted, and Betsy Lewin, *Elephant Quest* (P)

_____, *Gorilla Walk* (I)

Ling, Bill, *Pig* (N–P)

Ling, Mary, *Butterfly* (P)

_____, *Foal* (P)

Maas, Robert, *Garden* (P)

Machotka, Hana, *Breathtaking Noses* (N–P)

_____, *Outstanding Outsides* (N–P)

_____, *Terrific Tails* (N–P)

Maestro, Betsy, *How Do Apples Grow?* (P)

_____, *Take a Look at Snakes* (P)

Markle, Sandra, *Outside and Inside Bats* (P–I)

_____, *Outside and Inside Kangaroos* (P–I)

Matthews, Downs, *Arctic Foxes* (P)

McMillan, Bruce, *The Baby Zoo* (I)

_____, *My Horse of the North* (P)

_____, *Wild Flamingos* (P)

McNulty, Faith, *How Whales Walked into the Sea* (P)

_____, *When I Lived with Bats* (P)

Montgomery, Sy, *The Snake Scientist* (I)

Norell, Mark A., and Lowell Dingus, *A Nest of Dinosaurs: The Story of the Oviraptor* (I–A)

Patent, Dorothy Hinshaw, *The American Alligator* (I)

_____, *Deer and Elk* (I)

_____, *Ospreys* (I)

Payne, Katharine, *Elephants Calling* (I)

Pfeffer, Wendy, *From Tadpole to Frog* (P)

Pringle, Laurence, *Elephant Woman: Cynthia Moss Explores the World of Elephants* (I)

Rauzon, Mark J., *Horns, Antlers, Fangs, and Tusks* (P)

_____, *Skin, Scales, Feathers, and Fur* (P)

Riley, Linda Capus, *Elephants Swim* (P)

Rounds, Glen, *Beaver* (P)

Ryden, Hope, *Joey: The Story of a Baby Kangaroo* (P)

_____, *The Raggedy Red Squirrel* (P)

_____, *Wild Horses I Have Known* (I)

Sattler, Helen Roney, *The Book of North American Owls* (I)

Simon, Seymour, *Gorillas* (P)

_____, *Sharks* (P)

_____, *Wolves* (P)

Sinclair, Sandra, *Extraordinary Eyes: How Animals See the World* (I)

Smith, Roland, and Michael J. Schmidt, *In the Forest with the Elk* (I)

Thomas, Peggy, *Big Cat Conservation* (I)

Tresselt, Alvin, *The Gift of the Tree* (P)

Wallace, Karen, *Gentle Giant Octopus* (P)

Webb, Sophie, *My Season with Penguins: An Antarctic Journal* (P–I)

Wexler, Jerome, *Jack-in-the Pulpit* (I)

_____, *Wonderful Pussy Willows* (P)

ECOLOGY AND HABITATS

Ashabranner, Brent, *Morning Star, Black Sun: The Northern Cheyenne Indians and America's Energy Crisis* (I–A)

Bang, Molly, *Common Ground: The Water, Earth, and Air We Share* (P)

Brandenburg, Jim, *An American Safari: Adventures on the North American Prairie* (I)

_____, *Sand and Fog: Adventures in Southern Africa* (I)

Dewey, Jennifer Owings, *Mud Matters: Stories from a Mud Lover* (I)

Elkington, John, Julia Hailes, Douglas Hill, and Joel Makower, *Going Green: A Kid's Handbook to Saving the Planet* (I–A)

Gibbons, Gail, *Exploring the Deep, Dark Sea* (P)

Levenson, George, *Pumpkin Circle: Story of a Garden* (P)

Miles, Betty, *Save the Earth: An Action Handbook for Kids* (I)

Pringle, Laurence, *Living Treasure: Saving Earth's Threatened Biodiversity* (I–A)

Simon, Seymour, *Oceans* (P–I)

_____, *Wildfires* (P–I)

Smith, Roland, *Sea Otter Rescue: The Aftermath of an Oil Spill* (I–A)

Swineburne, Stephen R., *Once a Wolf: How Wildlife Biologists Fought to Bring Back the Grey Wolf* (I–A)

Taylor, Barbara, *Pond Life* (I)

_____, *Rain Forest* (I)

Viner, Michael, with Pat Hilton, *365 Ways for You and Your Children to Save the Earth One Day at a Time* (I–A)

SCIENCE AND TECHNOLOGY

Branley, Franklin, *The International Space Station* (P)

Cole, Joanna, *The Magic School Bus and the Electric Field Trip* (P)

Gallant, Roy A., *The Day the Sky Split Apart: Investigating a Cosmic Mystery* (A)

Lauber, Patricia, *You're Aboard Spaceship Earth* (P)

Macaulay, David, *The New Way Things Work* (I)

Ride, Sally, and Tam O'Shaughnessy, *The Mystery of Mars* (I)

_____, *The Third Planet: Exploring the Earth from Space* (I)

Rubin, Susan Goldman, *Toilets, Toasters, and Telephones: The How and Why of Everyday Objects* (I)

Scott, Elaine, *Close Encounters: Exploring the Universe with the Hubble Space Telescope* (I)

Simon, Seymour, *Comets, Meteors, and Asteroids* (I)

_____, *Destination: Jupiter* (I)

_____, *Destination: Mars* (I)

_____, *Mercury* (I)

_____, *Neptune* (I)

_____, *Our Solar System* (I)

_____, *Uranus* (I)

_____, *Venus* (I)

Skurzynski, Gloria, *Zero Gravity* (I)

Sonenklar, Carol, *Robots Rising* (I)

DINOSAURS AND OTHER SCIENCE TOPICS

Arnold, Caroline, *Dinosaurs All Around: An Artist's View of the Prehistoric World* (I)

Berger, Melvin, *Germs Make Me Sick!* (P)

_____, *Why I Sneeze, Shiver, Hiccup, and Yawn* (P)

Bishop, Nic, *Digging for Bird Dinosaurs: An Expedition to Madagascar* (I)

Blackstone, Margaret, and Elissa Haden Guest, *Girl Stuff: A Survival Guide to Growing Up* (I–A)

Bulla, Clyde Robert, *What Makes a Shadow?* (P)

Cole, Babette, *Hair in Funny Places: A Book About Puberty* (I)

Cole, Joanna, *How You Were Born* (P)

_____, *The Magic School Bus Explores the Senses* (P)

_____, *The Magic School Bus in the Time of the Dinosaurs* (P)

_____, *The Magic School Bus Inside a Hurricane* (P)

Cutchins, Judy, and Ginny Johnston, *Are Those Animals REAL? How Museums Prepare Wildlife Exhibits* (I)

Farrell, Jeanette, *Invisible Enemies: Stories of Infectious Disease* (I–A)

Floca, Brian, *Dinosaurs at the Ends of the Earth: The Story of the Central Asiatic Expeditions* (P)

Harris, Robie H., *It's Perfectly Normal: A Book About Changing Bodies, Growing Up, Sex, and Sexual Health* (I)

_____, *It's So Amazing! A Book About Eggs, Sperm, Birth, Babies, and Families* (I)

Henderson, Douglas, *Asteroid Impact* (I)

Jackson, Donna M., *The Bone Detectives: How Forensic Anthropologists Solve Crimes and Uncover Mysteries of the Dead* (I)

Jukes, Mavis, *It's a Girl Thing: How to Stay Healthy, Safe, and in Charge* (I)

Keller, Laurie, *Open Wide: Tooth School Inside* (P)

Lavies, Bianca, *Compost Critters* (I)

Miller, Margaret, *My Five Senses* (N–P)

Mullins, Patricia, *Dinosaur Encore* (P)

Patent, Dorothy Henshaw, *Fire: Friend or Foe?* (P)

Robbins, Ken, *Air: The Elements* (I)

_____, *Water: The Elements* (I)

Sattler, Helen Roney, *Stegosaurs: The Solar-Powered Dinosaurs* (I)

Selsam, Millicent E., *How to Be a Nature Detective* (P)

Simon, Seymour, *The Brain: Our Nervous System* (I)

_____, *Muscles: Our Muscle System* (I)

_____, *Weather* (P)

_____, *Winter Across America* (P)

Smith, Roland, *Inside the Zoo Nursery* (I)

Wexler, Jerome, *Everyday Mysteries* (P)

Zoehfeld, Kathleen Weidner, *What Is the World Made Of? All About Solids, Liquids, and Gases* (P)

Books for a Social Studies Curriculum

HISTORICAL EVENTS AND ERAS

Armstrong, Jennifer, *Shipwreck at the Bottom of the World: The Extraordinary True Story of Shackleton and the Endurance* (I)

Ashabranner, Brent, *A Strange and Distant Shore: Indians of the Great Plains in Exile* (I–A)

Barboza, Steven, *Door of No Return: The Legend of Goree Island* (I)

Bartoletti, Susan Campbell, *Kids on Strike!* (I)

Beller, Susan Provost, *Never Were Men So Brave: The Irish Brigade During the Civil War* (I–A)

Bial, Raymond, *The Underground Railroad* (I)

Blumberg, Rhoda, *Bloomers!* (P)

_____, *Full Steam Ahead: The Race to Build a Transcontinental Railroad* (I)

_____, *What's the Deal? Jefferson, Napoleon, and the Louisiana Purchase* (I)

Branch, Muriel Miller, *Juneteenth: Freedom Day* (P–I)

Bruchac, Joseph, *Lasting Echoes: An Oral History of Native American People* (I–A)

Burr, Claudia, Krystyna Libura, and Maria Christina Urritia, *Broken Shields* (I)

_____, *What the Aztecs Told Me* (I)

Calabro, Marian, *The Perilous Journey of the Donner Party* (A)

Colman, Penny, *Rosie the Riveter: Women Working on the Home Front in World War II* (I)

Cooper, Michael, *Indian School: Teaching the White Man's Ways* (I)

Curlee, Lynn, *Liberty* (I)

Denenberg, Barry, *Voices from Vietnam* (A)

Feelings, Tom, *The Middle Passage: White Ships/Black Cargo* (I–A)

Ferrie, Richard, *The World Turned Upside Down: George Washington and the Battle of Yorktown* (I)

Fisher, Leonard Everett, *The Oregon Trail* (I–A)

_____, *Tracks Across America: The Story of the American Railroad, 1825–1900* (I)

Fleischman, Paul, *Dateline: Troy* (I–A)

Freedman, Russell, *Give Me Liberty: The Story of the Declaration of Independence* (A)

_____, *An Indian Winter* (I)

_____, *Kids at Work: Lewis Hine and the Crusade Against Child Labor* (I)

Giblin, James Cross, *The Century That Was: Reflections on the Last One Hundred Years* (A)

_____, *The Riddle of the Rosetta Stone: Key to Ancient Egypt* (I)

Goodman, Susan E., *Stones, Bones, and Petroglyphs: Digging into the Southwest Archaeology* (I)

Greenfeld, Howard, *The Hidden Children* (I)

Greenwood, Barbara, *A Pioneer Sampler: The Daily Life of a Pioneer Family in 1840* (I)

Hamanaka, Sheila, *The Journey: Japanese Americans, Racism, and Renewal* (I–A)

Hampton, Wilborn, *Kennedy Assassinated! The World Mourns: A Reporter's Story* (A)

Jacobs, Francine, *The Tainos: The People Who Welcomed Columbus* (I)

Jones, Charlotte Foltz, *Yukon Gold: The Story of the Klondike Gold Rush* (I–A)

Katz, William Loren, *Black Pioneers: An Untold Story* (I–A)

Kimmel, Elizabeth Cody, *Ice Story: Shackleton's Lost Expedition* (I)

Landau, Elaine, *The New Nuclear Reality* (A)

Lavender, David, *Snowbound: The Tragic Story of the Donner Party* (I)

Lawlor, Laurie, *Window on the West: The Frontier Photography of William Henry Jackson* (A)

Levine, Ellen, *Darkness over Denmark* (A)

_____, *A Fence Away from Freedom: Japanese Americans and World War II* (A)

Levinson, Nancy Smiler, *Turn of the Century: Our Nation One Hundred Years Ago* (I)

Maestro, Betsy, and Giulio Maestro, *The Discovery of the Americas* (P–I)

_____, *More Perfect Union: The Story of Our Constitution* (P–I)

Marrin, Albert, *America and Vietnam: The Elephant and the Tiger* (A)

_____, *Cowboys, Indians, and Gunfighters: The Story of the Cattle Kingdom* (A)

_____, *Terror of the Spanish Main: Sir Henry Morgan and His Buccaneers* (A)

McKissack, Patricia C., and Fredrick L. McKissack, *Black Hands, White Sails: The Story of African American Whalers* (I–A)

_____, *Christmas in the Big House, Christmas in the Quarters* (I)

_____, *Red-Tail Angels: The Story of the Tuskegee Airmen of World War II* (I)

Meltzer, Milton, *The Amazing Potato: A Story in Which the Incas, Conquistadors, Marie Antoinette, Thomas Jefferson, Wars, Famines, Immigrants, and French Fries All Play a Part* (I)

_____, *Cheap Raw Material* (A)

_____, *Gold: The True Story of Why People Search for It, Mine It, Trade It, Steal It, Mint It, Hoard It, Shape It, Wear It, Fight and Kill for It* (I)

_____, *Witches and Witch Hunts: A History of Persecution* (A)

Millard, Anne, *A Street Through Time: A 12,000 Year Walk Through History* (I)

Murphy, Claire Rudolf, and Jane G. Haigh, *Children of the Gold Rush* (I–A)

Murphy, Jim, *Across America on an Emigrant Train* (I)

_____, *Blizzard: The Storm That Changed America* (A)

_____, *The Boys' War: Confederate and Union Soldiers Talk About the Civil War* (I–A)

_____, *The Great Fire* (I)

_____, *The Long Road to Gettysburg* (I)

Nieuwsma, Milton J., *Kinderlager: An Oral History of Young Holocaust Survivors* (A)

Opdyke, Irene Gut, *In My Hands: Memories of a Holocaust Rescuer* (A)

Parker, Nancy Winslow, *The President's Cabinet: And How It Grew* (I)

Ray, Delia, *Behind the Blue and Gray: The Soldier's Life in the Civil War* (A)

_____, *A Nation Torn: The Story of How the Civil War Began* (A)

Ritter, Lawrence S., *Leagues Apart: The Men and Times of the Negro Baseball Leagues* (I)

Robertson, James I., Jr., *Civil War! America Becomes One Nation* (I)

Rochman, Hazel, and Darlene Z. McCampbell, *Bearing Witness: Stories of the Holocaust* (A)

Rubin, Susan Goldman, *Fireflies in the Dark: The Story of Friedl Decker-Brandeis and the Children of Terezin* (I)

St. George, Judith, *In the Line of Fire: Presidents' Lives at Stake* (A)

_____, *Mason and Dixon's Line of Fire* (I–A)

Schlissel, Lillian, *Black Frontiers: A History of African-American Heroes in the Old West* (I)

Sewall, Marcia, *People of the Breaking Day* (I)

_____, *The Pilgrims of Plimoth* (I)

_____, *Thunder from the Clear Sky* (I)

Stanley, Jerry, *Big Annie of Calumet: A True Story of the Industrial Revolution* (I)

_____, *Children of the Dust Bowl: The True Story of the School at Weedpatch Camp* (I)

_____, *I Am an American: A True Story of Japanese Internment* (I)

Taylor, Maureen, *Through the Eyes of Your Ancestors: A Step by Step Guide to Uncovering Your Family's History* (I–A)

Tunnell, Michael O., and George W. Chilcoat, *The Children of Topaz: The Story of a Japanese-American Internment Camp* (I)

Viola, Herman J., *It Is a Good Day to Die: Indian Eyewitnesses Tell the Story of the Battle of the Little Bighorn* (I–A)

Zeinert, Karen, *The Lincoln Murder Plot* (A)

Ziff, John, *Espionage and Treason* (**Crime, Justice, and Punishment** series) (A)

PEOPLE AND PLACES

Aaseng, Nathan, *Cherokee Nation v. Georgia: The Forced Removal of a People* (**Famous Trials** series) (A)

_____, *The Impeachment of Bill Clinton* (**Famous Trials** series) (A)

Anderson, Joan, *Cowboys: Roundup on an American Ranch* (P)

Arnold, Caroline, *City of the Gods: Mexico's Ancient City of Teotihuacan* (I)

_____, *Easter Island: Giant Stone Statues Tell of a Rich and Tragic Past* (I)

Ashabranner, Brent, *A Date with Destiny: The Women in Military Service for America Memorial* (A)

_____, *Land of Yesterday, Land of Tomorrow: Discovering Chinese Central Asia* (A)

_____, *A New Frontier: The Peace Corps in Eastern Europe* (I)

Barner, Bob, *Which Way to the Revolution? A Book of Maps* (P)

Beil, Karen Magnuson, *Fire in Their Eyes: Wildfires and the People Who Fight Them* (I)

Bial, Raymond, *Cajun Home* (I)

_____, *Portrait of a Farm Family* (I)

Brown, Dan, *Alice Ramsey's Grand Adventure* (P)

Brown, Tricia, *Children of the Midnight Sun: Young Native Voices of Alaska* (I–A)

Budhos, Marina, *Remix: Conversations with Immigrant Teenagers* (A)

Burleigh, Robert, *Black Whiteness: Admiral Byrd Alone in the Antarctic* (I–A)

Carlson, Laurie, *Boss of the Plains: The Hat That Won the West* (P)

Cole, Joanna, *The New Baby at Your Home* (P)

Colman, Penny, *Girls: A History of Growing Up Female in America* (I–A)

Curlee, Lynn, *Into the Ice: The Story of Arctic Exploration* (I)

Deem, James M., *Bodies from the Bog* (I–A)

Fisher, Leonard Everett, *The Architects* (**Colonial Craftsmen** series) (I)

_____, *The Blacksmiths* (**Colonial Craftsmen** series) (I)

Ford, Michael Thomas, *Outspoken: Role Models from the Lesbian and Gay Community* (A)

Geisert, Bonnie, *Prairie Town* (P)

Goodman, Susan E., *Animal Rescue: The Best Job There Is* (P)

Hansen, Joyce, and Gary McGowen, *Breaking Ground, Breaking Silence: The Story of New York's African Burial Ground* (A)

Horenstein, Henry, *My Mom's a Vet* (I)

Hurmence, Belinda, *Slavery Time: When I was Chillun* (I)

Jaskol, Julie, and Brian Lewis, *City of Angels: In and Around Los Angeles* (P)

Jenkins, Steve, *The Top of the World: Climbing Mt. Everest* (P)

Lewin, Ted, *Sacred River* (P)

Macy, Sue, *Winning Ways: A Photohistory of American Women in Sports* (I–A)

McKee, Time, *No More Strangers Now: Young Voices from a New South Africa* (A)

McMillan, Bruce, *Salmon Summer* (P–I)

Mochizuki, Ken, *Passage to Freedom: The Sugihara Story* (P)

Mudd-Ruth, Maria, *Firefighting: Behind the Scenes* (I)

Murphy, Jim, *Gone a-Whaling: The Lure of the Sea and the Hunt for the Great Whale* (I–A)

Nash, Gary B., *Forbidden Love: The Secret History of Mixed-Race America* (A)

Provensen, Alice, *The Buck Stops Here: The Presidents of the United States* (I)

Ritter, Lawrence, *The Story of Baseball* (I–A)

Rounds, Glen, *Sod Houses on the Great Plains* (P)

Rylant, Cynthia, *Appalachia: The Voices of Sleeping Birds* (I)

Scott, Ann Herbert, *Cowboy Country* (P)

Severance, John B., *Skyscrapers: How America Grew Up* (I)

Sneve, Virginia Driving Hawk, *The Seminoles* (I)

Stewart, Gail B., *Teen Addicts* (**Other America** series) (A)

_____, *Teen Alcoholics* (**Other America** series) (A)

Tessendorf, K. C., *Over the Edge: Flying with the Arctic Heroes* (I–A)

Waters, Kate, *Tapenum's Day: A Wampanoag Indian Boy in Pilgrim Times* (P)

Watkins, Richard, *Gladiator* (I–A)

Yue, Charlotte, and David Yue, *The Wigwam and the Longhouse* (I)

Zaunders, Bo, *Crocodiles, Camels, and Dugout Canoes: 8 Adventurous Episodes* (I)

MISCELLANEOUS

Bial, Raymond, *Country Fair* (I)

Giblin, James Cross, *Be Seated: A Book About Chairs* (I)

Hamanaka, Sheila, *On the Wings of Peace* (I)

Hindley, Judy, *A Piece of String Is a Wonderful Thing* (P)

Wolf, Bernard, *Homeless* (P–I)

Books for a Mathematics Curriculum

COUNTING

Anno, Mitsumasa, *Anno's Counting Book* (P)

_____, *Anno's Magic Seeds* (P)

Bang, Molly, *Ten, Nine, Eight* (N–P)

Crews, Donald, *Ten Black Dots* (P)

Ehlert, Lois, *Fish Eyes: A Book You Can Count On* (N–P)

Feelings, Muriel, *Moja Means One: A Swahili Counting Book* (N–P)

Fleming, Denise, *Count!* (N–P)

Geisert, Arthur, *Roman Numerals I to MM (Numerabilia Romana Uno Ad Duo Mila): Liber De Difficillimo Computando Numerum* (I)

Giganti, Paul Jr., *How Many Snails?* (P)

Hoban, Tana, *Count and See* (P)

Hutchins, Pat, *1 Hunter* (P)

Kitchen, Bert, *Animal Numbers* (P–I)

Merriam, Eve, *12 Ways to Get to 11* (P)

Morozumi, Atsuko, *One Gorilla* (N–P)

Tafuri, Nancy, *Who's Counting?* (P)

Walsh, Ellen Stoll, *Mouse Count* (N–P)

ADDITION AND SUBTRACTION

Aruego, José, and Ariane Dewey, *Five Little Ducks* (P)

Burningham, John, *The Shopping Basket* (P)

Chorao, Kay, *Number One Number Fun* (P)

Christelow, Eileen, *Five Little Monkeys Jumping on the Bed* (N–P)

Peek, Merle, *Roll Over!* (P)

Pinczes, Elinor, *A Remainder of One* (P)

MULTIPLICATION AND DIVISION

Aker, Suzanne, *What Comes in 2's, 3's, and 4's?* (I)

Hulme, Joy, *Sea Squares* (I)

Hutchins, Pat, *The Doorbell Rang* (P)

Leedy, Loreen, *2 3 2 5 Boo! A Set of Spooky Multiplication Stories* (I)

FRACTIONS

Leedy, Loreen, *Fraction Action* (I)

McMillan, Bruce, *Eating Fractions* (P–I)

MONEY AND TIME

Anno, Mitsumasa, *All in a Day* (P–I)

Hoban, Tana, *Twenty-Six Letters and Ninety-Nine Cents* (N–P)

Hutchins, Pat, *Clocks and More Clocks* (P)

Schwartz, David, *How Much Is a Million?* (P–I)

_____, *If You Made a Million* (P–I)

MEASUREMENT AND SIZE

Adler, David A., *How Tall, How Short, How Faraway?* (P)

Hoban, Tana, *Is It Larger? Is It Smaller?* (N–P)

Markle, Sandra, *Measuring Up! Experiments, Puzzles, and Games Exploring Measurement* (I)

PROBLEM SOLVING

Anno, Masaichiro, and Mitsumasa Anno, *Anno's Mysterious Multiplying Jar* (I–A)

Scieszka, Jon, *Math Curse* (I)

Books About Language

Ammer, Christine, *It's Raining Cats and Dogs . . . and Other Beastly Expressions* (P–I)

Butterworth, Nick, *Nice or Nasty: A Book of Opposites* (I)

Heller, Ruth, *A Cache of Jewels and Other Collective Nouns* (I)

_____, *Many Luscious Lollipops: A Book About Adjectives* (I)

Koch, Michelle, *Just One More* (N–P)

Marcus, Leonard, *Author Talk: Conversations with Judy Blume, Bruce Brooks, Karen Cushman, Russell Freedman, Lee Bennett Hopkins, James Howe, Johanna Hurwitz, E. L. Konigsburg, Lois Lowry, Ann M. Martin, Nicholasa Mohr, Gary Paulsen, Jon Scieszka, Seymour Simon, and Laurence Yep* (A)

Terban, Marvin, *The Dove Dove* (I)

_____, *Guppies in Tuxedos: Funny Eponyms* (I)

_____, *Hey, Hay! A Wagonful of Funny Homonym Riddles* (I)

_____, *I Think, I Thought and Other Tricky Verbs* (I)

_____, *In a Pickle and Other Funny Idioms* (I)

_____, *Mad as a Wet Hen!* (I)

_____, *Punching the Clock: Funny Action Idioms* (I)

_____, *Time to Rhyme: A Rhyming Dictionary* (I)

_____, *Your Foot's on My Feet! And Other Tricky Nouns* (I)

Books About the Arts

Aliki, *William Shakespeare and the Globe* (I)

Ancona, George, *Cutters, Carvers, and the Cathedral* (I)

Bare, Colleen Stanley, *This Is a House* (P)

Berger, Melvin, *The Science of Music* (A)

_____, *The Story of Folk Music* (A)

Blizzard, Gladys S., *Come Look with Me: Animals in Art* (P–I)

_____, *Come Look with Me: Exploring Landscape Art with Children* (P–I)

Bolton, Linda, *Hidden Pictures* (P)

Brennan, Stephen Vincent, *Hit the Nerve: New Voices of the American Theater* (A)

Carter, David A., and James Diaz, *The Elements of a Pop-Up* (I)

Christelow, Eileen, *What Do Illustrators Do?* (P)

Cummings, Pat, *Talking with Artists: Volume 3* (I)

Curlee, Lynn, *Rushmore* (I)

Fleisher, Paul, *The Master Violinmaker* (P)

Florian, Douglas, *A Carpenter* (N–P)

_____, *A Potter* (N–P)

Granfield, Linda, *Circus: An Album* (I)

Greenberg, Jan, and Sandra Jordan, *The Painter's Eye: Learning to Look at Contemporary American Art* (A)

_____, *The Sculptor's Eye: Looking at Contemporary American Art* (A)

Guthrie, Woody, *This Land Is Your Land* (P)

Hayes, Ann, *Meet the Orchestra* (P–I)

Hoban, Tana, *Look Book* (N–P)

Isaacson, Philip M., *A Short Walk Around the Pyramids and Through the World of Art* (I)

Johnson, Dinah, *All Around Town: The Photographs of Richard Samuel Robert* (P)

Jones, Bill T., and Susan Kuklin, *Dance* (P)

Krementz, Jill, *A Very Young Dancer* (I)

_____, *A Very Young Musician* (I)

Kuklin, Susan, *From Head to Toe: How a Doll Is Made* (P)

LeTord, Bijou, *A Bird or Two: A Story About Henri Matisse* (P)

Marcus, Leonard S., *A Caldecott Celebration: Six Artists and Their Paths to the Caldecott Medal* (I)

Micklethwait, Lucy, *I Spy a Lion: Animals in Art* (P)

_____, *I Spy Two Eyes: Numbers in Art* (P)

Orozco, Jose-Luis, *Diez Peditos/Ten Little Fingers and Other Play Rhymes and Action Songs from Latin America* (N–P)

Price, Leontyne, *Aïda* (I–A)

Raboff, Ernest, *Albrecht Dürer* (I–A)

_____, *Pablo Picasso* (I–A)

_____, *Leonardo da Vinci* (I–A)

Raschka, Chris, *Mysterious Thelonious* (I)

Roalf, Peggy, *Children* (**Looking at Paintings** series) (I)

_____, *Flowers* (**Looking at Paintings** series) (I)

Schwarz, Amy, *Old MacDonald* (N–P)

Sills, Leslie, *In Real Life: Six Women Photographers* (A)

Tucker, Jean S., *Come Look with Me: Discovering Photographs with Children* (I)

Varriale, Jim, *Kids Dance: The Students of Ballet Tech* (I)

Venezia, M., *Francisco Goya* (I–A)

_____, *Picasso* (I–A)

_____, *Rembrandt* (I–A)

Ventura, Piero, *Great Composers* (I)

Westray, Kathleen, *A Color Sampler* (P)

_____, *Picture Puzzler* (I)

Woolf, F., *Picture This: A First Introduction to Paintings* (I)

Yenawine, Philip, *People* (P)

_____, *Places* (P)

chapter 11

Building a Culturally Diverse Literature Collection

Quinnie Blue, did you wear your hair in braids like mine? Wasn't it hard to sit for such a long time while your mama made you look like a princess?

—DINAH JOHNSON, *Quinnie Blue*

THERE IS A RAINBOW OF CHILDREN IN THE LIBRARY, ALL OF THEM looking for books. Many will make connections with the characters in those books, just as the young narrator of *Quinnie Blue* is seeking to understand the grandmother who shares her name. Emeka, from Nigeria, is delighted to find a book with his very own name in the title, Ifeoma Onyefulu's *Emeka's Gift*. He knows he will enjoy reading about a boy just about his age and from his home country. Jennie is from Korea, although she's lived in America since she was a baby. She's reading Katherine Paterson's *The Great Gilly Hopkins*. She'll connect with Gilly despite differences in cultural background and life experience; she always identifies with characters she cares about. Adam is a second-generation Italian American on his father's side, with a Polish grandfather and a born-and-bred Southern grandmother on his mother's side. He's lived in Europe and considers himself a citizen of the world. He's looking through books about Australian animals wishing he could go and see them for himself. There is no character to connect with, but he has placed himself in the middle of the outback. Tree is African American, and right now she loves books about African-American children; she's checking out Eloise Greenfield's *Night on Neighborhood Street*. She'll recognize scenes that echo her own experience, and she'll discover new ideas. Brie's family is from Wisconsin and Georgia; she's lived in Georgia all of her life. She's looking at Walter Dean Myers's *Brown Angels*, entranced by the old pictures. The fact that the pictures are of African-American children and she's European American makes little difference to her. Tamara's mother is Mexican, and Tamara is bilingual. Today she's deep into a **Boxcar Children** mystery; she's such a good reader that she can read any book in the library, English or Spanish. She selects books that reflect her abilities and her wide experience of the world.

All these children attend the same elementary school in a small city in the southeast. They all need books that reflect their own experiences and those of their peers, and they find them in this sunlit, welcoming library because the

Like Quinnie, children seek to understand the lives of those they care about, including the characters with which they connect.

librarian, Rosemary Belger, makes sure that her collection reflects the cultural diversity in the school. It is not a surprise to these children to find books about people from diverse cultures as they browse the fiction and nonfiction shelves. All children, from all cultures and in all places, need to see books that reflect themselves and their experiences as well as allow them the opportunity to discover the lives of others.

Defining Culturally Diverse Literature

How lucky we are to be able to explore the diversity and richness that marks children's literature today. As we discussed in Chapter 1, the field of children's books changed considerably during the last half of the twentieth century as it began to reflect the cultural diversity that marks North America and to include literature from around the world. Building a culturally diverse collection of books means that we seek to find books from many cultures to fill our shelves and to enrich the minds and hearts of our students.

There are many ways to think about diversity. Too often those in the mainstream make the mistake of thinking that *cultural diversity* refers only to people who are different

from them, but it does not! Everyone has a cultural heritage, often one that is woven from many diverse strands; we all live in families and communities that draw on a wealth of knowledge and skills to help them function (Moll and Greenberg, 1990). Much more than race, ethnicity, gender, sexual preference, or special needs, culture involves values, attitudes, customs, beliefs, and ethics. Teaching Idea 11.1 offers a way to begin to discuss this with your students. From this perspective, all children's books could be considered culturally diverse in relation to each other. The important task is to create a collection that is balanced in terms of diversity, that explores not just the culture of mainstream European Americans, which for so long dominated children's books, but also the rich cultures of Native Americans, African Americans, Asian Americans, Latinos, and others from around the world who contribute to the patchwork quilt of North American culture and the diversity of our world.

Teaching Idea 11 ☆ 1

Celebrate Your Cultural Heritage

Everybody has a culture, and any study of other cultures begins with the recognition that all individuals come from particular cultural groups. Cultural groups share a common heritage, and this heritage is often visible in social customs and rituals. For example, the holidays we celebrate and how we celebrate them, the traditional foods that we eat, the rituals we perform, and the traditional clothing that we wear all reflect our customs, beliefs, and values.

Ask students to research their own family's heritage and to record their findings. Then, work with students and their families to plan ways to share the information about their cultural heritage with classmates. This may include sharing the meaning of rituals, describing the work of historical figures, serving traditional foods, wearing ceremonial clothing, inviting guest speakers, creating an art project or drama, or producing a list of books that will inform others.

In Chapter 7, we talked about books that reflected the lives of people who were diverse in terms of sexual preference, special needs, and, of course, gender. In this chapter we look closely at another kind of diversity as it is reflected in children's books. Here, we focus on books from North American parallel cultures, defined by Virginia Hamilton as "groups formerly called minority [and used] to suggest . . . that so-called minorities—those blacks, browns, and yellows—make up a vast contingent in the world view" (1993, p. 372). We then explore books from international cultures.

While multicultural books continue to receive increased attention today, children's literature in America is still largely a literature of the mainstream—middle-class Caucasians. If we examine the status of multicultural publishing from the early part of this century to the present, however, we find some promising trends.

A study of children's picture books that present pluralistic, balanced racial and ethnic images of children shows that book publication figures seldom parallel census figures. Although immigrant, racial, and ethnic groups increased dramatically in number, few books representing those groups were published during the 1960s, 1970s, and 1980s. Sims Bishop (1994) estimates that only 3 to 4 percent of the children's books published in 1990, 1991, and 1992 related to people of color. Miller-Lachmann's (1992) *Our Family, Our Friends, Our World* shows the same slight increase in the publication of books by and about parallel cultures. Helbig and Perkins's *Many Peoples, One Land: A Guide to New Multicultural Literature for Children and Young Adults* (2001), lists 541 books that relate the experiences of parallel cultures, were published between 1994 and 1999, and are of high literary quality. These books range from those suitable for preschool readers to those suitable for high school readers. Since more than 5,000 books for children and young adults are published *each* year, this is still woefully inadequate. Further, given the rapid growth of immigrant, racial, and ethnic groups, we may be falling futher behind, and many groups are severely underrepresented.

Of the many cultures in North America, African Americans are presented more frequently and with more variety and fewer stereotypes than other cultural groups. Many recent books with African-American characters reflect middle-class American life. There are few strong images of Asian characters of cultures other than Chinese and Japanese. A recent, small increase in the number of books with Latino characters, an increasing number of bilingual English/Spanish books, new Latino writers, and an increase in Latino poetry are welcome indications that this literature will grow. Literature in the Native American tradition continues to be primarily oral, although there are a few notable new works of contemporary fiction as well.

Folktales still account for about 20 percent of the total number of titles about persons of color. The largest number of books about Asian Americans, Native Americans, and Latinos are folklore. While these folktales do reflect the values of the people who created them, they say little about the lives of contemporary members of these cultures (Sims Bishop, 1994).

Publishing houses that focus on culturally diverse literature—such as Children's Book Press, Lee and Low Books, Pinata, and Arte Publico—promise a continued increase in available books by and about people of color. A list of such specialized publishers, with addresses, appears in Appendix C. Special recognition of authors and illustrators of particular parallel cultures, such as the Coretta Scott King Awards and the Pura Belpre Award, also help support the production of culturally diverse literature. Winners of these awards are listed in Appendix A.

Diversity goes beyond the borders of any one country, and children's books reflect the global perspective of the 1990s, a view that will only intensify in the twenty-first century. Books from English-speaking countries such as Australia, New Zealand, Great Britain, South Africa, and Canada are now easily available in the United States, and an increasing number of books from non–English-speaking countries are available in translation. Publishers such as North-South Books and Kane/Miller are in the forefront of this effort, publishing excellent translations of books from other countries. Their addresses also appear in Appendix C.

Culturally Diverse Literature in Children's Lives

America has been a culturally mixed society since its beginnings and is becoming more diverse as we begin the twenty-first century. The U.S. population constitutes an enormous group of people who read and speak English as well as many others who speak, read, write, and study other languages. Approximately one-third of the students entering school are of African-American, Asian-American, or Latino backgrounds. Further, more than 30 million people 5 years of age and older speak a language other than English at home. Beyond the borders of America, technological advances make our global village ever smaller.

Readers shape their view of the world and of themselves partly through the books they read. If children never see themselves in books, that omission subtly tells these young people that they are not important enough to appear in books, that books are not for them. Stereotyped images of an ethnic group, gender, nationality, region, religion, or other subculture are harmful not only to the children of that group but also to others who get a distorted view. Culturally diverse literature informs us about ourselves and helps us to know each other. As we discuss in other chapters, literature can act as both mirror and window for its readers (Cullinan, 1982; Galda, 1980). Recently, Sims Bishop (1996) has applied this metaphor to culturally diverse literature. While it is true that literature allows readers to understand both themselves and those different from themselves, perhaps the best books offer an experience that is more like looking through a window as the light slowly darkens. At first one sees clearly through the window into another's world—but gradually, as the light fades, the image of oneself becomes reflected, too. Children's books at their best highlight the unique characteristics of the cultures represented by their characters but also speak to universal experiences. With them we can celebrate differences, call attention to commonly held values and experience, and promote empathy and a sense of common humanity. The goal of creating a more equitable society requires that people from many backgrounds learn to live together peaceably. If we understand people of other cultures and other nations, it is difficult to view them as being "on the other side" in times of conflict. Teaching Idea 11.2 offers some ways to encourage students to learn about characters from various cultures and compare their experiences to their own.

Children can begin to know people of other cultures through literature. They can recognize similarities between themselves and others; they can understand universal qualities of humankind. Although we do not expect literature to explicitly, teach lessons of tolerance, thinking about, talking about,

---

Teaching Idea 11 · 2

Find Cultural Similarities and Differences

Have your students read books set in various countries and cultures, noting similarities and differences between what is portrayed in the books and what they experience in their own lives. Discuss customs that may differ. Discuss feelings, attitudes, and relationships that may be similar. Use some of the following ideas to focus on specific areas:

* Ask students to rewrite or rethink one of the stories, making themselves the main character. How would the story change? Why? Is the change critical to the theme of the story?

* Ask students to imagine one of the book characters in their home or neighborhood. Would he or she be happy? Comfortable? Explain why or why not.

* Ask students to make a list of ways in which the characters are like them and ways in which they differ. Make a Venn diagram listing individual characteristics and ones that overlap.

---

and developing an understanding of others is a natural outgrowth of reading diverse literature. Further, children who do not have the opportunity to read books from many cultures miss a lot of wonderful writing by extraordinary authors.

Criteria for Evaluating Culturally Diverse Literature

Although we still do not have adequate representation of parallel cultures, today we do have greater diversity in children's books. Today all genres contain books from different cultures and perspectives. Because of this, it is now possible to make diversity a central tenet of the literature collection in your classroom and in your school library. Because books from all cultures should be a part of children's daily life at school we chose to discuss those books within individual genre chapters rather than separately. You will find culturally diverse books in each chapter. Here we focus the discussion on ways of thinking about diversity in relation to children's books. We explore how to use these books in a classroom setting in Chapters 13 and 14.

There are many aspects to consider when selecting books to build a culturally diverse collection. First, consider the importance of culture in a book. Some books have characters that are from a variety of cultures, often indicating diversity through visual information such as color, eye shape, or hair color and style, but presenting no cultural content. You might think of books of this type as "painted faces" books. In some, the inclusion of culturally diverse characters is merely gratuitous and often stereotyped; they should be avoided. In others, the diversity subtly reinforces the idea that we live in a culturally diverse world. One such book, Rebecca C. Jones's *Matthew and Tilly* (P), illustrated by Beth Peck, is a picture storybook about friends fighting and then resolving their differences. It happens that Matthew is a white male, while Tilly is a black female; this information comes through the illustrations. Culture, as such, is not an important aspect of this book, but the theme of friendship is broadened by the diversity depicted.

Other books are about culture; their theme or unifying idea is that culture is important, that people are different, yet the same. Many of these books explicitly state this idea, such as Mem Fox's *Wherever You Are* (P), or Aliki's *Marianthe's Story: Painted Words/Spoken Memories* (P).

Other books are culturally rich, depicting experiences that are explicitly embedded in a particular culture, with setting, plot, and characters inextricably tied to culture, such as Francisco Jimenez's *La Mariposa* (P–I) or Judith Ortiz Cofer's *The Year of Our Revolution: New and Selected Stories and Poems* (A). These are the books that allow readers to look through the window at characters just like or different from themselves, to recognize their own or learn about another culture. These are the books that offer the opportunity for a more than superficial experience with diverse characters.

No matter what role culture plays in a book, the depiction of culture should be accurate, authentic, and free from stereotypes. Culturally diverse literature portrays what is unique to an individual culture and universal to all cultures. It accurately portrays the nuances and variety of day-to-day living in the culture depicted. It does not distort or misrepresent the culture it reflects (Sims Bishop, 1992, p. 41).

Determining authenticity, accuracy, and the absence of stereotypes can be difficult if one is not of the culture being depicted. However, this judgment is also founded in a general evaluation of the literary quality of a book. In Chapters 2 through 10 we discuss the criteria for quality literature in each genre and give examples of books that reflect the best of the genre. Here we evaluate books not on genre criteria but on criteria that speak to the quality of the cultural content. If you think of the genre criteria as one lens through which to view children's books critically, think of cultural content as a second lens, one that is additional to rather than instead of the genre criteria. Each informs the other, and any book can and should be evaluated in terms of its

quality as an example of its genre and also in terms of its cultural authenticity. Further, a collection of books—whether in a classroom, a school library, or a public library—can be evaluated in light of the diversity that it represents in terms of both depth and breadth.

The Multicultural Booklist Committee of the National Council of Teachers of English periodically prepares an annotated bibliography of multicultural books (defined as books about people of color residing in the United States, Africa, Asia, South and Central America, the Caribbean, Mexico, Canada, and England) as well as books that focus on intercultural or interracial issues. As they read and evaluate books, the committee eliminates those that demonstrate stereotyped images in text or illustration, demeaning or inaccurate use of language, and inaccuracies in text or illustration. The committee does not consider books multicultural when culture is mere tokenism, or when it is reflected through the gratuitous inclusion of a sprinkling of words from another language or an occasional character of color in the illustrations (Sims Bishop, 1994).

Problems with perspective are another concern of the committee and also a source of debate among the children's literature community. Some argue that no one outside of a particular cultural group can hope to write with the understanding and knowledge of an insider and therefore should not try. Others grant that being an outsider makes it more difficult, but that good writers such as Paul Goble transcend their outsider status. A good book will "contribute in a positive way to an understanding of the people and cultures portrayed" (Sims Bishop, 1994, xx) whether its author is an insider or an outsider to the culture. However, it is important to note the perspective of the author when deciding on the quality of any book.

Books representing culturally diverse groups must represent them accurately and with depth. Look for books that avoid stereotypes, portray the values and the cultural group in an authentic way, use language that reflects cultural group usage, and validate readers' experiences while also broadening vision and inviting reflection. As you begin to evaluate books for their cultural authenticity, use a checklist such as that in Figure 11.1. You can also consult sources such as *Kaleidoscope* (available through the National Council of Teachers of English); *Open the Books and See All the People*, published by the Queens Borough, New York, Public Library; Harris's *Teaching Multicultural Literature in Grades K–8* and *Teaching with Multiethnic Literature, K–8*; Miller-Lachmann's *Our Family, Our Friends, Our World*; Helbig and Perkins's *Many Peoples, One Land: A Guide to New Multicultural Literature for Children and Young Adults*; or Tomlinson's *Children's Books from Other Countries*. A committee of the International Reading Association also generates a list of "Notable Books for a Global Society," published annually in the February issue of *The Reading Teacher*.

Figure 11 ✿ 1

Checklist for Evaluating Culturally Diverse Literature

✿ Does the book qualify as good literature?

✿ Is the culture accurately portrayed, demonstrating diversity within as well as across cultures if appropriate and avoiding stereotypes?

✿ Is the book a positive contribution to an understanding of the culture portrayed?

Literature from Parallel Cultures

Because books from parallel cultures have been less readily available than those from the mainstream culture, here we highlight information about children's literature from the major North American parallel cultures as well as international children's literature. While many of the books mentioned in this chapter are discussed in the appropriate genre chapters, here we feature them in light of their cultural diversity. A focus on these books and the authors and illustrators who produce them is useful in building a culturally diverse literature collection.

AFRICAN-AMERICAN LITERATURE

Books about African Americans reflect the wide range of African-American culture, including the experience and consequences of slavery, the civil rights movement, life in the inner city, life in the South in the twentieth century, and the middle-class African-American experience. Established authors continue to write, and new voices are being heard, such as that of Leon Walter Tillage, whose life story, *Leon's Story*, won the Boston Globe-Horn Book Award for nonfiction in 1998, and Christopher Paul Curtis, who won a Newbery honor for his first novel, *The Watsons Go to Birmingham, 1963*, and the Newbery Medal for his second, *Bud, Not Buddy* (both I). Further, the diversity within people of African descent is now becoming part of children's books, with books set in the Caribbean, the West Indies, England, and South Africa, as well as North America (Sims Bishop, 1994). Even though the percentages are small, the folklore, poetry, fiction, informational books, and biographies help children from all cultures recognize and appreciate the contributions, lives, and values of African Americans.

African-American literature spans the genres. Many African-American authors and illustrators are noted for their work in a particular genre while others write across genres. Some outstanding African-American authors and illustrators and their work are discussed here. Others are listed in the Booklist at the end of this chapter; many also can be found in Chapters 2 through 10.

Virginia Hamilton is one of the most influential and prolific African-American authors writing today. She writes in many genres. A noted folklorist, her outstanding collections like *The People Could Fly* and *In the Beginning* (both I–A) are an integral part of American folklore. She is also one of

© 1985 Leo and Diane Dillon

Leo and Diane Dillon's powerful illustrations capture the strength of the African-American spirit in Virginia Hamilton's **The People Could Fly.**

Profile ✳ The Pinkney Family

© Myles C. Pinkney

The Pinkney family has contributed a remarkable number of high-quality and award-winning books to children's literature. We include profiles on four of them (Jerry, Gloria, Brian, and Andrea Davis Pinkney) in this chapter.

Jerry Pinkney

I grew up in a small house in Philadelphia, Pennsylvania. I was a middle child of six. I started drawing as far back as I can remember, at the age of four or five. My brothers drew, and I guess in a way I was mimicking them. I found I enjoyed the act of putting marks on paper. It gave me a way of creating my own space and quiet time, as well as a way of expressing myself.

In first grade I had the opportunity to draw a large picture of a fire engine on the blackboard. I was complimented and encouraged to draw more. The attention felt good, and I wanted more. Drawing helped me build my

self-esteem and feel good about myself, and, with hard work, I graduated from elementary school with honors.

My formal art training started at Dobbins Vocational High School, and upon graduation I received a scholarship to the Philadelphia Museum College of Art. My major was advertising and design. The most exciting classes for me were drawing, painting, and printmaking. It is no wonder I turned to illustrating and designing books. For me the book represents the ultimate in graphics: first, as a designer, considering space, page size, number of pages, and type size; then, as an illustrator, dealing with the aesthetics of line, color, and form.

To capture a sense of realism for characters in my work, I use models that resemble the people I want to portray. My wife, Gloria Jean (also an author), and I keep a closet full of old clothes to dress up the models, and I have the models act out the story. Photos are taken to aid me in better understanding body language and facial expressions. Once I have that photo in front of me I have freedom, because the more you know, the more you can be inventive.

Jerry Pinkney's books have received numerous awards, including Caldecott Honor Book awards.

Marketing flyer, HarperCollins Children's Books

© Myles C. Pinkney

Gloria Jean Pinkney

Gloria Jean Pinkney was born in Lumberton, North Carolina. Her family moved to Philadelphia when she was quite young. Gloria has been involved with her husband Jerry Pinkney and his artistic life since they met and married. Their four children also work in publishing or in closely related fields.

Gloria helps Jerry with his work by doing research for his stories and maintaining a wardrobe of period clothing. When they work on a story, they use models that resemble the people they want to portray. The models dress in clothing from the period and act out the story; Jerry and Gloria take photographs for Jerry to use in his illustrations.

Gloria began telling her own family stories from childhood memories. Her first book, *Back Home*, describes a trip she took to visit her great uncle and other relatives in Lumberton, North Carolina.

the most distinguished and talented writers of children's fiction in the field today. She was the first African American to win the Newbery Medal and the world-renowned Hans Christian Andersen Award, an international award given for the body of her work. Her numerous honors include the National Book Award, the Coretta Scott King Award, the Boston Globe-Horn Book Award, and the International Board on Books for Young People (IBBY) Honor List, and she is the only children's writer ever to receive the prestigious MacArthur Grant. Her novels include fantasy, mystery, realistic fiction, historical fiction, and biographical works.

Julius Lester is another outstanding African-American author who writes in many genres. His fresh retellings of the Uncle Remus stories, such as *Further Tales of Uncle Remus*

(I), bring these trickster tales to life and highlight the connections between the tales and the people who told them. His recent version of *John Henry* (P–I) is a powerful prose retelling of the classic tall tale. He also writes outstanding historical fiction for older readers.

Folklore, biography, and historical nonfiction are genres in which Patricia C. McKissack has excelled. Her folklore picture books, like *Flossie and the Fox* and *Mirandy and Brother Wind* (both P), are wonderful retellings of stories she was told as a young girl. Her biography and nonfiction works, several of which we discuss in Chapters 9 and 10, are often written with her husband, Fredrick McKissack, and reflect careful scholarship, attention to detail, and a storyteller's voice.

A prequel, *Sunday Outing*, presents the events leading up to the trip described in her first book. She has written another book with two of her sons, J. Brian and Myles, *In the Forest of Your Remembrance*, due in September 2001 from Phyllis Fogelman Books.

J. Brian Pinkney

Brian Pinkney says, "I always knew I wanted to be an illustrator. I wanted to be just like my father." Brian's interest in art convinced his mother to provide him with his own small studio. He grew up drawing, painting, and sculpting everything from superheroes to robots.

Brian earned a bachelor's degree in fine art from the Philadelphia College of Art in 1983. When he began his career in illustrating children's books, he first worked in watercolors. Unlike his father, whose art often sublimates line to color and value, Brian was interested in

volume and lots of lines. It wasn't until he went for his master's degree at the School of Visual Arts in New York, however, that he found his own distinct style with the scratchboard technique—a technique that has earned him a special place in the children's book world.

Brian says, "When I scratch, the nib makes a percussive sound, much like drumming." He further explains that scratchboard begins with a white board covered with black ink. Sharp tools are used to scratch away the black ink from the surface. As the black ink is scratched away, the white board beneath emerges. An outline of the character is revealed. Rather than adding black lines to a white canvas or paper, he subtracts. He scrapes off the black ink and thereby creates white lines. Slowly, a hint of the white background can be seen. As he continues to scratch away the black ink, the white background surfaces. A few details on the face begin to come out. Then Brian concentrates on uncovering the face of the character. Finally, the character is fully revealed, ready to step off the page and into a book! Brian adds the color last. His new technique is to tint the black and white images with lama dyes, then paint on top of that with acrylic paint.

Brian says, "Working in scratchboard is like drawing, etching, and sculpting all at the same time." Brian has received Caldecott Honor Book awards for his illustration.

Marketing flyer, Hyperion Books

Andrea Davis Pinkney

Andrea Davis Pinkney earned a degree in journalism from Syracuse University and began her career as an editor for a home decorating magazine. She became senior editor at *Essence* magazine, where she managed the contemporary living department and wrote features on children, family, travel, and black history.

Andrea Davis Pinkney, currently a senior editor at Hyperion Books for Children, is the driving editorial force behind Jump at the Sun, an imprint that celebrates the beauties of black culture. She conducts thorough research for her books. She has written several biographies, novels, and an informational book on Kwanzaa. Her husband, Brian Pinkney, has illustrated several of her books in scratchboard.

Marketing brochure, Hyperion Books for Children

Historical fiction at its best is one way to describe Mildred Taylor's books. With the stories of her childhood and her family as her guides she continues to write books that are powerfully moving. Her Newbery Medal–winning *Roll of Thunder, Hear My Cry* (A), discussed in Chapter 8, is part of an outstanding series of books about the Logan family.

Young readers have devoured books by Walter Dean Myers since the 1970s. He writes across many genres for an upper elementary through young adult audience. His poetry, such as *Harlem* (I), short stories like those in *145th Street Stories* (A), novels such as the Prinz Award–winner *Monster* (A), and carefully researched biographies, such as *Malcolm X: By Any Means Necessary* (A), attest to his skill and versatility.

Jacqueline Woodson is a young African-American writer whose novels for older readers are quickly becoming "classics" in the field. Her latest, *Miracle's Boys* (A), won the Coretta Scott King Award. She has recently tried her hand at picture storybooks; *We Had a Picnic This Sunday Past* (P) is a delight.

Major poets writing African-American and Caribbean poetry include Ashley Bryan, Gwendolyn Brooks, Lucille Clifton, Maya Angelou, Monica Gunning, Eloise Greenfield, and Nikki Giovanni. Many of these poets write in other genres as well. Bryan is noted for his folklore retellings, Greenfield and Clifton for their picture books.

There are many authors who explore both contemporary and historical African-American experience and folk-

© 1994 Jerry Pinkney

Author Julius Lester and artist Jerry Pinkney brilliantly recreate this well-loved American tall tale.

lore in picture storybooks, transitional chapter books, and novels. Books by Jeanette Caines, Lucille Clifton, Angela Johnson, Angela Shelf Medearis, Mildred Pitts Walter, Eleanora Tate, and others provide wonderful reading experiences for elementary and middle school children.

Some outstanding African-American illustrators are Donald Crews, Leo Dillon, Tom Feelings, James Ransome, Jerry Pinkney, Brian Pinkney, Synthia Saint James, and John Steptoe. James Ransome has graced many books with his powerful oil paintings, including Dinah Johnson's **Quinnie Blue** (P) and Lesa Cline-Ransome's **Satchel Paige** (P–I). He won the Coretta Scott King Award for illustration with his brilliant evocation of James Weldon Johnson's **The Creation** (P–I–A).

Jerry Pinkney is one of the best-known African-American illustrators, having illustrated Lester's Uncle Remus tales, McKissack's **Mirandy and Brother Wind**, San Souci's **The Talking Eggs** (P–I), and Julius Lester's retelling of **John Henry** (I), all Caldecott Honor Books, as well as many others. Pinkney's son, Brian, is also a noted illustrator, having received a Caldecott Honor for San Souci's **The Faithful Friend** (I). The family also includes authors Gloria Pinkney and Andrea Davis Pinkney. Often, the husbands and wives team to produce brilliantly executed books, such as Andrea and Brian's collaborative effort, **Alvin Ailey** (I). The Pinkney family is the subject of the Profile in this chapter.

As you can see, the rich heritage of the African-American experience is indeed reflected in its literature for children and young adults. Although the number of books is limited, talented African-American writers and illustrators give all readers the gift of wonderful books. The Booklist at the end of this chapter contains titles that represent some of their best efforts.

ASIAN-AMERICAN LITERATURE

Although still disproportionately small, the number of high-quality books featuring Asian Americans is increasing. Most of the existing books focus on Asian Americans with Chinese or Japanese heritage, but some other Asian countries, such as Korea, Vietnam, Thailand, and the Pacific Islands are slowly being recognized. There is a significant amount of folklore from Asian countries available, but contemporary fiction dealing with Asian-American experiences still lags. There is some excellent historical fiction, much of which focuses on the Japanese-American internment during the Second World War, and several nonfiction books explore the lives of recent Asian immigrants to North America.

Laurence Yep, a Chinese-American writer who has been telling the stories of Asian Americans for over 20 years, chronicles some of the problems that beset Asian-American immigrant families in his historical novels, **The Star Fisher** and **Dream Soul** (both I–A), which are based on his Chinese mother's experiences growing up in West Virginia in 1927. In **Dragon's Gate** (I–A) he goes further back in time to tell the story of a young boy's experiences leaving China for North America and the building of the transcontinental railroad. The richness of cultural and social details in these novels add depth to the moving stories. Yep writes across genres, producing folktales, contemporary fiction, fantasy, and mysteries in addition to historical fiction. In many of his contemporary fiction novels, such as **The Cook's Family** (A) and **Thief of Hearts** (A), Yep explores problems of belonging and alienation in the lives of Asian-American and multiracial adolescents. His San Francisco Chinatown mystery series, beginning with **The Case of the Lion Dance** (I), is full of rich cultural details. He is also noted for the inclusion of fantasy elements based on Chinese lore in many of his novels.

Lensey Namioka also writes about relationships in a contemporary Chinese-American family in **Yang the Youngest and His Terrible Ear**, **Yang the Second and Her Secret Admirers**, and **Yang the Third and Her Impossible Family** (all I) while also exploring issues of adjusting to the new customs and experiences that accompany immigration. In a novel for older readers, **April and the Dragon Lady** (A), she explores intergenerational and intergender conflict in a Chinese-American family. Marie G. Lee's novels of contemporary Korean-American family life, such as **Necessary Roughness** (A) explore both cultural and intergenerational conflicts.

Allen Say's paintings portray his love for both America and Japan in Grandfather's Journey.

Yoshiko Uchida, a first-generation Japanese American living in California at the outbreak of World War II, tells the story of her childhood in *Journey to Topaz* and *Journey Home* (both I–A). These novels provide a vivid and compelling record of the experience of internment. They are complemented by Ken Mochizuki's *Baseball Saved Us* (I).

Janet Wong is a young, contemporary poet who writes of her experiences growing up as a multiracial young woman in *Good Luck Gold and Other Poems* and *A Suitcase of Seaweed and Other Poems* (both I).

Allen Say has written and illustrated several beautiful books about Japanese and Japanese-American experiences. His *Grandfather's Journey* (P–I) won the Caldecott Medal for its evocative illustrations of a man torn between two beautiful countries—North America and Japan. The text and illustrations portray love and longing in a way that transcends political boundaries. Some of his other works, such as *Tree of Cranes* and *Tea with Milk* (both P–I) explore the blending of cultures.

Several Asian-American artists illustrate folklore from Asian countries. Ed Young is a prolific illustrator who won the Caldecott Medal for *Lon Po Po: A Red Riding Hood Story from China* (P). His illustrations for Ai-Ling Louie's *Yeh-Shen: A Cinderella Story from China* (P–I) are richly evocative of the tale's origins.

Although few in number, a wide range of fiction, nonfiction, and poetry books explore the values and lives of Asian Americans. Some of the best of these books are listed in the Booklist at the end of this chapter.

LATINO LITERATURE

The number of books for children portraying Latino characters stands in stark contrast to the number of Latinos in the population. Only a tiny minority of all children's books published represent a Latino culture (Nieto, 1993). Compared to the number of Latino children who need to see themselves represented in books, and the number of other children who need to understand something of Latino cultures, there is a dearth of books available. Happily, the situation is changing, however slowly; there are many gifted writers producing high-quality work, such as Victor Martinez, whose novel *Parrot in the Oven: Mi Vida* (A) won the 1996 National Book Award. Francisco Jimenez's *The Circuit* (A), a collection of stories based on the author's own experiences as a child in a migrant farmworker family, won the 1998 Boston Globe-Horn Book Award for fiction. Contemporary fiction and poetry are expanding, and the number of Latino writers is increasing. With the increase in the number of Spanish-speaking children in school, there also has been an increase in the number of Spanish-language children's books. However, it is important to remember that many of these books, welcome as they are, are not books that reflect any Latino culture, but rather mainstream children's books translated from English into Spanish.

Like the literature of other cultures, Latino literature spans folklore, poetry, all types of fiction and nonfiction, and represents a rich array of subcultures. Gary Soto is one of the primary Latino voices in children's literature today. His work ranges from short stories to novels to poetry. *Baseball in April and Other Stories* and *Local News* (both I–A) are collections of short stories that explore growing up as Soto did, poor and Mexican American in central California. His many novels explore life for preadolescent and adolescent Latino boys.

Soto is also a gifted poet. His poems in *Neighborhood Odes* (I–A) center on his early life. Those in *Canto Familiar* (I–A) speak of childhood experiences that transcend cultural differences. He has also written several picture storybooks, including the fantasy *Chato's Kitchen* (P), playfully illustrated by Susan Guervara.

Nicholasa Mohr is a Puerto Rican author who explores contemporary issues in the lives of Puerto Rican youth growing up in North America. Her short stories and novels, such as *Going Home* and *Felita* (both A) and *The Magic Shell* (I) are beautifully written and powerful. Her fantasy picture book, *Old Letivia and the Mountain of Sorrows* (P), is set in Puerto Rico and based on classic folktale patterns.

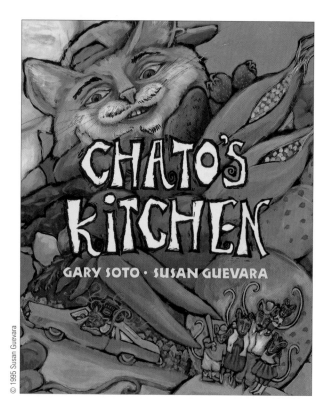

© 1995 Susan Guevara

Artist Susan Guevara captures the playful mood of Gary Soto's text in the engaging story Chato's Kitchen.

Pat Mora, a Mexican-American author, writes books that appeal to primary-grade children, such as *A Birthday Basket for Tia, Pablo's Tree, Tomas and the Library Lady*, as well as some lovely poetry, such as *Listen to the Desert, The Desert Is My Mother, This Big Sky*, and *Confetti: Poems for Children* (all P). A noted expert in Latino children's literature, Alma Flor Ada recounts stories of her Cuban family in *Where the Flame Trees Bloom* and *Under the Royal Palms: A Childhood in Cuba* (both I). Lucia Gonzalez retells *The Bossy Gallito/El Gallo de Bodas: A Traditional Cuban Folktale* and *Senor Cat's Romance and Other Favorite Stories from Latin America* (both P). Francisco X. Alarcon and Judith Ortiz Cofer add their poetic voices to an expanding body of Latino poetry. These and other books offer young readers a more diverse picture of Latino life and culture than was ever before available. It is still not enough. Other Latino authors and illustrators appear in the Booklist at the end of this chapter.

NATIVE AMERICAN LITERATURE

Native American experiences have been interpreted in literature for children by members of various tribal groups, anthropologists, folklorists, and others who have lived among Native Americans. Unfortunately, until the late 1970s much of the literature that portrayed Native Americans did so

with erroneous or stereotyped information and images. Literature by and about Native Americans came to the fore in the 1970s as Native American voices, so long suppressed, began to be heard and mainstream culture developed a new consciousness about Native Americans. Children now learn about several of the more than 500 different groups that comprise Native Americans.

Children's literature now includes Native American poetry and folklore, historical fiction, and biography, as well as historical nonfiction from a Native American perspective. There are a few books about contemporary Native American experiences, mostly nonfiction. As more Native American and other well-informed voices begin to be heard, the quality and quantity of the books available have increased. For example, a historical fiction novel for children, *Birchbark House* (I), by Louise Erdich, an award-winning and popular adult writer, recently was nominated for the National Book Award for children. An important resource regarding Native American literature, Slapin and Seale's *Through Indian Eyes: The Native Experience in Books for Children* offers essays, poems, and book reviews. Oyate, a Native organization, is another source for book reviews. Those at Oyate can help you judge authenticity in Native literature. Their Web site is www.oyate.org.

Some of the earliest pieces of fiction that truly expressed Native American values, Craig Kee Strete's *When Grandfather Journeys into Winter* and *The Bleeding Man and Other Science Fiction Stories* (both A) offer readers the opportunity to explore issues from a Native American perspective. A later novel, *Big Thunder Magic* (A), is a contemporary allegory set in city and pueblo. *The World in Grandfather's Hands* (A) is a more recent contemporary realistic novel of family life among urban Native Americans set in the Southwest.

Folklore and poetry from Native American cultures is available in anthology and picture book form. Among the contemporary anthologies available, Richard Erdoes's *The Sound of Flutes and Other Indian Legends*, John Bierhorst's *The Deetkatoo: Native American Stories About Little People* (I–A), *On the Road of Stars: Native American Night Poems and Sleep Charms* (P–I), and *The White Deer and Other Stories Told by the Lenape* (I–A) are rich resources. Hettie Jones's *The Trees Stand Shining: Poetry of the North American Indians* (P–I) is a classic collection that has been reissued.

Joseph Bruchac's Abenaki heritage is reflected in his collection, *Thirteen Moons on Turtle's Back: A Native American Year of Moons* (I). He also tells stories from other Native American groups, such as *The Boy Who Lived with the Bears and Other Iroquois Stories* (I), *The Story of the Milky Way* (I), a collaboration with Cherokee storyteller Gayle Ross, and *Gluskabe and the Four Wishes* (P), a Wabanaki tale. Michael Caduto and Bruchac's *Keepers of the Earth: Native American Stories and Environmental Activities for Children* (I) offers an organized volume of Native American folktales followed by ideas for discussion and activities. Bruchac's *Between Earth and Sky: Legends of Native Amer-*

ican Sacred Places and *Four Ancestors: Stories, Songs, and Poems from Native North America* (both I–A) range across Native American groups.

Bruchac also writes both contemporary and historical stories about Native American people. His contemporary fiction, such as *Eagle Song* (I), is a welcome addition to a genre almost devoid of Native American literature. We discuss his novel, *Sacajawea* (I–A) in Chapter 8. Other important historical fiction from a Native viewpoint includes Michael Dorris's *Guests, Sees Behind Trees,* and *Morning Girl* (all I); Dorris has also written a contemporary fiction novel, *The Window* (A).

Paul Goble is one of the most prolific authors and illustrators of Native American folklore. Although he is not Native American, his knowledge of the Lakota Sioux nation enables him to portray their culture accurately. His series of trickster stories, such as *Iktomi and the Buzzard* (P–I), and his beautiful retellings of more serious folktales and myths, such as *Buffalo Woman, The Girl Who Loved Wild Horses,* and *Star Boy* (all I), enable all children to enjoy the rich storytelling tradition of the Lakota Sioux.

Virginia Driving Hawk Sneve's *Dancing Teepees: Poems of American Indian Youth* (I–A) is an excellent collection of traditional and modern Native American poetry. She is also a talented writer of nonfiction, and her **First Americans** series, including *The Seminoles* (I), provides excellent information sources about many different Native American groups.

Diane Hoyt-Goldsmith's thoughtful photobiographies about contemporary Native American children and their traditions, such as *Cherokee Summer* and *Arctic Hunter* (both I) make the point that Native American children today share many similarities with children from other cultural groups in North America while also maintaining their rich cultural heritage. Other excellent nonfiction books about contemporary Native American culture include George Ancona's *Powwow* (I), a description of Montana's annual Crow Fair, part of the **We Are Still Here: Native Americans Today** series.

Shonto Begay, a Navajo artist and storyteller, displays his considerable talents in *Ma'ii and Cousin Horned Toad* (I), another trickster tale. His beautiful *Navajo: Visions and Voices Across the Mesa* (I–A) is a collection of chants, stories, and paintings that express the beliefs and traditions of the Navajo from ancient to contemporary times.

Shonto Begay captures the beauty of the Navajo nation in **Navajo: Visions and Voices Across the Mesa.**

George Littlechild, himself a member of the Plains Cree Nation, interprets the impact of white culture on his people through stunning collage paintings and powerful words in *This Land Is My Land* (P–I). These and other excellent books from the Native American tradition are listed in the Booklist at the end of this chapter.

While the number of books by and about people from parallel cultures in America is increasing, we must make special efforts to seek these books out, to include them in our classroom and school libraries and in our curriculum. When we do this, we help children see themselves as members of a larger community. Teaching Idea 11.3 is but one way of helping children explore culture through literature.

INTERNATIONAL LITERATURE

When Neil Armstrong was hurtling around the world in a capsule in outer space, he said that looking back at Earth was like looking at a big blue marble. His comment made us aware that our "marble" is not a very big one and that what happens in one part of it affects every other part. Viewing our world as a global village makes it clear that literature for children and young adults should reflect the interdependence of nations and people everywhere.

Books from around the world can give young readers the opportunity to travel to other lands and experience lives different from their own. Today a wide range of po-etry, folklore, fiction, and nonfiction from around the world is available in North America. The exchange of books among nations is becoming more widespread due to the ease of international travel and modern technology. Moreover, many authors and illustrators of children's books published in the United States live in England, Australia, Japan, Africa, and other parts of the globe. Publishers from all over the world meet at book fairs in Israel, Italy, Germany, Spain, Mexico, Argentina, Brazil, Colombia, and elsewhere to buy manuscripts and arrange for the copublication of the same book in several languages. Thus children in many countries may read the very same book written in their own native language. Children's literature has become truly international.

This exchange of books and the movement of people from country to country makes many wonderful experiences available to North American children. For example, Ifeoma Onyefulu, a Nigerian, brings Nigeria to North America in *A Is for Africa* and *Ogbo: Sharing Life in an African Village* (both P) with lucid writing and clear, full-color photographs. Kyoki Mori's novels *One Bird* and *Shizuko's Daughter* (both A) explore the opportunities and restrictions for women in contemporary Japan. Gaye Hicyilmaz's contemporary novel set during the war in Yugoslavia, *Smiling for Strangers* (A), follows 14-year-old Nina Topic as she escapes to England. Adeline Yen Mah tells of her own childhood in *Falling Leaves: The True Story of an Unwanted Chinese Daughter* (A). Christina Bjork takes young readers to Venice in *Vendela in Venice* (I), with help from illustrator Inga-Karin Eriksson. And Mette Newth's *The Transformation* (A) recreates the ancient Iceland and the clash between Native and Christian beliefs as well as between humans and nature.

People from the international community discuss books for children and young adults through their work in professional organizations—namely the International Board on Books for Young People (IBBY), the United States Board on Books for Young People (USBBY), the American Library Association (ALA), the American Booksellers Association (ABA), the Modern Language Association (MLA), and the International Reading Association (IRA), among others. The prestigious Hans Christian Andersen Awards, presented by IBBY, are given for the entire body of an author's and an illustrator's work. Nominees from all over the world are eligible. Winners are listed in Appendix A. The IBBY magazine, *Bookbird*, provides current information about children's literature from around the world.

The Mildred L. Batchelder Award is given in the United States annually to the publisher of the most outstanding book of the year, first published in another country, and published in translation in the United States. Batchelder Award winners are found in Appendix A. In Europe, the International Youth Library—located at Blutenburg Castle on the outskirts of Munich, Germany—is devoted to the col-

---

Teaching Idea 11 ☆ 3

Discover Common Folkloric Elements Across Cultures

Ask your students to read the folklore of several cultural groups. Discuss the following:

* ✻ What parallel characters appear? Who are the tricksters, the noodleheads, the ones who sacrifice for others?

* ✻ What kinds of animals appear? Which folklore includes ravens, eagles, wolves, bears, rabbits, turtles?

* ✻ Some cultures include magical objects in their stories. Discuss the kinds of objects and the powers they have, such as a rose, a ring, a spindle, an amulet, a bone and sinew of a caribou, a stone, a doll. See if the magical objects differ within and across cultural groups.

lection, study, and propagation of international children's literature.

When books present authentic images from another country, children learn an important lesson. They recognize that although all cultures are distinct and different, all people share universal needs for love, belonging, and acceptance. They learn that all people share the need for family, friends, and neighbors, and for food, clothing, and shelter. They learn to see themselves as citizens of the world. For example, readers of Mirjam Pressler's *Halinka* (A), translated from the German by Elizabeth D. Crawford, can't help but recognize themselves in this lonely and emotionally fragile young girl living in an orphanage in postwar Germany.

Culturally Diverse Literature in the Classroom

Another way to look at literature in terms of cultural diversity is to attempt to describe the possibilities inherent in the books themselves. That is, do the books simply contribute knowledge about a particular culture, or do they invite reader transformation and promote cross-cultural affective understanding? Do the books simply present differences or do they invite readers to explore alternative ways of thinking and living? Is a theme of cross-cultural understanding implicit or explicit?

In any classroom or school library collection, we need books from many cultures and across many genres. The titles in the Booklist at the end of this chapter offer a beginning as you continue to build your collection so that it truly represents the cultural diversity of our world. With these books in hand, you can offer your students experiences that will allow them to understand themselves and others.

TEACHING FOR DIVERSITY

Multicultural education has been widely studied and written about in the United States. Because the term *multicultural* refers to many cultures within one nation, we use the term *culturally diverse* here since we also include an international perspective. However, a discussion of teaching for diversity that includes an international perspective still can rely on the basic premises that multicultural educational reforms have developed.

There are four approaches to multicultural education that relate to teaching with culturally diverse literature. Banks and Banks (1993) distinguish among the contributions approach, the additive approach, the transformation

This powerful novel transcends time and international borders.

© 1998 Joseph Daniel Fiedler

approach, and the social action approach. The *contributions approach* is certainly the easiest way to incorporate culturally diverse literature into your curriculum. In this approach you select books that, for example, celebrate heroes and holidays from various cultures. Spending time reading about Dr. Martin Luther King in January is a common practice that falls into this category. In this approach culturally diverse books and issues are not integrated into the curriculum.

The *additive approach*, in which "content, concepts, themes, and perspectives are added to the curriculum without changing its basic structure" (Banks and Banks, 1993, p. 201), involves incorporating literature by and about people from diverse cultures into the mainstream curriculum without changing the curriculum. For example, Thanksgiving might still be part of a unit on holidays, but reading Michael Dorris's *Guests* (I), a slim novel about the first Thanksgiving told from the perspective of Moss, a young Native American boy whose family has invited the Pilgrims to feast with them, would be "adding" cultural diversity to the traditional view of Thanksgiving. This approach, like the contributions approach, does not fundamentally transform thinking.

The *transformation approach* "changes the basic assumptions of the curriculum and enables students to view concepts, issues, themes, and problems from several ethnic perspectives and points of view" (Banks and Banks, 1993, p. 203). In this approach the Thanksgiving unit would become a unit exploring cultural conflict. Students might read *Guests*, discuss the irony in the term *Thanksgiving*, study historical documents, and read Marcia Sewall's *People of the Breaking Day* (I–A). They would consider the colonization of America from the perspectives of those who were colonized as well as from the perspectives of those who came looking for a better life. This kind of experience can lead to the habit of considering ideas, issues, and events from a variety of perspectives—critical thinking. This kind of teaching is not occasional or superficial, but involves a consideration of diversity as a basic premise.

The fourth, or *social action approach*, adds striving for social change to the transformational approach. Here, students are taught to understand, question, and do something about important social issues. After reading a number of books, both fiction and nonfiction, about recent immigrants to North America, students might write letters to senators, representatives in Congress, and newspaper editors to express their opinions about some of the new immigration policies being discussed.

If you examine your own teaching it is easy to determine where you stand in your current practice. Wherever you are now in your development as a responsive teacher, you can alter your curriculum and classroom practices to include more diversity and sensitivity. Look at your classroom literature collection. How prevalent are books from parallel and international cultures? A first step toward change might entail the purchase of some of the books discussed in this chapter. Then look at your classroom practice. Is culture ever explicitly discussed? If so, is it discussed from an "us and them" perspective or explored as an interesting and integral part of life? Are events and ideas considered from a variety of perspectives, or just your own? A vivid example of this is seen in the many discussions bemoaning the destruction of the Amazon rain forest. Environmentally, this is a disaster for the world, but many of the native people of the region rely on jobs that are part of that destruction; without those jobs they and their families would starve. Reading books like Anna Lewington's *Antonio's Rain Forest* (I) results in a less ethnocentric view of the situation.

Once you have begun to build a culturally diverse literature collection, you can think of Banks's descriptions of the contributions and additive approaches as first steps toward transformation of the curriculum, if that is your goal.

Books offer students of all cultures the opportunity to see their own heroes, traditions, and experiences and those of their diverse peers. This is important for everyone, not just students of color or students in culturally diverse settings, but *all* students who will live and work in the global village of the twenty-first century. Even more powerful is to be able to see one's own and others' cultures as fundamentally important to a curriculum that teaches not only diverse content, but also diverse ways of thinking—leading to empowerment and social action.

Using children's literature to explore cultural diversity involves considering the quality of the books, the content of the books (what they are about and the perspective from which they are written, be it an insider's or an outsider's point of view), and the things you do with them. Teaching Idea 11.4 suggests turning a unit on regional books into a small culture study. To build cultural diversity into your curriculum, you must find books by and about many different kinds of people living different kinds of lives, evaluate those books on both their literary and cultural qualities, and then decide what you will do with students as they read and consider the virtual experiences and the cultural information the books offer.

Teaching Idea 11 ✳ 4

Study a Regional Culture

Every region of the United States has its natural beauty, cultural traditions, folklore, dialect, traditional foods, and unique manners or mannerisms. Your students will enjoy studying their region's characteristics through literature. For example, the culture of the southeastern Appalachian region of the United States is one that has been recreated in children's books across many genres. The folklore collections of Richard Chase; new retellings of old tales by authors such as William Hooks; poetry, picture books, and novels of authors like Cynthia Rylant, Gloria Houston, and Phyllis Reynolds Naylor—all evoke the unique culture of the region, both past and present.

Spend some time finding books that present the flavor of the region in which you teach and share these books with your students. You can simply enjoy books set in your part of the world or use them as the springboard to a culture study in which you and your students look for aspects of setting, characterization, and values that are common across books.

Summary

Books for children and young adults are beginning to reflect the diversity that characterizes North American and global society. As our country becomes more inclusive in attitude toward all peoples, rather than just the mainstream middle class, children's literature grows to include wonderful books by and about people of parallel cultures. Further, the notion of Earth as a global village is reflected in the thriving world of international children's books. Although we do not yet have a body of literature that reflects a diversity commensurate with the diversity in our population, we do have a good beginning. All classrooms and all libraries can contain collections that are balanced across cultural groups. Special attention to books from African-American, Asian-American, Latino, Native American, and international cultures can help bring balance to any collection of children's books. This balance makes it possible for teachers to teach for diversity through their careful selection of children's literature. After all, good books and good teaching can help change the world.

In the January/February 1999 issue of *The Horn Book Magazine*, Katherine Paterson writes about going to New Delhi to accept the Hans Christian Andersen Award, and Cathy Hirano discusses the challenges of translating from Japanese to English. Reading both of these articles can give you a deeper understanding of the international world of children's books. In the March/April 1999 issue of *The Horn Book Magazine*, Susan Dove Lempke reports on her informal survey of culturally diverse picture books, calling for more "high-quality literature showing a variety of people." Read her article, find some of the books she discusses, and then respond to her arguments.

Booklist

African-American Children's Books

FOLKLORE (SEE ALSO CHAPTER 5)

Hamilton, Virginia, *Her Stories: African American Folktales, Fairy Tales, and True Tales*, illustrated by Leo and Diane Dillon (I)

_____, *In the Beginning* (I–A)

_____, *The People Could Fly*, illustrated by Leo and Diane Dillon (I)

_____, *A Ring of Tricksters*, illustrated by Barry Moser (N–P)

_____, *When Birds Could Talk and Bats Could Sing*, illustrated by Barry Moser (N–P)

Haskins, James, *The Headless Haunt and Other African-American Ghost Stories*, illustrated by Ben Otero (I)

Hudson, Wade, and Cheryl Hudson, *How Sweet the Sound: African-American Songs for Children*, illustrated by Floyd Cooper (N–P)

Jaquith, Priscilla, *Bo Rabbit Smart for True: Tall Tales from the Gullah* (P)

Lester, Julius, *Further Tales of Uncle Remus: The Misadventures of Brer Rabbit, Brer Fox, Brer Wolf, the Doodang, and Other Creatures*, illustrated by Jerry Pinkney (P–I–A)

_____, *John Henry*, illustrated by Jerry Pinkney (I)

_____, *The Last Tales of Uncle Remus*, illustrated by Jerry Pinkney (P–I–A)

_____, *The Tales of Uncle Remus: The Adventures of Brer Rabbit*, illustrated by Jerry Pinkney (P–I–A)

Lyons, Mary E., *The Butter Tree: Tales of Bruh Rabbit* (P)

_____, *Raw Head, Bloody Bones: African-American Tales of the Supernatural* (I–A)

McKissack, Patricia C., *Flossie and the Fox* (P)

_____, *Mirandy and Brother Wind* (P)

Medearis, Angela Shelf, *The Freedom Riddle*, illustrated by John Ward (P–I)

_____, *Tailypo: A Newfangled Tall Tale*, illustrated by Sterling Brown (P–I)

San Souci, Robert, *Sukey and the Mermaid*, illustrated by Brian Pinkney (P–I)

_____, *The Talking Eggs*, illustrated by Jerry Pinkney (P–I)

Wahl, Jan, *Little Eight John*, illustrated by Wil Clay (P–I)

_____, *Tailypo!* illustrated by Wil Clay (P)

POETRY AND SONG (SEE ALSO CHAPTER 2)

Adedjouma, Davida, *The Palm of My Heart: Poetry by African American Children*, illustrated by Gregory Christie (P–I–A)

Adoff, Arnold, *The Basket Counts*, illustrated by Michael Weaver (I)

_____, *In for Winter, Out for Spring*, illustrated by Jerry Pinkney (P)

Barnwell, Ysaye M., *No Mirrors in My Nana's House*, illustrated by Synthia Saint James (N–P)

Bishop, Rudine Sims, *Wonders: The Best Poems of Effie Lee Newsome* (P–I)

Boyd, Candy Dawson, *Daddy, Daddy, Be There*, illustrated by Floyd Cooper (N–P–I)

Brooks, Gwendolyn, *Bronzeville Boys and Girls* (P–I)

Bryan, Ashley, *All Night, All Day: A Child's First Book of African-American Spirituals* (P–I–A)

_____, *Ashley Bryan's ABC of African American Poetry* (N–P–I–A)

_____, *Carol of the Brown King: Nativity Poems by Langston Hughes* (N–P–I–A)

_____, *Sing to the Sun* (P)

Clinton, Catherine, *I, Too, Sing America: Three Centuries of African American Poetry*, illustrated by Stephen Alcorn (P–I–A)

Feelings, Tom, *Soul Looks Back in Wonder* (N–P–I–A)

Giovanni, Nikki, *The Genie in the Jar*, illustrated by Chris Raschka (N–P)

_____, *Knoxville, Tennessee*, illustrated by Larry Johnson (P)

_____, *The Selected Poems of Nikki Giovanni* (A)

_____, *Shimmy Shimmy Shimmy Like My Sister Kate: Looking at the Harlem Renaissance Through Poems* (A)

_____, *Spin a Soft Black Song* (P–I)

_____, *The Sun Is So Quiet*, illustrated by Ashley Bryan (N–P–I)

Greenfield, Eloise, *Angels*, illustrated by Jan Spivey Gilchrist (N–P)

_____, *For the Love of the Game: Michael Jordan and Me*, illustrated by Jan Spivey Gilchrist (N–P–I)

_____, *Honey, I Love and Other Love Poems* (P–I)

_____, *Night on Neighborhood Street*, illustrated by Jan Spivey Gilchrist (P)

Grimes, Nikki, *A Dime a Dozen*, illustrated by Angelo (I–A)

_____, *It's Raining Laughter*, illustrated by Miles Pinkney (N–P)

_____, *Meet Danitra Brown*, illustrated by Floyd Cooper (N–P)

Hudson, Cheryl Willis, *Hold Christmas in Your Heart: African-American Songs, Poems, and Stories for the Holidays*, illustrated by Anna Rich, Cal Massey, Eric Battle, James Ransome, Ron Garnett, Sylvia Walker, and Higgins Bond (N–P)

Hughes, Langston, *Black Misery*, illustrated by Arouni (A)

_____, *The Block*, illustrated by Romare Bearden (A)

_____, *The Dream Keeper and Other Poems*, illustrated by Brian Pinkney (I)

Johnson, Angela, *The Other Side: Shorter Poems* (A)

Johnson, James Weldon, *The Creation*, illustrated by James Ransome (P–I–A)

_____, *Lift Ev'ry Voice and Sing*, illustrated by Jan Spivey Gilchrist (N–P–I–A)

Jones, Patricia Spears, *The Weather That Kills* (A)

Mathis, Sharon Bell, *Red Dog, Blue Fly: Football Poems*, illustrated by Jan Spivey Gilchrist (P–I)

McKissack, Patricia, and Fredrick McKissack, *Messy Bessey's School Desk*, illustrated by Dana Regan (N–P)

Medearis, Angela Shelf, *Rum-a-Tum-Tum*, illustrated by James Ransome (N–P–I)

_____, *Skin Deep and Other Teenage Reflections*, illustrated by Michael Bryant (A)

Myers, Walter Dean, *Angel to Angel: A Mother's Gift of Love* (N–P–I–A)

_____, *Brown Angels: An Album of Pictures and Verse* (P–I)

_____, *Harlem*, illustrated by Christopher Myers (P–I–A)

Okutoro, Lydia Omolola, *Quiet Storm: Voices of Young Black Poets* (A)

Parks, Gordon, *Arias in Silence* (I–A)

Strickland, Dorothy, and Michael Strickland, F*amilies: Poems Celebrating the African American Experience*, illustrated by John Ward (P–I)

Thomas, Joyce Carol, *Brown Honey and Broomwheat Tea*, illustrated by Floyd Cooper (P)

_____, *Cherish Me*, illustrated by Nneka Bennett (N)

_____, *Gingerbread Days*, illustrated by Floyd Cooper (P)

PICTURE BOOKS (SEE ALSO CHAPTERS 3 AND 4)

Adoff, Arnold, *Hard to Be Six*, illustrated by Cheryl Hanna (P)

Barber, Barbara E., *Allie's Basketball Dream*, illustrated by Darryl Ligasan (P)

_____, *Saturday at the New You*, illustrated by Anna Rich (P)

Barnwell, Ysaye M., *No Mirrors in My Nana's House*, illustrated by Synthia Saint James (P)

Battle-Lavert, Gwendolyn, *Off to School*, illustrated by Gershom Griffith (P)

_____, *The Shaking Bag*, illustrated by Aminah Brenda Lynn Robinson (P)

Belton, Sandra, *From Miss Ida's Porch*, illustrated by Floyd Cooper (I)

_____, *May'naise Sandwiches and Sunshine Tea*, illustrated by Gail Gordon Carter (P)

Clifton, Lucille, *Everett Anderson's Christmas Coming*, illustrated by Jan Spivey Gilchrist (P)

_____, *Three Wishes*, illustrated by Michael Hays (P)

Coleman, Evelyn, *White Socks Only*, illustrated by Tyrone Geter (I)

Cosby, Bill, *The Meanest Thing to Say*, illustrated by Varnette P. Honeywood (P)

Crews, Donald, *Bigmama's* (P)

_____, *Shortcut* (P)

Crews, Nina, *One Hot Summer Day* (P)

Cummings, Pat, *Carousel* (P)

_____, *Clean Your Room, Harvey Moon* (P)

Flournoy, Vanessa, and Valerie Flournoy, *Celie and the Harvest Fiddler*, illustrated by James Ransome (P–I)

Greenfield, Eloise, *Easter Parade* (P)

_____, *First Pink Light*, illustrated by Jan Spivey Gilchrist (P)

_____, *Grandpa's Face*, illustrated by Floyd Cooper (P)

_____, *William and the Good Old Days*, illustrated by Jan Spivey Gilchrist (P)

Grimes, Nikki, *Meet Danitra Brown*, illustrated by Floyd Cooper (P)

Hamilton, Virginia, *Drylongso*, illustrated by Jerry Pinkney (I–A)

Havill, Juanita, *Jamaica's Blue Marker*, illustrated by Anne Sibley O'Brien (P)

Herron, Carolivia, *Nappy Hair*, illustrated by Joe Cepeda (P)

Hopkinson, Deborah, *Sweet Clara and the Freedom Quilt*, illustrated by James Ransome (P–I)

Hort, Lenny, *How Many Stars in the Sky?*, illustrated by James Ransome (P)

Howard, Elizabeth Fitzgerald, *Mac and Marie and the Train Toss Surprise*, illustrated by Gail Gordon Carter (P)

_____, *Papa Tells Chita a Story*, illustrated by Floyd Cooper (P)

_____, *What's in Aunt Mary's Room?*, illustrated by Cedric Lucas (P–I)

Hudson, Wade, *Jamal's Busy Day*, illustrated by George Ford (P)

Johnson, Angela, *Do Like Kyla* (P)

_____, *The Leaving Morning*, illustrated by David Soman (P)

_____, *One of Three*, illustrated by David Soman (P)

_____, *When I Am Old with You*, illustrated by David Soman (P)

Johnson, Dinah, *Quinnie Blue*, illustrated by James Ransome (P)

_____, *Sunday Week*, illustrated by Tyrone Geter (P)

Johnson, Dolores, *The Best Bug to Be* (P)

_____, *Papa's Stories* (P)

_____, *Seminole Diary: Remembrances of a Slave* (P–I–A)

Lawrence, Jacob, *The Great Migration* (P–I–A)

Mathis, Sharon Bell, *The Hundred Penny Box*, illustrated by Leo and Diane Dillon (P–I)

McKissack, Patricia C., *Ma Dear's Aprons*, illustrated by Floyd Cooper (P)

_____, *A Million Fish . . . More or Less*, illustrated by Dena Schutzer (P–I)

Medearis, Angela Shelf, *The Adventures of Sugar and Junior* (P)

_____, *Dancing with the Indians*, illustrated by Samuel Byrd (P–I)

_____, *Haunts: Five Hair-Raising Tales*, illustrated by Trina Schart Hyman (I)

_____, *Our People*, illustrated by Michael Bryant (P)

_____, *Poppa's New Pants*, illustrated by John Ward (P)

Mitchell, Margaree King, *Granddaddy's Gift*, illustrated by Larry Johnson (P–I)

Myers, Walter Dean, *The Story of the Three Kingdoms*, illustrated by Ashley Bryan (P)

Nolen, Jerdine, *Harvey Potter's Balloon Farm*, illustrated by Mark Buehner (P)

Peterson, Jeanne Whitehouse, *My Mama Sings*, illustrated by Sandra Speidel (P)

Pinkney, Brian, *The Adventures of Sparrowboy* (P)

_____, *JoJo's Flying Side Kick* (P)

_____, *Paperboy* (P)

Pinkney, Brian, and Andrea Davis Pinkney, *I Smell Honey* (N)

Pinkney, Gloria Jean, *Back Home*, illustrated by Jerry Pinkney (P–I)

_____, *The Sunday Outing*, illustrated by Jerry Pinkney (P–I)

Ringgold, Faith, *Tar Beach* (I)

Smalls, Irene, *Dawn and the Round To-It*, illustrated by Tyrone Geter (P)

Smalls-Hector, Irene, *Ebony Sea*, illustrated by Jon Onye Lockard (I)

_____, *Jonathan and His Mommy*, illustrated by Michael Hays (P)

_____, *Louise's Gift or What Did She Give Me That For?* (P)

Steptoe, John, *Creativity* (P)

_____, *Stevie* (P)

Stroud, Bettye, *Down Home at Miss Dessa's*, illustrated by Felicia Marshall (P)

Tate, Eleanora E., *Front Porch Stories at the One-Room School*, illustrated by Eric Velasquez (I)

Thomas, Joyce Carol, *I Have Heard of a Land*, illustrated by Floyd Cooper (P–I)

Walter, Mildred Pitts, *Two and Too Much*, illustrated by Pat Cummings (P)

Wesley, Valerie Wilson, *Freedom's Gifts*, illustrated by Sharon Wilson (P–I)

Williams, Sherley Anne, *Girls Together*, illustrated by Synthia Saint James (P)

_____, *Working Cotton*, illustrated by Carole Byard (P–I)

Woodson, Jacqueline, *We Had a Picnic This Sunday Past* (P)

Wright, Courtni C., *Wagon Train: A Family Goes West in 1865*, illustrated by Gershom Griffith (I)

NOVELS (SEE ALSO CHAPTERS 6, 7, AND 8)

Banks, Jacqueline Turner, *Egg-Drop Blues* (I–A)

Boyd, Candy Dawson, *Chevrolet Saturdays* (I)

Curtis, Christopher Paul, *Bud, Not Buddy* (I)

_____, *The Watsons Go to Birmingham—1963* (I)

Davis, Ossie, *Just Like Martin* (A)

Draper, Sharon M., *Forged by Fire* (A)

_____, *Tears of a Tiger* (A)

Fenner, Carol, *Yolanda's Genius* (I–A)

Forrester, Sandra, *Sound the Jubilee* (A)

Greenfield, Eloise, *Koya DeLaney and the Good Girl Blues* (I)

Grimes, Nikki, *Jazmin's Notebook* (A)

Hamilton, Virginia, *The All Jahdu Storybook* (I)

_____, *Cousins* (I–A)

_____, *M. C. Higgins, the Great* (I–A)

_____, *Plain City* (A)

_____, *Planet of Junior Brown* (I–A)

_____, *Second Cousins* (I–A)

_____, *Zeely* (I)

Hansen, Joyce, *The Captive* (I–A)

_____, *I Thought My Soul Would Rise and Fly* (I–A)

Hyppolite, Joanne, *Seth and Samona* (I)

Johnson, Angela, *Gone from Home* (A)

_____, *Heaven* (A)

_____, *Humming Whispers* (A)

_____, *Songs of Faith* (A)

_____, *Toning the Sweep* (A)

Lester, Julius, *Long Journey Home: Stories from Black History* (A)

_____, *Pharoah's Daughter* (A)

McKissack, Patricia C., *A Picture of Freedom: The Diary of Clotee, a Slave Girl* (I–A)

_____, *Run Away Home* (I–A)

Moore, Yvette, *Freedom Songs* (A)

Myers, Walter Dean, *Fallen Angels* (A)

_____, *Fast Sam, Cool Clyde, and Stuff* (I–A)

_____, *The Glory Field* (A)

_____, *Monster* (A)

_____, *Slam!* (A)

_____, *Sniffy Blue, Ace Crime Detective: The Case of the Missing Ruby and Other Stories* (I)

_____, *Somewhere in the Darkness* (A)

_____, *The Young Landlords* (A)

_____, *145th Street Stories* (A)

Pinkney, Andrea Davis, *Hold Fast to Dreams* (I–A)

_____, *Raven in a Dove House* (A)

_____, *Silent Thunder: A Civil War Story* (I–A)

_____, *Solo Girl*, illustrated by Nneka Bennett (P–I)

Robinet, Harriette Gillem, *Forty Acres and Maybe a Mule* (I–A)

_____, *If You Please, President Lincoln* (I–A)

_____, *Mississippi Chariot* (I–A)

_____, *The Twins, the Pirates, and the Battle of New Orleans* (I–A)

_____, *Washington City Is Burning* (I–A)

Smothers, Ethel Footman, *Moriah's Pond* (I)

Tate, Eleanora E., *A Blessing in Disguise* (I–A)

_____, *Don't Split the Pole: Tales of Down-Home Folk Wisdom*, illustrated by Cornelius Van Wright and Ying-Hwa Hu (I–A)

_____, *The Secret of Gumbo Grove* (I)

_____, *Thank, You, Dr. Martin Luther King, Jr!* (I)

Taylor, Mildred D., *Mississippi Bridge* (I–A)

_____, *Roll of Thunder, Hear My Cry* (I–A)

_____, *The Well: David's Story* (I–A)

Turner, Glennette Tilley, *Running for Our Lives*, illustrated by Samuel Byrd (I–A)

Walter, Mildred Pitts, *Second Daughter: The Story of a Slave Girl* (A)

West, Dorothy, *The Richer, the Poorer: Stories, Sketches, and Reminiscences* (A)

Wilkinson, Brenda, *Definitely Cool* (I)

_____, *Ludell* (A)

Williams-Garcia, Rita, *Like Sisters on the Homefront* (A)

Wolf, Virginia Euwer, *Make Lemonade* (A)

Woodson, Jacqueline, *The Dear One* (A)

_____, *From the Notebooks of Melanin Sun* (A)

_____, *I Hadn't Meant to Tell You This* (A)

_____, *Last Summer with Maizon* (A)

_____, *Maizon at Blue Hill* (A)

_____, *Miracle's Boys* (A)

Wright, Richard, *Rite of Passage* (A)

NONFICTION (SEE ALSO CHAPTERS 9 AND 10)

Burns, Khephra, and William Miles, *Black Stars in Orbit: NASA's African American Astronauts* (I)

Cline-Ransome, Lesa, *Satchel Paige*, illustrated by James Ransome (I)

Cox, Clinton, *Undying Glory: The Story of the Massachusetts 54th Regiment* (I)

Golenbock, Peter, *Teammates*, illustrated by Paul Bacon (I)

Haskins, Francine, *I Remember "121"* (P)

Haskins, Jim, *Black Dance in America: A History Through Its People* (A)

_____, *Black Eagles: African Americans in Aviation* (I)

_____, *The Day Martin Luther King, Jr., Was Shot: A Photo History of the Civil Rights Movement* (I–A)

_____, *One More River to Cross: The Stories of Twelve Black Americans* (A)

Krull, Kathleen, *Wilma Unlimited: How Wilma Rudolph Became the World's Fastest Woman* (P–I)

McKissack, Fredrick, Jr., *Black Hoops: The History of African Americans in Basketball* (I)

McKissack, Patricia C., and Fredrick McKissack, Jr., *Black Diamond: The Story of the Negro Baseball Leagues* (A)

_____, *Christmas in the Big House, Christmas in the Quarters* (I–A)

Meltzer, Milton, *The Black Americans: A History in Their Own Words* (A)

Miller, Robert, *Reflections of a Black Cowboy: Book Four, Mountain Men*, illustrated by Richard Leonard (I)

_____, *The Story of Nat Love*, illustrated by Michael Bryant (P–I)

Miller, William, *Zora Hurston and the Chinaberry Tree*, illustrated by Cornelius Van Wright and Ying-Hwa Hu (P–I)

Monceaux, Morgan, *Jazz: My Music, My People* (I–A)

Myers, Walter Dean, *Now Is Your Time! The African-American Struggle for Freedom* (I–A)

_____, *Malcolm X: By Any Means Necessary* (A)

Parks, Rosa, with Jim Haskins, *Rosa Parks: My Story* (A)

Pinkney, Andrea Davis, *Alvin Ailey*, illustrated by Brian Pinkney (P–I)

_____, *Bill Pickett: Rodeo-Ridin' Cowboy*, illustrated by Brian Pinkney (P–I)

_____, *Dear Benjamin Banneker*, illustrated by Brian Pinkney (P–I)

_____, *Duke Ellington*, illustrated by Brian Pinkney (P–I)

_____, *Seven Candles for Kwanza*, illustrated by Brian Pinkney (P–I)

Rappaport, Doreen, *Escape from Slavery: Five Journeys to Freedom* (I–A)

Schroeder, Alan, *Sachmo's Blues*, illustrated by Floyd Cooper (P–I)

Walter, Mildred Pitts, *Kwanzaa: A Family Affair* (I)

_____, *Mississippi Challenge* (A)

Weatherford, Carole Boston, *Juneteenth Jamboree*, illustrated by Yvonne Buchanan (P–I)

Yarbrough, Camille, *The Little Tree Growin' in the Shade* (P)

Asian American Children's Books

FOLKLORE (SEE ALSO CHAPTER 5)

Chang, Margaret, and Raymond Chang, *The Beggar's Magic: A Chinese Tale*, illustrated by David Johnson (N–P)

Demi, *Buddha* (I–A)

_____, *The Dragon's Tale and Other Animal Fables of the Chinese Zodiac* (N–P)

_____, *The Stonecutter* (N–P)

Fang, Linda, *The Ch'I-lin Purse: A Collection of Ancient Chinese Stories*, illustrated by Jeanne M. Lee (P–I–A)

Han, Oki S., and Stephanie Haboush Plunkett, *Kongi and Potgi: A Cinderella Story from Korea* (N–P)

Ho, Mingfong, and Saphan Ros, *Brother Rabbit: A Cambodian Tale*, illustrated by Jennifer Hewitson

_____, *The Two Brothers*, illustrated by Jean Tseng and Mon-Sian Tseng (P–I)

Louie, Ai-Ling, *Yeh Shen: A Cinderella Story from China*, illustrated by Ed Young (I)

Namioka, Lensey, *The Loyal Cat*, illustrated by Aki Sogabe (P–I)

Uchida, Yoshiko, *The Wise Old Woman*, illustrated by Martin Springett (P–I)

Wang, Rosalind C., *The Treasure Chest: A Chinese Tale* (P–I)

Yee, Paul, *Tales from Gold Mountain: Stories of the Chinese in the New World* (I–A)

Yep, Laurence, *The Dragon Prince: A Chinese Beauty and the Beast Tale*, illustrated by Kam Mak (N–P–I)

_____, *The Khan's Daughter: A Mongolian Folktale*, illustrated by Jean Tseng and Mou-sien Tseng (N–P)

_____, *The Rainbow People* (A)

_____, *Tiger Woman*, illustrated by Robert Roth (N–P)

_____, *Tongues of Jade* (A)

Young, Ed, *Cat and Rat: The Legend of the Chinese Zodiac* (N–P)

_____, *Little Plum* (N–P)

_____, *Lon Po Po: A Red Riding Hood Story from China* (N–P)

_____, *The Lost Horse: A Chinese Folktale* (N–P)

_____, *Mouse Match* (N–P)

_____, *Night Visitors* (N–P–I)

Zhang, Song Nan, *Five Heavenly Emperors: Chinese Myths of Creation* (N–P–I)

POETRY AND SONG

Ho, Mingfong, *Maples in the Mist*, illustrated by Jean Tseng and Mou-sien Tseng (P–I–A)

Wong, Janet, *Good Luck Gold: And Other Poems* (I–A)

_____, *The Rainbow Hand: Poems About Mothers and Children* (I)

_____, *A Suitcase of Seaweed and Other Poems* (I)

PICTURE BOOKS (SEE ALSO CHAPTERS 3 AND 4)

Chinn, Karen, *Sam and the Lucky Money*, illustrated by Cornelius Van Wright and Ying-Hwa Hu (P–I)

Choi, Sook Nyul, *The Best Older Sister*, illustrated by Cornelius Van Wright and Ying-Hwa Hu (N–P)

_____, *Halmoni and the Picnic*, illustrated by Karen Dugan (P)

Friedman, Ina, *How My Parents Learned to Eat* (P)

Garland, Sherry, *The Lotus Seed*, illustrated by Tatsuro Kiuchi (P–I)

Hamanaka, Sheila, *Bebop-A-Do-Walk!*, illustrated by Sheila Hamanaka (N–P)

Heo, Yumi, *One Afternoon* (N–P)

Mochizuki, Ken, *Baseball Saved Us*, illustrated by Dom Lee (P–I)

_____, *Heroes*, illustrated by Dom Lee (P–I)

Narahashi, Keiko, *I Have a Friend* (N–P)

_____, *Is That Josie?* (N–P)

Nunes, Susan Miho, *The Last Dragon*, illustrated by Chris K. Soentpiet (P)

Sakai, Kimiko, *Sachiko Means Happiness*, illustrated by Tomie Arai (I)

Say, Allen, *El Chino* (I)

_____, *Grandfather's Journey* (P–I)

_____, *Tea with Milk* (P–I)

_____, *Tree of Cranes* (P–I)

Tan, Amy, *The Moon Lady*, illustrated by Gretchen Schields (I–A)

Wong, Janet, *Buzz*, illustrated by Margaret Chodos-Irvine (N–P)

Yee, Paul, *Roses Sing on New Snow: A Delicious Tale*, illustrated by Harvey Chan (I)

NOVELS (SEE ALSO CHAPTERS 6, 7, AND 8)

Carlson, Lori M., *American Eyes: New Asian-American Short Stories for Young Adults* (A)

Choi, Sook Nyul, *Gathering of Pearls* (A)

Lee, Marie G., *Finding My Voice* (A)

_____, *If It Hadn't Been for Yoon Jun* (A)

_____, *Necessary Roughness* (A)

_____, *Night of the Chupacabras* (I–A)

_____, *Saying Goodbye* (A)

Lord, Bette Bao, *In the Year of the Boar and Jackie Robinson* (I)

Namioka, Lensey, *April and the Dragon Lady* (A)

_____, *Yang the Second and Her Secret Admirers* (I)

_____, *Yang the Third and Her Impossible Family* (I)

_____, *Yang the Youngest and His Terrible Ear* (I)

Okimoto, Jean Davies, *Molly by Any Other Name* (A)

_____ *Talent Night* (A)

Uchida, Yoshiko, *Journey Home* (I–A)

_____, *Journey to Topaz* (I–A)

Yep, Laurence, *American Dragons: Twenty-Five Asian American Voices* (A)

_____, *The Case of the Lion Dance* (A)

_____, *Child of the Owl* (A)

_____, *The Cook's Family* (A)

_____, *Dragon's Gate* (I–A)

_____, *Dragonwings* (A)

_____, *Dream Soul* (I–A)

_____, *The Ghost Fox* (I–A)

_____, *Hiroshima* (A)

_____, *Mountain Light* (A)

_____, *Sea Glass* (I–A)

_____, *The Serpent's Children* (I–A)

_____, *The Star Fisher* (I–A)

_____, *Thief of Hearts* (A)

NONFICTION (SEE ALSO CHAPTERS 9 AND 10)

Brown, Tricia, *Konnichiwa! I Am a Japanese-American Girl*, illustrated by Kazuyoshi Arai (P)

_____, *Lee Ann: The Story of a Vietnamese-American Girl*, illustrated by Ted Thai (I)

Cha, Dia, *Dia's Story Cloth: The Hmong People's Journey of Freedom*, illustrated by Chue and Nhia Thao Cha (I)

Hamanaka, Sheila, *The Journey: Japanese Americans, Racism, and Renewal* (A)

Hoyt-Goldsmith, Diane, *Hoang Anh: A Vietnamese-American Boy*, illustrated by Lawrence Migdale (P)

Meltzer, Milton, *The Chinese Americans* (A)

Uchida, Yoshiko, *The Invisible Thread* (A)

Yep, Laurence, *The Lost Garden* (I–A)

LATINO CHILDREN'S BOOKS

FOLKLORE (SEE ALSO CHAPTER 5)

Ada, Alma Flor, *The Gold Coin*, illustrated by Neil Waldman (P)

Belpre, Pura, *Perez and Martina: A Puerto Rican Folktale/Perez y Martina*, illustrated by Carlos Sanchez (P)

Bernier-Grand, Carmen T., *Juan Bobo: Four Folktales from Puerto Rico*, illustrated by Ernesto Ramos Nieves (N–P)

Gonzalez, Lucia M., *The Bossy Gallito/El Gallo de Bodas: A Traditional Cuban Folktale*, illustrated by Lulu Delacre (N–P)

_____, *Senor Cat's Romance and Other Favorite Stories from Latin America*, illustrated by Lulu Delacre (N–P)

Jaffe, Nina, *The Golden Flower*, illustrated by Enrique O. Sanchez (P)

Mohr, Nicholasa, *The Song of el Coqui and Other Tales of Puerto Rico*, illustrated by Antonio Martorell (P–I)

Mora, Pat, *The Race of Toad and Deer*, illustrated by Maya Itzna Brooks (N–P)

Orozco, Jose-Luis, *De Colores and Other Latin-American Folk Songs for Children*, illustrated by Elisa Kleven (N–P)

Pitre, Felix, *Paco and the Witch*, illustrated by Christy Hale (N–P)

Schon, Isabel, *Dona Blanca and Other Hispanic Nursery Rhymes and Games* (P)

POETRY AND SONG (SEE ALSO CHAPTER 4)

Alarcon, Francisco X., *From the Bellybutton of the Moon and Other Summer Poems/Del Ombligo de la Luna y Otros Poemas de Verano: Poems/Poemas*, illustrated by Maya Christina Gonzalez (N–P)

_____, *Laughing Tomatoes and Other Spring Poems/Jitomates Risuenos y Otros Poemas de Primavera*, illustrated by Maya Christina Gonzalez (N–P)

Carlson, Lori M., *Barrio Streets Carnival Dreams: Three Generations of Latino Artistry* (A)

_____, *Cool Salsa: Bilingual Poems on Growing Up Latino in the United States* (A)

Cumpian, Carlos, *Latino Rainbow: Poems About Latino Americans*, illustrated by Richard Leonard (P–I)

Gonzalez, Ray, *Touching the Fire: Fifteen Poets of Today's Latino Renaissance* (A)

Mora, Pat, *Confetti: Poems for Children*, illustrated by Enrique O. Sanchez (N–P–I)

_____, *The Desert Is My Mother/El Desierto Es Mi Madre*, illustrated by Daniel Lechon (P)

_____, *Listen to the Desert/Oye al Desierto*, illustrated by Francisco X. Mora (P)

_____, *This Big Sky*, illustrated by Steve Jenkins (P)

_____, *Uno, Dos, Tres: One, Two, Three*, illustrated by Barbara Lavallee (N–P)

Ortiz Cofer, Judith, *Reaching for the Mainland and Selected New Poems* (A)

Soto, Gary, *Canto Familiar* (I)

_____, *A Fire in My Hands: A Book of Poems* (A)

_____, *Neighborhood Odes*, illustrated by David Diaz (I–A)

Picture Books (see also Chapters 3 and 4)

Ada, Alma Flor, *Gathering the Sun: An Alphabet in Spanish and English*, illustrated by Simon Silva (N–P)

Altman, Linda Jacobs, *Amelia's Road*, illustrated by Enrique O. Sanchez (P–I)

Anaya, Rudolfo, *The Farolitos of Christmas*, illustrated by Edward Gonzales (P–I)

Anzaldua, Gloria, *Prietita and the Ghost Woman/Prietita y la Llorona*, illustrated by Christina Gonzalez (P)

Cisneros, Sandra, *Hairs/Pelitos*, illustrated by Terry Ybanez (P)

Cordova, Amy, *Abuelita's Heart* (N–P–I)

Cruz, Martel, *Yagua Days* (P)

Delacre, Lulu, *Vejigante Masquerader* (P–I)

Delgado, Maria Isabel, *Chave's Memories: Los Recuerdos de Chave*, illustrated by Yvonne Symank (N–P)

Dorros, Arthur, *Abuela*, illustrated by Elisa Kleven (P)

_____, *Radio Man/Don Radio* (P)

Garza, Carmen Lomas, *My Family* (P)

Herrera, Juan Felipe, *Calling the Doves/El Canto de las Palomas*, illustrated by Elly Simmons (N–P–I–A)

Jiminez, Francisco, *La Mariposa*, illustrated by Simon Silva (P–I–A)

Lachtman, Ofelia Dumas, *Pepita Talks Twice/Pepita Habla Dos Veces*, illustrated by Alex Pardo (N–P)

Mohr, Nicholasa, *Old Letivia and the Mountain of Sorrows*, illustrated by Rudy Gutierrez (N–P)

Mora, Pat, *A Birthday Basket for Tia*, illustrated by Cecily Lang (P)

_____, *Pablo's Tree*, illustrated by Cecily Lang (P)

_____, *Tomas and the Library Lady*, illustrated by Raul Colon (N–P)

Nodar, Carmen Santiago, *Abuelita's Paradise/El Paraiso de Abuelita*, illustrated by Diane Paterson (P)

Reiser, Lynn, *Tortillas and Lullabies/Tortillas y Cancioncitas*, illustrated by "Corazones Valientes" (N–P)

Roe, Eileen, *Con Mi Hermano/With My Brother*, illustrated by Robert Casilla (P)

Rosa-Casanova, Sylvia, *Mama Provi and the Pot of Rice*, illustrated by Robert Roth (N–P)

Soto, Gary, *Big Bushy Mustache*, illustrated by Joe Cepeda (N–P)

_____, *Chato's Kitchen*, illustrated by Susan Guervara (N–P)

_____, *The Old Man and His Door*, illustrated by Joe Cepeda (N–P)

_____, *Snapshots from the Wedding*, illustrated by Stephanie Garcia (P–I)

NOVELS (SEE ALSO CHAPTERS 6, 7, AND 8)

Ada, Alma Flor, *My Name Is Maria Isabel* (P–I)

_____, *Under the Royal Palms* (P–I)

_____, *Where the Flame Trees Bloom*, illustrated by Antonio Martorell (I)

Beatty, Particia, *Lupita Manana* (A)

Belpre, Pura, *Firefly Summer* (A)

Bernardo, Anilu, *Fitting In* (I–A)

_____, *Jumping Off to Freedom* (A)

Bertrand, Diane Gonzales, *Alicia's Treasure* (A)

_____, *Sweet Fifteen* (A)

Cisneros, Sandra, *The House on Mango Street* (A)

Garcia, Lionel G., *To a Widow with Children* (A)

Garcia, Pelayo "Pete," *From Amigos to Friends* (A)

Hernandez, Irene Beltran, *The Secret of Two Brothers* (A)

Jimenez, Francisco, *The Circuit* (A)

Lachtman, Ofelia Dumas, *The Girl from Playa Blanca* (A)

_____, *Leticia's Secret*, illustrated by Roberta C. Morales (I–A)

Martinez, Floyd, *Spirits of the High Mesa* (I–A)

Martinez, Victor, *Parrot in the Oven: Mi Vida* (A)

Mohr, Nicholasa, *Felita* (A)

_____, *Going Home* (A)

_____, *The Magic Shell* (I)

Ortiz Cofer, Judith, *An Island Like You: Stories of the Barrio* (A)

_____, *The Year of Our Revolution: New and Selected Stories and Poems* (A)

Soto, Gary, *Baseball in April and Other Stories* (A)

_____, *Boys at Work* (I)

_____, *Buried Onions* (A)

_____, *Crazy Weekend* (A)

_____, *Jesse* (A)

_____, *Living Up the Street* (A)

_____, *Local News* (I–A)

_____, *Off and Running* (I–A)

_____, *Pacific Crossing* (A)

_____, *Petty Crimes* (A)

_____, *Pool Party* (I)

_____, *Summer on Wheels* (A)

_____, *Taking Sides* (A)

Tashlick, Phyllis, *Hispanic, Female and Young: An Anthology* (A)

Thomas, Piri, *Stories from el Barrio* (A)

Velasquez, Gloria, *Juanita Fights the School Board* (A)

_____, *Maya's Divided World* (A)

_____, *Tommy Stands Alone* (A)

NONFICTION (SEE ALSO CHAPTERS 9 AND 10)

Anastos, Phillip, and Chris French, *Illegal: Seeking the American Dream* (A)

Brimner, Larry Dane, *A Migrant Family* (I–A)

Hewett, Joan, *Hector Lives in the United States Now*, illustrated by Richard Hewett (P–I)

Hoobler, Dorothy, and Thomas Hoobler, *The Mexican American Family Album* (A)

Howlet, Bud, *I'm New Here* (P–I)

Hoyt-Goldsmith, Diane, *Day of the Dead: A Mexican-American Celebration*, illustrated by Lawrence Migdale (I)

Lomas Garza, Carmen, as told to Harriet Rohmer, *Family Pictures/Cuadros de Familia* (P–I)

Tillage, Leon Walker, *Leon's Story* (I)

Native American Children's Books

FOLKLORE (SEE ALSO CHAPTER 5)

Begay, Shonto, *Ma'ii and Cousin Horned Toad: A Traditional Navajo Story* (P)

Bierhorst, John, *The Deetkatoo: Native American Stories About Little People* (I–A)

_____, *Lightning Inside You: And Other Native American Riddles* (I)

_____, *Naked Bear: Folktales of the Iroquois* (I)

_____, *On the Road of Stars: Native American Night Poems and Sleep Charms*, illustrated by Judy Pedersen (N–P–I)

_____, *The People with Five Fingers: A Native Californian Creation Tale*, illustrated by Robert Andrew Parker (P)

_____, *The Sacred Path: Spells, Prayers and Power Songs of the American Indians* (I)

_____, *The White Deer: And Other Stories Told by the Lenape* (A)

Bruchac, Joseph, *Between Earth and Sky: Legends of Native American Sacred Places*, illustrated by Thomas Locker (I–A)

_____, *The Boy Who Lived with the Bears: And Other Iroquois Stories* (I)

_____, *Flying with the Eagle, Racing the Great Bear: Stories from Native America* (I–A)

_____, *Four Ancestors: Stories, Songs, and Poems from Native North America*, illustrated by S. S. Burrus, Murv Jacob, Jeffrey Chapman, and Duke Sine (P–I)

_____, *Gluskabe and the Four Wishes*, illustrated by Christine Nyburg Shrader (P)

Bruchac, Joseph, and Gayle Ross, *The Girl Who Married the Moon* (I–A)

_____, *The Story of the Milky Way: A Cherokee Tale*, illustrated by Virginia A. Stroud (P)

Caduto, Michael, and Joseph Bruchac, *Keepers of the Earth*, (I)

Dixon, Ann, *How Raven Brought Light to People*, illustrated by Jim Watts (P)

Erdoes, Richard, *The Sound of Flutes and Other Indian Legends* (I–A)

Goble, Paul, *Adopted by the Eagles: A Plains Indian Story of Friendship and Treachery* (I)

_____, *Buffalo Woman* (I)

_____, *Crow Chief: A Plains Indian Story* (I)

_____, *Dream Wolf* (I)

_____, *The Girl Who Loved Wild Horses* (I)

_____, *Iktomi and the Buzzard: A Plains Indian Story* (P–I)

_____, *The Legend of the White Buffalo Woman* (P–I)

_____, *Love Flute* (P–I)

_____, *Star Boy* (I)

Hausman, Gerald, *How Chipmunk Got Tiny Feet: Native American Animal Origin Stories*, illustrated by Ashley Wolff (P)

Lacapa, Michael, *The Flute Player: An Apache Folktale* (I)

Manitonquat (Medicine Story), *The Children of the Morning Light: Wampanoag Tales*, illustrated by Mary F. Arquette (I)

Martin, Rafe, *The Rough-Face Girl*, illustrated by David Shannon (I)

Oughton, Jerrie, *How the Stars Fell into the Sky: A Navajo Legend*, illustrated by Lisa Desimini (P–I)

_____, *The Magic Weaver of Rugs: A Tale of the Navajo*, illustrated by Lisa Desimini (P–I)

Pollock, Penny, *The Turkey Girl: A Zuni Cinderella Story*, illustrated by Ed Young (P)

Rodnas, Kristina, *Dance of the Sacred Circle: A Native American Tale* (I–A)

_____, *Dragonfly's Tale* (P)

_____, *The Eagle's Song: A Tale from the Pacific Northwest* (N–P)

_____, *Follow the Stars: A Native American Woodlands Tale* (N–P)

Ross, Gayle, *How Rabbit Tricked Otter and Other Cherokee Trickster Stories*, illustrated by Murv Jacob (I)

_____, *How Turtle's Back Was Cracked: A Traditional Cherokee Tale*, illustrated by Murv Jacob (N–P–I)

_____, *The Legend of the Windigo: A Tale from Native North America*, illustrated by Murv Jacob (N–P–I)

Rubalcaba, Jull, *Uncegila's Seventh Spot: A Lakota Legend*, illustrated by Irving Toddy (N–P–I)

Runningwolf, Michael B., and Patricia Clark Smith, *On the Trail of Elder Brother: Glous'gap Stories of the Micmac Indians*, illustrated by Michael B. Running Wolf (A)

Ude, Wayne, *Maybe I Will Do Something: Seven Coyote Tales*, illustrated by Abigail Rorer (I)

Yellow Robe, Rosebud, *Tonweya and the Eagles and Other Lakota Indian Tales* (I)

POETRY AND SONG (SEE ALSO CHAPTER 4)

Begay, Shonto, *Navajo: Visions and Voices Across the Mesa* (I–A)

Bruchac, Joseph, *The Earth Under Sky Bear's Feet: Native American Poems of the Land*, illustrated by Thomas Locker (I–A)

Bruchac, Joseph, and Jonathan London, *Thirteen Moons on Turtle's Back*, illustrated by Thomas Locker (I–A)

Harjo, Joy, *The Woman Who Fell from the Sky: Poems* (A)

Hirschfelder, Arlene, and Beverly Singer, *Rising Voices: Writings of Young Native Americans* (A)

Jones, Hettie, *The Trees Stand Shining: Poetry of the North American Indians*, illustrated by Robert Andrew Parker (P–I–A)

Sneve, Virginia Driving Hawk, *Dancing Teepees: Poems of American Indian Youth*, illustrated by Stephen Gammell (I–A)

Swamp, Chief Jake, *Giving Thanks: A Native American Good Morning Message*, illustrated by Erwin Printup, Jr. (P)

Tapahonso, Luci, *Blue Horses Rush In: Poems and Stories* (A)

PICTURE BOOKS (SEE ALSO CHAPTERS 3 AND 4)

Andrews, Jan, *Very Last First Time*, illustrated by Ian Wallace (P)

Baker, Olaf, *Where the Buffalo Begin*, illustrated by Stephen Gammell (P–I)

Erdrich, Louise, *Grandmother's Pigeon*, illustrated by Jim LaMarche (N–P–I)

Hobbs, Will, *Beardream*, illustrated by Jill Kastner (N–P)

McLerran, Alice, *The Ghost Dance*, illustrated by Paul Morin (I)

Oliviero, Jamie, *The Day Sun Was Stolen*, illustrated by Sharon Hitchcock (P–I)

Strete, Craig Kee, *Little Coyote Runs Away*, illustrated by Harvey Stevenson (N–P)

Strete, Criag Kee, and Michelle Netten Chacon, *How the Indians Bought the Farm* (N–P)

Stroud, Virginia A., *Doesn't Fall Off His Horse* (P–I)

_____, *The Path of Quiet Elk: A Native American Alphabet Book* (N–P)

NOVELS (SEE ALSO CHAPTERS 6, 7, AND 8)

Bruchac, Joseph, *The Arrow over the Door* (I–A)

_____, *Children of the Longhouse* (I–A)

_____, *Dog People: Native American Dog Stories* (I)

_____, *Eagle Song* (I–A)

_____, *Sacajawea* (I–A)

_____, *The Waters Between: A Novel of the Dawn Land* (A)

Dorris, Michael, *Guests* (I)

_____, *Morning Girl* (I)

_____, *Sees Behind Trees* (I)

_____, *The Window* (A)

Erdrich, Louise, *Birchbark House* (I)

Hill, Kirkpatrick, *Toughboy and Sister* (A)

_____, *The Year of Miss Agnes* (P–I)

Hobbs, Will, *Beardance* (A)

_____, *Bearstone* (A)

_____, *Far North* (A)

Hudson, Jan, *Dawn Rider* (A)

_____, *Sweetgrass* (A)

Martin, Nora, *The Eagle's Shadow* (I–A)

Mead, Alice, *Crossing the Starlight Bridge* (I)

O'Dell, Scott, and Elizabeth Hall, *Thunder Rolling in the Mountains* (A)

Oughton, Jerrie, *Music from a Place Called Half Moon* (I–A)

Robinson, Margaret A., *A Woman of Her Tribe* (A)

Roop, Peter, and Connie Roop, *Ahyoka and the Talking Leaves*, illustrated by Yoshi Miyake (I)

Sneve, Virginia Driving Hawk, *High Elk's Treasure*, illustrated by Oren Lyons (I)

_____, *The Trickster and the Troll* (P–I)

Spinka, Penina Keen, *Mother's Blessing* (A)

Strete, Craig Kee, *The Bleeding Man and Other Science Fiction Stories* (A)

_____, *Big Thunder Magic* (A)

_____, *When Grandfather Journeys into Winter* (I–A)

_____, *The World in Grandfather's Hands* (I–A)

NONFICTION (SEE ALSO CHAPTERS 9 AND 10)

Ancona, George, *Earth Daughter: Alicia of Acoma Pueblo* (I)

_____, *Powwow* (I)

Arnold, Caroline, *The Ancient Cliff Dwellers of Mesa Verde*, illustrated by Richard Hewett (I–A)

Broker, Ignatia, *Night Flying Woman: An Ojibway Narrative* (A)

Ekoomiak, Normee, *Arctic Memories* (I–A)

Erdoes, Richard, *Rain Dance People: The Pueblo Indians, Their Past and Present* (A)

Freedman, Russell, *Indian Chiefs* (I–A)

_____, *An Indian Winter*, illustrated by Karl Bodmer (I–A)

Hoyt-Goldsmith, Diane, *Arctic Hunter*, illustrated by Lawrence Migdale (I)

_____, *Cherokee Summer* (I)

_____, *Pueblo Storyteller*, illustrated by Lawrence Migdale (I)

_____, *Totem Pole*, illustrated by Lawrence Migdale (I)

Jacobs, Francine, *The Tainos: The People Who Welcomed Columbus*, illustrated by Patrick Collins (I–A)

Keegan, Marcia, *Pueblo Boy: Growing Up in Two Worlds* (I)

Kendall, Russ, *Eskimo Boy: Life in an Inupiaq Eskimo Village* (P–I)

King, Sandra, *Shannon: An Ojibway Dancer* (**We Are Still Here** series) (I)

Lazar, Jerry, *Red Cloud: Sioux War Chief* (**North American Indians of Achievement** series) (I)

Left hand Bull, Jacqueline, and Suzanne Haldane, *Lakota Hoop Dancer*, illustrated by Suzanne Haldane (P–I)

Littlechild, George, *This Land Is My Land* (P)

Meyer, Carolyn, *In a Different Light: Growing Up in a Yup'ik Eskimo Village in Alaska* (A)

Mitchell, Barbara, *Red Bird*, illustrated by Todd L. W. Doney (P–I)

Monroe, Jean Guard, and Ray A. Williamson, *First Houses: Native American Homes and Sacred Structures*, illustrated by Susan Johnston Carlson (I)

Peters, Russell M., *Clambake: A Wampanoag Tradition*, illustrated by John Madama (**We Are Still Here** series) (I)

Regguinti, Gordon, *The Sacred Harvest: Ojibway Wild Rice Gathering*, illustrated by Dale Kakkak (I)

Roessel, Monty, *Kinaalda: A Navajo Girl Grows Up* (**We Are Still Here** series) (I)

_____, *Songs from the Loom: A Navajo Girl Learns to Weave* (**We Are Still Here** series) (I)

Sewall, Marcia, *People of the Breaking Day* (I)

Seymour, Tryntje Van Ness, *The Gift of Changing Woman* (I–A)

Sneve, Virginia Driving Hawk, *The Cherokees*, illustrated by Ronald Himler (**First Americans** series) (P–I)

_____, *The Seminoles*, illustrated by Ronald Himler (**First Americans** series) (P–I)

Steltzer, Ulli, *Building an Igloo* (P–I)

Swentzell, Rina, *Children of Clay: A Family of Pueblo Potters*, illustrated by Bill Steen (**We Are Still Here** series) (I)

Tapahonso, Luci, and Eleanor Schick, *Navajo ABC* (P)

Thomson, Peggy, *Katie Henio: Navajo Sheepherder*, illustrated by Paul Conklin (I)

Wittstock, Laura Waterman, *Ininatig's Gift of Sugar: Traditional Native Sugarmaking*, illustrated by Dale Kakkak (**We Are Still Here** series) (I)

Wood, Ted, with Wanbli Numpa Afraid of Hawk, *A Boy Becomes a Man at Wounded Knee* (I–A)

International Children's Books

POETRY AND SONG

Agard, John, and Grace Nichols, *No Hickory, No Dickory, No Dock*, illustrated by Cynthia Jabar (P), Caribbean

Berry, James, *When I Dance*, illustrated by Karen Barbour (A), Caribbean/Britain

Bryan, Ashley, *Sing to the Sun* (P–I), Caribbean

Burgie, Irving, *Caribbean Carnival: Songs of the West Indies*, illustrated by Frané Lessac (P), Caribbean

Cassedy, Sylvia, and Kunihiro Suetake, translators, *Red Dragonfly on My Shoulder*, illustrated by Molly Bang (I–A), Japan

Delacre, Lulu, *Las Navidades: Popular Christmas Songs from Latin America* (P–I–A), Latin America

Demi, compiler, *In the Eyes of the Cat: Japanese Poetry for All Seasons*, translated by Tze-si Huang (I–A), Japan

Greenfield, Eloise, *The Sunday Tree*, illustrated by Mr. Amos Ferguson (P–I), Caribbean

Joseph, Lynn, *Coconut Kind of Day: Island Poems*, illustrated by Sandra Speidel (I), Caribbean

Lessac, Frané, *Caribbean Canvas* (P), Carribean

Mado, Michio, *The Animals: Selected Poems*, translated by Empress Michiko of Japan, illustrated by Mitsumasa Anno (P–I), Japan

Nye, Naomi Shihab, *The Tree Is Older Than You Are: A Bilingual Gathering of Stories and Poems from Mexico, with Paintings by Mexican Artists* (I–A), Mexico

Tagore, Rabindranath, *Paper Boats*, illustrated by Grayce Bochak (I), India

PICTURE BOOKS (SEE ALSO CHAPTERS 3 AND 4)

Alpin, Elaine Maria, *A Bear for Miguel*, illustrated by Joan Sandin (I), El Salvador

Ashley, Bernard, *Cleversticks*, illustrated by Derek Brazell (P), Britain/China

Atkins, Jeannine, *Aani and the Tree Huggers*, illustrated by Venantius J. Pinto (P–I), India

Axworthy, Anni, *Anni's India Diary* (I), India

Baille, Allan, *Rebel*, illustrated by Di Wu (P–I), Burma

Bjork, Christina, *Vendela in Venice* (I)

Bond, Ruskin, *Cherry Tree*, illustrated by Allan Eitzen (P), India

Bontemps, Arna, and Langston Hughes, *Popo and Fifina*, illustrated by E. Simms Campbell (I–A), Haiti

Brusca, Maria Cristina, *On the Pampas* (P), Argentina

Castaneda, Omar S., *Abuela's Weave*, illustrated by Enrique O. Sanchez (P–I), Guatemala

Daly, Niki, *Not So Fast, Songololo* (P), South Africa

Dorros, Arthur, *Tonight Is Carnaval*, illustrated by Club de Madras Virgin del Carmen of Lima, Peru (P–I), Peru

Edwards, Michelle, *Chicken Man* (P), Israel

Fox, Mem, *Possum Magic*, illustrated by Julie Vivas (P), Australia

Gajadin, Chitra, adapted by Rabindranath Tagore, *Amal and the Letter from the King*, illustrated by Helen Ong (I), India

Grifalconi, Ann, *Osa's Pride* (P), Cameroon

Grossman, Patricia, *Saturday Market*, illustrated by Enrique O. Sanchez (P), Mexico

Hayashi, Akiko, *Aki and the Fox* (P), Japan

Heide, Florence Parry, and Judith Heide Gilliland, *The Day of Ahmed's Secret*, illustrated by Ted Lewin (P), Egypt

_____, *Sami and the Time of the Troubles*, illustrated by Ted Lewin (P), Lebanon

Ikeda, Daisaku, translated by Geraldine McCaughrean, *The Cherry Tree*, illustrated by Brian Wildsmith (P), Japan

Isadora, Rachel, *At the Crossroads* (P), South Africa

_____, *Over the Green Hills* (P), South Africa

Joseph, Lynn, *An Island Christmas*, illustrated by Catherine Stock (P), Caribbean

Keller, Holly, *Grandfather's Dream* (P), Vietnam

_____, *Island Baby* (P), Caribbean

Krull, Kathleen, *Maria Molina and the Days of the Dead*, illustrated by Enrique O. Sanchez (P), Mexico

Kurtz, Jane, *Faraway Home*, illustrated by E. B. Lewis (P), Ethiopia

Lee, Jeanne M., *Silent Lotus* (I), Cambodia

Levinson, Riki, *Our Home Is the Sea* (P), Hong Kong

Lewin, Ted, *Amazon Boy* (P–I), South America

_____, *Sacred River* (P–I), India

Lewington, Anna, *Antonio's Rain Forest*, illustrated by Edward Parker (I), Brazil

Linden, Anne Marie, *Emerald Blue*, illustrated by Katherine Doyle (P), Barbados

McKay, Lawrence, Jr., *Caravan*, illustrated by Darryl Ligasan (P–I), Afghanistan

Mennen, Ingrid, and Niki Daly, *Somewhere in Africa*, illustrated by Nicolaas Maritz (P), South Africa

Merrill, Jean, *The Girl Who Loved Caterpillars: A Twelfth-Century Tale from Japan*, illustrated by Floyd Cooper (P), Japan

Mollel, Tololwa M., *Big Boy*, illustrated by E. B. Lewis (P), Tanzania/Masai

_____, *Subira Subira*, illustrated by Linda Saport (P), Tanzania

Onyefulu, Ifeoma, *A Is for Africa* (P)

_____, *Chidi Only Likes Blue: An African Book of Colors* (P)

_____, *Emeka's Gift* (P)

_____, *Ogbo: Sharing Life in an African Village* (P)

Oppenheim, Shulamith Levy, *The Hundredth Name* (P), Egypt

Orr, Katherine, *My Grandpa and the Sea* (P), Caribbean

Palacios, Argentina, *A Christmas Surprise for Chabelita*, illustrated by Lori Lohstoeter (P), Panama

Pomerantz, Charlotte, *The Chalk Doll*, illustrated by Frané Lessac (P), Jamaica

Reddix, Valerie, *Dragon Kite of the Autumn Moon*, illustrated by Jean and Mou-Sien Tseng (I), Taiwan

Schermbrucker, Reviva, *Charlie's House*, illustrated by Niki Daly (P), South Africa

Schur, Maxine Rose, *When I Left My Village*, illustrated by Brian Pinkney (I), Ethiopia

Stock, Catherine, *Armien's Fishing Trip* (P), South Africa

_____, *Where Are You Going, Manyoni?* (P), Zimbabwe

Tomioka, Chiyoko, *Rise and Shine Mariko-Chan*, illustrated by Yoshiharu Tsuchida (P), Japan

Topooco, Eusebio, *Waira's First Journey* (P–I), Bolivia

Williams, Karen Lynn, *Galimoto*, illustrated by Catherine Stock (P), South Africa/Malawi

NOVELS (SEE ALSO CHAPTERS 6, 7, 8)

Baille, Alan, *Little Brother* (A), Cambodia

Bawden, Nina, *Humbug* (A), England

Berry, James, *Ajeemah and His Son* (A), Jamaica

_____, *The Future-Telling Lady* (A), Jamaica

_____, *A Thief in the Village* (A), Jamaica

Bolden, Tonya, editor, *Rites of Passage: Stories About Growing Up by Black Writers from Around the World* (A)

Broome, Errol, *Dear Mr. Sprouts* (A), Australia

Cameron, Ann, *The Most Beautiful Place in the World*, illustrated by Thomas B. Allen (P–I), Guatemala

Case, Dianne, *92 Queens Road* (A), South Africa

Castaneda, Omar S., *Among the Volcanoes* (I), Guatemala/Mayan

Choi, Sook Nyul, *Year of Impossible Goodbyes* (A), North Korea

Crew, Gary, *Angel's Gate* (A), Australia

_____, *Strange Objects* (A), Australia

Dalokay, Vedat, *Sister Shako and Kolo the Goat* (I), Turkey

de Jenkins, Lyll Becerra, *The Honorable Prison* (A), Colombia

Disher, Garry, *The Bamboo Flute* (A), Australia

Doherty, Berlie, *Granny Was a Buffer Girl* (A), England

Farmer, Nancy, *Do You Know Me?*, illustrated by Shelley Jackson (I), Zimbabwe

Gee, Maurice, *The Fat Man* (A), New Zealand

_____, *The Fire-Raiser* (A), New Zealand

Gerstein, Mordicai, *The Wild Boy: A Novel Based on the Life of the Savage of Averyron* (A), France

Gordon, Sheila, *The Middle of Somewhere: A Story of South Africa* (A), South Africa

_____, *Waiting for the Rain: A Novel of South Africa* (A), South Africa

Harlow, Joan Hiatt, *Star in the Storm* (I), Newfoundland, Canada

Haugen, Tormod, *Keeping Secrets*, translated by David R. Jacobs (A), Norway

Hautzig, Esther, *The Endless Steppe* (A), Poland/Russia

Hicylimaz, Gaye, *Against the Storm* (I–A), Turkey

_____, *The Frozen Waterfall* (A), Turkey/Switzerland

_____, *Smiling for Strangers* (A), Yugoslavia/England

Hill, Anthony, *The Burnt Stick*, illustrated by Mark Sofilas (I), Australia/Aboriginal

Ho, Minfong, *The Clay Marble* (A), Thailand/Cambodia

_____, *Rice Without Rain* (A), Thailand

Hodge, Merle, *For the Life of Laetitia* (A), Trinidad

Holub, Josef, *The Robber and Me* (I–A), Germany

Huynh, Quang Nhuong, *The Land I Lost: Adventures of a Boy in Vietnam* (I–A), Vietnam

_____, *Water Buffalo Days: Growing Up in Vietnam* (I)

Jang, Ji-li, *Red Scarf Girl: A Memoir of the Cultural Revolution* (I–A), China

Jimenez, Juan Ramon, translated by Myra Cohn Livingston, *Platero y Yo/Platero and I*, illustrated by Antonia Frasconi (A), Spain

Jinks, Catherine, *Eye to Eye* (A), Australia

Kherdian, David, *The Road from Home: The Story of an Armenian Girl* (A), Turkey

Kidd, Diana, *Onion Tears* (A), Vietnam/Australia

Koehn, Ilse, *Mischling, Second Degree* (A), Germany

Kurtz, Jane, *The Storyteller's Beads* (A), Ethiopia

Laird, Elizabeth, *Kiss the Dust* (A), Iraq/Kurd

Maartens, Maretha, *Paper Bird* (A), South Africa

Mahy, Margaret, *24 Hours* (A), New Zealand

_____, *Underrunners* (A), New Zealand

Marsden, John, *Letters from the Inside* (A), Australia

Moeri, Louise, *The Forty-Third War* (A), Central America

Mori, Kyoko, *One Bird* (A), Japan

_____, *Shizuko's Daughter* (A), Japan

Naidoo, Beverley, *Chain of Fire* (A), South Africa

_____, *Journey to Jo'burg* (A), South Africa

Neville, Emily Cheney, *The China Year* (A), China

Newth, Mette, *The Dark Light* (A)

_____, *The Transformation* (A)

Orlev, Uri, *The Island on Bird Street* (A), Poland

_____, *The Man from the Other Side* (A), Poland

Oz, Amos, *Soumchi*, translated by Amos Oz and Penelope Farmer (A), Israel

Pausewang, Gudrun, *Fall-Out* (A), Germany

Pressler, Mirjam, *Halinka* (A), Germany

Rana, Indi, *The Roller Birds of Rampur* (A), India

Russell, Ching Yeung, *First Apple* (A), China

_____, *Water Ghost* (A), China

Schlein, Mirian, *The Year of the Panda* (I), China

Semel, Nava, translated by Hillel Halkin, *Flying Lessons* (A), Israel

Siegal, Aranka, *Upon the Head of the Goat* (A), Hungary

Staples, Suzanne Fisher, *Haveli* (A), Pakistan

_____, *Shabanu: Daughter of the Wind* (A), Pakistan

Temple, Frances, *Grab Hands and Run* (A), El Salvador

_____, *Taste of Salt* (A), Haiti

_____, *Tonight, By Sea* (A), Haiti

Watkins, Yoko Kawashima, *My Brother, My Sister, and I* (A), Japan

_____, *So Far from the Bamboo Grove* (A), Korea/Japan

Whelan, Gloria, *Good-Bye Vietnam* (A), Vietnam

_____, *Homeless Bird* (A), India

Wrightson, Patricia, *A Little Fear* (A), Australia

Yen Mah, Adeline, *Falling Leaves: The True Story of an Unwanted Chinese Daughter* (A)

Yumoto, Kazumi, *The Friends* (A), Japan

_____, *The Spring Tone* (A), Japan

Books That Celebrate Similarities and Differences

Adoff, Arnold, *All the Colors of the Race* (I)

_____, *Black Is Brown Is Tan* (P)

Aliki, *Marianthe's Story: Painted Words/Spoken Memories* (P)

Conrad, Pam, *Animal Lingo,* illustrated by Barbara Bustetter Falk (P)

Dabovich, Lydia, *The Keys to My Kingdom: A Poem in Three Languages* (P)

Dooley, Norah, *Everybody Cooks Rice* (P)

Dorros, Arthur, *This Is My House* (P)

Feder, Jane, *Table Chair Bear: A Book in Many Languages* (P)

Fox, Mem, *Wherever You Are* (P)

Greenspun, Adele Aron, *Daddies* (P)

Hamanaka, Sheila, *All the Colors of the Earth* (P)

Hollyer, Beatrice, *Wake Up World! A Day in the Life of Children Around the World* (P)

Jenness, Aylette, *Come Home with Me: A Multicultural Treasure Hunt* (I)

_____, *Families: A Celebration of Diversity, Commitment, and Love* (P)

Kindersley, Barnabas, and Annabel Kindersley, *Children Just Like Me* (P–I–A)

Knight, Margy Burns, *Talking Walls*, illustrated by Anne Sibley O'Brien (I)

Kroll, Virginia, *Hats Off to Hair!*, illustrated by Kay Life (P)

Lankford, Mary D., *Christmas Around the World*, illustrated by Karen Dugan (P)

_____, *Hopscotch Around the World*, illustrated by Karen Milone (P–I)

_____, *Jacks Around the World*, illustrated by Karen Dugan (P)

Lewin, Ted, *Market!* (P)

Lobel, Anita, *Away from Home* (P)

Mazer, Anne, *America Street: A Multicultural Anthology of Stories* (A)

Morris, Ann, *Houses and Homes*, illustrated by Ken Heyman (P)

_____, *Shoes Shoes Shoes* (P)

Nikola-Lisa, W., *Bein' with You This Way*, illustrated by Michael Bryant (P)

Nye, Naomi Shihab, *This Same Sky: A Collection of Poems from Around the World* (I)

Pomerantz, Charlotte, *If I Had a Paka: Poems in Eleven Languages* (P)

Priceman, Marjorie, *How to Make an Apple Pie and See the World* (P)

Rattigan, Jama Kim, *Dumpling Soup* (P)

Rosen, Michael, *Elijah's Angel: A Story for Chanukah and Christmas*, illustrated by Aminah Brenda Lynn Robinson (I)

Rosenberg, Maxine B., *Brothers and Sisters*, illustrated by George Ancona (P–I)

Rotner, Shelley, and Ken Kreisler, *Faces* (P)

Ryan, Pam Munoz, *One Hundred Is a Family* (P)

Schuett, Stacey, *Somewhere in the World Right Now* (P)

Tabor, Nancy Maria Grande, *Somos un Arco Iris/We Are a Rainbow* (P)

Thomas, Joyce Carol, *A Gathering of Flowers: Stories About Being Young in America* (A)

Yolen, Jane, editor, *Sleep Rhymes Around the World* (P–I)

_____, *Street Rhymes Around the World* (P–I)

PART TWO

Children and Books

Developing Responsive Readers

But the dam still stood, its great bulk defying the puny efforts of the Minnipins.

Glocken could not believe his eyes. His hand went out to the Whisper, and he struck it again, this time from the other side. And then again. And again. And again. And still the dam stood.

Until suddenly—it simply disappeared.

One moment it was there defying them. And the next moment it had gone into a thousand cracks. And the earth, the stone, the washed-limestone simply went to powder and slid away. With a roar, the released river shot out from under them, roaring down the valley, roaring across the waste, roaring to freedom!

In his excitement Glocken struck the Whisper one last time. There was a sudden fearful crack! over their heads.

Then the whole mountain fell down on top of them.

—CAROL KENDALL, *The Whisper of Glocken*, p. 218

ANNA, HER HEAD BENT FORWARD SO THAT HER DARK HAIR MAKES a tent around her face and the book she is reading, is totally engrossed in the world of *The Whisper of Glocken*. When she gets to the part where Silky finds a little gray creature and calls him Wafer, she looks up, sighs, and says, "Mom, Wafer is a perfect name for a gray kitten." She then goes back to her reading, once more lost to the world. Later, when she is finished with the book, she talks about it, wondering aloud how the Minnipins had the courage to leave their valley and venture out into the bigger world, questioning whether she would be that brave. From one book she's found the perfect name for her new gray kitten, has experienced a dangerous journey into an unknown land, and has thought about her personal courage, all without leaving her own living room.

She's been doing this forever. She careened down a hill in a buggy with Max, Rosemary Wells's captivating rabbit, even as she chewed the corners of the sturdy board book. She went with another Max in his private boat to the land of the wild things, played in the rain with Peter Spier's children, and learned to understand the natural world through Joanne Ryder's imaginative nonfiction. She's laughed, cried, absorbed information, experienced danger, engaged in adventures, solved mysteries, and learned a great deal about the world and about herself as she's read book after book. Anna's a lucky child. She's been engaged with wonderful children's books all of her life.

Memories of special books and of those who read them to us stay with us all of our lives. The experiences we have during our lives shape and are shaped by the books that are important to us. Like Anna, many children who love to read get so engrossed in their books that the real world disappears. Parents laugh about calling and calling their children to no avail, and then discovering them curled up somewhere reading, oblivious to what is going on around them. Teachers recognize that good books excite children about reading and encourage them to read widely. Librarians are aware that exciting read-alouds lure children into the library to check out books on their own. Teachers appreciate that a child's imagination is fostered by a story's invitation to pretend. But nonnarrative books also play an important role in children's lives. Teachers see how children seek out and devour nonfiction texts and how these books enliven any area of study. Britton (1970) talks of how the language models of well-written books—narrative, poetic, and infor-

mational texts—help form the language that children use in their own speaking and writing.

As children grow they learn to understand their world, using language and reasoning to make sense of their experiences, including their experiences with books. Children also develop socially as they come to understand their world, respond to people and books, and adopt feelings and beliefs about themselves. We search for an understanding of ourselves when we read. Literature fosters this development.

The culture in which children live also shapes both cognitive and social development as it influences how they perceive experience as well as what they experience. Culture shapes children's attitudes and understanding about books and the ways that books function in their lives. It also shapes the way the books themselves are written.

Yes, the books children read are formative influences in their lives; it is our responsibility to know their books. It is also our responsibility to know the children, their experiences, how they develop and learn, and how they read and respond to what they read. Useful criteria for choosing literature for children are based on knowledge of children's books and an understanding of children's development and experiences. In this chapter we explore children as readers, and we discuss practices that promote responsive reading. Further discussion of effective classroom practices appears in Chapters 13 and 14.

A critical reason for selecting appropriate books is to foster children's connections with the books they read. When we share excellent literature with children we must be sure to consider the age of the child. No matter how wonderful the book, children don't want to be seen reading what they consider to be "baby books." If we miss the golden years of 2 to 4 when Margaret Wise Brown's *Goodnight Moon* (N) strikes a responsive chord, children may never see the charm of it later. If we lose the chance to share Maurice Sendak's *Where the Wild Things Are* (P) when children are 5 to 7, they may never appreciate its magic. Fifth-grade students will not be caught reading Arnold Lobel's *Frog and*

© Lee Galda

Anna is totally absorbed in the book she is reading. A frequent traveler in the world of books, she knows the pathway well.

*Five- to seven-year-old children appreciate Max's fun during a wild rumpus. Sendak says his relatives used to come toward him and say "I'm going to eat you up." He used them as his models. Notice they are all smiling. (**Where the Wild Things Are** by Maurice Sendak.)*

Toad Are Friends (P), nor will older students be seen reading Natalie Babbitt's ***Tuck Everlasting*** (I), but what a shame if students miss them. There are more than 75,000 children's books in print. Children could read omnivorously and still never read an outstanding book. Most important, unless children read some of the really good books, they will probably not get hooked as lifelong readers.

We, as teachers, can observe children's responses to literature and other media, and thus become aware of the broad patterns of intellectual organization that structure their thinking. When we come to know the children in our classrooms, we also can learn to make judgments about the appropriateness of specific books for specific children. Most of all, when we begin to understand the cultural forces that shape our students' lives, we can begin to enlarge our perceptions of what is "appropriate" to include culturally diverse expressions of literacy. Figure 12.1 contains some guidelines for book selection that can help you make initial judgments about appropriate books. No guidelines, however, can substitute for knowing your students well.

A Transactional View of Reading

It is important to know your students well because who they are determines how they read. Readers construct meaning as they read (Goodman, 1985). Instead of absorbing "one right meaning" from a text (an elusive concept at best), readers rely on their own background knowledge

and create unique meanings (Rosenblatt, 1938/1976, 1978). Meaning does not reside in the text alone, waiting for a reader to unearth it; meaning is created in the transaction that occurs between a text and a reader. As a reader reads, personal experiences, feelings, preferences, and reasons for reading guide the selection and construction of meaning. At the same time, the text itself—the words on the page—guide and constrain the meaning that a reader builds. Engaged readers build meaning that is shaped by the text, no matter what kind of book they are reading.

Langer (1990) and others argue that reading is temporal in nature, that the meaning that they construct is fluid and changes during the act of reading. Readers begin by "being out and stepping into" their "envisionment" of the text. They then move through this envisionment, often stepping back and rethinking their previous understandings. Finally they step out of the envisionment and react to the reading experience (Langer, 1995). This process occurs with all types of text. However, the emphasis and reasoning processes that readers use to construct their envisionments vary, depending on whether the text is informative or narrative (Langer, 1995).

EFFERENT AND AESTHETIC READING

Efferent and aesthetic reading lie at either end of a continuum that describes how and why people read. When people want to find information about something, they usually look for an informational, or nonfiction, text. A person might read a recipe to discover how to prepare a new dish, a

Figure 12 ☆ 1

Guide to Book Selection

Characteristics of Children	Features of Books	Favorite Titles
INFANTS AND TODDLERS (BIRTH TO 2 YEARS)		
Explore world with eyes, ears, hands, feet, and mouth Enjoy bouncing rhymes, rhythm, music, and singing "Read" pictures as adult reads words; ask "What's that?"	Invite participation Have brief, rhythmic text Are colorful and sturdy	*Pat the Bunny* (Kunhardt) *Mother Goose Songbook* (Yolen) *Max's First Word* (Wells)
NURSERY–EARLY CHILDHOOD (2 TO 4 YEARS)		
Understand simple concepts, counting, and ABCs Want to "do it myself" Hold Book and "read" familiar story to self	Have clear, uncluttered pictures and simple concepts Present simple plots, songs, and verse Have melodic, lilting language, animal characters	ABC books; counting books *Goodnight Moon* (Brown) *Have You Seen My Duckling?* (Tafuri) *Rosie's Walk* (Hutchins)
PRIMARY (5 TO 8 YEARS)		
Become independent readers Have vivid imagination Demand strict moral judgments	Show eye-for-an-eye morality, strong friendships Present phrase structure for books to read alone Contain fantasy and realistic elements	*Where the Wild Things Are* (Sendak) *The Talking Eggs* (San Souci) *Chrysanthemum* (Henkes) *Frog and Toad Are Friends* (Lobel)
INTERMEDIATE (9 TO 12 YEARS)		
Like mystery, intrigue, and humor Develop strength in independent reading Form strong friendships outside the family	Present realistic view of the world Develop strong characters, memorable plots Stress growing-up themes	*Bridge to Terabithia* (Paterson) *Tuck Everlasting* (Babbitt) *Freaky Friday* (Rodgers)
ADVANCED (12 YEARS AND UP)		
Accepts responsibility for self and action Seeks role models and heroes Self-conscious; "everybody's looking at me"	Deal with social and personal problems Show the underside of people and society Develop complex plots and strong characterization	*Dicey's Song* (Voight) *A Wizard of Earthsea* (Le Guin) *The Wright Brothers* (Freedman) *A Wrinkle in Time* (L'Engle)

manual to learn how to assemble a bicycle, a factual text about dogs to discover how to care for a new puppy. Rosenblatt (1978) calls this *efferent* reading, reading that is done for the practical purpose of gaining knowledge from the text, much like your reading of this textbook. Just because this kind of reading has a practical purpose, however, does not mean that is isn't pleasurable. Many readers of all ages enjoy reading informational text in an efferent manner.

Stories and poems are also read for pleasure, but with a different purpose and in a different fashion. Rosenblatt calls this kind of reading *aesthetic*. Reading aesthetically involves being aware of the sound and feeling of a text, as well as identifying with characters and participating in the story world—virtually experiencing the story. Reading aesthetically gives readers the emotional space in which to evaluate the feelings, actions, and decisions of the story world, and thus to construct their own personal values (Britton, 1970). Reading aesthetically allows readers to make sense of their lives through books.

Efferent and aesthetic reading are not opposites, but lie at either end of a continuum, with most reading comprising a mixture of the two. While efferent reading relates mainly to public, cognitive aspects of meaning, aesthetic reading relates mainly to private, affective aspects of meaning, to the lived-through experience (Rosenblatt, 1991). Different genres signal a predominant stance to a reader, but it is a reader's individual purpose for reading that decides the stance. For example, a cookbook signals an efferent stance—information about how to cook is inside the covers. However, a reader might pick up an especially enticing cookbook and read it for pure pleasure, imagining how good the various dishes might taste and what dishes might go well together; another reader might enjoy the beautiful photographs of food or the accompanying humorous asides. It is a reader's purpose that determines the stance that a reader takes. Rosenblatt argues that while both efferent and aesthetic experiences can be present in any reading, it is important that we, as teachers, are clear about the primary stance appropriate for different purposes for reading. Stories and poems, for example, are meant to be read aesthetically. If a book is meant to be "'literature' for . . . students, it must be experienced" first (Rosenblatt, 1991, p. 447). Think, for example, about reading historical fiction. Certainly we learn facts about a historical period as we read, but the purpose for reading is not to learn the facts, but to virtually experience life in a particular time and place. The facts are secondary.

Readers connect with narratives, whether realistic or fantasy, by becoming involved with and caring about the characters, by being engrossed in the events of the story, by experiencing the story they are reading—by feeling as though they are there, in the story world. One young reader described being "inhaled by books," a metaphor that perfectly sums up the single-minded absorption that connecting with a book can provide (Galda, 1982). But just what happens when readers read aesthetically and respond to literature?

RESPONSE TO LITERATURE

Reading and responding to stories and poems is a complex process that involves readers, texts, and the contexts in which reading occurs. Who is reading, what is being read, the purposes for reading, and the social and cultural factors surrounding reading all influence what a particular reader creates while reading a particular text. Responses are influenced by many factors and come in many forms (Galda, 1988). A text that makes one reader cry might bore another; a book read as a 10-year-old brings a different kind of pleasure when read again as a 13-year-old; and the cultural values that permeate a text will trigger varying responses in culturally diverse readers.

Responses are often hard to preserve; they are present in the moment of reading and are only imperfectly captured later through writing, discussion, art, or dramatic activities. Young children in classrooms sometimes show their responses on their faces, in their bodies, in their laughter; older children often shield themselves by not expressing their responses unless encouraged to do so by a supportive classroom context.

Creating meaning with a literary text involves connecting life and text. And the act of creating meaning while reading a story or poem is at once highly individual and intensely social. This creation, however, always begins with a reader.

The Reader

Who readers are and what they have experienced influence their responses to the books they read. The places they have been, the people they know, the attitudes they hold, who they are, and the way they present themselves to the world all influence how readers read and respond. Research has shown that individuals seem to have "response styles," or characteristic ways of responding. For example, three fifth-grade girls with similar backgrounds and schooling were quite different in their approaches to books, but each was individually consistent (Galda, 1982). Four first- and second-grade students showed remarkably different response styles, with one reader exhibiting sensitivity toward the feelings of the story characters, and another reader using the story as a springboard for oral performance (Sipe, 1998).

Past experience with books, both inside and outside of the classroom, also influences how children read and respond. For example, years of reading stories in a classroom in which the teacher asks questions that prompt recall of specific information from stories and poems will force young readers away from their naturally aesthetic responses into an inappropriate, information-seeking stance. One parent, for instance, talking about how her son learned to hate reading in school, described how he first reads the questions that he has to answer at the end of each reading selection and then scans the story or poem to find the answers to those questions. Reading for information means he misses the story; never connecting with the story means he misses the pleasure that a story can bring. Missing that pleasure, he has not learned to like reading. Another middle school boy, an avid reader of long, complex animal fantasies at home, felt that he had become a "poor" reader because of his performance on the tests in a popular computer-based reading program. He had learned to read for the virtual experience, the pleasure; the tests asked for very specific, and often unimportant, details. Consequently, he chose less complex novels to read for his school reading.

In contrast, children who have had an array of pleasurable experiences with books will spontaneously compare stories, knowledgeably discuss authors, and bring their ideas about literature to their reading. Many researchers and teachers, such as Hickman (1981), Eeds and Wells (1989), Short and Pierce (1990), and Galda, Rayburn, and Stanzi (2000), have documented the richness of children's responses when children are in an environment that encourages exploration and consideration of books.

Readers' preferences and reading ability also influence the act of reading. Children who like science fiction approach a science fiction text with the expectation of pleasure (and with a storehouse of experience reading science fiction), whereas children who have not read and enjoyed science fiction approach the same text rather doubtfully. Children who read fluently read with an ease that enables them to concentrate fully on the story world they are creating; children who struggle with words often miss the meaning. A group of fourth-grade readers was discussing L'Engle's *A Wind in the Door* (I–A), a complex science fantasy that contains some difficult proper nouns, when one reader remarked: "I was doing okay; then I tried to figure out the names and got all mixed up." Another reader responded by describing how he had "replaced" the hard names with familiar ones because, as he put it, "it didn't make any difference to the story" (Galda, 1990, 1992, 1993).

Differences in concepts of story certainly influence response. What readers know about literature—its creations, its forms, its purposes, and its effects—influences the meaning that they create (Galda, 1982). Applebee (1978) describes how children's concepts of story grow in complexity as they mature. As they learn more about literature, children grow in their ability to appreciate different books for different reasons, to step back from their personal preferences and view books in the larger literary context. A third-grade reader who didn't especially enjoy **Charlotte's Web** (I) may learn later to appreciate the style and humor of E. B. White, even if animal fantasies are not a preferred genre.

CHILDREN'S COGNITIVE DEVELOPMENT Cognitive development and learning influence responses to literature. As children grow and learn they change as people, and certainly as readers. Piaget's theories of intellectual development offer a useful framework for analyzing changes underlying thought processes. He views the acquisition of knowledge as a gradual developmental process in which children actively experience and organize concepts about their environment. Therefore, the child is seen as an active, dynamic being who interacts with the environment to create knowledge.

Young children learn through their senses and motor movements; they feel, grasp, taste, touch, smell, see, and hear people and objects in their environment. Books that young children can hold (and chew) and that are congruent with real-life experiences make sense to them. Board books containing simple stories or pictures of familiar objects, and participation books, such as Kunhardt's *Pat the Bunny* (N) incorporate experiences appropriate for children up to 5 years old. Children are also learning language rapidly when they are very young; this language is learned in real-life contexts, because it serves real needs. Children learn language

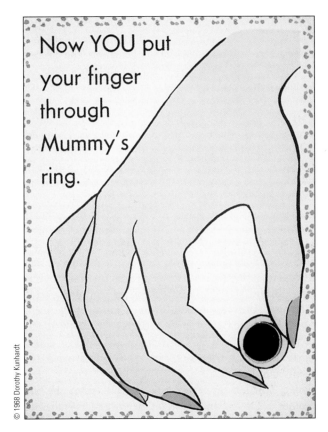

© 1968 Dorothy Kunhardt

Young children won't sit still for long unless they can join in the action. Pat the Bunny invites them to put a finger through Mummy's ring.

to tell people what they want, to relate to others, to find out about their world, and to play "let's pretend." Books provide infinite opportunities to engage children in talk about meaningful things.

During preschool and the primary grades children rapidly develop language, thought, and symbolic representation. Books provide children with rich and varied opportunities for exploring language in many ways, finding out about their worlds, and enjoying the many virtual experiences that stories can impart. At this age, children see stories as true, as presenting the world as it is—not as it might be. Generally, they believe in magic and do not question contradictions. Animal fantasies and folklore are often popular with this age child.

In elementary school, children quickly distinguish between reality and fantasy in literature. They frequently classify literature and can be quite systematic in the way they organize their storehouse of knowledge about their world. They also begin to tolerate contradictions in their own view of reality but, at the same time, are quite firmly attached to their own ideas of the way things are and should be. Books about the here and now, about children like themselves, are often popular at this age.

By the end of middle school children have developed their ability to reason logically, deal with abstractions, consider alternative ways of viewing a situation, and tolerate ambiguity. These developing abilities influence their responses to the books they read.

THE ROLE OF EXPERIENCE Development, of course, occurs in the context of our lives; *experience influences development.* Children who have many experiences with books bring a wealth of knowledge and ability to the texts they read. The intertwining of development and experience can be seen in the responses of fourth-, sixth-, and eighth-grade children who participated in a study by Cullinan, Harwood, and Galda (1983). The participants were interviewed individually and in groups of three after reading one realistic and one fantasy novel; they were asked to retell and discuss what they had read. In Katherine Paterson's realistic novel *Bridge to Terabithia* (I), Leslie, a central character, dies, but in their retellings, not a single fourth grader mentioned the death. When encouraged to tell more by nondirective probes, such as, "Anything else?" children added other details from the story but studiously avoided any mention of Leslie's death. When a child in the group questioned "whether she really died," others insisted she had "come back to life" and was right there with Jess at the end of the story. Their strong preference for a happy ending allowed them to create a happy ending even though one was not present in the text.

The sixth-grade boys were disdainful of the emotional intensity of the novel: They saw Jess as an emotional sissy and Leslie as a daredevil show-off. Some said the book sounded "like a Hollywood romance or a soap opera."

The eighth-grade girls read the novel as a romance and hoped that they might someday be the kind of friend to some boy, often a particular boy, that Leslie was to Jess. The eighth-grade boys, on the other hand, reacted very differently in the individual interview and the group discussion. Individually, they characterized the relationship between the boy and girl as idyllic, but, in the group, they demeaned both characters as "countrified" and immature. Their concern for their image affected their responses in front of their peers.

These comments demonstrate how children's development, their background of reading and life experiences, and their social milieu all are influential factors in their responses to literature, at least those that they are willing to express in public.

The context in which children read and respond makes a difference in the way they respond; supportive contexts allow children to stretch their ideas. Lehr (1991), for example, found that young children who are in literature-rich classrooms and have many experiences reading and discussing literature over time in a supportive context can, and do, discuss themes and character motivation and make generalizations about stories—behaviors usually associated with older children. Galda, Rayburn, and Stanzi (2000) demonstrated the depth of understanding evident in the discussions of second-grade readers in a safe, supportive literature-based classroom. While there are certainly differences between child and young adult cognition, these may be differences in degree rather than in kind. That is, young children may analyze and generalize, but not in an adult way and usually not without support from an adult or more competent peer.

All of the above are descriptions of general patterns of response. It is not the case that 8-year-old readers have no understanding of how texts work, or that 12-year-old girls read every book as a romance. In literature-rich kindergartens you will hear children earnestly discussing why Maurice Sendak didn't put any words on the wild rumpus pages in *Where the Wild Things Are* (P). Third-grade children who read with writer's eyes compare different authors' treatments of the same topic. And many seventh-grade girls read and enjoy difficult fantasy novels rather than popular teenage romances. Generic descriptions of how children of varying ages make sense of a story need to be considered in light of the texts the children read and the contexts in which they read and respond; they will always vary from child to child.

CHILDREN'S LANGUAGE DEVELOPMENT Descriptions of children's understandings about literature are based on what children tell us. For example, we make inferences about children's comprehension based on what they say about what they read. These inferences may be good—when what children say closely matches their understanding—or poor—when children understand but cannot express adequately their understandings through language. For example, young children may think about themes, or spontaneously compare texts to each other, but unless they know how to talk about these things, they may never be able to express their understandings.

Studies of children's language development provide a broad base for inferences about appropriate literary experiences (Britton, 1970). Three principles guide the way we view language and literature. First, children develop language naturally as they interact with language users—when they are immersed in language and expected to respond to it. Vygotsky's (1962, 1978) exploration of language and thought clearly demonstrates how human beings who are firmly embedded in a social world use language for social purposes and learn language in that social world. Children learn the use, function, and power of words because language users talk to them. Children learn about books by being read to (often when they are being held on a parent's lap) and by talking about what they are doing; they learn about books by seeing what others do with them. Stories told or read to children give them opportunities to hear words in use and, in the process, to support, expand, and stimulate their own experiments with language. As children listen to language they gradually understand meanings and eventually express meanings through their own sounds. Language development is a process of generalizing and discriminating finer meanings and sounds. As children learn, books can help at every stage to fulfill their need to make sense of language and the world.

Second, we also know that in language development comprehension generally exceeds production. Though they may not yet be using sentences in their talk, children understand sentences and draw meaning from the contexts in which they are heard. For example, when asked, "Where's your teddy bear?" a child can pick up the toy or point to it long before she can say the words. Similarly, the 6-year-old who responds to a question with "I know it in my head but I can't say it" understands more than he can communicate. Through experience, children assimilate meaning and expand the storehouse of words they use to express meaning. Books, which provide experience beyond the immediate environment, contribute to the meaning base of language. Through books we learn to comprehend more than we actually express in speaking or in writing. Books expand language by providing new words, experiences, and ideas in a context that helps children understand them. Books also provide language models in a variety of well-crafted styles.

Courtesy of John and Sarah Lewis

Parents and other caregivers who read to children provide a model of the pleasure of reading, what reading is, how language works, and new vocabulary.

Third, language learning never ends. As students mature, language skills increase and awareness grows in direct proportion to experiences. Students come to recognize that written material and society affect each other and that language is used in a variety of ways for a variety of purposes. Although they have been using language in any number of ways since their early years, students gradually come to understand and to be able to talk about the persuasive uses of language, the figurative uses of language, the existence of different points of view, and the influence of literature. From wide exposure to books and many other language experiences, students extend their ability to comprehend and appreciate the subtleties and ambiguities of language.

One way to see clearly how experience with books affects language development is to watch young children who learn to read without formal instruction. Children who are read to understand at an early age that books carry meaning and provide fun. Even very young children demonstrate this when they pick up their favorite nursery rhyme book and "read" it aloud to their stuffed animals or the family dog, relying on their memory of the words and the cues in the illustrations to tell them which rhyme belongs on which page. They also come to understand that the words, those black squiggles on the page, carry much of the meaning. They begin to ask questions like "What's that white space for?" and they note punctuation marks and follow along with their eyes as an adult reads aloud. As they listen to books they take in the lilt and cadence of book language, develop a sense of structure and form, and begin to recognize words. For many children who have extensive experience with books it is easy to move into independent reading. We discuss learning to read with literature in Chapter 13.

DEVELOPING A SENSE OF STORY Books also help children extend their understandings about story. Extensive experience with books gives children more resources to draw from as they build a concept of story. Children who hear many stories develop expectations about them; this is called *developing a sense of story*.

For example, research into the stories children tell shows that their ability to tell connected stories develops over time. Applebee (1978) found that children's stories change from disconnected strings to sequential orderings and eventually to focused, sequential stories containing distinct story markers. One such marker is evident when young children signal that they are telling a story by giving a title. Another appears when they begin their stories with a formal opening such as "once upon a time" and end with a closing such as "They lived happily ever after." Most children use recognizable opening and closing story frames by the time they are 5 years old. Many children at this age also use the past tense when they narrate action, and some alter their speaking tone into a dramatic "story voice," using the present tense when they are in a character role. The fact that these story markers appear regularly in children's oral language indicates the extent to which they have assimilated literature and dramatically illustrates the potential power of literature to affect language as well as cognitive and affective development.

You can see how children's sense of story works if you read Pat Hutchins's ***What Game Shall We Play?*** (P), a tightly structured story with a repetitive phrase, to a group of 5-year-olds. By the time you meet the third character the children will be "reading" it with you. Hearing only the first few pages, children can recognize the story structure and predict what is coming next. They do this with any highly patterned, repetitive text they hear. They are not memorizing the text, as so many very young children who "read and reread" their favorite story are doing (even when it is held upside down); rather, they know how the story works because of their prior experiences with stories.

In addition to developing an understanding of the sequential structure of stories, children learn to use the content of stories to organize what they encounter in the world. One well-read 5-year-old, living in a strange city for a brief period, thought she had figured out just where she was when she saw an old, vine-covered building and said, "Mommy, are we in Paris?" She, of course, had been reading Ludwig Bemelman's *Madeleine* (P).

Pat Hutchins invites children to join in saying the familiar phrase that is repeated in each episode of **What Game Shall We Play?**

Our vision of reality is shaped by the stories we tell ourselves. Telling ourselves stories is a primary human activity, one that adults as well as children engaged in (Bruner, 1987; Hardy, 1978). Each of us selectively perceives the world from a unique vantage point, and we tell ourselves stories about what we perceive. Children who are sent to bed in a dark room may fear the monsters that lie hidden there, and no amount of logical reassurance convinces them that the stories they have told themselves about the presence of monsters are unfounded. Philosophical treatises debate what "reality" actually is, but there is a consensus that one's own reality is what one perceives it to be; it is largely shaped by what we choose to believe and by the stories we tell ourselves.

As children mature and their experience with literature increases, their understanding about the relations between literature and life are affected. Galda (1993) found that one dimension that distinguished older readers (grades 8–9) from younger readers (grades 4–5) was that most of the older children consistently discussed the texts as works of art separate from life. The majority of the younger readers compared the characters in Betsy Byars's ***The Summer of the Swans*** (I) to their own lives. They complained of the lack of exact fit with their own worlds: The characters were "kind of like us," but "they don't act like we act at my house" and "They don't fight like real brothers and sisters." The older readers were more objective when they criticized the book; they understood how literature works. When one girl commented that Charlie's retardation "wasn't necessary" to the story, another countered with "Well, the story did need it because it sort of changed the relationship between Sara and Charlie." The eighth-grade readers in the Cullinan, Harwood, and Galda (1983) study had the same sort of discussion about ***Bridge to Terabithia*** (I). One said, "She shouldn't have died," and another replied, "But it wouldn't have been the story it was if she hadn't." Rather than dismissing those parts of the stories that they found extraneous, many of these older readers could go beyond their personal reactions to see how parts functioned in the story as a whole. In general, there was a more developed understanding of the interrelatedness of literary elements in the older readers than there was in the younger readers. Along with this was a diminishing tendency to judge a book according to its fit with one's personal perception of reality. Thus, even fantasy came to be understood as being about recognizable people with familiar problems, as being *true* even if not *actual*.

The Text

We have discussed how different kinds of texts signal different kinds of reading, with some texts written for a predominantly efferent stance, and others a predominately aesthetic stance. Reader preferences also influence the way that readers approach a book. We have already discussed how children change as readers over time, and certainly their appreciation for different kinds of books changes as well.

We can make some generalizations about children's interests and preferences, or about what they *might like* to read, or about what they *actually select* to read, but within each generalization lies a lot of individual variation. Many children, regardless of age, enjoy humor. Primary-grade children often enjoy stories with animal characters and are usually fond of folklore. There is a period of time during the elementary years when many readers are engrossed in mysteries and will read any book, by any author, as long as it's a mystery. As children enter the intermediate grades and begin to form important friendships outside of their immediate families, they often like to read realistic stories about children "just like" themselves, especially stories that are exciting and full of action. Many children and young adults are likely to choose books with characters a bit older than they are, using their reading to think about what life holds for them.

When Lehman (1989) compared books that were given the Children's Choice Award as well as awards bestowed by adults (such as the Newbery) with those that were honored by adults but not by children, she found that children preferred optimistic texts that were action-oriented, well paced, and offered clear resolutions of conflict. A book, no matter how high its literary quality, must also be engaging to children.

As children mature, boys and girls often show differences in reading interests. Many advanced-grade girls prefer romance and contemporary realistic novels to all other types of books; often, bright advanced-grade boys are immersed in the world of science fiction and fantasy, while others enjoy biography. These generalizations, however, are just that—generalizations. There are children who never truly like animal stories, children who do not get bitten by the mystery bug, and girls who disdain romance novels. As each individual reader matures and reads an increasing number of books with an increasing amount of understanding, the preferences of that individual will change along lines that reflect the individual's interests, development, and experiences.

As readers' preferences change, so, too, do their overall responses to literature. When children read widely they seem to develop an appreciation for a broad range of characters, styles, and genres, regardless of their own specific preferences. Experienced readers often look for interesting characters, and this focus seems to be linked to their developing ability to be "inhaled by books," regardless of character age or sex, and in spite of genre differences.

It is clear that successful guesses about what readers will enjoy reading are only possible if they are based on a clear understanding of individual children and a knowledge of a wide range of books. Even then, we, as teachers and librarians, can only encourage children to read books; it is entirely up to them to make books their own. In the Booklist at the end of this chapter we present selected books from the Children's Choices list. These are books that children across America have enjoyed.

The Context

It is vital to understand at least three things about the social nature of reading and responding to literature. First, learning occurs in a social context that is dependent upon interaction; literature plays an important role in that context. Second, children grow in their ability to understand literature as they gain experience with life and literature; this experience often occurs in the company of others. Third, a teacher's influence on children's response to literature is a powerful determinant of that response. How readers read and how they respond to the books they read are influenced by the contexts in which they are reading. Hearing a bedtime story is different from hearing a story at the library's 2:00 story hour; reading on a rainy Saturday afternoon in the most comfortable chair in the house is different from reading from 8:30 to 9:00 every morning at a school desk. Reading in a classroom that has plenty of books, that provides time to read them, and that includes other readers who support developing ideas is much different from reading for homework, punishment, or contests.

Children will become engaged readers when we surround them with opportunities to read and respond to a variety of genres, styles, and authors; when we appreciate individual differences and offer opportunities to explore and share diverse responses; and when we provide time and encouragement for responding in a variety of ways, such as spontaneous sharing, small- and large-group discussion, writing, art, drama, and movement.

While response is highly individualistic, it is also intensely social. Although reading books is often a solitary activity, the way we use and talk about books is a natural social response, one that we as readers all share. When we finish reading a good book it's quite natural to talk about it and we usually learn from that talk. Talking about books encourages readers to articulate their own responses to books and to find out how other readers responded. In many cases talking about books adds new dimensions to individual responses as the ideas of others provide new perspectives. As one young reader remarked, "I never thought about it that way, but now it makes a lot of sense"—a sentiment that anyone who has discussed books with friends can understand.

Children develop feelings and beliefs about themselves and their world through interactions with those around them; this includes their interactions around books. They find out who they are and what role they are to play by interpreting the verbal and nonverbal messages that significant others give them. Children develop a positive self-concept if people around them show them they are loved and valued.

In a similar way, they develop a positive attitude toward books if books are treated as a source of pleasure and knowledge. When children experience sharing books with a loving caregiver from early on, they develop positive feelings about books and the joy that can come from them. When children experience sharing books with peers and teachers in collaborative, supportive contexts, they develop positive feelings about books and about themselves as readers. The social and cultural context in which children grow and learn shapes their view of the world and the role of literature in it.

Children do not all experience the same social and cultural contexts. Heath (1982, 1983) documents how three very different home cultures—in the same city in North America—influence children's experiences with books and concepts about them and, in turn, their experiences in school. She argues that children learn at home how to define and enact book reading. In many cases this does not resemble how teachers expect children to read and respond in school. Sensitive teachers recognize individual differences and build on the oral and literate traditions that children bring to school from home, emphasizing a multifaceted conception of literacy. They also clearly explain the additional strategies that they expect children to use in school—demonstrating, for example, how they make connections between their lives

Profile ✴ Louise Rosenblatt

Courtesy of Louise Rosenblatt

Louise Rosenblatt is a remarkable woman with exceptional talent. Her work, which presents theories about the nature of reading and the literary experience, substantially shapes the teaching of English in schools and colleges.

Louise Rosenblatt brings a scholarly approach to literary criticism, combined with an active concern for the teaching of English. At a time when it was assumed that the reader's role was to passively receive a "ready-made" meaning from a text, she stressed the idea of the reader actively making meaning by engaging in a transaction with the text. This new vantage point helps us to understand that the reader's background and interests play an important part in the development of the ability to read. She also emphasized the difference between reading a poem or story with attention focused on what is being lived through (an aesthetic experience), and reading material with attention focused on what is to be carried away (an efferent experience), such as information or directions.

Louise Rosenblatt graduated with honors from Barnard College, Columbia University. After several years of graduate work in France (at the University of Grenoble and the Sorbonne, University of Paris), she received her doctorate in comparative literature from the Sorbonne. Her doctoral dissertation on the nineteenth-century aesthetic movement in England and France led her to see the necessity for a literate reading public. Postdoctoral work in anthropology with Franz Boas and Ruth Benedict at Columbia University inspired her feeling for the contributions of diverse cultures that encourage the creation of a democratic American society.

Louise Rosenblatt's primary professorship was at New York University, where she directed the doctoral program in English education. She also taught at Barnard College, Columbia University, Brooklyn College of the City University of New York, Northwestern University (summer sessions), and Rutgers University.

Louise Rosenblatt received the John Simon Guggenheim Fellowship (1943), the Great Teacher Award from New York University (1972), the Distinguished Service Award from the National Council of Teachers of English (1973), and the National Conference on Research in English Lifetime Award (1990). She was inducted into the Reading Hall of Fame by the International Reading Association in 1992. On the fiftieth anniversary of the publication of *Literature as Exploration*, the National Council of Teachers of English honored her with a full day of programs to celebrate her distinguished work. In another major text, *The Reader, the Text, the Poem*, she expands her theories and implications for practice.

In a letter dated February 7, 1993, Louise Rosenblatt states:

I believe that if in the early years youngsters get the feel of the aesthetic and efferent ways of reading, if the classroom atmosphere and teacher's interventions permit students to automatically adopt the appropriate stance, then all the other (efferent) things we do with literature—analyze, categorize, criticize, evaluate—will have real literary experiences as their subject or base. So many of the bright students who came into my freshman and sophomore classes at the university level had learned that one reads literature in school in order to do these efferent things (I have nothing against them in their proper place), and they had lost, if they ever had, the delight of aesthetic or literary experience. It's the cumulative effect over the years of the way literature is approached that I am concerned about.

Louise Rosenblatt was married to Sidney Ratner, scholar in philosophy and history, for more than 60 years. They have a grown son and a granddaughter.

and the books they read, or among various books. These teachers view reading as being shaped by one's individual experiences. They recognize that people have varied concepts regarding the functions of literature, the purposes for literature, and the appropriate stance to take toward literature.

As mentioned at the beginning of this chapter, just as literature is *shaped* by readers' views of the world, so, too, can literature help to *shape* readers' views of the world. Frye (1970) underscores the role of literature in "educating" the imagination and shows the necessity of imagination in creating a social vision. He believes that the fundamental job of the imagination in ordinary life is to produce, out of the society we *have* to live in, a vision of the society we *want* to live in. In this sense, we live in two worlds: our ordinary world and our ideal world. One world is around us, the other is a vision inside our minds, born and fostered by the imagination, yet real enough for us to try to make the world we see conform to its shape. Teachers can foster transforming experiences with literature through their own actions and through what they ask of their students.

Helping Children Grow as Responsive Readers

Activities described throughout this text are chosen to help readers develop a deeper understanding of and a greater appreciation for books. Because children's literature is so rich and varied, it can be used to enhance every area of the curriculum. The best kind of activity is one that is intended to bring readers back to books they've read and guide them to others. The Rosens state the case well:

> It is as though there is a deep lack of confidence in the power of literature to do its work and a profound conviction that unless literature can be converted into the hard currency of familiar school learning it has not earned its keep. What will take children more deeply into the experience of the book? This is the question we should be asking rather than by what means can I use this book as a launching-pad into any one of a dozen endeavors which leave the book further and further behind, at best a distant sound, at worst forgotten entirely. (1973, p. 195)

Linguist M.A.K. Halliday (1982) says that people *learn* language, *learn about* language, and *learn through* language. His model can be applied to literature, as well. When we read literature we learn language—the language of story, poem, and well-crafted nonfiction. As readers we also learn *about* language—how language is crafted to suit different purposes, how varied genres are structured, and how particular stylistic choices have different power and effect. And of course readers learn through literature; they read about other places, people, and ideas to broaden their knowledge and understanding. Beyond this, readers who are engaged with books learn about themselves and others; they consider the virtual experiences they have through story and construct their own value systems.

Children will, of course, learn many other things through literature. They can learn how to read, learn about innumerable topics, and learn to be better writers, among other things. They can learn all this, and more, in an atmosphere that does not lose sight of the fact that good books are important in and of themselves and don't always need to "teach" something. The challenge for educators is to teach with literature in a manner that preserves its integrity as well as the integrity of children's responses to it. It is not easy to keep the focus on children and their responses to the books they read. Indeed, children and books can easily get lost in a maze of goals, activities, and assessments if a literature-based curriculum is implemented without careful planning.

Natalie Babbitt (1990) speaks eloquently about some real dangers inherent in a poorly planned literature-based curriculum. One danger that she sees is what Rosenblatt (1978; 1991) and Goodman (1983) calls *basalizing literature.* Babbitt writes:

> I know that there is a movement underway to stop using texts for the teaching of reading and to start using works of fiction. In the beginning that seemed to me to be a good idea. But now I'm not so sure. The texts had related workbooks with sentences to complete, quizzes, questions to think about, and all kinds of suggested projects. The feeling has been, as I understand it, that these texts and workbooks were making a dry and tedious thing out of learning to read at the very time when concern about literacy levels was growing more and more serious. So it seemed sensible to try using real stories in the classroom— stories that could grab the children's fancies and show them what the joy of reading is all about. But what I see happening now is that these real stories are being used in the same way that the old texts were used. Every once in a while someone sends me something meant to accompany a classroom reading of my story, *Tuck Everlasting*, and here's what I find: a related workbook with sentences to complete, quizzes, questions to think about, and all kinds of suggested projects. I worry that this will make a dry and tedious thing out of fiction. (1990, pp. 696–697)

If teachers use trade books in the curriculum to interest children and to help them become literate in the fullest sense of the word, then it is crucial that we allow the books to be as interesting as they can be, that we not ruin the power of trade books by turning them into material for exercises.

Another concern centers on the individuality of emotional response. Stories and poems are about feelings, about meanings and significances, about questions rather than answers. Most authors write stories to raise questions rather than teach lessons. Certainly, stories deal with values, with morality, but teaching object lessons is not what they are about. Babbitt voices this concern in response to a discussion of the moral lessons in *Tuck Everlasting* when she says:

> I don't think any [young readers of *Tuck*] are coming away with a heightened sense of social responsibility. They could be made to, of course. You can come away from any book with that, if it's thrust upon you. But how sad for the book!
>
> . . . What children take away with them when they've finished a book will depend on each child's personal needs and personal quirks. (1990, p. 701)

Katherine Paterson, Marion Dane Bauer, and many other authors say the same thing: Their books are not meant to teach children morals, but are meant, rather, to engage readers, to allow children to discover, explore, and build their own values. The assumption that we can use books to inculcate morals in children, and the tendency to look at books in terms of what moral lessons they might "teach" lead only to practices that ruin the power of a good book.

The primary goal of a response-centered curriculum is to engage readers in the act of reading responsively. The focus is not on the works of literature, nor on the topics or skills, but on "the mind of the reader as it meets the book—the response" (Purves, Rogers, and Soter, 1990). A response-centered curriculum recognizes and encourages diversity among readers, recognizes and encourages connections among readers, and "recognizes that response is joyous" (Purves and Soter, 1990, p. 56). In this curriculum, the teacher provides a variety of books, time to read and explore them, time to talk and write about them, and time to draw and dramatize from them. In addition, teachers provide opportunities for students to enjoy the collaborative company of peers with whom to explore similarities and differences in responses. The teacher also helps students find the language with which to articulate their responses, and challenges them to understand why they respond as they do (Purves and Soter, 1990, p. 56). Figure 12.2 states some goals for a response-centered curriculum and some ways to achieve them.

A second goal is to build on the engagement that a response-centered curriculum fosters in order to develop children's awareness of "the family of stories" (Moss and Stott, 1986) and of how words work (Benton, 1984) in literature. This goal is focused on helping children learn language and learn about it and its use in literature through reading.

A third objective is to give children the opportunity to learn about themselves and their world through books, to learn *through* language. The virtual experiences possible

Figure 12 ✳ 2

Goals of a Response-Centered Curriculum

A Response-Centered Curriculum Helps Students To:

* Develop a lasting love of reading
* Establish the lifelong reading habit
* Feel secure in their responses to literature
* Make connections between literature and life
* See connections among texts (intertextuality)
* Recognize commonalities among responses
* See variations of meaning in stories and poems
* Recognize different purposes for reading
* Engage in aesthetic reading (reading to savor experience)
* Engage in efferent (reading to remember)
* Recognize different types of reading material—Informational/expository, narrative, poetic, and so on
* Learn about language and how it is used
* Understand how words work
* Appreciate the beauty of things well said
* Grasp subtleties of language

Ways To Achieve Goals Are To:

* Encourage students to interact with books
* Provide time to read and explore
* Give time to talk, write, draw, and dramatize
* Provide time to collaborate with peers
* Plan time to explore similarities and differences in their responses
* Accept and encourage diversity among readers
* Give students a choice of material to read
* Let them choose from ways to respond (talk, write, draw, dramatize, and so on)
* Provide ways to respond joyously
* Provide a variety of books
* Present motivation to read
* Give book talks to generate enthusiasm
* Integrate reading with other areas
* Create a rich literacy environment
* Help students find language to express responses
* Give students opportunities to learn language
* Help students realize their potential as learners, as language users, and as readers
* Give students the opportunity to learn about themselves and their world (learn through language)

through story, the emotional expansion that is possible with poetry, and the exposure to information about the child's world that comes from nonfiction all increase children's knowledge of themselves and their worlds. And this increased knowledge widens children's horizons and makes even more learning possible.

We advocate a response-centered literature curriculum because it is through such a curriculum that we as teachers can best help our students realize their potential as learners, as language users, and as readers. In an integrated, response-centered literature curriculum, books and readers are at the center of many types of learning. In Chapter 13 we detail specific ideas about a literature-based curriculum in the primary grades. In Chapter 14 we present ways of integrating literature study, reading, writing, oral language development, and other areas of the curriculum into the upper elementary and middle school grades. As a basis for the practices we detail in those chapters, here we broadly describe a response-based curriculum and three of its essential ingredients: time and choice, reading aloud, and activities that support children's developing understanding of literature. Students need time to read, choices about how they read and respond, many experiences hearing you read aloud, and your help as they grow in their understandings of how literature works.

TIME AND CHOICE

Children need both time to read and choices about what to read, how to read, and whom to read with.

> Allowing children time to be with books in the classroom, rather than assigning them to a certain number of books to be read on their own time, teaches them to value books. When time is set aside for reading and responding to literature, students know that this is viewed as important by their teacher. So, too, does reading to and with a class help to convince students of the value and the pleasures of reading. (Galda, 1988, p. 100)

In many classrooms Sustained Silent Reading (SSR) is one way that teachers build time for individual reading into their busy schedules. SSR is a plan wherein 20 to 30 minutes are set aside each day when everybody in the school reads— the principal, the custodian, the teachers, and all the students. There are many variations of the program: DEAR (Drop Everything and Read), USSR (Uninterrupted Sustained Silent Reading), and READ (Read Everything And Dream). Sometimes SSR operates within an individual classroom rather than throughout the entire school. These programs have consistently produced better readers. Even when students are not fluent independent readers, they need time to explore books independently.

We know that reading independently improves reading fluency, but research suggests that students do not have enough time to read in school. Many students spend up to 70 percent of the time allocated for reading instruction doing seatwork—workbooks and skill sheets, many of which are unrelated to reading and are actually detrimental to children's attitudes toward reading (Ingham, 1981).

A mother described her daughter storming in the door from school, complaining, "Mom, I *hate* reading!" Her mother countered, "But you love reading your Little House and Beverly Cleary books here at home." "Yes, I know that, but I *hate* reading!" What she hated was the class at school called Reading, which would have been more appropriately named Worksheets, and which obviously had nothing to do with really reading books. Classroom research shows that the amount of time devoted to worksheets does *nothing* to improve reading proficiency (Leinhardt, Zigmond, and Cooley, 1981; Rosenshine and Stevens, 1984). The amount of *independent* silent reading children do in school, however, is significantly related to gains in reading achievement (Allington, 1984). Researchers estimate that the typical primary school child reads silently only 7 or 8 minutes per day. By the middle grades, silent reading time still averages only 15 minutes per school day. No one can become skilled at anything practiced only 7 to 15 minutes a day.

We might think that we can solve the problem of tight schedules and too little time for reading in the classroom by assigning reading as homework. Research shows that children who averaged even 10 minutes per day of reading outside the classroom had significantly higher reading achievement scores than those who did not (Anderson, Wilson, and Fielding, 1988). However, few children read even 10 minutes per day. Fifty percent of the fifth-grade students studied read from books only 4 minutes a day or less, 30 percent 2 minutes a day or less, 10 percent not at all. Students were more likely to read outside of school if the teacher read aloud in school and if they had SSR during school. If we want students to read, we must tempt them with good stories, poems, and nonfiction, and show them that we value reading by devoting a significant amount of time to it in the classroom. Assign reading at home as homework, but make it classwork, too.

Not only is it vitally important that students have a significant amount of regularly scheduled time to read independently and with peers, and to respond to what they have read, but also it is important that they are given time to listen to you read aloud. There are as many ways to schedule reading time as there are classrooms. Reading time, either independent or teacher's oral reading, is often scheduled first thing in the morning, right after recess, or right after lunch as a way of calming and pulling a class together. Some teachers make use of lunchtime by encouraging students to take books with them and read while they eat. This also gives them something positive to do while they're waiting for lunch to end. Other teachers like to end the day by reading aloud to the whole class; ending on a cliff-hanger certainly encourages children to return tomorrow!

Students need opportunities to make choices. As we discuss above, responses and preferences are highly individualistic. Although you as a teacher need to be able to help students select books they will like—and certainly you can make suggestions and assign books and response activities—children need to be able to make their own choices about the books they read. They also should be able to make choices about what they want to do when they are finished with a book. Some children might like to paint, others to talk, and others to sit quietly and think.

Teachers help students become knowledgeable about themselves as readers by providing both guidance and the freedom to choose books. Teachers of young children might present many books to the class during read-aloud time; many of these books might be highly patterned stories or stories that might be familiar to the children. They can then read these stories independently during SSR time, approximating the teacher's reading and gradually developing their ability to read the text independently.

Older readers, too, benefit from hearing stories that the teacher and others enjoy. Reading aloud, and creating space and structures that allow children to read and talk with each other about books help promote reading while giving children ideas about books to read. Some teachers allow children a full range of choice; they can choose any book they would like to read. Others provide revolving classroom collections that support curricular study (discussed in Chapters 13 and 14) and ask children to choose from those books. Others carefully gather books that reflect the reading levels in the classroom. Whatever the approach, the idea that they can choose what they want to read has changed the way many children feel about reading.

As children become confident readers, they learn to recognize what books they can read and what books they might like to read. They begin to know which authors and illustrators they like. And they learn where to go for recommendations about books—to the teacher, the librarian, to family and friends, to other students in their class. Good readers know how to find books for themselves.

The value we place on books is also reflected in the physical environment of the classroom. The books that you have in your classroom should be easily accessible to students and attractively displayed, with many covers facing outward. Children can help devise a simple scheme to organize the books. Comfortable places to sit and relax with a book and attractive displays such as posters and book jackets also make reading inviting.

You as a teacher can show that you value literature by being a reader yourself, by reading along with the children during SSR, talking about books you like, reading bits of your own stories aloud to them, and of course, by reading aloud with pleasure and skill.

READING ALOUD

One primary way that teachers help children grow as engaged, responsive readers is to read aloud. Reading aloud is one of the most common and easiest means of sharing books and poetry. It is a pleasurable experience for all when done well, and it has a positive impact on students' reading development (Clark, 1976; Durkin, 1966; Wells, 1986). Reading aloud not only helps young children become readers, but also helps older children become better readers. Reading aloud extends students' horizons, introduces them to literature they might not read on their own, offers alternate worlds and lifestyles, increases their experiential base from which to view the world, and models good reading (Galda and Cullinan, 1991). Reading aloud to young children also demonstrates print and book handling concepts such as left to right and top to bottom directionality, page turning, and the role of print and pictures in telling a story or presenting a concept. The wealth of available evidence caused the Commission on Reading to conclude that "the single most important activity for building the knowledge required for

© Lee Galda

Children can understand books they cannot read on their own. Read books aloud that are slightly above their reading level to expand their literary experiences. Story time quickly becomes the favorite part of the school day.

eventual success in reading is reading aloud to children" (Anderson, Hiebert, Scott, and Wilkinson, 1985, p. 23). The many reasons for reading aloud are summarized here:

Reading Aloud . . .

Introduces new words (vocabulary)

Displays interesting sentence patterns

Presents a variety of forms of language

Shows various styles of written language

Develops a sense of story

Motivates children to read more

Provides ideas for students' writing

Enriches students' general knowledge

Models the sound of good reading for students

Adds pleasure to the day

There are some important guidelines to consider when selecting books to read aloud, the most important of which is to select books that are well written. Books of quality abound, and it is a waste of precious time to read second-rate materials. Good books pique children's interest and invite them to read them—or others like them—independently. Sometimes teachers will read an inferior book "because the children love it," but students will love good books even more. Select books that will influence and expand children's literary tastes.

Find out which books are already familiar by asking children to list their favorites, and then build from there, selecting books that children will probably not discover on their own. Save read-aloud time for the special books that you want your students to know. Introduce children to all of an author's books by reading aloud from one of them and telling them where to find the rest.

Reading from outstanding examples of all types of literature—realistic fiction, historical fiction, fantasy, science fiction, folklore, poetry, biography, nonfiction—can help expand children's literary tastes. Reading some books slightly above students' reading abilities extends their language; they usually comprehend more than they can read. However, as we have said earlier, a good book can be spoiled for children by reading it to them before they can understand its subtleties. Most books can be understood on several levels, but do consider the students' emotional maturity as you choose. Select books that you want to make part of the whole-class experience, books that you want to become part of the shared knowledge in your classroom.

When reading aloud to children, know your material before you begin. Practice reading is important, especially when reading poetry, where the phrasing and cadence carry so much of the meaning. Listen to recordings of poets reading their own work; they know how it should sound. One such recording, "Poetry Parade" (Weston Woods), offers David McCord, Aileen Fisher, Karla Kuskin, and Harry

Behn reading their poetry. Practice reading also helps you decide on the mood and tone that you want to set and allows you to learn special names or refrains so that you won't stumble over them and thus spoil the story.

It is important to be thoroughly familiar with the content of the material you read aloud. Some books contain words and incidents that might be offensive in some communities or that are best kept as a private interchange between author and individual reader. You can avoid embarrassment by being alert to sensitive issues. Not all books or all scenes from books are for oral group sharing.

When reading, use a natural voice, with inflections and modulations befitting the book. Avoid greatly exaggerated voice changes and overly dramatic gestures. Read slowly, enunciate clearly, project your voice directly, and maintain eye contact with your listeners as much as possible. Teachers who read aloud with their noses in the book soon lose their audience. Some brief guidelines for reading aloud are presented here.

Tips for Reading Aloud

1. Read the book ahead of time; be familiar with it.

2. Give a brief description of the book or character to establish a context for the listeners.

3. Begin reading aloud slowly; quicken the pace as listeners are drawn into the book.

4. Look up from the book frequently to maintain eye contact.

5. Interpret dialogue meaningfully.

6. Read entire books, if possible, or read a chapter or more per day to sustain meaning.

When it comes to reading picture books aloud to children, educators have different points of view. Some teachers believe that because the illustrations are integral to the text, children need to see them while hearing the words. Others read the text aloud and then explore the pictures with children later. Your decision will rest on the qualities of the particular book you choose. If you feel that the illustrations are needed to make sense of the story, hold the book open and to one side as you read. And there is nothing wrong with rereading a favorite book, either immediately or at another time; in fact, it is highly recommended.

Teachers who permit students to draw, read their own books, or do quiet seatwork during read-aloud time diminish the importance of reading aloud by implying that it does not deserve students' full attention. Instead, make read-aloud time a highlight of the day—something special you share. Your enthusiasm and extra preparations for the occasion set the tone; once you have begun, the magic of the book takes over.

Reading aloud is central to every school day and should continue at least through middle school. Nursery and primary

The kind of material to be read changes, but the practice of reading aloud to students continues throughout junior high school.

school teachers read aloud many times a day. Intermediate and advanced-grade teachers usually read aloud at one particular time. In one school during noon recess, different teachers read aloud from a novel, biography, or nonfiction book, and students choose the group they want to attend.

SUPPORTING CHILDREN'S GROWING LITERARY UNDERSTANDING

Sensitive teachers help children make connections between their own lives and the books they read. Cochran-Smith (1984) documented how one preschool teacher did this with her class as she demonstrated how to make connections between text and life, and between life and text. Heath and Wolf (1992) describe the way two children incorporate the literature that is read to them into their own lives. Many teachers across the grades see this as one of the most important things they do. Asking questions and making statements like "This story reminds me of the story that you told us about your cousin, Miguel" or "Has anyone ever had an

experience like this?" demonstrates to students that the stuff of their own lives is often mirrored in the books they read. This understanding helps them experience literature as a world of possibilities inextricably intertwined with their own lives.

While connections between life and text are still at the core of children's experiences with literature, connections among and between books are important as well. As children read and listen to stories, they begin to build their own personal storehouse of literary understanding. They begin to recognize thematic connections across stories, similarities in plot structures and characterization, and distinctive styles in text and illustration. Teachers can encourage this kind of understanding by drawing on their knowledge of how literature works, and planning a literature curriculum that contains books selected specifically to help students make connections among texts, connections that result in a deeper understanding of what literature is and how it works. Understanding and recognizing how authors manipulate literary elements to create outstanding texts of many genres allows teachers to plan questions and devise activities that encourage their students to explore literature more deeply. You will find examples of this kind of teaching in Chapters 13 and 14. Teaching Idea 12.1 presents some questions teachers can ask themselves that serve to heighten their awareness of literary structures and elements in the books they share with their students. This kind of teacher preparation helps children develop an understanding of the unity of all literature.

Teachers enhance their students' growing literary understandings when they structure opportunities for students to make links across books, or *intertextual* connections. Learning about the "family of stories" (Moss and Stott, 1986) is an ongoing process as students come to recognize similarities and differences in plot structures, characters, and themes. As with connecting books to life, connecting books to other books adds dimension to future reading and responding. Wide reading (many varied books) and deep reading (many books in a particular genre, by a particular author, with a particular structure, and so on) acquaint children with the world of literature and help them learn a lot about specific aspects of that world.

Talking about characters enables students to make comparisons among characters from various stories. These comparisons can lead to generalizations about character types that children will meet as they read widely. Discussing plot results in identification of various kinds of plots and in understandings about archetypal plots that underlie literature. For example, in a quest story a character begins at home, leaves in search of something important (an object, a person, self-knowledge), and returns home changed in some way. When students read and discuss such books, they can pinpoint characters' strengths and weaknesses, identify

Courtesy of Harcourt Brace and Company

Teaching Idea 12 ☆ 1

Questions to Ask Yourself While Reading

As you are rereading a book in preparation for class discussion, pay attention to what the author has done in terms of literary elements. Peterson and Eeds (1990) suggest that when teachers focus on literary elements as they read, they are better equipped to build upon tentative understandings that students might advance in discussions. Think about the following:

✳ *Plot.* What are the key events? How does the author build tension? Do the events occur chronologically, or does the author use other structures such as flashbacks?

✳ *Character.* How do characters emerge? Which are fully developed? How do the central characters grow and change? How does this connect with the events of the story? What influence do the characters have on the events? Which characters are static? Why might the author have done this?

✳ *Setting.* Are the characters and events influenced by the place and time? Do you know where and when this story is set? If so, how does the author reveal this?

✳ *Point of view.* Who is telling the story? How do you know this? What are the implications of this narrator? How does that influence what you, the reader, is able to know?

✳ *Theme.* What are the big ideas that unify the story? Are there symbols or extended metaphors that help build the themes?

problems that they must solve, discover similarities and differences in the characters' quests, and thus build an understanding of quest tales.

Finding similarities and differences in the underlying conflicts of stories also helps readers make connections among books. The connections build an understanding of literature. Some books revolve around several conflicts; others have only one or two central conflicts. Discussing these conflicts, or problems, helps readers notice their presence in stories and gives them another dimension along which to connect various stories.

Consideration of themes often brings about an important recognition of the various ways that different authors treat the same general theme. Readers read similar stories about particular themes in many different books.

Children who explore how literature works also learn to look at books as works of art crafted by a writer. They notice the language that the writer uses and learn to appreciate the nuances that distinguish one writer from another. Students use their knowledge about literature in their own writing, incorporating patterns, structures, themes, character types, and language that they have encountered. Books build upon books, stories lean on stories, and children become knowledgeable readers and writers.

However, the *study* of literature or of any topic related to the literature should not begin until after the literature is *experienced*: Someone tells, reads, or dramatizes a story, and a fortunate child just enjoys it. When the time comes for children to look at literature analytically and to make abstractions about its forms, structures, archetypes, and patterns, they have joyful experiences upon which to draw. Even with older children, enjoyment is still uppermost, and the study of literature is sensitively introduced only as it adds to their appreciation and insight. The study of literature does not replace the original literary experience; neither does study always need to follow the experience. There is a time and a place for both. As Northrop Frye explains,

> In all of our literary experience there are two kinds of response. There is the direct experience of the work itself, while we're reading a book, . . . especially for the first time. This experience is uncritical, or rather precritical. . . . Then there is the conscious, critical response we make after we've finished reading . . . where we compare what we've experienced with other things of the same kind, and form a judgment of value and proportion on it. This critical response, with practice, gradually makes our pre-critical responses more sensitive and accurate. . . . But behind our responses to individual works, there's a bigger response to our literary experience as a whole, as a total possession. (1970, pp. 104–105)

Perceptive readers develop by moving from unconscious enjoyment to self-conscious appreciation to conscious delight (Early, 1960). This kind of growth is not possible without a firm foundation in experiencing joy from books. Through carefully planned encounters with particular books, teachers build on this foundation of joy as they help their students delight in the artistry and interconnections in literature.

When children discover connections among books the excitement is palpable. This is evident in the following discussion by a group of sixth-grade students who had just finished reading Ursula Le Guin's **The Wizard of Earthsea** (A) and had previously read several books in **The Chronicles of Narnia** series (I) by C. S. Lewis and two of Madeleine L'Engle's space fantasies, *A Wrinkle in Time* (I–A) and *A Wind in the Door* (I–A).

MICHELLE: I liked **Narnia** best—it was so magicky.

JON-PAUL: Well, I liked it a lot, but not the best. For me, *A Wrinkle in Time* was best—"It," you know, the Naked Brain, and the shadowed planets, and all that.

TEACHER: There was a shadow in *A Wizard of Earthsea*, and the "black thing" caused shadowed or dark planets in *A Wrinkle in Time*. Somehow, the bad thing, the evil in several of the books we read, seems to be pictured in some way by blackness or shadows.

SARAH: Except for Narnia, and there it wasn't a black witch but a white witch. The evil spell was snow and winter.

HEDY: That's because nothing could grow or be alive then. Aslan brought the Spring.

SARAH: But still whatever it appeared like, there was a battle against the forces of evil.

TEACHER : What about *A Wizard of Earthsea*?

JON-PAUL: Well, like we read, the shadow that was following Ged was really the evil in himself, but he didn't recognize it until the end. I don't really understand that very well, but I understand it some.

TEACHER: In *A Wind in the Door* you could be "x-ed" if you weren't trying to be your real self. Again, the picture the author gives us to imagine in our own minds is rather similar: If you are "x-ed" what has happened to you?

JON-PAUL: You become annihilated. You don't exist any more. If you were a planet, where you used to be there was just a black hole of nothingness in the universe.

SARAH: And for Ged, if he didn't recognize that there *was* a bad side to his own nature, it could destroy them. He would be "x-ed" by his shadow, and he wouldn't be living any more, but just the power of evil could live in his body.

TEACHER: We talked a lot when we were reading the books by Madeleine L'Engle about the *theme* of her books—that the central idea was the battle between good and evil in the universe. What would you say is the theme of the other fantasies?

HEDY: Well, in **Narnia** it was sort of the same because Aslan was good and the White Witch was evil.

SARAH: I see it! I see it! I just finished reading Susan Cooper's *The Dark Is Rising*, and it's the same theme in that book, too. It's the light against the dark. It's good against evil. *They're all about the same thing!* (Anzul, 1978)

The other children sat in silence, mulling over this idea. They understood Sarah in a way. Certainly, they understood momentarily the words she was saying, though possibly they would soon forget them. They clearly would need time to read and reflect more. Listening to Sarah discover connections among the books she's read isn't the same as making those connections for themselves, but it did give them the idea that those connections are possible and exciting.

Sarah had taken one of those rare steps to a new level of understanding. From now on, every book she reads can not only be a delightful world in itself, but can also relate in some way to other books. She is on that threshold where every human experience she reads about and thus makes her own experience will begin to relate somehow to all human experience, and where human experience that is transmuted into literature begins to relate to all other literature.

Frye explains it this way:

All themes and characters and stories you encounter in literature belong to one big interlocking family. . . . You keep associating your literary experiences together: you're always being reminded of some other story you read or movie you saw or character that impressed you. For most of us, most of the time, this goes on unconsciously, but the fact that it does go on suggests that perhaps in literature you don't just read one novel or poem after another, but that there's a real subject to be studied, as there is in science, and that the more you read, the more you learn about literature as a whole. (1970, pp. 48–49)

When children link a particular work with others similar to it in some way, even at the primary school level, they begin to develop an understanding of the unity of all literature. Making connections helps children to understand and appreciate literature. It is also basic to learning; some cognitive psychologists have come to define learning as the search for patterns that connect.

ACTIVITIES TO HELP CHILDREN CONNECT WITH BOOKS

Research and practical experience show that most children who become involved in activities related to books read more than those who do not. As Figure 12.3 suggests, the phenomenon is cyclical—reading provides practice that makes a reader more proficient. Being a better reader leads to more pleasure and a willingness to practice more frequently.

Effective response activities allow children the time to savor and absorb books. It is important to ponder a book for a while before beginning another; students need a chance to linger in the spell cast by a good book. This may mean *doing nothing* or it may mean using creative learning activities. Response and reflection are important ingredients of a child's complete learning experience; give time for both.

Figure 12 ☆ 3

The Cyclical Nature of Reading

Practice
Pleasure
Proficiency

In classrooms where there are many books and where students are given time to read and respond to them, children may respond in many ways without specific prompting by the teacher. In a naturalistic study of response across the elementary grades, Hickman (1981) described seven different types of responses that occurred in the classrooms she observed. They can be summarized as follows:

1. Listening behaviors, such as laughter and applause
2. Contact with books, such as browsing, intent attention
3. Acting on the impulse to share, reading together
4. Oral responses, such as storytelling, discussion
5. Actions and drama, such as dramatic play
6. Making things like pictures, games, displays
7. Writing, by using literary models, summarizing, and writing about literature (p. 346)

Hickman makes the point that response doesn't have to be an activity. It can range from individual thoughtfulness, to simple sharing with another reader, to a formal activity such as a group depiction of an important scene from a book. The aesthetic nature of the reading experience requires personal involvement; therefore, the impact of the book determines the response a reader makes. Reading is both a social and a private affair that calls upon the emotions of the reader. Some books should be explored; others read, closed, and forever locked in the reader's heart. While some book encounters lead naturally into concrete projects, we should avoid overdoing a good thing, for in our zeal we may be engendering boredom instead of interest.

Children can be encouraged to respond to literature in many ways. They discover the pleasure in extended activities when there are many to choose from. Many of these choices involve social interaction; sharing responses with others often enlarges one's initial response. Structured and spontaneous opportunities for students to exchange and compare ideas with their peers and to build on the responses of others help children grow as responsive readers.

© Lee Galda

When classrooms keep reading with a central focus, students develop into communities of readers. They read books together and talk about books they read.

Teaching Idea 12 ✰ 2

Creative Ways to Share Books

* ✳ Devise a television or newspaper announcement to advertise a book. Include words and pictures.
* ✳ Make puppet characters, write a play about a book, and put on a puppet show.
* ✳ Choose a character from a book and write a new story about him or her.
* ✳ Write an account of what you would have done or how you would have acted had you been one of the characters in a book you read.
* ✳ Write about the author or illustrator of a book.
* ✳ Write a summary of a book, telling what you especially liked or disliked about it.
* ✳ Compare two books about the same subject.
* ✳ Compare two books by the same author.
* ✳ Write a story about the funniest incident in a book.

Source: Adapted from "Individualizing Book Reviews," by A. Pillar, 1975, *Elementary English* (now *Language Arts*), 52(4), pp. 467–469.

Teaching Idea 12 ✰ 3

Book Buddies

Cross-age sharing benefits both older and younger students. Similarly, when children talk about books it increases their understanding and improves their ability to express themselves orally. Participants also gain in reading and writing achievement and in self-esteem.

Classmate Book Buddies

To implement Book Buddies in your classroom, follow this procedure:

1. Students choose partners and the older student reads aloud.
2. After completing a book, partners go off to a quiet place to talk.
3. The reader gives a brief summary and the two discuss the book.

Cross-Age Book Buddies

To implement cross-age Book Buddies, ask a friend who teaches two or three grade levels higher to join you. Proceed as follows:

1. The older students come to visit and get acquainted. They can choose their partners.
2. The older students receive training in how to select books, read aloud, engage in discussion, and plan appropriate activities.
3. Book Buddies meet on a regular schedule to read together, talk about what they read, and do related activities.

Opportunities for formal book sharing are fun when they tap children's creative potential; they are valuable when they help children to understand a book better by clarifying thoughts and feelings. Above all, as in the activities described in this book, the prime goal is to develop in children an enduring love of literature; everything else is secondary and is aimed at achieving this goal. Being required to read a teacher-selected book and write a report about it has turned more children away from reading than perhaps any other activity. The traditional book reports we are force-fed—drudgery for the child who writes them, time-consuming for the teacher who reads and grades them, and boring for the children who must listen to them read aloud—subvert our main goal.

Book sharing should take children back to the book and give them a chance to reexperience the spell of a good story. Many ways of sharing books are enjoyable and meaningful to the child and valuable to the teacher who can discern from them what the child has gained from the book. Teaching Ideas 12.2 and 12.3 present some ideas for sharing books in a meaningful way.

Creative Ways to Share Books

Children can express themselves through reading, writing, listening, speaking, art, music, and movement. Some might want to respond on the computer; others won't. Remember, however, that children need choices. Some may like to put themselves in imaginative situations as they discuss books read; others may prefer just to talk about a book; and still others may choose to keep the reading experience personal. Be flexible. Encourage them to use your ideas as a springboard for other ideas that may be more important to them. It is illuminating to put yourself in their place; if you ask yourself what a particular idea is good for, you are on the right track. If it leads to thoughtful consideration of a book by the student or to further reading, then it has a place in your plans. Ask your students: "What do you want others to understand about your book?" and then ask "What could you do?" In a classroom that encourages many ways of responding, students will have many options for sharing books.

Oral Language

Oral language is central to many book extension activities. These range from the spontaneous recommendation of a book by its reader to structured panel discussions about books by one author. Effective oral-language response activities may be extensive or brief, but they always help children share and explore their responses to the books they read.

STORYTELLING BY CHILDREN Children's writing skills seldom match their oral language skills before the end of their elementary school years. Storytelling activities contribute to their sense of story and provide opportunities for developing and expanding language. A strong read-aloud program is vital; children will use the literary language they hear in creating their own stories.

Wordless books are an excellent stimulus to storytelling. Because the story line depends entirely upon the illustrations, children become much more aware of the details in the pictures; they do not make a quick scan of them. These books provide a story structure—plot, characters, theme—as do conventional books, and so provide the framework on which to build stories. Another excellent resource for storytelling activities is the folklore collection in your classroom. These structured stories, once told orally, are perfect for classroom storytelling. Beginning with familiar tales helps children feel confident of their ability to tell a story orally, and they soon experiment with new tales.

Children can tell such stories to each other, to a group, or into an audio or video recorder. Storytelling can be done with partners, in which case each partner takes the role of one or more of the characters as they interpret the story. In group storytelling, children take a role, each telling the story from one character's point of view. From the experience gained, children learn how the elements of the story interconnect and build on each other.

Tape recorders are indispensable for storytelling activities. When children record their stories, these become available for other children to listen to while looking at the book. Each storyteller's version of the book will be different, adding some variety to the classroom collection. In addition to using tape recorders for recording stories based on books, children can use them to dictate original stories, make background soundtracks for stories read aloud, record choral speaking, create dialogue for puppet shows, and carry out other dramatic activities. Camcorders or video recorders expand the possibilities. The Booklist at the end of this chapter contains a list of wordless books you can begin with. Folktales for storytelling are discussed in Chapter 5.

CHORAL SPEAKING Choral speaking—people speaking together—can be adapted for any age level. For the youngest it may mean joining in as a refrain is read aloud; for older students it may involve the group reading of a poem. Young children unconsciously chime in when you read aloud passages that strike a sympathetic chord. For example, children quickly pick up and repeat the refrain when you read Bill Martin and John Archambault's *Chicka Chicka Boom Boom* (P). Rhythm and repetition in language, both of which are conducive to choral speaking, are found in abundance in literature for every age group, especially in folklore, poetry, and patterned picture storybooks.

When introducing choral speaking, read aloud two or three times the story or poem you are using so that the rhythm of the language can be absorbed by your listeners. Encourage them to follow along with hand clapping until the beat is established. Favorite poems and refrains from stories—which become unconsciously committed to memory after repeated group speaking—stay in the mind as treasures to be savored for years.

Teachers use choral speaking for warm-up routines to get students to tune in to the task at hand. When we draw students together in a group speaking activity it not only focuses their attention but also gives them practice in using various patterns of oral language. Most often schools provide a great amount of practice in using written language but very little in using oral language. Choral speaking helps balance this inequity.

Students feel comfortable taking part in choral speaking; they are members of a group. Choral speaking supports unsure readers; they do not risk the embarrassment that comes from being singled out. Most important, the students become a community of learners. Joining together in group routines solidifies the sense of community.

As your students participate in choral speaking exercises they can decide how they want to say certain pieces. Rhythm, stress, pitch, and tempo can be adjusted until your students feel that they are capturing the meaning of the piece. This is especially effective with poetry, as much of the meaning in poetry relates to the sound of the poem. Teaching Idea 12.4 suggests a way to explore the relation of sound and meaning in poetry through choral speaking.

DRAMA Children engage in imaginative play instinctively. They re-create what they see on television, in everyday life, and in their books. "Let's pretend" games are a natural way for children to express their thoughts and feelings in the guise of characters and roles. Informal dramatic play capitalizes on children's natural desire to pretend and can be the forerunner of numerous drama experiences. These experiences can promote dialogue among students and between students and teachers that allows children to control and explore their responses to literature (Edmiston, Enciso, and King, 1987; O'Neill, 1989; Verriour, 1985). Dramatic activities provide opportunities to discuss and reflect on a book.

Many forms of drama can be explored in the classroom. Variations, often called creative dramatics, include pantomime, using body movements and expression but no words; interpreting, enacting, or recreating a story or a scene; and improvising, extending, and extrapolating beyond a story or a poem.

Pantomime is silent. In pantomime, a story or meaning is conveyed solely through facial expressions, shrugs, frowns, gestures, and other forms of body language. The situations, stories, or characters that are pantomimed should be ones that the children are familiar with, recognize easily, or want to explore further.

Re-enacting a story can immediately follow a read-aloud session. After reading aloud "The Three Billy Goats Gruff,"

Teaching Idea 12 ☆ 4

Using Choral Speaking to Explore Poetry

One effective way of introducing choral speaking to your class is to put one of your favorite poems on the overhead projector and explore how different ways of reading the same poem can create different effects. Even a simple tempo or stress change alters the effect and often the meaning of the poem. Here are some ways to explore the connections between meaning and sound in poetry:

✳ Vary the tempo. Read faster or slower and discuss the effect.

✳ Experiment with stress, discussing which words might be emphasized, and why.

✳ Play with tone; some poems seem to call for a deep, somber tone while others need a light tone.

✳ Try different groupings of voices. Poems can be read in many ways—in unison, with choruses, using single voices paired with other single or blended voices, or cumulatively, with voices blending to an increasingly powerful effect.

After you have worked with several poems this way, encourage your students to experiment in small groups with choral speaking as a way to explore meaning and sound in poetry. They might want to present several readings to the class or to other classes.

---

for example, the teacher might ask, "Who wants to be the Troll? . . . the big billy goat? . . . the middle billy goat? . . . the little billy goat?" Discuss with the children how the troll sounds when he asks, "Who's that tripping over my bridge?" Ask them to explain how he shows his anger, and how each of the billy goats sounds as he answers the troll. As children learn to enact stories they can do so without teacher guidance. Children who are working together in groups might decide to enact the story, or parts of the story, to explore character relationships, cause and effect, sequence, or any number of issues related to their story.

Interpretation involves an oral dramatic reading of a story that the children are interested in. This activity builds enthusiasm for reading and develops oral reading skills. It also encourages children to discuss characters, their personalities, and how they might talk given their personalities and the situations facing them in the story.

Improvisation goes beyond acting out the basic story line. It begins with a supposition, often about plot or characterization, that goes beyond the story itself. What happens after Snow White and her prince get married? What is Gilly Hop-

kins like after living with her grandmother for a year? Well-developed characters often inspire children to extensions into new situations. Improvisation can be particularly powerful as a way for older children to explore characterization.

Role-playing allows students to assume a role and interact with others in roles. It is usually done with short vignettes or with specific incidents from stories. This activity allows students to explore and discuss meaningful episodes in stories, various characters' point of view, and characters' motivation. Brief role-playing episodes often become scenes in more fully developed presentations.

In *Readers Theatre*, students read orally from student-generated scripts that are based on selections from literature. Performances are not formal: Lines are not memorized; there are virtually no sets, costumes, or staging; and participants do not move about the stage. A few gestures or changes in position are permitted but the real effect must come from the readers' oral interpretation of characters and the narration.

Sloyer (1982) suggests the following steps in preparing a Readers Theatre performance:

1. Select a story with lots of dialogue and a strong plot. The best stories have a taut plot with an "and then" quality to pique your interest and make you want to know what will happen next.

2. Discuss the number of characters needed, including one or more narrators who read the parts between the dialogue.

3. Adapt the story to a play script format, deleting unnecessary phrases like "he said," and assign roles.

4. Assign roles and allow students to practice. Students will not need to be coaxed into practicing their oral reading; they will do so on their own, especially if they can practice with a partner or a director who can advise them on whether the character is coming through in the reading.

5. For the finished production, have performers sit or stand side by side, with the narrators off to one side and slightly closer to the audience. Readers stand statue-still, holding their scripts. When not in a scene, readers may turn around or lower their heads.

Children learn a great deal about how stories work when they work closely with a text to make their own scripts. Titles listed in the Booklist at the end of this chapter are easily adapted to Readers Theatre.

Dramatization techniques differ depending upon the students and books involved and the purposes and goals of the experience—primarily according to whether it is done as a performance for others or for the benefit of the participants themselves. A guiding rule in this area, no less than in others, is to hold the children's benefit as the highest value. This is not to say that performances for others should not be given, only that they should not be given at the cost of exploiting children as performers. Remember that the dramatic activities that students engage in begin as ways of more fully exploring the stories and poems that they are reading. Keep the focus on the child and the story and dramatic activities will be memorable learning experiences for children.

DISCUSSION Books can become a valued stimulus for discussion. Teachers and librarians develop the ability to recognize when discussion is appropriate and when it is not. No rules can be given for this; it is sensed intuitively by those who base decisions on knowledge of children in the group. Children themselves can also determine whether or not discussion is appropriate.

When discussion is warranted, the purpose of the discussion determines how the discussion is organized, who participates, and what the focus is. It may be that a group of children spontaneously comes together to talk about a book or books that they have been reading. These spontaneous sharings may occur on the playground, at the water fountain, or during independent reading or reading workshop time. Teachers who encourage spontaneous discussions of books notice that they occur frequently and serve important purposes. Hepler and Hickman (1982) note that children tell each other about good books to read, organize their understanding of the content of a book, and clarify their interpretations as they talk together. All of this is done without the presence of a teacher.

In their description of the "grand conversations" that fifth-grade children had in their literature study groups, Eeds and Wells (1989) demonstrate how children construct meaning together, share personal stories, question what they read, and discuss an author's style during literature discussions. Other teachers and researchers write eloquently of how children help each other to become more thoughtful and discerning readers when they work together in book clubs or literature study groups (Galda, Rayburn, and Stanzi, 2000; McMahon and Raphael, 1997; Short and Pierce, 1990). These groups are sometimes led by teachers, but are often led by students who have learned to work together without the presence of a teacher. Teachers demonstrate and discuss with children the kinds of questions that can be considered and the procedures that might be followed; when students are ready to work together independently they do so. We discuss book clubs further in Chapter 14.

In many cases teachers first need to learn new ways of talking about books. For many years educators have been concerned with the types of questions that teachers ask of their students. Unfortunately, many of these questioning sessions take the form of brief oral examinations that end with a teacher evaluation (Cazden, 1988). This type of questioning is not conducive to generating real, interesting discussion about books.

Asking good questions is one way that teachers demonstrate what might happen in literature discussion groups; good questions elicit high-level thinking from children, and

poorly framed ones invite surface thinking. *Literal* questions elicit recall of factual information explicitly stated in the printed material. Such questions based on the familiar "Goldilocks and the Three Bears" might be: Where did the three bears go? What did Goldilocks do in their house?

Interpretive questions seek information inferred from text. They are best answered by reading between the lines and synthesizing information from two or more stated facts. Interpretive questions for the Goldilocks story could be: Why did Goldilocks go into the bears' house? Why did she choose to fall asleep in Baby Bear's bed? Interpretive questions have more than one right answer. They ask for educated guesses and hunches.

Critical questions intended to elicit evaluation of the book invite judgments about the quality of writing and authenticity of information (if nonfiction); they also encourage hypothesizing beyond the story. All of these are tasks that require higher-level thinking. This kind of questioning is not answered fully by giving one's personal opinion; the basis for the judgment must also be given. Critical questions for Goldilocks (where two versions have been read) could include: Which version do you like best and why? What is another possible ending for the story? What did Goldilocks tell her parents when she got home? Why do you think she told them that? Does the repetition of three (three bowls of porridge, three chairs, three beds) remind you of other folktales? What other stories use the same pattern?

For many years educators thought that teachers should proceed from literal to interpretive to critical questions, assuming that being able to answer literal questions is necessary before interpretation and critical evaluation can occur. This is not the case, however, as readers can have a powerful aesthetic experience with a book and be able to evaluate it critically without getting literal details (Rosenblatt, 1978).

Other kinds of questions that teachers can demonstrate involve exploring their own understanding of and responses to the books that they read. The goal of a discussion might be to clarify personal responses and extend those responses by talking with others. In this case teachers would share their own responses and encourage children to share their responses, expand on what they have said, and react to others' comments. The discussion of fantasy novels excerpted in this chapter is an excellent example of a clarifying discussion. Hynds (1992) suggests that teachers ask real questions, questions that they don't know the answers to, in discussions about books; encourage students to respond to each other by asking them to comment on others' ideas; and try to respond to the answers students give in a positive and supportive manner. In other words, teachers respond as readers interested in discussing a book they have read with others who also have read it.

As we discussed above, teachers can also ask themselves questions about the books they are reading, and then share these questions and answers with students during literary discussion groups. Discussion groups are wonderful opportunities for helping children learn about literature; they often present teachable moments that allow teachers to explore how literature works with interested students. Books can be explored in any number of ways. Eeds and Peterson (1991) suggest that teachers read a book twice to prepare for discussion, with the second reading focusing on structure, character, place, time, point of view, mood, and symbol as they apply to the book under consideration. Teaching Idea 12.1 presents their specific suggestions. Notes in the margins, Post-Its, notebooks, book markers, and other devices help teachers record what they have noticed and allow them to get ready for an exciting dialogue with students in literature discussions.

Questions are not the only way to organize discussions. Other strategies like webbing allow children to find a focus in their discussions without teacher questions. Webbing enhances comprehension and learning, links reading and writing together, and promotes enjoyment and appreciation of literature (Bromley, 1991). Creating a visual representation of ideas and information and their relationships can be a powerful tool for organizing and clarifying understanding. Webs can be used to explore characters, setting, artistic elements in picture books, relationships among books, plot, and just about anything that students are interested in exploring. Excellent examples of dynamic discussions appear in Chapters 13 and 14.

WRITING   The values of literature extend far beyond appreciation and enjoyment, although these are primary. When they read on their own, children build a storehouse of language possibilities. The stories, poems, and nonfiction texts they read and hear, created by skilled writers, serve as models for children in their own writing. When children write, they draw upon the literature they know as they select significant details, organize their thoughts, and express them with clarity. When children write, they also read differently, or, as Smith (1982) puts it, they "read like writers." They become sensitive to what other writers do and learn to read with a fine-tuned appreciation of the author's craft.

Writing in response to what is read helps readers to discover what they are thinking and feeling, and to make connections between life and text. Keeping a response journal helps children explore their own responses in a more private fashion than talking with peers. Journals are often an effective first step toward the more public response activities discussed above. Journals also serve as a record of what books students have read and how they felt about them, and they demonstrate how students grow as readers across time.

Keeping a journal can be an in-class or an at-home activity. Each journal entry should contain the date, the title, and the author of the book under consideration. Some teachers simply tell students to "Say whatever you want to say about the book that you are reading," whereas others give students general questions to answer, like, "What would you like to ask the author of this book?" or specific response prompts to follow (discussed in Chapter 14). Some teachers ask stu-

dents to write in their journals every day, establishing a regularly scheduled journal time, whereas others ask students to write in their journals whenever they finish a book. Teachers can read and respond to journals on a regular basis, either frequently or periodically, or can merely check to see that students are writing in their journals as requested. Some teachers make journals dialogic—writing letters back and forth with their students or having students write to each other. Experiment with what works best for you and your students.

ART   Art activities can be as extensive as your creativity and energy permit. Resources expand when you have access to an art specialist; in any case, your classroom should house numerous supplies and examples of children's artistic work. Art projects related to books should be used regularly, not saved for special occasions. A well-stocked art center leads to inventive projects in classrooms and libraries. Paper, fabric, yarn, buttons, socks, plastic bottles, paper bags, cardboard tubes, dowels, rods, wire, Styrofoam balls, egg cartons, toothpicks, and pipe cleaners all have potential in the hands of ingenious children and teachers. Needles and thread, glue and tape, and, of course, scissors, crayons, paints, paintbrushes, and markers are also needed. Items available free or for a nominal price can often be obtained from neighborhood shops, such as old wallpaper books from the local paint store. Art materials are often available to teachers who search grocery, hardware, discount, and other stores for them. Pizza rounds (cardboard trays), five-gallon ice cream drums, boxes, and display materials often make good classroom art supplies.

What you and your students do is not as important as how what you do fits the book that has sparked the project. Art can be a vehicle for thinking more deeply about a book. Many children express themselves better in art than in oral or written language; art becomes a way of responding, a way of exploring important aspects of the reading experience. Figure 12.4 provides an example of such a response. Children might labor painstakingly to depict an unusual and important setting, recreate a vivid scene, capture characterization in a portrait, or explore a favorite artist's technique. Like drama, art is a way for readers to discover what they know and how they feel about what they have read.

A technique called "Sketch to Stretch" (Harste, Short, and Burke, 1988) encourages children to explore their reading through art. After having read a common book, students are asked to sketch what the book meant to them or what they "made of the reading" (p. 354). After they complete the sketches they share them with others in the group, who discuss what they think the artist is trying to say. The artist then explains what he or she was trying to do. If several small groups are doing this, one sketch from each group can be put on an overhead and shared with the class. Harste and Short caution that this process may need to be repeated several times before students are comfortable with this procedure. Students could also respond through music or

Figure 12 ❖ 4

Student's Artistic Response

This first grader used both words and pictures to respond to the many nonfiction books he is reading about the natural world.

© Lee Galda

Teaching Idea 12 ❖ 5

Art Activities for Response

Getting children to express their response to literature through art activities invites creativity. Use the ideas here to come up with others of your own.

Collage

An arrangement of cut or torn paper or fabric. Use Ezra Jack Keats's books, like *The Snowy Day* or *Whistle for Willie*, as models for cut paper collages. Use Jeannie Baker's *Window* as a model for three-dimensional twigs and grass collages.

Wall Hanging

Large pieces of fabric decorated with scenes from a book and suspended from a dowel rod. Use a heavy fabric, such as burlap, for the background. Cut shapes of characters from other materials; attach to the background fabric.

Mosaic

Small bits of colored paper or tiles arranged into designs. Create figures from books. Use a book like Leo Lionni's *Pezzetino* as a model for mosaics.

Flannel Board

A piece of flannel cloth attached to fiberboard. Cut shapes of characters or objects from other pieces of flannel or material to move about as you tell the story. Stories like "The Gingerbread Boy," which have few characters and a brief, straightforward plot work well as flannel board stories.

Roller Movies

A story illustrated in scenes on a long piece of shelf paper with each end attached to a dowel rod. Use a cardboard carton to cut a TV screen; scroll the paper from one dowel to the other to show the appropriate scene as you tell the story.

Filmstrips and Slides

Pictures drawn on clear acetate film or slides to illustrate a story. Project them onto a screen as you tell the story.

Puppets

Figures made from paper bags, popsicle sticks, or plastic foam and fabric to represent characters. Shape the puppets to look like the characters and move them about as you say the dialogue for them.

movement by singing, playing, or dancing what a book meant to them.

Art can also be used as a way to present books to others. Talking and writing about a book are not the only ways of sharing books with others; many students enjoy sharing through art. This does not simply mean drawing a picture about a story, but using varied activities to capture the essence of a book. A wall hanging might be a perfect way to present a story with a strong episodic structure; a collage might be an effective portrayal of a character. Students need to know about and have the resources for a variety of artistic presentations. Teaching Idea 12.5 contains ideas for art projects that might be the perfect way to respond to a book. Allow your students the freedom to choose among them.

Teachers can do a great deal to help children connect with books. There are many more ideas for response activities than are presented here, and you will adapt many suggestions to suit the needs of your students. When you know your readers and the books they are reading, and when you provide a context that encourages them to explore and expand their connections with books, engaged and responsive readers flower.

Summary

Reading is a transaction that occurs between a reader and a text: The reader actively constructs the meaning, under the guidance of a text. Students bring experiences with life and literature to any act of reading; a text guides them as they use prior understandings to construct new meaning. Readers select their purpose for reading; it may be primarily efferent, in which a reader seeks to gain information, or aesthetic, in which they focus on what they are experiencing as they read. Factors inherent in readers and texts influence the aesthetic experience, as do social and cultural contexts.

Teachers can help children grow as responsive readers by allowing them time to read and respond, and by giving them choices about what they read, where they read, who they read with, and how they respond. Literature discussion groups, writing, informal sharing, dramatic activities, and art offer children opportunities for connecting with books.

Read Christine Heppermann's article "Reading in the Virtual Forest" in the November/December 2000 issue of *The Horn Book Magazine.* Then think about literary response and a response-centered curriculum. How might e-books alter how we respond and how we teach?

Booklist

Selected Books from Children's Choices, 2000

Agee, Jon, *Sit on a Potato Pan, Otis! More Palindromes* (I)

Blackwood, Gary, *Alien Astronauts* (A)

Cassie, Brian, *National Audubon Society First Field Guide: Trees* (I)

Child, Lauren, *Clarice Bean, That's Me* (P)

Cleary, Beverly, *Ramona's World* (I)

Cole, Babette, *Bad Habits* (P)

Dakos, Kali, *The Bug in Teacher's Coffee and Other School Poems* (P)

Davis, Katie, *I Hate to Go to Bed* (P)

Earle, Sylvia, *Dive! My Adventures in the Deep Frontier* (I)

Florian, Douglas, *Laugh-eteria* (I)

Gibbons, Gail, *Exploring the Deep, Dark Sea* (I)

Kehret, Peg, *Shelter Dogs: Amazing Stories of Adopted Strays* (A)

Layton, Neal, *Smile If You're Human* (I)

Martin, Bill, Jr., *A Beasty Story* (P)

McKean, Thomas, *Into the Candlelit Room and Other Strange Tales* (A)

Meddaugh, Susan, *The Best Place* (P)

Murphy, Mary, *Caterpillar's Wish* (P)

Paulsen, Gary, *Alida's Song* (A)

Peel, John, *2099: Doomsday* (A)

Pinkwater, Daniel, *Ice Cream Larry* (P)

Proimos, James, *The Loudness of Sam* (P)

Shannon, David, *David Goes to School* (P)

Sussex, Lucy, *Altered Voices: Nine Science Fiction Stories* (A)

Wallace, Karen, *Duckling Days* (P)

Wilson, Anthony, *How the Future Began: Communications* (A)

Wolinksy, Art, *Creating and Publishing Web Pages on the Internet* (A)

Yee, Wong Herbert, *Hamburger Heaven* (P)

Good Books to Read Aloud

Adoff, Arnold, *Black Is Brown Is Tan* (N)

Avi, *Poppy* (I)

_____, *Ereth's Birthday* (I)

_____, *Poppy and Rye* (I)

_____, *Ragweed* (I)

Babbitt, Natalie, *Tuck Everlasting* (I)

Bang, Molly, *Ten, Nine, Eight* (N)

_____, *When Sophie Gets Angry, Really, Really Angry* (N)

Barton, Byron, *Bones, Bones, Dinosaur Bones* (N)

Brown, Margaret Wise, *Goodnight Moon* (N)

_____, *The Runaway Bunny* (N)

Carle, Eric, *The Very Busy Spider* (P)

Clements, Andrew, *Frindle* (I)

_____, *Janitor's Boy* (I)

Cooper, Susan, *The Dark Is Rising* (A)

Coville, Bruce, *Jennifer Murdley's Toad* (I)

_____, *Jeremy Thatcher, Dragon Hatcher* (I)

Crews, Donald, *Light* (N)

dePaola, Tomie, *Nana Upstairs, Nana Downstairs* (P)

_____, *Strega Nona* (P)

DiCamillo, Kate, *Because of Winn Dixie* (I)

Farmer, Nancy, *The Ear, the Eye, and the Arm* (A)

Fleischman, Sid, *The Whipping Boy* (I)

Flournoy, Valerie, *The Patchwork Quilt* (P)

Fox, Mem, *Hattie and the Fox* (N)

_____, *Wilfrid Gordon McDonald Partridge* (P)

Goldstein, Bobbie, *Inner Chimes* (I)

Hall, Donald, *Ox-Cart Man* (P)

Hamilton, Virginia, *M.C. Higgins, the Great* (I)

Hopkins, Lee Bennett, *Good Books, Good Times* (P)

Howard, Elizabeth F., *Aunt Flossie's Hats* (P)

Hughes, Shirley, *Alfie Gives a Hand* (P)
Hunter, Mollie, *Sound of Chariots* (A)
Hutchins, Pat, *What Game Shall We Play?* (P)
Jacques, Brian, *Redwall* (A)
Lewis, C. S., *The Lion, the Witch, and the Wardrobe* (I)
Mathis, Sharon Bell, *The Hundred Penny Box* (I)
McCaffrey, Anne, *Dragonsong* (A)
McKinley, Robin, *The Blue Sword* (A)
Myers, Walter Dean, *Harlem* (A)
Naidoo, Beverly, *Chain of Fire* (A)
Naylor, Phyllis Reynolds, *Shiloh* (I)
O'Brien, Robert, *Mrs. Frisby and the Rats of NIMH* (I)
O'Dell, Scott, *Island of the Blue Dolphin* (A)
Orlev, Uri, *Island on Bird Street* (A)
_____, *Man from the Other Side* (A)
Peck, Richard, *A Long Way from Chicago* (A)
Polacco, Patricia, *Thank You, Mr. Falker* (P)
Pullman, Philip, *The Golden Compass* (A)
_____, *The Amber Spyglass* (A)
_____, *The Subtle Knife* (A)
_____, *I Was a Rat* (I)
Rathmann, Peggy, *Officer Buckle and Gloria* (P)
Sachar, Louis, *Holes* (I)
Steig, William, *Abel's Island* (I)
Taylor, Mildred, *Roll of Thunder, Hear My Cry* (A)
Voigt, Cynthia, *Homecoming* (A)
Yep, Laurence, *Dragonwings* (A)
_____, *The Star Fisher* (A)
Yolen, Jane, *Not One Damsel in Distress* (I)

Wordless Books

Baker, Jeannie, *Window* (P)
Briggs, Raymond, *The Snowman* (P)
Geisert, Arthur, *Oink* (P)
_____, *Oink Again* (P)
Goodall, John, *Naughty Nancy* (P)
_____, *The Story of an English Village* (P)
Hutchins, Pat, *Changes, Changes* (P)
Mayer, Mercer, *A Boy, a Dog, and a Frog* (P)
McCully, Emily Arnold, *New Baby* (P)

_____, *School* (P)
_____, *Picnic* (P)
_____, *First Snow* (P)
Ormerod, Jan, *Moonlight* (P)
_____, *Sunshine* (P)
Tafuri, Nancy, *Do Not Disturb* (P)
_____, *Early Morning in the Barn* (P)
_____, *Have You Seen My Duckling?* (P)
Turkle, Brinton, *Deep in the Forest* (P)
Wiesner, David, *Free Fall* (P)
_____, *Tuesday* (P)
_____, *June 29, 1996* (P)
Young, Ed, *The Other Bone* (P)
_____, *Up a Tree* (P)

Stories and Poems for Readers Theatre

FOLKLORE

Craig, M. Jean, *The Three Wishes* (P)
Galdone, Paul, *The Gingerbread Boy* (P)
_____, *Henny Penny* (P)
_____, *The Little Red Hen* (P)
Stevens, Janet, *The Three Billy Goats Gruff* (P)

POETRY

Harrison, David, *Somebody Catch My Homework* (P)
Kuskin, Karla, *Dogs and Dragons* (P)
_____, *Trees and Dreams* (P)

PICTURE BOOKS

Hutchins, Pat, *Changes, Changes* (P)
Johnson, Angela, *Tell Me a Story, Mama* (P)
Mayer, Mercer, *A Boy, a Dog, and a Frog* (P)
Sendak, Maurice, *Pierre* (P)

NOVELS

Byars, Betsy, *The Midnight Fox* (I)
Hunter, Mollie, *Mermaid Summer* (I)
MacLachlan, Patricia, *Sarah, Plain and Tall* (I)
_____, *Skylark* (I)

Literature-Based Instruction in Preschool and Primary Grades

Brown bear, brown bear, what do you see?
I see a red bird, looking at me.

—BILL MARTIN, ***Brown Bear, Brown Bear***

Everywhere you look in Betty's first-grade classroom you see children and books intermingled. Groups of children are sitting on the floor in the book corner, where most of the books are found. Many books are displayed with their covers facing outward, inviting children in. Other children are sitting on an elevated stage area, looking through cartons of books. There's a box of alphabet books that the children have been exploring over the past few weeks, and a box of books by Donald Crews, the author they are currently studying. The children have books with them during writing time. Some use them to find out how to spell words they want to use in their writing. Some use the story patterns as models for the original stories they are writing. During center time, too, children have books in their hands so they can re-enact favorite stories or recite poems that appeal to them.

Betty reads to the whole class several times a day: She does guided reading, shared reading, and choral reading with oversized books. She reads aloud to introduce new books into the classroom collection. She discusses story patterns, word choice, illustration style, authors, and illustrators. As a group the children sing songs found in book form, do choral readings of patterned stories, and repeat familiar phrases they love. They have many books on tape, such as Bill Martin's ***Brown Bear*** (N–P), so they can listen over and over again, following along in the book. Literature is a pervasive element in this classroom; children know that literature is fundamental to their lives.

A Literature-Based Literacy Curriculum

Betty's classroom practice is based on literature; learning about literature and learning through literature are essential to every school day. Teachers like Betty who implement a literature-based curriculum seek to increase their knowledge of the books available for today's children and to make these books an integral part of their teaching. They know that reading literature helps children learn to like to read; children then read more, and, in the process, become better readers and better language users (Anderson, Hiebert, Scott, and Wilkinson, 1985; Fielding, Wilson, and Anderson, 1984). They know that without learning to love reading, the children in their classrooms will not ever be avid readers. Teachers who base their literacy program on literature focus on the teaching of reading and writing, while also being concerned with engagement—the affective component of reading that supports learning.

Good literature provides a strong foundation for building a literacy curriculum in the preschool and primary grades. Students need good literature to feed their minds and to practice their developing reading skills. Betty's students are wonderful examples of how far good books can take children who are learning to read and think about themselves and their world. Teachers and librarians need good literature if they are to succeed in handing down the magic—a love of reading—while also teaching children how to be fluent readers, writers, and oral language users, as well as thoughtful people.

Literature provides a rich array of resources for preschool and primary-grade teachers. There are books for emergent readers that support their initial attempts at making sense of text. There are books that support newly independent readers as they build fluency. There are transitional chapter books that provide support for those readers who are ready to move beyond picture book–length texts. These books also support children as they learn to write; children quite naturally borrow patterns and structures from what they read as they create their own stories, poems, and nonfiction material. These same books also provide opportunities for oral language experiences such as drama, choral reading, storytelling, and discussion—opportunities for students to speak, as well as listen. Children's books provide a perfect opportunity for integrating the English language arts—reading, writing, listening, and speaking. Children's books also provide opportunities for children to develop their visual literacy skills as they learn to "read the pictures" in picture books. Teaching Idea 13.1 suggests ideas for helping children explore literature.

Books can be found which support any curriculum area; many literature-based teachers try to integrate not just the English language arts but also science, mathematics, and social studies, as well as art and music, through the use of children's books. Teachers who do this, link curriculum areas by teaching reading and writing in conjunction with a topic in a particular area. They select children's books about that area and use them as the texts through which they teach reading skills and strategies. For example, many primary grades focus on the community in their social studies curriculum. Using that focus to develop a thematic unit around the idea of belonging to a number of different communities can allow teachers to integrate their curriculum in a way that makes it meaningful to their students' lives. The books also become resources for students as they look for information and ideas, and models as students craft their own writing. Teaching Idea 13.2 presents guidelines for building a classroom library for the primary grades.

© Bernice E. Cullinan

A print-rich environment contains numerous books that invite students to read and write. In Joanne Payne Lionetti's third-grade classroom, books are not only accessible, they are unavoidable!

Teaching Idea 13 ✳ 1

Ways to Explore Literature

Exploring literature with students increases students' desire to read on their own. When the teacher reads aloud, tells stories, and gets students to talk about books, students respond by increasing the number of books they read.

✳ Read aloud. You are modeling what good reading is and exposing students to the high-quality literature you choose.

✳ Retell stories and poems. Retelling makes stories and poems a natural part of talk. Students will soon retell stories and poems to younger children and to their peers.

✳ Create a picture story. Tell a story in pictures as a sequence of drawings, comic strip style, collage, stylized frieze, or a story map inset with small pictures. This helps students recognize literary elements and structures, such as setting, plot, dialogue, and conclusion.

✳ Talk about books. Make talk about books a natural part of every day. Enthusiasm is contagious; share your enthusiasm for books.

✳ Recast old tales. List the basic elements of an old tale and ask your students to write their own stories using the same elements in a modern setting. Create a comparison chart with elements from their stories. Students will realize that basic stories can be retold endlessly.

✳ Dramatize scenes. Role-play characters confronting each other, working their way out of dilemmas. Improvisation makes literature memorable and helps students "own" it.

✳ Keep reading logs as a place to record books read.

✳ Identify themes, or big ideas. Encourage students to think about books that have similar themes. This helps students make connections among books and see patterns in literature.

✳ Organize a classroom library. Ask students to consider alternate ways to organize books. Discuss pros and cons of each way, and as a group decide which method works best.

✳ Draw story structures. Stories proceed in circular ways, along a straight line with rising action, in interrelated sequences of events. Discuss how the plot "looks" and draw or graph memorable events in a shape that makes the structure understandable.

Although you can certainly find curriculum guides and book study guides that provide step-by-step ideas for building a curriculum around literature, we encourage you to think for yourself. Think about your students—what they are interested in, what they know how to do, what they need to learn, and how they like to learn. Then think about your curriculum—what you need to teach, how much time you have to teach it, and what materials you have available. Consider how literature can help you create meaningful and effective learning experiences for your students.

There are many ways to enact a literature-based literacy curriculum. Such a curriculum varies along many dimensions, including curricular goals, learning activities, and selection of books. In a study of how literature-based programs look in various classrooms, Hiebert and Colt (1989) discovered that the programs vary along two main dimensions: The instructional format and the selection of literature. The variations are linked to the amount of teacher control in each dimension, ranging from teacher-led instruction to independent application in terms of instructional format, and from teacher-selected to student-selected material in terms of literature selection.

Some programs are marked by a high degree of teacher control; teachers select the materials and lead the instruc-

tion. Other programs are marked by student selection of materials and student direction of their own learning with less teacher intervention. All sorts of variations and combinations of student independence and teacher direction are possible. In some cases, you will want to select materials that will help students learn something they need to know in order to progress in the curriculum. In other cases, you and your students will negotiate what is to be explored, how it will be explored, and which materials will be used. Often, students will independently select books and decide what to do with them, either within parameters that you have set, or entirely on their own.

Many books have been written about the ways in which teachers have enacted a literature-based curriculum. Some of the best books about this topic are listed in Figure 13.1. Journals such as *Language Arts* and *The Reading Teacher* contain articles written by classroom teachers and by university researchers that inform us about the difficulties and the benefits of literature-based instruction. Many language arts and reading textbooks also explain in great detail ways of structuring such a curriculum. In this chapter we present the ways a few primary-grade teachers structured their curriculum using literature; we do the same for upper elementary and middle school in Chapter 14. As you read these chapters,

Teaching Idea 13 ⋅ 2

Create a Primary-Grade Classroom Library

Research shows that when there is a classroom library, students read 50 percent more books than when there is not. Classroom libraries provide easy access to books, magazines, and other materials. To make sure your classroom library is attractive and inviting, follow these guidelines.

Collect books that are

* Written about the curriculum topics being studied.
* Related to the current literature focus.
* Suitable for recreational reading.
* About diverse people and cultures.
* "Touchstone" books, enduring favorites.

Organize books

* In consultation with students.
* In a simple manner.

* In a way that accommodates routine changes in focus.
* So that book covers, not spines, are visible (when possible).

Include support materials such as

* Story props, including flannel boards and feltboard stories and figures.
* Tapes, filmstrips, VCR stories, CD-ROMs.
* Roller movies, puppets.
* Posters, bulletin boards, dust jackets.

Provide a comfortable, quiet space

* Where students can read privately or sit and relax.
* That is away from vigorous activity.
* That features an appealing display of books.

think about the children and the books that you know, and how you might adapt these ideas for your own classroom.

Using Literature with Emergent and Beginning Readers

Betty Shockley Bisplinghoff's class, depicted in the opening vignette, provided a good opportunity for watching many things that can happen with literature as first-grade students learn to read (Galda, Bisplinghoff, and Pellegrini, 1996; Galda, Bisplinghoff, Pellegrini, and Stahl, 1995). The school picture of Betty's class shows 17 children—African-American, Asian-American, and European-American—although across the school year the number of students ranges from 16 to 22. These students varied widely in their reading ability when they entered Betty's classroom: Some were reading fairly fluently, some were at a beginning first-grade level, but most were below grade level.

There are two adults in the picture, Betty and her aide. The school itself is a medium-sized K–5 school in which 74 percent of the students are eligible for free or reduced-fee lunch. Both school and classroom look like many others, but what happened in Betty's classroom was special, and the sound of children reading, writing, singing, and talking together was almost constant.

Generally, Betty organized her day around oral sharing time, writing workshop, independent reading, and whole-class reading instruction in the mornings, with afternoons devoted to math, science or social studies, and center time. Children's books were part of each segment of the day. Betty used picture books, some of which were highly patterned and thus predictable, and some of which had an oversized format; she also used transitional readers and early chapter books to support her students' developing abilities.

PICTURE BOOKS

Literally hundreds of picture books spilled from the shelves in Betty's classroom. There was a sumptuously stocked reading corner in the far right-hand corner, under some windows that looked out onto trees and grass. These books were always available for students to browse through during free time; children could also select them for their independent reading. Boxes of picture books sat on the stage. The stage was a place where Betty sat for whole-class instruction, where students sat to share their writing, and where students shared books by reading them, talking about them, telling stories, singing, and presenting dramas.

Betty read picture books aloud several times a day, for a variety of purposes. Sometimes, she read a book aloud simply because it was a good book and she wanted to share it with her students. Most often, any book read aloud connected in some way to something the children were studying,

Figure 13 ✧ 1

Good Books About a Literature-Based Curriculum

Bamford, R. A., & Kristo, J. V. (Eds.). (1998). *Making Facts Come Alive: Choosing Quality Nonfiction Literature K–8.* Norwood, MA: Christopher-Gordon.

Blatt, G. T. (Ed.). (1993). *Once Upon a Folktale: Capturing the Folklore Process with Children.* New York: Teachers College Press.

Campbell Hill, B., Johnson, N. J., & Schlick Noe, K. L. (Eds.). (1995). *Literature Circles and Response.* Norwood, MA: Christopher-Gordon.

Cullinan, B. E. (Ed.). (1992). *Invitation to Read: More Children's Literature in the Reading Program.* Newark, DE: International Reading Association.

Daniels, Harvey. (1994). *Literature Circles: Voice and Choice in the Student-Centered Classroom.* York, ME: Stenhouse.

Edinger, M. (1996). *Fantasy Literature in the Elementary Classroom: Strategies for Reading, Writing, and Responding.* New York: Scholastic.

Galda, L., Rayburn, J. S., & Stanzi, L. C. (2000). *Looking Through the Faraway End: Creating a Literature-Based Curriculum with Second Graders.* Newark, DE: International Reading Association.

Hancock, M. R. (2000). *A Celebration of Literature and Response: Children, Books, and Teachers in K–8 Classrooms.* Upper Saddle River, NJ: Prentice Hall.

Hefner, C. R., & Lewis, K. R. (1995). *Literature-Based Science: Children's Books and Activities to Enrich the K–5 Curriculum.* Phoenix: Oryx.

Hickman, J., & Cullinan, B. E. (1989). *Children's Literature in the Classroom: Weaving Charlotte's Web.* Norwood, MA: Christopher-Gordon.

Hickman, J., Cullinan, B. E., & Hepler, S. (1994). *Children's Literature in the Classroom: Extending Charlotte's Web.* Norwood, MA: Christopher-Gordon.

Holland, K., Hungerford, R., & Ernst, S. (Eds.). (1993). *Journeying: Children Responding to Literature.* Portsmouth, NH: Heinemann.

Laughlin, M. K., & Street, T. P. (1992). *Literature-Based Art & Music: Children's Books & Activities to Enrich the K–5 Curriculum.* Phoenix: Oryx.

McMahon, S. & Raphael, T. (Eds.). (1997). *The Book Club Connection: Literacy Learning and Classroom Talk.* New York: Teachers College Press.

Moss, J. F. (1996). *Teaching Literature in the Elementary School: A Thematic Approach.* Norwood, MA: Christopher-Gordon.

Peterson, R., & Eeds, M. (1990). *Grand Conversations: Literature Groups in Action.* New York: Scholastic.

Roser, N. L., & Martinez, M. G. (Eds.). (1995). *Book Talk and Beyond: Children and Teachers Respond to Literature.* Newark, DE: International Reading Association.

Samway, K. D., & Whang, G. (1996). *Literature Study Circles in a Multicultural Classroom.* York, ME: Stenhouse.

Short, K. (1997). *Literature as a Way of Knowing.* York, ME: Stenhouse.

Short, K., & Pierce, K. M. (Eds.). (1990). *Talking About Books: Creating Literate Communities.* Portsmouth, NH: Heinemann.

Sorensen, M., & Lehman, B. (Eds.). (1995). *Teaching with Children's Books: Paths to Literature-Based Instruction.* Urbana, IL: National Council of Teachers of English.

Wood, K. D., & Moss, A. (Eds.). (1992). *Exploring Literature in the Classroom: Contents and Methods.* Norwood, MA: Christopher-Gordon.

Zarnowski, M., and Gallagher, A. F. (Eds.). (1993). *Children's Literature and Social Studies: Selecting and Using Notable Books in the Classroom.* Washington, DC: National Council for the Social Studies.

---

whether that was frogs or patterns in writing, a particular author or illustrator, or a certain phonics pattern. Especially at the beginning of the year, the picture books that Betty selected were often patterned, predictable texts that supported the reading development of the many emergent and beginning readers in her classroom.

PATTERNED, PREDICTABLE TEXTS

We know that children become literate in different ways and at different rates of development; this was evident in Betty's classroom. We also know that children who have experience with literature before they come to school begin school with an advantage. They are already emergent readers, readers who have some concepts about how print works. One of the best ways that preschool and early elementary teachers can help children develop these concepts is to read to them. When the books that are read are highly patterned, and thus predictable, it is easier for children to figure out how print works (Holdaway, 1978).

Children search for patterns as they learn. They like to find things that match, words that rhyme, and phrases that are repeated. Many popular books contain repeated phrases, lines that rhyme, and natural-sounding language. Texts are predictable for a variety of reasons. Bill Martin (1972) identifies patterns that appear regularly in children's books, such as repetitive sequences, cumulative sequences, rhyme and rhythm, and familiar cultural sequences. Repetitive sequences make books predictable through repetition. Many books of folklore and poetry for young children are repetitive, and many contemporary authors use repetitive structures, as Bill Martin did in *Brown Bear, Brown Bear, What Do You See?* When meaning accumulates sentence by sentence, the predictability is cumulative; the popular old favorite, *Caps for Sale*, has a cumulative sequence. Rhyme and rhythm help children predict through sound—the rhyming of words in a regular beat, or rhythm. Familiar cultural sequences such as numbering, days of the week, or months of the year help children predict through their reliance on these patterns that children often already know.

Betty often read aloud from stories such as *Brown Bear, Brown Bear, What Do You See?* with its simple repetitive structure and repetitive text, or from stories such as *The Little Red Hen* (N–P) or *The Three Billy Goats Gruff* (N–P)— folktales that are full of repetition and have an obvious structure. As Betty read, the children would chime in when they knew what was coming, saying, "Then I'll do it all by myself!" during a reading of *The Little Red Hen,* or, "Trip trap, trip trap, who's that walking over my bridge?" during a reading of *The Three Billy Goats Gruff.* When books like this were available in enlarged editions known as "big books", the students could actually see the text and read chorally. As they did this, they also were making connections between sounds and print, learning about concepts of print such as top to bottom, left to right, and the functions of capitals, periods, and white spaces.

Big books allowed Betty to use literature to teach children phonics, word patterns, and reading strategies. When the text was rhymed, and the children could *see* the rhymes as well as hear them, talking about rhyming was an easy, natural thing to do. "I-n-g" words, first found in a big book text, were soon recognized everywhere. The months of the year became sight words after spending time with a big book version of Maurice Sendak's *Chicken Soup with Rice* (N–P). Betty had many big books, and she used them to structure meaningful phonics lessons and other reading strategy lessons throughout the year.

Patterned stories also formed the basis of rich oral language activities as students learned structures and patterns that they called upon to do storytelling and drama. In storytelling, children began by retelling familiar patterned stories. In this way they made the language of the story their own. Most of the students loved performing and would gladly entertain their peers with their own renditions of stories the whole class knew. The storytelling was quite interactive; if they forgot an important word or phrase, their peers were happy to supply it for them. Spontaneous dramatic activities also arose frequently in connection with these books. After hearing *The Three Billy Goats Gruff,* a group of students dragged a bench to the stage and proceeded to enact the story, complete with narrator and, of course, help from the audience.

These stories also made their way into the students' own stories, both oral and written. Sharing time, which once had focused on brief accounts of events from the children's lives, now featured elaborated accounts of these events, with students incorporating book language and patterns into their own stories. In their writing students often borrowed stock characters, basic plot structures, or literary phrases. These "borrowings" helped build their resources and abilities for both oral and written language production.

There is no substitute for time spent being captivated by a good book.

© Lee Galda

TRANSITIONAL BOOKS AND BEGINNING CHAPTER BOOKS

As is the case in many classrooms, Betty's students were not all at the same reading level, so her collection included picture books that were more difficult than the patterned, predictable texts discussed above. It also included transitional books for newly fluent readers (like the **Frog and Toad** series by Arnold Lobel and other titles mentioned in Chapter 4) and early chapter books, such as those mentioned in Teaching Idea 13.3. As the most advanced readers in the class grew ready for more extended text, Betty introduced the class to the **Frog and Toad** series by Arnold Lobel. After she read aloud from one of the books, she told students that several other books were written about the same characters; she made sure students knew where they were on the

Teaching Idea 13 ✩ 3

Use Chapter Books to Support Children's Development as Readers

When children are ready for the challenge—and the thrill—of reading a chapter book, begin with something simple, such as one of the several series of transitional chapter books such as Arnold Lobel's *Frog and Toad Are Friends*, Cynthia Rylant's *Henry and Mudge and the Forever Sea* or *Mr. Putter and Tabby Bake the Cake*, or Joan Robbins's *Addie Meets Max*. Encourage your students to form book clubs and read as many books in a series as possible, discussing them with members of their book clubs. When they and you are confident in their ability to read and comprehend these books, move them on to slightly longer and more challenging texts such as Ellen Conford's **Jenny Archer** series, Barbara Joosee's **Wild Willie** series, Barbara Park's **Junie B. Jones** series, Patricia Reilly Giff's **Polk Street School** series, or Johanna Hurwitz's **Aldo** books. Once students have mastered these, they can move on to Ann Cameron's *The Stories Julian Tells* and other books in that series, or Janice Lee Smith's *The Show-and-Tell War: And Other Stories About Adam Joshua* as well as other books in that series.

Books in a series help support newly fluent readers as they learn to read extended text. The continuity of character, setting, and style allow students to anticipate what will happen, thus making it easier for them to make accurate predictions as they read.

shelves. As the more advanced readers began to read them, they often had an attentive audience, with two or three of their peers gathered around them. As the students in the class came to know the stories well through repeated readings, the struggling readers were able to "read" them as well, calling on their memory and the illustrations to supplement their reading skills. By the end of the year everyone in the class had read through the series.

The more advanced readers moved from the **Frog and Toad** books to beginning chapter books. These are books that are still brief, with most being in the 40 to 60 page range, and that are arranged in a chapter book format. The illustrations, while helpful to readers trying to decode the text, are not integral to the text, as they are in picture books. These books gave more advanced readers the opportunity to read extended text over time. Because the texts of these books are arranged in chapters, these students felt a sense of accomplishment—they could now read chapter books. It also gave them practice in reading stories that were a bit more complex than many of the picture books they were familiar with. No students abandoned picture books altogether—Betty's collection was so extensive that even the most fluent reader could find a picture book with a challenging text—but those who could enjoyed their newly developed ability to read books with extended texts. As they became increasingly fluent, they moved on to longer versions of beginning chapter books, and eventually into novels that were episodic in structure. Books like this, such as Beverly Cleary's ever-popular **Ramona** series, have chapters that are self-contained stories yet are linked to each other to form a novel. These kinds of books offer children the opportunity to practice the kind of sustained reading that novels require, but their episodic structure makes comprehension less difficult.

MEDIA ADAPTATIONS OF CHILDREN'S BOOKS

Another way in which children can connect with books is through the media. Today's children respond delightedly to media presentations of literature. Today's teachers use media as a way of offering their students more and varied ways to connect with literature. Students can spend time listening repeatedly to a book, even if the teacher can't read it repeatedly, if the book is on tape. Rereading favorite books helps children in their attempts to read on their own, and a tape or CD-ROM recording offers unlimited practice. Many excellent audio versions of picture books are available for young readers; many teachers supplement these commercial versions with tapes they make themselves. Betty's students enjoyed listening to tapes, responding enthusiastically to an operatic version of Maurice Sendak's *Chicken Soup with Rice* (N–P). Videos also offer children the opportunity to see and hear stories they love. Some videos for young children reproduce the entire page of the book so that children can read the words as well as see the illustrations and listen to the story. Others omit the words but reproduce the illustrations, and still others recreate the story through drama or animation. CD-ROMs also offer children opportunities for exploring texts; David Macaulay's **The Way Things Work** CD-ROM, now in a second, updated version, offers children the opportunity to explore that text in an interactive fashion. Teaching Idea 13.4 offers suggestions for selecting media for the classroom.

Betty's literature-based literacy instruction offered her students the opportunity to read, write, speak, and listen for meaningful purposes. Quite often these purposes were related to the positive value that these students placed on being engaged with a good book.

Using Literature to Integrate the Curriculum

On the other side of town from Betty's classroom, Karen Bliss's first-grade class was experiencing literature-based instruction of a different kind. Using the science curriculum as a basis, Karen created and maintained a single theme across the year as she and her students explored the idea of interdependence. This theme involved a study of oceans for

Teaching Idea 13 ☆ 4

Select Media for Your Classroom

* Set your goals. Think about why you want to use media adaptations. If you want to extend your students' time with print, then you will want adaptations that are connected to books you have in your classroom library or those that include text. If you want to use media adaptations to help students practice visual literacy skills or to encourage them to compare across media, then you will want to find adaptations that suit these goals.

* Consider the literary value of the original work; a good film or tape or video cannot improve a bad book.

* Consider if the adaptation is appropriate to the literary work. Does it enrich and expand the work?

* Consider the audience. Are the literary work and its adaptation appropriate for your students? Adaptations that dilute a work of art to make it accessible to a younger audience are inauthentic and misleading.

* Consider the quality of the adaptation. Media materials should be technically excellent; clear sound and visual reproduction are vital.

© Lee Galda

These children are so involved in the story being read that the boy on the left is imitating the movement of one of the characters.

the first seven months of the school year. Her students were so interested in what they were doing that their reading, writing, listening, and speaking activities, as well as much of their social studies and science, were linked to their exploration of the oceans of the world. They learned geography, wrote extensively about the oceans and seas and the various continents they border, read extensively from fiction, non-fiction, and poetry, and painted many beautiful pictures of the oceans and their inhabitants. Their language activities were motivated and purposeful as they read books to research and wrote to explain. One of their big projects was a group-authored book on penguins, an animal they had become intrigued with during their studies. Working together and independently, they read children's books about penguins, wrote about penguins based on the models they found in the trade books they were reading, revised their writing, and published a class book about penguins. A parent made copies of the book for each student and for the classroom and school libraries. As they were learning about penguins, they were learning to read and write, speak and listen, with fluency and effectiveness.

It was only because the children wanted to explore the rain forests, an interest that grew when they began dis-

cussing the ecology of the oceans and their endangered habitats and species, that a new theme emerged in Karen's classroom. They worked on this new theme for the remaining two months of the school year. Also, while they were engaged in the study of these themes, the students did do other things. They pursued author studies, worked on holiday projects, and took advantage of opportunities for independent reading and writing. Karen's guided reading lessons were separate from the main thematic activity; she elected to work with the basal that the school system mandated. The day began with guided reading and math, and then the class moved into the thematic study.

By structuring the content of the learning tasks within a thematic framework as Karen did, and by exploring them through quality children's literature, you build in integration and meaningfulness. Themes create opportunities for purposeful language use as children employ oral and written language strategies to find out about the theme. Excellent children's books abound for almost any theme that might be chosen. For example, children's books about animals, a popular topic of study in the primary grades, are readily available. There is no shortage of books about special relationships between young and old people, about friendship, or

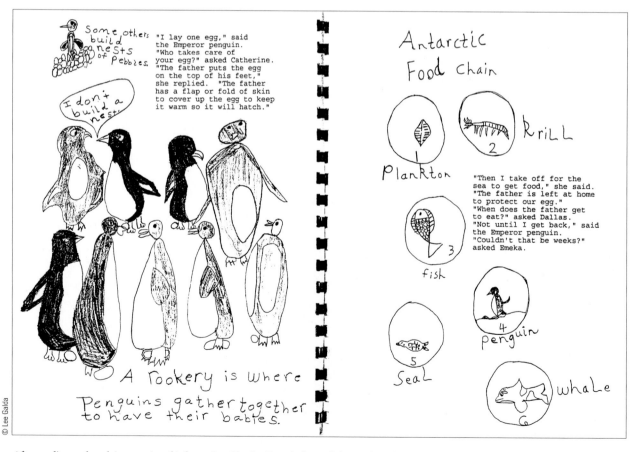

After reading and studying a series of informational books, Karen's class collaborated on their own book about penguins.

about families. There are books about weather, books about cultures and communities, and books about school.

There are also many books about writing and writers, and these can be interesting themes to explore. Fortunately, there are many fine autobiographies and biographies of writers whom children love to read. The Richard Owens series, mentioned in Chapter 9, with books such as Patricia Polacco's *Firetalking!* or Cynthia Rylant's *Best Wishes* (both P–I) are wonderful for exploring favorite writer's lives and their craft. Teaching Idea 13.4 offers suggestions for such a study and provides a list of books to get you started.

Literature provides a rich resource for any writing program. It can be used as a model for writing, providing examples of interesting language used well, and as a source for topics to write about. Karen used literature in this way. Some books illustrate unique formats: journals, letters, postcards, diaries, and autobiographies. Some books parody other forms of literature, some tell stories from different points of view, and some illustrate unique story patterns. No matter what point you want to illustrate about writing, there are books to help you make it clear.

Children who write are also interested in how writing happens in the real world—how a book gets made from beginning to end. There are many books about writing that allow primary-grade children to explore the "how" of the craft—how writers get ideas, how they work, how their books get illustrated, how they get published, and how they get to their audience. Figure 13.2 lists some books about writing, other than biographies, that primary-grade children find intriguing.

Whether you link your thematic study to the science and/or social studies curriculum, as Karen did, or to the language arts curriculum, a thematic organization offers children the opportunity to learn about language while they are learning through language.

Literature Study with Primary-Grade Readers

In yet another part of town, the children in Lisa Stanzi's second-grade reading group were learning about reading and writing, listening and speaking, as they engaged in the study of literature. Lisa's elementary school had an unusual way of organizing reading instruction: For 70 minutes each morning, students in a particular grade level were grouped according to ability, with each group receiving instruction from one teacher. Each of the two second-grade teachers worked with a group, and specialists worked with the other groups. Lisa's group consisted of five students from her class and six to seven from the other second-grade class; all were reading at or above grade level. In spite of this, the group was quite heterogeneous in many ways. Some were struggling at a second-grade reading level while others were fluent at a fourth-grade level. The students were from many parts of the world—China, India, and Africa, as well as the United States. Further, they all had varying levels of experience with books.

Lisa was in the process of moving from a basal-based reading curriculum into a more literature-based curriculum, hoping to transform her "reading" group into something that looked more like a book discussion group or literature-study group. To accomplish this, she gathered hundreds of trade books that supported the six themes that appeared in the system-mandated basal reader and planned her lessons around the literature in the basal, the books she offered the children for independent reading, and those she read aloud. The books ranged from very easy to more difficult picture books, fiction, poetry, and nonfiction, and

Figure 13 ✿ 2

Books About Writing and Publishing for Primary-Grade Children

Aliki, *How a Book Is Made*
Christelow, Eileen, *What Do Authors Do?*
Edwards, Michelle, *Dora's Book*
Gibbons, Gail, *Deadline! From News to Newspaper*
Goffstein, M. B., *A Writer*
Gottlieb, Dale, *My Stories by Hildy Calpurnia Rose*
Joyce, William, *The World of William Joyce Scrapbook*

Kehoe, Michael, *A Book Takes Root: The Making of a Picture Book*
Lester, Helen, *Author: A True Story*
Nixon, Joan Lowery, *If You Were a Writer*
Stevens, Janet, *From Pictures to Words: A Book About Making a Book*

included transitional books such as the **Frog and Toad** and **Henry and Mudge** series, and easy chapter books such as John Peterson's **The Littles** series. They also included brief chapter books such as Patricia MacLachlan's *Arthur, for the Very First Time, Sarah, Plain and Tall,* and **Skylark**, as well as James Howe's *The Celery Stalks at Midnight* and Sid Fleischman's *The Whipping Boy* (all I). When she introduced the first chapter book in November, Lisa read it aloud; by the end of the year the students were reading chapters at home in the evening in preparation for the next day's discussion. Every day for 70 minutes, her "literature group," as they called themselves, read, wrote, and talked about literature (Galda, Rayburn, and Stanzi, 2000).

Lisa taught reading through literature, using both the stories, poems, and nonfiction found in the basal and the hundreds of trade books that the children read. Oral discussion of literature was at the heart of her reading program, and she spent a significant amount of time helping her students learn to talk about books. Although Lisa worked on decoding skills and strategies with those students who needed this work, her focus was on comprehension strategies, which are directly linked to children being able to read and respond to a book. In this way she was much like Betty, incorporating reading instruction when her students were engaged in reading children's books, and responding to students' strengths and weaknesses. She also taught her students about literature by teaching them about literary elements, about how to make connections between what they were reading and their own lives, and about how to make connections among texts.

Lisa's students learned about what authors do by talking about the books they were reading. They studied authors and their work across the year, but they focused primarily on Patricia MacLachlan, reading three of her chapter books and all of her picture books. They began to understand how her love of the prairie infused her stories. Teaching Idea 13.5 gives you some ideas of how to begin author studies with your students.

Lisa's second-grade readers also explored genre characteristics and conventions, trying to distinguish between fantasy and realism, historical and contemporary settings, fiction and nonfiction. They did all of this by reading widely, writing in response journals, and discussing what they read. They delighted in noticing and discussing an author's particular use of a literary element such as plot, setting, or characterization.

On one spring morning a group of students talked about the relationships that the characters in *The Whipping Boy* (I) have with each other; they hypothesized about characters' motives for some of their actions. Sarah commented that she thought the Prince didn't want to go back to his castle. Chris added, "I think the prince likes Jemmy." Brett responded, "I think they're going to be friends." And Cameron moved the discussion to another level with his

Teaching Idea 13 ✷ 5

Study the Life and Work of an Author or Illustrator

Students become interested in authors' and illustrators' lives when they discover connections between the writers' and artists' life experiences and their work.

1. Choose an author or illustrator whose work students like and read as many of the person's books as possible.

2. Locate biographical information about the person. Look at the Richard Owen's series of autobiographies mentioned in Chapter 9, in *Something About the Author*, and on the Internet. Many children's book authors and illustrators have wonderful Web sites that you can find by typing in their names and then searching.

3. Read and discuss this information.

4. Make some generalizations about the person's work.

5. Make a comparison chart across books.

6. Make some generalizations about how the person's life influenced their work.

7. Compare incidents in the person's life to incidents in the books they write, places where the person has lived to the settings in their books, and so forth.

8. Prepare a display in which students can depict the connections they found between the person's life and work.

perceptive comment: "In the inside he likes him, but on the outside he's just mean." They went on to discuss the characters and their own lives as they wrestled with the idea that a person can be different on the inside from the way he or she is on the outside. Discussions like this prompted Chris to make a comment that revealed the heart of what Lisa did with books when he said, "In here we read differently. Here we think about what we read."

Lisa also helped her students develop their visual literacy skills as she taught them how to "read" the illustrations in their basal reader and in the books in the classroom. In many group discussions the children pored over illustrations as they sought to determine a mood, defend a theme, or describe a setting or character. For example, when one boy commented that the character in Anthony Browne's *Willy and Hugh* (P) was sad, another challenged this by pointing out that the words didn't say that Willy was sad.

The first child responded by showing an illustration in which Willy is walking with his shoulders slumped forward and his head down. At this point, Lisa talked about looking at illustrations for information. "Reading" illustrations is also important in determining genre, as when Lisa's students read Arthur Dorros's *Abuela* (P) and based their decision that the story was fantasy rather than realism on the illustrations. These kinds of discussions can lead to lessons about the art of illustrating, focusing on topics such as line, shape, color, white space, and media, things we discuss in Chapter 3.

Lisa's young readers spent the year honing their reading skills while engaging in often passionate discussions of the stories, poems, novels, and nonfiction books they read. They read many books, made many connections across books and with their own lives, and learned a lot about themselves and about literature. They were able to do this because their teacher, Lisa, created a literature-based reading program that was based on time, choice, and good books.

Assessment

When literature abounds in classrooms there is less time for traditional assessment procedures than when children are busy working on "gradable" products such as worksheets. There is, however, more opportunity for what some teachers describe as "authentic" assessment. This type of assessment involves observing children as they are reading and responding to literature, examining the work they produce as part of their reading and responding, and talking with them about what they are doing. It also involves assessing yourself as a teacher—looking critically at your planning, at the daily life of your classroom, and at your students' literacy development to determine what is and is not effective practice. The focus is on what children can and are doing, as teachers gather artifacts, observe student behaviors, listen to students talk, and record what goes on.

KEEP RECORDS

You will want to keep records that represent what your students are doing in the classroom and how they are performing. These records may include artifacts that children produce, such as reading logs or response journals. Children's response activities often involve products, such as pictures they paint or writing they produce. Save these so that you can inform yourself about students' understanding of and response to the books they are reading. Reading tests such as informal reading inventories or standardized tests become part of the record as well.

Notes from observation of students as they select books and as they read and respond to books provide a picture of what they are actually doing in the classroom—how they are performing the tasks that you have set for them. Watch to see if your students select books they can read and are likely to enjoy. If they are not yet reading fluently, see if they can retell the story through the illustrations. Find out how your students select books and whom they ask for suggestions. Discover whom they read with and where they like to read. Keep track of how your students respond to the books they read and examine the kinds of things they do. Notice the writing they do in response, and note how often they choose art or dramatic activities as response options. Watch students as they engage in these activities, looking for demonstrations of their engagement with and understanding of the books they read. As you observe, jot down brief notes about what you are seeing. If you use mailing labels to write on, you can affix them to a sheet of paper in each child's record. As you keep adding notes you build a picture of each child's reading behavior.

Notes from listening to their conversations about literature provide information about students' comprehension and response, just as an analysis of their oral reading provides information about their decoding strategies. Listening to children discuss books is a good way to assess their development as readers. Note the kinds of things they talk about, whether they attend to others' ideas, and whether others' ideas enrich their own reading and responding. This helps you know what you need to focus on in your instruction. Ask individual children to read aloud to you on a regular basis and note the skills and strategies they call upon as they decode unfamiliar text. This helps tell you what you need to teach.

As you engage in these assessment activities, you will find that you learn things about your students that inform the instructional decisions you make. You will find yourself teaching more effectively as you focus on students rather than on a standard curriculum. This focus is crucial to a literature-based literacy curriculum.

Summary

There are many ways to structure literature-based instruction for young children. Some teachers use literature to teach reading and writing, listening and speaking. They seek out patterned, predictable texts, transitional books, beginning chapter books, and media adaptations of literature to provide their students with rich literacy experiences. Other teachers use children's books to support a thematic organization that links several areas of the curriculum. The books become a resource for practicing the English language arts, and they provide learning content about a particular theme. Still other teachers teach students about literature through literature-based instruction, even as they teach them how to read, write, respond, and discuss the books they read. There are as many ways to structure literature-based instruction as there are teachers and classrooms. In all cases, however, teachers pay careful attention to what their students are doing as they assess their progress in order to plan instruction.

Read Christine Heppermann's article "Little Bear on the Air" in the May/June 1999 issue of *The Horn Book Magazine*, paying attention to her critique of children's book-related television cartoons. Then, study one of the books and watch the cartoon version, thinking about whether you agree or disagree with Heppermann. What kinds of artistic styles translate well to a television cartoon format? What kinds of stories? What might you want to do if your students are familiar with these cartoons?

chapter 14

Literature-Based Instruction in Intermediate Grades and Middle School

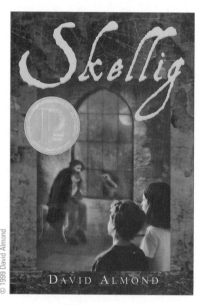

David Almond has written a powerful novel about life, death, hope, and goodwill that leaves young readers wondering.

© 1999 David Almond

Dr. Death faced me across the kitchen table. He touched my hand with his long curved fingers. I caught the scent of tobacco that surrounded him. I saw the black spots on his skin. Dad was telling him the story: my disappearance in the night, my sleepwalking. I heard in his voice how scared he still was, how he thought he'd lost me. I wanted to tell him again that I was all right, everything was all right.

—DAVID ALMOND, *Skellig*, p. 122

THE STUDENTS IN GEORGE'S SIXTH-GRADE CLASS ARE SCATTERED around the room in small groups, heatedly discussing David Almond's *Skellig* (1), a Michael L. Printz Honor Book. They have just finished the part where Michael and Mina visited Skellig in the night, and Michael's father awoke to find him gone. They are trying to decide just what or who Skellig is. Is he an angel? A vagrant? A figment of Mina and Michael's overactive imaginations? An apparition sent to comfort Michael during his newborn sister's medical crisis? Because there is so much to think and talk about, so many things to figure out, George is reading this brief novel aloud so that everyone is, quite literally, on the same page. The surreal story has gripped everyone, and students ask George to go back a few chapters to reread some of the earlier descriptions of Skellig. Many students have asked their parents to buy them their own copy of the book; others are hoping that it will be offered through the book club that their class participates in. Later, George will ask his students to talk about the genre that *Skellig* belongs in, another query that will provoke lively discussion.

Reading and talking together about books that provoke strong responses is making these sixth-grade students more avid readers. It is also helping them to become better readers, because their desire to understand and be able to participate in class discussions is strong. These students are lucky to have the opportunity to engage with good books on a regular basis, to have time to talk about them with their peers, and to have opportunities to respond in journals, projects, and more formal papers. Both fluent and still struggling readers are caught up in the ideas that Almond is exploring and are actively creating meaning as they read. And they're enjoying it!

There are many ways to make literature a central part of intermediate-grade and middle school instruction. Figure 13.1 lists many books that report on how various teachers incorporate literature in their curriculums. Here we explore different structures that allow teachers and students to read, think, and talk about books in a variety of ways and for a variety of purposes.

Reading Workshop

In the upper grades, and especially in middle and junior high schools, teachers often use the workshop as an organizing structure for reading and writing instruction. Atwell (1998) describes how the workshop runs in her classroom. She often begins each class with a brief lesson about literature, focusing on what she has noticed her students need to learn or what in the curriculum they are ready to learn. Her students then read independently. Following the reading, they write a letter or an entry in a dialogue journal to a peer or to her. These letters serve the social function that is so important to reading, as the recipient of the letter writes back. The partners engage in a written conversation about books. (As an alternative to the letters, students could discuss their books in pairs or small groups.)

The reading workshop integrates well with a writing workshop, as students learn to pace themselves in their reading and writing, to expect brief, explicit instruction from their teacher, and to interact with their peers in a structured manner. Teachers can allow their students to select their own books, or can offer students the opportunity to select from a collection that relates to the curriculum. This structure offers choice about what to read, allows time to read and respond, and provides someone to "talk" with about reading. Teaching Idea 14.1 suggests a way to get students engaged in sharing their responses to the books they are reading.

Book Club

Book Club (McMahon, Raphael, Goatley, and Pardo, 1997) was developed by classroom teachers in conjunction with university researchers. It is structured to include multiple opportunities for language use, and easily accommodates thematic studies in a language arts curriculum or links between language arts and other curricular areas.

Teaching Idea 14 · 1

Create a Classroom Reader's Choice Award

In order to help your students learn to rely on one another's opinions as they select books, create a classroom choice award file. Ask students to do the following:

1. Conduct a survey to determine favorite books.
2. Write the titles of books that they especially like on index cards.
3. Give book talks to promote the reading of their favorite books.
4. Create a file from the index cards for students to browse through when selecting books.
5. Rate each book read by marking the index card from 0 to 5 and adding a one-sentence comment.
6. At the end of the year, add up the ratings to determine the "best" books.
7. Share this list with students who will be in the classroom next year. It makes a great summer reading list!

Book Club is grounded in a sociocultural perspective on language and learning and response theory, discussed in Chapter 12. A sociocultural perspective reflects an understanding that language first develops through social interaction, and eventually becomes internalized as thought. During this interaction, learning occurs when individuals work on tasks in the company of more knowledgeable others who guide them. As this occurs, individuals develop their own sense of self and of others and learn to use language in particular forms within particular contexts (McMahon et al., 1997). Because readers are reading and responding to literature in Book Club, this perspective includes the idea that readers read within a social context and construct their responses over time as they read and share their thinking with others. These theoretical concepts shaped the structure that marks the Book Club. This includes reading, writing, small-group discussions, whole-class interactions, and multiple opportunities for instruction.

READING

If we want our students to read more, then we have to provide time for them to read during the school day. Book Club does just this. The reading in Book Club differs from independent reading in an S.S.R. format, because the books are selected by the teacher or by teacher and students to explore a theme or curricular area. Criteria for selection include age-appropriateness, thematic connection, literary quality, and substance; the book must be sufficiently engaging and stimulating that students will want to think, write, and talk about it.

The whole class may be reading the same book, or the class may divide into small groups, or book clubs, with each book club reading a different book, all relating to the unifying theme. Reading may be done individually, in pairs (often called buddy reading), through teacher read-alouds, or with the support of audiotapes. The point is that everyone has time to read an age-appropriate book so that he or she will

Nothing can replace time spent engaged in a good book.

be able to respond to it through writing and discussion. For struggling readers, this offers the opportunity to see what reading is all about—engaging with interesting ideas and compelling language—since many struggling readers never have the opportunity to work with age-appropriate texts.

WRITING

After reading, students have the opportunity to write about what they are reading. This writing may be unstructured journal writing but more often will be structured by the teacher through the use of "think sheets" or questions and tasks that both support students' developing responses and offer alternative ways for students to think and talk about books. Writing serves to help students articulate their developing understandings about text and to prepare them for an oral discussion of these texts. The writing component can also include more sustained writing activities.

TALKING ABOUT TEXT WITH PEERS: THE BOOK CLUB

After reading and writing, students meet in small, heterogeneous, peer-led discussion groups, or book clubs, to talk about their responses, to ask questions, and to compare ideas. These discussions offer students the opportunity to build on their personal responses within the social context of the group, to use oral language to talk about books in meaningful ways, to learn how to conduct themselves as a member of a group, and to serve as a resource for others.

COMMUNITY SHARE: WHOLE-CLASS INTERACTIONS

Both preceding and following the book club discussions, the class as a whole talks together about the book they are reading. This is called "community share." Before reading, the teacher might focus students on strategies and skills they might need as they read, write, and talk about their book. Specific literary elements might be presented to guide students in their understanding of an author's craft. Following book clubs, the teacher might bring up interesting ideas that have come up in book clubs, or raise questions that she would like the class to consider. At any time she might read aloud from another book that explores the focal theme and ask students to consider their developing ideas in light of this additional experience. These brief whole-class activities serve as means to maintain a community of readers that stretches across individual books clubs. They also add to the richness and diversity of the social interaction around the target book.

Teachers who use Book Club have various opportunities for instruction, including the writing and thinking tasks they set for their students and the focus they provide during community share. In some classrooms, this is enough. In others, there is a need for more extensive direct instruction in reading and language arts.

Recently, a group of teachers and university researchers developed what they call "Book Club Plus" in response to their need to ensure enough instructional time around reading. Book Club Plus provides a structured opportunity for reading and language arts instruction in guided reading groups. The texts read in these groups are thematically related to the Book Club book, but are at students' instructional level rather than at their age level. Thus students get practice thinking and talking about books that engage their emotions and also get intensive instructional support from their teacher (Raphael, Florio-Ruane, and George, in press).

Book Club and Book Club Plus provide a framework that is based on sound theory and research, yet is flexible enough that teachers can use the framework to support the needs of their students and the demands of their curriculum. The invariant structure of time to read, time to think and write, time to talk with peers, and time to interact as a whole class, coupled with multiple opportunities for instruction, supports the literacy learning of diverse students in diverse contexts. It allows teachers to present thematically focused units of study that provide students with opportunities to learn about themselves and others, and to grapple with powerful ideas, while at the same time developing their reading, writing, listening, and speaking skills and learning about how literature works.

Exploring the Civil War Through Book Club

As part of her graduate work, Deb Kruse-Field, a fifth–sixth-grade teacher, has developed a Book Club unit that serves as a resource for creating an instruction plan. She wants to use Book Club to link her social studies curriculum with her language arts/reading curriculum. This particular unit focuses on the Civil War, an important event in United States history. Deb has identified a variety of books and has developed whole-group lessons, individual activities, and thinking/writing prompts that she can select from as she tailors the unit to the needs and demands of a specific class. Here we present some of her ideas as an example of what ideas for a Book Club unit might look like.

Because she knows that she will have many kinds of learners in any class she teaches, Deb has selected a diverse array of books at a variety of levels. Her prime criterion is the quality of the literature, closely followed by the potential interest of her students. She has also selected literature that offers a variety of perspectives on the Civil War: female and male, Union and Confederate, immigrant and mill worker, slave and master. She has also selected diverse genres—novels, picture books, poetry, nonfiction, and biography—to add to her students' reading experiences as well as to enrich the potential activities and assignments she might select.

Deb divides the books she has selected into three types: books that might be read in common, books that might be read in small groups, and books that serve as extensions and resource material. Figure 14.1 lists the books she has selected. There are, of course, many more titles she could have chosen. Her choices reflect her resources and the needs and demands of curriculum and community.

After selecting the books, Deb generates a list of possibilities for whole-class lessons that focus on a particular topic but also address multiple skills. She decides to explore language, structure and time, characterization, conflict/cooperation/change, point of view, and also the focus of Book Club itself: asking good questions in order to have smart discussions.

Regarding structure and time, Deb plans to sequence events in one or two picture storybooks (*Pink and Say* and *Nettie's Trip South*) so that students can distinguish critical events and create a synopsis of either story. She may ask students to create a story map that reflects the unique shape of the books they are reading, and she is sure that she will ask students to create a class time line of events as they read the fiction and nonfiction that she has selected.

Deb plans to help her students explore language by looking at the beginnings and endings of the books they read, then analyze them for elements that make them "grabbers." Books such as *Moon over Tennessee* are packed with metaphorical language, and she plans to explore the similies, metaphors, and imagery the authors use. Many of the books she has selected have rich dialogue that brings the time and characters to life; she can explore dialogue through both texts and real-life experiences and have students work with dialogue to create brief dramas that could be used as a final project. *Moon over Tennessee* and *Bull Run* have strong language; she may use these books as sources from which her students can create "found" poems that express an appropriate mood or feeling about the time period.

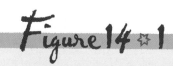

Bibliography for a Civil War Unit

Possible Texts to Read in Common

Crist-Evans, Craig, *Moon over Tennessee: A Boy's Civil War Journal*

Fleischman, Paul, *Bull Run*

McKissack, Patricia, and Fredrick McKissack, *Christmas in the Big House, Christmas in the Quarters*

Polacco, Patricia, *Pink and Say*

Turner, Ann, *Nettie's Trip South*

Whitman, Walt, *Leaves of Grass*

_____, *Specimen Days*

Possible Small-Group Texts

Armstrong, Jennifer, *The Dreams of Mairhe Mehan*

_____, *Steal Away*

Beatty, Patricia, *Charley Skedaddle*

_____, *Turn Homeward, Hannalee*

_____, *Who Comes with Cannons?*

Paulson, Gary, *Soldier's Heart*

Reeder, Carolyn, *Shades of Gray*

Possible Texts for Research and Extensions

Freedman, Russell, *Lincoln: A Photobiography*

Hamilton, Virginia, *Many Thousand Gone: African Americans from Slavery to Freedom*

Haskins, Jim, *Black, Blue, and Gray: African Americans in the Civil War*

_____, *Get on Board: The Story of the Underground Railroad*

Herbert, Janis, *The Civil War for Kids*

Hunt, Irene, *Across Five Aprils*

Lester, Julius, *To Be a Slave*

Marrin, Albert, *Unconditional Surrender: U. S. Grant and the Civil War*

Murphy, Jim, *The Boys' War: Confederate and Union Soldiers Talk About the Civil War*

Character maps and listing character traits will help her students explore characterization in the books they read and will help students understand how time and place shape character. Comparing fictional characters with the actual people described in some of the nonfiction Deb has selected will help students think about an author's process of character development. She may also ask students to examine the characters in their books with an eye toward the difference between an author "telling" and "showing" what a character is like.

Conflict, cooperation, and change can be explored by asking students to develop "once/now" statements about themselves and then about the characters they have met in their reading. For instance, the main character in *Charley Skedaddle* might be characterized by this statement: "Once, Charley loved a good fight. Now, he runs away." This is a perfect opportunity to discuss the impact of the Civil War and link it to character development as well as to explore juxtaposition, paradox, and comparison/contrast. Students might also use a graphic organizer to make note of how conflict, cooperation, and change operate in the books they read and in the actual events of the Civil War.

Point of view is an important issue in *Pink and Say* and in *Nettie's Trip South*, and Deb has deliberately selected novels that present different points of view about the war. This is a perfect opportunity to explore both literary and historical point of view and how it shapes the story being constructed. *Bull Run* is told in different points of view and lends itself to Reader's Theatre, which heightens the impact of various perspectives on one event in time. Finally, brief debates about central questions of the Civil War between students who have taken on the persona of characters will allow students to make intertextual connections, learn about the various perspectives regarding the Civil War, and hone their critical thinking and oral debating skills.

Most of these activities do double duty—they ask students to consider literary elements, structures, and processes, and they help students consider the historical period they are studying. Other activities center on the process of conducting book club discussions. Deb might ask students to distinguish between questions such as "Who won the war?"—which does not lead to an interesting discussion—and "When can war be good?"—which does.

WRITING PROMPTS

Deb has also generated a series of writing prompts for students to respond to individually in their journals or in whole-class exercises. These prompts are designed to compliment the whole-class lessons that she may teach and to fit well with the particular books the students will be reading. She also has prompts that reflect more generalizable ways to approach text, as well as some that help students focus on the historical period they are exploring. Offering students writing prompts gives Deb the opportunity to focus on skills, strategies, and content that she wants them to learn; it helps students see how they can "write to learn" as well. Some of these prompts are listed in Figure 14.2.

Figure 14 ✣ 2

Writing Prompts

Prediction

* Look at the cover and read the back of the book. What will this story be about? How will it end? What will be the book's point of view?
* After you finish reading a chapter or a group of chapters, predict what will happen next and explain why you think this will happen.

Characterization

* What good attributes does your character possess? Bad attributes? Use examples from the text that show these attributes in your character.
* What does your character care about most? How do you know?
* In what ways does your character change throughout the book or in a particular chapter? Give examples of specific changes. Would you consider these changes positive or negative?
* Compare your main character with a character from one of our community share books or from another book of your choice.
* What do you like about how your character solves problems? What would you do differently?
* If you were the main character of your book for a day, what would you do?
* Draw a symbol to represent your character. Why did you choose this particular image?

Point of View

* Whose perspective do you most relate to in the book? Why?
* How do characters look at issues differently in your book?

Setting and Time Period

* How do you picture the setting of the story? (Draw a picture if you want to.) How does the author create these images?
* Would you like to experience the story's setting? Why? Why not?
* Does the way this author writes about setting remind you of any other authors or settings?
* Draw a picture of an important scene.

Language

* Pick out wonderful first and last lines of chapters. How do they set the story's tone? Compare these phrases with first and last lines in another book. How are they similar or different?
* Find literary techniques in the story that are especially effective (for example, similes, metaphors, foreshadowing, juxtaposition). How do these techniques add to the story?

* What kinds of sentences does the author use? Short? Long? What about punctuation? Why would the author choose to write this way? Do you like this style?
* Find words that are extraordinary (words that you know and that you don't know are fine). Look up words you don't know. What catches you about the words? Why would the author choose them?
* Pick a passage that grabs you. Divide your paper into two columns. Write the page number and at least part of the passage on one side. Write your reaction to the passage on the other.

Conflict, Cooperation, and Change

* What are the two best examples of conflict in your book? Why?
* What are the two best examples of cooperation in your book? Why?
* When is change good in the story? When is conflict good? What about in your own life?

Sequence and Structure

* Make a chain of events that happen in a chapter or over several chapters.
* Are there flashbacks in your book? Why would the author use them? Do you like them?
* How many different story lines are in your book? What are they? Do they work together?
* Write a synopsis of a chapter or group of chapters in five sentences or less.

Author's Purpose and Process

* Why do you think the author wrote this book?
* What kind of research would the author have to do to write this story?

Civil War Power Questions

* How might our country be different if the Civil War had not occurred?
* What new ideas about the Civil War did you discover?
* Should the South have seceded?
* How else could the conflict have been solved?
* Should army deserters have been punished?
* Should blacks have been allowed to fight on either side in the war from the beginning?
* Should women have been allowed to fight?
* What was the biggest impact of the Civil War? Why do you think that?
* Was either the North or the South right about its cause? Why or why not?
* What else do you still want to know about this period?

CULMINATING AND EXTENSION ACTIVITIES

Finally, Deb has generated several ideas for cumulative and extension activities. Ideas for whole-group work include writing a play or a dialogue among characters from the novels the students have read, emphasizing points of view. If time permits, costumes can be added and performances can be given for parents and other students. A less time-consuming adaptation would be to have students write and perform a series of monologues, using *Bull Run* as a model. Another idea would be to have a debate or trial about a Civil War issue. Possible topics could include hiding slaves, or deserting during battle.

Individual and small-group projects include research, creative writing, and formal papers. These ideas are listed in Figure 14.3; Teaching Idea 14.2 also describes another type of project. Deb plans to select from these ideas according to the abilities and needs of her students, and to allow them to select from this less-extensive range of possibilities. As in her other lessons, activities, and writing prompts, these project ideas reflect her dual focus on the literature itself and the historical period, or, in curriculum terms, on English language arts and social studies. Note that none

---

Figure 14 ✩ 3

Small-Group and Individual Project Ideas

Research

EXTENDED RESEARCH

Research one Civil War aspect in depth, such as camp life, a battle, women in the war, leaders, abolitionists, prisons, and so on. Write about the topic and how it relates to what you learned from your reading in class. Also keep in mind conflict/cooperation/change and point of view. You may want to include maps or drawings if appropriate for your subject.

LINK TO CIVIL WAR WRITERS

Many writers, such as Walt Whitman, flourished during the time of the Civil War. Read some of Whitman or another Civil War writer and compare their writings to what you have learned in class. What is their point of view? How do they describe conflict/cooperation/change? How does their writing relate to the novel you read?

Creative Writing

TWO-SIDED JOURNAL

Write Civil War journal entries from at least two different points of view: Union/Confederate soldier, mother/soldier, slave/master, and so on. Your entries should reflect different perspectives, include conflict/cooperation/change, and be packed with "meat."

POETRY PAPER

Though it uses fewer words, poetry is not easier to write than prose. Create a series of poems that shows what you know about the Civil War. Think about your point of view in the poems, and include conflict/cooperation/change as you express your ideas.

NEWSPAPER

Create a newspaper about a day during the Civil War. You can include editorials, cartoons, news articles, advertisements, and so forth.

PICTURE BOOK

Patricia Polacco and Ann Turner have shown what powerful information can come from picture books. Create your own fiction or nonfiction picture book about the Civil War.

NEW ENDING OR NEW CHAPTER

Rewrite the ending of your novel or write a new chapter. Make sure your writing fits with the author's style and shows an understanding of the book and Civil War issues.

Formal Papers

ANALYZE BEGINNINGS AND ENDINGS

Choose several authors and explain how they effectively write beginning and ending lines of chapters. How do they grab the reader's attention? How do they tie up loose ends? Be sure to include quotes and page numbers.

ONCE/NOW ESSAY

Write a Once/Now essay (*Once* this character was X, but *now* this character is Y because . . .). This should be about one of the characters in your book and your ideas should be supported with examples from the text.

BOOK CRITIC

Be a book critic. Rate your book and explain how areas such as style, story structure, language, content, and message fit your rating. What could the author have done differently? Why would it have been better?

COMPARISON PAPER

Compare your book with at least one other book. Which book do you like better? Why? Think about style, point of view, story, content, structure, and characters.

Teaching Idea 14 ☆ 2

The Literature Newsletter

A classroom newsletter devoted to what students are reading is a good place to publish students' writing and also artwork that was prompted by their reading. It is a wonderful way to send home news of the classroom, and to make suggestions for books that can be read outside of school. The student-produced newsletter can include the following:

✳ Book reviews
✳ Editorials about issues raised in books
✳ Crossword puzzles using book knowledge
✳ An advice column directed to book characters
✳ Book-related cartoons
✳ Feature articles on authors

of her activities ask students to read inappropriately; that is, they are not asked to read a novel for facts about the Civil War, although they may certainly pick some up as they read!

Using Literature to Transform Curriculum

Not all teachers choose to use a Book Club structure as they combine curriculum areas through literature. Many choose to bring literature into a particular curriculum area simply by asking students to read or by reading aloud books that reflect issues and ideas concerning the curriculum. Doing this allows students to read more widely and deeply about the topics being taught. Reading widely allows students to discover what they are interested in and to delve deeply into that interest. This, in turn, means that they are more likely to discover differing perspectives and new ways to consider information. Reading widely also provides an important opportunity for critical reading and thinking, as discussed in Chapter 12. Through wise selection, teachers can transform their curriculum, as Banks and Banks (1993) suggest, so that their students consider knowledge as being shaped by culture, and learn to consider ideas, issues, and events within a framework that embraces diversity.

One fifth-grade teacher does this by finding books that reflect the themes and issues that she wants to explore in her

social studies curriculum. Judy's fifth-grade class is studying American history, from the days of early explorations to the present time. She has always combined language arts and social studies instruction through children's literature. This year, however, she decides to do more than select books to read that illuminate the historical periods she is covering. She organizes her social studies and language arts curriculum around the theme of progress and cultural conflict, hoping to create a climate in her classroom whereby her diverse students will question what we mean by "progress" and will begin to see the history of the United States from multiple perspectives. Because the notion of progress often includes environmental issues, she decides to connect her theme to that portion of the science curriculum that covers ecology and environmental issues.

Judy begins the year by starting at the beginning—at least from the mainstream perspective. A study of Columbus and his "discovery" of the Americas provides an interesting introduction to the importance of perspective in interpreting historical events. Books such as Maestro's *The Discovery of the Americas* (I), Yolen's *Encounter* (P–I), and Conrad's *Pedro's Journal* (I) add contrast to the account of the age of exploration in the social studies text. Classic biographies of Columbus, in which he is praised as a great man, such as d'Aulaire's *Christopher Columbus* (I), are compared to more recent texts such as Vicki Liestman's *Columbus Day* (I) and Milton Meltzer's *Columbus and the World Around Him* (A). This provides a perfect context for learning to critically assess nonfiction texts, an important life skill.

Simultaneously, the whole class is reading Dorris's *Morning Girl* (I), sometimes aloud, sometimes silently, and students are writing about the book and discussing it after each chapter. The fifth graders have really come to know Morning Girl and Star Boy as people, and they have begun to talk about what a gentle, peaceful life the Taino had. Then, the book ends with an excerpt from Columbus's journal in which he disparages the Taino as having no language and being fit for slavery. What a shock! This experience, perhaps more than any other, helps these children see the power of perspective and the conflict that "progress," in this case the exploration of new lands, can bring.

With this strong beginning, it is easy for students to continue to explore the idea of progress and cultural conflict through the social studies topics they study and the literature they read. Both the Civil War and the Westward Expansion are illuminated as historical periods when they are viewed as instances of cultural conflict, and they are made memorable through the reading and discussion of evocative books. Reading picture books like Turner's *Nettie's Trip South* (I–A), biographical novels like Lyons's *Letters from a Slave Girl* (I–A), Freedman's *Lincoln: A Photobiography* (I–A), and novels such as Beatty's *Who Comes with Cannons?* (A) becomes an important experience for these children as they discuss the ideas of states' rights and secession, slavery and emancipation

IBD NEWS

December 23, 1501   Year In Review
★★★
Winopegi, Pubs.   25 shells
★★★

GIRL FIGHTS FISH

Young Karana Winopegi caught and fought a huge black octopus. She used the strongest sinew and the finest stone for a hook. As the black devil swam towards the rocky shore, Karana was forced to let go of the sinew or be dashed on the rocks. Though she hopes to try to catch the octopus again, she'll have to find more sinew. Her words sum up her determination: "Though I haven't yet caught the black devil, I think that he will not live much longer for the hook was in his beak."

Karana fights octopus.

Karana was forced to take this action because she needed food. After The People left the island because they were seeking freedom and peace in another land, Karana had to feed and clothe herself. Starvation drove her to try to catch and eat the octopus.

Karana was alone on the island because her brother got bitten by a venomous snake and died. Since the death of her brother her only company has been wild dogs.

She was so tired of eating abalone over and over again that she went into the deep ocean to fish for octopus.

WILD DOG TAMED

Karana tamed a wild dog when she found him hurt in the gorge on the west side of the island. He had been hurt by another dominant male. The injured dog had been the leader of the group of dogs on the island. Now Karana keeps him in her cave on the west side of the island. She has built a fence of bones in front of the cave so the wild dogs can not get in and hurt him again. His wound healed slowly.

Karana named him Ronatu, which means "one with eyes of gold." He is solid gray with not a speck of white on him. He acts as her guard dog and tags along with her when she goes hunting.

Ronatu was severely injured in his fight with the black octopus and is fighting for his life at this time.

The injured Ronatu.

One of Judy's students used a newspaper format to respond to the book she was reading independently, Scott O'Dell's **Island of the Blue Dolphins.**

from a variety of perspectives. The Civil War becomes not just an event in the history of their country, but another example of cultural conflict and resolution.

The study of the Westward Expansion is given truth and impact through the reading of nonfiction books like Freedman's *Indian Winter* (A), Fisher's *The Oregon Trail* (A), and Brown's *Wounded Knee: An Indian History of the American West* (A), adapted by Amy Ehrlich for young readers from Brown's original *Bury My Heart at Wounded Knee.* These books, along with novels like Scott O'Dell and Elizabeth Hall's *Thunder Rolling in the Mountains* (A), the powerful story of the last days of the Nez Perce as a free people in 1877, help students to understand not only the exhilaration of moving to a new land, taming it, and making it your own, but also the agony of living through the destruction of your people, values, and way of life.

The story of immigration in America is also a story of cultural conflict and change, and Judy's class goes on to read and discuss books like Yep's *The Star Fisher* (A), which chronicles the difficulties of adjusting to a new culture. This becomes a subtheme that continues through the year and expands into family history projects.

By integrating social studies and literature within a meaningful thematic framework, Judy is able to transform her social studies curriculum from a study of history to a study of cultural conflict and progress in history. She also is able to incorporate the idea of cultural perspective in her science curriculum when the class studies ecology and the environment. Adding a Native American perspective to the discussion of the use of natural resources helps her students see that there are at least two sides to every issue. For example, although farming the prairie meant food for an expanding American population, it also meant severe loss of topsoil and destruction of the natural habitat for several species who were also destroyed as a result. This, in turn, led to the starvation of Native Americans who relied on hunting the prairie to feed their people. Faced with facts like these, it is easier to understand and admire alternate perspectives, such as the Native American attitude toward natural resources. Rather than being held up as an example of an "undeveloped" or naive cultural attitude, or a quaint and amusing belief, the Native American reverence for nature becomes a prophetic lesson for all.

Judy chooses books that she hopes will provoke discussions of cultural conflict and perspective—books to engage students who read at different levels, books from a variety of genres. She provides time to read and gives students the opportunity to think, write, and talk about what they are reading. By bringing students together around meaningful books, Judy gives them the opportunity to explore issues in history and science that are still important today. This, in turn, leads to discussions of contemporary issues, discussions that allow students to question previously held beliefs and form lasting values.

Connecting Literature Study and Writing

Other teachers do not have the opportunity or perhaps the desire to integrate literature across the curriculum, but nevertheless use literature as a foundation for their language arts curriculum. They might do as Lisa Stanzi, described in Chapter 13, does and ask students to read short stories, poems, fiction, and nonfiction that complement the basal series they use.

Many teachers also use literature as an important component of their writing program, teaching their students to read with appreciation of the wordsmithery demonstrated by the writers they admire, to explore structures and styles as they relate to mood and tone, or to use the books they read as models for their own writing. Students who write read differently from those who do not write. When students are learning the craft of writing, they are sensitive to what other writers do and adopt some of the strategies as their own.

Students who read are better writers than those who do not read. The only source of knowledge sufficiently rich and reliable for learning about written language is the writing already done by others. We learn to write by reading what others have written; we enrich our repertoire of language possibilities by reading what others have said. Hearing and reading good stories, poems, and nonfiction develops vocabulary, sharpens sensitivity to language, and fine-tunes a sense of writing styles. This may be especially important in regard to nonfiction. Students who read nothing but textbooks have no way of knowing just how graceful nonfiction writing can be, have no understanding of how structures can support concept development or build arguments. No wonder their research papers read like encyclopedia entries!

Teachers who integrate reading and writing through literature talk about how aspects of published writers' styles crop up in student writing, about how familiar structures are borrowed and used in new ways. Students of all ages do this—borrow from the books they read—to their great advantage. Teachers can capitalize on this by structuring lessons that focus students on exploring how language works in the books they are reading and how they can use their new-found knowledge to produce their own texts.

Students can observe how changing the point of view alters a story or the presentation of information. They can study how setting influences character and events, and how the same story can be told in a variety of ways. They can consider the words and the arrangements of those words in favorite stories, poems, and nonfiction texts. Structure can be explored in this way as well, as young readers experiment with the forms they find in the books they read. Students can notice and discuss the wide variety of topics that successful authors explore in poetry, fiction, and nonfiction, and consider the topics that they know about and are interested in exploring further through their own writing. No matter what point you might want to make about writing, there is a book to help you make it clear.

Books about writing have been written for students in intermediate grades and middle school; many are listed in Figure 14.4. These books complement those for younger students listed in Chapter 13.

Figure 14 ✿ 4

Good Books About the Writing Process

Bauer, Marion Dane, *Our Stories: A Fiction Workshop for Young Authors*

_____, *What's Your Story? A Young Person's Guide to Writing Fiction*

_____, *A Writer's Story: From Life to Fiction*

Esbensen, Barbara Juster, *A Celebration of Bees: Helping Children Write Poetry*

Fletcher, Ralph, *How Writers Work: Finding a Process That Works for You*

Graves, Donald, *Explore Fiction*

_____, *Explore Nonfiction*

_____, *Explore Poetry*

Grossman, Florence, *Listening to the Bells: Learning to Read Poetry by Writing Poetry*

Janeczko, Paul, *How to Write Poetry*

Livingston, Myra Cohn, *I Am Writing a Poem About: A Game of Poetry*

_____, *Poem-Making: Ways to Begin Writing Poetry*

Stanek, Lou Willett, *Thinking Like a Writer*

WORKING WITH POETRY

Being surrounded by good models of writing helps students learn to write well in a variety of genres. Students usually receive a great deal of exposure to stories, but are often asked to write reports or poems without much experience reading quality nonfiction or poetry. Textbooks in content areas are not always especially well written, and the poetry that students encounter in basal reading series is simply not enough. Susan, who teaches seventh graders, knows that she has to give students consistent and sustained opportunity to read and explore poetry before she can expect them to study it or write it. Consequently, from the beginning of the school year she makes poetry available for students to read and share. She regularly reads or recites poetry to her students, and she takes pains to find poetry that relates to other books they are reading to share with her students.

This time spent with poetry is necessary because many of Susan's students begin the year afraid of poetry; it is that funny kind of writing that they find difficult to understand and that they have learned to dislike because of excessive analysis or handwriting practice. Seven years of answering literal questions about poetry takes its toll. However, because Susan gives her students time to enjoy poetry, by the time she is ready to focus on poetry in her writing curriculum her students are ready to join her enthusiastically. Armed with many of the books on poetry that are listed in Figure 14.4, Susan devises a series of lessons that combine reading and discussing poetry, talking about form and poetic devices, and experimenting with writing various types of poetry using different poetic devices.

For six weeks her three seventh-grade classes spend their 50 minutes a day immersed in reading and writing poetry.

The boundaries between reading and writing workshops have blurred, and they are truly reading like writers—and writing like the readers they are. One student, an avid horse-lover, produced the following poem:

SHOW

We dance into the ring,
a flash of chestnut.
Together,
we can work miracles.
And she dances,
her hooves barely touching the ground.
At "X" we salute the judge.
She nods, and we move on.
At "C" we canter,
a rollicking gait,
and I dare not give her her head.
She, too, is strong.
When we are done
once more we salute the judge
and when we leave, there is also
a flash of blue.
Later, after the show,
I am alone with her in a yellow-green meadow.
We canter.
This time her head is free.
The wind spreads the grass afore us
like a race track.
And she is the horse
And she is winning.

Can you tell that this young woman has enjoyed reading the many books of free verse that Susan has placed in her classroom library?

Assessment

No matter how you structure your literature-based curriculum, assessment will be an important part of what you do. It is impossible to be a responsive teacher unless you are carefully observing what your students are doing. As we state in Chapter 13, a literature-based classroom provides many opportunities for assessment, even though it uses far fewer worksheets. Teachers understand that standardized tests are part of the school year, but they also develop assessment practices that can inform them of their students' progress on a regular, ongoing basis. Teaching Idea 14.3 lists some ideas that teachers can incorporate as part of an ongoing assessment.

One such idea is the "performance sample," a formal observation of students as they are doing what has been assigned. For example, a teacher can sit next to and formally observe a book club discussion group, evaluating the group's effectiveness based on predetermined criteria, criteria that are shared with the students beforehand. Most teachers develop an observation form that allows them to check off or briefly describe whatever it is they are observing.

The curriculum usually also includes gradable "products" that students generate. These, too, become an important component of any teacher's assessment. Students can evaluate their own success and/or progress by compiling a portfolio that reflects their best efforts. Asking students to look at their work and select materials that demonstrate what they have learned is a powerful step toward the practice of self-evaluation, a necessary skill for independent learners.

Summary

There are many ways to structure literature-based instruction in the intermediate grades and middle school. A reading and writing workshop is one structure that allows students time and choice about their reading as well as the opportunity to interact with peers around their reading and writing. Book Club is another structure that allows social interaction, time spent reading, writing about what is read, and talking with peers. One advantage of Book Club is the many opportunities for instruction. Teachers who don't use either of these structures simply infuse literature into their curriculum with the goal of encouraging students to read. Others work toward transforming the curriculum they teach through literature that provides students with alternative perspectives. Finally, many teachers combine literature study and writing, using the books students read as resources for and examples of good writing. All of these ways of incorporating literature into the curriculum are based on assessment practices that keep teachers informed about how their students are performing.

Teaching Idea 14 ☆ 3

Things to Observe About Reading Literature

* What books are your students reading, and how long does it take them to read them? Use reading logs, observe library behavior.

* How do your students decide what book to select? Observe library behavior, and ask students to describe their decision-making process in writing.

* How do your students feel about reading? Conduct a reading attitude survey.

* Are your students good conversationalists about books? Observe a group discussion, and ask students to self-evaluate their group behavior.

* Do your students comprehend the books they are reading? Are they engaged by the books? Observe students' comments during discussion. Review the artifacts that students produce, such as journal or log entries.

Students who read like writers are always interested in what good writers have to say about the writing process. In the September/October 2000 issue of *The Horn Book Magazine*, Jennifer Armstrong writes about writing in "The Writer's Page: Blood from a Stone." Donna Jo Napoli contributes her own perspective on the writing process in "The Writer's Page: What's Math Got to Do with It?" in the January/February 2001 issue. Read these features and start a file that contains contemporary writers' descriptions of the writing process so that you can share them with your students as the need arises. Other good sources for this kind of information include the Newbery Medal acceptance speeches that appear in the July/August issues of *The Horn Book Magazine*.

Selected Children's and Young Adult Book Awards

American Library Association Awards

THE JOHN NEWBERY MEDAL AND HONOR BOOKS

The John Newbery Medal, established in 1922 and named for an eighteenth-century British publisher and bookseller, the first to publish books for children, is given annually for the most distinguished contribution to literature for children published in the United States in the preceding year. This award is administered by the Association for Library Services for Children, a division of the American Library Association.

1922

The Story of Mankind by Hendrik Willem van Loon, Liveright

HONOR BOOKS: *The Great Quest* by Charles Hawes, Little, Brown; *Cedric the Forester* by Bernard Marshall, Appleton; *The Old Tobacco Shop* by William Bowen, Macmillan; *The Golden Fleece and the Heroes Who Lived Before Achilles* by Padraic Colum, Macmillan; *Windy Hill* by Cornelia Meigs, Macmillan

1923

The Voyages of Doctor Doolittle by Hugh Lofting, Harper

HONOR BOOKS: No Record

1924

The Dark Frigate by Charles Hawes, Little, Brown

HONOR BOOKS: No record

1925

Tales from Silver Lands by Charles Finger, Doubleday

HONOR BOOKS: *Nicholas* by Anne Carroll Moore, Putnam; *Dream Coach* by Anne Parrish, Macmillan

1926

Shen of the Sea by Arthur Bowie Chrisman, Dutton

HONOR BOOK: *Voyagers* by Padraic Colum, Macmillan

1927

Smoky, The Cowhorse by Will James, Scribner's

HONOR BOOKS: No record

1928

Gayneck, The Story of a Pigeon by Dhan Gopat Mukeri, Dutton

HONOR BOOKS: *The Wonder Smith and His Son* by Ella Young, Longmans; *Downright Dencey* by Caroline Snedeker, Doubleday

1929

The Trumpeter of Krakow by Eric P. Kelly, Macmillan

HONOR BOOKS: *Pigtail of Ah Lee Ben Loo* by John Benett, Longmans; *Millions of Cats* by Wanda Gág, Coward-McCann; *The Boy Who Was* by Grace Hallock, Dutton; *Clearing Weather* by Cornelia Meigs, Little, Brown; *Runaway Papoose* by Grace Moon, Doubleday; *Tod of the Fens* by Elinor Whitney, Macmillan

1930

Hitty, Her First Hundred Years by Rachel Field, Macmillan

HONOR BOOKS: *Daughter of the Seine* by Jeanette Eaton, Harper; *Pran of Albania* by Elizabeth Miller, Doubleday; *Jumping-Off Place* by Marian Hurd McNeely, Longmans; *Tangle-Coated Horse and Other Tales* by Ella Young, Longmans; *Vaino* by Julia Davis Adams, Dutton; *Little Blacknose* by Hildegarde Swift, Harcourt

1931

The Cat Who Went to Heaven by Elizabeth Coatsworth, Macmillan

HONOR BOOKS: *Floating Island* by Anne Parrish, Harper; *The Dark Star of Itza* by Alida Malkus, Harcourt; *Queer Person* by Ralph Hubbard, Doubleday; *Mountains Are Free* by Julia Davis Adams, Dutton; *Spice and the Devil's Cave* by Agnes Hewes, Knopf; *Meggy Macintosh* by Elizabeth Janet Gray, Doubleday; *Garram the Hunter* by Herbert Best, Doubleday; *Ood-Le-Uk the Wanderer* by Alice Lide and Margaret Johansen, Little, Brown

1932

Waterless Mountain by Laura Adams Armer, Longmans

HONOR BOOKS: *The Fairy Circus* by Dorothy P. Lathrop, Macmillan; *Calico Bush* by Rachel Field, Macmillan; *Boy of the South Seas* by Eunice Tietjens, Coward-McCann; *Out of the Flame* by Eloise Lownsbery, Longmans; *Jane's Island* by Marjorie Allee, Houghton; *Truce of the Wolf and Other Tales of Old Italy* by Mary Gould Davis, Harcourt

1933

Young Fu of the Upper Yangtze by Elizabeth Foreman Lewis, Winston

HONOR BOOKS: *Swift Rivers* by Cornelia Meigs, Little, Brown; *The Railroad to Freedom* by Hildegarde Swift, Harcourt; *Children of the Soil* by Nora Burglon, Doubleday

1934

Invincible Louisa by Cornelia Meigs, Little, Brown

HONOR BOOKS: *The Forgotten Daughter* by Caroline Snedeker, Doubleday; *Swords of Steel* by Elsie Singmaster, Houghton; *ABC Bunny* by Wanda Gág, Coward-McCann; *Winged Girl of Knossos* by Erik Berry, Appleton; *New Land* by Sarah Schmidt, McBride; *Big Tree of Buntahy* by Padraic Colum, Macmillan; *Glory of the Seas* by Agnes Hewes, Knopf; *Apprentice of Florence* by Ann Kyle, Houghton

1935

Dobry by Monica Shannon, Viking

HONOR BOOKS: *Pageant of Chinese History* by Elizabeth Seeger, Longmans; *Davy Crockett* by Constance Rourke, Harcourt; *A Day on Skates* by Hilda Van Stockum, Harper

1936

Caddie Woodlawn by Carol Ryrie Brink, Macmillan

HONOR BOOKS: *Honk, the Moose* by Phil Stong, Dodd, Mead; *The Good Master* by Kate Seredy, Viking; *Young Walter Scott* by Elizabeth Janet Gray, Viking; *All Sail Set* by Armstrong Sperry, Winston

1937

Roller Skates by Ruth Sawyer, Viking

HONOR BOOKS: *Phoebe Fairchild: Her Book* by Lois Lenski, Stokes; *Whistler's Van* by Idwal Jones, Viking; *Golden Basket* by Ludwig Bemelmans, Viking; *Winterbound* by Margery Bianco, Viking; *Audubon* by Constance Rourke, Harcourt; *The Codfish Musket* by Agnes Hewes, Doubleday

1938

The White Stag by Kate Sredy, Viking

HONOR BOOKS: *Pecos Bill* by James Cloyd Bowman, Little, Brown; *Bright Island* by Mabel Robinson, Random; *On the Banks of Plum Creek* by Laura Ingalls Wilder, Harper

1939

Thimble Summer by Elizabeth Enright, Rinehart

HONOR BOOKS: *Nino* by Valenti Angelo, Viking; *Mr. Popper's Penguins* by Richard and Florence Atwater, Little, Brown; *"Hello the Boat!"* by Phyllis Crawford, Holt; *Leader by Destiny: George Washington, Man and Patriot* by Jeanette Eaton, Harcourt; *Penn* by Elizabeth Janet Gray, Viking

1940

Daniel Boone by James Daugherty, Viking

HONOR BOOKS: *The Singing Tree* by Kate Seredy, Viking; *Runner of the Mountain Tops* by Mabel Robinson, Random; *By the Shores of Silver Lake* by Laura Ingalls Wilder, Harper; *Boy with a Pack* by Stephen W. Meader, Harcourt

1941

Call It Courage by Armstrong Sperry, Macmillan

HONOR BOOKS: *Blue Willow* by Doris Gates, Viking; *Young Mac of Fort Vancouver* by Mary Jane Carr, Harper; *The Long Winter* by Laura Ingalls Wilder, Harper; *Nansen* by Anna Gertrude Hall, Viking

1942

The Matchlock Gun by Walter D. Edmonds, Dodd, Mead

HONOR BOOKS: *Little Town on the Prairie* by Laura Ingalls Wilder, Harper; *George Washington's World* by Genevieve Foster, Scribner's; *Indian Captive: The Story of Mary Jemison* by Lois Lenski, Harper, *Down Ryton Water* by Eva Roe Gaggin, Viking

1943

Adam of the Road by Elizabeth Janet Gray, Viking

HONOR BOOKS: *The Middle Moffat* by Eleanor Estes, Harcourt; *Have You Seen Tom Thumb?* by Mabel Leigh Hunt, Harper

1944

Johnny Tremain by Esther Forbes, Houghton

HONOR BOOKS: *These Happy Golden Years* by Laura Ingalls Wilder, Harper; *Fog Magic* by Julia Sauer, Viking; *Rufus M.* by Eleanor Estes, Harcourt; *Mountain Born* by Elizabeth Yates, Coward-McCann

1945

Rabbit Hill by Robert Lawson, Viking

HONOR BOOKS: *The Hundred Dresses* by Eleanor Estes, Harcourt; *The Silver Pencil* by Alice Dalgliesh, Scribner's; *Abraham Lincoln's World* by Genevieve Foster, Scribner's; *Lone Journey: The Life of Roger Williams* by Jeanette Eaton, Harcourt

1946

Strawberry Girl by Lois Lenski, Harper

HONOR BOOKS: *Justin Morgan Had a Horse* by Marguerite Henry, Rand; *The Moved-Outers* by Florence Crannel Means, Houghton; *Bhimsa, the Dancing Bear* by Christine Weston, Scribner's; *New Found World* by Katherine Shippen, Viking

1947

Miss Hickory by Carolyn Sherwin Bailey, Viking

HONOR BOOKS: *Wonderful Year* by Nancy Barnes, Messner; *BigTree* by Mary and Conrad Buff, Viking; *The Heavenly Tenants* by William Maxwell, Harper; *The Avion My Uncle Flew* by Cyrus Fisher, Appleton; *The Hidden Treasure of Glaston* by Eleanore Jewett, Viking

1948

The Twenty-One Balloons by William Pene du Bois, Viking

HONOR BOOKS: *Pancakes-Paris* by Claire Huchet Bishop, Viking; *Li Lun, Lad of Courage* by Carolyn Treffinger, Abingdon; *The Quaint and Curious Quest of Johnny Longfoot* by Catherine Besterman, Bobbs; *The Cow-Tail Switch, and Other West African Stories* by Harold Courlander, Holt; *Misty of Chincoteague* by Marguerite Henry, Rand

1949

King of the Wind by Marguerite Henry, Rand McNally

HONOR BOOKS: *Seabird* by Holling C. Holling, Houghton; *Daughter of the Mountains* by Louise Rankin, Viking; *My Father's Dragon* by Ruth S. Gannett, Random; *Story of the Negro* by Arna Bontemps, Knopf

1950

The Door in the Wall by Marguerite de Angeli, Doubleday

HONOR BOOKS: *Tree of Freedom* by Rebecca Caudill, Viking; *The Blue Cat of Castle Town* by Catherine Coblentz, Longmans; *Kildee House* by Rutherford Montgomery, Doubleday; *George Washington* by Genevieve Foster, Scribner's, *Song of the Pines* by Walter and Marion Havighurst, Winston

1951

Amos Fortune, Free Man by Elizabeth Yates, Aladdin

HONOR BOOKS: *Better Known as Johnny Appleseed* by Mabel Leigh Hunt, Harper; *Gandhi; Fighter Without a Sword* by Jeanette Eaton, Morrow; *Abraham Lincoln, Friend of the People* by Clara Ingram Judson, Follett; *The Story of Appleby Capple* by Anne Parrish, Harper

1952

Ginger Pye by Eleanor Estes, Harcourt

HONOR BOOKS: *Americans Before Columbus* by Elizabeth Baity, Viking; *Minn of the Mississippi* by Holling C. Holling, Houghton; *The Defender* by Nicholas Kalashnikoff, Scribner's; *The Light at Tern Rock* by Julia Sauer, Viking; *The Apple and the Arrow* by Mary and Conrad Buff, Houghton

1953

Secret of the Andes by Ann Nolan Clark, Viking

HONOR BOOKS: *Charlotte's Web* by E. B. White, HarperCollins; *Moccasin Trail* by Eloise McGraw, Coward-McCann; *Red Sails to Capri* by Ann Weil, Viking; *The Bears on Hemlock Mountain* by Alice Dalgliesh, Scribner's; *Birthdays of Freedom*, Vol. 1, by Genevieve Foster, Scribner's

1954

. . . and now Miguel by Joseph Krumgold, HarperCollins

HONOR BOOKS: *All Alone* by Claire Huchet Bishop, Viking; *Shadrach* by Meindert DeJong, HarperCollins; *Hurry Home, Candy* by Meindert DeJong, HarperCollins; *Theodore Roosevelt, Fighting Patriot* by Clara Ingram Judson, Follett; *Magic Maize* by Mary and Conrad Buff, Houghton

1955

The Wheel on the School by Meindert DeJong, HarperCollins

HONOR BOOKS: *The Courage of Sarah Noble* by Alice Dalgliesh, Scribner's; *Banner in the Sky* by James Ullman, HarperCollins

1956

Carry on, Mr. Bowditch by Jean Lee Latham, Houghton Mifflin

HONOR BOOKS: *The Secret River* by Marjorie Kinnan Rawlings, Scribner's; *The Golden Name Day* by Jennie Linquist, HarperCollins; *Men, Microscopes, and Living Things* by Katherine Shippen, Viking

1957

Miracles on Maple Hill by Virginia Sorensen, Harcourt

HONOR BOOKS: *Old Yeller* by Fred Gipson, HarperCollins; *The House of Sixty Fathers* by Meindert DeJong, HarperCollins; *Mr. Justice Holmes* by Clara Ingram Judson, Follett; *The Corn Grows Ripe* by Dorothy Rhoads; Viking; *Black Fox of Lorne* by Marguerite de Angeli, Doubleday

1958

Rifles for Watie by Harold Keith, Crowell

HONOR BOOKS: *The Horsecatcher* by Mari Sandoz, Westminster; *Gone-Away Lake* by Elizabeth Enright, Harcourt Brace; *The Great Wheel* by Robert Lawson, Viking; *Tom Paine, Freedom's Apostle* by Leo Gurko, HarperCollins

1959

The Witch of Blackbird Pond by Elizabeth George Speare, Houghton Mifflin

HONOR BOOKS: *The Family Under the Bridge* by Natalie Savage Carlson, HarperCollins; *Along Came a Dog* by Meindert DeJong, HarperCollins; *Chucaro: Wild Pony of the Pampa* by Francis Kalnay, Harcourt Brace; *The Perilous Road* by William O. Steele, Harcourt Brace

1960

Onion John by Joseph Krumgold, HarperCollins

HONOR BOOKS: *My Side of the Mountain* by Jean George, Dutton: *America Is Born* by Gerald W. Johnson, Morrow; *The Gammage Cup* by Carol Kendall, Harcourt Brace

1961

Island of the Blue Dolphins by Scott O'Dell, Houghton Mifflin

HONOR BOOKS: *America Moves Forward* by Gerald W. Johnson, Morrow; *Old Ramon* by Jack Schaefer, Houghton Mifflin; *The Cricket in Times Square* by George Selden, Farrar, Straus and Giroux

1962

The Bronze Bow by Elizabeth George Speare, Houghton Mifflin

HONOR BOOKS: *Frontier Living* by Edwin Tunis, World; *The Golden Goblet* by Eloise McGraw, Coward-McCann; *Belling the Tiger* by Mary Stolz, HarperCollins

1963

A Wrinkle in Time by Madeleine L'Engle, Farrar, Straus and Giroux

HONOR BOOKS: *Thistle and Thyme* by Sorche Nic Leodhas, Holt; *Men of Athens* by Olivia Coolidge, Houghton

1964

It's Like This, Cat by Emily Cheney Neville, Harper

HONOR BOOKS: *Rascal* by Sterling North, Dutton; *The Loner* by Ester Wier, McKay

1965

Shadow of a Bull by Maia Wojciechowska, Atheneum

HONOR BOOK: *Across Five Aprils* by Irene Hunt, Follett

1966

I, Juan de Pareja by Elizabeth Borten de Treviño, Farrar, Straus and Giroux

HONOR BOOKS: *The Black Cauldron* by Lloyd Alexander, Holt; *The Animal Family* by Randall Jarrell, Pantheon; *The Noonday Friends* by Mary Stolz, Harper

1967

Up a Road Slowly by Irene Hunt, Follett

HONOR BOOKS: *The King's Fifth* by Scott O'Dell, Houghton; *Zlateh the Goat and Other Stories* by Isaac Bashevis Singer, Harper; *The Jazz Man* by Mary H. Weik, Atheneum

1968

From the Mixed-Up Files of Mrs. Basil E. Frankweiler by E. L. Konigsburg, Atheneum

HONOR BOOKS: *Jennifer, Hecate, Macbeth, William McKinley, and Me, Elizabeth* by E. L. Konigsburg, Atheneum; *The Black Pearl* by Scott O'Dell, Houghton; *The Fearsome Inn* by Isaac Bashevis Singer, Scribner's; *The Egypt Game* by Zilpha Keatley Snyder, Atheneum

1969

The High King by Lloyd Alexander, Holt

HONOR BOOKS: *To Be a Slave* by Julius Lester, Dial; *When Shlemiel Went to Warsaw and Other Stories* by Isaac Bashevis Singer, Farrar, Straus and Giroux

1970

Sounder by William H. Armstrong, Harper

HONOR BOOKS: *Our Eddie* by Sulamith Ish-Kishor, Pantheon; *The Many Ways of Seeing: An Introduction to the Pleasures of Art* by Janet Gaylord Moore, World; *Journey Outside* by Mary Q. Steele, Viking

1971

Summer of the Swans by Betsy Byars, Viking

HONOR BOOKS: *Kneeknock Rise* by Natalie Babbitt, Farrar, Straus and Giroux; *Enchantress from the Stars* by Sylvia Louise Engdahl, Atheneum; *Sing Down the Moon* by Scott O'Dell, Houghton

1972

Mrs. Frisby and the Rats of NIMH by Robert C. O'Brien, Atheneum

HONOR BOOKS: *Incident at Hawk's Hill* by Allan W. Eckert, Little, Brown; *The Planet of Junior Brown* by Virginia Hamilton, Macmillan; *The Tombs of Atuan* by Ursula K. Le Guin, Atheneum; *Annie and the Old One* by Miska Miles, Little, Atlantic; *The Headless Cupid* by Zilpha Keatley Snyder, Atheneum

1973

Julie of the Wolves by Jean Craighead George, Harper

HONOR BOOKS: *Frog and Toad Together* by Arnold Lobel, Harper; *The Upstairs Room* by Johanna Reiss, Harper; *The Witches of Worm* by Zilpha Keatley Snyder, Atheneum

1974

The Slave Dancer by Paula Fox, Bradbury

HONOR BOOKS: *The Dark Is Rising* by Susan Cooper, Atheneum, McElderry

1975

M. C. Higgins, the Great by Virginia Hamilton, Macmillan

HONOR BOOKS: *Figgs and Phantoms* by Ellen Raskin, Dutton; *My Brother Sam Is Dead* by James Lincoln and Christopher Collier, Four Winds; *The Perilous Guard* by Elizabeth Marie Pope, Houghton; *Philip Hall Likes Me. I Reckon Maybe* by Bette Greene, Dial

1976

The Grey King by Susan Cooper, Atheneum, McElderry

HONOR BOOKS: *The Hundred Penny Box* by Sharon Bell Mathis, Viking; *Dragonwings* by Laurence Yep, Harper

1977

Roll of Thunder, Hear My Cry by Mildred D. Taylor, Dial

HONOR BOOKS: *Abel's Island* by William Steig, Farrar, Straus and Giroux; *A String in the Harp* by Nancy Bond, McElderry

1978

Bridge to Terabithia by Katherine Paterson, Harper

HONOR BOOKS: *Ramona and Her Father* by Beverly Cleary, Morrow; *Anpao: An American Indian Odyssey* by Jamake Highwater, Harper

1979

The Westing Game by Ellen Raskin, Dutton

HONOR BOOKS: *The Great Gilly Hopkins* by Katherine Paterson, Harper

1980

A Gathering of Days: A New England Girl's Journal, 1830–32 by Joan Blos, Scribner's

HONOR BOOK: *The Road from Home: The Story of an Armenian Girl* by David Kherdian, Greenwillow

1981

Jacob Have I Loved by Katherine Paterson, Harper

HONOR BOOKS: *The Fledgling* by Jane Langton, Harper; *A Ring of Endless Light* by Madeleine L'Engle, Farrar, Straus and Giroux

1982

A Visit to William Blake's Inn: Poems for Innocent and Experienced Travelers by Nancy Willard, Harcourt

HONOR BOOKS: *Ramona Quimby, Age 8* by Beverly Cleary, Morrow; *Upon the Head of the Goat: A Childhood in Hungary, 1939–1944* by Aranka Siegel, Farrar, Straus and Giroux

1983

Dicey's Song by Cynthia Voigt, Atheneum

HONOR BOOKS: *The Blue Sword* by Robin McKinley, Greenwillow; *Dr. De Soto* by William Steig, Farrar, Straus and Giroux; *Graven Images* by Paul Fleischman, Harper; *Homesick: My Own Story* by Jean Fritz, Putnam; *Sweet Whispers, Brother Rush* by Virginia Hamilton, Philomel

1984

Dear Mr. Henshaw by Beverly Cleary, Morrow

HONOR BOOKS: *The Wish Giver: Three Tales of Coven Tree* by Bill Brittain, Harper; *A Solitary Blue* by Cynthia Voigt, Atheneum; *The Sign of the Beaver* by Elizabeth George Speare, Houghton; *Sugaring Time* by Kathryn Lasky, Macmillan

1985

The Hero and the Crown by Robin McKinley, Greenwillow

HONOR BOOKS: *The Moves Make the Man* by Bruce Brooks, Harper; *One-Eyed Cat* by Paula Fox, Bradbury; *Like Jake and Me* by Mavis Jukes, Knopf

1986

Sarah, Plain and Tall by Patricia MacLachlan, Harper

HONOR BOOKS: *Commodore Perry in the Land of Shogun* by Rhoda Blumberg, Lothrop; *Dogsong* by Gary Paulsen, Bradbury

1987

The Whipping Boy by Sid Fleischman, Greenwillow

HONOR BOOKS: *On My Honor* by Marion Dane Bauer, Clarion; *A Fine White Dust* by Cynthia Rylant, Bradbury; *Volcano* by Patricia Lauber, Bradbury

1988

Lincoln: A Photobiography by Russell Freedman, Clarion

HONOR BOOKS: *Hatchet* by Gary Paulsen, Bradbury; *After the Rain* by Norma Fox Mazer, Morrow

1989

Joyful Noise: Poems for Two Voices by Paul Fleischman, Harper

HONOR BOOKS: *In the Beginning: Creation Stories from Around the World* by Virginia Hamilton, Harcourt; *Scorpions* by Walter Dean Myers, Harper

1990

Number the Stars by Lois Lowry, Houghton

HONOR BOOKS: *Afternoon of the Elves* by Janet Taylor Lisle, Orchard; *Shabanu: Daughter of the Wind* by Suzanne Fisher Staples, Knopf; *The Winter Room* by Gary Paulsen, Orchard

1991

Maniac Magee by Jerry Spinelli, Little, Brown

HONOR BOOK: *The True Confessions of Charlotte Doyle* by Avi, Orchard

1992

Shiloh by Phyllis Reynolds Naylor, Atheneum

HONOR BOOKS: *Nothing but the Truth: A Documentary Novel* by Avi, Orchard; *The Wright Brothers: How They Invented the Airplane* by Russell Freeman, Holiday

1993

Missing May by Cynthia Rylant, Orchard

HONOR BOOKS: *What Hearts* by Bruce Brooks, Harper; *The Dark Thirty: Southern Tales of the Supernatural* by Patricia C. McKissack, Knopf; *Somewhere in the Darkness* by Walter Dean Myers, Scholastic

1994

The Giver by Lois Lowry, Houghton

HONOR BOOKS: *Crazy Lady!* by Jane Leslie Conley, Harper; *Dragon's Gate* by Laurence Yep, Harper; *Eleanor Roosevelt: A Life of Discovery* by Russell Freedman, Clarion

1995

Walk Two Moons by Sharon Creech, Harper

HONOR BOOKS: *Catherine, Called Birdy* by Karen Cushman, Clarion; *The Ear, the Eye and the Arm* by Nancy Farmer, Orchard

1996

The Midwife's Apprentice by Karen Cushman, Clarion

HONOR BOOKS: *The Great Fire* by Jim Murphy, Scholastic; *The Watsons Go to Birmingham—1963* by Christopher Paul Curtis, Delacorte; *What Jamie Saw* by Carolyn Coman, Front Street; *Yolanda's Genius* by Carol Fenner, McElderry

1997

The View from Saturday by E. L. Konigsburg, Karl/Atheneum

HONOR BOOKS: *A Girl Named Disaster* by Nancy Farmer, Jackson/Orchard; *The Moorchild* by Eloise McGraw, McElderry; *The Thief* by Megan Whalen Turner, Greenwillow; *Belle Prater's Boy* by Ruth White, Farrar, Straus and Giroux

1998

Out of the Dust by Karen Hesse, Scholastic Press

HONOR BOOKS: *Lilly's Crossing* by Patricia Reilly Giff, Delacorte; *Ella Enchanted* by Gail C. Levine, HarperCollins; *Wringer* by Jerry Spinelli, HarperCollins

1999

Holes by Louis Sachar, Farrar, Straus and Giroux

HONOR BOOK: *A Long Way from Chicago* by Richard Peck, Dial

2000

Bud Not Buddy by Christopher Paul Curtis, Delacorte

HONOR BOOKS: *Getting Near to Baby* by Audrey Coloumbis, Delacorte; *26 Fairmount Avenue* by Tomie dePaola, Putnam; *Our Only May Amelia* by Jennifer L. Holm, HarperCollins

2001

A Year Down Yonder by Richard Peck, Penguin Putnam Dial, Phyllis Fogelman Books

HONOR BOOKS: *Hope Was Here* by Joan Bauer, Putnam; *The Wanderer* by Sharon Creech, HarperCollins/Joanna Cotler Books; *Because of Winn-Dixie* by Kate DiCamillo, Candlewick; *Joey Pigza Loses Control* by Jack Gantos, Farrar, Straus and Giroux

THE RANDOLPH CALDECOTT MEDAL AND HONOR BOOKS

The Randolph Caldecott Medal, established in 1938 and named for a nineteenth-century British illustrator of books for children, is given annually to the illustrator of the most distinguished picture book for children published in the United States in the preceding year. This award is administered by the Association for Library Services for Children, a division of the American Library Association.

1938

Animals of the Bible by Helen Dean Fish, illus. by Dorothy P. Lathrop, Lippincott

HONOR BOOKS: *Seven Simeons* by Boris Artzybasheff, Viking; *Four and Twenty Blackbirds* by Helen Dean Fish, illus. by Robert Lawson, Stokes

1939

Mei Li by Thomas Handforth, Doubleday

HONOR BOOKS: *The Forest Pool* by Laura Adams Armer, Longmans; *Wee Gillis* by Munro Leaf, illus. by Robert Lawson, Viking; *Snow White and the Seven Dwarfs* by Wanda Gág, Coward; *Barkis* by Clare Newberry, Harper; *Andy and the Lion* by James Daugherty, Viking

1940

Abraham Lincoln by Ingri and Edgar Parin D'Aulaire, Doubleday

HONOR BOOKS: *Cock-a-Doodle Doo . . .* by Berta and Elmer Hader, Macmillan; *Madeline* by Ludwig Bemelmans, Viking; *The Ageless Story* by Lauren Ford, Dodd

1941

They Were Strong and Good by Robert Lawson, Viking

HONOR BOOK: *April's Kittens* by Clare Newberry, Harper

1942

Make Way for Ducklings by Robert McCloskey, Viking

HONOR BOOKS: *An American ABC* by Maud and Miska Petersham, Macmillan; *In My Mother's House* by Ann Nolan Clark, illus. by Velino Gerrera, Viking; *Paddle-to-the-Sea* by Holling C. Holling, Houghton; *Nothing at All* by Wanda Gág, Coward-McCann

1943

The Little House by Virginia Lee Burton, Houghton

HONOR BOOKS: *Dash and Dart* by Mary and Conrad Buff, Viking; *Marshmallow* by Clare Newberry, Harper

1944

Many Moons by James Thurber, illus. by Louis Slobodkin, Harcourt

HONOR BOOKS: *Small Rain: Verses from the Bible* selected by Jessie Orton Jones, illus. by Elizabeth Orton Jones, Viking; *Pierre Pigeon* by Lee Kingman, illus. by Arnold E. Bare, Houghton; *The Mighty Hunter* by Berta and Elmer Hader, Macmillan; *A Child's Good Night Book* by Margaret Wise Brown, illus. by Jean Charlot, Scott; *Good Luck Horse* by Chih-Yi Chan, illus. by Plao Chan, Whittlesey

1945

Prayer for a Child by Rachel Field, illus. by Elizabeth Orton Jones, Macmillan

HONOR BOOKS: *Mother Goose*, illus. by Tasha Tudor, Walck; *In the Forest* by Marie Hall Ets, Viking; *Yonie Wondernose* by Marguerite de Angeli, Doubleday; *The Christmas Anna Angel* by Ruth Sawyer, illus. by Kate Seredy, Viking

1946

The Rooster Crows . . . (traditional Mother Goose) illus. by Maud and Miska Petersham, Macmillan

HONOR BOOKS: *Little Lost Lamb* by Golden MacDonald, illus. by Leonard Weisgard, Doubleday; *Sing Mother Goose* by Opal Wheeler, illus. by Marjorie Torrey, Dutton; *My Mother Is the Most Beautiful Woman in the World* by Becky Reyher, illus. by Ruth Gannett, Lothrop; *You Can Write Chinese* by Kurt Weise, Viking

1947

The Little Island by Golden MacDonald, illus. by Leonard Weisgard, Doubleday

HONOR BOOKS: *Rain Drop Splash* by Alvin Tresselt, illus. by Leonard Weisgard, Lothrop; *Boats on the River* by Marjorie Flack, illus. by Jay Hyde Barnum, Viking; *Timothy Turtle* by Al Graham, illus. by Tony Palazzo, Viking; *Pedro, the Angel of Olvera Street* by Leo Politi, Scribner's; *Sing in Praise: A Collection of the Best Loved Hymns* by Opal Wheeler, illus. by Marjorie Torrey, Dutton

1948

White Snow, Bright Snow by Alvin Tresselt, illus. by Roger Duvoisin, Lothrop

HONOR BOOKS: *Stone Soup* by Marcia Brown, Scribner's; *McElligot's Pool* by Dr. Seuss, Random; *Bambino the Clown* by George Schreiber, Viking; *Roger and the Fox* by Lavinia Davis, illus. by Hildegard Woodward, Doubleday; *Song of Robin Hood* ed. by Anne Malcolmson, illus. by Virginia Lee Burton, Houghton

1949

The Big Snow by Berta and Elmer Hader, Macmillan

HONOR BOOKS: *Blueberries for Sal* by Robert McCloskey, Viking; *All Around the Town* by Phyllis McGinley, illus. by Helen Stone, Lippincott; *Juanita* by Leo Politi, Scribner's; *Fish in the Air* by Kurt Wiese, Viking

1950

Song of the Swallows by Leo Politi, Scribner's

HONOR BOOKS: *America's Ethan Allen* by Stewart Holbrook, illus. by Lynd Ward, Houghton; *The Wild Birthday Cake* by Lavinia Davis, illus. by Hildegard Woodward, Doubleday; *The Happy Day* by Ruth Krauss, illus. by Marc Simont, Harper; *Bartholomew and the Oobleck* by Dr. Seuss, Random; *Henry Fisherman* by Marcia Brown, Scribner's

1951

The Egg Tree by Katherine Milhous, Scribner's

HONOR BOOKS: *Dick Whittington and His Cat* by Marcia Brown, Scribner's; *The Two Reds* by William Lipkind, illus. by Nicholas Mordvinoff, Harcourt; *If I Ran the Zoo* by Dr. Seuss, Random; *The Most Wonderful Doll in the World* by Phyllis McGinley, illus. by Helen Stone, Lippincott; *T-Bone, the Baby Sitter* by Clare Newberry, Harper

1952

Finders Keepers by William Lipkind, illus. by Nicholas Mordvinoff, Harcourt

HONOR BOOKS: *Mr. T. W. Anthony Woo* by Marie Hall Ets, Viking; *Skipper John's Cook* by Marcia Brown, Scribner's; *All Falling Down* by Gene Zion, illus. by Margaret Bloy Graham, Harper; *Bear Party* by William Pène du Bois, Viking; *Feather Mountain* by Elizabeth Olds, Houghton

1953

The Biggest Bear by Lynd Ward, Houghton

HONOR BOOKS: *Puss in Boots* by Charles Perrault, illus. and tr. by Marcia Brown, Scribner's; *One Morning in Maine* by Robert McCloskey, Viking; *Ape in a Cape* by Fritz Eichenberg, Harcourt; *The Storm Book* by Charlotte Zolotow, illus. by Margaret Bloy Graham, Harper; *Five Little Monkeys* by Juliet Kepes, Houghton

1954

Madeline's Rescue by Ludwig Bemelmans, Viking

HONOR BOOKS: *Journey Cake, Ho!* by Ruth Sawyer, illus. by Robert McCloskey, Viking; *When Will the World Be Mine?* by Miriam Schlein, illus. by Jean Charlot, Scott; *The Steadfast Tin Soldier* by Hans Christian Anderson, illus. by Marcia Brown, Scribner's; *A Very Special House* by Ruth Krauss, illus. by Maurice Sendak, Harper; *Green Eyes* by A. Birnbaum, Capitol

1955

Cinderella, or the Little Glass Slipper by Charles Perrault, tr. and illus. by Marcia Brown, Scribner's

HONOR BOOKS: *Books of Nursery and Mother Goose Rhymes*, illus. by Marguerite de Angeli, Doubleday; *Wheel on the Chimney* by Margaret Wise Brown, illus. by Tibor Gergely, Lippincott; *The Thanksgiving Story* by Alice Dalgliesh, illus. by Helen Sewell, Scribner's

1956

Frog Went A-Courtin' ed. by John Langstaff, illus. by Feodor Rojankovsky, Harcourt

HONOR BOOKS: *Play with Me* by Marie Hall Ets, Viking; *Crow Boy* by Taro Tashima, Viking

1957

A Tree Is Nice by Janice May Udry, illus. by Marc Simont, Harper

HONOR BOOKS: *Mr. Penny's Race Horse* by Marie Hall Ets, Viking; *1 Is One* by Tasha Tudor, Walck; *Anatole* by Eve Titus, illus. by Paul Galdone, McGraw; *Gillespie and the Guards* by Benjamin Elkin, illus. by James Daughtery, Viking; *Lion* by William Pène du Bois, Viking

1958

Time of Wonder by Robert McCloskey, Viking

HONOR BOOKS: *Fly High, Fly Low* by Don Freeman, Viking; *Anatole and the Cat* by Eve Titus, illus. by Paul Galdone, McGraw

1959

Chanticleer and the Fox adapted from Chaucer and illus. by Barbara Cooney, Crowell

HONOR BOOKS: *The House That Jack Built* by Antonio Frasconi, Harcourt; *What Do You Say, Dear?* by Sesyle Joslin, illus. by Maurice Sendak, Scott; *Umbrella* by Taro Yashima, Viking

1960

Nine Days to Christmas by Marie Hall Ets and Aurora Labastida, illus. by Marie Hall Ets, Viking

HONOR BOOKS: *Houses from the Sea* by Alice E. Goudey, illus. by Adrienne Adams, Scribner's; *The Moon Jumpers* by Janice May Udry, illus. by Maurice Sendak, Harper

1961

Baboushka and the Three Kings by Ruth Robbins, illus. by Nicolas Sidjakov, Parnassus

HONOR BOOK: *Inch by Inch* by Leo Lionni, Obolensky

1962

Once a Mouse . . . by Marcia Brown, Scribner's

HONOR BOOKS: *The Fox Went Out on a Chilly Night* by Peter Spier, Doubleday; *Little Bear's Visit* by Else Holmelund Minarik, illus. by Maurice Sendak, Harper; *The Day We Saw the Sun Come Up* by Alice E. Goudey, illus. by Adrienne Adams, Scribner's

1963

The Snowy Day by Ezra Jack Keats, Viking

HONOR BOOKS: *The Sun Is a Golden Earring* by Natalie M. Belting, illus. by Bernarda Bryson, Holt; *Mr. Rabbit and the Lovely Present* by Charlotte Zolotow, illus. by Maurice Sendak, Harper

1964

Where the Wild Things Are by Maurice Sendak, Harper

HONOR BOOKS: *Swimmy* by Leo Lionni, Pantheon; *All in the Morning Early* by Sorche Nic Leodhas, illus. by Evaline Ness, Holt; *Mother Goose and Nursery Rhymes*, illus. by Philip Reed, Atheneum

1965

May I Bring a Friend? by Beatrice Schenk de Regniers, illus. by Beni Montresor, Atheneum

HONOR BOOKS: *Rain Makes Applesauce* by Julian Scheer, illus. by Marvin Bileck, Holiday; *The Wave* by Margaret Hodges, illus. by Blair Lent, Houghton; *A Pocketful of Cricket* by Rebecca Caudill, illus. by Evaline Ness, Holt

1966

Always Room for One More by Sorche Nic Leodhas, illus. by Nonny Hogrogian, Holt

HONOR BOOKS: *Hide and Seek Fog* by Alvin Tresselt, illus. by Roger Duvoisin, Lothrop; *Just Me* by Marie Hall Ets, Viking; *Tom Tit Tot* by Evaline Ness, Scribner's

1967

Sam, Bangs and Moonshine by Evaline Ness, Holt

HONOR BOOK: *One Wide River to Cross* by Barbara Emberley, illus. by Ed Emberley, Prentice

1968

Drummer Hoff by Barbara Emberley, illus. by Ed Emberley, Prentice

HONOR BOOKS: *Frederick* by Leo Lionni, Pantheon; *Seashore Story* by Taro Yashima, Viking; *The Emperor and the Kite* by Jane Yolen, illus. by Ed Young, World

1969

The Fool of the World and the Flying Ship by Arthur Ransome, illus. by Uri Shulevitz, Farrar, Straus and Giroux

HONOR BOOK: *Why the Sun and the Moon Live in the Sky* by Elphinstone Dayrell, illus. by Blair Lent, Houghton

1970

Sylvester and the Magic Pebble by William Steig, Windmill

HONOR BOOKS: *Goggles!* by Ezra Jack Keats, Macmillan; *Alexander and the Wind-Up Mouse* by Leo Lionni, Pantheon; *Pop Corn and Ma Goodness* by Edna Mitchell Preston, illus. by Robert Andrew Parker, Viking; *Thy Friend, Obadiah* by Brinton Turkle, Viking; *The Judge* by Harve Zemach, illus. by Margot Zemach, Farrar, Straus and Giroux

1971

A Story—A Story by Gail E. Haley, Atheneum

HONOR BOOKS: *The Angry Moon* by William Sleator, illus. by Blair Lent, Atlantic/Little; *Frog and Toad Are Friends* by Arnold Lobel, Harper; *In the Night Kitchen* by Maurice Sendak, Harper

1972

One Fine Day by Nonny Hogrogian, Macmillan

HONOR BOOKS: *If All the Seas Were One Sea* by Janina Domanska, Macmillan; *Moja Means One: Swahili Counting Book* by Muriel Feelings, illus. by Tom Feelings, Dial; *Hildidid's Night* by Cheli Duran Ryan, illus. by Arnold Lobel, Macmillan

1973

The Funny Little Woman retold by Arlene Mosel, illus. by Blair Lent, Dutton

HONOR BOOKS: *Anansi the Spider* adapted and illus. by Gerald McDermott, Holt; *Hosie's Alphabet* by Hosea, Tobias, and Lisa Baskin, illus. by Leonard Baskin, Viking; *Snow-White and the Seven Dwarfs* tr. by Randall Jarrell, illus. by Nancy Ekholm Burkert, Farrar, Straus and Giroux; *When Clay Sings* by Byrd Baylor, illus. by Tom Bahti, Scribner's

1974

Duffy and the Devil by Harve Zemach, illus. by Margot Zemach, Farrar, Straus and Giroux

HONOR BOOKS: *Three Jovial Huntsmen* by Susan Jeffers, Bradbury; *Cathedral: The Story of Its Construction* by David Macaulay, Houghton

1975

Arrow to the Sun adapted and illus. by Gerald McDermott, Viking

HONOR BOOK: *Jambo Means Hello* by Muriel Feelings, illus. by Tom Feelings, Dial

1976

Why Mosquitoes Buzz in People's Ears retold by Verna Aardema, illus. by Leo and Diane Dillon, Dial

HONOR BOOKS: *The Desert Is Theirs* by Byrd Baylor, illus. by Peter Parnall, Scribner's; *Strega Nona* retold and illus. by Tomie dePaola, Prentice

1977

Ashanti to Zulu: African Traditions by Margaret Musgrove, illus. by Leo and Diane Dillon, Dial

HONOR BOOKS: *The Amazing Bone* by William Steig, Farrar, Straus and Giroux; *The Contest* retold and illus. by Nonny Hogrogian, Greenwillow; *Fish for Supper* by M. B. Goffstein, Dial; *The Golem* by Beverly Brodsky McDermott, Lippincott; *Hawk, I'm Your Brother* by Byrd Baylor, illus. by Peter Parnall, Scribner's

1978

Noah's Ark illus. by Peter Spier, Doubleday

HONOR BOOKS: *Castle* by David Macaulay, Houghton; *It Could Always Be Worse* retold and illus. by Margot Zemach, Farrar, Straus and Giroux

1979

The Girl Who Loved Wild Horses by Paul Goble, Bradbury

HONOR BOOKS: *Freight Train* by Donald Crews, Greenwillow; *The Way to Start a Day* by Byrd Baylor, illus. by Peter Parnall, Scribner's

1980

Ox-Cart Man by Donald Hall, illus. by Barbara Cooney, Viking

HONOR BOOKS: *Ben's Trumpet* by Rachel Isadora, Greenwillow; *The Garden of Abdul Gasazi* by Chris Van Allsburg, Houghton

1981

Fables by Arnold Lobel, Harper

HONOR BOOKS: *The Bremen-Town Musicians* by Ilse Plume, Doubleday; *The Grey Lady and the Strawberry Snatcher* by Molly Bang, Four Winds; *Mice Twice* by Joseph Low, McElderry/Atheneum; *Truck* by Donald Crews, Greenwillow

1982

Jumanji by Chris Van Allsburg, Houghton

HONOR BOOKS: *Where the Buffaloes Begin* by Olaf Baker, illus. by Stephan Gammell, Warne; *On Market Street* by Arnold Lobel, illus. by Anita Lobel, Greenwillow; *Outside Over There* by Maurice Sendak, Harper; *A Visit to William Blake's Inn* by Nancy Willard, illus. by Alice and Martin Provensen, Harcourt

1983

Shadow by Blaise Cendrars, tr. and illus. by Marcia Brown, Scribner's

HONOR BOOKS: *When I Was Young in the Mountains* by Cynthia Rylant, illus. by Diane Goode, Dutton; *A Chair for My Mother* by Vera B. Williams, Greenwillow

1984

The Glorious Flight: Across the Channel with Louis Bleriot by Alice and Martin Provensen, Viking

HONOR BOOKS: *Ten, Nine, Eight* by Molly Bang, Greenwillow; *Little Red Riding Hood* retold and illus. by Trina Schart Hyman, Holiday

1985

St. George and the Dragon retold by Margaret Hodges, illus. by Trina Schart Hyman, Little, Brown

HONOR BOOKS: *Hansel and Gretel* retold by Rika Lesser, illus. by Paul O. Zelinsky, Dodd; *Have You Seen My Duckling?* by Nancy Tafuri, Greenwillow; *The Story of Jumping Mouse* by John Steptoe, Lothrop

1986

The Polar Express by Chris Van Allsburg, Houghton

HONOR BOOKS: *The Relatives Came* by Cynthia Rylant, illus. by Stephen Gammell, Bradbury; *King Bidgood's in the Bathtub* by Audrey Wood, illus. by Don Wood, Harcourt

1987

Hey, Al by Arthur Yorinks, illus. by Richard Egielski, Farrar, Straus and Giroux

HONOR BOOKS: *The Village of Round and Square Houses* by Ann Grifalconi, Little, Brown; *Alphabetics* by Suse MacDonald, Bradbury; *Rumplestiltskin* adapted and illus. by Paul O. Zelinsky, Dutton

1988

Owl Moon by Jane Yolen, illus. by John Schoenherr, Philomel

HONOR BOOK: *Mufaro's Beautiful Daughters: An African Tale* adapted and illus. by John Steptoe, Lothrop

1989

Song and Dance Man by Karen Ackerman, illus. by Stephen Gammell, Knopf

HONOR BOOKS: *The Boy of the Three Year Nap* by Allen Say, Houghton; *Free Fall* by David Wiesner, Lothrop; *Goldilocks and the Three Bears* adapted and illus. by James Marshall, Dial; *Mirandy and Brother Wind* by Patricia McKissack, illus. by Jerry Pinkney, Knopf

1990

Lon Po Po: A Red Riding Hood Story from China adapted and illus. by Ed Young, Philomel

HONOR BOOKS: *Bill Peet: An Autobiography* by Bill Peet, Houghton; *Color Zoo* by Lois Ehlert, Lippincott; *Hershel and the Hanukkah Goblins* by Eric Kimmel, illus. by Trina Schart Hyman, Holiday House; *The Talking Eggs* by Robert D. San Souci, illus. by Jerry Pinkney, Dial

1991

Black and White by David Macaulay, Houghton

HONOR BOOKS: *"More More More," Said the Baby: 3 Love Stories* by Vera B. Williams, Greenwillow; *Puss in Boots* by Charles Perrault, tr. by Malcolm Arthur, illus. by Fred Marcellino, Farrar, Straus and Giroux

1992

Tuesday by David Wiesner, Clarion

HONOR BOOK: *Tar Beach* by Faith Ringgold, Crown

1993

Mirette on the High Wire by Emily Arnold McCully, Putnam

HONOR BOOKS: *The Stinky Cheese Man* by Jon Scieszka and Lane Smith, Viking; *Working Cotton* by Sherley Anne Williams, illus. by Carole Byard, Harcourt; *Seven Blind Mice* by Ed Young, Philomel

1994

Grandfather's Journey by Allen Say, Houghton

HONOR BOOKS: *In the Small, Small Pond* by Denise Fleming, Holt; *Owen* by Kevin Henkes, Greenwillow; *Peppe the Lamplighter* by Elisa Bartone, illus. by Ted Lewin, Lothrop; *Raven: A Trickster Tale from the Pacific Northwest* by Gerald McDermott, Harcourt; *Yo! Yes?* by Chris Raschka, Orchard

1995

Smoky Night by Eve Bunting, illus. By David Diaz, Harcourt

HONOR BOOKS: *John Henry* by Julius Lester, illus. by Jerry Pinkney, Dial; *Swamp Angel* by Anne Isaacs, illus. by Paul O. Zelinsky, Dutton; *Time Flies* by Eric Rohmann, Crown

1996

Officer Buckle and Gloria by Peggy Rathmann, Putnam

HONOR BOOKS: *Alphabet City* by Stephen T. Johnson, Viking; *The Faithful Friend* by Robert D. San Souci, illus. by Brian Pinkney, Simon and Schuster; *Tops and Bottoms* by Janet Stevens, Harcourt; *Zin! Zin! Zin! A Violin* by Lloyd Moss, illus. by Marjorie Priceman, Simon and Schuster

1997

Golem by David Wisniewski, Clarion

HONOR BOOKS: *Hush! A Thai Lullaby* by Minfong Ho, illus. by Holly Meade, Kroupa/Orchard; *The Graphic Alphabet* by David Pelletier, Orchard; *The Paperboy* by Dav Pilkey, Jackson/Orchard; *Starry Messenger* by Peter Sís, Foster/Farrar.

1998

Rapunzel by Paul O. Zelinsky, Dutton

HONOR BOOKS: *Harlem* by Walter Dean Myers, illus. by Christopher Myers, Scholastic; *The Gardener* by Sarah Stewart, illus. by David Small, Farrar, Straus and Giroux; *There Was an Old Lady Who Swallowed a Fly* by Simms Taback, Viking

1999

Snowflake Bentley by Jacqueline Briggs Martin, illus. by Mary Azarian, Houghton

HONOR BOOKS: *Duke Ellington* by Andrea Davis Pinkney, illus. by Brian Pinkney, Hyperion; *No, David* by David Shannon, Scholastic; *Snow* by Uri Shulevitz, Farrar, Straus and Giroux; *Tibet Through the Red Box* by Peter Sís, Farrar, Straus and Giroux

2000

Joseph Had a Little Overcoat by Simms Taback, Viking

HONOR BOOKS: *The Ugly Duckling* by Hans Christian Andersen, illus. by Jerry Pinkney, Morrow; *A Child's Calendar* by John Updike, illus. by Trina Schart Hyman, Holiday; *Sector 7* by David Wiesner, Clarion; *When Sophie Gets Angry, Really, Really Angry* by Molly Bang, Scholastic

2001

So You Want To Be President? by Judith St. George, illus. by David Small, Philomel Books, Penguin Putnam

HONOR BOOKS: *Casey at the Bat: A Ballad of the Republic Sung in the Year 1888* by Ernest Lawrence Thayer, illus. by Christopher Bing, Handprint Books; *Click, Clack, Moo: Cows That Type* by Doreen Cronin, illus. by Betsy Lewin, Simon and Schuster; *Olivia* by Ian Falconer, Simon and Schuster, Atheneum, Anne Schwartz Books

THE CORETTA SCOTT KING AWARD AND HONOR BOOKS

The awards, administered by the Social Responsibilities Round Table and the American Library Association, recognize an outstanding African-American author and illustrator whose work commemorates and fosters the life, work, and dreams of Dr. Martin Luther King, Jr., and honors the courage and determination of Coretta Scott King to continue to work for peace and world brotherhood. Prior to 1974, the Coretta Scott King Award was given to authors only.

1970

AUTHOR AWARD: *Martin Luther King, Jr.: Man of Peace* by Lillie Patterson, Garrard

1971

AUTHOR AWARD: *Black Troubador: Langston Hughes* by Charlemae Rollins, Rand

1972

AUTHOR AWARD: *17 Black Artists* by Elton C. Fax, Dodd

1973

AUTHOR AWARD: *I Never Had It Made* by Jackie Robinson as told to Alfred Duckett, Putnam

1974

AUTHOR AWARD: *Ray Charles* by Sharon Bell Mathis, Crowell
ILLUSTRATOR AWARD: *Ray Charles*, illus. by George Ford, by Sharon Bell Mathis, Crowell

1975

AUTHOR AWARD: *The Legend of Africania* by Dorothy Robinson, Johnson Publishing
ILLUSTRATOR AWARD: No award given

1976

AUTHOR AWARD: *Duey's Tale* by Pearl Bailey, Harcourt
ILLUSTRATOR AWARD: No award given

1977

AUTHOR AWARD: *The Story of Stevie Wonder* by James Haskins, Lothrop
ILLUSTRATOR AWARD: No award given

1978

AUTHOR AWARD: *Africa Dream* by Eloise Greenfield, Crowell
AUTHOR HONOR BOOKS: *The Days When the Animals Talked: Black Folk Tales and How They Came to Be* by William J. Faulkner, Follett; *Marvin and Tige* by Frankcina Glass, St. Martin's; *Mary McCleod Bethune* by Eloise Greenfield, Crowell; *Barbara Jordan* by James Haskins, Dial; *Coretta Scott King* by Lillie Patterson, Garrard; *Portia: The Life of Portia Washington Pittman, the Daughter of Booker T. Washington* by Ruth Ann Stewart, Doubleday
ILLUSTRATOR AWARD: *Africa Dream*, illus. by Carole Bayard, by Eloise Greenfield, Crowell

1979

AUTHOR AWARD: *Escape to Freedom* by Ossie Davis, Viking
AUTHOR HONOR BOOKS: *Benjamin Banneker* by Lillie Patterson, Abingdon; *I Have a Sister, My Sister Is Deaf* by Jeanne W. Peterson, Harper; *Justice and Her Brothers* by Virginia Hamilton, Greenwillow; *Skates of Uncle Richard* by Carol Fenner, Random House
ILLUSTRATOR AWARD: *Something on My Mind*, illus. by Tom Feelings, by Nikki Grimes, Dial

1980

AUTHOR AWARD: *The Young Landlords* by Walter Dean Myers, Viking

AUTHOR HONOR BOOKS: *Movin' Up* by Berry Gordy, Harper; *Childtimes: A Three-Generation Memoir* by Eloise Greenfield and Lessie Jones Little, Harper; *Andrew Young: Young Man With a Mission* by James Haskins, Lothrop; *James Van Der Zee: The Picture Takin' Man* by James Haskins, Dodd; *Let the Lion Eat Straw* by Ellease Southerland, Scribner's

ILLUSTRATOR AWARD: *Cornrows*, illus. by Carole Bayard, by Camille Yarbrough, Coward

1981

AUTHOR AWARD: *This Life* by Sidney Poitier, Knopf

AUTHOR HONOR BOOK: *Don't Explain: A Song of Billie Holiday* by Alexis De Veaux, Harper

ILLUSTRATOR AWARD: *Beat the Story Drum, Pum-Pum* by Ashley Bryan, Atheneum

ILLUSTRATOR HONOR BOOKS: *Grandmama's Joy*, illus. by Carole Bayard, by Eloise Greenfield, Collins; *Count on Your Fingers African Style*, illus. by Jerry Pinkney, by Claudia Zaslavsky, Crowell

1982

AUTHOR AWARD: *Let the Circle Be Unbroken* by Mildred Taylor, Dial

AUTHOR HONOR BOOKS: *Rainbow Jordan* by Alice Childress, Coward-McCann; *Lou in the Limelight* by Kristin Hunter, Scribner; *Mary: An Autobiography* by Mary E. Mebane, Viking

ILLUSTRATOR AWARD: *Mother Crocodile* by John Steptoe, Delacorte

ILLUSTRATOR HONOR BOOK: *Daydreamers*, illus. by Tom Feelings, by Eloise Greenfield, Dial

1983

AUTHOR AWARD: *Sweet Whispers, Brother Rush* by Virginia Hamilton, Philomel

AUTHOR HONOR BOOK: *This Strange New Feeling* by Julius Lester, Dial

ILLUSTRATOR AWARD: *Black Child* by Peter Magubane, Knopf

ILLUSTRATOR HONOR BOOKS: *All the Colors of the Race*, illus. by John Steptoe, by Arnold Adoff, Lothrop; *I'm Going to Sing: Black American Spirituals*, illus. by Ashley Bryan, Atheneum; *Just Us Women*, illus. by Pat Cummings, by Jeanette Caines, Harper

1984

AUTHOR AWARD: *Everett Anderson's Goodbye* by Lucille Clifton, Holt

SPECIAL CITATION: *The Words of Martin Luther King, Jr.*, compiled by Coretta Scott King, Newmarket Press

AUTHOR HONOR BOOKS: *The Magical Adventures of Pretty Pearl* by Virginia Hamilton, Harper; *Lena Horne* by James Haskins, Coward-McCann; *Bright Shadow* by Joyce Carol Thomas, Avon; *Because We Are* by Mildred Pitts Walter

ILLUSTRATOR AWARD: *My Mama Needs Me*, illus. by Pat Cummings, by Mildred P. Walter, Lothrop

1985

AUTHOR AWARD: *Motown and Didi* by Walter Dean Myers, Viking

HONOR BOOKS: *Circle of Gold* by Candy Dawson Boyd, Apple, Scholastic; *A Little Love* by Virginia Hamilton, Philomel

ILLUSTRATOR AWARD: No award given

1986

AUTHOR AWARD: *The People Could Fly: American Black Folktales* by Virginia Hamilton, Knopf

AUTHOR HONOR BOOKS: *Junius Over Far* by Virginia Hamilton, Harper; *Trouble's Child* by Mildred Pitts Walter, Lothrop

ILLUSTRATOR AWARD: *The Patchwork Quilt*, illus. by Jerry Pinkney, by Valerie Flourney, Dial

ILLUSTRATOR HONOR BOOK: *The People Could Fly: American Black Folktales*, illus. by Leo and Diane Dillon, by Virginia Hamilton, Knopf

1987

AUTHOR AWARD: *Justin and the Best Biscuits in the World* by Mildred Pitts Walter, Lothrop

AUTHOR HONOR BOOKS: *Lion and the Ostrich Chicks and Other African Folk Tales* by Ashley Bryan, Atheneum; *Which Way Freedom* by Joyce Hansen, Walker

ILLUSTRATOR AWARD: *Half a Moon and One Whole Star*, illus. by Jerry Pinkney, by Crescent Dragonwagon, Macmillan

ILLUSTRATOR HONOR BOOKS: *Lion and the Ostrich Chicks and Other African Folk Tales* by Ashley Bryan, Atheneum; *C.L.O.U.D.S.* by Pat Cummings, Lothrop

1988

AUTHOR AWARD: *The Friendship* by Mildred Taylor, Dial
AUTHOR HONOR BOOKS: *An Enchanted Hair Tale* by Alexis De Veaux, Harper; *The Tales of Uncle Remus: The Adventures of Brer Rabbit* by Julius Lester, Dial
ILLUSTRATOR AWARD: *Mufaro's Beautiful Daughters: An African Tale* by John Steptoe, Lothrop
ILLUSTRATOR HONOR BOOKS: *What a Morning! The Christmas Story in Black Spirituals*, illus. by Ashley Bryan, selected by John Langstaff, Macmillan; *The Invisible Hunters: A Legend from the Miskito Indians of Nicaragua*, illus. by Joe Sam, compiled by Harriet Rohmer, et al., Children's Press

1989

AUTHOR AWARD: *Fallen Angels* by Walter Dean Myers, Scholastic
AUTHOR HONOR BOOKS: *A Thief in the Village and Other Stories* by James Berry, Orchard; *Anthony Burns: The Defeat and Triumph of a Fugitive Slave* by Virginia Hamilton, Knopf
ILLUSTRATOR AWARD: *Mirandy and Brother Wind*, illus. by Jerry Pinkney, by Patricia McKissack, Knopf
ILLUSTRATOR HONOR BOOKS: *Under the Sunday Tree*, illus. by Amos Ferguson, by Eloise Greenfield, Harper; *Storm in the Night*, illus. by Pat Cummings, by Mary Stolz, Harper

1990

AUTHOR AWARD: *A Long Hard Journey: The Story of the Pullman Porter* by Patricia and Frederick McKissack, Walker
AUTHOR HONOR BOOKS: *Nathaniel Talking* by Eloise Greenfield, illus. by Jan Spivey Gilchrist, Black Butterfly; *The Bells of Christmas* by Virginia Hamilton, Harcourt; *Martin Luther King, Jr., and the Freedom Movement* by Lillie Patterson, Facts on File
ILLUSTRATOR AWARD: *Nathaniel Talking*, illus. by Jan Gilchrist, by Eloise Greenfield, Black Butterfly Press
ILLUSTRATOR HONOR BOOK: *The Talking Eggs*, illus. by Jerry Pinkney, by Robert San Souci, Dial

1991

AUTHOR AWARD: *The Road to Memphis* by Mildred D. Taylor, Dial
AUTHOR HONOR BOOKS: *Black Dance in America* by James Haskins, Crowell; *When I Am Old with You* by Angela Johnson, Orchard
ILLUSTRATOR AWARD: *Aïda*, illus. by Leo and Diane Dillon, told by Leontyne Price, Harcourt

1992

AUTHOR AWARD: *Now Is Your Time! The African American Struggle for Freedom* by Walter Dean Myers, Harper
AUTHOR HONOR BOOK: *Night on Neighborhood Street* by Eloise Greenfield, illus. by Jan Spivey Gilchrist, Dial
ILLUSTRATOR AWARD: *Tar Beach* by Faith Ringgold, Crown
ILLUSTRATOR HONOR BOOKS: *All Night, All Day: A Child's First Book of African American Spirituals* by Ashley Bryan, Atheneum; *Night on Neighborhood Street*, illus. by Jan Spivey Gilchrist, by Eloise Greenfield, Dial

1993

AUTHOR AWARD: *The Dark Thirty: Southern Tales of the Supernatural* by Patricia C. McKissack, Knopf
AUTHOR HONOR BOOKS: *Mississippi Challenge* by Mildred Pitts Walter, Bradbury; *Sojourner Truth: Ain't I a Woman?* by Patricia C. and Frederick L. McKissack, Scholastic; *Somewhere in the Darkness* by Walter Dean Myers, Scholastic
ILLUSTRATOR AWARD: *The Origin of Life on Earth: An African Creation Myth*, illus. by Kathleen Atkins Wilson, retold by David Anderson, Sights Productions
ILLUSTRATOR HONOR BOOKS: *Little Eight John*, illus. by Wil Clay, by Jan Wahl, Lodestar; *Sukey and the Mermaid*, illus. by Brian Pinkney, text by Robert San Souci, Four Winds; *Working Cotton*, illus. by Carole Byard, by Sherley Anne Williams, Harcourt

1994

AUTHOR AWARD: *Toning the Sweep* by Angela Johnson, Orchard
AUTHOR HONOR BOOKS: *Brown Honey in Broom Wheat Tea* by Joyce Carol Thomas, illus. by Floyd Cooper, HarperCollins; *Malcolm X: By Any Means Necessary* by Walter Dean Myers, Scholastic; *Soul Looks Back in Wonder*, ed. by Phyllis Fogelman, illus. by Tom Feelings, Dial Books for Young Readers
ILLUSTRATOR AWARD: *Soul Looks Back in Wonder* by Tom Feelings, Dial
ILLUSTRATOR HONOR BOOKS: *Brown Honey in Broom Wheat Tea*, illus. by Floyd Cooper, by Joyce Carol Thomas, HarperCollins; *Uncle Jed's Barbershop*, illus. by James Ransome, by Margaree King Mitchell, Simon and Schuster

1995

AUTHOR AWARD: *Christmas in the Big House, Christmas in the Quarters* by Patricia C. and Fredrick L. McKissack, Scholastic
AUTHOR HONOR BOOKS: *The Captive* by Joyce Hansen, Scholastic; *I Hadn't Meant to Tell You This* by Jacqueline Woodson, Delacorte; *Black Diamond: Story of the Negro Baseball League* by Patricia C. and Fredrick L. McKissack, Scholastic
ILLUSTRATOR AWARD: *The Creation* illus. by James E. Ransome, by James Weldon Johnson, Holiday
ILLUSTRATOR HONOR BOOKS: *The Singing Man,* illus. by Terea Shaffer, by Angela Shelf Medearis, Holiday House; *Meet Danitra Brown,* illus. by Floyd Cooper, by Nikki Grimes, Lothrop, Lee and Shepard

1996

AUTHOR AWARD: *Her Stories: African American Folktales, Fairy Tales, and True Tales* by Virginia Hamilton, illus. by Leo and Diane Dillon, Blue Sky/Scholastic
AUTHOR HONOR BOOKS: *The Watsons Go to Birmingham—1963* by Christopher Paul Curtis, Delacorte; *Like Sisters on the Homefront* by Rita Williams-Garcia, Delacorte; *From the Notebooks of Melanin Sun* by Jacqueline Woodson, Scholastic/Blue Sky Press
ILLUSTRATOR AWARD: *The Middle Passage: White Ships Black Cargo* by Tom Feelings, Dial
ILLUSTRATOR HONOR BOOKS: *Her Stories,* illus. by Leo and Diane Dillon, by Virginia Hamilton, Scholastic/Blue Sky Press; *The Faithful Friend,* illus. by Brian Pinkney, by Robert San Souci, Simon and Schuster Books for Young Readers

1997

AUTHOR AWARD: *Slam* by Walter Dean Myers, Scholastic
AUTHOR HONOR BOOK: *Rebels Against Slavery: American Slave Revolts* by Patricia and Fredrick McKissack, Scholastic
ILLUSTRATOR AWARD: *Minty: A Story of Harriet Tubman* illus. by Jerry Pinkney, by Alan Schroeder, Dial
ILLUSTRATOR HONOR BOOKS: *The Palm of My Heart: Poetry by African American Children,* illus. by Gregorie Christie, ed. by Davida Adedjouma, Lee and Low Books; *Running The Road to ABC,* illus. by Reynold Ruffins, by Denize Lauture, Simon and Schuster Books for Young Readers; *Neeny Coming, Neeny Going,* illus. by Synthia Saint James, by Karen English, BridgeWater Books

1998

AUTHOR AWARD: *Forged by Fire* by Sharon M. Draper, Atheneum
AUTHOR HONOR BOOKS: *Bayard Rustin: Behind the Scenes of the Civil Rights Movement* by James Haskins, Hyperion; *I Thought My Soul Would Rise and Fly: The Diary of Patsy, A Freed Girl* by Joyce Hansen, Scholastic
ILLUSTRATOR AWARD: *In Daddy's Arms I Am Tall: African Americans Celebrating Fathers,* illus. by Javaka Steptoe, by Alan Schroeder, Lee and Low
ILLUSTRATOR HONOR BOOKS: *Ashley Bryan's ABC of African American Poetry* by Ashley Bryan, Jean Karl/Atheneum; *Harlem,* illus. by Christopher Myers, by Walter Dean Myers, Scholastic; *The Hunterman and the Crocodile* by Baba Wagué Diakité, Scholastic

1999

AUTHOR AWARD: *Heaven* by Angela Johnson, Simon and Schuster
AUTHOR HONOR BOOKS: *Jazmin's Notebook* by Nikki Grimes, Dial Books; *Breaking Ground, Breaking Silence: The Story of New York's African Burial Ground* by Joyce Hansen and Gary McGowan, Henry Holt and Company; *The Other Side: Shorter Poems* by Angela Johnson, Orchard Books
ILLUSTRATOR AWARD: *I See the Rhythm,* illus. by Michele Wood, by Toyomi Igus, Children's Book Press
ILLUSTRATOR HONOR BOOKS: *I Have Heard of a Land,* illus. by Floyd Cooper, by Joyce Carol Thomas, Joanna Cotler Books/HarperCollins; *The Bat Boy and His Violin,* illus. by E. B. Lewis, by Gavin Curtis, Simon and Schuster; *Duke Ellington: The Piano Prince and His Orchestra,* illus. by Brian Pinkney, by Andrea Davis Pinkney, Hyperion Books for Children

2000

AUTHOR AWARD: *Bud, Not Buddy* by Christopher Paul Curtis, Delacorte
AUTHOR HONOR BOOKS: *Francie* by Karen English, Farrar, Straus and Giroux; *Black Hands, White Sails: The Story of African-American Whalers* by Patricia C. and Frederick L. McKissack, Scholastic Press; *Monster* by Walter Dean Myers, HarperCollins
ILLUSTRATOR AWARD: *In the Time of the Drums,* illus. by Brian Pinkney, by Kim L. Siegelson, Jump at the Sun/Hyperion Books for Children
ILLUSTRATOR HONOR BOOKS: *My Rows and Piles of Coins,* illus. by E. B. Lewis, by Tololwa M. Mollel, Clarion Books; *Black Cat* by Christopher Myers, Scholastic

2001

AUTHOR AWARD: *Miracle's Boys* by Jacqueline Woodson, Putnam

AUTHOR HONOR BOOKS: *Let It Shine! Stories of Black Women Freedom Fighters* by Andrea Davis Pinkney, illus. by Stephen Alcorn, Gulliver Books, Harcourt

ILLUSTRATOR AWARD: *Uptown* by Bryan Collier, Henry Holt

ILLUSTRATOR HONOR BOOKS: *Freedom River* by Bryan Collier, Jump at the Sun/Hyperion; *Only Passing Through: The Story of Sojourner Truth*, illus. by R. Gregory Christie, by Anne Rockwell, Random House; *Virgie Goes to School with Us Boys*, illus. by E. B. Lewis, by Elizabeth Fitzgerald Howard, Simon and Schuster

THE PURA BELPRÉ AWARD

The Pura Belpré Award, established in 1996, is presented biennially to a Latino/Latina writer and illustrator whose work best portrays, affirms, and celebrates the Latino cultural experience in an outstanding work of literature for children and youth. It is co-sponsored by the Association for Library Service to Children, a division of the American Library Association, and the National Association to Promote Library Services to the Spanish Speaking, an ALA Affiliate. The award is named in honor of Pura Belpré, the first Latina librarian in the New York Public Library. As children's librarian, storyteller, and author, she enriched the lives of Puerto Rican children in the United States through her pioneering work of preserving and disseminating Puerto Rican folklore.

1996

NARRATIVE WINNER: *An Island Like You: Stories of the Barrio* by Judith Ortiz Cofer, Melanie Kroupa/Orchard Books, 1995

HONOR BOOKS FOR NARRATIVE: *The Bossy Gallito / El Gallo de Bodas: A Traditional Cuban Folktale* by Lucía González, illus. by Lulu Delacre, Scholastic, 1994; *Baseball in April, and Other Stories*, by Gary Soto, Harcourt, 1994

ILLUSTRATION WINNER: *Chato's Kitchen* illus. by Susan Guevara, by Gary Soto, Putnam, 1995

HONOR BOOKS FOR ILLUSTRATION: *Pablo Remembers: The Fiesta of the Day of the Dead* by George Ancona, Lothrop, 1993 (Also available in a Spanish-language edition: *Pablo Recuerda: La Fiesta de Dia de los Muertos*, Lothrop, 1993); *The Bossy Gallito/El Gallo de Bodas: A Traditional Cuban Folktale* illus. by Lulu Delacre, retold by Lucia Gonzalez, Scholastic, 1994; *Family Pictures/Cuadros de Familia* by Carmen Lomas Garza, Spanish text by Rosalma Zubizarreta, Children's Book Press, 1990

1998

NARRATIVE WINNER: *Parrot in the Oven: mi vida* by Victor Martinez, Joanna Cotler/HarperCollins, 1996

HONOR BOOKS FOR NARRATIVE: *Laughing Tomatoes and Other Spring Poems/Jitomates Risuenos y Otros Poemas de Primavera* by Francisco Alarcón, illus. by Maya Christina Gonzalez, Children's Book Press, 1997; *Spirits of the High Mesa* by Floyd Martinez, Arte Publico Press, 1997

ILLUSTRATION WINNER: *Snapshots from the Wedding*, illus. by Stephanie Garcia, by Gary Soto, Putnam, 1997

HONOR BOOKS FOR ILLUSTRATION: *In My Family/En mi familia* by Carmen Lomas Garza, Children's Book Press, 1996; *The Golden Flower: A Taino Myth from Puerto Rico*, illus. by Enrique O. Sánchez, by Nina Jaffe, Simon and Schuster, 1996; *Gathering the Sun: An Alphabet in Spanish and English*, illus. by Simon Silva, by Alma Flor Ada, English tr. by Rosa Zubizarreta, Lothrop, 1997

2000

NARRATIVE WINNER: *Under the Royal Palms: A Childhood in Cuba* by Alma Flor Ada, Atheneum, 1998

HONOR BOOKS FOR NARRATIVE: *From the Bellybutton of the Moon and Other Summer Poems/Del Ombligo de la Luna y Otro Poemas de Verano* by Francisco X. Alarcón, illus. by Maya Christina Gonzalez, Children's Book Press, 1998; *Laughing Out Loud, I Fly: Poems in English and Spanish* by Juan Felipe Herrera, illus. by Karen Barbour, HarperCollins, 1998

ILLUSTRATION WINNER: *Magic Windows* by Carmen Lomas Garza, Children's Book Press, 1999

HONOR BOOKS FOR ILLUSTRATION: *Barrio: Jose's Neighborhood* by George Ancona, Harcourt, 1998; *The Secret Stars*, illus. by Felipe Dávalos, by Joseph Slate, Marshall Cavendish, 1998; *Mama and Papa Have a Store* by Amelia Lau Carling, Dial, 1998

THE ROBERT F. SIBERT AWARD

The Robert F. Sibert Award, established in 2001, is sponsored by Bound to Stay Bound Books, Inc. in honor of its longtime president, Robert F. Sibert. It is administered by the Association of Library Service to Children, a division of the American Library Association, and seeks outstanding informational books written and illustrated to present, organize, and interpret verifiable, factual material for children.

2001

Sir Walter Ralegh and the Quest for El Dorado by Marc Aronson, Clarion Books

HONOR BOOKS: *The Longitude Prize* by Joan Dash, illus. by Susan Petricic, Frances Foster Books/Farrar, Straus and Giroux; *Blizzard* by Jim Murphy, Scholastic; *My Season with Penguins: An Antarctic Journal* by Sophie Webb, Houghton; *Pedro and Me: Friendship, Loss, and What I Learned* by Judd Winick, Henry Holt

THE LAURA INGALLS WILDER MEDAL

The Laura Ingalls Wilder Medal, established in 1954 and named for its first winner, the author of the **Little House** books, is given to an author or illustrator whose books, published in the United States, have made a substantial and lasting contribution to literature for children. Until 1980, the award was given every five years; currently it is awarded every three years. This award is administered by the Association for Library Service to Children, a division of the American Library Association.

1954	Laura Ingalls Wilder
1960	Clara Ingram Judson
1965	Ruth Sawyer
1970	E. B. White
1975	Beverly Cleary
1980	Theodor S. Geisel (Dr. Seuss)
1983	Maurice Sendak
1986	Jean Fritz
1989	Elizabeth George Speare
1992	Marcia Brown
1995	Virginia Hamilton
1998	Russell Freedman
2001	Milton Meltzer

THE MARGARET A. EDWARDS AWARD

The Margaret A. Edwards Award, established in 1988, honors an author's lifetime achievement for writing books that have been popular over a period of time. The annual award is administered by YALSA, Young Adult Library Services Association, a division of the American Library Association, and sponsored by *School Library Journal*. It recognizes an author's work in helping adolescents become aware of themselves and addressing questions about their role and importance in relationships, society, and in the world.

1988	S. E. Hinton
1990	Richard Peck
1991	Robert Cormier
1992	Lois Duncan
1993	M. E. Kerr
1994	Walter Dean Myers
1995	Cynthia Voigt
1996	Judy Blume
1997	Gary Paulsen
1998	Madeleine L'Engle
1999	Anne McCaffrey
2000	Chris Crutcher
2001	Robert Lipsyte

THE MICHAEL L. PRINTZ AWARD

The Michael L. Printz Award, established in 2000, is administered by the Young Adult Library Services Association, a division of the American Library Association. The award honors the author of an outstanding young adult book.

2000

Monster by Walter Dean Myers, HarperCollins

HONOR BOOKS: *Skellig* by David Almond, Delacorte Press; *Speak* by Laurie Halse Anderson, Farrar, Straus and Giroux; *Hard Love* by Ellen Wittlinger, Simon and Schuster

2001

Kit's Wilderness by David Almond, Delacorte Press

HONOR BOOKS: *Many Stones* by Carolyn Coman, Front Street Press; *The Body of Christopher Creed* by Carol Plum-Ucci, Harcourt; *Angus, Thongs, and Full-Frontal Snogging* by Louise Rennison, HarperCollins; *Stuck in Neutral* by Terry Trueman, HarperCollins

National Council of Teachers of English Awards

THE AWARD FOR EXCELLENCE IN POETRY FOR CHILDREN

The NCTE Award for Excellence in Poetry for Children, established in memory of Jonathan Cullinan (1969–1975) is given to a living American poet in recognition of an outstanding body of poetry for children. The award is administered by the National Council of Teachers of English and was given annually from 1977 to 1982; currently, the award is presented every three years. The poet receives a citation. A medallion designed by Karla Kuskin is available for use on dust jackets of all the poet's books. An archival collection of the poets' books is housed at the Children's Literature Research Center, Andersen Library, at the University of Minnesota. Another collection is housed at Boston Public Library in the David McCord Room.

1977 David McCord
1978 Aileen Fisher
1979 Karla Kuskin
1980 Myra Cohn Livingston
1981 Eve Merriam
1982 John Ciardi
1985 Lilian Moore
1988 Arnold Adoff
1991 Valerie Worth
1994 Barbara Esbensen
1997 Eloise Greenfield
2000 X. J. Kennedy

THE ORBIS PICTUS AWARD AND HONOR BOOKS

The Orbis Pictus Award, established in 1990, is administered by the National Council of Teachers of English and honors the author of an outstanding nonfiction book.

1990

The Great Little Madison by Jean Fritz, Putnam

HONOR BOOKS: *The Great American Gold Rush* by Rhoda Blumberg, Bradbury Press; *The News About Dinosaurs* by Patricia Lauber, Bradbury Press

1991

Franklin Delano Roosevelt by Russell Freedman, Clarion Books

HONOR BOOKS: *Arctic Memories* by Normee Ekoomiak, Henry Holt; *Seeing Earth from Space* by Patricia Lauber, Orchard Books

1992

Flight: The Journey of Charles Lindbergh by Robert Burleigh and Mike Wimmer, Philomel Books

HONOR BOOKS: *Now Is Your Time! The African America Struggle for Freedom* by Walter Dean Myers, HarperCollins; *Prairie Vision: The Life and Times of Solomon Butcher* by Pam Conrad, HarperCollins

1993

Children of the Dust Bowl: The True Story of the School at Weedpatch Camp by Jerry Stanley, Crown

HONOR BOOKS: *Talking with Artists* by Pat Cummins, Bradbury Press; *Come Back, Salmon* by Molly Cone, Sierra Club Books

1994

Across America on an Emigrant Train by Jim Murphy, Clarion Books

HONOR BOOKS: *To the Top of the World: Adventures with Arctic Wolves* by Jim Brandenburg, Walker and Company; *Making Sense: Animal Perception and Communication* by Bruce Brooks, Farrar, Straus and Giroux

1995

Safari Beneath the Sea: The Wonder of the North Pacific Coast by Diane Swanson, Sierra Club Books

HONOR BOOKS: *Wildlife Rescue: The Work of Dr. Kathleen Ramsay* by Jennifer Owings Dewey, Boyds Mills Press; *Kids at Work: Lewis Hine and the Crusade Against Child Labor* by Russell Freedman, Clarion Books; *Christmas in the Big House, Christmas in the Quarters* by Patricia McKissack and Fredrick McKissack, Scholastic

1996

The Great Fire by Jim Murphy, Scholastic

HONOR BOOKS: *Dolphin Man: Exploring the World of Dolphins* by Laurence Pringle, photos by Randall S. Wells, Atheneum; *Rosie the Riveter: Women Working on the Home Front in World War II* by Penny Colman, Crown

1997

Leonardo da Vinci by Diane Stanley, Morrow Junior Books

HONOR BOOKS: *Full Steam Ahead: The Race to Build a Transcontinental Railroad* by Rhoda Blumberg, National Geographic Society; *The Life and Death of Crazy Horse* by Russell Freedman, Holiday House; *One World, Many Religions: The Way We Worship* by Mary Pope Osborne, Knopf

1998

An Extraordinary Life: The Story of a Monarch Butterfly by Laurence Pringle, illus. by Bob Marstall, Orchard Books

HONOR BOOKS: *A Drop of Water: A Book of Science and Wonder* by Walter Wick, Scholastic; *A Tree Is Growing* by Arthur Dorros, illus. by S. D. Schindler, Scholastic; *Charles A. Lindbergh: A Human Hero* by James Cross Giblin, Clarion; *Kennedy Assassinated! The World Mourns: A Reporter's Story* by Wilborn Hampton, Candlewick; *Digger: The Tragic Fate of the California Indians from the Missions to the Gold Rush* by Jerry Stanley, Crown

1999

Shipwreck at the Bottom of the World: The Extraordinary True Story of Schackleton and the Endurance by Jennifer Armstrong, Crown

HONOR BOOKS: *Black Whiteness: Admiral Byrd Alone in the Antarctic* by Robert Burleigh, illus. by Walter Lyon Krudop, Atheneum; *Fossil Feud: The Rivalry of the First American Dinosaur Hunters* by Thom Holmes, Messner; *Hottest, Coldest, Highest, Deepest* by Steve Jenkins, Houghton; *No Pretty Pictures: A Child of War* by Anita Lobel, Greenwillow

2000

Through My Eyes by Ruby Bridges, Margo Lundell, Scholastic

HONOR BOOKS: *At Her Majesty's Request: An African Princess in Victorian England* by Walter Dean Myers, Scholastic; *Clara Schumann: Piano Virtuoso* by Susanna Reich, Clarion; *Mapping the World* by Sylvia A. Johnson, Atheneum; *The Snake Scientist* by Sy Montgomery, illus. by Nic Bishop, Houghton; *The Top of the World: Climbing Mount Everest* by Steve Jenkins, Houghton

International Reading Association Awards

THE IRA CHILDREN'S BOOK AWARD

The IRA Children's Book Award, established in 1975, sponsored by the Institute for Reading Research and administered by the International Reading Association, is presented for a children's book published in the preceding year by an author who shows unusual promise. Since 1987, the award has been presented for both picture books and novels. Books originating in any country are eligible. For books written in a language other than English, the IRA committee first determines if the book warrants an English translation and, if so, extends to it an additional year of eligibility.

1975

Transport 7–41 by T. Degens, Viking

1976

Dragonwings by Laurence Yep, Harper

1977

A String in the Harp by Nancy Bond, McElderry/Atheneum

1978

A Summer to Die by Lois Lowry, Houghton

1979

Reserved for Mark Anthony Crowder by Alison Smith, Dutton

1980

Words by Heart by Ouida Sebestyen, Atlantic/Little

1981

My Own Private Sky by Delores Beckman, Dutton

1982

Good Night, Mr. Tom by Michelle Magorian, Kestrel/Penguin, Great Britain, Harper, USA

1983

The Darkangel by Meredith Ann Pierce, Atlantic/Little

1984

Ratha's Creature by Clare Bell, Atheneum

1985

Badger on the Barge by Janni Howker, Greenwillow

1986

Prairie Songs by Pam Conrad, Harper

1987

PICTURE BOOK: *The Line Up Book* by Marisabina Russo, Greenwillow
NOVEL: *After the Dancing Days* by Margaret I. Rostkowski, Harper

1988

PICTURE BOOK: *Third Story Cat* by Leslie Baker, Little, Brown
NOVEL: *The Ruby in the Smoke* by Philip Pullman, Knopf

1989

PICTURE BOOK: *Rechenka's Eggs* by Patricia Polacco, Philomel
NOVEL: *Probably Still Nick Swansen* by Virginia Euwer Wolff, Holt

1990

PICTURE BOOK: *No Star Nights* by Anna Egan Smucker, Knopf
NOVEL: *Children of the River* by Linda Crew, Delacorte

1991

PICTURE BOOK: *Is This a House for Hermit Crab?* by Megan McDonald, Orchard
NOVEL: *Under the Hawthorn Tree* by Marita Conlon-McKenna, O'Brien Press

1992

PICTURE BOOK: *Ten Little Rabbits* by Virginia Grossman, Chronicle
NOVEL: *Rescue Josh McGuire* by Ben Mikaelsen, Hyperion

1993

PICTURE BOOK: *Old Turtle* by Douglas Wood, Pfeiffer-Hamilton
NOVEL: *Letters From Rifka* by Karen Hesse, Holt

1994

PICTURE BOOK: *Sweet Clara and the Freedom Quilt* by Deborah Hopkinson, illus. by James E. Ransome, Knopf
NOVEL: *Behind the Secret Window: A Memior of a Hidden Childhood* by Nelly S. Toll, Dutton

1995

PICTURE BOOK: *The Ledgerbook of Thomas Blue Eagle* by Gay Matthaei and Jewel Grutman, illus. by Adam Cvijanovic, Thomasson-Grant
NOVEL: *Spite Fences* by Trudy Krisher, Bantam
INFORMATION BOOK: *Stranded at Plimoth Plantation 1626* by Gary Bowen, Harper

1996

PICTURE BOOK: *More Than Anything Else* by Marie Bradby and Chris K. Soentpiet, Orchard
NOVEL: *The King's Shadow* by Elizabeth Adler, Farrar, Straus and Giroux
INFORMATION BOOK: *The Case of the Mummified Pigs and Other Mysteries in Nature* by Susan E. Quinlan, Boyds Mills

1997

PICTURE BOOK: *The Fabulous Flying Fandinis* by Ingrid Slyder, Cobblehill/Dutton
NOVEL: *Don't You Dare Read This, Mrs. Dunphrey* by Margaret P. Haddix, Simon and Schuster
INFORMATION BOOK: *The Brooklyn Bridge* by Elizabeth Mann, Mikaya Press

1998

YOUNGER READER: *Nim and the War Effort* by Milly Lee and Yangsook Choi, Farrar, Straus and Giroux
OLDER READER: *Moving Mama to Town* by Ronder Thomas Young, Orchard
INFORMATIONAL READER: *Just What the Doctor Ordered: The History of American Medicine* by Brandon Marie Miller, Lerner

1999

YOUNGER READER: *My Freedom Trip: A Child's Escape from North Korea* by Frances and Ginger Park, Boyds Mills Press
OLDER READER: *Choosing Up Sides* by John H. Ritter, Philomel Books
INFORMATIONAL READER: *First in the Field: Baseball Hero Jackie Robinson* by Derek T. Dingle Hyperion Books

2000

YOUNGER READER: *The Snake Scientist* by Sy Montgomery, Houghton Mifflin
YOUNGER READER: *Molly Bannaky* by Alice McGill, Houghton Mifflin
OLDER READER: *Bud, Not Buddy* by Christopher Paul Curtis, Delacorte Press, Random House; *Eleanor's Story: An American Girl in Hitler's Germany* by Eleanor Ramrath Garner, Peachtree

2001

YOUNGER READER: *Stranger in the Woods* by Carl R. Sams II and Jean Stoick, Carl R. Sams II Photography
YOUNGER READER: *My Season with Penguins* by Sophie Webb, Houghton Mifflin
OLDER READER: *Jake's Orphan* by Peggy Brooke, Dorling-Kindersley; *Girls Think of Everything* by Catherine Thimmesh, Houghton Mifflin

THE LEE BENNETT HOPKINS– IRA PROMISING POET AWARD

The Lee Bennett Hopkins–International Reading Association Promising Poet Award, established in 1995 and administered by the International Reading Association is presented every three years. The award is given to an American living poet who has had one book, but not more than two published. The award consists of an engraved trophy and a $500 honorarium.

1995	Deborah Chandra
1998	Kristine O'Connell George
2001	Craig Crist-Evans

International Awards

THE LIBRARY ASSOCIATION CARNEGIE MEDALLISTS

Instituted in 1936 to mark the centenary of the birth of Andrew Carnegie, philanthropist and benefactor of libraries, the Library Association Carnegie Medal is awarded annually for an outstanding book for children written in English receiving its first publication in the United Kingdom during the preceding year.

1936	Arthur Ransome, *Pigeon Post*
1937	Eve Garnet, *The Family from One End Street*
1938	Noel Streatfeild, *The Circus Is Coming*
1939	Eleanor Doorly, *The Radium Woman* (biography of Marie Curie)
1940	Kitty Barne, *Visitors from London*
1941	Mary Treadgold, *We Couldn't Leave Dinah*
1942	'B.B.' (D. J. Watkins-Pitchford), *The Little Grey Men*
1943	No award
1944	Eric Linklater, *The Wind on the Moon*
1945	No award
1946	Elizabeth Goudge, *The Little White Horse*
1947	Walter de la Mare, *Collected Stories for Children*
1948	Richard Armstrong, *Sea Change*
1949	Agnes Allen, *The Story of Your Home* (nonfiction)
1950	Elfrida Vipont, *The Lark on the Wing*

1951	Cynthia Harnett, *The Wool-Pack*
1952	Mary Norton, *The Borrowers*
1953	Edward Osmond, *A Valley Grows Up* (nonfiction)
1954	Ronald Welch, *Knight Crusaders*
1955	Eleanor Farjeon, *The Little Bookroom*
1956	C. S. Lewis, *The Last Battle*
1957	William Mayne, *A Grass Rope*
1958	Philippa Pearce, *Tom's Midnight Garden*
1959	Rosemary Sutcliff, *The Lantern Bearers*
1960	Ian W. Cornwall and Howard M. Maitland, *The Making of Man* (nonfiction)
1961	Lucy M. Boston, *A Stranger at Green Knowe*
1962	Pauline Clark, *The Twelve and the Genii*
1963	Hester Burton, *Time of Trial*
1964	Sheena Porter, *Nordy Bank*
1965	Philip Turner, *The Grange at High Force*
1966	No award
1967	Alan Garner, *The Owl Service*
1968	Rosemary Harris, *The Moon in the Cloud*
1969	K. M. Peyton, *The Edge of the Cloud*
1970	Edward Blishen and Leon Garfield, *The God Beneath the Sea*
1971	Ivan Southall, *Josh*
1972	Richard Adams, *Watership Down*
1973	Penelope Lively, *The Ghost of Thomas Kempe*
1974	Mollie Hunter, *The Stronghold*
1975	Robert Westall, *The Machine Gunners*
1976	Jan Mark, *Thunder and Lightnings*
1977	Gene Kemp, *The Turbulent Term of Tyke Tyler*
1978	David Rees, *The Exeter Blitz*
1979	Peter Dickinson, *Tulku*
1980	Peter Dickinson, *City of Gold*
1981	Robert Westall, *The Scarecrows*
1982	Margaret Mahy, *The Haunting*
1983	Jan Mark, *Handles*
1984	Margaret Mahy, *The Changeover*
1985	Kevin Crossley-Holland, *Storm*
1986	Berlie Doherty, *Granny Was a Buffer Girl*
1987	Susan Price, *The Ghost Drum*
1988	Geraldine McCaughrean, *A Pack of Lies*
1989	Anne Fine, *Goggle-Eyes*
1990	Gillian Cross, *Wolf*
1991	Berlie Doherty, *Dear Nobody*
1992	Anne Fine, *Flour Babies*
1993	Robert Swindells, *Stone Cold*
1994	Theresa Breslin, *Whispers in the Graveyard*
1995	Philip Pullman, *Northern Lights*
1996	Melvin Burgess, *Junk*
1997	Tim Bowler, *River Boy*
1998	David Almond, *Skellig*
1999	Aiden Chambers, *Postcards from No Man's Land*

THE HANS CHRISTIAN ANDERSEN AWARD

The Hans Christian Andersen Award, established in 1956, is given biennially and administered by the International Board on Books for Young People. It is given to one author and, since 1966, to one illustrator in recognition of his or her entire body of work. A medal is presented to the recipient.

1956

Eleanor Farjeon, Great Britain

1958

Astrid Lindgren, Sweden

1960

Erich Kästner, Germany

1962

Meindert DeJong, USA

1964

René Guillot, France

1966

AUTHOR: Tove Jansson, Finland
ILLUSTRATOR: Alois Carigiet, Switzerland

1968

AUTHORS: James Krüss, Germany, and José Maria Sanchez-Silva, Spain
ILLUSTRATOR: Jiri Trnka, Czechoslovakia

1970

AUTHOR: Gianni Rodari, Italy
ILLUSTRATOR: Maurice Sendak, USA

1972

AUTHOR: Scott O'Dell, USA
ILLUSTRATOR: Ib Spang Olsen, Denmark

1974

AUTHOR: Maria Gripe, Sweden
ILLUSTRATOR: Farshid Mesghali, Iran

1976

AUTHOR: Cecil Bodker, Denmark
ILLUSTRATOR: Tatjana Mawrina, USSR

1978

AUTHOR: Paula Fox, USA
ILLUSTRATOR: Otto S. Svend, Denmark

1980

AUTHOR: Bohumil Ríha, Czechoslovakia
ILLUSTRATOR: Suekichi Akaba, Japan

1982

AUTHOR: Lygia Bojunga Nunes, Brazil
ILLUSTRATOR: Zbigniew Rychlicki, Poland

1984

AUTHOR: Christine Nöstlinger, Austria
ILLUSTRATOR: Mitsumasa Anno, Japan

1986

AUTHOR: Patricia Wrightson, Australia
ILLUSTRATOR: Robert Ingpen, Australia

1988

AUTHOR: Annie M. G. Schmidt, Holland
ILLUSTRATOR: Dusan Kallay, Czechoslovakia

1990

AUTHOR: Tormod Haugen, Norway
ILLUSTRATOR: Lisbeth Zwerger, Austria

1992

AUTHOR: Virginia Hamilton, USA
ILLUSTRATOR: Kveta Pacovská, Czechoslovakia

1994

AUTHOR: Michio Mado, Japan
ILLUSTRATOR: Jörg Müller, Switzerland

1996

AUTHOR: Uri Orlev, Israel
ILLUSTRATOR: Klaus Ensikat, Germany

1998

AUTHOR: Katherine Paterson, USA
ILLUSTRATOR: Tomi Ungerer, France

2000

AUTHOR: Ana Maria Machado, Brazil
ILLUSTRATOR: Anthony Browne, United Kingdom

THE MILDRED L. BATCHELDER AWARD

The Batchelder Award, established in 1966, is given by the Association of Library Service to Children of the American Library Association to the publisher of the most outstanding book of the year that is a translation, published in the United States, of a book that was first published in another country. In 1990, Honor Books were added to this award. The original country of publication is given in parentheses.

1968

The Little Man by Erich Kastner, tr. by James Kirkup, illus. by Rick Schreiter, Knopf, Germany

1969

Don't Take Teddy by Babbis Friis-Baastad, tr. by Lise Somme McKinnon, Scribner's, Norway

1970

Wildcat Under Glass by Alki Zei, tr. by Edward Fenton, Holt, Greece

1971

In the Land of Ur by Hans Baumann, tr. by Stella Humphries, Pantheon, Germany

1972

Friedrich by Hans Peter Richter, tr. by Edite Kroll, Holt, Germany

1973

Pulga by S. R. Van Iterson, tr. by Alison and Alexander Gode, Morrow, Netherlands

1974

Petros' War by Aldi Zei, tr. by Edward Fenton, Dutton, Greece

1975

An Old Tale Carved Out of Stone by A. Linevsky, tr. by Maria Polushkin, Crown, Russia

1976

The Cat and Mouse Who Shared a House by Ruth Hurlimann, tr. by Anthea Bell, illus. by the author, Walck, Germany

1977

The Leopard by Cecil Bødker, tr. by Gunnar Poulsen, Atheneum, Denmark

1978

Konrad by Christine Nostlinger, illus. by Carol Nicklaus, Watts, Germany

1979

Rabbit Island by Jörg Steiner, tr. by Ann Conrad Lammers, illus. by Jörg Müller, Harcourt, Germany

1980

The Sound of the Dragons Feet by Alki Zei, tr. by Edward Fenton, Dutton, Greece

1981

The Winter When Time Was Frozen by Els Pelgrom, tr. by Maryka and Rafael Rudnik, Morrow, Netherlands

1982

The Battle Horse by Harry Kullman, tr. by George Blecherand Lone Thygesen-Blecher, Bradbury, Sweden

1983

Hiroshima No Pika by Toshi Maruki, Lothrop, Japan

1984

Ronia, the Robber's Daughter by Astrid Lindgren, tr. by Patricia Crampton, Viking, Sweden

1985

The Island on Bird Street by Uri Orlev, tr. by Hillel Halkin, Houghton, Israel

1986

Rose Blanche by Christophe Gallaz and Roberto Innocenti, tr. by Martha Coventry and Richard Graglia, Creative Education, Italy

1987

No Hero for the Kaiser by Rudolf Frank, tr. by Patricia Crampton, Lothrop, Germany

1988

If You Didn't Have Me by Ulf Nilsson, tr. by Lone Tygesen-Blecher and George Blecher, illus. by Eva Eriksson, McElderry, Sweden

1989

Crutches by Peter Hätling, tr. by Elizabeth D. Crawford, Lothrop, Germany

1990

Buster's World by Bjarne Reuter, tr. by Anthea Bell, Dutton, Denmark

1991

Two Long and One Short by Nina Ring Aamundsen, Houghton, Norway

1992

The Man from the Other Side by Uri Orlev, tr. by Hillel Halkin, Houghton, Israel

1993

No Award

1994

The Apprentice by Molina Llorente, tr. by Robin Longshaw, Farrar, Straus and Giroux, Spain

1995

The Boys from St. Petri by Bjarne Reuter, tr. by Anthea Bell, Dutton, Denmark

1996

The Lady with the Hat by Uri Orlev, tr. by Hillel Halkin, Houghton, Israel

1997

The Friends by Kazumi Yumoto, tr. by Cathy Hirano, Farrar, Straus and Giroux

1998

The Robber and Me by Josef Holub, edited by Mark Aronson and tr. by Elizabeth D. Crawford, Henry Holt, Germany

1999

Thanks to My Mother by Schoschana Rabinovici, tr. by James Skofield, Dial

2000

The Baboon King by Anton Quintana, tr. by John Nieuwenhuizen, Walker and Company, Holland

2001

Samir and Yonatan, tr. by Arthur A. Levine, Scholastic, Israel

Other Awards

THE EZRA JACK KEATS AWARD

This award, first presented in 1985, is administered by the Ezra Jack Keats Foundation and the New York Public Library. The award was given biennially to a promising new writer. Beginning in the year 2001 the award is given annually with an award to an illustrator as well as one to a writer. The award honors work done in the tradition of Ezra Jack Keats: appeal to young children, storytelling quality, relation between text and illustration, positive reflection of families, and the multicultural nature of the world. The award is presented at the Early Childhood Resource and Information Center of the New York Public Library. Funded by the Ezra Jack Keats Foundation, the recipient receives a monetary award and a medallion.

1985   *The Patchwork Quilt* by Valerie Flournoy, illus. by Jerry Pinkney, Dial

1987   *Jamaica's Find* by Juanita Havill, illus. by Anne Sibley O'Brien, Houghton

1989   *Anna's Special Present* by Yoriko Tsutsui, illus. by Akiko Hayashi, Viking Kestrel

1991   *Tell Me a Story, Mama* by Angela Johnson, illus. by David Soman, Orchard

1993   *Tar Beach* by Faith Ringgold, Crown

1995   *Taxi! Taxi!* by Cari Best, illus. by Dale Gottlieb, Little, Brown

1997 *Calling the Doves* Juan Felipe Herrara, illus. by Elly Simmons, Children's Book Press

1999 *Dear Juno* by Soyung Pak, illus. by Susan Kathleen Hartung, Viking

2001 TEXT: *Henry Hikes to Fitchburg* by D. B. Johnson, Houghton

ILLUSTRATION: *Uptown* by Bryan Collier, Henry Holt

THE BOSTON GLOBE–HORN BOOK AWARDS

The Boston Globe–Horn Book Awards have been presented annually since 1967 by *The Boston Globe* newspaper and *The Horn Book Magazine*. Through 1975, two awards were given, one for outstanding text and one for outstanding illustration. In 1976, the award categories were changed to fiction or poetry, nonfiction, and illustration. A monetary gift is awarded to the winner in each category.

1967

TEXT: *The Little Fishes* by Erik Christian Haugaard, Houghton
ILLUSTRATION: *London Bridge Is Falling Down!* illus. by Peter Spier, Doubleday

1968

TEXT: *The Spring Rider* by John Lawson, Harper
ILLUSTRATION: *Tikki Tikki Tembo* by Arlene Mosel, illus. by Blair Lent, Holt

1969

TEXT: *A Wizard of Earthsea* by Ursula K. Le Guin, Houghton, Parnassus
ILLUSTRATION: *The Adventures of Paddy Pork* by John S. Goodall, Harcourt

1970

TEXT: *The Intruder* by John Rowe Townsend, Harper
ILLUSTRATION: *Hi, Cat!* by Ezra Jack Keats, Macmillan

1971

TEXT: *A Room Made of Windows* by Eleanor Cameron, Little, Brown
ILLUSTRATION: *If I Built a Village* by Kazue Mizumura, Harper

1972

TEXT: *Tristan and Iseult* by Rosemary Sutcliff, Dutton
ILLUSTRATION: *Mr. Gumpy's Outing* by John Burningham, Holt

1973

TEXT: *The Dark Is Rising* by Susan Cooper, Atheneum, McElderry
ILLUSTRATION: *King Stork* by Trina Schart Hyman, Little, Brown

1974

TEXT: *M. C. Higgins, the Great* by Virginia Hamilton, Macmillan
ILLUSTRATION: *Jambo Means Hello* by Muriel Feelings, illus. by Tom Feelings, Dial

1975

TEXT: *Transport 7-41-R* by T. Degens, Viking
ILLUSTRATION: *Anno's Alphabet* by Mitsumasa Anno, Harper

1976

FICTION: *Unleaving* by Jill Paton Walsh, Farrar, Straus and Giroux
NONFICTION: *Voyaging to Cathay: Americans in the China Trade* by Alfred Tamarin and Shirley Glubok, Viking
ILLUSTRATION: *Thirteen* by Remy Charlip and Jerry Joyner, Four Winds

1977

FICTION: *Child of the Owl* by Laurence Yep, Harper
NONFICTION: *Chance, Luck and Destiny by* Peter Dickinson, Little, Brown
ILLUSTRATION: *Grandfa' Grig Had a Pig and Other Rhymes Without Reason from Mother Goose* by Wallace Tripp, Little, Brown

1978

FICTION: *The Westing Game* by Ellen Raskin, Dutton
NONFICTION: *Mischling, Second Degree: My Childhood in Nazi Germany* by Ilse Koehn, Greenwillow
ILLUSTRATION: *Anno's Journey* by Mitsumasa Anno, Philomel

1979

FICTION: *Humbug Mountain* by Sid Fleischman, Little, Brown
NONFICTION: *The Road from Home: The Story of an Armenian Girl* by David Kherdian, Greenwillow
ILLUSTRATION: *The Snowman* by Raymond Briggs, Random

1980

FICTION: *Conrad's War* by Andrew Davies, Crown
NONFICTION: *Building: The Fight Against Gravity* by Mario Salvadori, McElderry
ILLUSTRATION: *The Garden of Abdul Gasazi* by Chris Van Allsburg, Houghton

1981

FICTION: *The Leaving* by Lynn Hall, Scribner's
NONFICTION: *The Weaver's Gift* by Kathryn Lasky, Warne
ILLUSTRATION: *Outside Over There* by Maurice Sendak, Harper

1982

FICTION: *Playing Beatie Bow* by Ruth Park, Atheneum
NONFICTION: *Upon the Head of the Goat: A Childhood in Hungary 1939-1944* by Aranka Siegal, Farrar, Straus and Giroux
ILLUSTRATION: *A Visit to William Blake's Inn: Poems for Innocent and Experienced Travelers* by Nancy Willard, illus. by Alice and Martin Provensen, Harcourt

1983

FICTION: *Sweet Whisper, Brother Rush* by Virginia Hamilton, Philomel
NONFICTION: *Behind Barbed Wire: The Imprisonment of Japanese Americans During World War II* by Daniel S. Davis, Dutton
ILLUSTRATION: *A Chair for My Mother* by Vera B. Williams, Greenwillow

1984

FICTION: *A Little Fear* by Patricia Wrightson, Atheneum, McElderry
NONFICTION: *The Double Life of Pocahontas* by Jean Fritz, Putnam
ILLUSTRATION: *Jonah and the Great Fish* by Warwick Hutton, McElderry

1985

FICTION: *The Moves Make the Man* by Bruce Brooks, Harper
NONFICTION: *Commodore Perry in the Land of the Shogun* by Rhoda Blumberg, Lothrop
ILLUSTRATION: *Mama Don't Allow* by Thacher Hurd, Harper
SPECIAL AWARD: *1, 2, 3* by Tana Hoban, Greenwillow

1986

FICTION: *In Summer Light* by Zibby Oneal, Viking
NONFICTION: *Auks, Rocks, and the Odd Dinosaur: Inside Stories from the Smithsonian's Museum of Natural History* by Peggy Thomsen, Harper
ILLUSTRATION: *The Paper Crane* by Molly Bang, Greenwillow

1987

FICTION: *Rabble Starkey* by Lois Lowry, Houghton
NONFICTION: *The Pilgrims of Plimoth* by Marcia Sewall, Atheneum
ILLUSTRATION: *Mufaro's Beautiful Daughters* by John Steptoe, Lothrop

1988

FICTION: *The Friendship* by Mildred Taylor, Dial
NONFICTION: *Anthony Burns: The Defeat and Triumph of a Fugitive Slave* by Virginia Hamilton, Knopf
PICTURE BOOK: *The Boy of the Three-Year Nap* by Diane Snyder, Houghton

1989

FICTION: *The Village by the Sea* by Paula Fox, Orchard
NONFICTION: *The Way Things Work* by David Macaulay, Houghton
PICTURE BOOK: *Shy Charles* by Rosemary Wells, Dial

1990

FICTION: *Maniac Magee* by Jerry Spinelli, Little, Brown
NONFICTION: *The Great Little Madison* by Jean Fritz, Putnam
PICTURE BOOK: *Lon Po Po: A Red-Riding Hood Story from China* by Ed Young, Philomel
SPECIAL AWARD: *Valentine and Orson* by Nancy Ekholm Burkert, Farrar, Straus and Giroux

1991

FICTION: *The True Confessions of Charlotte Doyle* by Avi, Orchard
NONFICTION: *Appalachia: The Voices of Sleeping Birds* by Cynthia Rylant, Harcourt
PICTURE BOOK: *The Tale of the Mandarin Ducks* by Katherine Paterson, illus. by Haru Wells, Lodestar

1992

FICTION: *Missing May* by Cynthia Rylant, Orchard
NONFICTION: *Talking with Artists* by Pat Cummings, Bradbury
PICTURE BOOK: *Seven Blind Mice* by Ed Young, Philomel

1993

FICTION: *Ajeemah and His Son* by James Berry, Harper
NONFICTION: *Sojourner Truth: Ain't I a Woman?* by Patricia C. and Fredrick L. McKissack, Scholastic
PICTURE BOOK: *The Fortune Tellers* by Lloyd Alexander, illus. by Trina Schart Hyman, Dutton

1994

FICTION: *Scooter* by Vera B. Williams, Greenwillow
NONFICTION: *Eleanor Roosevelt: A Life of Discovery* by Russell Freedman, Clarion
PICTURE BOOK: *Grandfather's Journey* by Allen Say, Houghton

1995

FICTION: *Some of the Kinder Planets* by Tim Wynne-Jones, Orchard
NONFICTION: *Abigail Adams, Witness to a Revolution* by Natalie S. Bober, Atheneum
PICTURE BOOK: *John Henry* by Julius Lester, illus. by Jerry Pinkney, Dial

1996

FICTION: *Poppy* by Avi, illus. by Brian Floca, Jackson/Orchard
NONFICTION: *Orphan Train Rider: One Boy's True Story* by Andrea Warren, Houghton
PICTURE BOOK: *In the Rain with Baby Duck* by Amy Hest, illus. by Jill Barton, Candlewick

1997

FICTION AND POETRY: *The Friends* by Kazumi Yumoto, tr. by Cathy Hirano, Farrar
FICTION AND POETRY HONORS: *Lily's Crossing* by Patricia Reilly Giff, Delacourt; *Harlem* by Walter Dean Myers, illus. by Christopher Myers, Scholastic
NONFICTION: *A Drop of Water: A Book of Science and Wonder* by Walter Wick, Scholastic
NONFICTION HONORS: *Lou Gehrig: The Luckiest Man* by David A. Adler, illus. by Terry Widener, Gulliver/Harcourt; *Leonardo da Vinci* by Diane Stanley, Morrow
PICTURE BOOK: *The Adventures of Sparrowboy* by Brian Pinkney, Simon
PICTURE BOOK HONORS: *Home on the Bayou: A Coyboy's Story* by G. Brian Karas, Simon; *Potato: A Tale from the Great Depression* by Kate Lied, illus. by Lisa Campbell Ernst, National Geographic

1998

FICTION AND POETRY: *The Circuit: Stories from the Life of a Migrant Child* by Francisco Jiménez, University of New Mexico Press
FICTION AND POETRY HONORS: *While No One Was Watching* by Jane Leslie Conly, Holt; *My Louisiana Sky* by Kimberly Willis Holt, Holt
NONFICTION: *Leon's Story* by Leon Walter Tillage, illus. by Susan L. Roth, Farrar
NONFICTION HONORS: *Martha Graham: A Dancer's Life* by Russell Freedman, Clarion; *Chuck Close Up Close* by Jan Greenberg and Sandra Jordan, DK Ink
PICTURE BOOK: *And If the Moon Could Talk* by Kate Banks, illus. by Georg Hallensleben, Foster/Farrar
PICTURE BOOK HONORS: *Seven Brave Women* by Betsy Hearne, illus. by Bethanne Andersen, Greenwillow; *Popcorn: Poems* by James Stevenson, Greenwillow

1999

FICTION: *Holes* by Louis Sachar, Foster/Farrar
FICTION HONORS: *The Trolls* by Polly Horvath, Farrar; *Monster* by Walter Dean Myers, illus. by Christopher Myers, HarperCollins
NONFICTION: *The Top of the World: Climbing Mount Everest* by Steve Jenkins, Houghton
NONFICTION HONORS: *Shipwreck at the Bottom of the World: The Extraordinary True Story of Shackleton and the Endurance* by Jennifer Armstrong, Crown; *William Shakespeare and the Globe* by Aliki, HarperCollins
PICTURE BOOK: *Red-Eyed Tree Frog* by Joy Cowley, illus. by Nic Bishop, Scholastic Press
PICTURE BOOK HONORS: *Dance* by Bill T. Jones and Susan Kuklin, illus. by Susan Kuklin, Hyperion; *The Owl and the Pussycat* by Edward Lear, illus. by James Marshall, di Capua/HarperCollins
SPECIAL CITATION: *Tibet: Through the Red Box* by Peter Sís, Foster/Farrar

2000

FICTION: *The Folk Keeper* by Franny Billingsley, Atheneum
FICTION HONORS: *King of Shadows* by Susan Cooper, McElderry; *145th Street: Short Stories* by Walter Dean Myers, Delacorte
NONFICTION: *Sir Walter Ralegh and the Quest for El Dorado* by Marc Aronson, Clarion
NONFICTION HONORS: *Osceola: Memories of a Sharecropper's Daughter* collected and edited by Alan Govenar; illus. by Shane W. Evans, Jump at the Sun/Hyperion; *Sitting Bull and His World* by Albert Marrin, Dutton
PICTURE BOOK: *Henry Hikes to Fitchburg* by D. B. Johnson, Houghton
PICTURE BOOK HONORS: *Buttons* by Brock Cole, Farrar; *A Day, A Dog* by Gabrielle Vincent, Front Street

THE LEE BENNETT HOPKINS POETRY AWARD

The Lee Bennett Hopkins Poetry Award, established in 1993 and administered by Penn State University, is given annually for a volume of poetry—either an original collection or an anthology—to a living American poet. In 1999, the Penn State University group decided to choose Honor Books for the award.

1993

Sing to the Sun by Ashley Bryan, McElderry

1994

Spirit Walker by Nancy Wood, Doubleday

1995

Beast Feast by Douglas Florian, Greenwillow

1996

Dance with Me by Barbara Juster Esbensen, Harper

1997

Voices from the Wild by David Bouchard, Chronicle

1998

The Great Frog Race by Kristine O'Connell George, Clarion

1999

The Other Side: Shorter Poems by Angela Johnson, Orchard

HONOR BOOK: *A Crack in the Clouds* by Constance Levy, McElderry

2000

What Have You Lost? ed. by Naomi Shihab Nye, Greenwillow

HONOR BOOKS: *An Old Shell* by Tony Johnston, Farrar, Straus and Giroux; *The Rainbow Hand* by Janet S. Wong, McElderry

2001

Light Gathering Poems ed. by Liz Rosenberg, Henry Holt

HONOR BOOK: *Stone Bench in an Empty Park* edited by Paul Janeczko, Orchard

How to Update Current Listing and Find Other Awards

There are about 150–200 different awards given for children's and young adult books; each has its own unique selection process and criteria. Some awards are chosen by adults, some by children and some by young adults; some are international, some state or regional; some are for a lifetime of work, some are for one book. We used the comprehensive listing of various award winners in *Children's Books: Awards and Prizes*, published by the Children's Book Council. This publication is updated periodically. We also used Web sites of professional organizations for the most up-to-date information: www.ala.org, and www.reading.org, and www.ncte.org, among others.

appendix **B**

Resources

Book Selection Aids

Adventuring with Books: Grades Pre-K–6, 12th ed., edited by Kathryn Mitchell Pierce, National Council of Teachers of English, 1999. A comprehensive list of books selected for their merit and potential use in the classroom. Approximately 2,000 new books are annotated with several hundred from previous editions listed by genre. New editions are prepared periodically.

Best Science and Technology Reference Books for Young People, edited by H. Robert Malinowsky, Oryx, 1991. Reviews science and technology resources and recommends grade levels for sci-tech reference books.

Books to Help Children Cope with Separation and Loss, 2nd ed., compiled by Masha Rudman, Kathleen Gagne, and Joanne E. Bernstein, Bowker, 1993. 514 pages. Discussion of bibliotherapy with annotated lists of books grouped by categories such as adoption, divorce, and disabilities.

Children's Books: Awards and Prizes, compiled and edited by the Children's Book Council, 1996. 497 pages. A comprehensive list of honors awarded to children's books. Awards chosen by adults and children are grouped by state, national, and international designations.

Children's Books in Print, Bowker, annual. A comprehensive index of all children's books in print at time of publication. Author, title, and illustrator indexes give pertinent publishing information. A directory of publishers and addresses is included.

Children's Catalog, Wilson, annual. A comprehensive catalog classified by Dewey decimal system with nonfiction, fiction, short stories, and easy books. Five-year cumulations and annual supplements available.

Children's Literature Review, Gale Research. Since 1976, new volumes added periodically. Articles about authors and topics of interest with excerpts from reviews of the works of each author.

Continuum Encyclopedia of Children's Literature, edited by Bernice E. Cullinan and Diane G. Person, Giniger/Continuum International, 2001. A comprehensive collection of author and illustrator biographies, topic and genre entries about children's literature in the major English-speaking countries.

Elementary School Library Collection, 25th ed., edited by Linda Homa, Bro-Dart Co., 2000. Comprehensive bibliography of print and nonprint materials for school media collections. Dewey decimal subject classification, age level, and brief annotations.

For Reading Out Loud! by Margaret Mary Kimmel and Elizabeth Segel, Delacorte, 1983. A guide to selecting books for sharing with young people and techniques for sharing them. Subject, title, and author index.

Hey! Listen to This: Stories to Read Aloud, edited by Jim Trelease, Penguin, 1992. Selections from literature to read to primary-grade children. Trelease adds intriguing background information about each excerpt.

Jewish Children's Books: How to Choose Them, How to Use Them by Marcia Posner, Hadassah, 1986. 48 pages. Summaries, themes, discussion guides, questions and activities, and further resources are given for more than 30 books.

Kaleidoscope: A Multicultural Booklist for Grades K–8, 2nd ed., edited by Rosalinda Barrera, Verlinda D. Thompson, and Mark Dressman, National Council of Teachers of English, 1997. Nearly 600 fiction and nonfiction texts for elementary and middle school students that feature culturally diverse populations.

Library Services for Hispanic Children: A Guide for Public and School Librarians, edited by Adela Artola Allen, Oryx Press, 1987. 201 pages. Articles on professional issues related to library service for Hispanic children. Annotated bibliographies of children's books in English about Hispanics, recent noteworthy children's books in Spanish, computer software, and resources about Hispanic culture for librarians.

The New Read-Aloud Handbook, 4th ed., by Jim Trelease, Penguin, 1990. An enthusiastic argument for why we should read to children, techniques for reading aloud, and a treasury of over 300 books that work well as read-alouds.

Newbery and Caldecott Medals Books, 1986–2000: A Comprehensive Guide to the Winners, The Horn Book, Association for Library Service to Children, 2001. A continuing collaboration features book summaries, selected excerpts, reviews, acceptance speeches, and biographical essays about the winners.

Pass the Poetry, Please, 3rd ed., by Lee Bennett Hopkins, HarperCollins, 1998. A well-informed author describes engaging interviews with outstanding poets. Hopkins includes comments from interviews, insights into the poets' work, and suggests ways to use poetry with children.

Read to Me: Raising Kids Who Love to Read, 2nd ed., by Bernice E. Cullinan, Scholastic, 2000. A book that encourages parents to make reading a central part of children's lives and shows them how to do it.

Selected Jewish Children's Books, compiled by Marcia Posner, Jewish Book Council, 1991. Annotated list of books containing Jewish content and values categorized by topic and age levels.

Subject Guide to Children's Books in Print, Bowker, annual. Approximately 140,000 titles are grouped under 7,000 subject categories. This indispensable reference helps you find books on specific topics.

Subject Index to Poetry for Children and Young People, compiled by Violet Sell, Core Collection Books, 1982. 1,035 pages. An index of poetry organized by subject with a code for title and author.

With Women's Eyes: Visitors to the New World, 1775–1918, edited by Marion Tinling, Shoe String Press, 1993. 204 pages. Twenty-seven European women who visited America between 1775 and 1918 tell about their experiences.

Reference Books About Authors and Illustrators

The Art of Leo and Diane Dillon, edited by Byron Preiss, Ballantine Books, 1981. Introductory critical essay with 120 illustrations, including 8 color plates of the Dillons' art. The Dillons comment on the meaning, context, and techniques used in each painting.

The Art of Nancy Ekholm Burkert, edited by David Larkin, HarperCollins, 1977. 50 pages. Full-page color spreads of 40 Burkert paintings with an interpretive essay by Michael Danoff.

Author Talk: Conversations with Judy Blume, Bruce Brooks, Karen Cushman, Russell Freedman, Lee Bennett Hopkins, James Howe, Johanna Hurwitz, E. L. Konigsburg, Lois Lowry, Ann Martin, Nicholasa Mohr, Gary Paulsen, Jon Scieszka, Seymour Simon, and Laurence Yep, by Leonard S. Marcus, Simon & Schuster, 2000. Interviews with well-known children's writers.

Awakened by the Moon: Margaret Wise Brown, by Leonard Marcus, Beacon Press, 1992. A literary study of an outstanding author who helped establish modern picture books.

Boy: Tales of Childhood, by Roald Dahl, Puffin, Viking, 1984. 176 pages. An autobiography that describes the origins of one author's ideas.

Carl Larsson, by the Brooklyn Museum and the National Museum in Stockholm with the support of the Swedish Institute in Stockholm, the Brooklyn Museum, 1982. 96 pages. A catalog of Carl Larsson's paintings with commentary by critics. Chronology and selected bibliography.

Caldecott Medal Books: 1938–1957, by Bertha Mahony Miller and Elinor Whitney Field, Horn Book, 1958. Artists' acceptance speeches and biographical articles of the Caldecott Medal winners.

Celebrating Children's Books, edited by Betsy Hearne and Marilyn Kaye, Lothrop, Lee & Shepard, 1981. Articles about their craft by the foremost authors writing for children today. The essays in this collection appear in honor of Zena Sutherland.

Children's Book Illustration and Design, Volume One 1992; Volume Two 1998, edited by Julie Cummins, PBC International, Inc. Each book is a showcase for the work of about 80 illustrators of children's books selected by a knowledgeable critic.

From Writers to Students: The Pleasures and Pains of Writing, edited by Jerry Weiss, International Reading Association, 1979. 113 pages. Interviews with 19 noted authors who reveal the inside story on their writing, including Judy Blume, Mollie Hunter, Milton Meltzer, Mary Rodgers, Laurence Yep, and others.

Illustrators of Children's Books, 1744–1945, edited by Bertha E. Mahony, Louise Payson Latimer, and Beulah Folmsbee, Horn Book, 1947. 527 pages. *Illustrators of Children's Books, 1946–1956,* edited by Bertha Mahony Miller, Ruth Hill Viguers, and Marcia Dalphin, Horn Book, 1958. 229 pages. *Illustrators of Children's Books 1957–1966,* edited by Lee Kingman, Joanna Foster, and Ruth Giles Lontoft, Horn Book, 1968. 295 pages. *Illustrators of Children's Books 1967–1976,* edited by Lee Kingman, Grace Allen Hogarth, and Harriet Quimby. Horn Book, 1978. 290 pages. *Illustrators of Children's Books 1977–1986,* edited by Lee Kingman, Horn Book, 1987. Biographical sketches and discussion of artists' techniques.

Little by Little: A Writer's Education, by Jean Little, Viking, 1987. 233 pages. *Stars Come Out Within,* by Jean Little, Viking, 1992. A two-part autobiography by Canadian writer Jean Little.

Meet the Authors and Illustrators, by Deborah Kovacs and James Preller, Scholastic, 1991. Sixty creators of favorite children's books talk about their work.

Meet the Author Series, Richard C. Owen Publisher. Autobiographies by Verna Aardema, Frank Asch, Eve Bunting, Lois Ehlert, Jean Fritz, Paul Goble, Ruth Heller, Lee Bennett Hopkins, James Howe, Karla Kuskin, George Ella Lyon, Margaret Mahy, Rafe Martin, Patricia M. Kissack, Patricia Polacco, Laurence Pringle, Cynthia Rylant, Jane Yolen, and others. A continuing series suitable for students in primary and intermediate grades.

Newbery and Caldecott Medal Books: 1956–1965, edited by Lee Kingman, Horn Book, 1965. 300 pages. *Newbery and Caldecott Medal Books: 1966–1975,* edited by Lee Kingman, Horn Book, 1975. *Newbery and Caldecott Medal Books, 1976–1985,* edited by Lee Kingman, Horn Book, 1987. *Newbery Medal Books: 1922–1955,* edited by Bertha Mahony Miller and Elinor Whitney Field, Horn Book, 1955. Acceptance speeches and biographical sketches about the winners.

Oxford Companion to Children's Literature, compiled by Humphrey Carpenter and Mari Prichard, Oxford University Press, 1984. Includes nearly 2,000 entries, more than 900 of which are biographical sketches of authors, illustrators, printers, and publishers. Other entries cover topic and genre issues and plot summaries of major works.

Pauses: Autobiographical Reflections of 101 Creators of Children's Books, by Lee Bennett Hopkins, HarperCollins, 1995. Biographical information and excerpts from interviews with authors and illustrators.

Secret Gardens, by Humphrey Carpenter, Houghton Mifflin, 1985. A book about the authors who wrote during the years called the golden age of children's literature in the late nineteenth and early twentieth centuries.

Self-Portrait: Erik Blegvad, by Erik Blegvad, Addison-Wesley, 1979. 32 pages. Blegvad discusses himself, his life, and his work.

Self-Portrait: Trina Schart Hyman, by Trina Schart Hyman, Addison-Wesley, 1981. 32 pages. Hyman describes her life, friends, and family and their reflections in her painting.

Self-Portrait: Margot Zemach, by Margot Zemach, Addison-Wesley, 1978. 32 pages. Zemach talks about her life, her family, and her work.

Something About the Author, Gale Research. One hundred and twenty volumes give extensive biographical information, photographs, publication records, awards received, and quotations about thousands of authors and illustrators of children's books.

Speaking for Ourselves: Autobiographical Sketches by Notable Authors of Books for Young Adults, edited by Donald R. Gallo, National Council of Teachers of English, 1990. Includes brief first-person statements from writers about writing and a bibliography for each writer.

Speaking for Ourselves, Too, edited by Donald R. Gallo, National Council of Teachers of English, 1993. More autobiographical sketches by notable authors of books for young adults. Also includes brief first-person statements from writers about writing and a bibliography for each writer.

Speaking of Poets: Interviews with Poets Who Write for Children and Young Adults, edited by Jeffrey S. Copeland, National Council of Teachers of English, 1993. Contains brief biographies and substantial interviews with poets followed by individual bibliographies.

Speaking of Poets: Interviews with Poets Who Write for Children and Young Adults 2, edited by Jeffrey S. Copeland and Vicki L. Copeland, National Coucil of Teachers of English, 1994. More interviews with poets followed by individual bibliographies.

Starting from Home: A Writer's Beginnings, by Milton Meltzer, Viking, 1988. Meltzer's life story.

Talking with Artists, Volume One, 1992, *Volume Two,* 1995, edited by Pat Cummings, Bradbury. Children's book illustrators talk about their work.

Periodicals About Children's Literature

Bookbird: A Journal of International Children's Literature A refereed journal published quarterly by IBBY, the International Board on Books for Young People, Nonnenweg 12 Postfach, CH-4004 Basel, Switzerland. Incoming editors: Evelyn Freeman, Barbara Lehman, Patricia Scharer. Past editor-in-chief Meena G. Khorana. The journal provides a forum to exchange experience and information among readers and writers in 50 nations of the world. Includes analyses of children's literature in particular regions, for example, children's literature of Latin America.

Book Links: Connecting Books, Libraries, and Classrooms Editor Laura Tillotson, ltillotson@ala.org, American Library Association, published six times a year. Features booklists, interviews, teaching guides, and theme-related bibliographies to help teachers and librarians bring literature to children in ways to make connections across the curriculum.

Booklist Editor Bill Ott, American Library Association, published biweekly September through August; once each in July and August. Reviews children's, young adult, and adult books and nonprint materials. Periodic bibliographies on a specific subject, reference tools, and commentary on issues are invaluable.

Bulletin of the Center for Children's Books Published monthly, except August, by the Graduate School of Library and Information Science of the University of Illinois at Urbana-Champaign and distributed by the University of Illinois Press. A review journal now edited by Janice M. Del Negro that was initiated by Zena Sutherland and edited by Betsy Hearne. One of the few journals to include critical starred reviews of books rated as * (books of special distinction), R (recommended), Ad (additional), M (marginal), NR (not recommended), SpC (special collection), SpR (special reader). Curriculum use and developmental values are assigned when appropriate.

CBC Features   Children's Book Council, published semiannually. A newsletter about current issues and events, free and inexpensive materials, materials for Children's Book Week, topical bibliographies, and essays by publishers and authors or illustrators.

Children's Literature Association Quarterly   Children's Literature Association. Book reviews and articles on British and American children's literature, research, teaching children's literature, theater, and conference proceedings. Special sections on current topics of interest, poetry, censorship, awards, and announcements.

The Horn Book Magazine   Editor Roger Sutton, Horn Book, Inc., published bimonthly. A review journal with intelligent commentary by the editor and invited writers, articles by creators of children's books, publishers, critics, teachers, and librarians. Ratings include starred reviews for outstanding books and comprehensive reviews of recommended books. Also includes Newbery and Caldecott acceptance speeches, biographical sketches of winners, Boston Globe-Horn Book Award winners, and other notable awards. Announces children's literature conferences and events. Two cumulative indexes with ratings for all books published appear in *The Horn Book Guide.*

Scholastic Instructor   Editor Terry Cooper, published eight times a year by Scholastic. Teachers and librarians write feature articles about trends, new books, and authors and illustrators of note. Bernice E. Cullinan is editor of the primary-grade poetry column and Paul Janescko is editor of the intermediate-grade poetry column. An annual poetry writing contest for children is conducted.

Journal of Youth Services in Libraries   A refereed journal published quarterly by the Association of Library Services to Children and Young Adults, a division of the American Library Association. *Joys* is edited by members of ALSC and YALSA with the assistance of Lynn Hoffman. Two guest editors, Hedra Peterman and Jana Fine, will guide the issues this year. Articles of interest to teachers and librarians on current issues, specialized bibliographies, acceptance speeches by the Newbery and Caldecott Award winners, conference proceedings, and organizational news.

Language Arts   A journal published monthly from September through May by the National Council of Teachers of English. A book review column reviews current recommended books for children. Profiles on authors and illustrators, articles on using books in the classroom, response to literature, and writing as an outgrowth of reading literature.

The New Advocate   Editor-in-chief Violet Harris, University of Illinois, published four times a year by Christopher Gordon Publisher, Norwood, MA. This lively journal addresses current issues and topics of interest in the children's book world.

The New York Times Book Review   Includes occasional column of reviews written by authors, illustrators, or reviewers, plus a spring and fall special section featuring children's books plus an annual list of the 10 best-illustrated books of the year.

Primary Voices K–6   This journal is published four times a year by the National Council of Teachers of English. It addresses topics of importance to the literacy community.

Publisher's Weekly   Published by Cahners with a spring and fall special edition on children's books. Diane Roback is senior children's book editor, Jennifer M. Brown is forecasts editor, and Jason Britton is associate editor. Both positive and negative reviews of books and news articles of interest to publishers, teachers, librarians, and authors. Interviews with authors, illustrators, and publishers are regular features.

The Reading Teacher   Co-editors Priscilla L. Griffith and Carol Lynch Brown, published nine times a year by the International Reading Association. A column of reviews of current children's books is a regular feature. Articles appear on the use of books in the classroom, special bibliographies, cross-cultural studies, and research using children's books in reading programs.

Riverbank Review: Of Books for Young Readers   Published quarterly in affiliation with the School of Education at the University of St. Thomas. Editor Martha Davis Beck and a notable advisory board select outstanding writers and reviewers. Interviews with authors, illustrators discussing their work, and information to extend teachers' and parents' background knowledge about children's books.

School Library Journal   Editor-in-chief Julie Cummins, published 11 times a year by Cahners. Includes articles on current issues and reviews of children's books written by practicing librarians. Information is given about conferences and library services. Also includes an annual "Best Books of the Year" column and a cumulative index of starred reviews.

School Library Media Quarterly   Published quarterly by the American Association of School Librarians, American Library Association. It includes research articles on censorship, using books in the classroom, research, library services, and current issues.

Science and Health   Published by the National Science Teachers Association, published eight times per year. Monthly column of reviews of informational books on science topics, plus an annual list of recommended books chosen by NSTA/Children's Book Council Liaison Committee.

Note: Each professional organization and journal publisher has an online Web site. Check the Internet for listings of current events and features.

Publishers' Addresses

Abrams Books for Young Readers
100 Fifth Avenue
New York, NY 10011
www.abramsbooks.com

Addison Wesley Longman, Inc.
One Jacob Way
Reading, MA 01867-3999
www.awl.com

Africa World Press
11-D Princess Rd.
Lawrenceville, NJ 08648
E-mail: africawpress@nyo.com
http://africanworld.com

Arte Publico Press
University of Houston
4800 Calhoun
Houston, TX 77204-2090
http://bentley.uh.edu/arte_publico

Atheneum (*see* Simon & Schuster)

Avon Books
1350 Avenue of the Americas
New York, NY 10019
http://avonbooks.com

Bantam Doubleday Dell Books for
Young Readers
1540 Broadway
New York, NY 10036
http://www.bdd.com

Black Classic Press
P.O. Box 13414
Baltimore, MD 21203
E-mail: bcp@charm.net
http://www.blackclassic.com

Blue Sky (*see* Scholastic)

Boyds Mills Press
815 Church Street
Honesdale, PA 18431
http://www.boydsmillspress.com

Bradbury Press (*see* Simon & Schuster)

Camelot (*see* Avon)

Candlewick Press
2067 Massachusetts Avenue
Cambridge, MA 02140

Carolrhoda (*see* Lerner)

Cavendish Children's Books
Marshall Cavendish
99 White Plains Road
Tarrytown, NY 10591-9001
http://www.marshallcavendish.com

Children's Book Press
246 First Street
Suite 101
San Francisco, CA 94105
E-mail: cbookpress@igc.apc.org

Clarion (*see* Houghton Mifflin)

The Creative Co.
Box 227
123 South Broad Street
Mankato, MN 56001
E-mail: creativeco@aol.com

Cricket Books
Division of Carus Publishing
332 S. Michigan Ave
Suite 1100
Chicago, IL 60604
www.cricketmag.com

Crowell (*see* HarperCollins)

Crown (*see* Random House)

D K Publishing Inc.
Subsidiary of Dorling Kindersley Ltd.
95 Madison Avenue
New York, NY 10016
http://www.dk.com

Delacorte (*see* Bantam Doubleday Dell)

Dell (*see* Bantam Doubleday Dell)

Dial Books for Young Readers
(*see* Penguin Putnam)

Disney Press
Division of Walt Disney Co.
114 Fifth Avenue
New York, NY 10011
http://www.disneybooks.com

Doubleday (*see* Bantam Doubleday Dell)

Dutton (*see* Penguin Putnam)

Wm. B. Eerdmans Publishing Co.
255 Jefferson Ave. SE
Grand Rapids, MI 49503
E-mail: general@eerdmans.com
www.eerdmans.com/youngreaders

Farrar, Straus and Giroux
19 Union Square West
New York, NY 10003
212-206-5309

Phyllis Fogelman Books
(*see* Penguin Putnam)

Four Winds Press
(*see* Simon & Schuster)

Front Street Books Inc.
20 Battery Park Avenue
Asheville, NC 28801-2734
http://www.frontstreetbooks.com

David R. Godine Publisher Inc.
9 Hamilton Place
Boston, MA 02108
http://www.godine.com

Golden Books Children's Publishing
Group
888 Seventh Avenue
New York, NY 10106

Greenwillow (*see* HarperCollins)

Grolier Publishing
90 Sherman Turnpike
Danbury, CT 06816
http://publishing.grolier.com

Groundwood Books
325 Humber College Blvd.
Toronto, Ontario M9W 7C3
In the United States:
Publishers Group West
1700 Fourth Street
Berkeley, CA 94710
E-mail: mlundin@groundwood-dm.com

Grosset (*see* Penguin Putnam)

Harcourt Brace Children's Books
525 B Street, Suite 1900
San Diego, CA 92101
www.harcourtbooks.com

HarperCollins Children's Books
1350 Avenue of the Americas
New York, NY 10019
http://www.harperchildrens.com

Holiday House Inc.
425 Madison Avenue
New York, NY 10017
www.holidayhouse.com

Henry Holt & Co. Inc.
115 West 18th Street
New York, NY 10011
www.henryholt.com

Houghton Mifflin Co.
222 Berkeley Street
Boston, MA 02116-3764
http://www.hmco.com/trade

Hyperion (*see* Disney)

Jewish Publication Society
1930 Chestnut Street
Philadelphia, PA 19103-4599
http://www.jewishpub.org

Just Us Books Inc.
356 Glenwood Avenue, 3rd floor
East Orange, NJ 07017
E-mail: justusbook@aol.com

The Kane Press
222 East 46th Street
New York, NY 10017

Kane/Miller Book Publishers
Box 310529
Brooklyn, NY 11231-0529
E-mail: kanemill@aol.com

Kids Can Press Ltd.
85 River Rock Drive, Suite 202
Buffalo, NY 14207

Alfred A. Knopf (*see* Random House)

Lee & Low Books Inc.
95 Madison Avenue, Room 606
New York, NY 10016
http://www.leeandlow.com

Lerner Publications Co.
241 First Avenue North
Minneapolis, MN 55401
http://www.lernerbooks.com

Lippincott (*see* HarperCollins)

Little, Brown and Company, Inc.
Div. of Time Warner Trade Publishing
3 Center Plaza
Boston, MA 02108-2084
http://www.littlebrown.com

Lothrop (*see* HarperCollins)

Margaret McElderry Books
(*see* Simon & Schuster)

The Millbrook Press Inc.
2 Old New Milford Rd.
Brookfield, CT 06804

Mondo Publishing
One Plaza Road
Greenvale, NY 11548

Morrow (*see* HarperCollins)

National Geographic Society Book Div.
1145 17th Street NW
Washington, DC 20036

North South Books
1123 Broadway, Suite 800
New York, NY 10010
http://www.northsouth.com

Orchard Books (*see* Scholastic)

Richard C. Owen Publishers Inc.
Box 585
Katonah, NY 10536
E-mail: rcowen@worldnet.att.net

Oxford University Press
198 Madison Avenue
New York, NY 10016-4314
http://www.oup-usa.org

Pantheon (*see* Random House)

Peachtree Publishers Ltd.
494 Armour Circle NE
Atlanta, GA 30324-4088

Penguin Putnam Inc.
374 Hudson Street
New York, NY 10014
www.penguinputnam.com

Philomel books (*see* Penguin Putnam)

Pleasant Company Publications
Box 998
Middleton, WI 53562-0998
http://www.pleasantco.com

Rand McNally
8255 Central Park Avenue
Skokie, IL 60076
http://www.randmcnally.com

Random House
201 East 50th Street
New York NY 10022

Rizzoli International Publications Inc.
300 Park Avenue South, 3rd floor
New York, NY 10010-5399

Scholastic Inc.
555 Broadway
New York, NY 10012
http://www.scholastic.com

Sierra Club Books
85 Second Street
San Francisco, CA 94105
http://www.sierraclub.org/books

Silver Moon Press
160 Fifth Avenue
New York, NY 10010
http://www.silvermoonpress.com

Simon & Schuster
1230 Avenue of the Americas
New York, NY 10020
www.SimonSaysKids.com

Third World Press
7822 Dobson
Chicago, IL 60619
http://www.thirdworldpress.com

Viking (*see* Penguin Putnam)

Waldman House Press
525 N. Third Street
Minneapolis, MN 55401

Walker & Co.
435 Hudson Street
New York, NY 10014

Frederick Warne (*see* Penguin Putnam)

Franklin Watts Inc. (*see* Grolier)

Albert Whitman & Co.
6340 Oakton Street
Morton Grove, IL 60053-2723

Winston-Derek Publishers Group Inc.
101 French Landing Drive
Nashville, TN 37228

Wordsong (*see* Boyds Mills Press)

Paperback Book Clubs

Scholastic Book Clubs
555 Broadway
New York, NY 10012-3999
www.scholastic.com

Troll Book Clubs
100 Corporate Drive
Mahwah, NJ 07430

Trumpet Book Club (*see* Scholastic)

Professional Organizations

American Library Association
50 East Huron Street
Chicago, IL 60611
www.ala.org

Children's Book Council
12 West 37th Street, 2nd floor
New York, NY 10018
www.cbcbooks.org

International Reading Association
800 Barksdale Road
Newark, DE 19714
www.reading.org

National Council of Teachers of English
1111 Kenyon Road
Urbana, IL 61801
www.ncte.org

Children's Magazines and Newspapers

Chickadee

Age range: 4–9. Introduces the world of science, nature, and technology to young children through engaging stories and well-developed illustrations. Chickadee Magazine, 25 Boxwood Lane, Buffalo, NY 14227-2780

Click: Opening Windows for Young Minds

Age range: 3–7. Published 10 times a year by the publishers of *Cricket Magazine* and *Smithsonian Magazine,* and contains 36 pages that visualize a child's world.
Cricket Magazine Group, Box 7434, Red Oak, IA 51591-0434

Cobblestone

Age range: 8–14. This is a magazine of American history containing stories of the past for middle school students. Cobblestone, 7 School Street, Peterborough, NH 03458

Cricket

Age range: 9–14. Contains quality literature in folktales, fantasy, science fiction, history, biographies, poems, science, and sports stories. Cricket Magazine Group, Box 7434, Red Oak, IA 51591-2434

Current Events

Age range: 11–16. Contains articles on current events that students in social studies classes in middle, junior, and early senior high schools can understand. Weekly Reader Corporation, 3001 Cindel Drive, Delran, NJ 08370

Current Science

Age range: 11–16. Filled with current science discoveries and issues that students in middle, junior, and early senior high schools can understand. Weekly Reader Corporation, 3001 Cindel Drive, Delran, NJ 08370

Faces

Age range: 8–14. Anthropologists of the American Museum of Natural History advise editors about the lifestyles, beliefs, and customs of cultures throughout the world. Cobblestone Publishing Inc., 7 School Street, Peterborough, NH 03458 http://www.cobblestonepub.com

Highlights for Children

Age range: 2–12. The flagship general interest magazine that combines learning and fun in 42 pages filled with stories, poems, information, hidden pictures, cartoons, and crafts. Highlights for Children, Box 269, Columbus, OH 43272-0002

Junior Scholastic

Age range: Grades 6–8. A classroom magazine published 18 times during the school year that features social studies events and issues. Scholastic Inc., 2931 E. McCarty Street, Box 3710, Jefferson City, MO 65102-9957

Ladybug

Age range: 2–6. Contains a collection of stories, poems, songs, and games for young children. A parent's companion suggests additional activities, crafts, and books. Cricket Magazine Group, Box 7434, Red Oak, IA 51591-2434

Merlyn's Pen: The National Magazine of Student Writing

Age range: Grades 6–9. Published four times a year, the magazine contains stories, poems, and expository pieces written by teens in the United States. Merlyn's Pen Inc., 4 King Street, Box 910, East Greenwich, RI 02818, E-mail: merlynspen@aol.com

Merlyn's Pen Senior Edition

Age range: Grades 9–12. Published four times a year, the magazine contains stories, poems, letters, plays, and essays written by students in grades 9–12. Merlyn's Pen, Inc., 4 King Street, Box 910, East Greenwich, RI 02818, E-mail: merlynspen@aol.com

The Mini Page

Age range: 5–12. A four-page educational newspaper inserted in 500 newspapers, often part of Newspaper in Education Week programs. Universal Press Syndicate, Box 419150, Kansas City, MO 64141

National Geographic World

Age Range: 8–14. Contains natural history, science, diverse cultural groups, and outdoor adventure captured in excellent photographs and engaging writing. National Geographic Society, Box 2330, Washington, DC 20013-2330

Odyssey

Age range: 814. Features current events about space exploration and astronomy in each 48-page, fully illustrated, theme-related issue. Cobblestone Publishing, Inc., 7 School Street, Peterborough, NH 03458

Owl: The Discovery Magazine for Kids

Age range: 8 and up. Each 32-page issue contains nature, science, animals, technology, games, puzzles, pull-out poster, and a comic strip. Owl Magazine, 25 Boxwood Lane, Buffalo, NY 14227-2780

Ranger Rick

Age range: 6–12. Each 48-page issue contains nature stories, information, poems, animal life histories, natural history, riddles, crafts, and activities in well-illustrated pages. Animal lovers are regular readers. National Wildlife Federation, 8925 Leesburg Pike, Vienna, VA 22184-0001

Science World

Age range: Grades 7–10. This 24-page news magazine is published biweekly during the school year. It features current research in life, earth, astronomy, space, physical, and health sciences. Scholastic Inc., 2931 E. McCarty Street, Box 3710, Jefferson City, MO 65102-9957, E-mail: scienceworld@scholastic.com

Sesame Street

Age range: 2–6. This appealing magazine features stories, games, and activities to introduce the alphabet, numbers, and problem solving. Its stories reinforce social skills using characters from the television program. Sesame Street Magazine, Box 52000, Boulder, CO 80321-2000

Spider

Age range: 6–9. Intended for independent readers, the magazine contains stories, poems, informational articles, multicultural tales, activities, and well-illustrated pages that appeal to primary-grade readers. Cricket Magazine Group, Box 7434, Red Oak, IA 51591-2434

Sports Illustrated for Kids

Age range: 8–14. This magazine, modeled on its adult predecessor, introduces young readers to professional and amateur sports events and sports heroes. Time Life, Inc., Box 830609, Birmingham, AL 35283

Stone Soup: The Magazine by Young Writers and Artists

Age range: 6–14. This magazine publishes poems, stories, art, and expository pieces written by children. Children's Art Foundation, Box 83, Santa Cruz, CA 95063

Storyworks Magazine

Age range: Grades 3–5. Good stories, poems, plays, nonfiction, word games, author interviews, news briefs about books, and student-written book reviews excite readers and teachers. Scholastic, Inc., 2931 E. McCarty Street, Box 3710, Jefferson City, MO 65101-3710

3-2-1 Contact

Age range: 8–12. This is a science, nature, technology magazine that introduces young people to the science in the world around them through stories, nonfiction, puzzles, games, math-related activities, and information on computer programming. 3-2-1 Contact, Box 51177, Boulder, CO 80322-1177

Time for Kids

Age range: Grades 4–6. This weekly classroom news magazine presents current events in language that intermediate-grade students can understand. A teacher's edition suggests ways to extend the learning. Time for Kids, Box 30609, Tampa, FL 33630-0609

U*S* Kids

Age range: 8–13. Stories, articles, and activities in this 42-page full-color magazine interest children in their world and the people who live in it. Games, interactive activities, and puzzles with a historical focus combine learning and pleasure. U*S* Kids, Box 7133, Red Oak, IA 51591-0133

Weekly Reader

Age range: Grades K–6. This graded series of classroom newspapers contains current news, activities, and recreational reading. Weekly Reader Corp., Box 2791, Middletown, CT 06457-9291

Your Big Backyard

Age range: 8–12. Outstanding photography and illustrations attract readers to this nature and conservation magazine. The National Wildlife Federation, 8925 Leesburg Pike, Vienna, VA 22184

Zillions: The Consumer Report for Kids

Age range: 8–14. The place kids learn how to determine when a bargain is a bargain; they become wise consumers. Zillions Subscription Dept., Box 51777, Boulder, CO 80321-1777

Reference

Magazines for Kids and Teens: A Resource for Teachers, Parents, Librarians, and Kids. Editor Don Stoll. Foreword by Jim Trelease. Published by International Reading Association and EdPress Association, 1997.

The History of Children's Literature

The Evolution of Childhood

Children's books, produced as early as four hundred years ago, have changed dramatically across time. Literature never grows in a vacuum; it grows as a part of the surrounding world of thought, economics, and customs. Children's literature is no exception. The prevailing concept of childhood and what children should be taught determines the kinds of books published for them. Therefore, we find in children's books a record of the ideals and standards each generation wants to teach their young.

Historically, Europeans viewed children as miniature adults and made few concessions for *their* differences. In the seventeenth and eighteenth centuries, adults were concerned about saving children's souls and guaranteeing their entrance into heaven. Books praised pious children. Beginning in the nineteenth century and evolving in the twentieth century, the idea grew that children are developmentally distinct from adults; they have different needs and abilities. This vision of childhood led to a demand for books unique to children's needs and interests; thereafter, children's book publishing flourished.

Fifteenth- and Sixteenth-Century Children's Literature

THE ORAL TRADITION

During the 1500s and 1600s, literature for children was primarily oral folktales, fables, and Bible stories told in family circles, or ballads and epics told by wandering performers. Life was harsh.

Everyone, including children, worked long hours. During dark winter months, light to read by was a luxury.

Fables, brief allegorical narratives that illustrate a moral or satirize human behavior, were widely told. The oldest known fables are those from the Sanskrit collection *Pachatantra,* but many fables are attributed to the Greek Aesop. Very little is known about Aesop, but one legend says he was a slave of Samos in the sixth century B.C. He is associated with wild adventures. Aesop's fables were preserved mainly through Babrius, a Greek fabulist; Phaedrus, a first-century Latin writer; and Planudes Maximus, a Byzantine scholar circa 1260–1330.

Canterbury became the spiritual center of England when St. Augustine arrived from Rome to convert people to Christianity in 597. He founded an abbey at Canterbury and became the first archbishop of Canterbury. The early cathedral was burned and rebuilt several times (in 1011, 1067, and 1174). After the murder of Thomas Becket in 1170 and the penance of Henry II, Canterbury became famous as the object of a pilgrimage. Chaucer's *Canterbury Tales* are based on stories of the travelers.

Stories of King Arthur and the Knights of the Round Table were told from the sixth century onward. The origins of the tales are lost in antiquity; origins are irrelevant, however, for the tales serve as symbols of courage, goodness, and gallantry today. Over the years additions include the exploits of Tristram, Gawaine, Lancelot, and Merlin as well as the quest for the Holy Grail—the cup used by Christ at the Last Supper. The stories still enjoy an enthusiastic audience today.

THE INVENTION OF PRINTING

A German, Johann Gutenberg (1397–1468), is believed to be the first European to print with movable type cast in molds. Similar printing had been done earlier in China but there is no evidence that this printing was known in Europe in Gutenberg's time. Gutenberg's name does not appear on any printing attributed to him and details of his life are cloudy. Gutenberg lived in Strasbourg and there is some evidence that in 1436 or 1437 he made his great invention there. He returned to his birthplace, Mainz near Frankfort, where the printing attributed to him was produced. The masterpiece from his printing press was known as the *Gutenberg Bible.* In order to produce the Bible he borrowed money that he was unable to repay. He lost his press and types. The Gutenberg Museum in Mainz has examples of his work but not of his features; these are unknown.

William Caxton, an English businessman, went to Cologne, Germany, to learn the printing trade. Caxton set up his first printing press in England around 1476 and published *A Book of Curtesey* (1477), *The Historye of Reynart the Foxe* (1481), and *Aesop's Fables* (1484). Caxton published Thomas Malory's version of the Arthurian legends, *Le Morte d'Arthur,* in 1485.

HORNBOOKS *Hornbooks* are small wooden paddles with attached lesson sheets covered by transparent cow's horn (like very heavy plastic) tacked down with brass strips. They were first used around 1550 to teach children the alphabet, syllables, vowels, the Lord's Prayer, and short verses. The verses had a religious message, such as "In Adam's fall, we sinned all" used to illustrate the letter 'A.' The ultimate goal of learning was religious salvation.

CHAPBOOKS *Chapbooks,* crudely printed little books or pamphlets sold by itinerant peddlers (chapmen), first appeared in the late 1500s but became widely popular in the seventeenth and eighteenth centuries. Chapbooks containing fairy tales, nursery rhymes, and retold stories, were usually anonymous and undated. Despite their cheap quality, they circulated widely, created a readership, and preserved the tales and rhymes for later publication.

Seventeenth- and Eighteenth-Century Children's Literature

MORAL LESSONS

Bookmaking in America was a slow, costly process. Not many colonists owned books. If they did own one, it was likely the Bible or another religious book. Books for pleasure reading were virtually nonexistent; there was little distinction between books for children and books for adults. The primary purpose of books was to lead readers toward religious salvation. The few books available

---

Figure 1

Landmarks of the Colonial Period and the Seventeenth and Eighteenth Centuries

Colonial Period

1484	*Aesop's Fables*
1550	Hornbooks (small wooden paddle with lesson sheet attached)
1636	*Youth's Behavior*
1646	John Cotton, *Milk for Babes, drawn out of the breasts of both Testaments, chiefly for the spiritual nourishment of Boston babes in either England, but may be of like use for any children*

Seventeenth Century

1658	John Amos Comenius, *Orbis Sensualium Pictus*
1665	Henry Winstanly, *All the Principal Nations of the World*
1672	James Janeway, *A Token for Children*
1678	John Bunyan, *Pilgrim's Progress*
1697	Charles Perrault, *Contes de ma Mere l'Oye (Tales of Mother Goose)*
1679	Benjamin Harris, *The New England Primer*

Eighteenth Century

1702	Cotton Mather, *A Token for the Children of New England, or some examples of children in whom the fear of God was remarkably budding before they died*
1715	Isaac Watts, *Divine and Moral Songs for Children*
1719	Daniel Defoe, *Robinson Crusoe*
1740	Chapbooks
1744	John Newbery, *A Little Pretty Pocket-book: Intended for the Instruction and Amusement of Little Master Tommy and Pretty Miss Polly*
1765	Oliver Goldsmith, *The History of Little Goody Two Shoes*
1769	Battledores
1778	Anna Laetitia Barbauld, *Lessons for Children*
1786	Sarah Trimmer, *Fabulous Histories, History of the Robins*
1783	Noah Webster, *Webster's Blue-Backed Speller*

to children were moralistic, didactic, and riddled with sanctions. Through books of catechism and lists of duties, children were instructed to live spiritual lives, to obey their parents, to prepare for death, and to avoid incurring the wrath of God. Books glorified saintly lives and pious deaths. Images of fire and brimstone burned brightly in books for children.

John Cotton (1584–1652), an outspoken Puritan clergyman in England, was summoned to appear before the High Court of Commission (1632) for his nonconformist statements. Instead of appearing, he resigned and fled with his parishioners to the Massachusetts Bay Colony in 1633. He was a firm believer in the minister's right to dictate to the congregation. His *Milk for Babes* (1646), a well-known catechism for children, asked questions such as "How did God make you?" to be answered, "I was conceived in sin and born in iniquity."

John Bunyan (1628–1688), an English author, son of a tinsmith, read chapbooks as a child but as he grew older and more religious he turned to the Bible and its teachings. His fiery sermons caused him to be locked up for unlicensed preaching and nonconformity to practices of the Church of England. While in jail, he wrote about Christian and Christiana, troubled souls, who make a pilgrimage from the City of Destruction to everlasting life in Celestial City in *Pilgrim's Progress* (Part I, 1678; Part II, 1684). Bunyan's early experiences reading fairy tales influenced his storytelling so that the pilgrimages read like fairy-tale heroes fighting enemies with symbolic names, such as Giant Despair. The books, written for adults, contained a great deal of theology, but children were attracted to the good stories underlying the preaching.

BOOKS FOR FORMAL INSTRUCTION

Children attended "dame schools" conducted in private homes while the teacher carried on her household duties. Neighborhood children sat at the kitchen table to read and recite their lessons while the teacher (dame) continued to bake bread and prepare meals. The curriculum included reading, writing, spelling, arithmetic, prayers, hymns, and catechism read from hornbooks, the Bible, and a few other books.

Battledores, made from folded heavy paper, had a cover embellished with crude woodcuts of animals, while the inside was filled with alphabets, numerals, and simple reading lessons. They were intended to instruct and amuse and contained only vague references to religion. Battledores were popular in England and North America from the mid-1700s well into the 1800s.

The New England Primer provided religious education in language children could understand. First published in London as *The Protestant Tutor,* its author, Benjamin Harris, was sent to the pillory in 1681 for printing the book, one of the first to omit the traditional religious catechism. Harris escaped to Boston where he reissued the book in 1690. *The New England Primer* was illustrated with crude woodcuts and gruesome accounts of hangings and burnings. *The New England Primer* was published in several editions, all containing the alphabet, couplets advising virtuous and mannerly behavior, the catechism, and various hymns and prayers. Children were expected to study it until they memorized it word-for-word.

CHANGING IDEAS OF EDUCATION

While the colonists were learning to live in an untamed land, educators in Europe were moving away from stern Puritan morality. John Amos Comenius (1592–1670), John Locke (1632–1704), and Jean-Jacques Rousseau (1712–1778) directed educational thought toward a child-centered view.

John Amos Comenius wrote a compendium of the information he believed every child should know in *Orbis Sensualium Pictus (Illustrated World of the Senses).* Comenius, a Moravian churchman, advocated relating education to everyday life by emphasizing contact with objects in the environment and systematizing all knowledge. Teaching was to be done in the vernacular (language or dialect native to a region) instead of Latin and language was to be learned in a conversational method, not through rote repetition. His book, *Orbis Pictus,* was the first book in which pictures were as important as the text. (See Appendix A: The Orbis Pictus Award.)

John Locke held the view that a child is born as a *tabula rasa,* a blank slate ready to have life experiences written on it.

Jean-Jacques Rousseau believed that a child is born with an innate sense of right and wrong and, left to his own natural impulses, the "noble savage" would grow into a superior adult. Rousseau set forth his ideas in *Emile* (1762), giving rise to the image of a mentor and student sitting on a log as the ideal teaching/learning situation.

BEGINNINGS OF CHILDREN'S BOOK PUBLISHING

In 1744, a London merchant, John Newbery (1713–1767), opened a shop called The Bible and Sun (originally called The Bible and Crown) near St. Paul's churchyard. Newbery offered for sale, along with medicines, the first book specifically designed to entertain as well as to instruct children. *A Little Pretty Pocket-Book: Intended for the Instruction and Amusement of Little Master Tommy and Pretty Miss Polly* was the first attempt to teach children the alphabet by way of diversion. John Newbery earned a spot in history because of his notable act of selling children's books. The Newbery Medal, named in his honor, is given annually for the most distinguished contribution to literature for children published in the United States. (See Appendix A.) Later, in 1765, Newbery published *The History of Little Goody Two Shoes,* a book attributed to Oliver Goldsmith and one that established the image of a pious, virtuous child.

MOVING BEYOND RELIGION: ENTERTAINMENT AND DIDACTICISM

Once started, the movement toward publishing books for children's pleasure began. The "teachy-preachy" books with virtuous, religious characters gradually gave way to fanciful stories, poetry, and picture books for entertainment. Despite the desire for pure pleasure in stories, authors tucked lessons underneath a thin plot line. For example, children would ask questions such as "Pray Papa, what is a camel?" and adults would respond with an uninterrupted barrage of factual information.

At the end of the eighteenth century, children in books were polite, diligent, dutiful, and prudent. Well-behaved boys and girls searched relentlessly for information. Parents, teachers, ministers, and librarians were unquestioned as sources of information and translators of God's prescription for behavior.

In an attempt to expand the bookselling market started by John Newbery, some publishers commissioned people to write expressly for children. Most of the writers were women; among them, Mrs. Sarah Kirby Trimmer (1741–1810), Mrs. Laetitia Aiken Barbauld (1743–1825), and Maria Edgeworth (1767–1849). Mrs. Trimmer, mother of twelve, wrote about a family of robins to teach moralistic lessons. Mrs. Barbauld created stories for her adopted son to express her belief that there was a proper, rigid, respectful order for parents and children to follow. Maria Edgeworth, the eldest daughter in a large Irish family, learned firsthand what children liked and disliked. Maria's mother died a few years after her birth; her father remarried three times and fathered 21 children, 18 of whom survived infancy. Maria wrote stories to entertain the ever-expanding brood. She wrote the stories, tried them out on her siblings, revised them, and copied them over in ink (Goldstone, 1984, p. 48). One of Maria Edgeworth's stories, *The Purple Jar* (1796), illustrates the subtle message of obeying elders.

After the American Revolution (1775–1781), Americans struggled to unite their nation and were eager to show that they no longer belonged to England. Writers praised their new land to develop a sense of national pride. Many books claimed that Americans were more fortunate than people from other lands; others were pitied because they could not live in America. Books for children featured adventure stories of travel on the American frontier and courageous battles with the Indians. The books were as didactic as the earlier "teachy-preachy" books, but they added history and geography lessons to the new American ethic of "work hard and make good."

Nineteenth-Century Children's Literature

Early in the nineteenth century, righteous teachings still prevailed in children's books, but they were made a little more palatable under the guise of entertainment. Mary Poppins's rule "A little bit of sugar makes the medicine go down" worked for books as well as discipline. During the early 1800s, stories written expressly for children's enjoyment grew.

Children sought adventure in books such as *Robinson Crusoe, Gulliver's Travels,* and *The Swiss Family Robinson,* originally written for adults but taken over by children. Books written specifically for children slowly made their way to America although a stern work ethic condemned frivolity. Fairy tales collected by Charles Perrault, *Histories ou Contes du Temps Passe' avec Moralite's (Stories or Tales of Times Past with Morals)* and *Contes de ma Mere l'Oye (Tales of Mother Goose),* which included "Sleeping Beauty," "Little Red Riding Hood," "Blue Beard," "Puss in Boots," "Cinderella," and "Tom Thumb," were considered silly fluff. Puritanical adults did not want children to waste time on them because they thought they were a dangerous corrupting influence. Good behavior and knowledge were highly valued.

Between 1825 and 1850, Samuel Goodrich, who believed books could guide children along the right path, collaborated with other writers, such as Nathaniel Hawthorne, to produce the **Peter Parley**

Figure 2

Landmark Books of the Nineteenth Century

1801	Marie Edgeworth, *Early Lessons*	1858	Jacob Abbott, *Rollo in Rome*
1801	Marie Edgeworth, *Moral Tales*	1858	Jacob Abbott, *Rollo's Tour in Europe*
1812	Johann Wyss, *The Swiss Family Robinson*	1865	Lewis Carroll, *Alice in Wonderland*
1822	Samuel and Charles Goodrich, *Peter Parley's History of the United States*	1867	Martha Farquharson Finley, *Elsie Dinsmore*
1826	James Fenimore Cooper, *The Last of the Mohicans*	1868	Louisa May Alcott, *Little Women*
1827	Samuel and Charles Goodrich, *Tales of Peter Parley About America*	1868	Horatio Alger, *Ragged Dick*
1834	Jacob Abbott, *Rollo Learning to Talk*	1876	Mark Twain, *The Adventures of Tom Sawyer*
1834	*McGuffy's Eclectic Readers*	1880	Margaret Sidney, *The Five Little Peppers and How They Grew*
1843	Charles Dickens, *A Christmas Carol*	1883	Robert Lewis Stevenson, *Treasure Island*
		1891	C. Collodi, *Pinocchio*

series. Peter Parley is a distinguished elderly gentleman who answers children's questions about history, science, and geography in *Tales of Peter Parley About America* (1827) and in more than a hundred titles that followed. Although some Peter Parley books were designed as textbooks, most were intended for out-of-school reading and called "toy books." They were simple, well illustrated, clearly printed, and inexpensive. Despite wide approval of the information and codes of conduct, the books were criticized because people believed they made children imaginative and indolent (Perkinson, 1978). Nevertheless, the Peter Parley books were forerunners of a type of literature popular with children—series books.

Once begun, series books flourished. Children read them avidly as alternatives to textbooks. Jacob Abbott's series is about a boy who learns all that he can about the world while remaining aware of his supposedly superior American heritage. The series, **Rollo's Tour in Europe,** reads like a travelogue, with wise Uncle George serving as a mentor to young Rollo. Rollo eventually returns to America satisfied that he hails "from a land superior to those inhabited by foreigners" (Jordan, 1983, pp. 48–49). Authors felt obliged to tell readers they were lucky to live in the budding democracy of America.

BOOKS FOR FORMAL INSTRUCTION

The New England Primer continued to be a popular textbook for children during the first half of the 1800s. It was revised several times to reflect changing American values. For example, immediately following the American Revolution, textbook authors tried to develop a pure American education and get rid of any reference to England. Books stressed practicality and loyalty. Noah Webster led the way with his spelling book, *Webster's Blue-Backed Speller,* a standard used to judge an educated person.

The United States was 60 years old when the first system of public education was established in Massachusetts under the leadership of Horace Mann. The young nation expanded westward but organized public education was slow to follow. Decades passed before all children had access to public schools. Textbooks were the primary resource for education. School attendance was sporadic because children worked; children most often learned their lessons at home. Textbooks were the one constant in a pupil's education. Students reported their progress by telling how far they had read in textbooks: They had completed the Primer or were halfway through Webster. The method of study was always the same: Students memorized the lessons and recited them to the teacher.

McGuffey's Eclectic Readers, first appearing in 1834, were a series of books of increasing difficulty filled with stories, poems, and information written by many authors—America's first basal readers. They provided a national literature and a national curriculum for people who wanted to unify Americans by giving them common experiences.

THE NEED FOR FANTASY

Children had little time to be children in the mid-nineteenth century. Social and economic conditions dictated that many young people work, often in horrendous circumstances. The Industrial Revolution created the need for a plentiful supply of cheap labor. Women, children, and immigrants were enticed to cities to live lives filled with unremitting drudgery and a considerable amount of danger. Women and children worked in the mills 12 hours a day, 6 days a week where gruesome accidents were common (Holland, 1970; Paterson, *Lyddie* [I–A], 1991).

The society that tolerated grim conditions for children developed a literature that provided a fantasy escape from the harsh workaday world while still giving a justification for the work ethic. Much of the fanciful literature came from England but hard-working American children welcomed it with open arms.

Alice's Adventures in Wonderland (1865) and *Through the Looking Glass* (1871) by Charles Dodgson are the first significant works of fantasy for children. Dodgson, a clergyman and scholarly math professor at Oxford, chose a pen name (Lewis Carroll) to avoid being identified with his books for children—the very reason he is remembered today. The legend says that Dodgson often told stories to the three Liddell girls, daughters of a minister friend. One afternoon, Alice asked for a story with nonsense. The story she heard that day became the world-famous one. He wrote it down for her the following Christmas.

The complicated nonsense and word play Alice Liddell loved intrigues readers who become "curiouser and curiouser" as Alice follows a white rabbit down a hole. The story of memorable madness, read by generations of children and adults alike, is filled with subtleties that poke fun at English social customs. Some of the satire eludes modern readers, but the cleverness of the story and the word play still charms them.

THE DEVELOPMENT OF POETRY

Mother Goose verses were the earliest poetic forms to delight the ear and tickle the tongue and imagination of children. Doggerel, sentimental lines, riddles, and traditional rhymes were plentiful. Poetry written especially for children began to show up around the middle of the 1800s.

Some truly great works, though written for adults, preceded the flowering of poetry written for children. For example, the English poet William Blake (1757–1827) captured the spirit of childhood in verse. Barely noticed in his lifetime, his *Songs of Innocence* (1789) and *Songs of Experience* (1794) live on. The poems in *Songs of Innocence* portray the human mind with a childlike quality. In the introduction, Blake begins:

> *Piping down the valleys wild,*
> *Piping songs of pleasant glee,*
> *On a cloud I saw a child,*
> *And he laughing said to me.*
> *Pipe a song about a Lamb.*

PUBLIC DOMAIN,
REPRINTED 1925, P. 65

Blake's poems show the child as refreshingly curious and responding intuitively to unfathomable beauty. They are a benchmark for subsequent poetry for children.

Ann Taylor (1782–1866) and Jane Taylor (1783–1824) began writing verses quite young. When Ann was 22 and Jane 21, they published *Original Poems for Infant Minds by Several Young Persons* (1804). Their verses reflected a childlike spirit despite subtle lessons. "Twinkle, twinkle, little star" by Jane Taylor is a song that children sing today. This and other early poems, such as "Mary had a little lamb" (1830) by Sarah Josepha Hale and "'Will you walk into my parlor?' said the Spider to the Fly" in *Fireside Verses* by Mary Howitt (1799–1888), were spread so widely it is difficult to remember they are not folklore.

Most nineteenth-century poets still had a strong desire to teach lessons, but some went beyond preachy moralistic verses. A few early English poets portrayed life from a child's point of view and sang the pleasures of childhood as children saw them. The tradition begun by William Blake led to poetic conventions we draw upon today. Early poets include William Roscoe, *The Butterfly's Ball* (1806); Edward Lear, *A Book of Nonsense* (1846); William Allingham, *In Fairyland* (1870); Robert Louis Stevenson, *A Child's Garden of Verses* (1885); and A. A. Milne, *When We Were Very Young* (1924) and *Now We Are Six* (1927).

An American, Clement C. Moore, wrote *A Visit from St. Nicholas* (1823), a poem that keeps the magic of Christmas alive even today. Written for his own children, it appeared anonymously in the Troy (N.Y.) *Sentinel* on December 23, 1823. It is a rarity completely free from the didactic teachings of the time. Children's delight in the imaginative vision that Clement C. Moore's words created caused them to take the poem for their own and, as an owner's right, to rename it "The Night Before Christmas," which it shall forever remain. The words by Moore invite us "To the top of the porch, to the top of the wall! Now, dash away, dash away, dash away all!" (Public Domain, 1823; 1971) may have been a signal to move toward the boundless visions future poets would paint. Moore could never have predicted the growth of poetry from a slender branch into the center of the school curriculum: not as an add-on, but as the basic material for children learning to read, to write, to speak, and to listen.

THE DEVELOPMENT OF BOOK ILLUSTRATION

The illustration of picture books has developed into a fine art through the growth of publishing. Picture book art is the first and perhaps the only art children ever see; it has a lasting effect on their developing taste. Today's children need to understand pictures because we are surrounded by visual information texts using pictures and symbols as well as words. Visual texts are accessible to a wider range of readers than word texts.

Children's book illustration developed rapidly after 1850, although bright spots appeared earlier. Illustrated books actually began with artless, anonymous woodcuts used on catechism pages. Printers used any woodcuts they happened to have lying about the shop, not necessarily pictures connected to the text they were printing.

George Cruikshank (1792–1878), an early outstanding artist, illustrated *Grimm's Fairy Tales* in 1823. His unforgettable, luxuriant but delicate, art for the tenacious tales extended the fancy and became the standard by which other art was judged. Cruikshank's distinctive style appears in the four volumes of *George Cruikshank's Fairy Library* (1853–54).

Prior to 1850, artists merely decorated a text with designs or occasional illustrations to fill gaps in a page or to emphasize crucial moments in a story. Because of technical limitations they seldom achieved a perfect match between picture images and literary images. In the 1860s, Edmund Evans, a talented printer and bookmaker, began to make vast improvements in picture books by perfecting color printing. Evans joined artist Walter Crane, the son of a portrait painter, in criticizing the poor quality of art in children's books. They worked together to implement the use of color. The pair brought out Walter Crane's first alphabet books, *Railroad Alphabet* and *Farm Yard Alphabet* in 1865. Nursery song picture books—*Sing a Song of Sixpence, The House That Jack Built, Dame Trot and Her Comical Cat,* and *The History of Cock Robin and Jenny Wren*—followed in 1867 and 1869, establishing Crane's productive career. Walter Crane's toy book, *Sleeping Beauty* illustrates the fairy tales that followed.

Improved photo-engraving processes in the 1880s freed artists from the tyranny of the hand-engraved (and distorted) translations of their art. Full-fledged color illustrations by Walter Crane, Kate Greenaway, and Randolph Caldecott, and skillfully crafted black-and-white art by John Tenniel flourished. Artists became partners in storytelling. The combination of an increasing literacy and improvements in printing lowered the cost of books. This led to wider distribution of books toward the end of the century.

Randolph Caldecott (1846–1886) contributed sketches to magazines in England and America, but the turning point in his career came in *The Diverting History of John Gilpin* (1878). His art showed vitality, movement, and humor; it immortalized Caldecott in the field of children's literature. The Caldecott Medal for outstanding illustration is named in his honor; the medal carries a scene from *John Gilpin* (see Appendix A).

Kate Greenaway (1846–1901) made a living decorating greeting cards with prim, well-groomed children playing in flower gardens. She turned her considerable talent to books in *Under the Window* (1878), her first picture book. Greenaway's distinguished career merited having the Greenaway Medal—the award for the most distinguished illustrated book in England—named in her honor (see Appendix A).

John Tenniel left his artistic mark on Lewis Carroll's *Alice's Adventures in Wonderland* (1865) and *Through the Looking Glass* (1871). His vision of Alice is so distinctive that we find it difficult to think of her without Tenniel's art.

THE GROWTH OF REALISM

The desire to indoctrinate children in the American work ethic was evident in a series begun by Horatio Alger in 1868. Alger created characters who worked hard but were well paid for their efforts. Horatio Alger wrote more than 100 stories in which male characters acquired power and wealth through great effort, courage, and impeccable morality. The stories were dramatic: Alger's hero would snatch a baby from a burning building or rescue a damsel from the heels of a runaway horse. Children read the books avidly. Alger set *Ragged Dick* (1868) in a New York slum rather than in the usual rural surroundings. Subtitled "Street Life in New York with the Boot Blacks," *Ragged Dick,* like other books in the series, traces a poor boy's progress from poverty to wealth and respectability. The author's name, Horatio Alger, invokes the same work ethic today. A contemporary Horatio Alger Award is given to honor a person who works hard and succeeds.

Books for boys differed from books for girls. Boys' books were filled with adventure, travel, and the desire to succeed, but girls' books had characters who practiced the genteel arts of homemaking, caring for others, and piety. Martha Farquharson (Finley) described female behavior melodramatically in the **Elsie Dinsmore** series, wherein tears, fainting spells, and prayers were called forth regularly. Elsie Dinsmore is a link in the chain of tearful, saintly girls that includes *Little Goody Two Shoes* and Rosamond (of *The Purple Jar*).

Gradually a new type of literature appeared in which characters were portrayed more realistically. Priggishness gave way to devilment as boys—but not yet girls—acted more like real children. Thomas Bailey Aldrich's autobiographical *The Story of a Bad Boy* (1870) acknowledges tricks, pranks, and mischievous behavior in a "boys will be boys" spirit. The book began an era of "bad-boy literature" that peaked in Mark Twain's *The Adventures of Huckleberry Finn* (1884). The trend continues today.

Girls were given an alternative to Elsie Dinsmore's overly dramatic fainting spells when Louisa May Alcott wrote *Little Women* in 1868. Alcott began her career by writing and selling potboilers to magazines to support her family. Although considered too worldly by fundamentalist leaders at the time, *Little Women* has been called the century's most significant piece of fiction. Alcott's substantial work focused on the homespun virtues of a wholesome American family. We are still finding some of her long-lost fiction, for example *A Long Fatal Love Chase.*

Girls took pleasure in a series of family stories by Margaret Sidney (pseudonym of Harriet M. Lothrop). *The Five Little Peppers and How They Grew* (1880) begins a sentimental series about a widowed mother's brave struggle to raise her five children. Generosity, humility, and proper manners are rewarded in the stories of a family without money but lots of love.

The last half of the nineteenth century brought forth a surfeit of inexpensive, aesthetically weak, mass-produced series written to formula. The series books, printed on poor-quality paper, had little literary distinction to recommend them, but children devoured them with the same enthusiasm as readers of today's series books. The Immortal Four—Finley, Alger, Adams, and Fosdick—all used a variety of pseudonyms under which they ground out hundreds of books. This wave of fast-paced, cheap, and extremely popular books provoked adult objections, but they were popular entertainment for children.

Writers built on the success of the Horatio Alger and Elsie Dinsmore series by producing other fast-moving adventure stories. One entrepreneur, Edward Stratemeyer, developed a syndicate of hack writers to produce millions of cheap juvenile books—some still available today. Mass marketing made it possible for children to obtain books without adult supervision; inexpensive production made books dispensable.

Edward Stratemeyer wrote for pulp magazines and, shortly after the Spanish-American War, wrote *Under Dewey at Manila.* He enjoyed writing war stories and wrote several series with America's wars as background. As his sales increased, Stratemeyer outlined plots and hired hack writers to produce the **Colonial Boys** series, the **Mexican War** series, and **Pan American** series. He developed other series, including the **Rover Boys,** the **Motor Boys, Tom Swift,** the **Hardy Boys,** and the **Bobbsey Twins**—using the pseudonyms Arthur Winfield, Clarence Young, Victor Appleton, Franklin W. Dixon, and Laura Lee Hope, respectively. Stratemeyer produced 68 different series under 46 pseudonyms. After his death in 1935, his daughter, Harriet Stratemeyer Adams, took over the massive operation that still produces books including the **Nancy Drew** series under the pseudonym Carolyn Keene. Harriet Stratemeyer died at age 89 in 1982 but the series continues to be published under the editorial direction of Simon and Schuster.

Eventually Americans could envision a world beyond native shores; provincialism waned and authors wrote about children in other lands. For example, Mary Mapes Dodge's *Hans Brinker; or The Silver Skates* (1865) popularized a story about a Dutch boy who saved Holland by putting his finger in a hole in a dike, a levee built to prevent the sea from flooding the land. Johanna Spyri wrote *Heidi* (1884) as a glimpse of life in Switzerland, but children loved it for its portrayal of a girl's relationship with her grandfather.

EARLY MAGAZINES

Many magazines for children began as Sunday School periodicals. *The Encourager* (Methodist), *The Children's Magazine* (Episcopal), *The Juvenile Instructor* (Mormon), and *Catholic Youth's Magazine* contained religious stories and Biblical verse. Secular magazines such as *Frank Leslie's Chatterbox* (1879–1886) advertised that they could "improve the mind, diffuse knowledge," and provide healthy, interesting literature for the young. Sketches conveyed morals or useful information in purified language.

St. Nicholas (1873–1943), a high-quality journal for children that survived for 70 years, was a breath of fresh air due to its good stories and warm, informal tone communicated by editor Mary Mapes Dodge. Dodge sought excellent writers; she included work by Louisa May Alcott, Frances Hodgson Burnett, Joel Chandler Harris, Rudyard Kipling, Howard Pyle, Laura Richards, Mark Twain, and Frank Stockton, who became associate editor. Many of the magazine's short stories were reprinted as books or in anthologies; some of the serialized novels remain classics today. Frances Hodgson Burnett's *Sara Crewe* (1888), Frank Stockton's *America's Birthday Party* (1876), Susan Coolidge's *What Katy Did* (1872), Louisa May Alcott's *Jo's Boys* (1873), *An Old-Fashioned Girl* (1870), and *Eight Cousins* (1875), Rudyard Kipling's *The Jungle Book* (1894), and Lucretia P. Hale's *The Peterkin Papers* (1880) first appeared in the pages of *St. Nicholas.*

The Youth's Companion (1827–1929) was published for 102 years, longer than any other children's magazine in America. In 1929, it merged with *The American Boy* which ceased publication in 1941.

Editorial policy demanded that its content remain seemly; parents could give the magazine to children without fear of introducing them to any untoward subject. A distinguished list of contributors—Sarah Orne Jewett, Jack London, Theodore Roosevelt, Henry Wadsworth Longfellow, Alfred Lord Tennyson, James M. Barrie, H. G. Wells, and Oliver Wendell Holmes—wrote for the magazine.

The first children's magazine published in America, *The Juvenile Miscellany* (1826–1834), edited by Lydia Maria Child, became an immediate success. Lydia Maria Child, a former teacher, wanted children to learn to read with material they could enjoy, but found very little to fulfill this requirement. She filled the void with *The Juvenile Miscellany*. When she spoke out vehemently against slavery, however, sales dropped so drastically that the magazine was forced to stop publication in 1834. Sarah Josepha Hale's "Mary Had a Little Lamb" first appeared in this magazine.

Twentieth-Century Children's Literature

The new century brought forth new stories for children. Moral overtones were not forgotten, but most books contained humor, adventure, spirit, imagination, and enough rough-and-tumble to satisfy readers who liked real live action.

1900–1920: FANTASY AND REALISM

Boys read adventure stories: George Grinnell's *Jack Among the Indians* (1900) and George Henty's *With Kitchener in the Soudan* (1903). Girls read quiet home and family stories: Kate Douglas Wiggin's *Rebecca of Sunnybrook Farm* (1903), Lucy M. Montgomery's *Anne of Green Gables* (1908), Frances Hodgson Burnett's *The Secret Garden* (1911). One story, *Pollyanna* (1912), by Eleanor Porter, became so well loved that the character's name continues to symbolize her joyful optimistic disposition. Fantasy continued to flourish; the classic story-play *Peter Pan* (1904) by J. M. Barrie is still loved by adults and children everywhere.

Picture books as we know them today flourished around the turn of the century, when many of today's classics were published. Arthur Rackham illustrated Barrie's *Peter Pan in Kensington Gardens* (1906) and Beatrix Potter created *The Tale of Peter Rabbit* (1902). W. W. Denslow drew pictures for Frank Baum's *Wizard of Oz* (1900) and L. Leslie Brooke illustrated *The Golden Goose Book* (1905). The works earned the artists a place beside Cruikshank, Crane, Tenniel, Greenaway, and Caldecott as outstanding illustrators of early children's books.

1920–1940: PICTURE BOOKS

The American school of illustration developed during the 1920s and 1930s. Prior to 1920 most picture books originated in England. Wanda Gág's *Millions of Cats* (P), published in 1928, showed the work of an artist who used sophisticated printing technology to produce her unique vision (Meigs, Eaton, Nesbitt, & Viguers, 1969).

Public libraries opened children's rooms and children flocked to them. *The Horn Book Magazine,* a review journal of children's

books, appeared in 1924. Publishers created children's departments and inaugurated promotional activities such as Children's Book Week. The demand for children's books grew. During these decades Laura Ingalls Wilder began her **Little House** (I) series, and J.R.R. Tolkien wrote *The Hobbit* (I–A) (1938).

During the Holocaust and World War II, talented artists and authors escaped from Europe to live and work in America. American children's literature was enriched by the work of Ingri and Edgar Parin d'Aulaire (*Abraham Lincoln,* 1939) (P), Ludwig Bemelmans (*Madeline,* 1939) (P), and Roger Duvoisin (*White Snow, Bright Snow* by Alvin Tresselt, 1947) (P).

1940–1960: QUALITY FICTION

During the 1940s and 1950s, children's books became an important part of libraries, schools, homes, and publishing houses. Books published during this period, such as Robert McCloskey's *Make Way for Ducklings* (1941) (P), Eleanor Estes's *The Moffats* (1941) (I), *Johnny Tremain* (1943) (I–A) by Esther Forbes, *Charlotte's Web* (1952) (I) by E. B. White, *My Side of the Mountain* (1959) (I) by Jean George, and the **Narnia** (1950) (I–A) series by C. S. Lewis remain popular today.

1960–1980: GOVERNMENT FUNDING

The 1960s and 1970s were a time of growth in children's literature. Congress passed the National Defense Education Act of 1958 with Title II to provide federal funds for the purchase of children's science and mathematics books. The Elementary and Secondary School Education Act of 1965 brought another wave of federal funds for non-textbook purchases. Teachers used children's books in the classroom to enrich the curriculum and to encourage students to read. School and public librarians guided students to books for information and books for pleasure. Public librarians served more—and younger—children in story hours, summer reading programs, after-school programs, and author visits. Literacy organizations held conferences and established journals to study literature and to promote reading. High fantasy, such as Susan Cooper's *The Dark Is Rising* (1966) (A) and Lloyd Alexander's *The Book of Three* (1964) (I–A) enriched the field. Outstanding picture books such as Ezra Jack Keats's *Snowy Day* (1962) (P), Leo Lionni's *Swimmy* (1963) (P), and Maurice Sendak's *Where the Wild Things Are* (1963) (P) enjoyed great popularity. Authors and illustrators from minority groups made major contributions, such as Virginia Hamilton's *M. C. Higgins, the Great* (1974) (I–A) and Laurence Yep's *Dragonwings* (1975) (I–A). Television programs based on children's books—*Reading Rainbow* and *After School Specials*—attracted children to reading.

1980–2000: NEW MARKETS

Children's-only bookstores mushroomed in the 1980s, while large chain supermarket stores opened in the 1990s. Barnes & Noble, Borders, and Little Professor chains, for example, devote an unprecedented amount of floor space to children's books.

Enthusiasm for children's books runs high and sales of children's books hold steady.

Multimedia products—CD-ROMs and interactive game adaptations of stories and informational books—are sold everywhere. David Macaulay published *The Way Things Work* (1988) (I–A) as an informational book but it soon became available on CD-ROM. Students can enter a museum and step back 250 million years to search for buried dinosaur bones in *Dinosaur Hunter,* an Eyewitness Virtual Reality CD-ROM. It seems miraculous to obtain a 30-volume set encyclopedia that shows such things as volcanoes erupting and mushrooms growing right before our eyes on one CD-ROM!

Poetry received a vote of confidence when the 1982 Newbery Medal was awarded to *A Visit to William Blake's Inn* (1982) (I–A) by Nancy Willard and the 1989 Newbery Medal was awarded to *Joyful Noise: Poems for Two Voices* by Paul Fleischman.

Literature-based programs became a driving force in shifting teaching practice away from isolated skill instruction toward integrated reading, writing, listening, and speaking. Library materials are no longer used primarily as supplementary material; they have become central to teaching and learning. Now teachers and librarians work together to develop thematic units, to introduce concepts across content areas, and to make connections among subject areas. In fact, the role of the school media specialist evolved into a literature and curriculum consultant. Literature-based instruction engages students in active inquiry where they not only develop research skills, but develop the library habit.

Students ask for flexible scheduling so they can have free access to libraries and their resources. Teacher–librarians recognize the need for books and collaborative planning as critical; they often spend their own money on books when public funds are not available.

Enthusiasm for children's books has created new markets; new markets have led to increased production. Whereas approximately 2,000 children's books were published each year in the 1960s, in the 1990s more than 5,000 were published annually. In addition to teachers and librarians who spend money on children's books, parents are discovering their role in children's reading. Parents understand that children of any age learn when adults read to them. As a result, publishers produce books for children at every developmental stage—from infants and toddlers to young adults. Marketing departments create products to accompany children's books—dolls, stuffed animals, jewelry, clothing, toys, and memorabilia. Children's books mean business—big business—for writers, illustrators, publishers, booksellers, and literary agents.

Illustrated folklore, fantasy, realism, and poetry marked the beginning of the twentieth century. Toy books, picture books, series books, science fiction, biography, historical fiction, and nonfiction and an increasing paperback market set the tone for the twenty-first century. The genres change across time. As the world changes, so, too, does literature for children. The ease of world travel and communication has turned children's books into a global industry. International book fairs lead to co-publishing among many nations. Children's books truly have universal appeal.

Glossary of Literary Terms

Alliteration Repetition of initial consonant.

Antagonist Character directly opposed to protagonist or hero.

Anthropomorphism Gives human qualities to animals or objects.

Character A personality in literature.

Characterization Means by which an author establishes credibility of person or creature created by words, for example, physical description, or character's actions, words, thoughts, and feelings.

Chronological order Events related in order of happening.

Classic Literary work from past generation that retains popularity over time.

Cliché Expression used so often it loses its freshness and clarity. Overused term that loses meaning.

Cliffhanger Suspenseful plot structure.

Climax Peak of action that brings about resolution of conflict.

Conflict Central problem or struggle; person against self, person against person, person against society, person against nature.

Connotation Emotional meaning of a word.

Convention Formulas and elements taken from folklore.

Denotation Dictionary meaning of a word.

Denouement Closing action after climax and resolution.

Didactic Preachy, moralistic.

End papers Insides of front and back covers.

Episodic plot Independent chapters.

Folklore Myths, legends, proverbs, nursery rhymes, stories handed down by word of mouth from generations past.

Folksong Song of unknown authorship preserved and transmitted by oral tradition.

Folktale Short narrative handed down through oral tradition.

Format Physical makeup of a book including page size, typeface, margins, paper, and binding.

Flashback Earlier scene out of sequence.

Foreshadowing Hints of things to come.

Genre Category of literature.

Hyperbole Exaggeration and overstatement.

Imagery Words that appeal to senses.

Jacket Dust jacket. Paper cover on hardbound book.

Language style Choice and arrangement of words to tell a story or poem that express the individuality, the ideas, and the intent of the author.

Metaphor Implied comparison.

Motif Recurring element in literature; a conventional situation, device, or incident; prevailing idea or design.

Omniscient narrator All-knowing narrator tells story in third person.

Onomatopoeia Words sound like their meaning: boom!

Parody Composition designed to ridicule in humorous fashion another piece of work or its author. Burlesque or humorous imitation of a work.

Pattern Repeated structure or device, for example, use of three.

Personification Gives human traits to inanimate objects.

Plot Sequence and relationship of events.

Plot structure Way a story is organized, the arrangements of the incidents, the ordering of events, the sequence, the story pattern. Types of plots: episodic, cumulative, flashbacks, chronological, cyclical.

Point of view Perspective from which an author tells a story or a poet speaks: first person, third person, omniscient narrator. Vantage point the author chooses.

Protagonist Central character; hero.

Resolution Action following climax; solution of the central problem.

Rhythm Recurring flow of strong and weak beats in the language of prose or poetry.

Setting Time and place of the story events.

Simile Stated comparison.

Symbol Element with figurative and literal meaning.

Tall tale Humorous tale of American frontier that recounts extravagantly impossible happenings.

Theme Central or dominating idea. In nonfiction, it may be the topic. In poetry, fiction, drama, it is an abstract concept that is made vivid through character, plot, and image.

Unity Coordination of text and illustration.

Variant Different version of the same folktale.

Verisimilitude Appearance or semblance of truth.

Verse Unit of poetry; a metrical composition.

Professional References

Ada, A. F. (1990). *A magical encounter: Spanish language children's literature in the classroom.* San Francisco: Santillana.

Alexander, L. (1970). Identifications and identities. *Wilson Library Bulletin, 45*(2), 144–148.

Alexander, L. (1981). The grammar of story. In B. Hearne & M. Kaye (Eds.), *Celebrating children's books* (pp. 3–13). New York: Lothrop.

Allington, R. L. (1984). Oral reading. In P. D. Pearson (Ed.), *Handbook of reading research* (pp. 829–864). New York: Longmans.

Anderson, R. C., Hiebert, E. H., Scott, J. A., & Wilkinson, I.A.G. (1985). *Becoming a nation of readers: The report of the commission on reading.* Washington, DC: National Institute of Education.

Anzul, M. (1988). Exploring literature with children within a transactional framework. *Dissertation Abstracts International, 49,* 08, 2132A.

Applebee, A. N. (1978). *The child's concept of story.* Chicago: University of Chicago Press.

Applebee, A. N. (1979). Children and stories: Learning the rules of the game. *Language Arts 56,* 645.

Atwell, N. (1998). *In the middle: New understandings about writing, reading, and learning.* Portsmouth, NH: Boynton/Cook, Heinemann.

Babbitt, N. (1990). Protecting children's literature. *The Horn Book Magazine, 66,* 696–703.

Banks, J. A., & Banks, C.A.M. (1993). Multicultural education: Issues and perspectives (3rd ed.). Boston: Allyn & Bacon.

Barrera, R. B., Thompson, V. D., Dressman, M. (2001). *Kaleidoscope: A multicultural booklist for grades K–8.* Urbana, IL: National Council of Teachers of English.

Baumann, J. F., & Kameenui, E. J. (1991). Research on vocabulary instruction: Ode to Voltaire. In J. Flood, J. M. Jensen, D. Lapp, & J. R. Squire (Eds.), *Handbook on teaching the English language arts* (pp. 604–632). New York: Macmillan.

Benton, M. (1984). The methodology vacuum in teaching literature. *Language Arts, 61,* 265–275.

Bettelheim, B. (1976). The uses of enchantment: *The meaning and importance of fairy tales.* New York: Knopf.

Birkman, M. (1973). *Children's responses to free verse.* Unpublished doctoral dissertation, Purdue University, West Lafayette, Indiana.

Blos, J. (1992). Perspectives on historical fiction. In R. Ammon & M. Tunnell (Eds.), *The story of ourselves: Teaching history through children's literature* (pp. 11–17). Portsmouth, NH: Heinemann.

Booth, David, & Moore, Bill. (1998). *Poems please! Sharing poetry with children.* Markham, Ont.: Pembroke.

Botkin, B. A. (1944). *A treasury of American folklore.* New York: Crown.

Britton, J. (1970). *Language and learning.* London: Penguin.

Bromley, K. D. (1991). *Webbing with literature: Creating story maps with children's books.* Boston: Allyn & Bacon.

Bruner, J. S. (1987). *Actual minds, possible worlds.* Cambridge, MA: Harvard University Press.

Bryant, P. E., Bradley, L., Maclean, M., & Crossland, J. (1989). Nursery rhymes, phonological skills and reading. *Journal of Child Language, 16,* 407–428.

Calder, J. W. (1984). The effects of story structure instruction on third-graders' concept of story, reading comprehension, response to literature, and written composition. *Dissertation Abstracts International, 46,* 02, 387A.

Cameron, E. (1969). *The green and burning tree.* New York: Atlantic, Little, Brown.

Carr, J. (1981). What do we do about bad biographies? *School Library Journal, 27*(9), 19–21.

Cazden, C. (1988). *Classroom discourse.* Portsmouth, NH: Heinemann.

Chukovsky, K. (1963). (Morton, M., Trans. & Ed). *From two to five.* Berkeley: University of California.

Cianciolo, P. J. (1976). *Illustrations in children's books.* Dubuque, IA: Brown.

Cianciolo, P. J. (1997). *Picture books for children* (4th ed.). Chicago: American Library Association.

Cianciolo, P. J., & Quirk, B. A. (1993). *Teaching and learning critical aesthetic response to literature: An instructional improvement study in grades K–5.* East Lansing, MI: The Center for the Learning and Teaching of Elementary Subjects, Institute for Research on Teaching, Michigan State University.

Clark, M. M. (1976). *Young fluent readers.* London: Heinemann.

Cochran-Smith, M. (1984). *The making of a reader.* Norwood, NJ: Ablex.

Cole, J. (1996). *On the bus with Joanna Cole: A creative autobiography.* Portsmouth, NH: Heinemann.

Cooper, S. (1981). Escaping into ourselves. In B. Hearne & M. Kaye (Eds.), *Celebrating children's books* (pp. 14–23). New York: Lothrop.

Corso, G. (1983). Comment. In P. Janeczko (Ed.), *Poetspeak* (p. 11). New York: Bradbury.

Cox, M. R. (1893). *Cinderella: Three hundred and forty-five variants.* New York: David Nutt/The Folklore Society.

Cullinan, B. E. (Ed.). (1992). *Invitation to read.* Newark, DE: International Reading Association.

Cullinan, B. E. (Ed.). (1996). *A jar of tiny stars: Poems by NCTE award-winning poets.* Honesdale, PA: Boyds Mills/NCTE.

Cullinan, B. E., Harwood, K., & Galda, L. (1983). The reader and the story: Comprehension and response. *Journal of Research and Development in Education, 16*(3), 29–38.

Cullinan, B. E., & Person, D. (2001). *The continuum encyclopedia of children's literature.* New York: Continuum International.

Cullinan, B. E., Scala, M., & Schroder, V. (1995). *Three voices: An invitation to poetry across the curriculum.* New York: Stenhouse.

Darton, F.J.H. (1982). *Children's books in England* (3rd ed.). London: Cambridge University Press.

de la Mare, W. (1942). *Peacock pie.* London: Faber & Faber.

de la Mare, W. (1962). Cited in W. S. Baring-Gould & C. Baring-Gould, *The annotated Mother Goose.* New York: Bramhall.

Demers, P., & Moyles, C. (1982). *From instruction to delight: An anthology of children's literature to 1850.* Toronto: Oxford University Press.

Donaldson, M. (1978). *Children's minds.* New York: Norton.

Durkin, D. (1966). *Children who read early.* New York: Teachers College Press.

Early, M. J. (1960). Stages of growth in literary appreciation. *English Journal, 49,* 161–167.

Edmiston, B., Enciso, P., & King, M. L. (1987). Empowering readers and writers through drama: Narrative theater. *Language Arts, 64,* 219–229.

Edmonds, L. (1986). The treatment of race in picture books for young children. *Book Research Quarterly, 2*(3), 30–41.

Eeds, M., & Peterson, R. (1991). Teacher as curator: Learning to talk about literature. *The Reading Teacher, 45,* 118–126.

Eeds, M., & Wells, D. (1989). Grand conversations: An exploration of meaning construction in literature study groups. *Research in the Teaching of English, 23,* 4–29.

Egoff, S. A. (1981). *Thursday's child: Trends and patterns in contemporary children's literature.* Chicago: American Library Association.

Farmer, P. (1979). *Beginnings: Creation myths of the world.* New York: Atheneum.

Favat, F. A. (1977). *Child and tale: The origins of interest.* Urbana, IL: National Council of Teachers of English.

Feitelsen, D., Kita, B., & Goldstein, Z. (1986). Effects of listening to series stories on first graders' comprehension and use of language. *Research in the Teaching of English, 20,* 339–356.

Fielding, L., Wilson, P. T., & Anderson, R. (1984). A new focus on free reading: The role of trade books in reading instruction.

In T. E. Raphael & R. E. Reynolds (Eds.), *The contexts of school-based literacy* (pp. 149–160). New York: Random.

Fisher, A. (2001). *Sing of the earth and sky: Poems about our planet and the wonders beyond.* Illus. by K. Thompson. Honesdale, PA: Boyds Mills.

Fisher, C. J., & Natarella, M. (1982). Young children's preferences in poetry: A national survey of first, second and third graders. *Research in the Teaching of English, 16*(4), 339–354.

Freedman, R. (1988, July/August). Newbery medal acceptance. *Horn Book Magazine,* 444–451.

Fritz, J. (1976). George Washington, my father, and Walt Disney. *Horn Book Magazine, 52*(2), 191–198.

Frye, N. (1963). *The well-tempered critic.* Bloomington: Indiana University Press.

Frye, N. (1970). *The educated imagination.* Bloomington: Indiana University Press.

Galda, L. (1982). Assuming the spectator stance: An examination of the responses of three young readers. *Research in the Teaching of English, 16,* 1–20.

Galda, L. (1983). Research in response to literature. In H. Agee & L. Galda (Eds.), *Response to literature: Empirical and theoretical studies (Journal of Research and Development in Education), 16*(3), 1–7.

Galda, L. (1988). Readers, texts, and contexts: A response-based view of literature. *The New Advocate, 1,* 92–102.

Galda, L. (1990). A longitudinal study of the spectator stance as a function of age and genre. *Research in the Teaching of English, 24,* 261–278.

Galda, L. (1992). Evaluation as a spectator: Changes across time and genre. In J. Many & C. Cox (Eds.), *Reader stance and literary understanding: Exploring the theories, research, and practice* (pp. 127–142). Norwood, NJ: Ablex.

Galda, L. (1993). How preferences and expectations influence evaluative responses to literature. In K. E. Holland, R. Hungerford, & S. Ernst (Eds.), *Journeying: Children responding to literature* (pp. 302–315). Portsmouth, NH: Heinemann.

Galda, L., Bisplinghoff, B. S., & Pellegrini, A. D. (1996). Literacy in transition: Home and school influences. Reading Research Report No. 62, Athens, GA: National Reading Research Center.

Galda, L., & Cullinan, B. (1991). Literature for literacy: What research says about the benefits of using trade books in the classroom. In J. Flood, J. M. Jensen, D. Lapp, & J. R. Squire (Eds.), *Handbook of research on teaching the English language arts* (pp. 529–535). New York: Macmillan.

Galda, L., Cullinan, B. E., & Strickland, D. (1997). *Language, literacy and the child.* (2nd ed.). Fort Worth, TX: Harcourt.

Galda, L., Rayburn, J. S., & Stanza, L. C. (2000). *Looking through the faraway end: Creating a literature-based reading curriculum with 2nd graders.* Newark, DE: International Reading Association.

Galda, L., Shockley, B., & Pellegrini, A. D. (1995). Sharing lives: Reading, writing, talking, and living in a first grade classroom. *Language Arts, 72,* 334–339.

Gardner, D. (1965). Emotions: A basis for learning. *Feelings and learning.* Washington, DC: Association for Childhood Education International.

Giblin, J. C. (1986, July). *Children's literature in the eighties.* Second Annual Highlights Foundation Writer's Workshop, Chautauqua, NY, p. 14.

Giniger, K. S. (1989). *The distribution and sale of foreign language books in the United States.* Alexandria, VA: International Publishing Newsletter.

Goldstone, B. P. (1984). *Lessons to be learned: A study of eighteenth-century English didactic children's literature (American University Studies Series),* New York: Peter Lang, XIV, Vol. 1.

Goodman, K. S. (1985). Transactional psycholinguistics model: Unity in reading. In H. Singer & R. B. Ruddell (Eds.), *Theoretical models and processes of reading* (3rd ed.) (pp. 813–840). Newark, DE: International Reading Association.

Goodman, K. S., & Goodman, Y. (1983) Reading and writing relationships: Pragmatic functions. *Language Arts, 69,* 590–599.

Grimal, P. (1965). *Larousse world mythology.* Secaucus, NJ: Chartwell.

Grossman, F. (1991). *Listening to the bells: Learning to read poetry by writing poetry.* Portsmouth, NH: Heinemann.

Hall, S. (1994). *Using picture storybooks to teach literary devices: Recommended books for children and young adults.* Phoenix, AZ: Oryx Press.

Halliday, M.A.K. (1982). Three aspects of children's language development: Learning language, learning through language, and learning about language. In Y. Goodman, M. Huassle, & D. S. Strickland (Eds.), *Oral and written language development research: Impact on the schools* (pp. 7–19). Urbana, IL: National Council of Teachers of English.

Hardy, B. (1978). Towards a poetics of fiction: An approach through narrative. In M. Meek, A. Warlow, & G. Barton (Eds.), *The cool web* (pp. 12–23). New York: Atheneum.

Harris, V. (Ed.). (1992). *Teaching multicultural literature in grades K–8.* Norwood, MA: Christopher-Gordon.

Harris, V. (Ed.). (1997). *Using multiethnic literature in the K–8 classroom.* Norwood, MA: Christopher-Gordon.

Harrison, D., & Cullinan, B. (1999). *Easy poetry lessons that dazzle and delight.* New York: Scholastic.

Harste, J. C., Short, K. C., & Burke, C. (1996). *Creating classrooms for writers and inquirers* (2nd ed.). Portsmouth, NH: Heinemann.

Harwayne, S. (1992). *Lasting impressions: Weaving literature into the writing workshop.* Portsmouth, NH: Heinemann.

Hazard, P. (1967). *Books, children, and men.* Boston: Horn Book.

Heard, G. (1989). *For the good of the earth and the sun: Teaching poetry.* Portsmouth, NH: Heinemann.

Heard, G. (1995). Writing toward home: Tales and lessons to find your way. Portsmouth, NH: Heinemann.

Heath, S. B. (1982). What no bedtime story means: Narrative skills at home and school. *Language and Society, 11,* 49–75.

Heath, S. B. (1983). *Ways with words: Language, life, and work in communities and classrooms.* Cambridge, MA: Cambridge University Press.

Heath, S. B. (1993). Report to the English Standards Board. Chicago: CSR, NCTE, IRA Standards Project.

Heinlein, R. A. (1953, July). Ray guns and rocket ships. *Library Journal, 78,* 1188.

Helbig, A. K., & Perkins, A. R. (2000). *Many peoples, one land: A guide to multicultural literature for children and young adults.* Westport, CT: Greenwood.

Hepler, S. I., & Hickman, J. (1982). The book was okay, I love you—Social aspects of response to literature. *Theory Into Practice, 21,* 278–283.

Herman, G. B. (1978). "Footprints in the sands of time": Biography for children. *Children's Literature in Education, 9(2),* 85–94.

Hickman, J. (1981). A new perspective on response to literature: Research in an elementary school setting. *Research in the Teaching of English, 15,* 343–354.

Hiebert, E. H., & Colt, J. (1989). Patterns of literature-based reading instruction. *The Reading Teacher, 43,* 14–20.

Hodges, M., & Steinfirst, S. (1980). *Elva S. Smith's history of children's literature.* Chicago: American Library Association.

Holland, R. (1970). *Mill child: The story of child labor in America.* New York: Macmillan.

Hopkins, L. B. (1998). *Pass the poetry please!* New York: HarperCollins.

Hunter, M. (1976). *Talent is not enough: Mollie Hunter on writing for children.* New York: Harper.

Hynds, S. (1992). Challenging questions in the teaching of literature. In J. A. Langer (Ed.), *Literature instruction: A focus on student response* (pp. 78–100). Urbana, IL: National Council of Teachers of English.

Ingham, J. (1981). *Books and reading development.* London: Heinemann.

Jackson, J. (1992). Paper presented at the Holmes-Hunter Lecture. University of Georgia, Athens.

Jagendorf, M. A. (1957). *Noodlehead stories from around the world.* New York: Vanguard.

Jordan, A. (1983). *From Rollo to Tom Sawyer, and other papers.* Boston: Horn Book.

Jung, C. G. (1991). *Psychology of the unconscious.* Princeton, NJ: Princeton University Press.

Kamil, M., Mosenthal, P. B., Pearson, P. D., & Barr, R. (2000). *Handbook of reading research (Volume III).* Mahwah, NJ: Erlbaum.

Kiefer, B. Z. (1986). The child and the picture book: Creating live circuits. *Children's Literature Association Quarterly, 11,* 63–68.

Kimmel, E. A. (1977). Confronting the ovens: The Holocaust and juvenile fiction. *Horn Book Magazine, 53(1).*

Langer, J. A. (1990). The process of understanding: Reading for literary and informative purposes. *Research in the Teaching of English, 24,* 229–260.

Langer, J. A. (1995). *Envisioning literature: Literary understanding and literature instruction.* New York: Teachers College Press.

Larrick, N. (1965, September 11). The all-white world of children's books. *Saturday Review,* 63–65.

Larrick, N. (1991). *Let's do a poem.* New York: Delacorte.

Lehman, B. (1989). Child reader and literary work: Children's literature merges two perspectives. *Children's Literature Association Quarterly, 14*(3), 123–128.

Lehr, S. S. (1991). *The child's developing sense of theme: Responses to literature.* New York: Teacher's College Press.

Leinhardt, G., Zigmond, N., & Cooley, W. W. (1981). Reading instruction and its effects. *American Educational Research Journal, 18,* 343–361.

Livingston, Myra Cohn. (1990). Climb into the bell tower: Essays on poetry. New York: Harper.

Luthi, M. (1970). *Once upon a time: On the nature of fairy tales.* New York: Ungar.

Maclean, M., Bryant, P. E., & Bradley, L. (1987). Rhymes, nursery rhymes and reading in early childhood. *Merrill-Palmer Quarterly, 33,* 255–281.

Marcus, Leonard S. (1991). *Margaret Wise Brown: Awakened by the moon.* Boston: Beacon Press.

Martin, Bill, Jr. (1972). *Sounds of Laughter (Teachers' Edition).* New York: Holt Reinhart & Winston.

May, J. (1984). Editorial: Judy Blume as Archie Bunker. *Children's Literature Association Quarterly, 9*(1), 2.

McClure, A. (1985). *Children's responses to poetry in a supportive literary context.* Unpublished doctoral dissertation, Ohio State University.

McClure, A., Harrison, P., & Reed, S. (1990). *Sunrises and songs: Reading and writing poetry in an elementary classroom.* Portsmouth, NH: Heinemann.

McMahon, S., & Raphael, T. E. (1993). Literature and the reading program: Why and how. *Michigan Reading Journal, 26*(3), 28–39.

McMahon, S., Raphael, T. E., Goatley, V. J., & Pardo, L. S. (1997). *The book club connection: Literacy learning and classroom talk.* New York: Teachers College.

McPhail, D. (1996). *In flight with David McPhail: A creative autobiography.* Portsmouth, NH: Heinemann.

McVitty, W. (1992). *Word magic: Poetry as a shared adventure.* Primary English Teaching Association.

Meek, M., Warlow, A., & Barton, G. (1978). *The cool web: The pattern of children's reading.* New York: Atheneum.

Meigs, C., Eaton, A. T., Nesbitt, E., & Viguers, R. H. (1969). *A critical history of children's literature.* New York: Macmillan.

Meltzer, M. (1976). Where do all the prizes go? The case for nonfiction. *Horn Book Magazine, 52*(1), 21–22.

Meltzer, M. (1989). The social responsibility of the writer. *The New Advocate, 2*(3), 155–157.

Merriam, E. (1981). Acceptance speech, National Council of Teachers of English Award for Excellence in Poetry for Children.

Miller-Lachman, L. (1992). *Our family, our friends, our world.* New Providence, NJ: Bowker.

Moffett, J. (1983). *Teaching the universe of discourse.* Boston: Houghton.

Monson, D. L., & Sebesta, S. L. (1991). Reading preferences. In J. Flood, J. M. Jensen, D. Lapp, & J. R. Squire (Eds.), *Handbook of research on teaching the English language arts* (pp. 664–673). New York: Macmillan.

Moss, A., & Stott, J. C. (1986). *The family of stories: An anthology of children's literature.* New York: Holt.

National Council of Teachers of English. (1983). Statement on censorship and professional guidelines. *The Bulletin, 9*(1–2), 17–18.

Naylor, P. R. (1992, July/August). Newbery acceptance speech. *Horn Book Magazine,* 404–411.

Nodelman, P. (1988). *Words about pictures.* Athens: University of Georgia Press.

O'Neill, C. (1989). Dialogue and drama: The transformation of events, ideas, and teachers. *Language Arts, 66,* 147–158.

Opie, I., & Opie, P. (1951). *The Oxford dictionary of nursery rhymes.* London: Oxford University Press.

Opie, I., & Opie P. (1974). *Classic fairy tales.* London: Oxford University Press.

Paterson, K. (1986). The secret life of Katherine Clements Womeldorf. In *Once upon a time* (pp. 18–19). New York: Putnam.

Perkinson, H. J. (1978). American textbooks and educational change. In National Institute of Education, *Early American Textbooks 1775–1900* (pp. 21–57). Washington, DC: Alvina Treut Burrows Institute.

Pillar, A. M. (1983). Aspects of moral judgment in response to fables. *Journal of Research and Development in Education, 16*(3), 37–46.

Posner, M. (1987). The broad range of Jewish children's books. *A. B. Bookman's Weekly, 79,* 1225–1233.

Pringle, L. (1986, July). *Science writing.* Second Annual Highlights Foundation Writer's Workshop, Chautauqua, NY, p. 26.

Purves, A. C., Rogers, T., & Soter, A. D. (1990). *How porcupines make love II: Teaching a response-centered literature curriculum.* New York: Longmans.

Raphael, T. E., Florio-Ruane, S., & George, M. (in press). Book club plus: A conceptual framework to organize literacy instruction. *Language Arts.*

Ravitch, D. (1985). *The schools we deserve: Reflections on the educational crises of our times.* New York: Basic.

Rollock, Barbara. (1988). *Black authors and illustrators of children's books.* New York: Garland.

Rosen, C., & Rosen, H. (1973). *The language of primary school children.* London: Penguin.

Rosenbach, A.S.W. (1966). *Early American children's books.* Millwood, NY: Kraus Reprint (Original work published 1933).

Rosenblatt, L. M. (1938/1976). *Literature as exploration.* New York: Noble & Noble (Original work published 1938).

Rosenblatt, L. M. (1978). *The reader, the text, the poem: The transactional theory of the literary work.* Carbondale: Southern Illinois University Press.

Rosenblatt, L. M. (1991). Literature—S.O.S.! *Language Arts, 68,* 444–448.

Rosenshine, B., & Stevens, R. (1984). Classroom instruction in reading. In P. D. Pearson (Ed.), *Handbook of reading research* (pp. 745–798). New York: Longmans.

Roser, N., & Frith, M. (1983). *Children's choices: Teaching with books children like.* Newark, DE: International Reading Association.

Saul, W. (1986, October). Living proof: Children's biographies of Marie Curie. *School Library Journal, 33,* 103–108.

Sawyer, R. (1962). *The way of the storyteller.* New York: Viking.

Schlager, N. (1978). Predicting children's choices in literature: A developmental approach. *Children's Literature in Education, 9,* 136–142.

Sears, Peter. (1990). *Gonna bake me a rainbow: A student guide to writing poetry.* New York: Scholastic.

Short, K. G., & Pierce, K. M. (1990). *Talking about books: Creating literate communities.* Portsmouth, NH: Heinemann.

Sims Bishop, R. (1997). *Kaleidoscope: A multicultural booklist for grades K–8.* Urbana, IL: National Council of Teachers of English.

Sims Bishop, R. (1982a). Profile: Lucille Clifton. *Language Arts, 59*(2), 160–167.

Sims Bishop, R. (1982b). *Shadow and substance: Afro-American experience in contemporary children's fiction.* Urbana, IL: National Council of Teachers of English.

Sims Bishop, R. (1985). Children's books about blacks: A mid-eighties status report. *Children's Literature Review, 8,* 9–14. Detroit: Gale Research.

Sims Bishop, R. (1987). Extending multicultural understanding through children's books. In B. E. Cullinan (Ed.), *Children's literature in the reading program* (pp. 60–67). Newark, DE: International Reading Association.

Sims Bishop, R. (1992). Multicultural literature for children: Making informed choices. In V. J. Harris (Ed.), *Teaching multicultural literature in grades K–8* (p. 41). Norwood, MA: Christopher-Gordon.

Sipe, L. (1998). Individual literary response styles of first and second graders. In T. Shanahan & F. V. Rodriguez-Brown (Eds.), *National Reading Conference Yearbook, 47* (pp. 76–89). Chicago: National Reading Conference.

Sloyer, S. (1982). *Readers theatre: Story dramatization in the classroom.* Urbana, IL: National Council of Teachers of English.

Smith, F. (1978). *Understanding reading* (2nd ed.). New York: Holt.

Smith, F. (1982). *Writing and the writer.* New York: Holt.

Smith, P. (1992). Poetry supplement. Houston, TX: Cypress-Fairbanks School District.

Smith, W. J. (1980). *Laughing time.* New York: Delacorte.

Stott, J. C. (1981). Teaching literary criticism in the elementary grades: A symposium. *Children's Literature in Education, 12,* 192–206.

Straparola, G. (1894). *The nights of Straparola.* London: Lawrence and Bullen.

Sutcliff, R. (1973). History is people. In V. Haviland (Ed.), *Children and literature: Views and reviews* (pp. 307–308). Glenview, IL: Scott, Foresman.

Sutherland, Z. (1984). *The Scott, Foresman anthology of children's literature.* Reading, MA: Addison-Wesley.

Sutherland, Zena, & Livingston, Myra Cohen. (1984). *The Scott, Foresman anthology of children's literature.* Glenview, IL: Scott, Foresman.

Taxel, J. (1984). The American revolution in children's fiction: An analysis of historical meaning and narrative structure. *Curriculum Inquiry, 14*(1), 7–55.

Taxel, J. (1992). The politics of children's literature: Reflections on multiculturalism, political correctness, and Christopher Columbus. In V. Harris (Ed.), *Teaching multicultural literature in grades K–8* (pp. 1–36). Norwood, MA: Christopher-Gordon.

Terry, A. (1974). *Children's poetry preferences: A national survey of upper elementary grades.* Urbana, IL: National Council of Teachers of English.

Tomlinson, C. M. (Ed.) (1998). *Children's books from other countries.* Lanham, MD: Scarecrow.

Trelease, J. (1991). *The new read-aloud handbook.* New York: Penguin.

Tway, E. (1970). A study of the feasibility of training teachers to use the literature rating scale in evaluating children's fiction writing. *Dissertation Abstracts International, 31,* 11, 5918A.

Verriour, P. (1985). Face to face: Negotiating meaning through drama. *Theory Into Practice, 24,* 181–186.

Vygotsky, L. S. (1962). *Thought and language.* Cambridge, MA: MIT Press.

Vygotsky, L. S. (1978), *Mind in society.* Cambridge, MA: Harvard University Press.

Wells, G. (1976). *The meaning makers: Children learning language and using language to learn.* Portsmouth, NH: Heinemann.

Wells, G. (1986). *The meaning makers.* Portsmouth, NH: Heinemann.

White, E. B. (1979). *Essays of E. B. White.* New York: Harper.

Wolf, S. A., & Heath, S. B. (1992). *The braid of literature: Children's worlds of reading.* Cambridge, MA: Harvard.

Wolf, W., Huck, C. S., & King, M. L. (1967). *Critical reading ability of elementary school children* (Contract No. OE-4-10-187). Report No. 5-1040. Washington, DC: United States Department of Education.

Yolen, J. (1981). *Touch magic: Fantasy, faerie and folklore in the literature of childhood.* New York: Philomel.

Children's Literature References

Aardema, Verna (Reteller). (1988). *Princess Gorilla and a New Kind of Water.* Illus. Victoria Chess. New York: Dial.

Aardema, Verna (Reteller). (1989). *Rabbit Makes a Monkey of Lion: A Swahili Tale.* Illus. Jerry Pinkney. New York: Dial.

Aardema, Verna. (1975). *Why Mosquitoes Buzz in People's Ears: A West African Tale.* Illus. Leo and Diane Dillon. New York: Dial.

Aardema, Verna. (1981). *Bringing the Rain to Kapiti Plain.* Illus. Beatriz Vidal. New York: Dial.

Aardema, Verna. (1991). *Borreguita and the Coyote: A Tale from Ayutila, Mexico.* Illus. Petra Mathers. New York: Knopf.

Aardema, Verna. (1992). *Traveling to Tondo: A Tale of the Nkundo of Zaire.* Illus. Will Hillenbrand. New York: Knopf.

Aardema, Verna. (1993). *A Bookworm Who Hatched.* Katonah, NY: Richard C. Owen.

Aardema, Verna. (1994). *Misoso: Once Upon a Time Tales from Africa.* Illus. Reynold Ruffins. New York: Knopf.

Aardema, Verna. (1996). *The Lonely Lioness and the Ostrich Chicks.* New York: Knopf.

Aaseng, Nathan. (1997). *Black Inventors.* New York: Facts on File.

Aaseng, Nathan. (2000). *Cherokee Nation v. Georgia: The Forced Removal of a People* (**Famous Trials** Series*).* New York: Lucent.

Aaseng, Nathan. (2000). *The Impeachment of Bill Clinton.* New York: Lucent.

Abbott, Jacob. (1834). *Rollo Learning to Talk.* Boston: Reynolds.

Abbott, Jacob. (1858). *Rollo in Rome.* Boston: Reynolds.

Abbott, Jacob. (1858). *Rollo's Tour of Europe.* Boston: Reynolds.

Abelove, Joan. (1998). *Go and Come Back.* New York: DK Publishing.

Ackerman, Karen. (1988). *Song and Dance Man.* Illus. Stephen Gammell. New York: Knopf.

Ada, Alma Flor. (1993). *My Name Is Maria Isabel.* New York: Simon & Schuster.

Ada, Alma Flor. (1994). *The Gold Coin.* Illus. Neil Waldman. New York: Aladdin.

Ada, Alma Flor. (1994). *Where the Flame Trees Bloom.* New York: Simon & Schuster.

Ada, Alma Flor. (1995). *Mediopollito/Half Chicken.* New York: Doubleday.

Ada, Alma Flor. (1997). *Gathering the Sun: An Alphabet in Spanish and English.* Illus. Simon Silva. New York: Lothrop, Lee & Shepard.

Ada, Alma Flor. (1998). *Under the Royal Palms: A Childhood in Cuba.* New York: Atheneum.

Ada, Alma Flor. (1999). *Three Golden Oranges.* Illus. Reg Cartwright. New York: Atheneum.

Adams, Richard. (1974). *Watership Down.* New York: Macmillan.

Adedjouma, Davida (Ed.). (1996). *The Palm of My Heart: Poetry by African American Children.* New York: Lee and Low.

Adler, C. S. (1999). *Not Just a Summer Crush.* New York: Clarion.

Adler, David A. (1981). *Cam Jansen and the Mystery of the Dinosaur Bones.* New York: Viking.

Adler, David A. (1986). *Martin Luther King, Jr.: Free at Last.* New York: Holiday House.

Adler, David A. (1989). *Jackie Robinson: He Was the First.* New York: Holiday House.

Adler, David A. (1989). *A Picture Book of Martin Luther King Jr.* New York: Holiday House.

Adler, David A. (1990). *A Picture Book of Benjamin Franklin.* New York: Holiday House.

Adler, David A. (1990). *A Picture Book of Thomas Jefferson.* New York: Holiday House.

Adler, David A. (1992). *A Picture Book of Jesse Owens.* Illus. Robert Casilla. New York: Holiday House.

Adler, David A. (1994). *A Picture Book of Robert E. Lee.* Illus. John Wallner. New York: Holiday House.

Adler, David A. (1994). *A Picture Book of Sojourner Truth.* New York: Holiday House.

Adler, David A. (1995). *One Yellow Daffodil: A Hanukkah Story.* San Diego: Harcourt.

Adler, David A. (1999). *How Tall, How Short, How Faraway.* Illus. Nancy Tobin. New York: Holiday House.

Adler, David. (1999). *The Babe and I.* Illus. Terry Widener. San Diego: Harcourt.

Adoff, Arnold. (1973). *Black Is Brown Is Tan.* Illus. Emily A. McCully. New York: HarperCollins.

Adoff, Arnold. (1979). *Eats: Poems.* Illus. Susan Russo. New York: Lothrop, Lee & Shepard.

Adoff, Arnold. (1982). *All the Colors of the Race.* Illus. John Steptoe. New York: Lothrop, Lee & Shepard.

Adoff, Arnold. (1986). *Sports Pages.* Illus. Steve Kuzma. New York: HarperCollins.

Adoff, Arnold. (1988). *Greens.* New York: Lothrop, Lee & Shepard.

Adoff, Arnold. (1989). *Chocolate Dreams.* Illus. Turi Maccombie. New York: Lothrop, Lee & Shepard.

Adoff, Arnold. (1990). *Hard to Be Six.* New York: Lothrop, Lee & Shepard.

Adoff, Arnold. (1991). *In for Winter, Out for Spring.* Illus. Jerry Pinkney. San Diego: Harcourt.

Adoff, Arnold. (1995). *Street Music: City Poems.* New York: HarperCollins.

Adoff, Arnold. (2000). *The Basket Counts.* Illus. Michael Weaver. New York: Simon & Schuster.

Aesop. (1991). *Androcles and the Lion.* Adapter and Illus. Janet Stevens. New York: Morrow/Avon.

Afanasyev, Alexander Nikolayevich. (1990). *The Fool and the Fish.* Illus. Gennady Spirin. Reteller Lenny Hort. New York: Dial.

Agard, John, & Nichols, Grace. (1994). *No Hickory, No Dickory, No Dock.* Illus. Cynthia Jabar. Cambridge: Candlewick.

Agee, Jon. (1988). *The Incredible Painting of Felix Clousseau.* New York: Farrar, Straus & Giroux.

Agee, Jon. (1999). *Sit on a Potato Pan, Otis! More Palindromes.* New York: Farrar, Straus & Giroux.

Agee, Jon. (2000). *Elvis Lives! And Other Anagrams.* New York: Farrar, Straus & Giroux.

Ahlberg, Allen. (2000). *The Bravest Bear Ever.* Illus. Paul Howard. Cambridge: Candlewick.

Ahlberg, Janet, & Ahlberg, Allan. (1979). *Each Peach Pear Plum.* New York: Viking.

Ahlberg, Janet, & Ahlberg, Allan. (1981). *Peek-A-Boo.* New York: Viking.

Aker, Suzanne. (1990). *What Comes in 2's, 3's, and 4's?* New York: Simon & Schuster.

Alarcon, Francisco X. (1997). *Laughing Tomatoes and Other Spring Poems/Jitomates Risuenos y Otro Poemas de Primavera.* Illus. Maya Christina Gonzales. San Francisco: Children's Book Press.

Alarcon, Francisco X. (1998). *From the Bellybutton of the Moon and Other Summer Poems/Del Ombligo de las Luna y Otros Poemas de Verano: Poems/Poemas.* Illus. Maya Christina Gonzales. San Francisco: Children's Book Press.

Alcock, Vivien. (1987). *Ghostly Companions.* New York: Delacorte.

Alcock, Vivien. (1988). *Monster Garden.* New York: Delacorte.

Alcock, Vivien. (1998). *Stranger at the Window.* Boston: Houghton.

Alcott, Louisa May. (1868; 1968 Reissue). *Little Women.* Illus. Jessie Willcox Smith. Boston: Little, Brown.

Alcott, Louisa May. (1869; 1971 Reissue). *An Oldfashioned Girl.* New York: Grosset and Dunlap.

Alcott, Louisa May. (1870; 1977 Reissue). *Eight Cousins.* New York: Webster, Golden.

Alcott, Louisa May. (1886; 1971 Reissue). *Jo's Boys.* New York: Grosset and Dunlap.

Alcott, Louisa May. (1995). *A Long Fatal Love Chase.* New York: Random House.

Aldrich, Thomas Bailey. (1870; 1976 Reissue). *The Story of a Bad Boy.* New York: Garland.

Alexander, Lloyd. (1964; 1999). *The Book of Three (The Pyrdain Chronicles).* New York: Holt.

Alexander, Lloyd. (1965; 1999). *The Black Cauldron.* New York: Holt.

Alexander, Lloyd. (1966; 1999). *The Castle of Llyr.* New York: Holt.

Alexander, Lloyd. (1967; 1999). *Taran Wanderer.* New York: Holt.

Alexander, Lloyd. (1968; 1999). *The High King.* New York: Holt.

Alexander, Lloyd. (1973). *The Foundling and Other Tales of Prydain.* New York: Holt.

Alexander, Lloyd. (1988). *The Drackenburg Adventure.* New York: Dutton.

Alexander, Martha. (1993). *Willy's Boot.* New York: Candlewick.

Alexander, Sue. (1983). *Nadia the Willful.* New York: Pantheon.

Alger, Horatio. (1868). *Ragged Dick.* Boston: Loring.

Aliki. (1968). *Hush Little Baby: A Folk Lullaby.* New York: Simon & Schuster.

Aliki. (1983). *A Medieval Feast.* New York: HarperCollins.

Aliki. (1986). *Go Tell Aunt Rhody.* New York: Macmillan.

Aliki. (1986). *How a Book Is Made.* New York: HarperCollins.

Aliki. (1989). *Many Lives of Benjamin Franklin.* New York: Simon & Schuster.

Aliki. (1995). *Tabby: A Story in Pictures.* New York: HarperCollins.

Aliki. (1997). *My Visit to the Zoo.* New York: HarperCollins.

Aliki. (1999). *Marianthe's Story: Painted Words/Spoken Memories.* New York: Greenwillow.

Aliki. (1999). *William Shakespeare and the Globe.* New York: HarperCollins.

Allen, Thomas B. (1989). *On Grandaddy's Farm.* New York: Knopf.

Allingham, William. (1870). *In Fairyland.* London: Longmans.

Almond, David. (1999). *Skellig.* New York: Delacorte.

Alphin, Elaine Maria. (1996). *A Bear for Miguel.* New York: HarperCollins.

Altman, Linda Jacobs. (1993). *Amelia's Road.* Illus. Enrique O. Sanchez. New York: Lee and Low.

Ammer, Christine. (1989). *It's Raining Cats and Dogs. And Other Beastly Expressions.* New York: Paragon.

Anastos, Phillip, & French, Chris. (1991). *Illegal: Seeking the American Dream.* New York: Rizzoli.

Anaya, Rudolfo. (1995). *The Farolitos of Christmas.* Illus. Edward Gonzales. New York: Hyperion.

Anaya, Rudolfo. (2000). *My Land Sings: Stories from the Rio Grande.* Illus. Amy Cordova. New York: Morrow/Avon.

Ancona, George. (1987). *Turtle Watch.* New York: Macmillan.

Ancona, George. (1989). *Handtalk Zoo.* New York: Simon & Schuster.

Ancona, George. (1992). *Man and Mustang.* New York: Macmillan.

Ancona, George. (1993). *Powwow.* San Diego: Harcourt.

Ancona, George. (1994). *The Piñata Maker/El Piñatero.* San Diego: Harcourt.

Ancona, George. (1995). *Cutters, Carvers, and the Cathedral.* New York: Lothrop, Lee & Shepard.

Ancona, George. (1995). *Earth Daughter: Alicia of Acoma Pueblo.* New York: Simon & Schuster.

Andersen, Hans Christian. (1979). *The Steadfast Tin Soldier.* Illus. Paul Galdone. New York: Clarion.

Andersen, Hans Christian. (1979). *Thumbelina.* Illus. Susan Jeffers. New York: Dial.

Andersen, Hans Christian. (1982). *The Emperor's New Clothes.* Reteller and Illus. Anne Rockwell. New York: HarperCollins.

Andersen, Hans Christian. (1993). *The Snow Queen.* Illus. Mary Engelbreit. New York: Workman.

Anderson, Joan. (1996). *Cowboys: Roundup on an American Ranch.* New York: Scholastic.

Anderson, Laurie Halse. (1999). *Speak.* New York: Farrar, Straus & Giroux.

Anderson, Lena. (1989). *Stina.* New York: Greenwillow.

Anderson, Matthew T. (1999). *Burger Wuss.* Illus. David Butler. Cambridge: Candlewick.

Anderson, Rachel. (1992). *The Bus People.* New York: Holt.

Anderson, Rachel. (1993). *Paper Faces.* New York: Holt.

Andreasen, Dan. (2000). *Rose Red and the Bear Prince.* New York: HarperCollins.

Andreson, Laurie Halse. (2000). *Fever 1793.* New York: Simon & Schuster.

Andrews, Jan. (1986). *Very Last First Time.* Illus. Jan Wallace. New York: Simon & Schuster.

Angell, Judie. (1985). *One Way to Ansonia.* New York: Simon & Schuster.

Angelou, Maya. (1993). *Soul Looks Back in Wonder.* New York: Dial.

Anholt, Catherine. (1995). *What Makes Me Happy?* New York: Candlewick.

Anholt, Catherine, & Anholt, Laurence. (1992). *All About You.* New York: Viking.

Anno, Mitsumasa. (1975). *Anno's Alphabet.* New York: HarperCollins.

Anno, Mitsumasa. (1977). *Anno's Counting Book.* New York: HarperCollins.

Anno, Mitsumasa. (1978). *Anno's Journey.* New York: Philomel.

Anno, Mitsumasa. (1982). *Anno's Britain.* New York: Philomel.

Anno, Mitsumasa. (1983). *Anno's Mysterious Multiplying Jar.* New York: Philomel.

Anno, Mitsumasa. (1987). *Anno's Math Games.* New York: Philomel.

Anno, Mitsumasa. (1989). *Anno's Aesop: A Book of Fables by Aesop and Mr. Fox.* New York: Scholastic.

Anno, Mitsumasa. (1990). *All in a Day.* New York: Philomel.

Anno, Mitsumasa. (1993). *Anno's Twice-Told Tales: The Fisherman and His Wife and the Four Clever Brothers.* New York: Philomel.

Anno, Mitsumasa. (1995). *Anno's Magic Seeds.* New York: Philomel.

Anzaldua, Gloria. (1996). *Prietita and the Ghost Woman/Prietita y la Llorona.* Illus. Christina Gonzales. San Francisco: Children's Book Press.

Archer, Jules. (1991). *Breaking Barriers: The Feminist Revolution from Susan B. Anthony to Margaret Sanger to Betty Friedan.* New York: Viking.

Archer, Jules. (1994). *A House Divided: The Lives of Ulysses S. Grant and Robert E. Lee.* New York: Scholastic.

Ardizzone, Edward. (1956). *Tim All Alone.* New York: Oxford University.

Ardizzone, Edward. (1961; 2000 Reprint). *Little Tim and the Brave Sea Captain.* New York: Morrow/Avon.

Armstrong, Jennifer. (1992). *Steal Away.* New York: Orchard/Jackson.

Armstrong, Jennifer. (1995). *Black-Eyed Susan.* New York: Crown.

Armstrong, Jennifer. (1996). *The Dreams of Mairhe Mehan.* New York: David McKay.

Armstrong, Jennifer. (1997). *Mary Mehan Awake.* New York: Knopf.

Armstong, Jennifer. (1999). *Shipwreck at the Bottom of the World: The Extraordinary True Story of Shackleton and the Endurance.* New York: Random House.

Arnold, Caroline. (1985). *Saving the Peregrine Falcon.* Minneapolis, MN: Carolrhoda.

Arnold, Caroline. (1987). *Giraffe.* Photog. Richard Hewett. New York: Morrow/Avon.

Arnold, Caroline. (1987). *Zebra.* Photog. Richard Hewett. New York: Morrow/Avon.

Arnold, Caroline. (1988). *Llama.* Photog. Richard Hewett. New York: Morrow/Avon.

Arnold, Caroline. (1989). *Cheetah.* Photog. Richard Hewett. New York: Morrow/Avon.

Arnold, Caroline. (1989). *Hippo.* Photog. Richard Hewett. New York: Morrow/Avon.

Arnold, Caroline. (1989). *The Terrible Hodag.* Illus. Lambert Davis. San Diego: Harcourt.

Arnold, Caroline. (1990). *Orangutan.* New York: Morrow/Avon.

Arnold, Caroline. (1990). *Wild Goats.* New York: Morrow/Avon.

Arnold, Caroline. (1991). *Snakes.* New York: Morrow/Avon.

Arnold, Caroline. (1992). *The Ancient Cliff Dwellers of Mesa Verde.* Boston: Houghton.

Arnold, Caroline. (1992). *Camel.* New York: Morrow/Avon.

Arnold, Caroline. (1993). *Dinosaurs All Around: An Artist's View of the Prehistoric World.* New York: Clarion.

Arnold, Caroline. (1993). *Elephant.* New York: Morrow/Avon.

Arnold, Caroline. (1994). *Killer Whale.* New York: Morrow/Avon.

Arnold, Caroline. (2000). *Easter Island: Giant Stone Statues Tell of a Rich and Tragic Past.* Boston: Clarion.

Arnold, Katya. (1993). *Baba Yaga: A Russian Folktale.* New York: North-South.

Arnosky, Jim. (1995). *I See Animals Hiding.* New York: Scholastic.

Arnosky, Jim. (1996). *All About Owls.* New York: Scholastic.

Arnosky, Jim. (1997). *All About Rattlesnakes.* New York: Scholastic.

Arnosky, Jim. (1997). *Watching Water Birds.* Washington, DC: National Geographic.

Arnosky, Jim. (1998). *Watching Desert Wildlife.* Washington, DC: National Geographic.

Aronson, Marc. (1999). *Sir Walter Ralegh and the Quest for El Dorado.* New York: Clarion.

Arrington, Frances. (2000). *Bluestem.* New York: Philomel.

Aruego, José. (1988). *Look What I Can Do.* New York: Macmillan.

Asbjørnsen, Peter Christian, & Moe, Jorgen E. (1972). *The Three Billy Goats Gruff.* Illus. Marcia Brown. San Diego: Harcourt.

Asbjørnsen, Peter Christian, & Moe, Jorgen E. (1975). *The Squire's Bride.* Illus. Marcia Sewall. New York: Simon & Schuster.

Asbjørnsen, Peter Christian, & Moe, Jorgen E. (1980 o.p.). *The Runaway Pancake.* Illus. Otto S. Svend. London: Pelham Books.

Asch, Frank. (1997). *One Man Show.* Katonah, NY: Richard C. Owen.

Ashabranner, Brent. (1982). *Morning Star, Black Sun: The Northern Cheyenne Indians and America's Energy Crisis.* Photog. Paul Conklin. New York: Putnam.

Ashabranner, Brent. (1990). *The Time of My Life: A Memoir.* New York: Dutton.

Ashabranner, Brent. (1992). *Land of Yesterday, Land of Tomorrow: Discovering Chinese Central Asia.* New York: Cobblehill.

Ashabranner, Brent. (1995). *A New Frontier: The Peace Corps in Eastern Europe.* New York: Cobblehill.

Ashabranner, Brent. (1996). *A Strange and Distant Shore: Indians of the Great Plains in Exile.* New York: Cobblehill/Penguin.

Ashabranner, Brent. (2000). *A Date with Destiny: The Women in Military Service for America Memorial.* New York: 21st Century.

Ashbe, Jeanne. (2000). *What's Inside.* La Jolla: Kane/Miller Book Publishers.

Ashby, Ruth, & Ohrn, Deborah Gore (Eds.). (1995). *Herstory: Women Who Changed the World.* New York: Viking.

Asher, Sandy. (1987). *Where Do You Get Your Ideas? Helping Young Writers.* Illus. Susan Hellard. New York: Walker.

Ashley, Bernard. (1992). *Cleversticks.* Illus. Derek Brazell. New York: Crown.

Asimov, Isaac. (1961). *Words from the Myths.* Illus. William Barss. Boston: Houghton.

Asimov, Isaac. (1966). *Fantastic Voyage: A Novel.* Boston: Houghton.

Asimov, Isaac. (1983). *Norby the Mixed-Up Robot.* New York: Walker.

Asimov, Isaac, Greenberg, Martin, & Waugh, Charles (Eds.). (1984). *Time Warp.* Milwaukee: Raintree.

Atkins, Jeannine. (1995). *Aani and the Tree Huggers.* Illus. Venantius J. Pinto. New York: Lee and Low.

Atwater, Richard. (1938). *Mr. Popper's Penguins.* Illus. Richard and Florence Atwater. Boston: Little, Brown.

Atwood, Ann. (1979). *Haiku: The Mood of Earth.* Illus. Ann Atwood. New York: Scribner's.

Auch, Mary Jane. (1998). *Frozen Summer.* New York: Holt.

Avi. (1979). *Night Journeys.* New York: Morrow/Avon.

Avi. (1980). *Encounter at Easton.* New York: Morrow/Avon.

Avi. (1980). *The History of Helpless Harry: To Which Is Added a Variety of Amusing and Entertaining Adventures.* New York: Morrow/Avon.

Avi. (1983). *Smuggler's Island.* New York: Morrow/Avon.

Avi. (1984). *The Fighting Ground.* New York: HarperCollins.

Avi. (1986). *S. O. R. Losers.* New York: Morrow/Avon.

Avi. (1991). *Nothing But the Truth: A Documentary Novel.* New York: Scholastic.

Avi. (1992). *Who Was That Masked Man, Anyway?* New York: Scholastic.

Avi. (1994). *The Barn.* New York: Scholastic.

Avi. (1997). *Poppy.* Illus. Brian Floca. Danbury, CT: Orchard.

Avi. (1999). *Abagail Takes the Wheel.* Illus. Don Bolognse. New York: HarperCollins.

Avi. (1999). *Poppy and Rye.* Illus. Brian Floca. New York: Camelot.

Avi. (2000). *Ereth's Birthday.* Illus. Brian Floca. New York: HarperCollins.

Avi. (2000). *Poppy.* New York: Camelot.

Avi. (2000). *Ragweed: A Tale for Dimwood Forest.* Illus. Brian Floca. New York: HarperCollins.

Axelrod, Alan. (1991). *Songs of the Wild West.* Contributor Dan Fox. New York: Simon & Schuster.

Axworthy, Anni. (1992). *Anni's India Diary.* Dallas: Whispering Coyote.

Aylesworth, Jim. (1992). *Old Black Fly.* Illus. Stephen Gammell. New York: Holt.

Aylesworth, Jim. (1992). *The Folks in the Valley: A Pennsylvania Dutch ABC.* Illus. Stefano Vitale. New York: HarperCollins.

Azarian, Mary. (2000). *A Gardner's Alphabet.* Boston: Houghton.

Babbitt, Natalie. (1969). *The Search for Delicious.* New York: Farrar, Straus & Giroux.

Babbitt, Natalie. (1975). *Tuck Everlasting.* New York: Farrar, Straus & Giroux.

Bach, Alice, & Exum, J. Cheryl. (1989). *Moses's Ark: Stories from the Bible.* Illus. Leo and Diane Dillon. New York: Delacorte.

Bach, Alice, & Exum, J. Cheryl. (1991). *Miriam's Well: Stories About Women in the Bible.* Illus. Leo and Diane Dillon. New York: Delacorte.

Bach, Alice. (1978). *Millicent the Magnificent.* New York: HarperCollins.

Baer, Edith. (1998). *Walk the Dark Streets: A Novel.* New York: Farrar, Straus & Giroux.

Baer, Gene. (1989). *Thump, Thump, Rat-A-Tat-Tat.* Illus. Lois Ehlert. New York: HarperCollins.

Bagert, Brod. (1992). *Let Me Be the Boss.* Illus. G. L. Smith Honesdale, PA: Boyds Mills.

Bagert, Brod. (1993). *Chicken Socks and Other Contagious Poems.* Honesdale, PA: Boyds Mills.

Bagert, Brod. (1995). *Elephant Games and Other Playful Poems to Perform.* Honesdale, PA: Boyds Mills.

Baillie, Allan. (1992). *Little Brother.* New York: Viking.

Baillie, Allan. (1994). *Rebel.* Illus. Di Wu. New York: Ticknor & Fields.

Baker, Jeannie. (1991). *Window.* New York: Greenwillow.

Baker, Jeannie. (2000). *The Hidden Forest.* New York: Greenwillow.

Baker, Leslie. (1987). *The Third Story Cat.* Boston: Little, Brown.

Baker, Leslie. (1992). *The Antique Store Cat.* Boston: Little, Brown.

Baker, Olaf. (1989). *Where the Buffaloes Begin.* Illus. Stephen Gammell. New York: Viking.

Bang, Molly. (1976). *Wiley and the Hairy Man.* New York: Macmillan.

Bang, Molly. (1983). *Ten, Nine, Eight.* New York: Greenwillow.

Bang, Molly. (1997). *Common Ground: The Water, Earth, and Air We Share.* New York: Scholastic.

Bang, Molly. (1999). *When Sophie Gets Angry, Really, Really Angry.* New York: Scholastic.

Banks, Jacqueline Turner. (1995). *Egg-Drop Blues.* Boston: Houghton.

Banks, Kate. (2000). *Howie Bowles, Secret Agent.* Illus. Isaac Millman. New York: Farrar, Straus & Giroux.

Banks, Lynne Reid. (2000). *Alice-By-Accident.* New York: Morrow/Avon.

Banyai, Istvan. (1995). *Re-Zoom.* New York: Viking.

Banyai, Istvan. (1995). *Zoom.* New York: Viking.

Barasch, Lynne. (2000). *Radio Rescue.* New York: Farrar, Straus & Giroux.

Barber, Barbara E. (1994). *Saturday at the New You.* Illus. Anna Rich. New York: Lee and Low.

Barber, Barbara E. (1996). *Allie's Basketball Dream.* Illus. Darryl Ligasan. New York: Lee and Low.

Barboza, Steven. (1994). *Door of No Return: The Legend of Goree Island.* New York: Cobblehill.

Bare, Colleen Stanley. (1989). *Never Kiss an Alligator!* New York: Cobblehill/Dutton.

Bare, Colleen Stanley. (1992). *This Is a House.* New York: Dutton.

Barner, Bob. (1998). *Which Way to the Revolution? A Book of Maps.* New York: Holiday House.

Barnwell, Ysaye. (1998). *No Mirrors in My Nana's House.* Illus. Synthia Saint James. San Diego: Harcourt.

Barrett, Tracy. (1999). *Anna of Byzantium.* New York: Delacorte.

Barrie, James H. (1906). *Peter Pan in Kensington Gardens.* Illus. Arthur Rackham. Weathervane Scribner's.

Barrie, James M. (1988). *Peter Pan.* Illus. Jan Ormerod. (Original work published in 1904.). New York: Viking.

Barth, Edna. (1979). *Balder and the Mistletoe: A Story for the Winter Holidays.* New York: Clarion.

Barth, Edna. (1979). *Cupid and Psyche: A Love Story.* New York: Clarion.

Bartoletti, Susan Campbell. (1999). *Kids on Strike!* Boston: Houghton.

Barton, Byron. (1988). *I Want to Be an Astronaut.* New York: HarperCollins.

Barton, Byron. (1990). *Bones, Bones, Dinosaur Bones.* New York: HarperCollins.

Barton, Byron. (1991). *The Three Bears.* New York: HarperCollins.

Bartone, Elisa. (1993). *Peppe the Lamplighter.* Illus. Ted Lewin. New York: Lothrop, Lee & Shepard.

Base, Graeme. (1987). *Animalia.* New York: Abrams.

Bash, Barbara. (1993). *Shadows of Night: The Hidden World of the Little Brown Bat.* San Francisco: Sierra Club.

Bat-Ami, Miriam. (1999). *Two Suns in the Sky. Arden: Front Street.*

Battle-Lavert, Gwendolyn. (1995). *Off to School.* Illus. Gershom Griffith. New York: Holiday House.

Battle-Lavert, Gwendolyn. (2000). *The Shaking Bag.* Illus. Aminah B. Robinson. Morton Grove, IL: Whitman.

Bauer, Caroline Feller. (1986). *Snowy Day Stories and Poems.* New York: Lippincott.

Bauer, Cat. (2000). *Harley, Like a Person.* New York: Winslow.

Bauer, Joan. (1998). *Rules of the Road.* New York: Puffin.

Bauer, Joan. (1999). *Backwater.* New York: Putnam.

Bauer, Joan. (2000). *Hope Was Here.* New York: Putnam.

Bauer, Joan. (2000). *Rules of the Road.* New York: Puffin.

Bauer, Marion Dane. (1985). *Like Mother, Like Daughter.* New York: Clarion.

Bauer, Marion Dane. (1986). *On My Honor.* New York: Clarion.

Bauer, Marion Dane. (1992). *Ghost Eye.* New York: Scholastic.

Bauer, Marion Dane. (1992). *What's Your Story: A Young Person's Guide to Writing Fiction.* New York: Clarion.

Bauer, Marion Dane. (1994). *Am I Blue? Coming Out from the Silence.* New York: HarperCollins.

Bauer, Marion Dane. (1996). *A Writer's Story: From Life to Fiction.* New York: Clarion.

Bawden, Nina. (1973). *Carrie's War.* New York: HarperCollins.

Bawden, Nina. (1992). *The House of Secrets.* New York: Clarion.

Bawden, Nina. (1992). *Humbug.* Boston: Houghton.

Baylor, Byrd. (1975, 1986). *The Desert Is Theirs.* Illus. Peter Parnall. New York: Scribner's.

Baylor, Byrd. (1976). *Hawk, I'm Your Brother.* Illus. Peter Parnall. New York: Scribner's.

Baylor, Byrd. (1983). *The Best Town in the World.* Illus. Ronald Himler. New York: Scribner's.

Baylor, Byrd. (1986). *I'm in Charge of Celebrations.* Illus. Peter Parnall. New York: Scribner's.

Baynes, Pauline. (1988). *Noah and the Ark.* New York: Holt.

Beard, Darleen Bailey. (1998). *The Flimflam Man.* Illus. Eileen Christelow. New York: Farrar, Straus & Giroux.

Beatty, John, & Beatty, Patricia. (1974). *Master Rosalind.* New York: Morrow/Avon.

Beatty, Patricia. (1972). *O the Red Rose Tree.* New York: Morrow/Avon.

Beatty, Patricia. (1981). *Lupita Mañana.* New York: Morrow/Avon.

Beatty, Patricia. (1984). *Turn Homeward, Hannalee.* New York: Morrow/Avon.

Beatty, Patricia. (1987). *Charlie Skedaddle.* New York: Morrow/Avon.

Beatty, Patricia. (1990). *Wait for Me, Watch for Me, Eula Bea.* New York: Morrow/Avon.

Beatty, Patricia. (1991). *Jayhawker.* New York: Morrow/Avon.

Beatty, Patricia. (1992). *Who Comes with Cannons?* New York: Morrow/Avon.

Beatty, Patricia. (1993). *The Nickle-Plated Beauty.* New York: Morrow/Avon.

Bechard, Margaret. (1999). *If It Doesn't Kill You.* New York: Viking.

Begay, Shonto. (1992). *Ma'ii and Cousin Horned Toad: A Traditional Navajo Story.* New York: Scholastic.

Begay, Shonto. (1995). *Navajo: Visions and Voices Across the Mesa.* New York: Scholastic.

Beil, Karen Magunson. (1999). *Fire in Their Eyes: Wildfires and People Who Fight Them.* San Diego: Harcourt.

Bell, Claire. (1987). *Ratha's Creature.* New York: Dell.

Bellairs, John. (1975). *The Figure in the Shadows.* Illus. Mercer Mayer. New York: Dial.

Bellairs, John. (1976). *The Letter, the Witch, and the Ring.* New York: Dial.

Bellairs, John. (1993). *The Ghost in the Mirror.* New York: Dial.

Beller, Susan Provost. (1998). *Never Were Men So Brave: The Irish Brigade During the Civil War.* New York: McElderry.

Belpré, Pura. (1961). *Perez and Martina: A Puerto Rican Folktale/Perez y Martina.* New York: Warne.

Belpré, Pura. (1969; o.p.). *Santiago.* Illus. Symeon Shimin. New York: Warne.

Belpré, Pura. (1996). *Firefly Summer.* Houston: Arte Publico.

Belton, Sandra. (1993). *From Miss Ida's Porch.* New York: Simon & Schuster.

Bemelmans, Ludwig. (1939; 1962). *Madeline.* New York: Viking.

Beneduce, Ann Keay. (1993). *A Weekend with Winslow Homer.* New York: Rizzoli.

Berger, Melvin. (1976). *The Story of Folk Music.* Chatham, NY: Phillips.

Berger, Melvin. (1985). *Germs Make Me Sick!* New York: HarperCollins.

Berger, Melvin. (1989). *The Science of Music.* New York: HarperCollins.

Berger, Melvin. (2000). *Why I Sneeze, Shiver, Hiccup, and Yawn (A Lot . . .).* Illus. Paul Meisel. New York: HarperCollins.

Bergman, Tamar. (1988). *Boy from over There.* Boston: Houghton.

Bernardo, Anilu. (1996). *Fitting In.* Houston: Arte Publico.

Bernardo, Anilu. (1996). *Jumping Off to Freedom.* Houston: Arte Publico.

Bernhard, Emery. (1994). *Eagles: Lions of the Sky.* New York: Holiday House.

Bernhard, Emery. (1995). *Salamanders.* New York: Holiday House.

Bernhard, Emery. (1997). *Prairie Dogs.* Illus. Durga Bernhard. San Diego: Harcourt.

Bernier-Grand, Carmen T. (1994). *Juan Bobo: Four Tales from Puerto Rico.* New York: HarperCollins.

Bernos De Gasztold, Carmen. (1992). *Prayers from the Ark: Selected Poems.* Trans. Rumer Godden. Illus. Barry Moser. New York: Viking.

Berry, James. (1988). *A Thief in the Village.* New York: Scholastic.

Berry, James. (1991). *When I Dance.* Illus. Karen Barbour. San Diego: Harcourt.

Berry, James. (1992). *Ajeemah and His Son.* New York: HarperCollins.

Berry, James. (1993). *The Future-Telling Lady.* New York: HarperCollins.

Bertrand, Diane Gonzales. (1995). *Sweet Fifteen.* Houston: Arte Publico.

Bertrand, Diane Gonzales. (1996). *Alicia's Treasure.* Houston: Arte Publico.

Besson, Jean-Louis. (1995). *October 45: Childhood Memories of the War.* San Diego: Harcourt.

Betancourt, Jeanne. (1993). *My Name Is Brain Brian.* New York: Scholastic.

Bial, Raymond (Author/Photographer). (1992). *County Fair.* Boston: Houghton.

Bial, Raymond. (1995). *Portrait of a Farm Family.* Boston: Houghton.

Bial, Raymond. (1995). *The Underground Railroad.* Boston: Houghton.

Bial, Raymond. (1998). *Cajun Home.* Boston: Houghton.

Bider, Djemma. (1989). *A Drop of Honey.* Illus. Armen Kojoyian. New York: Simon & Schuster.

Bierhorst, John. (1971). *In the Trail of the Wind: American Indian Poems and Ritual Orations.* New York: Farrar, Straus & Giroux.

Bierhorst, John. (1983). *The Sacred Path: Spells, Prayers, and Power Songs of the American Indians.* New York: Morrow/Avon.

Bierhorst, John. (1987). *The Naked Bear: Folktales of the Iroquois.* Illus. Dirk Zimmer. New York: Morrow/Avon.

Bierhorst, John. (1990). *Spirit Child: A Story of the Nativity.* Illus. Barbara Cooney. New York: Morrow/Avon.

Bierhorst, John. (1992). *Lightning Inside You: And Other Native American Riddles.* New York: Morrow/Avon.

Bierhorst, John. (1994). *On the Road of the Stars: Native American Night Poems and Sleep Charms.* New York: Simon & Schuster.

Bierhorst, John (Ed.). (1995). *The White Deer and Other Stories Told by the Lenape.* New York: Morrow/Avon.

Bierhorst, John. (1998). *The Deetkatoo: Native American Stories About Little People.* Illus. Ron Hilbert Coy. New York: Morrow/Avon.

Bierhorst, John. (2000). *The People with Five Fingers: A Native Californian Creation Tale.* Illus. Robert Andrew Parker. New York: Marshall Cavendish.

Billingsley, Franny. (1999). *The Folk Keeper.* New York: Atheneum.

Birdseye, Tom. (1988). *Air Mail to the Moon.* Illus. Stephen Gammell. New York: Holiday House.

Birdseye, Tom. (1993). *Just Call Me Stupid.* New York: Holiday House.

Bishop, Claire Huchet. (1938). *The Five Chinese Brothers.* Illus. Kurt Weise. New York: Coward.

Bishop, Gerald (Ed.). (1993). *Ranger Rick.* Washington, DC: National Wildlife Federation.

Bishop, Nic. (2000). *Digging for Bird-Dinosaurs: An Expedition to Madagascar.* Boston: Houghton.

Bjork, Christina. (1987). *Linnea in Monet's Garden* (Joan Sandin, Trans.). Illus. Lena Anderson. New York: Farrar, Straus & Giroux.

Bjork, Christina. (1988). *Linnea's Windowsill Garden* (Joan Sandin, Trans.). Illus. Lena Anderson. New York: Farrar, Straus & Giroux.

Blackstone, Margaret, & Guest, Elissa Haden. (2000). *Girl Stuff: A Survival Guide to Growing Up.* San Diego: Harcourt.

Blackwood, Alan. (1993). *Orchestra: An Introduction to the World of Classical Music.* Brookfield, CT: Millbrook.

Blackwood, Gary. (1998). *Alien Astronauts (Secrets of the Unexplained, Group 1).* Tarrytown: Marshall Cavendish.

Blackwood, Gary. (1998). *The Shakespeare Stealer.* New York: Dutton.

Blades, Ann. (1971). *Mary of Mile 18.* Plattsburgh, NY: Tundra.

Blair, Walter. (1987). *Tall Tale America: A Legendary History of Our Humorous Heroes.* Illus. Glen Rounds. Chicago: University of Chicago Press.

Blake, William. (1789; 1966 Reissue). *Songs of Innocence.* Illus. Ellen Raskin. New York: Doubleday.

Blake, William. (1794; 1927 Reissue). *Songs of Experience.* London: Beun.

Bland, Celia. (1995). *Peter MacDonald: Former Chairman of the Navajo Nation.* New York: Chelsea.

Blegvad, Lenore. (1996). *A Sound of Leaves.* New York: McElderry.

Blizzard, Gladys S. (1992). *Come Look with Me: Animals in Art.* Charlottesville, VA: Thomasson-Grant.

Blizzard, Gladys S. (1992). *Come Look with Me: Exploring Landscape Art with Children.* Charlottesville, VA: Thomasson-Grant.

Block, Francesca Lia. (1995). *Baby Be-Bop.* New York: HarperCollins.

Bloor, Edward. (1999). *Crusader.* San Diego: Harcourt.

Blos, Joan. (1979). *A Gathering of Days: A New England Girl's Journal, 1830–32.* New York: Macmillan.

Blumberg, Rhoda (Ed.). (1998). *What's the Deal: Jefferson, Napoleon, and the Lousiana Purchase.* Washington, DC: National Geographic.

Blumberg, Rhoda. (1985). *Commodore Perry in the Land of the Shogun.* New York: Lothrop, Lee & Shepard.

Blumberg, Rhoda. (1991). *The Remarkable Voyages of Captain Cook.* New York: Bradbury.

Blumberg, Rhoda. (1993). *Bloomers!* New York: Bradbury.

Blumberg, Rhoda. (1996). *Full Steam Ahead: The Race to Build a Transcontinental Railroad.* Washington, DC: National Geographic.

Blume, Judy. (1970). *Are You There God? It's Me, Margaret.* New York: Bradbury.

Blume, Judy. (1971). *Then Again, Maybe I Won't.* New York: Bradbury.

Blume, Judy. (1972). *Tales of a Fourth Grade Nothing.* New York: Dutton.

Blume, Judy. (1980). *Superfudge.* New York: Dutton.

Bober, Natalie. (1995). *Abigail Adams: Witness to a Revolution.* New York: Atheneum.

Bodecker, N. M. (1991). *Water Pennies: And Other Poems.* Illus. Erik Blegvad. New York: McElderry.

Bolden, Tonya (Ed.). (1994). *Rites of Passage: Stories About Growing Up by Black Writers from Around the World.* New York: Hyperion.

Bolton, Linda. (1995). *Hidden Pictures.* New York: Dutton.

Bonafoux, Pascal. (1992). *A Weekend with Rembrandt.* New York: Rizzoli.

Bond, Nancy. (1994). *Truth to Tell.* New York: Simon & Schuster.

Bond, Ruskin. (1991). *Cherry Tree.* Honesdale, PA: Boyds Mills.

Bontemps, Arna, & Hughes, Langston. (1932). *Popo and Fifina.* New York: Macmillan.

Boock, Paula. (1999). *Dare Truth or Promise.* Boston: Houghton.

Bosse, Malcolm. (1980). *Cave Beyond Time.* New York: HarperCollins.

Bosse, Malcolm. (1994). *The Examination.* New York: Farrar, Straus & Giroux.

Bosse, Malcolm. (1995). *Tusk and Stone.* Arden, NC: Front Street.

Boston, Lucy. (1955). *The Children at Green Knowe.* New York: Harcourt.

Botkin, B. A. (1944; o.p.). *Treasury of American Folklore.* New York: Crown.

Boudalika, Litsa. (1998). *If You Could Be My Friend: Letters of Mervet Akram Sha'bar and Galit Fink.* Danbury, CT: Orchard.

Boulton, Jane. (1994). *Only Opal: The Diary of a Young Girl.* Illus. Barbara Cooney. New York: Philomel.

Bowdish, Lynea. (2000). *Brooklyn, Bugsy, and Me.* Illus. Nancy Carpenter. New York: Farrar, Straus & Giroux.

Bowen, Betsy. (1993). *Tracks in the Wild.* Boston: Little, Brown.

Bowen, Betsy. (1998). *Gentle Giant Octopus.* Illus. Mike Bostock. Cambridge: Candlewick.

Bowen, Gary. (1994). *Stranded at Plimoth Plantation 1626.* New York: HarperCollins.

Boyd, Candy Dawson. (1993). *Chevrolet Saturdays.* New York: Simon & Schuster.

Boyd, Candy Dawson. (1998). *Daddy, Daddy, Be There.* Illus. Floyd Cooper. New York: Penguin.

Branch, Muriel Miller. (1998). *Juneteenth: Freedom Day.* Photog. Willis Branch. New York: Cobblehill.

Brandenburg, Jim. (1993). *To the Top of the World: Adventures with Arctic Wolves.* New York: Walker.

Brandenburg, Jim. (1994). *Sand and Fog: Adventures in Southern Africa.* New York: Walker.

Brandenburg, Jim. (1997). *An American Safari: Adventures on the North American Prairie.* New York: Walker.

Branford, Henrietta. (1999). *The Fated Sky.* Illus. Cythia Von Buhler. Cambridge: Candlewick.

Branley, Franklyn M. (1986). *Snow Is Falling: Let's Read-And-Find-Out Science Book.* New York: Crowell.

Bray, Rosemary L. (1995). *Martin Luther King.* New York: Greenwillow.

Brenner, Barbara, & Garelick, May. (1992). *The Tremendous Tree Book.* Honesdale, PA: Boyds Mills.

Brenner, Barbara, and Takaya, Julia. (1996). *Chibi: A True Story from Japan.* New York: Clarion/Houghton.

Brett, Jan. (1985). *Annie and the Wild Animals.* Boston: Houghton.

Brett, Jan. (1989). *Beauty and the Beast.* New York: Clarion.

Brett, Jan. (1990). *The Mitten: A Ukranian Folktale.* New York: Putnam.

Brett, Jan. (1991). *Berlioz the Bear.* New York: Putnam.

Brett, Jan. (1994). *Town Mouse, Country Mouse.* New York: Putnam.

Bridges, Ruby. (1999). *Through My Eyes.* New York: Scholastic.

Briggs, Raymond. (1989). *The Snowman.* New York: Random House.

Brimner, Larry Dane. (1992). *A Migrant Family.* Minneapolis, MN: Lerner.

Brinckloe, Julie. (1985). *Fireflies.* New York: Macmillan.

Brink, Carol Ryrie. (1973). *Caddie Woodlawn.* New York: Macmillan.

Brittain, Bill. (1994). *Wizards and the Monster.* New York: HarperCollins.

Broker, Ignatia. (1983). *Night Flying Woman: An Ojibway Narrative.* St. Paul: Minnesota Historical Society.

Brooke, L. Leslie. (1903; 1986 Reprint). *Johnny Crow's Garden.* New York: Warne.

Brooke, L. Leslie. (1905; 1977 Reprint). *The Golden Goose Book.* New York: Warne.

Brooke, L. Leslie. (1922). *Ring O' Roses: A Nursery Rhyme Picture Book.* New York: Clarion.

Brooke, William J. (1992). *Untold Tales.* New York: HarperCollins.

Brooks, Bruce. (1984). *The Moves Make the Man.* New York: HarperCollins.

Brooks, Bruce. (1986). *Midnight Hour Encores.* New York: HarperCollins.

Brooks, Bruce. (1989). *No Kidding.* New York: HarperCollins.

Brooks, Bruce. (1990). *Everywhere.* New York: HarperCollins.

Brooks, Bruce. (1992). *What Hearts.* New York: HarperCollins.

Brooks, Bruce. (1996). *Asylum for Nightface.* New York: HarperCollins.

Brooks, Bruce. (1999). *Vanishing.* New York: HarperCollins.

Brooks, Gwendolyn. (1967). *Bronzeville Boys and Girls.* New York: HarperCollins.

Brooks, Martha. (2000). *Being with Henry.* New York: DK Publishing.

Broome, Errol. (1993). *Dear Mr. Sprouts.* New York: Knopf.

Brown, Craig. (1995). *Tractor.* New York: Greenwillow.

Brown, Don. (1998). *Alice Ramsey's Grand Adventure.* Boston: Houghton.

Brown, Laurie Krasny, & Brown, Marc Tolan. (1997). *What's the Big Secret? Talking About Sex with Girls and Boys.* Boston: Little, Brown.

Brown, Marc. (1987). *Play Rhymes.* New York: Dutton.

Brown, Marcia. (1961). *Once a Mouse.* New York: Scribner's.

Brown, Margaret Wise. (1947). *Goodnight Moon.* Illus. Clement Hurd. New York: HarperCollins.

Brown, Margaret Wise. (1992). *Red Light, Green Light.* Illus. Leonard Weisgard. New York: Scholastic.

Brown, Margaret Wise. (1995). *The Days Before Now.* New York: Simon & Schuster.

Brown, Mary Barrett. (1992). *Wings Along the Waterway.* New York: Scholastic.

Brown, Susan Taylor. (1999). *Can I Pray with My Eyes Open?* Illus. Garin Baker. New York: Hyperion.

Brown, Tricia. (1991). *Lee Ann: The Story of a Vietnamese-American Girl.* Photog. Ted Thai. New York: Putnam.

Brown, Tricia. (1995). *Konnichiwa! I Am a Japanese-American Girl.* New York: Holt.

Brown, Tricia. (1998). *Children of the Midnight Sun: Young Native Voices of Alaska.* Photog. Roy Corral. Portland, OR: Graphic Arts Center Publishing Company.

Browne, Anthony. (1985). *Gorilla.* New York: Knopf.

Browne, Anthony. (1986). *Piggybook.* New York: Knopf.

Browne, Anthony. (1989). *I Like Books.* New York: Knopf.

Browne, Anthony. (1989). *Things I Like.* New York: Knopf.

Browne, Anthony. (1990). *The Tunnel.* New York: Knopf.

Browne, Anthony. (1991). *Changes.* New York: Knopf.

Browne, Anthony. (1991). *Willy and Hugh.* New York: Knopf.

Bruchac, Joseph. (1993). *Flying with the Eagle, Racing the Great Bear.* Illus. Murv Jacob. Mahwah, NJ: Bridgewater.

Bruchac, Joseph. (1994). *The Great Ball Game: A Muskogee Story.* New York: Dial.

Bruchac, Joseph. (1994). *On the Road of Stars: Native American Night Poems and Sleep Chants.* New York: Macmillan.

Bruchac, Joseph. (1995). *A Boy Called Slow: The True Story of Sitting Bull.* New York: Philomel.

Bruchac, Joseph. (1995). *The Boy Who Lived with the Bears and Other Iroquois Stories.* New York: HarperCollins.

Bruchac, Joseph. (1995). *Dog People: Native American Dog Stories.* Illus. Murv Jacob. New York: Fulcrum.

Bruchac, Joseph. (1995). *The Earth Under Sky Bear's Feet: Native American Poems of the Land.* New York: Philomel.

Bruchac, Joseph. (1995). *Gluskabe and the Four Wishes.* New York: Cobblehill/Dutton.

Bruchac, Joseph. (1996). *Between Earth and Sky: Legends of Native American Sacred Places.* San Diego: Harcourt.

Bruchac, Joseph. (1996). *Children of the Longhouse.* New York: Dial.

Bruchac, Joseph. (1996). *Legends of Native American Sacred Places.* San Diego: Harcourt.

Bruchac, Joseph. (1997). *Four Ancestors: Stories, Songs, and Poems from Native North America.* Illus. S. S. Burrus, Murv Jacob, Jeffrey Chapman, and Duke Sine. Mahwah, NJ: Bridgewater.

Bruchac, Joseph. (1997). *Lasting Echoes: An Oral History of Native American People.* Illus. Paul Morin. San Diego: Harcourt.

Bruchac, Joseph. (1998). *The Arrow over the Door.* Illus. James Watling. New York: Dial.

Bruchac, Joseph. (1998). *Children of the Longhouse.* New York: Puffin.

Bruchac, Joseph. (1999). *Eagle Song.* Illus. Dan Andreasen. New York: Puffin.

Bruchac, Joseph. (1999). *The Waters Between: A Novel of the Dawn Land.* Hanover: University Press of New England.

Bruchac, Joseph. (2000). *Crazy Horse's Vision.* Illus. S. D. Nelson. New York: Lee and Low.

Bruchac, Joseph. (2000). *Sacajawea: The Story of Bird Woman and the Lewis Clark Expedition.* New York: Silver Whistle.

Bruchac, Joseph, & London, Jonathan. (1992). *Thirteen Moons on Turtle's Back: A Native American Year of Moons.* Illus. Thomas Locker. New York: Philomel.

Bruchac, Joseph, & Ross, Gayle. (1995). *The Story of the Milky Way.* New York: Dial.

Bruchac, Joseph, & Ross, Gayle. (1996). *The Girl Who Married the Moon: Tales from Native North America.* New York: Troll.

Brusca, Maria Christina. (1991). *On the Pampas.* New York: Holt.

Brusca, Maria Cristina, & Wilson, Tona. (1995). *Pedro Fools the Gringo and Other Tales of a Latin American Trickster.* New York: Holt.

Brusca, Maria Cristina, & Wilson, Tona. (1995). *When Jaguars Ate the Moon and Other Stories About Animals and Plants of the Americas.* New York: Holt.

Bryan, Ashley. (1985). *The Cat's Purr.* New York: Atheneum.

Bryan, Ashley. (1986). *Lion and the Ostrich Chicks and Other African Folktales.* New York: Atheneum.

Bryan, Ashley. (1989). *Turtle Knows Your Name.* New York: Atheneum.

Bryan, Ashley. (1991). *All Night, All Day: A Child's First Book of African-American Spirituals.* New York: Atheneum.

Bryan, Ashley. (1992). *Sing to the Sun.* New York: McElderry.

Bryan, Ashley. (1997). *Ashley Bryan's ABC of African American Poetry.* New York: Simon & Schuster.

Bryan, Ashley. (1998). *Carol of the Brown King: Nativity Poems by Langston Hughes.* New York: Atheneum.

Bryant, Jennifer Fisher. (1994). *Louis Braille: Inventor.* New York: Chelsea.

Bucknall, Caroline. (1987). *Three Little Pigs.* New York: Dial.

Budiansky, Satephen. (2000). *The World According to Horses: How They Run, See, and Think.* New York: Holt.

Buffet, Jimmy, & Buffett, Savannah Jane. (1988). *The Jolly Mon.* Illus. Lambert Davis. San Diego: Harcourt.

Bulla, Clyde Robert. (1962). *What Makes a Shadow?* New York: HarperCollins.

Bulla, Clyde Robert. (1963; o.p.). *Viking Adventure.* New York: HarperCollins.

Bulla, Clyde Robert. (1981). *A Lion to Guard Us.* New York: HarperCollins.

Bunting, Eve. (1986). *The Mother's Day Mice.* Illus. Jan Brett. New York: Clarion.

Bunting, Eve. (1987). *Ghost's Hour, Spook's Hour.* Illus. Donald Carrick. New York: Clarion.

Bunting, Eve. (1988). *Is Anybody There?* New York: Lippincott.

Bunting, Eve. (1990). *The Wall.* Illus. Ronald Himler. Boston: Houghton.

Bunting, Eve. (1991). *Fly Away Home.* Illus. Ronald Himler. New York: Clarion.

Bunting, Eve. (1994). *Smoky Night.* Illus. David Diaz. San Diego: Harcourt.

Bunting, Eve. (1995). *Dandelions.* Illus. Greg Shed. San Diego: Harcourt.

Bunting, Eve. (1995). *Once Upon a Time.* Katonah, NY: Richard C. Owen.

Bunting, Eve. (1995). *Spying on Miss Müller.* New York: Clarion/Houghton.

Bunting, Eve. (1998). *So Far from the Sea.* Illus. Chris K. Soentpiet. Boston: Clarion.

Bunyan, John. (1678, 1684; 1979 Reprint). *The Pilgrim's Progress.* New York: Dodd, Mead.

Burchard, Peter. (1995). *Charlotte Forten: A Black Teacher in the Civil War.* New York: Crown.

Burges, Melvin. (1998). *Smack.* New York: Holt.

Burgess, Barbara Hood. (1994). *The Fred Field.* New York: Delacorte.

Burgie, Irving. (1992). *Carribbean Carnival: Songs of the West Indies.* New York: Morrow/Avon.

Burkert, Nancy Ekholm. (1989). *Valentine and Orson.* New York: Farrar, Straus & Giroux.

Burks, Brian. (1995). *Runs with Horses.* San Diego: Harcourt.

Burks, Brian. (1998). *Walks Alone.* San Diego: Harcourt.

Burleigh, Robert. (1998). *Black Whiteness: Admiral Byrd Alone in the Antarctic.* New York: Simon & Schuster.

Burleigh, Robert, & Wimmer, Mike. (1991). *Flight: The Journey of Charles Lindbergh.* New York: Philomel.

Burnett, Frances Hodgson. (1888; 1963 Revised). *Sara Crewe.* Revised as the *Little Princess.* New York: HarperCollins.

Burnett, Frances Hodgson. (1911; 1988 Reissue). *The Secret Garden.* Illus. Tasha Tudor. New York: Viking.

Burnford, Sheila. (1961). *The Incredible Journey.* Illus. Carl Burger. Boston: Little, Brown.

Burningham, John. (1971). *Mr. Gumpy's Outing.* New York: Holt.

Burningham, John. (1978). *Time to Get Out of the Bath, Shirley.* New York: HarperCollins.

Burningham, John. (1980). *The Shopping Basket.* New York: HarperCollins.

Burns, Khepra, & Miles, William. (1995). *Black Stars in Orbit: NASA's African American Astronauts.* San Diego: Harcourt.

Burr, Claudia, Libura, Krystyna, & Urrutia, Maria. (1997). *Broken Shields.* Toronto: Groundwood Books.

Burr, Claudia, Libura, Krystyna, & Urrutia, Maria. (1997). *What the Aztecs Told Me.* Toronto: Groundwood Books.

Burton, Jane. (1992). *Fox.* Illus. Mary Ling. New York: Dorling Kindersley.

Burton, Virginia Lee. (1939). *Mike Mulligan and His Steam Shovel.* Boston: Houghton.

Burton, Virginia Lee. (1942). *The Little House.* Boston: Houghton.

Butler, Stephen. (1991). *Henny Penny.* New York: Morrow/Avon.

Butterworth, Nick, & Inkpen, Mick. (1987). *Nice or Nasty: A Book of Opposites.* Boston: Little, Brown.

Byars, Betsy. (1970). *Summer of the Swans.* New York: Viking.

Byars, Betsy. (1986). *Blossoms Meet the Vulture Lady.* New York: Delacorte.

Byars, Betsy. (1986, 1989). *The Golly Sisters Go West.* New York: HarperCollins.

Byars, Betsy. (1987). *Blossoms and the Green Phantom.* New York: Delacorte.

Byars, Betsy. (1990). *Bingo Brown, Gypsy Lover.* New York: Viking.

Byars, Betsy. (1991). *The Moon and I.* Englewood Cliffs, NJ: Simon & Schuster, Messner.

Byars, Betsy. (1994). *The Dark Stairs: A Herculeah Jones Mystery.* New York: Viking.

Byars, Betsy. (1995). *Tarot Says Beware.* New York: Viking.

Byars, Betsy. (1996). *The Midnight Fox.* Illus. Ann Grifalcon. New York: Viking.

Bynum, Janie. (2000). *Otis.* San Diego: Harcourt.

Cadnum, Micheal. (2000). *The Book of the Lion.* New York: Viking.

Caduto, Michael J. , & Bruchac, Joseph. (1988). *Keepers of the Earth: Native American Stories and Environmental Activities for Children.* Golden, CO: Fulcrum.

Cajacob, Thomas, & Burton, Theresa. (1986). *Close to the Wild: Siberian Tigers in a Zoo.* Minneapolis, MN: Carolrhoda.

Calabro, Marian. (1999). *The Perilous Journey of the Donner Party.* Boston: Houghton.

Caldecott, Randolph. (1878; 1978 Reissue). *The Diverting History of John Gilpin.* Available as Randolph Caldecott's *John Gilpin and Other Stories.* New York: Warne.

Calvert, Patricia. (1994). *Bigger.* New York: Scribner's.

Calvert, Patricia. (1998). *Great Lives: The American Frontier.* New York: Atheneum.

Cameron, Ann. (1981). *Stories Julian Tells.* New York: Pantheon.

Cameron, Ann. (1986). *More Stories Julian Tells.* New York: Pantheon.

Cameron, Ann. (1987). *Julian's Glorious Summer.* New York: Pantheon.

Cameron, Ann. (1988). *The Most Beautiful Place in the World.* Illus. Thomas B. Allen. New York: Knopf.

Cameron, Ann. (1995). *The Kidnapped Prince: The Life of Olaudah Equiano.* New York: Knopf.

Cameron, Ann. (2000). *Gloria's Way.* Illus. Lis Toft. New York: Farrar, Strauss & Giroux.

Cameron, Eleanor. (1969). *The Green and Burning Tree.* Boston: Little, Brown.

Cameron, Eleanor. (1971). *A Room Made of Windows.* Boston: Little, Brown.

Cameron, Eleanor. (1977). *Julia and the Hand of God.* New York: Dutton.

Cameron, Eleanor. (1982). *That Julia Redfern.* New York: Dutton.

Cameron, Eleanor. (1984). *Julia's Magic.* New York: Dutton.

Cameron, Eleanor. (1988). *The Private Worlds of Julia Redfern.* New York: Dutton.

Caple, Kathy. (2000). *The Friendship Tree.* New York: Holiday House.

Caraker, Mary. (1991). *Faces of Ceti.* Boston: Houghton.

Caras, Roger. (1994). *A World Full of Animals: A Roger Caras Story.* San Francisco: Chronicle.

Carle, Eric. (1968). *1, 2, 3 to the Zoo.* New York: Philomel.

Carle, Eric. (1989). *The Very Busy Spider.* New York: Philomel.

Carle, Eric. (1991). *Dragons and Other Creatures That Never Were.* Compiler Laura Whipple. New York: Philomel.

Carle, Eric. (1991). *Eric Carle's Dragons Dragons and Other Creatures That Never Were.* New York: Penguin Putnam.

Carle, Eric. (1995). *The Very Lonely Firefly.* New York: Philomel.

Carle, Eric. (1996). *The Art of Eric Carle.* New York: Putnam.

Carlson, Laurie. (1998). *Boss of the Plains: The Hat That Won the West.* Illus. Holly Meade. New York: DK Publishing.

Carlson, Lori. (1994). *American Eyes: New Asian-American Short Stories for Young Adults.* New York: Holt.

Carlson, Lori. (1994). *Cool Salsa: Bilingual Poems on Growing Up Latino in the United States.* New York: Holt.

Carlson, Lori. (1996). *Barrio Streets, Carnival Dreams: Three Generations of Latino Artistry.* New York: Holt.

Carlstrom, Nancy White. (1986). *Jesse Bear, What Will You Wear?* Illus. Bruce Degen. New York: Macmillan.

Carlstrom, Nancy White. (1988). *Better Not Get Wet, Jesse Bear.* Illus. Bruce Degen. New York: Macmillan.

Carr, Jan. (1995). *Dark Day, Light Night.* Illus. James Ransome. New York: Hyperion.

Carrick, Carol. (1976). *The Accident.* Illus. Donald Carrick. New York: Clarion.

Carrick, Carol. (1982). *Sleep Out.* Illus. Donald Carrick. New York: Clarion.

Carrick, Carol. (1987). *Lost in the Storm.* Illus. Donald Carrick. New York: Clarion.

Carrick, Carol. (1988). *Left Behind.* Illus. Donald Carrick. New York: Clarion.

Carrick, Donald. (1984). *Dark and Full of Secrets.* Boston: Houghton.

Carroll, Lewis. (1865; 1992). *The Adventures of Alice in Wonderland.* New York: Morrow/Avon.

Carroll, Lewis. (1871; 1977 Reissue). *Through the Looking Glass.* Illus. John Tenniel. New York: St. Martin's.

Carter, Alden. (2000). *Crescent Moon.* New York: Holiday House.

Carter, Ann (Compiler). (1991). *Birds, Beasts, and Fishes: A Selection of Animal Poems.* Illus. Reg Cartwright. New York: Macmillan.

Carter, David A., & Diaz, James. (1999). *The Elements of Pop-Up.* New York: Little Simon.

Carter, Dorothy. (1987). *His Majesty, Queen Hatshepsut.* New York: HarperCollins.

Case, Dianne. (1995). *92 Queens Road.* New York: Farrar, Straus & Giroux.

Caseley, Judith. (1991). *Harry and Willy and Carrothead.* New York: Greenwillow.

Caseley, Judith. (1994). *Starring Dorothy Kane.* New York: Greenwillow.

Cassedy, Sylvia. (1994). *Behind the Attic Wall.* New York: Camelot.

Cassedy, Sylvia, & Suetake, Kunihiro. (1992). *Red Dragonfly on My Shoulder.* New York: HarperCollins.

Cassedy, Sylvia. (1983). *Behind the Attic Wall.* New York: HarperCollins.

Cassedy, Sylvia. (1987). *M. E. and Morton.* New York: HarperCollins.

Cassedy, Sylvia. (1989). *Lucie Babbidge's House.* New York: HarperCollins.

Cassedy, Sylvia. (1990). *In Your Own Words: A Beginner's Guide to Writing.* (Rev. ed.). New York: HarperCollins.

Cassedy, Sylvia. (1993). *Zoomrimes: Poems About Things That Go.* New York: HarperCollins.

Cassie, Brian. (1999). *National Audubon Society First Field Guide: Trees.* New York: Scholastic.

Castaneda, Omar S. (1991). *Among the Volcanoes.* New York: Dutton.

Castaneda, Omar S. (1993). *Abuela's Weave.* New York: Lee and Low.

Cather, Willa. (1949 Reprint). *My Ántonia.* New York: Random House.

Cauley, Lorinda Bryan (Reteller and Illus.). (1988). *The Pancake Boy: An Old Norwegian Folktale.* New York: Putnam.

Cauley, Lorinda Bryan. (1984). *The Town Mouse and the Country Mouse.* New York: Putnam.

Caxton, William. (1477). *A Book of Curtesey.*

Caxton, William. (1481; 1960). *The History of Reynard the Fox.* Cambridge: Harvard University Press.

Caxton, William. (1484). *Aesop's Fables.*

Cazet, Denys. (1987). *A Fish in His Pocket.* New York: Scholastic.

Cech, John. (1994). *Jacques-Henri Lartigue: Boy with a Camera.* New York: Simon & Schuster.

Cecil, Laura. (1995). *Frog Princess.* New York: Greenwillow.

Cedeno, Maria E. (1993). *Cesar Chavez: Labor Leader (Hispanic Heritage Series).* Brookfield, CT: Millbrook.

Celsi, Teresa. (1990). *The Fourth Little Pig.* New York: Raintree.

Cendrars, Blaise. (1982). *Shadow.* Trans. Marcia Brown. Illus. Marcia Brown. New York: Scribner's.

Cerullo, Mary M. (1994). *Lobsters: Gangsters of the Sea.* New York: Cobblehill.

Ceserani, Gian Paolo. (1982). *Marco Polo.* New York: Putnam.

Cha, Dia. (1996). *Dia's Story Cloth: The Hmong People's Journey of Freedom.* New York: Lee and Low.

Chalk, Gary. (1993). *Yankee Doodle.* New York: Dorling Kindersley.

Chalk, Gary. (1994). *Mr. Frog Went A-Courting: Discover the Secret Story.* New York: Dorling Kindersley.

Chang, Ina. (1991). *A Separate Battle: Women and the Civil War.* New York: Dutton.

Chang, Margaret, & Chang, Raymond. (1997). *The Beggar's Magic: A Chinese Tale.* Illus. David Johnson. New York: McElderry.

Charles, Donald. (1989). *Paddy Pig's Poems.* New York: Simon & Schuster.

Charlip, Remy. (1985). *Thirteen.* New York: Simon & Schuster.

Chase, Richard (Ed.). (1943). *Jack Tales.* Boston: Houghton.

Chaucer, Geoffrey. (1988). *Canterbury Tales.* Trans. Barbara Cohen. Illus. Trina Schart Hyman. New York: Lothrop, Lee & Shepard.

Cherry, Lynne. (1992). *A River Ran Wild.* New York: Dutton.

Child, Lauren. (1999). *Clarice Bean, That's Me.* Cambridge: Candlewick.

Child, Lydia Marie. (1989). *Over the River and Through the Wood.* Illus. Iris Van Rynback. Boston: Little, Brown.

Chinn, Karen. (1995). *Sam and the Lucky Money.* New York: Lee and Low.

Chocolate, Deborah M. Newton. (1998). *The Piano Man.* Illus. Eric Velasquez. New York: Walker.

Choi, Sook Nyul. (1991). *Year of Impossible Goodbyes.* Boston: Houghton.

Choi, Sook Nyul. (1993). *Halmoni and the Picnic.* Boston: Houghton.

Choi, Sook Nyul. (1994). *Gathering of Pearls.* Boston: Houghton.

Choi, Sook Nyul. (1997). *The Best Older Sister.* Illus. Cornelius Van Wright and Ying-Hwa Hu. New York: Bantam.

Chorao, Kay. (1995). *Number One, Number Fun.* New York: Holiday House.

Chorao, Kay. (2000). *Pig and Crow.* New York: Holt.

Christelow, Eileen. (1990). *Five Little Monkeys Jumping on the Bed.* New York: Clarion.

Christelow, Eileen. (1995). *What Do Authors Do?* New York: Clarion.

Christelow, Eileen. (2000). *What Do Illustrators Do?* Boston: Houghton.

Christiansen, C. B. (1994). *I See the Moon.* New York: Atheneum.

Christopher, John. (1967). *The City of Gold and Lead.* New York: Macmillan.

Christopher, John. (1967). *The White Mountains.* New York: Macmillan.

Christopher, John. (1970). *The Pool of Fire.* New York: Macmillan.

Christopher, John. (1990). *When the Tripods Came.* New York: Simon & Schuster.

Christopher, Matt. (1964). *Catcher with a Glass Arm.* Illus. Foster Caddell. Boston: Little, Brown.

Ciardi, John. (1962). *You Read to Me, I'll Read to You.* New York: Lippincott.

Ciardi, John. (1989). *The Hopeful Trout and Other Limericks.* Illus. Susan Meddaugh. Boston: Houghton.

Ciardi, John. (1991). *The Monster Den.* Illus. Edward Gorey. Honesdale, PA: Boyds Mills.

Ciardi, John. (1993). *Someone Could Win a Polar Bear.* Illus. Edward Gorey. Honesdale, PA: Boyds Mills.

Ciardi, John. (1994). *The Reason for the Pelican.* Honesdale, PA: Boyds Mills.

Cisneros, Sandra. (1988). *The House on Mango Street.* Houston: Arte Publico.

Cisneros, Sandra. (1994). *Hairs/Pelitos.* New York: Knopf.

Cisneros, Sandra. (1997). *Pelitos/Hairs.* Illus. Terry Ybanez. New York: Random House.

Clapp, Patricia. (1987). *The Witch's Children.* New York: Puffin.

Clark, Margaret (Reteller). (1990). *The Best of Aesop's Fables.* Illus. Charlotte Voake. Boston: Little, Brown.

Clayton, Gordon. (1992). *Foal.* Illus. Mary Ling. New York: Dorling Kindersley.

Clayton, Gordon. (1993). *Calf.* New York: Dorling Kindersley.

Clearly, Brian P. (2000). *Hairy, Scary, Ordinary: What Is an Adjective?* Illus. Jenya Prosmitsky. Minneapolis, MN: Carolrhoda.

Cleary, Beverly. (1965). *The Mouse and the Motorcycle.* New York: Morrow/Avon.

Cleary, Beverly. (1977). *Ramona and Her Father.* New York: Morrow/Avon.

Cleary, Beverly. (1979). *Ramona and Her Mother.* New York: Morrow/Avon.

Cleary, Beverly. (1988). *A Girl from Yamhill.* New York: Morrow/Avon.

Cleary, Beverly. (1991). *Strider.* New York: Morrow/Avon.

Cleary, Beverly. (1995). *My Own Two Feet: A Memoir.* New York: Morrow/Avon.

Cleary, Beverly. (1998). *Ramona's World.* Illus. Alan Tiegreen. New York: Morrow/Avon.

Clements, Andrew. (1999). *The Landry News.* New York: Simon & Schuster.

Clements, Andrew. (2000). *Frindle: Janitor's Boy.* New York: Simon & Schuster.

Clifford, Eth. (1992). *Will Somebody Please Marry My Sister?* Boston: Houghton.

Clifton, Lucille. (1970). *Some of the Days of Everett Anderson.* Illus. Evaline Ness. New York: Holt.

Clifton, Lucille. (1980). *My Friend Jacob.* Illus. Thomas Di Grazia. New York: Dutton.

Clifton, Lucille. (1991). *Everett Anderson's Christmas Is Coming.* Illus. Jan Gilchrist. New York: Holt.

Clifton, Lucille. (1992). *Three Wishes.* New York: Doubleday.

Climo, Shirley. (1987). *A Month of Seven Days.* New York: HarperCollins.

Climo, Shirley. (1989). *The Egyptian Cinderella.* Illus. Ruth Heller. New York: HarperCollins.

Climo, Shirley. (1993). *The Korean Cinderella.* New York: HarperCollins.

Climo, Shirley. (1994). *Stolen Thunder: A Myth.* New York: Clarion.

Climo, Shirley. (1995). *Atalanta's Race: A Greek Myth.* New York: Clarion.

Climo, Shirley. (1995). *The Little Red Ant and the Great Big Crumb: A Mexican Fable.* New York: Clarion.

Climo, Shirley. (1996). *The Irish Cinderella.* New York: HarperCollins.

Cline-Ransome, Lesa. (2000). *Satchel Paige.* Illus. James Ransome. New York: Simon & Schuster.

Clinton, Catherine. (1998). *I, Too, Sing America: Three Centuries of African American Poetry.* Boston: Houghton.

Cobb, Vicki. (1989). *Writing It Down.* Illus. Marylin Hafner. New York: HarperCollins.

Coerr, Eleanor. (1986). *The Josefina Story Quilt.* New York: HarperCollins.

Coerr, Eleanor. (1995). *Buffalo Bill and the Pony Express.* New York: HarperCollins.

Cohat, E. (1995). *Seashore.* New York: Scholastic.

Cohen, Barbara. (1980). *The Donkey's Story: A Bible Story.* Illus. Susan Jeanne Cohen. New York: Lothrop, Lee & Shepard.

Cohen, Caron L. (1985). *Sally Ann Thunder Ann Whirlwind Crockett.* New York: Greenwillow.

Cohen, Caron L. (1992). *Pigeon, Pigeon.* New York: Dutton.

Cohen, Miriam. (1967). *Will I Have a Friend?* Illus. Lillian Hoban. New York: Macmillan.

Cohen, Miriam. (1988). *It's George!* Illus. Lillian Hoban. New York: Greenwillow.

Cohen, Miriam. (1989). *See You in Second Grade!* Illus. Lillian Hoban. New York: Greenwillow.

Cole, Babette. (1999). *Bad Habits! (Or the Taming of Lucretcia Crum)*. UK: Penguin.

Cole, Babette. (2000). *Hair in Funny Places: A Book About Puberty.* New York: Hyperion.

Cole, Brock. (1992). *The Goats.* New York: Farrar, Straus & Giroux.

Cole, Henry. (1998). *I Took a Walk.* New York: Greenwillow.

Cole, Joanna. (1984). *A New Treasury of Children's Poetry: Old Favorites and New Discoveries.* New York: Doubleday.

Cole, Joanna. (1984). *How You Were Born.* New York: Morrow/Avon.

Cole, Joanna. (1986). *Magic School Bus at the Water Works.* Illus. Bruce Degen. New York: Scholastic.

Cole, Joanna. (1989). *A Gift from Saint Francis: The First Crèche.* Illus. Michele Lemieux. New York: Morrow/Avon.

Cole, Joanna. (1989). *It's Too Noisy.* New York: HarperCollins.

Cole, Joanna. (1994). *The Magic School Bus in the Time of Dinosaurs.* New York: Scholastic.

Cole, Joanna. (1995). *The Magic School Bus Inside a Hurricane.* New York: Scholastic.

Cole, Joanna. (1995). *My New Kitten.* New York: Morrow/Avon.

Cole, Joanna. (1999). *The Magic School Bus and the Electric Field Trip.* Illus. Bruce Degan. New York: Scholastic.

Cole, Joanna. (1999). *The Magic School Bus Explores the Senses.* New York: Scholastic.

Cole, Joanna. (2000). *The New Baby at Your House.* New York: Morrow/Avon.

Cole, William. (1992). *A Zooful of Animals.* Boston: Houghton.

Coleman, Evelyn. (1998). *The Riches of Oseola McCarty.* Illus. Daniel Minter. Morton Grove, IL: Whitman.

Coleman, Michael. (1999). *Weirdo's War.* Danbury, CT: Orchard.

Coles, Robert. (1995). *The Story of Ruby Bridges.* New York: Scholastic.

Collier, James Lincoln, & Collier, Christopher. (1974). *My Brother Sam Is Dead.* New York: Macmillan.

Collier, James Lincoln, & Collier, Christopher. (1983). *War Comes to Willy Freeman.* New York: Delacorte.

Collier, James Lincoln, & Collier, Christopher. (1994). *With Every Drop of Blood.* New York: Delacorte.

Collodi, C. (1993). *Pinocchio.* Illus. Lorenzo Mattotti. (Original work published in 1883). New York: Lothrop, Lee & Shepard.

Colman, Hila. (1988). *Rich and Famous Like My Mom.* New York: Crown.

Colman, Penny. (1995). *Rosie the Riveter: Women Working on the Home Front in World War II.* New York: Crown.

Colman, Penny. (2000). *Girls: A History of Growing Up Female in America.* New York: Scholastic.

Colum, Padraic. (1983). *Golden Fleece and Heroes Who Lived Before Achilles.* New York: Macmillan.

Colum, Padraic. (1984). *Children of Odin: The Book of Northern Myths.* (Original work published in 1920). New York: Macmillan.

Coman, Carolyn. (2000). *Many Stones.* Arden, NC: Front Street.

Comenius, John Amos. (1659; 1970 Reissue). *Orbis Sensualiaum Pictus.* Menston, England: Scolar.

Conford, Ellen. (1983). *If This Is Love, I'll Take Spaghetti.* New York: Simon & Schuster.

Conford, Ellen. (1989). *Jenny Archer, Author.* Boston: Little, Brown.

Conford, Ellen. (1998). *Crush: Stories.* New York: HarperCollins.

Conly, Jane Leslie. (1993). *Crazy Lady!* New York: Geringer/Harper.

Conly, Jane Leslie. (1995). *Trout Summer.* New York: Holt.

Conly, Jane Leslie. (1998). *While No One Was Watching.* New York: Hing.

Conly, Jane Leslie. (2000). *What Happened on Planet Kid.* New York: Holt.

Connolly, James E. (Collector). (1985). *Why the Possum's Tail Is Bare and Other North American Indian Nature Tales.* Illus. Adrienne Adams. Owings Mills, MD: Stemmer.

Conover, Chris (Reteller and Illus.). (1989). *Mother Goose and the Sly Fox.* New York: Farrar, Straus & Giroux.

Conrad, Pam. (1984). *I Don't Live Here!* New York: Dutton.

Conrad, Pam. (1986). *Prairie Songs.* New York: HarperCollins.

Conrad, Pam. (1989). *The Tub People.* Illus. Richard Egielski. New York: HarperCollins.

Conrad, Pam. (1990). *Stonewords: A Ghost Story.* New York: HarperCollins.

Conrad, Pam. (1991). *Pedro's Journal: A Voyage with Christopher Columbus, August 3, 1492–February 14, 1493.* Illus. Peter Koeppen. Honesdale, PA: Boyds Mills.

Conrad, Pam. (1991). *Prairie Visions: The Life and Times of Solomon Butcher.* New York: HarperCollins.

Conrad, Pam. (1995). *Animal Lingo.* New York: HarperCollins.

Conrad, Pam. (1995). *Call Me Ahnighito.* New York: Geringer/Harper.

Coolidge, Susan. (1872; 1977 Reprint). *What Katy Did.* New York: Dent.

Cooney, Barbara (Adapter and Illus.). (1958). *Chanticleer and the Fox.* New York: HarperCollins.

Cooney, Barbara. (1982). *Miss Rumphius.* New York: Viking.

Cooney, Barbara. (1988). *Island Boy.* New York: Viking.

Cooney, Barbara. (1990). *Hattie and the Wild Waves.* New York: Viking.

Cooney, Barbara. (1996). *Eleanor.* New York: Viking.

Cooper, Floyd. (1994). *Coming Home: From the Life of Langston Hughes.* New York: Philomel.

Cooper, Floyd. (1996). *Mandela: From the Life of the South African Statesman.* New York: Philomel.

Cooper, James Fenimore. (1962). *The Last of the Mohicans.* New York: Dutton.

Cooper, Michael. (1999). *Indian School: Teaching the White Man's Ways.* Boston: Houghton.

Cooper, Susan. (1966). *Over Sea, Under Stone.* San Diego: Harcourt.

Cooper, Susan. (1973). *The Dark Is Rising.* Illus. Alan E. Cober. New York: Atheneum.

Cooper, Susan. (1973). *Greenwitch.* New York: McElderry.

Cooper, Susan. (1974). *The Grey King.* New York: McElderry.

Cooper, Susan. (1977). *Silver on the Tree.* New York: McElderry.

Cooper, Susan (Reteller). (1991). *Tam Lin.* Illus. Warwick Hutton. New York: McElderry.

Cooper, Susan. (1999). *King of Shadows.* New York: McElderry.

Corbett, Scott. (1981). *Deadly Hoax.* New York: Dutton.

Corcoran, Barbara. (1993). *Wolf at the Door.* New York: Simon & Schuster.

Cordova, Amy. (1997). *Abuelita's Heart.* New York: Simon & Schuster.

Cormier, Robert. (1990). *Other Bells for Us to Ring.* New York: Delacorte.

Cormier, Robert. (1999). *Frenchtown Summer.* New York: Delacorte.

Cosby, Bill. (1997). *The Meanest Thing to Say: Little Bill Books for Beginning Readers.* Illus. Varnette P. Honeywood. New York: Scholastic.

Cotton, John. (1646). *Milk for Babes.* London: Overton.

Couloumbis, Audrey. (1999). *Getting Near to Baby.* New York: Putnam.

Cousins, Lucy. (1991). *Farm Animals.* New York: Morrow/Avon.

Cousins, Lucy. (1996). *Katy Cat and Beaky Boo.* New York: Candlewick.

Coville, Bruce. (1991). *Jeremy Thatcher, Dragon Hatcher.* San Diego: Harcourt.

Coville, Bruce. (1992). *Jennifer Murdley's Toad.* Illus. Gary Lippincott. San Diego: Harcourt.

Coville, Bruce. (1993). *Aliens Ate My Homework.* New York: Simon & Schuster.

Covington, Dennis. (1991). *Lizard.* New York: Delacorte.

Cowcher, Helen. (1990). *Antarctica.* New York: Farrar, Straus & Giroux.

Cowcher, Helen. (1991). *Tigress.* New York: Farrar, Straus & Giroux.

Cowcher, Helen. (1993). *La Tigresa.* New York: Farrar, Straus & Giroux.

Cowley, Joy. (1999). *Red-Eyes Tree Frog.* Photog. Nic Bishop. New York: Scholastic.

Cox, Clinton. (1991). *The Undying Glory.* New York: Scholastic.

Coy, John. (1996). *Night Driving.* Illus. Peter McCarty. New York: Holt.

Coy, John. (1996). *Night Driving.* New York: Holt.

Craft, M. Charlotte. (1996). *Cupid and Psyche.* New York: Morrow/Avon.

Craig, Helen. (1992). *The Town Mouse and the Country Mouse.* New York: Candlewick.

Craig, Helen. (1993). *I See the Moon, and the Moon Sees Me.* New York: HarperCollins.

Crane, Walter. (1865). *Dame Trot and Her Comical Cat.* London: Warne.

Crane, Walter. (1865). *The House That Jack Built.* London: Warne.

Crane, Walter. (1865). *Railroad Alphabet.* London: Routledge.

Crane, Walter. (1866). *The History of Cock Robin and Jenny Wren.* London: Warne.

Crane, Walter. (1867). *Sing a Song of Sixpence.* London: Warne.

Crane, Walter. (1874). *Farmyard Alphabet.* London: Routledge.

Crane, Walter. (1876). *Sleeping Beauty in the Wood.* London: Routledge.

Creech, Sharon. (1995). *Absolutely Normal Chaos.* New York: HarperCollins.

Creech, Sharon. (1996). *Walk Two Moons.* New York: HarperCollins.

Creech, Sharon. (2000). *The Wanderer.* Illus. David Diaz. New York: HarperCollins.

Creech, Susan. (1999). *Bloomability.* New York: HarperCollins.

Crew, Gary. (1993). *Strange Objects.* New York: Simon & Schuster.

Crew, Gary. (1995). *Angel's Gate.* New York: Simon & Schuster.

Crew, Linda. (1995). *Fire on the Wind.* New York: Delacorte.

Crews, Donald. (1980). *Truck.* New York: Greenwillow.

Crews, Donald. (1984). *School Bus.* New York: Greenwillow.

Crews, Donald. (1986). *Ten Black Dots.* New York: Greenwillow.

Crews, Donald. (1991). *Bigmama's.* New York: Greenwillow.

Crews, Donald. (1992). *Shortcut.* New York: Greenwillow.

Crews, Nina. (1995). *One Hot Summer Day.* New York: Greenwillow.

Crist-Evans, Craig. (1999). *Moon Over Tennessee: A Boy's Civil War Journal.* Illus. Bonnie Christensen. New York: Houghton.

Cristini, Ermano, & Puricelli, Luigi. (1985). *In My Garden.* Saxonville, MA: Picture Books Studio.

Cristini, Ermano, & Puricelli, Luigi. (1985). *In the Woods.* Saxonville, MA: Picture Books Studio.

Cronin, Doreen. (2000). *Click, Clack, Moo: Cows That Type.* Illus. Betsy Lewin. New York: Simon & Schuster.

Cross, Gillian. (1999). *Tightrope.* New York: Holiday House.

Crossley-Holland, Kevin. (1981). *Norse Myths.* New York: Pantheon.

Crossley-Holland, Kevin. (1988). *Beowulf.* Illus. Charles Keeping. New York: Oxford University Press.

Cruikshank, George. (1853–1854). *George Cruikshank's Fairy Library.* (4 Vols.). London: David Bogue.

Crutcher, Chris. (1986). *Running Loose.* New York: Dell.

Crutcher, Chris. (1995). *Ironman.* New York: Greenwillow.

Crutcher, Chris. (1995). *Staying Fat for Sarah Byrnes.* New York: Dell.

Cruz, Martel. (1987; o.p.). *Yagua Days.* Illus. Jerry Pinkney. New York: Dial.

Cullinan, Bernice (Ed.). (1996). *A Jar of Tiny Stars: Poems by NCTE Award-Winning Poets.* Honesdale, PA: Boyds Mills.

Cummings, Pat (Ed.). (1992). *Talking with Artists.* (Vol. 1). New York: Simon & Schuster.

Cummings, Pat (Ed.). (1995). *Talking with Artists.* (Vol. 2). New York: Simon & Schuster.

Cummings, Pat (Ed.). (1999). *Talking with Artists.* (Vol. 3). Boston: Houghton.

Cummings, Pat. (1991). *Clean Your Room, Harvey Moon.* New York: Simon & Schuster.

Cummings, Pat. (1994). *Carousel.* New York: Simon & Schuster.

Cummings, Pat. (2000). *Angel Baby.* New York: Lothrop, Lee & Shepard.

Cumpian, Carlos. (1994). *Latino Rainbow: Poems About Latino Americans.* Illus. Richard Leonard. Danbury, CT: Children's Press.

Curlee, Lynn. (1998). *Into the Ice: The Story of Arctic Exploration.* Boston: Houghton.

Curlee, Lynn. (1999). *Rushmore.* New York: Scholastic.

Curlee, Lynn. (2000). *Liberty.* New York: Atheneum.

Curry, Jane Louise. (1999). *A Stolen Life.* New York: McElderry.

Curtis, Christopher Paul. (1995). *The Watsons Go to Birmingham—1963.* New York: Delacorte.

Curtis, Christopher Paul. (1997). *The Watsons Go to Brimingham—1963.* New York: Bantam.

Curtis, Christopher Paul. (1999). *Bud, Not Buddy.* New York: Delacorte.

Cushman, Doug. (2000). *Inspector Hopper.* New York: HarperCollins.

Cushman, Karen. (1994). *Catherine, Called Birdy.* New York: Clarion/Houghton.

Cushman, Karen. (1995). *The Midwife's Apprentice.* New York: Clarion/Houghton.

Cushman, Karen. (1996). *The Ballad of Lucy Whipple.* New York: Clarion/Houghton.

Cushman, Karen. (2000). *Matilda Bone.* Boston: Clarion.

Cutchins, Judy, & Johnston, Ginny. (1995). *Are Those Animals Real? How Museums Prepare Wildlife Exhibits.* New York: Morrow/Avon.

Cutler, Jane. (1994). *No Dogs Allowed.* New York: Farrar, Straus & Giroux.

Cutler, Jane. (1996). *Rats!* New York: Farrar, Straus & Giroux.

Cutler, Jane. (1999). *'Gator Aid.* Illus. Tracy Campbell Pearson. New York: Farrar, Straus & Giroux.

Dabcovich, Lydia. (1992). *The Keys to My Kingdom: A Poem in Three Languages.* New York: Lothrop, Lee & Shepard.

Dahl, Roald. (1961). *James and the Giant Peach.* Illus. Nancy Ekholm Burkert. New York: Knopf.

Dahl, Roald. (1964). *Charlie and the Chocolate Factory.* Illus. Joseph Schindelman. New York: Knopf.

Dahl, Roald. (1984). *Boy: Tales of Childhood.* New York: Farrar, Straus & Giroux.

Dahl, Roald. (1988). *Matilda.* New York: Viking.

Dakos, Kalli. (1999). *The Bug in the Teacher's Coffee and Other School Poems.* Illus. Mike Reed. New York: HarperCollins.

Dalokay, Vedat. (1994). *Sister Shako and Kolo the Goat.* New York: Lothrop, Lee & Shepard.

Danziger, Paula. (1994). *Amber Brown Is Not a Crayon.* New York: Putnam.

Danziger, Paula. (1995). *You Can't Eat Your Chicken Pox, Amber Brown.* New York: Putnam.

D'Aulaire, Ingri, & D'Aulaire, Edgar Parin. (1957). *Abraham Lincoln.* New York: Doubleday.

D'Aulaire, Ingri, & D'Aulaire, Edgar Parin. (1980). *Ingri and Edgar Parin D'Aulaire's Book of Greek Myths.* New York: Doubleday.

D'Aulaire, Ingri. (1955). *Christoper Columbus.* New York: Doubleday.

D'Aulaire, Ingri. (1986). *Norse Gods and Giants.* New York: Doubleday.

Davidson, Margaret. (1986). *I Have a Dream: The Story of Martin Luther King.* New York: Scholastic.

Davis, Katie. (1999). *I Hate to Go to Bed.* San Diego: Harcourt.

Davis, Ossie. (1992). *Just Like Martin.* New York: Simon & Schuster.

Davis, Russell, & Ashabranner, Brent K. (1994). *The Choctaw Code.* North Haven: Shoe String.

Davol, Marguerite W. (2000). *The Loudest, Fastest, Best Drummer in Kansas.* Illus. Cat Bowman Smith. Danbury, CT: Orchard.

Dayrell, Elphinstone. (1977). *Why the Sun and the Moon Live in the Sky: An African Folktale.* Boston: Houghton.

De Angeli, Marguerite. (1954). *Book of Nursery and Mother Goose Rhymes.* Illus. Marguerite De Angeli. New York: Doubleday.

De Angeli, Marguerite. (1989). *The Door in the Wall.* New York: Doubleday.

De Beaumont, Marie Leprince. (1990). *Beauty and the Beast.* New York: Simon & Schuster.

De Brunhoff, Jean. (1967). *Story of Babar, the Little Elephant.* New York: Random House.

De Fina, Allan A. (1997). *When a City Leans Against the Sky.* Illus. Ken Condon. Honesdale, PA: Boyds Mills.

De Gasztold, Carmen, B. (1962). *Prayers from the Ark.* New York: Viking.

De Gerez, Toni. (1986). *Louhi, Witch of North Farm.* Illus. Barbara Cooney. New York: Viking.

De Jenkins, Lyll Becerra. (1988). *The Honorable Prison.* New York: Dutton.

De La Mare, Walter. (1969). *Peacock Pie.* Illus. Louise Brierly. New York: Holt.

DePaola, Tomie (Reteller). (1988). *The Legend of the Indian Paintbrush.* New York: Putnam.

DePaola, Tomie. (1977). *Helga's Dowry.* San Diego: Harcourt.

DePaola, Tomie. (1977; 1984). *The Quicksand Book.* New York: Holiday House.

DePaola, Tomie. (1978). *Pancakes for Breakfast.* San Diego: Harcourt.

DePaola, Tomie. (1978). *The Popcorn Book.* New York: Holiday House.

DePaola, Tomie. (1980). *The Lady of Guadalupe.* New York: Holiday House.

DePaola, Tomie. (1983). *The Legend of the Bluebonnet: A Tale of Old Texas.* New York: Putnam.

DePaola, Tomie. (1985). *Tomie DePaola's Mother Goose.* New York: Putnam.

DePaola, Tomie. (1986). *Tomie DePaola's Favorite Nursery Tales.* New York: Putnam.

DePaola, Tomie. (1987). *Tomie DePaola's Book of Christmas Carols.* New York: Putnam.

DePaola, Tomie. (1988). *Tomie DePaola's Book of Poems.* New York: Putnam.

DePaola, Tomie. (1989). *The Art Lesson.* New York: Putnam.

DePaola, Tomie. (1989). *Tony's Bread.* New York: Putnam.

DePaola, Tomie. (1990). *Francis: The Poor Man of Assisi.* New York: Holiday House.

DePaola, Tomie. (1992). *Bonjour, Mr. Satie.* New York: Putnam.

DePaola, Tomie. (1994). *Christopher: The Holy Giant.* New York: Holiday House.

DePaola, Tomie. (1994). *The Legend of the Poinsetta.* New York: Putnam.

DePaola, Tomie. (1995). *Mary: The Mother of Jesus.* New York: Holiday House.

DePaola, Tomie. (1995). *Tomie DePaola's Book of the Old Testament: New International Version.* New York: Putnam.

DePaola, Tomie. (1996). *The Baby Sister.* New York: Putnam.

DePaola, Tomie. (1998). *Nana Upstairs, Nana Downstairs: Strega Nona.* New York: Puffin.

DePaola, Tomie. (2000). *Here We All Are.* New York: Putnam.

DePaola, Tomie. (2000). *Jamie O'Rourke and the Pooka.* New York: Putnam.

DePaola, Tomie. (2001). *On My Way: A 26 Fairmount Avenue Book.* New York: Putnam.

De Regniers, Beatrice Schenk (Compiler). (1988). *Sing a Song of Popcorn: Every Child's Book of Poems.* New York: Scholastic.

De Regniers, Beatrice Schenk. (1985). *So Many Cats!* Illus. Ellen Weiss. New York: Clarion.

De Regniers, Beatrice Schenk. (1988). *The Way I Feel Sometimes.* Illus. Susan Meddaugh. New York: Clarion.

De Regniers, Beatrice Schenk. (1990). *Red Riding Hood.* Illus. Edward Gorey. New York: Aladdin.

DeClements, Barthe (1998). *Liar, Liar.* New York: Cavendish.

Deem, James M. (1998). *Bodies from the Bog.* Boston: Houghton.

Defelice, Cynthia. (1994). *Lostman's River.* New York: Macmillan.

Defelice, Cynthia. (1999). *Nowhere to Call Home.* New York: Farrar, Straus & Giroux.

Defoe, Daniel. (1719; 1920 Reprint). *Robinson Crusoe.* Illus. N. C. Wyeth. New York: Scribner's.

Degens, T. (1979, 1991). *Transport 7-41-R.* New York: Viking.

Degroat, Diane. (1999). *Trick or Treat, Smell My Feet.* New York: Morrow/Avon.

Delacre, Lulu (Selector and Illus.). (1989). *Arroz Con Leche: Popular Songs and Rhymes from Latin America.* English Lyrics by Elena Paz. Musical Arrangements by Ana-Maria Rosada. New York: Scholastic.

Delacre, Lulu. (1990). *Las Navidades: Popular Christmas Songs from Latin America.* New York: Scholastic.

Delacre, Lulu. (1993). *Vejigante Masquerader.* New York: Scholastic.

Delgado, Maria Isable. (1996). *Chave's Memories: Los Recuerdos De Chave.* Illus. Yvonne Symank. Houston: Arte Publico.

Delton, Judy. (1999). *Angel Spreads Her Wings.* Illus. Jill Weber. Boston: Houghton.

Demi. (1990). *The Empty Pot.* New York: Holt.

Demi. (1990). *The Magic Boat.* New York: Holt.

Demi. (1991). *Chingis Khan.* New York: Holt.

Demi. (1992). *In the Eyes of the Cat: Japanese Poetry for All Seasons.* Trans. Tze-Si Huang. New York: Holt.

Demi. (1994). *The Firebird.* New York: Holt.

Demi. (1996). *Buddha.* New York: Holt.

Demi. (1996). *The Dragon's Tale and Other Animal Fables of the Chinese Zodiac.* New York: Holt.

Demi. (1998). *The Dali Lama: A Biography of the Tibetan Spiritual and Political Leader.* New York: Holt.

Demi. (1998). *The Stonecutter.* New York: Random House.

Demi (Reteller). (2000). *The Emperor's New Clothes: A Tale Set in China.* New York: McElderry.

Denzel, Justin. (1988). *The Boy of the Painted Cave.* New York: Philomel.

Deschamps-Adams, Helene. (1995). *Spyglass.* New York: Holt.

Deschamps-Adams, Helene. (1995). *Spyglass: An Autobiography.* New York: Holt.

Dessen, Sarah. (1998). *Someone Like You.* New York: Viking.

Dessen, Sarah. (2000). *Dreamland.* New York: Penguin.

Deuker, Carl. (1994). *Heart of a Champion.* New York: Morrow/Avon.

Deuker, Carl. (2000). *Night Hoops.* Boston: Houghton.

Devito, Cara. (1993). *Where I Want to Be.* Boston: Houghton.

Dewey, Ariane. (1983). *Pecos Bill.* New York: Greenwillow.

Dewey, Ariane. (1987). *Gib Morgan, Oilman.* New York: Greenwillow.

Dewey, Ariane. (1994). *Cowgirl Dreams: A Western Childhood.* Honesdale, PA: Boyds Mills.

Dewey, Jennifer Owings. (1998). *Mud Matters: Stories from a Mud Lover.* Illus. Stephen Trimble. New York: Cavendish.

Dewey, Jennifer Owings. (1998). *Poison Dart Frogs.* Honesdale, PA: Boyds Mills.

Dexter, Catherine. (1989). *Mazemaker.* New York: Morrow/Avon.

Dexter, Catherine. (1995). *Alien Game.* New York: Morrow/Avon.

Diaz, Jorge Ancona. (1993). *Pablo Recuerda: La Fiesta del Dia de los Muertos.* New York: Lothrop, Lee & Shepard.

Dicamillo, Kate. (2000). *Because of Winn-Dixie.* Cambridge: Candlewick.

Dickens, Charles. (1843). *A Christmas Carol.* San Diego: Harcourt.

Dickinson, Emily. (1996). *Poems for Youth.* Boston: Little, Brown.

Dickinson, Peter. (1989). *Eva.* New York: Delacorte.

Dickinson, Peter. (1998). *Suth's Story (The Kin).* Illus. Nehad Jakesvic. New York: Grosset and Dunlap.

Dionetti, Michelle. (1991). *Coal Mine Peaches.* Illus. Anita Riggio. New York: Scholastic.

Disher, Gary. (1993). *The Bamboo Flute.* New York: Ticknor & Fields.

Dixon, Ann. (1992). *How Raven Brought Light to People.* Illus. James Watts. New York: McElderry.

Dodge, Mary Mapes. (1865; 1975 Reprint). *Hans Brinker; Or, the Silver Skates.* Illus. Hilda Van Stockum. Philadelphia: Collins.

Doherty, Berlie. (1988). *Granny Was a Buffer Girl.* New York: Scholastic.

Doherty, Berlie. (1992). *Dear Nobody.* New York: Scholastic.

Dolphin, Laurie. (1993). *Oasis of Peace/Neve Shalom/Wahat Al-Salam.* New York: Scholastic.

Dooley, Norah. (1991). *Everybody Cooks Rice.* Minneapolis, MN: Carolrhoda.

Dorris, Michael. (1992). *Morning Girl.* New York: Hyperion.

Dorris, Michael. (1994). *Guests.* New York: Hyperion.

Dorris, Michael. (1996). *Sees Behind Trees.* New York: Hyperion.

Dorris, Michael. (1999). *The Window.* New York: Hyperion.

Dorros, Arthur. (1991). *Abuela.* Illus. Elisa Kleven. New York: Dutton.

Dorros, Arthur. (1991). *Tonight Is Carnaval.* New York: Dutton.

Dorros, Arthur. (1992). *This Is My House.* New York: Scholastic.

Dorros, Arthur. (1993). *Radio Man/Don Radio.* New York: HarperCollins.

Dorros, Arthur. (1995). *Isla.* New York: Dutton.

Dotlich, Rebecca Kai. (1996). *Sweet Dreams of the Wild: Poems for Bedtime.* Honesdale, PA: Boyds Mills.

Dotlich, Rebecca. (1998). *Lemonade Sun: and Other Summer Poems.* Illus. Jan Spivey Gilchrist. Honesdale, PA: Boyds Mills.

Doucet, Sharon Arms. (2000). *Fiddle Fever.* Boston: Houghton.

Dowden, Anne Ophelia. (1988). *The Blossom on the Bough: A Book of Trees.* New York: Ticknor & Fields.

Dowden, Anne Ophelia. (1994). *Poisons in Our Path: Plants That Harm and Heal.* New York: HarperCollins.

Downs, Belinda. (1996). *A Stitch in Rhyme: A Nursery Rhyme Sampler with Embroidered Illustrations.* New York: Knopf.

Dragonwagon, Crescent. (1990). *Home Place.* Illus. Jerry Pinkney. New York: Macmillan.

Draper, Sharon M. (1994). *Tears of a Tiger.* New York: Simon & Schuster.

Draper, Sharon. (1998). *Forged by Fire.* New York: Aladdin.

Drucker, Malka, & Halperon, Michael. (1994). *Jacob's Rescue: A Holocaust Story.* New York: Dell.

Duder, Tessa. (1991). *In Lane Three, Alex Archer.* New York: Bantam.

Duder, Tessa. (1992). *Alex in Rome.* Boston: Houghton.

Duffey, Betsy. (1994). *Coaster.* New York: Viking.

Duffey, Betsy. (1999). *Cody Unplugged.* Illus. Ellen Thompson. New York: Viking.

Duffey, Betsy. (1999). *Spotlight on Cody.* Illus. Ellen Thompson. New York: Viking.

Duffy, Carol Ann. (1996). *Stopping for Death: Poems of Death and Loss.* New York: Holt.

Dugan, Barbara. (1994). *Good-Bye, Hello.* New York: Greenwillow.

Dumbleton, Mike. (1991). *Dial-A-Croc.* Illus. Ann James. New York: Scholastic.

Duncan, Lois. (1981). *Stranger with My Face.* Boston: Little, Brown.

Duncan, Lois. (1996). *The Magic of Spider Woman.* New York: Scholastic.

Dunlop, Eileen. (1995). *Webster's Leap.* New York: Holiday House.

Dunn, Danielle, & Dunn, Jessica. (1997). *A Teen's Guide to Getting Published.* Waco, TX: Profoch Press.

Dunning, Stephen (Compiler). (1966). *Reflections on a Gift of Watermelon Pickle and Other Modern Verse.* New York: Lothrop, Lee & Shepard.

Dunrea, Olivier. (1995). *The Painter Who Loved Chickens.* New York: Farrar, Straus & Giroux.

Durell, Ann (Compiler). (1989). *The Diane Goode Book of American Folk Tales and Songs.* Illus. Diane Goode. New York: Dutton.

Dyer, Jane. (1996). *Animal Crackers: A Delectable Collection of Pictures, Poems, and Lullabies for the Very Young.* Boston: Little, Brown.

Dyer, T. A. (1990). *A Way of His Own.* Boston: Houghton.

Dygard, Thomas J. (1996). *The Rebounder.* New York: Puffin.

Earle, Sylvia. (1999). *Dive! My Adventures in the Deep Frontier.* Washington, DC: National Geographic.

Early, Margaret. (1993). *Sleeping Beauty.* New York: Abrams.

Ebensen, Barbara. (2000). *The Night Rainbow.* Illus. Helen K. Davis. Boston: Orchard.

Edens, Cooper (Selector). (1988). *The Glorious Mother Goose.* Illus. with reproductions. New York: Atheneum.

Edgeworth, Maria. (1796). *The Purple Jar.* London: Routledge.

Edgeworth, Maria. (1801). *Early Lessons.* London: Routledge.

Edgeworth, Maria. (1801). *Moral Tales.* New York: Gilley.

Edwards, Michelle. (1991). *Chicken Man.* New York: Lothrop, Lee & Shepard.

Edwards, Michelle. (1992). *Alef-Bet: A Hebrew Alphabet Book.* New York: Lothrop, Lee & Shepard.

Edwards, Michelle. (1993). *Dora's Book.* New York: First Avenue Editions.

Ehlert, Lois. (1989). *Color Zoo.* New York: HarperCollins.

Ehlert, Lois. (1989). *Eating the Alphabet.* San Diego: Harcourt.

Ehlert, Lois. (1990). *Color Farm.* New York: HarperCollins.

Ehlert, Lois. (1990). *Feathers for Lunch.* San Diego: Harcourt.

Ehlert, Lois. (1990). *Fish Eyes: A Book You Can Count On.* San Diego: Harcourt.

Ehlert, Lois. (1991). *Red Leaf, Yellow Leaf.* San Diego: Harcourt.

Ehlert, Lois. (1992). *Circus.* New York: HarperCollins.

Ehlert, Lois. (1994). *Mole's Hill.* San Diego: Harcourt.

Ehlert, Lois. (1995). *Snowballs.* New York: Harcourt.

Ehlert, Lois. (1996). *Moon Rope.* San Diego: Harcourt.

Ehlert, Lois. (1996). *Under My Nose.* Katonah, NY: Richard C. Owen.

Ehrlich, Amy. (1974). *Wounded Knee: An Indian History of the American West.* New York: Holt.

Ekoomiak, Normee. (1988). *Arctic Memories.* New York: Holt.

Elish, Dan. (1994). *James Meredith and School Desegregation.* Brookfield, CT: Millbrook.

Elkington, John, Hailes, Julia, Hill, Douglas, & Makower, Joel. (1990). *Going Green: A Kid's Handbook to Saving the Planet.* New York: Viking.

Elledge, Scott (Ed.). (1990). *Wider Than the Sky: Poems to Grow Up With.* New York: HarperCollins.

Emberley, Barbara. (1967). *Drummer Hoff.* Illus. Ed Emberley. Englewood Cliffs, NJ: Prentice.

Emberley, Barbara. (1987). *One Wide River to Cross.* Boston: Little, Brown.

Engdahl, Sylvia. (1989). *Enchantress from the Stars.* New York: Atheneum.

Engel, Dean, & Freedman, Florence B. (1995). *Ezra Jack Keats: A Biography with Illustrations.* New York: Silver Moon.

English, Karen. (1996). *Neeny Coming, Neeny Going.* Mahwah, NJ: Bridgewater.

English, Karen. (1999). *Francie.* New York: Farrar, Straus & Giroux.

Enzenberger, Hans Magnus. (2000). *Lost in Time.* New York: Holt.

Erdoes, Richard. (1976). *The Rain Dance People: The Pueblo Indians, Their Past and Present.* New York: Knopf.

Erdoes, Richard. (1976). *The Sound of Flutes and Other Indian Legends.* New York: Pantheon.

Erdrich, Louise. (1999). *Grandmother's Pigeon.* Illus. Jim Lamarche. New York: Hyperion.

Erdrich, Louise. (1999). *The Birchbark House.* New York: Hyperion.

Ernst, Lisa Campbell. (1995). *Little Red Riding Hood: A Newfangled Prairie Tale.* New York: Simon & Schuster.

Esbensen, Barbara Juster (Reteller). (1989). *Ladder to the Sky: How the Gift of Healing Came to the Ojibway Nation.* Boston: Little, Brown.

Esbensen, Barbara Juster. (1986). *Words with Wrinkled Knees: Animal Poems.* Illus. John Stadler. New York: HarperCollins.

Esbensen, Barbara Juster. (1990). *Great Northern Diver: The Loon.* Boston: Little, Brown.

Esbensen, Barbara Juster. (1992). *Who Shrank My Grandmother's House?* Illus. Eric Beddows. New York: HarperCollins.

Esbensen, Barbara Juster. (1993). *Playful Slider: The North American River Otter.* Boston: Little, Brown.

Esbensen, Barbara Juster. (1995). *Dance with Me.* New York: HarperCollins.

Esbensen, Barbara Juster. (1996). *Echoes for the Eye: Poems to Celebrate Patterns in Nature.* New York: HarperCollins.

Espeland, Pamela. (1980). *Story of Cadmus.* Minneapolis, MN: Carolrhoda.

Estes, Eleanor. (1941). *The Moffats.* San Diego: Harcourt.

Everett, Gwen. (1992). *Li'l Sis and Uncle Willie: A Story Based on the Life and Paintings of William H. Johnson.* New York: Rizzoli.

Everett, Gwen. (1993). *John Brown: One Man Against Slavery.* New York: Rizzoli.

Evslin, Bernard. (1984). *Hercules.* New York: Morrow/Avon.

Faber, Doris. (1985). *Eleanor Roosevelt: First Lady of the World.* New York: Viking.

Faber, Doris. (1992). *Calamity Jane: Her Life and Her Legend.* Boston: Houghton.

Facklam, Margery. (1989). *Partners for Life: The Mysteries of Animal Symbiosis.* Boston: Little, Brown.

Facklam, Margery. (1993). *What Does the Crow Know? The Mysteries of Animal Intelligence.* San Francisco: Sierra Club.

Facklam, Margery. (1996). *Creepy, Crawly Caterpillars.* Boston: Little, Brown.

Fang, Linda. (1997). *The Ch'i-Lin Purse: A Collection of Ancient Chinese Stories.* Illus. Jeanne M. Lee. New York: Farrar, Straus & Giroux.

Farber, Norma. (1979). *How Does It Feel to Be Old?* Illus. Trina Schart Hyman. New York: Dutton.

Farjeon, Eleanor. (1951). *Poems for Children.* New York: Lippincott.

Farjeon, Eleanor. (1986). *Morning Has Broken.* New York: Franklin Watts.

Farley, Walter. (1941). *The Black Stallion.* Illus. Keith Ward. New York: Random House.

Farmer, Nancy. (1994). *The Ear, the Eye, and the Arm: A Novel.* New York: Scholastic.

Farmer, Nancy. (1995). *The Warm Place.* New York: Scholastic.

Farrell, Jeanette. (1998). *Invisible Enemies: Stories of Infectious Disease.* New York: Farrar, Straus & Giroux.

Farrell, Mame. (1998). *Bradley and the Billboard.* New York: Farrar, Straus & Giroux.

Faulkner, William J. (1995). *Brer Tiger and the Big Wind.* New York: Morrow/Avon.

Fearnley, Jan. (2000). *Mr. Wolf's Pancakes.* Waukesha, WI: Little Tiger.

Feder, Jane. (1995). *Table Chair Bear: A Book in Many Languages.* New York: Ticknor & Fields.

Feelings, Muriel. (1974). *Jambo Means Hello.* Illus. Tom Feelings. New York: Dial.

Feelings, Muriel. (1975). *Moja Means One: A Swahili Counting Book.* Illus. Tom Feelings. New York: Dial.

Feelings, Tom. (1993). *Soul Looks Back in Wonder.* New York: Dial.

Feelings, Tom. (1995). *The Middle Passage: White Ships/Black Cargo.* New York: Dial/Penguin.

Fenner, Carol. (1999). *The King of Dragons.* New York: McElderry.

Fenner, Carol. (1999). *Yolanda's Genius.* New York: McElderry.

Ferrie, Richard. (1999). *The World Turned Upside Down: George Washington and the Battle of Yorktown.* New York: Holiday House.

Ferris, Jean. (1998). *Bad.* New York: Farrar, Straus & Giroux.

Ferris, Jean. (1999). *Love Among the Walnuts.* San Diego: Harcourt.

Ferris, Jeri. (1994). *What I Had Was Singing: The Story of Marian Anderson.* Minneapolis, MN: Lerner.

Fiedler, Lisa. (1998). *Lucky Me.* Boston: Houghton.

Field, Rachel. (1988). *General Store.* Illus. Nancy Winslow Parker. New York: Greenwillow.

Fields, Julia. (1988). *Green Lion of Zion Street.* Illus. Jerry Pinkney. New York: McElderry.

Fienberg, Anna. (2000). *Borrowed Light.* New York: Delacorte.

Filipovic, Zlata. (1994). *Zlata's Diary: A Child's Life in Sarajevo.* New York: Viking.

Fine, Anne. (1994). *Flour Babies.* New York: Bantam Doubleday Dell.

Finley, Martha. (1867; 1981 Reissue). *Elsie Dinsmore.* Eds. Alison Lurie and Justin G. Schiller. New York: Garland.

Fisher, Aileen. (1991). *Always Wondering.* Illus. Joan Sandin. New York: HarperCollins.

Fisher, Leonard Everett. (1981). *The Seven Days of Creation.* New York: Holiday House.

Fisher, Leonard Everett. (1984). *Olympians: Great Gods and Goddesses of Ancient Greece.* New York: Holiday House.

Fisher, Leonard Everett. (1989). *The Wailing Wall.* New York: Macmillan.

Fisher, Leonard Everett. (1990). *The Oregon Trail.* New York: Holiday House.

Fisher, Leonard Everett. (1991). *The ABC Exhibit.* New York: Macmillan.

Fisher, Leonard Everett. (1992). *Galileo.* New York: Macmillan.

Fisher, Leonard Everett. (1992). *Tracks Across America: The Story of the American Railroad, 1825–1900.* New York: Holiday House.

Fisher, Leonard Everett. (1993). *Gutenberg.* New York: Simon & Schuster.

Fisher, Leonard Everett. (1994). *Marie Curie.* New York: Simon & Schuster.

Fisher, Leonard Everett. (1999). *Alexander Graham Bell.* New York: Atheneum.

Fisher, Leonard Everett. (1999). *The Architects.* New York: Benchmark.

Fisher, Leonard Everett. (1999). *The Blacksmiths.* New York: Benchmark.

Flack, Marjorie. (1933). *The Story About Ping.* Illus. Kurt Wiese. New York: Viking.

Fleischman, Paul. (1986). *I Am Phoenix: Poems for Two Voices.* Illus. Ken Nutt (Eric Beddows). New York: HarperCollins.

Fleischman, Paul. (1988). *Joyful Noise: Poems for Two Voices.* Illus. Eric Beddows. New York: HarperCollins.

Fleischman, Paul. (1991). *The Borning Room.* New York: HarperCollins.

Fleischman, Paul. (1991). *Time Train.* Illus. Claire Ewart. New York: HarperCollins.

Fleischman, Paul. (1992). *Townsend's Warbler.* New York: HarperCollins.

Fleischman, Paul. (1993). *Bull Run.* Illus. David Frampton. New York: HarperCollins.

Fleischman, Paul. (1996). *Dateline: Troy.* Cambridge: Candlewick.

Fleischman, Paul. (1996). *Saturnalia.* New York: HarperCollins.

Fleischman, Paul. (1999). *Seedfolks.* New York: HarperCollins.

Fleischman, Sid. (1986). *The Whipping Boy.* New York: Greenwillow.

Fleischman, Sid. (1987). *Scarebird.* Illus. Peter Sis. New York: Greenwillow.

Fleischman, Sid. (1992). *McBroom's Wonderful One-Acre Farm: Three Tall Tales.* New York: Greenwillow.

Fleischman, Sid. (1998). *Bandit's Moon.* Illus. Joseph A. Smith. New York: Greenwillow.

Fleisher, Paul. (1993). *The Master Violinmaker.* Boston: Houghton.

Fleishman, Paul. (1998). *Whirligig.* New York: Holt.

Fleishman, Sid. (2000). *Big Talk: Poems for Four Voices.* Illus. Beppe Giacobbe. Cambridge: Candlewick.

Fleming, Candace. (1998). *The Hatmaker's Saga: A Story by Benjamin Franklin.* Illus. Robert Andrew Parker. Danbury, CT: Orchard.

Fleming, Denise. (1991). *In the Tall, Tall Grass.* New York: Holt.

Fleming, Denise. (1992). *Count!* New York: Holt.

Fleming, Denise. (1993). *In the Small, Small Pond.* New York: Holt.

Fleming, Denise. (1994). *Barnyard Banter.* New York: Holt.

Fletcher, Ralph. (1994). *I Am Wings: Poems About Love.* New York: Bradbury.

Fletcher, Ralph. (1999). *Flying Solo.* New York: Clarion.

Fletcher, Susan. (1998). *Shadow Spinner.* New York: Aladdin.

Floca, Brian. (2000). *Dinosaurs at the Ends of the Earth: The Story of the Central Asiatic Expeditions.* New York: DK Publishing.

Florian, Douglas. (1991). *A Carpenter.* New York: Greenwillow.

Florian, Douglas. (1991). *A Potter.* New York: Greenwillow.

Florian, Douglas. (1992). *At the Zoo.* New York: Greenwillow.

Florian, Douglas. (1996). *On the Wing: Bird Poems and Paintings.* San Diego: Harcourt.

Floiran, Douglas. (1999). *Laugh-Eteria.* San Diego: Harcourt.

Florian, Douglas. (2000). *Mammalabilia.* San Diego: Harcourt.

Flournoy, Valerie. (1985). *The Patchwork Quilt.* Illus. Jerry Pinkney. New York: Dial.

Flournoy, Valerie. (1995). *Tanya's Reunion.* New York: Dial.

Forbes, Esther. (1969). *Johnny Tremain.* Illus. Lynd Ward. New York: Dell.

Ford, Michael Thomas. (1998). *Outspoken: Role Models from the Lesbian and Gay Community.* New York: Morrow/Avon.

Ford, Miela. (1995). *Sunflower.* New York: Greenwillow.

Foreman, Michael. (1992). *Michael Foreman's Mother Goose.* San Diego: Harcourt.

Foreman, Michael. (1993). *War Game.* New York: Arcade.

Forest, Antonia. (1970). *The Player's Boy.* London: Faber.

Forest, Heather. (1993). *The Baker's Dozen: A Colonial American Tale.* Illus. Susan Gaber. San Diego: Harcourt.

Forrester, Sandra. (1997). *Sound the Jubilee.* New York: Puffin.

Fox, Mem. (1985). *Wilfrid Gordon McDonald Partridge.* Illus. Julie Vivas. Brooklyn, NY: Kane Miller.

Fox, Mem. (1988). *Hattie and the Fox.* Illus. Patricia Mullins. New York: Bradbury.

Fox, Mem. (1990, 1992). *Dear Mem Fox: I Have Read All Your Books Even the Pathetic Ones.* San Diego: Harcourt.

Fox, Mem. (1993). *Radical Reflections.* San Diego: Harcourt.

Fox, Mem. (1993). *Time for Bed.* San Diego: Harcourt.

Fox, Mem. (1997). *Wherever You Are.* Illus. Leslie Staub. San Diego: Harcourt.

Fox, Paula. (1982). *The Slave Dancer.* New York: Bradbury.

Fox, Paula. (1984). *One-Eyed Cat.* New York: Bradbury.

Fox, Paula. (1991). *Monkey Island.* New York: Scholastic.

Fox, Paula. (1995). *The Eagle Kite.* New York: Scholastic.

Fox, Paula. (1995). *Western Wind: A Novel.* New York: Dell.

Fraden, Dennis Brindell, & Fraden, Judith Bloom. (2000). *Ida B. Wells: Mother of the Civil Rights Movement.* New York: Clarion.

Frank, E. R. (2000). *Life Is Funny.* New York: DK Publishing.

Frank, Lucy. (1995). *I Am an Artichoke.* New York: Holiday House.

Franklin, Kristine L. (1995). *Eclipse.* New York: Candlewick.

Fraustino, Lisa Rowe. (1995). *Ash.* New York: Scholastic.

Freedman, Russell. (1987). *Indian Chiefs.* New York: Holiday House.

Freedman, Russell. (1989). *Lincoln: A Photobiography.* New York: Clarion.

Freedman, Russell. (1990). *Franklin Delano Roosevelt.* Boston: Houghton.

Freedman, Russell. (1991). *The Wright Brothers: How They Invented the Airplane.* Illus. Wilbur and Orville Wright. New York: Holiday House.

Freedman, Russell. (1992). *An Indian Winter.* Illus. Karl Bodmer. New York: Holiday House.

Freedman, Russell. (1993). *Eleanor Roosevelt: A Life of Discovery.* New York: Clarion.

Freedman, Russell. (1994). *Kids at Work: Lewis Hine and the Crusade Against Child Labor.* New York: Clarion.

Freedman, Russell. (1996). *The Life and Death of Crazy Horse.* New York: Holiday House.

Freedman, Russell. (1998). *Martha Graham: A Dancer's Life.* New York: Clarion.

Freedman, Russell. (1999). *Babe Didrikson Zaharias: The Making of a Champion.* Boston: Clarion.

Freeman, Don. (1968). *Corduroy.* New York: Viking.

Freeman, Suzanne. (1994). *Ida B. Wells-Barnette and the Antilynching Crusade.* Brookfield, CT: Millbrook.

French, Jackie. (1995). *Somewhere Around the Corner.* New York: Holt.

French, Vivian. (1993). *Caterpillar, Caterpillar.* Cambridge: Candlewick.

French, Vivian. (2000). *Growing Frogs.* Illus. Alison Bartlett. Cambridge: Candlewick.

Friedman, Ina. (1984). *How My Parents Learned to Eat.* Boston: Houghton.

Fritz, Jean. (1958). *The Cabin Faced West.* Illus. Feodor Rojankovsky. New York: Putnam.

Fritz, Jean. (1960). *Brady.* New York: Putnam.

Fritz, Jean. (1967). *Early Thunder.* New York: Putnam.

Fritz, Jean. (1973). *And Then What Happened, Paul Revere?* Illus. Margot Tomes. New York: Putnam.

Fritz, Jean. (1974). *Why Don't You Get a Horse, Sam Adams?* Illus. Trina Schart Hyman. New York: Putnam.

Fritz, Jean. (1975). *Where Was Patrick Henry on the 29th of May?* New York: Putnam.

Fritz, Jean. (1975). *Who's That Stepping on Plymouth Rock?* Illus. J. B. Handelsman. New York: Putnam.

Fritz, Jean. (1976). *What's the Big Idea, Ben Franklin?* Illus. Margot Tomes. New York: Putnam.

Fritz, Jean. (1976). *Will You Sign Here, John Hancock?* Illus. Trina Schart Hyman. New York: Putnam.

Fritz, Jean. (1979). *Stonewall.* Illus. Stephen Gammell. New York: Putnam.

Fritz, Jean. (1981). *Traitor: The Case of Benedict Arnold.* New York: Putnam.

Fritz, Jean. (1981). *Where Do You Think You're Going, Christopher Columbus?* Illus. Margot Tomes. New York: Putnam.

Fritz, Jean. (1982). *Can't You Make Them Behave, King George?* Illus. Tomie DePaola. New York: Putnam.

Fritz, Jean. (1982). *Homesick: My Own Story.* New York: Putnam.

Fritz, Jean. (1983). *The Double Life of Pocahontas.* New York: Putnam.

Fritz, Jean. (1985). *China Homecoming.* New York: Putnam.

Fritz, Jean. (1986). *Make Way for Sam Houston.* New York: Putnam.

Fritz, Jean. (1989). *The Great Little Madison.* New York: Putnam.

Fritz, Jean. (1991). *Bully for You, Teddy Roosevelt.* New York: Putnam.

Fritz, Jean. (1993). *Surprising Myself.* Katonah, NY: Richard C. Owen.

Fritz, Jean. (1994). *Around the World in a Hundred Years: From Henry the Navigator to Magellan.* New York: Putnam.

Fritz, Jean. (1994). *Harriet Beecher Stowe and the Beecher Preachers.* New York: Putnam.

Fritz, Jean. (1995). *You Want Women to Vote, Lizzie Stanton?* New York: Putnam.

Fritz, Jean. (1999). *Why Not, Lafayette?* New York: Putnam.

Froman, Robert. (1974). *Seeing Things.* New York: HarperCollins.

Frost, Robert. (1959). *You Come Too: Favorite Poems for Young Readers.* New York: Holt.

Frost, Robert. (1978). *Stopping by Woods on a Snowy Evening.* Illus. Susan Jeffers. New York: Dutton.

Frost, Robert. (1982). *Swinger of Birches: Poems of Robert Frost for Young People.* Owings Mills, MD: Stemmer.

Frost, Robert. (1988). *Birches.* Illus. Ed Young. New York: Holt.

Fukuda, Hanako. (1970; o.p.). *Wind in My Hand: The Story of Issa.* San Carlos, CA.: Golden Gate.

Gaeddert, Louann. (1994). *Breaking Free.* New York: Atheneum.

Gág, Wanda. (1928). *Millions of Cats.* New York: Putnam

Gajadin, Chitra. (1992). *Amal and the Letter from the King.* Honesdale, PA: Boyds Mills.

Galdone, Paul. (1975). *The Gingerbread Boy.* New York: Clarion.

Galdone, Paul. (1979). *The Three Little Pigs.* New York: Clarion.

Galdone, Paul. (1983). *The Little Red Hen.* New York: Clarion.

Galdone, Paul. (1984). *Henny Penny.* Boston: Houghton.

Galdone, Paul. (1984). *The Elves and the Shoemaker.* New York: Clarion.

Gallant, Roy A. (1995). *The Day the Sky Split Apart: Investigating a Cosmic Mystery.* New York: Atheneum.

Gallico, Paul. (1940). *The Snow Goose.* New York: Knopf.

Galloway, Patricia. (1995). *Truly Grim Tales.* New York: Delacorte.

Gammell, Stephen. (2000). *Once Upon MacDonald's Farm.* New York: Simon & Schuster.

Ganer, Anita. (1996). *Out of the Ark: Stories from the World's Religions.* San Diego: Harcourt.

Gantos, Jack. (1998). *Joey Pigza Swallowed the Key.* New York: Farrar, Straus & Giroux.

Gantos, Jack. (1999). *Jack on the Tracks: Four Seasons of Fifth Grade.* New York: Farrar, Straus & Giroux.

Gantos, Jack. (2000). *Joey Pigza Loses Control.* New York: Farrar, Straus & Giroux.

Garcia, Lionel G. (1994). *To a Widow with Children.* Houston: Arte Publico.

Garcia, Pelayo. (1997). *From Amigos to Friends.* Houston: Arte Publico.

Garden, Nancy. (1995). *Dove and Sword: A Novel of Joan of Arc.* New York: Farrar, Straus & Giroux.

Garden, Nancy. (2000). *Holly's Secret.* New York: Farrar, Straus & Giroux.

Garland, Michael. (1995). *Dinner at Magritte's.* New York: Dutton.

Garland, Sherry. (1993). *The Lotus Seed.* San Diego: Harcourt.

Garland, Sherry. (1995). *Indio.* San Diego: Harcourt.

Gates, Doris. (1982). *Lord of the Sky: Zeus.* New York: Penguin.

Gates, Doris. (1983). *Two Queens of Heaven: Aphrodite and Demeter.* Illus. Trina Schart Hyman. New York: Penguin.

Gauch, Patricia Lee. (1974; 1992). *This Time, Tempe Wick?* New York: Putnam.

Gauch, Patricia Lee. (1990). *Thunder at Gettysburg.* New York: Putnam.

Gauch, Patricia Lee. (1994). *Noah.* New York: Philomel.

Gauch, Patricia Lee. (1994). *Tanya and Emily in a Dance for Two.* New York: Philomel.

Gauthier, Gail. (1998). *A Year with Butch and Spike.* New York: Putnam.

Gee, Maurice. (1986). *The Fire-Raiser.* Boston: Houghton.

Geisert, Arthur. (1991). *Oink.* Boston: Houghton.

Geisert, Arthur. (1992). *Pigs from 1 to 10.* Boston: Houghton.

Geisert, Arthur. (1993). *Oink, Oink.* Boston: Houghton.

Geisert, Arthur. (1996). *Roman Numerals I to MM (Numerabilia Romana Uno ad Duo Mila): Liber de Difficillimo Computando Numerum.* Boston: Houghton.

Geisert, Bonnie. (1998). *Prairie Town.* Illus. Arthur Geis. Boston: Houghton.

George, Jean Craighead. (1959). *My Side of the Mountain.* New York: Dutton.

George, Jean Craighead. (1971; 1991). *Who Really Killed Cock Robin? An Ecological Mystery.* New York: HarperCollins.

George, Jean Craighead. (1972). *Julie of the Wolves.* Illus. John Schoenherr. New York: HarperCollins.

George, Jean Craighead. (1980). *The Cry of the Crow.* New York: HarperCollins.

George, Jean Craighead. (1983). *One Day in the Desert.* New York: HarperCollins.

George, Jean Craighead. (1994). *Julie.* Illus. Wendell Minor. New York: HarperCollins.

George, Jean Craighead. (2000). *How to Talk to Your Cat.* Illus. Paul Meisel. New York: HarperCollins.

George, Jean Craighead. (2000). *How to Talk to Your Dog.* Illus. Sue Treasdell. New York: HarperCollins.

George, Lindsay Barrett. (1999). *Around the World: Who's Been Here?* New York: Greenwillow.

Gershator, Phillis. (2000). *Tiny and Bigman.* Illus. Lynne Cravath. New York: Cavendish.

Gershator, Phyllis. (1994). *Tukama Tootles the Flute: A Tale from the Antilles.* New York: Scholastic.

Gerson, Mary-Joan (Reteller). (1992). *Why the Sky Is Far Away.* Illus. Carla Golembe. Boston: Little Brown.

Gerson, Mary-Joan (Reteller). (1995). *People of Corn: A Mayan Story.* Boston: Little, Brown.

Gherman, Beverly. (1992). *E. B. White: Some Writer.* New York: Atheneum.

Gherman, Beverly. (1994). *The Mysterious Rays of Dr. Röntgen.* New York: Simon & Schuster.

Gibbons, Gail. (1981). *Trucks.* New York: HarperCollins.

Gibbons, Gail. (1987). *Deadline! From News to Newspaper.* New York: HarperCollins.

Gibbons, Gail. (1987). *Zoo.* New York: HarperCollins.

Gibbons, Gail. (1988). *Farming.* New York: Holiday House.

Gibbons, Gail. (1995). *Bicycle Book.* New York: Holiday House.

Gibbons, Gail. (1999). *Bats.* New York: Holiday House.

Gibbons, Gail. (1999). *Exploring the Deep, Dark Sea.* Boston: Little, Brown.

Giblin, James Cross. (1987). *From Hand to Mouth.* New York: HarperCollins.

Giblin, James Cross. (1990). *The Riddle of the Rosetta Stone: Key to Ancient Egypt.* New York: HarperCollins.

Giblin, James Cross. (1992). *George Washington: A Picture Book Biography.* New York: Scholastic.

Giblin, James Cross. (1993). *Be Seated: A Book About Chairs.* New York: HarperCollins.

Giblin, James Cross. (1994). *Thomas Jefferson: A Picture Book Biography.* New York: Scholastic.

Giblin, James Cross. (1997). *Charles A. Lindberg: A Human Hero.* New York: Clarion.

Giblin, James Cross. (2000). *The Amazing Life of Benjamin Franklin.* New York: Scholastic.

Giblin, James Cross. (2000). *The Century That Was: Reflections on the Last One Hundred Years.* New York: Atheneum.

Giblin, Jim. (2000). *The Amazing Life of Benjamin Franklin.* New York: Scholastic.

Giff, Patricia Reilley. (2000). *Nory Tyan's Song.* New York: Bantam.

Giganti, Paul, Jr. (1988). *How Many Snails? A Counting Book.* Illus. Donald Crews. New York: Greenwillow.

Gilden, Mel. (1989). *Outer Space and All That Junk.* New York: HarperCollins.

Gilliand, Judith Heide. (2000). *Steamboat! The Story of Captain Blanche Leathers.* New York: DK International/Kroupa.

Gilson, Jamie. (1987). *Hobie Hanson, You're Weird.* Illus. Elise Primavera. New York: Lothrop, Lee & Shepard.

Ginsburg, Mirra (Adapter). (1988). *The Chinese Mirror.* San Diego: Harcourt.

Ginsburg, Mirra. (1980). *Good Morning, Chick.* Adapter Kornei Chukovsky. Illus. Byron Barton. New York: Greenwillow.

Ginsburg, Mirra. (1992). *Asleep, Asleep.* Illus. Nancy Tafuri. New York: Greenwillow.

Giovanni, Nikki. (1987). *Spin a Soft Black Song.* New York: Farrar, Straus & Giroux.

Giovanni, Nikki. (1994). *Knoxville, Tennessee.* New York: Scholastic.

Giovanni, Nikki. (1996). *The Selected Poems of Nikki Giovanni.* New York: Morrow/Avon.

Giovanni, Nikki. (1996). *Shimmy, Shimmy, Shimmy Like My Sister Kate.* New York: Holt.

Giovanni, Nikki. (1996). *The Sun Is So Quiet.* Illus. Ashley Bryan. New York: Holt.

Giovanni, Nikki. (1998). *The Genie in the Jar.* Illus. Chris Raschka. New York: Holt.

Girnis, Meg. (2000). *ABC for You and Me.* Morton Grove, IL: Whitman.

Glaser, Isabel Joshlin. (1995). *Dreams of Glory: Poems Starring Girls.* New York: Atheneum.

Glassman, Judy. (1990). *The Morning Glory War.* New York: Dutton.

Glassman, Miriam. (1998). *Box Top Dreams.* New York: Delacorte.

Gleitzman, Morris. (1995). *Blabber Mouth.* San Diego: Harcourt.

Goble, Paul. (1982). *The Girl Who Loved Wild Horses.* New York: Macmillan.

Goble, Paul. (1982). *Star Boy.* New York: Bradbury.

Goble, Paul. (1984). *Buffalo Woman.* New York: Bradbury.

Goble, Paul. (1987). *Death of the Iron Horse.* New York: Bradbury.

Goble, Paul. (1988). *Her Seven Brothers.* New York: Bradbury.

Goble, Paul. (1989). *Iktomi and the Berries: A Plains Indian Story.* New York: Scholastic.

Goble, Paul. (1990). *Dream Wolf.* New York: Bradbury.

Goble, Paul. (1992). *Crow Chief: A Plains Indian Story.* New York: Scholastic.

Goble, Paul. (1992). *Love Flute.* New York: Simon & Schuster.

Goble, Paul. (1993). *The Lost Children: The Boys Who Were Neglected.* New York: Bradbury.

Goble, Paul. (1994). *Adopted by the Eagles: A Plains Indian Story of Friendship and Treachery.* New York: Bradbury.

Goble, Paul. (1994). *Hau Kola 5 Hello Friend.* Katonah, NY: Richard C. Owen.

Goble, Paul. (1994). *Iktomi and the Buzzard: A Plains Indian Story.* New York: Scholastic.

Goble, Paul. (1998). *The Legend of the White Buffalo Woman.* Washington, DC: National Geographic.

Goblin, James Cross. (1999). *The Mystery of the Mammoth Bones and How It Was Solved.* New York: HarperCollins.

Godwin, Laura. (1998). *Forest.* Illus. Stacey Schuett. New York: HarperCollins.

Godwin, Laura. (2000). *Barnyard Prayers.* Illus. Brian Selnick. New York: Hyperion.

Godwin, Laura. (2000). *The Doll People.* Illus. Brian Selznick. New York: Hyperion.

Goedecke, Christopher J. (1992). *The Wind Warrior: The Training of a Karate Champion.* Photog. Rosmarie Hauserr. New York: Simon & Schuster.

Goennel, Heidi. (1989). *My Dog.* New York: Scholastic.

Goennel, Heidi. (1992). *The Circus.* New York: Morrow/Avon.

Goennel, Heidi. (1993). *Heidi's Zoo: An Un-Alphabet Book.* New York: Tambourine.

Goffstein, M. B. (1994). *A Writer.* New York: HarperCollins.

Gold, Alison Leslie. (2000). *A Special Fate: Chiune Sugihara: Hero of the Holocaust.* New York: Scholastic.

Goldstein, Bobbye S. (Selector). (1992). *Inner Chimes: Poems on Poetry.* Illus. Jane Breskin Zalben. Honesdale, PA: Boyds Mills.

Golenbock, Peter. (1990). *Teammates.* San Diego: Harcourt.

Gonzales, Lucia M. (1997). *Senor Cat's Romance and Other Favorite Stories from Latin America.* Illus. Lulu Delacre. New York: Scholastic.

Gonzales, Lucia M. (1999). *The Bossy Gallito/El Gallo de Bodas: A Traditional Cuban Folktale.* Illus. Lulu Delacre. New York: Scholastic.

Gonzales, Ray. (1998). *Touching the Fire: Fifteen Poets of Today's Latino Renaissance.* New York: Doubleday.

Goodall, John. (1979). *The Story of an English Villiage.* New York: Atheneum.

Goodall, John. (1988). *Little Red Riding Hood.* New York: McElderry.

Goodall, John. (1999). *Naughty Nancy.* New York: McElderry.

Goode, Diane. (1989). *Diane Goode's Book of American Folktales and Songs.* New York: Dutton.

Goode, Diane. (1994). *Diane Goode's Book of Scary Stories and Songs.* New York: Dutton.

Goodman, Susan E. (1998). *Stones, Bones, and Petroglyphs: Digging into the Southwest's Archaeology.* Photog. Michael Doolittle. New York: Atheneum.

Goodman, Susan E. (2000). *Animal Rescue: The Best Job There Is.* New York: Simon & Schuster.

Goodrich, Samuel G. (1822). *Peter Parley's History of the United States of America.* New York: Garland.

Goodrich, Samuel G. , & Goodrich, Charles. (1827; 1976 Reissue). *Tales of Peter Parley About America.* New York: Garland.

Gorbachev, Valeri. (1999). *Where Is the Apple Pie?* New York: Philomel.

Gordon, Amy. (1999). *When JFK Was My Father.* Boston: Houghton.

Gordon, Gaelyn. (1992). *Duckat.* Illus. Chris Gaskin. New York: Scholastic.

Gordon, Jeffie Ross. (1992). *Six Sleepy Sheep.* Illus. John O'Brien. Honesdale, PA: Boyds Mills.

Gordon, Ruth. (1991). *Time Is the Longest Distance.* New York: HarperCollins.

Gordon, Ruth. (1995). *Pierced by a Ray of Sun: Poems About the Times We Feel Alone.* New York: HarperCollins.

Gordon, Sheila. (1987). *Waiting for the Rain: A Novel of South Africa.* New York: Scholastic.

Gordon, Sheila. (1990). *The Middle of Somewhere: A Story of South Africa.* New York: Scholastic.

Gorman, Carol. (1999). *Dork in Disguise.* New York: HarperCollins.

Gottlieb, Dale. (1991). *My Stories by Hildy Calpurnia Rose.* New York: Knopf.

Govenar, Alan (Collector, Ed.). (2000). *Osceola: Memories of a Share-Cropper's Daughter.* New York: Hyperion.

Grabowski, John. (1992). *Sandy Koufax.* New York: Chelsea.

Graham, Bob. (1989). *Has Anyone Here Seen William?* Boston: Little, Brown.

Grahame, Kenneth. (1908; 1940; 1961). *Wind in the Willows.* New York: Scribner's.

Gramatky, Hardie. (1939). *Little Toot.* New York: Putnam.

Grande Tabor, Nancy M. (1996). *Somos un Arco Iris/We Are a Rainbow.* Waterton, MA: Charlesbridge.

Granfield, Linda. (1998). *Circus: An Album.* New York: DK Publishing.

Grassby, Donna. (2000). *A Seaside Alphabet.* Montreal: Tundra.

Gravelle, Karen. (1998). *What's Going on Down There? Answers to Questions Boys Find Hard to Ask.* Illus. Robert Leighton. New York: Walker.

Graves, Donald. (1995). *Baseball, Snakes, and Summer Squash.* Honesdale, PA: Boyds Mills.

Gray, Elizabeth Vining. (1942; 1987). *Adam of the Road.* New York: Viking.

Greaves, Margaret. (1990). *Tattercoats.* New York: Potter.

Green, Connie Jordan. (1992). *Emmy.* New York: Simon & Schuster.

Greenaway, Elizabeth. (1994). *Cat Nap.* New York: Random House.

Greenaway, Kate. (1878). *Under the Window.* London: Warne.

Greenberg, Jan, & Jordan, Sandra. (1991). *The Painter's Eye: Learning to Look at Contemporary American Art.* New York: Delacorte.

Greenberg, Jan, & Jordan, Sandra. (1993). *The Sculptor's Eye: Looking at Contemporary American Art.* New York: Delacorte.

Greenberg, Jan, & Jordan, Sandra. (1995). *The American Eye: Eleven Artists of the Twentieth Century.* New York: Delacorte.

Greenberg, Jan & Jordan, Sandra. (2000). *Frank O. Gehry: Outside In.* New York: DK Publishing.

Greenberg, Keith Elliot. (1992). *Magic Johnson: Champion with a Cause.* Minneapolis, MN: Lerner.

Greene, Bette. (1974). *Philip Hall Likes Me. I Reckon Maybe.* New York: Dial.

Greene, Carol. (1992). *The Golden Locket.* San Diego: Harcourt.

Greene, Carol. (1992). *Katherine Dunham: Black Dancer.* Chicago: Children's Book Press.

Greene, Constance. (1975). *I Know You, Al.* New York: Viking.

Greene, Constance. (1979). *Beat the Turtle Drum.* New York: Dell.

Greene, Constance. (1986). *Just Plain Al.* New York: Viking.

Greene, Constance. (1992). *Al(exandra) the Great.* New York: Viking.

Greene, Ellin (Reteller). (1996). *Ling-Li and the Phoenix Fairy: A Chinese Folktale.* New York: Clarion.

Greene, Ellin. (2000). *The Little Golden Lamb.* Illus. Rosanne Litzinger. Boston: Clarion.

Greene, Jacqueline Dembar. (1988). *Out of Many Waters.* New York: Walker.

Greene, Jacqueline Dembar. (1994). *One Foot Ashore.* New York: Walker.

Greene, Stephanie. (1999). *Owen Foote, Frontiersman.* Illus. Martha Weston. New York: Clarion.

Greene, Stephanie. (2000). *Owen Foote, Money Man.* Boston: Houghton.

Greenfeld, Howard. (1989). *Books: from Writer to Reader.* New York: Crown.

Greenfeld, Howard. (1993). *The Hidden Children.* New York: Ticknor & Fields.

Greenfeld, Howard. (1993). *Paul Gauguin.* New York: Abrams.

Greenfield, Eloise, & Little, Lessie Jones. (1979). *Childtimes: A Three-Generation Memoir.* New York: HarperCollins.

Greenfield, Eloise. (1973). *Rosa Parks.* New York: Crowell.

Greenfield, Eloise. (1974). *She Come Bringing Me That Little Baby Girl.* Philadelphia: Lippincott.

Greenfield, Eloise. (1974). *Sister.* New York: Crowell.

Greenfield, Eloise. (1975). *Me and Nessie.* New York: Crowell.

Greenfield, Eloise. (1975). *Paul Robeson.* New York: Crowell.

Greenfield, Eloise. (1976). *First Pink Light.* New York: HarperCollins.

Greenfield, Eloise. (1977). *Mary McLeod Bethune.* New York: HarperCollins.

Greenfield, Eloise. (1978). *Honey, I Love and Other Love Poems.* Illus. Leo and Diane Dillon. New York: HarperCollins.

Greenfield, Eloise. (1978). *Talk About a Family.* New York: Lippincott.

Greenfield, Eloise. (1988). *Nathaniel Talking.* New York: Writers and Readers.

Greenfield, Eloise. (1988). *Under the Sunday Tree.* Illus. Amos Ferguson. New York: HarperCollins.

Greenfield, Eloise. (1991). *Grandpa's Face.* Illus. Floyd Cooper. New York: Putnam.

Greenfield, Eloise. (1991). *Night on Neighborhood Street.* Illus. Jan Spivey Gilchrist. New York: Dial.

Greenfield, Eloise. (1992). *Koya Delaney and the Good Girl Blues.* New York: Scholastic.

Greenfield, Eloise. (1997). *For the Love of the Game: Michael Jordan and Me.* Illus. Jan Spivey. New York: HarperCollins.

Greenfield, Eloise. (1998). *Angels: An African-American Treasury.* New York: Hyperion.

Greenfield, Eloise. (1998). *Easter Parade.* New York: Disney.

Greenspun, Adele Aron. (1991). *Daddies.* New York: Philomel.

Greenwald, Sheila. (1980). *It All Began with Jane Eyre.* Boston: Little, Brown.

Greenwald, Sheila. (1989). *Rosy's Romance.* Boston: Little, Brown.

Greenwood, Barbara. (1994). *A Pioneer Sampler: The Daily Life of a Pioneer Family in 1840.* New York: Ticknor & Fields.

Gregor, C. Shana. (1996). *Cry of the Benu Bird: An Egyptian Creation Story.* Boston: Houghton.

Gretchen, Sylvia (Adapter). (1990). *Hero of the Land of Snow.* Illus. Julia Weaver. Berkeley, CA: Dharma.

Griego, Margot C., Bucks, Betsy L., Gilbert, Sharon S., & Kimball, Laurel H. (1991). *Tortillitas Para Mama and Other Spanish Rhymes.* Illus. Barbara Cooney. New York: Holt.

Grifalconi, Ann. (1986). *The Village of Round and Square Houses.* Boston: Little, Brown.

Grifalconi, Ann. (1987). *Darkness and the Butterfly.* Boston: Little, Brown.

Grifalconi, Ann. (1990). *Osa's Pride.* Boston: Little, Brown.

Griffin, Adele. (1999). *Dive.* New York: Hyperion.

Griffith, Helen V. (1987). *Grandaddy's Place.* Illus. James Stevenson. New York: Greenwillow.

Griffith, Helen. (1999). *Cougar.* New York: Greenwillow.

Grimes, Nikki. (1994). *Meet Danitra Brown.* New York: Lothrop, Lee & Shepard.

Grimes, Nikki. (1997). *It's Raining Laughter.* Illus. Miles Pinkney. New York: Penguin.

Grimes, Nikki. (1998). *A Dime a Dozen.* Illus. Angelo. New York: Dial.

Grimes, Nikki. (2000). *Jasmin's Notebook.* New York: Puffin.

Grimm, Jacob, & Grimm, Wilhelm. (1972). *Snow White and the Seven Dwarfs.* New York: Farrar, Straus & Giroux.

Grimm, Jacob, & Grimm, Wilhelm. (1973). *The Juniper Tree and Other Tales from Grimm.* (2 Vols.) (Lore Segal and Randall Jarrell, Trans.). Illus. Maurice Sendak. New York: Farrar, Straus & Giroux.

Grimm, Jacob, & Grimm, Wilhelm. (1977; 1823 Reprint). *Grimm's Fairy Tales.* Illus. George Cruikshank. San Diego: Green Tiger.

Grimm, Jacob, & Grimm, Wilhelm. (1979). *Hansel and Gretel.* Trans. Elizabeth Crawford. Illus. Lisbeth Zwerger. New York: Morrow/Avon.

Grimm, Jacob, & Grimm, Wilhelm. (1982). *Rapunzel.* Illus. Trina S. Hyman. New York: Holiday House.

Grimm, Jacob, & Grimm, Wilhelm. (1983). *Little Red Riding Hood.* Reteller and Illus. Trina Schart Hyman. New York: Holiday House.

Grimm, Jacob, & Grimm, Wilhelm. (1988). *Hansel and Gretel.* Illus. Anthony Browne. New York: Knopf.

Grimm, Jacob, & Grimm, Wilhelm. (1992). *The Bremen Town Musicians.* Illus. Bernadette Watts. New York: North-South.

Grimm, Jacob, & Grimm, Wilhelm. (1995). *The Golden Goose.* New York: Farrar, Straus & Giroux.

Grimm, Jacob. (1983). *Little Red Cap.* Trans. Elizabeth Crawford. Illus. Lizbeth Zwerger. New York: Morrow/Avon.

Grimm, Jacob. (1984). *Hansel and Gretel: A Tale from the Brothers Grimm.* New York: Putnam.

Grimm, Jacob. (1986). *Rumpelstiltskin.* Reteller and Illus. Paul O. Zelinsky. New York: Dutton.

Grimm, Jacob. (1988). *Hansel and Gretel.* Illus. Anthony Browne. New York: Knopf.

Grinnell, George. (1900). *Jack Among the Indians.* Boston: Stokes.

Grossman, Florence. (1991). *Listening to the Bells: Learning to Read Poetry by Writing Poetry.* Portsmouth, NH: Heinemann.

Grossman, Virginia. (1991). *Ten Little Rabbits.* Illus. Sylvia Long. San Francisco: Chronicle.

Grossman, Virginia. (1994). *Saturday Market.* New York: Lothrop, Lee & Shepard.

Grove, Vicki. (1998). *Reaching Dustin.* New York: Putnam.

Guarino, Deborah. (1989). *Is Your Mama a Llama?* Illus. Steven Kellogg. New York: Scholastic.

Gunning, Monica. (1993). *Not a Copper Penny in Me House.* Illus. Frané Lessac. Honesdale, PA: Boyds Mills.

Gutenberg, Johannes. (1437). *The Bible.*

Haas, Jessie. (1993). *A Horse Like Barney.* New York: Greenwillow.

Haas, Jessie. (1994). *Uncle Daney's Way.* New York: Greenwillow.

Haas, Jessie. (1995). *A Blue for Beware.* New York: Greenwillow.

Haas, Jessie. (1996). *Beware the Mare.* New York: Greenwillow.

Haas, Jessie. (1999). *Beware and Stogie.* New York: Greenwillow.

Haas, Jessie. (1999). *Unbroken.* Illus. Deborah Lanino. New York: Morrow/Avon.

Haas, Jessie. (2000). *Hurry!* Illus. Jos. A. Smith. New York: Greenwillow.

Hadithi, Mwenye. (1987). *Crafty Chameleon.* Illus. Adrienne Kennaway. Boston: Little, Brown.

Hague, Kathleen, & Hague, Michael. (1981). *The Man Who Kept House.* San Diego: Harcourt.

Hahn, Mary Downing. (1991). *Stepping on the Cracks.* Boston: Houghton.

Hahn, Mary Downing. (1996). *Following My Own Footsteps.* Boston: Clarion.

Haigh, Jane, & Murphy, Claire Rudolf. (1999). *Children of the Gold Rush.* New York: Reinhart.

Hale, Lucretia. (1880; 1960 Reprint). *The Peterkin Papers.* Boston: Houghton.

Hale, Lucretia. (1989). *The Lady Who Put Salt in Her Coffee.* Adapter and Illus. Amy Schwartz. San Diego: Harcourt.

Hale, Sarah Josepha Buell. (1995). *Mary Had a Little Lamb.* Illus. Salley Mavor. New York: Scholastic.

Haley, Gail (Reteller). (1986). *Jack and the Bean Tree.* New York: Crown.

Haley, Gail (Reteller). (1992). *Mountain Jack Tales.* New York: Dutton.

Haley, Gail. (1970). *A Story, a Story.* New York: Atheneum.

Haley, Gail. (1973; o.p.). *Jack Jouett's Ride.* New York: Viking.

Hall, Donald (Ed.). (1990). *The Oxford Book of Children's Verse in America.* New York: Oxford University.

Hall, Donald. (1942; 1994). *The Farm Summer.* New York: Dial.

Hall, Donald. (1979). *Ox-Cart Man.* Illus. Barbara Cooney. New York: Viking.

Hall, Donald. (1992). *The Farm Summer 1942.* Illus. Barry Moser. New York: Dial.

Hall, Donald. (1995). *Lucy's Summer.* San Diego: Harcourt.

Hall, Donald. (2000). *When Willard Met Babe Ruth.* Illus. Barry Moser. San Diego: Harcourt.

Hall, Lynn. (1991). *Dagmar Schultz and the Green-Eyed Monster.* New York: Macmillan.

Hall, Lynn. (1994). *The Soul of the Silver Dog.* New York: Knopf.

Hamanaka, Sheila. (1990). *The Journey: Japanese Americans, Racism, and Renewal.* New York: Scholastic.

Hamanaka, Sheila. (1994). *All the Colors of the Earth.* New York: Morrow/Avon.

Hamanaka, Shelia. (1995). *Bebop-A-Do-Walk!* New York: Simon & Schuster.

Hamanaka, Sheila. (1995). *On the Wings of Peace.* New York: Clarion.

Hamilton, Virginia. (1967). *Zeely.* Illus. Symeon Shimin. New York: Macmillan.

Hamilton, Virginia. (1968). *House of Dies Drear.* New York: Macmillan.

Hamilton, Virginia. (1971). *Planet of Junior Brown.* New York: Macmillan.

Hamilton, Virginia. (1974). *M. C. Higgins, the Great.* New York: Macmillan.

Hamilton, Virginia. (1982). *Sweet Whispers, Brother Rush.* New York: Philomel.

Hamilton, Virginia. (1983). *The Magical Adventures of Pretty Pearl.* New York: HarperCollins.

Hamilton, Virginia. (1984). *A Little Love.* New York: Philomel.

Hamilton, Virginia. (1985). *The People Could Fly: American Black Folk Tales.* Illus. Leo and Diane Dillon. New York: Knopf.

Hamilton, Virginia. (1988). *Anthony Burns: The Defeat and Triumph of a Fugitive Slave.* New York: Knopf.

Hamilton, Virginia. (1988). *In the Beginning: Creation Stories from Around the World.* Illus. Barry Moser. San Diego: Harcourt.

Hamilton, Virginia. (1990). *Cousins.* New York: Putnam.

Hamilton, Virginia. (1990). *The Dark Way: Stories from the Spirit World.* Illus. Lambert Davis. San Diego: Harcourt.

Hamilton, Virginia. (1991). *The All Jahdu Storybook.* San Diego: Harcourt.

Hamilton, Virginia. (1992). *Drylongso.* Illus. Jerry Pinkney. San Diego: Harcourt.

Hamilton, Virginia. (1993). *Many Thousand Gone: African Americans from Slavery to Freedom.* Illus. Leo and Diane Dillon. New York: Knopf.

Hamilton, Virginia. (1993). *Plain City.* New York: Scholastic.

Hamilton, Virginia. (1995). *Her Stories: African American Folktales, Fairy Tales, and True Tales.* New York: Scholastic.

Hamilton, Virginia. (1995). *When Birds Could Talk and Bats Could Sing.* New York: Scholastic.

Hamilton, Virginia. (1997). *A Ring of Tricksters.* Illus. Barry Moser. New York: Scholastic.

Hamilton, Virginia. (1998). *Second Cousins.* New York: Scholastic.

Hamilton, Virginia. (1999). *Bluish.* New York: Scholastic.

Hamilton, Virginia. (1999). *Second Cousins.* New York: Scholastic.

Hampton, Wilborn. (1997). *Kennedy Assassinated! The World Mourns: A Reporter's Story.* Cambridge: Candlewick.

Han, Oki S., & Plunkett, Stephanie Haboush. (1996). *Kongi and Potgi: A Cinderella Story from Korea.* New York: Dial.

Hansen, Joyce, & McGowen, Gary. (1998). *Breaking Ground, Breaking Silence: The Story of New York's African Burial Ground.* New York: Holt.

Hansen, Joyce. (1988). *Out from This Place.* Madison, WI: Turtleback

Hansen, Joyce. (1992). *Which Way Freedom?* New York: Camelot.

Hansen, Joyce. (1994). *The Captive.* New York: Scholastic.

Hansen, Joyce. (1997). *I Thought My Soul Would Rise and Fly.* New York: Scholastic.

Hansen, Joyce. (1999). *The Heart Calls Home.* New York: Walker.

Harjo, Joy. (1996). *The Woman Who Fell from the Sky: Poems.* New York: Norton.

Harnett, Cynthia. (1959). *Caxton's Challenge.* Tulsa: World Publishing.

Harris, Benjamin. (1679). *The Protestant Tutor.* London: Benjamin Harris.

Harris, Benjamin. (1690). *The New England Primer.* Boston: Benjamin Harris.

Harris, Joel Chandler. (1986). *Jump: The Adventures of Brer Rabbit.* (Van Dyke Parks and Malcolm Jones, Eds.). Illus. Barry Moser. San Diego: Harcourt.

Harris, Joel Chandler. (1987). *Jump Again! More Adventures of Brer Rabbit.* Illus. Barry Moser. San Diego: Harcourt.

Harris, Joel Chandler. (1989). *Jump on Over! The Adventures of Brer Rabbit and His Family.* Adapter Van Dyke Parks. Illus. Barry Moser. San Diego: Harcourt.

Harris, Robie H. (1994). *It's Perfectly Normal: Changing Bodies, Growing Up, Sex, and Sexual Health.* New York: Candlewick.

Harris, Robie H. (1999). *It's So Amazing! A Book About Eggs, Sperm, Birth, Babies, and Families.* Illus. Michael Emberley. Cambridge: Candlewick.

Harrison, Barbara, & Terris, Daniel. (1992). *A Twilight Struggle: The Life of John Fitzgerald Kennedy.* New York: Lothrop, Lee & Shepard.

Harrison, Barbara. (1999). *Theo.* Boston: Clarion.

Harrison, David. (1992). *Somebody Catch My Homework.* Illus. Betsy Lewin. Honesdale, PA: Boyds Mills.

Harrison, David. (1994). *The Boy Who Counted Stars.* Honesdale, PA: Boyds Mills.

Harrison, David. (1996). *A Thousand Cousins.* Honesdale, PA: Boyds Mills.

Harrison, Michael. (1998). *It's My Life.* New York: Holiday House.

Harshman, Marc. (1990). *Snow Company.* New York: Dutton.

Hart, Jane (Compiler). (1982). *Singing Bee: A Collection of Children's Songs.* Illus. Anita Lobel. New York: Lothrop, Lee & Shepard.

Harvey, Brett. (1986). *My Prairie Year: Based on the Diary of Elenore Plaisted.* Illus. Deborah Kogan Ray. New York: Holiday House.

Harvey, Brett. (1987). *Cassie's Journey: Going West in the 1860s.* Illus. Deborah Kogan Ray. New York: Holiday House.

Harvey, Brett. (1990). *My Prairie Christmas.* New York: Holiday House.

Harwayne, Shelley. (1992). *Lasting Impressions: Weaving Literature Into the Writing Workshop.* Portsmouth, NH: Heinemann.

Haseley, Dennis. (1994). *Getting Him.* New York: Farrar, Straus & Giroux.

Haskins, Francine. (1991). *I Remember "121".* San Francisco: Children's Book Press.

Haskins, James. (1990). *Black Dance in America: A History Through Its People.* New York: HarperCollins.

Haskins, James. (1992). *One More River to Cross: The Stories of Twelve Black Americans.* New York: Scholastic.

Haskins, James. (1992). *The Day Martin Luther King, Jr., Was Shot: A Photo History of the Civil Rights Movement.* New York: Scholastic.

Haskins, James. (1992). *Thurgood Marshall: A Life for Justice.* New York: Holt.

Haskins, James. (1994). *The Headless Haunt and Other African-American Ghost Stories.* New York: HarperCollins.

Haskins, James. (1995). *Black Eagles: African Americans in Aviation.* New York: Scholastic.

Haskins, James. (1995). *Get on Board: The Story of the Underground Railroad.* New York: Scholastic.

Haskins, James. (1998). *Black, Blue, and Gray: African Americans in the Civil War.* New York: Simon & Schuster.

Hastings, Selina (Reteller). (1993). *The Firebird.* New York: Candlewick.

Hastings, Selina. (1988). *A Selection from the Canterbury Tales.* New York: Holt.

Hastings, Selina. (1991). *Reynard the Fox.* Illus. Graham Percy. New York: Tambourine.

Haugaard, Erik Christian. (1984). *The Samurai's Tale.* Boston: Houghton.

Haugen, Tormod. (1991). *Keeping Secrets.* New York: HarperCollins.

Hausherr, Rosmarie. (1992). *What Instrument Is This?* New York: Scholastic.

Hausman, Gerald (Reteller). (1996). *Eagle Boy: A Traditional Navajo Legend.* New York: HarperCollins.

Hausman, Gerald. (1995). *How Chipmunk Got Tiny Feet: Native American Stories.* New York: HarperCollins.

Hautman, Pete. (1998). *Stone Cold.* Illus. Owen Smith. New York: Simon & Schuster.

Hautzig, Esther. (1968). *The Endless Steppe: Growing Up in Siberia.* New York: Crowell.

Havill, Juanita. (1995). *Jamacia's Blue Marker.* Illus. Anne Sibley O'Brian. Boston: Houghton.

Havill, Juanita. (1999). *Jamacia and the Substitute Teacher.* Boston: Houghton.

Hawkins, Colin, & Hawkins, Jacqui. (1992). *Hey Diddle Diddle.* New York: Candlewick.

Hawthorne, Nathaniel. (1992). *King Midas and the Golden Touch.* New York: Simon & Schuster.

Hayashi, Akiko. (1991). *Aki and the Fox.* New York: Doubleday.

Hayes, Ann. (1991). *Meet the Orchestra.* Illus. Karmen Thompson. San Diego: Harcourt.

Hayes, Joe. (2000). *Little Gold Star/Estrellita de Oro: A Cinderella Cuento.* Illus. Gloria Osuna Perez and Lucia Angela Perez. El Paso: Cinco Puntos Press.

Hayes, Sarah. (1989). *This Is the Bear.* Illus. Helen Craig. Boston: Little, Brown.

Hayes, Sarah. (1995). *This Is the Bear and the Bad Little Girl.* Cambridge: Candlewick.

Heard, Georgia. (1989). *For the Good of the Earth and the Sun: Teaching Poetry.* Portsmouth, NH: Heinemann.

Heard, Georgia. (1992). *Creatures of Earth, Sea, and Sky.* Illus. Jennifer Owings Dewey. Honesdale, PA: Boyds Mills.

Heard, Georgia. (1995). *Writing Toward Home: Tales and Lessons to Find Your Way.* Portsmouth, NH: Heinemann.

Hearne, Betsy. (1996). *Eliza's Dog.* New York: McElderry.

Heide, Florence Parry, & Gilliland, Judith Heide. (1990). *The Day of Ahmed's Secret.* Illus. Ted Lewin. New York: Lothrop, Lee & Shepard.

Heide, Florence Parry, & Gilliland, Judith Heide. (1992). *Sami and the Time of the Troubles.* New York: Clarion.

Heines, Ethel (Reteller). (1995). *The Cat and the Cook and Other Fables of Krylov.* New York: Greenwillow.

Heinlein, Robert A. (1957). *Door Into Summer.* New York: Dutton.

Heinlein, Robert A. (1987). *Citizen of the Galaxy.* New York: Macmillan.

Heinlein, Robert A. (1988). *Tunnel in the Sky.* New York: Macmillan.

Heller, Ruth. (1989). *Cache of Jewels and Other Collective Nouns.* New York: Putnam.

Heller, Ruth. (1989). *Many Luscious Lollipops: A Book About Adjectives.* New York: Putnam.

Heller, Ruth. (1991). *Up, Up and Away: A Book About Adverbs.* New York: Grosset.

Heller, Ruth. (1996). *Fine Lines.* Katonah, NY: Richard C. Owen.

Hendershot, Judith. (1987). *In Coal Country.* Illus. Thomas B. Allen. New York: Knopf.

Hendershot, Judith. (1993). *Up the Tracks to Grandma's.* New York: Knopf.

Henderson, Kathy. (1999). *The Storm.* Cambridge: Candlewick.

Henkes, Kevin. (1987). *Sheila Rae, the Brave.* New York: Greenwillow.

Henkes, Kevin. (1990). *Julius, the Baby of the World.* New York: Greenwillow.

Henkes, Kevin. (1991). *Chrysanthemum.* New York: Greenwillow.

Henkes, Kevin. (1995). *Protecting Marie.* New York: Greenwillow.

Henkes, Kevin. (1996). *Lilly's Purple Plastic Purse.* New York: Greenwillow.

Henkes, Kevin. (1999). *The Birthday Room.* New York: Greenwillow.

Henkes, Kevin. (2000). *Wemberly Worried.* New York: Greenwillow.

Hennessy, B. G. (1990). *Jake Baked the Cake.* Illus. Mary Morgan. New York: Viking.

Hennessy, B. G. (1993). *The First Night.* New York: Viking.

Henry, Marguerite. (1947). *Misty of Chincoteague.* Illus. Wesley Dennis. New York: Macmillan.

Henty, George. (1903). *With Kitchener in the Soudan: A Story of Atbara and Omdurman.* London: Blackie.

Heo, Yumi. (1994). *One Afternoon.* Danbury, CT: Orchard.

Heo, Yumi. (1995). *Father's Rubber Shoes.* New York: Scholastic.

Herbert, Janis. (1999). *The Civil War for Kids.* Chicago: Chicago Review Press.

Herman, John. (1998). *Deep Waters.* New York: Penguin.

Hermes, Patricia. (1995). *On Winter's Wind: A Novel.* Boston: Little, Brown.

Hermes, Patricia. (1998). *Cheat the Moon: A Novel.* Boston: Little, Brown.

Hernandez, Irene Beltran. (1995). *The Secret of Two Brothers.* Houston: Arte Publico.

Herrara, Juan Felipé. (1996). *Calling the Doves: El Canto de las Palomas.* Illus. Elly Simmons. San Francisco: Children's Book Press.

Herrara, Juan Felipé. (2000). *The Upside Down Boy/El Nino de Cabeza.* Illus. Elizabeth Gomez. San Francisco: Children's Book Press.

Herron, Carolivia. (1997). *Nappy Hair.* Illus. Joe Cepeda. New York: Knopf.

Herson, Kathleen. (1989). *The Half Child.* New York: Simon & Schuster.

Heslewood, Juliet. (1993). *Introducing Picasso.* Boston: Little, Brown.

Hesse, Karen. (1994). *Sable.* New York: Holt.

Hesse, Karen. (1997). *Out of the Dust.* New York: Scholastic.

Hesse, Karen. (1999). *A Light in the Storm: The Civil War Diary of Amelia Martin (Dear Ann).* New York: Scholastic.

Hesse, Karen. (2000). *Stowaway.* Illus. Robert Andrew Parker. New York: Simon & Schuster.

Hest, Amy. (1991). *Love You, Soldier.* New York: Macmillan.

Hest, Amy. (1995). *In the Rain with Baby Duck.* New York: Candlewick.

Hest, Amy. (1995). *The Private Notebook of Katie Roberts, Age 11.* New York: Candlewick.

Hest, Amy. (1998). *The Great Green Notbook of Katie Roberts Who Just Turned 12 on Monday.* Illus. Sonja Lamut. Cambridge: Candlewick.

Hewett, Joan. (1990). *Hector Lives in the United States Now.* New York: HarperCollins.

Hewett, Lorri. (1998). *Lives of Our Own.* New York: Dutton.

Hewett, Lorri. (1999). *Dancer.* New York: Dutton.

Hewitt, Kathryn. (1987). *King Midas and the Golden Touch.* San Diego: Harcourt.

Heyer, Marilee (Reteller and Illus.). (1986). *Weaving of a Dream: A Chinese Folktale.* New York: Viking.

Hicyilmaz, Gaye. (1992). *Against the Storm.* Boston: Little, Brown.

Hicyilmaz, Gaye. (1993). *The Frozen Waterfall.* New York: Farrar, Straus & Giroux.

Hicyilmaz, Gaye. (2000). *Smiling for Strangers.* New York: Farrar, Straus & Giroux.

Higginson, William J. (1992). *Wind in the Tall Grass: A Collection of Haiku.* New York: Simon & Schuster.

High, Linda Oatman. (1995). *Maizie.* New York: Holiday House.

Hildick, E. W. (1984). *Ghost Squad Breaks Through.* New York: Dutton.

Hilgartner, Beth. (1986). *A Murder for Her Majesty.* Boston: Houghton.

Hill, Anthony. (1994). *The Burnt Stick.* Boston: Houghton.

Hill, Eric. (1980). *Where's Spot?* New York: Putnam.

Hill, Eric. (1984). *Spot Goes Splash!* New York: Putnam.

Hill, Kirkpatrick. (1990). *Toughboy and Sister.* New York: McElderry.

Hill, Kirkpatrick. (2000). *The Year of Miss Agnes.* New York: Simon & Schuster.

Hillert, Margaret. (1996). *The Sky Is Not So Far Away.* Honesdale, PA: Boyds Mills.

Hindley, Judy. (1993). *A Piece of String Is a Wonderful Thing.* New York: Candlewick.

Hines, Anna Grosnickle. (1987). *It's Just Me, Emily.* New York: Clarion.

Hirschfelder, Arlene, & Singer, Beverly. (1992). *Rising Voices: Writings of Young Native Americans.* New York: Scribner's.

Hirschi, Ron. (1990). *Spring.* Illus. Thomas D. Mangelsen. New York: Cobblehill.

Hitchcock, Alfred. (1983). *Alfred Hitchcock's Supernatural Tales of Terror and Suspense.* New York: Random House.

Ho, Minfong. (1990). *Rice without Rain.* New York: Lothrop, Lee & Shepard.

Ho, Minfong. (1991). *The Clay Marble.* New York: Farrar, Straus & Giroux.

Ho, Minfong, & Ros, Saphan. (1995). *The Two Brothers.* Illus. Jean Tseng and Mon-Sian Tseng. New York: Lothrop, Lee & Shepard.

Ho, Minfong, & Ros, Saphan. (1997). *Brother Rabbit: A Cambodian Tale.* Illus. Jennifer Hewitson. New York: Lothrop, Lee & Shepard.

Hoban, Russell. (1964; 1986). *Bread and Jam for Frances.* Illus. Lillian Hoban. New York: HarperCollins.

Hoban, Tana. (1972). *Count and See.* New York: Simon & Schuster.

Hoban, Tana. (1985). *Is It Larger? Is It Smaller?* New York: Greenwillow.

Hoban, Tana. (1985). *What Is It?* New York: Greenwillow.

Hoban, Tana. (1987). *Dots, Spots, Speckles, and Stripes.* New York: Greenwillow.

Hoban, Tana. (1987). *Twenty-Six Letters and Ninety-Nine Cents.* New York: Greenwillow.

Hoban, Tana. (1989). *Of Colors and Things.* New York: Greenwillow.

Hoban, Tana. (1990). *Exactly the Opposite.* New York: Greenwillow.

Hoban, Tana. (1995). *Colors Everywhere.* New York: Greenwillow.

Hoban, Tana. (1996). *Just Look.* New York: Greenwillow.

Hobbs, Valerie. (2000). *Charlie's Run.* New York: Farrar, Straus & Giroux.

Hobbs, Will. (1989). *Bearstone.* New York: Simon & Schuster.

Hobbs, Will. (1993). *Beardance.* New York: Simon & Schuster.

Hobbs, Will. (1997). *Beardream.* Illus. Jill Kastner. New York: Atheneum.

Hobbs, Will. (1997). *Far North.* New York: Camelot.

Hobbs, Will. (1998). *The Maze.* New York: Camelot.

Hobbs, Will. (1999). *Jason's Gold.* New York: Morrow/Avon.

Hoberman, Mary Ann. (1976). *Bugs: Poems.* New York: Viking.

Hoberman, Mary Ann. (1978; 1982). *A House Is a House for Me.* Illus. Betty Fraser. New York: Viking.

Hoberman, Mary Ann. (1991). *Fathers, Mothers, Sisters, Brothers.* Illus. Marylin Hafner. Boston: Little, Brown.

Hoberman, Mary Ann. (1995). *The Cozy Book.* New York: Viking.

Hoberman, Mary Ann (Adapter). (2000). *The Eensy-Weensy Spider.* Illus. Nadine Bernard Westcott. Boston: Little Brown.

Hodges, Margaret, & Evernden, Margery. (1993). *Of Swords and Sorcerers: The Adventures of King Arthur and His Knights.* New York: Scribner's.

Hodges, Margaret. (1980). *The Little Humpbacked Horse: A Russian Tale Retold.* Illus. Chris Conover. New York: Farrar, Straus & Giroux.

Hodges, Margaret. (1989). *Arrow and the Lamp.* Boston: Little, Brown.

Hodges, Margaret. (1990). *Saint George and the Dragon.* Illus. Trina Schart Hyman. Boston: Little, Brown.

Hodges, Margaret. (1990). *The Kitchen Knight: A Tale of King Arthur.* Illus. Trina Schart Hyman. New York: Holiday House.

Hodges, Margaret. (1991). *Brother Francis and the Friendly Beasts.* Illus. Ted Lewin. New York: Scribner's.

Hodges, Margaret. (1991). *St. Jerome and the Lion.* Illus. Barry Moser. New York: Scholastic.

Hodgkins, Fran. (2000). *Animals Among Us: Living with Suburban Wildlife.* New York: Linnett.

Hoffman, Mary. (1991). *Amazing Grace.* Illus. Caroline Binch. New York: Dial.

Hogrogian, Nonny. (1965). *Always Room for One More.* New York: Holt.

Hogrogian, Nonny. (1971). *One Fine Day.* New York: Simon & Schuster.

Hogrogian, Nonny. (1976). *The Contest.* New York: Greenwillow.

Hogrogian, Nonny. (1986). *Noah's Ark.* New York: Knopf.

Holabird, Katharine. (1984). *Angelina and Alice.* Illus. Helen Craig. New York: Potter.

Holabird, Katharine. (1989). *Angelina's Birthday Surprise.* Illus. Helen Craig. New York: Potter.

Holder, Heide. (1981). *Aesop's Fables.* Illus. Heide Holder. New York: Viking.

Holling, Holling C. (1957). *Pagoo.* Boston: Houghton.

Hollyer, Beatrice. (1999). *Wake Up, World! A Day in the Life of Children Around the World.* New York: Holt.

Holm, Jennifer. (1999). *Our Only May Amelia.* New York: HarperCollins.

Holman, Felice. (1974). *Slake's Limbo.* New York: Scribner's.

Holt, Kimberly Willis. (1998). *Mister and Me.* Illus. Leonard Jenkins. New York: Putnam.

Holt, Kimberly Willis. (1998). *My Louisana Sky.* New York: Holt.

Holt, Kimberly Willis. (1999). *When Zachary Beaver Came to Town.* New York: Holt.

Honey, Elizabeth. (2000). *Don't Pat the Wombat!* Illus. William Clarke. New York: Knopf.

Hoobler, Dorothy, & Hoobler, Thomas. (1994). *The Mexican American Family Album.* New York: Oxford University.

Hooks, William H. (1987). *Moss Gown.* Illus. Donald Carrick. New York: Clarion.

Hooks, William H. (1995). *Freedom's Fruit.* Illus. James Ransome. New York: Knopf.

Hooks, William H. (Reteller). (1989). *The Three Little Pigs and the Fox.* Illus. S. D. Schindler. New York: Macmillan.

Hoover, H. M. (1984). *The Shepherd Moon.* New York: Viking.

Hoover, H. M. (1987). *Orvis.* New York: Viking.

Hoover, H. M. (1990). *Away Is a Strange Place to Be.* New York: Dutton.

Hoover, H. M. (1992). *Only Child.* New York: Dutton.

Hoover, H. M. (1995). *Winds of Mars.* New York: Dutton.

Hopkins, Lee Bennett (Ed.). (2000). *My America: A Poetry Atlas of the United States.* Illus. Stephen Alcorn. New York: Simon & Schuster.

Hopkins, Lee Bennett (Selector). (1988; o.p.). *Voyages: Poems by Walt Whitman.* San Diego: Harcourt.

Hopkins, Lee Bennett (Selector). (1989). *Still as a Star: A Book of Nighttime Poems.* Illus. Karen Milone. Boston: Little, Brown.

Hopkins, Lee Bennett. (1986). *Surprises.* Illus. Megan Lloyd. New York: HarperCollins.

Hopkins, Lee Bennett. (1988). *Side by Side: Poems to Read Together.* New York: Simon & Schuster.

Hopkins, Lee Bennett. (1990). *Good Books, Good Times.* Illus. Harvey Stevenson. New York: HarperCollins.

Hopkins, Lee Bennett. (1993). *Ragged Shadows: Poems of Halloween Night.* Boston: Little, Brown.

Hopkins, Lee Bennett. (1993). *The Writing Bug.* Katonah, NY: Richard C. Owen.

Hopkins, Lee Bennett. (1994). *Hand in Hand: An American History Through Poetry.* New York: Simon & Schuster.

Hopkins, Lee Bennett. (1995). *Been to Yesterdays: Poems of a Life.* Honesdale, PA: Boyds Mills.

Hopkins, Lee Bennett. (1995). *Blast Off! Poems About Space.* New York: HarperCollins.

Hopkins, Lee Bennett. (1996). *Opening Days; Sports Poems.* San Diego: Harcourt.

Hopkinson, Deborah. (1993). *Sweet Clara and the Freedom Quilt.* Illus. James Ransome. New York: Knopf.

Hopkinson, Deborah. (1999). *A Band of Angels: A Story Inspired by the Jubilee Singers.* New York: Atheneum.

Horenstein, Henry. (1994). *My Mom's a Vet.* Cambridge: Candlewick.

Hort, Lenny. (1991). *How Many Stars in the Sky?* New York: Morrow/Avon.

Hort, Lenny. (2000). *The Seals on the Bus.* Illus. G. Brian Karas. New York: Holt.

Horvath, Polly. (1999). *The Trolls.* New York: Farrar, Straus & Giroux.

Hotze, Sollace. (1991). *Summer Endings.* New York: Clarion.

Houston, Gloria. (1988). *The Year of the Perfect Christmas Tree.* Illus. Barbara Cooney. New York: Dial.

Houston, Gloria. (1990). *Littlejim.* Illus. Thomas B. Allen. New York: Philomel.

Houston, Gloria. (1992). *But No Candy.* New York: Philomel.

Houston, Gloria. (1992). *My Great-Aunt Arizona.* New York: HarperCollins.

Houston, Gloria. (1998). *Bright Freedom's Song: A Story of the Underground Railroad.* San Diego: Harcourt.

Howard, Elizabeth F. (1989). *Chita's Christmas Tree.* New York: Simon & Schuster.

Howard, Elizabeth F. (1991). *Aunt Flossie's Hats (And Crab Cakes Later).* Illus. James Ransome. New York: Clarion.

Howard, Elizabeth F. (1995). *Papa Tells Chita a Story.* New York: Simon & Schuster.

Howard, Elizabeth Fitzgerald. (1996). *What's in Aunt Mary's Room.* Illus. Cedric Lucas. New York: Clarion.

Howard, Ellen. (1987). *Edith Herself.* New York: Atheneum.

Howard, Ellen. (1990). *Sister.* New York: Atheneum.

Howard, Ellen. (1991). *The Chickenhouse House.* New York: Atheneum.

Howarth, Lesley. (1995). *Weather Eye.* New York: Candlewick.

Howe, James. (1983). *The Celery Stalks at Midnight.* New York: Simon & Schuster.

Howe, James, & Howe, Deborah. (1979). *Bunnicula: A Rabbit Tale Mystery.* New York: Simon & Schuster.

Howe, James. (1985). *What Eric Knew.* New York: Atheneum.

Howe, James. (1994). *Playing with Words.* Katonah, NY: Richard C. Owen.

Howe, John. (1989). *Jack and the Beanstalk.* Boston: Little, Brown.

Howker, Janni. (1995). *The Topiary Garden.* New York: Scholastic.

Howlett, Bud. (1993). *I'm New Here.* Boston: Houghton.

Hoyt-Goldsmith, Diane, & Migdale, Lawrence. (1991). *Pueblo Storyteller.* New York: Holiday House.

Hoyt-Goldsmith, Diane. (1992). *Arctic Hunter.* New York: Holiday House.

Hoyt-Goldsmith, Diane. (1992). *Hoang Anh: A Vietnamese-American Boy.* Photog. Lawrence Migdale. New York: Holiday House.

Hoyt-Goldsmith, Diane. (1993). *Cherokee Summer.* New York: Holiday House.

Hoyt-Goldsmith, Diane. (1994). *Day of the Dead: A Mexican-American Celebration.* New York: Holiday House.

Hoyt-Goldsmith, Diane. (1995). *Apache Rodeo.* New York: Holiday House.

Huck, Charlotte. (1989). *Princess Furball.* Illus. Anita Lobel. New York: Greenwillow.

Huck, Charlotte. (1993). *Secret Places.* Illus. Lindsay George. New York: Greenwillow.

Huck, Charlotte. (1996). *Toads and Diamonds.* Illus. Anita Lobel. New York: Greenwillow.

Hudson, Cheryl Willis. (1992). *Goodnight Baby.* New York: Scholastic.

Hudson, Cheryl Willis. (1995). *Hold Christmas in Your Heart: African-American Songs, Poems, and Stories for the Holidays.* Illus. Anna Rich, Cal Massey, Eric Battle, James Ransome, Ron Garnett, Sylvia Walker, and Higgins Bond. New York: Cartwheel.

Hudson, Jan. (1989). *Sweetgrass.* New York: Philomel.

Hudson, Jan. (1990). *Dawn Rider.* New York: Philomel.

Hudson, Wade. (1991). *Jamal's Busy Day.* Orange, NJ: Just Us Books.

Hudson, Wade, & Hudson, Cheryl. (1995). *How Sweet the Sound: African-American Songs for Children.* New York: Scholastic.

Hudson, Wade, & Hudson, Cheryl. (1999). *How Sweet the Sound: African-American Ghost Stories.* Illus. Floyd Cooper. New York: Scholastic.

Hughes, Langston. (1962). *Dreamkeeper and Other Poems.* New York: Knopf.

Hughes, Langston. (1994). *Black Misery.* New York: Oxford University.

Hughes, Langston. (1995). *The Block.* New York: Viking.

Hughes, Monica. (1990). *Invitation to the Game.* New York: Simon & Schuster.

Hughes, Monica. (1995). *The Golden Aquarians.* New York: Simon & Schuster.

Hughes, Shirley. (1990). *The Snow Lady.* New York: Lothrop, Lee & Shepard.

Hughes, Shirley. (1991). *Wheels.* New York: Lothrop, Lee & Shepard.

Hughes, Shirley. (1995). *Rhymes for Annie Rose.* New York: Lothrop, Lee & Shepard.

Hughes, Shirley. (1998). *Alfie and the Birthday Surprise.* New York: Lothrop, Lee & Shepard.

Hull, Mary. (1994). *Rosa Parks.* New York: Chelsea.

Hulme, Joy. (1991). *Sea Squares.* Illus. Carol Schwartz. New York: Hyperion.

Hunt, Irene. (1964). *Across Five Aprils.* Chicago: Follett.

Hunt, Jonathan. (1989). *Illuminations.* New York: Bradbury.

Hunter, C. W. (1992). *The Green Gourd: A North Carolina Folktale.* New York: Putnam.

Hunter, Mollie. (1998). *The Mermaid Summer.* New York: HarperCollins.

Hunter, Mollie. (2000). *The King's Swift Rider: A Novel of Robert the Bruce.* New York: HarperCollins.

Hurd, Edith Thacker. (2000). *Starfish (Let's Read-And-Find Out Science* Series). Illus. Robin Brickman. New York: HarperCollins.

Hurd, Thatcher. (1992). *The Quiet Evening.* New York: Greenwillow.

Hurmence, Belinda. (1984). *Tancy.* New York: Clarion.

Hurmence, Belinda. (1997). *Slavery Times When I Was Chillun.* New York: Penguin.

Hurwitz, Johanna. (1981). *Aldo Ice Cream.* New York: Morrow/Avon.

Hurwitz, Johanna. (1983). *Rip-Roaring Russell.* New York: Morrow/Avon.

Hurwitz, Johanna. (1985). *Russell Rides Again.* New York: Morrow/Avon.

Hurwitz, Johanna. (1987). *The Adventures of Ali Baba Bernstein.* Illus. Gail Owens. New York: Scholastic.

Hurwitz, Johanna. (1987). *Russell Sprouts.* Illus. Lillian Hoban. New York: Morrow/Avon.

Hurwitz, Johanna. (1990). *Aldo Peanut Butter.* New York: Morrow/Avon.

Hurwitz, Johanna. (1992). *School's Out.* New York: Morrow/Avon.

Hurwitz, Johanna. (1994). *School Spirit.* New York: Morrow/Avon.

Hurwitz, Johanna. (1995). *Roz and Ozzie.* New York: Morrow/Avon.

Hurwitz, Johanna. (1998). *A Dream Come True.* New York: Owen.

Hurwitz, Johanna. (1998). *Faraway Summer.* Illus. Mary Azarian. New York: Morrow/Avon.

Hurwitz, Johanna. (1998). *Starting School (Class Clown).* Illus. Karen Dugan. New York: Morrow/Avon.

Hurwitz, Johanna. (2000). *One Small Dog.* Illus. Diane Degroat. New York: Morrow/Avon.

Hutchins, Pat. (1942; 1996). *Titch and Daisy.* New York: Greenwillow.

Hutchins, Pat. (1970). *Clocks and More Clocks.* New York: Macmillan.

Hutchins, Pat. (1971). *Changes, Changes.* New York: Macmillan.

Hutchins, Pat. (1978). *Happy Birthday, Sam.* New York: Greenwillow.

Hutchins, Pat. (1982). *1 Hunter.* New York: Greenwillow.

Hutchins, Pat. (1985). *Very Worst Monster.* New York: Greenwillow.

Hutchins, Pat. (1988). *Where's the Baby?* New York: Greenwillow.

Hutchins, Pat. (1990). *What Game Shall We Play?* New York: Greenwillow.

Huth, Holly Young. (2000). *The Son of the Sun and the Daughter of the Moon: A Saami Folktale.* Illus. Anna Vojtech. New York: Athenuem.

Hutton, Warwick (Adapter). (1987). *Adam and Eve: The Bible Story.* New York: McElderry.

Hutton, Warwick. (1990). *Theseus and the Minotaur.* New York: Macmillan.

Hutton, Warwick. (1992). *The Trojan Horse: Retold.* New York: Simon & Schuster.

Hutton, Warwick. (1994). *Persephone.* New York: Macmillan.

Hutton, Warwick. (1995). *Odysseus and the Cyclops.* New York: McElderry.

Huynh, Quang Nhuong. (1986). *The Land I Lost: Adventures of a Boy in Vietnam.* New York: HarperCollins.

Hyatt, Patricia Rusch. (1995). *Coast to Coast with Alice.* Minneapolis, MN: Carolrhoda.

Hyman, Trina Schart. (1983). *Little Red Riding Hood.* New York: Holiday House.

Hyman, Trina Schart. (1984). *Saint George and the Dragon.* Boston: Little, Brown.

Hyppolite, Joanne. (1995). *Seth and Samona.* New York: Dell.

Ibbotson, Eva. (2000). *Island of the Aunts.* Illus. Kevin Hawkes. New York: Dutton.

Ikeda, Daisaku. (1991). *The Cherry Tree.* New York: Knopf.

Ingold, Jeanette. (1999). *Airfield.* San Diego: Harcourt.

Ingold, Jeanette. (2000). *Pictures 1918.* New York: Puffin.

Innocenti, Robert, & Gallaz, Christophe. (1986). *Rose Blanche.* Trans. Richard Graglia and Martha Coventry. Mankato, MN: Creative Education

Irwin, Hadley. (1994). *Jim-Dandy.* New York: McElderry.

Isaacs, Anne. (1994). *Swamp Angel.* New York: Dutton.

Isaacs, Ann. (2000). *Torn Thread.* New York: Scholastic.

Isaacson, Philip M. (1993). *A Short Walk Around the Pyramids and Through the World of Art.* New York: Knopf.

Isadora, Rachel. (1989). *The Princess and the Frog.* New York: Greenwillow.

Isadora, Rachel. (1990). *Babies.* New York: Greenwillow.

Isadora, Rachel. (1991). *At the Crossroads.* New York: Greenwillow.

Isadora, Rachel. (1992). *Over the Green Hills.* New York: Greenwillow.

Isadora, Rachel. (2000). *ABC Pop!* New York: Viking.

Ishii, Momoko (Reteller). (1987). *The Tongue-Cut Sparrow.* Trans. Katherine Paterson. Illus. Suekichi Akaba. New York: Lodestar.

Ish-Kishor, Sulamith. (1969). *Our Eddie.* New York: Knopf.

Issa. (1969; o.p.). *Don't Tell the Scarecrow.* New York: Simon & Schuster.

Jackson, Donna M. (1996). *The Bone Detectives: How Forensic Anthropologists Solve Crimes and Uncover Mysteries of the Dead.* Boston: Little, Brown.

Jackson, Donna. (2000). *The Wildlife Detectives: How Forensic Scientists Fight Crimes Against Nature.* Boston: Houghton.

Jacobs, Francine. (1992). *The Tainos: The People Who Welcomed Columbus.* New York: Putnam.

Jacobs, Joseph (Reteller). (1923). *English Fairy Tales.* New York: Putnam.

Jacobs, Joseph (Reteller). (1989). *Tattercoats.* Illus. Margot Tomes. New York: Putnam.

Jacobs, William J. (1990). *Ellis Island: New Hope in a New Land.* New York: Scribner's.

Jacobs, William J. (1991). *Washington.* New York: Scribner's.

Jacobs, William J. (1996). *World Religions: Great Lives.* New York: Atheneum.

Jacques, Brian. (1986). *Redwall.* New York: Philomel.

Jacques, Brian. (1988). *Mossflower.* New York: Putnam.

Jacques, Brian. (1990). *Mattimeo.* New York: Putnam.

Jacques, Brian. (1991). *Mariel of Redwall.* New York: Putnam.

Jacques, Brian. (1994). *Martin the Warrior.* New York: Philomel.

Jacques, Brian. (1995). *The Bellmaker.* New York: Philomel.

Jaffe, Nina. (1996). *The Golden Flower: A Taino Myth from Puerto Rico.* New York: Simon & Schuster.

Jaffe, Nina. (1997). *A Voice of the People: The Life and Work of Harold Courtlander.* New York: Holt.

Jaffrey, Madhur (Adapter). (1985). *Seasons of Splendour: Tales, Myths, and Legends of India.* Illus. Michael Foreman. New York: Atheneum.

Jakes, John. (1986). *Susanna of the Alamo: A True Story.* San Diego: Harcourt.

Jakoubek, Robert. (1994). *James Farmer and the Freedom Rides.* Brookfield, CT: Millbrook.

Jakoubek, Robert. (1994). *Walter White and the Power of Organized Protest.* Brookfield, CT: Millbrook.

James, Elizabeth, & Barkin, Carol. (1991). *How to Write a Great School Report.* New York: Morrow/Avon.

James, Elizabeth, & Barkin, Carol. (1991). *How to Write Your Best Book Report.* New York: Morrow/Avon.

James, Mary. (1990). *Shoebag.* New York: Scholastic.

Janeczko, Paul, & Nye, Naomi Shihab (Eds.). (1996). *I Feel a Little Jumpy Around You: A Book of Her Poems and His Poems Collected in Pairs.* New York: Simon & Schuster.

Janeczko, Paul B. (1990). *The Place My Words Are Looking For: What Poets Say About and Through Their Work.* New York: Bradbury.

Janeczko, Paul B. (1993). *Looking for Your Name: A Collection of Contemporary Poems.* New York: Scholastic.

Janeczko, Paul. (1983). *Poetspeak: in Their Work, About Their Work.* New York: Atheneum.

Janeczko, Paul. (1985). *Pocket Poems.* New York: Simon & Schuster.

Janeczko, Paul. (1988). *The Music of What Happens: Poems That Tell Stories.* New York: Scholastic.

Janeczko, Paul. (1989). *Brickyard Summer.* Illus. Ken Rush. New York: Scholastic.

Janeczko, Paul B. (Selector). (1991). *Preposterous: Poems of Youth.* New York: Scholastic.

Janeczko, Paul B. (1993). *Stardust Otel.* New York: Scholastic.

Janeczko, Paul B. (1995). *Poetry from A to Z: A Guide for Young Writers.* New York: Bradbury.

Janeczko, Paul B. (1995). *Wherever Home Begins: 100 Contemporary Poems.* New York: Scholastic.

Janeczko, Paul. (1998). *That Sweet Diamond: Baseball Poems.* Illus. Carole Katchen. New York: Atheneum.

Janeway, James. (1672; 1976 Reprint). *A Token for Children: Being an Exact Account of the Conversation, Holy and Exemplary Lives, and Joyful Deaths of Several Young Children.* New York: Garland.

Jansson, Tove. (1995). *Tales from Moominvalley.* New York: Farrar, Straus & Giroux.

Jansson, Tove. (1996). *Finn Family Moomintroll.* New York: Farrar, Straus & Giroux.

Jaquith, Priscilla. (1995). *Bo Rabbit Smart for True: Tall Tales from the Gullah.* New York: Philomel.

Jarrell, Randall. (1995). *Animal Family.* New York: HarperCollins.

Jaskol, Julie, & Lewis, Brian. (1999). *City of Angels: In and Around Los Angeles.* Illus. Elisa Kleven. New York: Dutton.

Jeffers, Susan. (1991). *Brother Eagle, Sister Sky: A Message from Chief Seattle.* New York: Dial.

Jenkins, Steve. (1995). *Biggest, Strongest, Fastest.* Boston: Houghton.

Jenkins, Steve. (1995). *Looking Down.* Boston: Houghton.

Jenkins, Steve. (1999). *The Top of the World: Climbing Mt. Everest.* Boston: Houghton.

Jenness, Aylette. (1990). *Families: A Celebration of Diversity, Commitment, and Love.* Boston: Houghton.

Jenness, Aylette. (1993). *Come Home with Me: A Multicultural Treasure Hunt.* New York: North-South.

Jenning, Patrick. (1999). *Putnam and Pennyroyal.* New York: Scholastic.

Jennings, Richard W. (2000). *Orwell's Luck.* New York: Walter Lorraine.

Jessel, Camilla. (1991). *The Kitten Book.* Cambridge: Candlewick.

Jessel, Camilla. (1994). *The Puppy Book.* Cambridge: Candlewick.

Jiménez, Francisco. (1998). *La Mariposa.* Illus. Simon Silva. Boston: Houghton.

Jiménez, Francisco. (1999). *The Circuit: Stories from the Life of a Migrant Child.* New York: Houghton

Jiménez, Juan Ramon. (1994). *Platero y Yo/Platero and I.* New York: Clarion.

Jocelyn, Marthe. (2000). *Earthly Astonishments.* New York: Dutton.

Johnson, Angela. (1989). *Tell Me a Story, Mama.* Illus. David Soman. Danbury, CT: Orchard.

Johnson, Angela. (1990). *Do Like Kyla.* New York: Scholastic.

Johnson, Angela. (1990). *When I Am Old with You.* Illus. David Soman. New York: Scholastic.

Johnson, Angela. (1991). *One of Three.* Illus. David Soman. New York: Scholastic.

Johnson, Angela. (1992). *The Leaving Morning.* New York: Scholastic.

Johnson, Angela. (1993). *Toning the Sweep.* New York: Scholastic.

Johnson, Angela. (1995). *Humming Whispers.* New York: Scholastic.

Johnson, Angela. (1998). *Gone from Home.* New York: DK Publishing.

Johnson, Angela. (1998). *Heaven.* New York: Simon & Schuster.

Johnson, Angela. (1998). *Songs of Faith.* Danbury, CT: Orchard.

Johnson, Angela. (2000). *Gone from Home: Short Takes.* New York: Knopf.

Johnson, Angela. (2000). *The Other Side: Shorter Poems.* Illus. Paul Werstine. Danbury, CT: Orchard.

Johnson, D. B. (2000). *Henry Hikes to Fitchburg.* Boston: Houghton.

Johnson, Dinah. (2000). *All Around the Town: The Photographs of Richard Samuel Robert.* New York: Holt.

Johnson, Dinah. (2000). *Queenie Blue.* Illus. James Ransome. New York: Holt.

Johnson, Dolores. (1992). *The Best Bug to Be.* New York: Simon & Schuster.

Johnson, Dolores. (1993). *Now Let Me Fly: The Story of a Slave's Family.* New York: Simon & Schuster.

Johnson, Dolores. (1994). *Papa's Stories.* New York: Simon & Schuster.

Johnson, Dolores. (1994). *Seminole Diary: Remembrances of a Slave.* New York: Atheneum.

Johnson, James Weldon. (1993). *The Creation.* Boston: Little, Brown.

Johnson, James Weldon. (1995). *Lift Every Voice and Sing.* Illus. Jan Spivey Gilchrist. New York: Scholastic.

Johnson, Paul Brett. (1999). *Old Dry Frye: A Deliciously Funny Tall Tale.* New York: Scholastic.

Johnson, Stephen T. (1995). *Alphabet City.* New York: Viking.

Johnson, Sylvia. (1994). *A Beekeeper's Year.* Boston: Little, Brown.

Johnson, Sylvia. (1995). *Raptor Rescue! An Eagle Flies Free.* New York: Dutton.

Johnston, Julie. (1993). *Hero of Lesser Causes.* Boston: Little, Brown.

Johnston, Julie. (1994). *The Only Outcast.* Montreal: Tundra.

Johnston, Tony (Adapter). (1990). *The Badger and the Magic Fan.* Illus. Tomie DePaola. New York: Putnam.

Johnston, Tony. (1985). *The Quilt Story.* Illus. Tomie DePaola. New York: Putnam.

Johnston, Tony. (1988). *Yonder.* Illus. Lloyd Bloom. New York: Dial.

Johnston, Tony. (1995). *Alice Nizzy Nazzy: The Witch of Santa Fe.* Illus. Tomie DePaola. New York: Putnam.

Johnston, Tony. (1996). *My Mexico/Mexico Mio.* New York: Putnam.

Johnston, Tony. (1996). *The Wagon.* New York: Morrow/Avon.

Jonas, Ann. (1989). *Color Dance.* New York: Greenwillow.

Jonas, Ann. (1990). *Aardvarks, Disembark!* New York: Greenwillow.

Jones, Charlotte Foltz. (1998). *Yukon Gold: The Story of the Klondike Gold Rush.* New York: Holiday House.

Jones, Hettie (Ed.). (1971). *The Trees Stand Shining: Poetry of the North American Indians.* Illus. Robert Andrew Parker. New York: Dial.

Jones, Hettie. (1995). *Big Star Fallin' Mama: Five Women in Black Music.* New York: Viking.

Jones, Patricia Spears. (1995). *The Weather That Kills: Poems.* New York: Coffeehouse.

Jones, Rebecca C. (1995). *Matthew and Tilly.* Illus. Beth Peck. New York: Puffin.

Joosse, Barbara. (1991). *Mama, Do You Love Me?* Illus. Barbara Lavallee. San Francisco: Chronicle.

Joosse, Barbara. (1995). *The Morning Chair.* New York: Clarion.

Joosse, Barbara. (1998). *Ghost Trap: A Wild Willie Mystery.* Illus. Sue Truesdall. Boston: Clarion.

Joseph, Lynn. (1990). *A Coconut Kind of Day.* New York: Lothrop, Lee & Shepard.

Joseph, Lynn. (1992). *An Island Christmas.* New York: Clarion.

Joyce, William. (1992). *Bentley and Egg.* New York: HarperCollins.

Joyce, William. (1997). *The World of William Joyce Scrapbook.* New York: HarperCollins.

Jukes, Mavis. (1996). *It's a Girl Thing: How to Stay Healthy, Safe, and in Charge.* New York: Knopf.

Jukes, Mavis. (1999). *Planning the Impossible.* New York: Delacorte.

Juster, Norton. (1961). *The Phantom Tollbooth.* New York: Knopf.

Juster, Norton. (1982). *Otter Nonsense.* New York: Morrow/Avon.

Kajikawa, Kimiko. (2000). *Yoshi's Feast.* Illus. Yumi Heo. New York: DK Publishing.

Kalman, Maira. (1992). *Max in Hollywood, Baby.* New York: Viking.

Kamen, Gloria. (1996). *Hidden Music: The Life of Fanny Mendelsohn.* New York: Atheneum.

Kandoian, Ellen. (1989). *Is Anybody Up?* New York: Putnam.

Karas, G. Brian. (2000). *Bebe's Bad Dream.* New York: Greenwillow.

Karr, Kathleen. (1990). *It Ain't Always Easy.* New York: Farrar, Straus & Giroux.

Karr, Kathleen. (1992). *Oh, Those Harper Girls!* New York: Farrar, Straus & Giroux.

Karr, Kathleen. (1998). *The Great Turkey Walk.* New York: Farrar, Straus & Giroux.

Karr, Kathleen. (1999). *Man of the Family.* New York: Farrar, Straus & Giroux.

Karr, Kathleen. (2000). *The Boxer.* New York: Farrar, Straus & Giroux.

Karr, Kathleen. (2000). *Skullduggery.* Illus. Troy Howell. New York: Hyperion.

Katz, Michael Jay. (1990). *Ten Potatoes in a Pot: And Other Counting Rhymes.* Illus. June Otani. New York: HarperCollins.

Katz, Susan. (1998). *Snowdrops for Cousin Ruth.* New York: Simon & Schuster.

Katz, William Loren. (1999). *Black Pioneers: An Untold Story.* New York: Atheneum.

Kay, Verla. (1999). *Gold Fever.* Illus. S. D. Schindler. New York: Putnam.

Kay, Verla. (1999). *Iron Horses.* Illus. Michael McCurdy. New York: Putnam.

Keats, Ezra Jack. (1962). *The Snowy Day.* New York: Viking.

Keats, Ezra Jack. (1964). *Whistle for Willie.* New York: Viking.

Keats, Ezra Jack. (1967). *Peter's Chair.* New York: HarperCollins.

Keats, Ezra Jack. (1973). *Pssst! Doggie.* New York: Watts.

Keegan, Marcia. (1991). *Pueblo Boy: Growing Up in Two Worlds.* New York: Dutton.

Kehoe, Michael. (1982). *The Puzzle of Books.* Minneapolis, MN: Carolrhoda.

Kehoe, Michael. (1997). *A Book Takes Root: The Making of a Picture Book.* New York: First Avenue Editions.

Kehret, Peg. (1999). *Shelter Dogs: Amazing Stories of Adopted Strays.* Photog. Greg Farrar. Morton Grove, IL: Whitman.

Keith, Harold. (1957). *Rifles for Watie.* New York: HarperCollins.

Keller, Holly. (1991). *Horace.* New York: Greenwillow.

Keller, Laurie. (2000). *Open Wide: Tooth School Inside.* New York: Holt.

Kellogg, Steven. (1973). *The Island of the Skog.* New York: Dial.

Kellogg, Steven. (1976; 1996). *Yankee Doodle.* New York: Aladdin.

Kellogg, Steven. (1979). *Pinkerton, Behave.* New York: Dial.

Kellogg, Steven. (1984). *Paul Bunyan, a Tall Tale.* New York: Morrow/Avon.

Kellogg, Steven. (1986). *Pecos Bill.* New York: Morrow/Avon.

Kellogg, Steven. (1987). *Aster Aardvark's Alphabet Adventures.* New York: Morrow/Avon.

Kellogg, Steven. (1987). *Prehistoric Pinkerton.* New York: Dial.

Kellogg, Steven. (1988). *Johnny Appleseed.* New York: Morrow/Avon.

Kellogg, Steven. (1991). *Jack and the Beanstalk.* New York: Morrow/Avon.

Kellogg, Steven. (1992). *Mike Fink.* New York: Morrow/Avon.

Kelly, Eric. (1973). *The Trumpeter of Krakow.* New York: Macmillan.

Kendall, Carol. (1959). *The Gammage Cup.* New York: Harcourt.

Kendall, Carol. (2000). *The Whisper of Glocken: A Novel of the Minnipins.* Illus. Imero Gobotto. New York: Odyssey.

Kendall, Martha E. (1987). *Elizabeth Cady Stanton.* Edina, MN: Highland.

Kendall, Russ. (1992). *Eskimo Boy: Life in an Inupiaq Eskimo Village.* New York: Scholastic.

Kennedy, X. J. (1978). *One Winter Night in August and Other Nonsense Jingles.* New York: McElderry.

Kennedy, X. J. (1985). *The Forgetful Wishing Well: Poems for Young People.* New York: McElderry.

Kennedy, X. J. (1989). *Ghastlies, Goops, and Pincushions: Nonsense Verse.* Illus. Ron Barrett. New York: McElderry.

Kennedy, X. J. (1990). *Fresh Brats.* Illus. James Watts. New York: McElderry.

Kennedy, X. J. (1991). *Kite That Braved Old Orchard Beach.* New York: McElderry.

Kennedy, X. J. (1993). *Drat These Brats!* New York: McElderry.

Kennedy, X. J. (1997). *Uncle Switch: Loony Limericks.* Illus. John O'Brien. New York: Simon & Schuster.

Kennedy, X. J., & Kennedy, Dorothy. (1985). *Knock at a Star: A Child's Introduction to Poetry.* Boston: Little, Brown.

Kennedy, X. J., & Kennedy, Dorothy. (1992). *Talking Like the Rain: A First Book of Poems.* Illus. Jane Dyer. Boston: Little, Brown.

Kerby, Mona. (1990). *Amelia Earhart: Courage in the Sky.* New York: Viking.

Kerr, Judith. (1972). *When Hitler Stole Pink Rabbit.* New York: Putnam.

Kerr, M. E. (1994). *Deliver Us from Evie.* New York: HarperCollins.

Kerr, M. E. (2000). *What Became of Her.* New York: HarperCollins.

Key, Alexander. (1968). *Escape to Witch Mountain.* Philadelphia: Westminster, John Knox.

Key, Francis Scott. (1973). *The Star Spangled Banner.* Illus. Peter Spier. New York: Doubleday.

Khalsa, Dayal Kaur. (1989). *How Pizza Came to Queens.* New York: Potter.

Kherdian, David. (1992). *Feathers and Tails: Animal Fables from Around the World.* New York: Philomel.

Kherdian, David (Ed.). (1995). *Beat Voices: An Anthology of Beat Poetry.* New York: Holt.

Kidd, Diana. (1991). *Onion Tears.* New York: Scholastic.

Killien, Christi. (1992). *The Daffodils.* New York: Scholastic.

Kimmel, Elizabeth Cody. (1999). *Ice Story: Shackleton's Lost Expedition.* Boston: Clarion.

Kimmel, Eric. (1988). *Anansi and the Moss-Covered Rock.* Illus. Janet Stevens. New York: Holiday House.

Kimmel, Eric. (1993). *Anansi Goes Fishing.* Illus. Janet Stevens. New York: Holiday House.

Kimmel, Eric. (1995). *The Adventures of Hershel of Ostropol.* New York: Holiday House.

Kimmel, Eric. (1996). *Count Silvernose: A Story from Italy.* New York: Holiday House.

Kimmel, Eric. (2000). *Grizz!* Illus. Andrew Glass. New York: Holiday House.

Kimmel, Eric. (2000). *The Two Mountains: An Aztec Legend.* Illus. Leonard Everett Fisher. New York: Holiday House.

Kimmell, Elizaeth Code. (1999). *Visiting Miss Caples.* Illus. David Kah. New York: Dial.

King, Elizabeth. (1993). *Backyard Sunflower.* New York: Dutton.

King, Sandra. (1993). *Shannon: An Ojibway Dancer.* Minneapolis, MN: Lerner.

King-Smith, Dick. (1985). *Babe, the Gallant Pig.* New York: Crown.

King-Smith, Dick. (1988). *Martin's Mice.* New York: Crown.

King-Smith, Dick. (1993). *All Pigs Are Beautiful.* Cambridge: Candlewick.

King-Smith, Dick. (1994). *I Love Guinea Pigs.* Cambridge: Candlewick.

King-Smith, Dick. (1996). *The Topsy-Turvy Storybook.* London: Gollancz UK.

Kinsey-Warnock, Natalie. (1991). *The Night the Bells Rang.* New York: Dutton.

Kiode, Tan. (2000). *May We Sleep Here Tonight?* Illus. Yasuko Koide. New York: McElderry.

Kipling, Rudyard. (1894; 1964 Reissue). *The Jungle Book.* Illus. Robert Shore. New York: Macmillan.

Kipling, Rudyard. (1985). *How the Camel Got His Hump.* New York: Peter Bedrick.

Kipling, Rudyard. (1987). *How the Rhinoceros Got His Skin.* New York: Peter Bedrick.

Kipling, Rudyard. (1987). *The Just-So Stories.* Illus. Safaya Salter. New York: Holt.

Kismaric, Carole (Adapter). (1988). *The Rumor of Pavel Paali: A Ukranian Folktale.* Illus. Charles Mikolaycak. New York: HarperCollins.

Kitamura, Satoshi. (1992). *From Acorn to Zoo: And Everything in Between in Alphabetical Order.* New York: Farrar, Straus & Giroux.

Kitamura, Satoshi. (2000). *Me and My Cat?* New York: Farrar, Straus & Giroux.

Kitchen, Bert. (1987). *Animal Numbers.* New York: Dial.

Klausner, Janet. (1990). *Talk About English: How Words Travel and Change.* New York: Crowell.

Klausner, Janet. (1993). *Sequoyah's Gift: A Portrait of the Cherokee Leader.* New York: HarperCollins.

Klein, Robin. (1996). *The Sky in Silver Lace.* New York: Viking.

Knight, Margy Burns. (1992). *Talking Walls.* Illus. Anne Sibley O'Brien. Gardner, ME: Tilbury.

Knutson, Barbara. (1987). *Why the Crab Has No Head.* Minneapolis, MN: Carolrhoda.

Koch, Michelle. (1989). *Just One More.* New York: Greenwillow.

Koehn, Ilse. (1977). *Mischling, Second Degree.* New York: Greenwillow.

Kogawa, Joy. (1986). *Naomi's Road.* New York: Oxford University.

Konigsburg, Elaine. (1967). *From the Mixed-Up Files of Mrs. Basil E. Frankweiler.* New York: Macmillan, Atheneum.

Konigsburg, Elaine. (1973). *A Proud Taste for Scarlet and Miniver.* New York: Atheneum.

Konigsburg, Elaine. (1996). *The View from Saturday.* New York: Atheneum.

Koss, Amy Goldman. (1999). *The Ashwater Experiment.* New York: Dial.

Kovalski, Maryann. (1987). *The Wheels on the Bus.* Boston: Little, Brown.

Kraft, Betsy Harvey. (1995). *Mother Jones: One Woman's Fight for Labor.* New York: Clarion.

Kraus, Robert. (1994). *Fables Aesop Never Wrote.* New York: Viking.

Krauss, Ruth. (1953). *A Very Special House.* Illus. Maurice Sendak. New York: HarperCollins.

Krementz, Jill. (1986). *A Very Young Dancer.* New York: Dell.

Krementz, Jill. (1991). *A Very Young Musician.* New York: Simon & Schuster.

Krensky, Stephen. (1995). *The Printer's Apprentice.* New York: Delacorte.

Kroeber, Theodora. (1964). *Ishi, Last of His Tribe.* Berkeley: Parnassus.

Kroeger, Mary Kay, & Borden, Louise. (1996). *Paperboy.* New York: Clarion/Houghton.

Kroll, Steven. (1994). *Lewis and Clark: Explorers of the American West.* New York: Holiday House.

Kroll, Virginia. (1995). *Hats Off to Hair!* Waterton, MA: Charlesbridge.

Krudop, Walter Lyon. (2000). *The Man Who Caught Fish.* New York: Farrar, Straus & Giroux.

Krull, Kathleen. (1992). *Gonna Sing My Head Off!* Illus. Allen Garns. New York: Knopf.

Krull, Kathleen. (1994). *Lives of the Writers: Comedies, Tragedies (And What the Neighbors Thought).* San Diego: Harcourt.

Krull, Kathleen. (1994). *Maria Molina and the Days of the Dead.* New York: Simon & Schuster.

Krull, Kathleen. (1995). *Lives of the Artists: Masterpieces, Messes (And What the Neighbors Thought).* San Diego: Harcourt.

Krull, Kathleen. (1996). *Wilma Unlimited: How Wilma Rudolph Became the World's Fastest Woman.* San Diego: Harcourt.

Krull, Kathleen. (1998). *Lives of the Presidents: Fame, Shame (And What the Neighbors Thought).* San Diego: Harcourt.

Kuklin, Susan. (1994). *From Head to Toe: How a Doll Is Made.* New York: Hyperion.

Kunhardt, Dorothy. (1940). *Pat the Bunny.* Racine, WI: Western.

Kurtz, Jane. (1998). *The Storyteller's Beads.* New York: Gulliver.

Kurtz, Jane. (1999). *I'm Sorry, Almera Ann.* Illus. Susan Havice. New York: Holt.

Kurtz, Jane. (2000). *River Friendly, River Wild.* Illus. Neil Brennan. New York: Simon & Schuster.

Kuskin, Karla. (1959). *Just Like Everyone Else.* New York: HarperCollins.

Kuskin, Karla. (1975). *Near the Window Tree.* New York: HarperCollins.

Kuskin, Karla. (1980). *Dogs and Dragons, Trees and Dreams.* New York: HarperCollins.

Kuskin, Karla. (1987). *Jerusalem, Shining Still.* Illus. David Frampton. New York: HarperCollins.

Kuskin, Karla. (1990). *Roar and More.* New York: HarperCollins.

Kuskin, Karla. (1992). *Soap Soup.* New York: HarperCollins.

Kuskin, Karla. (1995). *James and the Rain.* New York: Simon & Schuster.

Kuskin, Karla. (1995). *Thoughts, Pictures, and Words.* Katonah, NY: Richard C. Owen.

Kuskin, Karla. (1997). *The Upstairs Cat.* Boston: Houghton.

Kuskin, Karla. (1998). *The Sky Is Always the Sky.* New York: HarperCollins.

Kuskin, Karla. (2000). *I Am Me.* New York: Simon & Schuster.

La Fontaine, Jean De. (1980). *The Rich Man and the Shoemaker.* Illus. Brian Wildsmith. New York: Oxford University Press.

La Fontaine, Jean De. (1987). *The Hare and the Tortoise.* Illus. Brian Wildsmith. New York: Oxford University Press.

La Fontaine, Jean De. (1987). *The Lion and the Rat.* Illus. Brian Wildsmith. New York: Oxford University Press.

La Fontaine, Jean De. (1987). *The North Wind and the Sun.* Illus. Brian Wildsmith. New York: Oxford University Press.

Lacapa, Michael. (1990). *The Flute Player: An Apache Folktale.* Flagstaff: Northland.

Lachtman, Ofelia Dumas. (1995). *Pepita Talks Twice/Pepita Habla Dos Veces.* Illus. Alex Pardo Delange. Houston: Arte Publico.

Lachtman, Ofelia Dumas. (1997). *Letici's Secret.* Illus. Robert C. Morales. Houston: Arte Publico.

Lachtman, Ofelia Dumas. (1999). *The Girl from Playa Blanca.* Houston: Arte Publico.

Lacome, Julie. (2000). *Ruthie's Big Old Coat.* Cambridge: Candlewick.

Laird, Christa. (1990). *Shadow of the Wall.* New York: Greenwillow.

Laird, Christa. (1995). *But Can the Phoenix Sing?* New York: Greenwillow.

Laird, Elizabeth. (1987). *The Road to Bethlehem: An Ethiopian Nativity.* New York: Holt.

Laird, Elizabeth. (1991). *Kiss the Dust.* New York: Dutton.

Lalicki, Barbara. (1994). *If There Were Dreams to Sell.* New York: Simon & Schuster.

Landau, Elaine. (2000). *The New Nuclear Reality.* New York: 21st Century.

Lang, Andrew (Ed.). (1948; 1994). *The Blue Fairy Book.* New York: Fine Communications.

Langley, John. (1996). *Little Red Riding Hood.* Hauppauge, NY: Barron's.

Langstaff, John. (1987). *What a Morning! The Christmas Story in Black Spirituals.* Illus. Ashley Bryan. New York: McElderry.

Langstaff, John. (1991). *Climbing Jacob's Ladder: Heroes of the Bible in African-American Spirituals.* Illus. Ashley Bryan. Music arranged by John Andrew Ross. New York: McElderry.

Lankford, Mary. (1992). *Hopscotch Around the World.* Illus. Karen Milone. New York: Morrow/Avon.

Lankford, Mary. (1995). *Christmas Around the World.* New York: Morrow/Avon.

Lankford, Mary. (1996). *Jacks Around the World.* New York: Morrow/Avon.

Larrick, Nancy. (1988). *Bring Me All of Your Dreams.* New York: M. Evans.

Lasker, Joe. (1974). *He's My Brother.* Niles, IL: Whitman.

Lasker, Joe. (1978). *Merry Ever After: The Story of Two Medieval Weddings.* New York: Viking.

Lasky, Kathryn, & Knight, Meribah. (1993). *Searching for Laura Ingalls: A Reader's Journey.* New York: Macmillan.

Lasky, Kathryn. (1993). *Monarchs.* San Diego: Harcourt.

Lasky, Kathryn. (1994). *Beyond the Burning Time.* New York: Scholastic.

Lasky, Kathryn. (1994). *Days of the Dead.* New York: Hyperion.

Lasky, Kathryn. (1995). *She's Wearing a Dead Bird on Her Head!* New York: Hyperion.

Lasky, Kathryn. (1998). *A Brilliant Streak: The Making of Mark Twain.* San Diego: Harcourt.

Lasky, Kathryn. (1999). *Elizabeth I: Red Rose of the House of Tutor (Royal Diaries).* New York: Scholastic.

Lasky, Kathryn. (1999). *She's Wearing a Dead Bird on Her Head.* New York: Farrar, Straus & Giroux.

Lasky, Kathryn. (2000). *The Journal of Augustus Pelletier: The Lewis and Clark Expedition.* New York: Scholastic.

Lathrop, Dorothy D. (Helen Dean Fish). (1937; 1938). *Animals of the Bible.* New York: HarperCollins.

Lattimore, Deborah Nourse. (1988). *The Prince and the Golden Ax.* New York: HarperCollins.

Lattimore, Deborah Nourse. (1989). *Why There Is No Arguing in Heaven: A Mayan Myth.* New York: HarperCollins.

Lattimore, Deborah Nourse. (1990). *The Dragon's Robe.* New York: HarperCollins.

Lattimore, Deborah Nourse. (1994). *Frida Maria: A Story of the Old Southwest.* San Diego: Harcourt.

Lauber, Patricia. (1987). *Get Ready for Robots.* Illus. True Kelley. New York: HarperCollins.

Lauber, Patricia. (1988). *Lost Star: The Story of Amelia Earhart.* New York: Scholastic.

Lauber, Patricia. (1988). *Snakes Are Hunters.* Illus. Holly Keller. New York: HarperCollins.

Lauber, Patricia. (1990). *Seeing Earth from Space.* New York: Scholastic.

Lauber, Patricia. (1995). *Who Eats What? Food Chains and Food Webs.* New York: HarperCollins.

Lauber, Patricia. (1996). *Hurricanes: Earth's Mightiest Storms.* New York: Scholastic.

Lauber, Patricia. (1996). *You're Aboard Spaceship Earth.* New York: HarperCollins.

Lavender, David. (1996). *Snowbound: The Tragic Story of the Donner Party.* New York: Holiday House.

Lavies, Bianca. (1990). *Backyard Hunter: The Praying Mantis.* New York: Dutton.

Lavies, Bianca. (1992). *The Atlantic Salmon.* New York: Dutton.

Lavies, Bianca. (1993). *Compost Critters.* New York: Dutton.

Lavies, Bianca. (1993). *A Gathering of Garter Snakes.* New York: Dutton.

Lawlor, Laurie. (1999). *Window on the West: The Frontier Photography of William Henry Jackson.* New York: Holiday House.

Lawrence, Jacob. (1993). *The Great Migration: An American Story.* New York: HarperCollins.

Lawrence, Jacob. (1993). *Harriet and the Promised Land.* New York: Simon & Schuster.

Lawrence, Louise. (1978). *Star Lord.* New York: HarperCollins.

Lawrence, Louise. (1991). *Andra.* New York: HarperCollins.

Lawson, Robert. (1939). *Ben and Me: A New and Astonishing Life of Benjamin Franklin as Written by His Good Mouse Amos.* Boston: Little, Brown.

Lawson, Robert. (1944). *Rabbit Hill.* New York: Viking.

Layton, Neal. (1999). *Smile If You're Human.* Eds. Cecile Goyette and Toby Sherry. New York: Dial.

Lazar, Jerry. (1995). *Red Cloud: Sioux War Chief.* New York: Chelsea.

Lazo, Caroline E. (1990). *Endangered Species.* New York: Macmillan.

Lazo, Caroline E. (1994). *Elie Wiesel.* New York: Dillon.

Lazo, Caroline. (1994). *Martin Luther King, Jr.* New York: Dillon.

Le Guin, Ursula K. (1968). *The Wizard of Earthsea.* Illus. Ruth Robbins. Boston: Houghton.

Le Guin, Ursula K. (1971). *The Tombs of Atuan.* New York: Atheneum.

Le Guin, Ursula K. (1972). *The Farthest Shore.* New York: Atheneum.

Le Guin, Ursula K. (1990). *Tehanu: The Last Book of Earthsea.* New York: Atheneum.

Le Tord, Bijou. (1995). *A Blue Butterfly: A Story About Claude Monet.* New York: Doubleday.

Lear, Edward. (1846; 1976 Reprint). *A Book of Nonsense.* New York: Garland.

Lear, Edward. (1992). *The Complete Nonsense of Edward Lear.* New York: Knopf.

Lear, Edward. (1995). *The Pelican Chorus and Other Nonsense.* New York: HarperCollins.

Lears, Laurie. (1998). *Ian's Walk: A Story of Autism.* Illus. Karen Ritz. Morton Grove, IL: Whitman.

Lee, Dennis. (1979). *Alligator Pie.* Boston: Houghton.

Lee, Jeanne. (1987). *Ba-Nam.* New York: Holt.

Lee, Jeanne. (1991). *Silent Lotus.* New York: Farrar, Straus & Giroux.

Lee, Marie G. (1994). *Finding My Voice.* New York: Laureleaf.

Lee, Marie G. (1994). *Saying Goodbye.* Boston: Houghton.

Lee, Marie G. (1995). *If It Hadn't Been for Yoon Jun.* New York: Morrow/Avon.

Lee, Marie G. (1996). *Necessary Roughness.* New York: HarperCollins.

Lee, Marie G. (1999). *Night of the The Chupacabras.* New York: Camelot.

Leedy, Loreen. (1994). *Fraction Action.* New York: Holiday House.

Leedy, Loreen. (1995). *2 × 2 = Boo! A Set of Spooky Multiplication Stories.* New York: Holiday House.

Left Hand Bull, Jacqueline, & Haldane, Suzanne. (1999). *Lakota Hoop Dancer.* New York: Dutton.

L'Engle, Madeleine. (1962). *A Wrinkle in Time.* New York: Farrar, Straus & Giroux.

L'Engle, Madeleine. (1965). *The Arm of the Starfish.* New York: Farrar, Straus & Giroux.

L'Engle, Madeleine. (1973). *A Wind in the Door.* New York: Farrar, Straus & Giroux.

L'Engle, Madeleine. (1978). *A Swiftly Tilting Planet.* New York: Farrar, Straus & Giroux.

Lenssen, Ann. (1992). *A Rainbow Balloon: A Book of Concepts.* New York: Cobblehill.

Lent, Blair. (1964). *The Wave.* Boston: Houghton.

Leonard, Laura. (1989). *Saving Damaris.* New York: Simon & Schuster.

Leonard, Laura. (1991). *Finding Papa.* New York: Simon & Schuster.

Lerner, Carol. (1993). *Plants That Make You Sniffle and Sneeze.* New York: Morrow/Avon.

Lerner, Carol. (1994). *Backyard Birds of Winter.* New York: Morrow/Avon.

Lerner, Carol. (1996). *Backyard Birds of Summer.* New York: Morrow/Avon.

Lerner, Carol. (1999). *My Indoor Garden.* New York: Morrow/Avon.

Leslie, Amanda. (1992). *Play Kitten Play: Ten Animal Fingerwiggles.* New York: Candlewick.

Leslie-Spinks, Tim, & Andres, Alice. (1993). *Treasures of Trinkamalee.* North York, ON : Annick Press.

Lessac, Frané. (1987; 1994). *Caribbean Canvas.* Honesdale, PA: Boyds Mills.

Lessie, Pat. (1999). *Fablesauce: Aesop Reinterpreted in Rhymed Couplets.* Illus. Karen Gaudette. Athol: Haley's.

Lester, Alison. (1998). *The Quicksand Pony.* Boston: Houghton.

Lester, Helen. (1993). *Author: A True Story.* Boston: Houghton.

Lester, Julius. (1968). *To Be a Slave.* New York: Dial.

Lester, Julius. (1972). *Long Journey Home: Stories from Black History.* New York: Dial.

Lester, Julius. (1987). *The Tales of Uncle Remus: The Adventures of Brer Rabbit.* Illus. Jerry Pinkney. New York: Dial.

Lester, Julius. (1988). *More Tales of Uncle Remus: Further Adventures of Brer Rabbit, His Friends, Enemies, and Others.* Illus. Jerry Pinkney. New York: Dial.

Lester, Julius. (1989). *How Many Spots Does a Leopard Have?* Illus. David Shannon. New York: Scholastic.

Lester, Julius. (1990). *Further Tales of Uncle Remus: The Misadventures of Brer Rabbit, Brer Fox, Brer Wolf, the Doodang, and Other Creatures.* Illus. Jerry Pinkney. New York: Dial.

Lester, Julius. (1994). *The Last Tales of Uncle Remus.* New York: Dial.

Lester, Julius. (1995). *Long Journey Home: Stories from Black History.* New York: Dial.

Lester, Julius. (1999). *John Henry.* New York: Penguin.

Lester, Julius. (2000). *Pharaoh's Daughter: A Novel of Ancient Egypt.* San Diego: Harcourt.

Lester, Mike. (2000). *A Is for Salad.* New York: Putnam.

Letord, Bijou. (2000). *A Bird or Two: A Story About Henri Matisse.* Grand Rapids: Eerdmans.

Levenson, George. (1999). *Pumpkin Circle: Story of a Garden.* Illus. Shmuel Thaler. Berkeley: Tricycle Press.

Leverich, Kathleen. (1991). *Best Enemies Again.* New York: Greenwillow.

Levi, Steven C. (1996). *Cowboys of the Sky: The Story of Alaska's Bush Pilots.* New York: Walker.

Levin, Betty. (1995). *Fire in the Wind.* New York: Greenwillow.

Levin, Betty. (1998). *Look Back, Moss.* New York: Greenwillow.

Levin, Betty. (1999). *Creature Crossing.* Illus. Joseph A. Smith. New York: Greenwillow.

Levine, Arthur. (1994). *The Boy Who Drew Cats: A Japanese Folktale.* New York: Dial.

Levine, Ellen. (1995). *A Fence Away from Freedom: Japanese Americans and World War II.* New York: Putnam.

Levine, Ellen. (2000). *Darkness over Denmark.* New York: Holiday House.

Levine, Gail Carson. (1998). *Ella Enchanted.* New York: HarperCollins.

Levine, Gail Carson. (1999). *Dave at Night.* New York: HarperCollins.

Levinson, Nancy Smiler. (1994). *Turn of the Century: Our Nation One Hundred Years Ago.* New York: Dutton.

Levinson, Riki. (1985). *Watch the Stars Come Out.* Illus. Diane Goode. New York: Dutton.

Levinson, Riki. (1986). *I Go with My Family to Grandma's.* Illus. Diane Goode. New York: Dutton.

Levinson, Riki. (1988). *Our Home Is the Sea.* New York: Dutton.

Levinson, Riki. (1992). *Boys Here—Girls There.* New York: Dutton.

Levitin, Sonia. (1987). *Journey to America.* New York: Simon & Schuster.

Levitin, Sonia. (1989). *Silver Days.* New York: Atheneum.

Levitin, Sonia. (1998). *The Singing Mountain.* New York: Simon & Schuster.

Levitin, Sonia. (1999). *Boom Town.* Illus. Cat Bowman Smith. Danbury, CT: Orchard.

Levitin, Sonia. (1999). *Taking Charge.* Illus. Cat Bowman Smith. Danbury, CT: Orchard.

Levy, Constance. (1994). *A Tree Place and Other Poems.* New York: McElderry.

Levy, Elizabeth. (1979). *Something Queer Is Going On.* New York: Delacorte.

Lewin, Ted. (1993). *Amazon Boy.* New York: Simon & Schuster.

Lewin, Ted. (1994). *The Reindeer People.* New York: Simon & Schuster.

Lewin, Ted. (1995). *Sacred River.* New York: Clarion.

Lewin, Ted. (1996). *Market!* New York: Morrow/Avon.

Lewin, Ted, & Lewin, Betsy. (1999). *Gorilla Walk.* New York: Lothrop, Lee & Shepard.

Lewington, Anna. (1992). *Antonio's Rain Forest.* Minneapolis, MN: Carolrhoda.

Lewis, C. S. (1994). *The Horse and His Boy.* New York: HarperCollins.

Lewis, C. S. (1994). *The Last Battle.* New York: HarperCollins.

Lewis, C. S. (1994). *The Lion, the Witch, and the Wardrobe.* Illus. Pauline Baynes. New York: HarperCollins.

Lewis, C. S. (1994). *The Magician's Nephew.* Illus. Pauline Baynes. New York: HarperCollins.

Lewis, C. S. (1994). *Prince Caspian.* New York: HarperCollins.

Lewis, C. S. (1994). *The Silver Chair.* New York: HarperCollins.

Lewis, C. S. (1994). *The Voyage of the "Dawn Treader. "* New York: Harper.

Lewis, J. Patrick. (1990). *A Hippopotamusn't: And Other Animal Verses.* Illus. Victoria Chess. New York: Dial.

Lewis, J. Patrick. (1995). *Black Swan, White Crow.* Illus. Chris Manson. New York: Atheneum.

Lewis, J. Patrick. (1996). *Ridicholas Nicholas: Animal Poems.* New York: Dial.

Lewis, J. Patrick. (1998). *Riddle-Lightful: Oodles of Little Riddle Poems.* Illus. Debbie Tilley. New York: Knopf.

Lewis, Kim. (1999). *Just Like Floss.* Cambridge: Candlewick.

Lewis, Maggie. (1999). *Morgy Makes His Move.* Illus. Martha Chesworth. Boston: Houghton.

Lewis, Richard. (1965). *In a Spring Garden.* Illus. Ezra Jack Keats. New York: Dial.

Lewis, Richard. (1991). *All of You Was Singing.* Illus. Ed Young. New York: Atheneum.

Lewison, Wendy C. (1992). *Going to Sleep on the Farm.* Illus. Juan Wijngaard. New York: Dial.

Liestman, Vicki. (1991). *Columbus Day.* Minneapolis, MN: Carolrhoda.

Lindbergh, Anne. (1992). *Three Lives to Live.* Boston: Little, Brown.

Lindbergh, Anne. (1992). *Travel Far, Pay No Fare.* New York: HarperCollins.

Lindbergh, Reeve. (1990). *Johnny Appleseed: A Poem.* Illus. Kathy Jacobsen. Boston: Little, Brown.

Linden, Ann Marie. (1994). *Emerald Blue.* New York: Simon & Schuster.

Lindgren, Astrid. (1950). *Pippi Longstocking.* New York: Viking.

Lindgren, Astrid. (1985). *Ronia, the Robber's Daughter.* New York: Viking.

Lindquist, Susan Hart. (1999). *Summer Soldiers.* New York: Delacorte.

Ling, Mary. (1992). *Butterfly.* New York: Dorling Kindersley.

Ling, Mary. (1992). *Foal.* New York: Dorling Kindersley.

Lingard, Joan. (1990). *Tug of War.* New York: Dutton.

Lingard, Joan. (1991). *Between Two Worlds.* New York: Dutton.

Lionni, Leo. (1959). *Little Blue and Little Yellow.* New York: Astor.

Lionni, Leo. (1963). *Swimmy.* New York: Knopf.

Lionni, Leo. (1970; 1987). *Fish Is Fish.* New York: Knopf.

Lionni, Leo. (1975). *Pezzetino.* New York: Pantheon.

Lipsyte, Robert. (1967). *The Contender.* New York: HarperCollins.

Lipsyte, Robert. (1991). *The Brave.* New York: HarperCollins.

Lipsyte, Robert. (1994). *Joe Louis: A Champ for All America.* New York: HarperCollins.

Lipsyte, Robert. (1994). *Michael Jordan: A Life Above the Rim.* New York: HarperCollins.

Lisle, Janet Taylor. (1989). *Afternoon of the Elves.* New York: Scholastic.

Lisle, Janet Taylor. (1991). *Lampfish of Twill.* New York: Scholastic.

Lisle, Janet Taylor. (1993). *Forest.* New York: Scholastic.

Lisle, Janet Taylor. (2000). *The Art of Keeping Cool.* New York: Atheneum.

Little, Jean. (1962). *Mine for Keeps.* Boston: Little, Brown.

Little, Jean. (1972). *From Anna.* New York: HarperCollins.

Little, Jean. (1977; 1991). *Listen for the Singing.* New York: HarperCollins.

Little, Jean. (1985). *Mama's Going to Buy You a Mockingbird.* New York: Viking.

Little, Jean. (1986). *Different Dragons.* New York: Viking.

Little, Jean. (1987). *Little by Little: A Writer's Education.* New York: Viking.

Little, Jean. (1989). *Hey World, Here I Am.* New York: HarperCollins.

Little, Jean. (1992). *Stars Come Out Within.* New York: Viking.

Little, Jean. (1995). *His Banner Over Me.* New York: Viking.

Little, Jean. (1998). *Emma's Magic Winter.* Illus. Jennifer Plecas. New York: HarperCollins.

Littlechild, George. (1993). *This Land Is My Land.* San Francisco: Children's Book Press.

Littlefield, Bill. (1993). *Champions: Stories of Ten Remarkable Athletes.* Boston: Little, Brown.

Livingston, Myra Cohn. (1984). *Sky Songs.* Illus. Leonard Everett Fisher. New York: Holiday House.

Livingston, Myra Cohn. (1986). *Sea Songs.* Illus. Leonard Everett Fisher. New York: Holiday House.

Livingston, Myra Cohn. (1987). *I Like You, If You Like Me.* New York: Macmillan.

Livingston, Myra Cohn. (1988). *Space Songs.* Illus. Leonard Everett Fisher. New York: Holiday House.

Livingston, Myra Cohn. (1990). *Dog Poems.* Illus. Leslie Morrill. New York: Holiday House.

Livingston, Myra Cohn. (1991). *Lots of Limericks.* New York: McElderry.

Livingston, Myra Cohn. (1991). *Poem Making.* New York: HarperCollins.

Livingston, Myra Cohn. (1992). *If You Ever Meet a Whale.* New York: Holiday House.

Livingston, Myra Cohn. (1992). *Let Freedom Ring: A Ballad of Martin Luther King.* New York: Holiday House.

Livingston, Myra Cohn. (1994). *Abraham Lincoln: A Man for All the People: A Ballad.* New York: Holiday House.

Livingston, Myra Cohn. (1994). *Keep on Singing: A Ballad of Marian Anderson.* New York: Holiday House.

Livingston, Myra Cohn. (1995). *Call Down the Moon: Poems of Music.* New York: McElderry.

Livingston, Myra Cohn. (1995). *Roll Along: Poems on Wheels.* New York: McElderry.

Llewellyn, Claire. (1992). *My First Book of Time.* New York: Dorling Kindersley.

Llorente, Pilar Molina. (1994). *The Apprentice.* Trans. Robin Longshaw. Illus. Juan Ramon Alonso. New York: Farrar, Straus & Giroux.

Lobel, Anita. (1990). *Alison's Zinnia.* New York: Greenwillow.

Lobel, Anita. (1991). *The Dwarf Giant.* New York: Holiday House.

Lobel, Anita. (1994). *Away from Home.* New York: Greenwillow.

Lobel, Anita. (2000). *No Pretty Pictures: A Child of War.* New York: Camelot.

Lobel, Arnold. (1970). *Frog and Toad Are Friends.* New York: HarperCollins.

Lobel, Arnold. (1972). *Frog and Toad Together.* New York: HarperCollins.

Lobel, Arnold. (1976). *Frog and Toad All Year.* New York: HarperCollins.

Lobel, Arnold. (1979). *Days with Frog and Toad.* New York: HarperCollins.

Lobel, Arnold. (1980). *Fables.* New York: HarperCollins.

Lobel, Arnold. (1981). *On Market Street.* Illus. Anita Lobel. New York: Greenwillow.

Lobel, Arnold. (1986). *The Random House Book of Mother Goose.* New York: Random House.

Lobel, Arnold. (1988). *The Book of Pigericks.* New York: HarperCollins.

Locker, Thomas. (1984). *Where the River Begins.* New York: Dial.

Locker, Thomas. (1985). *Mare on the Hill.* New York: Dial.

Locker, Thomas. (1987). *The Boy Who Held Back the Sea.* New York: Dial.

Locker, Thomas. (1988). *Family Farm.* New York: Dial.

Locker, Thomas. (1990). *Snow Towards Evening: A Year in a River Valley: Nature Poems.* New York: Dial.

Lofting, Hugh. (1988). *The Story of Doctor Doolittle.* (Original work published in 1920). New York: Dell.

Logue, Mary. (2000). *Dancing with an Alien.* New York: HarperCollins.

Loh, Morag. (1987). *Tucking Mommy In.* Illus. Donna Rawlins. New York: Scholastic.

Lomas Garza, Carmen. (1990). *Family Pictures/Cuadros de Familia.* San Francisco: Children's Book Press.

Longfellow, Henry Wadsworth. (1983). *Hiawatha.* Illus. Susan Jeffers. New York: Dial.

Longfellow, Henry Wadsworth. (1984). *Hiawatha's Childhood.* Illus. Errol Le Cain. New York: Farrar, Straus & Giroux.

Longfellow, Henry Wadsworth. (1985). *Paul Revere's Ride.* Illus. Nancy Winslow Parker. New York: Greenwillow.

Longfellow, Henry Wadsworth. (1990). *Paul Revere's Ride.* Illus. Ted Rand. New York: Dutton.

Look, Lenore. (1999). *Love as Strong as Ginger.* Illus. Stephen T. Johnson. New York: Atheneum.

Lord, Bette Bao. (1982; o.p.). *Spring Moon.* New York: Morrow/Avon.

Lord, Bette Bao. (1984). *In the Year of the Boar and Jackie Robinson.* New York: HarperCollins.

Louie, Ai-Ling. (1990). *Yeh-Shen: A Cinderella Story from China.* Illus. Ed Young. New York: Philomel.

Louise, Lawrence. (1985). *Children of the Dust.* New York: HarperCollins.

Love, D. Anne. (1999). *I Remember the Alamo.* New York: Holiday House.

Lovelace, Maude Hart. (1940). *Betsy-Tacy.* New York: HarperCollins.

Lovelace, Maude Hart. (1941). *Betsy-Tacy and Tib.* New York: HarperCollins.

Lowell, Susan. (2000). *Cindy Ellen: A Wild Western Cinderella.* Illus. Jane Manning. New York: HarperCollins.

Lowry, Lois. (1977). *A Summer to Die.* Boston: Houghton.

Lowry, Lois. (1978). *Find a Stranger, Say Goodbye.* Boston: Houghton.

Lowry, Lois. (1980). *Autumn Street.* Boston: Houghton.

Lowry, Lois. (1981). *Anastasia Again!* Boston: Houghton.

Lowry, Lois. (1982). *Anastasia at Your Service.* Boston: Houghton.

Lowry, Lois. (1983). *The 100th Thing About Caroline.* Boston: Houghton.

Lowry, Lois. (1983). *Taking Care of Terrific.* Boston: Houghton.

Lowry, Lois. (1984). *Us and Uncle Fraud.* Boston: Houghton.

Lowry, Lois. (1985). *Anastasia Has the Answers.* Boston: Houghton.

Lowry, Lois. (1985). *Anastasia on Her Own.* Boston: Houghton.

Lowry, Lois. (1987). *Anastasia's Chosen Career.* Boston: Houghton.

Lowry, Lois. (1987). *Rabble Starkey.* Boston: Houghton.

Lowry, Lois. (1989). *Number the Stars.* Boston: Houghton.

Lowry, Lois. (1990). *Your Move, J. P.* Boston: Houghton.

Lowry, Lois. (1991). *Anastasia at This Address.* Boston: Houghton.

Lowry, Lois. (1993). *The Giver.* Boston: Houghton.

Lowry, Lois. (1998). *Looking Back: A Book of Memories.* Boston: Houghton.

Lowry, Lois. (1999). *Zooman Sam.* Illus. Diane Degroat. Boston: Houghton.

Lowry, Lois. (2000). *Gathering Blue.* Boston: Houghton.

Lucas, Barbara M. (1993). *Snowed In.* New York: Simon & Schuster.

Lucas, Eileen. (1992). *Jane Goodall: Friend of the Chimp.* Brookfield, CT: Millbrook.

Ludwig, Warren. (1991). *Old Noah's Elephants: An Israeli Folktale.* New York: Whitebird, Putnam.

Lunn, Janet. (2000). *The Hollow Tree.* New York: Viking.

Lurie, Alison. (1980). *Clever Gretchen and Other Forgotten Folktales.* New York: HarperCollins.

Lynch, Chris. (1995). *Ice Man.* New York: HarperCollins.

Lynch, Chris. (1995). *Shadow Boxer.* New York: HarperCollins.

Lynn, Joseph. (2000). *The Color of My Words.* New York: HarperCollins.

Lyon, George Ella. (1989). *Red Rover, Red Rover.* New York: Scholastic.

Lyon, George Ella. (1990). *Come a Tide.* Illus. Stephen Gammell. New York: Scholastic.

Lyon, George Ella. (1993). *Dreamplace.* New York: Scholastic.

Lyon, George Ella. (1994). *Here and Then.* New York: Scholastic.

Lyon, George Ella. (1996). *A Wordful Child.* Katonah, NY: Richard C. Owen.

Lyon, George Ella. (1999). *A Traveling Cat.* Illus. Paul Brett Johnson. Danbury, CT: Orchard.

Lyon, George Ella. (2000). *One Lucky Girl.* Illus. Irene Trivas. New York: DK Publishing.

Lyons, Mary E. (1990). *Sorrow's Kitchen: The Life and Folklore of Zora Neale Hurston.* New York: Scribner's.

Lyons, Mary. (1991). *Raw Head, Bloody Bones: African American Tales of the Supernatural.* New York: Scribner's.

Lyons, Mary. (1992). *Letters from a Slave Girl: The Story of Harriet Jacobs.* New York: Scribner's.

Lyons, Mary. (1993). *Starting Home: The Story of Horace Pippin, Painter.* New York: Scribner's.

Lyons, Mary. (1993). *Stitching Stars: The Story Quilts of Harriet Powers.* New York: Scribner's.

Lyons, Mary. (1994). *Master of Mahogany: Tom Day, Free Black Cabinetmaker.* New York: Scribner's.

Lyons, Mary. (1995). *Keeping Secrets: The Girlhood Diaries of Seven Women Writers.* New York: Holt.

Lyons, Mary. (1995). *The Butter Tree: Tales of Bruh Rabbit.* New York: Holt.

Lyttle, Richard. (1989). *Pablo Picasso: The Man and His Image.* New York: Atheneum.

Maartens, Maretha. (1991). *Paper Bird.* Boston: Houghton.

Maass, Robert. (1998). *Garden.* New York: Holt.

Macaulay, David. (1973). *Cathedral: The Story of Its Construction.* Boston: Houghton.

Macaulay, David. (1975). *Pyramid.* Boston: Houghton.

Macaulay, David. (1977). *Castle.* Boston: Houghton.

Macaulay, David. (1987). *Why the Chicken Crossed the Road.* Boston: Houghton.

Macaulay, David. (1988). *The Way Things Work.* Boston: Houghton.

Macaulay, David. (1990). *Black and White.* Boston: Houghton.

Macaulay, David. (1995). *Shortcut.* Boston: Houghton.

Macaulay, David. (Revised 1998). *The New Way Things Work.* Boston: Houghton.

Maccarone, Grace. (2000). *A Child Was Born: A First Nativity Book.* Illus. Sam Williams. New York: Scholastic.

MacDonald, Amy. (1990). *Little Beaver and the Echo.* New York: Putnam.

MacDonald, Amy. (1990). *Rachel Fister's Blister.* Illus. Marjorie Priceman. Boston: Houghton.

MacDonald, Amy. (1992). *Let's Pretend.* New York: Candlewick.

MacDonald, Caroline. (1989). *The Lake at the End of the World.* New York: Dial.

MacDonald, Golden. (1946). *The Little Island.* Illus. Leonard Weisgard. Garden City, NY: Doubleday.

MacDonald, Suse. (1986). *Alphabatics.* New York: Bradbury.

MacDonald, Suse. (1990). *Once Upon Another: The Tortoise and the Hare—The Lion and the Mouse.* Retellers and Illus. Suse MacDonald and Bill Oakes. New York: Doubleday.

Machotka, Hana. (1990). *What Do You Do at a Petting Zoo?* New York: Morrow/Avon.

Machotka, Hana. (1992). *Breathtaking Noses.* New York: Morrow/Avon.

Machotka, Hana. (1993). *Outstanding Outsides.* New York: Morrow/Avon.

Machotka, Hana. (1994). *Terrific Tales.* New York: Morrow/Avon.

Macht, Norman L. (1991). *Christy Mathewson.* New York: Chelsea.

MacLachlan, Patricia. (1980). *Arthur, for the Very First Time.* Illus. Lloyd Bloom. New York: HarperCollins.

MacLachlan, Patricia. (1984). *Unclaimed Treasures.* New York: HarperCollins.

MacLachlan, Patricia. (1985). *Sarah, Plain and Tall.* New York: HarperCollins.

MacLachlan, Patricia. (1988). *The Facts and Fictions of Minna Pratt.* New York: HarperCollins.

MacLachlan, Patricia. (1991). *Journey.* New York: Delacorte.

MacLachlan, Patricia. (1991). *Three Names.* New York: HarperCollins.

MacLachlan, Patricia. (1994). *Skylark.* New York: HarperCollins.

MacLachlan, Patricia. (1995). *Baby.* New York: Bantam Doubleday Dell.

MacLachlan, Patricia. (1995). *What You Know First.* New York: Cotler/Harper.

Macy, Sue. (1996). *Winning Ways: A Photohistory of American Women in Sports.* New York: Holt.

Mado, Michio. (1992). *The Animals: Selected Poems.* New York: Simon & Schuster.

Maestro, Betsy, & Maestro, Giulio. (1987). *More Perfect Union: The Story of Our Constitution.* New York: Lothrop, Lee & Shepard.

Maestro, Betsy. (1989). *Snow Day.* New York: Scholastic.

Maestro, Betsy. (1992). *How Do Apples Grow?* New York: HarperCollins.

Maestro, Betsy. (1992). *Take a Look at Snakes.* New York: Scholastic.

Maestro, Betsy, & Maestro, Giulio. (1991). *The Discovery of the Americas.* New York: Lothrop, Lee & Shepard.

Magorian, Michelle. (1982). *Good Night, Mr. Tom.* New York: HarperCollins.

Magorian, Michelle. (1984). *Back Home.* New York: HarperCollins.

Maguire, Gregory. (1999). *The Good Liar.* Boston: Houghton.

Mahy, Margaret. (1984). *The Changeover.* New York: Simon & Schuster.

Mahy, Margaret. (1986). *Aliens in the Family.* New York: Scholastic.

Mahy, Margaret. (1987). *17 Kings and 42 Elephants.* Illus. Patricia Maccarthy. New York: Dial.

Mahy, Margaret. (1989). *The Great White Man-Eating Shark: A Cautionary Tale.* Illus. Jonathan Allen. New York: Dial.

Mahy, Margaret. (1992). *The Horrendous Hullabaloo.* Illus. Patricia Maccarthy. New York: Viking.

Mahy, Margaret. (1992). *Underrunners.* New York: Viking.

Mahy, Margaret. (1994). *The Greatest Show Off Earth.* New York: Viking.

Mahy, Margaret. (1995). *My Mysterious World.* Katonah, NY: Richard C. Owen.

Mahy, Margaret. (2000). *24 Hours.* Illus. David Loew. New York: McElderry.

Malnig, Anita. (1985). *Where the Waves Break: Life at the Edge of the Sea.* Minneapolis, MN: Carolrhoda.

Malory, Sir Thomas. (1988). *Le Morte D'Arthur.* New York: Crown.

Manes, Stephen. (1982). *Be a Perfect Person in Just Three Days.* New York: Clarion.

Manitonquat (Medicine Story). (1994). *The Children of the Morning Light: Wampanoag Tales.* New York: Simon & Schuster.

Manley, Joan B. (1995). *She Flew No Flags.* Boston: Houghton.

Manniche, Lise. (1982). *The Prince Who Knew His Fate.* New York: Putnam.

Many, Paul. (2000). *My Life, Take Two.* New York: Walker.

Marahashi, Keiko. (1994). *Is That Josie?* New York: McElderry.

Marchetta, Melina. (1999). *Looking for Alibrandi.* Danbury, CT: Orchard.

Marcus, Leonard, & Schwartz, Amy. (1990). *Mother Goose's Little Misfortunes.* Illus. Amy Schwartz. New York: Bradbury.

Margolis, Richard. (1984). *Secrets of a Small Brother.* Illus. Donald Carrick. New York: Simon & Schuster.

Marin, Nora. (1997). *The Eagle's Shadow.* New York: Scholastic.

Marino, Jan. (1994). *For the Love of Pete: A Novel.* New York: Morrow/Avon.

Maris, Ron. (1992). *Ducks Quack.* New York: Candlewick.

Markle, Sandra. (1994). *Outside and Inside Birds.* New York: Bradbury.

Markle, Sandra. (1995). *Measuring Up! Experiments, Puzzles, and Games Exploring Measurement.* New York: Simon & Schuster.

Markle, Sandra. (1997). *Outside and Inside Bats.* New York: Atheneum.

Markle, Sandra. (1999). *Outside and Inside Kangaroos.* New York: Atheneum.

Marrin, Albert. (1987). *Hitler.* New York: Viking.

Marrin, Albert. (1992). *America and Vietnam: The Elephant and the Tiger.* New York: Viking.

Marrin, Albert. (1993). *Cowboys, Indians, and Gunfighters: The Story of the Cattle Kingdom.* New York: Simon & Schuster.

Marrin, Albert. (1994). *Unconditional Surrender: U. S. Grant and the Civil War.* New York: Simon & Schuster.

Marrin, Albert. (1994). *Virginia's General: Robert E. Lee and the Civil War.* New York: Simon & Schuster.

Marrin, Albert. (1995). *The Sea King: Sir Francis Drake and His Times.* New York: Simon & Schuster.

Marrin, Albert. (1999). *Terror of the Spanish Main: Sir Henry Morgan and His Buccaneers.* New York: Dutton.

Marrin, Albert. (2000). *Sitting Bull and His World.* New York: Dutton.

Marsden, John. (1995). *Tomorrow, When the War Began.* Boston: Houghton.

Marsden, John. (1996). *Letters from the Inside.* New York: Dell.

Marshall, Edward. (1982). *Space Case.* New York: Dial.

Marshall, James. (1986). *Merry Christmas, Space Case.* New York: Dial.

Marshall, James. (1988). *Goldilocks and the Three Bears.* New York: Dial.

Marshall, James. (1989). *The Three Little Pigs.* New York: Dial.

Marshall, James. (1990). *Hansel and Gretel.* New York: Dial.

Marshall, James. (1991). *Old Mother Hubbard and Her Wonderful Dog.* New York: Farrar, Straus & Giroux.

Marshall, James. (1992). *The Cut-Ups Crack Up.* New York: Viking.

Marshall, James. (1992). *Pocketful of Nonsense.* Racine, WI: Western.

Marshall, Janet. (1995). *Look Once, Look Twice.* New York: Ticknor & Fields.

Martin, Ann. (1993). **Baby-sitters Club** Series. New York: Scholastic.

Martin, Bill, Jr. (1964; 1992). *Brown Bear, Brown Bear, What Do You See?* Illus. Eric Carle. New York: Holt.

Martin, Bill, Jr. (1991). *Polar Bear, Polar Bear, What Do You Hear?* Illus. Eric Carle. New York: Holt.

Martin, Bill, Jr. (1999). *A Beastly Story.* Illus. Steven Kellogg. San Diego: Silver Whistle.

Martin, Bill, Jr., & Archambault, John. (1985). *The Ghost-Eye Tree.* Illus. Ted Rand. New York: Holt.

Martin, Bill, Jr., & Archambault, John. (1987). *Here Are My Hands.* Illus. Ted Rand. New York: Holt.

Martin, Bill, Jr., & Archambault, John. (1987). *Knots on a Counting Rope.* New York: Holt.

Martin, Bill, Jr., & Archambault, John. (1989). *Chicka Chicka Boom Boom.* Illus. Lois Ehlert. New York: Simon & Schuster.

Martin, C.L.G. (1988). *The Dragon Nanny.* Illus. Robert Rayevsky. New York: Simon & Schuster.

Martin, Jacqueline Briggs. (1996). *Grandmother Bryant's Pocket.* Boston: Houghton.

Martin, Rafe. (1985). *Foolish Rabbit's Big Mistake.* Illus. Ed Young. New York: Putnam.

Martin, Rafe. (1989). *Will's Mammoth.* Illus. Stephen Gammell. New York: Putnam.

Martin, Rafe. (1992). *The Rough-Face Girl.* Illus. David Shannon. New York: Putnam.

Martin, Rafe. (1992). *A Storyteller's Story.* Photog. Jill Krementz. Katonah, NY: Richard C. Owen.

Martinez, Victor. (1998). *Parrot in the Oven: Mi Vida.* New York: HarperCollins.

Maruki, Toshi. (1982). *Hiroshima, No Pika.* New York: Lothrop, Lee & Shepard.

Marzollo, Jean, & Marzollo, Claudio. (1982). *Jed's Junior Space Patrol.* Illus. David Rose. New York: Dial.

Marzollo, Jean. (1984). *Ruthie's Rude Friends.* New York: Dial.

Marzollo, Jean. (1989). *Jed and the Space Bandits.* New York: Dial.

Marzollo, Jean. (1990). *Pretend You're a Cat.* Illus. Jerry Pinkney. New York: Dial.

Matas, Carol. (1993). *Daniel's Story.* New York: Scholastic.

Matas, Carol. (1996). *After the War.* New York: Simon & Schuster.

Matas, Carol. (1998). *Greater Than Angels.* New York: Simon & Schuster.

Matas, Carol. (2000). *In My Enemy's House.* New York: Simon & Schuster.

Mather, Cotton. (1749). *A Token for the Children of New England, or Some Examples of Children in Whom the Fear of God Was Remarkably Budding Before They Died.* Philadelphia: Franklin and Hall.

Mathers, Petra. (1991). *Sophie and Lou.* New York: HarperCollins.

Mathers, Petra. (2000). *A Cake for Herbie.* New York: Atheneum.

Mathis, Sharon Bell. (1975). *The Hundred Penny Box.* Illus. Leo and Diane Dillon. New York: Viking.

Mathis, Sharon Bell. (1991). *Red Dog, Blue Fly: Football Poems.* New York: Viking.

Matthews, Downs. (1995). *Arctic Foxes.* New York: Simon & Schuster.

Matthews, Mary. (1996). *Magid Fasts for Ramadan.* New York: Clarion.

Matthews, Tom L. (1998). *A Light Shining Through the Mist: A Photobiography of Diane Fossey.* Washington, DC: National Geographic.

Matthews, Tom L. (1999). *Always Inventing: A Photobiography of Alexander Graham Bell.* Washington, DC: National Geographic.

Mayer, Marianna. (1988). *Iduna and the Magic Apples.* Illus. Laszlo Gal. New York: Simon & Schuster.

Mayer, Marianna. (1994). *Baba Yaga and Vasilisa the Brave.* New York: Morrow/Avon.

Mayer, Marianna. (1998). *Young Mary of Nazareth.* New York: Morrow/Avon.

Mayer, Mercer. (1974). *Frog Goes to Dinner.* New York: Dial.

Mayer, Mercer, & Mayer, Marianna. (1986). *A Boy, a Dog, and a Frog.* New York: Dutton.

Mayerson, Evelyn. (1990). *The Cat Who Escaped from Steerage.* New York: Simon & Schuster.

Mayo, Margaret. (2000). *Brother Sun, Sister Moon: The Life and Stories of St. Frances.* Boston: Little Brown.

Mazer, Harry. (1998). *The Wild Kid.* Illus. Debra Lanino. New York: Farrar, Straus & Giroux.

Mazer, Norma Fox. (1999). *Goodnight, Maman.* New York: Harcourt.

Mazur, Anne. (1993). *American Street: A Multicultural Anthology of Stories.* New York: Persea.

McCaffrey, Anne. (1976). *Dragonsong.* New York: Simon & Schuster.

McCaffrey, Anne. (1977). *Dragonsinger.* New York: Simon & Schuster.

McCaffrey, Anne. (1979). *Dragondrums.* New York: Simon & Schuster.

McCaffrey, Anne. (1996). *Black Horses for the King.* San Diego: Harcourt.

McCaughrean, Geraldine. (1993). *Greek Myths.* New York: McElderry.

McClain, Ellen Jaffe. (1994). *No Big Deal.* New York: Dutton.

McCloskey, Robert. (1941). *Make Way for Ducklings.* New York: Viking.

McCloskey, Robert. (1948). *Blueberries for Sal.* New York: Viking.

McCloskey, Robert. (1952). *One Morning in Maine.* New York: Viking.

McCloskey, Robert. (1957). *Time of Wonder.* New York: Viking.

McCord, David. (1977; 1986 Reissue). *One at a Time.* Boston: Little, Brown.

McCord, David. (1986). *All Small.* Boston: Little, Brown.

McCord, David. (1999). *Every Time I Climb a Tree.* Boston: Little, Brown.

McCully, Emily Arnold. (1984). *Picnic.* New York: HarperCollins.

McCully, Emily Arnold. (1985). *First Snow.* New York: HarperCollins.

McCully, Emily Arnold. (1987). *School.* New York: HarperCollins.

McCully, Emily Arnold. (1988). *New Baby.* New York: HarperCollins.

McCully, Emily Arnold. (1992). *Mirette on the High Wire.* New York: Putnam.

McCully, Emily Arnold. (2000). *Monk Camps Out.* New York: Scholastic.

McCurdy, Michael. (1994). *Escape from Slavery: The Boyhood of Frederick Douglass in His Own Words.* New York: Knopf.

McDermott, Dennis. (2000). *The Golden Goose.* New York: Morrow/Avon.

McDermott, Gerald. (1973). *The Magic Tree: A Tale from the Congo.* New York: Holt.

McDermott, Gerald. (1978). *The Stonecutter: A Japanese Folktale.* New York: Penguin.

McDermott, Gerald. (1984). *Daughter of the Earth: A Roman Myth.* New York: Delacorte.

McDermott, Gerald. (1990). *Tim O'Toole and the Wee Folk.* New York: Viking.

McDermott, Gerald. (1993). *Raven: A Trickster Tale from the Pacific Northwest.* San Diego: Harcourt.

McDermott, Gerald. (1999). *The Fox and the Stork.* San Diego: Harcourt.

McDonald, Megan. (1990). *Is This a House for Hermit Crab?* Illus. S. D. Schindler. New York: Scholastic.

McDonald, Megan. (1991). *The Potato Man.* Illus. Ted Lewin. New York: Scholastic.

McDonnell, Christine. (1998). *It's a Deal, Dogboy.* Illus. G. Brian Karas. New York: Viking.

McGiel, Alice. (1999). *Alice Molly Bannaky.* Illus. Chris K. Soentpiet. Boston: Houghton.

McGovern, Ann. (1987). *Secret Soldier: The Story of Deborah Sampson.* New York: Simon & Schuster.

McGraw, Eloise. (1985). *Mara, Daughter of the Nile.* New York: Viking.

McGrory, Anik. (2000). *Mouton's Impossible Dream.* San Diego: Harcourt.

McGuffey, William H. (1837; Reprint 1982). *McGuffey's Eclectic Readers.* Milford, MI: Mott.

McKay, David. (1969). *A Flock of Words: An Anthology of Poetry for Children and Others.* Illus. Margery Gill. San Diego: Harcourt.

McKay, Hilary. (1997). *Dolphin Luck.* Illus. Alex Ayliffe. New York: McElderry.

McKay, Hilary. (1998). *The Exiles in Love.* New York: McElderry.

McKay, Lawrence, Jr. (1995). *Caravan.* New York: Lee and Low.

McKean, Thomas. (1999). *Into the Candlelit Room and Other Strange Tales.* New York: Penguin.

McKee, Tim. (1998). *No More Strangers Now: Young Voices from a New South Africa.* Illus. Anne Blackshaw. New York: DK Publishing.

McKenzie, Ellen Kindt. (1994). *The Perfectly Orderly House.* New York: Holt.

McKinley, Robin (Adapter). (1988). *The Outlaws of Sherwood.* New York: Greenwillow.

McKinley, Robin. (1982). *The Blue Sword.* New York: Greenwillow.

McKinley, Robin. (1984). *The Hero and the Crown.* New York: Greenwillow.

McKinley, Robin. (1994). *A Knot in the Grain and Other Stories.* New York: Greenwillow.

McKinley, Robin. (1997). *Rose Daughter.* New York: Greenwillow.

McKinley, Robin. (1999). *Beauty.* New York: HarperCollins.

McKinley, Robin. (2000). *Spindle's End.* New York: Putnam.

McKissack, Patricia C. (1986). *Flossie and the Fox.* Illus. Rachel Isadora. New York: Dial.

McKissack, Patricia C. (1988). *Mirandy and Brother Wind.* Illus. Jerry Pinkney. New York: Knopf.

McKissack, Patricia C. (1989). *Jesse Jackson: A Biography.* New York: Scholastic.

McKissack, Patricia C. (1991). *Mary McLeod Bethune: A Great Teacher.* Illus. Ned Ostendorf. Hillside, NJ: Enslow.

McKissack, Patricia C. (1992). *A Million Fish . . . More or Less.* New York: Knopf.

McKissack, Patricia C. (1997). *A Picture of Freedom: The Diary of Clotee, a Slave Girl.* New York: Scholastic.

McKissack, Patricia C. (1997). *Can You Imagine?* Katonah, NY: Richard C. Owen.

McKissack, Patricia C. (1997). *Ma Dear's Aprons.* Illus. Floyd Cooper. New York: Atheneum.

McKissack, Patricia C. (1997). *Run Away Home.* New York: Scholastic.

McKissack, Patricia C. , & McKissack, Fredrick. (1992). *Sojourner Truth: Ain't I a Woman?* New York: Scholastic.

McKissack, Patricia C. , & McKissack, Fredrick. (1994). *African-American Scientists.* Brookfield, CT: Millbrook.

McKissack, Patricia C. , & McKissack, Fredrick. (1994). *Black Diamond: The Story of the Negro Baseball Leagues.* New York: Scholastic.

McKissack, Patricia C. , & McKissack, Fredrick. (1994). *Christmas in the Big House, Christmas in the Quarters.* New York: Scholastic.

McKissack, Patricia C. , & McKissack, Fredrick. (1995). *Red-Tail Angels: The Story of the Tuskegee Airmen of World War II.* New York: Walker.

McKissack, Patricia, & McKissack, Frederick. (1999). *Black Hands and White Sails: The Story of African-American Whalers.* New York: Scholastic.

McKissack, Patricia, & McKissack, Fredrick. (1998). *Messy Bessey's School Desk.* Illus. Dana Regan. Danbury, CT: Children's Press.

McLerran, Alice. (1995). *The Ghost Dance.* New York: Clarion.

McLerran, Alice. (1991). *Roxaboxen.* Illus. Barbara Cooney. New York: Lothrop, Lee & Shepard.

McLerran, Alice. (1996). *The Year of the Ranch.* Illus. Kimberly Bulcken Root. New York: Penguin.

McMahon, Patricia. (1992). *Chi-Hoon: A Korean Girl.* Photog. Michael F. O'Brien. Honesdale, PA: Boyds Mills.

McMillan, Bruce. (1989). *Super, Super Superwords.* New York: Morrow/Avon.

McMillan, Bruce. (1991). *Eating Fractions.* New York: Scholastic.

McMillan, Bruce. (1992). *The Baby Zoo.* New York: Scholastic.

McMillan, Bruce. (1992). *Beach Ball—Left, Right.* New York: Holiday House.

McMillian, Bruce. (1997). *My Horse of the North.* New York: Scholastic.

McMillan, Bruce. (1997). *Wild Flamingos.* Boston: Houghton.

McMillan, Bruce. (1998). *Salmon Summer.* Boston: Houghton.

McMullan, Kate. (2000). *Papa's Song.* Illus. Jim McMullan. New York: Farrar, Straus & Giroux.

McNeal, Tom, & McNeal, Laura. (1999). *Crooked.* New York: Knopf.

McNulty, Faith. (1999). *How Whales Walked Into the Sea.* Illus. Ted Lewin. New York: Scholastic.

McNutly, Faith. (1999). *When I Lived with Bats.* Illus. Lena Shiffman. New York: Scholastic.

McPhail, David. (1984). *Fix-It.* New York: Dutton.

McPhail, David. (1985). *Emma's Pet.* New York: Dutton.

McPhail, David. (1987). *Emma's Vacation.* New York: Dutton.

McPhail, David. (1990). *Lost!* Boston: Little, Brown.

McPhail, David. (1990). *Pig Pig Gets a Job.* New York: Dutton.

McPhail, David. (1992). *Farm Boy's Year.* New York: Simon & Schuster.

McVitty, Walter (Reteller). (1988). *Ali Baba and the Forty Thieves.* Illus. Margaret Early. New York: Abrams.

Mead, Alice. (1994). *Crossing the Starlight Bridge.* New York: Simon & Schuster.

Mead, Alice. (1995). *Junebud.* New York: Farrar, Straus & Giroux.

Mead, Alice. (1998). *Junebug and the Reverend.* New York: Farrar, Straus & Giroux.

Meddaugh, Susan. (1995). *Hog-Eye.* Boston: Houghton.

Meddaugh, Susan. (1999). *The Best Place.* Boston: Houghton.

Medearis, Angela Shelf. (1991). *Dancing with the Indians.* Illus. Samuel Byrd. New York: Holiday House.

Medearis, Angela Shelf. (1994). *Dare to Dream: Coretta Scott King and the Civil Rights Movement.* New York: Dutton.

Medearis, Angela Shelf. (1994). *Little Louis and the Jazz Band: The Story of Louis "Satchmo" Armstrong.* New York: Dutton.

Medearis, Angela Shelf. (1994). *Our People.* New York: Atheneum.

Medearis, Angela Shelf. (1994). *Singing Man: Adapted from a West African Folktale.* New York: Holiday House.

Medearis, Angela Shelf. (1995). *The Adventures of Sugar and Junior.* Illus. Nancy Poydar. New York: Holiday House.

Medearis, Angela Shelf. (1995). *The Freedom Riddle.* New York: Lodestar.

Medearis, Angela Shelf. (1995). *Skin Deep and Other Teenage Reflections.* Illus. Michael Bryant. New York: Macmillan.

Medearis, Angela Shelf. (1995). *Too Much Talk.* New York: Candlewick.

Medearis, Angela Shelf. (1996). *Haunts: Five Hair-Raising Tales.* Illus. Trina Schart Hyman. New York: Holiday House.

Medearis, Angela Shelf. (1996). *Tailypo: A Newfangled Tall Tale.* Illus. Sterling Brown. New York: Holiday House.

Medearis, Angela Shelf. (1997). *Rum-A-Tum-Tum.* Illus. James Ransome. New York: Holiday House.

Meltzer, Milton. (1967). *Bread—And Roses: The Struggle of American Labor.* New York: Knopf.

Meltzer, Milton. (1969). *Brother, Can You Spare a Dime?* New York: Knopf.

Meltzer, Milton. (1980). *The Chinese Americans.* New York: HarperCollins.

Meltzer, Milton. (1982). *The Hispanic Americans.* New York: HarperCollins.

Meltzer, Milton. (1984). *The Black Americans: A History in Their Own Words, 1619–1983.* New York: HarperCollins.

Meltzer, Milton. (1986). *George Washington and the Birth of Our Nation.* New York: Watts.

Meltzer, Milton. (1986). *Poverty in America.* New York: Morrow/Avon.

Meltzer, Milton. (1986). *Winnie Mandela: The Soul of South Africa.* New York: Viking.

Meltzer, Milton. (1987). *The American Revolutionaries: A History in Their Own Words.* New York: HarperCollins.

Meltzer, Milton. (1988). *Starting from Home: A Writer's Beginnings.* New York: Viking.

Meltzer, Milton. (1989). *Voices from the Civil War.* New York: HarperCollins.

Meltzer, Milton. (1990). *The Bill of Rights: How We Got It and What It Means.* New York: HarperCollins.

Meltzer, Milton. (1990). *Columbus and the World Around Him.* New York: Watts.

Meltzer, Milton. (1991). *Thomas Jefferson: The Revolutionary Aristocrat.* New York: Watts.

Meltzer, Milton. (1992). *The Amazing Potato: A Story in Which the Incas, Conquistadors, Marie Antoinette, Thomas Jefferson, Wars, Famines, Immigrants, and French Fries All Play a Part.* New York: HarperCollins.

Meltzer, Milton. (1993). *Gold: The True Story of Why People Search for It, Mine It, Trade It, Steal It, Mint It, Hoard It, Shape It, Wear It, Fight and Kill for It.* New York: HarperCollins.

Meltzer, Milton. (1993). *Lincoln: In His Own Words.* San Diego: Harcourt.

Meltzer, Milton. (1994). *Cheap Raw Material: How Our Youngest Workers Are Exploited and Abused.* New York: Viking.

Meltzer, Milton. (1995). *Frederick Douglass: In His Own Words.* San Diego: Harcourt.

Meltzer, Milton. (1995). *Hold Your Horses! A Feedbag Full of Fact and Fable.* New York: HarperCollins.

Meltzer, Milton. (1998). *Langston Hughes: An Illustrated Edition.* Brookfield, CT: Millbrook.

Meltzer, Milton. (1999). *Witches and Witch-Hunts: A History of Persecution.* Illus. Barry Mozer. New York: Scholastic.

Mendez, Phil. (1989). *The Black Snowman.* New York: Scholastic.

Mennen, Ingrid, & Daly, Niki. (1991). *Somewhere in Africa.* Illus. Nicolaas Maritz. New York: Dutton.

Merriam, Eve. (1985). *Blackberry Ink.* New York: Morrow/Avon.

Merriam, Eve. (1987). *Halloween ABC.* Illus. Lane Smith. New York: Simon & Schuster.

Merriam, Eve. (1988). *You Be Good and I'll Be Night.* New York: Morrow/Avon.

Merriam, Eve. (1989). *A Poem for a Pickle: Funnybone Verses.* Illus. Sheila Hamanaka. New York: Morrow/Avon.

Merriam, Eve. (1993). *12 Ways to Get to 11.* New York: Simon & Schuster.

Merriam, Eve. (1994). *Higgle Wiggle: Happy Rhymes.* New York: Morrow/Avon.

Merrill, Jean. (1992). *The Girl Who Loved Caterpillars.* Illus. Floyd Cooper. New York: Putnam.

Metaxas, Eric. (1991). *Jack and the Beanstalk.* New York: Simon & Schuster.

Metzger, Lois. (1992). *Barry's Sister.* New York: Simon & Schuster.

Metzger, Lois. (1995). *Ellen's Case.* New York: Simon & Schuster.

Metzger, Lois. (1999). *Missing Girls.* New York: Viking.

Meyer, Carolyn. (1992). *Where the Broken Heart Still Beats: The Story of Cynthia Ann Parker.* San Diego: Harcourt.

Meyer, Carolyn. (1996). *In a Different Light: Growing Up in a Yup'ik Eskimo Village in Alaska.* New York: McElderry.

Micklethwait, Lucy. (1993). *A Child's Book of Art.* New York: Dorling Kindersley.

Micklethwait, Lucy. (1993). *I Spy Two Eyes: Numbers in Art.* New York: Greenwillow.

Micklethwait, Lucy. (1994). *I Spy a Lion: Animals in Art.* New York: Greenwillow.

Micklethwait, Lucy. (1996). *I Spy a Freight Train: Transportation in Art.* New York: Greenwillow.

Miles, Betty. (1991). *Save the Earth: An Action Handbook for Kids.* Illus. Nelle Davis. New York: Knopf.

Miles, Shapiro. (1994). *Maya Angelou.* New York: Chelsea.

Millard, Anne. (1999). *A Street Through Time: 12,000 Year Walk Through History.* Illus. Steve Noon. New York: DK Publishing.

Miller, Margaret. (1988). *Whose Hat?* New York: Greenwillow.

Miller, Margaret. (1994). *My Five Senses.* New York: Simon & Schuster.

Miller, Robert H. (1991). *The Buffalo Soldiers.* Parsippany, NJ: Silver.

Miller, Robert H. (1992). *Reflections of a Black Cowboy.* Englewood Cliffs, NJ: Silver.

Miller, Robert H. (1995). *The Story of Nat Love.* Parsippany, NJ: Silver.

Miller, William. (1994). *Zora Hurston and the Chinaberry Tree.* New York: Lee and Low.

Miller, William. (1995). *Frederick Douglass: The Last Day of Slavery.* New York: Lee and Low.

Mills, Claudia. (1998). *Standing Up to Mr. O.* New York: Farrar, Straus & Giroux.

Mills, Claudia. (1999). *Gus, Grandpa, and the Two-Wheeled Bike.* Illus. Catherine Stock. New York: Farrar, Straus & Giroux.

Mills, Claudia. (1999). *You're a Brave Man, Julius Zimmerman.* New York: Farrar, Straus & Giroux.

Mills, Judy. (1998). *Robert Kennedy.* Morton Grove, IL: Whitman.

Mills, Lauren. (1993). *Tatterhood and the Hobgoblins: A Norwegian Folktale.* Boston: Little, Brown.

Milne, A. A. (1924). *When We Were Very Young.* Illus. E. H. Shepard. New York: Dutton.

Milne, A. A. (1926). *Winnie the Pooh.* Illus. E. H. Shepard. New York: Dutton.

Milne, A. A. (1927). *Now We Are Six.* Illus. E. H. Shepard. New York: Dutton.

Minarik, Else. (1959). *Father Bear Comes Home.* Illus. Maurice Sendak. New York: HarperCollins.

Minarik, Else. (1968). *A Kiss for Little Bear.* New York: HarperCollins.

Mitchell, Barbara. (1996). *Red Bird.* Illus. Todd Doney. New York: Lothrop, Lee & Shepard.

Mitchell, Margaree King. (1993). *Uncle Jed's Barbershop.* New York: Simon & Schuster.

Mitchell, Margaree King. (1998). *Grandaddy's Gift.* Illus. Larry Johnson. New York: Troll.

Mochizuki, Ken. (1989). *Baseball Saved Us.* New York: Lee and Low.

Mochizuki, Ken. (1995). *Heroes.* New York: Lee and Low.

Mochizuki, Ken. (1997). *Passage to Freedom: The Sugihara Story.* New York: Lee and Low.

Moea, Pat (Ed.). (1996). *Confetti: Poems for Children.* Illus. Enrique O. Sanchez. New York: Lee and Low.

Moeri, Louise. (1981). *Save Queen of Sheba.* New York: Dutton.

Moeri, Louise. (1989). *The Fifty-Third War.* Boston: Houghton.

Mohr, Joseph. (1999). *Silent Night, Holy Night: A Christmas Carol.* Illus. Maja Dusikova. New York: North-South.

Mohr, Nicholasa, and Martorell, Antonio. (1995). *The Song of El Coquí: And Other Tales of Puerto Rico.* New York: Viking.

Mohr, Nicholasa. (1979). *Felita.* New York: Dial.

Mohr, Nicholasa. (1986). *Going Home.* New York: Dial.

Mohr, Nicholasa. (1994). *Nicholasa Mohr: Growing Up Inside the Sanctuary of My Imagination.* New York: Messner.

Mohr, Nicholasa. (1996). *Old Letivia and the Mountain of Sorrows.* Illus. Rudy Gutierrez. New York: Viking.

Molina Llorente, Pilar. (1993). *The Apprentice.* New York: Farrar, Straus & Giroux.

Mollel, Tololwa M. (1990). *The Orphan Boy: A Maasai Story.* Illus. Paul Morin. New York: Clarion.

Mollel, Tololwa M. (1995). *Big Boy.* New York: Clarion.

Mollel, Tololwa M. (2000). *Subria Subira.* Illus. Linda Saport. Boston: Clarion.

Monceaux, Morgan. (1994). *Jazz: My Music, My People.* New York: Knopf.

Monceaux, Morgan, & Ruth Katcher. (1999). *My Heroes, My People: African Americans and Native Americans in the West.* New York: Farrar, Straus & Giroux.

Monjo, F. N. (1970). *The Drinking Gourd.* Illus. Fred Brenner. New York: HarperCollins.

Monjo, F. N. (1973). *Poor Richard in France.* Illus. Brinton Turkle. New York: Dell.

Monjo, F. N. (1990). *Grand Papa and Ellen Aroon.* New York: Dell.

Monjo, F. N. (1991). *The House on Stink Alley.* New York: Dell.

Montgomery, Lucy M. (1908; 1983 Reprint). *Anne of Green Gables.* New York: Putnam.

Montgomery, Sy. (1999). *The Snake Scientist.* Illus. Nic Bishop. Boston: Houghton.

Moon, Pat. (1991). *Earth Lines: Poems for the Green Age.* New York: Greenwillow.

Moore, Clement Clark. (1991). *Grandma Moses' Night Before Christmas.* New York: Random House.

Moore, Clement Clarke. (1992). *Twas the Night Before Christmas: A Visit from St. Nicholas.* (Original work published in 1823). Boston: Houghton.

Moore, Lilian. (1995). *I Never Did That Before.* New York: Atheneum.

Moore, Martha. (1995). *Under the Mermaid Angel.* New York: Delacorte.

Moore, Yvette. (1991). *Freedom Songs.* New York: Scholastic.

Mora, Pat. (1992). *A Birthday Basket for Tia.* New York: Simon & Schuster.

Mora, Pat. (1994). *The Desert Is My Mother/El Desierto es Mi Madre.* Houston: Arte Publico.

Mora, Pat. (1994). *Listen to the Desert/Oye al Desierto.* New York: Clarion.

Mora, Pat. (1994). *Pablo's Tree.* New York: Simon & Schuster.

Mora, Pat. (1995). *The Race of Toad and Deer.* Illus. Maya Itzna Brooks. Danbury, CT: Orchard.

Mora, Pat. (1996). *Uno, Dos, Tres: One, Two, Three.* New York: Clarion.

Mora, Pat. (1997). *Tomas and the Library Lady.* New York: Random House.

Mora, Pat. (1998). *This Big Sky.* New York: Scholastic.

Morgenstern, Susie. (1998). *Secret Letters from 0 to 10.* Illus. Gil Rosen. New York: Viking.

Mori, Kyoko. (1993). *Shizuko's Daughter.* New York: Holt.

Mori, Kyoko. (1995). *One Bird.* New York: Holt.

Morimoto, Junko. (1990). *My Hiroshima.* New York: Viking.

Morley, Jacqueline. (1999). *Egyptian Myths.* Illus. Giovanni Caselli. Lincolnwood: NTC/Contemporary Publishing Company.

Morozumi, Atsuko. (1993). *One Gorilla.* New York: Farrar, Straus & Giroux.

Morpurgo, Michael. (1991). *Waiting for Anya.* New York: Viking.

Morris, Ann. (1995). *Shoes Shoes Shoes.* New York: Morrow/Avon.

Morrison, Lillian. (1977; o.p.). *Sidewalk Racer and Other Poems of Sports and Motion.* New York: Morrow/Avon.

Morrison, Lillian. (1989). *Best Wishes, Amen: Autograph Verse.* New York: HarperCollins.

Morrison, Lillian. (1992). *Whistling the Morning In.* Illus. Joel Cook. Honesdale, PA: Boyds Mills.

Morrison, Taylor. (1996). *Antonio's Apprenticeship: Painting a Fresco in Renaissance Italy.* New York: Holiday House.

Moses, Will. (1995). *The Legend of Sleepy Hollow.* New York: Philomel.

Moss, Jeff. (1989). *The Butterfly Jar.* Illus. Chris Demarest. New York: Bantam.

Most, Bernard. (2000). *ABC T Rex.* San Diego: Harcourt.

Mother Goose. (1987). *The Real Mother Goose.* Illus. Blanche Fisher Wright. (Reproduction of 1916 edition, Checkerboard Press). New York: Macmillan.

Muhlberger, Richard. (1990). *The Christmas Story: Told Through Paintings.* San Diego: Harcourt.

Muller, Jorg. (1977). *The Changing City.* New York: McElderry.

Muller, Jorg. (1977). *The Changing Countryside.* New York: McElderry.

Mullins, Patricia. (1993). *Dinosaur Encore.* New York: HarperCollins.

Mullins, Patricia. (1994). *V for Vanishing: An Alphabet of Endangered Species.* New York: HarperCollins.

Murphy, Jim. (1990). *The Boy's War: Confederate and Union Soldiers Talk About the Civil War.* Boston: Houghton.

Murphy, Jim. (1992). *The Long Road to Gettysburg.* New York: Clarion.

Murphy, Jim. (1993). *Across America on an Emigrant Train.* New York: Clarion.

Murphy, Jim. (1995). *The Great Fire.* New York: Scholastic.

Murphy, Jim. (1995). *Into the Deep Forest with Henry David Thoreau.* New York: Clarion.

Murphy, Jim. (1998). *Gone-A-Whaling: The Lure of the Sea and the Hunt for the Great Whale.* Boston: Clarion.

Murphy, Mary. (1999). *Caterpillar's Wish.* New York: DK Publishing.

Murray, Peter. (1993). *The Amazon.* Plymouth, MN: Child's World.

Musleah, Rahel. (2000). *Why on This Night? A Passover Haggadah for Family Celebration.* Illus. Louise August. New York: Simon & Schuster.

Myers, Anna. (1994). *Rosie's Tiger.* New York: Walker.

Myers, Anna. (1995). *Graveyard Girl.* New York: Walker.

Myers, Christopher. (1999). *Black Cat.* New York: Scholastic.

Myers, Laurie. (1993). *Earthquake in the Third Grade.* Boston: Houghton.

Myers, Walter Dean. (1975). *Fast Sam, Cool Clyde, and Stuff.* New York: Viking.

Myers, Walter Dean. (1988). *Fallen Angels.* New York: Scholastic.

Myers, Walter Dean. (1989). *The Young Landlords.* New York: Viking.

Myers, Walter Dean. (1991). *Now Is Your Time: The African-American Struggle for Freedom.* New York: HarperCollins.

Myers, Walter Dean. (1992). *Somewhere in the Darkness.* New York: Scholastic.

Myers, Walter Dean. (1993). *Brown Angels: An Album of Pictures and Verse.* New York: HarperCollins.

Myers, Walter Dean. (1993). *Malcolm X: By Any Means Necessary.* New York: Scholastic.

Myers, Walter Dean. (1994). *Darnell Rock Reporting.* New York: Delacorte.

Myers, Walter Dean. (1994). *The Glory Field.* New York: Scholastic.

Myers, Walter Dean. (1994). *Me, Mop, and the Moondance Kid.* New York: Dell.

Myers, Walter Dean. (1995). *The Story of the Three Kingdoms.* New York: HarperCollins.

Myers, Walter Dean. (1996). *Slam.* New York: Scholastic.

Myers, Walter Dean. (1996). *Smiffy Blue, Ace Crime Detective: The Case of the Missing Ruby and Other Stories.* Illus. David Sims. New York: Scholastic.

Myers, Walter Dean. (1997). *Harlem.* Illus. Christopher Myers. New York: Scholastic.

Myers, Walter Dean. (1997). *Harlem: A Poem.* Illus. Christopher Myers. New York: Scholastic.

Myers, Walter Dean. (1998). *Angel to Angel: A Mother's Gift of Love.* New York: HarperCollins.

Myers, Walter Dean. (2000). *Malcom X: A Fire Burning Brightly.* New York: HarperCollins.

Myers, Walter Dean. (2000). *Monster.* Illus. Christopher Myers. New York: HarperCollins.

Myers, Walter Dean. (2000). *145th Street Stories.* New York: Delacorte.

Nabwire, Constance, & Montgomery, Bertha. (1990). *Cooking the African Way.* Minneapolis, MN: Lerner.

Naidoo, Beverley. (1988). *Journey to Jo'burg.* New York: HarperCollins.

Naidoo, Beverley. (1990). *Chain of Fire.* New York: HarperCollins.

Namioka, Lensey. (1992). *Yang the Youngest and His Terrible Ear.* Boston: Little, Brown.

Namioka, Lensey. (1994). *April and the Dragon Lady.* New York: Browndeer.

Namioka, Lensey. (1995). *Yang the Third and Her Impossible Family.* Boston: Little, Brown.

Namioka, Lensey. (2000). *Yang the Second and Her Secret Admirers.* New York: Yearling.

Napoli, Donna Jo. (1994). *The Prince of the Pond: Otherwise Known as de Fawg Pin.* Illus. Judith Byron Schachner. New York: Puffin.

Napoli, Donna Jo. (1996). *Zel.* New York: Dutton.

Napoli, Donna Jo. (1997). *Stones in Water.* New York: Dutton.

Napoli, Donna Jo. (1999). *Crazy Jack.* New York: Delacorte.

Napoli, Donna Jo. (1999). *Spinners.* New York: Dutton.

Napoli, Donna Jo. (2000). *Beast.* New York: Atheneum.

Narahashi, Keiko. (1999). *I Have a Friend.* New York: McElderry.

Nash, Gary B. (1999). *Forbidden Love: The Secret History of Mixed-Race America.* New York: Holt.

Nash, Ogden. (1973). *Custard the Dragon.* Boston: Little, Brown.

Nash, Ogden. (1991). *The Adventures of Isabel.* Illus. James Marshall. Boston: Little, Brown.

Navasky, Bruno. (1993). *Festival in My Heart: Poems by Japanese Children.* New York: Abrams.

Naylor, Phyllis Naylor. (2000). *The Grooming of Alice.* Illus. Mark Eliott. New York: Atheneum.

Naylor, Phyllis R. (1998). *Achingly Alice.* New York: Atheneum.

Naylor, Phyllis Reynolds. (1989). *Alice in Rapture, Sort Of.* New York: Simon & Schuster.

Naylor, Phyllis Reynolds. (1991). *Shiloh.* New York: Simon & Schuster.

Naylor, Phyllis Reynolds. (1994). *Alice in Between.* New York: Simon & Schuster.

Naylor, Phyllis Reynolds. (1995). *Alice the Brave.* New York: Simon & Schuster.

Naylor, Phyllis Reynolds. (1999). *Alice on the Outside.* New York: Atheneum.

Naylor, Phyllis Reynolds. (2000). *Walker's Crossing.* New York: Atheneum.

Neil, Philip. (1994). *King Midas.* Illus. Isabelle Brent. Boston: Little, Brown.

Neitzel, Shirley. (1989). *The Jacket I Wear in the Snow.* Illus. Nancy Winslow Parker. New York: Greenwillow.

Neitzel, Shirley. (1995). *The Bag I'm Taking to Grandma's.* New York: Greenwillow.

Nelson, Theresa. (1989). *And One for All.* New York: Scholastic.

Nelson, Theresa. (1994). *Earthshine.* New York: Scholastic.

Nelson, Theresa. (1998). *The Empress of Elsewhere.* New York: DK Publishing.

Nelson, Vaunda Micheaux. (1993). *Mayfield Crossing.* New York: Putnam.

Nelson, Vaunda Micheaux. (1995). *Possibles.* New York: Putnam.

Nerlove, Miriam. (1996). *Flowers on the Wall.* New York: McElderry.

Ness, Evaline. (1966). *Sam, Bangs, and Moonshine.* New York: Holt.

Neville, Emily Cheney. (1991). *The China Year.* New York: HarperCollins.

Newbery, John. (1744; 1967 Reissue). *A Little Pretty Pocket-Book: Intended for the Instruction and Amusement of Little Master Tommy and Pretty Miss Polly.* San Diego: Harcourt.

Newbery, John. (1765). *The History of Little Goody Two Shoes.* London: John Newbery.

Newlands, Anne. (1988). *Meet Edgar Degas.* New York: HarperCollins.

Newth, Mette. (1998). *The Dark Light.* Trans. Faith Ingwersen. New York: Farrar, Straus & Giroux.

Newth, Mette. (2000). *The Transformation.* New York: Farrar, Straus & Giroux.

Nichol, Barbara. (1994). *Beethoven Lives Upstairs.* New York: Scholastic.

Nickens, Bessie. (1994). *Walking the Log: Memories of a Southern Childhood.* New York: Rizzoli.

Nieuwsma, Milton J. (Ed.). (1999). *Kinderlager: An Oral History of Young Holocaust Survivors.* New York: Holiday House.

Nikola-Lisa, W. (1994). *Bein' with You This Way.* New York: Lee and Low.

Nimmo, Jenny. (2000). *Esmerelda and the Children Next Door.* Illus. Paul Howard. Boston: Houghton.

Nims, Bonnie Larkin. (1992). *Just Beyond Reach and Other Riddle Poems.* Photog. George Ancona. New York: Scholastic.

Nixon, Joan Lowery. (1988). *If You Were a Writer.* Illus. Bruce Degen. New York: Simon & Schuster.

Nixon, Joan Lowery. (1995). *Spirit Seeker.* New York: Bantam Doubleday Dell.

Nixon, Joan Lowery. (1998). *The Haunting.* New York: Delacorte.

Noble, Trina Hakes. (1980). *The Day Jimmy's Boa Ate the Wash.* Illus. Steven Kellogg. New York: Dial.

Nodar, Carmen Santiago. (1992). *Abuelita's Paradise/El Paraiso de Abuelita.* Morton Grove, IL: Whitman.

Nolen, Jerdine. (1994). *Harvey Potter's Balloon Farm.* Illus. Mark Buehner. New York: Lothrop, Lee & Shepard.

Nolen, Jerdine. (2000). *Big Jabe.* Illus. Kadir Nelson. New York: Lothrop, Lee & Shepard.

Noll, Sally. (1990). *Watch Where You Go.* New York: Greenwillow.

Norell, Mark A., & Dingus, Lowell. (1999). *A Nest of Dinosaurs: The Story of the Oviraptor.* New York: Doubleday.

Norton, Mary. (1953). *The Borrowers.* Illus. Beth and Joe Krush. San Diego: Harcourt.

Nunes, Susan Miho. (1995). *The Last Dragon.* Illus. Chris K. Soentpiet. Boston: Clarion.

Nye, Naomi Shihab. (1992). *This Same Sky: A Collection of Poems from Around the World.* New York: Simon & Schuster.

Nye, Naomi Shihab. (1995). *The Tree Is Older Than You Are: A Bilingual Gathering of Stories and Poems from Mexico, with Paintings by Mexican Artists.* New York: Simon & Schuster.

Nye, Naomi Shihab. (1999). *What Have You Lost?* New York: HarperCollins.

Nye, Naomi Shihab (Ed.). (2000). *Salting the Ocean.* Illus. Ashley Bryan. New York: HarperCollins.

O'Connor, B. (1999). *Me and Rupert Goody.* New York: Farrar, Straus & Giroux.

O'Brien, Robert C. (1971). *Mrs. Frisby and the Rats of Nimh.* New York: Atheneum.

O'Brien, Robert C. (1975). *Z for Zachariah.* New York: Atheneum.

O'Dell, Scott. (1980). *Sarah Bishop.* Boston: Houghton.

O'Dell, Scott. (1987). *Island of the Blue Dolphins.* New York: Dell.

O'Dell, Scott, & Hall, E. (1992). *Thunder Rolling in the Mountains.* Boston: Houghton.

Okimoto, Jean Davies. (2000). *Molly by Any Other Name.* New York: Universe.

Okimoto, Jean Davies. (2000). *Talent Night.* Lincoln, NE: iuniverse.com.

Olaleye, Isaac. (1995). *The Distant Talking Drum.* Honesdale, PA: Boyds Mills.

Oliviero, Jamie. (1995). *The Day Sun Was Stolen.* New York: Hyperion.

Olson, Arielle. (1992). *Noah's Cats and the Devil's Fire.* Illus. Barry Moser. New York: Scholastic.

Oneal, Zibby. (1985). *In Summer Light.* New York: Viking.

Oneal, Zibby. (1986). *Grandma Moses: Painter of Rural America.* New York: Viking.

Oneal, Zibby. (1990). *A Long Way to Go.* New York: Viking.

O'Neill, Mary. (1973; 1989). *Hailstones and Halibut Bones.* Illus. John Wallner. New York: Doubleday.

Onyefulu, Ifeoma. (1975). *Emeka's Gift.* New York: Dutton.

Onyefulu, Ifeoma. (1993). *A Is for Africa.* New York: Dutton.

Onyefulu, Ifeoma. (1996). *Ogbo: Sharing Life in an African Village.* San Diego: Harcourt.

Onyefulu, Obi. (1994). *Chinye: A West African Folk Tale.* New York: Viking.

Opie, Iona. (1996). *My Very First Mother Goose.* Illus. Rosemary Wells. Cambridge: Candlewick.

Opie, Iona (Ed.). (1999). *Here Comes Mother Goose.* Illus. Rosemary Wells. Cambridge: Candlewick.

Opie, Iona, & Opie, Peter. (1951). *The Oxford Dictionary of Nursery Rhymes.* New York: Oxford University.

Opie, Iona, & Opie, Peter. (1955). *The Oxford Nursery Rhyme Book.* New York: Oxford University.

Opie, Iona, & Opie, Peter (Compilers). (1988). *Tail Feathers from Mother Goose: The Opie Rhyme Books.* Illus. various artists. Boston: Houghton.

Opkyke, Irene Gut. (1999). *In My Hands: Memories of a Holocaust Rescuer.* Contributor Jennifer Armstrong. New York: Knopf.

Oppenheim, Shulamith Levey. (1992). *The Lily Cupboard.* Illus. Ronald Himler. New York: HarperCollins.

Oppenheim, Shulamith Levey. (1995). *The Hundredth Name.* Honesdale, PA: Boyds Mills.

Orgel, Doris. (1994). *Ariadne, Awake!* New York: Viking.

Orlev, Uri. (1993). *Lydia, the Queen of Palestine.* Boston: Houghton.

Orlev, Uri. (1995). *The Lady with the Hat.* Boston: Houghton.

Ormerod, Jan, & Lloyd, David (Retellers). (1990). *The Frog Prince.* Illus. Jan Ormerod. New York: Lothrop, Lee & Shepard.

Ormerod, Jan. (1981). *Moonlight.* New York: Lothrop, Lee & Shepard.

Ormerod, Jan. (1981). *Sunshine.* New York: Lothrop, Lee & Shepard.

Ormerod, Jan. (1991). *When We Went to the Zoo.* New York: Lothrop, Lee & Shepard.

Ormerod, Jan. (1994). *Jan Ormerod's to Baby with Love.* New York: Lothrop, Lee & Shepard.

Orozco, Jose-Luis. (1994). *De Colores and Other Latin-American Folk Songs for Children.* New York: Dutton.

Orr, Katherine. (1990). *My Grandpa and the Sea.* Minneapolis, MN: Carolrhoda.

Ortiz Cofer, Judith. (1995). *An Island Like You: Stories of the Barrio.* New York: Scholastic.

Ortiz Cofer, Judith. (1995). *Reaching for the Mainland and Selected New Poems.* Tempe: Bilingual Press.

Ortiz Cofer, Judith. (1998). *The Year of Our Revolution: New and Selected Stories and Poems.* Houston: Arte Publico.

Osborne, Mary Pope. (1990). *The Many Lives of Benjamin Franklin.* New York: Dial.

Osborne, Mary Pope. (1991). *American Tall Tales.* New York: Knopf.

Osborne, Mary Pope. (1996). *Favorite Norse Myths.* New York: Scholastic.

Osborne, Mary Pope. (2000). *Adeline Falling Star.* New York: Scholastic.

Osborne, Mary Pope. (2000). *Kate and the Beanstalk.* Illus. Giselle Potter. New York: Atheneum.

Osofsky, Audrey. (1996). *Free to Dream: The Making of a Poet: Langston Hughes.* New York: Lothrop, Lee & Shepard.

Oughton, Jerrie. (1992). *How the Stars Fell Into the Sky: A Navajo Tale.* Illus. Lisa Desimini. Boston: Houghton.

Oughton, Jerrie. (1994). *Magic Weaver of Rugs: A Tale of the Navajo.* Boston: Houghton.

Oughton, Jerrie. (1995). *Music from a Place Called Half Moon.* Boston: Houghton.

Owens, Mary Beth. (1990). *A Caribou Alphabet.* New York: Farrar, Straus & Giroux.

Oxenbury, Helen. (1972). *ABC of Things.* New York: Delacorte.

Oxenbury, Helen. (1986). *I Can. I Hear. I See. I Touch.* (Boxed set). New York: Random House.

Oxenbury, Helen. (1991). *Mother's Helper.* New York: Dial.

Oxenbury, Helen. (1992). *Good Night, Good Morning.* New York: Dial.

Oxenbury, Helen. (1994). *The Important Visitor.* New York: Puffin.

Oz, Amos (Trans.). (1995). *Soumchi.* San Diego: Harcourt.

Paek, Min. (1988). *Aekyung's Dream.* San Francisco: Children's Book Press.

Palacios, Argentina. (1993). *A Christmas Surprise for Chabelita.* Mahwah, NJ: Bridgewater.

Paladino, Catherine. (1993). *Land, Sea, and Sky: Poems to Celebrate the Earth.* Boston: Little, Brown.

Panzer, Nora. (1995). *Celebrate America in Poetry and Art.* New York: Hyperion.

Parish, Peggy. (1977). *Teach Us, Amelia Bedelia.* Illus. Lynn Sweat. New York: Greenwillow.

Parish, Peggy. (1988). *Scruffy.* Illus. Kelly Oechsli. New York: HarperCollins.

Park, Barbara. (2000). *The Graduation of Jake Moon.* Illus. Paul Colin. New York: Atheneum.

Park, Linda Sue. (2000). *The Kite Fighters.* Illus. Eung Won Park. Boston: Houghton.

Parker, Nancy Winslow. (1991). *The President's Cabinet: And How It Grew.* New York: HarperCollins.

Parks, Gorday. (1994). *Arias in Silence.* Boston: Little Brown.

Parks, Rosa. (1992). *Rosa Parks: My Story.* New York: Dial.

Parley, Peter. (1827). *Tales of Peter Parley About America.* Mineola, NY: Dover Publications.

Parnall, Peter. (1991). *Marsh Cat.* New York: Macmillan.

Pascal, Francine. **Sweet Valley High** Series. New York: Bantam.

Patent, Dorothy Hinshaw. (1990). *Gray Wolf, Red Wolf.* Illus. William Munoz. Boston: Houghton.

Patent, Dorothy Hinshaw. (1991). *Way of the Grizzly.* New York: Clarion.

Patent, Dorothy Hinshaw. (1993). *Osprey.* New York: Clarion.

Patent, Dorothy Hinshaw. (1994). *The American Alligator.* New York: Clarion.

Patent, Dorothy Hinshaw. (1994). *Deer and Elk.* New York: Clarion.

Patent, Dorothy Hinshaw. (1998). *Fire: Friend or Foe?* Illus. William Munoz. Boston: Clarion.

Paterson, Katherine. (1973). *Sign of the Chrysanthemum.* Illus. Peter Lenda. New York: Crowell.

Paterson, Katherine. (1976). *Bridge to Terabithia.* Illus. Donna Diamond. New York: HarperCollins.

Paterson, Katherine. (1978). *The Great Gilly Hopkins.* New York: HarperCollins.

Paterson, Katherine. (1980). *Jacob Have I Loved.* New York: HarperCollins.

Paterson, Katherine. (1988). *Park's Quest.* New York: Lodestar.

Paterson, Katherine. (1989). *The Tale of the Mandarin Ducks.* New York: Lodestar.

Paterson, Katherine. (1991). *Lyddie.* New York: Dutton, Lodestar.

Paterson, Katherine. (1996). *Flip-Flop Girl.* New York: Puffin.

Paterson, Katherine. (1996). *The Angel and the Donkey.* New York: Clarion.

Paterson, Katherine. (1996). *Jip: His Story.* New York: Lodestar.

Paterson, Katherine. (2000). *Preacher's Boy.* Boston: Houghton.

Paton Walsh, Jill. (1978). *Chance Child.* New York: Farrar, Straus & Giroux.

Paton Walsh, Jill. (1978). *Children of the Fox.* New York: Farrar, Straus & Giroux.

Paton Walsh, Jill. (1982). *The Green Book.* New York: Farrar, Straus & Giroux.

Patrick, Denise Lewis. (1997). *The Adventures of Midnight Son.* New York: Holt.

Patrick, Denise Lewis. (1999). *The Longest Ride.* New York: Holt.

Paul, Ann Whitford. (1991). *Eight Hands Round: A Patchwork Alphabet.* Illus. Jeanette Winter. New York: HarperCollins.

Paul, Ann Whitford. (1999). *Everything to Spend the Night from A to Z.* Illus. Maggie Smith. New York: DK Publishing.

Paulsen, Gary. (1985). *Dogsong.* New York: Bradbury.

Paulsen, Gary. (1991). *The Winter Room.* New York: Scholastic.

Paulsen, Gary. (1993). *Harris and Me: A Summer Remembered.* San Diego: Harcourt.

Paulsen, Gary. (1994). *Mr. Tucket.* New York: Delacorte.

Paulsen, Gary. (1995). *Call Me Francis Tucket.* New York: Delacorte.

Paulsen, Gary. (1996). *Brian's Winter.* New York: Bantam Doubleday Dell.

Paulsen, Gary. (1998). *Soldier's Heart: A Novel of the Civil War.* New York: Delacorte.

Paulsen, Gary. (1999). *Alida's Song.* New York: Delacorte.

Paulsen, Gary. (1999). *Brian's Return.* New York: Delacorte.

Paulsen, Gary. (2000). *Hatchet.* New York: Simon & Schuster Children's Publishing.

Pausewang, Gudrun. (1994). *Fall-Out.* New York: Viking.

Paxton, Tom (Reteller). (1988). *Aesop's Fables.* New York: Morrow/Avon.

Paxton, Tom (Reteller). (1990). *Belling the Cat: And Other Aesop's Fables.* Illus. Robert Rayevsky. New York: Morrow/Avon.

Payne, Katherine. (1992). *Elephants Calling.* New York: Crown.

Pearce, Philippa. (1958; 1984). *Tom's Midnight Garden.* New York: HarperCollins.

Pearce, Philippa. (1981). *Who's Afraid? And Other Strange Stories.* New York: Greenwillow.

Pearce, Philippa. (1987). *Emily's Own Elephant.* Illus. John Lawrence. New York: Greenwillow.

Pearson, Gayle. (1993). *The Fog Doggies and Me.* New York: Simon & Schuster.

Pearson, Kit. (1990). *The Sky Is Falling.* New York: Viking.

Pearson, Kit. (1993). *The Lights Go on Again.* New York: Viking.

Peck, Richard. (1991). *Anonymously Yours.* Englewood Cliffs, NJ: Simon & Schuster, Messner.

Peck, Richard. (1998). *A Long Way from Chicago: A Novel in Stories.* New York: Dial.

Peck, Richard. (1998). *Strays Like Us.* Illus. Robert Hunt. New York: Dial.

Peck, Richard. (1999). *Amanda Miranda.* Illus. Robert Hunt. New York: Dial.

Peek, Merle. (1981). *Roll Over! A Counting Song.* New York: Clarion.

Peel, John. (1999). *2099: Doomsday.* New York: Scholastic.

Peet, Bill. (1989). *Bill Peet: An Autobiography.* Boston: Houghton.

Pelz, Ruth. (1989; o.p.). *Black Heroes of the Wild West.* Seattle: Open Hand.

Pennebaker, Ruth. (2000). *Both Sides Now.* New York: Holt.

Perham, Molly. (1993). *King Arthur: The Legends of Camelot.* New York: Viking.

Perkins, Lynne Ray. (1999). *All Alone in the Universe.* New York: Greenwillow.

Perrault, Charles. (1697; 1925). *Histoires ou Contes du Temps Passé avec Moralités (Stories of Long Ago with Morals).* London: Nonesuch.

Perrault, Charles. (1794). *Contes de Ma Mère L'oye (Tales of Mother Goose).* Haverhill, MA: Peter Edes.

Perrault, Charles. (1952). *Puss in Boots.* Illus. Marcia Brown. New York: Scribner's.

Perrault, Charles. (1954). *Cinderella.* Illus. Marcia Brown. New York: Scribner's.

Perrault, Charles. (1965). *Little Red Riding Hood.* Illus. Beni Montresor. New York: Knopf.

Perrault, Charles. (1980). *The Story of Sleeping Beauty.* New York: Harper Audio.

Perrault, Charles. (1989). *Cinderella and Other Tales from Perrault.* New York: Holt.

Perrault, Charles. (1990). *Puss in Boots.* Illus. Fred Marcellino. New York: Farrar, Straus & Giroux.

Perrault, Charles. (2000). *Cinderella, Puss in Boots, and Other Favorite Tales.* Trans. A. E. Johnson. New York: Abrams.

Peters, Lisa Westberg. (2000). *Cold Little Duck, Duck, Duck.* Illus. Sam Williams. New York: Greenwillow.

Peters, Russell. (1992). *Clambake: A Wampanoag Tradition.* Photog. John Madama. Minneapolis, MN: Lerner.

Peterson, Jeanne Whitehouse. (1994). *My Mama Sings.* New York: HarperCollins.

Petry, Ann. (1988). *Tituba of Salem Village.* New York: HarperCollins.

Pfeffer, Wendy. (1994). *From Tadpole to Frog.* New York: HarperCollins.

Philbrick, W. R. (1993). *Freak the Mighty.* New York: Scholastic.

Philbrick, W. R. (1998). *Max the Mighty.* New York: Scholastic.

Philip, Neil. (1987). *Tale of Sir Gawain.* New York: Philomel.

Philip, Neil. (1991). *Fairy Tales from Eastern Europe.* Illus. Larry Wilkes. New York: Clarion.

Philip, Neil. (1995). *Singing America: Poems That Define a Nation.* New York: Viking.

Philip, Neil. (1995). *Songs Are Thoughts: Poems of the Inuit.* New York: Scholastic.

Philip, Neil. (2000). *Celtic Fairy Tales.* Illus. Isabelle Brent. New York: Viking.

Pierce, Meredith Ann. (1982). *Dark Angel.* Boston: Little, Brown.

Pierce, Meredith Ann. (1985). *A Gathering of Gargoyles.* New York: Tor.

Pierce, Meredith Ann. (1990). *The Pearl of the Soul of the World.* Boston: Little, Brown.

Pierce, Tamora. (1983). *Alanna, the First Adventure.* New York: Atheneum.

Pierce, Tamora. (1984). *In the Hand of the Goddess.* New York: Atheneum.

Pierce, Tamora. (1986). *The Woman Who Rides Like a Man.* New York: Atheneum.

Pierce, Tamora. (1988). *Lionness Rampant.* New York: Atheneum.

Pierce, Tamora. (1992). *Wild Magic: The Immortals.* New York: Atheneum.

Pierce, Tamora. (1994). *Wolf Speaker.* New York: Atheneum.

Pierce, Tamora. (1995). *The Emperor Mage.* New York: Atheneum.

Pilkey, Dav. (2000). **Captain Underpants** Series. New York: Scholastic.

Pinczes, Elinor. (1995). *A Remainder of One.* Boston: Houghton.

Pinkney, Andrea Davis. (1993). *Alvin Ailey.* New York: Hyperion.

Pinkney, Andrea Davis. (1993). *Seven Candles for Kwanzaa.* Illus. Brian Pinkney. New York: Dial.

Pinkney, Andrea Davis. (1994). *Dear Benjamin Banneker.* San Diego: Harcourt.

Pinkney, Andrea Davis. (1995). *Hold Fast to Dreams.* New York: Morrow/Avon.

Pinkney, Andrea Davis. (1997). *Solo Girl.* Illus. Nneka Bennett. New York: Disney.

Pinkney, Andrea Davis. (1998). *Bill Pickett: Rodeo-Ridin' Cowboy.* Illus. Brian Pinkney. San Diego: Harcourt.

Pinkney, Andrea Davis. (1998). *Duke Ellington.* Illus. Brian Pinkney. New York: Disney.

Pinkney, Andrea Davis. (1998). *Raven in a Dove House.* New York: Gulliver.

Pinkney, Andrea Davis. (1999). *Silent Thunder: A Civil War Story.* New York: Hyperion.

Pinkney, Brian. (1995). *Jo Jo's Flying Sidekick.* New York: Simon & Schuster.

Pinkney, Brian. (1997). *The Adventures of Sparrowboy.* New York: Simon & Schuster.

Pinkney, Brian. (2000). *Cosmo and the Robot.* New York: Greenwillow.

Pinkney, Gloria. (1992). *Back Home.* New York: Dial.

Pinkney, Gloria. (1994). *The Sunday Outing.* New York: Dial.

Pinkney, Jerry. (2000). *Aesop's Fables.* New York: North-South.

Pinkwater, Daniel. (1978). *Alan Mendelsohn, the Boy from Mars.* New York: Dutton.

Pinkwater, Daniel. (1998). *The Education of Robert Nifkin.* New York: Farrar, Straus & Giroux.

Pinkwater, Daniel. (1999). *Ice Cream Larry.* Illus. Jill Pinkwater. New York: Cavendish.

Pinkwater, Manus. (1976; 1988). *Lizard Music.* New York: Bantam.

Pitcher, Caroline. (2000). *Mariana and the Merchild: A Folk Tale from Chile.* Illus. Jackie Morris. Grand Rapids: Eerdmans.

Pitre, Felix. (1995). *Paco and the Witch.* Illus. Christy Hale. New York: Lodestar.

Plotz, Helen (Ed.). (1988). *Week of Lullabies.* Illus. Marisabina Russo. New York: Greenwillow.

Plummer, Louise. (1995). *The Unlikely Romance of Kate Bjorkman.* New York: Bantam Doubleday Dell.

Plummer, Louise. (2000). *A Dance for Three.* New York: Bantam.

Poe, Edgar Allen. (1987). *Annabel Lee.* New York: Tundra.

Pohrt, Tom. (1995). *Coyote Goes Walking.* New York: Farrar, Straus & Giroux.

Polacco, Patricia. (1988). *The Keeping Quilt.* New York: Simon & Schuster.

Polacco, Patricia. (1994). *Pink and Say.* New York: Philomel.

Polacco, Patricia. (1995). *Babushka's Mother Goose.* New York: Philomel.

Polacco, Patricia. (1996). *Aunt Chip and the Great Triple Creek Dam Affair.* New York: Philomel.

Polacco, Patricia. (1998). *Thank You, Mr. Falker.* New York: Philomel.

Politi, Leo. (1949). *Song of the Swallows.* New York: Scribner's.

Pollock, Penny. (1996). *The Turkey Girl: A Zuni Cinderella Story.* Boston: Little, Brown.

Pomerantz, Charlotte. (1982; o.p.). *If I Had a Paka: Poems in Eleven Languages.* New York: Greenwillow.

Pomerantz, Charlotte. (1984). *One Duck, Another Duck.* New York: Greenwillow.

Pomerantz, Charlotte. (1989). *The Chalk Doll.* Illus. Frané Lessac. New York: HarperCollins.

Pomerantz, Charlotte. (1989). *Flap Your Wings and Try.* Illus. Nancy Tafuri. New York: Greenwillow.

Pomerantz, Charlotte. (1993). *Halfway to Your House: Poems.* New York: Greenwillow.

Poole, Josephine. (1998). *Joan of Arc.* Illus. Angela Barrett. New York: Knopf.

Pope, Elizabeth Marie. (1999). *The Perilous Gard.* Illus. Richard Cuffari. New York: Puffin.

Porte, Barbara. (1989). *Harry in Trouble.* Illus. Yossi Abolafia. New York: Greenwillow.

Porte, Barbara. (1994). *Harry's Birthday.* New York: Greenwillow.

Porte, Barbara. (1994). *Something Terrible Happened.* New York: Scholastic.

Porter, Eleanor. (1912). *Pollyanna.* Boston: Parnassus.

Potok, Chaim. (1998). *Zebra: and Other Stories.* New York: Knopf.

Potter, Beatrix. (1902). *The Tale of Peter Rabbit.* New York: Warne.

Potter, Beatrix. (1989). *The Journal of Beatrix Potter: 1881–1897.* New York: Warne.

Potter, Beatrix. (1995). *Beatrix Potter's Nursery Rhyme Book.* New York: Warne.

Powell, Randy. (1999). *Tribute to Another Dead Rock Star.* New York: Farrar, Straus & Giroux.

Powzyk, Joyce. (1988). *Tracking Wild Chimpanzees in Kibira National Park.* New York: Lothrop, Lee & Shepard.

Pratt, Kristin Joy. (1992). *A Walk in the Rain Forest.* Neveda City, CA: Dawn.

Pratt, Kristin Joy. (1994). *A Swim Through the Sea.* Neveda City, CA: Dawn.

Prelutsky, Jack. (1974). *Circus.* New York: Macmillan.

Prelutsky, Jack. (1976). *Nightmares: Poems to Trouble Your Sleep.* Illus. Arnold Lobel. New York: Greenwillow.

Prelutsky, Jack. (1978). *The Mean Old Mean Hyena.* Illus. Arnold Lobel. New York: Greenwillow.

Prelutsky, Jack (Selector). (1983). *The Random House Book of Poetry.* Illus. Arnold Lobel. New York: Random House.

Prelutsky, Jack. (1984). *The New Kid on the Block.* Illus. James Stevenson. New York: Greenwillow.

Prelutsky, Jack (Compiler). (1986). *Read-Aloud Rhymes for the Very Young.* Illus. Marc Brown. New York: Knopf.

Prelutsky, Jack. (1989). *The Baby Uggs Are Hatching.* New York: Greenwillow.

Prelutsky, Jack (Selector). (1989). *Poems of A. Nonny Mouse.* Illus. Henrik Drescher. New York: Knopf.

Prelutsky, Jack. (1990). *Beneath a Blue Umbrella.* Illus. Garth Williams. New York: Greenwillow.

Prelutsky, Jack. (1990). *Something Big Has Been Here.* Illus. James Stevenson. New York: Greenwillow.

Prelutsky, Jack (Selector). (1991). *For Laughing Out Loud: Poems to Tickle Your Funnybone.* Illus. Marjorie Priceman. New York: Knopf.

Prelutsky, Jack (Selector). (1993). *A. Nonny Mouse Writes Again: Poems.* New York: Knopf.

Prelutsky, Jack. (1993). *Dragons Are Singing Tonight.* New York: Greenwillow.

Prelutsky, Jack. (1996). *A Pizza the Size of the Sun.* New York: Greenwillow.

Pressler, Mirjam. (1998). *Halinka.* Trans. Elizabeth D. Crawford. New York: Holt.

Pressler, Mirjam. (2000). *Anne Frank: A Hidden Life.* Trans. Anthea Bell. New York: Dutton.

Pressler, Mirjam. (2000). *Halinka.* Trans. Elizabeth D. Crawford. New York: Laureleaf.

Price, Leontyne. (1990). *Aïda.* Illus. Leo and Diane Dillon. San Diego: Harcourt.

Priceman, Marjorie. (1994). *How to Make an Apple Pie and See the World.* New York: Knopf.

Pringle, Laurence. (1977). *Elephant Woman: Cynthia Moss Explores the World of Elephants.* New York: Atheneum.

Pringle, Laurence. (1990). *Saving Our Wildlife.* Hillside, NJ: Enslow.

Pringle, Laurence. (1991). *Living Treasure: Saving Earth's Threatened Biodiversity.* Illus. Irene Brady. New York: Morrow/Avon.

Priomos, James. (1999). *The Loudness of Sam.* San Diego: Harcourt.

Proddow, Penelope. (1979; o.p.). *Art Tells a Story: Greek and Roman Myths.* New York: Doubleday.

Propp, Vera. (1999). *When the Soldiers Were Gone.* New York: Putnam.

Provensen, Alice. (1990). *The Buck Stops Here: The Presidents of the United States.* New York: HarperCollins.

Provensen, Alice, & Provensen, Martin. (1976 Reissue). *The Mother Goose Book.* New York: Random House.

Provensen, Alice, & Provensen, Martin. (1984). *Leonardo Da Vinci: The Artist, Inventor, Scientist in Three-Dimensional Movable Pictures.* New York: Viking.

Pryor, Bonnie. (1988). *Seth of the Lion People.* New York: Morrow/Avon.

Pryor, Bonnie. (1996). *The Dream Jar.* New York: Morrow/Avon.

Pullman, Philip. (1997). *The Subtle Knife.* New York: Random House.

Pullman, Philip. (2000). *The Amber Spyglass.* New York: Knopf.

Pullman, Philip. (2000). *I Was a Rat.* Illus. Kevin Hawkes. New York: Knopf.

Pyle, Howard. (1903; 1968). *The Story of King Arthur and His Knights.* Illus. N. C. Wyeth. New York: Scribner's.

Pyle, Howard. (1913; 1968). *The Merry Adventures of Robin Hood of Great Renown in Nottinghamshire.* New York: Scribner's.

Qualey, Marsha. (1993). *Revolutions of the Heart.* Boston: Houghton.

Qualey, Marsha. (1995). *Hometown.* Boston: Houghton.

Quayle, Eric (Reteller). (1989). *The Shining Princess and Other Japanese Legends.* Boston: Arcade.

Rabin, Staton. (1994). *Casey Over There.* Illus. Greg Shed. San Diego: Harcourt.

Raboff, Ernest. (1987). *Leonardo Da Vinci.* New York: HarperCollins.

Raboff, Ernest. (1987). *Pablo Picasso.* New York: HarperCollins.

Raboff, Ernest. (1988). *Albrecht Dürer.* New York: HarperCollins.

Raboff, Ernest. (1988). *Michelangelo Buonarroti.* New York: HarperCollins.

Radin, Ruth Yaffee. (1989). *High in the Mountains.* Illus. Ed Young. New York: Macmillan.

Radinovici, Schoschana. (2000). *Thanks to My Mother.* Trans. James Skofield. New York: Dial.

Rael, Elsa Okon. (1993). *Marushka's Egg.* New York: Simon & Schuster.

Raffi. (1992). *Five Little Ducks.* Illus. José Aruego and Ariane Dewey. New York: Crown.

Raffi. (1995). *Raffi's Top Ten Songs to Read.* New York: Crown.

Raimondo, Lois. (1994). *The Little Llama of Tibet.* New York: Scholastic.

Rana, Indi. (1991). *The Roller Birds of Rambur.* New York: Holt.

Randle, Kristen D. (1999). *Breaking Rank.* New York: Morrow/Avon.

Randsom, Candace F. (2000). *Danger at Sand Cave.* Illus. Den Schofield. Minneapolis, MN: Carolrhoda.

Rankin, Laura. (1991). *The Handmade Alphabet.* New York: Dial.

Ransome, Arthur (Reteller). (1968). *The Fool of the World and the Flying Ship: A Russian Tale.* Illus. Uri Shulevitz. New York: Farrar, Straus & Giroux.

Rappaport, Doreen. (1988). *The Boston Coffee Party.* Illus. Emily Arnold McCully. New York: HarperCollins.

Rappaport, Doreen. (1991). *Escape from Slavery: Five Journeys to Freedom.* New York: HarperCollins.

Raschka, Chris. (1996). *The Blushful Hippopotamus.* New York: Jackson/Orchard.

Raskin, Ellen. (1966). *Nothing Ever Happens on My Block.* New York: Atheneum.

Raskin, Ellen. (1978). *The Westing Game.* New York: Dutton.

Rathmann, Peggy. (1995). *Good Night, Gorilla.* New York: Putnam.

Rathmann, Peggy. (1995). *Officer Buckle and Gloria.* New York: Putnam.

Rattigan, Jama Kim. (1993). *Dumpling Soup.* Boston: Little, Brown.

Rauzon, Mark J. (1993). *Horns, Antlers, Fangs, and Tusks.* New York: Lothrop, Lee & Shepard.

Rauzon, Mark J. (1993). *Skin, Scales, Feathers, and Fur.* New York: Lothrop, Lee & Shepard.

Ray, Deborah Kogan. (1990). *My Daddy Was a Soldier.* New York: Holt.

Ray, Delia. (1990). *A Nation Torn: The Story of How the Civil War Began.* New York: Dutton.

Ray, Delia. (1991). *Behind the Blue and Gray: The Soldier's Life in the Civil War.* New York: Dutton.

Ray, Jane. (1990). *Noah's Ark: Words from the Book of Genesis.* New York: Dutton.

Ray, Mary Lyn. (1994). *Alvah and Arvilla.* San Diego: Harcourt.

Ray, Mary Lyn. (1994). *Shaker Boy.* San Diego: Harcourt.

Ray, Mary Lyn. (1999). *Basket Moon.* Boston: Little, Brown.

Rayevsky, Inna (Reteller). (1990). *The Talking Tree: An Old Italian Tale.* Illus. Robert Rayevsky. New York: Putnam.

Recorvitz, Helen. (1999). *Goodbye, Walter Malenski.* Illus. Lloyd Bloom. New York: Foster.

Reddix, Valerie. (1991). *Dragon Kite of the Autumn Moon.* New York: Lothrop, Lee & Shepard.

Reeder, Carolyn. (1989). *Shades of Gray.* New York: Macmillan.

Reeder, Carolyn. (1991). *Grandpa's Mountain.* New York: Macmillan.

Reeder, Carolyn. (1993). *Moonshiner's Son.* New York: Macmillan.

Reef, Catherine. (1995). *Walt Whitman.* New York: Clarion.

Regguinti, Gordon. (1992). *The Sacred Harvest: Ojibway Wild Rice Gathering.* Minneapolis, MN: Lerner.

Reid, Barbara. (1993). *Two by Two.* New York: Scholastic.

Reiser, Lynn. (1998). *Tortillas and Lullabies/Tortillas y Cancioncitas.* Illus. Corazones Valientes. New York: Greenwillow.

Reiss, Johanna. (1976). *The Journey Back.* New York: Crowell.

Reiss, Johanna. (1987). *The Upstairs Room.* New York: HarperCollins.

Reisser, Lynn. (1995). *Two Mice in Three Fables.* New York: Greenwillow.

Reit, Seymour. (1989). *Behind Rebel Lines: The Incredible Story of Emma Edmonds, Civil War Spy.* San Diego: Harcourt.

Rennison, Louise. (2000). *Angus, Thongs and Full Frontal Snoggings: Confessions of Georgia Nicolson.* New York: HarperCollins.

Reuter, Bjarne. (1994). *The Boys from St. Petri.* New York: Dutton.

Rey, Margaret, & Rey, H. A. (2000). *Whiteblack the Penguin Sees the World.* Boston: Houghton.

Rice, Edward. (1978). *Ten Religions of the East.* New York: Simon & Schuster.

Richler, Mordecai. (1975; 1998). *Jacob Two-Two Meets the Hooded Fang.* Illus. Franz Wegner. Montreal: Tundra.

Richmond, Robin. (1992). *Introducing Michelangelo.* Boston: Little, Brown.

Ride, Sally. (1986). *To Space and Back.* New York: Lothrop, Lee & Shepard.

Ride, Sally, & O'Shaughnessey, Tam. (1999). *The Mystery of Mars.* New York: Crown.

Ride, Sally, & O'Shaughnessy, Tam. (1994). *The Third Planet: Exploring the Earth from Space.* New York: Crown.

Ridlon, Marci. (1996). *Sun Through the Window.* Honesdale, PA: Boyds Mills.

Riley, Linda Capus. (1995). *Elephants Swim.* Boston: Houghton.

Rinaldi, Ann. (1986). *Time Enough for Drums.* New York: Holiday House.

Rinaldi, Ann. (1992). *A Break with Charity: A Story About the Salem Witch Trials.* San Diego: Harcourt.

Rinard, Judith E. (1987). *Wildlife, Making a Comeback: How Humans Are Helping.* Washington, DC: National Geographic.

Ringgold, Faith. (1991). *Tar Beach.* New York: Crown.

Ringgold, Faith. (1995). *My Dream of Martin Luther King.* New York: Crown.

Ringgold, Faith, Freeman, Linda, & Roucher, Nancy. (1996). *Talking to Faith Ringgold.* New York: Crown.

Ritter, Lawrence S. (1995). *Leagues Apart: The Men and Times of the Negro Baseball Leagues.* New York: Morrow/Avon.

Ritter, Lawrence S. (1999). *The Story of Baseball.* New York: Morrow/Avon.

Roalf, Peggy. (1992). *Dancers (Looking at Paintings).* New York: Hyperion.

Roalf, Peggy. (1993). *Children (Looking at Paintings).* New York: Hyperion.

Roalf, Peggy. (1993). *Flowers (Looking at Paintings).* New York: Hyperion.

Robart, Rose. (1987). *The Cake That Mack Ate.* Illus. Maryann Kovalski. Boston: Little Brown.

Robbins, Ken. (1990). *A Flower Grows.* New York: Dial.

Robbins, Ken. (1994). *Water: The Elements.* New York: Holt.

Robbins, Ken. (1995). *Air: The Elements.* New York: Holt.

Robbins, Ken. (1996). *Fire: The Elements.* New York: Holt.

Roberts, Bethany. (1995). *A Mouse Told His Mother.* Boston: Little, Brown.

Roberts, Willo Davis. (1975). *The View from the Cherry Tree.* New York: Atheneum.

Roberts, Willo Davis. (1989). *What Could Go Wrong?* New York: Atheneum.

Roberts, Willo Davis. (1996). *Twisted Summer.* New York: Atheneum.

Robertson, James I., Jr. (1997). *Civil War! America Becomes One Nation.* New York: Knopf.

Robinet, Harriette Gillem. (1995). *If You Please, President Lincoln.* New York: Atheneum.

Robinet, Harriette Gillem. (1996). *Washington City Is Burning.* Illus. Gabriela Gonzalez Dellosso. New York: Atheneum.

Robinet, Harriette Gillem. (1997). *Mississippi Chariot.* Madison: Turtleback Books.

Robinet, Harriette Gillem. (1997). *The Twins, the Pirates and the Battle of New Orleans.* Illus. Keinyo White. New York: Atheneum.

Robinet, Harriette Gillem. (2000). *Forty Acres and Maybe a Mule.* New York: Aladdin.

Robinson, Margaret A. (1990). *A Woman of Her Tribe.* New York: Scribner's.

Rochman, Hazel, & McCampbell, Darlene Z. (1995). *Bearing Witness: Stories of the Holocaust.* New York: Scholastic.

Rockwell, Anne. (1973). *My Doctor.* New York: Macmillan.

Rockwell, Anne. (2000). *The Boy Who Wouldn't Obey: A Mayan Legend.* New York: Greenwillow.

Rockwell, Harlow. (1987). *My Nursery School.* New York: Puffin.

Rockwell, Thomas. (1973). *How to Eat Fried Worms.* New York: Watts.

Rodanas, Kristina. (1991). *Dragonfly's Tale.* New York: Clarion.

Rodanas, Kristina. (1994). *Dance of the Sacred Circle: A Native American Tale.* Boston: Little, Brown.

Rodari, Florian. (1992). *A Weekend with Picasso.* New York: Rizzoli.

Rodari, Florian. (1993). *A Weekend with Velázquez.* New York: Rizzoli.

Rodari, Florian. (1994). *A Weekend with Matisse.* New York: Rizzoli.

Rodnas, Kristina. (1995). *The Eagle's Song: A Tale from the Pacific Northwest.* Boston: Little, Brown.

Rodnas, Kristina. (1998). *Follow the Stars: A Native American Woodlands Tale.* New York: Cavendish.

Rodowsky, Colby. (1994). *Hannah in Between.* New York: Farrar, Straus & Giroux.

Rodowsky, Colby. (1995). *Sydney, Invincible.* New York: Farrar, Straus & Giroux.

Rodowsky, Colby. (1999). *Not My Dog.* New York: Farrar, Straus & Giroux.

Roe, Eileen. (1991). *Con Mi Hermano: With My Brother.* New York: Bradbury.

Roessel, Monty. (1993). *Kinaaldá: A Navajo Girl Grows Up.* New York: Lerner.

Roessel, Monty. (1995). *Songs from the Loom: A Navajo Girl Learns to Weave.* New York: Lerner.

Rogasky, Barbara. (1994). *Winter Poems.* New York: Scholastic.

Rogers, Jean. (1988). *Runaway Mittens.* Illus. Rie Munoz. New York: Greenwillow.

Rollins, Charlemae Hill. (1963; 1993). *Christmas Gif': An Anthology of Christmas Poems, Songs, and Stories Written by and About African Americans.* New York: Morrow/Avon.

Rood, Ronald. (1993). *Tide Pools.* New York: HarperCollins.

Roop, Peter, & Roop, Connie. (1986). *Buttons for General Washington.* Minneapolis, MN: Carolrhoda.

Roop, Peter, & Roop, Connie. (1992). *Ahyoka and the Talking Leaves.* New York: Lothrop, Lee & Shepard.

Roop, Peter, & Roop, Connie. (1999). *Girl of the Shining Mountains: Sacagawea's Story.* New York: Hyperion.

Rosa-Casanova, Sylvia. (1997). *Mama Provia and the Pot of Rice.* Illus. Robert Roth. New York: Atheneum.

Roscoe, William. (1807). *The Butterfly's Ball.* London: Harris.

Rosen, Michael J. (1992). *Elijah's Angel: A Story for Chanukah and Christmas.* Illus. Aminah Brenda Lynn Robinson. San Diego: Harcourt.

Rosen, Michael J. (1992). *How the Animals Got Their Colors: Animal Myths from Around the World.* San Diego: Harcourt.

Rosen, Michael J. (1992). *The Greatest Table: A Banquet to Fight Against Hunger.* San Diego: Harcourt.

Rosen, Michael. (1989). *We're Going on a Bear Hunt.* New York: Macmillan, McElderry.

Rosenberg, Maxine B. (1991). *Brothers and Sisters.* Photog. George Ancona. Boston: Houghton.

Rosenberg, Maxine B. (1994). *Hiding to Survive: Fourteen Jewish Children and the Gentiles Who Rescued Them from the Holocaust.* New York: Clarion.

Rosenberry, Vera. (1999). *Vera's First Day of School.* New York: Holt.

Ross, Adrienne. (2001). *In the Quiet.* New York: Bantam.

Ross, Amy Goldman. (2000). *The Girls.* Illus. Cliff Nielsen. New York: Dial.

Ross, Gayle. (1994). *How Rabbit Tricked Otter and Other Cherokee Trickster Stories.* New York: HarperCollins.

Ross, Gayle. (1995). *How Turtle's Back Was Cracked: A Traditional Cherokee Tale.* New York: Dial.

Ross, Gayle. (1996). *The Legend of the Windigo: A Tale from Native North America.* Illus. Murv Jacob. New York: Dial.

Rostkowski, Margaret. (1986). *After the Dancing Days.* New York: HarperCollins.

Rostkowski, Margaret. (1989). *The Best of Friends.* New York: HarperCollins.

Roth, Susan. (1990). *Marco Polo: His Notebook.* New York: Doubleday.

Rotner, Shelley. (1993). *Ocean Day.* New York: Macmillan.

Rotner, Shelley. (1995). *Wheels Around.* Boston: Houghton.

Rotner, Shelley, & Kreisler, Ken. (1994). *Faces.* New York: Macmillan.

Rounds, Glen. (1984). *The Morning the Sun Refused to Rise: An Original Paul Bunyan Tale.* New York: Holiday House.

Rounds, Glen. (1995). *Sod Houses on the Great Plains.* New York: Holiday House.

Rounds, Glen. (1999). *Beaver.* New York: Holiday House.

Rousseau, Jean-Jacques. (1762). *Émile.*

Rowling, J. K. (1998). *Harry Potter and the Sorcerer's Stone.* Illus. Mary Grandpre. New York: Scholastic.

Rowling, J. K. (1999). *Harry Potter and the Chamber of Secrets.* Illus. Mary Grandpre. New York: Scholastic.

Rowling, J. K. (1999). *Harry Potter and the Prisoner of Azkeban.* Illus. Mary Grandpre. New York: Scholastic.

Rowling, J. K. (2000). *Harry Potter and the Goblet of Fire.* Illus. Mary Grandpre. New York: Scholastic.

Rubalcaba, Jull. (1995). *Uncegila's Seventh Spot: A Lakota Legend.* Illus. Irving Toddy. Boston: Clarion.

Rubenstein, G. (1988). *Space Demons.* New York: Dial.

Rubenstein, G. (1995). *Galax-Arena: A Novel.* New York: Simon & Schuster.

Rubin, Susan Goldman. (1998). *Toilets, Toaster, and Telephones: The How and Why of Everyday Objects.* Illus. Elsa Warnick. San Diego: Harcourt.

Rubin, Susan Goldman. (2000). *Fireflies in the Dark: The Story of Freidl Decker-Brandeis and the Children of Terezen.* New York: Holiday House.

Ruby, Lois. (1994). *Steal Away Home.* New York: Macmillan.

Ruby, Lois. (2000). *Soon Be Free.* New York: Simon & Schuster.

Runningwolf, Michael B., & Smith, Patricia Clark. (2000). *On the Trail of Elder Brother: Glous'gap Stories of the Micmac Indians.* Illus. Michael B. Running Wolf. New York: Persea.

Rupert, Janet. (1994). *The African Mask.* Boston: Houghton.

Russell, Ching Yeung. (1994). *First Apple.* Honesdale, PA: Boyds Mills.

Russell, Ching Yeung. (1995). *Water Ghost.* Honesdale, PA: Boyds Mills.

Russell, William F. (1989). *Classic Myths to Read Aloud.* New York: Crown.

Ruth, Maria Mudd. (1998). *Firefighting Behind the Scenes.* Boston: Houghton.

Ryan, Pam Munoz. (1994). *One Hundred Is a Family.* New York: Hyperion.

Ryan, Pam Munoz. (1999). *Amelia and Eleanor Go for a Ride.* Illus. Brian Selznick. New York: Scholastic.

Ryden, Hope. (1992). *The Raggedy Red Squirrel.* New York: Dutton.

Ryden, Hope. (1994). *Joey: The Story of a Baby Kangaroo.* New York: Tambourine.

Ryden, Hope. (1999). *Wild Horses I Have Known.* Boston: Clarion.

Ryder, Joanne. (1982). *The Snail's Spell.* New York: Warne.

Rylant, Cynthia. (1982). *When I Was Young in the Mountains.* Illus. Diane Goode. New York: Dutton.

Rylant, Cynthia. (1984). *Waiting to Waltz: A Childhood.* Illus. Stephen Gammell. New York: Bradbury.

Rylant, Cynthia. (1985). *Every Living Thing.* Illus. S. D. Schindler. New York: Bradbury.

Rylant, Cynthia. (1985). *The Relatives Came.* New York: Bradbury.

Rylant, Cynthia. (1986). *A Fine White Dust.* New York: Bradbury.

Rylant, Cynthia. (1987). *Henry and Mudge in the Green Time.* New York: Bradbury.

Rylant, Cynthia. (1987). *Henry and Mudge Under the Yellow Moon.* New York: Bradbury.

Rylant, Cynthia. (1987). *Henry and Mudge: The First Book.* Illus. Suçie Stevenson. New York: Bradbury.

Rylant, Cynthia. (1988). *All I See.* Illus. Peter Catalanotto. New York: Scholastic.

Rylant, Cynthia. (1989). *But I'll Be Back Again: An Album.* New York: Scholastic.

Rylant, Cynthia. (1989). *Henry and Mudge Get the Cold Shivers.* Illus. Suçie Stevenson. New York: Bradbury.

Rylant, Cynthia. (1991). *Appalachia: The Voices of Sleeping Birds.* Illus. Barry Moser. San Diego: Harcourt.

Rylant, Cynthia. (1991). *Henry and Mudge and the Bedtime Thumps.* Illus. Suçie Stevenson. New York: Bradbury.

Rylant, Cynthia. (1991). *Henry and Mudge Take the Big Test.* Illus. Suçie Stevenson. New York: Bradbury.

Rylant, Cynthia. (1992). *Best Wishes.* Illus. Carlo Ontal. Katonah, NY: Richard C. Owen.

Rylant, Cynthia. (1992). *Henry and Mudge and the Long Weekend.* Illus. Suçie Stevenson. New York: Bradbury.

Rylant, Cynthia. (1992). *Missing May.* New York: Scholastic.

Rylant, Cynthia. (1993). *I Had Seen Castles.* San Diego: Harcourt.

Rylant, Cynthia. (1994). *Henry and Mudge and the Careful Cousin: The 13th Book of Their Adventures.* New York: Bradbury.

Rylant, Cynthia. (1994). *Mr. Putter and Tabby Walk the Dog.* San Diego: Harcourt.

Rylant, Cynthia. (1995). *Henry and Mudge and the Best Day of All: The 14th Book of Their Adventures.* New York: Macmillan.

Rylant, Cynthia. (1996). *The Old Woman Who Named Things.* San Diego: Harcourt.

Rylant, Cynthia. (2000). *Henry and Mudge and Annie's Perfect Pet: The Twentieth Book of Their Adventures.* Illus. Suçie Stevenson. New York: Simon & Schuster.

Sabuda, Robert. (1992). *Saint Valentine.* New York: Atheneum.

Sabuda, Robert. (1995). *Arthur and the Sword.* New York: Atheneum.

Sachar, Louis. (1987). *There's a Boy in the Girl's Bathroom.* New York: Knopf.

Sachar, Louis. (1998). *Holes.* New York: Farrar, Straus & Giroux.

Sachar, Louis. (1999). **Marvin Redpost** Series. New York: Random House.

Sachs, Marilyn. (1987). *Bear's House.* New York: Dutton.

Sachs, Marilyn. (1987). *Fran Ellen's House.* New York: Dutton.

Sachs, Marilyn. (1995). *Thirteen Going on Seven.* New York: Puffin.

Sachs, Marilyn. (1998). *Surprise Party.* New York: Dutton.

Sage, Alison (Reteller). (1991). *Rumpelstiltskin.* Illus. Gennady Spirin. New York: Dial.

Sakai, Kimiko. (1990). *Sachiko Means Happiness.* San Francisco: Children's Book Press.

Salisbury, Graham. (1998). *Jungle Dogs.* New York: Delacorte.

Salkin, Jeffery K. (1998). *For Kids—Putting God on Your Guest List: How to Claim the Spiritual Meaning of Your Bar or Bat Mitzvah.* New York: Jewish Lights.

Samton, Sheila. (1991). *Jenny's Journey/El Viaje de Jenny.* New York: Viking.

San Jose, Christine. (1994). *Cinderella.* Honesdale, PA: Boyds Mills.

San Souci, Robert. (1990). *The Talking Eggs: A Folktale from the American South.* Illus. Jerry Pinkney. New York: Dial.

San Souci, Robert. (1991). *Larger Than Life: The Adventures of American Legendary Heroes.* New York: Doubleday.

San Souci, Robert. (1992). *Sukey and the Mermaid.* Illus. Brian Pinkney. New York: Simon & Schuster.

San Souci, Robert. (1993). *Cut from the Same Cloth: American Women of Myth, Legend, and Tall Tale.* New York: Philomel.

San Souci, Robert. (1993). *Young Guinevere.* New York: Doubleday.

San Souci, Robert. (1994). *Sootface: An Ojibwa Cinderella Story.* New York: Doubleday.

San Souci, Robert. (1995). *The Faithful Friend.* Illus. Brian Pinkney. New York: Simon & Schuster.

San Souci, Robert. (1995). *Kate Shelley: Bound for Legend.* New York: Dial.

Sancha, Sheila. (1989). *Walter Dragun's Town: Crafts and Trade in the Middle Ages.* New York: HarperCollins.

Sandburg, Carl. (1995). *Poetry for Young People.* New York: Sterling.

Sanders, Scott. (1989). *Aurora Means Dawn.* Illus. Jill Kastner. New York: Bradbury.

Sandin, Joan. (1981). *The Long Way to a New Land.* New York: HarperCollins.

Sandin, Joan. (1989). *The Long Way Westward.* New York: HarperCollins.

Sanfield, Steve. (1995). *Strudel, Strudel, Strudel.* New York: Scholastic.

Sargent, Sara. (1986). *Watermusic.* New York: Clarion.

Sattler, Helen Roney. (1990). *Giraffes, the Sentinels of the Savannas.* Illus. Christopher Santoro. New York: Lothrop, Lee & Shepard.

Sattler, Helen Roney. (1992). *Stegosaurs: The Solar-Powered Dinosaurs.* New York: Lothrop, Lee & Shepard.

Sattler, Helen Roney. (1995). *The Book of North American Owls.* New York: Clarion.

Sauerwein, Leigh. (1994). *The Way Home.* New York: Farrar, Straus & Giroux.

Sawyer, Ruth. (1936). *Roller Skates.* New York: Viking.

Sawyer, Ruth. (1994). *The Remarkable Christmas of the Cobbler's Sons.* New York: Viking.

Say, Allen. (1982). *Bicycle Man.* Boston: Houghton.

Say, Allen. (1989). *Lost Lake.* Boston: Houghton.

Say, Allen. (1990). *El Chino.* Boston: Houghton.

Say, Allen. (1991). *Tree of Cranes.* Boston: Houghton.

Say, Allen. (1993). *Grandfather's Journey.* Boston: Houghton.

Say, Allen. (1996). *Emma's Rug.* New York: Lorraine/Houghton.

Say, Allen. (1999). *Tea with Milk.* Boston: Houghton.

Schaefer, Lola M. (2000). *This Is the Sunflower.* New York: Greenwillow.

Schermbrucker, Reviva. (1991). *Charlie's House.* Illus. Niki Daly. New York: Viking.

Schertle, Alice. (1994). *How Now, Brown Cow?* San Diego: Harcourt.

Schertle, Alice. (1995). *Down the Road.* San Diego: Harcourt.

Schlein, Miriam. (1990). *The Year of the Panda.* Illus. Kam Mak. New York: HarperCollins.

Schlissel, Lillian. (1993). *The Way West: Journal of a Pioneer Woman.* New York: Simon & Schuster.

Schlissel, Lillian. (1995). *Black Frontiers: A History of African American Heroes in the Old West.* New York: Simon & Schuster.

Schnur, Steven. (1994). *The Shadow Children.* New York: Morrow/Avon.

Schon, Isabel. (1983). *Dona Blanca and Other Hispanic Nursery Rhymes and Games.* Minneapolis, MN: Denison.

Schorsch, Nancy T. (1991). *Saving the Condor.* New York: Watts.

Schroeder, Alan. (1989). *Ragtime Tumpie.* Illus. Bernie Fuchs. Boston: Little, Brown.

Schroeder, Alan. (1996). *Minty: A Story of Young Harriet Tubman.* Illus. Jerry Pinkney. New York: Dial.

Schroeder, Alan. (1996). *Satchmo's Blues.* New York: Doubleday.

Schroeder, Alan. (1999). *The Tale of Willie Monroe.* Illus. Andrew Glass. Boston: Clarion.

Schuett, Stacey. (1995). *Somewhere in the World Right Now.* New York: Knopf.

Schur, Maxine. (1994). *Day of Delight: A Jewish Sabbath in Ethiopia.* New York: Dial.

Schur, Maxine. (1996). *When I Left My Village.* New York: Dial.

Schwartz, Alvin. (1973). *Witcracks: Jokes and Jests from American Folklore.* Illus. John O'Brien. New York: HarperCollins.

Schwartz, Alvin. (1975; 1990). *Whoppers: Tall Tales and Other Lies.* New York: HarperCollins.

Schwartz, Alvin. (1980). *Flapdoodle: Pure Nonsense from American Folklore.* New York: HarperCollins.

Schwartz, Alvin. (1989). *I Saw You in the Bathtub and Other Folk Rhymes.* Illus. Syd Hoff. New York: HarperCollins.

Schwartz, Alvin. (1992). *And the Green Grass Grew All Around.* Illus. Sue Truesdell. New York: HarperCollins.

Schwartz, Amy. (1988). *Annabelle Swift, Kindergartner.* New York: Scholastic.

Schwartz, Amy. (1999). *Old MacDonald.* New York: Scholastic.

Schwartz, David. (1985). *How Much Is a Million?* Illus. Steven Kellogg. New York: Lothrop, Lee & Shepard.

Schwartz, David. (1989). *If You Made a Million.* Illus. Steven Kellogg. New York: Lothrop, Lee & Shepard.

Schwartz, Howard, & Rush, Barbara. (1992). *The Sabbath Lion: A Jewish Folktale from Algeria.* New York: HarperCollins.

Scieszka, Jon. (1989). *The True Story of the Three Little Pigs.* Illus. Lane Smith. New York: Viking.

Scieszka, Jon. (1991). *The Frog Prince Continued.* Illus. Steve Johnson. New York: Viking.

Scieszka, Jon. (1991). *Knights of the Kitchen Table.* New York: Viking.

Scieszka, Jon. (1991). *The Not-So-Jolly Roger.* New York: Viking.

Scieszka, Jon. (1992). *The Good, the Bad, and the Goofy.* New York: Viking.

Scieszka, Jon. (1992). *The Stinky Cheese Man: And Other Fairly Stupid Tales.* Illus. Lane Smith. New York: Viking.

Scieszka, Jon. (1993). *Your Mother Was a Neanderthal.* New York: Viking.

Scieszka, Jon. (1995). *Math Curse.* New York: Viking.

Scieszka, Jon. (1997). *2095.* New York: Puffin.

Scieszka, Jon. (1998). *Summer Reading Is Killing Me.* New York: Viking.

Scieszka, Jon. (1998). *Tut Tut.* New York: Turtleback.

Scieszka, Jon. (1999). *It's All Greek to Me.* New York: Viking.

Scott, Ann Herbert. (1993). *Cowboy Country.* New York: Clarion.

Scott, Elaine. (1998). *Close Encounters: Exploring the Universe with the Hubble Space Telescope.* New York: Disney.

Scott, Jack Denton. (1988). *Swans.* Photog. Ozzie Sweet. New York: Putnam.

Segal, Lore. (1970). *Tell Me a Mitzi.* Illus. Harriet Pincus. New York: Farrar, Straus & Giroux.

Segal, Lore. (1977). *Tell Me a Trudy.* Illus. Rosemary Wells. New York: Farrar, Straus & Giroux.

Segal, Lore. (1987). *The Book of Adam to Moses.* Illus. Leonard Baskin. New York: Schocken.

Selden, George. (1960). *Cricket in Times Square.* New York: Farrar, Straus & Giroux.

Selden, George. (1969). *Tucker's Countryside.* New York: Farrar, Straus & Giroux.

Selden, George. (1987). *Old Meadow.* New York: Farrar, Straus & Giroux.

Selsam, Millicent E. (1976). *Popcorn.* New York: Morrow/Avon.

Selsam, Millicent E. (1995). *How to Be a Nature Detective.* New York: HarperCollins.

Semel, Nava. (1995). *Flying Lessons.* New York: Simon & Schuster.

Sendak, Maurice. (1962). *Pierre: A Cautionary Tale in Five Chapters and a Prologue.* New York: HarperCollins.

Sendak, Maurice. (1963). *Where the Wild Things Are.* New York: HarperCollins.

Sendak, Maurice. (1981). *Outside Over There.* Illus. Janeyee Young. New York: HarperCollins.

Sendak, Maurice, & Margolis, Matthew. (1976). *Some Swell Pup: Or, Are You Sure You Want a Dog?* New York: Farrar, Straus & Giroux.

Serfozo, Mary. (1988). *Who Said Red?* Illus. Keiko Narahashi. New York: McElderry.

Service, Pamela. (1988). *Stinker from Space.* New York: Scribner's.

Service, Pamela. (1992). *Weirdos of the Universe, Unite!* New York: Atheneum.

Service, Pamela. (1993). *Stinker's Return.* New York: Scribner's.

Seuss, Dr. (1958). *Yertle the Turtle.* New York: Random House.

Seuss, Dr. (1961). *Sneetches and Other Stories.* New York: Random House.

Seuss, Dr. (1971). *The Lorax.* New York: Random House.

Seuss, Dr. (1990). *Oh, the Places You'll Go!* New York: Random House.

Severance, John B. (1999). *Einstein: Visionary Scientist.* New York: Clarion.

Severance, John B. (2000). *Skyscrapers: How America Grew Up.* New York: Holiday House.

Sewall, Marcia. (1986). *The Pilgrims of Plimoth.* New York: Atheneum.

Sewall, Marcia. (1990). *People of the Breaking Day.* New York: Atheneum.

Sewall, Marcia. (1995). *Thunder from the Clear Sky.* New York: Atheneum.

Seymour, Tryntje Van Ness. (1993). *The Gift of Changing Woman.* New York: Holt.

Shannon, David. (1999). *David Goes to School.* New York: Scholastic.

Shannon, George. (1993). *Climbing Kansas Mountain.* New York: Bradbury.

Shannon, George. (1994). *Still More Stories to Solve: Fourteen Folktales from Around the World.* New York: Greenwillow.

Shannon, George. (1996). *Tomorrow's Alphabet.* New York: Greenwillow.

Shapiro, Miles. (1994). *Maya Angelou.* New York: Chelsea.

Sharmat, Marjorie W. (1981). *Nate the Great and the Missing Key.* New York: Putnam.

Sharon, Lois, and Sharon, Bram (Compilers). (1989). *Elephant Jam.* (Rev. ed.). Illus. David Shaw. New York: Crown.

Shaw, Alison. (1995). *Until I Saw the Sea: A Collection of Seashore Poems.* New York: Holt.

Shaw, Nancy. (1988). *Sheep in a Shop.* Illus. Margot Apple. Boston: Houghton.

Shea, Pegi Deitz. (1995). *The Whispering Cloth.* Illus. Anita Riggio. Honesdale, PA: Boyds Mills.

Sheffield, Margaret. (1973). *Where Do Babies Come From?* Illus. Sheila Bewley. New York: Knopf.

Shepard, Aaron. (1993). *Legend of Slappy Hooper: An American Tall Tale.* New York: Scribner's.

Sherman, Josepha (Reteller). (1988). *Vassilisa the Wise: A Tale of Medieval Russia.* Illus. Daniel San Souci. San Diego: Harcourt.

Sherrow, Victoria. (1994). *Mohandas Gandhi: The Power of the Spirit.* Brookfield, CT: Millbrook.

Shreve, Susan. (1984). *The Flunking of Joshua T. Bates.* New York: Knopf.

Shreve, Susan. (1993). *Joshua T. Bates Takes Charge.* New York: Knopf.

Shulevitz, Uri. (1974). *Dawn.* New York: Farrar, Straus & Giroux.

Shumate, Jane. (1994). *Chief Gall: Sioux War Chief.* New York: Chelsea.

Shute, Linda (Reteller). (1988). *Clever Tom and the Leprechaun.* New York: Lothrop, Lee & Shepard.

Sidney, Margaret. (1880; 1976 Reprint). *The Five Little Peppers and How They Grew.* New York: Lothrop, Lee & Shepard.

Siebert, Diane. (1988). *Mojave.* Illus. Wendell Minor. New York: HarperCollins.

Siebert, Diane. (1994). *Plane Song.* New York: HarperCollins.

Siegal, Aranka. (1981). *Upon the Head of a Goat: A Childhood in Hungary 1939–1944.* New York: Farrar, Straus & Giroux.

Siegel, Beatrice. (1995). *Marian Wright Edelman: The Making of a Crusader.* New York: Simon & Schuster.

Sierra, Judy. (1996). *Nursery Tales Around the World.* New York: Clarion.

Sierra, Judy. (1996). *Wiley and the Hairy Man.* New York: Lodestar/Dutton.

Sierra, Judy. (2000). *The Beautiful Butterfly: A Folktale from Spain.* Illus. Victoria Chess. Boston: Clarion.

Sills, Leslie. (1993). *Visions: Stories About Women Artists.* Morton Grove, IL: Whitman.

Silverstein, Shel. (1974). *Where the Sidewalk Ends.* New York: HarperCollins.

Silverstein, Shel. (1981). *A Light in the Attic.* New York: HarperCollins.

Silverstein, Shel. (1996). *Falling Up.* New York: HarperCollins.

Simon, Seymour. (1968). *Animals in Field and Laboratory.* New York: McGraw.

Simon, Seymour. (1971). *The Paper Airplane Book.* New York: Viking.

Simon, Seymour. (1980). *Einstein Anderson: Science Sleuth.* New York: Puffin.

Simon, Seymour. (1985). *Jupiter.* New York: Morrow/Avon.

Simon, Seymour. (1985). *Saturn.* New York: Morrow/Avon.

Simon, Seymour. (1987; 2000). *Destination: Mars.* New York: HarperCollins.

Simon, Seymour. (1987). *Icebergs and Glaciers.* New York: Morrow/Avon.

Simon, Seymour. (1987). *Mars.* New York: Morrow/Avon.

Simon, Seymour. (1987). *Uranus.* New York: Morrow/Avon.

Simon, Seymour. (1988). *Galaxies.* New York: Morrow/Avon.

Simon, Seymour. (1988). *Volcanoes.* New York: Morrow/Avon.

Simon, Seymour. (1990). *Oceans.* New York: Morrow/Avon.

Simon, Seymour. (1991). *Neptune.* New York: Morrow/Avon.

Simon, Seymour. (1992). *Mercury.* New York: Morrow/Avon.

Simon, Seymour. (1992). *Our Solar System.* New York: Morrow/Avon.

Simon, Seymour. (1992). *Venus.* New York: Morrow/Avon.

Simon, Seymour. (1993). *Weather.* New York: Morrow/Avon.

Simon, Seymour. (1993). *Wolves.* New York: HarperCollins.

Simon, Seymour. (1994). *Comets, Meteors, and Asteroids.* New York: Morrow/Avon.

Simon, Seymour. (1994). *Winter Across America.* New York: Hyperion.

Simon, Seymour. (1995). *Sharks.* New York: HarperCollins.

Simon, Seymour. (1996). *The Heart: Our Circulatory System.* New York: Morrow/Avon.

Simon, Seymour. (1996). *Spring Across America.* New York: Hyperion.

Simon, Seymour. (1996). *Wildfires.* New York: Morrow/Avon.

Simon, Seymour. (1998). *Destination Jupiter.* New York: Morrow/Avon.

Simon, Seymour. (1998). *Muscles: Our Muscle System.* New York: Morrow/Avon.

Sinclair, Sandra. (1992). *Extraordinary Eyes: How Animals See the World.* New York: Dial.

Singer, Isaac Bashevis. (1967). *Mazel and Shlimazel, or the Milk of the Lioness.* New York: Farrar, Straus & Giroux.

Singer, Isaac Bashevis. (1973). *Why Noah Chose the Dove.* Illus. Eric Carle. New York: Farrar, Straus & Giroux.

Singer, Marilyn. (1989). *Turtle in July.* Illus. Jerry Pinkney. New York: Macmillan.

Singer, Marilyn. (1999). *Stay True: Short Stories for Strong Girls.* New York: Scholastic.

Sis, Peter. (1991). *Follow the Dream: The Story of Christopher Columbus.* New York: Knopf.

Sis, Peter. (1996). *Starry Messenger.* New York: Farrar, Straus & Giroux.

Sis, Peter. (2000). *Dinosaur!* New York: Greenwillow.

Skira-Venturi, Rosabianca. (1994). *A Weekend with Van Gogh.* New York: Rizzoli.

Skolsky Mindy Warshaw. (2000). *Hannah and the Whistling Teakettle.* New York: DK Publishing.

Skurzynski, Gloria. (1983). *The Tempering.* New York: Clarion.

Skurzynski, Gloria. (1992). *Goodbye, Billy Radish.* New York: Bradbury.

Skurzynski, Gloria. (1993). *Get the Message: Telecommunications in Your High-Tech World.* New York: Bradbury.

Skurzynski, Gloria. (1994). *Zero Gravity.* New York: Bradbury.

Skurzynski, Gloria. (1996). *Good-Bye, Billy Radish.* Illus. John Collier. New York: Aladdin.

Sky-Peck, Kathryn. (1991). *Who Has Seen the Wind? An Illustrated Collection of Poetry for Young People.* New York: Rizzoli.

Slate, Joseph. (1996). *Miss Bindergarten Gets Ready for Kindergarten.* Illus. Ashley Wolff. New York: Dutton/Penguin.

Sleator, William. (1988). *Duplicate.* New York: Dutton.

Sleator, William. (1993). *Others See Us.* New York: Dutton.

Slepian, Jan. (1990). *Risk N' Roses.* New York: Putnam.

Slepian, Jan. (1995). *Pinocchio's Sister.* New York: Philomel.

Slier, Debby. (1993). *The Real Mother Goose: Book of American Rhymes.* New York: Scholastic.

Slier, Deborah. (1989). *Baby's Places.* New York: Checkerboard.

Sloat, Teri. (1989). *From Letter to Letter.* New York: Dutton.

Slobodkina, Esphyr. (1947). *Caps for Sale.* Glenview, IL: Scott, Foresman.

Slote, Alfred. (1978). *My Trip to Alpha I.* New York: HarperCollins.

Slote, Alfred. (1983). *Omega Station.* Illus. Anthony Kramer. New York: HarperCollins.

Slote, Alfred. (1990). *The Trading Game.* New York: HarperCollins.

Slote, Alfred. (1991). *Finding Buck McHenry.* New York: HarperCollins.

Smalls, Irene. (1996). *Ebony Sea.* Illus. Jon Onye Lockard. Ann Arbor: Borders Press.

Smalls, Irene. (1996). *Louise's Gift.* Boston: Little, Brown.

Smalls-Hector, Irene. (1992). *Jonathan and His Mommy.* Boston: Little, Brown.

Smith, Barry. (1991). *Minnie and Ginger.* New York: Crown.

Smith, D. James. (1999). *Fast Company.* New York: DK Publishing.

Smith, Doris Buchanan. (1986). *Return to Bitter Creek.* New York: Viking.

Smith, Doris Buchanan. (1989). *Voyages.* New York: Viking.

Smith, Janice Lee. (1981). *The Monster in the Third Dresser Drawer.* New York: HarperCollins.

Smith, Janice Lee. (1984). *The Kid Next Door and Other Headaches.* New York: HarperCollins.

Smith, Janice Lee. (1989). *It's Not Easy Being George.* New York: HarperCollins.

Smith, Robert Kimmel. (1989). *Bobby Baseball.* New York: Delacorte.

Smith, Roland, & Schmidt, Michael J. (1998). *In the Forest with the Elephants.* San Diego: Harcourt.

Smith, Roland. (1990). *Sea Otter Rescue: The Aftermath of an Oil Spill.* New York: Dutton.

Smith, Roland. (1992). *Snakes in the Zoo.* Brookfield, CT: Millbrook.

Smith, Roland. (1993). *Inside the Zoo Nursery.* New York: Dutton.

Smith, Susan Mathias. (1994). *The Booford Summer.* New York: Clarion.

Smith, T. H. (1986). *Cry to the Night Wind.* New York: Viking.

Smith, William Jay, & Ra, Carol. (1992). *Behind the King's Kitchen: A Roster of Rhyming Riddles.* Illus. Jacques Hnizdovsky. Honesdale, PA: Boyds Mills.

Smith, William Jay. (2000). *Around My Room.* Illus. Erik Blegvad. New York: Farrar, Straus & Giroux.

Smothers, Ethel F. (1995). *Moriah's Pond.* New York: Knopf.

Sneve, Virginia Driving Hawk. (1972). *High Elk's Treasure.* New York: Holiday House.

Sneve, Virginia Driving Hawk. (1989). *Dancing Tepees.* Illus. Stephen Gammell. New York: Holiday House.

Sneve, Virginia Driving Hawk. (1994). *The Seminoles.* New York: Holiday House.

Sneve, Virginia Driving Hawk. (1996). *The Cherokees.* New York: Holiday House.

Sneve, Virginia Driving Hawk. (1997). *The Trickster and the Troll.* Lincoln: University of Nebraska.

Snyder, Zilpha Keatley. (1994). *Cat Running.* New York: Delacorte.

Sobol, Donald. (1991). *Encyclopedia Brown Takes the Cake.* New York: Scholastic.

Sonenklar, Carol. (1999). *Robots Rising.* New York: Henry Holt.

Sorel, Edward. (1998). *Johnny on the Spot.* San Francisco: Children's Book Press.

Sorensen, Henri. (1995). *New Hope.* New York: Lothrop, Lee & Shepard.

Soto, Gary. (1991). *Baseball in April and Other Stories.* San Diego: Harcourt.

Soto, Gary. (1991). *A Fire in My Hands.* Illus. James M. Cardillo. New York: Scholastic.

Soto, Gary. (1991). *A Summer Life.* New York: Dell.

Soto, Gary. (1991). *Taking Sides.* San Diego: Harcourt.

Soto, Gary. (1992). *Living Up the Street.* New York: Dell.

Soto, Gary. (1992). *Neighborhood Odes.* Illus. David Diaz. San Diego: Harcourt.

Soto, Gary. (1992). *Pacific Crossing.* San Diego: Harcourt.

Soto, Gary. (1993). *Local News.* San Diego: Harcourt.

Soto, Gary. (1993). *The Pool Party.* New York: Delacorte.

Soto, Gary. (1994). *Crazy Weekend.* New York: Scholastic.

Soto, Gary. (1994). *Jesse.* San Diego: Harcourt.

Soto, Gary. (1995). *Boys at Work.* New York: Delacorte.

Soto, Gary. (1995). *Canto Familiar.* San Diego: Harcourt.

Soto, Gary. (1995). *Chato's Kitchen.* Illus. Susan Guervara. New York: Putnam.

Soto, Gary. (1995). *Summer on Wheels.* New York: Scholastic.

Soto, Gary. (1996). *Off and Running.* Illus. Velasquez. New York: Delacorte.

Soto, Gary. (1997). *The Elements of San Joaquin.* San Diego: Harcourt.

Soto, Gary. (1998). *Big Bushy Mustache.* Illus. Joe Cepeda. New York: Random House.

Soto, Gary. (1998). *The Old Man and His Door.* Illus. Joe Cepeda. New York: Paper Star.

Soto, Gary. (1998). *Petty Crimes.* San Diego: Harcourt.

Soto, Gary. (1999). *Buried Onions.* New York: HarperCollins.

Souhami, Jessica. (1995). *The Leopard's Drum: An Asante Tale from West Africa.* Boston: Little, Brown.

Souhami, Jessica. (1996). *Old MacDonald.* New York: Scholastic.

Souhami, Jessica. (2000). *No Dinner! The Story of the Old Woman and the Pumpkin.* New York: Cavendish.

Speare, Elizabeth George. (1958). *The Witch of Blackbird Pond.* Boston: Houghton.

Speare, Elizabeth George. (1961). *The Bronze Bow.* Boston: Houghton.

Speare, Elizabeth George. (1983). *The Sign of the Beaver.* Boston: Houghton.

Speed, Toby. (2000). *Brave Potatoes.* Illus. Barry Root. New York: Putnam.

Spiegelman, Art. (1986). *Maus I.* New York: Pantheon.

Spiegelman, Art. (1991). *Maus II.* New York: Pantheon.

Spier, Peter. (1961; 1989). *The Fox Went Out on a Chilly Night.* New York: Doubleday.

Spier, Peter. (1967). *To Market! to Market!* New York: Doubleday.

Spier, Peter. (1977). *Noah's Ark.* New York: Doubleday.

Spier, Peter. (1982). *Rain.* New York: Doubleday.

Spinelli, Eileen. (1996). *Where Is the Night Train Going? Bedtime Poems.* Honesdale, PA: Boyds Mills.

Spinelli, Eileen. (2000). *Night Shift Daddy.* New York: Hyperion.

Spinelli, Jerry. (1991). *There's a Girl in My Hammerlock.* New York: Simon & Schuster.

Spinelli, Jerry. (1996). *Crash.* New York: Knopf.

Spinelli, Jerry. (1998). *Knots in My Yo-Yo String: The Autobiography of a Kid.* New York: Knopf.

Spinelli, Jerry. (2000). *Stargirl.* New York: Knopf.

Spinka, Penina Keen. (1992). *Mother's Blessing.* New York: Macmillan.

Spires, Elizabeth. (1995). *With One White Wing: Puzzles in Poems and Pictures.* New York: McElderry.

Spires, Elizabeth. (1999). *Riddle Road: Puzzles in Poems and Pictures.* Illus. Erik Blegvad. New York: McElderry.

Springer, Nancy. (1998). *I Am Mordred: A Tale from Camelot.* New York: Philomel.

Spyri, Johanna. (1884; 1984 Reprint). *Heidi.* New York: Knopf.

St. George, Judith. (1991). *Mason and Dixon's Line of Fire.* New York: Putnam.

St. George, Judith. (1992). *Dear Dr. Bell—Your Friend, Helen Keller.* New York: Putnam.

St. George, Judith. (1999). *In the Line of Fire: Presidents' Lives at Stake.* New York: Holiday House.

St. George, Judith. (2000). *So You Want to Be President?* Illus. David Small. New York: Philomel.

Staines, Bill (Author and Composer). (1989). *All God's Critters Got a Place in the Choir.* Illus. Margot Zemach. New York: Dutton.

Standiford, Natalie. (1991). *Space Dog, the Hero.* New York: Morrow/Avon.

Stanley, Diane. (1986). *Peter the Great.* New York: Macmillan.

Stanley, Diane. (1996). *Saving Sweetness.* Illus. G. Brian Karas. New York: Putnam.

Stanley, Diane. (1997). *Rumpelstiltskin's Daughter.* New York: Morrow/Avon.

Stanley, Diane. (1998). *Joan of Arc.* New York: Morrow/Avon.

Stanley, Diane, & Vennema, Peter. (1988). *Shaka: King of the Zulus.* New York: Morrow/Avon.

Stanley, Diane, & Vennema, Peter. (1990). *Good Queen Bess: The Story of Elizabeth I of England.* New York: Simon & Schuster.

Stanley, Diane, & Vennema, Peter. (1992). *Bard of Avon: The Story of William Shakespeare.* New York: Morrow/Avon.

Stanley, Diane, & Vennema, Peter. (1994). *Cleopatra.* New York: Morrow/Avon.

Stanley, Jerry. (1992). *Children of the Dust Bowl: The True Story of the School at Weedpatch Camp.* New York: Crown.

Stanley, Jerry. (1994). *I Am an American: A True Story of Japanese Internment.* New York: Crown.

Stanley, Jerry. (1996). *Big Annie of Calumet: A True Story of the Industrial Revolution.* New York: Crown.

Staples, Suzanne Fisher. (1989). *Shabanu.* New York: Knopf.

Staples, Suzanne Fisher. (1993). *Haveli.* New York: Knopf.

Steele, William O. (1979; o.p.). *The Magic Amulet.* San Diego: Harcourt.

Steig, Jeanne. (1988). *Consider the Lemming.* Illus. William Steig. New York: Farrar, Straus & Giroux.

Steig, Jeanne. (1998). *A Handful of Beans: Six Fairy Tales Retold.* Illus. William Steig. New York: HarperCollins.

Steig, William. (1969; 1988). *Sylvester and the Magic Pebble.* New York: Simon & Schuster.

Steig, William. (1971). *Amos and Boris.* New York: Farrar, Straus & Giroux.

Steig, William. (1977). *Caleb and Kate.* New York: Farrar, Straus & Giroux.

Steig, William. (1982). *Dr. De Soto.* New York: Farrar, Straus & Giroux.

Steig, William. (1986). *Brave Irene.* New York: Farrar, Straus & Giroux.

Steig, William. (1988). *Spinky Sulks.* New York: Farrar, Straus & Giroux.

Steig, William. (1992). *Doctor De Soto Goes to Africa.* New York: HarperCollins.

Steptoe, John. (1969). *Stevie.* New York: HarperCollins.

Steptoe, John. (1980). *Daddy Is a Monster. Sometimes.* Philadelphia: Lippincott.

Steptoe, John. (1987). *Mufaro's Beautiful Daughters: An African Tale.* New York: Lothrop, Lee & Shepard.

Steptoe, John. (1997). *Creativity.* Illus. E. B. Lewis. New York: Clarion.

Stevens, Bryna. (1992). *Frank Thompson: Her Civil War Story.* New York: Macmillan.

Stevens, Janet (Reteller and Illus.). (1990). *How the Manx Cat Lost Its Tail.* San Diego: Harcourt.

Stevens, Janet. (1984). *The Tortoise and the Hare: An Aesop Fable.* New York: Holiday House.

Stevens, Janet. (1987). *The Three Billy Goats Gruff.* San Diego: Harcourt.

Stevens, Janet. (1987). *The Town Mouse and the Country Mouse: An Aesop Fable.* New York: Holiday House.

Stevens, Janet. (1995). *From Pictures to Words: A Book About Making a Book.* New York: Holiday House.

Stevens, Janet. (1995). *Tops and Bottoms.* San Diego: Harcourt.

Stevens, Janet. (1996). *Old Bag of Bones: A Coyote Tale.* New York: Holiday House.

Stevenson, James. (1988). *We Hate Rain!* New York: Greenwillow.

Stevenson, James. (1994). *Fun/No Fun.* New York: Greenwillow.

Stevenson, James. (1995). *The Bones in the Cliff.* New York: Greenwillow.

Stevenson, James. (1995). *I Had a Lot of Wishes.* New York: Greenwillow.

Stevenson, James. (1996). *Sweet Corn: Poems.* New York: Greenwillow.

Stevenson, Robert Louis. (1883; 1981). *Treasure Island.* Illus. N. C. Wyeth. New York: Scribner's.

Stevenson, Robert Louis. (1885; 1985). *A Child's Garden of Verses.* Illus. Michael Foreman. New York: Delacorte.

Stevenson, Robert Louis. (1905). *A Child's Garden of Verses.* Illus. Jessie Willcox Smith. New York: Macmillan.

Stevenson, Robert Louis. (1988). *The Land of Nod: And Other Poems for Children.* Selector and Illus. Michael Hague. New York: Holt.

Stewart, Elisabeth. (1994). *On the Long Trail Home.* New York: Clarion.

Stewart, Gail B. (2000). *Teen Addicts/Teen Alcoholics* (**Other America** Series). New York: Lucent.

Stewart, Sarah. (1995). *Library.* New York: Farrar, Straus & Giroux.

Still, James. (1997). *Jack and the Wonder Beans.* New York: Putnam.

Stine, R. L. (1992). *Goosebumps: Welcome to Dead House.* New York: Scholastic.

Stobbs, William. (1983). *The House That Jack Built.* New York: Oxford University.

Stock, Catherine (Author and Illus.). (1990). *Armien's Fishing Trip.* New York: Morrow/Avon.

Stock, Catherine. (1993). *Where Are You Going, Manyoni?* New York: Morrow/Avon.

Stockton, Frank. (1876). *America's Birthday Party.* New York: The Century Co.

Stojic, Manya. (2000). *Rain.* New York: Crown.

Stolz, Mary. (1989). *Storm in the Night.* Illus. Pat Cummings. New York: HarperCollins.

Stolz, Mary. (1990). *Bartholomew Fair.* New York: Greenwillow.

Stolz, Mary. (1996). *Coco Grimes.* New York: HarperCollins.

Storr, C. (1997). *Androcles and the Lion.* Chatham, NJ: Raintree Steck-Vaughn.

Stoutenberg, Adrien. (1976). *American Tall Tales.* Illus. Richard M. Powers. New York: Puffin.

Stow, Jenny. (1992). *The House That Jack Built.* New York: Dial.

Stratemeyer, Edward. (1898). *Under Dewey at Manilla.* Boston: Lothrop.

Strete, Craig Kee. (1974). *The Bleeding Man and Other Science Fiction Stories.* New York: Greenwillow.

Strete, Craig Kee. (1979). *When Grandfather Journeys Into Winter.* Illus. Hal Frenck. New York: Greenwillow.

Strete, Craig Kee. (1990). *Big Thunder Magic.* New York: Greenwillow.

Strete, Craig Kee. (1995). *The World in Grandfather's Hands.* New York: Clarion.

Strete, Craig Kee. (1997). *Little Coyote Runs Away.* Illus. Harvey Stevenson. New York: Putnam.

Strete, Craig Kee, & Chacon, Michelle Netten. (1996). *How the Indians Bought the Farm.* New York: Greenwillow.

Strickland, Dorothy, & Strickland, Michael. (1994). *Families: Poems Celebrating the African-American Experience.* Honesdale, PA: Boyds Mills.

Strickland, Michael. (1997). *My Own Story.* Honesdale, PA: Boyds Mills.

Strommen, Judith Bernie. (1993). *Champ Hobarth.* New York: Holt.

Stroud, Bettye. (1996). *Down Home at Miss Dessa's.* New York: Lee and Low.

Stroud, Virginia. (1994). *Doesn't Fall Off His Horse.* New York: Dial.

Stroud, Virginia. (1996). *The Path of Quiet Elk: A Native American Alphabet Book.* New York: Dial.

Sturges, Philemon. (1995). *Ten Flashing Fireflies.* New York: North-South.

Sturgis, Alexander. (1994). *Introducing Rembrandt.* Boston: Little, Brown.

Stuve-Bodeen, Stephanie. (2000). *Mama Elizabeti.* Illus. Christy Hale. New York: Lee and Low.

Sufrin, Mark. (1991). *George Catlin: Painter of the Indian West.* New York: Atheneum.

Sussex, Lucy (Compiler). (1999). *Altered Voices: Nine Science Fiction Stories.* New York: Scholastic.

Sutcliff, Rosemary. (1960). *Knights Fee.* New York: Henry Z. Walck.

Sutcliff, Rosemary. (1970). *The Witch's Brat.* New York: Henry Z. Walck.

Sutcliff, Rosemary. (1979). *Song for a Dark Queen.* New York: HarperCollins.

Sutcliff, Rosemary. (1992). *The Shining Company.* New York: Farrar, Straus & Giroux.

Sutcliff, Rosemary. (1993). *The Eagle of the Ninth.* New York: Farrar, Straus & Giroux.

Sutcliff, Rosemary. (1993). *The Silver Branch.* New York: Farrar, Straus & Giroux.

Sutcliff, Rosemary. (1994). *The Lantern Bearers.* New York: Farrar, Straus & Giroux.

Sutcliff, Rosemary. (1994). *The Light Beyond the Forest.* New York: Puffin.

Sutcliff, Rosemary. (1994). *The Road to Camlann: The Death of King Arthur.* Illus. Shirley Felts. New York: Puffin.

Sutcliff, Rosemary. (1994). *The Sword and the Circle: King Arthur and the Knights of the Round Table.* New York: Puffin.

Sutcliff, Rosemary. (1996). *The Wanderings of Odysseus: The Story of the Odyssey.* New York: Delacorte.

Sutcliff, Rosemary. (1994). *Warrior Scarlet.* Illus. Charles Keeping. New York: Farrar, Straus & Giroux.

Suteyev, Vladimir. (1972; 1988). *Chick and the Duckling.* (Mirra Ginsburg, Trans.). Illus. José Aruego and Ariane Dewey. New York: Macmillan.

Sutherland, Zena (Selector). (1990). *The Orchard Book of Nursery Rhymes.* Illus. Faith Jaques. New York: Scholastic.

Swamp, Chief Jake. (1995). *Giving Thanks: A Native American Good Morning Message.* New York: Lee and Low.

Swartz, Larry. (1993). *Classroom Events Through Poetry.* Markham, Ont.: Pembroke.

Swentzell, Rina. (1992). *Children of Clay: A Family of Pueblo Potters.* Minneapolis, MN: Lerner.

Swift, Jonathan. (1726; 1952 Reprint). *Gulliver's Travels.* Illus. Arthur Rackham. New York: Dutton.

Swineburne, Stephen R. (1999). *Once a Wolf: How Wildlife Biologists Fought to Bring Back the Grey Wolf.* Illus. Jim Brandenburg. Boston: Houghton.

Swope, Sam. (2000). *Gotta Go! Gotta Go!* Illus. Sue Riddle. New York: Farrar, Straus & Giroux.

Taback, Simms. (1999). *Joseph Had a Little Overcoat.* New York: Viking.

Tafuri, Nancy. (1983). *Early Morning in the Barn.* New York: Morrow/Avon.

Tafuri, Nancy. (1988). *Spots, Feathers, and Curly Tails.* New York: Greenwillow.

Tafuri, Nancy. (1996). *Have You Seen My Duckling?* New York: HarperCollins.

Tagore, Rabindranath (Reteller). (1992). *Amal and the Letter from the King.* Honesdale, PA: Boyds Mills.

Tagore, Rabindranath. (1992). *Paper Boats.* Honesdale, PA: Boyds Mills.

Talbert, Marc. (1992). *The Purple Heart.* New York: HarperCollins.

Talbert, Marc. (1999). *Star of Luis.* Boston: Houghton.

Tallchief, Maria. (1999). *Tallchief: America's Prima Ballerina.* New York: Viking.

Tan, Amy. (1992). *The Moon Lady.* New York: Macmillan.

Tapahonso, Luci, & Schick, Eleanor. (1995). *Navajo ABC.* New York: Simon & Schuster.

Tapahonso, Luci. (1997). *Blue Horses Rush In: Poems and Stories.* Tucson: Unviersity of Arizona Press.

Tarcov, Edith H. (1993). *Frog Prince.* New York: Scholastic.

Tashjian, Janet. (1999). *Multiple Choice.* New York: Holt.

Tate, Eleanora E. (1987). *The Secret of Gumbo Grove.* New York: Watts.

Tate, Eleanora E. (1990). *Thank You, Dr. Martin Luther King Jr.* New York: Watts.

Tate, Eleanora E. (1992). *Front Porch Stories at the One-Room School.* New York: Bantam.

Tate, Eleanora E. (1995). *A Blessing in Diguise.* New York: Delacorte.

Tate, Eleanora E. (1999). *Don't Split the Pole: Tales of Down-Home Folk Wisdom.* Illus. Cornelius Van Wright and Ying-Hwa Hu. New York: Delacorte.

Taylor, Ann, & Taylor, Jane. (1804; 1977 Reprint). *Original Poems for Infant Minds.* New York: Garland.

Taylor, Barbara. (1992). *Pond Life.* New York: Dorling Kindersley.

Taylor, Barbara. (1992). *Rain Forest.* New York: Dorling Kindersley.

Taylor, Kim. (1992). *Butterfly.* Illus. Mary Ling. New York: Dorling Kindersley.

Taylor, Kim. (1992). *Owl.* Illus. Mary Ling. New York: Dorling Kindersley.

Taylor, Maureen. (1999). *Through the Eyes of Your Ancestors: A Step by Step Guide to Uncovering Your Family's History.* Boston: Houghton.

Taylor, Mildred. (1976). *Roll of Thunder, Hear My Cry.* New York: Dial.

Taylor, Mildred. (1981). *Let the Circle Be Unbroken.* New York: Dial.

Taylor, Mildred. (1985). *Song of the Trees.* New York: Dial.

Taylor, Mildred. (1987). *The Friendship.* New York: Dial.

Taylor, Mildred. (1987). *The Gold Cadillac.* New York: Dial.

Taylor, Mildred. (1990). *Mississippi Bridge.* New York: Dial.

Taylor, Mildred. (1990). *The Road to Memphis.* New York: Dial.

Taylor, William. (1999). *The Blue Lawn.* New York: Consortium.

Tchudi, Susan, & Tchudi, Stephen. (1984). *The Young Writer's Handbook: A Practical Guide for the Beginner Who Is Serious About Writing.* New York: Scribner's.

Tejima, Keizaburo. (1987). *Owl Lake.* New York: Philomel.

Temple, Frances. (1993). *Grab Hands and Run.* New York: Scholastic.

Temple, Frances. (1994). *The Ramsay Scallop.* Danbury, CT: Orchard.

Temple, Frances. (1994). *Taste of Salt.* New York: Scholastic.

Temple, Frances. (1995). *Tonight, By Sea.* New York: Scholastic.

Temple, Frances. (1996). *The Beduin's Gazelle.* New York: Scholastic.

Terban, Marvin. (1983). *In a Pickle.* New York: Clarion.

Terban, Marvin. (1984). *I Think I Thought And Other Tricky Verbs.* New York: Clarion.

Terban, Marvin. (1986). *Your Foot's on My Feet! And Other Tricky Nouns.* New York: Clarion.

Terban, Marvin. (1987). *Mad as a Wet Hen and Other Funny Idioms.* New York: Clarion.

Terban, Marvin. (1988). *The Dove Dove.* New York: Clarion.

Terban, Marvin. (1988). *Guppies in Tuxedos: Funny Eponyms.* Illus. Giulio Maestro. Boston: Houghton.

Terban, Marvin. (1990). *Punching the Clock: Funny Action Idioms.* Boston: Houghton.

Terban, Marvin. (1991). *Hey, Hay! A Wagonful of Funny Homonym Riddles.* New York: Clarion.

Terban, Marvin. (1993). *Time to Rhyme: A Rhyming Dictionary.* Honesdale, PA: Boyds Mills.

Tessendorf, K. C. (1998). *Over the Edge: Flying with the Arctic Heroes.* New York: Atheneum.

Thaler, Mike. (1989). *The Teacher from the Black Lagoon.* New York: Scholastic.

Thayer, Ernest L. (1888; 1989). *Casey at the Bat.* Illus. Wallace Tripp. New York: Putnam.

Thesman, Jean. (1990). *Rachel Chance.* Boston: Houghton.

Thesman, Jean. (1991). *The Rain Catchers.* Boston: Houghton.

Thesman, Jean. (1993). *Molly Donnelly.* Boston: Houghton.

Thesman, Jean. (1996). *The Ornament Tree.* Boston: Houghton.

Thesman, Jean. (1999). *Tree of Bells.* Boston: Houghton.

Thimmesh, Catherine. (2000). *Girls Think of Everything: Stories of Ingenious Inventions by Women.* Illus. Melissa Sweet. Boston: Houghton.

Thisman, Jean. (2000). *Calling the Swan.* New York: Penguin.

Thomas, Jane Resh. (1998). *Behind the Mask: The Life of Queen Elizabeth.* New York: Clarion.

Thomas, Joyce Carol. (1990). *A Gathering of Flowers: Stories About Being Young in America.* New York: HarperCollins.

Thomas, Joyce Carol. (1993). *Brown Honey in Broomwheat Tea.* New York: HarperCollins.

Thomas, Joyce Carol. (1995). *Gingerbread Days: Poems.* New York: HarperCollins.

Thomas, Joyce Carol. (1998). *Cherish Me.* Illus. Nneka Bennett. New York: HarperCollins.

Thomas, Joyce Carol. (1998). *I Have Heard of a Land.* Illus. Floyd Cooper. New York: HarperCollins.

Thomas, Joyce Resh. (1994). *Lights on the River.* New York: Hyperion.

Thomas, Peggy. (2000). *Big Cat Conservation 21st Century: Science of Saving Animals, Series I.* Illus. Robin Brickman. New York: HarperCollins.

Thomas, Piri. (1992). *Stories from El Barrio.* New York: Knopf.

Thomas, Rob. (1997). *Slave Day.* Illus. Aaron Meshon. New York: Simon & Schuster.

Thomas, Shelley Moore. (2000). *Good Night, Good Knight.* Illus. Jennifer Plecas. New York: Dutton.

Thompson, Lauren. (2000). *Love One Another: The Last Days of Jesus.* Illus. Elizabeth Uyehara. New York: Scholastic.

Thomson, Peggy. (1995). *Katie Henio: Navajo Sheepherder.* New York: Cobblehill.

Thurber, James. (1933). *My Life and Hard Times.* New York: HarperCollins.

Thurber, James. (1994). *The Great Quillow.* San Diego: Harcourt.

Thwaite, Ann. (1994). *The Brilliant Career of Winnie-The-Pooh: The Definitive History of the Best Bear in All the World.* New York: Dutton.

Tillage, Leon Walter. (1997). *Leon's Story.* Illus. Susan L. Roth. New York: Farrar, Straus & Giroux.

Todd, Kathleen. (1982). *Snow.* Reading, MA: Addison.

Tolhurst, Marilyn. (1991). *Somebody and the Three Blairs.* Illus. Simone Abel. New York: Scholastic.

Tolkien, J.R.R. (1938). *The Hobbit.* Boston: Houghton.

Tolkien, J.R.R. (1979 Reprint). *The Lord of the Rings.* Winchester, MA: Allen and Unwin.

Tomioka, Chiyoko. (1992). *Rise and Shine, Mariko-Chan!* Illus. Yoshiharu Tsuchida. New York: Scholastic.

Topooco, Eusebio. (1993). *Waira's First Journey.* New York: Lothrop, Lee & Shepard.

Towle, Wendy. (1993). *The Real McCoy: The Life of an African American Inventor.* New York: Scholastic.

Trease, Geoffrey. (1941). *Cue for Treason.* New York: Vanguard Press.

Trease, Geoffrey. (1983). *Bows Against the Barons.* Illus. C. Walter Hodges. London: Hodder and Stoughton.

Tresselt, Alvin (Reteller). (1989). *The Mitten: An Old Ukranian Folktale.* Illus. Yaroslava. New York: Morrow/Avon.

Tresselt, Alvin. (1947; 1989). *White Snow, Bright Snow.* Illus. Roger Duvoisin. New York: Lothrop, Lee & Shepard.

Tresselt, Alvin. (1992). *The Gift of the Tree.* New York: Lothrop, Lee & Shepard.

Trivizas, Eugene. (1993). *Three Little Wolves and the Big Bad Pig.* New York: McElderry.

Troughton, Joanna. (1986). *How Rabbit Stole the Fire: A North American Indian Folktale.* London: Bedrick.

Troughton, Joanna. (1986). *How the Birds Changed Their Feathers: A South American Indian Folktale.* London: Bedrick.

Troughton, Joanna. (1990). *How Stories Came Into the World: A Folk Tale from West Africa.* London: Bedrick.

Trueman, Terry. (2000). *Stuck in Neutral.* New York: HarperCollins.

Tsutsui, Yoriko. (1987). *Anna's Secret Friend.* Illus. Akiko Hayashi. New York: Viking.

Tucker, Jean S. (1994). *Come Look with Me: Discovering Photographs with Children.* Charlottesville, VA: Thomasson-Grant.

Tudor, Tasha. (1996). *1 Is One.* New York: Simon & Schuster.

Tunis, John R. (1990). *Highpockets.* New York: Morrow/Avon.

Tunnell, Michael O. (1997). *Mailing May.* Illus. Ted Rand. New York: Tambourine.

Tunnell, Michael O. , & Chilcoat, George W. (1996). *The Children of Topaz: The Story of a Japanese American Internment Camp.* New York: Holiday House.

Turkle, Brinton. (1976). *Deep in the Forest.* New York: Dutton.

Turner, Ann, & Blake, Robert J. (1992). *Rainflowers.* New York: HarperCollins.

Turner, Ann. (1985). *Dakota Dugout.* New York: Macmillan.

Turner, Ann. (1987). *Nettie's Trip South.* Illus. Ronald Himler. New York: Macmillan.

Turner, Ann. (1987). *Time of the Bison.* Illus. Beth Peck. New York: Macmillan.

Turner, Ann. (1989). *Grasshopper Summer.* New York: Macmillan.

Turner, Ann. (1992). *Katie's Trunk.* Illus. Ron Himler. New York: Macmillan.

Turner, Ann. (1994). *Sewing Quilts.* Illus. Thomas B. Allen. New York: Simon & Schuster.

Turner, Ann. (1995). *Dust for Dinner.* New York: HarperCollins.

Turner, Ann. (1999). *Red Flower Goes West.* Illus. Dennis Nolin. New York: Hyperion.

Turner, Ann. (2000). *Learning to Swim: A Memoir.* New York: Scholastic.

Turner, Glennette Tilley. (1994). *Running for Our Lives.* New York: Holiday House.

Turner, Megan Whalen. (1995). *Instead of Three Wishes.* New York: Greenwillow.

Turner, Robyn M. (1991). *Georgia O'Keeffe.* Boston: Little, Brown.

Turner, Robyn M. (1992). *Mary Cassatt.* Boston: Little, Brown.

Twain, Mark. (1876; 1989 Reissue). *The Adventures of Tom Sawyer.* New York: Penguin.

Twain, Mark. (1888; 1986 Reissue). *The Adventures of Huckleberry Finn.* New York: Penguin.

Uchida, Yoshiko. (1949). *The Dancing Kettle.* New York: Harcourt.

Uchida, Yoshiko. (1955). *The Magic Listening Cap.* New York: Harcourt.

Uchida, Yoshiko. (1978). *Journey Home.* Illus. Charles Robinson. New York: McElderry.

Uchida, Yoshiko. (1981). *A Jar of Dreams.* New York: McElderry.

Uchida, Yoshiko. (1985). *Journey to Topaz.* Illus. Donald Carrick. San Francisco: Creative Arts.

Uchida, Yoshiko. (1991). *The Invisible Thread: A Memoir by the Author of the Best Bad Thing.* Englewood Cliffs, NJ: Messner.

Uchida, Yoshiko. (1994). *The Wise Old Woman.* Illus. Martin Springett. New York: McElderry.

Ude, Wayne. (1993). *Maybe I Will Do Something: Seven Coyote Tails.* Boston: Houghton.

Udry, Janice. (1961). *Let's Be Enemies.* New York: HarperCollins.

Udry, Janice. (1962). *The Mean Mouse and Other Mean Stories.* Illus. Ed Young. New York: HarperCollins.

Vail, Rachel. (1995). *Ever After.* New York: Morrow/Avon.

Vail, Rachel. (1996). *Daring To Be Abigail.* New York: Scholastic.

Vail, Rachel. (1998). *If You Only Knew.* New York: Scholastic.

Vail, Rachel. (1998). *Not That I Care.* New York: Scholastic.

Vail, Rachel. (1998). *Please, Please, Please.* New York: Scholastic.

Van Allsburg, Chris. (1979). *The Garden of Abdul Gasazi.* Boston: Houghton.

Van Allsburg, Chris. (1981). *Jumanji.* Boston: Houghton.

Van Allsburg, Chris. (1982). *Ben's Dream.* Boston: Houghton.

Van Allsburg, Chris. (1983). *The Wreck of the Zephyr.* Boston: Houghton.

Van Allsburg, Chris. (1984). *The Mysteries of Harris Burdick.* Boston: Houghton.

Van Allsburg, Chris. (1985). *The Polar Express.* Boston: Houghton.

Van Allsburg, Chris. (1986). *The Stranger.* Boston: Houghton.

Van Allsburg, Chris. (1988). *Two Bad Ants.* Boston: Houghton.

Van Allsburg, Chris. (1991). *The Wretched Stone.* Boston: Houghton.

Van Allsburg, Chris. (1992). *The Widow's Broom.* Boston: Houghton.

Van Allsburg, Chris. (1995). *Bad Day at Riverbend.* Boston: Houghton.

Van Der Rol, Ruud, & Verhoeven, Rian. (1993). *Anne Frank: Beyond the Diary.* New York: Viking.

Van Laan, Nancy. (1995). *Sleep, Sleep, Sleep: A Lullaby for Little Ones Around the World.* Illus. Holly Meade. Boston: Little, Brown.

Van Leeuwen, Jean. (1987). *Oliver, Amanda, and Grandmother Pig.* Illus. Ann Schweninger. New York: Dial.

Van Leeuwen, Jean. (1990). *Oliver Pig at School.* Illus. Ann Schweninger. New York: Dial.

Van Leeuwen, Jean. (1992). *Going West.* Illus. Thomas B. Allen. New York: Dial.

Van Leeuwen, Jean. (1994). *Bound for Oregon.* New York: Dial.

Van Loon, Hendrik Willem. (1972). *The Story of Mankind.* (Original work published in 1922). New York: Liveright.

Vandraanen, Wendelin. (1998). *Sammy Keyes and the Hotel Thief.* New York: Random House.

Vandraanen, Wendelin. (1998). *Sammy Keyes and the Skelteton Man.* New York: Knopf.

Varriale, Jim, and Feld, Eliot. (1999). *Kids Dance: The Students of Ballet Tech.* New York: Dutton.

Velasquez, Gloria. (1995). *Maya's Divided World.* Houston: Arte Publico.

Velasquez, Gloria. (1995). *Tommy Stands Alone.* Houston: Arte Publico.

Velasquez, Gloria. (1997). *Juanita Fights the School Board.* Houston: Arte Publico.

Venezia, Mike. (1988). *Picasso.* San Francisco: Children's Book Press.

Venezia, Mike. (1988). *Rembrandt.* San Francisco: Children's Book Press.

Venezia, Mike. (1991). *Francisco Goya.* San Francisco: Children's Book Press.

Ventura, Piero. (1989). *Great Composers.* New York: Putnam.

Ventura, Piero. (1992). *1492: The Year of the New World.* New York: Putnam.

Ventura, Piero. (1995). *Darwin: Nature Reinterpreted.* Boston: Houghton.

Vicq De Cumpitch, Roberto De. (2000). *Bembo's Zoo: An Animal ABC Book.* New York: Holt.

Vincent, Gabrielle. (1984). *Merry Christmas, Ernest and Celestine.* New York: Greenwillow.

Vincent, Gabrielle. (2000). *A Day, a Dog.* New York: Front Street.

Viola, Herman J. (1998). *It Is a Good Day to Die: Indian Eyewitnesses Tell the Story of Battle of Little Bighorn.* New York: Crown.

Viorst, Judith. (1969). *I'll Fix Anthony.* New York: HarperCollins.

Vivas, Julie (Illus.). (1988). *The Nativity.* San Diego: Harcourt.

Viorst, Judith. (1971). *The Tenth Good Thing About Barney.* New York: Atheneum.

Viorst, Judith. (1972). *Alexander and the Terrible, Horrible, No Good, Very Bad Day.* New York: Atheneum.

Viorst, Judith. (1974). *Rosie and Michael.* Illus. Lorna Tomei. New York: Atheneum.

Viorst, Judith. (1990). *Earrings!* Illus. Nola Langner Malone. New York: Atheneum.

Vivas, Julie (Illus.). (1998). *The Nativity.* San Diego: Harcourt.

Vogel, Carole Garbuny. (1999). *Legends of Landforms: Native American Lore and the Geology of the Land.* Brookfield, CT: Millbrook.

Vogt, Gregory L. (1994). *The Search for the Killer Asteroid.* Brookfield, CT: Millbrook.

Voigt, Cynthia. (1985). *The Runner.* New York: Atheneum.

Voigt, Cynthia. (1986). *Izzy Willy-Nilly.* New York: Atheneum.

Voigt, Cynthia. (1987). *The Callendar Papers.* New York: Fawcett.

Voigt, Cynthia. (1987). *Came a Stranger.* New York: Atheneum.

Voigt, Cynthia. (1988). *Tree by Leaf.* New York: Atheneum.

Voigt, Cynthia. (1996). *Bad Girls.* New York: Scholastic.

Vos, Ida. (1991). *Hide and Seek.* Boston: Houghton.

Vos, Ida. (1993). *Anna Is Still Here.* Boston: Houghton.

Vos, Ida. (1995). *Dancing on the Bridge of Avignon.* Boston: Houghton.

Vozar, David. (1993). *Yo, Hungry Wolf! A Nursery Rap.* New York: Doubleday.

Waber, Bernard. (1965). *Lyle, Lyle, Crocodile.* Boston: Houghton.

Waber, Bernard. (1995). *Do You See a Mouse?* Boston: Houghton.

Waddell, Martin. (1996). *Owl Babies.* New York: Candlewick.

Wadsworth, Ginger. (1991). *Rachel Carson: Voice for the Earth.* Minneapolis, MN: Lerner.

Wahl, Jan (Reteller). (1991). *Tailypo!* New York: Holt.

Wahl, Jan. (1992). *Little Eight John.* New York: Dutton.

Walker, Alice. (1974). *Langston Hughes, American Poet.* New York: HarperCollins.

Walker, Kate. (1991). *Peter.* Boston: Houghton.

Walker, Lou Ann. (1994). *Roy Lichtenstein: The Artist at Work.* New York: Lodestar.

Walker, Paul Robert. (1988). *Pride of Puerto Rico: The Life of Roberto Clemente.* San Diego: Harcourt.

Walker, Paul Robert. (1993). *Big Men, Big Country: A Collection of American Tall Tales.* San Diego: Harcourt.

Walker, Sally M. (1998). *The 18 Penny Goose.* Illus. Ellen Beier. New York: HarperCollins.

Wallace, Karen. (1999). *Duckling Days.* New York: Dorling Kindersley.

Wallis, Diz. (1991). *Something Nasty in the Cabbages: A Tale from Roman De Renard.* Honesdale, PA: Boyds Mills.

Wallner, Alexandra. (1994). *Betsy Ross.* New York: Holiday House.

Wallner, Alexandra. (1995). *Beatrix Potter.* New York: Holiday House.

Wallner, Alexandra. (1997). *Laura Ingalls Wilder.* New York: Holiday House.

Walsh, Ellen. (1989). *Mouse Paint.* San Diego: Harcourt.

Walsh, Ellen. (1991). *Mouse Count.* San Diego: Harcourt.

Walsh, Jill Patton. (1986). *The Green Book.* New York: Farrar, Straus & Giroux.

Walsh, Melanie. (2000). *Do Donkeys Dance?* Boston: Houghton.

Walsh, Melanie. (2000). *Do Monkeys Tweet?* Boston: Houghton.

Walsh, Melanie. (2000). *Do Pigs Have Stripes?* Boston: Houghton.

Walter, Mildred Pitts. (1990). *Two and Too Much.* New York: Bradbury.

Walter, Mildred Pitts. (1992). *Mississippi Challenge.* New York: Bradbury.

Walter, Mildred Pitts. (1995). *Kwanzaa: A Family Affair.* New York: Lothrop, Lee & Shepard.

Walter, Mildred Pitts. (1996). *Second Daughter: The Story of a Slave Girl.* New York: Scholastic.

Walter, Mildred Pitts. (1999). *Suitcase.* Illus. Teresa Flavin. New York: Lothrop, Lee & Shepard.

Wang, M. L. (1989). *The Ant and the Dove: An Aesop Tale Retold.* San Francisco: Children's Book Press.

Wang, Rosalind C. (1995). *The Treasure Chest: A Chinese Tale.* New York: Holiday House.

Ward, Helen. (1999). *The Hare and the Tortoise: A Fable from Aesop.* Brookfield, CT: Millbrook.

Warner, Lucille Schulberg. (1976). *From Slave to Abolitionist: The Life of William Wells Brown.* New York: Dial.

Waters, Kate. (1989). *Sarah Morton's Day: A Day in the Life of a Pilgrim Girl.* New York: Scholastic.

Waters, Kate. (1996). *Tapenum's Day: A Wampanoag Indian Boy in Pilgrim Times.* New York: Scholastic.

Watkins, Richard. (1997). *Gladiator.* Boston: Houghton.

Watkins, Yoko Kawashima. (1986). *So Far from the Bamboo Grove.* New York: Lothrop, Lee & Shepard.

Watkins, Yoko Kawashima. (1994). *My Brother, My Sister, and I.* New York: Bradbury.

Watson, Clyde. (1971). *Father Fox's Pennyrhymes.* Illus. Wendy Watson. New York: HarperCollins.

Watson, Clyde. (1991). *Father Fox's Feast of Songs.* Illus. Wendy Watson. Honesdale, PA: Boyds Mills.

Watson, Wendy. (1989). *Wendy Watson's Mother Goose.* New York: Lothrop, Lee & Shepard.

Watts, Bernadette. (1992). *The Wind and the Sun: An Aesop Fable.* New York: North-South.

Watts, Bernadette. (2000). *The Lion and the Mouse: An Aesop Fable.* New York: North-South.

Waugh, Sylvia. (1993). *The Mennyms.* New York: Greenwillow.

Weatherford, Carole Boston. (1995). *Juneteenth Jamboree.* New York: Lee and Low.

Weaver, Will. (1995). *Farm Team.* New York: HarperCollins.

Webster, Noah. (1783). *Webster's Blue-Backed Speller.* Hartford, CT: Hudson & Goodwin.

Weeks, Sarah. (1999). *Regular Guy.* New York: HarperCollins.

Weeks, Sarah. (2000). *Guy Time.* New York: HarperCollins.

Weil, Lisl. (1986). *Pandora's Box.* New York: Atheneum.

Weisman, David. (1990). *Jeremy Visick.* Boston: Houghton.

Weiss, Nicki. (1962). *On a Hot, Hot Day.* New York: Putnam.

Weissberg, Ted. (1993). *Arthur Ashe.* New York: Chelsea.

Weitzman, Jacqueline Preiss. (2000). *You Can't Take a Balloon into the National Gallery.* New York: Dial.

Welch, Willy. (1995). *Playing Right Field.* New York: Scholastic.

Wells, Rosemary. (1995). *Lassie Come Home: Eric Knight's Original 1938 Classic.* Illus. Susan Jeffers. New York: Holt.

Wells, Rosemary. (1979). *Max's First Word. Max's New Suit. Max's Ride.* (Boxed set of board books). New York: Dial.

Wells, Rosemary. (1980). *When No One Was Looking.* New York: Dial.

Wells, Rosemary. (1985). *Max's Breakfast.* New York: Dial.

Wells, Rosemary. (1989). *Max's Chocolate Chicken.* New York: Dial.

Wells, Rosemary. (1991). *Max's Dragon Shirt.* New York: Dial.

Wells, Rosemary. (1992). *Shy Charles.* New York: Dial.

Wells, Rosemary. (1993). *Waiting for the Evening Star.* New York: Dial.

Wells, Rosemary. (1995). *Edward in Deep Water.* New York: Dial.

Wells, Rosemary. (1995). *Edward Unready for School.* New York: Dial.

Wells, Rosemary. (1995). *Edward's Overwhelming Overnight.* New York: Dial.

Wells, Rosemary. (1995). *Max and Ruby's Midas: Another Greek Myth.* New York: Dial.

Wells, Rosemary. (1999). *Mary on Horseback: Three Mountain Stories.* New York: Viking.

Wells, Rosemary. (2000). *Emily's First 100 Days of School.* New York: Hyperion.

Wensel, Ulises. (1994). *They Followed a Bright Star.* New York: Putnam.

Werlin, Nancy. (1998). *The Killer's Cousin.* New York: Delacorte.

Wesley, Valerie Wilson. (1997). *Freedom's Gifts: A Juneteenth Story.* Illus. Sharon Wilson. New York: Simon & Schuster.

West, Alan. (1994). *José Martí: Man of Poetry, Soldier of Freedom.* Brookfield, CT: Millbrook.

West, Dorothy. (1996). *The Richer, the Poorer: Stories, Sketches, and Reminiscences.* New York: Anchor.

Westall, Robert. (1991). *Echoes of War.* New York: Farrar, Straus & Giroux.

Westall, Robert. (1991). *The Kingdom by the Sea.* New York: Farrar, Straus & Giroux.

Westall, Robert. (1994). *The Witness.* New York: Dutton.

Westall, Robert. (1997). *The Machine Gunners.* Madison, WI: Turtleback

Westray, Kathleen. (1993). *A Color Sampler.* New York: Ticknor & Fields.

Westray, Kathleen. (1994). *Picture Puzzler.* New York: Ticknor & Fields.

Westrup, Hugh. (1994). *Maurice Strong: Working for Planet Earth.* Brookfield, CT: Millbrook.

Wexler, Jerome. (1992). *Wonderful Pussy Willows.* New York: Dutton.

Wexler, Jerome. (1993). *Jack-In-The-Pulpit.* New York: Dutton.

Wexler, Jerome. (1995). *Everyday Mysteries.* New York: Dutton.

Whelan, Gloria. (1987). *Next Spring an Oriole.* New York: Random House.

Whelan, Gloria. (1992). *Goodbye Vietnam.* New York: Knopf.

Whelan, Gloria. (2000). *Homeless Bird.* New York: HarperCollins.

Whipple, Laura (Compiler). (1989). *Eric Carle's Animals Animals.* New York: Putnam.

Whippo, Walt. (2000). *Little White Duck.* Illus. Joan Paley. Boston: Little Brown.

White, E. B. (1952). *Charlotte's Web.* Illus. Garth Williams. New York: HarperCollins.

White, Linda Arms. (2000). *Comes a Wind.* Illus. Tom Curry. New York: DK Publishing.

White, Ruth. (1996). *Belle Prater's Boy.* New York: Farrar, Straus & Giroux.

White, Ruth. (2000). *Memories of Summer.* New York: Farrar, Straus & Giroux.

Whitelaw, Nancy. (1995). *Mr. Civil Rights: The Story of Thurgood Marshall.* Greensboro, NC: Morgan.

Whitmore, Arvella. (1990). *The Bread Winner.* Boston: Houghton.

Whittier, John Greenleaf. (1992). *Barbara Frietchie.* (Original work published in 1864). New York: Greenwillow.

Wibberley, Leonard. (1968). *Attar of the Ice Valley.* New York: Farrar, Straus & Giroux.

Wibberley, Leonard. (1986). *John Treegate's Musket.* New York: Farrar, Straus & Giroux.

Wiesner, David. (1988). *Free Fall.* New York: Lothrop, Lee & Shepard.

Wiesner, David. (1991). *Tuesday.* New York: Clarion.

Wiesner, David. (1992). *June 29, 1996.* New York: Clarion.

Wiggin, Kate Douglas. (1903; 1962 Reprint). *Rebecca of Sunnybrook Farm.* New York: Macmillan.

Wild, Margaret. (1991). *Let the Celebrations Begin.* Illus. Julie Vivas. New York: Scholastic.

Wild, Margaret. (1993). *Going Home.* New York: Scholastic.

Wilder, Laura Ingalls. (1941; 1953). *Little Town on the Prairie.* Illus. Garth Williams. New York: HarperCollins.

Wilder, Laura Ingalls. (1962; 1995). *On the Way Home: The Diary of a Trip from South Dakota to Mansfield, Missouri, in 1894.* New York: HarperCollins.

Wilder, Laura Ingalls. (1995). *West from Home: Letters of Laura Ingalls Wilder, San Francisco, 1915.* New York: HarperCollins.

Wildsmith, Brian. (1998). *A Christmas Story.* New York: Eerdmans.

Wilkinson, Brenda. (1975). *Ludell.* New York: HarperCollins.

Wilkinson, Brenda. (1993). *Definitely Cool.* New York: Scholastic.

Willard, Nancy. (1981). *A Visit to William Blake's Inn: Poems for Innocent and Experienced Travelers.* Illus. Alice and Martin Provensen. San Diego: Harcourt.

Willard, Nancy. (1987). *Voyage of the Ludgate Hill: Travels with Robert Louis Stevenson.* Illus. Alice and Martin Provensen. San Diego: Harcourt.

Willard, Nancy. (1991). *Pish, Posh, Said Hieronymous Bosch.* Illus. Leo and Diane Dillon. San Diego: Harcourt.

Willard, Nancy. (1993). *Starlit Somersault Downhill.* Boston: Little, Brown.

Williams, Barbara. (1975). *Kevin's Grandma.* Illus. Kay Chorao. New York: Dutton.

Williams, Carol Lynch. (1999). *My Angelica.* New York: Delacorte.

Williams, David. (1993). *Grandma Essie's Covered Wagon.* New York: Knopf.

Williams, Karen Lynn. (1990). *Galimoto.* Illus. Catherine Stock. New York: Lothrop, Lee & Shepard.

Williams, Lori Aurelia. (2000). *When Kambia Elaine Flew in from Neptune.* Illus. Jack Louth. New York: Simon & Schuster.

Williams, Marcia. (1996). *King Arthur and the Knights of the Round Table.* Cambridge: Candlewick.

Williams, Margery. (1922; 1991 Reprint). *The Velveteen Rabbit.* Illus. William Nicholson. New York: Doubleday.

Williams, Sherley Anne. (1992). *Working Cotton.* Illus. Carole Byard. San Diego: Harcourt.

Williams, Sheron. (1992). *And in the Beginning.* New York: Atheneum.

Williams, Sue. (1990). *I Went Walking.* San Diego: Harcourt.

Williams, Vera. (1982). *A Chair for My Mother.* New York: Greenwillow.

Williams, Vera. (1988). *Stringbean's Trip to the Shining Sea.* Illus. Vera and Jennifer Williams. New York: Greenwillow.

Williams, Vera. (1990). *"More More More," Said the Baby.* New York: Greenwillow.

Williams, Vera. (1993). *Scooter.* New York: Greenwillow.

Williams-Garcia, Rita. (1995). *Like Sisters on the Homefront.* New York: Dutton.

Williamson, Ray A. (1993). *First Houses: Native American Homes and Sacred Structures.* Boston: Houghton.

Willner-Pardo, Gina. (1995). *Jason and the Losers.* New York: Clarion.

Willner-Pardo, Gina. (1999). *Jumping into Nothing.* Illus. Thomas Yezerski. New York: Farrar, Straus & Giroux.

Wilner, Isabel. (1995). *B Is for Bethlehem: A Christmas Alphabet.* New York: Penguin.

Wilson, Anthony. (1999). *How the Future Began: Communications.* New York: Larousse Kingfisher Chambers.

Wilson, Budge. (1992). *The Leaving.* New York: Philomel.

Wilson, Budge. (1995). *The Dandelion Garden: And Other Stories.* New York: Putnam.

Wilson, Elizabeth B. (1994). *Bibles and Bestiaries: A Guide to Illuminated Manuscripts.* New York: Farrar, Straus & Giroux.

Windham, Sophie. (1994). *The Mermaid and Other Sea Poems.* New York: Scholastic.

Winner, David. (1990). *Desmond Tutu.* Ridgefield, CT: Morehouse.

Winter, Jeanette. (1988). *Follow the Drinking Gourd.* New York: Knopf.

Winter, Jeanette. (1998). *Georgia.* New York: Silver Whistle.

Winter, Jeanette. (2000). *The House That Jack Built.* New York: Dial.

Winter, Kathryn. (1998). *Katarina: A Novel.* New York: Farrar, Straus & Giroux.

Winthrop, Elizabeth (Adapter). (1991). *Vasilissa the Beautiful.* Illus. Alexander Koshkin. New York: HarperCollins.

Winthrop, Elizabeth. (1983). *A Child Is Born: The Christmas Story.* Illus. Charles Mikolaycak. New York: Holiday House.

Winthrop, Elizabeth. (1985). *Castle in the Attic.* New York: Holiday House.

Winthrop, Elizabeth. (1989). *The Best Friends Club: A Lizzie and Harold Story.* Illus. Martha Weston. New York: Lothrop, Lee & Shepard.

Winton, Tim. (1999). *Lockie Leonard Scumbuster.* New York: McElderry.

Wiseman, David. (1981). *Jeremy Visick.* Boston: Houghton.

Wisler, G. Clifton. (1993). *Jericho's Journey.* New York: Lodestar.

Wisniewski, David. (1989). *The Warrior and the Wise Man.* New York: Lothrop, Lee & Shepard.

Wisniewski, David. (1990). *Elfwyn's Saga.* New York: Lothrop, Lee & Shepard.

Wisniewski, David. (1992). *Sundiata: Lion King of Mali.* New York: Clarion.

Wisniewski, David. (1994). *Wave of the Sea-Wolf.* New York: Clarion.

Wisniewski, David. (1996). *Golem.* New York: Clarion.

Withers, Carl (Compiler). (1988). *A Rocket in My Pocket.* Illus. Susanne Suba. New York: Holt.

Wittlinger, Ellen. (1999). *Hard Love.* New York: Simon & Schuster.

Wittlinger, Ellen. (2000). *What's in a Name?* Illus. John Mathias. New York: Simon & Schuster.

Wittstock, Laura Waterman. (1993). *Ininatig's Gift of Sugar: Traditional Native Sugarmaking.* Minneapolis, MN: Lerner.

Wolf, Bernard. (1995). *Homeless.* New York: Scholastic.

Wolff, Virginia Euwer. (1993). *Make Lemonade.* New York: Holt.

Wolff, Virginia Euwer. (1998). *Bat 6.* New York: Scholastic.

Wolinsky, Art. (1999). *Creating and Publishing Web Pages on the Internet.* Berkeley Heights, NJ: Enslow.

Wolkstein, Diane. (1996). *Esther's Story.* New York: Morrow/Avon.

Wolman, Bernice. (1992). *Taking Turns: Poetry to Share.* New York: Atheneum.

Wong, Janet S. (1994). *Good Luck Gold and Other Poems.* New York: McElderry.

Wong, Janet. (1996). *A Suitcase of Seaweed and Other Poems.* New York: McElderry.

Wong, Janet. (1999). *The Rainbow Hand: Poems About Mothers and Children.* Illus. Jennifer Hewitson. New York: McElderry.

Wong, Janet. (2000). *Buzz.* Illus. Margaret Chodos-Irvine. San Diego: Harcourt.

Wood, Audrey. (1984). *The Napping House.* Illus. Don Wood. San Diego: Harcourt.

Wood, Audrey. (1992). *Silly Sally.* San Diego: Harcourt.

Wood, Nancy. (1993). *Spirit Walker.* New York: Doubleday.

Wood, Ted (with Wanbli Numpa Afraid of Hawk). (1995). *A Boy Becomes a Man at Wounded Knee.* New York: Walker.

Woodruff, Elvira. (1994). *Dear Levi: Letters from the Overland Trail.* Illus. Beth Peck. New York: Random House.

Woodson, Jacqueline. (1991). *The Dear One.* New York: Delacorte.

Woodson, Jacqueline. (1992). *Last Summer with Maizon.* New York: Dell.

Woodson, Jacqueline. (1992). *Maizon at Blue Hill.* New York: Delacorte.

Woodson, Jacqueline. (1994). *I Hadn't Meant to Tell You This.* New York: Delacorte.

Woodson, Jacqueline. (1995). *From the Notebooks of Melanin Sun.* New York: Scholastic.

Woodson, Jacqueline. (2000). *Miracle's Boys.* New York: Putnam.

Woolf, Felicity. (1990). *Picture This: A First Introduction to Paintings.* New York: Doubleday.

Worth, Valerie. (1976; 1986). *More Small Poems.* Illus. Natalie Babbitt. New York: Farrar, Straus & Giroux.

Worth, Valerie. (1987). *All the Small Poems.* Illus. Natalie Babbitt. New York: Farrar, Straus & Giroux.

Wosmek, Frances. (1985, 1993). *A Brown Bird Singing.* Illus. Ted Lewin. New York: Lothrop, Lee & Shepard.

Wrede, Patricia C. (1990). *Dealing with Dragons.* San Diego: Harcourt.

Wright, Betty Ren. (1994). *The Ghost Comes Calling.* New York: Scholastic.

Wright, Betty Ren. (1998). *A Ghost in the Family.* New York: Scholastic.

Wright, Blanche Fisher (Illus.). (1916). *The Real Mother Goose.* New York: Rand/Checkerboard.

Wright, Courtni Crump. (1994). *Journey to Freedom: A Story of the Underground Railroad.* Illus. Gershom Griffith. New York: Holiday House.

Wright, Courtni Crump. (1994). *Jumping the Broom.* Illus. Gershom Griffith. New York: Holiday House.

Wright, Richard. (1994). *Rite of Passage.* New York: HarperCollins.

Wrightson, Patricia. (1983). *A Little Fear.* New York: Atheneum.

Wrightson, Patricia. (1986). *The Nargun and the Stars.* New York: McElderry.

Wynne-Jones, Diana. (1995). *Cart and Cwidder.* New York: Greenwillow.

Wynne-Jones, Diana. (1995). *The Crown of Dalemark.* New York: Greenwillow.

Wynne-Jones, Diana. (1995). *Drowned Ammet.* New York: Greenwillow.

Wynne-Jones, Diana. (1995). *The Spellcoats.* New York: Greenwillow.

Wynne-Jones, Tim. (1995). *Some of the Kinder Planets.* New York: Scholastic.

Wynne-Jones, Tim. (1998). *Stephen Fair.* New York: DK Publishing.

Wynot, Jillian. (1990). *The Mother's Day Sandwich.* Illus. Maxie Chambliss. New York: Scholastic.

Wyss, Johann. (1812; 1949 Reprint). *The Swiss Family Robinson.* Illus. Lynd Ward. New York: Grosset and Dunlap.

Yaccarino, Dan. (2000). *Deep in the Jungle.* New York: Atheneum.

Yacowitz, Caryn (Adapter). (1992). *The Jade Stone: A Chinese Folktale.* Illus. Ju-Hong Chen. New York: Holiday House.

Yamanaka, Lois-Ann. (1999). *Name Me Nobody.* New York: Hyperion.

Yarbro, Chelsea Quinn. (1984). *Locadio's Apprentice.* New York: HarperCollins.

Yarbrough, Camille. (1996). *The Little Tree Growing in the Shade.* New York: Putnam.

Yates, Diana. (1992). *Chief Joseph: Thunder Rolling Down from the Mountains.* New York: Ward.

Yee, Brenda Shannon. (1999). *Sand Castle.* New York: Greenwillow.

Yee, Paul. (1990). *Tales from Gold Mountain: Stories of the Chinese in the New World.* New York: Macmillan.

Yee, Paul. (1991). *Roses Sing on New Snow: A Delicious Tale.* New York: Macmillan.

Yee, Wong Herbert. (1999). *Hamburger Heaven.* Boston: Houghton.

Yektai, Niki. (1992). *The Secret Room.* New York: Scholastic.

Yellow Robe, Rosebud. (1979). *Tonweya and the Eagles, and Other Lakota Indian Tales.* New York: Dial.

Yen Mah, Adeline. (1999). *Chinese Cinderella: True Story of an Unwanted Daughter.* New York: Delacorte.

Yenawine, Philip. (1991). *Lines.* New York: Museum of Modern Art.

Yenawine, Philip. (1993). *People.* New York: Delacorte.

Yenawine, Philip. (1993). *Places.* New York: Museum of Modern Art.

Yep, Laurence. (1975). *Dragonwings.* New York: HarperCollins.

Yep, Laurence. (1977). *Child of the Owl.* New York: HarperCollins.

Yep, Laurence. (1979). *Sea Glass.* New York: HarperCollins.

Yep, Laurence. (1984). *The Serpent's Children.* New York: HarperCollins.

Yep, Laurence. (1985). *Mountain Light.* New York: HarperCollins.

Yep, Laurence. (1989). *The Rainbow People.* Illus. David Wiesner. New York: HarperCollins.

Yep, Laurence. (1991). *The Lost Garden: A Memoir by the Author of Dragonwings.* Englewood Cliffs, NJ: Messner.

Yep, Laurence. (1991). *The Star Fisher.* New York: Morrow/Avon.

Yep, Laurence. (1991). *Tongues of Jade.* Illus. David Wiesner. New York: HarperCollins.

Yep, Laurence. (1993). *American Dragons: Twenty-Five Asian American Voices.* New York: HarperCollins.

Yep, Laurence. (1993). *Dragon's Gate.* New York: HarperCollins.

Yep, Laurence. (1995). *Hiroshima.* New York: Scholastic.

Yep, Laurence. (1995). *Thief of Hearts.* New York: HarperCollins.

Yep, Laurence. (1995). *Tiger Woman.* Illus. Robert Roth. New York: Bridgewater.

Yep, Laurence. (1997). *The Ghost Fox.* Illus. Jean Tseng and Mou-Sien Tseng. New York: Little Apple.

Yep, Laurence. (1997). *The Kahn's Daughter: A Mongolian Folktale.* Illus. Jean Tseng and Mou-Sien Tseng. New York: Scholastic.

Yep, Laurence. (1998). *The Case of the Lion Dance.* New York: HarperCollins.

Yep, Laurence. (1998). *The Cook's Family.* New York: Putnam.

Yep, Laurence. (1999). *The Dragon Prince: A Chinese Beauty and the Beast Tale.* Illus. Kam Mak. New York: HarperCollins.

Yep, Laurence. (2000). *Dream Soul.* New York: HarperCollins.

Yolen, Jane. (1980). *Commander Toad in Space.* New York: Putnam.

Yolen, Jane. (1982). *Dragon's Blood.* New York: Delacorte.

Yolen, Jane. (1986). *The Lullaby Songbook.* Arranger Adam Stemple. Illus. Charles Mikolaycak. San Diego: Harcourt.

Yolen, Jane. (1987). *Owl Moon.* Illus. John Schoenherr. New York: Putnam.

Yolen, Jane. (1987). *Piggins.* New York: Harcourt.

Yolen, Jane. (1988). *The Devil's Arithmetic.* New York: Viking.

Yolen, Jane. (1988). *The Emperor and the Kite.* Illus. Ed Young. New York: Putnam.

Yolen, Jane. (1988). *Piggins and the Royal Wedding.* Illus. Jane Dyer. San Diego: Harcourt.

Yolen, Jane. (1989). *Things That Go Bump in the Night: A Collection of Original Stories.* New York: HarperCollins.

Yolen, Jane. (1990). *The Dragon's Boy.* New York: HarperCollins.

Yolen, Jane. (1991). *All in the Woodland Early.* Illus. Jane Breskin Zalben. Honesdale, PA: Boyds Mills.

Yolen, Jane. (1991). *All Those Secrets of the World.* Illus. Leslie Baker. Boston: Little, Brown.

Yolen, Jane. (1991). *Wings.* San Diego: Harcourt.

Yolen, Jane. (1992). *A Letter from Phoenix Farm.* Photog. Jason Stemple. Katonah, NY: Richard C. Owen.

Yolen, Jane. (1992). *Jane Yolen's Mother Goose Songbook.* Illus. Rosekrans Hoffman. Music by Adam Stemple. Honesdale, PA: Boyds Mills.

Yolen, Jane. (1993). *Sleep Rhymes Around the World.* Illus. Native Artists. Honesdale, PA: Boyds Mills.

Yolen, Jane. (1993). *Weather Report.* Illus. Annie Gusman. Honesdale, PA: Boyds Mills.

Yolen, Jane. (1995). *Alphabestiary.* Honesdale, PA: Boyds Mills.

Yolen, Jane. (1995). *Camelot: A Collection of Original Arthurian Stories.* New York: Philomel.

Yolen, Jane. (1995). *Water Music: Poems for Children.* Illus. Jason Stemple. Honesdale, PA: Boyds Mills.

Yolen, Jane (Ed.). (1996). *Mother Earth, Father Sky.* Illus. Jennifer Hewitson. Honesdale, PA: Boyds Mills.

Yolen, Jane. (1996). *Passager.* San Diego: Harcourt.

Yolen, Jane. (1996). *Sea Watch.* New York: Philomel.

Yolen, Jane. (1996). *Sky Scrape/City Scape.* Honesdale, PA: Boyds Mills.

Yolen, Jane. (1997). *Once Upon a Bedtime Story.* Illus. Ruth Tietjen Councell. Honesdale, PA: Boyds Mills.

Yolen, Jane. (1997). *Once Upon Ice and Other Frozen Poems.* Honesdale, PA: Boyds Mills.

Yolen, Jane. (1998). *Snow Snow: Winter Poems for Children.* Illus. Jason Stemple. Honesdale, PA: Boyds Mills.

Yolen, Jane. (2000). *Color Me a Rhyme: Nature Poems for Young People.* Illus. Jason Stemple. Honesdale, PA: Boyds Mills.

Yolen, Jane. (2000). *Not One Damsel in Distress: World Folktales for Strong Girls.* Illus. Susan Guevara. San Diego: Harcourt.

Yolen, Jane, & Harris, Robert. (2000). *The Queen's Own Fool.* Illus. Cynthia Von Buhler. New York: Philomel.

Yorinks, Arthur. (1980). *Louis the Fish.* New York: Farrar, Straus & Giroux.

Yorinks, Arthur. (1986). *Hey, Al.* Illus. Richard Egielski. New York: Farrar, Straus & Giroux.

Yorinks, Arthur. (1989). *Oh, Brother.* Illus. Richard Egielski. New York: Farrar, Straus & Giroux.

Yoshida, Toshi. (1989). *Young Lions.* New York: Philomel.

Young, Ed. (1984). *The Other Bone.* New York: HarperCollins.

Young, Ed. (1989). *Lon Po Po: A Little Red Riding Hood Story from China.* New York: Philomel.

Young, Ed. (1992). *Seven Blind Mice.* New York: Philomel.

Young, Ed. (1994). *Little Plum.* New York: Putnam.

Young, Ed. (1995). *Donkey Trouble.* New York: Atheneum.

Young, Ed. (1995). *Night Visitors.* New York: Philomel.

Young, Ed. (1997). *Mouse Match.* San Diego: Harcourt.

Young, Ed. (1998). *Cat and Rat: The Legend of the Chinese Zodiac.* New York: Holt.

Young, Ed. (1998). *The Lost Horse: A Chinese Folktale.* New York: Silver Whistle.

Young, Ronder Thomas. (1993). *Learning by Heart.* Boston: Houghton.

Younger, Barbara. (1998). *Purple Mountain Majesties: The Story of Katharine Lee Bates and "America the Beautiful."* New York: Dutton.

Yue, Charlotte, & Yue, David. (2000). *The Wigwam and the Longhouse.* Boston: Houghton.

Yumoto, Kazumi. (1997). *The Friends.* Trans. Cathy Hirano. New York: Farrar, Straus & Giroux.

Yumoto, Kazumi. (1999). *The Spring Tree.* New York: Farrar, Straus & Giroux.

Zaunders, Bo. (1999). *Crocodiles, Camels, and Dugout Canoes: Eight Adventureous Episodes.* Illus. Roxie Munro. New York: Dutton.

Zeifert, Harriet. (2000). *Little Red Riding Hood.* Illus. Emily Bolam. New York: Viking.

Zelinsky, Paul O. (1986). *Rumpelstiltskin.* New York: Dutton.

Zelinsky, Paul O. (1991). *The Wheels on the Bus.* New York: Dutton.

Zelinsky, Paul O. (1997). *Rapunzel.* New York: Dutton.

Zemach, Harve, & Zemach, Margot. (1975). *Mommy Buy Me a China Doll.* New York: Farrar, Straus & Giroux.

Zemach, Harve. (1973). *Duffy and the Devil.* Illus. Margot Zemach. New York: Farrar, Straus & Giroux.

Zemach, Margot. (1981). *Hush, Little Baby.* New York: Dutton.

Zemach, Margot. (1988). *The Three Little Pigs: An Old Story.* New York: Farrar, Straus & Giroux.

Zemser, Amy Browen. (1998). *Beyond the Mango Tree.* New York: Greenwillow.

Zhang, Song Nan. (1994). *Five Heavenly Emperors: Chinese Myths of Creation.* Montreal: Tundra.

Zhensun, Zheng, & Low, Alice. (1991). *A Young Painter: The Life and Paintings of Wang Yani—China's Extraordinary Young Artist.* Photog. Zheng Zhensun. New York: Scholastic.

Ziefert, Harriet. (1992). *Big to Little, Little to Big.* Illus. Susan Baum. New York: HarperCollins.

Ziefert, Harriet. (1992). *Clothes On, Clothes Off.* Illus. Susan Baum. New York: HarperCollins.

Ziefert, Harriet. (1992). *Empty to Full, Full to Empty.* Illus. Susan Baum. New York: HarperCollins.

Ziefert, Harriet. (1995). *The Gingerbread Boy.* New York: Viking.

Ziefert, Harriet. (2000). *Little Red Riding Hood.* Illus. Emily Bolam. New York: Viking.

Zienert, Karen. (1999). *The Lincoln Murder Plot.* North Haven, CT: Shoe String.

Ziff, John. (2000). *Espionage and Treason.* Philadelphia: Chelsea.

Zindel, Paul. (1992). *The Pigman and Me.* New York: HarperCollins.

Zoenfeld, Kathleen Weidner. (1998). *What Is the World Made Of? All About Solids, Liquids, and Gasses.* Illus. Paul Meisel. New York: HarperCollins.

Zolotow, Charlotte. (1963). *The Quarreling Book.* New York: HarperCollins.

Zolotow, Charlotte. (1972; 1999). *The Beautiful Christmas Tree.* Illus. Yan Nascimbene. Boston: Houghton.

Zolotow, Charlotte. (1978). *Someone New.* Illus. Erik Blegvad. New York: HarperCollins.

Zolotow, Charlotte. (1993). *Snippets: A Gathering of Poems, Pictures, and Possibilities.* New York: HarperCollins.

Zolotow, Charlotte. (1995). *The Old Dog.* New York: HarperCollins.

Text Credits

Illustration Credits

CHAPTER 1

6 *Harry Potter*, characters, names and all related indicia are trademarks of Warner Bros. © 2001. Reprinted with permission. 7 Bernice Cullinan. 10 "Dragonfly" from *Lemonade Sun: And Other Summer Poems* by Rebecca Kai Dotlitch, illustrations © 1998 Jan Spivey Gilchrist. Published by Wordsong/Boyds Mills Press, Inc. 10 Copyright © 1997 by X. J. Kennedy. First appeared as *Uncle Switch: Loony Limericks*, published by Margaret K. McElderry Books, a division of Simon & Schuster Children's Books. Text reprinted by permission of Curtis Brown, Ltd. 10 From *Color Me a Rhyme: Nature Poems for Young People* by Jane Yolen, photographs © 2000 by Jason Stemple. Published by Wordsong/Boyds Mills Press, Inc. 11 From *Whiteblack the Penguin*, Copyright © 2000, written and illustrated by H. A. Rey. Published by Houghton Mifflin Company. 12 Illustration from *Rapunzel* by Paul O. Zelinsky. Copyright © 1997 by Paul O. Zelinsky. Used by permission of Dutton Children's Books, an imprint of Penguin Books for Young Readers, a division of Penguin Putnam, Inc. 13 Illustration from *Joseph Had a Little Overcoat* by Simms Taback. Copyright © 1999 by Simms Taback. Used by permission of Viking Penguin, an imprint of Penguin Putnam Books for Young Readers, a division of Penguin Putnam, Inc. 13 Illustration from *Golem* by David Wisniewski. Copyright © 1996 by David Wisniewski. Reprinted by permission of Clarion Books/Houghton Mifflin Company. All rights reserved. 15 Illustration from *Smoky Night* by Eve Bunting. Illustration copyright © 1994 by David Diaz. Reproduced by permission of Harcourt, Inc. 15 Illustration from *Hairs = Pelitos* by Sandra Cisneros. Text copyright © 1984, 1994 by Sandra Cisneros, illustrations copyright © 1994 by Terry Ybáñez. Published by Dragonfly Books, an imprint of Alfred A. Knopf, Inc. 17 Illustration from *So You Want To Be President?* by Judith St. George. Text copyright © 2000 by Judith St. George, illustrations copyright © 2000 by David Small. Used by permission of Viking Penguin, an imprint of Penguin Putnam Books for Young Readers, a division of Penguin Putnam, Inc. 19 The Louisa May Alcott Memorial Association. 22 Reprinted with permission of Simon & Schuster Books for Young Readers, an imprint of Simon & Schuster Children's Publishing Division. From *River Friendly, River Wild* by Jane Kurtz, illustrated by Neil Brennan. Illustrations copyright © 2000 by Neil Brennan. 23 Bernice Cullinan.

CHAPTER 2

34 Illustration from *Mammalabilia*, copyright © 2000 by Douglas Florian, reproduced by permission of Harcourt, Inc. 35 "Eagle Flight" from *Creatures of Earth, Sea, and Sky* by Georgia Heard. Illustration copyright © 1993 by Jennifer Owings Dewey. Published by Wordsong/Boyds Mills Press. 37 Courtesy of HarperCollins Publishers. 39 Courtesy Curtis Brown, Ltd. 40 Courtesy Little, Brown and Company. 42 "Sky Scrape/City Scape" from *Sky Scrape/City Scape* by Jane Yolen. Illustration copyright © 1996 by Ken Condon. Published by Wordsong/Boyds Mills Press. 43 Piper Productions. Courtesy of HarperCollins Publishers. 45 Photo by Bachrach. 45 Courtesy of HarperCollins Publishers. 46 Courtesy Temple Studios. 47 Photo by Peterson Portrait, courtesy of HarperCollins

Publishers. 48 Photo by Marilyn Sanders. 50 Cover from *Hush Songs: African American Lullabies* by Joyce Carol Thomas. Copyright 2000 by Joyce Carol Thomas, illustrations © 2000 by Brenda Joysmith. Reprinted by permission of Hyperion Books for Children. 51 Endpaper photographs from *Been to Yesterdays* by Lee Bennett Hopkins. Copyright © 1995 by Lee Bennett Hopkins. Published by Wordsong/Boyds Mills Press, Inc. 52 Courtesy of HarperCollins Publishers. 53 Cover from *Stone Bench in an Empty Park* by Paul B. Janeczko, photographs by Henri Silberman. Published by Orchard Books, a division of Scholastic, Inc. Text copyright © 2000 by Paul B. Janeczko, photographs copyright © 2000 by Henri Silberman. Reprinted by permission. 54 Reprinted with the permission of Atheneum Books for Young Readers, an imprint of Simon & Schuster Children's Publishing Division from *Doodle Dandies* by J. Patrick Lewis, illustrated by Lisa Desimini. Text copyright © 1998 J. Patrick Lewis. Illustrations copyright © 1998 Lisa Desimini. 54 "Old Man of Peru" by James Marshall from *Pocketful of Nonsense* © 1992 James Marshall, illustration © 1992 James Marshall. Published by Golden Books Publishing Company, Inc. 60 Courtesy of Thomas V. Crowell. 61 Courtesy Houghton Mifflin Company.

CHAPTER 3

68 Illustration from *Rapunzel* by Paul O. Zelinsky. Copyright © 1997 by Paul O. Zelinsky. Used by permission of Dutton Children's Books, an imprint of Penguin Books for Young Readers, a division of Penguin Putnam, Inc. 71 Illustration From *The Starry Night* by Neil Waldman, illustrations © 1999 by Neil Waldman. Published by Caroline House, an imprint of Boyds Mills Press, Inc. 71 Cover from *Molly Bannaky* by Alice McGill, illustrations by Chris Soentpiet. Jacket art copyright © 1999 by Chris Soentpiet. Reprinted by permission of Houghton Mifflin Company. All rights reserved. 73 Illustration from *One Sunday Morning* by Yumi Heo. Published by Orchard Books, a division of Scholastic, Inc. Copyright © 1999 by Yumi Heo. Reprinted by permission. 73 Illustration from *The Whispering Cloth: A Refugee's Story* by Pegi Deitz Shea. Text copyright © 1995 by Pegi Deitz Shea, illustrations copyright © 1995 by Anita Riggio. Published by Caroline House, an imprint of Boyds Mills Press, Inc. 74 From *Bembo's Zoo: An Animal ABC Book* by Roberto de Vicq de Cumptich. Copyright © 2000 by Roberto de Vicq de Cumptich. Reprinted by permission of Henry Holt and Company, LLC. 75 Illustration from *Alphabet City* by Stephen T. Johnson. Copyright © 1995 by Stephen T. Johnson. Used by permission of Viking Kestrel, an imprint of Penguin Putnam Books for Young Readers, a division of Penguin Putnam, Inc. 75 From *Out of Sight: Pictures of Hidden Worlds* by Seymour Simon. Copyright © 2000 by Seymour Simon. Used with permission of SeaStar Books, a division of North-South Books, Inc., New York. 76 Cover illustration from *Wilma Unlimited: How Wilma Rudolph Became the World's Fastest Woman* by Kathleen Krull. Illustration copyright © 1996 by David Diaz. Reproduced by permission of Harcourt, Inc. 77 Cover illustration from *The Babe and I* by David A. Adler. Illustration copyright © 1999 by Terry Widener. Reproduced by permission of Harcourt, Inc. 78 Illustration from *Stevie*

CHAPTER 4

CHAPTER 5

CHAPTER 6

162 Reprinted with the permission of Margaret K. McElderry Books, an imprint of Simon & Schuster Children's Publishing Divison from *The Dark Is Rising* by Susan Cooper. Illustrated by Alan E. Cober. Illustrations copyright © 1973 Alan E. Cober. **165** Jacket illustration from *Tuck Everlasting* by Natalie Babbitt. Copyright © 1975 by Natalie Babbitt. Reprinted by permission of Farrar, Straus & Giroux, Inc. **167** Cover from *The Giver* by Lois Lowry. Copyright © 1993 by Lois Lowry. Reprinted by permission of Houghton Mifflin Co. All rights reserved. **169** Courtesy of Houghton Mifflin. **170** Reprinted with the permission of Atheneum Books for Young Readers, an imprint of Simon & Schuster Children's Publishing Division from *The Wind in the Willows* by Kenneth Grahame, illustrated by Ernest H. Shephard. Color pictures copyright © 1959 Ernest H. Shephard. **171** Cover illustration copyright © 1999 by Lane Smith, from *It's All Greek to Me: The Time Warp Trio* by Jon Scieszka. Used by permission of Viking Penguin, an imprint of Penguin Putnam Books for Young Readers, a division of Penguin Putnam, Inc. **172** Cover from *Beast* by Donna Jo Napoli. Cover illustration © 2000 by Rafal Olbinski. Published by Atheneum Books for Young Readers, an imprint of Simon & Schuster Children's Publishing Division. Reprinted with permission. **173** Cover illustration by Eric Rohmann, copyright © 1996 by Eric Rohmann, from *The Golden Compass* by Philip Pullman. Used by permission of Alfred A. Knopf Children's Books, a division of Random House, Inc. **175** Cover from *Gathering Blue* by Lois Lowry. Copyright © 2000 by Lois Lowry. Reprinted by permission of Houghton Mifflin Company. All rights reserved.

CHAPTER 7

187 Cover of *Shiloh* by Phyllis Reynolds Naylor. Jacket illustration Lynne Dennis. Copyright © 1991 Lynne Dennis. Reprinted by permission of Dilys Evans Fine Illustration. **189** Courtesy Katherine Lambert Photography. **190** From *Owl Moon* by Jane Yolen, illustrated by John Schoenherr, copyright © 1988 by John Schoenherr. Published by Philomel Books, an imprint of Penguin Putnam Books for Young Readers, a division of Penguin Putnam, Inc. **191** Cover from *The Wanderer* by Sharon Creech. Text copyright © 2000 by Sharon Creech, cover illustration copyright © 2000 by David Diaz. Published by Joanna Cotler Books, an imprint of HarperCollins Publishers. **192** Jacket design from *Not My Dog* by Colby Rodowsky, pictures by Thomas F. Yezerski. Copyright © 1999 by Colby Rodowsky. Illustration copyright © 1999 by Thomas F. Yezerski. Reprinted by permission of Farrar, Straus and Giroux, LLC. **195** Cover from *Homeless Bird* by Gloria Whelan. Text copyright © 2000 by Gloria Whelan, cover illustration copyright © 2000 by Robert Crawford. Published by HarperCollins Publishers. **198** Cover from *Seedfolks* by Paul Fleischman. Text copyright © 1997 by Paul Fleischman, cover illustration copyright © 1997 by Judy Pedersen. Published by Joanna Cotler Books, an imprint of HarperCollins Publishers.

CHAPTER 8

205 From *Bud, Not Buddy* by Christopher Paul Curtis. Used by permission of Random House Children's Books, a division of Random House, Inc. **209** Illustration from *Molly Bannaky* by Alice McGill, illustrations by Chris Soentpiet. Illustrations copyright © 1999 by Chris Soentpiet. Reprinted by permission of Houghton Mifflin Company. All rights reserved. **211** From *Roll of Thunder, Hear My Cry* by Mildred D. Taylor. Puffin cover illustration by Max Ginsberg. Copyright © 1991 by Max Ginsberg, cover illustration. Used by permission of Puffin Books, a division of Penguin Books USA, Inc. **212** Photo by Jack Ackerman. **213** Illustration from *Pink and Say* by Patricia Polacco, copyright © 1994 by Babushka, Inc. Used by permission of Philomel Books, an imprint of Penguin Putnam Books for Young Readers, a division of Penguin Putnam, Inc. **216** Cover from *Arrow Over the Door* by Joseph Bruchac. Illustrated by James Watling, copyright © 1998 by James Watling, illustrations. Used by permission of Dial Books for Young Readers, an imprint of Penguin Putnam Books for Young Readers, a division of Penguin Putnam, Inc. **217** From *I Have Heard of a Land* by Joyce Carol Thomas. Illustrations copyright © 1998 by Floyd Cooper. Used by permission of HarperCollins Publishers. **220** Cover art from *Nowhere to Call Home* by Cynthia DeFelice, illustration by Michael Dooling. Copyright © 1999 by Cynthia DeFelice. Illustration copyright © 1999 by Michael Dooling. Reprinted by permission of Farrar, Straus and Giroux, LLC. **222** Cover from *The Year of Miss Agnes* by Kirkpatrick Hill, illustrated by Peter Knorr. Illustrations copyright © 2000 Peter Knorr. Published by Margaret K. McElderry Books, an imprint of Simon & Schuster Children's Publishing Division.

CHAPTER 9

233 Illustration by Michael Dooling from *The Amazing Life of Benjamin Franklin*. Published by Scholastic Press, a division of Scholastic, Inc. Illustration copyright © 2000 by Michael Dooling. Reprinted by permission. **236** *Zora Hurston and the Chinaberry Tree* by William Miller, illustrated by Cornelius Van Wrights and Ying-Hwa Hu © 1994. Permission arranged by Lee & Low Books, Inc. New York, NY 10016. **238** Photograph by Charles Osgood. Copyright © 1988, Chicago Tribune Co. **239** From *Martin Luther King* by Rosemary L. Bray. Illustrations copyright © 1995 by Malch Zeldis. Used by permission of HarperCollins Publishers. **242** The Royal Archives © 1998 Her Majesty Queen Elizabeth II. **243** Jacket photo courtesy of the Sugihara Family.

CHAPTER 10

252 From *Red-Eyed Tree Frog* by Joy Cowley. Published by Scholastic Press, a division of Scholastic, Inc. Jacket photograph copyright © 1999 by Nic Bishop. Reprinted by permission. **255** Photo by William Gottlieb, courtesy of Harcourt Brace. **256** Photo © Joe McDonald. **257** Illustration by Leonid Gore from *Blizzard!* by Jim Murphy. Published by Scholastic Press, a division of Scholastic Inc. Cover illustration copyright © 2000 by Scholastic Inc. Reprinted by permission. **258** From *Shipwreck at the Bottom of the World* by Jennifer Armstrong, copyright © 1998 by Jennifer M. Armstrong. Used by permission of Crown Children's Books, a Division of Random House, Inc. **259** NASA. **260** Cover from *The Wigwam and the Long House* by Charlotte & David Yue. Jacket art copyright © 2000 by David Yue. Reprinted by permission of Houghton Mifflin Company. All rights reserved. **261** *Mapping the World* jacket art: upper left, upper right, and lower left from the Library of Congress. Lower right, Dr. Walter H. F. Smith, National Oceanic and Atmospheric Administration. **263** Reprinted with the permission of Little Simon, an imprint of Simon & Schuster Children's Publishing Division from *The Elements of Pop-Up* by David A. Carter and James Diaz. Copyright © 1999 David A. Carter and James Diaz.

CHAPTER 11

275 From *Quinnie Blue* by Dinah Johnson, illustrated by James Ransome. Illustrations copyright, © 1998 by James Ransome. Reprinted by permission of Henry Holt and Company, LLC. **279** Illustration by Leo and Diane Dillon, illustration copyright © 1985 by Leo and Diane Dillon, from *The People Could Fly: American Black Folktales* by Virginia Hamilton, illustrated by Leo and Diane Dillon. Used by permission of Alfred A. Knopf Children's Books, a division of Random House, Inc. **280** Photo by Myles C. Pinkney. **280** Photo by Myles C. Pinkney. **281** Photo by Rick Osentoski, courtesy of *Jump at the Sun*, Hyperion Books. **281** Photo by Dwight Carter, courtesy of *Jump at the Sun*, Hyperion Books. **282** Illustration from *John Henry* by Julius Lester, illustrated by Jerry Pinkney, copyright © 1994 by Jerry Pinkney, illustrations. Used by permission of Dial Books for Young Readers, an imprint of Penguin Putnam Books for Young Readers, a division of Penguin Putnam, Inc. **283** Illustration from *Grandfather's Journey*. Copyright © 1993 by Allen Say. Reprinted by permission of Houghton Mifflin Company. All rights reserved. **284** Cover from *Chato's Kitchen* by Gary Soto, illustrations by Susan Guevara, copyright © 1995 by Susan

Guevara, illustrations. Published by G. P. Putnam's Sons, an imprint of Penguin Putnam Books for Young Readers, a division of Penguin Putnam, Inc. **285** From *Navajo: Visions and Voices Across the Mesa* by Shonto Begay. Copyright © 1995 by Shonto Begay. Reprinted by permission of Scholastic, Inc. **287** Cover from *Halinka* by Mirjam Pressler. Cover illustration and hand lettering © 1998 by Joseph Daniel Feidler. Published by Henry Holt and Company.

CHAPTER 12

305 Lee Galda. **306** From *Where the Wild Things Are* by Maurice Sendak, copyright © 1963 by Maurice Sendak. Reprinted by permission of HarperCollins Publishers. **309** From *Pat the Bunny* by Dorothy Kunhardt © 1940, renewed 1968 by Dorothy Kunhardt. Used by permission of Golden Books Publishing Company, Inc. All rights reserved. **311** Courtesy of John

and Sarah Lewis, Cambridge, Massachusetts. **312** From *What Game Shall We Play* by Pat Hutchins. Copyright © 1990 by Pat Hutchins. Used by permission of HarperCollins Publishers. **314** Photo courtesy of L. Rosenblatt. **318** Lee Galda. **320** Courtesy of Harcourt Brace and Company. **323** Lee Galda.

CHAPTER 13

335 Bernice E. Cullinan. **339** Lee Galda. **341** Lee Galda. **342** Lee Galda.

CHAPTER 14

348 Cover from *Skellig* by David Almond. Copyright © 1999 by David Almond. Published by Delacorte Press, an imprint of Dell Yearling, Random House Children's Books. **350** © PhotoDisc. **356** Lee Galda.

Author and Title Index

Subject Index

Notes

Notes

Notes

Notes

Notes

Notes

Notes

Notes

Touchstones in the History of Children's Literature

1950s

1959 PHILIPPA PEARCE
Tom's Midnight Garden

1957 DR. SEUSS
The Cat in the Hat

1956 GWENDOLYN BROOKS
Bronzeville Boys and Girls

1952 ANNE FRANK
*Anne Frank:
The Diary of a Young Girl*

1952 MARY NORTON
The Borrowers
ILLUS. BETH & JOE KRUSH

1952 E. B. WHITE
Charlotte's Web
ILLUS. GARTH WILLIAMS

1950 BEVERLY CLEARY
Henry Huggins

1950 C. S. LEWIS
*The Lion, the Witch,
and the Wardrobe*

1940s

1947 MARGARET WISE BROWN
Goodnight Moon
ILLUS. CLEMENT HURD

1947 ALVIN TRESSELT
White Snow, Bright Snow
ILLUS. ROGER DUVOISIN

1945 LOIS LENSKI
Strawberry Girl

1944 ROBERT LAWSON
Rabbit Hill

1943 JAMES THURBER
Many Moons
ILLUS. MARC SIMONT

1942 VIRGINIA LEE BURTON
The Little House

1941 ROBERT MCCLOSKEY
Make Way for Ducklings

1941 H. A. REY
Curious George

1930s

1939 LUDWIG BEMELMANS
Madeline

1939 VIRGINIA LEE BURTON
*Mike Mulligan and
His Steam Shovel*

1937 J. R. R. TOLKIEN
The Hobbit

1935 CAROL RYRIE BRINK
Caddie Woodlawn

1934 PAMELA TRAVERS
Mary Poppins

1932 LAURA INGALLS WILDER
*Little House in the
Big Woods*
ILLUS. GARTH WILLIAMS

1920s

1926 A. A. MILNE
Winnie-the-Pooh
ILLUS. E. H. SHEPARD

1922 MARGERY WILLIAMS
The Velveteen Rabbit
ILLUS. WILLIAM NICHOLSON

1900s

1911 FRANCES HODGSON
BURNETT
The Secret Garden

1908 LUCY M. MONTGOMERY
Anne of Green Gables

1908 KENNETH GRAHAME
The Wind in the Willows

1904 JAMES M. BARRIE
Peter Pan

1903 KATE DOUGLAS WIGGIN
*Rebecca of
Sunnybrook Farm*

1903 LESLIE BROOKE
Johnny Crow's Garden

1902 BEATRIX POTTER
The Tale of Peter Rabbit

1900 L. FRANK BAUM
The Wizard of Oz
ILLUS. W. W. DENSLOW

1800s

1899 E. NESBIT
*The Story of the
Treasure Seekers*

1894 RUDYARD KIPLING
The Jungle Book

1891 CARLO COLLODI
Pinocchio

1891 JAMES WHITCOMB RILEY
Rhymes of Childhood

1888 ROBERT BROWNING
The Pied Piper of Hamelin

Expand Your Learning into a Multimedia Environment

The enclosed CD-ROM includes the following integrated components:

A dynamic searchable database of booklists, relevant links to popular children's Web sites, updates on the latest happenings in children's literature, as well as postings of winners of the Newbury and Caldecott awards and InfoTrac College Edition exercises.

Use your CD-ROM to take your learning online!

INSTALLATION:

1. Insert your *Literature and the Child* CD into your CD-ROM drive.
2. Double click on the "Start_here.htm" file located on the CD-ROM. This will launch your browser.

Questions about using this CD-ROM? Please contact our Academic Resource Center at 1-800-423-0563 or via email at support@kdc.com.